Indonesia
a travel survival kit

Robert Storey
Dan Spitzer
Richard Nebesky
James Lyon
Tony Wheeler

Indonesia – a travel survival kit

3rd edition

Published by
 Lonely Planet Publications
 Head Office: PO Box 617, Hawthorn, Vic 3122, Australia
 Branches: PO Box 2001A, Berkeley, CA 94702, USA and London, UK

Printed by
 Colorcraft Ltd, Hong Kong

Photographs by

Joe Cummings (JC)	James Lyon (JL)	Tamsin O'Neill (TO)	Paul Steel (PS)
Hugh Finlay (HF)	Pauline Lyon (PL)	Alan Samagalski (AS)	Phil Weymouth (PW)
Lance Hart (LH)	Richard Nebesky (RN)	Dan Spitzer (DS)	Tony Wheeler (TW)
Joost Hoetjes (JH)	John Noble (JN)		

Front cover: Harvesting rice, International Photographic Library Pty Ltd

First Published
 1986

This Edition
 October 1992

Although the authors and publisher have tried to make the information as accurate as possible, they accept no responsibility for any loss, injury or inconvenience sustained by any person using this book.

National Library of Australia Cataloguing in Publication Data

Wheeler, Tony, 1946-
 Indonesia – a travel survival kit.

 3rd ed.
 Includes index.
 ISBN 0 86442 163 X.

 1. Indonesia – Guidebooks. I. Title. (Series: Lonely Planet travel
 survival kit).

915.980439

text & maps © Lonely Planet 1992
photos © photographers as indicated 1992

Robert Storey

Vagabond and mountain climber extraordinaire, Robert has had a number of distinguished careers, including monkey-keeper at a zoo and slot machine repairman in a Las Vegas casino. After running out of funds in Taiwan, Robert settled down there, learned to speak Chinese, and wrote Lonely Planet's Taiwan guide. He's updated several other LP guides, among them China, Hong Kong, Macau & Canton and North-East Asia. For this edition, Robert wandered through eastern Indonesia, demonstrated how to catch dysentery by drinking unboiled water and made the first recorded ascent of Gunung Rinjani with a laptop computer.

Dan Spitzer

Dan received a BA from the University of Michigan, undertook graduate studies at Berkeley and earned a PhD in Latin American Studies from the University of Michigan. After teaching Caribbean studies, political theory and political economy at a small college in Vermont, he began a career as a journalist and author, spending five years in Asia, Africa and Latin America in the process. This Indonesian update is Dan's seventh travel book. Among his other books are *Wanderlust*, *Asia Overland* and the 1989 Lonely Planet guide to Mexico. Dan lives in Berkeley, California.

Richard Nebesky

Richard was born in Prague, Czechoslovakia. He left there after the Soviet-led invasion in 1968 and settled in Australia. He has a BA in politics and history, and has travelled and worked in Europe, Asia, North America and Africa. He joined Lonely Planet in 1987 and has also worked on *Australia – a travel survival kit*.

James Lyon

James is by nature a sceptic, by training a social scientist, and by trade an editor at Lonely Planet's Melbourne office. He first visited Asia in the 1970s, and has been back on several trips. He has travelled in Bali with his wife, Pauline, and their two young children, but returned by himself to update this book and to explore the boondocks of Lombok.

Tony Wheeler

Tony was born in England but spent most of his youth overseas. He returned to England to do a university degree in engineering, worked as an automotive engineer, returned to university to complete an MBA then dropped out on the Asian overland trail with his wife Maureen. They've been travelling, writing and publishing guidebooks ever since, having set up Lonely Planet Publications in the mid-70s.

This Edition

This is the third edition of Lonely Planet's Indonesia guide. The monumental task of compiling the first edition was the collective work of Alan Samagalski, who roamed the far reaches of the archipelago, Ginny Bruce, who covered Java, and Mary Covernton, who did Sumatra and Bali. For the second edition, Alan went to Sumatra and Sulawesi, Tony Wheeler explored Bali and Lombok as well as covering Sumatra, John Noble and Susan Forsyth island-hopped through Nusa Tenggara and Maluku, and Joe Cummings went to Java and Kalimantan.

For this edition, Robert Storey oversaw the project and researched Nusa Tenggara, Maluku and Sulawesi. Dan Spitzer updated Java and Kalimantan, Richard Nebesky went to Sumatra, and Bali was covered by Tony Wheeler along with James Lyon, who also explored Lombok.

We are also indebted to a number of Indonesian residents and travellers out on the road, who devoted time and energy to making this edition far more coherent than otherwise would have been the case. Among those we'd like to specially thank, and with apologies to anyone left out, are: Lucky Pangemanan, Palu; Roy & Pingkan Kader, Manado; Lawrence Blair, Bali; Lois Pederson, Jayapura; Justinus Daby, Wamena; Dominggus Rohi, Kupang; Jeff & Ruthie Gucker, Waingapu; Baginda Batangtaris, Jakarta; and Huub Kistermann, the Netherlands. Special thanks also to Paul Greening for his many accurate and detailed letters.

From the Publisher

This 3rd edition of *Indonesia – a travel survival kit* was edited at the offices of Lonely Planet in Australia by Kay Waters, Katie Cody and Peter Turner. Jane Hart was responsible for design, illustrations, maps and cover design. Thanks to Vicki Beale for additional mapping.

Thanks also to Sharon Wertheim for indexing, and to Diana Saad and Simone Calderwood for proofreading.

Warning & Request

Things change – prices go up, schedules change, good places go bad and bad ones go bankrupt – nothing stays the same. So if you find things better or worse, recently opened or long since closed, please write and tell us and help make the next edition better.

Your letters will be used to help update future editions and, where possible, important changes will also be included in a Stop Press section in reprints.

We greatly appreciate all information sent to us by travellers. Back at Lonely Planet we employ a hardworking readers' letters team to sort through the many letters we receive. The best ones will be rewarded with a free copy of the next edition or another Lonely Planet guide if you prefer. We give away lots of books, but, unfortunately, not every letter/postcard does receive one.

See page 936 for a list of travellers who have written to us.

Contents

BALI 333

SUMATRA...466

Map Legend

BOUNDARIES

— · — · — · —	........International Boundary
—— · · ——	................Internal Boundary
++++++++++++	....National Park or Reserve
- - - - - - - -	........................The Equator
····················	.........................The Tropics

SYMBOLS

◉ NEW DELHI	........................National Capital
● BOMBAY	.........Provincial or State Capital
● Pune	..............................Major Town
◆ Barsi	..............................Minor Town
■	..........................Places to Stay
▼	..............................Places to Eat
⬒	....................................Post Office
✈	....Airport
i	......................Tourist Information
⊖	.............Bus Station or Terminal
66	............Highway Route Number
⚲ ☩ ⛪	...... Mosque, Church, Cathedral
∴	...........................Temple or Ruin
✚	....Hospital
✳	....Lookout
⚐	..............................Camping Area
⊓	...................................Picnic Area
⌂	...............................Hut or Chalet
▲	........................Mountain or Hill
	..........................Railway Station
	...............................Road Bridge
	...........................Railway Bridge
	..................................Road Tunnel
	..............................Railway Tunnel
	...................Escarpment or Cliff
	....Pass
	.............Ancient or Historic Wall

ROUTES

————	.......Major Road or Highway
- - - - - - -	.........Unsealed Major Road
————	........................Sealed Road
- - - - - -	.....Unsealed Road or Track
════	...........................City Street
+++++++++++	...............................Railway
●━◉━●	..............................Subway
··················	...............................Walking Track
- - - - - - -	...............................Ferry Route
++++++++++	........Cable Car or Chair Lift

HYDROGRAPHIC FEATURES

	....................River or Creek
	..............Intermittent Stream
	........Lake, Intermittent Lake
	............................Coast Line
	...................................Spring
	.............................Waterfall
	..................................Swamp
	................Salt Lake or Reef
	...............................Glacier

OTHER FEATURES

	Park, Garden or National Park
	........................Built Up Area
	... Market or Pedestrian Mall
	.........Plaza or Town Square
	............................Cemetery

Note: not all symbols displayed above appear in this book

Introduction

Like a string of jewels in a coral sea, the 13,000-plus islands of the Indonesian archipelago stretch almost 5000 km from the Asian mainland into the Pacific Ocean. And like jewels the islands have long represented wealth. A thousand years ago the Chinese sailed as far as Timor to load up cargoes of sandalwood and beeswax; by the 16th century the spice islands of the Moluccas were luring European navigators in search of cloves, nutmeg and mace, once so rare and expensive that bloody wars were fought for control of their production and trade. The Dutch ruled for almost 350 years, drawing their fortunes from the islands whose rich volcanic soil could produce two crops of rice a year, as well as commercially valuable crops like coffee, sugar, tobacco and teak.

Endowed with a phenomenal array of natural resources and strange cultures, Indonesia became a magnet for every shade of entrepreneur from the West – a stamping ground for proselytising missionaries, unscrupulous traders, wayward adventurers,

inspired artists. It has been overrun by Dutch and Japanese armies; surveyed, drilled, dug up and shipped off by foreign mining companies; littered with the 'transmigrants' of Java and Bali; poked and prodded by ethnologists, linguists and anthropologists turning fading cultures into PhD theses.

Now there is a new breed of visitor – the modern-day tourist. The government, ever eager to rake in foreign exchange, designated 1991 as 'Visit Indonesia Year'. A special logo resembling a hamburger was designed for the occasion, and appeared everywhere throughout the archipelago. Whether the Visit Indonesia Hamburger drew in more tourists is questionable, but there is no doubt that some parts of the country now receive large numbers of visitors. Places like Bali, Lombok, Torajaland, and the Hindu-Buddhist monuments of Borobudur and Prambanan in Central Java attract huge numbers of visitors. On the other hand, much of the country remains barely touched by mass tourism. Many travellers still consider

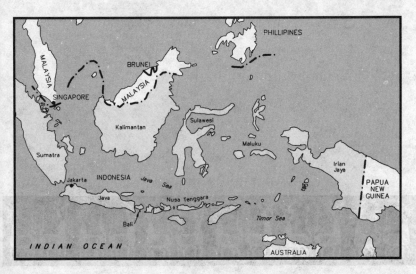

the outer islands to be too expensive to reach or too difficult or time-consuming to travel in. Both views are out of date. Travel in some parts of the outer islands can still be tedious, but over the last 10 years things have improved considerably; there are more roads and more buses, more ferry, shipping and air connections between the islands, and even a few tourist information offices – making it easier to travel than ever before.

Indonesia possesses some of the most remarkable sights in South-East Asia and there are things about this country you will never forget: the flaming red and orange sunsets over the mouth of the Sungai (river) Kapuas in Kalimantan; standing on the summit of Keli Mutu in Flores and gazing at the coloured lakes that fill its volcanic craters; the lumbering leather-skinned dragons of Komodo Island; expatriates in Yogyakarta using an Asian language –

Bahasa Indonesia – as the common means of communication; the funeral ceremonies of the Torajas in the highlands of Central Sulawesi; the Dani tribesmen of Irian Jaya wearing little else but feathers and penis gourds; the wooden *wayang golek* puppets manipulated into life by the puppet-masters of Yogyakarta; the brilliant coral reefs off Manado on the north coast of Sulawesi.

You can lie on your back on Kuta Beach in Bali and soak up the ultraviolet rays, paddle a canoe down the rivers of Kalimantan, surf at Nias off the coast of Sumatra, trek in the high country of Irian Jaya, catch giant butterflies in Sulawesi, eat your way through a kaleidoscope of fruit from one end of the archipelago to the other, stare down the craters of live volcanoes, learn the art of batik in Yogyakarta or kite-making from any Indonesian kid – almost anything you want, Indonesia has got!

Facts about the Country

HISTORY
In the Beginning

It's generally held that the earliest inhabitants of the Indonesian archipelago came from India or Burma, while later migrants, known as 'Malays', came from southern China and Indochina. This second group is reckoned to have entered the Indonesian archipelago gradually over several thousand years.

Among its phases, it's thought, was what's known as the Dongson Culture, which originated in Vietnam and southern China about 3000 years ago and spread to Indonesia, bringing with it techniques of irrigated rice growing, ritual buffalo sacrifice, bronze casting, the custom of erecting large monumental stones (megaliths) and some of the peculiar *ikat* weaving methods found in pockets of Indonesia today. Some of these practices have survived only in isolated islands or areas which were little touched by later arrivals and cultural currents – such as the Batak areas of Sumatra, Tanatoraja in Sulawesi, parts of Kalimantan and several islands of Nusa Tenggara.

From the 7th century BC – approximately the time of the Dongson arrival – there were well-developed and organised societies in the Indonesian archipelago. The inhabitants knew how to irrigate rice fields, domesticate animals, use copper and bronze, and had some knowledge of sea navigation. There were villages – often permanent ones – where life was linked to the production of rice, the staple crop.

These early Indonesians were animists, believing that all animate and inanimate objects have their own particular life force, *semangat* or soul. Certain people had more semangat than others – such as the tribal and village leaders, and the shamans or priests who had magical powers and could control the spirit world. The spirits of the dead had to be honoured because their semangat could still help the living; there was a belief in the afterlife, and weapons and utensils would be left in tombs for use in the next world. Supernatural forces were held responsible for natural events, and evil spirits had to be placated by offerings, rites and ceremonies. In a region where earthquakes, volcanic eruptions and torrential rainstorms are common events, a belief in malevolent spirits is hardly surprising.

Villages, at least in Java, developed into embryonic towns and, by the 1st century AD, small kingdoms (little more than collections of villages subservient to petty chieftains) evolved with their own ethnic and tribal religions. The climate of Java, with its hot, even temperature, plentiful rainfall and volcanic soil was ideal for the wet-field method of rice cultivation, known as *sawah* cultivation. The well-organised society it required may explain why the people of Java and Bali developed a more sophisticated civilisation than those of the other islands. The dry field or *ladang* method of rice cultivation is a much simpler form of agriculture and requires no elaborate social structure.

The social and religious duties of the rice-growing communities were gradually refined to form the basis of *adat* or customary law. This traditional law was to persist through waves of imported religious beliefs – Hinduism, Buddhism, Islam and Christianity – and still remains a force in Indonesia today.

The Coming of Hinduism & Buddhism

One of the puzzles of Indonesian history is how the early kingdoms on Sumatra, Java, Kalimantan and Bali were penetrated by Hinduism and Buddhism. The oldest works of Hindu art in Indonesia, statues from the 3rd century AD, come from Sulawesi and Sumatra. The earliest Hindu inscriptions, in Sanskrit, have been found in West Java and eastern Kalimantan and date from the early 5th century AD.

Several theories regarding the influx of

Hinduism and Buddhism have been proposed. Large-scale immigration from India is generally ruled out and there is no evidence for the theory that Indian princes, defeated in wars in India, fled to the islands of South-East Asia and established kingdoms on the Indian model. Certainly Indian traders brought Tamil, the language of southern India, but only Brahmins could have brought Sanskrit, the language of religion and philosophy. Some Brahmins may have followed the traders as missionaries – although Hinduism is not a proselytising religion. On the other hand, Buddhism *is* a proselytising religion and was carried far from its Indian homeland.

Another theory holds that the early Indonesians were attracted to the cultural life of India in much the same way as the Elizabethan English were to that of Italy. The Indonesian aristocracy may have played an active role in transferring Indian culture to Indonesia by inviting Brahmin priests to their courts. Possibly it was hoped that the new religions could provide occult powers and a mythological sanction for the Indonesian rulers – as had happened in India. This theory fits in well with the mythological and mystical view of history which has persisted since the beginning of recorded Indonesian civilisation. In the Hindu period the kings were seen as incarnations of Vishnu. Even after the arrival of Islam the dynasties traced their lineage on one side back to Mohammed and from there to the prophets and Adam – but on the other side it was traced to the heroes of the *wayang*, the indigenous puppet theatre of Java, and to gods which orthodox Muslims considered pagan. One Sumatran dynasty even claimed descent from Alexander the Great and as late as the second half of the 19th century the rulers of Solo were boasting of a special alliance with Nyai Lara Kidul, the Goddess of the South Seas, and with Sunan Lawu, the ruler of the spirits on Gunung (Mt) Lawu.

The Development of Early Sea Trade
Foreign traders were attracted by the Indonesian archipelago's unique local products. Foremost were spices, which were used as flavourings and also to preserve food (meat in particular). Sumatra was famous for gold, pepper and benzoin (an aromatic gum valued especially by the Chinese) but the real 'Spice Islands' were the tiny specks in the region now known as Maluku (the Moluccas): the islands of Ternate and Tidore off the coast of Halmahera, Ambon and Banda. These islands grew nutmeg and cloves, which could be used for spices and preservatives in the manufacture of perfumes, and for medicinal purposes. By the 1st century AD Indonesian trade was firmly established with other parts of Asia, including China and India. Indian trade, the more active of the two, linked India, China and Indonesia with Greece and Rome – Ptolemy mentions the islands of Indonesia in his writings as early as 165 AD.

The Early Kingdoms
The Sumatran Hindu-Buddhist kingdom of Srivijaya rose in the 7th century AD and, while its power has been romanticised, it nevertheless maintained a substantial international trade – run by Tamils and Chinese. It was the first major Indonesian commercial seapower, able to control much of the trade in South-East Asia by virtue of its control of the Straits of Melaka between Sumatra and the Malay peninsula.

Merchants from Arabia, Persia and India brought goods to the coastal cities to exchange for both local products and goods from China and the spice islands. Silk, porcelain, and Chinese rhubarb (peculiar for its medicinal properties) came from China in return for ivory, tortoise shell, rhinoceros horn, cloves, cardamom and pepper, as well as precious wood like ebony and camphor wood, perfumes, pearls, coral, camphor oil, amber and the dull reddish-white precious stone known as cornelian or chalcedony. Exports to Arabia included aloes for medicinal uses, camphor oil, sandalwood, ebony and sapanwood (from which a red dye is made), ivory, tin and spices. By the 13th century woollen and cotton cloth, as well as iron and rice, were imported to Sumatra.

Meanwhile, on Java, the Buddhist Shailendra and the Hindu Mataram dynasties flourished on the plains of Central Java between the 8th and 10th centuries. While Srivijaya's trade brought it wealth, these land-based states had far greater human labour at their disposal and left magnificent remains, particularly the vast Buddhist monument of Borobudur and the huge Hindu temple complex of Prambanan.

Thus two types of states evolved in Indonesia. The first, typified by Srivijaya, were the mainly Sumatran coastal states – commercially oriented, their wealth derived from international trade and their cities highly cosmopolitan. In contrast, the inland kingdoms of Java, separated from the sea by volcanoes (like the kingdom of Mataram in the Sungai Solo region), were agrarian cultures, bureaucratic and conservative, with a marked capacity to absorb and transform the Indian influences.

By the end of the 10th century, the centre of power had moved from Central to East Java where a series of kingdoms held sway until the rise of the Majapahit kingdom. This is the period when Hinduism and Buddhism were syncretised and when Javanese culture began to come into its own, finally spreading its influence to Bali. By the 12th century Srivijaya's power seems to have declined and the empire broke up into smaller kingdoms.

The Hindu Majapahit Kingdom

One of the greatest of Indonesian states and the last important kingdom to remain predominantly Hindu until its extinction was Majapahit. Founded in East Java in 1293, the kingdom had a brief period of conquering glory but in the late 14th century the influence of Majapahit began to decline.

The power of the kingdom was largely due to the rigorous action of one of its early prime ministers, Gajah Mada. Gajah Mada was a royal guard who put down an anti-royalist revolt in the 1320s and then, during the reign of Hayam Wuruk, brought parts of Java and other areas under control. The kingdom has often been portrayed as an Indonesian

version of Rome, with its own vast empire, but it is now thought that its power did not extend beyond Java, Bali and the island of Madura. If Gajah Mada did have some control over the other islands he did not govern them as the Romans governed Europe or the Dutch governed Indonesia. Instead it's likely to have been trade which linked these regions, and at the Majapahit end this trade was probably a royal monopoly.

Hayam Wuruk's reign is usually referred to as an Indonesian Golden Age, comparable with the Tang Dynasty of China. One account, by the court poet Prapanca, credits the Majapahits with control over much of the coastal regions of Sumatra, Borneo, Sulawesi, Maluku, Sumbawa and Lombok, and also states that the island of Timor sent tribute. The kingdom is said to have maintained regular relations with China, Vietnam, Cambodia, Annam and Siam. However, by 1389 (25 years after the death of Gajah Mada) the kingdom was on the decline, and the coastal dependencies in northern Java were in revolt.

The Penetration of Islam

Islam first took hold in north Sumatra, where traders from Gujarat (a western state in India) stopped en route to Maluku and China. Settlements of Arab traders were established in the latter part of the 7th century, and in 1292 Marco Polo noted that the inhabitants of the town of Perlak (present day Aceh) on Sumatra's north tip had been converted to Islam.

The first Muslim inscriptions in Java date back to the 11th century and there may even have been Muslims in the Majapahit court at the zenith of its power in the mid-14th century. But it was not until the 15th and 16th centuries that Indonesian rulers turned to Islam and it became a state religion. It was then superimposed on the mixture of Hinduism and indigenous animist beliefs to produce the peculiar hybrid religion which predominates in much of Indonesia, especially Java, today.

By the time of Majapahit's final collapse

at the beginning of the 16th century, many of its old satellite kingdoms had declared themselves independent Muslim states. Much of their wealth was based on their position as transhipment points for the growing spice trade with India and China. Islam spread across the archipelago from west to east and followed the trade routes. It appears to have been a peaceful transformation – unlike Arab and Turkish conversions made at the point of the sword. The spread of Islam in Indonesia is often described like some contagious disease, as if it happened simply because it was Islam.

While pockets of the Indonesian population are fundamentalist Muslims, such as the Acehnese in northern Sumatra, the success of Islam was due, on the whole, to its ability to adapt to local customs. The form of Islam followed in much of Indonesia today is not the austere form of the Middle East, but has more in common with Sufism. This is a mystical variant of Islam brought to India from Persia and possibly carried into Indonesia by wandering Sufi holymen and mystics.

The Rise of Melaka & Makassar
By the 15th century the centre of power in the archipelago had moved to the south-west of the Malay peninsula, where the trading kingdom of Melaka (also spelt Malacca) was reaching the height of its power. The rise of Melaka, and of trading cities along the north coast of Java, coincided with the spread of Islam through the archipelago – the Melaka kingdom accepted Islam in the 14th century. Though centred on the peninsula side of the Straits, the Melaka kingdom controlled both sides, based its power and wealth on trade, and gathered the ports of northern Java within its commercial orbit. By the 16th century it was the principal port of the region, possibly one of the biggest in the world.

By the end of the 16th century a seapower had risen in the Indonesian archipelago – the twin principalities of Makassar and Gowa in south-west Sulawesi. These regions had been settled by Malay traders who also sailed to Maluku and beyond. In 1607 when Torres sailed through the strait which now bears his name, he met Makassar Muslims in west New Guinea. Other Makassar fleets visited the north Australian coast for several hundred years, introducing the Aborigines to metal tools, pottery and tobacco.

The Portuguese Arrive
When the first Europeans arrived in the Indonesian archipelago they found a varying collection of principalities and kingdoms. These kingdoms were occasionally at war with each other, but were also linked by the substantial inter-island and international trade over which successive powerful kingdoms – Srivijaya, Majapahit and Melaka – had been able to exert control by virtue of their position or their seapower.

European influence from the 16th to 18th centuries was due to the penetration of individuals and organisations into the complex trading network of the archipelago. Marco Polo and a few early missionary-travellers aside, the first Europeans to visit Indonesia were the Portuguese. Vasco de Gama had led the first European ships round the Cape of Good Hope to Asia in 1498; by 1510 the Portuguese had captured Goa on the west coast of India and then pushed on to South-East Asia. The principal aim of the first Portuguese to arrive in the Indonesian archipelago was the domination of the valuable spice trade in Maluku – the Molucca Islands. Under Alfonso d'Albuquerque they captured Melaka in 1511, and the following year arrived in the Maluku.

Portuguese control of trade in Indonesia was based on their fortified bases, such as Melaka, and on their supremacy at sea due to the failure of their various foes to form a united front against them. This allowed them to exercise a precarious control of the strategic trading ports that stretched from Maluku to Melaka, Macau, Goa, Mozambique and Angola. From a European point of view the Portuguese were pioneers who opened up the trade routes from Europe to Asia, forerunners of European expansionism. From an Indonesian point of view they were just

Indonesia

| 0 | 250 | 500 | 750 km |

SULU
SEA

Philippines

PACIFIC

CELEBES
SEA

Tarakan

MOLUCCA
SEA

OCEAN

Manado

Halmahera

Gorontalo

Equator

M
A
L
U
K
U

inda
pan
Palu Poso

Biak

Jayapura

SULAWESI

Buru *Seram*

I R I A N   J A Y A

Papua New Guinea

ndang

BANDA SEA

FLORES
SEA

bok

Flores

NUSA TENGGARA

Dilli

ARAFURA

Merauke

Sumba

Timor

Kupang

SEA

Darwin

Australia

another group of traders who found their way to the spice islands. The coming of the Portuguese to Indonesia did not represent a fundamental alteration of Indonesian society or trade – even the capture of Melaka did not change anything. The face and the colour of the rulers changed, but local traders took no notice of political boundaries and allegiances if they did not affect trade.

The initial Portuguese successes encouraged other European nations to send ships to the region – notably the English, the Dutch and the Spanish. The latter established themselves at Manila in 1571. By the time these new forces appeared on the horizon, the Portuguese had suffered a military defeat at Ternate and were a spent force. It was the Dutch who would eventually lay the foundations of the Indonesian state we know today.

The Coming of the Dutch

A badly led expedition of four Dutch ships, under the command of Cornelius de Houtman, arrived at Banten in West Java in 1596 after a 14-month voyage in which more than half of the 249 crew died. A Dutch account of Banten at the time gives a lively picture:

There came such a multitude of Javanese and other nations such as Turks, Chinese, Bengali, Arabs, Persians, Gujarati, and others that one could hardly move...that each nation took a spot on the ships where they displayed their goods the same as if they were in a market. Of which the Chinese brought of all sorts of silk woven and non-woven, spun and non-spun, with beautiful earthenware, with other strange things more. The Javanese brought chickens, eggs, ducks, and many kinds of fruits. Arabs, Moors, Turks, and other nations of people each brought of everything one might imagine.

The Dutch got off to a poor start. They made a bad impression on the Javanese by killing a prince and some of his retainers, concluded a meaningless treaty of friendship with the ruler of Banten and lost one of their ships when attacked by the Javanese north of Surabaya. Nevertheless they returned to Holland with goods that yielded a small profit for their backers. Other independent expeditions followed and met with varying success – some ships were captured by the Spanish and Portuguese. The behaviour of the Dutch was uneven and so was their reception but Dutch trade expanded quickly. This was partly because regional Indonesian leaders took advantage of the higher prices which the Dutch and Portuguese competition generated.

Then in 1580, Spain, the traditional enemy of Holland, occupied Portugal and this prompted the Dutch government to take an interest in the Far East. The government amalgamated the competing merchant companies into the United East India Company, or the VOC (Vereenigde Oost-Indische Compagnie). The intention was to create a force to bring military pressure to bear on the Portuguese and the Spanish. Dutch trading ships were replaced by heavily armed fleets with instructions to attack Portuguese bases. By 1605 the Dutch had defeated the Portuguese at Tidore and Ambon and occupied the territory themselves – but it was another 36 years before they captured Melaka.

The Foundation of a Dutch Empire

The founder of the Dutch empire in the Indies was Jan Pieterszoon Coen, an imaginative but ruthless man. Amongst his achievements was the near-total extermination of the indigenous population of the Banda Islands in Maluku. Coen developed a grandiose plan to make his capital in Java the centre of the intra-Asian trade from Japan to Persia, and to develop the spice plantations using Burmese, Madagascan and Chinese labourers.

While the more grandiose plans were rejected he nevertheless acted vigorously in grabbing a monopoly on the spice trade as he had been instructed. An alliance with Ternate in 1607 gave the Dutch control over the source of cloves, and their occupation of Banda from 1609-21 also gave them control of the nutmeg trade. As the Dutch extended their power they forced a reduction in spice production by destroying excess clove and nutmeg plantations, thus ruining the livelihoods of the local inhabitants but keeping

European prices and profits high. After capturing Melaka from the Portuguese in 1641 the Dutch became masters of the seas in the region. They not only held a monopoly of the clove and nutmeg trade, they also had a hold on the Indian cloth trade, and on Japanese copper exports. By the middle of the century they had made their capital Batavia, on the island of Java, the centre of trade on a route from Japan to Persia via Ceylon and India. They defeated Makassar in 1667 and secured a monopoly of its trade, and eventually brought the Sumatran ports under their sway. The last of the Portuguese were expelled in 1660 and the English in 1667.

The first effect of Dutch power in the Indies was the disruption of the traditional pattern of trade by their attempts – with some success – to achieve a monopoly of the spice trade at its source. The company's policy at this stage was to keep to its trading posts and avoid expensive territorial conquests. An accord with the Susuhunan (literally 'he to whose feet people must look up') of Mataram, the dominant kingdom in Java, was established. It permitted only Dutch ships, or those with permission from the VOC, to trade with the spice islands and the regions beyond them.

Then, perhaps unintentionally, but in leaps and bounds, the Dutch developed from being one trading company among many to the masters of a colonial empire centred on their chief trading port at Batavia. Following a 'divide and rule' strategy the Dutch exploited the conflicts between the Javanese kingdoms and, in 1678, were able to make the ruler of Mataram their vassal and dominate his successors.

They had already put Banten under their control by helping the ruler's ambitious son to overthrow his father. In 1755 the Dutch split the Mataram kingdom into two – Yogyakarta and Surakarta (Solo). These new states and the five smaller states on Java were only nominally sovereign; in reality they were dominated by the Dutch East India Company. Fighting amongst the princes was halted, and peace was brought to East Java by the forced cessation of invasions and raids

from Bali. Thus Java was united – what the native kings had failed to do for centuries had been achieved towards the end of the 18th century by a foreign trading company with an army that totalled only 1000 Europeans and 2000 Asians.

The Decline of the VOC

Despite some dramatic successes, the fortunes of the VOC were on the decline by the middle of the 18th century. The Dutch monopoly of the spice trade was finally broken, after the Dutch-English war of 1780-84, by the Treaty of Paris which permitted free trade in the east. Dutch trade in China was outstripped by European rivals, and in India much of their trade was diverted by the British to Madras. In addition, the emphasis of European trade with the east began to shift from spices to Chinese silk, Japanese copper, coffee, tea and sugar – over which it was impossible to establish a monopoly.

Dutch trading interests gradually contracted more and more around their capital of Batavia. The Batavian government increasingly depended for its finances on customs dues and tolls on goods coming into Batavia, and on taxes from the local Javanese population. Increased smuggling and the illicit private trade carried on by company employees helped to reduce profits. The mounting expense of wars within Java and of administering the additional territory acquired after each new treaty also played a part in the decline.

The VOC turned to the Dutch government at home for support and the subsequent investigation of VOC affairs revealed corruption, bankruptcy and mismanagement. In 1800 the VOC was formally wound up, its territorial possessions became the property of the Netherlands government and the trading empire was gradually transformed into a colonial empire.

The British Occupation

In 1811, during the Napoleonic Wars when France occupied Holland, the British occupied several Dutch East Indies posts, including Java. Control was restored to the

Dutch in 1816 and a treaty was signed in 1824 under which the British exchanged their Indonesian settlements (such as Bengkulu in Sumatra) for Dutch holdings in India and the Malay Peninsula. While the two European powers may have settled their differences to their own satisfaction, the Indonesians were of another mind. There were a number of wars or disturbances in various parts of the archipelago during the early 19th century, but the most prolonged struggles were the Paderi War in Sumatra (1821-38) and the famous Java War (1825-30) led by Prince Diponegoro. In one sense the Java War was yet another war of succession, but both wars are notable because Islam became the symbol of opposition to the Dutch.

In 1814, Diponegoro, the eldest son of the Sultan of Yogya, had been passed over for the succession to the throne in favour of a younger claimant who had the support of the British. Having bided his time, Diponegoro eventually vanished from court and in 1825 launched a guerrilla war against the Dutch. The courts of Yogya and Solo largely remained loyal to the Dutch but many of the Javanese aristocracy supported the rebellion. Diponegoro had received mystical signs that convinced him that he was the divinely appointed future king of Java. News spread among the people that he was the long-prophesied Ratu Adil, the prince who would free them from colonial oppression.

The rebellion finally ended in 1830 when the Dutch tricked Diponegoro into peace negotiations, arrested him and exiled him to Sulawesi. The five-year war had cost the lives of 8000 European and 7000 Indonesian soldiers of the Dutch army. At least 200,000 Javanese died, most from famine and disease, and the population of Yogyakarta was halved.

Dutch Exploitation of Indonesia

For 350 years, from the time the first Dutch ships arrived in 1596 to the declaration of independence in 1945, there was little stability in Indonesia. The first Dutch positions in the archipelago were precarious, like the first Portuguese positions. Throughout the 17th century the VOC, with its superior arms and Buginese and Ambonese mercenaries, fought everywhere in the islands. Despite Dutch domination of Java, many areas of the archipelago – including Aceh, Bali, Lombok and Borneo – remained independent.

Fighting continued to flare up in Sumatra and Java, and between 1846 and 1849 expeditions were sent to Bali in the first attempts to subjugate the island. Then there was the violent Banjarmasin War in south-east

Expansion of Dutch Control

Dutch Control
1619-1898
1898-1942

Malaysia

Malaysia

Sumatra

Kalimantan

Maluku

Sulawesi

Dutch Controlled
Area by 1619

Java

Borneo, during which the Dutch defeated the reigning sultan. The longest and most devastating war was the one in Aceh which had remained independent under British protection (the two had an active trade). In 1871 the Dutch negotiated a new treaty in which the British withdrew objections to a possible Dutch occupation of Aceh. The Dutch declared war on Aceh in 1873. The war lasted for 35 years until the last Aceh guerrilla leaders finally surrendered in 1908.

Even into the 20th century Dutch control outside Java was still incomplete. Large-scale Indonesian piracy continued right up until the middle of the 19th century and the Dutch fought a war in Sulawesi against the Buginese. Dutch troops occupied southwest Sulawesi between 1900 and 1910, and Bali in 1906. The 'bird's head' of West Irian did not come under Dutch administration until 1919-20. Ironically, just when the Dutch finally got it all together they began to lose it. By the time Bali was occupied the first Indonesian nationalist movements were getting under way.

The determined exploitation of Indonesian resources by the Dutch really only began in 1830. The cost of the Java and Paderi wars meant that, despite increased returns from the Dutch system of land tax, Dutch finances were severely strained. When the Dutch lost Belgium in 1830 the home country itself faced bankruptcy and any government investment in the Indies *had* to make quick returns. From here on Dutch economic policy in Indonesia falls into three overlapping periods: the period of the so-called 'Culture' System, the Liberal Period, and the Ethical Period.

The Culture System

A new governor-general, Johannes Van den Bosch, fresh from experiences of the slave labour of the West Indies, was appointed in 1830 to make the East Indies pay their way. He succeeded by introducing a new agricultural policy called the *cultuurstelsel* or Culture System. It was really a system of government-controlled agriculture or, as

Indonesian historians refer to it, the *Tanam Paksa* (Compulsory Planting).

Forced labour was not new in Java – the Dutch merely extended the existing system by forcing the peasants to produce particular crops, including coffee, which the Dutch introduced. Instead of land rent, usually assessed at about two-fifths of the value of the crop, the Culture System proposed that a portion of peasants' land and labour be placed at the government's disposal. On this land a designated crop, suitable for the European market, was to be grown.

In practice things did not work out that way and the system produced fearful hardship. The land required from each peasant was sometimes as much as a third or even a half of their total land. In some cases the new crops demanded more labour than the maximum allowed for, and the government did not bear the losses of a bad harvest. Often the Culture System was applied on top of the land tax rather than in place of it. When the cash crops failed the peasants had no money to buy the rice they would otherwise have planted on their land. In some regions the population starved because the Javanese regents (princes) and their Chinese agents forced the peasants to use almost all their rice land to grow other crops. In the 1840s there was severe famine in some areas because of the encroachments on rice lands.

The system was never applied to the whole population – by 1845 it involved only about 5% of the total cleared land, so its impact on the Javanese was very uneven. Amongst the crops grown was indigo (from which the deep blue dye is extracted), which required arduous cultivation, and sugar, which took twice the labour required of rice fields. The Culture System was, however, a boon to the Dutch and to the Javanese aristocracy. The profits made Java a self-sufficient colony and saved The Netherlands from bankruptcy. That this gain was made by appropriating all available profits and making the peasants bear all the losses was irrelevant to the Dutch. They believed that the function of a colony was to benefit the coloniser and that the welfare of the indigenous people should not interfere with this.

The Liberal Period

In the 10 years after 1848, efforts were made to correct the worst abuses of the Culture System. The liberals in the Dutch parliament attempted to reform the system, while at the same time retaining the profits and alleviating the conditions of the peasants.

They were committed to reducing government interference in economic enterprises and were therefore opposed to the system of government-controlled agriculture in Indonesia. Their policies advocated opening up the country to private enterprise – in the belief that once the peasant was freed from compulsion, productivity would increase and everyone would be swept to prosperity by the forces of a free economy. But to make the archipelago safe for individual capitalists and to free the Indonesians from oppression were, in fact, two conflicting aims.

From the 1860s onwards, the government abolished monopolies on crops which were no longer profitable anyway. Things moved more slowly for other crops; in 1870 a law was passed by which control of sugar production would be relinquished over a 12-year period from 1878 onwards, while the monopoly of the most profitable crop, coffee, was retained right up until 1917.

The 1870 Agrarian Law and other new policies proved profitable for the Dutch but brought further hardships to the Indonesians. Sugar production doubled in 1870-85, new crops like tea and cinchona flourished, and a start was made with rubber, which eventually became a valuable export. At the same time oil produced in south Sumatra and Kalimantan became a valuable export, a response to the new industrial demands of the European market.

The exploitation of Indonesian resources was no longer limited to Java but had filtered through to the outer islands. As Dutch commercial interests expanded, so did the need to protect them. More and more territory was taken under direct control of the Dutch government and most of the outer islands came under firm Dutch sovereignty.

The Ethical Policy

At the turn of the century there were two increasingly vocal groups in the Dutch parliament – those who had a humanitarian interest in the welfare of the Indonesian people, and those who wanted to raise the purchasing power of the Indonesians in order to widen the market for consumer goods. The group who aimed at improving the welfare of the Indonesian people approached the task with a strong sense of a moral mission.

New policies were to be implemented, foremost among them irrigation, transmigration from heavily populated Java to lightly populated islands, and education. There were also plans for improved communications, credit facilities for Indonesians, agricultural advice, flood control, drainage, extension of health programmes, industrialisation and the protection of native industry. Other policies aimed for the decentralisation of authority with greater autonomy for the Indonesian government, as well as greater power to local government units within the archipelago.

There were four main criticisms of these new policies. As they were implemented they improved the lot of the Europeans in Indonesia, not the Indonesians themselves; those programmes which did benefit the Indonesians only reached a small percentage of the population; the programmes were carried out in a paternalistic, benevolent fashion which continued to regard the Indonesians as inferiors; and some of the policies were never implemented at all. Industrialisation was never implemented, because it was never seriously envisaged that Indonesia would compete with European industry, and because it was also feared that industrial development would result in the loss of a market for European goods.

Throughout all three periods, the exploitation of Indonesia's wealth contributed to the industrialisation of The Netherlands. Large areas of Java became plantations whose products, cultivated by Javanese peasants and collected by Chinese intermediaries, were sold on the overseas markets by European merchants. Before WW II, Indonesia supplied most of the world's quinine and pepper, over a third of its rubber, a quarter of its coconut products, and almost a fifth of its tea, sugar, coffee and oil. Indonesia made The Netherlands one of the major colonial powers.

Indonesian Nationalist Movements

Of all the policies of the Ethical Period, it was the education policies which were to have the least predictable and the most far-reaching effects. The diversification of economic activity and the increasing scope and range of government activity, banks and business houses, meant a growing need for Indonesians with some Western education to do the paperwork. As educational opportunities increased and some Indonesians attained higher levels of education, an educated elite developed which became increasingly aware and resentful of European rule.

The first Indonesian nationalist movements of the 20th century had their roots in educational organisations. Initially the nationalist organisations largely concerned the upper and middle class Indonesians whose education and contact with Western culture had made them more conscious of their own cultural traditions and critical of the injustices of the colonial system. Then mass movements began to develop, drawing support from the peasants and the urban working class.

The Islamic Association The first truly mass movement was Sarekat Islam (Islamic Association), which had its origins in a trading society formed in 1909 to protect Indonesians against Chinese dealers. It quickly became one of the most significant of the early nationalist movements. It was the first movement attempting to bridge the gap between the villagers and the new Western-educated elite.

The Indonesian Communist Party Created in 1914, this small Marxist group, later

known as the PKI (Perserikatan Kommunist Indonesia – the United Indonesian Communists) built up influence in the Islamic Association until a showdown in 1921 forced the Communists out. The Communists organised strikes in urban businesses and in the sugar factories but Communist-led revolts in Java (1926) and Sumatra (1927) were both suppressed by the Dutch. The PKI was effectively destroyed for the rest of the colonial period, with its leaders imprisoned or self-exiled to avoid arrest.

The Indonesian Nationalist Party The Partai Nasional Indonesia (PNI) was formed (under a different name) in 1927 and advocated an independent Indonesia as its ultimate objective. The party was chaired by and had arisen out of the Bandung Study Group which was formed by Achmed Sukarno, who later become the first president of independent Indonesia.

The PNI became the most powerful nationalist organisation. Its early success was partly a result of Sukarno's skill as an orator and his understanding of the common people from whom the party drew and built up its mass support. The Dutch quickly recognised the threat from the PNI, and Sukarno and three other PNI leaders were imprisoned in 1930. The party was outlawed and its membership split into factions.

Other nationalist groups arose. In 1932, Mohammed Hatta and Sutan Sjahrir, who were to become important figures in the nationalist movement, returned from university in The Netherlands and established their own nationalist group. Sukarno was released and then re-arrested in 1933, and Hatta and Sjahrir were arrested in 1934. None of the three leaders were freed until the Japanese invasion of 1942.

As the 1930s progressed, the question of cooperation or non-cooperation with the Dutch in the face of growing European and Japanese fascism was raised. While some nationalist leaders attempted to formulate an anti-fascist solidarity pact with the Dutch in return for Indonesian independence, at no time – even after the Nazi occupation of The Netherlands – did the Dutch encourage the Indonesians to believe that their cooperation was needed, or that their independence aims would be recognised.

The Japanese Invasion & Occupation

The first Japanese landings in Indonesia were in January 1942. The Dutch forces eventually surrendered, and to some extent the Japanese were hailed by the Indonesians as liberators. Sjahrir commented that:

...for the average Indonesian the war...was simply a struggle in which the Dutch colonial rulers finally would be punished by Providence for the evil, the arrogance and the oppression they had brought to Indonesia.

An ancient prophesy was revived which predicted that Indonesia would be ruled by a white buffalo (interpreted as meaning the Dutch) and then by a yellow chicken (the Japanese) which would stay only for 'a year of corn' before independence was again achieved. The Japanese occupation lasted for 3½ years.

Japanese control was very much dependent on goodwill. Believing the anti-Dutch sentiments of the Indonesians to be stronger than any anti-Japanese sentiments, the Japanese were prepared to work with the Indonesian nationalists. Sukarno and Hatta, the best known nationalists, worked above ground and collaborated with the Japanese. Sjahrir led one of the underground groups, among which were people who later became prominent in Indonesian politics.

The period of Japanese occupation was immensely important in the development of the nationalist movement and there is little doubt that it grew in strength. The Japanese sponsored mass organisations based on Islam and anti-Western sentiments. Sukarno and Hatta were allowed to travel about addressing gatherings of Indonesians, and Sukarno used these occasions to spread nationalist propaganda.

In 1943, the Japanese formed the Volunteer Army of Defenders of the Fatherland, a home defence corps which Indonesians joined in large numbers. Sukarno and Hatta were allowed to address the recruits and the corps soon became a hotbed of nationalism, later forming the backbone of the Indonesian forces fighting the Dutch after WW II.

The Independence Struggle

In mid-1945, with the tide of war against them, the Japanese set up a committee of Indonesian nationalists entitled the 'Investigating Body for the Preparation of Indonesian Independence'. This committee represented an important point in the history of the nationalist movement because it outlined the geographical limits of a future independent Indonesia.

It also set out the philosophical basis which would underlie the government and social structure of the new state. This was based on a speech Sukarno made on 1 June to the committee announcing the *Pancasila* or 'Five Principles' on which an independent Indonesia would be based: Faith in God, Humanity, Nationalism, Representative Government and Social Justice. As Sukarno put it, it was a synthesis of Western democratic ideas, Islam, Marxism and indigenous village customs and traditions of government.

Three plans were drawn up for territorial boundaries and the vote came out strongly in favour of including all the territories of the Dutch East Indies, plus the territories of North Borneo, Brunei, Sarawak, Portuguese Timor, Malaysia, New Guinea and surrounding islands. Sukarno, according to a book by Hatta, argued for the inclusion of Malaysia in the belief that the interests of Indonesia would not be secure unless both sides of the Straits of Melaka were under its control. Despite majority feeling, the Japanese seemed to have influenced the Indonesians into accepting one of the other plans which claimed only the former territory of the Dutch East Indies.

On 6 August 1945 the USA dropped the atomic bomb on Hiroshima. On 9 August the second atomic bomb was dropped on Nagasaki, and the next day Japan surrendered.

Japan was no longer in a position to grant or guarantee Indonesian independence, but it still controlled the archipelago. The underground movements were now determined to rise against the Japanese and take over the administration. In the early morning of 16 August a group of students – including Adam Malik, the future foreign minister of the Republic of Indonesia – kidnapped Sukarno, his wife and children, and Hatta, and held them outside Jakarta. The following day, outside his Jakarta home, Sukarno proclaimed the formation of an independent Indonesia. An Indonesian government consisting of 16 ministers was formed on 31 August, with Sukarno as president and Hatta as vice-president.

In September 1945, the first British and Australian troops landed in Jakarta, and from October onwards began arriving throughout the territories. They had three main tasks – to disarm the Japanese troops and send them back to Japan, rescue Allied prisoners of war and, lastly, to hold the Indonesian nationalists down until the Dutch could return to the archipelago and reassert their 'lawful' sovereignty.

Most of the 'British' troops were in fact Indians – the soldiers of one colony being used to help restore colonialism in another – and many deserted to the Indonesian side. Japanese troops tried to recapture towns held by the Indonesians, such as Bandung. Heavy fighting, which lasted for 10 days, broke out in Surabaya between Indonesians and the Indian troops led by British officers.

Against this background of turbulence, attempts were made to begin negotiations between the Dutch and the nationalists but the Dutch failed to recognise that their colonial empire was finished. Hatta said:

The Dutch are graciously permitting us entry into the basement while we have climbed all the way to the top floor and up to the attic. Indonesia today has achieved her own administration as a result of her own efforts. And what earthly reason is there for Indonesia to return to her former status as a colony of a foreign nation which did practically nothing to defend her from the Japanese? The Dutch should not remain under the delusion that they can thwart Indonesia's desire to remain independent.

The last British troops left at the end of November 1946, by which time 55,000 Dutch troops had landed in Java. In Bogor (Java) and in Balikpapan (Kalimantan) Indonesian republican officials were imprisoned. Bombing raids on Palembang and Medan in Sumatra prepared the way for the Dutch occupation of these cities. In southern Sulawesi Captain Westerling was accused of pacifying the region by murdering 40,000 Indonesians in a few weeks. Elsewhere the Dutch were attempting to form puppet states among the more amenable ethnic groups.

The next three years saw a confusing struggle – half diplomatic and half military. Despite major military operations in 1947 and 1948 the nationalists continued to hold out, world opinion swayed heavily against the Dutch and it became obvious that only a concerted and costly campaign could defeat the nationalist forces. The Dutch were finally forced out by international pressure, particularly from the USA, which threatened the Dutch with economic sanctions. In December 1949, after negotiations in The Netherlands, the Dutch finally transferred sovereignty over the former Dutch East Indies to the new Indonesian republic.

Economic Depression & Disunity

The threat of external attacks from the Dutch had helped to keep the nationalists mostly united in the first five years or so after the proclamation of independence. With the Dutch gone the divisions in Indonesian society began to reassert themselves. Sukarno had tried to hammer out the principles of Indonesian unity in his Pancasila speech of 1945 and while these, as he said, may have been 'the highest common factor and the lowest common multiple of Indonesian thought', the divisive elements in Indonesian society could not be swept away by a single speech. Regional differences in customs (adat), morals, tradition, religion, the impact of Christianity and Marxism, and fears of political domination by the Javanese all contributed to disunity.

In the early years of the republic there were a number of separatist movements which sprang out of the religious and ethnic diversity of the country. These included the militant Darul Islam (Islamic Domain) which proclaimed an Islamic State of Indonesia and waged guerrilla warfare in west Java against the new Indonesian Republic from 1949 to 1962. There was also an attempt by former Ambonese members of the Royal Dutch Indies Army to establish an independent republic in Maluku, and there were revolts in Minahasa (the northern limb of Sulawesi) and in Sumatra.

Against this background lay divisions in the leadership elite, and the sorry state of the new republic's economy. When the Republic of Indonesia came into being the economy was in tatters after almost 10 years of Japanese occupation and war with the Dutch. The population was increasing and the new government was unable to boost production of foodstuffs and clothing to keep pace with, let alone overtake, this increase in population. Most of the population was illiterate; there were few schools and few teachers. While there was a sufficiently large elite of Western-educated Indonesians to fill top levels of government there were insufficient middle-level staff, technicians and people with basic skills such as typing and accountancy. Inflation was chronic, smuggling cost the central government badly needed foreign currency, and many of the plantations had been destroyed during the war.

Political parties proliferated and deals between parties for a share of cabinet seats resulted in a rapid turnover of coalition governments. There were 17 cabinets for the period 1945 to 1958. The frequently postponed elections were finally held in 1955 and the PNI – regarded as Sukarno's party – topped the poll. There were also dramatic increases in support for the Communist PKI but no party managed more than a quarter of the votes and short-lived coalitions continued.

Sukarno Takes Over – Guided Democracy

By 1956 President Sukarno was openly criticising parliamentary democracy. Its most serious weakness, he said, was that it was 'based upon inherent conflict' thus running counter to the Indonesian concept of harmony as the natural state of human relationships.

Sukarno sought a system based on the traditional village system of discussion and deliberation upon a problem in an attempt to find common ground and a consensus of opinion under the guidance of the village elders. He argued that the threefold division – nationalism *(nasionalisme)*, religion *(agaman)* and communism *(komunisme)* – would be blended into a cooperative government, or what he called a *Nas-A-Kom* government.

In February 1957, at a large meeting of politicians and others, Sukarno proposed a cabinet representing all the political parties of importance (including the PKI). This was

Sukarno

his attempt to overcome the impasse in the political system, but it was not an attempt to abolish the parties. Sukarno then proclaimed 'guided democracy' and brought Indonesia's period of Western parliamentary democracy to a close. This was achieved with support from his own party, and with some support from regional and military leaders grown weary of the political merry-go-round in Jakarta.

The Sumatra & Sulawesi Rebellions

As a direct result of Sukarno's actions, rebellions broke out in Sumatra and Sulawesi in 1958. Led by senior military and civilian leaders of the day, these rebellions were partly a reaction against Sukarno's usurpation of power and partly against the growing influence of the Communist Party which was winning increasing favour with Sukarno. The rebellions were also linked to the growing regional hostility to the mismanagement, inefficiency and corruption of the central government. This was intensified by Java's declining share in the export trade, while the foreign earnings of the other islands were used to import rice and consumer goods for Java's increasing population.

The central government, however, effectively smashed the rebellion by mid-1958, though guerrilla activity continued for three years. Rebel leaders were granted amnesty, but the two political parties which they had been connected with were banned and some of the early nationalist leaders were discredited. Sjahrir and others were arrested in 1962.

The defeat of the rebellion was a considerable victory for Sukarno, his supporters and the army, led by General Nasution, which had gained administrative authority throughout the country. The Communist Party had also benefited because it had been a target of criticism by the rebels. Sukarno was now able to exercise enormous personal influence and set about reorganising the political system in order to give himself *real* power.

In 1960 the elected parliament was dis-solved and replaced by a parliament appointed by the president. It had no authority over the president and enacted laws subject to his agreement. A new body, the Supreme Advisory Council, with 45 members including a president who appointed the others, was established and became the chief policy-making body. An organisation called the National Front was set up in September 1960 to 'mobilise the revolutionary forces of the people'. The Front was presided over by the president and became a useful adjunct to the government in organising 'demonstrations' – such as sacking embassies during the period of 'Confrontation' with Malaysia.

Sukarno – Revolution & Nationalism

With his assumption of power, Sukarno set Indonesia on a course of stormy nationalism. During the early 1960s he created a strange language of capital letters: the world was divided between the NEFOS (New Emerging Forces) and the OLDEFOS (Old Established Forces), in which Westerners were the NEKOLIM (the Neo-Colonial Imperialists).

His speeches were those of a romantic revolutionary and they held his people spellbound. *Konfrontasi* become a term to juggle with. Malaysia would be confronted, as would its protector, Britain. The USA would be confronted, as would the whole Western world. The people sometimes called Sukarno *bapak* – father – but he was really *bung*, the daring older brother who carried out the outrageous schemes they wished they could do themselves.

The Western world remembers Sukarno's flamboyance and his contradictions. No other Asian leader has so keenly offended the puritan values of the West; abstinence, monogamy and other virtues were conspicuously undervalued by Sukarno. His notorious liking for women and his real and/or alleged sexual exploits were certainly advantageous to him in Indonesia, where he was not expected to be the good family man, faithful to his wife in the best traditions of Western politics.

He claimed to be a believer in God and also a Marxist – this peculiar blending of contradictory philosophies sprang from the time when he was trying to find common ground against the Dutch. Sukarno set himself up as a conciliator between the nationalist groups because he knew that unity was vital in order to achieve independence. He also made appeals to the emotions and mysticism of the Javanese because these were their characteristics.

Economic Deterioration

What Sukarno could not do was create a viable economic system that would lift Indonesia out of its poverty. Sukarno's corrosive vanity burnt money on a spate of status symbols meant to symbolise the new Indonesian identity. They included the Merdeka (Freedom) Monument, a mosque designed to be the biggest in the world, and a vast sports stadium built with Russian money. Unable to advance beyond revolution to the next stage of rebuilding, with its slow and unspectacular processes, Sukarno's monuments became substitutes for real development.

Richard Nixon, who became the US President in 1968, visited Indonesia in 1953 and presented this image of Indonesia under Sukarno:

In no other country we visited was the conspicuous luxury of the ruler in such striking contrast to the poverty and misery of his people. Jakarta was a collection of sweltering huts and hovels. An open sewer ran through the heart of the city, but Sukarno's palace was painted a spotless white and set in the middle of hundreds of acres of exotic gardens. One night we ate off gold plate to the light of a thousand torches while musicians played on the shore of a lake covered with white lotus blossoms and candles floating on small rafts.

A more aggressive stance on foreign affairs also became a characteristic of Sukarno's increased authority. Sukarno believed that Asia had been humiliated by the West and had still not evened the score. He sought recognition of a new state that was once a 'nation of coolies and a coolie amongst

nations'. Indonesia was also surrounded, and from Sukarno's view threatened, by the remnants of Western imperialism: the British and their new client state of Malaysia; the hated Dutch who continued to occupy West Irian; and the Americans and their military bases in the Philippines.

From this point of view Sukarno's efforts to take over West Irian and his Confrontation with Malaysia – if inadvisable – make some sense. Indonesia walked out of the United Nations in January 1965 after Malaysia had been admitted to the Security Council. Under Sukarno, Indonesia turned its attention towards attaining those territories it had claimed in August 1945. First on the agenda was West Irian, still under Dutch rule. An arms agreement with the Soviet Union in 1960 enabled the Indonesians to begin a diplomatic as well as military confrontation with the Dutch over West Irian. It was pressure from the United States on the Dutch that finally led to the Indonesian takeover in 1963.

The same year Indonesia embarked on Confrontation with the new nation of Malaysia, formed from a federation of the Malay peninsula and the states in northern Borneo which bordered on Indonesian Kalimantan. For Indonesia the formation of Malaysia meant the consolidation of British military power on its own doorstep. Sukarno and Indonesian military leaders also suspected that the British and the Americans had aided the separatist rebels in the archipelago. It took three years for the Confrontation to run its course. It tied up 50,000 British, Australian and New Zealand soldiers in military action along the Kalimantan-Malaysia border, but was never really a serious threat to the survival of Malaysia.

The critical effects of Confrontation were economic. The eight-year economic plan announced in 1963 was intended to increase revenue from taxes, stabilise consumer prices and strengthen the currency. The plan miscarried, in part due to half-heartedness and corruption on the part of military leaders and administrators but mainly because of the runaway inflation caused by the expenses of

Confrontation. Foreign aid dried up because the USA withdrew its aid when Indonesia launched Confrontation.

Without finance the government had to look elsewhere for money. Government subsidies in several areas of the public sector were abolished, leading to massive increases in rail freight, and rail, bus and air fares. Similar increases occurred in electricity, tap water, post and telegraph charges. These rises flowed on to the market, with large increases in the price of basic consumer goods like rice, beef, fish, eggs, salt and soap. Salaries were increased in this period but not enough to keep up with the ever-mounting prices.

Sukarno, the Army & the Communists

Confrontation also alienated Western nations, and Indonesia came to depend more and more on support from the Soviet Union, then increasingly from Communist China. Meanwhile, tensions grew between the Indonesian Army and the PKI (Communist Party). Though Sukarno often talked as if he held absolute power, his position actually depended on maintaining a balance between the different political powers in Indonesia at the time, primarily between the army and the PKI. Sukarno is often described as the great *dalang* or puppet master, who balanced the forces of the left and right just as competing forces are balanced in the Javanese shadow puppet shows.

The PKI was the third largest communist party in the world, outside the Soviet Union and China. By 1965 it claimed to have three million members, it controlled the biggest trade union organisation in Indonesia (the Central All-Indonesian Workers Organisation) and the largest peasant group (the Indonesian Peasant Front). It also had an influence in the major mass organisation (the National Front). The membership of affiliate organisations of the PKI was said to be 15 to 20 million. Except for the inner cabinet, it penetrated the government apparatus extensively.

It is possible that the successes of the party in the 1955 election suggested to Sukarno

that the PKI could be the force that would end centuries of economic oppression of the Indonesian peasant – by feudal lords, the Dutch, the modern upper class, the army, and the superstitions of the people – and to that end he gave the PKI his support.

Guided democracy under Sukarno was marked by an attempt to give the peasants better social conditions but attempts to give tenant farmers a fairer share of their rice crops and to redistribute land led to more confusion. The PKI often pushed for reforms behind the government's back and encouraged peasants to seize land without waiting for decisions from land reform committees. In 1964 these tactics led to violent clashes in Central and East Java and Bali, and the PKI got a reputation as a troublemaker.

The PKI was dissatisfied with what had been achieved domestically and wanted more control of policy making. It also wanted the workers and peasants armed in self-defence units. The pressure increased in 1965 with growing tension between the PKI and the army. The crunch came with the proposal to arm the Communists. The story goes that after a meeting with Zhou Enlai in Jakarta in April 1965, Sukarno secretly decided to accelerate the progress of the Communist Party. He created a 'fifth force' – an armed militia independent of the four branches of the armed forces (the army, navy, air force and police) and arranged for 100,000 rifles to be brought in secretly from China.

Slaughter of the Communists

In the early hours of the morning of 1 October 1965, six of the Indonesian Army's top generals were murdered after military rebels raided their houses. They were the Army Commander and Army Minister, Lieutenant-General Ahmad Yani, who had all Indonesian troops under his control and who opposed the establishment of a fifth force, and members of the Army Central High Command. Three of the generals – Yani, Harjono and Pandjaitan – were shot dead at their homes. Their bodies and the three other generals were taken to the rebel headquarters at Halim air force base outside Jakarta, where those still alive were killed. The home of the Defence Minister, General Nasution, was also attacked but he managed to escape. His five-year-old daughter was killed, and his adjutant Lieutenant Tendean (presumably mistaken for Nasution) was taken to Halim where he was shot with the generals.

Other rebel units occupied the national radio station and the telecommunications building on Merdeka Square, and took up positions around the Presidential Palace, yet there appears to have been little or no attempt to coordinate further revolt in the rest of Java, let alone in the rest of the archipelago. Within a few hours of the beginning of the coup, General Suharto, head of the army's Strategic Reserve, was able to mobilise army forces to take counteraction. By the evening of 1 October the coup had clearly failed, but it was not clear who had been involved or what its effects would be.

It has been argued that the coup was primarily an internal army affair, led by younger officers against the older leadership. The official Indonesian view is that it was an attempt by leaders of the PKI to seize power. There are some who think the Communists were entirely to blame for the coup and support the Indonesian Army's assertion that the PKI plotted the coup and used discontented army officers to carry it out. Another view is that military rebels and the PKI took the initiative separately and then became partners. And then there are those who believe that Sukarno himself was behind the coup – and yet another story that Suharto was in the confidence of one of the conspirators. There is also a theory that Suharto himself provoked the coup as a means of clearing out his rivals in the army as well as Sukarno and seizing power himself – advocates of this theory point out that Suharto was not on the rebels' execution list although he was more important than some of those who were killed.

If the Communists *were* behind the attempted coup then for what reason is anybody's guess. They had been fairly successful up until then, gaining mass support

and influence in government, and had no apparent reason to risk it all on one badly organised escapade. It's been suggested that they may have reacted to Sukarno's apparently deteriorating health and, fearing a military coup once Sukarno was out of the way, decided to act. Yet there's no way that the Communists, if they were behind the coup, could have fought the army even if the 100,000 guns from China had arrived.

Whatever the PKI's real role in the coup, the effect on its fortunes was devastating. With the defeat of the coup, a wave of anti-Communism swept Indonesia; thousands upon thousands of Communists and their sympathisers were slaughtered and more imprisoned. The party and its affiliates were banned, its leaders were killed, imprisoned or went into hiding. Aidit, Chairman of the Party, was eventually shot by government soldiers in November 1965.

Estimates of just how many people were killed vary widely. Adam Malik, the future Foreign Minister under Suharto, said that a 'fair figure' was 160,000; and there are other estimates of 200,000 and 400,000. Army units were organised to kill villagers suspected of being PKI, and anti-Communist civilians were given arms to help with the job. Private grudges were settled and petty landlords seized the opportunity to rid themselves of peasants who, under local PKI leadership, had taken over fields in an attempt to enforce the government's ineffectual land reforms. Debtors also used the opportunity to rid themselves of their creditors. On top of this, perhaps 250,000 people were arrested and sent to prison camps for allegedly being involved in some way with the coup.

Sukarno's Fall & Suharto's Rise

General Suharto took the lead in putting down the attempted coup with remarkable speed. He took over leadership of the armed forces, ended the Confrontation with Malaysia, and carried on a slow and remarkably patient, but not entirely peaceful, duel with Sukarno.

By mid-October 1965 Suharto was in such

Suharto

a strong position that Sukarno appointed him Commander-in-Chief of the armed forces. Army units, under the command of Colonel Sarwo Edhie, began the massacre of the PKI and their supporters in Central Java. Sukarno was aghast at the killings and into the early part of the following year continued to make public statements in support of the Communists. He sacked General Nasution from his position as Defence Minister and Army Chief of Staff. The army responded by organising violent demonstrations made up largely of adolescents. One demonstration tried to storm the Presidential Palace and another ransacked the Foreign Ministry.

Sukarno still had dedicated supporters in all the armed forces and it seemed unlikely that he would topple, despite the street riots and the violence in the countryside. Suharto obviously believed it was time to increase the pressure. On 11 March, after troops loyal to Suharto had surrounded the Presidential Palace, Sukarno signed the 11 March Order

– a vague document which, while not actually handing over the full powers of government to Suharto, officially allowed Suharto to act on his own initiative rather than on directions from the president. While always deferring to the name of Sukarno and talking as if he was acting on Sukarno's behalf, Suharto now set the wheels moving for his own outright assumption of power. The PKI was officially banned. Suharto's troops occupied newspaper houses, radio, cable, telex and telephone offices, and the following day again blockaded the Presidential Palace. Pro-Sukarno officers, men in the armed forces and a number of cabinet ministers were arrested. A new six-man inner cabinet including Suharto and two of his nominees, Adam Malik and Sultan Hamengkubuwono of Yogyakarta, was formed.

Suharto then launched a campaign of intimidation to blunt any grass roots opposition to his steadily increasing power. Thousands of public servants were dismissed as PKI sympathisers, putting thousands more in fear of losing their jobs. Suharto intensified his efforts to gain control of the People's Consultative Congress, the body whose function it was to elect the president. The arrest or murder after the abortive coup of 120 of its 609 members had already ensured a certain amount of docility but despite further pressure, Sukarno managed to hang onto the presidency into 1967. In March of that year, the Congress elected Suharto acting president. On 27 March 1968 it 'elected' him president. One of Suharto's first acts was to break diplomatic relations with China.

The New Order
Suharto wanted the new regime to at least wear the clothes of democracy, and in 1971 general elections were held. Suharto used the almost defunct Golkar party as the spearhead of the army's election campaign. Having appointed his election squad, the old parties were then crippled by being banned, by the disqualification of candidates and by disenfranchising voters. Predictably, Golkar swept to power with 236 of the 360 elective

seats – the PNI was shattered and won just 20 seats. The new People's Consultative Congress also included 207 Suharto appointments and 276 armed forces officers.

Suharto then enforced the merger of other political parties. The four Muslim parties were merged into the Development Union Party, and the other parties into the Indonesian Democratic Party. Political activity between elections and below the district level – ie, in the villages – was prohibited. Since most people lived in the villages this meant there would be no political activity at all outside election campaigns. Effectively, it was the end of Indonesian democracy.

Under Suharto, Indonesia turned away from its isolationist stance and rejoined the United Nations. It joined in the formation of the Association of South-East Asian Nations (ASEAN), reflecting an acceptance of its immediate neighbours in marked contrast to Sukarno's Confrontation with Malaysia. It made a determined effort to attract foreign investment. The largest proportion now comes from Japan, which is also Indonesia's biggest trading partner.

Unfortunately, Indonesia's invasion of East Timor in 1975 not only committed the country to a seemingly interminable war against the Fretilin guerrillas but also strained relations with Australia. This again conjured up the shadow of Confrontation and the image of Indonesia as a potential aggressor. The Indonesians are also continually troubled by Irian Jaya's guerrillas, who have never accepted the Indonesian takeover of the province, consequently straining Indonesian relations with neighbouring Papua New Guinea.

Politically, Indonesia is much more stable but this is mainly because the government's authority rests squarely on a foundation of military power. Opposition has either been eliminated or is kept suppressed and muted. The government sees opposition from several sources including Muslim extremists, university students, Communists, racial tension (particularly anti-Chinese sentiment which could spill over into attacks on the Chinese who run the business enterprises of

Suharto and the other generals) and various dissident groups.

The Communist bogeyman has also failed to disappear. In mid-1985 three members of the East Java branch of the PKI, who had been in prison since the 1965 coup, were executed. In late 1986, nine more former members of the PKI were executed in Jakarta; all had been in prison since the time of the coup. At the time of writing a number of other former PKI members are also awaiting possible execution.

In spite of continued anti-Communist rhetoric, Indonesia restored diplomatic relations with China in 1990 after a 23-year gap. This was a high-profile event in which China's Premier Li Peng visited Jakarta and Suharto went to Beijing later the same year. Singapore – which had no diplomatic relations with China in deference to Indonesia's wishes – restored official ties with China just two months after Indonesia. For China, it was regarded as a major diplomatic coup since the Chinese were desperate to break out of their political isolation, imposed after the bloody 1989 crackdown on prodemocracy demonstrators in Beijing.

GEOGRAPHY

The Republic of Indonesia is the world's most expansive archipelago, stretching almost 5000 km from Sabang off the northern tip of Sumatra, to a little beyond Merauke in south-eastern Irian Jaya. It stretches north and south of the equator for a total of 1770 km, from the border with Sabah to the small island of Roti off the southern tip of Timor.

Officially, the archipelago contains 13,677 islands – from specks of rock to huge islands like Sumatra and Borneo – 6000 of which are inhabited. The five main islands are Sumatra, Java, Kalimantan (Indonesian Borneo), Sulawesi and Irian Jaya (the western part of New Guinea). Most of the country is water; the Indonesians refer to their homeland as *Tanah Air Kita*, which means literally 'Our Earth and Water'. While the total land and sea area of Indonesia is about 2½ times greater than the land area of Australia, Indonesia's total land area is only

1,900,000 sq km, or a little larger than Queensland.

Most of these islands are mountainous; in Irian Jaya there are peaks so high they're snow-capped all year round. North-central Kalimantan and much of central Sulawesi are also mountainous, but in most other parts of Indonesia volcanoes dominate the skyline. Running like a backbone down the western coast of Sumatra is a line of extinct and active volcanoes which continues through Java, Bali and Nusa Tenggara and then loops around through the Banda Islands of Maluku to north-eastern Sulawesi. Some of these have erupted, with devastating effects – the massive blow out of Krakatau in 1883 produced a tidal wave killing 30,000 people, and the 1963 eruption of Gunung Agung on Bali wasted large areas of the island. To many Balinese the eruption of this sacred mountain was a sign of the wrath of the gods, and in East Java the Tenggerese people still offer a propitiatory sacrifice to the smoking Bromo crater which dominates the local landscape. It is also the ash from these volcanoes that has provided Indonesia with some of the finest, richest and most fertile stretches of land on the planet.

Unlike the large sunburnt neighbour to the south, Indonesia is a country of plentiful rainfall, particularly in west Sumatra, north-west Kalimantan, West Java and Irian Jaya. A few areas of Sulawesi and some of the islands closer to Australia – notably Sumba and Timor – are considerably drier but they're exceptions. The high rainfall and the tropical heat make for a very humid climate – but also for a very even one. The highlands of Java and Irian Jaya can get very cold indeed but on the whole most of Indonesia is warm and humid year-round.

Because of this high rainfall and year-round humidity, nearly two-thirds of Indonesia is covered in tropical rainforest – most of it on Sumatra, Kalimantan, Sulawesi and Irian Jaya. Most of the forests of Java disappeared centuries ago as land was cleared for agriculture. Today the rest of Indonesia's rainforest, which is second only to Brazil's in area and makes up 10% of all

the rainforest in the world, is disappearing at a rate of at least 5000 sq km a year – roughly the area of Bali (some estimates say 15,000 sq km). The main culprits are local and foreign timber companies, which carry out little reafforestation, and the government which, to say the least, doesn't discourage the companies. Indonesia is the world's largest wood exporter, selling about US$2 billion worth each year, much of it plywood. Other contributing factors are the clearing of forest for agriculture, transmigration settlements and mining.

In 1983 Indonesia was the scene of probably the greatest forest fire ever recorded, when 30,000 sq km of rainforest were destroyed in the Great Fire of Kalimantan, which lasted nine months. The government blamed shifting 'slash-and-burn' cultivators for this, but outside experts say the fire was triggered by the waste wood and debris left by loggers, setting off peat and coal fires beneath the ground which burned for months.

Along the east coast of Sumatra, the south coast of Kalimantan, Irian Jaya, and much of the northern coast of Java, there is swampy, low-lying land often covered in mangroves. In many areas the over-clearing of natural growth has led to a continual erosion as topsoil is washed down the rivers by heavy rains, simultaneously wreaking havoc with the Indonesian roads.

The tropical vegetation, the mountainous terrain and the break up of the country into numerous islands, has always made communication difficult between islands and between different parts of each island. But it is these factors which have had a marked effect on its history and culture, and also explain some of the peculiarities of the country and its people.

Firstly, Indonesia straddles the equator between the Indian Ocean to the west and the Pacific Ocean to the east. To the north are China and Japan, to the north-west India and beyond that Arabia. Because of this central position the Indonesian islands – particularly Sumatra and Java – and the Malay peninsula have long formed a stopover and staging ground on the sea routes between India and China, a convenient midway point where merchants of the civilised world met and exchanged goods.

Secondly, the regular and even climate (there are some exceptions – in some of the islands east of Java and Bali the seasonal differences are pronounced, and even within Java some districts have a sufficiently marked dry season to suffer drought at times) means that a rhythm of life for many Indonesian farmers is based less on the annual fluctuations of the seasons than on the growth pattern of their crops. In areas with heavy rainfall and terraced rice field cultivation there is no set planting season or harvest season, but a continuous flow of activity where at any one time one hillside may demonstrate the whole cycle of rice cultivation, from ploughing to harvesting.

Politically, Indonesia is divided into 27 provinces for administration by the central government. Java has five provinces: Jakarta Raya, West Java, Central Java, Yogyakarta and East Java. Sumatra has eight provinces – Aceh, North Sumatra, West Sumatra, Riau, Jambi, Bengkulu, South Sumatra and Lampung. Kalimantan has West, Central, South and East provinces. Sulawesi has North, Central, South and South-Eastern provinces. Other provinces are: Bali, West Nusa Tenggara (Lombok and Sumbawa), East Nusa Tenggara (Sumba, West Timor, Flores, and the Solor and Alor Archipelagos), East Timor, the Moluccas (Maluku) and Irian Jaya.

Java is the hub of Indonesia and its most heavily populated island. The capital of Indonesia, Jakarta, is located on the island's north-western coast. While the Javanese are the dominant group in Indonesian politics and in the military, their control over the other islands is a tenuous one for the reasons already mentioned. The diversity of the archipelago's inhabitants and the break-up of the country into numerous islands helps to fuel separatism – and since the formation of the republic in 1949 the central administration in Jakarta has fought wars against separatists in West Java, Sumatra, Minahasa

in northern Sulawesi, West Irian and Maluku.

Indonesia shares borders with Malaysia and Papua New Guinea. Relations with Malaysia were unhappy during the Sukarno era and the period of 'Confrontation' but since then they have very much improved. Trouble with Papua New Guinea results from continuing problems with the OPM (Free West Papua) guerrillas who refuse to recognise Indonesian sovereignty over West Irian and take refuge in Papua New Guinea. East Timor remained a colony of Portugal up until independence but was invaded by Indonesia in 1975.

CLIMATE

Straddling the equator, Indonesia tends to have a fairly even climate all year round. There are no seasons comparable with the four that Westerners are familiar with, and you do not get the extremes of winter and summer as you do in Europe or some parts of Asia such as China and northern India.

Indonesians distinguish between a wet season and a dry season. In most parts of Indonesia the wet season falls between October and April, and the dry season between May and September. In some parts you don't really notice the difference – the hot season just seems to be slightly hotter and not quite so wet as the wet season; moreover the rain comes in sudden tropical downpours. In other parts – like Maluku – you really do notice the additional water; it rains almost non-stop and travelling during this period becomes more than difficult.

The Indonesians may tell you it gets cold in their country – you'll often see them running around in long-sleeved shirts and even winter coats in the stifling heat! In fact, it's invariably hot and generally humid during the day and warm during the night. Once you get up into the hills and mountains the temperature drops dramatically – in the evenings and during the night it can be amazingly cold! Camp out at night atop Gunung Rinjani in Lombok without a sleeping bag, and you'll be as stiff as those wood carvings they sell in Bali. Sleeping out at night on the deck of a small boat or ship can also be bitterly cold, no matter how oppressive the heat may be during the day. You don't exactly need Antarctic survival gear, but bring jeans and some warm clothes. There is a 'cold season' if you want to call it that, mainly July and August, but you're only likely to notice it in the 'deep south' (about 10° south of the equator) and again, mostly in the highlands.

At the other end of the thermometer, an hour's walk along Kuta Beach in the middle of the day will roast you a nice bright red – bring a hat, sunglasses and some sunscreen (UV) lotion.

Java

Across the island the temperature throughout the year averages 22 to 29°C (78 to 85°F) and humidity averages a high 75%, but the north coastal plains are usually hotter (up to 34°C (94°F) during the day in the dry season) and more oppressively humid than anywhere else. Generally the south coast is a bit cooler than the north coast, and the mountainous regions inland are very much cooler.

The wet season is between October and the end of April. The rain comes as a tropical downpour, falling most afternoons during the wet season and intermittently at other times of the year. The heaviest rains are usually around January-February. Although the climate is generally hot and wet, there are some surprising variations across the island. Large areas of West Java average over 3000 mm (166 inches) of rain a year while East Java, particularly in the lowlands, has a rainfall of only 35 inches and occasional droughts. The dry season in Java is between May and September, and probably the best time to visit the island is June, July and August.

Bali

Here it is much like Java; the dry season is between April and September. The coolest months of the year are generally May, June and July with the average temperature around 28°C (82°F). The rainy season is between October and March but the tropical

showers alternate with clear skies and sunshine; the hottest months of the year are generally February and March, with the average temperature around 30°C (86°F). Overall, the best time to visit the island is in the dry and cooler months between May and August, with cool evenings and fresh breezes coming in off the sea.

Sumatra

The climate of Sumatra resembles that of Java and is hot and extremely humid. The equator cuts this island into two roughly equal halves and, since the winds of northern Sumatra differ from those of the rest of the archipelago, so does the timing of the seasons, though temperatures remain pretty constant year-round. North of the equator the heaviest rainfall is between October and April and the dry season is May to September. South of the equator the heaviest rainfall is in December to February, though it will have started raining in September. In Sumatra heavy rains can make bad roads impassable.

Nusa Tenggara

In the islands east of Bali the seasonal differences are more pronounced. The driest months are August and September, and the wettest months are November to February. However, the duration of the seasons varies from island to island. The seasons on Lombok are more like those on Bali, with a dry season from April to September and a wet season from October to March. Much the same applies to Sumbawa and Flores. The duration of the dry season increases the closer you get to Australia – the rusty landscapes of Sumba and Timor are a sharp contrast to well-vegetated Flores. At 11° south latitude, Timor is also the only island in Indonesia far enough from the equator to get typhoons (cyclones), but these are rare. Nearby northern Australia is not so lucky.

Sulawesi

The wettest months here tend to be from around November-December to March-April but in central and northern Sulawesi the rainfall seems to be a bit more evenly spread throughout the year. In the mountainous regions of central Sulawesi, even in the dry season it may rain by late afternoon – likewise in the northern peninsula. The south-eastern peninsula is the driest part of the island.

Temperatures drop quite considerably going from the lowlands to the mountains. Average temperatures along the coast range from around 26 to 30°C, but in the mountains the average temperature drops by 5°C.

Except in south-western Sulawesi and the Minahasa region of the north (or in odd places where foreign mining companies operate) the wet season turns the mostly unsurfaced roads into excruciatingly frustrating vehicle-bogging mud. It makes travel by road in some parts of the island either impossible or tedious at these times – there's some improvement being made to the roads so check out the current situation when you get there – be prepared to fly, skirt the coast in ships or even do some walking.

Kalimantan

Permanently hot and damp; the wettest period is October to March, and the driest period is July to September. Although the sun predominates between April and September be prepared for heavy tropical downpours during this period.

Maluku (The Moluccas)

Maluku is the big exception to the rules in Indonesia. Whilst the wet season everywhere else is from October to April, in Maluku the wet season is April through to July, and may even carry on to the end of August. Travelling in Maluku during the wet is hardly worth contemplating; the sea is too rough during this time for small boats, so there are fewer inter-island connections. Even when you do get to wherever it is you want to go you'll end up spending most of your time there sheltering in your hotel from the elements. The best time to visit is September to March.

Irian Jaya

Irian Jaya is hot and humid in the coastal regions. In the highlands it's warm by day, but can get very cold by night – and the higher you go the colder it gets! August and September in the highlands will be gloomy and misty. In the northern part of Irian Jaya, May to October is the drier season and May is the hottest month. Southern Irian Jaya has a much more well-defined season than the northern part of the island.

FLORA & FAUNA

Indonesia harbours one of the world's richest natural environments, where diverse plant and animal species thrive.

The western part of the country was once linked to the Asian mainland, and as a result some large Asian land animals, including elephants, tigers, rhinoceros and leopards, still survive (barely).

One of Indonesia's most famous animals is the Komodo dragon, the world's largest lizard, found only on the island of Komodo and a few neighbouring islands. Kalimantan is well-known for its orang-utan, a primate which more closely resembles humans than any other. Sumatra has the world's largest flower, the Rafflesia, which can grow up to a metre in diameter.

The offshore coral reefs provide a luxuriant haven for abundant species of marine life, as well as providing opportunities for snorkelling and scuba diving.

The tropical rainforests of Kalimantan and Irian Jaya probably harbour rare plant and animal species which have not yet even been identified. Unfortunately, the impact of

Sunda rhinoceros

human development, especially logging and agriculture, is no doubt having adverse effects on the environment. The sad reality is that some species are destined to disappear before they've even been discovered by the humans who have doomed them.

Even 'common' domestic animals have an unusual twist in Indonesia. Many travellers have noticed that Indonesian cats usually have broken, bent or missing tails. Fortunately, this is not due to some maniac running around the country attacking cats with a meat cleaver – it's simply a genetic trait.

Sea Turtles

Sea turtles are found in the waters around Bali and throughout Indonesia, and are a popular delicacy, particularly for feasts. In several places they are herded before being slaughtered. Bali is the site of the most intensive slaughter of green sea turtles in the world. Green sea turtles are killed mainly for their meat, and the shells of the hawksbill turtle are used to make jewellery, haircombs and other trinkets, which are sold to tourists. It's estimated that more than 20,000 turtles are killed in Bali each year.

The environmental group Greenpeace has long campaigned to protect Indonesia's sea turtles. It appeals to travellers to Indonesia not to eat turtle meat or buy any sea-turtle products, including tortoiseshell items, stuffed turtles or turtle-leather goods. Indonesia is a signatory to the Convention on International Trade in Endangered Species (CITES) and as such bans the import and export of products made from endangered species. It is therefore illegal to export any products made from green sea turtles or turtle shells from Indonesia. And in many countries including Australia, the USA, the UK and other EC countries it's illegal to import turtle products without a permit. So, in the interests of conservation, as well as conformity to customs laws, please don't buy turtle-shell or any other turtle products.

National Parks

Although environmentalists have blasted

Indonesia's government for its logging and transmigration development schemes, it's only fair to mention that the past decade has seen a rapid increase in the number of national parks, nature reserves and historical sites. While it's true that loggers, farmers and hunters have even violated national parks, there has been a sincere effort to enforce the rules – no easy task in a country with so much sparsely inhabited jungle. All the large islands – Sumatra, Java, Kalimantan, Sulawesi and Irian Jaya – have national parks, and there are other parks to protect special places like Komodo. Some of these parks are enormous in size, have few or no roads and are mostly accessible by foot, boat or an aircraft landing on lakes.

The Indonesian national park service, PHPA (Perlindungan Hutan dan Pelestarian Alam) maintains information offices at various points around the country. You may have to visit these offices occasionally to obtain required permits for a few remote areas. The staff are generally friendly and can usually supply helpful information about the park you want to visit. You'll find the locations of the local PHPA offices mentioned in the relevant sections of this book.

GOVERNMENT

Executive power rests with the president, who is head of state and holds office for a period of five years. Officially, highest authority rests with the People's Consultative Congress (MPR) which sits at least once every five years and is responsible for electing the president. The congress is composed of all the members of the House of Representatives (which sits once a year) along with those appointed by the president to represent various groups and regions. Technically, the president is responsible only to the People's Consultative Congress, which elects him and the vice-president. The president appoints ministers to his cabinet and they are responsible only to him.

Party politics, what there is of it, continues under the one 'group' and two-party system devised by Suharto in the early 1970s. This involves the government-run Golkar which is technically not a political party, the Muslim United Development Party (PPP) and the Indonesian Democratic Party (PDI). Distinctions between the parties are deliberately being blurred. The enforced acceptance of the Pancasila philosophy as the sole philosophical base for all political, social and religious organisations is also aimed partly at defusing, and partly at suppressing, dissent.

Suharto has shown himself to be remarkably resilient. His rule is certainly not unopposed but he has continually sought to reaffirm his authority and has successfully met any challenges. Being president of Indonesia is like riding a tiger – the succession problem looms closer and closer with each passing year and, unless Suharto dies in the saddle, his real problem is to make sure he doesn't get eaten if he decides to step down.

The big issue dominating Indonesian politics in the early 1990s has been the succession of Suharto. In 1988, he was 'elected' to his 5th five-year term. While he has made no public declaration of his intentions to stand for re-election again in 1993 (when he will be 72 years old), there is little doubt that he is already manoeuvring to secure a sixth term.

Opposition is building. Even prominent members of the military have suggested that he ought to retire when his current term ends, provoking strong verbal threats from Suharto. The press – which has become increasingly daring in 1991, with the military's support – has become more critical of Suharto.

An interesting trend is that Suharto has started to sound more and more 'Islamic' in his public pronouncements – interesting because he has devoted much of his career to extolling secularism while suppressing Islamic fundamentalists, who he considers the greatest threat to Indonesia's political stability. Because there is growing opposition from the military to Suharto seeking yet another presidential term in 1993, some speculate that he is ready to play the 'Muslim card' to hang on to power. In 1990, a petition by 21 prominent Muslim leaders was circulated, endorsing Suharto for another presidential term. In 1991, Suharto made his first-ever pilgrimage to Mecca. Golkar Party MPs who have dared to criticise Suharto have found themselves dropped from the list of candidates who can run for re-election (they need the party's permission) and replaced with candidates with impeccable Muslim credentials. Suharto's new strategy is clearly a gamble – he is alienating the army, the final 'trump card' in Indonesian politics.

The Army

For most of his career, Suharto and the army have been as close as lips and teeth. It was the military that swept Suharto into power, and it is largely the military that has kept him there. Suharto's presently deteriorating relations with the military could be his undoing.

The present cabinet contains only a minority of military men but they hold some important ministerial positions. The Defence Minister, General Benny Murdani, for example, is probably the second most powerful man in Indonesia today. Despite its minority in the cabinet, and the fact that Suharto prefers a civilian image in public, the army is where political power in Indonesia rests. Both the political and the military philosophy of the Indonesian army positively encourages involvement in politics, and the army hardly regards itself as having usurped power that somehow 'rightfully' belongs to civilians. It was General Nasution who was largely responsible for developing the idea of the army having a social and political as well as a military role.

This idea was taken and developed at the Army Staff & Command School in the late '50s and early '60s (when the then Colonel Suharto was a student there). It was decided that national defence policy was to be based on the army, since the navy and air force would never be strong enough to block an invasion. The army would have to be one that could continue, in the last resort, an indefinite guerrilla struggle. To be successful in such a war the army would have to be accepted and supported by the people.

Therefore, to prepare for this eventuality, the army would have to be permanently in contact with the people at a local level so as to build up and sustain their goodwill. Thus developed the idea and the subsequent implementation of 'Territorial Management', the establishment of a parallel administration down to village level where resident army personnel could supervise and prod the civil authorities. There is the assumption within the Indonesian army that it *should* play a central role in uniting the nation and guiding its development.

The President

Suharto was born in 1921 and spent his childhood amongst peasants in small villages in Central Java and in Solo, his father ensuring that he got a primary and middle school education. The time he spent from the age of 15 living in the house of a *dukun* (faith healer) appears to have imbued him with a sense of traditional Javanese mysticism which has lasted to this day. He joined the Royal Dutch Indies Army in 1940 and quickly became a sergeant. He served with the Japanese during the occupation and became an officer in the Japanese-sponsored Volunteer Army of Defenders of the Motherland. He led attacks against the Dutch during the independence struggle after WW II and rose rapidly through the ranks.

In 1962 he was promoted to Major-General by Sukarno and was put in charge of the forces which were set up to take West Irian from the Dutch. In 1961 he became commander of the army's Strategic Reserve (later to be known as KOSTRAD). This was an important posting because the reserve, set up by Nasution, was a well-equipped, highly mobile fighting force directly at the disposal of the General Staff, thus avoiding any argument or even outright opposition from regional commanders.

Just why Suharto took the role of overthrowing Sukarno is unclear – perhaps it was personal ambition, a reaction to the attempted coup, unease at the growing strength of the PKI, a reaction to the deterioration of the economy under Sukarno, or a mixture of all four. Certainly Suharto cut through his opponents with exceptional determination.

One thing is certain – Suharto, and his relatives, have become very rich since he came to power. For example, in 1991, the president's son, Tommy Suharto, was granted the lucrative clove monopoly. In Suharto's 1989 autobiography, the president stated that his family's financial dealings were simply 'social work'.

The Pancasila Democracy

The present regime calls its rule the 'Pancasila democracy'. Since it was first expounded by Sukarno in 1945 the Pancasila (Five Principles) have remained the philosophical backbone of the Indonesian state. It was meant by Sukarno to provide a broad philosophical base on which a united Indonesian state could be formed. All over Indonesia you'll see the Indonesian coat of arms (illustrated on the next page) with its symbolic incorporation of the Pancasila, hung on the walls of government offices and the homes of village heads, on the covers of student textbooks or immortalised on great stone tablets. These principles are:

1. Faith in God – symbolised by the star. It doesn't matter which God – Allah, Vishnu, Buddha or whoever – but all Indonesians must believe in God.

2. Humanity – symbolised by the chain. This represents the unbroken unity of humankind, and Indonesia takes its place amongst this family of nations.

3. Nationalism – symbolised by the head of the buffalo. All ethnic groups in Indonesia must unite.

4. Representative government – symbolised by the banyan tree. As distinct from the Western brand of parliamentary democracy, Sukarno envisaged a form of Indonesian democracy based on the village system of deliberation (*permusyawaratan*) among representatives to achieve consensus (*mufakat*).

The Western system of 'majority rules' is considered a means by which 51% oppress the other 49%.

5. Social justice – symbolised by the sprays of rice and cotton. A just and prosperous society gives adequate supplies of food and clothing for all – these are the basic requirements of social justice.

While the Pancasila was originally designed as a means of uniting the Indonesians, in practice different political groups have sought to interpret the five principles to serve their own purposes. The attempt by Sukarno to satisfy all religious groups in the archipelago by affirming belief in an unspecified God was not entirely successful, as many Muslims insisted that the only valid religion was Islam and the only true God was Allah.

Pancasila crest

ECONOMY

Indonesia is potentially one of the wealthiest countries in the world, as it is endowed with substantial natural resources. The Indonesian government gets something like 60 to 65% of its revenue from oil taxes, and 70 to 80% of export earnings comes from oil. Indonesia is the world's eighth largest oil producer and the largest exporter of liquefied natural gas. Its vast, though disappearing, rainforests produce plenty of timber and wood products like furniture, much of which is exported. There are also large reserves of tin, coal, copper and bauxite, substantial cash crops like rubber, coffee and copra, and there is now a determined effort to attract the tourist dollar. The problem is utilising these resources effectively; the dependence on oil and natural gas exports makes Indonesia particularly vulnerable to any slump in the world economy, while other raw materials are shipped out of the country with minimal benefit to the local people except a few tycoons with government connections.

During the Suharto era the Indonesian economy has largely been governed by an alliance between army leaders and Western-educated economists. Rigorous economic measures were taken in the first years of the regime designed to get Indonesia back on its feet after the economic mismanagement of the Sukarno years. Sufficiently large cuts were made in government expenditure to balance the budget; the plunge of the rupiah was halted; rice prices were kept temporarily in check by establishing a reserve which reduced speculation; inflation was dramatically reduced; and there was some success in stabilising the price of other basic commodities.

Under Suharto's rule the Planning Body for National Development *(Bappenas)* has implemented a series of Five Year Development Plans designed to rehabilitate and improve the economy. The acronym for these plans is Pelita, *pelita* also being the word for a lamp which illuminates a wayang performance. While there has been overall improvement, the Indonesian economy over the last 20 years has been racked by incompetence, mismanagement and corruption.

Corruption

There is one seemingly static, permanent feature of the Indonesian economy – corruption. High-placed government officials, and their families, routinely become quite wealthy during their terms in office.

It would certainly be an understatement to say that the army and the economy of Indonesia are closely knit; military leaders head or are mixed up with an incredible range of business enterprises. The reason for this can partly be found in the 1950s when conventional sources of revenue for the army were so inadequate that other sources had to be found for army leaders to keep their units going. The army was not the only poorly paid institution; civil servants and professional people were taking second jobs and running private businesses to supplement inadequate official pay packets.

In 1957 Dutch assets in Indonesia were seized as part of the government's anti-Dutch nationalisation policy of the time. The seizures were carried out by the army and it left the officers in charge of running factories, trading companies and plantations. Some profits were directed back to their units and in areas with export produce, smuggling flourished. The problem with this sort of system is where philanthropy ends and corruption begins, where bonds of mutual loyalty mean that associates get promoted at the expense of competence, and where the army starts using its muscle – such as martial law powers – to help its profitable business enterprises keep making a profit.

Official kleptomania is not new under Suharto – it was normal under the Dutch rule, the rule of the VOC and during the rule of the Indonesian princes who farmed out monopolies and revenue-collecting agencies to favoured court clients. During the first years of independence one needed friends in key bureaucratic positions, and on a small scale this meant cash payments to petty officials. For big business it required an alliance with a minister or senior bureaucrat. When the regime changed in 1965-67 many business fiefdoms also changed – the Mercedes Benz dealership, for example, passed from a PNI-linked businessman to an army trading company, and when that collapsed it went into the hands of General Ibnu Sutowo, who ran the Pertamina oil conglomerate.

While corruption is not a new problem in Indonesia it has certainly been worsened by the political changes since 1965. These changes are the extension of the parallel military administration, and the removal of any counterbalancing political forces. These forces are needed to keep in check the often united front of military and civilian administrators, security officials and other local notables.

The Pertamina Debacle

The classic example of kleptocracy and mismanagement under the Suharto government was the near-collapse of the oil company Pertamina and the industrial empire which had grown out of it under the control of Lieutenant-General Ibnu Sutowo (originally appointed to his position by President Sukarno).

The company originated from an oil company under army control which was established in 1957 to develop the north Sumatra oilfields. By 1967 Pertamina had taken over management and control of the nation's oil production. By 1974 Pertamina's interests moved into all sorts of other enterprises: petrochemical production, fertilisers, shipping and real estate, steel manufacture, rice production in Sumatra, even an airline (Pelita).

Sutowo had turned Pertamina into a private financial and industrial complex accountable to nobody but him. In one of the last-gasp efforts of what was left of the free press in 1969, Sutowo was accused by the newspaper *Indonesia Raja* of frittering away loans and oil revenue on irrelevant ventures including a mosque at the University of Indonesia, a US$2.5 million sports stadium at Palembang, a travel office and two hotels in Jakarta, and a restaurant in New York. He was also making profits from his position as a director of a Hong Kong insurance company he had set up to insure Pertamina's ships. He sold mining concessions to friends for nominal fees who resold them for huge profits; he collected what amounted to presents from foreigners worth US$60 million; he devised contracts by which Indonesia actually lost money by selling oil through Japanese trading companies. The paper listed the names, prices and market values of five second-hand tankers which Pertamina was supposed to have bought – on Sutowo's instructions – for more than they were worth, the implication being that someone got a kickback.

Pertamina's schemes were financed by heavy borrowing from overseas and by the early 1970s it had got out of hand. Loans were being repaid with other loans and an enormous debt had accumulated. Finally the Japanese and US banks came to their senses and loans to Pertamina dried up. Pertamina finally crashed in early 1975 and the government had to bail it out. The government took over the responsibility of repaying Pertamina's debts and also determined that in future all borrowing for state enterprises should be through the Bank of Indonesia or the Ministry of Finance. Sutowo was replaced as head of Pertamina in 1976. Pertamina's total debts were then estimated at US$10.5 billion – greater than the total 1976-77 national budget and two-thirds of the gross domestic product!

Foreign Stakes

The USA and Japan have the biggest economic stakes in Indonesia. Their interests in the archipelago increased significantly between WW I and II although their investments were still well behind the Dutch and British. Japanese and US interests included tin and rubber – they looked to Indonesia as a source of natural rubber, as an alternative supplier to British-controlled Malaya – and they tried to gain a foothold in the Indonesian oil industry. There had been little exploitation of Indonesia's resources before WW II but they remained a factor in US thinking and policy concerning South-East Asia.

With the fall of Sukarno, Suharto made a determined effort to attract foreign aid and investment. Old debts were recognised by the Indonesian government, nationalised estates of former foreign owners were restored, and laws were passed to encourage foreign capital investments. Foreign investors have indeed been active in Indonesia – familiar Western brand names like Coca-Cola and Bayer make this obvious. Most Western products you see on sale all over Indonesia are not imported – rather, they are manufactured locally under licence or as joint-venture operations.

On the other hand, bureaucracy, corruption and a host of restrictions have discouraged many foreign companies from setting up operations in Indonesia. The area in which Indonesia has been most successful in attracting foreign capital is not in joint ventures, but in loans – Indonesia has run up an enormous foreign debt. Theoretically, such loans should have been used to develop export industries which would generate foreign capital to service the debt. This is the development model that has worked so successfully in South Korea, for instance. In practice, Indonesia has developed very little manufacturing capability and instead relies on exports of oil, natural gas and coffee to pay off creditors. Disasters like the Pertamina debacle haven't helped. So far, Indonesia has managed to pay its bills, but with much difficulty.

The Rural Sector

Although Indonesia produces a range of agricultural products, including exotic introductions from Latin America thanks to the early Spanish and Portuguese settlers, the staple produce remains rice. As you move across the archipelago you also find other staples including maize (corn) and sago in the extreme east.

Rice cultivation in terraced sawah fields has been known for over 2000 years. In sparsely populated areas of Sumatra, Kalimantan and West Java, where the peasants moved from one place to another, a form of shifting cultivation or ladang was developed. In ladang cultivation the jungle is burned off to speed up the normal process of decomposition and enrich the soil in preparation for planting, but the soil quickly loses its fertility.

With the exception of Bali and most of Java, plus a few much smaller patches across the archipelago, the soil is just as poor in Indonesia as it is elsewhere in the tropics.

When the top cover of forest is removed the intense heat and heavy rain soon leach the soil of its fertility. As a result settled agriculture is impossible without the continuous addition of soil nutrients.

The difficulties of making any improvement in the rural sector are immense and various schemes introduced in the late '60s and '70s often had poor results due to poor planning, official bungling or corruption. Some schemes, while increasing productivity or improving the lot of the land-owning farmers, completely missed other sectors of the population such as the landless farm labourers, or actually made them worse off. The introduction of high-yield varieties of rice from 1968, however, has made a great difference.

Deregulation & Privatisation

As in many Third-World countries, Indonesian business grew up behind a protective wall of barriers. Import and export monopolies were granted to favoured clients (including Suharto's relatives and cronies), tariffs kept out imports, and restrictions were placed on foreign ownership. The government had monopoly control over key industries like banking, oil refining, airlines, TV, radio, telephones and toll roads. These measures were supposedly designed to protect the economy.

Instead, these rules gave birth to a bungling and corrupt bureaucracy. Protected industries like banks were so inefficient they could charge usurious interest rates. Keeping out foreign investment meant Indonesia had to instead seek foreign loans to develop its own industries, resulting in a build-up of debt. High import taxes and government-sanctioned import monopolies meant Indonesian companies found the cost of foreign-made components so high that they couldn't develop export industries. Export monopolies meant that coffee farmers, for example, could look forward to low prices while the exporter got rich.

From the late 1980s onwards there has been a change in attitudes. Following world trends – largely inspired by the 'Thatcher revolution' in Britain – deregulation is the word. The banking industry was thrown open to foreign joint ventures, resulting in a sharp drop in interest rates and a boom in investment. Import monopolies have been mostly eliminated, resulting in lower prices to consumers and export-oriented manufacturers. While foreigners are not permitted to own land in Indonesia, a deregulation measure implemented in 1989 permitted foreigners to establish industrial manufacturing estates. As a result, foreign money has started pouring in, much of it to the island of Batam, a free-trade zone 20 km south of Singapore. Rules on stock trading were liberalised in 1989, causing the Jakarta Stock Exchange to become Asia's hottest market for the year, drawing in plenty of capital for new investment.

The government still controls about 200 companies, but privatisation is gaining speed. There are now private TV stations. Toll roads in Jakarta are private ventures. Competition has entered the telecommunications industry, which has seen an explosion of 'Warpostal' agencies: private companies offering 24-hour fax, telex, telephone and mail service. Government-owned hotels, built to attract tourists but often poorly-managed and falling apart, are now being sold off.

All this has made a visible improvement in economic growth and living standards in the past few years. However, it has also exacerbated the highly visible economic gap between the 'haves' and 'have-nots'.

Tourism

Indonesians have long recognised the importance of foreign tourism. In 1989 the government announced that it had passed its target of 1¼ million visitors a year, bringing in more than US$1 billion of foreign exchange – then promptly set a new goal of 2½ to three million by 1994! It's the up-market foreign cash cows that Indonesia really wants to pull in. On the other hand, much to the consternation of Indonesia's neighbours, Indonesians must pay a 250,000 rp exit tax when leaving the country. This effectively reduces to a trickle the flow of Indonesian tourists visiting nearby Singapore, Malaysia and Thailand.

Western Europe is still regarded as the steadiest source of longer-staying visitors, followed by the USA. Countries in the region – like Australia, Singapore, Japan and Malaysia – are also important sources of tourists. In Bali the Japanese are the second biggest group of foreign visitors – trooping in behind the Australians, who often appear to have co-evolved there with surfboards and motorcycles.

Amongst other ideas aimed at stimulating the tourist trade are: campaigns to attract conventions; more hotel rooms in Jakarta and Bali; the new airport in Jakarta; promotion of 'marine tourism' including the great rivers of Sumatra and Kalimantan; even roadside inns along the Trans-Sumatran Highway with a view to developing tours of the island by car. But perhaps the best achievement of the push for more tourists is another deregulation measure – the two-month tourist pass, which eliminates the need for a visa, as long as you enter the country through specific airports or seaports, and makes travel in Indonesia much easier than it was in the past.

Poverty & Prospects for the Future

Government-sponsored and financed irrigation projects, fertiliser subsidies and cheap agricultural credit enabled Indonesia to become self-sufficient in rice production by 1982, and thus reduce its risky dependency on food imports. While this was a significant step forward, attempts to alleviate poverty have met with a mixed bag of successes and failures.

To help assure access to essential goods, both the Sukarno and the Suharto governments operated a nationwide system of subsidies and price controls for necessities, including rice, wheat, sugar, cooking kerosene and gasoline. Increasing financial stringency in recent years has forced cutbacks on subsidies, plus the recognition that low prices hurt production. The free market is being given a freer hand, but the adjustments will be painful. In particular the domestic price of oil has risen, forcing up the price of everything else. Nevertheless, consumption of oil continues to increase, a worrying prospect, as Indonesia's oil reserves are showing signs of exhaustion and the country could well become a net oil importer in 10 or 20 years.

Health care has received high priority with considerable expansion in the number of health centres. One sign of general improvement has been a significant drop in the infant mortality rate – from 14% in the early 1970s to 9% today (by comparison the Australian infant mortality rate is 1% and the Japanese is 0.7%). Education also has a high priority and, except for some isolated areas, nearly all children have access to primary school education. However, many drop out early, there is a shortage of qualified teachers and in rural areas the quality of education doesn't ensure that the majority of children will leave school literate.

Privatisation has enabled the establishment of new industries and increased employment opportunities, but mostly in the cities. The production of these industries and the employment they offer reaches only a small proportion of the population, which is still overwhelmingly rural, with a large proportion working on small farms. The average Indonesian farm labourer gets by on very little. Similarly, textile workers, *bemo* (a small 'truck' used as local transport) drivers, teachers and civil servants are all poorly paid.

While rural productivity has increased, so has rural unemployment. The introduction of sickles, rotary weeders replacing hand weeding, and even Japanese hand-tractors has reduced the need for farm labour and benefited the larger farmers at the expense of the labourers. Unemployed rural residents tend to migrate to the cities in search of the elusive pot of gold, but with poor education and skills they often wind up as squatters in the slums of Jakarta and other cities.

As elsewhere in the Third World, the rich get richer and the poor get children. Although initially a burden, children are regarded as an economic asset because they provide a form of social security for the parents. High birth rates are highest among the poor. The unfortunate result is that the fastest growing segment of the population is the least educated and least likely to succeed economically. Campaigns in support of the two-child family go largely unheeded (a failing hardly unique to the Indonesian government).

Because political activity and organisations are now banned at village level (except during the staged elections held every five years) the rural poor – the labourers and those with minimal holdings – are completely unprotected by any sort of legislation, political party, union or other organisation. There may not be any organised resistance but every so often some sporadic outburst of violence is reported in the Indonesian press, such as: West Javanese villagers burning down a caustic-soda factory whose acid discharge had poisoned their paddy fields and fish ponds; attacks by canoe-fishermen on trawlers intruding into their fishing grounds; wrecking of tractors, and 'night harvests' on the fields of landed farmers.

Although Indonesia is better off than it was 20 years ago, the fruits of this economic growth are very unevenly distributed. Yet somehow even the poorest of Indonesians show a remarkable resilience and capacity to survive. They sell food, clothing, plastic shoes, sit on the side of the street all day flogging off a few combs or a couple of bunches of bananas, jump on crowded buses to hawk ice blocks, pineapple chunks, or single cigarettes. They sift through garbage, recycle the tobacco from cigarette ends, pedal *becaks* (trishaws), shine shoes, mind parked cars or scratch some of the money from the tourist industry as touts. And if they come home with nothing then their family or neighbours will help them to survive another day.

POPULATION

Indonesia's total population is around 180 million. Java alone has about 108 million people.

Indonesia's population is growing at a rate of about 1.8% per year. If it continues at that rate it will have almost 200 million people by the turn of the century. By the year 2035 the population will be around 300 million. Overpopulation, however, is largely a Javanese and, to some extent, a Balinese problem. Java's population was estimated as six million in 1825, 9.5 million in 1850, 18 million in 1875, 28 million in 1900, 36 million in 1925, 63 million in 1961 and 99 million in 1985.

Java and the island of Madura off Java's north coast have a total area of 130,000 sq km or about 1½ times the area of the UK. Java's population density is more than 800 people per sq km, more than twice that of either England or Holland (the two most densely populated countries in Europe) and more than twice that of Japan. Population in Indonesia is very unevenly distributed.

Island(s)	Area	Population
Bali & Nusa Tenggara	4.61%	5.7%
Java	6.89%	60.7%
Kalimantan	28.11%	4.7%
Maluku & Irian Jaya	25.87%	1.8%
Sulawesi	9.85%	7.1%
Sumatra	24.67%	19.9%

Population Control

Each year over three million people are added to the Indonesian population, most of them in Java. However, there are birth control programmes operating in Indonesia but whether they have had much success is debatable.

After taking power Suharto reversed Sukarno's policies of continued population expansion to provide a work force to develop the outer islands. He set up a National Family Planning Co-ordinating Board which greatly expanded the network of private clinics providing free contraceptive services. Efforts were concentrated on Bali and Java at first and noticeable drops in the birth rate were reported. It was also reported that over 80% of the people who took part in the scheme were the wives of peasants, fisherpeople and labourers – the poorer end of the scale who normally have the most children.

There has been lesser success in highly traditional areas (like Yogyakarta) and in the more strongly Muslim areas. A major obstacle to change amongst the latter group is the popular belief that Allah will take care of a family's needs no matter how big it grows.

The board's most noticeable propaganda is the Happy Family symbol – a couple with two children – on the five rupiah coin, which is the smallest coin in circulation. There has also been a blitz of slogan propaganda; *Kami keluarga kecil yang bahagia dan sejahtera*, for example, means 'We are a small family, which is content and doing fine'. Whether anyone actually takes any notice is hard to say; personal experience suggests that large families are still the rule in Indonesia.

Transmigration

As well as reducing the birth rate, attempts are also being made to take the pressure off heavily populated areas, particularly Java and Bali, by moving people out to less populated areas like Sumatra, Kalimantan, Irian Jaya and Maluku. These *transmigrasi* programmes started with Dutch efforts to relieve population pressure in Java in 1905. The Suharto government's first Five Year Plan moved 182,000 people out of Java, Bali and Lombok – below target by only 8000. The second Five Year Plan aimed to move over a million people in the five years from 1974, but by 1976 the target figure had to be reduced by half. The third and fourth Five Year Plans (1979-1984 and 1984-89) ambitiously aimed at shifting 500,000 and 750,000 families respectively – more than five million people.

So far, however, the transmigrasi programmes seem to have had little effect on the population burden of Java. The main problem is that insufficient numbers of people can physically be moved to offset the growth in population. Furthermore, transmigration settlements have developed a poor reputation – one of the underlying faults has been the tendency to attempt wet-rice cultivation in unsuitable areas. Settlers have frequently ended up as subsistence farmers no better off than they were back in Java, if not because of poor soil and water then because of inadequate support services and isolation from markets.

In addition, most government-sponsored transmigrants are not experienced farmers; two-thirds of transmigrants are landless peasants, the poorest of the countryside, and another 10% are homeless city dwellers. Up until 1973, the urban poor of Jakarta were often virtually press-ganged into moving out of Java – they turned out to be the least successful transmigrants, often returning to the towns they came from. The most successful transmigrants are often those who move 'spontaneously' – because they emigrate on their own initiative to the outer islands, and because they can choose where to live. Transmigration is a voluntary programme but as officials strain to meet new targets, there is increasing pressure on people to sign up.

Transmigration takes its toll on the natural environment through destruction of rainforest, loss of topsoil and degraded water supplies. Tension, even conflict, with the indigenous people in some settled areas is not uncommon.

PEOPLE

The rugged, mountainous terrain and the fact that the country is made up of many islands has separated groups of people from each other and resulted in an extraordinary differentiation of language and culture across the archipelago. Indonesians are divided – according to one classification – into approximately 300 ethnic groups which speak some 365 languages and dialects.

Indonesia's national motto is *Bhinneka Tunggal Ika*, an old Javanese phrase meaning 'They are many; they are one', which usually gets translated as 'Unity in diversity'. The peoples of the archipelago were not 'Indonesian' until 1949, when a line was drawn on the map enclosing a group of islands which housed a remarkably varied collection of people.

Most Indonesians are of Malay stock,

descended from peoples who originated in China and Indochina and spread into Indonesia over several thousand years. The other major grouping is the darker-skinned, fuzzy-haired Melanesians who inhabit much of easternmost Indonesia.

Despite the Malay predominance, the culture and customs of the various islands are often quite different. There are different languages and dialects, different religions, and differences in adat, the unwritten village law which regulates the behaviour of everyone in every village in Indonesia. The Indonesian terrain is partly responsible for the incredible diversity; mountains and jungles cut off tribes and groups on certain islands from the outside world – like the Kubu tribe of south Sumatra, thought to be descendants of the original settlers from Sri Lanka. They were barely known to outsiders until guerrillas fighting against the Dutch came into contact with them. Other isolated groups have included the Papuan Dani people of the Balim Valley in Irian Jaya, and the Dayaks – the collective name given to the people who inhabit the interior of Borneo. There are also the Baduis of West Java who withdrew to the highlands as the Islamic religion spread through the island, and have had little contact with outsiders. Other distinctive groups, like the Balinese and Javanese, have had considerable contact with the outside world but nevertheless have managed to maintain their traditional cultures intact.

The Overseas Chinese

Of all the ethnic minorities in Indonesia, few have had a larger impact on the country than the Chinese, or 'overseas Chinese' as they are commonly known. Although they are believed to make up less than 3% of the population, the Chinese are the major force in the economy, operating everything from small shops, hotels and restaurants to major banks and telecommunications agencies.

Talk to the average Indonesian and you will hear much anti-Chinese resentment. The Chinese are accused of being both capitalistic exploiters and communists (a seeming contradiction) and disloyal to the Indonesian nation. Much of this resentment is based on pure jealousy – the Chinese are by far the wealthiest ethnic group in the country. More bizarre is the fact that most Indonesians are envious of the physical appearance of the Chinese – the Chinese have lighter skin (considered beautiful in Indonesia). Look at any advertisement in Indonesia and the models are almost sure to be Chinese.

Indonesia's love-hate relationship with the Chinese has had some bitter consequences. In the slaughter following the 1965 coup attempt, many of the victims were Chinese. A large number of Chinese fled the country at the time, many winding up in China, Hong Kong and Macau where they still live today. The government shut down all Chinese schools in 1965 and they have not been allowed to reopen, so few young Chinese-Indonesians can speak, read or write Chinese. Chinese newspapers and signs in Chinese characters are still banned. All Chinese festivals remain prohibited, most temples have been closed and the Chinese have been encouraged to abandon their traditional religions (Taoism and Buddhism) and convert to Christianity or Islam (most choose Christianity). The Chinese must take Indonesian names. The government's policy is clearly to make the Chinese assimilate and disappear as a visible minority. Ironically, the government clearly recognises the Chinese work ethic and has tried to encourage them in business – Suharto's own banker is Chinese.

Nor is this odd situation limited to Indonesia. Throughout South-East Asia, the Chinese are both respected and hated for their business abilities, and envied for their physical appearance which the locals find so attractive. In Thailand, Malaysia and the Philippines, the Chinese are the major force in business. The Chinese dominated the economy of Vietnam until 1969 when their businesses were seized and they were expelled en masse. Tiny Singapore, a mere city-state smaller than Jakarta, is 80% Chinese and by far the wealthiest place in South-East Asia.

EDUCATION

Although there have been improvements, education is one of Indonesia's weak points. Schooling is not free in Indonesia, not even at the primary level, though government schools charge only about 1200 rp per month. Unfortunately, many families cannot afford even this, and send the children out to work rather than to school. There is also a disturbing tendency for the government to use the educational system for propaganda purposes. The literacy rate in 1988 (the last year for which figures are available) was 26%.

There are plenty of private schools, many operated by mosques and churches. Private schools generally have higher standards, and this is where the upper crust educate their children. Of course, private schools are more expensive.

Going to university is expensive and only a few can afford it. Tuition costs have increased rapidly in recent years, and are currently around 150,000 rp per semester. Higher education is concentrated in Java. Number one and biggest in Indonesia is UI (Universitas Indonesia) in Jakarta, a government-run university. Yogya is Indonesia's main educational centre, famous for its Universitas Gajah Mada. Bandung has the major high-tech school, ITB (Institut Teknologi Bandung). Lesser universities are located in the outlying provinces, such as Sulawesi's UNHAS (Universitas Hassanuddin) in Ujung Pandang.

ARTS

Crafts

Indonesia produces some find woodcarvings, and you'll see plenty of impressive examples all over the archipelago. Don't be surprised to find woodcarving salesmen wandering into your hotel or restaurant touting their wares.

The art of applying wax to cloth and then tie-dying in spectacular pictures and designs is known in Indonesia as *batik*. The centre of this activity is Yogyakarta. See the Java chapter for details.

In Nusa Tenggara, especially on the

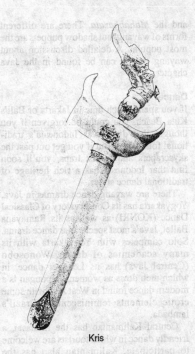

Kris

islands of Sumba and Flores, you will have ample opportunity to see *ikat*, a type of weaving with tie-dyed threads. This is one form of artwork which has attracted a great deal of interest in the West, and many visitors flock to these islands just to buy ikat. A detailed discussion can be found in the introduction of the Nusa Tenggara chapter.

Songket is silk cloth with gold or silver threads woven into it, though these days imitation silver or gold is often used. Songket is most commonly found in West Sumatra, but can be seen in parts of Kalimantan and Bali.

The *kris* (dagger) is a fine piece of artwork, often decorated with jewels and endowed with mystical powers. It's found mainly in Java and Bali.

Theatre

Javanese *wayang* (puppet) plays have their origins in the Hindu epics, the *Ramayana* and the *Mahabharata*. There are different forms of wayang, but shadow puppets are the most popular. A detailed discussion about wayang theatre can be found in the Java chapter.

Dance

If you spend much time in Jakarta or Bali's Kuta Beach, you could be forgiven if you thought that disco was Indonesia's traditional folk dance. But if you get out past the skyscrapers and tourist traps, you'll soon find that Indonesia has a rich heritage of traditional dance styles.

There are wayang dance dramas in Java. Yogyakarta has its Conservatory of Classical Dance (KONRI) as well as its Ramayana Ballet, Java's most spectacular dance drama. Solo competes with Yogyakarta with its many academies of dance. Wonosobo (Central Java) has its Lengger dance, in which men dress as women. Jaipongan is a modern dance found in West Java with some erotic elements reminiscent of Brazil's lambada.

Central Kalimantan has the Manasai, a friendly dance in which tourists are welcome to participate. Kalimantan also has the Mandau dance, performed with knives and shields.

Some of the most colourful performances of all, including the Barong, Kechak, Topeng, Legong and Baris dances are found in Bali. For more information on these and other dances, see the Bali chapter.

Music

Indonesia produces a lot of indigenous pop music, most of which does not suit Western tastes. One thing you can be certain of is that Indonesians like their music *loud*.

Traditional *gamelan* orchestras are found primarily in Java and Bali. The orchestras are composed mainly of percussion instruments including drums, gongs and shake-drums (*angklung*), along with flutes and xylophones. See the Java chapter for more detail.

Western rock music – both modern and vintage stuff from the 1960s – is also popular. Michael Jackson and the Rolling Stones have given concerts to packed audiences at the Senayan football stadium in south Jakarta.

Currently, Indonesia's rock idol is Iwan Fals and his band Kantata Takwa. Fals has a definite anti-Establishment and anti-government bent; his songs have gotten him arrested several times. However, he always seems to get released fairly quickly, probably because his father is a general in the Indonesian army.

CULTURE

Indonesia has a diverse mix of cultures rather than a single one, but the effects of mass education, mass media and a policy of government-orchestrated nationalism have created a sort of Indonesian national culture.

Traditional Lifestyle

'Keeping face' is important to Indonesians and they are generally extremely courteous – criticisms are not spoken directly and they will usually agree with what you say rather than offend. They will also prefer to say something rather than appear as if they don't know the answer. They mean well but when you ask how to get somewhere, you may often find yourself being sent off in the wrong direction!

Taboos

Indonesians will accept any lack of clothing on the part of poor people who cannot afford them; but for Westerners, thongs, bathing costumes, shorts or strapless tops are considered impolite except perhaps around places like Kuta. Elsewhere you have to look vaguely respectable.

Women are better off dressing modestly – revealing tops are just asking for trouble. Short pants are marginally acceptable if they are the baggy type which almost reach the knees.

While places of worship are open to all, permission should be requested to enter, particularly when ceremonies are in progress, and you should ensure that you're decently dressed.

Avoiding Offence

Asians resent being touched on the head – the head is regarded as the seat of the soul and is therefore sacred. In traditional Javanese culture, a lesser person should not have their head above that of a senior person, so you may sometimes see Javanese duck their heads when greeting someone, or walk past with dropped shoulders as a mark of respect.

When handing over or receiving things remember to use the right hand – the left hand is often used as a substitute for toilet paper. To show great respect to a high-ranking or elderly person, hand something to them using both hands. Talking to someone with your hands on your hips is impolite and is considered a sign of contempt, anger or aggressiveness – it's the same stance taken by characters in traditional dance and operas to signal these feelings to the audience. Hand shaking is customary for both men and women on introduction and greeting.

The correct way to beckon to someone is with the hand extended and a downward waving motion of all the fingers (except the thumb). It looks almost like waving goodbye. The Western method of beckoning, with the index finger crooked upward, won't be understood and will most likely be considered rude.

Avoid writing letters or notes to people using a red pen. This is considered unfriendly in most east Asian countries. Any other colour will do.

As in other Asian countries, limited English on the part of the locals means that there's a set of stock questions that everybody asks you. It's hard to know how to react when you're sitting on a bus or boat and someone asks you 'Where are you going?'. The usual stock questions in Indonesia are: Where are you from? Where are you going? What is your name? How long have you been in Indonesia? Are you married? What is your religion?

The question to be careful of is the one on religion; Indonesians presume that Westerners are Christian. If you are an atheist you'll be better off not telling them; in Indonesia the logic is that Communists are atheists, and therefore if you are an atheist you must be a Communist.

The question about marriage should be treated carefully too. Indonesians find it absurd that anyone would not want to be married, and being divorced is a great shame. Your social relations will go more smoothly if you say you are 'already married' or 'not yet married'. If you are over age 30, it's better to be 'married' or else people will assume there must be some defect in your personality. If you really can't handle being 'married', you could say your spouse is dead, which is considered less of a tragedy than being divorced.

Sport

Pencak silat, a form of martial arts, is most popular in West Java and West Sumatra. This form of fighting uses not only hands, but also some weapons including sticks and knives.

These days, badminton is the most popular sport. Indonesian Susi Susanti is reputed to be the best female badminton player in the world. Alan Budikusuma is a world-famous Indonesian male badminton player.

Soccer is the second most popular sport, often shown on national TV. Tennis is catching on too, and Indonesia has produced one world-famous female tennis player, Yayu Basuki from Yogya.

RELIGION

The early Indonesians were animists and practised ancestor and spirit worship. The social and religious duties of the early agricultural communities that developed in the archipelago were gradually refined to form a code of behaviour which became the basis of adat, or customary law. When Hindu-Buddhism spread into the archipelago it was overlaid on this already well developed spiritual culture.

Although Islam was to become the predominant religion of the archipelago it was really only a nominal victory. What we see in ostensibly Islamic Indonesia today is actually Islam rooted in Hindu-Buddhism, adat and animism. Old beliefs carry on and in

Java, for example, there are literally hundreds of holy places where spiritual energy is said to be concentrated; amongst them are the Sendang Semanggi spring near Yogya, the Gua Sirandil sea-cave near Cilacap, and the misty uplands of the Dieng Plateau – all places where, with patient meditation and self-denial, the spiritual force may be absorbed. Today a holy stone on Gunung Bromo in East Java still receives regular offerings from some Tenggerese villagers as it did when animism was the predominant religion.

As for Christianity, despite the lengthy colonial era the missionaries have only been successful in converting pockets of the Indonesian population – the Bataks of Sumatra, the Minahasans and Toraja of Sulawesi, some of the Dayaks of Kalimantan, the Florinese, Ambonese and some of the West Irianese. Christian beliefs are also usually bound up with traditional religious beliefs and customs.

There are still a few pockets where animism survives virtually intact, such as in west Sumba and some parts of Irian Jaya.

Hinduism

Outside India, Hindus predominate only in Nepal and Bali. It is one of the oldest extant religions, its roots extending back beyond 1000 BC, in the civilisation which grew up along the Indus River Valley in what is now modern-day Pakistan.

The Hindus believe that underlying a person's body, personality, mind and memories there is something else – it never dies, it is never exhausted, it is without limit of awareness and bliss. What confuses Westerners is the vast pantheon of gods found in Hinduism – you can look upon these different gods as representations of the many attributes of an omnipresent god. The symbols and images of Hinduism are meant to introduce the worshipper to what they *represent* – the images should not be mistaken with idolatry, and the multiplicity of them with polytheism. The three main physical representations of the one omnipresent god are Brahma the creator, Vishnu the preserver and Shiva the destroyer.

Central to Hinduism is the belief that we will all go through a series of rebirths or reincarnations. Eventual freedom from this cycle depends on your karma – bad actions during your present life result in bad karma and this results in a lower reincarnation. Conversely, if your deeds and actions have been good you will be reincarnated on a higher level and you'll be a step closer to eventual freedom from rebirth. Hinduism specifies four main castes: the highest is the Brahmin priest caste; next is the Kshatriyas, who are soldiers and governors; the Vaisyas are tradespeople and farmers; and lowest are the Sudras, who are menial workers and craftspeople. You cannot change your caste – you're born into it and are stuck with it for the rest of that lifetime.

Centuries ago Hinduism pervaded Java and spread to Bali. Today, Hinduism in Bali bears only a vague resemblance to the form practised on the Indian sub-continent. In Indonesia Hinduism survives in a much more tangible form in the remains of great temples like Prambanan near Yogyakarta and those on the Dieng Plateau, and in stories and legends still told in dance and in the wayang puppet performances of both Bali and Java.

These stories are drawn from a number of ancient Hindu texts including the *Bhagavad Gita*, a poem credited to the philosopher-soldier Krishna in which he explains the duties of a warrior to Prince Arjuna. The *Bhagavad Gita* is contained in the *Mahabharata*, which tells of a great battle said to have taken place in northern India. The *Ramayana* is another story and tells of Prince Rama's expedition to rescue his wife, Sita, who had been carried away by the demon prince Rawana. In this epic Rama is aided by the monkey god Hanuman and by an army of monkeys. Rama is regarded as the personification of the ideal human and as an incarnation of the god Vishnu. Vishnu has visited the earth a number of times, the seventh time as Rama, and the eighth time as Krishna.

Ganesh

The gods are also depicted in statues and reliefs in the ancient Hindu temples of Java. Often they can be identified by the 'vehicle' upon which they ride; Vishnu's vehicle is Garuda, the half-man half-eagle after whom Indonesia's international airline is named. Of all the Hindu gods, Shiva the destroyer is probably the most powerful and the most worshipped, but out of destruction comes creation and so the creative role of Shiva is frequently represented as the lingam – a phallic symbol. Shiva's consort is Parvati, by whom he had two children, one of whom is Ganesh the elephant-headed god. Coming back from a long trip, Shiva discovered Parvati in her room with a young man and, not pausing to think that their son might have grown up during his absence, lopped his head off! He was then forced by Parvati to bring his son back to life but could only do so by giving him the head of the first living thing he saw – which happened to be an elephant. Ganesh's vehicle is the rat.

Buddhism

Buddhism was founded in India around the 6th century BC by Siddhartha Gautama. He was a prince brought up in luxury, but in his twenties he despaired of ever finding fulfilment on the physical level since the body was inescapably involved with disease, decrepitude and death. At around the age of 30 he made his break from the material world and plunged off in search of 'enlightenment'. After various unsuccessful stratagems, one evening he sat beneath a banyan tree in deep meditation and achieved enlightenment.

Buddha founded an order of monks and for the next 45 years preached his ideas until his death around 480 BC. To his followers he was known as Sakyamuni. Gautama Buddha is not the only Buddha, but the fourth, and he is not expected to be the last one.

Buddha taught that all life is suffering and that happiness can only be achieved by overcoming this suffering through following the 'eight-fold path' to *nirvana*, a condition beyond the limits of the mind, where one is no longer oppressed by earthly desires. Strictly speaking, Buddhism is more of a philosophy and a code of morality than a religion, because it is not centred on a god. Buddhism appears to retain some of the Hindu concepts, such as the idea of reincarnation and karma.

Hinduism & Buddhism in Indonesia

It remains one of the puzzles of Indonesian history how the ancient kingdoms of the archipelago were penetrated by Hinduism and Buddhism. The evidence of Hindu-Buddhist influence is clear enough in different parts of Indonesia, where there are Sanskrit inscriptions dating back to the 5th century AD, and many Hindu and Buddhist shrines and statues have been found in the archipelago. Disentangling the two is difficult, because there is usually a blending of Hindu and Buddhist teachings with older religious beliefs. It's been suggested, for instance, that the wayang puppet shows of Java have their roots in primitive Javanese ancestor worship, though the wayang stories that have been passed on are closely linked with later Hindu mythology or with Islam.

The elements of Indian religion and culture which had the greatest influence in

Indonesia were those to do with courts and government: the Indian concept of the god-king, the use of Sanskrit as the language of religion and courtly literature and the intro-duction of Indian mythology. Even the events and people recorded in epics like the *Ramayana* and the *Mahabharata* have all been shifted out of India to Java. Various Hindu and Buddhist monuments were built in Java, of which the Buddhist stupa of Borobudur and the Hindu temple complex at Prambanan are the most impressive. The Sumatran-based Srivijaya kingdom, which arose in the 7th century, was the centre of Buddhism in Indonesia.

Bali's establishment as a Hindu enclave dates from the time when the Javanese Hindu kingdom of Majapahit, in the face of Islam, virtually evacuated Java to the neighbouring island – taking with them their art, literature and music as well as their religion and rituals. It's a mistake, however, to think that this was purely an exotic seed planted on virgin soil. The Balinese probably already had strong religious beliefs and an active cultural life and the new influences were simply overlaid on the existing practices – hence the peculiar Balinese variant of Hinduism. The Balinese worship the Hindu trinity of Brahma the creator, Shiva the destroyer and Vishnu the preserver but they also have a supreme god, Sanghyang Widhi. In Bali, unlike in India, the threesome is always alluded to, never seen – a vacant shrine or an empty throne says it all. Second-ary Hindu gods, such as Ganesh, may occasionally appear, but there are many other purely Balinese gods, spirits and enti-ties. Other aspects of Balinese Hinduism separate it from Indian Hinduism – like the widow-witch Rangda. She bears a close resemblance to Durga, the terrible side of Shiva's wife Parvati, but the Balinese Barong dance (in which she appears) cer-tainly isn't part of Indian Hinduism.

Islam

Islam is the most recent and widespread of the Asian religions. The founder of Islam was the Arab prophet Mohammed but he merely transmitted the word of God to his people. To call the religion 'Mohammed-anism' is wrong, since it implies that the religion centres around Mohammed and not around God. The proper name of the religion is Islam, derived from the word *salam* which means primarily 'peace', but in a secondary sense 'surrender'. The full connotation is something like 'the peace which comes by surrendering to God'. A person who follows *Islam* is a *Muslim*.

The prophet was born around 570 AD and came to be called Mohammed, which means 'highly praised'. His descent is traditionally traced back to Abraham. There have been other true prophets before Mohammed – among them Moses, Abraham and Jesus – but Mohammed is regarded as the culmina-tion of them, as there will be no more prophets.

Mohammed taught that there is one all-powerful, all-pervading God, Allah. 'There is no God but Allah' is the fundamental tenet of the Islamic religion. The initial reaction to Mohammed's message was one of hostility; the uncompromising monotheism conflicted with the pantheism and idolatry of the Arabs. Apart from that, Mohammed's moral teach-ings conflicted with what he believed was a corrupt and decadent social order, and in a society afflicted with class divisions Mohammed preached a universal humanity in which all people are equal in the eyes of God. Mohammed and his followers were forced to flee from Mecca to Medina in 622 AD, and there Mohammed built up a politi-cal base and an army which eventually defeated Mecca, although Mohammed died two years later in 632 AD.

Mohammed's teachings are collected in the Koran (or Qur'an), the holy book of Islam, compiled after Mohammed's death. Much of the Koran is devoted to codes of behaviour, and much emphasis is placed on God's mercy to humankind. Mohammed's teachings are heavily influenced by two other religions, Judaism and Christianity, and there are some extraordinary similarities including belief in hell and heaven, belief in a judgement day, and a creation theory almost identical to the Garden of Eden and myths like Noah's Ark and Aaron's Rod.

Islam hangs on four pegs: God, creation, humankind, and the day of judgement. Everything in Islam centres on the fact of God or Allah but the distinctive feature of Islam is the appreciation of the value of the individual. In Hinduism and Buddhism the individual is just a fleeting expression with no permanence or value but the Islamic religion teaches that individuality, as expressed in the human soul, is eternal, because once created the soul lives forever. For the Muslim, life on earth is just a forerunner to an eternal future in heaven or hell as appropriate.

Islam is a faith that demands unconditional surrender to the wisdom of Allah. It involves total commitment to a way of life, philosophy and law. Theoretically it is a democratic faith in which devotion is the responsibility of the individual, unrestricted by hierarchy and petty social prerequisites, and concerned with encouraging initiative and independence in the believer. Nor, in theory, is it bound to a particular locale – the faithful can worship in a rice field at home, in a mosque or on a mountain. It is also a fatalistic faith in that everything is rationalised as the will of Allah.

It is a moralistic religion and has its own set of rituals and laws, such as worshipping five times a day, recitation of the Koran, almsgiving, and fasting annually during the month of Ramadan. Making the pilgrimage to Mecca is the foremost ambition of every devout Muslim – those who have done this, called *haji* if they are men or *haja* if women, are deeply respected. Other Muslim customs include scrupulous attention to cleanliness, including ritualistic washing of hands and face. The pig is considered unclean and is not kept or eaten by strict Muslims.

Islam also called on its followers to spread the word – by the sword, if necessary. In succeeding centuries Islam was to expand over three continents. By the time a century had passed the Arab Muslims had built a huge empire which stretched all the way from Persia to Spain. The Arabs, who first propagated the faith, developed a reputation as ruthless opponents but reasonable masters, so people often found it advisable to surrender to them.

At an early stage Islam suffered a fundamental split that remains to this day. The third Caliph, successor to Mohammed, was murdered and followed by Ali, the prophet's son-in-law, in 656 AD. Ali was assassinated in 661 by the Governor of Syria, who set himself up as Caliph in preference to the descendants of Ali. Most Muslims today are Sunnites, followers of the succession from the Caliph, while the others are Shias or Shi'ites, who follow the descendants of Ali.

Islam only travelled west for a hundred years before being pushed back at Poitiers in France in 732, but it continued east for centuries. It regenerated the Persian Empire which was then declining from its protracted struggles with Byzantium. In 711, the same year in which the Arabs landed in Spain, they sent dhows up the Indus River into India. This was more a raid than a full-scale invasion but in the 11th century all of north India fell into Muslim hands. From India the faith was carried into South-East Asia by Arab and Indian traders.

Islam in Indonesia

Islam made its first appearance in Indonesia with the establishment of Arabic settlements in the latter part of the 7th century. How it managed to gain a hold over the region is, like the spread of Hindu-Buddhism, a mystery. One theory holds that Islam was introduced through the missionary activity of the Sufis – Muslims who practised forms of mysticism and could thus confront the mystics of the earlier Hindu and animist religions on equal terms. The Sufis were probably more tolerant of adat law which, on a strictly literal interpretation, could have been seen as conflicting with Islamic law.

The state of Pasai in Aceh adopted Islam near the end of the 13th century; the founder of Melaka had accepted the faith in the early part of the 15th century and within 50 years Melaka was renowned as a centre for the teaching of Islam as well as a centre of

South-East Asian trade. Possibly the spread of Islam in the next few years was related to the territorial expansion and increasing political influence of Melaka. Trading ships carried the new religion to Java, from where it spread to the spice islands of eastern Indonesia via Makassar (now Ujung Pandang) in Sulawesi. Islam caught on in Java in the 16th and 17th centuries, and at about the same time Aceh developed as a major Islamic power and the religion took root in west and south Sumatra, in Kalimantan and Sulawesi.

By the 15th and 16th centuries, centres for the teaching of Islam along the northern coast of Java may have played an important role in disseminating the new religion, along with previously established centres of Hindu learning, which adopted elements of Islam. Javanese tradition holds that the first propagators of Islam in Java were nine holy men, the *wali songo*, who possessed a deep knowledge of Islamic teaching as well as exceptional supernatural powers. Another theory holds that Islam was adopted by various Javanese princes who sought a supernatural sanction for their rule, and that the common people followed suit in much the same way as Europeans adopted the religions of their kings.

Whatever the reasons for the spread of Islam, today it is the professed religion of 90% of Indonesians and its traditions and rituals affect all aspects of their daily life. Like Hinduism and Buddhism before it, Islam also had to come to terms with older existing traditions and customs.

Indonesian Islam is rather different from the austere form found in the Middle East; customs in Indonesia often differ from those of other Muslim countries. Respect for the dead throughout most of Indonesia is not expressed by wearing veils but in donning traditional dress. Muslim women in Indonesia are allowed more freedom and shown more respect than their counterparts in other Muslim countries. They do not have to wear facial veils, nor are they segregated or considered to be second-class citizens. Muslim men in Indonesia are only allowed to marry two women and even then must have the

consent of their first wife – Muslims in other parts of the world can have as many as four wives. Throughout Indonesia it is the women who initiate divorce proceedings. The Minangkabau society of Sumatra, for example, is a strongly Muslim group but their adat laws allow matriarchal rule, which conflicts strongly with the assumption of male supremacy inherent in Islam.

Like other Muslims, Indonesian Muslims practise circumcision. The laws of Islam require that all boys be circumcised and in Indonesia this is usually done somewhere between the ages of six and 11.

One of the most important Islamic festivals is Ramadan, a month of fasting prescribed by Islamic law, which falls in the ninth month of the Muslim calendar. It's often preceded by a cleansing ceremony, Padusan, to prepare for the coming fast. Traditionally, during Ramadan people get up at 4 am to eat and then fast until sunset. During Ramadan many Muslims visit family graves and royal cemeteries, recite extracts from the Koran, sprinkle the graves with holy water and strew them with flowers. Special prayers are said at mosques and at home. The first day of the 10th month of the Muslim calendar is the end of Ramadan. Mass prayers are held in the early morning and these are followed by two days of feasting. Extracts from the Koran are read and religious processions take place; gifts are exchanged and pardon is asked for past wrongdoings in this time of mutual forgiveness.

Islam not only influences routine daily living but also Indonesian politics. It was with the Diponegoro revolt in the 19th century that Islam first became a rallying point in Indonesia. In the early part of the 20th century Sarekat Islam became the first mass political party. Its philosophy was derived from Islam and its support was derived from the Muslim population. In post-independence Indonesia it was an Islamic organisation, the Darul Islam, which launched a separatist movement in West Java. Despite the Islamic background of the country and the predominance of Muslims in the government, the Indonesian government has not followed the trend towards a more fundamentalist Islamic state.

The Mosque A mosque is an enclosure for prayer. The word *mesjid* means 'to prostrate oneself in prayer'. Mosques can be differentiated according to function: the *jami mesjid* is used for the Friday prayer meetings; the *musalla* is one that is used for prayer meetings but not for Friday prayer meetings; the 'memorial mosque' is for the commemoration of victorious events in Islamic history; and a *mashad* is found in a tomb compound. There are also prayer houses which are used by only one person at a time, not for collective worship – you'll often find that larger hotels and airport terminals in Indonesia have a room set aside for this purpose.

The oldest mosques in Indonesia – in Cirebon, Demak and Palembang, for example – have roofs with two, three or five storeys. It is thought that these multi-storeyed roofs were based on Hindu *meru* (shrines) that you'll still see in Bali. Today's mosques are often built with a high dome over an enclosed prayer hall. Inside there are five main features. The *mihrab* is a niche in a wall marking the direction to Mecca. The *mimbar* is a raised pulpit, often canopied, with a staircase. There is also a stand to hold the Koran, a screen to provide privacy for important persons praying, and a fountain, pool or water jug for ablutions. Outside the building there is often a *menara* – a minaret, or tower, from which the *muezzin* summons the community to prayer.

Apart from these few items the interior of the mosque is empty. There are no seats and no decorations – if there is any ornamentation at all it will be quotations of verses from the Koran. The congregation sits on the floor.

Friday afternoons are officially decreed as the time for believers to worship and all government offices and many businesses are closed as a result. All over Indonesia you'll hear the call to prayer from the mosques, but the muezzin of Indonesia are now a dying breed – the wailing will usually be performed by a cassette tape.

LANGUAGE

The 300-plus languages spoken throughout Indonesia, except those of the North Halmahera and most of Irian Jaya, belong to the Malay-Polynesian group. Within this group are many different regional languages and dialects. There are, in fact, five main language groups in Sumatra alone: Acehnese, Batak, Minangkabau, Lampung and the language spoken along the east coast, originating in southern Sumatra and from which Bahasa Indonesia is derived. Sulawesi has at least six distinct language groups and the tiny island of Alor in Nusa Tenggara no fewer than seven. The languages of the Kalimantan interior form their own distinct sub-family.

Java has three main languages: Sundanese, spoken in West Java; Javanese, spoken in Central and East Java; and Madurese, spoken on the island of Madura (off the north coast of Java) and parts of East Java. The Balinese have their own language. An interesting feature of the Balinese, Javanese and Sundanese languages is their division into many levels – different words may be used when speaking to an inferior, an equal or a superior. In Javanese, yet another courtly level exists for use when speaking to the Sultan. These levels are more than simply the difference between polite or formal usage and everyday speech, for they have different words even for everyday things.

Bahasa Indonesia

Today, the national language of Indonesia is Bahasa Indonesia, which is basically the same as Malay. Pure Malay, as spoken by the Malaysians, is confined in Indonesia to Sumatra but it has long been the common language of the Indonesian archipelago, having been the language of inter-island trade for centuries. As spoken, Bahasa Indonesia is close enough to the language spoken on the Malay peninsula for Malay and Indonesian to be mutually intelligible. *Bahasa* means 'language', so Bahasa Indonesia is simply the 'language of Indonesia'.

Javanese, with its 'high' and 'low' forms, was too complicated to become a national language – even if it was used by the main ethnic group of the archipelago. Although educated Indonesians used Dutch as their common language during the colonial era, it was Malay which was taken up by the nationalist movements as a means of mass communication. They used the slogan 'one country, one people, one language' even before national independence was achieved. The use of a single, common language was part of the attempt to achieve unity amongst the diverse peoples of the archipelago.

Indonesian is a language with many foreign words mixed in, indicating the long history of contact the archipelago has had with other cultures. Sanskrit words include *angsa* (duck), *gembala* (shepherd) and *kaca* (mirror). The Portuguese left signs of their presence with words like *mentega* (butter), *pesta* (festival), *gereja* (church), *meja* (table) and even the name of the island of Flores, which is Portuguese for 'flowers'. Indonesian can be a very musical and evocative language – the sun is *mata hari*, derived from the words for day *(hari)* and eye *(mata)*; thus mata hari is the 'eye of day'.

A very interesting phenomenon has been the development of a dialect known as Bahasa Prokem. Used by rebellious young people mostly in Jakarta since the early 1980s, Prokem is trendy mainly because it's almost unintelligible to the older generation. Novels written in Prokem have become instantly popular and, being non-political, so far the government hasn't banned them. It appears that Indonesia has a sizable generation gap.

Communicating

Bahasa Indonesia is now actively promoted as the national language. Almost anywhere you go in Indonesia people will speak Bahasa Indonesia as well as their own local language. Amongst the older generation, there are still quite a number of Dutch-speaking people. Today, English is the first foreign language and a lot of Indonesians know a few phrases of English but rarely much beyond 'Hello mister!' In more isolated areas you may find that only younger people and children know Bahasa Indonesia, because they're taught it in school, but that some of the older people don't understand it. Outside Java, Bali and other touristy areas, it's essential to know some Indonesian.

Like any language Bahasa Indonesia has its simplified colloquial form and its more developed literate language. For the visitor who wants to pick up just enough to get by, the common language – *pasar*, or market Indonesian – is very easy to learn. It's rated as one of the simplest languages in the world as there are no tenses, no genders, and often one word can convey the meaning of the whole sentence. There are often no plurals – you just say the word twice. It's an easy language to pronounce, with no obscure rules and none of the tonal complications that make some Asian languages, such as Thai and Chinese, difficult. Finally, the use of Roman script makes learning to read a simple task for most Westerners.

You can learn enough Bahasa Indonesia to get by within a month. Once you get deep into the language it's as complicated as any other, but for everyday use it's easy to learn and pronounce. And even if you can't understand much of what people say to you, not having to resort to phrase books to communicate your needs is half the battle won.

Apart from the ease of learning a little Bahasa Indonesia, there's another very good reason for trying to pick up at least a few words and phrases – few people are as delighted with foreigners learning their language as the Indonesians. They don't criticise you if you mangle your pronunciation or tangle your grammar. They make you feel like you're an expert if you know only a handful of words, and bargaining is a lot easier when you do it in their language. And once you know some Bahasa Indonesia you can start picking up bits and pieces of the regional languages – which can be fun, although you're best off putting your efforts into learning Bahasa Indonesia.

Some of the basics of the language are shown in the next section. For a more comprehensive overview, get Lonely Planet's *Indonesian phrasebook* by Paul Woods. It's

set out with a view to teaching the basics of the language, rather than just listing endless phrases.

An English/Indonesian and Indonesian/English dictionary is also very useful. They're sold quite cheaply in Indonesia, and you can also get bilingual dictionaries in French, German, Dutch and Japanese. Western secondary school Indonesian textbooks are worth buying before you leave and taking with you.

Get some children's reading books in Indonesia, since they'll be graded from beginner up; Indonesian comic books are also good because the pictures will help you work out the meaning of the words. The Indonesians themselves are enthusiastic and amazingly patient teachers.

Pronunciation

Most sounds are the same as in English although a few vowels and consonants differ. The sounds are nearly the same every time.

a like the 'a' in 'father'.

e like the 'e' in 'bet' when unstressed, as in *besar* (big), and sometimes is hardly pronounced at all, as in the greeting *selamat*, which sounds like 'slamat' when spoken quickly. When stressed it is like the 'a' in 'may', as in *becak* (rickshaw). There is no general rule as to when the 'e' is stressed or unstressed.

i like the 'ee' sound in 'meet'

o like the 'oa' in 'boat'

u like the 'u' in 'flute'

ai like 'i' as in 'line'
au like a drawn out 'ow' as in 'cow'

ua at the start of a word, like a 'w' – such as *uang* (money), pronounced 'wong'.

The pronunciation of consonants is very straightforward. Most sound like English consonants except:

c like the 'ch' in 'chair'

g like the 'g' in 'garden'

ng like 'ng' in 'singer'

ngg like 'ng' in 'anger'

j like the 'j' in 'join'

r like Spanish trilled r, achieved by rolling your tongue. *Apa kabar* (how are you?) is pronounced 'apa kabarrr'

h like English 'h', but a bit more strongly (as if you were sighing) though almost silent at the end of a word

k like the English 'k' except when it appears at the end of the word, in which case you just stop short of actually saying the 'k'

ny is a single sound like the beginning of 'new', before the 'oo' part of that word

Stress

There is no strong stress in Indonesian, and nearly all syllables have equal emphasis, but a good approximation is to stress the second-last syllable. The main exception to the rule is the unstressed 'e' in words such as *besar* (big), pronounced be-SARRR.

Grammar

Articles are not used in Indonesian – there's no 'the' or 'a'. The verb 'to be' is not used before an adjective. Thus, where we would say 'the room is dirty' in Indonesian it is simply *kamar kotor* – 'room dirty'. To make a word plural in some cases you double it – thus 'child' is *anak*, 'children' *anak anak* – but in many other cases you simply use the same singular form and the context or words such as 'many' *(banyak)* indicate the plurality.

Probably the greatest simplification in Indonesian is that verbs are not conjugated nor are there different forms for past, present and future tenses. Instead words like 'already' *(sudah)*, 'yesterday' *(kemarin)*, 'will' *(akan)* or 'tomorrow' *(besok)* are used to indicate the tense. *Sudah* is the all-purpose past tense indicator: 'I eat' is *saya makan* while 'I have already eaten' is simply *saya sudah makan*.

Except for the adjectives 'all' *(semua)*, 'many' *(banyak)* and 'a little' *(sedikit)*, adjectives follow the noun. Thus a 'big bus' is *bis besar*.

Pronouns

I	*saya*
you (sing)	*saudara*
he/she/it	*dia/ia*
we	*kita/kami*
you (pl)	*saudara*
they	*mereka*

Pronouns are often dropped when the meaning is clear from the context. This is just as well because more than a dozen words for 'you' are used, depending on the age, status or sex of the person addressed.

Speaking to an older man (especially anyone old enough to be your father) or to show respect for a man of high status, it's common to call them *bapak*, 'father' or simply *pak*. Similarly an older woman is *ibu*, 'mother' or simply *bu*. Using other forms such as *saudara* when talking to someone who is obviously your senior may well cause offence.

Tuan is a respectful term, like 'sir', and is often used to address officials. *Nyonya* is the equivalent for a married woman and *nona* for

an unmarried woman. When in doubt, use these forms to avoid causing offence.

You can call someone slightly older or of the same age either *abang* (older brother) or *kakak* (older sister). *Kamu* (or simply *mu*) and *engkau* are used only among friends or to address children.

Saudara is a more formal, less-used word for people of roughly the same age or status who you do not know well. *Anda* is the egalitarian form designed to overcome the plethora of words for the second person. It is often seen in written Indonesian and is becoming more common in everyday speech.

Greeting & Civilities

good morning (until 11 am)	*selamat pagi*
good day (11 am to 3 pm)	*selamat siang*
good afternoon (3 to 7 pm)	*selamat sore*
good night	*selamat malam*
good night (to someone going to bed)	*selamat tidur*
welcome	*selamat datang*
goodbye (said by the person who is leaving to the person who is staying)	*selamat tinggal*
goodbye (said by the person who is staying to the person who is going)	*selamat jalan*

Morning is *pagi* and extends from about 7 to 11 am. Pagi pagi is early morning - before 7 am. *Siang* is the middle of the day, around 11 am to 3 pm. *Sore* is the afternoon, around 3 to 7 pm. Night is *malam* and only really starts when it gets dark.

thank you	*terima kasih*
thank you very much	*terima kasih banyak*
you're welcome	*kembali*
please (asking for help)	*tolong*

please open the door	tolong buka pinta
please (giving permission)	silakan
please come in	silakan masuk
sorry	ma'af
excuse me	permisi
how are you?	apa kabar?
I'm fine	kabar baik
what is your name?	siapa nama saudara?
my name is...	nama saya...
another, one more	satu lagi
good, fine, OK	baik
nice, good	bagus
yes	ya
not, no – the negative	tidak/bukan

The negative *tidak* is used with verbs, adjectives and adverbs, whilst *bukan* is used with nouns and pronouns.

Questions & Comments

what is this?	apa ini?
what is that?	apa itu?
how much?	berapa?
how much is the price?	berapa harga?
how much money?	berapa uang?
expensive	mahal
how many kilometres?	berapa kilometer?
where is?	di mana ada?
which way?	ke mana?
I don't understand	saya tidak mengerti
this/that	ini/itu
big/small	besar/kecil
finished	habis
open/closed	buka/tutup

Transport

I want to go to...	mau pergi ke...
ticket	karcis, tiket
refund a ticket	membatalkan tiket
airport	lapangan udara
domestic air terminal	terminal dalam negeri
international air terminal	terminal luar negeri
rubber time	jam karet

bus	bis
train	kereta api
ship	kapal
motorcycle	sepeda motor
station	stasiun
here	di sini
stop (verb)	berhenti
straight on	terus
right	kanan
left	kiri
slow	pelan-pelan
driving around	keleling

Places

bank	bank
post office	kantor pos
immigration office	kantor imigrasi
tourist office	kantor parawisata

Map Reading

map	peta
north	utara
south	selatan
east	timur
west	barat
central	tengah
beach	pantai
big	besar
bridge	jembatan
cave	gua
church	gereja
city	kota
crater (in volcano)	kawah
forest	hutan
fortress	benteng
garden	kebun
island	pulau
lake	danau
mosque	mesjid
mountain	gunung
park	taman
province	propinsi
regency	kabupaten
river	sungai
road	jalan
sand	pasir
sea	laut
small	kecil
village	desa, kampung

Accommodation

price list	*daftar harga*
discount	*potongan harga*
economy room	*ruang ekonomi*
standard room	*ruang standard*
VIP room	*ruang VIP*
quiet room	*ruang tenang*
with private bath	*kamar mandi didalam*
with shared bath	*kamar mandi diluar*
please wash my clothes	*tolong cucikan pakaian saya*
towel	*handuk*
I want to pay now	*saya mau bayar sekarang*
my bed has bedbugs	*ranjang saya ada kutubusuk*

Numbers

1	*satu*	6	*enam*
2	*dua*	7	*tujuh*
3	*tiga*	8	*delapan*
4	*empat*	9	*sembilan*
5	*lima*	10	*sepuluh*

After the numbers one to 10, the 'teens' are *belas*, the 'tens' are *puluh*, the hundreds are *ratus* and the thousands *ribu*. Thus:

11	*sebelas*
12	*duabelas*
13	*tigabelas*
20	*duapuluh*
21	*duapuluh satu*
25	*duapuluh lima*
30	*tigapuluh*
90	*sembilanpuluh*
99	*sembilanpuluh sembilan*
100	*seratus*
200	*duaratus*
250	*duaratus limapuluh*
254	*duaratus limapuluh empat*
888	*delapanratus delapanpuluh delapan*
1000	*seribu*
1050	*seribu limapuluh*

A half is *setengah*, which is pronounced

'stenger', so half a kilo is 'stenger kilo'. 'Approximately' is *kira-kira*.

Time

when?	*kapan?*
tomorrow/yesterday	*besok/kemarin*
hour	*jam*
week	*minggu*
month	*bulan*
year	*tahun*
what time?	*jam berapa?*
how many hours?	*berapa jam?*
7 o'clock	*jam tujuh*
five hours	*lima jam*
5 o'clock	*jam lima*

Days of the Week

Monday	*Hari Senin*
Tuesday	*Hari Selasa*
Wednesday	*Hari Rabu*
Thursday	*Hari Kamis*
Friday	*Hari Jumat*
Saturday	*Hari Sabtu*
Sunday	*Hari Minggu*

Necessities

bathroom	*kamar mandi*
battery	*batu baterei*
candle	*lilin*
chemist/drugstore	*apotik*
cigarette lighter	*geratan*
flashlight	*senter*
insect repellent	*obat nyamuk*
matches	*korik api*
mosquito coil	*ombat nyamuk*
postage stamp	*perangko*
sanitary pad and/ or tampon	*pembalut wanita*
sanitary pads (Kotex)	*Softex*
soap	*sabun*
sunblock (UV lotion)	*Pabanox*
telephone card	*kartu telepon*
telephone number	*nomor telepon*
toilet	*kamar kecil WC*
(pronounced 'way say')	
toilet paper	*kertas WC*
toothpaste	*pasta gigi*

Emergency

I'm sick	*saya sakit*
hospital	*rumah sakit*
call the police	*pangil polisi*
I'm lost	*salah jalan*

help!	*tolong*!
thief!	*pencuri*!
fire!	*kebakaran*!
don't pinch my children	*jangan cubit anak saya*

Facts for the Visitor

VISAS & EMBASSIES

For many nationalities, a visa is not necessary for entry and a stay of up to two months. This includes, but is not limited to, the following: Argentina, Australia, Austria, Belgium, Brazil, Canada, Chile, Denmark, Finland, France, Germany, Greece, Iceland, Ireland, Italy, Japan, Liechtenstein, Luxemburg, Malaysia, Malta, Mexico, Morocco, The Netherlands, New Zealand, Norway, the Philippines, Singapore, South Korea, Spain, Sweden, Switzerland, Thailand, the UK, the USA, Venezuela and Yugoslavia.

If you're from one of these countries you'll be issued a two-month tourist pass (which is a stamp in your passport) when you enter Indonesia, and there's no need to obtain a visa beforehand. However, you must have an ongoing ticket and enter and exit through one of the following airports or seaports (remembering that the approved gateways often change):

Airports
Bali
    Denpasar, Ngurah Rai Airport
Irian Jaya
    Biak, Frans Kaisiepo Airport
Java
    Jakarta, Sukarno-Hatta & Halim Perdana Kusuma airports
    Surabaya, Juanda Airport
Kalimantan
    Balikpapan, Sepinggan Airport
    Pontianak, Soepadio Airport
Maluku
    Ambon, Pattimura Airport
Riau
    Batam Island, Batu Besar Airport
Sulawesi
    Manado, Sam Ratulangi Airport
Sumatra
    Medan, Polonia Airport
    Pekanbaru, Simpang Tiga Airport
    Padang, Tabing Airport
Timor
    Kupang, El Tari Airport

Seaports
Bali
    Denpasar, Benoa Seaport
Java
    Jakarta, Tanjung Priok Seaport
    Surabaya, Tanjung Perak Seaport
    Semarang, Tanjung Mas Seaport
Maluku
    Ambon, Yos Sudarso Seaport
Riau
    Batam Island, Batu Ampar & Sekupang seaports
    Bintan, Tanjung Pinang Seaport
Sulawesi
    Manado, Bitung Seaport
Sumatra
    Medan, Belawan Seaport
    Bengkulu, Padang Bai Seaport

Some travellers do arrive in Indonesia without a ticket and, in this case, immigration will require that you buy an onward ticket right at the airport, which often costs more than a discount return ticket you could have bought in Singapore or elsewhere. If you're not sure where you'll be exiting Indonesia from, try getting a cheap onward ticket such as Medan to Penang. If you don't want to use it you should be able to get a refund, but if you can't get a refund, you won't be too much out of pocket.

The tourist pass is valid for two months from the date of entry. This needs some clarification – if you entered Indonesia on, say, 25 January, you must depart no later than 24 March. Many travellers have the mistaken idea that they could depart on 25 March – quite a few people have gotten into trouble this way by overstaying by one day.

The tourist pass is supposedly not extendible. Your passport must be valid for at least a further six months at the time of your arrival in Indonesia. However, apart from money, there's nothing to stop you from going out to, say, Singapore, and then re-entering Indonesia for another two-month stay – you can do this as often as you like.

If you're not on the list of nationalities who can get the two-month tourist pass, or if you want to enter Indonesia through a place which isn't on the list of designated ports, you will need an Indonesian visa before you enter the country. These can be obtained at Indonesian consulates and embassies abroad and are usually valid for 30 days, though they *might* be difficult to get if you are only visiting Indonesia as a tourist. Two photos are required. You'll probably – but not necessarily – be able to extend your initial visa at an immigration office *(kantor imigrasi)* in Indonesia. You also usually need a visa if you are going to *leave* Indonesia through a non-designated port, even if you entered through a designated one – details on the situation in some of these places are given in the relevant town sections of this book.

If you are intending to work in Indonesia, you'll probably need a special working visa – see your employer about it. We've heard reports that the Indonesian embassy in Singapore is most troublesome for issuing working visas.

Indonesian Embassies

Australia
Embassy, 8 Darwin Avenue, Yarralumla, ACT 2600 (☎ (06) 2733222)
Consulate-General, Piccadilly Court, 3rd Floor, 222 Pitt St, Sydney, NSW 2000 (☎ (02) 2642976, 2195, 2323, 2508, 2712)
Consulate, 7 Bennet St, Darwin, NT 0800 (☎ (089) 819352)
Consulate, 3rd Floor, 52 Albert Rd, South Melbourne, Vic 3205 (☎ (03) 6907811)
Consulate, 133 St George's Terrace, Perth, WA 6000, (☎ (09) 3219821)
Brunei
Jalan Kumbang Pasang LB 711, Bandar Seri Begawan
Canada
Embassy, 287 Maclaren St, Ottawa, Ontario KIP 6A9 (☎ (613) 236-7403 to 5)
Consulate, 470 Granville St, Vancouver, BC
Consular office in Toronto, Ontario
Denmark
Embassy, Orehoj Alle 12900, Hellerup, Copenhagen (☎ (02) 96 72 44)
France
4749 Rue Cortambert 75116, Paris (☎ (1) 45030760 or 45041371)
Germany
Embassy, 2 Bernakasteler Strasse, 5300 Bonn 2 (☎ (228) 382990)

Consulate, 26 Wiesenhuttenplatz, Frankfurt
Consular offices in Berlin, Bremen, Dusseldorf, Hamburg, Hannover, Kiel, Munich and Stuttgart
Hong Kong
Consulate-General, 127-129 Leighton Rd, Causeway Bay, Hong Kong (☎ 8904421)
India
50-A Chanakyapuri, New Delhi
Italy
53 Via Campania, Rome (☎ 475 9251)
Japan
9-2 Higashi Gotanda 5 Chome, Shinagawa-ku, Tokyo
Malaysia
Embassy, Jalan Pekeliling 233, Kuala Lumpur (☎ 421011, 421141, 421228)
Consulate, 37 Northam Rd, Penang (☎ 25162, 3, 4, 8)
Consulate, Jalan Sagunting 1, Kota Kinabalu, Sabah (☎ 54100, 54245, 55110)
Netherlands
Embassy, 8 Tobias Asserlaan, 2517 KC Den Haag (☎ 070-4696/7)
New Zealand
Embassy, 9-11 Fitzherbert Terrace, Thordon, Wellington (☎ 736 669)
Norway
Embassy, Inkonitogata 8, Oslo 2 (☎ (2) 44 19 13)
Papua New Guinea
Embassy, Henao Drive Section 67, Lot 6, Gordon Estate, Boroko, Port Moresby (☎ 253116, 253118, 253544)
Philippines
Embassy, 185/187 Salcedo St, Legaspi Village, Makati, Manila (☎ (2) 85-50-61 to 68, 88-03-01 to 07)
Consular office in Davao
Singapore
Embassy, Wisma Indonesia, 435 Orchard Rd, Singapore 0923 (☎ (73) 77422)
Spain
13 Caile del Cinca, Madrid
Sweden
Embassy, Strandvagen 47/V, 11456 Stockholm (☎ (08) 63 54 70, 74)
Switzerland
Embassy, 51 Elfenauweg, 3006 Bern
Thailand
Embassy, 600-602 Petchburi Rd, Bangkok (☎ 252 3135 to 40)
UK
Embassy, 38 Grosvenor Square, London W1X 9AD (☎ (071) 4997661)
USA
Embassy, 2020 Massachussetts Ave NW, Washington DC 20036 (☎ (202) 293-1745)
Consulate, 645 South Mariposa, Los Angeles, CA 90005
Consulate, Pri Tower, 833 Bishop St, Honolulu,

Hawaii
Consular offices in Chicago, Houston, New York and San Francisco

Visa Extensions

Although the authorities frown on it, you can extend your two-month tourist pass for up to one week if you can come up with a good excuse, like missed flight connections or illness. Proof of these circumstances is usually not required, but dress well and be very polite when you visit the immigration office. Extensions beyond one week are almost impossible to get unless you have connections (or, some would say, pay bribes – not that we're suggesting you do this!). Of course, if you're in the hospital in critical condition and can prove it, a longer extension should be possible.

Whatever you do, do not simply show up at the airport with an expired visa or tourist pass and expect to be able to board your flight. If you've overstayed your visa by even one day and didn't bother to get an extension, you will probably not be allowed to board your flight, and instead will be sent back to the local immigration office where you'll have to clear the matter up. You might be asked to 'pay a fine'. If you overstay and immigration takes a disliking to you, they could stamp your passport so you can't re-enter Indonesia.

Foreign Embassies in Indonesia

Countries with diplomatic relations with Indonesia will generally have their consular offices in Jakarta, the capital. Australia, Finland, France, Germany, Italy, Japan, The Netherlands, Sweden and Switzerland have representatives in Bali – see the Bali chapter for details. Some of the more useful foreign embassies in Jakarta include:

Australia
Jalan Thamrin 15 (☎ 323109)
Austria
Jalan Diponegoro 44 (☎ 3338090)
Belgium
Jalan Cicurug 4 (☎ 351682)

Brunei
9th Floor, Central Plaza Building, Jalan Jenderal Sudirman (☎ 517990)
Burma (Myanmar)
Jalan H Augus Salim 109 (☎ 320440)
Canada
5th Floor, Wisma Metropolitan I, Jalan Jenderal Sudirman, Kav 29 (☎ 510709)
Denmark
Bina Mulya Building, 4th Floor, Jalan Rasuna Said, Kav 10 (☎ 5204350)
Finland
Bina Mulya Building, 10th Floor, Jalan Rasuna Said, Kav 10 (☎ 5176480)
France
Jalan Thamrin 20 (☎ 332807)
Germany
Jalan Thamrin 1 (☎ 323908)
India
Jalan Rasuna Said 51, Kuningan (☎ 5204150)
Italy
Jalan Diponegoro 45 (☎ 337422)
Japan
Jalan Thamrin 24 (☎ 324308)
Malaysia
Jalan Imam Bonjol 17 (☎ 323750)
Netherlands
Jalan Rasuna Said, Kav S-3, Kuningan (☎ 511515)
New Zealand
Jalan Diponegoro 34 (☎ 338081)
Norway
Bina Mulya Bldg, 4th Floor, Jalan Rasuna Said, Kav 10 (☎ 517140)
Pakistan
Jalan Teuku Umar 50 (☎ 344825)
Papua New Guinea
6th Floor, Panin Bank Centre, Jalan Jenderal Sudirman (☎ 711218)
Philippines
Jalan Imam Bonjol 6-8 (☎ 348917)
Poland
Jalan Diponegoro 65 (☎ 320509)
Singapore
Jalan Rasuna Said, Block X, Kav 2 No 4 (☎ 5201489)
South Korea
Jalan Jenderal Gatot Subroto, Kav 57-58 (☎ 512309)
Spain
Wisma Kosgoro, 6th Floor, Jalan Thamrin 53 (☎ 320257)
Sri Lanka
Jalan Diponegoro 70 (☎ 321018)
Sweden
Jalan Taman Cut Mutiah 12 (☎ 333061)
Switzerland
Jalan Rasuna Said, B-1, Kav X-3 (☎ 516061)

Taiwan
    Chinese Chamber of Commerce to Jakarta, Jalan
    Banyumas 4, (☎ 351212)
Thailand
    Jalan Imam Bonjol 74 (☎ 343762)
UK
    Jalan Thamrin 75 (☎ 330904)
USA
    Jalan Merdeka Selatan 5 (☎ 360360)
Russia
    Jalan Thamrin 13 (☎ 327007)
Vietnam
    Jalan Teuku Umar 25 (☎ 347325)

DOCUMENTS

A passport is essential and, if yours is within a few months of expiration, you should get a new one now – many countries will not issue a visa if your passport has less than six months of validity remaining. Also, be sure it has plenty of space for visas and entry and exit stamps. It could be embarrassing to run out of blank pages when you are too far away from an embassy to get a new passport issued or extra pages added.

Losing your passport is very bad news – getting a new one means a trip to your embassy or consulate and usually a long wait while they send faxes or telexes (at your expense) to confirm that you exist. If you're going to be spending a long time in Indonesia, many embassies will allow you to register your passport, which makes replacement easier. Registered or not, it helps if you have a separate record of passport number, issue date, and a photocopy of your old passport or birth certificate. While you're compiling that info add the serial numbers of your travellers' cheques, details of health insurance and US$200 or so as emergency cash – and keep all that material totally separate from your passport, cheques and other cash.

If you plan to be driving abroad get an International Driving Permit from your local automobile association. They are valid for one year only.

An International Youth Hostel Association (IYHA) card is of very limited use in Indonesia, but there are a few hostels which will recognise it and give a slight discount.

If you plan to pick up some cash by working, photocopies of university diplomas, transcripts and letters of recommendation could prove helpful. If you're travelling with your spouse, a photocopy of your marriage licence just might come in handy should you become involved with the law, hospitals or other bureaucratic authorities. Useful (though not essential) is an International Health Certificate – see the Health section for more details.

The International Student Identity Card (ISIC) can perform all sorts of miracles, such as getting you a discount on some international and domestic flights, as well as discounts at a few museums. Small wonder there is a worldwide trade in fake cards, but the authorities have tightened up on the abuse of student cards in several ways. You may be required to provide additional proof of student status – such as 'student' in your passport, or a letter from your university or college stating that you are a student. In additional, there are now maximum age limits (usually 26) for some concessions, and the fake-card dealers have been clamped down on. Nevertheless, fake cards are still widely available and usable, but some are of quite poor quality.

Remember that a student is a very respectable thing to be, and if your passport has a blank space for occupation you are much better off having 'student' there than something nasty like 'journalist' or 'photographer'.

CUSTOMS

Customs allow you to bring in a maximum of two litres of alcoholic beverages, 200 cigarettes or 50 cigars or 100 grams of tobacco, and a 'reasonable' amount of perfume per adult. Bringing narcotics, arms and ammunition, cordless telephones, TV sets, radio receivers, pornography, fresh fruit, printed matter in Chinese characters and Chinese medicines into the country is prohibited. The rules state that 'film, pre-recorded video tape, video laser disc, records, computer software must be screened by the Censor Board', presumably to control pornography. You are permitted to bring in one radio or cassette recorder as long as you take it out on departure. Officially, your personal goods are not supposed to have a value exceeding US$250, but they don't seem to care about your camera and Walkman.

Despite all these onerous-sounding rules, Indonesian customs are by no means heavy-handed with foreigners. Some entry points might be stricter or more conscientious than others, but probably all they'll do is have you open your bags for a brief rummage around, and often not even that – at least if you have a Western face. People with Asian features are scrutinised more closely.

MONEY

Try and bring as much money as possible, preferably in relatively safe travellers' cheques issued by a major bank. Also bring at least a few hundred US dollars in cash – there are a few odd towns where banks do not accept travellers' cheques.

Changing money in places like Jakarta, Yogya and Kuta, where there are large numbers of foreign tourists, is generally very easy and the exchange rate is favourable. Touristy places have lots of moneychangers as well as the banks and their exchange rates are very similar to, and often better than, bank rates.

If you intend travelling extensively around Indonesia then bring US dollars – either in cash or in travellers' cheques from a major US company such as American Express, Citicorp or Bank of America – or you'll be sorry. Australian dollars are second-best, but you may have trouble even with these. In major cities like Jakarta and Denpasar, it's also easy to change major European currencies such as Deutschmarks, pounds sterling, Netherlands guilders, French or Swiss francs. Slightly more obscure major currencies such as Canadian dollars can be easily changed in Kuta, but even in Jakarta just about the only place you can change the stuff is at the American Express office.

The banks which normally handle foreign exchange include Bank Expor Impor Indonesia, Bank Rakyat Indonesia, Bank Dagang Negara and Bank Negara Indonesia. However, not all branches change money.

Some banks may give better exchange rates than others. You usually get a slightly

better rate on cash than with travellers' cheques. There is a 500 rp 'stamp duty' (tax) if changing more than 100,000 rp, and a 1000 rp stamp duty if changing over one million rp.

If you're going to really remote places, carry stacks of rupiah because there won't be anywhere to change foreign cash or cheques. Places where you can change cash and travellers' cheques are noted in the relevant sections.

There are other problems to consider; it's often difficult to change big notes – breaking a 10,000 rp note in a small city can be a major hassle and out in the villages it's damn near impossible. Secondly, away from the major centres notes tend to stay in circulation much longer and tend to get very tatty – when they get too dog-eared and worn-looking they're difficult to spend. Torn notes or ones held together with adhesive tape won't be accepted by anyone and you should try and avoid having them passed onto you – the only place you'll be able to get rid of them is at the bank.

Credit cards are of limited usefulness. They can be used if you stay in the big hotels; some city shops and restaurants will accept them, as will international airlines. Garuda and Merpati take credit cards for domestic flights and some travel agents will accept them too.

Currency

The unit of currency in Indonesia is the rupiah (rp) – like the lira in Italy there is nothing else. You get coins of 25, 50 and 100 rp. There used to be 5 and 10 rp coins, but they seem to have vanished. Notes come in 100, 500, 1000, 5000 and 10,000 rp denominations.

There is no restriction on the import or export of foreign currencies in cash, travellers' cheques or any other form – you can take in and take out as much as you like. However, there is a restriction on the movement of Indonesian currency; you're not allowed to take in or take out more than 50,000 rp.

Exchange Rates

Australia	A$1	=	1576 rp
Britain	UK£1	=	3788 rp
Canada	C$1	=	1739 rp
Germany	DM1	=	1444 rp
Hong Kong	HK$1	=	268 rp
Japan	Y100	=	1619 rp
Malaysia	R1	=	814 rp
Netherlands	G1	=	1151 rp
New Zealand	NZ$1	=	1123 rp
Philippines	P1	=	85 rp
Singapore	S$1	=	1263 rp
Sweden	Kr1	=	359 rp
Switzerland	SFr1	=	1433 rp
Thailand	B1	=	80 rp
USA	US$1	=	2067 rp

The rupiah has a floating rate, and in recent years it has tended to fall by about 4% a year against the US dollar.

Costs

How much it will cost to travel in Indonesia is largely up to the individual and depends on what degree of comfort you desire or what degree of discomfort you're prepared to put up with. It also depends on how much travelling you do. But most importantly in Indonesia it's where you go that makes or breaks the budget – some parts of the country cost *much* more to travel through than others.

If you follow the well-beaten tourist track through Bali, Java and Sumatra you'll find Indonesia is one of the cheapest places in South-East Asia (exceptions like Jakarta apart) in which to travel. Travellers' centres like Bali, Yogyakarta and Lake Toba are excellent value for food and accommodation, while Nusa Tenggara is marginally more expensive than Bali but cheap by any standards.

On the other hand, once you get to some of the outer provinces, like Kalimantan, Maluku or Irian Jaya, you could be paying five or more times what you paid in Kuta Beach for equivalent accommodation. In Kuta, you can get some pretty decent accommodation starting at about 3000 rp per night for a single room, but in Ambon (Maluku) the room prices start from around 10,000 rp per night. Food prices don't vary as much as room prices, though food quality deteriorates in eastern Indonesia.

Transport expenses also increase once you get into the outer provinces. On Bali, Java, Sumatra and Nusa Tenggara there's very little need to take to the air, while in the interior of Irian Jaya you have no choice but to fly. In the outer islands like Maluku, you really can't rely on ships – there may be only one ship every week or two between any two islands. If you're not prepared to fly you'll spend a good deal of your two-month tourist pass just waiting around in port towns.

If you confine yourself to Sumatra, Java, Bali and Nusa Tenggara, rock-bottom budget travel works out to around US$10 per day, not including what you spent to reach Indonesia in the first place. Multiply that figure by at least five if you're heading towards Maluku and Irian Jaya – multiply again by two or three if you need such luxuries as air-conditioning and tour guides, or want to buy woodcarvings, batik paintings and other souvenirs. You should keep in mind that in places like Kuta, where living expenses are low, there are more things to buy: massages, admission charges to discos, copious quantities of alcohol to consume, and tours and dance performances in abundance. Before you go out of your way to set new records for austerity, you should remember that travelling is not meant to be some sort of endurance test. If you want to find out how long you can stay away and how little money you can spend doing it, go ahead, but it's not going to earn you any credit in heaven. It is slightly silly to go overseas in order to spend several months in a permanent state of discomfort.

Tipping

Tipping is not a normal practice in Indonesia so please don't try to make it one. Jakarta taxi drivers, however, seem to expect (demand?) a tip. If you must tip, 500 rp would be enough. Hotel porters expect a couple of hundred rupiah per bag. Officially, the sign in Jakarta's airport says that porters should receive 400 rp for up to 50 kg of luggage, and 800 rp for over 50 kg. Unofficially, if you've got over 50 kg of luggage, you'd better have a mule.

Bargaining

Many everyday purchases in Indonesia require bargaining. This applies particularly to handicrafts, clothes and artwork but can also apply to almost anything you buy in a shop. Restaurant meals, transport and, often, accommodation are generally fixed in price – restaurants usually have their menus and prices posted up on the wall and hotels usually have a price list. Sometimes when supply exceeds demand hotels may be willing to bend their prices rather than see you go next door. Though transport prices are fixed, bemos throughout Indonesia have a well-earned reputation for charging Westerners whatever they're willing to pay – or even more than they're willing to pay!

Your first step should be to establish a starting price. It's usually easiest to ask them their price rather than make an initial offer, unless you know very clearly what you're willing to pay. As a rule of thumb your starting price could be anything from a third to two-thirds of the asking price – assuming that the asking price is not completely crazy. Then with offer and counter-offer you move closer to an acceptable price. Don't show too much interest when bargaining, and if you can't get an acceptable price walk away. You will often be called back and offered a lower price.

A few rules apply to good bargaining. First of all it's not a question of life or death, where every rupiah you chisel away makes a difference. Don't pass up something you really want that's expensive or unobtainable at home because the seller won't come down a few hundred rupiah more – it is nothing compared with the hundreds of dollars you spent on the airfare! Secondly, when your offer is accepted you have to buy it – don't then decide you don't want it after all. Thirdly, while bargaining may seem to have a competitive element in it, it's a mean victory knocking a poor becak driver down from 400 to 350 rp for a ride.

Bargaining is sometimes fun – and often not. A lot depends on whether you and the vendor are smiling or yelling at each other. Sometimes it seems as if people don't want your money if they can't overcharge you. Sometimes they will ask ludicrous prices and will get very upset if you offer a ridiculously low price back, even if you mean it as a joke. This also works in the other direction; there is a nauseating category of Westerner on the Asian trail who will launch into lengthy bitch sessions about being overcharged five cents for an orange.

The locals are usually a good source of information about current prices. If you don't know what the right price for transport is you might try asking another passenger what the regular price (*harga biasa*) is. Then you offer the correct fare. There's not much point doing this when you're buying something in a shop or at a market – onlookers naturally side with their own people, so you don't get past square one.

Don't get hassled by bargaining. Remember that no matter how good you are at it or how inept, there's always going to be someone who is better or will boast about how much cheaper they got something than you did. Don't go around feeling that you're being ripped off all the time – too many people do. In Indonesia you can still buy a lot of stuff cheaper than you would back home.

WHEN TO GO

The cool, dry season from April to October is the best time to visit much of Indonesia, but there are also distinct tourist seasons which alter the picture in some parts. Bali is Australia's favourite Asian getaway and everyone is duty-bound to make the pilgrimage eventually. The Christmas holiday period brings a wave of migratory Australians – and air fares from Australia are also higher at this time. The May and August school holidays also get them flocking in. The European summer holidays bring crowds – July for the Germans, August for the French. The second big influx of tourists is into Torajaland in Sulawesi – practically a French and German colony during the European summer holidays.

WHAT TO BRING

Bring as little as possible. It is much better to buy something you've left behind than to have to throw things away because you've got too much to carry. If you have to get something it shouldn't be too hard to pick it up in Indonesia – there are many well-stocked shops everywhere. The only problem is that Indonesian clothes, particularly shoes, only seem to be available in small sizes.

Before deciding what to bring, decide what you're going to carry it in. For budget travellers the backpack is still the best single piece of luggage. Adding some thief-deterrent by sewing on a few tabs so you can shut your pack with a padlock is a good idea. On the other hand, packs can be cumbersome and difficult to get onto crowded bemos. One innovation is the travel-pack, which can be used as either a backpack or a carry bag.

If you're into hiking then you've got heaps of opportunity in Indonesia, so a large pack with a frame may come in handy. For most people though, a small to medium-sized soft pack, with no frame or with a semi-rigid frame, is much better all round. A pack with zippered compartments – as opposed to one which loads from the top – is a little more theft-proof, and zippers make it easier to load and unload the contents. Shoulder bags are easier to wield on crowded buses and trains, but they're hard to carry for any distance – so if you've got any walking to do you're better off with a pack. A small day-pack is very useful. Whatever you bring, try and make it small; in some parts of Indonesia bemos are packed to the hilt with passengers and there's next to no space left over to stow baggage.

You really need only two sets of clothes – the one on your body and another set to wear while you're washing the first set. Clothing is quite cheap in Indonesia and you can always buy more, at least as long as you're not too large.

Temperatures are uniformly tropical year-round in Indonesia so short-sleeved shirts and T-shirts are the order of the day. Bring at least one long-sleeved shirt for the cool evenings. A few places in Indonesia get bloody cold at night – the Balim Valley in Irian Jaya, Kintamani in Bali and the Dieng Plateau in Java, for example. You don't need Antarctic survival gear, but long jeans, shoes and possibly a jacket are necessary. If you travel in passenger trucks or boats at night you'll be surprised just how much the temperature drops.

Modesty prevails. If you must wear shorts, they should be the loose-fitting type which come down almost to the knees, but even that will be unacceptable to many Indonesians. Higher dress standards apply particularly whenever you're visiting a government office – if you wear shorts, you will probably not be allowed in the building. You see signs up around Kuta showing how you should and should not dress during these formal occasions.

Dark-coloured clothes hide the dirt better. Artificial fibres like rayon and nylon are too hot and sticky in this climate; drip-dry cotton or silk are best. You need clothes which will dry fairly quickly in the humidity – thicker jeans are a problem in this regard. You'll need some heavy clothing if you travel by motorcycle.

A hat and sunglasses are absolutely essential, and don't forget sunscreen (UV) lotion. A water bottle is a good idea but you can easily buy water in plastic throwaway bottles.

Some travellers find a sarong useful. Besides wearing it, a sarong can serve as an impromptu blanket during cold evenings; or lie on it on a white-sand beach; wrap it round your head to counter the pounding sun; use it as a top sheet or, alternatively, as a barrier between yourself and an unhealthy-looking mattress in an unhealthy-looking hotel; pin it up over the window of your hotel room to block the outside lights that burn fiercely all night long; even use it as a towel – if it still seems clean enough.

A sleeping bag is really only useful if you intend doing a lot of high-altitude camping.

Toiletries like soap, shampoo, conditioner, toothpaste and toilet paper are all readily available in Indonesia. Dental floss and shaving cream are hard to find, however, and tampons can be found with some difficulty.

Stock up on some passport or visa photos – these are readily obtained at photographic shops in Indonesia but you can never find these shops when you need them. A couple of places in Indonesia require permits to visit (like the interior of Irian Jaya) and photos are needed.

The following is a checklist of things you might consider packing, but don't feel obligated to bring everything on this list:

Passport, money, air ticket, address book, namecards, visa & passport photos, Swiss army knife, electric immersion coil (for making hot water), cup, padlock, camera & accessories, sunglasses, alarm clock, leakproof water bottle, torch (flashlight) with batteries, comb, compass, daypack, long pants, short pants, long shirt, T-shirt, nylon jacket, sweater, raincover for backpack, rainsuit or poncho, razor, razor blades, shaving cream, sewing kit, spoon, sunhat, sunscreen, toilet paper, tampons, toothbrush, toothpaste, dental floss, deodorant, shampoo, underwear, socks, thongs, nail clipper, tweezers, mosquito repellent, vitamins, Panadol (Tylenol), laxative, Lomotil, birth control and any special medications you use.

A final thought: airlines do lose bags from time to time – you've got a much better chance of not losing your bag if it is tagged with your name and address *inside* as well as outside. Other tags can always fall off or be removed.

TOURIST OFFICES
Local Tourist Offices
Unlike many other Asian countries, Indonesia has neither an excellent tourist information service pumping out useful brochures, nor well-equipped offices with all the facts at their fingertips.

The Indonesian national tourist organisation, the Directorate General of Tourism (which has its base in Jakarta) maintains tourist offices called Kanwil Pariwisata in each province. The regional tourist offices are called DIPARDA or BAPPARDA. The sign on the building is usually written only in Indonesian.

The usefulness of the tourist offices varies greatly from place to place. This happens in Java, where the city tourist offices (sometimes called 'Visitors Information Centres') in Jakarta, Yogya, Solo attract lots of tourists and provide excellent maps and information about the city and its immediate vicinity, while offices in the less-visited areas may have nothing at all – they'll always try to help, but it's pretty hopeless if they don't speak English and you don't speak Indonesian. For more details of local offices read the information sections listed under the main cities. Literature is sometimes not displayed so ask to see what they've got. Sometimes their stocks are severely limited and they can't give anything away – but you could borrow it from them and whip down the road to a shop with a photocopier and get a copy. Useful publications are the *Tourist Map of Indonesia* and the *Calendar of Events* for the whole country.

Overseas Reps

There are a number of Indonesian Tourist Promotion Offices (ITPO) abroad where you can get some brochures and information about Indonesia. The ITPO headquarters is at the Directorate General of Tourism, Jalan Kramat Raya 81, PO Box 409, Jakarta. There are also offices in San Francisco, Tokyo, Singapore and Frankfurt. Overseas, Garuda Airlines offices are also worth trying for information.

USEFUL ORGANISATIONS

When it comes to useful organisations, many travellers think first of their nation's embassy. In fact, embassies often prove to be a disappointment. If you lose your passport your embassy can issue a new one, and if you die they'll probably pass the message on to your next of kin eventually, but if you've got

malaria or all your money gets stolen, it's likely you'll be left twisting in the wind. Still, you've nothing to lose by giving them a call – there are a few embassy staff who actually take their job seriously.

Tim Sar (☎ 5501111) in Jakarta is the search and rescue organisation. In other cities, Tim Sar is listed on the first page of the telephone book, often just with the heading 'SAR'.

The Summer Institute of Linguistics (or Bible Translators) is an international missionary organisation with branches in 56 countries. Whether or not you are interested in their religious activities, they do linguistics courses and operate medical clinics around Indonesia. They also dispense vaccinations and medical advice, and can keep you informed of the latest epidemics ravaging the country. You can ring them in Jakarta (☎ (21) 330710) or write to PO Box 373 KBY, JKSMG, Jakarta 12001. Their head office is in Huntington Beach, California, USA.

BUSINESS HOURS & HOLIDAYS

Most government offices are open Monday to Thursday from 8 am to 3 pm, Friday from 8 to 11.30 am, and Saturday from 8 am to 2 pm.

Private business offices have staggered hours: Monday to Friday from 8 am to 4 pm or 9 am to 5 pm, with a lunch break in the middle of the day. Some offices are also open on Saturday mornings until about noon.

Banks are open Monday to Friday, usually from 8 am to noon (sometimes until 2 pm), and on Saturdays usually from 8 to 11 am. Most post offices have similar opening hours. Bank branches in hotels stay open longer, and moneychangers in places like Kuta Beach stay open until the evening.

Shops tend to open around 8 am and stay open until around 9 pm. Sunday is a public holiday but some shops and many airline offices open for at least part of the day. In the big cities, shopping complexes, supermarkets and department stores stay open from 8.30 am to 8 pm every day and often on Sunday.

Muslim Holidays

Ramadan (Bulan Puasa) is the traditional Muslim month of daily fasting from sunrise to sunset. It falls in the ninth month of the Muslim calendar. It's a good time to avoid fervent Muslim areas of Indonesia – you get woken up in your losmen at 3 am in the morning to have a meal before the fasting period begins. Many restaurants shut down during the day, leaving you searching the backstreets for a restaurant that's open.

Lebaran (Idul Fitri) marks the end of Ramadan, and is a noisy celebration at the end of a month of gastronomic austerity. It's a national public holiday of two days' duration.

The Alquran is a Muslim Javanese and Sumatran-oriented sacrificial ceremony. Idul Adha is a festival commemorating Abraham's willingness to sacrifice his son, Isaac, celebrated with prayers and feasts. Maulud Nabi Mohammed (Hari Natal) is the birthday of the Prophet Mohammed. Isra Miraj Nabi Mohammed celebrates the ascension of the Prophet.

National Public Holidays

In addition to Muslim holidays, there are also a few national public holidays celebrated by everybody:

Kartini Day falls on 21 April and commemorates the birthday of Raden Ajeng Kartini, who was born in 1879. She was the daughter of the Regent of Jepara in Java and started a school for the daughters of regents aimed at giving them a Western-style education. In letters to Dutch friends (which have been published) she poured out her feelings about the burdens and restrictions of Javanese and Islamic customs, and her writings also had a strong nationalist bent to them. She is considered not only an early nationalist but also the first Indonesian women's emancipationist.

Independence Day (Hari Proklamasi Kemerdekaan) commemorates the fact that on 17 August 1945 Sukarno proclaimed Indonesian independence in Jakarta. Every year on this day celebrations of the event are held all over the country but particularly in Jakarta where there are parades, a flag-raising ceremony and a reading of the original text of the declaration.

Christmas Day & New Year's Day need no introduction. They are national public holidays in Indonesia.

CULTURAL EVENTS

With such a diversity of people in the archipelago there are many local holidays, festivals and cultural events. On Sumba, for example, mock battles and jousting matches harking back to the era of internecine warfare are held in February and March. The Balinese have the Galungan festival, during which time all the gods, including the supreme deity Sanghyang Widi, come down to earth to join in. In Tanatoraja in central Sulawesi the end of the harvest season is the time for funeral and house-warming ceremonies. In Java, Bersih Desa takes place at the time of the rice harvest – houses and gardens are cleaned, village roads and paths repaired. This festival was once enacted to remove evil spirits from the village but it's now used to express gratitude to Dewi Sri, the rice goddess. Because most Indonesians are Muslims, many holidays and festivals are associated with the Islamic religion. Muslim festivals are affected by the lunar calendar and dates move back 10 or 11 days each year, so it's not easy to list what month they will fall in.

A regional *Calendar of Events* is generally available from the appropriate regional tourist office. It lists national holidays, festivals particular to that region and many of the music, dance and theatre performances held throughout the year. There's also an *Indonesia Calendar of Events* booklet which covers holidays and festivals throughout the archipelago. You should be able to pick up a copy from any of the overseas Indonesian Tourist Promotion Offices, or overseas Garuda offices.

POST & TELECOMMUNICATIONS
Postal Rates

Domestic letters cost 100 rp within the same city, 200 rp for any place within Indonesia, or

500 rp for express mail. For international post, a special discount rate applies for countries which are members of the Association of South-East Nations (ASEAN), which includes Singapore, Malaysia, Thailand, Brunei and the Philippines. International airmail rates for letters(20g), postcards and aerograms are as follows:

Destination	Letter (20g)	P'card	A'gram
Australia & Pacific	1000 rp	700 rp	700 rp
USA, Canada & Europe	1100 rp	800 rp	800 rp
ASEAN countries	450 rp	300 rp	300 rp

Parcels up to a maximum weight of 10 kg can be sent by sea mail. If you have more than that, break it up into several parcels. The rates to Canada, Europe and the USA are:

Destination	Weight	Rates
Canada	0-3 kg	27,000 rp
Europe	3-5 kg	48,000 rp
USA	5-10 kg	76,000 rp

Parcel post rates to Australia and New Zealand are about 10% cheaper.

Sending Mail

Letters and small packets bound for overseas or domestic delivery may be registered for an extra fee at any post office branch. There are also two forms of express service available for mail within Indonesia: blue *kilat* envelopes are for regular airmail; yellow *kilat khusus* are for airmail express. These envelopes, plus aerogrammes, can be bought at all post offices.

Overseas parcels can be posted, insured and registered (*tercatat*), from a main post office but they'll usually want to have a look at the contents first so there's not much point in making up a nice tidy parcel before you get there. If you're going to Singapore you'll find it considerably cheaper to post overseas packages and parcels from there than from Indonesia.

Receiving Mail

The postal service in Indonesia is generally pretty good and the poste restantes at Indonesian *kantor pos* – at least in major travellers' centres like Jakarta, Yogya, Bali, Medan and Lake Toba – are efficiently run. Expected mail always seems to arrive. Have your letters addressed to you with your surname in capitals and underlined, the poste restante, Kantor Pos, and city in question. 'Lost' letters may have been misfiled under Christian names so always check under both your names.

Telephone

The telecom offices (*kantor telepon dan telegrap*) are often open 24 hours in major cities, and increasingly offer fax service as well as telephone and telegraph. However, the best service of all is provided by the private telecommunications agencies, usually called Warpostal, Warparpostel or Wartel, found throughout the country. Hours of operation at many of these offices are from around 7.30 am until midnight, but sometimes 24 hours.

Public pay phones are still rare, but are

gradually becoming more common. They can be found in some post offices, at the airports and in public phone booths in the major cities and towns. They are blue in colour and take 50 rp and 100 rp coins. On the street, they cost 50 rp for three minutes, but in many hotels and restaurants there are private pay phones where you get only one minute for 100 rp. When the phone begins to beep, feed in more coins or you'll be cut off. With private pay phones, normally you must dial the number first and drop the coin into the slot *after* the other party has answered – otherwise, you will be able to hear them but they won't be able to hear you!

Telephone cards *(kartu telepon)* are a recent innovation. You insert the magnetic card into a special telephone *(telepon kartu)* and dial. A local call requires one unit, which works out to 82.50 rp. Telephone cards are sold in the following denominations: 20 units (1650 rp); 60 units (4950 rp); 80 units (6600 rp); 100 units (8250 rp); 280 units (23,100 rp); 400 units (33,000 rp); 680 units (56,100 rp).

Domestic calls are charged according to a system of zones. For example, if you're ringing from Biak in Irian Jaya, Zones I, II and III include the local area around Biak plus Nabire and Manok; Zone IV is the rest of Irian Jaya plus Ambon and Ternate; and Zone V is Java, Sumatra, Sulawesi, Nusa Tenggara and Kalimantan. The rates per minute are: zone I, 900 rp; zone II, 1000 rp; zone III, 1200 rp; zone IV, 1500 rp; zone V, 2000 rp. There is a 50% discount on calls placed between 9 pm and 6 am.

There are two types of calls: normal *(biasa)* and immediate *(segera)*. The latter is a type of express call that gets you through faster than a normal call. Express calls cost twice as much as normal calls.

There is now international direct dialling (IDD) to many countries. To make an IDD call, first dial 00, then the country code, area code (minus the initial zero if it has one) and then the number you want to reach. The country code for dialling to Indonesia is 62.

As with domestic calls, international calls are charged according to zones.

IDD Rates Rates for IDD telephone calls are:

Zone I: Singapore, Malaysia and Brunei; 2800 rp per minute.
Zone II: Hong Kong, Thailand and the Philippines; 3800 rp per minute.
Zone III: Australia, New Zealand, Japan, South Korea, India and the USA; 4550 rp per minute.
Zone IV: Canada and the UK; 5200 rp per minute.
Zone V: Western Europe (minus the UK), Alaska, South America and Africa; 6180 rp per minute.

For most countries, there is a 25% discount for IDD calls placed between midnight and 6 am. For a few countries, this discount is in effect from 9 pm until 6 am. Check with the phone company to see which night-time discount, if any, applies to the country you wish to call.

With operator assistance, you can reverse charges. Another way to reverse charges is to use Home Country Direct Dialling, available from special telephones in a few airports and luxury hotels. These phones can be used for placing collect calls only to specified countries. Just press the button for your country (Australia, USA, etc) and an operator from that country will come on the line. Home Country Direct Dialling is currently available for the following countries only: Australia, Italy, Japan, The Netherlands, New Zealand, Singapore, South Korea and the USA.

Some useful numbers include:

Directory assistance, local:	108
Directory assistance, long-distance:	106
Operator assistance, domestic:	100
Operator assistance, international:	101

Fax, Telex & Telegraph
You can send messages by fax, telex and telegraph from the government-run telecommunications office in most cities and many mid-sized towns. However, the privately operated Warpostal agencies offer better service.

The cost for sending an international fax is:

Zone I: Singapore, Malaysia and Brunei; 4400 rp per page.

Zone II: Hong Kong, Thailand and the Philippines; 6600 rp per page.
Zone III: Australia, New Zealand, Japan, South Korea, India and the USA; 7700 rp per page.
Zone IV: Canada and the UK; 8800 rp per page.
Zone V: Western Europe (minus the UK), Alaska, South America and Africa; 10,450 rp per page.

For international telexes, you are charged for a minimum of three minutes. Telex rates are:

Australia, Asia, Canada, Europe, New Zealand and the USA (minus Alaska); 17,347 rp for three minutes. Alaska, South America and Africa; 22,495 rp for three minutes.

There is a minimum of 10 words per telegram, including the address. International telegram charges (per word) are: Australia and New Zealand 520 rp; Canada and the USA 650 rp; Europe 650 rp.

TIME
There are three time zones in Indonesia. Sumatra, Java, and West and Central Kalimantan are on Western Indonesian Time which is seven hours ahead of GMT. Bali, Nusa Tenggara, South and East Kalimantan, and Sulawesi are on Central Indonesian Time, which is eight hours ahead of GMT. Irian Jaya and Maluku are on East Indonesian Time, which is nine hours ahead of GMT. In a country straddling the equator, there is of course no daylight saving time.

Allowing for variations due to daylight saving, when it is 12 noon in Jakarta it is 1 pm in Ujung Pandang, 2 pm in Jayapura, 5 am in London, 3 pm in Melbourne or Sydney, 12 midnight in New York and 9 pm

the previous day in San Francisco or Los Angeles. Because of a detour in the time zones Singapore is one hour ahead of Sumatra and Java.

Strung out along the equator, Indonesian days and nights are approximately equal in length, and sunrises and sunsets occur very rapidly with almost no twilight. Sunrise is around 5.30 to 6 am and sunset is around 5.30 to 6 pm, varying slightly depending on distance from the equator.

ELECTRICITY
Electricity is usually 220 volts, 50 cycles AC, but a few places are still wired for 110 volts – so check first before you plug in a foreign electrical appliance! Sockets are designed to accommodate two round prongs of the European variety; there is no third pin for earth (ground). Electricity is usually pretty reliable in cities, but occasional blackouts are common in rural areas. It's wise to keep a torch (flashlight) handy for such occasions (don't forget extra batteries), and candles could also prove useful (don't forget the cigarette lighter or matches!).

In some small towns, or even in parts of larger towns, electricity is still a fairly futuristic thing – you find the odd isolated hotel where lighting is provided with oil lamps. Even where there is electricity you're likely to find the lighting can be very dim. Electricity is expensive (for most Indonesians), so cheaper hotels have light bulbs of such low wattage that you can almost see the electricity crawling laboriously around the filaments. If you can't get by with just 25

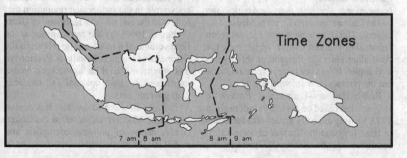

watts then it might be worth carrying a more powerful light bulb with you.

Street lighting can also be a problem – sometimes there's very little, sometimes none at all. Walking down dark, pot-holed streets in some Indonesian cities is like walking through a minefield. Falling into a sewage canal is a real drag, so be sure you bring a torch.

LAUNDRY

Virtually every hotel – from the smallest to the largest – has a laundry service, and in most places this is very inexpensive. About the only thing you need be concerned about is the weather – clothes are dried on the line, so a hot, sunny day is essential. Give them your laundry in the morning – they like to wash clothes before 9 am so it has sufficient time to dry before sunset.

WEIGHTS & MEASURES

Indonesia has fully adopted the international metric system.

BOOKS & MAPS

Indonesia is not a straightforward country. Its history, economics, politics and culture – and their bizarre interactions – are wide open to interpretation, and different writers come up with astoundingly different interpretations of events. If you read about Java or Bali you'll be suffocated beneath the literature – but trying to find out anything about the outer islands is like putting together bits and pieces of a jigsaw.

People & Society

Indonesians: Portraits from an Archipelago by Ian Charles Stewart (Concept Media, Singapore, 1983) is a photographic essay on Indonesian life and culture which took the Australian photographer/author three years to compile. It's a very large, expensive book but the photographs are very fine.

Robin Hanbury-Tenison's *A Pattern of Peoples* was based on his trip to Indonesia in 1973, visiting minority groups like the Danis of Irian Jaya and the Torajas of Sulawesi. It comments on the effects that tourism and other developments have had on what were – until recently – isolated peoples.

A compilation of some of the intriguing religious, social and mystical customs of the diverse peoples of Indonesia is Lee Khoon Choy's *Indonesia: Between Myth & Reality* (Federal Publications, Singapore, 1977). It's a journalistic travelogue, derived from the author's short spells in the country as a journalist and politician and his stay as Singapore's Ambassador to Indonesia from 1970 to 1975.

The best account of the top echelons of the Indonesian government and military is Australian journalist David Jenkin's *Suharto and his Generals: Indonesian Military Politics 1975-1983* (Monograph Series No 64, Cornell Modern Indonesia Project, South East Asia Program, Cornell University, 1984). Jenkins interviewed many of Indonesia's leading generals, including those both in and out of power. The final product is an intriguing and illuminating work.

Christopher Koch's *The Year of Living Dangerously* is an evocative reconstruction of life in Jakarta during the final chaotic months of the Sukarno period and a sympathetic portrayal of the Indonesians and their culture and society. The movie by Australian director Peter Weir packs a feel for the place that few other movies could ever hope to achieve.

The Fugitive, by Pramoedya Ananta Toer (Penguin, 1992), is set in East Java in WW II. Pramoedya wrote the book while at Bukit Duri Prison, a forced labour camp, where he was imprisoned from 1947 to 1949 for his active role in the Indonesian revolution that followed the end of WW II. *House of Glass* (Penguin, 1992), by the same author, is the final volume of a quartet of novels set in the Indonesia of Dutch colonialism. Pramoedya has spent more than seventeen years imprisoned by both colonial and independent governments.

Twilight in Jakarta by the Indonesian journalist, Mochtar Lubis, is an outspoken condemnation of political corruption and one of the the most vivid documentations of life in the capital at the beginning of the 1960s, particularly of Jakarta's lower depths – the prostitutes, becak drivers and rural immigrants. Lubis is well known for his forthright views and he was twice imprisoned during the Sukarno regime for his political convictions. The book goes on and off the ban list in Indonesia, but at present the Oxford in Asia paperback (Oxford University Press, Malaysia, 1983) is on sale in Jakarta.

Pramoedya Ananta Toer, a Javanese author, has written four novels about life in colonial Indonesia. The first two – *This Earth of Mankind* and *Child of All Nations* – are available in Penguin paperback. Both novels were bestsellers in Indonesia but the Suharto government banned them in 1981, claiming that, while they might be skilful accounts of the colonial era, they were also subtle Marxist parodies of President Suharto's Indonesia. The author has been in and out of prison ever since he started writing: the Dutch jailed him during the independence struggle; he was briefly detained by the Army in the 1960s, as an anti-Sukarno move, and his history of the Chinese in Indonesia was banned; in 1965 he was jailed by Suharto's New Order government and exiled to Baru Island for 14 years. Pramoedya now lives in Jakarta under house arrest.

History

A good general history that pieces together some of the jigsaw is *A History of Modern Indonesia* (Macmillan, 1981) by M C Ricklefs, Professor of History at Monash University in Melbourne, Australia. It takes you through from 1300 and while it mainly concerns itself with Java and the Dutch conquest it also ties in what was happening in the outer islands.

Indonesia – an Alternative History by academics Malcolm Caldwell and Ernst Utrecht, is an interesting book. Utrecht was once a member of Indonesia's Supreme Advisory Council which Sukarno set up to advise him on government policy. In a blow-by-blow account of Dutch economic policy

in Indonesia, they argue that it is the Dutch who are responsible for Indonesia's economic problems. They also criticise the Western attitude which sees Indonesia only as a cornerstone of defence against Communism and as a lucrative place of investment.

Australian journalist Bruce Grant's *Indonesia* (Melbourne University Press, Melbourne, 1964) gives background info about the country and takes you through the tumultuous Sukarno years. The book was first published in 1964, with later reprints taking in the events just after the attempted coup of 1965. His biography of the leader and translations of some of Sukarno's speeches make for some fascinating reading.

An interesting and very readable account of the Suharto years is *Suharto's Indonesia* (Fontana, 1980) by Australian journalist Hamish McDonald, who worked as a freelance correspondent in Jakarta from 1975 to 1978.

One of the more evocative books on contemporary Indonesia is *The Indonesian Tragedy* (Routledge & Kegan Paul, UK, 1978) by Australian journalist Brian May. Much of the book, as May himself says, 'is a tale of Western-aided despotism' that Indonesia has suffered under Suharto's rule. It also gives a rather more sympathetic account of Sukarno than has generally been afforded.

Travel Guides

If you think travel through the outer islands of Indonesia is time-consuming now, then just read Helen & Frank Schreider's *Drums of Tonkin* (published 1965) – they overcame the lack of transport by island-hopping all the way from Java to Timor in a tiny amphibious jeep, defying landslides, oncoming monsoons, hostile (or just over-enthused?) native inhabitants and the strange propensity Jakarta soldiers once had to shoot at vehicles making illegal turns.

Whilst the Schreiders took only their pet dog with them, zoologist-TV personality David Attenborough left the UK with practically nothing and returned from the archipelago with an orang-utan, a couple of pythons, civets, parrots and assorted other birds and reptiles. The whole saga of the enterprise, eventually to be dignified by the title 'expedition', is recounted in his book *Zoo Quest for a Dragon*, published in 1957.

The Tropical Traveller by John Hatt (Pan Books, London) is a good general introduction to travel in the tropics.

If you intend trekking, camping out or heading off to the great outdoors beyond everything, or are just interested in doing something different, get Christina Dodwell's *An Explorer's Handbook – Travel, Survival & Bush Cookery* (Hodder & Stoughton, London).

Other Lonely Planet guides covering Indonesia are *South-East Asia on a Shoestring* and *Bali & Lombok – a travel survival kit*.

Bookshops

If you want to read, bring your own books. US and British paperbacks in English are available from the bookshops in some of the larger hotels in the main cities, sometimes from airport shops, but they're expensive and the supply and range are extremely limited. There are second-hand bookshops in well-touristed places like Kuta, Sanur or Ubud in Bali.

Maps

The most widely available series of maps, both within and without Indonesia, seems to be by Nelles of Germany, also distributed by Periplus. Besides an overall map of Indonesia, there are more detailed Nelles maps of Sumatra, Java and Nusa Tenggara, Bali, Kalimantan, Sulawesi, and Irian Jaya and Maluku.

Some other maps available outside Indonesia include *Bartholomew's Asia, South-East*, *Hildebrand's Travel Map Western Indonesia* and *Apa Maps Western Indonesia*.

Some other maps can only be found within Indonesia. A useful map of all Indonesia is published by P T Pembina (☎ 813886), Jalan D I Panjaitan 45, Jakarta. They also have very good individual maps of Java, Sumatra, Kalimantan and Sulawesi. The *Jawa-Bali Kilometer & Tourist Map* published by P T Pembina isn't *absolutely* accurate in fine detail but it's the best general map available for Java.

The Directorate General of Tourism publishes a useful give-away information booklet, the *Indonesia Tourist Map*, which includes maps of Java, Bali, Sumatra and Sulawesi, and a good overall map of Indonesia. Maps of major Javanese, Sumatran and Balinese cities are easy enough to come by – ask at the tourist offices or try bookshops, airports and major hotels, particularly in Jakarta, Denpasar and Kuta.

In the outer islands the odd good map may pop up but quite often you'll be lucky to come across anything at all, or else only fairly simple maps. Hotels often have a good, detailed map of the town or city hanging on the wall of their foyer. The local police station should have a good map and will often allow foreigners to photocopy it.

Virtually every town and city has a *kantor pekerjaan umum*, usually just known as *kantor PU*. This office is responsible for mapping the city in question, and sometimes they have copies for sale. If not, they will probably allow you to make photocopies of their master map.

MEDIA

The news media is expected to – and does – practise self-censorship. While stories of corruption, wastage of funds and government ineptitude are frequently run, care is always taken not to point the finger too closely. Most importantly, criticism of Suharto and his immediate family is not tolerated. In one way or another the Indonesian government keeps criticism down to a tolerable, non-threatening level. However, in the past year or so, the press has become increasingly bold, apparently with support from some high-ranking military figures who have become disillusioned with the current state of Indonesian politics.

Newspapers & Magazines

Whenever you buy newspapers and magazines in Indonesia, take a close look at the date. It is not uncommon for vendors to try to sell old news from two or three weeks ago. This doesn't happen so much in Jakarta, but is a common practice elsewhere. They will do this even if they have more recent editions.

Domestic The English-language press is limited mostly to the *Jakarta Post*, published daily and available around the country. While subject to the same 'self-censorship' as other Indonesian publications, it manages to tell you quite a lot about Indonesia – and the rest of the world – in a roundabout way.

The *Indonesia Times*, an 'independent newspaper' according to the slogan printed on top, appears to be an English-language mouthpiece for the government. We've never seen it on sale anywhere, but it's handed out freely to foreign passengers on some international and domestic flights. A similar situation exists for the *Indonesian Observer*. The *Surabaya Post* is another English-language newspaper rumoured to exist, although we haven't seen a copy in years.

The English-language magazine *What's On* has a pretty self-descriptive title – it's all about food, fashion, nightlife, and things to see and do in Indonesia. It's most readily found in magazine shops in large hotels in Jakarta and Bali.

For the official government line there are a number of regular publications issued by the Centre for Strategic and International Studies (CSIS) in Jakarta. You should be able to pick up their publications in the bookshops in major tourist hotels in Jakarta.

Of course, Indonesian-language newspapers are on sale throughout the country. Two of the leading newspapers are the Jakarta daily *Sinar Harapan* and the Catholic newspaper *Kompas*. *Suara Karya* is the mouthpiece of Golkar, the government political party.

One of the main non-government organisations in Indonesia which researches and attempts to influence the Indonesian government to develop alternative social and economic policies is the Institute for Social and Economic Research, Education and Information . This organisation was founded in 1971, mainly by a group of Jakarta intellectuals, many of them Western-trained academics. The institute's monthly journal is called *Prisma* and articles from it are translated and published in an English-language quarterly called *Prisma – The Indonesian Indicator*. You should be able to find it in the bookshops in the larger tourist hotels in Jakarta.

Foreign For information on what's happening in Indonesia today (including Indonesian politics, history and culture) take out a subscription to *Inside Indonesia* published in Australia at PO Box 190, Northcote, Vic 3070, Australia. Excellent articles cover everything from powerplays within the army, to the environment, and it discusses issues not raised in the Indonesian media and rarely covered overseas.

The *International Herald-Tribune* and *Asian Wall Street Journal* are sold in Indonesia.

Western magazines like *Time*, *Newsweek*,

The Economist and the excellent Hong Kong-published *Far Eastern Economic Review* are available in Indonesia. In the past, these were often bizarrely censored, with articles unfavourable to the Indonesian government blotted out, but this practice seems to have lapsed since 1989.

Radio & TV

Radio Republik Indonesia (RRI) is the national radio station, which broadcasts 24 hours in Indonesian from every provincial capital. Radio Pemerintah Daerah (RPD) serves a similar function but is broadcast from the capitals of regencies. In large cities like Jakarta there are also privately run stations.

Thanks to satellite broadcasting, TV can be received everywhere in Indonesia. You'll see plenty of satellite dish antennas around the country, aimed almost straight up, as broadcast satellites are put in geostationary orbit – they travel around the equator at the same speed the earth rotates at. You'll also see plenty of Indonesians in geostationary orbit around the TV set in any hotel – they are among the world's foremost TV addicts.

Rajawali Citra Televisi Indonesia (RCTI) is a privately owned station which broadcasts in Jakarta and East Java. Many shows are in English. It operates daily from around 1 pm until 2 am. A decoding device is needed to receive this station.

Televisi Republik Indonesia (TVRI) is the government-owned Indonesian-language TV station, which is broadcast in every province. The broadcasts start at around 4 pm and run until midnight.

Televisi Pendidikan Indonesia (TPI) is a government-owned educational station. It broadcasts from around 6 am until noon and can be received in every province.

The daily English-language newspaper, the *Jakarta Post*, carries a listing of all TV programmes in the Jakarta area.

FILM & PHOTOGRAPHY

Indonesia is an incredibly photogenic country and you can easily whip through large quantities of film! As in most Asian countries, the locals prefer colour print film to anything else, so slide film is relatively rare. Black and white film is also not especially popular. Nevertheless, in Jakarta and Bali you can usually find most types of film, even Polaroid film, movie film and video tape. Kodachrome is rarely seen outside the main tourist centres. Although various types of Western and Japanese film are available in Indonesia the cost is usually higher than in the West. If you're entering Indonesia from Singapore stock up on film there, where it's relatively cheap.

In the small towns and particularly in the outer islands or where few tourists go, many types of film aren't available at all. Turnover of stock is often slow, so it's best to check the expiry date of the film. The most readily available film will generally be Fujicolor, along with Indonesian-made or some types of Kodak black and white film.

Developing and printing is quite good and much cheaper than in the West. You can get Ektachrome and Fujichrome slide film developed in two or three days and colour print film can be done same day through photographic shops in major Indonesian towns all across the archipelago. Many of these have machines which churn out prints in 45 minutes, and the quality is usually very good.

Kodachrome transparencies (or other films where the cost of purchase includes the processing cost) need to be sent overseas.

Film manufacturers warn that films should be developed as quickly as possible once exposed – although in practice they seem to last for months without deterioration even in Asia's summer heat.

Camera batteries and other accessories are readily available from photographic shops.

Technical Problems

Shoot early or late – from 10 am to 1 or 2 pm the sun is uncomfortably hot and high overhead, and you're likely to get a bluish washed-out look to your pictures. A polarising filter helps reduce glare and darkens an otherwise washed-out sunlit sky. A lens hood will reduce your problems with reflections and direct sunlight on the lens. Beware of the sharp differences between sun and shade – if you can't get reasonably balanced overall light you may have to opt for exposing only one area or the other correctly. Or use a fill-in flash.

Those lush, green rice fields come up best if backlit by the sun. For those sunset shots at Kuta, Kalibukbuk or Pontianak set your exposure on the sky without the sun making an appearance – then shoot at the sun. Photography from fast-moving trains and buses doesn't work well unless you use a fast shutter speed. Dust can be a problem – hazy days will make it difficult to get sharp shots.

Be wary of X-rays at airports, which may fog your film. Some airports have signs warning you that the machine is not film safe – many do not. Generally speaking, X-ray machines only damage high-speed film, but if there's any doubt it's wise to keep your film away from the things!

People Photos

You get a fantastic run for your money in Indonesia – not only are there 180 million or so portraits to choose from but the variation in ethnic types is phenomenal.

Few people expect payment for their photos, the Balim Valley in Irian Jaya being an odd exception. What Indonesians *will* go for is a copy of the photo – if you hang around Indonesia long enough you'll wind up with a pocketful of bits of paper with addresses of people to send their photos to.

There are three basic approaches to photographing people: one is to be polite, ask permission and pose the shot; another is the no-holds-barred and upset everyone approach; the other is surreptitious, standing half a km away with a metre-long telescopic lens. Some Indonesians will shy away from having their photo taken and duck for cover; some are shy but only too pleased to be photographed; some are proud and ham it up for the camera; others won't get out of the way of the bloody lens when you want them too!

Whatever you do, photograph with discretion and manners. Hardly surprisingly, many people don't like having a camera lens shoved down their throats – it's always polite to ask first and if they say no then don't. A gesture, a smile and a nod are all that is usually necessary. In some places you may come up against religious barriers to taking photographs – such as trying to photograph Muslim women in the more devoutly Islamic parts of the archipelago. The taboo might also apply to the minority groups. In Bali, for example, you should not take photographs at public bathing places; just because the Balinese bathe in streams, rivers, lakes or other open places doesn't mean they don't think of them as private places – intruding with your camera is no different to sneaking up to someone's bathroom window and pointing your camera through. Remember, wherever you are in Indonesia, the people are *not* exotic Birds of Paradise and the village priest is *not* a photographic model. And finally, don't be surprised if Indonesian people turn the tables on you – they have become fond of sneaking up on Westerners and shooting a few exotic photos to show their friends!

Prohibited Subjects

Be careful of what you photograph in Indonesia – they're touchy about places of military importance and this can include airports (like the one at Malang in Java which is an air force base but also handles civilian flights), bridges, railway terminals and stations, seaports and any military installations or bases. Ask if in doubt.

HEALTH

Being a tropical country with a low level of sanitation and a high level of ignorance, Indonesia is a fairly easy place to get ill. The climate provides a good breeding ground for quaint creatures like malarial mosquitoes, but the biggest hazards by far come from contaminated food and water, and traffic accidents. You should not worry excessively about all this – a condition some travellers call 'safety fatigue'. Nevertheless, arming yourself with some knowledge, vaccinations and common sense can mean the difference between spending your holiday relaxing on the beach, or spending it in the emergency room.

The Traveller's Health Guide by Dr Anthony C Turner (Roger Lascelles, London) or *Staying Healthy in Asia* (Volunteers in Asia Publications) are guides to staying healthy while travelling, or what to do if you fall ill. For the technically oriented, the classical medical reference is the *Merck Manual*, a weighty volume which covers virtually every illness known to humanity.

Children, particularly babies and unborn children, present their own peculiar problems when travelling. Lonely Planet's *Travel with Children* by Maureen Wheeler gives a rundown on health precautions to be taken with kids, or if you're pregnant and travelling.

In most cases you can buy virtually any medicine across the counter in Indonesia without a prescription. If you need some special medication, take it with you. However, you shouldn't have any trouble finding common Western medicines in Indonesia, at least in big cities like Jakarta and Denpasar where there are lots of well-stocked pharmacies (apotik). Out in rural areas, pharmacies are scarce, but grocery stores will gladly sell you all sorts of dangerous drugs, often long beyond their expiration dates. Many of the big tourist hotels also have drugstores. Chinese shops often sell Chinese herbal medicines.

In each apotik there is an English-language copy of the IIMS (Indonesian Index of Medical Specialities), a guide to pharmaceutical preparations available to doctors in Indonesia. It's updated three times a year and it lists drugs by brand name, generic name, manufacturer's name and therapeutic action. A problem with buying medicines in Indonesia is that the labels are in Indonesian and you may have trouble figuring out what the appropriate dose is. Drugs may not be of the same strength as in other countries or may have deteriorated due to age or poor storage conditions.

The Chinese are regarded as the masters of herbal medicine, but Indonesia has its own home-grown variety known as *jamu*. For the most part, it's consumed by women who believe it will keep them young and beautiful, but jamu is also touted as a miracle cure for just about everything. It's sold at the same pharmacies that carry Western medicines. Our own experiences with herbal medicines indicate that they sometimes work, but often don't; their effectiveness depends in large part on what illness you're treating and your knowledge of how to use the stuff. This is a complex topic which requires a book in itself.

As for medical treatment, Catholic or missionary hospitals are often pretty good, and in remote areas may be your only hope other than prayer beads and chanting. Missionary hospitals frequently have English-speaking staff. Back in the developed world, you can often locate competent doctors and hospitals by asking at hotels or offices of foreign companies in places where large expatriate communities work. In the towns and cities there seems to be a fair supply of doctors and dentists to choose from. In Bahasa Indonesia a doctor is *dokter* and a dentist is *dokter gigi*. In the outback of places like Irian Jaya there are the clinics set up by the missionaries. There are also public hospitals *(rumah sakit)* in the cities and towns.

Hospitals are open during the day, but private clinics operate mostly in the evening, from 6 pm. It's first come, first served, so go early and be prepared to wait.

In Jakarta or Denpasar, you could try waking up the staff at your embassy or consulate – they just might be able to refer you to some competent medical facility.

In south Jakarta, most expatriates use Pondok Indah (☎ 7500157), Jalan Metro Duta Kav UE, a perfectly modern hospital that rivals the best hospitals in the West, although it charges modern prices. In south Jakarta there is also the Rumah Sakit Pertamina (☎ 7200290), Jalan Kyai Maja 43, Kebayoran – if your illness doesn't kill you, just wait until you see the bill. Better known hospitals in central Jakarta (near Jalan Jaksa) are the Rumah Sakit Cipto Mangunkusumo (☎ 330808), Jalan Diponegoro 71, a government public hospital (reasonably priced but very crowded); and St Carolus Hospital (☎ 4214426), Jalan Salemba Raya 41, a private Catholic hospital charging mid-range prices.

Also popular is Medical Scheme (☎ 515597) in the Setiabudi Building, Jalan H Rasuna Said, Kuningan. It's a private practice but they deal with all emergencies, and vaccinations are given to non-members for a small fee. Doctors speak English and Dutch.

The Metropolitan Medical Center (☎ 320408) is in the Hotel Wisata, Jalan Thamrin – behind the Hotel Indonesia. Hours at this practice vary so it's best to ring first. Dr Darmiyanti & Associates (☎ 346823) is at Jalan Lombok 57, Menteng. Some English is spoken and they have branch practices in a number of major hotels.

Predeparture Preparations

Very few people will be required to have vaccinations but several are certainly recommended. If you're arriving within six days after leaving or transiting a yellow fever infected area then a vaccination is required.

Vaccinations against typhoid and paratyphoid are recommended by the Indonesian government. Typhoid and paratyphoid are both diseases of insanitation spread by contaminated food. A very useful vaccination is TABT, which provides protection against typhoid, paratyphoid A and B, and tetanus. Tetanus is due to a bacillus which usually enters the blood system through a cut, or as the result of a skin puncture by a rusty nail, wire, etc. It is worth being vaccinated against tetanus because there is more risk of contracting the disease in warm climates where cuts take longer to heal. A tetanus booster shot should be given every five years.

Cholera is a disease of insanitation and usually comes in epidemics – vaccinations provide protection for six months and are recommended, but not required.

Polio is also a disease spread by insanitation and is found more frequently in hot climates. A booster every five years is recommended by many doctors.

You should have your vaccinations recorded in an International Health Certificate.

Get your teeth checked and any necessary dental work done before you leave home. Always carry a spare pair of glasses or your prescription in case of loss or breakage.

Health Insurance Although you may have medical insurance in your own country, it is probably not valid in Indonesia. A travel insurance policy is a very good idea – to protect you against cancellation penalties on advance purchase flights, against medical costs through illness or injury, against theft or loss of possessions, and against the cost of additional air tickets if you get really sick and have to fly home. Read the small print carefully since it's easy to be caught out by exclusions. For example, a travel insurance policy widely used in Australia specifically excludes motorcycle injuries if you don't hold a current Australian motorcycle licence. It's obviously designed to cut out all those people who obtain Balinese licences, but it could also catch people travelling through Australia and then on to Indonesia who hold, say, a British or US licence.

If you purchase an International Student Identity Card (ISIC) or Teacher Card (ISTC), you may be automatically covered depending on which country you purchased the card in. Check with the student travel office to be sure. If you're neither a student or a teacher, but you're between the ages of 15 and 25, you can purchase an International Youth Identity Card (YIEE) which entitles you to the same benefits. Some student travel offices also sell insurance to others who don't hold these cards.

Medical Kit You should assemble some sort of basic first aid kit. You won't want it to be too large and cumbersome for travelling, but some items which could be included are: Band-Aids or gauze bandage with plaster (adhesive tape); a thermometer; tweezers; scissors; antibiotic ointment; an antiseptic agent (Dettol or Betadine); Caladryl (for sunburn and itchy bites); insect repellent; multi-vitamins; water sterilisation tablets;

anti-malarial tablets; any medication you're already taking (plus prescription); diarrhoea medication (Lomotil or Imodium); paracetamol (Panadol), for pain and fever; a course of antibiotics (probably tetracycline, but check with your doctor, and bring the prescription); and contraceptives, if necessary. Most of these medications are available in Indonesia at low cost, but it's still not a bad idea to come prepared.

Basic Rules

Food & Water Much of the water that comes out of the tap in Indonesia is little better than sewage water. Drink it and you'll reap the whirlwind! Depending on how dirty it is and how sensitive you are, it might not even be safe to brush your teeth with tap water. It might seem like a needless expense to use bottled or boiled water for brushing your teeth, but getting sick can be expensive too, not to mention occasionally fatal.

Bottled water is widely available in Indonesia. It's expensive at hotels and restaurants, but is reasonably priced in grocery stores or supermarkets. You can boil your own water if you carry an electric immersion coil and a large metal cup (plastic will melt), both of which are available in department stores in Indonesia (check out the basement of Sarinah in Jakarta). For emergency use, water purification tablets will help. Water is more effectively sterilised by iodine than by chlorine tablets, because iodine kills amoebic cysts. However, iodine is not safe for prolonged use, and also tastes horrible. Bringing water to a boil is sufficient to kill most bacteria, but 20 minutes of boiling is required to kill amoebic cysts. Fortunately, amoebic cysts are relatively rare and you should not be overly concerned about these. If you have nothing to boil or purify your water with, you have to consider the risks of drinking possibly contaminated water against the risks of dehydrating – the first is possible, the second is definite.

It's a good idea to carry a water bottle with you. You are dehydrating if you find you are urinating infrequently or if your urine turns a deep yellow or orange; you may also find yourself getting headaches. Dehydration is a real problem if you go hiking in Indonesia – if you can't find water along the way or can't carry enough with you, then you will soon learn just how hot this place really is!

Fruit juices, soft drinks, tea and coffee will not quench your thirst – when it's really hot, you need water – *clean* water.

When it comes to food, use your best judgement. To be absolutely safe, everything should be thoroughly cooked – you can get dysentery from salads and unpeeled fruit. Fish, meat and dairy products are generally OK provided they are fresh – if they spoil, you could become violently ill. Fish can also be a problem if they lived in contaminated water. Fish from the 'black rivers' of Indonesia are the fastest ticket to the hepatitis clinic.

Other Precautions Sunglasses not only give you that fashionable Hollywood look, but will protect your eyes from the scorching Indonesian sun. Amber and grey are said to be the two most effective colours for filtering out harmful ultraviolet rays.

Sunburn is also a problem, particularly with people just off the plane in Denpasar who can't wait to hit the beach. Bring sunscreen (UV) lotion and something to cover your head. You can also buy sunscreen in better Indonesian pharmacies – two popular brands are Pabanox and Parasol.

If you're sweating profusely, you're going to lose a lot of salt and that can lead to fatigue and muscle cramps for some people. If necessary you can make it up by putting extra salt in your food (a teaspoon a day is plenty), but don't increase your salt intake unless you also increase your water intake.

Take good care of all cuts and scratches. In this climate they take longer to heal and can easily get infected. Treat any cut with care; wash it out with sterilised water, preferably with an antiseptic (Betadine), keep it dry and keep an eye on it – they really can turn into tropical ulcers! It would be worth bringing an antibiotic cream with you, or you can buy one in Indonesia ('NB' ointment). Cuts on your feet and ankles are particularly troublesome – a new pair of sandals can quickly give you a nasty abrasion which can be difficult to heal. For the same reason, try not to scratch mosquito bites.

The climate may be tropical, but you *can* catch a cold in Indonesia. One of the easiest ways is leaving a fan on at night when you go to sleep, and air conditioners are even worse. You can also freeze your hide by sleeping out on the decks of ships at night, or going up to mountainous areas without warm clothes. Procold, available over the counter in Indonesia, can give symptomatic relief, but the way to cure a cold is to rest, drink lots of liquids, keep warm (easy to do in Indonesia!) and wait it out.

Medical Problems & Treatment

Diarrhoea Diarrhoea is often due simply to a change of diet. A lot depends on what you're used to eating and whether or not you've got an iron gut. If you do get diarrhoea, the first thing to do is wait – it rarely lasts more than a few days.

Diarrhoea will cause you to dehydrate, which will make you feel much worse. The solution is not simply to drink water, since it will run right through you. You'll get much better results by mixing your water with oral rehydration salts, which are available at pharmacies. The most common brand is Oralit, but the generic term is *bubuk glukosa elektrolit* (glucose electrolyte powder). Dissolve the powder in *cool* water (never hot!) and drink, but don't use it if the powder is wet. The quantity of water is specified on the packet. Oralit is also useful for treating heat exhaustion caused by excessive sweating.

If the diarrhoea persists then the usual treatment is Lomotil or Imodium tablets. The maximum dose for Lomotil is two tablets three times a day. Both Lomotil and Imodium are prescription drugs in the West, but are available over the counter in most Asian countries, though apparently not in Indonesia. Fortunately, Indonesia has its own local brands – a good one to look for is Entrostop. Anti-diarrhoeal drugs don't cure anything, but slow down the digestive system so that the cramps go away and you

don't have to go to the toilet all the time. Excessive use of these drugs is not advised, as they can cause dependency and other side effects. Furthermore, the diarrhoea serves one useful purpose – it helps the body expel unwanted bacteria.

Activated charcoal, while not actually considered a drug, can provide much relief from diarrhoea and is a time-honoured treatment. A local brand available in Indonesia is Norit, also known generically as 'carbotablet'.

Fruit juice, tea and coffee can aggravate diarrhoea – again, water with oral rehydration salts is the best drink. It will help tremendously if you eat a light, fibre-free diet. Yoghurt and boiled eggs with salt are basic staples for diarrhoea patients. Later you may be able to tolerate plain white rice, and rice porridge with chicken *(bubur ayam)* is also very good for this condition. Keep away from vegetables, fruits and greasy foods for awhile. If you go out and have a big plate of greasy noodles with hot sauce, you'll be back to square one. If the diarrhoea persists for a week or more, it's probably not simple travellers' diarrhoea – it could be dysentery and it might be wise to see a doctor.

Dysentery Dysentery is considerably more serious than the usual garden variety diarrhoea. Dysentery causes diarrhoea, often accompanied by fever, blood and pus in the stool. The victim usually feels faint, totally lacking in energy, can barely eat and can hardly get out of bed. It's a real drag! Dysentery comes in two varieties, amoebic and bacillary.

Diarrhoea with blood or pus and fever is usually bacillary dysentery. It's quite common in Indonesia and many travellers fall prey to it. Since it's caused by bacteria infecting the gut, it can be treated with antibiotics like tetracycline, or a sulfa drug. You can buy tetracycline over the counter in Indonesia, and it's a useful thing to throw into your first-aid kit. The usual dose is 250 mg tablets, taken four times daily for about a week. It's important that once you start a course of antibiotics, you finish it. If you stop taking the antibiotics after one or two days, a complete relapse is more than likely. In most cases, bacillary dysentery will eventually clear up without treatment, but in some cases it's actually fatal, especially in children. Be sure to use water and Oralit (see previous section on Diarrhoea) to prevent dehydration.

Antibiotics are heavy artillery, so don't start swallowing tetracycline at the first sign of diarrhoea. The main problem is that antibiotics upset the balance of intestinal flora. The problem is more serious for women since this can lead to yeast infections, and tetracycline is also contraindicated in women who are pregnant or breastfeeding.

Diarrhoea with blood or pus but without fever is usually amoebic dysentery. This is a disease you should not neglect because it will not go away by itself. In addition, if you don't wipe out the amoebae while they are still in your intestine, they will eventually migrate to the liver and other organs, causing abscesses which could require surgery.

There are several ways to cure this disease. If you treat it promptly, the amoebae will still be restricted only to the intestine. In this case, tetracycline is effective. The dosage is 250 mg, four times daily for a *minimum* of 10 days.

The most sure-fire cure for amoebic dysentery is metronidazole (Flagyl), an anti-amoebic drug. It will wipe out amoebae no matter where they reside in the body, even in the liver and other organs. The dosage is three 250 mg tablets (750 mg) three times daily for seven to 10 days. Flagyl is also available in 500 mg tablets, so in that case you take 1½ tablets per dose. If you take Flagyl, do *not* under any circumstances consume alcohol at the same time – not a drop! Flagyl and alcohol together can cause a severe reaction.

Herbal medicine fanatics will be pleased to know that dried papaya seeds can actually cure amoebic dysentery, but only if it hasn't gone beyond the intestine. The dosage is one heaped tablespoon daily for eight days. If you're really worried about catching amoebic dysentery, papaya seeds can be used as a preventive measure – one heaped tablespoon weekly is usually effective. Remember that the seeds must be thoroughly dried and that they taste awful. But just because something is 'natural' doesn't mean it's harmless – papaya seeds can cause miscarriage in pregnant women and they may have other unknown side effects. Treat papaya seeds as you would any other medicine – with caution.

Giardiasis This is another type of amoeba which causes severe diarrhoea, nausea and weakness, but doesn't produce blood in the stool or cause fever. Giardiasis is very common in Indonesia.

Although the symptoms are similar to those of amoebic dysentery, there are some important differences. On the positive side, giardia will not migrate to the liver and other organs – it stays in the intestine and therefore is much less likely to cause long-term health problems.

The bad news is that tetracycline and papaya seeds are no help whatsoever. It can only be cured with an anti-amoebic drug like metronidazole (Flagyl) – again, never drink alcohol while taking Flagyl. Without treatment, the symptoms may subside and you might feel fine for a while, but the illness will return again and again, making your life miserable.

To treat giardiasis, the proper dosage of Flagyl is different than for amoebic dysentery. Take one 250 mg tablet three times daily for 10 days. It can sometimes be difficult to rid yourself of giardiasis, so you might need laboratory tests to be certain you're cured.

Cholera Cholera vaccination is not very effective. However, outbreaks of cholera are generally widely reported, so you can avoid such problem areas. The disease is characterised by a sudden onset of acute diarrhoea with 'rice water' stools, vomiting, muscular cramps and extreme weakness. You need medical help – but treat for dehydration, which can be extreme, and if there is an appreciable delay in getting to hospital then begin taking tetracycline. See the Dysentery section for dosages and warnings.

Typhoid Typhoid fever is another gut infection that travels the faecal-oral route – ie, contaminated water and food are responsible. Vaccination against typhoid is not totally effective and it is one of the most dangerous infections, so medical help must be sought.

In its early stages typhoid resembles many other illnesses: sufferers may feel like they have a bad cold or flu on the way, as early symptoms are a headache, a sore throat and a fever which rises a little each day until it is around 40°C or more. The victim's pulse is often slow relative to the degree of fever present and gets slower as the fever rises – unlike a normal fever where the pulse increases. There may also be vomiting, diarrhoea or constipation.

In the second week the high fever and slow pulse continue and a few pink spots may appear on the body; trembling, delirium, weakness, weight loss and dehydration are other symptoms. If there are no further complications, the fever and other symptoms will slowly go during the third week. However, you must get medical help before this because pneumonia (acute infection of the lungs) or peritonitis (burst appendix) are common complications, and because typhoid is very infectious.

The fever should be treated by keeping the victim cool and dehydration should also be watched for. Chloramphenicol is the recommended antibiotic but there are fewer side affects with ampicillin. The adult dosage is two 250 mg capsules, four times a day. Children aged between eight and 12 years should have half the adult dose; younger children should have ⅓ the adult dose.

Patients who are allergic to penicillin should not be given ampicillin.

Malaria The parasite that causes this disease is spread by the bite of the *Anopheles* mosquito. The disease has a nasty habit of recurring in later years, even if you're cured at the time, and it can kill you.

There are four different types of malaria,

but 95% of all cases are one of two varieties. The most serious of these two types is falciparum malaria, which is widespread in the tropics, including Indonesia.

The illness develops 10 to 14 days after being bitten by the mosquito and symptoms consist of high fever with alternate shivering and sweating, intense headaches, and usually nausea or vomiting. Without treatment the condition is fatal within two weeks in up to 25% of cases. It is this variety of malaria which is now showing widespread resistance to the most common anti-malarial drug, chloroquine. The problem is especially serious in Irian Jaya.

Vivax malaria is the other main type and the two rarer types are similar to vivax. Vivax malaria may be severe, but is not dangerous to life. However, the illness will continue to recur, causing chronic ill-health, if not adequately treated.

Malaria is a risk year-round throughout all of Indonesia below 1200 metres. Some areas, like Bali, are low-risk and at some times of the year you don't see any mosquitoes at all, but it's wise to take precautions anyway.

It is not (yet) possible to be inoculated against malaria but protection is simple – either a daily or weekly tablet depending on which variety your doctor recommends. The tablets kill the parasites if they get into your bloodstream. You usually have to start taking

the tablets about two weeks before entering the malarial zone and continue taking them for at least one month after you've left it. You may be prescribed two drugs to be taken simultaneously – chloroquine and maloprim for example – in order to guard against resistance to either one.

If you're travelling with children or if you're pregnant then the story with anti-malarial tablets is more complex. For a rundown see Lonely Planet's *Travel with Children*. Basically, the story is that some anti-malarials may stay in your system for up to a year after the last dose is taken and may cause birth defects. So if you get pregnant or are planning to get pregnant within 12 months of taking anti-malarials your unborn child could be endangered. With newer drugs there's not much information around on the effects of long-term use. You should try and find out whether there is resistance to the drug you are prescribed.

Another precaution is to avoid being bitten in the first place. Some Indonesian hotels (not many) have mosquito nets. In the evenings when mosquitoes are most active, cover bare skin, particularly the ankles. Use an insect repellent – any brand that contains the magic ingredient diethyl-toluamide ('deet') should work well. Autan and Off! are two such popular brands widely available in Indonesia. From our experience, we've found that the bottles this stuff comes in often leak eventually, making for a rather messy backpack – at least keep it wrapped in a plastic bag. Alternatively, try Tiger Balm, a cure-all sold in Chinese medicine shops all over the world that seems to work as a mosquito repellent. Mosquito coils are readily available in Indonesia, though the smoke they produce is not good for the lungs or eyes. Having an electric fan blowing on you while you sleep is very effective at keeping the mossies away, but you might wind up with a cold instead. Finally, it's been found that large doses of vitamin B complex are excreted through the skin and seem to act as a mild mosquito repellent, but don't count on this alone.

Treating malaria is complicated and some-thing you should not undertake yourself except in an emergency. Blood tests are needed to determine whether you in fact have malaria rather than dengue fever (see next section), and the choice of drugs depends on how well you react to them. However, if you are far from hospitals and doctors, you may have no alternative to self-treatment, except to die. In that case, the simplest treatment is a single dose of three Fansidar tablets, taken all at once. It's not a panacea – in Irian Jaya, the malaria bug now has considerable resistance to Fansidar too. If this treatment fails, then the drug of choice is quinine *(kina* in Bahasa Indonesia) – instructions are printed on the bottle. Note that these drugs are not candy – allergic reactions can occur and are sometimes serious. Even if you think you've cured yourself, you still need to get to a hospital and have blood tests – otherwise there is the strong possibility of relapse.

Dengue Fever This is a mosquito-born disease which resembles malaria, but is not fatal and doesn't recur once the illness has passed.

A high fever, severe headache and pains in the joints are the usual symptoms – the aches are so bad that the disease is also called breakbone fever. The fever usually lasts two to three days, then subsides, then comes back again and takes several weeks to pass. People who have had this disease say it feels like imminent death.

Despite the malaria-like symptoms, anti-malarial drugs have no effect whatsoever on dengue fever. Only the symptoms can be treated, usually with complete bed rest, aspirin, codeine and an intravenous drip. There is no means of prevention other than to avoid getting bitten by mosquitoes, but once you've had dengue fever, you're immune for about a year. The patient should be kept under a mosquito net until after the fever passes – otherwise there is the risk of infecting others.

Eye Infections Trachoma is a common eye infection; it's easily spread by contaminated towels which are handed out by restaurants and even airlines. The best advice about wiping your face is to use disposable tissue paper. If you think you have trachoma, you need to see a doctor – the disease can damage your vision if untreated. Trachoma is normally treated with antibiotic eye ointments for about four to six weeks.

Hepatitis A Hepatitis is a disease which affects the liver. There are several varieties, mostly commonly hepatitis A and B. Hepatitis A occurs in countries with poor sanitation, of which Indonesia is definitely one. It's spread from person to person via infected food or water, or contaminated cooking and eating utensils. Salads which have been washed in infected water, or fruit which has been handled by an infected person, might carry the disease.

Symptoms appear 15 to 50 days after infection (generally around 25 days) and consist of fever, loss of appetite, nausea, depression, complete lack of energy, and pains around the bottom of your rib cage (the location of the liver). Your skin turns progressively yellow and the whites of your eyes change from white to yellow to orange.

The best way to detect hepatitis is to watch the colour of your urine, which will turn a deep orange no matter how much liquid you drink. If you haven't drunk much liquid and/or you're sweating a lot, don't jump to conclusions since you may just be dehydrated.

The severity of hepatitis A varies; it may last less than two weeks and give you only a few bad days, or it may last for several months and give you a few bad weeks. You could feel depleted of energy for several months afterwards. If you get hepatitis, rest and good food is the only cure; don't use alcohol or tobacco because that only gives your liver more work to do. It's important to keep up your food intake to assist recovery.

AIDS & Hepatitis B Everyone has heard of AIDS by now, so it needn't be elaborated on here. What is less known is hepatitis B, which is transmitted in the same three ways as the AIDS virus: by sexual intercourse; by contaminated needles; or by being inherited (by an infant) from an infected mother. Indonesian 'health clinics' often reuse needles without proper sterilisation – no one knows how many people have been infected this way. Innocent use of needles – ear piercing, tattooing and acupuncture – can also spread the disease. As for the 'health clinics', you can buy needles and syringes over the counter in Indonesia, and it's not a bad idea to do this if you need injections or must have blood samples taken.

There is no vaccine for AIDS, but there is one for hepatitis B. The vaccine must be given before you've been exposed. Once you've got the virus, you're a carrier for life and the vaccine is useless. Therefore, you need a blood test before the vaccine is administered, to determine whether you're a carrier. The vaccine requires three injections, each a month apart. Unfortunately, the vaccine is expensive.

Rabies Even if you're a devout dog lover, you aren't likely to go around petting the stray dogs you encounter in Indonesia. Third World dogs are not like the cute little fluffy creatures that play with children in the backyards of Western suburbia – they are often half-starved, badly mistreated and have been known to take a bite out of Western tourism.

Fido is likely to be even less friendly if infected with rabies. Although your chances of getting it are small, rabies is a disease worth guarding against. A vaccination is available but few people bother to get it. The vaccine requires three injections – once a week for three weeks – and is good for about two years. However, if you're bitten, the vaccine by itself is *not* sufficient to prevent rabies; it will only increase the time you have to get treatment, and you will require fewer injections if you've been vaccinated.

The rabies virus infects the saliva of the animal and is usually transferred when the rabid animal bites you and the virus passes through the wound into your body. That also means that if you have a scratch, cut or other break in the skin you could catch rabies if an infected animal licks that break in the skin. If you are bitten or licked by a possibly rabid animal you should wash the wound thoroughly (but without scrubbing, as this may push the infected saliva deeper into the your body) and then start on a series of injections which will prevent the disease developing. Once it reaches the brain, rabies has a 100% fatality rate. The new rabies vaccines have fewer side effects than the older animal-derived serums and vaccines.

The incubation period for rabies depends on where you're bitten. If on the head, face or neck then it's as little as 10 days; on the arms it's 40 days; on the legs, 60 days. This allows plenty of time to be given the vaccine and for it to have a beneficial effect. With proper treatment, given quickly after having been bitten, rabies will not develop.

Bilharzia Bilharzia (schistosomiasis) is not very common in Indonesia but occasional cases have been reported. The type found in Indonesia is somewhat less severe than the African variety. Bilharzia is carried in water by minute worms. The larvae infect certain varieties of freshwater snails, found in rivers, streams, lakes and particularly behind dams. The worms multiply and are eventually discharged into the water surrounding the snails.

They attach themselves to your intestines or bladder, where they produce large numbers of eggs. The worm enters through the skin, and the first symptom may be a tingling and sometimes a light rash around the area where it entered. Weeks later, when the worm is busy producing eggs, a high fever may develop. A general feeling of being unwell may be the first symptom; once the disease is established abdominal pain and blood in the urine are other signs.

Avoiding swimming or bathing in freshwater where bilharzia is present is the main method of preventing the disease. Even deep water can be infected. If you do get wet, dry off quickly and dry your clothes as well. Seek medical attention if you have been exposed to the disease and tell the doctor your suspicions, as bilharzia in the early stages can be confused with malaria or typhoid. If you cannot get medical help immediately, Niridazole is the recommended treatment. The recommended adult dosage is 750 mg (1½ tablets) taken twice daily for a week. Children aged between eight and 12 years should be given 500 mg (one tablet) twice daily for a week.

Prickly Heat & Fungus You sweat profusely in Indonesia; the sweat can't evaporate because the air itself is already moist, and before long you'll be dripping in it. Prickly heat is a common problem for people from temperate climates. Small red blisters appear on the skin where your sweat glands have been unable to cope with the amount of sweat you're generating. The problem is exacerbated because the sweat fails to evaporate. To prevent (or cure it), wear clothes which are light and leave an air space between the material and the skin; don't wear synthetic clothing since it can't absorb the sweat; dry well after bathing and use calamine lotion or a zinc-oxide based talcum powder. Anything that makes you sweat more – exercise, tea, coffee, alcohol – only makes the condition worse. You can also keep your skin dry with air-conditioning, electric fans or a trip to the cool mountains.

Fungal infections (gatal) also occur more frequently in this sort of climate – men sometimes get patches of infection on the inside of the thigh. It itches like hell but is easy to clear up with an anti-fungal cream and powder (bedak). In Indonesia, a popular anti-fungal cream is Canesten.

Fungal ear infections usually result from swimming or washing in unclean water – Aquaear drops, available over the counter in Australia, are a preventative to be used before you enter or wash in the water. Some travellers carry a broad-spectrum antibiotic like Septrim to cure fungal infections. This is not a bad idea, although antibiotics can lower your resistance to other infections.

Athlete's foot is also a fungal infection, usually occurring between the toes. Wearing open-toed sandals will often solve the problem without further treatment because this permits the sweat to evaporate. Cleaning between the toes with a warm soapy water and an old toothbrush also helps.

Roundworm, Threadworm & Hookworm

In warmer climates where hygiene standards are low there are many forms of worm infestation. Some are spread by infected meat, some by infected fish, some by infected water and others by faecally infected earth or food.

If you get roundworm, threadworm or hookworm, treatment is straightforward. Mebendazole, marketed in Indonesia under the brand names Vermox, Vermoran and Totamin, is most effective – you just take one pill, which is good for three months. Somewhat less effective, but also very good, is Combantrin. Children under six months old, nursing mothers and pregnant women should not take it without first consulting a doctor.

Ascaris, or roundworm, is the most common worm infestation that plagues foreigners. The eggs are usually ingested through vegetables that have been grown using human faeces as manure, and which have not been properly washed; the eggs hatch in the stomach and then the larvae burrow through the intestines, enter the bloodstream and make their way through the liver to the heart, from where they work their way up to the lungs and the windpipe. They are then coughed up, swallowed and deposited in the intestines where they mature and grow to 20-35 cm (eight to 14 inches) long. The most common symptom of adult roundworm infestation is abdominal discomfort increasing to acute pain due to intestinal blockage.

Threadworm eggs, when swallowed, hatch in the stomach. The worms enter the intestine where they grow and mate; the mature female worms make their way through the bowel to the anus where the depositing of their sticky eggs causes intense itching. One way to diagnose the presence of worms is to stretch a piece of adhesive tape over a flat stick, with the sticky area on the outside, and press it into the area around the anus. If there is an infestation you may be able to see worms and eggs on the tape – the mature worms look like little strands of cotton thread about 1.3 cm (half an inch) long.

Hookworms can be picked up by walking around in bare feet, in soil littered with infected faeces. The eggs hatch in the soil and then the larvae enter the bloodstream by burrowing through the skin, following much the same internal route as the roundworm, until they reach the intestine and hook onto the lining. By feeding on the host's blood, hookworms can grow up to 1.3 cm (half an inch) long. The most common result of hookworm infestation is anaemia, although they can also do damage to the organs they come into contact with. The best prevention is to wear shoes unless on the beach. Even with shoes on, if you walk through muddy water there is a chance of getting it. Hookworms can also be absorbed by drinking infected water or eating uncooked and unwashed vegetables.

Snakes We speak here not of bemo drivers, but of legless animals that crawl around on their bellies and make hissing noises. In Bahasa Indonesia, they are called *ular*.

Indonesia has several poisonous snakes, the most famous being the cobra *(ular sendok)*. There are many other poisonous species. *All* sea snakes are poisonous and are readily identified by their flat tails.

Although not poisonous, giant-sized pythons lurk in the jungle. They do not generally consume humans, but have been known to do so. They do frequently eat pigs, and are thus an enemy of non-Muslim farmers.

Fortunately, even poisonous snakes tend to be shy. Most snake-bite victims are those who accidentally step on a snake. Be careful about walking through tropical areas with a lot of underbrush. Boots give a little more protection than running shoes.

Should you be unfortunate enough to get bitten, try to remain calm (sounds easier than it really is) and not run around. The conventional wisdom is to rest and allow the poison to be absorbed slowly. Tying a rag or towel around the limb to apply pressure slows down the poison, but the use of tourniquets is not advisable because it can cut off circulation and cause gangrene. Cutting the skin and sucking out the poison has also been widely discredited. Immersion in cold water is also considered useless.

Treatment in a hospital with an antivenin would be ideal. However, getting the victim to a hospital is only half the battle – you will also need to identify the snake. In this particular case, it might be worthwhile to kill the snake and take its body along, but don't attempt that if it means getting bitten again. Try to transport the victim on a makeshift stretcher.

All this may sound discouraging, but the simple fact is that there is very little first-aid treatment you can give which will do much good. Fortunately, snake bite is rare and the vast majority of victims survive even without medical treatment.

Jellyfish Heeding local advice is the best way of avoiding contact with these sea creatures with their stinging tentacles. The box jellyfish found in inshore waters in some parts of Indonesia is potentially fatal, but stings from most jellyfish are simply rather painful. Dousing in vinegar will deactivate any stingers which have not 'fired'. Calamine lotion, antihistamines and analgesics may reduce the reaction and relieve the pain.

Wasps & Bees Wasps, which are common in the tropics, are a more serious hazard than snakes because they are more aggressive and will chase humans when stirred up. They won't attack unless they feel threatened, but if they do attack, they usually do so en masse. This is not just uncomfortable, it can be fatal. If you're out hiking and see a wasp nest, the best advice is to move away quietly. A few brainless people like to see how skilful they are at throwing rocks at wasp nests – this is not recommended. Should you be attacked, the only sensible thing to do is run like hell.

It would take perhaps 100 wasp or bee stings to kill a normal adult, but a single sting can be fatal to someone who is allergic. In fact, death from wasp and bee stings is more common than death from snakebite. People who are allergic to wasp and bee stings are also allergic to bites by red ants. If you happen to have this sort of allergy, you'd be wise to throw an antihistamine and epinephrine into your first-aid kit. Epinephrine is most effective when injected, but taking it in pill form is better than nothing.

Women's Health
Gynaecological Problems Poor diet, lowered resistance due to the use of antibiotics for stomach upsets and even contraceptive pills can lead to vaginal infections when travelling in hot climates. Keeping the genital area clean, and wearing skirts or loose-fitting trousers and cotton underwear will help to prevent infections.

Yeast infections, characterised by a rash, itch and discharge, can be treated with a vinegar or even lemon-juice douche or with yoghurt. Nystatin suppositories are the usual medical prescription. Trichomoniasis is a more serious infection; symptoms are a discharge and a burning sensation when urinating. Male sexual partners must also be treated, and if a vinegar-water douche is not effective medical attention should be sought. Flagyl is the prescribed drug.

Pregnancy Most miscarriages occur during the first three months of pregnancy, so this is the most risky time to travel. The last three months should also be spent within reasonable distance of good medical care, as quite serious problems can develop at this time. Pregnant women should avoid alcohol and all unnecessary medication, but vaccinations should still be taken where possible. Additional care should be taken to prevent illness and particular attention should be paid to diet and nutrition.

WOMEN TRAVELLERS
Indonesia is a Muslim society and very much male-oriented. Nevertheless, lots of Western women travel in Indonesia either alone or in pairs – most seem to enjoy the country and

its people, most seem to get through the place without any problems, or else suffer only a few minor hassles with the men. Your genetic make-up plays a part – blonde-haired, blue-eyed women seem to have more hassles than dark women. Some cities are worse than others – a lot of women have complained about Yogyakarta. There are some things you can do to avoid being harassed; dressing modestly helps a lot.

Indonesians, both men and women, are generally not comfortable being alone – even on a simple errand they are happier having a friend along. Travelling alone is considered an oddity – women travelling alone, even more of an oddity. Nevertheless, for a woman travelling alone or with a female companion, Indonesia can be easier going than some other Asian countries.

You might spare a thought for Indonesian women, who are given the privilege of doing backbreaking labour and raising children, but never trusted in positions of authority. The whole concept of feminism, equality between the sexes etc, would seem absurd to most Indonesians.

DANGERS & ANNOYANCES
Theft

Foreigners are regarded by many Indonesians as walking bank accounts, from which they would like to make a withdrawal. There is really very little violent crime, but pickpockets are very common. Losing your cash is one thing, but it's much worse to have your passport and/or travellers' cheques stolen because it often means a long trek back to Jakarta to get them replaced. There is, however, an Australian consulate and also a US consular agent in Bali. Some travellers' cheque companies also have an office in Bali.

A money belt is the safest way to carry your valuables. The only problem with money belts, particularly in hot, humid climates, is that they are very uncomfortable to wear! A vest (waistcoat) with two large zip-up pockets inside to keep your valuables in is a good idea. Other people wear small

leather pouches with a strap looped around their neck and under their clothes.

Sealing your pockets closed with velcro will make it harder for a thief to pick your pocket. This method is not 100% theft-proof, but it helps. Crowded buses and trains are the most likely venue for getting your pocket picked. The thieves are very skilful – a gang of about five 'accidentally' bump into you, go through your pockets in about three seconds and then they're out the door with your wallet.

One precaution you can take, which will help if you do lose your valuables, is to leave a small stash of money (say US$100) in your hotel room (perhaps hidden in a secret pocket inside your backpack), with a record of the travellers' cheque serial numbers and your passport number; you'll need the money if you've got a long trip to a replacement office. If you get stuck try telephoning your consulate or embassy. It's a sensible precaution to carry more than one type of travellers' cheque with you. Make sure that the company you buy your cheques from has a replacement office in Indonesia. Also ensure that you keep your original receipt of purchase separate from the cheques themselves – without the receipt you may have to wait weeks for replacement and may not even get any at all. Another thing worth making a copy of before you leave home is your address book.

It's a depressing reality that sometimes it's your fellow travellers who rip you off. If you do stay in dorms (there are a few in Jakarta) or share your hotel room with strangers, don't leave valuables like your passport, travellers' cheques, money, credit cards and air tickets lying around.

Some hotels have rooms that are locked with a padlock, but it's best to use your own padlock.

If you check out of a hotel and forget to return the key, *do not* hand it to some 'trustworthy' person like a bemo driver who says he can return it for you. They could just as well use the key to rob the next guest who stays in that room. We know of at least one case where this happened. You're better off mailing the key back to the hotel or throwing it away – hotels always have copies.

Drugs

In much of Indonesia, recreational plants and chemicals are utterly unheard of. Bali used to be the place to float around sky-high, but that image has faded considerably. There aren't so many drugs about now and the authorities are much heavier-handed. The Bali drug scene was basically marijuana and mushrooms, but neither are so readily available now and it's unsafe to buy from a local supplier unless you know the person very well. Hotel owners are quick to turn you in as well. There are a number of Westerners soaking up the sunshine in the prison at the back end of Legian.

Crocodiles

The situation here is much like in northern Australia. Crocodiles *(buaya)* mostly inhabit low swampy jungle areas and slow-moving rivers near the sea coast. They wisely avoid contact with humans since they are liable to be turned into fashionable handbags. They *can* be dangerous, but unless you go stomping around the swamps of Irian Jaya, you probably won't see one. Still, if you intend to jump into any rivers for a refreshing swim, it would be wise to first make local enquiries.

Noise

If you're deaf, there's no problem. If you're not deaf, you might be after a few months in Indonesia. The major sources of noise are radios and TVs – Indonesians always set the volume knob to maximum. You can easily escape the racket at remote beaches and other rural settings by walking away, but there isn't much you can do on a bus with a reverberating stereo system pumping out wretched music. In hotels, the lobby often contains a booming TV set, but if you choose your room carefully, you might be able to avoid the full impact. If you complain about the noise, it's likely the TV or radio will be turned down, but then turned back up again five minutes later.

Another major source of noise is the mosques, which start broadcasting the calls to prayer at 4 am, repeating the procedure four more times during the day. Again, choose your hotel room carefully.

'Hello Mister' Fatigue

This is the universal greeting given to foreigners regardless of whether the person being addressed is male or female. The less advanced English students know only 'Mister', which they will enthusiastically *scream* in your ear every five seconds – 'Mister Mister Mister!' Most have no idea what it means, but they have been told by their school teachers that this is the proper way to greet foreigners. After two months of listening to this, some foreigners go over the edge. Try to remember that they think it's polite. It's much less of a problem in Jakarta, where foreigners are ubiquitous and English-speaking abilities are higher.

Other Hassles

You tend to get stared at in Indonesia, particularly in places where few foreigners go. But on the whole the Indonesians stand back and look, rather than gather round you. Those who do come right up to you are usually kids, though some teenagers also do this. Getting stared at is nothing new; almost 500 years ago when the first Portuguese arrived in Melaka the *Malay Annals* recorded that:

the people of Melaka...came crowding to see what the Franks (Portuguese) looked like; and they were all astonished and said, 'These are white Bengalis!' Around each Frank there would be a crowd of Malays, some of them twisting his beard, some of them fingering his head, some taking off his hat, some grasping his hand.

The insatiable curiosity of Indonesians manifests itself in some peculiar ways. Many Indonesians take their holidays in Bali not for the beach, but just so they can stare at foreigners. Sometimes you get people who start following you on the street just to look at you – such people are called *buntut*. If you read a book or write something down, it's not unusual for people to poke their nose right into your book or writing pad, or take it from your hands so that they can have a better look.

The other habit which is altogether ordinary to Indonesians is touching. The Indonesians are an extraordinarily physical people; they'll balance themselves on your knee as they get into a bemo, or reach out and touch your arm while making a point in conversation, or simply touch you every time they mean to speak to you or when they want to lead you in a new direction if they're showing you around a house or museum. All this is considered friendly – some Indonesians just have to be friendly regardless of the time or situation, even if it means waking you from your peaceful slumber!

While casual touching among members of the same sex is regarded as OK, body contact between people of different sexes is not. Walking down the street holding hands with a member of the opposite sex will provoke stares, pointing, loud comments and shouting. Public displays of affection (like kissing) may incur the wrath of moral vigilantes.

Really irritating to many foreigners are some of the younger guys who hang around bus stations, outside cinemas and ferry docks with not much else to do except stir foreigners. They'll crack jokes, laugh, try and pinch your bum and sometimes make obscene gestures. If it happens don't give them their entertainment by chucking a fit. Just leave and come back some other time.

On the whole you'll find the Indonesians (including the army and the police, despite the nasty reputation they have with the locals) *extraordinarily* hospitable and very easy to get on with.

Travelling With Children

Travelling anywhere with children requires energy and organisation. The Indonesians are generally very friendly and receptive to children. Of course some areas of Indonesia are hard going, probably too hard for most people to want to tackle with the additional burden of small children. Other areas, such as Bali, are easy.

A real problem exists with little children

who have blond hair and blue eyes. Many Indonesians just can't resist pinching them on the cheek and, while no harm is meant, most children don't like it and will start crying.

For more information on travelling in Asia with children see LP's *Travel with Children*.

WORK

It is possible for foreigners to work in Indonesia, provided you are willing to make some long-term commitments. Although Indonesia is still a Third-World country, in some situations you can be paid well. Given the low cost of living, you could eventually save quite a bundle if you don't live extravagantly.

People with valuable technical skills, like engineers, computer programmers and the like can easily find jobs with foreign multinational corporations. Most budget travellers do not fall into this category.

There are a few jobs available for Westerners as bartenders in five-star hotels. The pay is good, but note that these jobs are for men only.

For most travellers, both male and female, the easiest way to pick up decent work is to teach English. There are good opportunities for doing this in large cities like Jakarta, Surabaya, Bandung and Yogya, and somewhat fewer opportunities in tourist centres like Bali. The best paying jobs by far are in Jakarta. Salaries start at 30,000 rp per hour, and can go as high as 50,000 rp per hour if you teach at banks, five-star hotels and other large companies. It's not quite as good as it sounds though. Most banks and big companies will not offer you full-time work – you'll have to do some commuting between jobs in Jakarta's insane traffic if you want to work 20 hours a week, which is about as much as most teachers can stand. Also, it takes connections to get the really plumb jobs.

To get good-paying work, there are a few qualifiers. First of all, you have to look 'decent' – forget the thongs, T-shirts and short pants. To teach at a bank, men will probably need a white shirt and tie, while women will be expected to wear a dress. Scraggly beards and punk haircuts will not impress your potential employers. Academic credentials and letters of reference will help, but are not essential. Finally, companies prefer someone who has been around awhile, not a traveller who just fell off the plane at Denpasar with a guitar and a surfboard. But if you're persistent, you can usually find something.

You'll also have to consider your visa. The words 'employment prohibited' are stamped on your two-month tourist pass and most other visas. It is possible to get a working visa, but that involves more bureaucracy. Although enforcement of the regulations has not been rigid, you are vulnerable to getting fined and booted out of the country if the authorities take a dim view of your activities. Sometimes your employer will help you to deal with the immigration authorities, but usually you're on your own. Some foreigners have paid bribes to get work visas, but we aren't recommending that you do this. If you do get a work visa, you may have to pay taxes. All this is worth keeping in mind.

ACTIVITIES

Surfing

Bali has long had a reputation as something of a surfing Mecca, an image created in part by those surfing-travelling films. For details on surfing and what to bring with you (apart from your board) see *Bali & Lombok – a travel survival kit*. Apart from Bali, Nias off the west coast of Sumatra has long had a reputation as Indonesia's second surfing Mecca and we've even met people hunting waves on Sumba Island in Nusa Tenggara.

Western surfers have certainly had an influence on local attitudes – as late as the 1960s, virtually no Balinese would set foot in the water, believing that there were 'devils' lurking in the waves. Today, the Balinese have taken to surfing too. Or rather, the men have. In all our travels through the country, we've never seen an Indonesian woman even swimming, let alone surfing.

Windsurfing

Obviously, Bali is the place where windsurfing is most common, followed by Lombok. It's caught on in Manado in North Sulawesi too. Indonesians windsurf the Sungai (river) Kapuas at Pontianak in West Kalimantan, and there's a place at Pantai Waiara near Maumere on Flores that rents windsurfers.

Scuba Diving

With so many islands and so much coral, Indonesia presents all sorts of possibilities for diving. In Bali, the coral reefs off Pulau Menjangan (island) – which lies off the north-west corner of Bali – are a popular diving spot. Tulamben on the north-east coast has a reef with a sheer drop of 800 metres – a second attraction here is the US ship SS *Liberty*, sunk by the Japanese in 1942 and offering fascinating diving at depths between 10 and 40 metres. Further afield there are the brilliant coral reefs around Bunaken Island off Manado in northern Sulawesi, and around the Bandas in the Maluku. In several of these places you can get trips out to the reefs including the use of diving equipment, but it's advisable to bring your own regulator.

Snorkelling

If diving is beyond your budget then try snorkelling. There are beautiful coral reefs on almost every coastline in Indonesia. Whilst you can usually buy or rent the gear when you need it, packing your own snorkel, mask and fins is a good idea.

Trekking

For information about trekking see the Walking section in the Getting Around chapter.

Whitewater Rafting

Although the art of floating down raging rivers is not very well-developed in Indonesia, there is great potential. A few commercial operators now cater to this peculiar Western custom. The Sungai Hamputung in Kalimantan offers a fairly easy float down a river with an impressive jungle canopy above. The canyon of the Sungai Sadan in Torajaland, Sulawesi, is becoming popular. There are a number of other rivers in Central Sulawesi which are also attracting Western tour groups. Enquire with local travel agents if interested.

Whitewater enthusiasts get quite a thrill out of being the first to raft a particular river, and in this regard Indonesia offers quite a few opportunities. There are a number of unrafted rivers in Irian Jaya, but tackling these will require expedition-style preparations – roads are nonexistent, crocodiles will probably find Western food delightful and there may be unexpected surprises like waterfalls. But if you survive all this, it will certainly be the adventure of a lifetime.

HIGHLIGHTS

Indonesia has so many outstanding attractions that it really becomes difficult to define the country's 'highlights'. Judging by the number of tourists, the beaches of Bali and Lombok are certainly highly regarded, but fine beaches are found throughout the archipelago.

Not that you need be the least bit interested in sand or surf. Volcano worshippers will certainly want to visit Krakatau, probably the most active volcano in the world. Easily accessible Gunung Bromo in east Java is the most popular volcano with visitors. Java has the largest collection of active volcanoes, though Sumatra, Bali and Flores also have some fine specimens.

Then there is Keli Mutu in Flores, one of the most bizarre sights in the world with its three multicoloured crater lakes. For sheer size and beauty, few lakes in the world can match Lake Toba in northern Sumatra. There's a very different sort of lake near the summit of 3726-metre Gunung Rinjani in Lombok, and the strenuous climb to get there takes you through an area of incredible natural beauty.

Culture buffs will find plenty of interest in Torajaland, southern Sulawesi. Art lovers covet the batik of Yogyakarta and the ikat of Sumba. Few temples in the world are more magnificent than Borobudur.

If you're interested in seeing ancient, exotic cultures, and magnificent wilderness untrammelled by civilisation, nothing quite matches the splendour of the Balim Valley in Irian Jaya.

ACCOMMODATION

One thing you'll have to learn to deal with is the *mandi*. The word mandi simply means to bath or to wash. A mandi is a large water tank beside which you'll find a plastic saucepan. The popularity of the mandi is mainly due to a frequent lack of running water in Indonesia – sometimes the tank is refilled by a hose attached to a hand-pump. Climbing into the mandi is very bad form indeed – it's your water supply and it's also the supply for every other guest that comes after you, so the idea is to keep the water clean. What you're supposed to do is scoop water out of the mandi and pour it over yourself. Some of the better tourist hotels might actually have bathtubs, showers and hot water, but such luxuries are still relatively rare.

Another thing which may require adjustments to your way of thinking are Indonesian toilets. These are basically holes in the ground, footrests on either side, over which you squat and aim. In some tourist areas,

Asian toilets are fading away as more places install Western-style toilets. The lack of running water makes flushing toilets a problem, so what you do is reach for that plastic saucepan again, scoop water from the mandi and flush it that way.

As for toilet paper, you'll seldom find it supplied in public places, though you can easily buy your own. In fact, Indonesians seldom use the stuff. This is partly to save money, but mainly because Indonesian plumbing systems don't handle toilet paper too well and easily become plugged up. The Indonesian method is to use the left hand and copious quantities of water – again, keep that saucepan handy. Some Westerners easily adapt to this method, but many do not. If you need to use toilet paper, see if there is a wastebasket next to the toilet. If there is, then that's where the paper should go, not down the toilet. If you plug up the hotel's plumbing with toilet paper, the management is going to get really angry.

Kamar kecil is Bahasa Indonesia for toilet, but they usually understand 'way-say' (WC). *Wanita* means women and *pria* means men.

Camping

While there are no established public or private camping grounds, there are plenty of opportunities for back-country camping. It is important that you camp away from civilisation, unless you want Indonesian spectators all night.

You can probably get by without a sleeping bag below 1000 metres, but at higher elevations you'll certainly need one. Rain is a possibility even in the dry season, especially as you gain altitude, so bring some sort of tent or rainfly. You'll also want to guard against insects and other things that crawl and slither in the night, so a tent or mosquito net would be appropriate.

Hostels

Indonesia doesn't have much in the way of hostels, mainly because there are so many low-cost hotels. An exception is Jakarta, where accommodation is relatively dear, so there are a number of places offering cheap dormitory accommodation. There are a handful of hostels in a few other places, like Surabaya and Kupang, but it's entirely possible to travel through Indonesia on a tight budget without ever staying in a hostel.

The main thing to be cautious about in hostels is security. Few places provide lockers, and it's not just the Indonesians you must worry about – foreigners have been known to subsidise their vacation by helping themselves to other people's valuables. While it's not a huge problem, it is something to be aware of.

If you want to avoid nocturnal visits by rats, don't put food in your room, or at least have it sealed in ratproof jars or containers. Rats have a keen sense of smell, and they can and will chew through a backpack to get at food.

Bedbugs are occasionally a problem in this climate. Examine the underside of the mattress carefully before retiring. If you find it crawling with bugs, either change rooms or have the management spray copious quantities of poison which, hopefully will eliminate the bugs rather than you.

Hotels

Hotels in Indonesia comes in different grades of price and comfort. At the bottom end of the scale is the 'homestay' *(penginapan)*. A slightly more upmarket penginapan is called a *losmen*. Other names applied to inexpensive hotels are *wisma* and *pondok*.

The Indonesian government has embarked on a campaign to get all penginapan, losmen, wisma and pondok to change their names to 'hotel'. Not all the hotel owners are happy about this, since the old naming system gave potential guests some idea of the price.

By way of compensation, there is now an official rating system: a hotel can be either a flower *(melati)* hotel, which is relatively low standard, or a star *(bintang)* hotel, which is more luxurious. A hotel at the bottom of the barrel would be one-star *(melati satu)* whereas a five-star hotel *(lima bintang)* occupies the top end. In the future, all hotels will be required to post signs indicating how many flowers or stars they deserve. In addition, many hotels now hit you with a 10% tax, and upper-crust places charge a whopping 21% tax and service charge.

The real budget homestays are spartan places with shared bath, costing as little as 2500 rp per person. The five-star hotels can match the best in the West, with prices piercing the 200,000 rp level. Mid-range hotel rooms often come with private bath and typically cost about 15,000 rp for a single. But in Indonesia, what you pay depends more on where you are; the cost of accommodation varies considerably across the archipelago. If you follow the well-beaten tourist track through Bali to Java and Sumatra you'll find Indonesia one of the cheapest places in South-East Asia (exceptions like Jakarta apart). Travellers' centres like Bali, Yogyakarta and Danau Toba are good value for food and accommodation. Nusa Tenggara is marginally more expensive than Bali, but cheap by any standards. On the other hand, once you get to some of the outer provinces, like Kalimantan, Maluku, or Irian Jaya, you could be paying five to 10 times as much as you'd pay in Yogyakarta or Kuta Beach for equivalent accommodation.

If you get into a town and the cheap places mentioned in this book have closed down, or you have no information on cheap places to stay, then ask taxi drivers, becak drivers or even the police what's available. Other travellers who have come from where you're heading are also good sources of information.

Often you have to bargain for your room price just as you do for other purchases. Rather than argue, the most polite way to do this is to simply ask for a discount. Ironically, it's the high-class places that bargain most – if you ask for a discount, they'll often say 'OK' and knock off 10 to 20%. The existence of a printed price list (*daftar harga*) doesn't mean the price is fixed. Some hotels routinely ask for more than they expect – you're a mug if you don't push for a discount.

On the whole it's cheaper if two people travel together and split the cost of the room – the price for a two-person room is nearly always well below the cost of two singles. You rarely get dormitory accommodation in Indonesia, although there are a few hotels catering to Western budget travellers, notably in Jakarta, that provide dorm beds.

Even the cheapest hotels tend to be reasonably clean, if spartan, though some stand out as long overdue for demolition. Some places can be abominably noisy, with the inevitable television booming in the passageway outside your room or punching up through the floorboards until after midnight. Other hotels are just several layers of hot little sweat boxes and slimy bathrooms. The tendency in the last few years has been to tear down the old firetraps and replace them with more wholesome accommodation, but of course prices have risen to reflect the improved conditions. The best way to survive some of the more dismal places is to go to Indonesia with a level of saintly tolerance, a good pair of earplugs, or enough money to afford some upper-market accommodation now and then and avoid the worst places

How good a time you have in Indonesia often depends on where you're staying – ie, the friendliness and location of your hotel. If you want to enjoy yourself or learn something about the country then there's no point incarcerating yourself in the large tourist hotels. If you want to meet the local people and/or other travellers then you've got to stay in the cheap places. So pick your hotel carefully; while some places may not have such comfy beds the people you meet more than make up for it.

Staying in Villages

In many places in Indonesia you'll often be welcome to stay in the villages. Ask for the village head – the *kepala desa* or *kepala kampung*. They're generally very hospitable and friendly, offering you not only a roof over your head but also meals. Obviously you don't get a room of your own, just a bed. What you pay for this depends on the bargain you reach with the kepala desa. Sometimes he may offer it to you for nothing but more often some payment will be expected: about

2000 or 3000 rp a night as rule-of-thumb. If you intend to stay with a kepala desa it's a good idea to have one or two gifts to offer – cigarettes, postcards and photographs are popular.

Staying with the Police

In places where there's no accommodation available you can often stay in the local police station. Indonesian police and military are actually quite friendly to foreigners – how they treat the locals is another matter.

Rental

Given the wide assortment of cheap hotels, it almost doesn't pay to bother with renting a house or apartment. However, if you're working in Indonesia for a long time, you may eventually want to get your own place, at least to enjoy the benefits of privacy and quietness.

Rents vary wildly depending on where you want to live. In Jakarta, a decent apartment could be had for around 150,000 rp per month. If you require such amenities as swimming pools, tennis courts and security guards, the tariff could easily come to two million rp or more.

Elsewhere in the country, prices will be lower. More than a few foreigners have taken up semipermanent residence in Bali, either renting houses on long-term lease or leasing the land and building their own homes.

Generally speaking, finding a place to rent is not too difficult and a deposit is seldom required. However, negotiating a proper price may take some time, and it's wise to obtain the help of an Indonesian friend.

FOOD

You'll generally eat well in most parts of Indonesia. There are some gastronomic voids in the more poverty-stricken areas, but the variety is stunning in cities like Jakarta and touristy regions like Bali. There are occasional surprises too, like mid- year in Tanatoraja (Sulawesi), when harvest and funeral ceremonies are at their height and you can try pig and buffalo meat barbecued in bamboo tubes, washed down with copious quantities of white and red alcoholic *tuak* tapped from a palm tree. Of course, food like this is not available from your average push-cart.

Many general books on Asian food include a section on Indonesian cuisine, including *South-East Asia Food* by Rosemary Brissenden (Penguin). *Indonesian Cookery* by David Scott with Surya Winata (Rider) is a good introduction to Indonesian cooking. *Cooking the Indonesian Way* by Alec Robeau (A H & A W Reed) is another useful introduction to the art and includes interesting legends and stories from various islands of the archipelago.

Jalan Malioboro in Yogyakarta is the longest restaurant in the world – lined in the evening with innumerable food stalls serving up genuine Yogya food, which you eat while sitting on mats laid out on the footpath. Pontianak and Samarinda in Kalimantan have the biggest river prawns you've probably ever seen in your life; Jayapura has the best selection of barbecued fish *(ikan bakar)*.

Interestingly, many Dutch travellers will tell you that the best Indonesian food to be had is in Amsterdam. One thing we can tell you for sure is that the best Indonesian food *cannot* be had in the eastern provinces of Indonesia, like Nusa Tenggara, Irian Jaya and Maluku. In these areas, there's a real lack of food variety – definitely no place for gourmets! Carrying vitamin pills and milk powder is a good idea in the backwaters, particularly if you're a vegetarian.

Restaurants

At the bottom of the barrel in terms of price are the *warungs*. These are the poor persons' restaurants, and they can be seen everywhere in Indonesia. They're usually just a rough table and bench seats, surrounded by sheets or canvas strung up to act as walls. In Yogya on Jalan Malioboro they're basically food trolleys and you sit on mats laid out on the footpath. Often the food is as drab as the warung looks, but occasionally you find something outstanding. One thing you can be sure about is that warungs are cheap. A night market (*pasar malam*) is often a congregation point for warungs.

One step up from the warungs, sometimes in name only, is the *rumah makan* – literally the 'house to eat', often only distinguished from the warung by its fixed position and the addition of solid walls – but many such places call themselves warungs so it's a hazy distinction.

A *restoran* is a restaurant – once again often nothing more than the name distinguishes it from a rumah makan. But in many cases a restoran will be an up-market place, often Chinese-run and with a Chinese menu. Chinese food is nearly always more expensive than Indonesian food, but there is usually a more varied menu.

Kuta Beach and Jakarta are the two main places in Indonesia where Western food has grabbed hold. In Kuta you would be forgiven if you thought there was no such thing as Balinese cooking – while the food you get around Kuta is good and cheap, traditional Balinese food has just about dropped out of the picture, and Indonesian food is succumbing to the onslaught of hamburgers, steaks, yoghurt, fish & chips, banana muesli and – for homesick Aussies – vegemite on toast, mate!

Jakarta has the most cosmopolitan range of culinary delights in Indonesia, from European and Mexican to Indian, Chinese, Thai, Korean and Japanese. Parts of Indonesia where there are large expatriate communities working for foreign firms – Balikpapan for example – are also sources of foreign food.

Kentucky Fried Chicken has come to roost in Jakarta, Yogya and Kuta Beach, complete with air-conditioning, laminex tables and a statue of the ever-smiling Colonel. If you made as much money as he has, you'd smile too. Indonesia also has a growing contingent of McDonald's, Pizza Hut and Burger King outlets.

In spite of the wide variety of food, many travellers lose weight, and some say a trip through Indonesia is the best crash diet they know of. This has more to do with illness than lack of tasty food, so take care – in some places, 'hygiene' is just a slogan. As a general guide, the cleanliness of a warung or restaurant is a good indicator as to how sanitary its kitchen is likely to be. A bad meal at the local Rumah Makan Dysentery can spoil your trip – be wary of uncooked vegetables and fruits, rubbery seafood and 'boiled' drinking water straight from the tap.

Snacks

The Indonesians are keen snackers and everywhere you'll find lots of street stall snacks such as peanuts in palm sugar, shredded coconut cookies or fried bananas. Potatoes and other starchy roots are eaten as a snack – either steamed, with salt and grated coconut added, or thinly sliced and fried.

Main Dishes

Food in Indonesia – particularly meat dishes – is generally Chinese-influenced, although there are a number of purely Indonesian dishes. Pork is not widely used since it is regarded by Muslims as unclean, but it sometimes appears in Chinese dishes. Javanese cooking uses fresh spices and a mixture of ingredients, the chilli mellowed by the use of sugar in many dishes. Sumatran cooking, on the other hand, blends fresh and dry spices to flavour the main ingredient. The types of fresh spices that Indonesians use are known to most Westerners only as dried ground powders. There is also some Dutch influence in the use of vegetables from temperate zones in some recipes.

Rice is the basis of the meal, with an assortment of side dishes, some hot (with chilli) and spicy, and some just spicy. Many dishes are much like soup, the water being used to moisten the large quantity of rice eaten. Salad is usually served, along with *sambal* (a spicy side dish) and *acar* (pickles). Many dishes are cooked in *santan*, the liquid obtained when grated coconut is squeezed. *Bumbu* is a combination of pounded ingredients used to flavour a dish. Indonesians use every part of a plant, including the leaves of cassavas, papayas, mangoes and beans.

A few basic words and phrases will help make ordering a meal easier.

makan	to eat
minum	to drink
makanan	food
nasi bungkos	take-away food
minuman	drink
makan pagi	breakfast
makan siang	lunch
makan malam	dinner
saya mau makan	I want to eat
enak	delicious!
daftar makanan	the menu
rekening	the bill
manis	sweet
pedas	spicy hot
asam manis	sweet and sour
dingin	cold
panas	hot (temperature)
goreng	fried
bakar	barbecued
rebus	boiled
pisau	knife
garpu	fork
sendok	spoon

Some of the dishes you're likely to encounter in Indonesia are listed here:

abon – spiced and shredded dried meat often sprinkled over nasi rames or nasi rawon

acar – pickle; cucumber or other vegetables in a mixture of vinegar, salt, sugar and water

apam – delicious pancake filled with nuts and sprinkled with sugar

ayam – chicken; *ayam goreng* is fried chicken

babi – pork. Since most Indonesians are Muslim, pork is generally only to be found in market stalls and restaurants run by Chinese, and in areas where there are non-Muslim populations such as in Bali, Irian Jaya and Tanatoraja.

bakmi – rice-flour noodles, either fried (*bakmi goreng*) or in soup

bakso or *ba'so* – meatball soup

bawang – onion

bubur ayam – Indonesian porridge with chicken. The porridge is generally sweetened and made from rice, black sticky rice or mung beans.

bubur kacang – mung bean porridge cooked in coconut milk

buncis – beans

cap cai – usually pronounced 'chop chai'. This is a mix of fried vegetables, although it sometimes comes with meat as well.

cassava – Known as tapioca to Westerners, this is a long, thin, dark brown root which looks something like a shrivelled turnip.

daging babi – pork

daging sapi – beef

daging kambing – goat or mutton

dragonflies – a popular Balinese snack, caught with sticky sticks and then roasted!

emping – powdered and dried *melinjo* nuts, fried as a snack to accompany a main meal

es krim – ice cream. In Indonesia you can get Western brands like Flipper's and Peters, and also locally manufactured varieties.

fu yung hai – a sort of sweet & sour omelette

gado-gado – another very popular Indonesian dish of steamed bean sprouts, various vegetables and a spicy peanut sauce

garam – salt

gula – sugar

gula gula – lollies (sweets, candy)

gulai/gule – thick curried-meat broth with coconut milk

ikan – fish. Understandably there's a wide variety to choose from in Indonesia: *ikan laut* is saltwater fish, *ikan danau* is freshwater fish and *ikan cumi* is squid. *Ikan asam manis* is sweet and sour fish and *ikan bakar* is barbecued fish. If you're buying fresh fish (you can often buy these at a market and get your hotel to cook them up), the gills should be a deep red colour, not brown, and the flesh should be firm to touch.

ikan belut – eels. Another Balinese delicacy; kids catch them in the rice paddies at night.

jahe – ginger

kacang – peanuts or beans

kacang hijau – mung bean sprouts. These can be made into a sweet filling for cakes and buns.

kare – curry; as in *kare udang* (prawn curry)

kecap asin – salty soy sauce

kecap manis – sweet soy sauce

keju – cheese

kentang – potatoes; usually the size found in the West and used in various ways including dishes of Dutch origin and as a salad ingredient

kepiting – crab; features in quite a few dishes, mostly of Chinese origin

kodok – frog; plentiful in Bali and caught in the rice paddies at night

kroket – mashed potato cake with minced meat filling

krupuk – is made of shrimp and cassava flour or of fish flakes and rice dough, cut in slices and fried to a crisp

krupuk melinjo (emping) – is made of the seeds of the melinjo fruit *(gnetum-gnemon)*, pounded flat, dried and fried to make a crisp chip and served as a snack with a main course

kueh – cake

lemper – sticky rice with a small amount of meat inside, wrapped up and boiled in a banana leaf; a common snack found throughout the country

lombok – chilli. There are various types: *lombok merah* (large, red); *lombok hijau* (large, green) and *lombok rawit* (rather small but deadliest of them all, often packaged with *tahu*, etc).

lontong – rice steamed in a banana leaf

lumpia – spring rolls; small pancake filled with shrimp and bean sprouts and fried

madu – honey. The best Indonesian honey is said to come from Sumbawa Island.

martabak – found on food trolleys all over the archipelago. A martabak is basically a pancake but there are two varieties. The one that seems to be everywhere is the sickeningly sweet version guaranteed to set your dentist's bank account soaring when you get back home. But (at least in Java) you can also get a delicious savoury martabak stuffed with meat, egg and vegetables. Some people think the sweet version isn't all that bad.

mentega – butter

mentimun – cucumber

merica – pepper

mie goreng – fried wheat-flour noodles, served sometimes with vegetables, sometimes with meat

mie kuah – noodle soup

mentega – butter

nasi campur – steamed rice topped with a little bit of everything – some vegetables, some meat, a bit of fish, a krupuk or two – a good, usually tasty and filling meal

nasi goreng – This is the most common of Indonesian dishes; almost like hamburgers are to Americans, meat pies to Australians, fish & chips to the British – popular at any time of day, including breakfast time. Nasi goreng simply means fried (goreng) rice (nasi) – a basic nasi goreng may be little more than fried rice with a few scraps of vegetable to give it some flavour, but sometimes it includes some meat. *Nasi goreng istemewa* (special) usually means nasi goreng with a fried egg on top. The dish can range from dull and dreary to very good.

nasi gudeg – unripe jackfruit cooked in santan and served up with rice, pieces of chicken and spices

nasi Padang – Padang food, from the Padang region of Sumatra, is popular all over Indonesia. It's usually served cold and consists of the inevitable rice, with a whole variety of side dishes including beef, fish, fried chicken, curried chicken, boiled cabbage, sometimes fish and prawns. The dishes are laid out before you and your final bill is calculated by the number of empty dishes when you've finished eating. Nasi Padang is traditionally eaten with the fingers and it's also traditionally very hot (pedas not panas) – sometimes hot enough to burn your fingers, let alone your tongue! It's sometimes wonderful, like the stuff you get up in Balikpapan, and sometimes very dull. It's also one of the more expensive ways to eat in Indonesia and you generally end up spending a couple of thousand rupiah on a meal, although it can be well worth it.

nasi pecel – similar to gado-gado, with boiled papaya leaves, tapioca, bean sprouts, string beans, fried soybean cake, fresh cucumber, coconut shavings and peanut sauce

nasi putih – white (putih) rice – usually steamed; glutinous rice is mostly used in snacks and cakes

nasi rames – rice with a combination of egg, vegetables, fish or meat

nasi rawon – rice with spicy hot beef soup, fried onions and spicy sauce

nasi uduk – rice boiled in coconut milk or cream

opor ayam – chicken cooked in coconut milk

pete – a huge broad bean, quite spicy, which is often served in the pod

pisang goreng – fried banana fritters; a popular street-side snack

rijstaffel – Dutch for 'rice table'; Indonesian food with a Dutch interpretation, it consists of lots of individual dishes with rice. Rather like a glorified nasi campur or a hot nasi Padang. Bring a big appetite.

roti – bread. The stuff you get in Indonesia is nearly always snow white and sweet.

sago – a starchy, low protein food extracted from a variety of palm tree. Sago is the staple diet of the Maluku islands.

sambal – a hot spicy chilli sauce served as an accompaniment with most meals

sate – One of the best known of Indonesian dishes, satay (sate) are small pieces of various types of meat on a skewer served with a spicy peanut sauce. Street sate-sellers carry their charcoal grills around with them and cook the sate on the spot.

saus tomat – tomato sauce; ketchup

sayur – vegetables

sayur-sayuran – vegetable soup with coconut milk

sembal pedis – hot sauce

sop – clear soup with mixed vegetables and meat or chicken

soto – meat and vegetable broth, often a main meal eaten with rice and a side dish of sambal

tahu – tofu, or soybean curd; soft bean cake made from soybean milk. It varies from white and yellow to thin and orange-skinned. It's found as a snack in the food stalls and is sometimes sold with a couple of hot chillies or with a filling of vegetables

tempe – made of whole soybeans fermented into cake, wrapped in plastic or a banana leaf; rich in vegetable protein, iron and vitamin B. Tempe goreng is pieces of tempe (tempeh) fried with palm sugar and chillies.

telur – egg

ubi – sweet potato; spindle-shaped to spherical with a pulpy yellow or brown skin and white to orange flesh

udang – prawns or shrimps

udang karang – lobster

Desserts
Fresh fruit is used as dessert.

Fruit
It's almost worth making a trip to Indonesia just to sample the tropical fruit – apples and bananas curl and die before the onslaught of nangkas, rambutans, mangosteens, salaks and zurzats.

apel – apple

apokat – Avocados are plentiful and cheap. Try an avocado and ice-cream combo.

belimbing – The 'starfruit' is a cool, crispy, watery tasting fruit – if you cut a slice you'll immediately see where the name comes from.

durian – the most infamous tropical fruit, the durian is a large green fruit with a hard, spiky exterior. Inside are pockets of creamy white fruit. Stories are told of an horrific stench emanating from an opened durian – hotels and airlines often ban them because of their foul odour. Some don't smell so bad – unpleasant yes, but certainly not like holding your nose over an overflowing sewer. It's worth noting that the juice leaves a permanent stain on your clothing. The durian season is in the later part of the year.

jambu – guava. The crispy, pink-skinned, pear- shaped ones are particularly popular. Others have pale green or white skin. The small seeds should not be eaten. Many Asians like to dip the cut fruit in thick soy sauce with sliced chilli before eating

jeruk – the all-purpose term for citrus fruit. There are several kinds available. The main ones include the huge *jeruk muntis* or *jerunga*, known in the West as the pomelo. It's larger than a grapefruit but has a very thick skin, tastes sweeter, more like an orange and has segments that break apart very easily. Regular oranges are known as *jeruk manis* – sweet jeruk. The small tangerine-like oranges which are often quite green are *jeruk baras*. Lemons are *jeruk nipis*.

kelapa – coconut; as plentiful as you would expect! *Kelapa mudah* means young coconut and you'll often get them straight from the tree. Drink the milk and then scoop out the flesh.

mangga – mango. The mango season is the second half of the year.

manggis – mangosteen. One of the most famous of tropical fruits, this is a small purple-brown fruit. The outer covering cracks open to reveal pure-white segments with an indescribably fine flavour. Queen Victoria once offered a reward to anyone able to transport a mangosteen back to England while still edible. From November to February is the mangosteen season.

nangka – Also known as jackfruit this is an enormous yellow-green fruit that can weigh over 20 kg. Inside are individual segments of yellow fruit, each containing a roughly egg-shaped seed. The segments

Custard apple

Pineapple

Durian

Coconuts

Starfruit

Jackfruit

are held together by strong white fibres. The fruit is moist and fairly sweet, with a slightly rubbery texture. As each nangka ripens on a tree it may be individually protected in a bag. The skin of a nangka is green when young, yellow when ripe.

nanas – pineapple

papaya – or paw paw are not unusual in the West. It's actually a native of South America and was brought to the Philippines by the Spanish, and from there spread to other parts of South-East Asia.

pisang – banana. The range in Indonesia is astonishing – from midgets to specimens well over a foot long. A bunch of bananas, by the way, is *satu sisir pisang*.

rambutan – a bright red fruit covered in soft, hairy spines – the name means hairy. Break it open to reveal a delicious white fruit closely related to the lychee. From November to February is the rambutan season.

salak – Found chiefly in Indonesia, the salak is immediately recognisable by its perfect brown 'snakeskin' covering. Peel it off to reveal segments that, in texture, are like a cross between an apple and a walnut but in taste are quite unique. Each segment contains a large, brown oval-shaped seed. Bali salaks are much nicer than any others.

sawo – brown-skinned, looks like a potato and has honey-flavoured flesh

zurzat – Also spelt *sirsat* or *sirsak* and sometimes called white mango, the zurzat is known in the West as custard apple or soursop. The Indonesian variety is one of the best. The warty green skin of the zurzat covers a thirst-quenching, soft, white, pulpy interior with a slightly lemonish, tart taste. You can peel it off or slice it into segments. Zurzats are ripe when the skin has begun to lose its fresh green colouring and become darker and spotty. It should then feel slightly squishy rather than firm.

Self-Catering

In any medium to large-sized city, you'll find well-stocked supermarkets. It's here that you'll find a wide variety of both local and imported foods. The other alternative is to explore the outdoor markets where you find fresh fruits, vegetables, eggs, chickens (both living and having recently passed away), freshly ground coffee and just about anything else. There are no price tags in the market and bargaining is often necessary.

An easy guide to the identification of weird-looking food is *A Jakarta Market* by Kaarin Wall, published by the American Women's Association – it should be possible for you to pick up a copy in Jakarta. It's got pictures and descriptions of vegetables, roots and herbs, dry goods, fish, fresh fruit and other foods you'll find in the markets in Jakarta, which are also relevant to the rest of Indonesia.

Betel Nut

Not exactly a food, betel nut *(sirih* in Bahasa Indonesia) is popular, especially in the villages. It's what causes that red stain on what's left of their teeth and gums. The betel nut *pinang* is chewed in combination with sirih leaf, *kapor sirih* (powdered lime) and a brown substance called *gambir*.

DRINKS

Indonesians have enthusiastically embraced Western soft drink culture. In a country where delicious, fresh fruit juices are sold you can still rot your teeth on Coca Cola, 7-Up, Sprite and Fanta. Prices are typically around 750 rp and up for a bottle, and from 1000 rp for a can.

There is a saying that while the British built roads in their colonies, the Dutch built breweries. Many of these still exist and, while beer is comparatively expensive (normally 2500 rp, often more), it's also good. The three popular brands are San Miguel, Anker and Bintang – the latter two are manufactured locally. Bintang is the most popular. Some other popular Indonesian drinks, both alcoholic and non-alcoholic, include:

air – water. You usually get a glass of it at the end of a restaurant meal. It should have been boiled (and may not have cooled down since), but often it won't be boiled at all! Many Indonesians find it hard to understand that Westerners want water that has been boiled and cooled down as opposed to just heated: *air putih* (literally white water) is a phrase that should bring the right result. *Mendidih duapuluh menit* means 'boil 20 minutes' – don't believe it. Good luck.

air jeruk – citrus fruit juice. *Jeruk manis* is orange juice and *jeruk sitrun* is lemon juice.

air minum – drinking water

arak – a stage on from brem (distilled rice wine). It's usually home-produced, although even the locally bottled brands look home-produced. It makes quite a good drink mixed with 7-Up or Sprite. Taken in copious quantities it has a similar effect to being hit on the head with an elephant.

Aqua – the most common brand of mineral water. It usually comes in litre bottles and is highly recommended if you're dubious about drinking other water, although it's not cheap, at 1000 rp or more for a 1½ litre bottle.

brem – rice wine; either home-produced or there's the commercially bottled 'Bali Brem'. A bit of an acquired taste, but not bad after a few bottles!

es juice – Although you should be a little careful about ice and water the delicious fruit drinks are irresistible. Just take one or two varieties of tropical fruit, add crushed ice and pass it through a blender. You can make mind-blowing combinations of orange, banana, pineapple, mango, jackfruit, zurzat or whatever else is available.

es buah – more a dessert than a drink; a curious combination of crushed ice, condensed milk, shaved coconut, syrup, jelly and fruit. Sickening say some, wonderful say others.

Green Sands – a pleasant soft drink, made not from sand, but from malt, apple and lime juice.

kopi – coffee. Excellent coffee is grown in Indonesia. It's usually very sweet and served with the coffee granules floating on top.

lassi – a refreshing yoghurt-based drink. Some people regard it as divine.

stroop – cordial

susu – milk; not common in Indonesia although you can get long-life milk in cartons and powdered milk (Dancow is a common brand) in packets. Cans of condensed Indomilk, 'prepared from the rich, creamy milk of Australian cows' according to the label, are also sold in Indonesia and are very sweet. Another common one is Bear Brand canned milk from every Third World country's favourite multinational, Nestlé. Fresh milk *(susu segar)* can be found in Yogya and Solo.

teh – tea; Some people are not enthusiastic about Indonesian tea but if you don't need strong, bend-the-teaspoon-style tea you'll probably find it's quite OK. *Teh tawar* or *teh pahit* is tea without sugar and *teh gula* is tea with sugar.

tuak – an alcoholic drink fermented from the sap tapped from a type of palm tree.

TOBACCO

If you're an anti-smoking activist, you'll have your work cut out for you in Indonesia. Most Indonesian men (rarely women) smoke like chimneys. Some say Indonesian chain smokers only need one match a day – they light the first cigarette in the morning, and then continue to light the next cigarette with the one currently being smoked, ad infinitum.

If you have the habit yourself, you might be pleased by the local selection of tobacco products. Indonesia is justly famous for its unique 'kretek' cigarettes, produced by blending cloves with tobacco. The fragrant odour is quite unlike any you've ever smelled before. There are plenty of brands on the market, among them Gudang Garam, Djarum, Bentoel, Sampoerna, Wismilak, Kansas, Ardath, Commodore and Dji Sam Soe. Imported cigarettes like Dunhill, Lucky Strike and Marlboro are available but more expensive.

ENTERTAINMENT

Cinemas

Indonesians are great movie fans and cinemas can be found in all but the smallest village. In large cities like Jakarta, Surabaya, Denpasar, etc, the latest Western films can be seen, usually with English dialogue and Indonesian subtitles. As one gets into the backwaters, the films tend to be of vintage age – old hits from the 1960s are still being shown! Besides Western movies, there are plenty of violent kung fu epics from Hong Kong and weird science-fiction films from Japan. Indonesia's own film industry is still in the infant stage, but there are a few home-grown movies, though most Westerners don't find them especially inspiring.

Cinemas usually only operate in the evening, starting from 5 pm, but a few places open on Sunday around 1 pm. In large cities, the movies are advertised in the newspapers. Cinemas have different classes: 3000 rp for a cheap cinema, or around 7000 rp for a high-class place.

Discos

Young Indonesians have taken to disco dancing like ants to honey. Obviously, discos are easiest to find in large cities like Jakarta and resort areas like Kuta Beach in Bali. Some discos are independent, but many are located in five-star hotels. Prices vary, but in general there's a small cover charge and expensive drinks. In Jakarta, a cheap disco would have a 5000 rp cover charge but would charge 7000 rp for a beer.

Nightclubs

For those who would prefer something more sedate than the thump of disco music, nightclubs offer an alternative. Mostly, they are found in large cities or tourist resorts, and are usually associated with big hotels.

Spectator Sports

Most of Indonesia's live spectator sports are male-oriented and associated with gambling. You'll certainly have plenty of chance to see cockfighting, especially in Bali and Kalimantan. Other tastes that can be catered for include boxing, soccer and horse racing. TV stations broadcast tennis and badminton championships.

THINGS TO BUY

Souvenir vendors positively swarm around touristy places like Kuta Beach and Yogyakarta. Off the beaten track, shopping is more relaxed. If you're an art collector, you'll find plenty of chances to stock up on unusual items. Wood carvings are on sale everywhere. Batik (see the Yogyakarta section) and ikat (see the Nusa Tenggara chapter) attract a steady stream of foreign art enthusiasts. Good pottery is available, mostly in Java.

If you have little or no interest in art, there are still plenty of more practical, everyday items that make good buys. Sarinah Department Store in Jakarta, and other various upmarket shops, have export-quality clothing in large sizes for dirt cheap prices. You can even find jackets, ski caps and other winter clothing.

If you can figure out a way to get it home, rattan and bamboo furniture is a very cheap and practical item to buy in Indonesia.

Many foreigners get addicted to Indonesian coffee, which is superb. Kapal Api is a popular brand name for packaged coffee, but the best coffee is the stone-ground stuff you buy in markets. If you're going to keep it a long time, it's best to buy whole coffee beans and grind it yourself when you're ready to drink it. Cheap coffee grinders can also be bought in Indonesia.

Getting There & Away

Jakarta remains the principal gateway for entry by air and Bali also has an international airport. Five international airlines have direct flights to Bali – the Indonesian national airline Garuda, the Australian airline Qantas, Air New Zealand, Singapore Airlines and Thai International. There are also international flights to various cities in the outer islands and a couple of possible land and sea entry routes.

Depending on where you're starting from, it's often cheaper to buy an air ticket to Singapore, from where you can enter Indonesia by air or ship, or by flying from nearby Penang in Malaysia.

It's useful to see what's available and become familiar with airline ticketing jargon. One of the best sources of information is the monthly magazine *Business Traveller*, available from newsstands in most developed countries, or direct from 60/61 Fleet St, London EC4Y 1LA, UK.

The discounted ticket possibilities to Indonesia include advance purchase fares or more straightforward discounts on regular fares. When you're looking for bargain fares go to a travel agent rather than directly to the airline, as the latter can only sell fares by the book. Travel agents often hesitate to sell you the cheapest ticket available, not necessarily because they want to cheat you, but because many budget tickets come with lots of restrictions which you may find inconvenient. If you want the cheapest ticket, be sure to tell this to the travel agent and then ask what restrictions, if any, apply. Make sure you get details in writing of the flights you've requested (before you pay for the ticket), check whether all your money will be refunded if the flight is cancelled, and ask about any extra charges (eg surcharges). Check how long the ticket is valid for, the minimum period of stay and the cancellation fees. If you change your date of travel, amendment fees could apply. Plenty of dis-

count tickets are valid for 12 months, allowing multiple stopovers with open dates. These tickets allow for a great deal of flexibility. Some cheaper fares can limit your choice of stopovers – a higher fare may allow more stopovers.

Advance Purchase Excursion, or APEX, tickets are sold at a discount but will lock you into a rigid schedule. Such tickets must be purchased two or three weeks ahead of departure, do not permit stopovers and may have minimum and maximum stays as well as fixed departure and return dates. Unless you definitely must return at a certain time, it's best to purchase APEX tickets on a one-way basis only. There are stiff cancellation fees if you decide not to use your APEX ticket.

'Round-the-world' tickets are usually offered by an airline or combination of airlines, and let you take your time (six months to a year) moving from point to point on their routes for the price of one ticket. The main restriction is that you have to keep moving in the same direction; a drawback is that because you are usually booking individual flights as you go, and can't switch carriers, you can get caught out by flight availabilities and have to spend more or less time in a place than you want to.

Some airlines offer discounts of up to 25% on their tickets to student-card holders. If buying an international ticket in Indonesia, an official-looking letter from the school is also needed. You also must be aged 26 or younger. These discounts are generally only available on ordinary economy-class fares. You wouldn't get one, for instance, on an APEX or a round-the-world ticket, as these are already discounted.

Airlines usually carry babies up to two years of age at 10% of the relevant adult fare; a few may carry them free of charge. Reputable international airlines usually provide nappies (diapers), tissues, talcum and all the other paraphernalia needed to keep babies clean, dry and half-happy. For children between the ages of four and 12 the fare on international flights is usually 50% of the regular fare, or 67% of a discounted fare. These days most fares are likely to be discounted.

'Frequent flyer' plans have proliferated in recent years and are now offered by most airlines, even some budget ones. Basically, these allow you a free ticket if you chalk up so many km with the same airline. The plans aren't always as good as they sound – some airlines require you to acquire and use all your frequent flyer credits within one year or you lose the lot. Sometimes you find yourself flying on a particular airline just to get frequent flyer credits, but the ticket is considerably more expensive than what you might have gotten from a discount airline without a frequent flyer bonus. When you purchase the ticket, be sure to give the travel agent or airline your frequent flyer membership number. A common complaint seems to be that airlines 'forget' to record your frequent flyer credits when you fly with them – save all your ticket receipts and be prepared to push if no bonus is forthcoming. This applies as much to big-name airlines as it does to Third-World ones.

One thing to avoid is a 'back-to-front' ticket. These are best explained by example – if you want to fly from Japan (where tickets are very expensive) to Indonesia (where tickets are significantly cheaper), you can pay by cheque or credit card and have a friend or travel agent in Indonesia mail the ticket to you. The problem is that the airlines have computers and will know that the ticket was issued in Indonesia rather than Japan, and they will refuse to honor it. Consumer groups have filed lawsuits over this practice, with mixed results, but in most countries the law protects the airlines, not consumers. In short, the ticket is only valid starting from the country where it was issued.

To/From Australia

During peak seasons – school holidays and especially the christmas break – flights to and from Australia are very heavily booked,

so you must plan well ahead if you want to fly to Indonesia then.

You can fly direct to Jakarta and/or Bali (Denpasar) from Sydney, Melbourne, Brisbane, Adelaide, Perth, Port Hedland and Darwin. Only Garuda/Merpati operate the Darwin flights, while Garuda and Qantas operate flights (three to seven a week) on the other sectors. From time to time there have been charters between Darwin in Australia and Maluku. Flight time from Melbourne to Denpasar is about 5½ to 6½ hours. For West Australians, Bali is almost a local resort. Perth to Denpasar flying time is just 3½ hours, less time than it takes to go from Perth to the east coast of Australia.

Qantas and Garuda offer almost exactly the same fares and conditions for flights to Bali and Jakarta. Tickets have limited validity, and high (December and January) and low (February to December) seasons. There are no APEX air fares available from Australia to Indonesia. Below are sample air fares (in A$) from Australia to Bali and Java. Cheaper prices may be available from discount travel agents or wholesalers, on special promotional fares, or as part of a package.

From	To	Return	One Way
East coast	Denpasar	900-1100	700-800
East coast	Jakarta	1100-1300	800-900
West coast	Denpasar	700-800	400-450
West coast	Jakarta	800-1000	500-550
Darwin	Jakarta	800	500

A very interesting alternative to the Garuda or Qantas flights is to take Merpati (☎ (089) 411030) from Darwin to Kupang on the island of Timor. From Kupang there are regular flights to Bali or you can island-hop through the Nusa Tenggara archipelago to Bali. Natrabu (☎ 813695), at 12 Westlane Arcade off Smith St Mall, is a Merpati agent in Darwin. You do not need a visa to enter or leave Indonesia through Kupang, but require an onward ticket from Indonesia if you wish to buy a one-way ticket to Kupang.

Merpati's low-season Darwin-Kupang return fare is A$350; the high-season fare is A$400. The one-way fare is about A$200.

Darwin to Denpasar on Garuda costs about A$650 low season, or A$750 high. The one-way fare from Kupang to Denpasar is A$170.

A round-the-world ticket going Melbourne-Bali-London and returning via the USA, Honolulu and New Zealand would cost around A$2000, but there are hundreds of possible configurations, so ask around.

You might get best value from an accommodation-inclusive package. These include air fares and pre-booked accommodation. Check the major newspapers for ads by discount shops. As an example, you could get 10 nights' accommodation at a three-star hotel in Bali, transfers, daily continental breakfast, and full dinner on the last day, flying return from Melbourne to Denpasar with Garuda, for A$1000, which is hardly more than you would pay for the air fare alone. Conditions usually apply – eg two people must travel together, in high season, and pay at least 45 days in advance. Flight times cannot usually be altered, so make sure your insurance covers the cost of unexpected cancellation or alteration of your flight plans. Because holiday air fares like this are so cheap, some people buy a holiday package and then don't bother to use the accommodation. Normally, package tours require you to pre-book accommodation for your whole stay, but if you want to do some independent travelling and still take advantage of a cheap package deal, your travel agent may be able to base a package on the more flexible excursion fares, so you can defer your return flight without having to book accommodation in advance for the extra nights. This is an ideal combination, but you'll have to shop around to find an agent who will do it.

Remember that, in general, fares vary widely according to the season, the airline and the agent, so shop around for the best deal. For good fares to Indonesia try STA and Flight Centres International offices in the main cities, or the various agents who advertise in the Yellow Pages and in the travel pages of the main newspapers.

To/From New Zealand
Garuda and Air New Zealand have twice-weekly services from Auckland to Indonesia. Air New Zealand's fares are generally a little lower than Garuda's. Conditions apply (eg Air New Zealand requires you to pay 14 days in advance; Garuda applies a 10% cancellation fee). The return economy air fare from Auckland to Denpasar or Jakarta is about NZ$1400 to NZ$1550. The one-way fare is about NZ$1000.

Check the latest fare developments and discounts with the airlines, or shop around a few travel agents for possible deals. As in Australia, STA and Flight Centres International are popular travel agents.

To/From the UK
Air-ticket discounting is a long-running business in the UK and it's wide open. The various agents advertise their fares and there is nothing under-the-counter about it at all. To find out what's going, a number of magazines in Britain have good information about flights and agents. These include: *Trailfinder*, free from the Trailfinders Travel Centre in Earls Court; and *Time Out* and *City Limits*, the London weekly entertainment guides widely available in the UK. Also check the Sunday papers and *Exchange & Mart* for ads.

Discount tickets are almost exclusively available in London. You won't find your friendly travel agent out in the country offering cheap deals. The danger with discounted tickets in Britain is that some of the 'bucket shops' (as ticket-discounters are known) are unsound. Sometimes the backstairs over-the-shop travel agents fold up and disappear after you've handed over the money and before you've got the tickets. Get the tickets before you hand over the cash.

Most British travel agents are registered with ABTA (Association of British Travel Agents). If you have paid for your flight to an ABTA-registered agent who then goes out of business, ABTA will guarantee a refund or an alternative. Unregistered bucket shops are riskier but also sometimes cheaper.

Two reliable London bucket shops are Trailfinders in Earls Court, and the Student Travel Association with several offices.

It's relatively easy to find cheap fares to Australia with stopovers in Indonesia. It's not, however, such a bargain to go just to Bali or Bali return. From London, the fare to Bali is around £350 one way or £650 return. A London-Australia (Perth) ticket with stopovers in Singapore and Bali costs around £450 one way. A return ticket to Melbourne or Sydney with stopovers in Singapore, Bali and Bangkok costs around £900. A circle Asia fare from London to Singapore, Jakarta, Bali, Hong Kong and back to London would cost around £850, or via Bangkok, Bali and Singapore around £750.

Another alternative is to fly London-Singapore for around £300 one way or £500 return and then make your own way down to Bali by air, or sea and land.

To/From Europe

The Netherlands, Brussels and Antwerp are good places for buying discount air tickets. In Antwerp, WATS has been recommended. In Zurich try SOF Travel and Sindbad. In Geneva try Stohl Travel. In The Netherlands, NBBS is a reputable agency.

Currently, the best deals going are with Czechoslovak Airlines. Good value can be gotten on the Russian airline Aeroflot, the Polish airline LOT and the Rumanian airline Tarom, but none of these fly into Jakarta, though they can get you to Bangkok or Singapore. Most East European airlines have a reputation for poor safety and lost luggage.

Garuda has flight connections between Jakarta and several European cities: Paris, Amsterdam, Zurich, Frankfurt and Rome.

To/From the USA

There are some very good open tickets which remain valid for six months or one year (opt for the latter), but don't lock you into any fixed dates of departure. For example, there are cheap tickets between the US west coast and Singapore with stopoffs in Japan, Korea, Taiwan, Hong Kong and Bangkok for very little extra money – the departure dates can be changed and you have one year to complete the journey. However, be careful during the peak season (summer and Chinese New Year) because seats will be hard to come by unless reserved months in advance.

Usually, and not surprisingly, the cheapest fare to whatever country is offered by a bucket shop owned by someone of that particular ethnic origin. San Francisco is the bucket shop capital of the USA, though some good deals can be found in Los Angeles, New York and other cities. Bucket shops can be found through the Yellow Pages or the major daily newspapers. Those listed in both Roman and Oriental scripts are invariably discounters. The *New York Times*, the *LA Times*, the *Chicago Tribune* and the *San Francisco Examiner* all produce weekly travel sections in which you'll find any number of travel agents' ads. The magazine *Travel Unlimited* (PO Box 1058, Allston,

Mass 02134) publishes details of the cheapest air fares to destinations all over the world from the USA.

A more direct way is to wander around San Francisco's Chinatown, where most of the shops are – especially in the Clay St and Waverly Place area. Many of these are staffed by recent arrivals from Hong Kong and Taiwan who speak little English. Enquiries are best made in person.

It's not advisable to send money (even cheques) through the post unless the agent is very well established – some travellers have reported being ripped off by fly-by-night mail order ticket agents.

Council Travel is the largest student travel organisation and, although you don't have to be a student to use them, they do have specially discounted student tickets. Council Travel has an extensive network in all major US cities and is listed in the telephone book. There are also Student Travel Network offices which are associated with Student Travel Australia.

One of the cheapest and most reliable travel agents on the west coast is Overseas Tours (☎ (800) 3238777 in California, (800) 2275988 elsewhere), 475 El Camino Real, Room 206, Millbrae, CA 94030. Another good agent is Gateway Travel (☎ (214) 9602000, (800) 4411183), 4201 Spring Valley Rd, Suite 104, Dallas, TX 75244, who seem to be reliable for mail order tickets.

From the US west coast you can get to Hong Kong, Bangkok or Singapore for about US$1000 to US$1300 return and get a flight from there to Bali.

Alternatively, Garuda has a Los Angeles-Honolulu-Biak-Denpasar route which is an extremely interesting back door route into Indonesia. Biak is a no-visa entry point so that's no problem, and from there you can explore Irian Jaya. The return fare from Los Angeles to Bali is about US$1500.

To/From Canada
Getting discount tickets in Canada is much the same as in the USA – go to the travel agents and shop around until you find a good deal. Again, you'll probably have to fly into Hong Kong or Singapore and carry on from there to Indonesia.

CUTS is Canada's national student bureau and has offices in a number of Canadian cities including Vancouver, Edmonton, Toronto and Ottawa – you don't necessarily have to be a student. There are a number of good agents in Vancouver for cheap tickets, CP-Air are particularly good for fares to Hong Kong.

The *Toronto Globe & Mail* and the *Vancouver Sun* carry travel agents' ads. The magazine *Great Expeditions* (PO Box 8000-411, Abbotsford BC V2S 6H1) is useful.

To/From Singapore
There are direct flights from Singapore to Jakarta, Denpasar and several cities in Sumatra. There are also some flights to Kalimantan and to the Riau Archipelago, which is the cluster of small Indonesian islands immediately south of Singapore.

You can get a return ticket with Garuda from Singapore to Jakarta for about S$700 (minimum stay five nights, maximum 30), or to Denpasar for S$900.

Singapore is also a good place to buy a cheap air ticket if you're leaving South-East Asia for the West. Cheap air tickets from Singapore are available at Airmaster Travel Centre. Also try Student Travel Australia. Other agents advertise in the *Straits Times* classified columns.

Fares from Singapore to the West vary with when you want to fly and who you want to fly with. The cheapest fares are likely to be with various East European or Middle East airlines. There are also cheap fares available on various South-East Asian airlines to other parts of South-East Asia and to the West.

To/From Malaysia
You can fly from Penang to Medan in Sumatra with Garuda (US$60), Sempati Air (US$45) or Malaysian Air Service (MAS). This flight is one of the most popular routes into Indonesia. You can also fly from Kuala Lumpur to Medan for around US$80 with Garuda or MAS.

MAS has a twice-weekly flight between Pontianak (in Kalimantan) and Kuching (Malaysia). Bouraq and MAS fly between Tarakan (Kalimantan) and Tawau (Malaysia).

To/From Hong Kong

There are direct flights between Hong Kong and Jakarta, with connections to Denpasar. Hong Kong is a good place for air fare bargains. Travel agents advertise in the classified sections of the *South China Morning Post* and the *Hong Kong Standard* newspapers but some are definitely more reliable and helpful than others.

Major competitors in the budget ticket business include: *Travel Expert* (☎ 5432770, fax 5447055), Room 708, Haleson Building, 1 Jubilee St, Central, or try their Kowloon office (☎ 3670963), Room 803, Metropole Building, 57 Peking Rd, Tsimshatsui; *Shoestring Travel* (☎ 7232306), flat A, 4th floor, Alpha House, 27-33 Nathan Rd, Tsimshatsui; *Traveller Services* (☎ 3674127, fax 3110387), Room 704, Metropole Building, 57 Peking Rd, Tsimshatsui; *Phoenix Services* (☎ 7227378) in Room B, 6th floor, Milton Mansion, 96 Nathan Rd, Tsimshatsui. If you're really student with an ISIC card, try Hong Kong Student Travel Bureau (☎ 7303269), Room 1021, 10th floor, Star House, Tsimshatsui. Whatever you do, shop around and compare prices before you buy!

Typical bargain-basement one-way/return fares from Hong Kong are Jakarta HK$2000/3350 or Denpasar HK$3100/4800. You can also find interesting fares from Hong Kong through Indonesia to Australia.

To/From Japan

Expensive! Your best bet might be to take a boat over to nearby South Korea and buy your ticket there. If you have to buy a ticket in Japan there are often ads for specialist travel agents in the English-language papers and magazines aimed at resident foreigners. Council Travel (☎ (03) 35817581) has an office at the Sanno Grand Building, Room 102, 14-2 Nagata-cho, 2-chome, Chiyoda-ku, Tokyo 100. STA (☎ (03) 32211733) is at Sanden Building, 3-5-5 Kojimachi, Chiyoda-ku, Tokyo.

To/From South Korea

The best deals are available from the Korean International Student Exchange Society (KISES) (☎ (02) 7339494), Room 505, YMCA building, Chongno 2-ga, Seoul. Discount fares from Seoul to Jakarta are US$530.

To/From Taiwan

For a level of competence and cheap fares rarely seen in Taiwan, try Jenny Su Travel Service (☎ (02) 5951646), 10th floor, 27 Chungshan N Rd, Section 3, Taipei. Quoted one-way/return air fares from Taipei to Jakarta were US$450/750 on Garuda Airlines. Prices on tickets bought in Jakarta are about the same.

To/From Papua New Guinea

From Papua New Guinea there is a once-weekly flight between Wewak and Jayapura in Irian Jaya (via Vanimo). For more details see the Irian Jaya chapter.

LAND

Land crossings between Kalimantan and eastern Malaysia are possible. See the Kalimantan chapter for more details.

SEA

Surprisingly for an island country, there are few opportunities to arrive in Indonesia by sea.

The most feasible route is the Jakarta-Tanjung Pinang-Singapore service – see the Jakarta Getting There & Away section in the Java chapter for more details.

A twice-weekly catamaran service operates between Medan (Sumatra) and Penang (Malaysia) for M$90 in economy class. See Getting There & Away in the Sumatra chapter for more information.

Alternatively, from Singapore you can take a boat to Batam and another to Tanjung Pinang, an Indonesian island a few hours south of Singapore. From Tanjung Pinang you can catch a boat to Pekanbaru or Medan. For more details of these routes – plus other possibilities for getting to or from Sumatra – see the Sumatra chapter.

An interesting new twist is the planned boat service between Davao in the Philippines, and Manado in Northern Sulawesi. If you find yourself in either of these two cities, make enquiries at the respective tourist offices.

With a bit of effort it's still possible to get yacht rides around South-East Asia. Very often, yacht owners are travellers too and need another crew member or two; willingness to give it a try is often more important than experience and often all it costs you is the contribution to the food kitty. As for where to look – well, anywhere that yachts pass through or in towns with Western-style yacht clubs. We've had letters from people who have managed to get rides from Singapore, Penang, Phuket (in Thailand) and Benoa (in Bali). Other popular yachting places include the main ports in Papua New Guinea and Hong Kong. Every August there is a Darwin to Ambon (capital of the Maluku Islands) yacht race.

TOURS

Most tours are oriented towards Bali. There are so many tours that it's impossible to list them all here. While none are cheap, there are different price ranges according to standard of accommodation. Some of the more deluxe tours also include luxurious boat trips to neighbouring islands. One note of caution – the more upmarket tours may be comfortable and fun, but some of the staged ceremonies you'll be shown are basically little more than theatre. We ran into one tour group on the island of Lembata while they were attending a 'traditional ceremony' imported from Hawaii, complete with female dancers in grass skirts and flower necklaces, moving to the beat of bongo drums. Nice, but not exactly authentic Indonesian culture.

LEAVING INDONESIA

Cheap, discount air tickets out of Indonesia can be bought from various travel agents in Jakarta, and at Kuta Beach and Legian on Bali. At budget travel agencies, you usually save at least 3% if you pay cash rather than using a credit card.

You can also buy tickets in Bali for departure from Jakarta and Singapore to other parts of South-East Asia, as well as to Auckland, Honolulu, the US west coast or London. You can hook up with the UTA trans-Pacific services out of Jakarta with flights to Noumea, Papeete, the US west coast and New York.

In Jakarta, the other place for cheap tickets, one of the cheapest travel agents is Seabreeze Travel (☎ 326675), Jalan Jaksa 43, near all the budget hotels. There are several other travel agents on Jalan Jaksa, but none quoted fares as low as Seabreeze. Travel International (☎ 330103) in the President Hotel on Jalan Thamrin is also a good place for cheap tickets, as is Vayatour (☎ 3100720) next door to Travel International. There are two reasonably priced travel agents in the Hotel Borobudur Intercontinental (near the GPO): Mantili Travel and Pacto Ltd, both using the same telephone number (☎ 3805555).

To Asian destinations, quoted discount fares include: Singapore US$80 (on Sempati), Bangkok US$290, Calcutta US$450, Hong Kong US$370, Manila US$280, Seoul US$530, Taipei US$470 and Tokyo US$550. To Australia, you can fly to Perth for US$330, Melbourne for US$490 and Sydney for US$490. There are discount flights to London for US$580 and Los Angeles for US$690.

Departure Tax

Airport tax on international flights is 15,000 rp. On domestic flights, airport tax is between 1500 and 6000 rp, depending on the airport, but this is normally included in the ticket price.

Getting Around

AIR

Indonesia has a variety of airlines, a bizarre collection of aircraft and an extensive network of flights that make some pretty remote corners of the country easily accessible. The main airlines are Garuda, Mandala, Merpati, Bouraq and Sempati, and there are several smaller ones. Not all domestic air fares are equal – Garuda has the most expensive fares, though they also have a discount air pass which is useful if you make frequent flights over a short period of time.

Each airline publishes a nationwide timetable – definitely worth picking up if you're going to do a lot of flying. Garuda and Merpati both hand out timetables like confetti, but other airlines are pretty stingy with theirs. With any airline, you should be able to obtain a timetable by visiting the head office in Jakarta, though you might be able to acquire these top-secret documents in Bali too.

Don't rely on this book to tell you every flight that's available to or from a given place. There are so many flights – sometimes with two or three airlines covering the same route – that it's impossible to list them all here! All we can give you here is the main flights, or those which are probably most useful to tourists, together with some idea of the fares involved. Get the timetables (but don't always believe them!) and check with the local airline offices about what's available.

Airport tax on domestic flights varies from about 1500 to 6000 rp and should be included on your ticket. On most flights, baggage is limited to 20 kg, sometimes to 10 kg on the smaller planes, so check first. Sometimes they charge you excess baggage and sometimes they don't.

On the more popular routes, try to book as far in advance as possible, especially in the peak tourist season around July and August when flights can be fully booked two or three weeks in advance. Don't expect to be able to

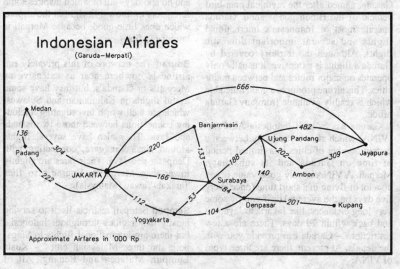

Indonesian Airfares
(Garuda–Merpati)

Approximate Airfares in '000 Rp

make a booking in advance in one town and then buy your ticket at the departure point. If you don't buy the ticket when you make a booking, then you don't have a booking! It's also prudent to reconfirm your flight the day before departure. Bookings have to go through the airline office in the city of departure. In the outer islands, this can mean a long wait while contact is made by short-wave radio – try to sit with the operator to make sure your booking has been made.

On top of the basic fares, a 10% tax is charged, as well as insurance and baggage charges (usually no more than 1500 rp). The charges and departure tax on domestic flights are normally paid when you buy the ticket.

Most airlines offer student discounts of up to 25%. You need a valid International Student Identity Card (ISIC) to take advantage of this, as well as a letter from the school or institution. For domestic flights, there is no age limit for claiming to be a student, but for international flights the age limit is 26.

Local Air Services

Garuda The major national airline is Garuda, named after the mythical man-bird vehicle of the Hindu god Vishnu. Garuda operate most of Indonesia's international flights and several important domestic flights. Although the territory covered by Garuda's flights is extensive, it usually only operates on major routes and between major cities. This airline produces a good timetable which is readily available from any Garuda office.

Garuda has a 'Visit Indonesia Air Pass' (VINA) which allows you to fly between a certain number of cities in a limited period of time on Garuda and its subsidiary, Merpati. A VINA is only good value if you do a lot of flying in a short time (once every five days on the average) or if you fly some very long distances, like Jakarta to Jayapura and back within 20 days. There are a few restrictions – Garuda can provide you with the details. At present, there are three types of VINA:

Pass	Validity	Cities	Price
VINA	120 days	4	US$350
VINA	230 days	8	US$500
VINA	360 days	12	US$600

On top of these prices, there is a 10% value-added tax and airport departure tax at each city.

Merpati This was once an independent airline but was taken over by Garuda and since 1989 has been integrated into Garuda's network. Merpati runs a mind-boggling collection of aircraft – everything from modern jets to single-engine eggbeaters. The intention is that they should run services to obscure locations, and they're most useful in some out-of-the-way places like Irian Jaya and Nusa Tenggara. Merpati also flies a few back-door international routes, including Darwin-Kupang and Pontianak-Kuching (Malaysia). The Garuda timetable lists Merpati's flights, but Merpati also publishes its own timetable. From our experience, Merpati operates on 'rubber time' with flights being late by an average of two hours. They usually make no announcement that a flight is going to be late, offer no explanation and no apology – all of which inspires some foreigners to throw a fit right in the airport, which does little good, because Merpati is immune to fits.

Bouraq The network of this privately run airline is nowhere near as extensive as Merpati's or Garuda's, but they have some useful flights in Kalimantan and Sulawesi which are well worth investigating, including connections between those two islands and Java. They also have several flights around Nusa Tenggara, connecting with Denpasar and Java. Their fares are slightly lower than Merpati's. Bouraq also flies Tarakan-Tawau (Malaysia).

Sempati Sempati restricts itself to serving mostly major cities throughout Indonesia, but there are international flights to Singapore and three Malaysian cities – Kuala Lumpur, Malacca and Penang. All of

Sempati's aircraft are modern jets. Sempati produces a decent timetable, but getting your hands on one will require luck or connections.

Mandala In this dull jumbo-jet age, Mandala's four-engined prop-planes make an interesting change. They serve a couple of main routes connecting Jakarta with Ambon, Medan, Padang, Surabaya and Ujung Pandang. Mandala's air fares are about 20% cheaper than Garuda's.

Other There are some intriguing possibilities for flying in Indonesia. The mission aircraft which operate in places like Kalimantan, Central Sulawesi and Irian Jaya fly to some really remote parts of the interior of these islands and will take *paying* passengers if they have room. You're most likely to use the flights around Irian Jaya – see the Irian Jaya chapter for details.

Privately run air freight companies like Airfast will take paying passengers if they have room. Cargo aircraft owned by the Indonesian military will sometimes carry well-connected Indonesian people, but never foreigners.

Various aircraft and helicopters are used by the foreign mining and oil companies – if you meet the right people in the right place, if they like the look of your face, and if they're not yet sick of every self-proclaimed Marco Polo looking for a free ride, you never know where you could end up.

Other airlines include Bali Air which is owned by Bouraq and operates charter flights, and Indoavia which is owned by Merpati and flies to some isolated islands.

BUS

Once upon a time, getting from point A to point B by road in much of Indonesia involved intermittent days of pure hell jolting over roads constructed of trenches big enough to swallow half a truck. Things are gradually improving – Java and Bali have some excellent surfaced highways, but in remote backwaters like Irian Jaya, a 'road' is often little more than a set of tire tracks in the mud. In Indonesia the further off the beaten track you get, the more beaten-up the track becomes.

Some of the bus companies offer door-to-door service. This is more of a curse than a blessing – they'll go all around town picking up passengers who have already bought tickets, or searching out additional business. This, of course, can take a considerable amount of time since they won't finally leave until the bus is reasonably full, and you seem to drive around town endlessly in circles. At the end of the trip they'll take each passenger to whatever particular part of town he or she wants to go to – and again if you're the last one they drop off this can also take a considerable amount of time. This driving around in circles is known as *keliling*. In most large cities, keliling is now prohibited, but in smaller cities expect at least one hour of keliling on each end.

Regardless of what type of bus you're travelling on, bring as little luggage as possible – there is rarely any room to store anything, even under the seats! A large pack with a frame will be a positive abomination to find a space for – so if you can travel with a small bag, do so.

Classes

In the more developed parts of Indonesia, buses may be air-conditioned with built-in video systems to entertain the passengers. On the other hand, rural backwaters are served by some antique buckets-of-bolts with bald tires and failing brake systems, and often piloted by kamikaze drivers who like to see how close to the edge of the cliff they can come. It such places, you may have to share the bus with goats, pigs and chickens. On Gili Sawu, we even had to share the back of the bus with a cow. Luggage and animals are usually tied onto the roof (not possible with the cow), so you have to watch to make sure your backpack isn't being used as 'kitty (or goat) litter'.

In many parts of Indonesia buses don't usually run at night. However, there are night buses between Bali and Java and with improvements in the roads on the other islands, more and more companies are putting on night services. These buses are usually very comfortable, always with air-conditioning and often with video tape recorders playing movies or karaoke melodies. The more luxurious night buses even have toilets on board.

No matter how old or new the bus is, one thing you can count on is an eardrum-shattering stereo system playing some of the most wretched music this side of the equator. Other than riding on the roof with the goats, your only defence against this evil noise is to try to find a seat that is not directly under a speaker. Some travellers swear that the mind-numbing music is being used by the government to brainwash people. This, of course, is not true; TV is the main vehicle for brainwashing.

Reservations

For short routes on good roads you'll probably find frequent vehicles departing all through the day. For longer routes you'll have to get down to the station early in the morning to get a vehicle; on bad roads there'll be fewer vehicles, so buying a ticket beforehand can be a good idea. In many places the bus companies will have an office from where you can buy a ticket and reserve a seat; there may be shops which act as agents (or own the buses) from where you can buy tickets in advance. Often, hotels will act as agents or will buy a ticket for you and arrange to have the bus pick you up at the hotel – sometimes they will charge a few hundred rupiah for this service but it's easily worth it.

Costs

The daytime buses that depart early in the morning – carrying chickens, pigs and goats – are usually the cheapest. You'll rarely have to pay more than 6000 rp for a full-day journey.

By way of comparison, the more luxurious overnight buses from Jakarta to Bali cost around 40,000 rp, including the ferry crossing. Jakarta to Medan (Sumatra) takes over two days and costs 78,000 rp, also with ferry included.

TRUCK

One of the great ironies of Indonesia is that farm animals ride in buses and people ride in the backs of farm trucks! Trucks come in many different varieties. The luxurious ones operate with rows of bench seats in the tray at the back to sit on. More likely, you will have to sit on the floor or stand. In remote backwaters like Lembata, we've had to ride on the roof and dodge tree branches! If you are on a truck – and that implies a rough road ahead – it's imperative to try and get a seat in front of the rear axle, otherwise every time the truck hits a pothole you get to find out what it's like to be a ping-pong ball. This is even more distressing if you're riding on the roof.

Safety is not a strong point with the trucks. If the truck drives over the edge of a cliff, it could ruin your whole day. In general, you're better off sticking with the buses if they are available.

BEMO

Bemos are the most popular form of land transport, used both as local transport around cities and towns and on short intercity runs. Originally a bemo was a small pickup truck with a row of seats down each side. These days, they are rapidly being replaced by small minibuses, usually a Toyota Commando or a Mitsubishi Colt. Bemos are also known as *opelets* or *mikrolets* or *colts*, but the difference is largely semantic.

Most bemos operate a standard route, picking up and dropping off people and goods anywhere along the way. Within cities, there is usually a standard fare no matter how long or short the distance. On longer routes between cities, you may have to bargain a bit.

Bemo drivers often try to overcharge foreigners – more in some places than in others. It's best to ask somebody about the *harga biasa* (normal price) before you get on. You can also ask other bemo passengers once you've gotten on board, but they may side with the bemo driver. If you know the fare is 200 rp and they try and charge you 400 rp just hand over the right fare; if they really insist that 400 rp is the correct fare then it most likely is – the fares will likely have gone up since this book was published, so use the prices given as a rough guide only! The other thing to remember is that the difference between 200 rp and 400 rp is only 10 cents (US money) – if your budget is so tight that you really feel you have to argue passionately about being overcharged by 10 cents then it's time to either go home or walk.

Beware of getting on an empty bemo; you may end up chartering it! One annoying problem you come across time and time again in Indonesia is wandering into the bemo station to search out a bemo going where you want to go, and being told by driver after driver how much it will cost you to charter it! On the other hand, sometimes chartering a bemo is worth considering – between a group of half a dozen people it can work out cheaper than hiring a motorcycle by the day and much cheaper than hiring a car. It can also be much more convenient for some straightforward point A to point B trips. For example, to travel by regular bemo between Kuta Beach and Sanur in Bali you have to take one bemo into Denpasar, transfer to another bemo station and then take another bemo out. With a bit of bargaining half a dozen people could charter a bemo directly for the same cost; it's faster, more convenient and you get to-the-door service at your destination. Regular bemos carry around 12 people, so multiplying the usual fare by 12 should give you a rough idea of what to pay. Smaller bemos are, of course, cheaper than big ones. If you find yourself in the sticks without any wheels you'll either have to try and charter a bemo or bus, camp out or find the kepala desa (head of the village) and ask to be put up for the night.

As with all public transport in Indonesia, the drivers wait until their vehicles are crammed to capacity before they contemplate moving. Often there are people, produce, chickens, stacks of sarongs, laden baskets, even bicycles hanging out the windows and doors and at times it seems you're in danger of being crushed to death or at least asphyxiated. There's no such thing as air-conditioning on any of these vehicles. Indonesians don't travel well; many people have amazingly weak stomachs that chuck up last night's gado-gado the first time the vehicle crosses a ripple in the road.

TRAIN

Train travel in Indonesia is restricted solely to Java and Sumatra – for full details see those chapters. Briefly, there is a pretty good railway service running from one end of Java to the other – in the east it connects with the ferry to Bali, and in the west with the ferry to Sumatra. There are a few lines tacked down in Sumatra, but most of that island is reserved for buses. There are no railways on any of the other islands.

Classes

Trains vary – there are slow, miserable, cheap ones, fast, comfortable, expensive ones and in-between ones. Some major towns like Jakarta and Surabaya have several railway stations so check where you'll be going to and where you have to leave from.

Reservations

Jakarta's Gambir station has a special tourist information office where the English-speaking staff makes reservations, sell tickets and smiles at foreigners. This is certainly preferable to battling the long lines where the Indonesians must buy their tickets from cheerless, overworked ticket clerks. However, in most railway stations you'll have to slug it out with everyone else. It's best to buy your train tickets one day in advance to be assured of getting a seat.

Costs

Costs vary not only according to class but also according to which train you take. To give some idea, Jakarta to Yogyakarta in economy class costs only 5000 rp, while business class is 15,000 rp and executive class up to 37,000 rp. Student discounts are available, but they tend to vary too, from about 10% to 25%.

CAR & MOTORBIKE

Hiring or bringing your own motorbike could be one of the most interesting ways to travel through Indonesia. They've long been a favourite means of getting around Bali but they're also suited to many other parts of the country – particularly where there are poor, unsurfaced roads on which large vehicles get bogged. In fact, you'll avoid a bone-shattering ride on some of these roads if you can hire a trail bike! Outside Java and Bali, traffic is generally not heavy until you hit the cities and towns. Ferries and ships between the islands are more regular these days and will transport motorcycles.

Motorcycles definitely have their pluses and minuses: the minus points are danger and distance. Another disadvantage is that on a motorcycle you forsake many opportunities to get to grips with Indonesia. You don't meet people the way you do on a bemo, you don't see life as it's lived, you just rush round keeping your eye on the road. Furthermore, motorcycles are an unpleasant intrusion in many places – noisy, distracting, annoying and unwanted. But by the same token, the major plus is the enormous flexibility a motorcycle gives you, allowing you to get to places that people without their own transport have to walk to, and it saves having to wait endlessly for transport. And if you see something you like you can stop and continue on 10 minutes or 10 hours later. With a bemo you're likely to just shoot straight by – perhaps without even seeing it.

There is no denying the dangers of bike riding in Indonesia – combined with all the normal hazards of motorcycle riding are narrow roads, unexpected potholes, crazy drivers, buses and trucks which (through size alone) reckon they own the road, children who dart onto the road, bullocks that lumber in, dogs and chickens that run around in circles, and unlit traffic at night. Take it slowly and cautiously around curves to avoid hitting oncoming traffic – this includes very large and heavy buses, buffaloes, herds of stray goats, and children. Rocks, boulders and landslides on poor stretches of roads are another hazard. Watch out for animals that are tethered to one side of the road and then wander over to the other side, stretching their ropes across the road at neck height for a motorcyclist.

Roadworks are another hazard – you round a corner and come slap up against a grader, rocks piled into the middle of the road or 55-gallon drums of tar. They rarely, if ever, put up warning signs that there are roadworks in progress. Up in the mountains there are perilous and unprotected drops down sheer cliff faces to the valleys below – this limits your opportunities for swerving round these obstacles!

At home, most people would never dream of hopping on a motorcycle in shorts and thongs and without a crash helmet – but in Bali they take one rudimentary test, stick their bikes in first gear and their brains in reverse and charge off. Indonesia is no place to learn how to ride a motorcycle.

Road Rules

Basically, there aren't any. People in Indonesia drive on the left (usually!) of the road, as in Australia, Japan, Britain and most of South-East Asia. Opportunities for driving yourself are fairly limited in Indonesia unless you bring your own vehicle with you, except in Bali and Java – see the Bali and Java chapters for more details. In other places where tourists congregate, you can usually hire a jeep or minibus with driver included.

Punctures are usually repaired at roadside stands known as *tambal ban*. Whatever you do, try not to have an accident – if you do, as a foreigner it's *your* fault.

Rental

If you're willing to throw caution to the wind, motorcycles can be hired in Java, and more easily in Bali. Those for hire in Bali are almost all between 90 and 125 çc, with 100 cc as the usual size. You really don't need anything bigger – the distances are short and the roads are rarely suitable for going very fast. Anyway, what's the hurry? In any case, for long-distance travel, a small bike is better if it breaks down or runs out of gas and you have to push – particularly if it breaks down on some of those hilly islands like Flores or Sumbawa where it's a long way between service stations! If you have to load and unload the thing on and off boats, it's much easier with a small bike.

Rental charges vary with the bike and the period of hire. The longer the hire period, the lower the rate: the bigger or newer the bike, the higher the rate. Typically, in Bali you can expect to pay at least 10,000 rp per day. A newish 125 cc in good condition might cost you 15,000 rp a day for short periods. It's virtually impossible to hire a bike in Bali and take it to another island. You need to have a licence, but in Bali getting that is as easy as opening a cornflakes packet. See the Bali chapter for details of how to rent a motorcycle there and how to get a licence.

The price for hiring a car varies according to both location and vehicle. In Jakarta, a car without driver costs 100,000 rp per day, or 150,000 rp with a driver. In Bali, you can get a self-drive jeep for as little as 35,000 rp, or a minibus for slightly more. Elsewhere, the vehicle usually comes with a driver. In most cases, the price includes unlimited mileage but you supply the petrol.

In Jakarta there are a number of car rental agencies: Hertz, Mandarin Oriental Hotel (☎ 321397, ext 1268); Avis, Jalan P Diponegoro 25 (☎ 334495); Indo Rent, Jalan Hayam Wuruk 6 (☎ 355326). National Car Rental has offices in a number of cities: Jakarta (☎ 333423), Bandung (☎ 433025), Yogyakarta (☎ 87078), Medan (☎ 327641) Surabaya (☎ 60527) and Denpasar (☎ 71906). There are plenty of other places that rent vehicles and, if you're in a city that has a government tourist information centre, it's not a bad idea to enquire there first.

Petrol is reasonably cheap in Indonesia – it's currently around 550 rp a litre – slightly over US$1 a gallon. There are petrol stations around the larger towns, but out in the villages it can be hard to find. If you intend going to out-of-the-way places it may be advisable to take some with you, as long as you can carry it safely. If not, it's available from small wayside shops and hawkers on the streets, sometimes sold in Coca-Cola bottles – look for signs that read *press ban*, or crates of bottles with a sign saying *bensin*. Some of the stuff off the roadside stands is said to be of dubious quality, so it's probably best to refill whenever you see a Pertamina petrol station *(pompa bensin)* – although they're few and far between in some areas.

BICYCLE

The story on bicycle hire is much the same. Bicycles can be rented in the main centres of Java, Bali and also Lombok, but they're not used very much by Indonesians or by travellers. A few odd places like Yogyakarta are exceptions, with plenty of bicycles in common use. Also be prepared to do some maintenance work on the rusty old hulks you'll find in Indonesia.

The main advantage of cycling is the quality of the experience. You can cover many more km by bemo, bus or motorcycle but you really don't see more. Bicycles also tend to bridge the time gap between the rush of the West and the calm of rural Asia – without the noise of a motorcycle engine you can hear the wind rustling in the rice paddies, or the sound of a gamelan practising as you pass a village in Bali.

The main problems with seeing Indonesia by bicycle are the traffic in Java and the hills everywhere, which make it rather impractical or tough going to ride all over Indonesia. Seeing Bali by pushbike has become much more popular in recent years. More people are giving it a try and more places are renting bikes. At all the main sights in Java there are bicycle parking areas (usually 100 rp) where an attendant keeps an eye on your bicycle.

Some people even bring their bikes with them. You can usually bring your pushbike with you as baggage and some airlines (like Qantas) may carry it for free. However, it's an intrusive piece of luggage that will complicate hopping between islands. Some travellers think a bike is the best way to tour around the world, while others see it as a stone around their neck.

HITCHING

Yes, you can even hitchhike in Indonesia. You meet a lot of nice people, and enjoying the scenery from the roof of a truck is an experience you won't forget! If you survive, the only problem is that it might take a very long time to get anywhere. There aren't many private cars on the roads (even in Java) and the trucks can be too crowded or moving too fast to stop anyway. You're probably more likely to get short rides on the backs of motorcycles.

WALKING

Indonesia is too large to seriously consider walking across the country, but there are numerous trekking possibilities.

If you hike at high-altitude locations like Gunung Rinjani in Lombok or Puncak Trikora in Irian Jaya, you must be prepared for unstable mountain weather. Sudden rainstorms are common at high altitudes, and Indonesia is no longer tropical once you get above 3000 metres. The rain will not only make you wet, but freezing cold. Forget umbrellas – a good rain poncho is essential. Bring warm clothing, but dress in layers so you can peel off each item of clothing as the day warms up. Proper footwear is essential. A compass could be a real life-saver if you're caught in the fog.

Be sure to bring sunscreen (UV) lotion – it's even more essential at high altitudes than in the lowlands.

It should go without saying that you must bring sufficient food and water. Don't underestimate your need for water – figure on about two litres per day, more in extreme heat.

If you haven't done much long-distance walking or jogging recently, work up to it gradually rather than trying to 'get in shape' all at once. Do a few practice runs at home before disappearing into the Indonesian jungles.

Guides

A big decision is whether or not you need a guide. If you do need one, be prepared to haggle over the price. Guides in Indonesia sometimes ask for ridiculous amounts of money. Unless hired through a travel agency, a guide will typically cost around 10,000 rp per day. A travel agency may ask 10 times this amount, or more. Take some time to talk to your guide to make sure he (Indonesian guides are always male) really understands the route and won't simply help you get lost.

The Indonesian government has a policy of licensing guides. Licensed guides are not necessarily better than unlicensed ones, but usually are. If a guide is licensed, he is almost certainly a local, not a transient just passing through looking to pick up some quick cash from tourists. In any event, if your guide claims to be licensed, you should ask to see the licence and copy down his name and number. That way, if you encounter some really big problems (eg the guide abandons you on a mountainside, or rips off your camera and disappears) you can report him. On the other hand, if your guide turns out to be exceptionally good, you can then recommend him to other travellers you meet.

BOAT

Along with the roads, the shipping connections between the various islands of the archipelago have also improved greatly over the last few years, particularly in Nusa Tenggara. There are regular ferries connecting Sumatra and Java, Bali and Java, and almost all the islands of Nusa Tenggara – see the relevant chapters in this book for details. These ferries run either daily or several times a week so there's no longer any need to spend days in sleepy little port towns, reading big thick books, waiting for the elusive piece of driftwood to take you to the next island. Some of these ferries can transport large vehicles, and all of them will take motorcycles.

Inter-island & Coastal Shipping

Along with the more regular ferry hops, inter-island and coastal shipping have also improved greatly, with more modern passenger-carrying ships on regular runs. There are seven main passenger ships commonly used by travellers, all run by the national shipping line Pelni (P T Pelayaran Nasional Indonesia). They run loop trips and follow regular timetables, stopping at various ports depending on the ship.

Ships typically have a capacity of 100 people in 1st class, 200 in 2nd, 300 in 3rd, 400 in 4th and 500 in economy. Economy class, previously known as deck class, consists of a long, low platform divided into 10 two-metre by one-metre sections by small plastic pegs. Each section is numbered and assigned with an overhead luggage rack. These are located at the rear of the ship on decks three, four and five (there are typically nine decks in all). Deck three is near the waterline – it's advisable to request deck five as it's less stuffy and there are fewer vibrations. Lucky you – economy class even comes with a colour TV set and videos each night. The bathrooms have hot and cold water. Four meals are served each day – economy class meals may include rice, fish, vegetables or meat and a hard-boiled egg, all served on a plastic dish with a plastic spoon

and cup in a tidy cardboard box. Billycans are filled three times a day with hot water and hot tea.

At the other end of the ship, 1st class has two single beds in a small air-con room, and the 1st-class restaurant has white tablecloths. In 2nd class, accommodation consists of a larger room with four bunks each – there are male and female rooms. Rambo movies on the video, lifeboat drill and perpetual English lessons notwithstanding, it should be an unforgettable trip!

To give some idea of relative costs, the journey by ship from Tanjung Priok (port of Jakarta) to Ambon (Maluku Islands) is priced as follows: 1st class 320,000 rp; 2nd class 233,000 rp; 3rd class 171,000 rp; 4th class 132,000 rp; economy class 84,000 rp. By way of comparison, a straight Jakarta-Ambon air ticket from Merpati costs 421,200 rp. The ship takes four days, the flight takes five hours, but flights run daily while the ship runs once every two weeks. On most Pelni ships, there is a 25% discount for children.

Important seaports to know include Belawan (port of Medan, Sumatra), Bima (Sumbawa), Bitung (port of Manado, Sulawesi), Dilli (east Timor), Ende (Flores),

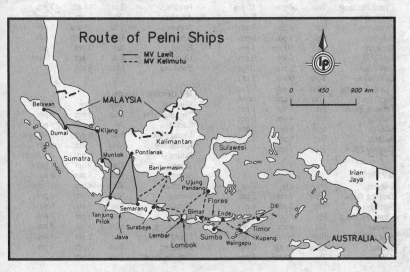

Route of Pelni Ships
—— MV Lawit
--- MV Kelimutu

Kijang (Riau Islands), Kupang (west Timor), Kwandang (near Gorontalo, Sulawesi), Lembar (Lombok), Pantoloan (port of Palu, Sulawesi), Sibolga (north-west Sumatra), Tanjung Priok (port of Jakarta), Ternate (north Maluku) and Waingapu (Sumba).

The following are the basic routes and schedules of the main Pelni passenger ships. Each ship takes between two and 2½ weeks to do a return trip.

MV Lawit

Seaport	Day	Arr	Dep
Tanjung Priok	Wed	6 am	4 pm
Muntok	Thu	noon	4 pm
Kijang	Fri	9 am	1 pm
Dumai	Sat	8 am	11 am
Belawan	Sun	8 am	1 pm
Dumai	Mon	10 am	1 pm
Kijang	Tue	9 am	1 pm
Muntok	Wed	6 am	9 am
Tanjung Priok	Thu	5 am	11 am
Pontianak	Fri	5 pm	8 pm
Semarang	Sun	5 am	9 am
Pontianak	Mon	6 pm	9 pm
Tanjung Priok	Wed	6 am	

MV Kerinci

Seaport	Day	Arr	Dep
Tanjung Priok	Tue	7 am	5 pm
Surabaya	Wed	2 pm	6 pm
Ujung Pandang	Thu	6 pm	10 pm
Balikpapan	Fri	4 pm	8 pm
Pantoloan	Sat	6 am	9 am
Toli-Toli	Sat	5 pm	9 pm
Tarakan	Sun	10 am	4 pm
Toli-Toli	Mon	6 am	9 am
Pantoloan	Mon	5 pm	10 pm
Balikpapan	Tue	9 am	1 pm
Ujung Pandang	Wed	6 am	10 am
Surabaya	Thu	8 am	noon
Tanjung Priok	Fri	9 am	1 pm
Padang	Sat	4 pm	7 pm
Sibolga	Sun	6 am	9 am
Padang	Sun	8 am	11 pm
Tanjung Priok	Tue	7 am	

MV Rinjani

Seaport	Day	Arr	Dep
Tanjung Priok	Wed	9 am	5 pm
Surabaya	Thu	2 pm	6 pm
Ujung Pandang	Fri	6 pm	10 pm
Baubau	Sat	noon	3 pm
Ambon	Sun	noon	6 pm
Sorong	Mon	11 am	5 pm
Ambon	Tue	10 am	6 pm

Baubau	Wed	2 pm	5 pm
Ujung Pandang	Thu	6 am	10 am
Surabaya	Fri	8 am	noon
Tanjung Priok	Sat	9 am	1 pm
Belawan	Mon	9 am	1 pm
Tanjung Priok	Wed	9 am	

MV Kambuna

Seaport	Day	Arr	Dep
Tanjung Priok	Wed	9 am	5 pm
Surabaya	Thu	2 pm	6 pm
Ujung Pandang	Fri	6 pm	10 pm
Balikpapan	Sat	4 pm	8 pm
Pantoloan	Sun	6 am	9 am
Bitung	Mon	9 am	4 pm
Pantoloan	Tue	5 pm	10 pm
Balikpapan	Wed	9 am	1 pm
Ujung Pandang	Thu	6 am	10 am
Surabaya	Fri	9 am	noon
Tanjung Priok	Sat	9 am	1 pm
Belawan	Mon	9 am	1 pm
Tanjung Priok	Wed	9 am	

MV Tidar

Seaport	Day	Arr	Dep
Surabaya	Mon	8 am	4 pm
Ujung Pandang	Tue	4 pm	9 pm
Balikpapan	Wed	2 pm	5 pm
Tarakan	Thu	2 pm	5 pm
Balikpapan	Fri	2 pm	5 pm
Ujung Pandang	Sat	8 am	noon
Surabaya	Sun	10 am	4 pm
Ujung Pandang	Mon	4 pm	9 pm
Baubau	Tue	11 am	3 pm
Ambon	Wed	1 pm	6 pm
Ternate	Thu	11 am	5 pm
Ambon	Fri	10 am	6 pm
Baubau	Sat	3 pm	6 pm
Ujung Pandang	Sun	7 am	10 am
Surabaya	Mon	8 am	

MV Umsini – Route A

Seaport	Day	Arr	Dep
Tanjung Priok	Thu	2 pm	9 pm
Surabaya	Fri	6 pm	9 pm
Ujung Pandang	Sat	9 pm	midnight
Kwandang	Mon	5 am	8 am
Bitung	Mon	6 pm	midnight
Ternate	Tue	9 am	1 pm
Sorong	Wed	5 am	8 am
Jayapura	Thu	4 pm	11 pm
Sorong	Sat	8 am	1 pm
Ternate	Sun	5 am	8 am
Bitung	Sun	3 pm	7 pm
Kwandang	Mon	5 am	8 am
Ujung Pandang	Tue	1 pm	4 pm
Surabaya	Wed	2 pm	5 pm
Tanjung Priok	Thu	2 pm	

MV Umsini – Route B

Seaport	Day	Arr	Dep
Tanjung Priok	Thu	2 pm	9 pm
Surabaya	Fri	6 pm	9 pm
Ujung Pandang	Sat	9 pm	midnight
Kwandang	Mon	5 am	8 am
Bitung	Mon	6 pm	midnight
Ternate	Tue	9 am	1 pm
Manokwari	Wed	2 pm	5 pm
Jayapura	Thu	4 pm	11 pm
Sorong	Sat	8 am	1 pm
Ternate	Sun	5 am	8 am
Bitung	Sun	3 pm	7 pm
Kwandang	Mon	5 am	8 am
Ujung Pandang	Tue	1 pm	4 pm
Surabaya	Wed	2 pm	5 pm
Tanjung Priok	Thu	2 pm	

MV Kelimutu – Route A

Seaport	Day	Arr	Dep
Semarang	Sun	11 am	1 pm
Banjarmasin	Mon	2 pm	4 pm
Surabaya	Tue	10 am	4 pm
Lembar	Wed	noon	2 pm
Ujung Pandang	Thu	noon	4 pm
Bima	Fri	7 am	9 am
Waingapu	Fri	7 pm	10 pm
Ende	Sat	5 am	8 am
Kupang	Sat	6 pm	11 pm
Dilli	Sun	11 am	5 pm
Kupang	Mon	5 am	9 am
Ende	Mon	7 pm	10 pm
Waingapu	Tue	5 am	7 am

Bima	Tue	5 pm	6 pm
Ujung Pandang	Wed	10 am	1 pm
Lembar	Thu	10 am	11 am
Surabaya	Fri	6 am	11 am
Banjarmasin	Sat	7 am	9 am
Semarang	Sun	8 am	11 am

MV Kelimutu – Route B

Seaport	Day	Arr	Dep
Semarang	Sun	8 am	11 am
Banjarmasin	Mon	noon	2 pm
Surabaya	Tue	7 am	4 pm
Lembar	Wed	noon	2 pm
Ujung Pandang	Thu	noon	6 pm
Bima	Fri	10 am	5 pm
Waingapu	Sat	5 am	9 am
Ende	Sat	4 pm	8 pm
Kupang	Sun	6 am	7 pm
Ende	Mon	5 am	8 am
Waingapu	Mon	3 pm	7 pm
Bima	Tue	5 am	8 am
Ujung Pandang	Wed	6 am	10 am
Lembar	Thu	8 am	10 am
Surabaya	Fri	6 am	10 am
Banjarmasin	Sat	6 am	8 am
Semarang	Sun	7 am	10 am

Apart from these seven ships, getting a boat is generally a case of hanging around a port until something comes by. Check with the shipping offices, Pelni, the harbour master's office, and anyone else you can think of.

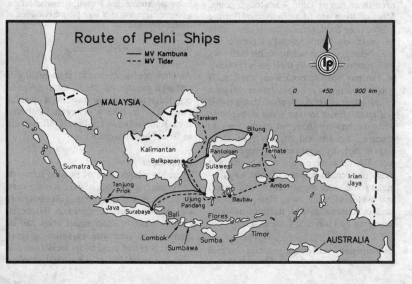

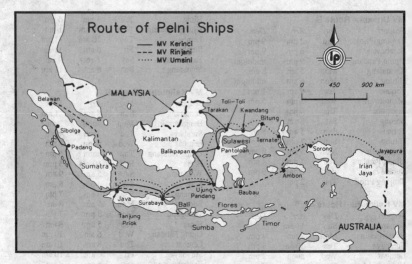

Route of Pelni Ships
— MV Kerinci
--- MV Rinjani
····· MV Umsini

Tickets can be bought at shipping offices, although for some ships and in some ports (big ones like Jakarta and Surabaya aside) it may be possible and cheaper to negotiate your fare on-board rather than buy tickets from the office in advance.

Unscheduled cargo and passenger ships – even those run by Pelni – are tough going. Most of them are filthy, with overflowing toilets, poor food, and the decks covered in an intricately lumpy carpet of people and their belongings, often fencing off their own little patch of deck with their cases, bunches of bananas and the occasional chicken. If you're travelling deck class then unroll your sleeping bag and make yourself comfortable – a good idea is to take some newspapers with you and lay them out on the floor to cover up the dirt and chicken crap. Deck class in the rainy season can be very cold and wet. The crew have their own cabins and they often rent these out – it's one way they make some extra money. Bring some food and water of your own. Here are some readers' comments and recommendations regarding boat travel in Indonesia:

Unless it's really wet I reckon deck class is as good as cabin but get as high in the ship as possible. Privacy

and security are major considerations. If you want fresh air in your cabin you get a lot of Indonesian faces too. If you keep your ultra-valuables on you an official will give you somewhere to stick your pack. Cabins get very hot, windows often don't help. Rats and cockroaches do not abound on the higher decks...

If you're travelling in a cabin take 1st class – very little more than 2nd class, but you get reasonable food, a private cabin and your own private collection of cockroaches and mice!

Definitely a once-only experience...

Another possibility worth investigating is getting a passage on one of those magnificent Bugis schooners you see lined up at the Pasar Ikan in Jakarta. They sail between Java, Kalimantan and Sulawesi, often going as far as Nusa Tenggara.

Small Boat

There's a whole range of floating tubs you can use to hop between islands, across rivers, down rivers and over lakes. Just about any sort of vessel can be rented in Indonesia. Fishing boats or other small boats can be chartered to take you to small offshore islands. Some of these boats are *not* reliable – engine trouble is an occasional problem

Top: Gunung Agung, Bali (PL)
Left: Working on the ships at Sunda Kelapa, Jakarta (PW)
Right: Clay pots, Lombok (JL)

Top: Sultan's Palace, Yogyakarta, Java (JH)
Left: Dieng Children, Java (JH)
Right: Bird Market, Yogyakarta, Java (JH)

and departures may depend on how much the captain had to drink the night before . Check out the boat before you rent it – it would be nice if it had a two-way radio and a lifeboat, just in case.

The *longbot* (longboat) is a long, narrow boat powered by a couple of outboard motors, with bench seats on either side of the hull for passengers to sit on. You find these mainly on the rivers of Kalimantan where they're a common means of transport.

Outrigger canoes powered by an outboard motor are a standard form of transport for some short inter-island hops – like the trip out from Manado in northern Sulawesi to the coral reefs surrounding nearby Pulau Bunaken. On Lombok these elegant, brilliantly painted fishing boats, looking rather like exotic dragonflies, are used for the short hop from Bangsal Harbour to the offshore islands of Gili Air and Gili Trawangan. There are standard fares for standard routes, and you can charter these boats.

Speedboats are not all that common, although they are used on some routes on the rivers of Kalimantan, or for some short inter-island hops in some parts of Indonesia. They are, of course, considerably faster than longbots or river ferries, but considerably more expensive.

River ferries are commonly found in Kalimantan, where the rivers *are* the roads. They're large, bulky vessels that carry people and goods up and down the water network.

LOCAL TRANSPORT
To/From the Airport

There are generally taxis waiting outside the airports – even if the taxi has no meter there will usually be a fixed fare into town; tickets for the journey can be bought from the taxi desk in the airport terminal. From the town to the airport you just have to bargain a fare with the driver – Jakarta's airport is the worst in the whole country for overcharging by taxi drivers. In other towns, local buses or bemos may pass within walking distance of the airport; they are considerably cheaper than taking a taxi. In some of the smaller outer

islands, like those of Nusa Tenggara, where some of the airports are quite far from the town and have no regular road transport between them, the airlines have taxis or bemos to take passengers to the airport. The cost of these airline taxis is not included in the ticket so you have to pay extra, but often it's the only reliable way of getting to your flight.

Bus

Large buses aren't used much as a means of local transport except in Java, perhaps because most Indonesian towns aren't that big; smaller vehicles suffice.

There's quite an extensive system of buses in Jakarta and these are universally cheap (about 200 rp), but be *very* careful about pickpockets. These guys usually work in gangs and can empty your pockets faster than you can say gado-gado.

Train

As of yet, no city in Indonesia has a mass-transit rail system, but Jakarta is building one. The first line is scheduled for completion sometime in 1993, and will run from the city centre to Bogor in the south. It remains to be seen how efficient this system will be and how much it will help relieve traffic congestion in the city. There is much talk of building a second line, but so far it hasn't got off the drawing board.

Taxi

You can readily find metered taxis in Jakarta, Surabaya, Bandung, Semarang, Solo and Yogyakarta. Elsewhere, you may have to bargain the fare in advance, but metered taxis are becoming more and more common.

Metered taxis charge about 800 rp at flagfall for the first km, and about 400 rp for each additional km.

Bemo

Bemos are the usual form of transport around Indonesian towns and cities – most run on standard routes with standard fares.

Becak

These are three-wheeler cycle-rickshaws. Unlike the version found in India where the driver sits in front of you, or the Filipino version with the driver at the side, in Indonesia the driver sits at the rear, nosing your life ever forwards into the traffic. Many drivers rent their machines, but those who own them add personal touches: brightly painted pictures, tinkling bells or whirring metal discs strung across the undercarriage. In Yogyakarta one guy peddled furiously around the streets at night with a tiny flashing light-bulb on the point of his coolie hat! Whilst becaks are now banned from the main streets of large Javanese cities (they are banned from Jakarta altogether), in just about any town of any size in Java as well as in some other parts of Indonesia (like Ujung Pandang in Sulawesi), they're the most basic form of transport – for people and anything else that has to be shifted.

Bargain your fare *before* you get into the becak! And make sure, if there are two of you, that it covers both people – otherwise you'll be in for an argument when you get to your destination. Indonesian becak drivers are hard bargainers – they have to be to survive! But they will usually settle on a reasonable fare – say 200 rp per km, but expect to pay extra for every piece of luggage you stow on board and every hill that has to be peddled over. Hiring a becak by time or for a round-trip often makes good sense if you're planning to cover a lot of ground in one day, particularly in large places like Yogyakarta or Solo.

Bajaj

These are neat little three-wheeled vehicles with a driver at the front, a small motorbike engine below and seats for two passengers behind. They're a common form of local transport in Jakarta, but you don't see them very often elsewhere.

Dokar

Dokars are the jingling, horse-drawn carts found all over Indonesia. The two-wheeled carts are usually brightly coloured with dec-

Dokar

orative motifs and fitted with bells which chime when they're in motion. The small horses or ponies that pull them are often equipped with long tassles attached to their gear. A typical dokar has bench seating on either side, which can comfortably fit three people, four if they're all slim; their owners generally pack in as many people as possible plus bags of rice and other paraphernalia. It's a picturesque way of getting around if you don't get upset by the ill-treatment of animals – although generally the ponies are looked after pretty well since they mean the difference between starvation and survival. The price depends on the colour of your skin – the bidding starts at around 1000 rp. After negotiations, count on paying about 200 rp per person per km.

In Java you also see the *andong* or *delman* which is a larger horse-drawn wagon designed to carry six people. In some parts of Indonesia like Gorontalo and Manado in northern Sulawesi you also see the *bendi*, which is like a small dokar, designed to carry two people.

Other

There are various other ways of getting around. In many of the hill resorts in Java you can hire horses. Likewise, just about anywhere in Indonesia where horses are raised it's often possible to hire one – this is possibly the ideal solution to getting over some of that rough terrain and actually enjoying those abominable roads! In Jakarta, bicycles with little seats at the rear are used as a taxi service – see them near the Pasar Ikan. Guys with motorcycles are permanent fixtures at some large city bus stations around Indonesia – they'll take you to anywhere in town (and probably beyond) for a bargainable price.

TOURS

A wide range of tours can be booked from travel agents within Indonesia. Most of these take in places where tourists are numerous, such as Jakarta, Yogyakarta, Bali, Lombok, Komodo and Lake Toba.

You can be absolutely certain that taking a tour will work out to be more expensive than going by yourself, but tours may occasionally be worth the money. For example, the one-day Jakarta city tour for 53,000 rp is popular – it includes lunch, transport and entrance fees. Or you can join a half-day Jakarta tour for 30,000 rp. Given the traffic chaos and confusing public transport system in Jakarta, it's money well spent.

Tours are normally much less expensive if you book through a hotel rather than through a travel agent. For example, in Waikabubak (Sumba), hotels can arrange a jeep with tour guide/driver for 75,000 rp per day for three people, and this is probably the best way of visiting villages in the area. In Labuhanbajo (west Flores), one hotel runs a six-day boat and snorkelling tour of the area for 250,000 rp per person, which includes all transport, accommodation, food and equipment rental. There are plenty of these bargain tours available – make enquiries at your hotel.

There are, of course, expensive all-inclusive tours available from travel agencies in Jakarta, Bali and elsewhere. There are zillions of these agents; a well-known one is Vayatour (☎ 3100720) in the President Hotel, Jalan Thamrin, Jakarta. Also in Jakarta is Pacto (☎ 347447), 8 Jalan Surabaya, or contact their Bali branch (☎ 88096), Jalan Tanjungsari, Sanur. You can find many other agents by looking in the yellow pages of the telephone directory. Most travel agents have some economy tours, but they prefer to sell packages with accommodation at a luxurious hotel like the Hilton or Sheraton, banquet-style meals and prices beginning at around 200,000 rp per day.

Java

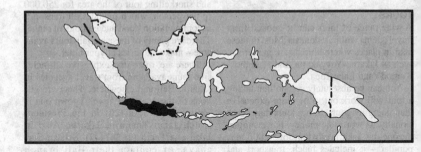

There is a Javanese myth which opens with Semar (the wise clown of the wayang shadow-puppet plays) speaking with a powerful Hindu-Muslim priest, the first of Java's long line of colonisers. The priest asks Semar to tell him the story of Java before there were people on the island. Semar replies that in those days the whole island was covered with primeval forest except for the small patch of rice fields he himself cultivated at the foot of Gunung Merbabu, a volcano in central Java, where he lived peacefully tilling the soil for thousands of years.

Then the startled priest, exclaiming that no man could live for so long, demands that Semar tell him what sort of being he actually is. 'In truth,' says Semar, 'I am not a man, I am the guardian spirit – the *danjang* – of Java. I am the oldest spirit of Java, and I am the king and ancestor of all the spirits, and through them of all men.' Then Semar continues in a changed tone: 'I have also a question to ask you. Why are you ruining my country? Why have you come here and driven my children and grandchildren out? The spirits, overcome by your greater spiritual power and religious learning, are slowly being forced to flee into the craters of the volcanoes or to the depths of the Southern Sea. Why are you doing this?'

The priest replies that he has been ordered by his king, in a country to the west of Java,

to fill the island with people, to clear the forests for rice fields, to set up villages and to settle thousands of families there as colonists. Those of the spirits who protect the colonists may continue to live on Java, and Semar will be the spiritual adviser and magical supporter of all the kings and princes to come, the chief danjang of Java.

HISTORY

In this story Javanese history begins with a migration, rather than a creation, myth. Considering the successive movements of people from South-East Asia into the Indonesian archipelago this is hardly surprising. The harmful spirits which inhabited Java were pushed into the mountains and forests or into the ocean and the helpful ones were adopted as protectors and advisers.

The island's exceptional fertility allowed the development of an intensive sawah agriculture, which in turn required close cooperation between villages for the maintenance of the irrigation systems. From this first need for local government small kingdoms eventually developed but the first major principality appears to have been that of King Sanjaya's; around the beginning of the 8th century he founded the kingdom of Mataram, which controlled much of central Java. Mataram's religion centred on the Hindu god Shiva, and the kingdom produced some of the earliest of Java's Hindu temples on the Dieng Plateau.

Sanjaya's Hindu kingdom was followed by a Buddhist interlude under the Shailendra dynasty; it was during this time that Mahayana Buddhism was established in Java and work began (probably around 780 AD) on Borobudur. Either Hinduism continued to exist alongside Buddhism or else there was a Hindu renaissance. In either case the massive Hindu Prambanan complex was built and consecrated around 856 AD. Despite the Hindu resurgence Buddhism continued to flourish.

Mataram eventually fell, possibly as a result of conflict with the Sumatra-based Srivijaya kingdom which invaded Java in the 11th century. Srivijaya, however, also suffered attacks from the Chola kingdom of southern India and Javanese power revived under King Airlangga, a semi-legendary figure who brought much of Java under his control and formed the first royal link between Java and Bali. Airlangga divided his kingdom between his two sons, resulting in the formation of the Kediri and Janggala kingdoms.

In the early 13th century, the commoner Ken Angrok usurped the throne of Singosari (a part of the Janggala kingdom), defeated Kediri and then brought the rest of Janggala under his control. He founded a new kingdom of Singosari which expanded its power during the 13th century. The reign of its last king, Kertanagara, ended when he was murdered around 1292 but his son-in-law, Wijaya, established the Majapahit kingdom, the greatest kingdom of the Hindu-Javanese period. During the 14th century the Majapahit kingdom claimed sovereignty over the entire Indonesian archipelago, although its territorial sovereignty was probably restricted to Java, Madura and Bali.

The Majapahits did something which no previous Javanese kingdom had done: while previous kingdoms had based their power on the control of the rich Javanese agricultural areas, the Majapahits established the first Javanese commercial empire by taking control of Java's main ports and the shipping lanes throughout Indonesia. The memory of Majapahit lives on in Indonesia and the kingdom is sometimes seen as having established a precedent for the present political boundaries of the Indonesian republic.

The Majapahit kingdom began to decline soon after the death of Gajah Mada, the strongman prime minister who had been responsible for its territorial conquests. Various principalities began breaking away from Majapahit rule and adopting Islam. Although the usual view is that Islam in Java originally represented a religious and political force opposed to the Majapahit, there is evidence that Islam was making converts amongst the Majapahit elite even at the height of the kingdom's power. Exactly how or why Islam spread to Java is unknown, but around the 15th and 16th centuries new kingdoms which professed Islam rather than Hinduism were arising on the island.

By the end of the 16th century a Muslim kingdom calling itself Mataram had taken control of central and eastern Java. The last remaining independent principalities, Surabaya and Cirebon, were eventually subjugated, leaving only Mataram and Bantam (in West Java) to face the Dutch in the 17th century. The conquest of Java by the Dutch need not be recounted here, but by the end of the 18th century practically all of the island was under Dutch control.

During the Dutch period there were strong Muslim powers in Java, most notably Mataram. The Javanese were great warriors who continually opposed the Dutch but they were never a united force. If they weren't quarrelling amongst themselves they were at odds with the Sundanese or the Madurese. The last remnants of the Mataram kingdom survived as the principalities of Surakarta (Solo) and Yogyakarta until the foundation of the Indonesian republic. Javanese kings claimed to rule with divine authority and the Dutch helped to preserve the vestiges of a traditional Javanese aristocracy by confirming them as regents, district officers or sub-district officers in the European administration.

It has been said that Suharto is much more

a Javanese king than an 'elected' president, and Indonesia much more a Javanese kingdom than a republic. Admirers of Suharto compare him to the wise kings of the wayang puppet shows, who turn chaos into order and bring prosperity to the kingdom. Critics respond that he rules much more like a Javanese king or sultan, with systems of palace-centred patronage, favouritism and officially sponsored corruption.

There are many sensitive subjects in Indonesia: Muslim extremists, Communism, racial problems (particularly anti-Chinese sentiment), human rights, East Timor, Irian Jaya, students (seen as potential subversives), the military, and the business enterprises of Suharto, his wife and the Indonesian military leaders. The ultimate base for Suharto's authority is always the military, which is overwhelmingly Javanese at the top level.

A strong consciousness of ancient religious and mystical thought carries over into modern-day Java and is believed to reach right up to the top Javanese in the Indonesian government. Sukarno identified with Bima, the strong-willed prince of the wayang. Suharto is said to identify strongly with the clown-god Semar, who in the traditional wayang plays often steps in to save the situation when more refined characters have failed. Suharto is even thought to meditate occasionally in one of the caves on the Dieng Plateau, said to be a dwelling place of the god, in order to revitalise his spiritual energy.

Java plays an extraordinary role in Indonesia today. It is more than simply the geographical centre of Indonesia. Much of Indonesian history was hacked out on Javanese soil. The major battles of the independence movement took place on Java and two of the strongest political parties in the first decade of independence – the Nationalist Party (PNI) and the Communist Party (PKI) – drew their support from the Javanese. To a large extent the rebellions of the

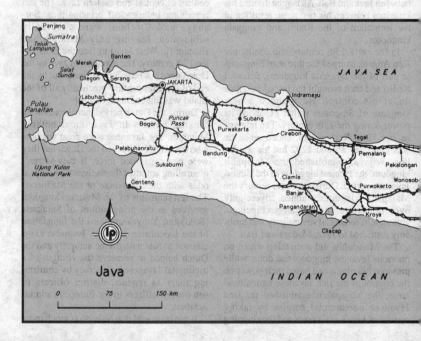

Java

0   75   150 km

Sumatrans, Minahasans and Ambonese in the 1950s and 1960s were rebellions against Javanese domination. Furthermore the Darul Islam rebellion against the new republic broke out in West Java. The abortive Communist coup of 1965 started in Jakarta and some of its most dramatic and disastrous events took place in Java. Arguably the transmigration programme – of dubious benefit to solving the problem of Javanese overpopulation – is really just a systematic Javanese colonisation of the outer islands.

ECONOMY & GEOGRAPHY

Socially, Java is an island of contrasts, while geographically it is an island of great and varied beauty. Java provides leadership in politics and trade, an abundant labour force and great potential markets. In terms of population pressure, however, it also provides the nation's greatest economic problems. In the late '60s foreign investment went initially to the area surrounding booming Jakarta. Today, Java has Indonesia's three largest commercial cities, secondary industries are developing and Java is tapping the hydro-electric and geothermal potential of its rivers and volcanic lakes. Fishing is a major occupation and the many small fishermen are protected by the prohibition of trawlers in coastal waters. The country, however, remains overwhelmingly rural. About 70% of the workforce is engaged in agriculture, but Java's long-established hothouse style of wet-rice cultivation is barely efficient enough to support families on small holdings diminishing in size on overcrowded land.

Java is predominantly a land of mountain peaks and smoking volcanoes (34% of the world's active volcanoes are found in Indonesia), fertile green fields and terraces, but to the north is the flat coastal plain and the sluggish Java Sea. The south coast faces the onslaught of the crashing waves of the Indian Ocean. It's a land of strong contrasts: wealth

and squalor; majestic, open country and crowded, filthy cities; quiet, rural scenes and hustling, modern traffic.

Java is a long, narrow island which can be conveniently divided into three sections. In West Java is the capital, Jakarta, a city which seems to epitomise all of Indonesia's problems. Tourist attractions like Bandung (the cultural centre of the Sundanese), Cirebon, Pangandaran and the Ujong Kulon National Park are also found in West Java. In Central Java you will find temples and royal cities that tell of the rise and fall of the Hindu, Buddhist and Muslim kingdoms. Here too the old Javanese-Hindu traditions were least altered by the Muslims and outside influences and this region remains the vital centre of Javanese culture. Java is people and lots of them. Wherever you go it's hard to escape the fact that this is one of the most densely populated areas in the world; but there are isolated places where you can find yourself out of sight and sound of other people. There's the huge Dieng Plateau in the beautiful central highlands and, in East Java, the area around the spectacular Gunung Bromo volcano is as wild and desolate as you could hope for.

THE JAVANESE

Although the inhabitants of the whole island of Java are often referred to as Javanese, it is more correct to distinguish the Javanese proper from other major groups like the Sundanese and Madurese and from minor groups like the Tenggerese and Badui. The Sundanese are concentrated in West Java; the Madurese on the island of Madura off the north coast of Java and on the adjacent coast; the Badui in a pocket in the mountains of West Java; and the Tenggerese are centred on Gunung Bromo in East Java. The Javanese proper inhabit the central and eastern parts of the island.

All of them are Malay people – their differences seem to be mainly cultural. The Sundanese and the Madurese retained much less of the Hindu influence than the people of central and eastern Java. The Badui and the Tenggerese are distinguished by their

history of resistance to Islam. India has had probably the most profound and enduring influence on religion in Java, yet the Indian poet Rabindranath Tagore, when visiting the country, said: 'I see India everywhere, but I do not recognise it.'

Although the Javanese are nominally Muslim, their religion is a mixture of pre-Hindu animism, Hinduism and Islam. The current division between the *santri* (the devout Muslim) and the *abangan* (the nominal Muslim whose real beliefs stem from older and more accommodating mysticism) reflects the Javanese ability to absorb different beliefs. There is a continuing and very real belief in ghosts and numerous benevolent and malevolent spirits. Graveyards are generally thought to be haunted. When the Solo municipal cemeteries were relocated in 1981 many of the living relatives, before exhuming the bodies, consulted soothsayers to determine whether the spirits of the dead were still present in or near the graves. Magical power can be concentrated in amulets and heirlooms (especially the Javanese dagger known as the kris), in parts of the human body like the nails and the hair, and in sacred musical instruments. The traditional medicine man, or dukun, is still consulted when illness strikes.

To be Javanese literally means to be civilised; the Javanese ideal is to be polite and refined. Loud displays of emotion and flamboyant behaviour of any kind are considered *kasar* (coarse and rough, bad manners). Reserve is a Javanese trait, and stems from an unwillingness to make anyone else feel uncomfortable or ashamed. It is impolite to point out mistakes, embarrassments, sensitive or negative areas, or to directly criticise authority. Even the Javanese language reinforces this deferral to authority. Like Balinese, Javanese has 'high' and 'low' forms; different words are used when speaking to superiors, elders, equals or inferiors. This underlines differences in status, rank, relative age, and the degree of acquaintance between the two people talking.

While the Javanese developed probably the most refined culture in Indonesia, Java, particularly Jakarta, is also home to some of the poorest people in the archipelago. However, somehow the people continue to find means of survival – they sell food and clothing, sit all day on the streetside selling combs or a few bunches of bananas, or jump on a crowded bus hawking ice-creams, pine-apple chunks and single cigarettes. They recycle trash or cigarette ends, pedal becaks, shine shoes, mind parked cars, become pros-titutes, beg or tout. And if they return with nothing at the end of the day then their family or neighbours will always help them to survive.

Someone operating a pushcart warung on a street in Jakarta might work 16 hours a day to make 3000 to 4000 rp. In a provincial town a fish carter (delivering basketloads of fish) might make only 1500 to 4000 rp a day. The cities are less than half of the story; the rest of the population are engaged in agriculture, most of them working tiny rice plots barely sufficient to meet their daily needs. Others seek outside income – like many of the becak drivers who work in the cities – or sell up their land and then either move to the cities and towns or work as farm labourers. At the other end of the scale are the Indonesian elite, who can afford to buy an imported leg of lamb (at around 35,000 rp) or imported grapes (around 27,000 rp a kg) from Jakarta's Sarinah department store to serve to their dinner guests in the high-fenced mansions of Jakarta's Pondok Indah district.

CULTURE – WAYANG

Javanese culture is a product of pre-Hindu, Hindu and Islamic influences. The rise of the 16th-century Islamic states brought a rich new cultural heritage but the Hindu heritage also managed to continue its influence.

The Javanese shadow-puppet (wayang) theatre has been a major means of preserving the Hindu-Buddhist heritage in Java. The main wayang form is the *wayang kulit*; the word wayang means shadow, and the word *kulit* means leather. Thus the wayang kulit indicates a form of shadow theatre using puppets made of leather. In the wider sense the word 'wayang' refers to all dramatic plays.

Wayang Kulit

The shadow-puppet theatre, in which perfo-rated leather figures are manipulated behind an illuminated cotton screen, is the best known of the wayang forms. The stories are usually based on the Hindu epics, the *Ramayana* and the *Mahabharata*, although other pre-Islamic stories are also performed. In a traditional performance a whole night might be devoted to just one drama *(lakon)* from a legend. A single puppeteer (the dalang) animates the puppets and narrates and chants through the entire night to the accompaniment of the gamelan orchestra.

The real origin of the wayang kulit is unknown. Shadow-puppet theatre is not

Wayang kulit puppet

unique to Java; it can also be found in Turkey, India, China and parts of South-East Asia. Strangely enough, given that the wayang kulit tells stories from pre-Islamic days, Javanese tradition credits the creation of the wayang to the nine *walis*, the semi-legendary apostles of Islam in Java. Many wayang kulit figures and even whole stories have a specific mystical function; certain stories are performed for the purpose of protecting a rice crop (these incorporate the rice goddess Dewi Sri), the welfare of a village or even individuals.

By the 11th century wayang performances with leather puppets were flourishing in Java and by the end of the 18th century the wayang kulit had developed most of the details of puppet design and performance techniques we see today. The standardisation of the puppet designs is traditionally attributed to King Raden Patah of Demak (an Islamic kingdom on the site of modern-day Semarang), who reigned in the first half of the 16th century.

The puppets are made of leather, water buffalo leather from a young animal being the most favoured material. The outline of the puppet is cut using a thin knife and the fine details carved out using small chisels and a hammer. When the carving is finished the movable arms are attached and the puppet is painted. Lines are drawn in and accentuated with black ink, which is also used to increase the contrast of the carved holes. The *cempurit*, the stick of horn used to hold the puppet upright, is then attached.

The leaf-shaped *kayon* is meant to represent the 'tree' or 'mountain of life' and is used to end scenes or to symbolise wind, mountains, obstacles, clouds or the sea. Made of the same flexible hide as the other puppets, the kayon might be waved softly behind the cloth screen while a puppet figure is held horizontally – a surprisingly effective way of indicating flight through the cloudy sky. There are a number of symbolic decorations on the kayon including the face in the centre of the tree which symbolises the danger and risk that all people must confront in life.

The characters in wayang are brought to life by the dalang. To call the dalang a puppeteer belittles the extraordinary range of talents he or she must possess. Sitting cross-legged on a mat before the white screen the dalang might manipulate dozens of figures in the course of a performance.

The dalang recounts events spanning centuries and continents, improvising from the basic plot a complex network of court intrigues, great loves, wars, philosophy, magic, mysticism and comedy. The dalang must be a linguist capable of speaking both the language of the audience and the ancient *kawi* language spoken by the aristocratic characters of the play. The dalang must also be a mimic capable of producing a different voice for each of the characters, and have great physical stamina to sustain a performance which will last from the evening until the early hours of the morning. He or she must be a musician, able to direct the village's gamelan orchestra which accompanies the performance, be versed in history, and have a deep understanding of philosophy and religion. The puppet master must be a poet capable of creating a warm or terrifying atmosphere, but must also be a comedian able to introduce some comic relief into the performances. Understandably, the dalang has always been regarded as a very special type of person. Most dalang are men but today there are a number of female dalang in Java.

The dalang directs the gamelan orchestra using a system of cues, often communicating the name of the composition to be played using riddles or puns. The player of the *kendang* (drum) acts as the liaison between the dalang and the other gamelan players, in setting the proper tempo and changes of tempo for each piece, and in executing the important signals for ending pieces. The dalang may communicate with the orchestra using signals tapped out with the wooden *cempala* (a mallet) held in the left hand. Or there may be other types of cues – for example, one of the clowns in the performance may announce that a singing contest is to be held, then announce the song he intends singing and the gamelan will play that song.

The mass of the audience sits in front of the screen to watch the shadow figures, but some also sit behind the screen with the dalang, to watch the expert at work.

Wayang Golek

These three-dimensional wooden puppets have movable heads and arms and are manipulated in the same way as shadow puppets – but without using a shadow screen. Although wayang golek is found in Central Java it is most popular amongst the Sundanese of West Java. Sometimes a wayang golek puppet is used right at the end of a wayang kulit play to symbolise the transition back from the world of two dimensions to the world of three.

Wayang golek uses the same stories as the wayang kulit, including the *Mahabharata* and the *Ramayana*, as well as stories about the mythical Javanese King Panji and other legendary kings. It also has its own set of stories, for which there is some direct Islamic inspiration. These include the elaborate romances inspired by legends about the Prophet Mohammed's uncle Amir Hamzah.

Wayang Klitik

In East Java the wayang kulit is replaced by the *wayang klitik* or *keruchil*, a flat wooden puppet carved in low relief; this type of wayang is performed without a shadow screen. The wayang klitik is associated with the Damar Wulan stories which are of particular historical relevance to East Java. The stories relate the adventures of a handsome prince and his rise to become ruler of the Majapahit kingdom.

Wayang Orang

Also known as *wayang wong*, the *wayang orang* is a dance drama in which real people dance the part of the wayang characters, imitating the movements and speech of the puppets.

Wayang Topeng

The *wayang topeng* is similar to wayang orang but uses masks. The two forms of dance drama were cultivated at varying times in the courts of Central Java. Wayang topeng is the older of the two and dates back as far the Majapahit kingdom. In more recent times wayang wong was the official court dance drama, while wayang topeng was also performed outside the walls of the palace. The stylisation of human features seen in the shadow puppets is also seen in the wayang topeng masks; elongation and refinement are the key notes of the noble *(halus)* characters, while grotesque exaggeration denotes the vulgar *(kasar)* characters.

THE MAHABHARATA & RAMAYANA

Ancient India, like ancient Greece, produced two great epics. The *Ramayana* describes the adventures of a prince who is banished from his country and wanders for many years in the wilderness. The *Mahabharata* is based on the legends of a great war. The first story is a little reminiscent of the *Odyssey*, which relates the adventures of Ulysses as he struggles to return home from Troy; the second has much in common with the *Iliad*.

When Hinduism came to Java so did the *Ramayana* and the *Mahabharata*. The Javanese shifted the locale to Java; Javanese children were given the names of the heroes and by tradition the kings of Java were descendants of the epic heroes.

The Mahabharata

The great war portrayed in the *Mahabharata* is believed to have been fought in northern India around the 13th or 14th century BC. The war became a centre of legends, songs and poems and at some point the vast mass of stories accumulated over the centuries were gathered together into a narrative called the 'Epic of the Bharata Nation (India)' – the *Mahabharata*. Over the following centuries more was added to it until it was seven times the size of the Iliad and the Odyssey combined!

The central theme of the *Mahabharata* is the power struggle between the Kurava brothers and their cousins, the Pandava brothers. Important events along the way include: the appearance of Krishna, an incarnation of Lord Vishnu, who becomes the adviser of the Pandava; the marriage of Prince Arjuna of the Pandavas to the Princess Drupadi; the Kuravas' attempt to kill the Pandavas; and the division of the kingdom into two in an attempt to end the rivalry between the cousins. Finally, after 13 years in exile and hiding, the Pandavas realise there is no alternative but war, the great war of the *Mahabharata*, which is a series of bloody clashes between the cousins.

It is at this time that the Pandava warrior Arjuna becomes despondent at the thought of fighting his own flesh and blood, so Krishna, his charioteer and adviser, explains to him the duties and obligations of the warrior in a song known as the 'Bhagavad Gita'. Krishna explains that the soul is indestructible and that whoever dies shall be reborn and so there is no cause to be sad; it is the soldier's duty to fight and he will be accused of cowardice if he runs away.

In the course of the battles many of the great heroes from both sides are slain one by one; many others also lose their lives but in the end the Pandavas are victorious over the Kuravas.

The Ramayana

The *Ramayana*, the story of Prince Rama, is thought to have been written after the *Mahabharata*. Long before Prince Rama was born the gods had determined that his life would be that of a hero – but like all heroic lives it would be full of grave tests. Rama is an incarnation of the god Vishnu, and it will be his destiny to kill the ogre king Rawana (also known as Dasamuka and Dasakhantha).

Due to scheming in the palace, Rama, his wife the beautiful Sita and his brother Laksamana are all exiled to the forest, where Sita is abducted by the ogre king. Rama begins his search for Sita, and is joined by the monkey god Hanuman and the monkey king Sugriwa. Eventually a full-scale assault is launched on the evil king and Sita is rescued.

Performances & Characters

The *Mahabharata* and the *Ramayana* are the basis of the most important wayang stories, particularly in the wayang kulit, and also appear in Balinese dances, especially the Kechak. While they often come across like ripping yarns, both are essentially moral tales, which for centuries have played a large part in establishing traditional Javanese values. In the *Mahabharata*, the Kuravas are essentially the forces of greed, evil and destruction, while the Pandavas represent refinement, enlightenment and civilised behaviour.

The division between good and evil is never absolute; the good heroes have bad traits and vice versa. Take, for example, Yudistra, the eldest of the Pandava brothers. His moral integrity is high, but his great fault is his extravagant generosity. Although the forces of good usually triumph over evil, more often than not the victory is an ambivalent one; both sides suffer grievous loss and though a king may win a righteous war he may lose all his sons in the process. In the *Mahabharata*, when the great battle is over and the Pandavas are victorious, one of their enemies sneaks into the encampment and kills all the Pandava women and children.

Bima Bima is the second-eldest of the Pandavas. He is physically big, burly, aggressive, not afraid to act on what he believes; he can be rough, even using the language of the man of the street to address the gods. He is able to fly and is the most powerful warrior on the battlefield, but he also has infinite kindness and a firm adherence to principle which makes him a heroic figure who can't really be criticised for his faults.

Arjuna Arjuna is the handsome and refined ladies' man, a representative of the noble class, whose eyes look at the ground because it's kasar to stare into people's faces. He can also be fickle and selfish, and that is his weakness. He has one single quality which outweighs his failings; he is halus – a Javanese word which means refined in manner, never speaking ill to offend others, polite and humble, patient, careful, the direct opposite of kasar. Arjuna's charioteer is Krishna, a spiritual adviser but also a cunning and ruthless politician.

Semar A purely Javanese addition to the story is Arjuna's servant, the dwarf clown Semar. An incarnation of a god, Semar is a great source of wisdom and advice to Arjuna – but his body is squat with an enormous posterior, bulging belly, and he sometimes has an uncontrollable disposition for farting. Semar has three sons: Gareng with his misshapen arms, crossed eyes, limp and speech impediment; Petruk with his hilarious long nose, enormous smiling mouth, and a general lack of proportion both in physical stature and thinking; and Bagong, the youngest of the three, who speaks as though he has a mouthful of marbles. Though they are comic figures, they play the important role of interpreting the actions and speech of the heroic figures in the wayang kulit plays. Despite their bumbling natures and gross appearance they are the mouthpieces of truth and wisdom.

Kurava Characters On the Kurava side is Duryudana, a handsome and powerful leader, but too easily influenced by the prevailing circumstances around him and thus often prey to the evil designs of his uncle and adviser, Sangkuni. Karna is the good man on the wrong side, whose loyalty is divided between the Kuravas and the Pandavas. He is actually a Pandava but was brought up a Kurava; adhering to the code of the warrior he stands by his king as a good Javanese should and, as a result, he dies at the hands of Arjuna.

Ramayana Characters The characters of the *Ramayana* are a little more clear-cut. Like Arjuna, Rama is the epitome of the ideal man – a gentle husband, a noble prince, a kindly king, a brave leader. His wife Sita is the ideal wife who remains totally devoted to her husband. But elements of the *Mahabharata* can also be found in the

Ramayana: Rawana's warrior brother knows that the king is evil but is bound by the ethics of the Ksatria warrior and remains loyal to his brother to the end, consequently dying a horrible death by dismemberment.

Wayang Kulit Performances It's fairly easy to tell the kasar figures from the halus figures. The halus figures tend to be smaller in size and more elegant in proportion; their legs are slender and close together, and their heads are tilted downwards presenting an image of humility and self-effacement. The kasar characters are often enormous, muscular and hairy, with their heads upturned. Eye shape and the colour of the figures, particularly on the faces, are of great importance. Red often indicates aggressiveness, greed, impatience, anger or simply a very forthright personality. Black, and often blue, indicates calmness, spiritual awareness and maturity. Gold and yellow are reserved for kings and the highest nobles. White can symbolise purity or virtue, high moral purpose and the like. Hair styles, ornamentation and clothing are all important in identifying a particular puppet.

A traditional wayang kulit performance transmits the desirable values and characteristics of the heroes of the *Ramayana* and *Mahabharata* – inner control, dedication and self-sacrifice – and stresses the importance of refined behaviour over the violent and crude. One's passions, desires, lust and anger must be disciplined; in the 'Bhagavad Gita' Krishna tells Arjuna that these cause people to do evil, even against their own will. All is clouded by desire, says Krishna, as a fire by smoke, as a mirror by dirt. The performance portrays the forces upon which all life depends, the meaning and purpose of life, the inconsistencies, weakness and greatness of its epic heroes and, by implication, human society as a whole.

Although the wayang theatre still teaches the traditional Javanese values it's difficult to determine its current direction. Some argue that its ritual function seems to be disappearing and that it's becoming more and more purely a form of entertainment, with much of the mystical aura and traditional philosophy being lost. In the past the skills of the dalang were handed down from father to son, but for years now there have been schools in Java – some more traditional than others – which also teach the techniques. Even puppet design is changing and on TV for 15 minutes each Sunday morning characters from the wayang cackle, sing and shriek about such matters as paying taxes on time, birth control and agricultural development.

THE GAMELAN

The musical instruments of Indonesia can be grouped into four main strata: those from pre-Hindu days; those from the Hindu period from the first centuries AD until about the 15th century; the Islamic period from about the 13th century AD; and the last from the 16th century, which is associated with Christian and European influences.

The oldest known instruments in Indonesia are the bronze 'kettle drums' belonging to the Dongson culture which developed in what is now northern Vietnam and spread into the Indonesian archipelago – they are not really drums as they have bronze rather than membrane heads. These instruments have been found in Sumatra, Java, Bali, Kalimantan and other parts of South-East Asia; amongst the most curious examples are those of the island of Alor in Nusa Tenggara.

Other instruments, particularly those made of bamboo (like flutes and reed pipes), are also thought to be very old. By the time of the Hindu period there was a wealth of metallic as well as wooden and bamboo instruments played in Java, and these are depicted on the stone reliefs of Borobudur and Prambanan, and other shrines. On Borobudur there are reliefs of drums (waisted, hourglass, pot and barrel-shaped), two-stringed lutes, harps, flutes, mouth organs, reed pipes, a keyed metallophone (saron), xylophone, cymbals and others. Some of these instruments are direct imports from India, whilst others resemble the instruments now used in the Javanese gamelan orchestra.

One interesting and ancient instrument is the calung, a Sundanese instrument which is also found in a few places in Java and in southern Thailand. The basic version consists of a set of bamboo tubes, one end of each tube closed off by the natural node of the bamboo, and the other end pared down for part of its length like a goose-quill pen. The instrument is played with one or two sickle-shaped wooden hammers (panakol) padded with cotton or rubber. The calung is still commonly found in Java.

The oldest instruments still in use include drums, gongs, various wind instruments and plucked strings. The large Javanese gamelan, whose total complement comprises from 60 to 80 instruments, has sets of suspended and horizontal gongs, gong chimes, drums, flutes, bowed and plucked string instruments, metallophones and xylophones.

Gamelan Instruments

The word 'gamelan' is derived from the Javanese word gamel, which means a type of hammer, like a blacksmith's hammer. The orchestra is composed almost entirely of percussion instruments, played by being struck. Javanese tradition credits a god with the invention of the gamelan orchestra, used to summon the other gods to his palace at the summit of Gunung Lawu, between Solo and Madiun.

There are two types of gamelan styles: a soft style for indoor use and a loud style for outdoor functions, the difference being in the instruments used. Around the 17th century, the two styles were blended to form the modern gamelan. It was mainly because of the different ways in which the two styles were mixed and balanced that variations between the gamelan music found in Bali, Central Java and West Java were created. The gong, kempul, kenong, ketuk and kempyang belong to both the loud and soft styles. The saron, bonang, and kendang belong to the loud style. The slentem, gender, gambang, celempung, sitar, suling and rebab belong to the soft style.

Gong Ageng The *gong ageng* or *gong gede* is suspended on a wooden frame. There is at least one such gong, sometimes more, in a gamelan orchestra. The gong is made of bronze and is about 90 cm in diameter. It performs the crucial task of marking the end of the largest phrase of a melody.

Kempul This is a small hanging gong, and marks a smaller musical phrase than the big gong.

Kenong The kenong is a small gong laid horizontally on crossed cord and sitting inside a wooden frame.

Ketuk The ketuk is a small kenong tuned to a certain pitch, which marks subdivisions of phrases; it is played by the kenong player. The sound of the ketuk is short and dead compared with the clearer, resonant tone of the kenong.

Saron This is the basic instrument-type of the gamelan, a xylophone with bronze bars which are struck with a wooden mallet. There are three types of saron: high, medium and low-pitched. The high one is called *saron panerus* or *saron peking* and is played with a mallet made of buffalo horn rather than wood.

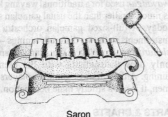

Saron

Bonang The bonang consists of a double row of bronze kettles (like small kenongs) resting on a horizontal frame; there are three kinds, although the lowest in pitch is no longer used in gamelan orchestras. The bonang is played with two long sticks bound with red cord at the striking end. Although in modern Javanese gamelan the bonang has

two rows of bronze kettles, originally it had only one row, as it still does in Bali.

Kendang These drums are all double-ended and beaten by hand (with the exception of the giant drum, the *bedug*, which is beaten with a stick). The drum is an important leading instrument; they are made from the hollowed tree-trunk sections of the jackfruit (nangka) tree with cow or goat skin stretched across the two ends. There are various types of drums but the middle-sized *kendang batangan* or *kendang ciblon* is chiefly used to accompany dance and wayang performances; the drum patterns indicate specific dance movements or movements of the wayang puppets.

Slentem The slentem carries the basic melody in the soft ensemble, as the saron does in the loud ensemble. It consists of thin bronze bars suspended over bamboo resonating chambers; it is struck with a padded disc on the end of a stick.

Gender This is similar to a slentem in structure, but there are more bronze keys and the keys and bamboo chambers are smaller. The gender is played with two disc-shaped hammers, smaller than those used for the slentem. The hand acts as a damper, so that each hand must simultaneously hit a note and damp the preceding one.

Gambang The gambang is the only gamelan instrument with bars made not of bronze, but of hardwood, and laid over a wooden frame. They are struck with two sticks made of supple buffalo horn, each ending with a small, round, padded disc. Unlike the gender keys the gambang keys do not need to be damped.

Celempung This is a plucked, stringed instrument, looking somewhat like a zither. It has 26 strings arranged in 13 pairs. The strings are stretched over a coffin-shaped resonator which stands on four legs; the strings are plucked with the thumb nails. The sitar is a smaller version of the celempung, with fewer strings and a higher pitch; the body is box-shaped and without legs.

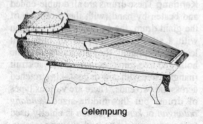

Celempung

Suling The suling, or flute, is the only wind instrument in the gamelan orchestra. It is made of bamboo and played vertically.

Rebab The rebab is a two-stringed bowed instrument of Arabic origin. It has a wooden body covered with fine, stretched skin. The moveable bridge is made of wood. The bow is made of wood and coarse horsehair tied loosely, not stretched tight like the bows of Western instruments. The rebab player sits cross-legged on the floor behind the instrument.

In a piece of gamelan music, the gong ageng marks the end of each of the largest phrases of the melody, the saron instruments play the main melody at various ranges of pitches and speeds, and the bonang play their own rippling configurations at a faster speed than the main melody. The gamelan also uses male and female singers – traditionally they make up part of the soft ensemble. The gamelan orchestra does not accompany the singer as Western orchestras do; rather, the singer in a gamelan is really just another instrument, no more or less important than any of the instruments.

Traditionally, gamelan players learnt to play by ear, beginning on the simpler instruments and moving forward as their repertoire and technique developed. A musician did not use notation when playing, although there are systems of written notation. The palaces at Solo and Yogyakarta had developed their own systems of notation, but in the late 19th century the *kepatihan* system, now used in Java, was developed and numbers were used for the notes (just as Western music uses letters). The older notation systems are found only in palace records of older music.

The saron and the slentem are the only instruments which can play exactly what is written down, the notation being just a skeleton of everything that is going on in a performance. The phrase- making instruments – the ketuk, kempul, kenong and gong – give some order and form to these notes, the gong marking the end of the longest musical phrase and the other instruments elaborating on the basic skeleton.

In the loud ensemble the drummer is the leader, the conductor of all the instruments, controlling the tempo, speeding up or slowing down the orchestra, signalling the entrance of the elaborating instruments and shifting the emphasis from the loud to the soft ensemble. Apart from signalling changes within one piece of music the drummer also signals a change from one piece of music to another, because usually at least two or three pieces are combined to form a medley. The rebab ornaments the music and its line is closely related to the singing.

A gamelan orchestra always accompanies a wayang performance although the *gamelan wayangan* used for a traditional wayang kulit is much smaller than the usual gamelan seen today. A full-sized gamelan orchestra has instruments with two different tunings – the *slendro* and the *pelog*. A gamelan wayangan only uses instruments with the slendro tuning. Although most gamelan players are men, it is not a strictly male occupation.

ARTS & CRAFTS

Indonesia has produced a range of performing and visual arts, and apart from the gamelan and the wayang, the ornamented kris (dagger) and the batik technique have reached a particularly high standard on Java.

Kris

Some think the Javanese kris – from the word *iris*, to cut – is derived from the bronze daggers produced by the Dongson culture around the 1st century AD. Bas-reliefs of a kris appear in the 14th century Panataran temple-complex in east Java, and the carrying of the kris as a custom in Java was noted in 15th century Chinese records. The kris is still an integral part of men's formal dress on ceremonial and festive occasions. A dalang will wear his kris while giving a wayang performance, and the kris is still part of the uniform of the guards at the palace in Yogyakarta.

The kris is no ordinary knife. It is said to be endowed with supernatural powers; adat law requires that every father furnish his son with a kris upon his reaching manhood, preferably an heirloom kris enabling his son to draw on the powers of his ancestors stored in the sacred weapon. Distinctive features and the number of curves in the blade, and the damascening, are read to indicate good or bad fortune for its owner. Damascening is a technique whereby another metal is hammered onto the blade of the kris to produce a design. The number of curves in the blade also has symbolic meaning: five curves symbolise the five Pandava brothers of the *Mahabharata* epic; three stand for fire, ardour or passion. Although the blade is the most important part of the kris, the hilt and scabbard are also beautifully decorated.

Before the arrival of Islam, Hindu-inspired images were often used to decorate the wooden hilts – the mythological Garuda was a popular figure. After the spread of Islam such motifs were discouraged, but were often preserved in stylised forms. In any case, the origins and symbolism of the kris lay too deep in Javanese mysticism to be eradicated by the laws of Islam.

Batik

Indonesian textiles come in a dazzling variety of fabrics, materials, techniques, colours and motifs. Basically there are three major textile groupings, which roughly parallel three cultural groups within Indonesia – a loose generalisation but a useful one.

The first is ikat, a form of tie-dyeing patterns onto the threads before weaving them together; this technique is associated with the proto-Malay people of the archipelago such as the various ethnic groups of Nusa Tenggara (see the Nusa Tenggara chapter for more on ikat). The techniques of silk weaving and songket (where gold or silver threads are woven into the silk cloth) are strongest where Islam has made most impact, in places like Aceh in Sumatra and amongst the Malays of coastal Kalimantan. The third group is batik, the alternate waxing and dyeing technique most clearly associated with those parts of central Java where the great Javanese kingdoms were established. It was also taken up in Bali, Madura and in Jambi in Sumatra, all of which have been subject to considerable Javanese influence.

The technique of applying wax or some other type of dye-resistant substance (like rice-paste) to cloth to produce a design is found in many parts of the world. The Javanese were making batik cloth at least as early as the 12th century but its origins are hard to trace. Some think the skills were brought to Java from India, others that the Javanese developed the technique themselves. The word 'batik' is an old Javanese word meaning 'to dot'.

The development of batik in Indonesia is usually associated with the flowering of the creative arts around the royal courts – it's likely that the use of certain motifs was the preserve of the aristocracy. The rise of Islam in Java probably contributed to the stylisation of batik patterns and the absence of representations of living things from most designs. More recently batik has grown from an art mainly associated with the royal courts, into an important industry with a number of noted production centres.

In the older method of making batik the wax is applied hot to the smooth cloth with the *canting*, a pen-like instrument with a small reservoir of liquid wax. The design is first traced out onto the prepared cloth and the patterns drawn in wax on the white cloth, or on a cloth previously dyed to the lightest colour required in the finished product. The wax-covered areas resist colour change when immersed in a dye bath. The waxing and dyeing are continued with increasingly dark shades until the final colours are achieved. Wax is added to protect previously dyed areas or scraped off to expose new areas to the dye. Finally, all the wax is scraped off and the cloth boiled to remove all traces of the wax. The wax mixture usually includes beeswax, paraffin, resins and fats mixed in varying proportions. This type of batik is called *batik tulis* or 'written batik', because the patterns are drawn onto the cloth in free-hand style.

From the mid-19th century production was speeded up by applying the wax with a metal stamp called a *cap*. The cap technique can usually be identified by the repetition of identical patterns, whereas in the freer composition using the canting even repeated geometric motifs vary slightly. Some batik combines the cap technique with canting work for the fine details. It's worth noting that batik cap is true batik; don't confuse it with screen-printed cloth which completely bypasses the waxing process and is often passed off as batik.

BOOKS

The classic book on Javanese religion, culture and values is *The Religion of Java* by Clifford Gertz, perhaps a rather dated book (it was based on research done in the 1950s), but nevertheless fascinating reading. Also worth reading is *Indonesia: Between Myth & Reality* by Lee Khoon Choy (London: Nile & Mackenzie 1976). Choy was the Singaporean ambassador to Indonesia from 1970 to 1975 and has written a readable journalistic account of the customs, traditions and spirituality of Indonesia. The chapters on Kebatinan (Javanese spiritualism) and Java's isolated minorities (the Badui and the Tenggerese) are particularly interesting.

The 'Oxford in Asia' paperback series (Oxford University Press) has a number of excellent books including *Javanese Wayang Kulit – An Introduction* by Edward C van Ness and Shita Prawirohardjo (1980), *Javanese Gamelan* by Jennifer Lindsay

(1979) and *Borobudur* by Jacques Dumarcay (1978).

An excellent way to become familiar with the *Ramayana* and *Mahabharata* epics is to read the English adaptations written by William Buck. Buck's inspired versions read like fantasy novels and will give you a greater appreciation of these Indian epics. His *Ramayana* and *Mahabharata* are published separately by The New English Library in the UK and by The New American Library in the USA and are available in paperback. They make good train and bus reading.

GETTING THERE & AWAY

Air

Jakarta is Indonesia's busiest entrance point for overseas airlines and, though not in the same class as Singapore, it's a good place to shop around for cheap international air tickets.

Jakarta is also the hub of the domestic airline network. Garuda/Merpati are the main airlines serving the outer islands from Java. Bouraq has services to Bali, Kalimantan, Sulawesi and Ternate (in Maluku). Mandala has services to Sumatra, Sulawesi and Ambon (in Maluku). Sempati, with major investments from the Suharto family, has expanded its domestic routes and internationally now offers the cheapest flights to Singapore.

Sea

There are, of course, shipping services from other Indonesian islands to Java but there is only one international connection – and even that isn't a real international connection, since it goes to the Indonesian island of Tanjung Pinang near Singapore.

You can travel indirectly from Jakarta to Singapore by taking the *Lawit* to Tanjung Pinang (36 hours, 88,000 rp 2nd class). From there you take a 40,000 rp hydrofoil to Batam where you clear Indonesian immigration and go on from there to Singapore. There's an additional 2000 rp port charge at Tanjung Pinang. There's also a cheaper, but slower ferry service between Tanjung Pinang and

Singapore which takes five or six hours instead of the faster 2½ hour hydrofoil service.

Take care in Tanjung Pinang coming from Singapore; there are various 'travel agents' in cahoots with hotel owners who will try to ensure that you miss the boat or give up trying to buy a ticket because it's 'full' so that you'll stay in Tanjung Pinang. Also be on watch for pickpockets arriving or departing Tanjung Priok, since they work overtime during the congested stampede to or from the ship.

Pelni liners operate from Jakarta's Tanjung Priok harbour. There are also a number of private freight-shipping lines operating from Jakarta's Sunda Kelapa harbour to Tanjung Pinang (and other islands) which will take passengers; fares are generally lower than Pelni's. For details of ships out of Jakarta see the Getting There & Away section of Jakarta.

To/From Bali

Bali is the one place you can get to by bus or train. Well, almost – the ferry connection across the narrow strait separating Bali from Java is included in the bus or train ticket. You can take buses from Yogyakarta or, more popularly, Surabaya direct to Denpasar. Or from Surabaya there are tickets available on the *Mutiara Timur* train straight through to Denpasar. This entails first taking a train to Banyuwangi/Ketapang harbour, then a ferry and bus to Denpasar. There are two trains departing Surabaya daily, at 9.30 am and 11 pm, and the trip takes roughly 15 hours.

The express *Bima* and *Mutiara* night trains from Jakarta link up with the morning train from Surabaya to Denpasar and it's possible to buy a ticket to cover the whole Jakarta-Bali trip. For more information on travelling between Java and Bali, see the Getting There & Away section of the Bali chapter.

GETTING AROUND

Most travellers going through Java follow the well-worn route from Jakarta to Bogor, Bandung, Yogyakarta, Solo, Surabaya and on to Bali, with short diversions from points along that route.

Air

There's no real need to fly around Java unless you're in a real hurry or have money to burn, as there's so much transport at ground level. If you do take to the air you'll get some spectacular views of Java's many mountains and volcanoes – try to get a window seat!

To/From the Airport

Apart from those in Jakarta there are no official airline buses to the airports but local city buses sometimes pass within easy walking distance. There are always taxis and, if the taxi has no meter, there is usually a fixed fare from the city to the airport.

Bus

Java has to be one of the easiest places in the world to get around by bus. Buses run all over the island, including to places not accessible by train, and just about anywhere you might stand on the roadside is as good as a bus stop. Fares are cheap and, where the buses run a parallel service to the railways, they are sometimes also faster. The main advantage of buses over trains is that buses go so often.

Train

Java has a pretty good rail service running from one end of the island to the other. In the east (at Ketapang/Banyuwangi) it connects with the ferry to Bali and in the west (at Merak) it connects with the ferry to Sumatra. The two main lines run between Jakarta and Surabaya and trains between the two cities either take the longer central route via Yogyakarta and Solo or the shorter northern route via Semarang.

One good thing about train stations is that they're centrally located (bus stations generally aren't) and there's nearly always a hotel just around the corner. Travelling by train can be less tiring and more comfortable than by bus, particularly on long hauls. However, there are a number of factors to consider: train services vary a great deal, schedules change with reasonable frequency and, although trains nearly always leave on-the-second, they nearly always arrive late – sometimes very late. Some cities, such as Jakarta and Surabaya, have several stations and some of these are more convenient than others.

You should be able to pick up a regional timetable at any of the main stations. Ask for a *jadwal perjalanan*; it's a free leaflet and· lists major train services throughout Java, local trains and connecting ferry services. A separate *tarif* booklet listing all the fares is also available. The complete timetable and fares booklet, the *buku petunjuk tarif dan jadwal perjalanan*, costs 1800 rp. It's available from Jakarta's Gambir railway station, but it may be more difficult to find elsewhere.

Trains in Java vary widely – there are expensive 1st and 2nd-class expresses, reasonably cheap and fast 2nd and 3rd-class trains, and slow and uncomfortable 3rd class-only trains. Student discounts, from 10 to 25%, are generally available but not for the expensive *Bima* and *Mutiara* night expresses.

In 1st class (air-con) and 2nd class (fan-cooled) you have a seat or sleeper assigned to you. At the top end of the scale are the deluxe, air-con night expresses that do the Jakarta-Surabaya run. The *Bima*, which runs via Yogyakarta, has 1st-class two-berth sleepers and 2nd-class three-berth sleepers. The *Mutiara*, which runs via Semarang, has 1st and 2nd-class reclining chairs.

Third-class travel is unreserved, but in the more expensive 2nd and 3rd-class trains even 3rd class is reasonable.

What you don't want for any length of time is a *langsam* train. They're peak hour commuter trains to the big cities and crammed not only with people but also with market vegetables, cattle, the lot.

Buying tickets can be a frustrating and chaotic experience. If the queue is miles long or even if the train is officially booked out, see the station master *(kepala stasiun)* and plead your case – he may be able to help. Tickets cannot generally be bought from the

station before the day of your departure, but tickets for the *Bima* and *Mutiara* trains are available the night before or on the same day before 9 am.

Train tickets can be bought and reservations made from one to three days in advance at some travel agencies in main cities. There is a charge for this service which varies depending on the train and class, but it can definitely be worth the money to save the time and the hassle of fighting the crowds at the stations.

Sector by sector the main train routes through Java are as shown below.

Jakarta-Yogyakarta All trains between Jakarta and Yogyakarta pass through Cirebon on the north coast. From Jakarta to Yogyakarta takes from nine to 12 hours with fares from 5000 rp in 3rd class *(Cepat Siang)*, 15,000 rp in 2nd *(Senja Utama)*.

The fast *Bima Express* costs 44,000 rp or 49,000 rp with sleeping berth, 1st class only. It departs Jakarta (Kota) at 4 pm and arrives in Yogya at 12.27 am then continues on to Surabaya. In the other direction it leaves Surabaya at 4.10 pm, goes through Yogya at 9.10 pm and arrives in Jakarta at 7.30 am the next day. A better schedule if you don't mind spending the night in a reclining seat is aboard the *Senja Utama*, which leaves Jakarta at 7.30 pm and arrives in Yogya at 4.43 am; it's 15,000 rp for 2nd *(bisnis)* class.

At the other end of the comfort scale are the 3rd class-only *Gaya Baru Malam Selatan* and *Cepat Siang* at 7700 rp and 5000 rp from Jakarta to Yogya; the Gaya Baru Malam Selatan continues from Yogya to Surabaya. In comparison, the cheapest bus fare is 10,000 rp from Java to Yogyakarta and takes about 14 hours.

Jakarta-Surabaya Trains between Jakarta and Surabaya either take the shorter northern route via Semarang or the longer southern route via Yogyakarta.

One of the two luxury trains is the deluxe *Bima Express*, via Yogya, which departs Jakarta (Kota) at 4 pm and arrives in Surabaya (Gubeng) at 7.40 am. Returning, it leaves Surabaya at about 4 pm and arrives Jakarta at about 7.30 am. Fare is 50,000 rp for a seat or 54,000 with sleeper, 1st class only.

The deluxe *Mutiara Utara* takes the northern route from Jakarta (Kota) to Surabaya (Pasar Turi). The 15-hour trip costs 54,000 rp 1st class with sleeper on this very comfortable train.

The cheapest service is the 3rd class-only *Gaya Baru Malam Utara* (also north coast), which goes from Jakarta's Pasar Senen to Surabaya's Pasar Turi and costs 7700 rp. Officially it takes 14 hours but in practice it can take from 22 to 24 hours or longer. The *Gaya Baru Malam Selatan* takes the longer southern route via Yogya. By comparison, non-air-con buses between Jakarta and Surabaya cost around 12,250 rp (15 hours by night bus).

Yogyakarta-Surabaya There are about half a dozen trains a day between Yogya and Surabaya. The trip takes from 5½ to 7½ hours and costs from 3300 rp in 3rd class. The deluxe *Bima Express* between Jakarta and Surabaya operates through Yogyakarta. Solo is on the main route from Yogyakarta to Surabaya. Non air-con buses between Yogya and Surabaya cost around 6000 rp.

Car

Rates are very expensive although there are lower weekly or monthly rates. A typical small car might be a Ford Laser, Toyota Corolla or Suzuki Jeep. A medium car could be a Toyota Corona, Mitsubishi Lancer or Renault 18. To hire a car you must have a valid local or international driving licence, and you must be at least 25 years of age to hire an Avis car, or 19 for a National car. Avis is substantially more expensive than National.

National Car Rental (☎ 332006), is at Kartika Plaza Hotel, Jalan Thamrin 10, Jakarta. Small cars are 76,000 rp a day, large cars 88,000 rp a day.

Avis (☎ 341964), Jalan Diponegoro 25,

Jakarta. Avis is also represented at the Borobudur Hotel (☎ 370108 ext 2153), Hotel Sari Pacific (☎ 323707 ext 1281) and at Sukarno-Hatta International Airport.

It's also possible to hire chauffeur-driven cars or minibuses quite easily through the car-rental companies and some travel agents and hotels in main cities. Rates vary but it's likely to be around 10,000 rp an hour for a minimum of two hours, or a flat rate for a set route. Blue Bird Transport in Jakarta (☎ 333461) offers chauffeur-driven cars starting at 110,000 rp per day for a Toyota Corona, up to 250,000 rp per day for a Mercedes.

Many taxis operate as 'hire cars' too and charge in the same way. Privately it's possible to hire cars and drivers outside of Jakarta for somewhat lower rates – in most cities in Java for about 70,000 rp per day with driver.

Taxi

Taxi drivers in Jakarta are a disreputable lot, although they *do* have meters. Elsewhere there are unmetered taxis in most cities (taxis in Yogya and Surabaya are metered), usually to be found around hotels and at airport, train and bus terminals. Many are private 'hire cars'; they generally charge 10,000 rp to 15,000 rp an hour for a minimum of two hours within city limits; out of town charges are according to distance.

Bajaj

The *bajaj* (pronounced 'ba-jai') is found only in Jakarta and operates only in certain zones of that city. It's a motorised three-wheeler for two people and, as for becaks, fares have to be agreed on.

Boat

There are plenty of ferries and boats from Java to the outer islands but there is also a boat trip across the inland sea between Cilacap and Kalipucang on the south coast which is really worth doing. If you're travelling between Central Java and Pangandaran in West Java the boat is an excellent alternative to taking the bus and/or train all the way.

There is a daily boat service to Pulau

Bidadari (island) in the Bay of Jakarta, but trips to the small islands off the coast usually involve chartering a fishing boat – an outrigger vessel with sails or a motorised boat – and are dependent on the weather. There are regular daily ferries between Java and Madura, Bali and Sumatra.

Jakarta

Trying to characterise Jakarta is like being caught in a riptide: you're pulled in one direction by Western-style high-rise glass-and-concrete urbanisation and an elite of Indonesian academics and intellectuals, only to find yourself bogged down in the poverty of the kampungs of immigrant peasants who have come into the city in search of work. Jakarta is a city which asks for neither affection nor commitment; other than to scratch out a living peddling things – bodies, political power, diplomacy or becaks – there is no reason to stay here and certainly little reason to actually like the place for itself. Yet this is where the rest of the archipelago gets its marching orders; this is where they decide how many transmigrants will be sent to colonise the outer islands, or which former colony (eg West Irian, East Timor) gets thumped this year; or which foreign company gets to dig up rocks in the middle of the Sulawesi or devastate Kalimantan's rainforest.

Sukarno had a completely different image of what Jakarta could be. He wanted to transform it into a city of grand structures more in keeping with his conception of Jakarta as a world centre. The 14-storey Jakarta Hotel broke the skyline, the six-lane Jalan Thamrin was constructed and a massive sports stadium was erected for the 1962 Asian Games. Work on Jakarta's massive mosque was begun, and the Merdeka Monument took root. 'But like the jungle,' wrote Bruce Grant back in 1964, 'the ragged millions of crowded Java are hard to keep at bay. Already they blur the lines of these grand structures, setting up their portable stalls along the highways, next to a concrete pillar, against a wall.'

With Sukarno's architectural ambitions cut short in 1965, the job of sorting out the city was left to Lieutenant General Ali Sadikin, who held the post of governor of Jakarta from 1966 to 1977. Although he is credited with rehabilitating the roads and bridges, building several hospitals and a large number of new schools, he also drew criticism for attempting to eliminate becaks from various parts of the city and banning street pedlars – policies aimed at reducing the amount of work available in the city and thus curtailing its attraction to rural immigrants. Starting in 1969 Sadikin also tried to halt migration into the city, moving out homeless people and forcibly removing squatters. He basically had little choice if the crowding and poverty were not to get worse. New arrivals from the countryside, without Jakarta residence permits, constantly face the possibility of expulsion from the city, but in the meantime even a becak rider can send back maybe 20,000 to 30,000 rp a month to his village after covering his own expenses.

Appropriately called by locals 'The Big Durian', Jakarta is often a squalid and dirty city that many travellers try to give a miss (you should have seen/smelled it 20 years ago, say the old hands!) but it actually has a lot to offer. Apart from a few interesting museums and Sukarno's collection of terrible public monuments, Jakarta has some fine old Dutch architecture and the most impressive reminder of the age of sailing ships to be seen anywhere in the world. Visit Kota, the old town of Batavia to get some appreciation of this era.

History

Jakarta has been the centre of colonial and independent government since the 17th century. There have been at least three towns in the area of Kota or 'Old' Jakarta, all of them centred around the present-day port of Sunda Kelapa at the mouth of Sungai Ciliwung. The earliest known settlement was called Sunda Kelapa. It was a major port town of the last Hindu kingdom of West Java ruled by the Pajajaran dynasty and it was here that the Portuguese first made contact with Java in 1522. The second city was created by Gunungjati, the Muslim general of Demak who took control of Sunda Kelapa in 1527. Known as Jayakarta, 'victorious' in Javanese, it survived unmolested for almost a century as a fief of the Banten sultanate, but today none of the structures of this old town remain. What there is, dates from the Dutch period.

At the beginning of the 17th century both Dutch and English merchants had trading posts in Jayakarta. It became a centre of rivalry between these imperial powers, which was further confused by intrigue between local rulers. Late in 1618 the British, backed by the Bantenese and the Jayakartans, besieged the Dutch VOC (Vereenigde Oost-Indische Compagnie) fortress. Early the following year, however, the Bantenese turned against the British and the Jayakartans and occupied the town. Nothing much happened over the next few months but the VOC personnel, holding out in their fortified post, decided to rename the place 'Batavia' after an ancient Germanic tribe of The Netherlands.

In May 1619 the Dutch, under Jan Pieterszoon Coen, stormed the town and reduced it to ashes. A stronger shoreline fortress was built and Batavia eventually became the capital of the Dutch East Indies. It had to be defended on a number of occasions, against Banten in the west and Mataram in the east, but it was never conquered by an Indonesian power. Although the long-running Dutch struggle with Mataram began when Sultan Agung attacked Batavia in 1628, the Javanese suffered enormous losses and finally withdrew after executing their failed commanders. Agung's second siege in 1629 was an even greater debacle, and after this devastating defeat, Batavia was never again threatened by an army of Mataram.

Within the walls of Batavia, the prosperous Dutch built tall stuffy houses and pestilential canals on virtual swampland and by the early 18th century Batavia was suffering growing pains. Batavia grew rapidly as Indonesians and especially Chinese were attracted by its commercial prospects, but by the early 18th century the growing Chinese population was creating unrest and violence broke out. In October 1740 a general massacre of Chinese took place and a year later Chinese inhabitants were moved to Glodok, outside the city walls. Other Batavians, discouraged by the severe epidemics between 1735 and 1780, moved when they could and the city began to spread far south of the port. The Koningsplein, now Merdeka Square, was finished in 1818 and Merdeka Palace in 1879; Kebayoran Baru was the last residential area to be laid out by the Dutch after WW II.

Dutch colonial rule came to an end when the Japanese occupied Java and the name 'Jakarta' was restored to the city. The republican government of the revolution retreated to Yogyakarta when the Dutch returned after the war but in 1950, when Indonesian independence was finally secured, Jakarta was made the capital of the new republic.

In 1945 Jakarta had a population of 900,000; since then there has been a continual influx of migrants from depressed rural areas and newcomers continue to crowd into the urban slums. Today the population is nearly seven million. Sukarno concentrated on prestigious projects and monumental buildings for Jakarta, and the Suharto government too has met criticism for its seeming neglect of the city's impoverished people. The massive Taman Mini project in particular was widely condemned as a waste of the nation's resources. Overall, however, Jakarta is a much better- looking place than it was 10 years ago.

Orientation

Jakarta sprawls out in every direction but Sukarno's towering gold-tipped Monas monument in Merdeka Square serves as an excellent landmark for the city. Most areas of interest in Jakarta are to the north and

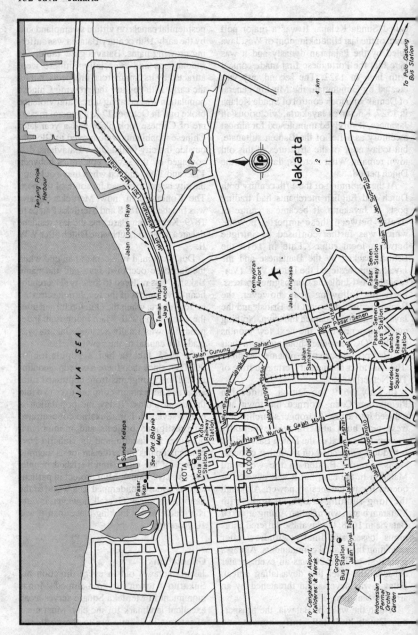

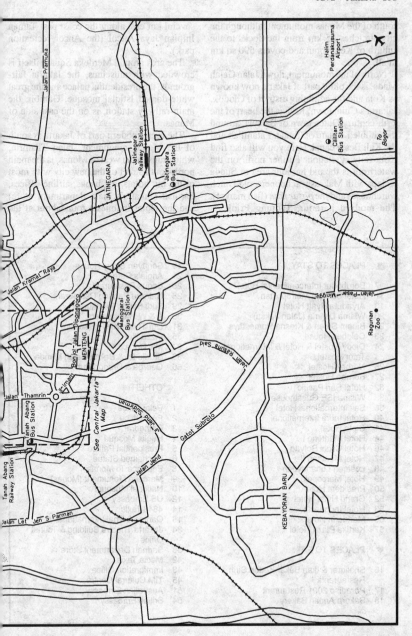

south of the Monas monument, although the city stretches 25 km from the docks to the suburb of Kebayoran and covers 590 sq km in all.

North of the monument, down Jalan Gajah Mada, is the older part of Jakarta now known as Kota and the adjoining district of Glodok, Jakarta's Chinatown. Kota is the heart of the 17th-century Dutch town of Batavia, around the cobbled square of Taman Fatahillah and the Kali Besar canal. Here you will also find Kota railway station. Further north on the waterfront is the old harbour area of Sunda Kelapa with Makassar schooners, old Dutch warehouses and the *pasar ikan* (fish market). The modern harbour, Tanjung Priok, is

several km east along the coast past Taman Impian Jaya Ancol (the Ancol recreation park).

The area around Merdeka Square itself is crowded with museums, the Jakarta fairgrounds, the presidential palace and the great white-domed Istiqlal mosque. Gambir, the main railway station, is on the east side of Monas.

The more modern part of Jakarta is south of the Monas monument. Jalan Thamrin, which runs to the west of Monas, is the main north-south street of the new city with most of the big hotels, big banks, airline offices, Sarinah (Jakarta's main department store) and the Hotel Indonesia roundabout at the

■ PLACES TO STAY

7	Borobudur Intercontinental Hotel
11	Hotel Sabang Metropolitan
13	Aryaduta Hyatt Hotel
20	Wisma Delima (Jalan Jaksa)
22	Bloem Steen & Kresna Homestays
23	Celebes House
24	Djody Hostel & Hotel & International Tator Hostel
26	Norbek Hostel
27	Borneo Hostel
32	Hotel Sari Pacific
33	Wisma ISE Guesthouse
36	Bali International Hotel
40	Hotel Indra International
41	Cipta Hotel
44	Hotel Menteng I
46	Hotel Cikini Sofyan
47	Hotel Menteng II
48	Losmen Luhandydan
49	Hotel Marcopolo
50	President Hotel
52	Grand Hyatt Hotel
53	Hotel Indonesia
55	Mandarin Hotel
57	Kartika Plaza Hotel

▼ PLACES TO EAT

15	Shalimar & Ikan Bakar Kebon Sirih Restaurants
17	Paradiso 2001 Restaurant
18	Sakura Anpan Bakery
19	Senayan Satay House
21	Angie's Cafe
25	Bagus Restaurant
28	Natrabu Padang Restaurant
29	Budi Bundo Restaurant
30	A & W Hamburgers
31	Lim Thiam Kie Restaurant
35	Pizza Hut
37	MacDonald's
39	Studio 21 & Bakmi Gajah Manda
56	George & Dragon Pub

OTHER

1	Pelni Office
2	Post Office
3	Cathedral
4	Istiqlal Mosque
5	Presidential Palace
6	Unchained Statue
8	Entrance To Monas
9	Merdeka Monument (Monas)
10	National Museum
12	US Embassy
14	4848 Taxis
16	Qantas & Thai International
34	Jakarta Theatre Building & Tourist Office
38	Sarinah Department Store
42	Media Taxis
43	Immigration Office
45	TIM Cultural Centre
51	Australian Embassy
54	British Embassy

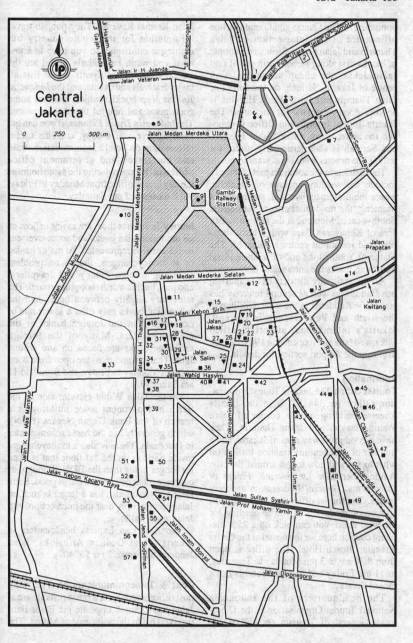

Central Jakarta

0   250   500 m

Jl Hayam Wuruk

Jl Gajah Mada

Jl Pecenongan

Jalan Ir H Juanda

Jalan Veteran

Jalan Pos Utara

Jalan Dr Sutomo

Jalan Medan Merdeka Utara

Jalan Medan Mederka Barat

Jalan Medan Merdeka Timur

Jalan Senen Raya

Gambir Railway Station

Jalan Abdul Muis

Jalan Prapatan

Jalan Medan Mederka Selatan

Jalan Kwitang

Jalan M H Thamrin

Jalan Kebon Sirih

Jalan Jaksa

Jalan Menteng Raya

Jalan H A Salim

Jalan Wahid Hasyim

Jalan Cokroaminoto

Jalan Cikini Raya

Jalan K H Mas Mansyur

Jalan Teuku Umar

Jalan Condangdia Lema

Jalan Kebon Kacang Raya

Jalan Sultan Syahrir

Jalan Prof Moham Yamin SH

Jalan Jend Sudirman

Jalan Imam Bonjol

Jalan Diponegoro

bottom of it. The Qantas and Garuda airline offices are at the intersection of Jalan Thamrin and Jalan Kebon Sirih, and a couple of blocks east along Kebon Sirih you'll find Jalan Jaksa, the cheap accommodation centre of Jakarta. Sarinah, on the corner of Jalan Thamrin and Jalan Wahid Hasyim, is another good landmark for this area. The Jakarta Tourist Information Office is opposite the store, across Jalan Wahid Hasyim, and Sarinah is also particularly useful for telling bus drivers where you want to go.

The districts in the southern part of the city include the wealthy enclave of Menteng, where the diplomats live and, south-east of Menteng, the residential area of Jatinegara. South-west of Menteng is the new suburban area of Kebayoran Baru with a busy shopping and restaurant centre at Blok M. The Statue of Youth at the end of Jalan Jenderal Sudirman marks the entrance to Kebayoran.

All the main city districts have suburban bus stations, as well as several intercity bus stations – Kalideres in the west, Cililitan in the south and Pulo Gadung in the east. Jakarta's international airport is called Sukarno-Hatta and it opened in 1985. See the To/From the Airport section for details.

Information

Tourist Office The Jakarta Tourist Information Office (☎ 344117) is in the Jakarta Theatre building on the corner of Jalan Wahid Hasyim and Jalan Thamrin. They have a good giveaway map of Jakarta, and a number of excellent information leaflets on what to see and how to get around the city. Among them *See for Yourself, Places of Interest* and *General Information* are very useful. The tourist office can also help you find accommodation. If you're heading for the west coast, you can pick up a 25% discount coupon here for the hostel at the Carita Krakatau Beach Hotel. The office is open from 8.30 am to 3 pm Monday to Thursday, to 11 am Friday and to 1 pm Saturday; it's closed Sunday.

The headquarters of the Indonesia National Tourist Organisation is the Directorate-General of Tourism (☎ 359001), at Jalan Kramat Raya 81. They publish travel information for the whole country but nothing is on display so you have to know what you want. Particularly useful are the annual *Calendar of Events* which lists all major festivals and events, and the *Indonesia Tourist Map* booklet which includes some good maps and helpful travel information. The *Indonesia Travel Planner*, if you can get them to give you a copy, contains useful information on hotel accommodation, train and bus travel, and government office addresses. It's open during the same hours as the city tourist office from Monday to Friday, but it closes at 2 pm Saturday.

Money In Jakarta there are major offices of all the Indonesian banks and some overseas banks are also represented. At major banks, or at moneychangers, there's no problem changing foreign money and travellers' cheques, but it's worth shopping around. The rates vary slightly between banks and the Indonesian banks may offer a lower rate of exchange than the foreign banks or the moneychangers. Many of the foreign exchange banks are found on and around Jalan Thamrin and most are open from 8 am to noon Monday to Friday, and from 8 to 11 am Saturday.

On the Jalan Wahid Hasyim side of the Sarinah department store building is a branch of the Bank Dagan Negara (BDN), which generally has the best exchange rates in Indonesia. There is also a moneychanger inside Sarinah on the 1st floor that is open for longer hours than the BDN although, of course, exchange rates are not as good. Bank Dagang Negara also has a larger branch on Jalan Kebon Sirih, near the intersection with Jalan Agus Salim.

The American Express headquarters in Jakarta are at Gedung Arthaloka, Jalan Jenderal Sudirman 2 (☎ 587409)

Post & Telecommunications The main post office and Jakarta's poste restante are at Jalan Pos Utara 2, opposite the Pasar Baru (market) off to the north-east of Monas. The poste restante here is pretty efficient – they give you the whole bundle from your pigeon-hole to look through and will willingly give you all the newly arrived mail that hasn't been sorted yet as well. There is a 50 rp charge for each letter from poste restante. It is open from 8 am to 4 pm Monday to Friday and until 1 pm on Saturday. For ordinary stamp sales and postmarking there are always a few windows open from 6 am to 10 pm Monday to Saturday (and closed from 11 am to noon Friday) and from 9 am to 4 pm Sunday. It's a good half-hour walk from the centre of town, or you can take a No 12 bus from Jalan Thamrin. There's also a small post office inside the Sarinah department store, which is open from 9 am to 2.30 pm Monday to Thursday, from 9 am to noon Friday and from 9 am to 12.30 pm Saturday; it's closed Sunday.

To make international and intercity phone calls you can try the telecom centre opposite the tourist office in the Jakarta Theatre building. It's open 24 hours and is very efficient. There are some public telephones for local calls in the same building but they're so often in need of repair that you're better off using public phones in the large hotels.

Convenient for those staying around Jalan Jaksa is the privately run RTQ Warparpostel, Jalan Jaksa 15C, opposite the Bagus Restaurant. This place offers international and domestic postal, telephone, fax, telex and telegram services. Operating hours are from around 6 am until midnight and, being privately run, it's exceedingly efficient compared with the government-run telecom services.

Immigration Office The Directorate-General of Immigration is fairly central at Jalan Teuku Umar 1 in Menteng. The office is open from 8 am daily except Sunday and closes at 3 pm Monday to Thursday, at noon Friday and at 2 pm Saturday.

Travel Agencies For international flights, one of the cheapest agents is Seabreeze Travel (☎ 326675), Jalan Jaksa 43. Travel International (☎ 330103) in the President Hotel on Jalan Thamrin is also a good place for cheap tickets, as is Vayatour (☎ 3100720) next door to Travel International. Other agents worth checking are Natrabu (☎ 331728), Jalan Agus Salim 29A (near Jalan Jaksa) and Pacto Ltd (☎ 320309) at Jalan Cikini Raya 24.

The agent for STA (Student Travel Australia) (☎ 6392703) is Indo Shangrila Travel, Jalan Gajah Mada 219G. Any student with an international student card is entitled to their fares, which are usually cheaper than a normal student discount of 25%. For more information on domestic bucket shops in Jakarta see the Getting There & Away chapter.

Bookshops Books – particularly imported ones – are expensive but if you want to stock up on paperbacks or look for Indonesian books then Jakarta is the best hunting ground. The large illustrated books on Borobudur, for example, that are sold at the temple site itself (published by Djambatan and Intermasa) are about 2500 rp cheaper in Jakarta.

Ayumas, at Jalan Kwitang 6, near Pasar Senen, is one of the largest bookshops in Jakarta and has a fair range of English paperbacks and Indonesian books, as well as a good selection of maps and books on Indonesia. Sarinah department store also has a fairly good book·and map section. Other bookshops include the Toko Buku Gramedia shops at Jalan Gajah Mada 109 and Jalan Melawai IV/13 Blok M, at Gunung Agung, Jalan Kwitang 24-25 and at Gunung Mulia next door at 22-23. And there are, of course, bookstalls in most of the large hotels where you'll find paperbacks, magazines, and foreign and Indonesian newspapers. In fact, probably the best selection of English-language reading in Jakarta, or anywhere in Indonesia for that matter, is available at the Hotel Indonesia and Borobudur Hotel.

Mochtar Lubis' controversial study *Twilight in Jakarta* has been on and off the ban list in Indonesia but for the moment it's available as an *Oxford in Asia* paperback in the National Museum shop. You'll also find a number of other interesting books on Indonesia here.

Maps If you're planning to stay a long time in Jakarta it could be worth investing in a detailed city map. The *Falk City Map* and the *PT Pembina Guide & Map of Jakarta* cost about 7000 rp.

Film & Photography Jalan Agus Salim, just east of and parallel to Jalan Thamrin, is a good place for your photographic supplies. The other good place to look is 'Blok M' near the pasar (market) which lies between Jalan Sultan Hasanuddin and Jalan Melawai in the Kebayoran Baru district in south-west Jakarta.

There are numerous Kodak-only stores in Jakarta. The distributor and laboratory for Kodak is at Jalan Kwitang 10. Jalan Kwitang lies roughly south-east of the Merdeka Monument; it is an eastwards continuation of Jalan A R Hakim, which is a continuation of Jalan Wahid Hasyim. If you can't find the stuff you want in the stores, then try this place. Nirwana Photo Company, Jalan Krekot Raya 67B, is the distributor for Sakuracolor. Modern Photo Film Company, at various addresses in Jakarta, is the Fuji distributor.

Colour prints cost around 200 or 250 rp each at places offering same-day processing. Try Jakarta Foto on Jalan Agus Salim and Globe Photo on Jalan Melawai V 26, Blok M, Kebayoran Baru.

Libraries & Organisations The Ganesha Society, an organisation of volunteer museum workers, holds weekly lectures or films about Indonesia at the Erasmus Huis (☎ 772325) on Jalan Rasuna Said, beside the Dutch Embassy in South Jakarta. Admission is around 1500 rp. The National Museum (☎ 360976) has their schedule, or ask the Ganesha guides who work there part-time.

The Indonesian/American Cultural Center (Perumpunan Persahabatan Indonesia Amerik) (☎ 881241), Jalan Pramuka Kav 30, has exhibits, films and lectures related to Indonesia each week. The Australian Cultural Centre (Pusat Kebudayaan Australia), in the Citibank building on Jalan Thamrin, has a good library. It's open from 9 am to 2 pm Monday to Thursday and until noon Friday. The British Council's library is open from 9 am to 1 pm and is in the Widjoyo Centre, Jalan Jenderal Sudirman 56. There are also cultural centres from Czechoslovakia, France, Germany, India, Italy and Japan.

National Parks/Nature Reserves Jakarta no longer has a branch office of the PHPA (Perlindungan Hutan dan Pelestarian Alam), the Directorate-General of Forest Protection and Nature Conservation. For detailed information on Indonesia's parks and reserves, you'll have to visit the national PHPA headquarters in Bogor, where there is a special office for National Park and Forestry Tourism. The address is Jalan Ir H Juanda 9, Bogor (☎ (0251) 21014). Dr Sophie speaks English and can be contacted at this office.

There is no need to go to the Bogor headquarters for entry permits to national parks and/or reserves. Permits can be acquired directly from local offices located on-site throughout Indonesia.

Airlines Addresses of international airlines that fly to and from Jakarta include:

Air Canada
    Jalan Jenderal Sudirman Kav 21, Chase Plaza, Ground Floor (☎ 588185)
Air India
    Sari Pacific Hotel, Jalan Thamrin 6 (☎ 325470)
Asiana Airlines
    Plaza Indonesia, Level 1
    Jalan Thamrin 28-30 (☎ 326885, 333363)
British Airways
    Jalan Jenderal Sudirman Kav 29, Wisma Metropolitan I, 10th Floor (☎ 5703742)
Canadian Airlines International
    Jalan Riau 19A (☎ 323730)
Cathay Pacific
    Borobudur Hotel, 3rd Floor, Jalan Lapangan Banteng Selatan (☎ 3806660)
China Airlines
    Jalan Jenderal Sudirman Kav 32, Wisman Dharmala Sakti (☎ 5704003)
Delta Airlines
    Jalan Jenderal Sudirman Kav 32, Wisma Dharmala Sakti 11th Floor (☎ 5704024)

EVA Airways
    Tamara Centre, Suite 102
    Jalan Jenderal Sudirman Kav 24 (☎ 5206456)
Garuda Indonesian Airways
    BDN Building, Jalan Thamrin 5 (☎ 334425).
    Also at Borobudur Hotel (☎ 359901) and Hotel
    Indonesia (☎ 310-0568)
Japan Airlines
    President Hotel, Jalan Thamrin 59 (☎ 322207)
KLM
    Hotel Indonesia, Jalan Thamrin (☎ 320034)
Lufthansa
    Panin Centre Building, Jalan Jenderal Sudirman
    1 (☎ 710247)
MAS
    Hotel Indonesia, Jalan Thamrin (☎ 320909)
Philippine Airlines
    Borobudur Hotel (☎ 370108 ext 2310)
Qantas
    BDN Building, Jalan Thamrin 5 (☎ 326707)
Royal Brunei
    Plaza Indonesia, Level I/93 (☎ 337985)
Singapore Airlines
    Sahid Jaya Hotel, Jalan Jenderal Sudirman 86
    (☎ 584021)
Thai Airways International
    BDN Building, Jalan Thamrin 5 (☎ 325176)
United Airlines
    Borobudur Hotel, Jalan Lapangan Banteng
    Selatan (☎ 362707)
UTA
    Jaya Building, Jalan Thamrin (☎ 323609)

Other Information The daily *Jakarta Post*
gives a useful run down of what is on, temporary exhibitions and cinema programmes.
The swimming pools at Ancol are great but
you could also try some of the hotel pools
closer at hand. Many of the hotels do open
their pools to the public for a small admission
– the Hotel Marcopolo is one.

Indonesian National Museum
On the west side of Merdeka Square, the
National Museum was built in 1862. It is
probably the best museum in Indonesia and
one of the best in South-East Asia. Its collection includes a huge ethnic map of Indonesia
and an equally big relief map on which you
can pick out all those volcanoes you have
climbed. It has an enormous collection of
cultural objects of the various ethnic groups
– costumes, musical instruments, model
houses and so on – and numerous fine
bronzes from the Hindu-Javanese period, as

well as many interesting stone pieces sal-
vaged from Central Javanese and other
temples. There's also a superb display of
Chinese ceramics dating back to the Han
dynasty (300 BC to 220 AD) which was
almost entirely amassed in Indonesia.

Just outside the museum is a bronze elephant which was presented by the King of
Thailand in 1871; thus the museum building
is popularly known as the Gedung Gajah or
Elephant House. As in most museums
throughout Indonesia, exhibit labels are
either absent or in Indonesian only, so unless
you're an art historian or can read Bahasa
Indonesia you'll occasionally be left guessing.

The museum is open from 8.30 am to 2
pm on Tuesday to Thursday, to 11 am on
Friday, to 1.30 pm on Saturday, and to 3 pm
on Sunday. It's closed on Monday. The entry
fee is 300 rp for adults and 150 rp for children. It's well worth a visit, for here you will
find some reminder of almost anywhere you
have been in Indonesia. On Tuesday,
Wednesday and Thursday there are useful
guided tours in English (free) at 9.30 am.
Gamelan performances are held every
Sunday between 9.30 and 10.30 am. On
Sunday the museum also opens its 'treasure'
room of gold and silver.

Other Museums
Jakarta has a number of other museums apart
from the excellent National Museum and
those in old Batavia. North-west of the
National Museum is the Taman Prasati
Museum, or Park of Inscription, on Jalan
Tanah Abang. This was once called the
Kebon Jahe Cemetery and a number of
important figures of the colonial era are
buried here, including Olivia Raffles, wife of
British Governor-General Sir Stamford
Raffles, who died in 1814. The cemetery is
open from 8 am to 3 pm Monday to Thurs-
day, to 11 am on Friday, and until 6 pm on
Saturday. It's closed on Sunday and holi-
days.

The Textile Museum is housed in a Dutch
colonial house on Jalan Satsuit Tubun 4, near
the Tanah Abang district bus station. It has a

large collection of batiks and woven cloth from all over Indonesia, as well as looms and batik-making tools, and it's well worth a visit. This museum is open from 9 am daily, except Monday, until 2 pm Tuesday to Thursday, 11 am on Friday, 1 pm on Saturday and 3 pm on Sunday. Admission is 250 rp.

The Abri Satriamandala Army Museum, on Jalan Gatot Subroto, has an enormous display of weapons and endless dioramas glorifying the Indonesian armed forces in their battles for independence. It's open from 9 am to 4 pm daily except Monday, and admission is 250 rp.

If you're a stamp collector, you might want to check out the Musium Prangko (Stamp Museum) at Taman Mini. Not only is there a historical exhibition of Indonesian stamps, but also dioramas depicting the designing/printing of stamps, as well as the homy satisfactions of philatelics. The Musium Prangko is open daily from 8 am until 4 pm Monday to Saturday, and until 3 pm on Sunday and holidays.

Old Batavia (Kota)

The old town of Batavia, known as Kota today, at one time contained Coen's massive shoreline fortress, the Kasteel, and was surrounded by a sturdy defensive wall and a moat. In the early 19th century Governor-General Daendels did a good job of demolishing much of the unhealthy city but there is still a Dutch flavour to this old part of town. A few of Batavia's old buildings remain in active use, although others were restored during the 1970s and have become museums. Cleaning up the stinking canals though is a superhuman task and these days gallons of deodorant are poured into the putrid waters.

The centre of old Batavia is the cobblestone square known as Taman Fatahillah. A block west of the square is the Kali Besar, the great canal along Sungai Ciliwung. This was once the high-class residential area of Batavia and on the west bank overlooking the canal are the last of the big private homes dating from the early 18th century. The Toko Merah or Red Shop, now occupied by the

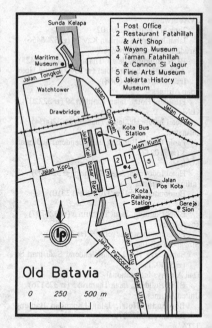

Old Batavia

1 Post Office
2 Restaurant Fatahillah & Art Shop
3 Wayang Museum
4 Taman Fatahillah & Cannon Si Jagur
5 Fine Arts Museum
6 Jakarta History Museum

0   250   500 m

Dharma Niaga company, was formerly the home of Governor-General van Imhoff. The north end of the Kali Besar canal is marked by a small Dutch drawbridge called the Chicken Market Bridge.

There are two booklets about Old Batavia which are worth buying for background information and further detail. They're extracts from the *Historical Sites of Jakarta* by A Heuken and entitled *The City Hall & its Surroundings* and *Gereja Portugis*. The booklets cost 2200 rp from the Jakarta History Museum in Kota, but only 1200 rp from the National Museum on Merdeka Square!

Jakarta History Museum On the south side of Taman Fatahillah Square, the museum is housed in the old town hall of Batavia, which is probably one of the most solid reminders of Dutch rule to be found anywhere in Indonesia. This large bell-towered hall, built in 1627 and added to between 1707 and 1710, served the administration of the city. It was

Top: Istiqlal Mosque, Jakarta, Java (AS)
Bottom: Puncak Pass between Bogor & Bandung, West Java (DS)

Top: Travellers arriving by becak at the Cilacap jetty, Java (TW)
Bottom: Segara Anakan, Central Java (JC)

also used by the city law courts and its dungeons were the main prison compound of Batavia. In 1830 the Javanese hero Prince Diponegoro was imprisoned here for a time on his way into exile in Menado.

Today it contains lots of heavy, carved furniture and other memorabilia from the Dutch period and there are sections for the earlier kingdoms that ruled the Jakarta area. Amongst the more interesting exhibits is a series of gloomy portraits of all the Dutch governors-general (which seems to set the mood for this place!), early pictures of Batavia, and models of inscribed stones from the Hindu Tarumanegara kingdom of West Java.

In the courtyard at the back of the building there is a strange memorial stone to one Pieter Erbervelt, who was put to death in 1722 for allegedly conspiring to massacre the Dutch inhabitants of Batavia.

The museum is open every day but Monday. It opens at 9 am and closes at 2 pm Tuesday to Thursday, at 11 am on Friday, at 1 pm on Saturday and at 2 pm on Sunday. Entrance costs 250 rp.

Wayang Museum Also on Taman Fatahillah, this museum has one of the best collections of wayang puppets in Java and includes puppets not only from Indonesia but also China, Malaysia, India and Cambodia. Among the more interesting items is a very fine chess set of wayang golek figures (Rama and his monkeys versus Rawana and his giants) and a number of wayang kulit puppets used in the Yogyakarta Family Planning Programme. Formerly the Museum of Old Batavia, the building itself was constructed in 1912 on the site of the Dutch Church of Batavia which was demolished by Daendels in 1808. In the downstairs courtyard there are some interesting memorials to the Dutch governors-general once buried here. These include some mention of Jan Pieterszoon Coen, founder of Batavia, who died of cholera in 1629 during the siege by Mataram.

Closed on Monday, the museum is open on Tuesday to Sunday from 9 am to 2 pm,

except Friday when it closes at 1 pm. Wayang golek or wayang kulit performances are put on at the museum every Sunday morning between 10 am and 1.30 pm. Entrance costs 250 rp.

Balai Seni Rupa (Art Museum) Built between 1866 and 1870, the Palace of Justice now houses Jakarta's principal art gallery. There's a permanent exhibition of works by Indonesia's most prominent painters, including Raden Saleh and Affandi, and a section for the Chinese ceramic collection of Indonesia's former vice-president, Adam Malik.

Closed on Monday, the museum is open from Tuesday to Sunday at 9 am, closing at 2 pm on Tuesday to Thursday, at 11 am on Friday and at 1 pm on Saturday and Sunday. Entrance costs 250 rp.

Cannon Si Jagur This huge bronze cannon is one of the most intriguing sights of old Batavia. Its outer surface is adorned with a Latin inscription *Ex me ipsa renata sum* which means 'Out of myself I was reborn' and the cannon tapers at one end into a large clenched fist. In Indonesia the fist is a sexual symbol and for that reason childless women at one time used to visit the cannon. They would offer flowers to their talisman and complete the ritual by sitting on top of the cannon. This must have upset the authorities a great deal for Si Jagur was shifted to a museum for some years to counteract the superstition. Si Jagur is a Portuguese cannon brought to Batavia as a trophy of war after the fall of Melaka in 1641 but the Javanese, naturally, have a mystical story to tell.

The legend relates that a king of Sunda had a dream in which he heard the thundering sound of a strange weapon. He ordered his prime minister, Kyai Setomo, to find a similar weapon, threatening him with death if he failed. Kyai Setomo discussed his fateful task with his wife, Nyai Setomi, and they both did some meditation. Days passed and the king grew so impatient that he visited Kyai Setomo's home, only to discover that the couple had been transformed into two large cannons! Sultan Agung then heard about the great weapons and ordered them to be brought to his court at Mataram but the male cannon, Kyai Setomo, refused to go. Instead he fled at night to Batavia where he had to remain outside the locked gates of the city. The people of Batavia were of course quite surprised to find a cannon sitting at their gates and came to regard him/it as holy. They gave him/it a little paper umbrella as protection from the sun and called him/it Kyai Jagur, Mr Fertility.

Gereja Sion On Jalan Pangeran Jayakarta, near Kota railway station, this church dates from 1695 and is the oldest remaining church in Jakarta. Also known as Gereja Portugis or Portuguese Church, it was built just outside the old city walls for the so-called 'black Portuguese' – the Eurasians and natives captured from Portuguese trading ports in India and Malaya and brought to Batavia as slaves. Most of these people were Catholics but they were given their freedom on the condition that they joined the Dutch Reformed Church, and the converts became known as the Mardijkers or 'liberated ones'. The exterior of the church is very plain, but inside there are copper chandeliers, the original organ and a baroque pulpit. Although in the year 1790 alone, more than 2000 people were buried in the graveyard here, very few tombs remain. One of the most interesting is the ornate bronze tombstone of Governor-General Zwaardecroon, who died in 1728 and, as was his wish, was buried among the 'ordinary' folk.

Sunda Kelapa
At the old port of Sunda Kelapa you can see more sailing ships, the magnificent Makassar schooners called *pinisi*, than you ever thought existed. This is undoubtedly one of the finest sights in Jakarta. Entry to the docks is only 110 rp but ultra-skinflints can avoid this by cutting through the Pasar Ikan (the fish market across the bridge) to the gateway of Luar Batang village on the water's edge. Small boats ferry the local people across from Luar Batang to the docks

and there are plenty of boatmen around wanting to take you out on the water. You can spend a good half-hour or so rowing around the schooners, avoiding decapitation by mooring ropes and gangplanks and occasionally having rubbish thrown on you from the ships! If you get out to the Thousand Islands (Pulau Seribu) in the Bay of Jakarta you will probably see Makassar schooners under sail.

The best time to visit the Pasar Ikan is around dawn when the day's catch is sold in an intense, colourful scene of busy crowds.

Museum Bahari (Maritime Museum) At the entrance to the Pasar Ikan, one of the old Dutch East India Company warehouses has been turned into a maritime museum. Exhibits are fairly meagre but include large models of boats from various islands and it's worth a short wander. The museum is open every day but Monday. It opens at 9 am, closing at 2 pm Tuesday to Thursday, at 11 am on Friday and at 1 pm on Saturday. Entrance is 250 rp. You can ascend the old watchtower back near the bridge for free; there is a good view over the harbour from the top.

Glodok
After the Chinese massacre of 1740, the Dutch decided there would be no repetition and all Chinese were prohibited from residing within the town walls, or even from being there after sundown. In 1741 a tract of land just to the south-west of Batavia was allocated as Chinese quarters. The area became Glodok, Jakarta's Chinatown, and the city's flourishing commercial centre. It's now bounded to the east by Jalan Gajah Mada, a wide road lined with offices, restaurants and modern shopping plazas. But if you walk in from Jalan Pancoran, beside the Glodok Plaza, you'll find a small part of old Glodok still consists of winding lanes, narrow crooked houses with balconies, slanting red-tiled roofs and tiny obscure shops. In between there are numerous eating places, markets, street hawkers and half the city's becak population! It can be a fascinating area to wander around and, just south of Jalan

Pancoran, near the Petak Sembilan fish market, you'll find the Chinese Dharma Jaya Temple – one of the most interesting in Jakarta. Built in 1650, it was the chief temple for the Chinese of Batavia and was once known for its casino and Chinese wayang kulit. At present this is the largest Buddhist temple in Jakarta.

If you're walking from Glodok back along Jalan Gajah Mada, it's worth pausing to have a glance at two old Jakarta buildings along this street. The Candra Naya, at No 188, was once the home of the Chinese 'captain' employed by the Dutch to manage the affairs of Batavia's Chinese community. Since 1946 the building has housed the offices of a social work society but you may be able to have a short wander inside. Further south at No 111, the National Archives building dates from 1760 and was formerly the country house of Governor-General Reinier de Klerk.

Taman Impian Jaya Ancol

Along the bay-front between Kota and Tanjung Priok, the people's 'Dreamland' is built on land reclaimed in 1962. This huge landscaped recreation park, providing non-stop entertainment, has hotels, nightclubs, theatres and a variety of sporting facilities.

Ancol's prime attractions include the Pasar Seni (art market) (see Things to Buy), its many sidewalk cafes and a gallery where there are often interesting exhibitions of modern Indonesian art and photography. Near the Pasar Seni there's an oceanarium (gelanggang samudra) and an amazing swimming pool complex, including a wave pool and slide pool (gelanggang renang). Jakarta's sports hall for jai alai, said to be the 'fastest ball game in the world', is also within the park and matches can be seen at 7 pm every evening. The Ancol beach, so close to the city, is hardly likely to be a pleasant place to swim but you can take a boat from the marina here for day trips to some of Jakarta's Pulau Seribu islands.

The latest addition to Jaya Ancol is Dunia Fantasi or 'Fantasy Land', a Disneyland type of park that's great for kids. It's open daily, on Monday to Friday from 2 to 9 pm, on Saturday from 2 to 10 pm, and on Sunday and holidays from 10 am to 9 pm. The basic entry fee for Dunia Fantasi is 1000 rp from Monday to Friday, 1200 rp on Saturday, and 1500 rp on Sunday and holidays. There are additional fees for the park's Disneyesque rides and you may purchase a pass entitling you to unlimited rides for 7,500 rp – a bargain.

Basic admission to Ancol is 850 rp on Monday to Thursday, 1000 rp on Friday and Saturday, and 1200 rp on Sunday and holidays. The Pasar Seni is open from 9 am to 10 pm daily, and the swimming pool complex from 7 am to 9 pm daily. It costs an additional 3500 rp to use the pools from Monday to Thursday, 5000 rp on Friday and Saturday, and 6000 rp on Sunday and holidays. Admission to the oceanarium is 800 rp Monday to Thursday, and 1000 rp on the other days. Children's rates for all attractions are less than half the price of adult admission. Apart from being more expensive the park can be very crowded on weekends, but on weekdays it's fairly quiet and a great place to escape from the hassles of the city. From the Kota bus station you can get there on a No 64 or 65 bus or an M15 minibus. For more information, call 681511 in Jakarta.

National Monument (Monas)

This 132-metre high column towering over Merdeka Square is both Jakarta's principal landmark and the most famous architectural extravagance of Sukarno. Commenced in 1961, the monument was not completed until 1975, when it was officially opened by Suharto. Architecturally it is pretty much a phallic symbol topped by a glittering flame symbolising the nation's independence and strength (and, some would argue, Sukarno's virility). It is constructed 'entirely of Italian marbles' according to a tourist brochure and the flame is gilded with 35 kg of gold leaf. In the base of Monas there is a museum with a series of dioramas giving a rundown of Indonesia's history and there is a fine view from the top of the column. Close to the monument's entrance on the square's northern side is a statue of the freedom fighter,

Prince Diponegoro, astride his horse. During the annual Jakarta Fair, the entrance shifts to the north-east side of the monument.

The monument is open daily from 9 am to 4.30 pm. It costs 2000 rp (850 rp for students) to go to the top of Monas and queues can be lengthy – tourists on weekends, schoolkids on weekdays. If you want to avoid hanging around it's probably best to go early. There's an additional 500 rp (250 rp for students) entry fee to the museum which, according to one traveller, is 'so atrocious it shouldn't be missed', although another visitor felt it did 'give a fair description of Indonesian history'. Although there's a nice view from the top, unless you've got nothing better to do, you wouldn't be missing much if you skipped the monument.

Other Sukarno Monuments
Inspired tastelessness – in the Russian 'heroes of socialism' style – best describes the plentiful supply of statues Sukarno left to Jakarta. All of them have acquired descriptive nicknames, including the gentleman at Kebayoran holding the flaming dish, who is known as 'the mad waiter'. There's also the Statue of Welcome – Hansel and Gretel – which was built by Sukarno as a symbol of Indonesian friendliness for the 1962 Asian Games held in Jakarta.

Istiqlal Mosque
On the north-eastern corner of Merdeka Square is Jakarta's principal place of Muslim worship. Recently completed, the modernistic Istiqlal mosque is reputedly the largest in South-East Asia.

All Saints Anglican Church
Due south-east of Merdeka Square, across from the Hyatt Arduta Hotel, this is probably the oldest remaining British institution in Indonesia. The origins of this church date back to the more humble beginnings of the London Missionary Society which constructed a small bamboo chapel here in 1822. The present building was constructed on the same site in 1829 and there are still some interesting old tombstones in its graveyard.

The hand-painted windows of the church were taken from the WW II prisoner of war camp chapel in Tanjung Priok.

Gedung Perintis Kemerdekaan
Independence was proclaimed on the site of the former home of Sukarno at Jalan Proklamasi 56 in Menteng and there is a monument to President Sukarno and Vice President Hatta here.

Taman Ismail Marzuki
On Jalan Cikini Raya, not far from Jalan Jaksa, the Taman Ismail Marzuki (TIM) (☎ 322606) is Jakarta's cultural showcase. There is a performance almost every night and here you might see anything from Balinese dancing to poetry readings, gamelan concerts to overseas jazz groups, an Indonesian PKI film to a New Zealand film festival! The TIM monthly programme is available from the tourist office, the TIM office and major hotels, and events are also listed in the *Jakarta Daily Post*.

There are also two art galleries within the compound – the Gallery Graphics and the Cipta Art Gallery, which exhibit contemporary Indonesian art. Both galleries are open from 9 am to 1 pm and from 5 to 9 pm Monday to Saturday. Jakarta's Planetarium is also here but shows are generally given in Indonesian. For information about shows in English, phone them (☎ 337530). The whole complex is open from morning until midnight and there are good outdoor cafes here, so it can be a useful place. The No 34 bus from Jalan Thamrin stops nearby.

Zoo
Jakarta's Ragunan Zoo is about 10 km south of the city centre in the Pasar Minggu area. The zoo has komodo dragons, orang-utans and other interesting Indonesian wildlife and it's open daily from 9 am to 6 pm. Admission is 700 rp on weekdays, 850 rp on weekends and holidays; it's half-price for children.

Taman Mini Indonesia Indah
In the south-east of the city, past Cililitan, Taman Mini is another of those 'whole

country in one park' collections which every South-East Asian country seems to be acquiring. The idea behind the park was conceived by Mme Tien Suharto in 1971, the families inhabiting the land were cleared out to make way for the project (then estimated to cost the awesome total of US$26 million) and the park was duly opened in 1975.

This 100-hectare park has 27 full-scale traditional houses from the 27 provinces of Indonesia with displays of regional handicrafts and clothing, and a large 'lagoon' where you can row around the islands of the archipelago or take a cable car across for a bird's eye view. There are also museums, theatres, restaurants, an orchid garden and a bird park with a huge walk-in aviary. There's even a mini Borobudur. The 'Indonesia Indah' is a three-dimensional screen show of the Indonesian panorama which takes place at the Keong Mas (Golden Snail) Theatre. In 30 minutes the film packs a lot in but it's special effects all the way – there's no subtlety about it at all! Admission is 1500 rp and there are showings at noon, 2 and 4 pm Monday to Friday, and every hour between 11 am and 5 pm on Saturday and Sunday.

You can walk or drive your own car around Taman Mini. Or you can go by horse and cart or take the mini train service that shuttles around the park dropping people off and picking them up. The park is open from 8 am to 5 pm daily, the houses and Museum Indonesia from 9 am to 4 pm. Admission is 600 rp (children 400 rp, cars 500 rp) and the train service costs an additional 200 rp, horse and cart 400 rp. The park is quite good value and of course Indonesians will tell you that if you see this there's no need to go anywhere else in the country! On Sunday mornings there are free cultural performances in most regional houses from 10 am to 2 pm. For other cultural events here, check the Taman Mini monthly programme available from the Tourist Office.

Taman Mini is about 10 km from the centre so you need to allow about 1½ hours to get out there and then about three hours to look round. From Banteng take a No 40, 41 or 401 bus to Cililitan and from there a T55

metro-mini to the park entrance. For additional information call 801905 in Jakarta.

Lubang Buaya
There is a memorial to the six generals and the army officer killed here by the Communists in 1965, called Pancasila Cakti, a few km east from Taman Mini. *Lubang buaya* means 'crocodile hole'.

Other Attractions
Jakarta has a number of gardens specialising in cultivating orchids and the **Indonesian Permai Orchid Gardens** in Slipi, near the Grogol bus station, is the best place to see them. There are 35,000 square metres of orchids, open from 9 am to 5 pm daily. There's also the **Taman Anggrek Ragunan Orchid Gardens** near the zoo.

Taman Buaya Pluit is a crocodile farm with about 500 of the friendly beasts. It's at Jalan Bandengan Utara 27, north-west of Kota. The **Pasar Burung**, on Jalan Pramuka in Jatinegara, is Jakarta's market for captive birds from all over Indonesia.

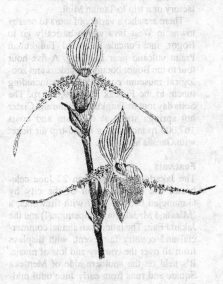

Orchid

The **Bharata Theatre** is on Jalan Kalilio near the Pasar Senen bus station. There are wayang orang performances from 8.15 pm to midnight every evening, except Monday and Thursday when there are *ketoprak* (popular comedy) performances. Tickets cost from 2500 rp. **Wayang kulit/golek** puppet shows are held outdoors in the Jakarta Fair area every second Saturday of the month during the Jakarta Fair in late June and July. These all-night performances start around 9 pm and admission is about 500 rp.

Organised Tours

Numerous travel agents offer daily tours of Jakarta but they tend to be expensive. Information on many of them is available from the tourist office and major hotels. They include Vayatour (☎ 3800202), Nitour (☎ 346347) and Setia Tours (☎ 6390008). All tour buses pick up from the major hotels, and tour prices and sights are very similar. A four-hour morning city tour, for example, costs about 20,000 rp and, starting at 9 am, includes the National Museum, National Monument, Sunda Kelapa and a batik factory or a trip to Taman Mini.

There are also a variety of tours to nearby towns in West Java which basically go to Bogor, the Puncak Pass and Tangkuban Prahu volcano near Bandung. A five-hour tour to the Bogor botanical gardens and zoological museum costs 49,000 rp including lunch; to the Puncak costs 69,000 rp. The Setia day tour to Tangkuban Prahu and Ciater hot springs starts at 6.30 am and costs 167,000 rp including a round-trip air ticket with Garuda and lunch.

Festivals

The Jakarta Anniversary on 22 June celebrates the establishment of the city by Gunungjati back in 1527 with fireworks, a 'Miss and Mr Jakarta' competition(!) and the Jakarta Fair. The latter is an annual commercial and country fair event, with displays from all over the country and lots of music. It's held on the southern side of Merdeka Square and runs from early June until mid-July.

Places to Stay – bottom end

Jakarta's cheap accommodation centre is Jalan Jaksa, a small street centrally located in the newer part of Jakarta and just south of that useful landmark, the Monas monument. It runs between Jalan Kebon Sirih and Jalan Wahid Hasyim, a few blocks over from Jakarta's main drag – Jalan Thamrin – and about 10 to 15 minutes' walk from Gambir railway station.

The *Wisma Delima*, Jalan Jaksa 5, has been Jakarta's most popular resting place for so long that simply asking for 'Jalan Jaksa' will probably get you here. There are both pros and cons to staying at Wisma Delima. It is small and they've certainly converted every available inch into room space, so rooms are rather cramped and stuffy, but otherwise it's OK and it is the cheapest place on Jalan Jaksa. The Lawalata family who run Wisma Delima remain unfailingly helpful and calm in the face of non-stop demand for space. Despite the pressure, it's a friendly place and a good contact point. The only problem is that it is very often full and when that happens, service and sanitation may deteriorate. There are two dormitories with fans, and beds cost 3000 rp (or 2500 rp with a YHA card). Singles/doubles cost 10,000/11,000 rp and there are triples at 15,000 rp. Food, cold drinks and cheap beer are available – good value for Jakarta.

If you don't have any luck here or don't like the place, there is an increasing number of good alternatives springing up along or close to Jalan Jaksa. *Norbeck Hostel* (☎ 330392), Jalan Jaksa 14, is very popular of late, probably because of its high visibility and cosy garden in front. There are tight security rules in effect here, welcomed by many travellers given Jakarta's growing incidence of thievery. Norbeck has perhaps the cheapest air-con rooms in Jakarta, tiny warrens with shared bath for only 10,000 rp. In addition, this quite clean establishment has rooms with fans for 9000 rp, doubles with private bath for 15,000 and larger air-con rooms with private bath for 22,000 rp. Food is available.

Across the street from Norbeck at 15C, you

can enjoy the warmth of an Indonesian homestay by lodging with the delightful *Marzuky* family. Mrs Marzuky rents out two basic rooms with shared bath for 8,000/15,000 rp for singles/doubles.

At No 27 is another old and popular standby, *Djody Hostel*. Beds in less than immaculate dormitories cost 7500 rp, rather airless rooms cost 15,000 to 18,000 rp. There are open sitting areas at front and back, and the showers and toilets are shared. Mosquitoes can be a problem, but mosquito nets are provided. Like most places on Jalan Jaksa, what it lacks most is ventilation. Further down on the same side of the street at No 35 is the slightly more upscale *Djody Hotel*, with fan-cooled rooms at 17,000/19,000 rp for singles/doubles, rooms with private bath for 24,000 rp and a couple of air-con rooms for 30,000 rp. The staff at both Djody locations are friendly and helpful. At No 37, you will find the basic but acceptable *International Tator Hostel* (☎ 325124) offering rooms with shared bath for 12,000 rp, doubles with private bath for 15,000 to 19,000 rp, and air-con rooms from 25,000 to 29,000 rp.

At No 35 on Kebon Sirih Barat Dalam, a small lane running west off Jalan Jaksa, is the *Borneo Hostel* (☎ 320095). It has a fan-cooled dormitory with beds at 4000 rp, rooms at 12,000 rp and 17,500 rp for a room with attached mandi. Kitchen facilities and a fridge are available. Some people think it 'looks cleaner and not so stuffy' as the Wisma Delima and that it's a useful addition to the cheap hotel scene. Others insist that it's unfriendly and expensive. If you continue along this lane, you will find similarly priced places such as the *Bintang Kejora* at No 52, the *Tiara* at No 33, the *Pondok Wisata* at No 16 and the *Pondok Wisata Jaya* at No 10.

On Gang 1, Jalan Kebon Sirih Timur Dalam (east off Jalan Jaksa) there are two other popular places. The *Bloem Steen* at No 173 is an attractive bungalow with several rooms. It's often full but is good value with rooms at 6000/12,000 rp for singles/doubles with good shared showers and a fine garden

terrace. Drinks, breakfast and other meals are available at reasonable prices. Next door, the *Kresna* at No 175 has decent doubles with fan for 11,000 rp or 14,000 rp with bath. Both of these places offer basic lodging, but some travellers prefer to stay in them because it's quiet on this lane.

If you walk to the south end of Jalan Jaksa, turn right onto Jalan Wahid Hasyim and cross Jalan Thamrin, you'll eventually come to the *Wisma ISE Guesthouse* (☎ 333463) at No 168, right side of the street. It looks plain, but is good value for Jakarta with clean singles/doubles at 11,500/15,500 rp. You can also get breakfast for 2500 rp. The management is very friendly and there's a pleasant balcony/bar on the top floor where you can look out over quite a bit of Jakarta. There are always some Indonesians staying at Wisma ISE since it serves as the Jakarta mess for Telecom workers from Bandung – it's a good place to practise Bahasa Indonesia.

Another recommended budget lodge, within walking distance of Gambir station on a small lane parallel to Jalan Kebon Sirih, is *Celebes House* at Jalan Menteng Raya 35. Rooms with fan cost 11,000 to 18,000 rp, air-con rooms are 27,5000. Reasonably priced meals are available.

Places to Stay – middle

There are a number of middle-bracket hotels in the Jalan Jaksa area. The *Hotel Karya* (☎ 320484) at Jalan Jaksa 32-34 has rather dismal economy rooms with fan and bathroom for 29,000 rp. Slightly better are air-con rooms at 35,000 rp with private bath and hot water. Rates include a rather basic toast-and-jam breakfast. Also close to Jalan Jaksa, but more expensive, is the *Hotel Wisma Indra* (☎ 334556) at Jalan Wahid Hasyim 63. Although you might be tempted to stay here because the price seems good for Jakarta, beginning with air-con singles with private bath for 40,000 rp, save your money and go elsewhere. Here the air-con is faulty at best and the hot water next to non-existent.

Although pricey for the locale, the all air-con *Cipta Hotel*, conveniently situated at Jalan Wahid Hasyim 61 where it intersects with Jalan Jaksa, offers clean, pleasant rooms starting at 75,000 rp, as well as a moderately priced cafe.

The larger *Sabang Metropolitan Hotel* (☎ 373933), Jalan H A Salim 11, once a good value for this price bracket, has been renovated, with a corresponding increase in rates. Air-con rooms range from two hard-to-get single/double mini-rooms at 75,000/95,000 rp to standard singles/doubles from 95,000 to 130,000 rp (plus 15% tax and service). The hotel has a not-so-special swimming pool and coffee shop, but the service is fair and it's in a good location.

Moving to the Menteng area, south of Jalan Thamrin and close to the TIM Cultural Centre, is a small three-hotel chain representing good mid-range value. *Hotel Menteng I* (☎ 357635) is at Jalan Gondangdia Lama 28, the *Hotel Menteng II* (☎ 325543) is at Jalan Cikini Raya 105 and the *Grand Menteng* (☎ 882153) is a bit further south on the next avenue to the east, at Jalan Matraman Raya 21. All three offer air-con rooms with private bathrooms and hot water, piped muzak, coffee shop, bar and swimming pool. The Grand Menteng also has a modest fitness centre. Prices start at 55,000 rp for an economy room and there are standard singles/doubles from 67,000/78,000 rp (plus 15% tax & service).

The *Hotel Marcopolo* (☎ 325409), at Jalan T Cik Ditiro 19, has air-con rooms with bathroom at 60,000 rp (hot water in the morning and evening). The hotel has a swimming pool, nightclub, bar and restaurants serving Indonesian, Chinese and European food.

Also in the Menteng area is a family-run hotel recommended by a Dutch reader. *Losmen Luhandydan* (☎ 371865), at Jalan Sawo 15, has four double rooms with fan and attached mandi and toilet for 23,000 rp per person including breakfast. The proprietors are friendly and they speak Dutch and English. The house has a pleasant garden and good lunches, and dinners are available at 5500 rp each.

Airport Area The Sukarno-Hatta Airport is such a distance from Jakarta's centre that some travellers with flights in the wee hours of the morning might consider lodging at the nearby *Cengkareng Transit Hotel* (☎ 611964), Jalan Jurumudi (Km 2.5). Note that although it's just opposite the runways, it takes a while to reach the hotel by road. Fortunately, there's a free minibus and hotel reps comb the airport for prospective clients. Basic air-con rooms cost 47,000/63,000 rp and there is a 24-hour coffee house on the premises.

Places to Stay – top end
Most of the 'international-class' hotels are in the city centre, on or around the main boulevard of Jalan Thamrin. The *Hotel Indonesia*, built for the Asian Games which Jakarta hosted in 1962, heralded a new era for hotel development in Indonesia – at 14 storeys it was the first 'skyscraper' in the archipelago and it was to be the largest, most modern hotel in South-East Asia. A number of luxury hotels with superb facilities followed, spurred on in part by the boom that brought troupes of business travellers to the capital. The economic recession, however, seems to have put a stop to this frenetic building and perhaps due to lack of competition, prices for Jakarta's luxury hotels are staggeringly steep. Rates quoted below are before a 10 to 15% 'luxury tax' and a 5 to 10% 'service charge'. Special weekend rates are generally for Indonesian residents only but better rates are often available through travel agents. You can also try asking for a discount at the reception desk – this often nets an immediate 10 to 20% discount. The hotels listed here are among the more important ones.

The *Borobudur Intercontinental Hotel* (☎ 370333) is on Jalan Lapangan Banteng Selatan, between Merdeka Square and the *pasar senen*. It is Jakarta's biggest hotel and offers everything from a health club, an olympic-size swimming pool, a jogging track, tennis and squash courts to restaurants and full air-con. The room tariff starts here at 333,000 rp and spirals ever upward.

The *Aryaduta Hyatt Hotel* (☎ 363202) is central at Jalan Prapatan 44/46. Recently renovated, its singles/doubles cost from 245,000 rp.

The *Hotel Indonesia* (☎ 320008) is on the Statue of Welcome roundabout, Jalan Thamrin. Major renovations in 1985 resulted in renewed splendour and higher rates. It has restaurants, a bar, a colourful aviary and an olympic-size swimming pool. Singles/doubles cost from 196,000/225,000 rp.

The *Jakarta Hilton* (☎ 587991) at Jalan Jenderal Gatot Subroto, on the outskirts of Kebayoran Baru, is the latest luxury hotel. It has large grounds, an attractive shopping bazaar, and is generally considered to have the best facilities and decor. Singles/doubles cost from 275,000/314,000 rp.

The *Mandarin Hotel* (☎ 321307), across from the Hotel Indonesia on Jalan Thamrin, has all the usual luxuries and services, a swimming pool and health centre but no grounds. It rivals the Borobudur Interconti-nental for swank. Singles/doubles cost from 313,000/343,000 rp.

The *President Hotel* (☎ 320508) is at Jalan Thamrin 59. It's a smaller and rather more old-fashioned looking hotel with no sports facilities. It was recently taken over by the Nikko chain – most of the guests are Japanese businessmen. Singles/doubles cost from 180,000/202,000 rp.

The *Sahid Jaya Hotel* (☎ 587031) is at Jalan Jenderal Sudirman, halfway between Jalan Thamrin and the Hilton, at No 86. It's a big hotel with a rooftop restaurant and a coffee shop, which is also owned by the Nikko chain. Singles/doubles cost from 245,000/275,000 rp.

The *Hotel Sari Pacific* (☎ 323707) is conveniently located about midway down Jalan Thamrin at number 6. It's popular for good service and good food and there's a disco and large swimming pool. Singles/doubles cost from 245,000/275,000 rp.

Places to Eat

Jakarta probably has the best selection of restaurants of any major Indonesian city, although a meal in a better-class restaurant tends to be expensive. Plenty of street hawkers and night markets cater for cheaper meals.

Jalan Jaksa Area There are plenty of places to eat around the Jalan Jaksa area. Meals at some of Jalan Jaksa's hotels are among the best deals going, but the *Bagus Restaurant*, near the Norbek Hostel, is currently the most popular. Despite the restaurant's mediocre fare and sometimes cold service, budget travellers meet at this open air eatery, whose food is reasonably cheap. Inside, the Bagus shows videos, with the schedule signposted in front of the restaurant.

On the opposite side of Jalan Jaksa, you will find *Anedja KPPD Cafe*, serving so-so north Indian dishes and some Indonesian fare at moderate prices. *Angies* at Jalan Jaksa 16 is a small cafe with a few tables in the front garden and more inside. It's popular for its cheap Western breakfasts and fruit salads. Standard Indonesian dishes are also cheap, 1200 rp for basic nasi or mie goreng.

There are cheap Indonesian warungs at either end of Jalan Jaksa, but be a little wary about cleanliness if you've just arrived and are not used to the local food standards. The alley between and parallel to Jalan Jaksa and Jalan H A Salim has a number of warungs as well.

Out on Jalan Kebon Sirih, to the north of Jalan Jaksa, there are several eating possibilities. On the corner of Jalan Jaksa and Jalan Kebon Sirih, the *Senayan Satay House* is more expensive than anything on Jalan Jaksa but good value. It has a varied menu including seafood, noodles and particularly good satay. Most dishes cost from 4000 rp to 6000 rp, it's comfortably air-conditioned and patronised mainly by expats and middle-class Chinese Indonesians.

At Jalan Kebon Sirih 40, tasty tandoori dishes are served at the *Shalimar* Indian restaurant (far superior, albeit more expensive fare than that offered by the Anedja KPPD Cafe). Situated above the Shalimar in the same building is the *Ikan Bakar Kebon Sirih*, a more up-scale Indonesian restaurant than those you will find along Jalan Jaksa. Try the house specialty, savory *ikan bakar*,

Makassar-style roast fish. Both restaurants at this location charge from 5000 to 8000 rp for a meal.

There is a string of restaurants along both sides of Jalan H A Salim, just a block over towards Jalan Thamrin. The shiny *Sakura Anpan*, a Japanese bakery at No 25/27, is a good, reasonably priced place for a quick snack, cold drink or ice cream. The popular *Natrabu Padang Restaurant* specialises in Padang/Minang food or there's the *Budi Bundo* which is cheaper and also good. *Lim Thiam Kie* at No 53 has excellent Chinese food and most dishes average around 2500 rp. Down a little alley close to the A&W is the *Paradiso 2001*, an interesting little vegetarian restaurant with good food advertised as having 'no cholesterol.' The Paradiso boasts that they're 'a restaurant for men of the future'. Women and children of the future can eat there too.

Jalan H A Salim was once known as Jalan Sabang and is still often called Sabang by locals. Throughout Java, Jalan Sabang is known as the satay capital of Indonesia because there are so many traditional food trolleys *(gerobak makanan* in Indonesian) hawking satay on this street. On a good night you may see as many as a hundred of them and the pungent smoke from their charcoal braziers will fill the street. It's ironic then, that in spite of all the delicious satay ayam cooking away right there at the curb, several different fast-food chicken places have opened their glass doors on Jalan Salim. Take your pick of *El Pollo Loco* at the corner of Salim and Jalan Wahid Hasyim, *Kentucky Fried Chicken* next door to Natrabu, and *Jakarta Ayam Goreng* at the top of the street. Around the corner at the Jakarta Theatre building, there's a *California Fried Chicken* joint as well as a *Pizza Hut*. Pizzas here range from 4500 rp for a small to 9000 rp and up for a large. Upstairs in the theatre building, you will find the quick-service *Cafe A&A*. Back on Jalan Salim, there are still more fast-food eateries: *A&W* (burgers from 2000 rp to 5000 rp) across from Kentucky Fried and *Kim's Hamburgers* on the other side of A&W.

In the Jakarta Theatre building, the *Green Pub* features Mexican food with meals averaging about 10,000 rp and a happy hour from 3 to 6 pm with half-price drinks. In the evening, the place is jammed, as Indonesians turn out to enjoy a local live band perform in Mexicano cowboy garb!

Across the road, the *Sarinah* department store on Jalan Thamrin has an excellent, if fairly expensive, bakery and snack counter – their *tahu Jakarta* is a tasty snack filled with spiced vegetables for a few hundred rupiah. And for those who simply can't live without a taste of home, there is a *McDonald's* at the front of the Sarinah. Prices here are roughly comparable with what you would pay at home. If you continue down Jalan Thamrin, you'll find other fast-food emporia at the shopping centre under the Grand Hyatt, including a *Swenson's Ice Cream*, a *Burger King*, a *Kentucky Fried Chicken*, and a *Del Taco*.

The well-known and very popular *Bakmi Gajah Mada* has a branch in the Studio 21 Theatre complex on Jalan Thamrin. They have an extensive menu of Chinese noodle and rice dishes starting at 4000 rp for an excellent bakmi goreng. If you plan to come for lunch, you may have to wait for a table as it can get very crowded.

The Markets There are lots of stalls set up around the central area of the city, as well as in Old Jakarta. Jalan Kebon Sirih and Jalan Wahid Hasyim have a collection of food stalls but some of them look remarkably dirty. After dark the parking lot behind Sarinah turns into *Selara Nusantara*, a kind of Singapore food centre where you can eat from any stall you choose and take a seat at any one of the tables scattered amongst them. It's fairly tame but there's plenty of choice and it is reasonably cheap – satay for 2000 rp, fish 2500 for rp, nasi gudeg at 1550 rp, fruit juices 900 rp and beer (large bottle) 2700 rp.

If you go west along Jalan Wahid Hasyim from Wisma ISE, heading towards the Tanah Abang bus station, you'll come to a good collection of cheap and very popular night warungs.

Jakarta is well known for good seafood and the lively Chinese-seafood night market on Jalan Pecanongan is excellent. Prices tend to be a bit higher though – a good meal for two (fish, rice and beer) might cost 7000 rp. Jalan Pecanongan is directly north of the Monas monument, about a three-km walk from Jalan Jaksa. Stalls start setting up here at around 5 pm. During the Jakarta Fair in June and July there are many other stalls operating in Merdeka Square.

There's also the *Pasar Boplo* night market, north of the main post office. *Jalan Mangga Besar*, off Jalan Hayam Wuruk in northern Jakarta, is a good night market area for Chinese, Indian and Padang food. *Pasar Senen* shopping centre, one km east of Merdeka Square, has a wide selection of food stalls – but only during the daytime. This is a particularly busy area for pickpockets, so take care.

South of the Hotel Indonesia roundabout, there's a string of interesting stalls including a good Korean barbecue along Jalan Kendal – if you walk south past the massage parlours on Jalan Blora, you turn left (where the transvestites hang out) along Jalan Kendal, which runs parallel to the railway line. At Blok M, Kebayoran, the *Pasar Kaget* is a night market run by people from Central and East Java.

Elsewhere Away from the Jalan Jaksa hotel enclave, along Jalan Gajah Mada there are numerous restaurants, bakeries, and fast-food and ice-cream parlours. The original *Bakmi Gajah Mada* noodle house is at Jalan Gajah Mada 92. If you just want a snack or a cheap drink and somewhere cool to drink it, try the air-conditioned Gajah Mada Plaza shopping centre. There are very good milk-shakes, sundaes and superb ice-cream flavours (a bit expensive at 2700 rp) at the US *Swensen's*. Chinese eating places abound in Glodok but this area really comes to life at night, at which time it's best to get there by taxi.

The Blok M shopping centre in Kebay-

oran, around the Aldiron Plaza and Kebayoran market, has a wide variety of places to eat. There's another *Swensen's* branch on Jalan Melawai Raya 16 and, above the ice cream parlour, there's a canteen serving cheap Indonesian 'fast foods'. The modern *Restaurant Melawai*, Jalan Melawai 1/92, is clean and has a wide variety of Indonesian dishes for 3500 to 15,000 rp. There's yet another *Bakmi Gajah Mada* noodle house at Jalan Melawai IV/No 25 and the *Ratu Bahari* has good Chinese seafood at reasonable prices. Other places include the English-style *King's Head* pub and *Rugantino's*, Jalan Melawai Raya 28, where you can get good Italian food.

More Expensive Restaurants Many of Jakarta's ritzy hotels, including the *Sari Pacific*, offer a rijstaffel buffet 'special' for around 15,000 to 20,000 rp. The *President Hotel* has a range of restaurants that mostly cater to Japanese tastes for steak and seafood. There's also a good pastry shop here and the views from the *Cocktail Bar* on the 30th floor of the adjacent Nusantara Building are superb.

The *Omar Khayam* (☎ 356719) at Jalan Antara 5-7, near the post office, is reputed to have excellent Indian curries and they also do a special all-you-can-eat buffet lunch. For southern Indian cuisine served in banana leaves, *Mutu Curry*, located adjacent to the Tanamur Disco on Jalan Tanah Abang Timur is recommended by locals.

Jakarta has a particularly good selection of Chinese seafood restaurants and some say the *Jun Njan* (☎ 364063), Jalan Batu Ceper 69 at the north end of Jalan Pecanongan, has the best seafood in Indonesia. It has a small menu, with most dishes at 6000 to 10,000 rp, but we'd recommend it as an excellent place for a splurge. Try the fried squid in oyster sauce or the fried prawns in butter sauce. Reservations are recommended. They also have a branch in south Jakarta at Jalan Panglima Polim Raya 77. The Jun Njan is closed on Mondays. More upscale, the *Spice Garden* in the Mandarin Oriental Hotel

(☎ 321307) on Jalan Thamrin serves savory Szechuan cuisine at Western prices.

The *George & Dragon Pub* off the southern sector of Jalan Thamrin on Jalan Teluk Betung has English-style pub food. You can even indulge yourself in sausage & mash there! The pub also serves some tasty Indian fare. A couple of doors down, the *Korea House* has good Korean barbecue food.

The historic *Oasis Bar & Restaurant* (☎ 327818) on Jalan Raden Saleh 47 is housed in a large, old Dutch villa and has the feel of an extravagant 1930s Hollywood film set, with prices to match – more than a dozen waitresses serve up a traditional rijstaffel (36,000 rp!), while you are serenaded by a group of Batak singers from Sumatra. Reservations are recommended. It's closed on Sundays.

The best and most upscale of Jakarta's French and Italian restaurants may be found in luxury hotels. Fine French cuisine is served in the Mandarin Oriental Hotel at the *Club Room* (☎ 321307), and superb Italian dining may be enjoyed at the Hyatt's *Ambiente* (☎ 376008). The posh *Nelayan* (☎ 370333) in the Borobudur Intercontinental is famous for seafood.

Entertainment

Jakarta's cheapest entertainment is to walk to the Taman Ria at Merdeka Square. It's open daily from 5 pm to midnight and admission is 850 rp. The fairground lights up and the merry-go-round turns but few people visit so take your own crowd. There are local pop bands and singers but it's more lively on Saturdays. The annual Jakarta Fair is held here.

Air Mancur Menari, on the western side of Monas, is the dancing fountain – coloured lamps produce movements, depending on the music, from 7 to 10 pm. There's an image of a naked woman in the flame from the north side.

The bar at the Hotel Indonesia has a happy hour from 6 to 8 pm with half-price drinks and free hors d'oeuvres. The Hyatt has the same with live chamber music from 7 to 9 pm. The Tavern Pub at the Hyatt has live music nightly featuring local bands like Galactic Band, The Big Kids and the Syncopators. The Pitstop at the Sari Pacific Hotel is a popular discotheque for locals and visitors alike. Note that there is a dress code – no jeans allowed. The Sari Pacific also sports the Melati Lounge, where jazz is played in a most interesting fashion over traditional anklung instruments. The Jaya Pub in the Jaya building at Jalan Thamrin 12 has live pub music most evenings.

Batak musicians and singers are popular entertainers in much of Java and Sumatra. They may be found every night at the Oasis Restaurant, Tuesday nights at the Hilton Pizzaria, and about 7 pm each evening at the mezzanine lounge of the Mandarin Hotel.

Of Jakarta's numerous discos, perhaps the most amusing is the Earthquake Discotheque on Monas Square, where the floor electronically quakes and shakes to the beat. Among the upscale discos are the Oriental in the Hilton and the Music Room in the Borobudur. Note that there are dress codes – no jeans – at the posher discos of the luxury hotels. For a venture on the somewhat sleazy side, the infamous Tanamur Disco at Jalan Tanah Abang Timur 14 is jammed nightly with gyrating revellers and innumerable ladies of the night. Wear what you like here.

The best cinema house in Jakarta is the relatively new Studio Twenty-One on Jalan Thamrin, four buildings south of the Sarinah department store. The Jakarta Theatre is showing its age and has a visible population of rats.

Films, lectures and discussions of Indonesian culture are often sponsored by foreign embassies and the Ganesha Society, a volunteer organization devoted to affording an appreciation of the nation's rich cultural heritage. Check the entertainment pages of the *Jakarta Post* for events, times and locations.

Things to Buy

Good buys in Jakarta include batik and antiques but probably the most important thing about Jakarta is that you can find things from almost anywhere in Indonesia. If this is

Batik motif

your first stop, it's a good place to get an overall view of Indonesian crafts and, if it's your last stop, then it's always a last chance to find something that you missed elsewhere in the country.

A good place to start is Sarinah on Jalan Thamrin. The 4th floor of this large building is devoted to batik and another to handicrafts from all over the country. It's a little variable – you might find some areas poorly represented – but items are generally good quality and reasonably priced. The batik floor is divided into different concessions sponsored by the big batik manufacturers like Batik Keris and Batik Danar Hadi. Check the basement for bargains. The Pasar Seni at Ancol recreation park is an excellent place to look for regional handicrafts and to see many of them actually being made. Whether it's woodcarvings, paintings, puppets, leather, batik or silver you'll find it all here. The Indonesian Bazaar is another craft market but this is an extension of the Hilton Hotel shopping arcade so it's likely to be expensive.

In Menteng, Jalan Surabaya is Jakarta's famous fleamarket. Here you'll find jewellery, batik, oddities like old typewriters and many (sometimes instant) antiques. It attracts a lot of tourists these days but it's worth a visit. Either early morning or late afternoon would probably be best, when they want to make last sales and go home. Menteng also hosts the air-conditioned Jakarta Handicrafts Centre which, like the Sarinah, carries handicrafts from all over the archipelago. There are many other shops for antiques and curios along Jalan Kebon Sirih Timur Dalam and Jalan H A Salim, both in the Jalan Jaksa area. The Duta Suara shop on Jalan H A Salim has a good range of Western and Indonesian tapes at around 6000 rp each. Pirate tapes are available in Indonesia despite the 1 June 1988 law to enforce international music copyright.

Getting There & Away

Jakarta is the main international gateway to Indonesia and for details on arriving there from overseas see the introductory Getting There & Away section at the start of the Java chapter. Travel agencies worth trying for discounted air fares on international flights out of Jakarta are listed under Information, at the start of the Jakarta section.

A number of travel agencies offer discounted air fares on domestic flights (Merpati and Mandala flights in particular). For flights to Nusa Tenggara, Sulawesi, Sumatra and Bali you can get as much as 25% discount. The Mitra Kercana Tour & Travel Service (☎ 349699, 361366) at Jalan Pintu Air 20A, Pasar Baru district near the Pelni office, is one.

Jakarta is also a major centre for domestic travel, with extensive bus, rail, air and sea connections.

Air International and domestic flights both operate from the Sukarno-Hatta International Airport. Airport tax is 11,000 rp on international departures, 5500 rp on domestic flights. The domestic tax may already be included in the ticket. Domestic airlines in Jakarta are:

Garuda (☎ 334425), BDN Building, Jalan Thamrin 5. Open 8 am to 12.30 pm and 1.30 to 4 pm Monday to Friday; 8 am to 1 pm Saturday, 9 am until 1 pm Sunday and holidays. Garuda also has offices in the Hotel Indonesia and Borobudur Intercontinental Hotel. Garuda flights depart from Jakarta to all the main cities in Java and to places all over the archipelago.

Bourag (☎ 6295150), Jalan Angkasa 1, Kemayoran. Open 8 am to 4 pm daily.

Mandala (☎ 368107), Jalan Veteran I No 34. Open 8 am to 4 pm Monday to Friday, 8 am to 1 pm Saturday, 9 am until 1 pm Sunday.

Merpati (☎ 413608), Jalan Angkasa 2, Kemayoran. Open 7 am to 4 pm Monday to Friday, 7 am to 2 pm Saturday, 8 am until 1 pm Sunday and holidays. Garuda has absorbed Merpati and you can therefore purchase Merpati tickets and make reservations at all Garuda offices in Indonesia.

Sempati (☎ 348760), Jalan Merdeka Timur 7, Sempati has undergone the most substantial expansion of any of Indonesia's private carriers. Most travel agents can book Sempati. Sempati has the cheapest flights to Singapore, twice daily at US$75, and also flies to Tanjung Pinang, Kalimantan, and Bangka Island, near Sumatra.

Bus Jakarta has three major bus stations. They are in the outer suburbs but are linked by city bus to the various district bus stations in central Jakarta. The bus stations are:

Kalideres Buses to the west go from the Kalideres station which is several km north-west of Merdeka Square. Buses to Merak, via Serang, depart roughly every 10 minutes and there are frequent buses to Labuhan and Carita.

Cililitan Buses depart from Cililitan to areas south of Jakarta. Popular buses include Bogor for 800 rp (if you take the toll road designated 'Jalan Toll' buses, you will save at least 15 minutes, making it a 30 minute trip), Puncak, Bandung for 2600 rp (4½ hours) and Banjar for 4700 rp (nine hours).

Pulo Gadung This is the station for buses to destinations east. Both public and private night buses operate from here. There are frequent services daily to Cirebon.

Destination	Time	Fare (rp)
Cirebon	5 hours	3850, 6100*
Semarang	12 hours	7200, 13,600*
Yogyakarta	12 hours	15,200, 21,000* 24,250**
Solo	11 hours	8300, 13,250* 13,250*
Surabaya	15 hours	12,250, 19,500* 29,950**
Malang	18 hours	15,600, 22,400*
Denpasar	25½ hours	21,850, 28,850* 38,600**

*air-con buses
**deluxe air-con buses with toilet and reclining seats

Bus companies operating to Sumatra are found along Jalan K H Mansyur. The best buses with aircraft seats, toilets, air-con (and video) are Bintang Kejora; next best is ANS. If you buy tickets from the offices they'll arrange free transport to the Kalideres bus station. Fares include Bukittinggi 22,700 rp, 36,200 with air-con, and 55,530 rp with air-con, toilet and reclining seat. Buses with toilets stop less frequently so they're faster.

Train Jakarta has four major railway stations. Gambir, on the east side of Merdeka Square and most convenient for Jalan Jaksa, handles trains to the south and east, plus most services through to Surabaya via Yogya. Pasar Senen, further east of Gambir, has most services to Surabaya via Semarang. If you're going west to Merak, for Sumatra, then the trains will be from Tanah Abang station, which is directly to the west of Jalan Thamrin. Beware of pickpockets at all of Jakarta's train stations, but particularly Gambir.

Note that the super deluxe night express trains to Surabaya – the *Bima Express* (via Yogya) and the *Mutiara Utara* (via Semarang) – do not depart from Gambir or from Pasar Senen but from Kota, which is north of Merdeka Square in Old Jakarta. If you're departing from Kota station you should allow adequate time to wind your way through the rush hour traffic snarls. From Jalan Thamrin you can take a No 70 or P11 bus to Kota station for just 200 or 500 rp. On the return journey, the *Bima* and *Mutiara* trains stop at Gambir and then continue on to Kota.

Tickets for the *Bima* and *Mutiara* can be purchased from the station ticket counter one day before departure. Tickets for other trains can usually only be bought a couple of hours before the train leaves, when collection is nearly always chaotic. If queues are hopelessly long or if trains are 'officially full', it's always worth trying the station master (kepala stasiun) for tickets. If you want to be certain of a sleeper or a seat, bookings (with the exception of 3rd class-only trains) can be made at some travel agents for a small charge. Carnation Tours & Travel (☎ 344027) at Jalan Menteng Raya 24, on the corner of Jalan Kebon Sirih, handles bookings and the office is open from 8 am to 3 pm Monday to Friday, from 8 am to 2 pm on Saturday and from 9 am to 1 pm on Sunday. Bhayangkara Tours & Travel, Jalan Kebon Sirih 23, also handle railway bookings.

From Gambir station trains depart every hour to Bogor and take 1½ hours at a cost of 500 rp in 3rd class-only. Although it takes quite awhile to reach the Cililitan bus station from Jalan Jaksa, it is nonetheless generally faster to take the bus. Exceptions to this are the express *Pakuan* trains, costing 1200 rp and departing Gambir at 10.40 am and 16.50 pm, reaching Bogor an hour later. The *Parahiyangan* is a comfortable express train from Gambir to Bandung. There are nine trains daily, the first departing at 5.30 am and arriving three hours later. The fares are 16,500 rp in 1st class and 11,000 rp in 2nd class. Trains to Merak depart Tanah Abang station at 6 am and 5 pm and take four hours, costing 1550 rp 3rd class-only.

Trains to Yogya take from 10 hours and fares vary from 5000 rp in the cheapest 3rd class, or 15,000 rp in 2nd, to 49,000 rp in 1st with a sleeper. From Jakarta to Surabaya, an 859-km trip, takes 12-14 hours on the best trains; the fares start at 7700 rp in the 3rd-class Gaya Baru trains. The *Bima Express* sleeper train, through to Surabaya, is marginally slower (two hours) than the *Mutiara Utara*. These deluxe trains cost 50,000 rp in 1st-class for a reclining seat or 54,000 rp with sleeper.

Taxi There are also intercity taxis and minibuses to Bandung that will pick you up and drop you off at your hotel. Fares start at 12,000 rp per person; they're fast and convenient but taxis will only depart when they have five passengers. Parahiyangan (☎ 353434) is at Jalan Wahid Hasyim 13. The 4848 taxi office is at Jalan Prapatan 34 (☎ 348048) and Jalan Kramat Raya 23 (☎ 368488).

Boat Pelni has lots of services out of Jakarta. Ships link Jakarta to Tanjung Pinang (from 38,000 rp economy class), Padang (from 34,500 rp economy class), Ujung Pandang (from 50,000 rp economy class), Belawan (from 51,500 rp economy class), Pontianak (33,500 rp economy class) and via Semarang and Surabaya to other destinations in Kalimantan and Sulawesi.

The Pelni ticket office (☎ 358398) is at Jalan Pintu Air 1 behind the Istiqlal Mosque. It's open from 8.30 am to noon and 1 to 2 pm on Monday to Friday, and from 8.30 am to noon Saturday.

Cargo Boat The Pelni cargo ship to Pontianak sometimes takes passengers (28,000 rp economy class), but it depends on the cargo carried and there's never a regular service. For details, check with the Pelni office at Tanjung Priok harbour (☎ 491014, 493184) but tickets have to be bought from the Pintu Air office.

The best place to get information on non-Pelni cargo boats is the old harbour, Sunda Kelapa. The staff at the harbour master's office (*kantor syahbander*) are the people to see first. Most of them speak excellent English and they're very helpful. It's also worth going around all the ships at the dock. The Pulau Indah company, for example, has a boat to Tanjung Pinang once a month; it costs 30,000 rp and takes three days. At least one cargo ship a day goes to Pontianak in Kalimantan; the going passenger rate is a bargain at about 23,000 rp. Conditions on board these cargo ships are spartan. Usually you have to sleep on a sheltered deck. Occasionally, there's a small cabin for hire for an additional 5000 to 10,000 rp or so.

Getting Around

To/From the Airport In 1985 Jakarta's old central Kemayoran domestic airport and Halim International Airport were both superseded by the Sukarno-Hatta International Airport, 35 km west of the centre. A toll road links the airport to the city and a journey between the two takes 45 minutes to an hour, although it can take longer in the rush hour.

There's a Damri Airport bus every 30 minutes to Gambir station (near Jalan Jaksa) and four other points in Jakarta. It costs 3000 rp per person. Alternatively a taxi to Jalan Thamrin would cost about 25,000 rp. You can do it more cheaply if you can stop the driver from taking the toll-road (3000 rp) but this takes longer. Going to the airport, you can sometimes negotiate with a driver to take you for a flat 20,000 rp including the toll. Most of the budget hotels on Jalan Jaksa can book this for you.

Many hotels have shared minibus services to the airport for about 10,000 rp. The Sabang Metropolitan Hotel on Jalan H A Salim has a 9000 rp minibus to the airport daily at 1 pm but you must book a day in advance.

To/From Tanjung Priok Harbour The Pelni ships all arrive at (and depart from) Pelabuhan or Dock No 1. It's two km from the dock – past the Pelni office – to the Tanjung Priok bus station, from where you can take a No 63 bus or pale blue minibus M15 to the Kota city bus terminal. From Kota you can then take a No 70 or P1 bus to Jalan Thamrin. Take care, because these buses are notorious for pickpockets. The harbour is 20 km from the centre of the city so allow an hour, at least, to get there, particularly on public transport. A taxi should cost around 6000 rp but eliminates the concern about thievery en route.

Bus In Jakarta everything is at a distance. It's hot and humid and hardly anybody walks – you will need to use some form of transport to get from one place to another. Jakarta has probably the most comprehensive city bus network of any major Indonesian city. Its buses, however, tend to be hopelessly crowded, particularly during rush hours. Jakarta's pickpockets are notoriously adept and they're great bag slashers too. Rip-offs are regularly reported on buses No 70, 700, P1 and P11. So take care. Indeed, if you are carrying a camera or anything else of value, you would be wise to spring for a taxi.

Around town there are lots of big regular

city buses charging a fixed 200 rp fare. The big express 'Patas' buses charge 500 rp and their air-con buses cost 1000 rp; these are usually less crowded – well, less so by Jakarta's standards. These services are supplemented by orange toy-sized buses which cost 250 rp and, in a few areas, by pale blue Mikrolet buses which cost 300 rp. You need to be a midget for the latter though.

If you'll be using city buses then a copy of *See for Yourself* (from the Jakarta Tourist Office) will be useful as it contains a fairly comprehensive list of the city bus routes. Sarinah department store on Jalan Thamrin is a good landmark for Jalan Jaksa, and some of the more useful buses that will drop you there include:

408, P11	Cililitan bus station to Jalan Thamrin
59	Pulo Gadung bus station to Jalan Thamrin
16	Kalideres bus station to Jalan Thamrin
70, P1, P11	Kota railway station to Jalan Thamrin
10	Pasar Senen railway station to Jalan Thamrin
34	Jalan Thamrin to 'TIM' on Jalan Cikini Raya
10, 12, 16	Jalan Thamrin to Blok M, Kebayoran
507	Jalan Kebon Sirih to Pulo Gadung bus station

'P' equals 'Patas', express
10, 12 and 110 go by the post office

Taxi Taxis in Jakarta have real working meters and most drivers use them these days without having to be asked. Jakarta has a large fleet of taxis and it's usually not too difficult to find one. Many residents swear by Bluebird cabs (pale blue) which have a radio call service (☎ 325607) and well-maintained cars. Steady Safe (☎ 356322) also has a good reputation. There are several other companies with acceptable service; the only one to avoid is President Taxi, which is famous for its surly drivers, poorly maintained vehicles and refusal to use the meter from bus stations. Occasionally, you might encounter a taxi driver with an otherwise reputable company who will try to con you into a set price rather than going by meter. It's best to simply get out and hail another taxi; there are plenty of them.

Flagfall is 900 rp for the first km, then 50 rp each additional 100 metres, and most trips will cost between 3000 and 5000 rp. Tanjung Priok to Jalan Thamrin, for example, should cost around 4200 rp. It's worth carrying plenty of small notes – another favourite game is 'sorry, no change'. It is customary to let the driver keep any change under 100 rp.

Bajaj & Other Bajajs (pronounced ba-jai) are nothing less than Indian auto-rickshaws – orange or green three-wheelers that carry two passengers (three at a squeeze if you're all dwarf-size) and sputter around powered by noisy two-stroke engines. Always agree on the price beforehand. Short trips – Jalan Jaksa to the post office, for example – will cost between 800 rp and 1000 rp. They're good value, especially during rush hours. Note that bajajs are not allowed along main streets such as Jalan Thamrin, so make sure they won't be simply dropping you off at the border.

Jakarta also has some weird and wonderful means of getting around – like the 'Morris' bemos that run mainly down Jalan Gajah Madah and are all old English Morris vans. And near the Pasar Ikan in Kota there are pushbikes with a padded 'kiddy carrier' on the back!

Car If you feel up to driving yourself around, Jakarta has branches of three major rent-a-car operators. National Car Rental (☎ 332006) is in the Kartika Plaza Hotel, Jalan Thamrin 10. Avis Rental Car (☎ 341964) is at Jalan Diponegoro 25 and they also have a desk at the Hotel Sari Pacific (☎ 3203707 ext 1281) on Jalan Thamrin. Hertz Car Rental (☎ 371208) is at the Mandarin Hotel on Jalan Thamrin.

Becak Becaks (pedal-powered rickshaws) are a rare sight around Jakarta these days but not so very long ago they were probably the biggest source of employment in the city. Since becaks were first introduced by the Japanese and used for hauling goods within the old city their use has spread all over Java and in the 1960s there were about 400,000 in Jakarta alone.

Over the last 15 years or so, Jakarta's becak men have been pushed back to side-streets by regulations aimed at tidying up the city. Permits for becaks are not renewed once they expire and whole fleets of becaks have been shipped out to country towns. Becaks are banned from the city centre before 10 pm but they survive in the less accessible kampongs and you'll find a surprising number of becaks in areas like Glodok. In fact, it's estimated that there are probably about 24,000 still in the city. They rarely venture onto Jakarta's heavily trafficked streets but late at night the odd solitary becak man can even be seen pedalling down Jakarta's main boulevard, Jalan Thamrin.

AROUND JAKARTA
Pulau Seribu/Thousand Islands

Scattered across the Java Sea to the north of Jakarta are these tropical islands, called Pulau Seribu or Thousand Islands, although they are actually only 112 in number. The entire island group has a population of 13,000 and almost half of these people live on just one island, Pulau Kelapa. So far only a few of the islands have been developed as tourist attractions, such as Pulau Bidadari, Pulau Pelangi and Pulau Putri. Some of the others are privately owned but many of them have no permanent population at all, and there are some beautiful beaches and good opportunities for scuba diving or simply exploring.

Jakarta's 'offshore' islands start only a few km out, in the Bay of Jakarta. Best known of these is Pulau Bidadari, which has been developed into a locally popular resort. It attracts a few tourists on day trips but it has been a big hit with Jakartans, particularly on weekends when it can be very crowded. The sea around Bidadari is not so clear. From Bidadari you can visit other nearby islands like Pulau Untung Jawa, Pulau Kahyangan,

Pulau Kelor (which has the ruins of an old Dutch fort), or Pulau Onrust where the remains of an old shipyard from the 18th century can be explored. Bidadari has bungalow accommodation, a restaurant, a bar and a small shop. There are camping sites on Pulau Kahyangan and Untung Jawa.

Islands good for swimming and diving include Pulau Damar, Pulau Tikus and Pulau Pari. They're within reasonable day-tripping distance of Jakarta and also reached from the Ancol Marina, but boats have to be chartered. You can also charter boats from Sunda Kelapa harbour – Pulau Panggang, for example, is a four-hour trip and you can reach other islands from there.

Getting There & Away To get to Bidadari take a boat from the Marina at Ancol. The round trip is 8200 rp and it takes about one hour to get out there. On weekdays a boat departs at 10.30 am, returning at 3 pm. On Saturdays there are departures at 10.30 am and 2 pm but only one service back at 4 pm. On Sundays and holidays boats depart at 8 and 10.30 am, returning from Bidadari at 2 and 4 pm.

Pulau Seribu Paradise

Much further north, among the more unpeopled islands and some of Indonesia's most beautiful coral reefs, four islands have been developed as Jakarta's tropical paradise. Pulau Putri, Pulau Pelangi, Pulau Perak and Pulau Papa Theo all cater for the affluent traveller, although skin diving enthusiasts will find slightly (just) cheaper accommodation and a 'serious dive camp' at the latter island.

On Pulau Putri and Pulau Pelangi there are small native-style huts and larger bungalows with air-conditioning, all overlooking the sea. Pulau Papa Theo dive camp has 10 huts and there are also two lodges for groups of up to 10 people. It's possible to take a hut for one night for from US$80 on weekdays/weekends but there are package trips offered which work out more cheaply. Rates include accommodation and three meals but

not transport to the islands. Pulau Perak is for day trips from the other three islands, but if you bring camping gear you can spend the night there for a nominal charge.

Scuba diving costs US$25 per dive or US$55 per day, including equipment and guide. Basic scuba instruction leading to a certificate is US$40.

Getting There & Away Transport is by boat or light aircraft. A daily boat trip from Ancol Marina takes four hours, US$60 round trip. Daily flights connect Jakarta with Pulau Panjang. The flight takes 25 minutes and then there's a 25-minute boat transfer from the air strip on Pulau Panjang to the other islands, for a total round-trip fare of US$160. For further details and bookings visit the Putri Pulau Seribu Paradise office (☎ 359333) in the Jakarta Theatre building or contact Pulau Seribu Paradise (☎ 515884), Setia Budi Building, Block C1, Jalan H R Rasuna Said, Jakarta. Alternatively, contact dive shops such as Dive Indonesia (☎ 370108 ext 76024) or the Jakarta Dive School (☎ 583051 ext 9037) and they will be happy to organise your transport and supply your diving equipment.

West Java

The province of West Java has a population of 32.5 million, an area of 46,300 sq km and Bandung as its capital. It is historically known as Sunda, the home of the Sundanese people and their culture. West Java is also the region of perhaps the most extreme contrasts. It is here, on the flattest, hottest coastline, that you will find the 'special territory' of Jakarta and all the noise, confusion and squalor of Indonesia's largest city. Yet geographically the rest of the province merges imperceptibly into Central Java. It is predominantly mountainous and agricultural, with lush green valleys and high volcanic peaks surrounding the capital, Bandung, at the core of the region. West Java is also strongly Islamic, yet in the remote

Kendeng mountains there is still a small isolated community known as the Baduis, believed to be descendants of the ancient Sundanese who fled from Islam more than 400 years ago. The name Sunda is of Sanskrit origin and means 'pure' or 'white'.

For travellers, West Java has tended to be a place to whiz through between Jakarta and destinations east but, apart from its historic and cultural centres, West Java offers one of the best beaches in Indonesia at Pangandaran and a fine backwater trip along the coastal lagoons to Central Java. Other major attractions, though remote and isolated, are the famous Krakatau Islands off the west coast and the unique Ujung Kulon National Park in the south-west of the province.

History

Early in its history, Sunda, unlike the great land-based Javanese kingdoms, was primarily dependent on overseas trade. It was not only an important spice centre in its own right but also a transhipment point for trade with Asia. West Java was the first contact point in Indonesia for the Dutch and earlier it was one of the first regions to come into contact with Indian traders and their culture. Ancient stone inscriptions record an early Hindu influence during the reign of King Purnawarman of Taruma and one of his rock edicts can be seen near Bogor. In the 7th century Taruma was destroyed by the powerful Sumatran-based Buddhist kingdom of Srivijaya. Much later, Hinduism reasserted itself alongside Buddhism when the Pajajarans ruled the region. They're chiefly remembered for constructing the first trading settlement on the site of Old Batavia when it was called Sunda Kelapa, and for establishing trading relations with the Portuguese.

The first half of the 16th century saw the military expansion of the Muslim state of Demak and in 1524 Muslim power first made itself felt in West Java. In that year Demak's general, Sunan Gunungjati, took the port of Banten and then Sunda Kelapa. Some time after 1552 he became the first of the kings of Cirebon, which today is the least visited and thus the most surprising of Java's

surviving sultanates. Banten, on the other hand, was the maritime capital of the only Muslim state to remain independent of the great Javanese power, Mataram, but today it is little more than a small fishing village.

After the fall of Melaka in 1511 Chinese, Arabs and Indians poured into Banten and it became a major trading centre for Muslim merchants who made use of the Sunda Straits (Selat Sunda) to avoid the Portuguese. Gunungjati's successor, Hasanuddin, spread Banten's authority to the pepper-producing district of Lampung in south Sumatra. His son, Maulana Yusuf, finally conquered the inland Hindu kingdom of Pajajaran in 1579 and so carved out a huge slice of Sunda as Banten's own domain.

Towards the end of the century Banten felt the first impact of a new force – the Europeans. In 1596 the Dutch made their first appearance at Banten, in 1600 the English established an East India Company trading post and two years later the Dutch formed a counterpart company, the VOC. Banten naturally became a centre of fierce Anglo-Dutch competition and the Dutch soon moved out and seized Jakarta instead, henceforth to be their capital as Batavia.

The VOC's most formidable opponent was the Mataram empire which was extending its power over parts of West Java but Banten, so close to their own headquarters, remained a troublesome rival. It not only harboured foreign competitors but a powerful ruling house. Hostilities reached their peak with the accession of Banten's greatest ruler, Sultan Agung, in 1651. With the help of European captains Agung established an impressive trading network. He defied both Mataram and the VOC on more than one occasion before civil war within the ruling house led to Dutch intervention and his defeat and capture in 1683.

By the end of the 17th century Dutch power had taken a great step forward in the west, and throughout the colonial era West Java remained under more direct control than the rest of the country. It was closer to Batavia but, more importantly, much of the land was ceded to the Dutch by Mataram in

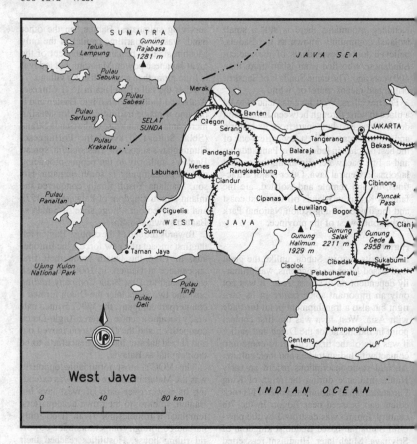

West Java

0   40   80 km

return for military aid, while in Central and East Java the kingdoms became Dutch protectorates.

Sundanese Arts

Music The most characteristic Sundanese instrument is the *kecapi*, accompanied by the suling. The kecapi is a type of lute (it looks a bit like a dulcimer, actually) which is plucked; the suling is a soft-toned bamboo flute which fades in and out of the long vibrating notes of the kecapi. Another traditional instrument is the angklung – a device of bamboo pieces of differing lengths and diameter loosely suspended in a bamboo frame – which is shaken to produce hollow echoing sounds. Originally the angklung was tuned to a five-note scale but it's being revived using Western octaves and can be played by a single performer or a large orchestra. In Cirebon there's a variation on Bandung-style kecapi-suling music, called *tarling* because it makes use of gui*tar* and su*ling*.

Another traditional Sundanese music form is *gamelan degung*. This dynamic gamelan style is played by a small ensemble similar to the Central Javanese gamelan with

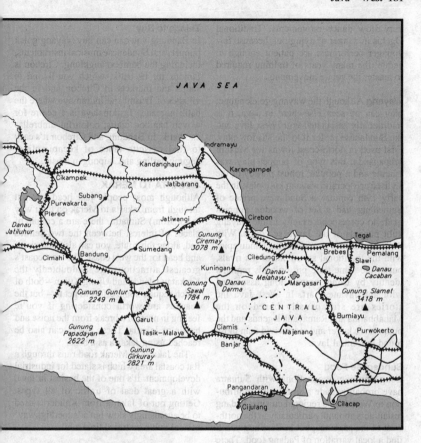

the addition of the *degung*, which is a set of small suspended gongs, and the suling. It is less somnambulant and more rhythmic than Central Javanese gamelan music, yet not as hectic as the Balinese forms.

Nowadays, West Java is famous for the more modern music and dance form called Jaipongan, which is found mostly in Bandung and Jakarta. Jaipongan features dynamic drumming coupled with erotic and sometimes humorous dance movements that include elements of *silat* (Indonesian martial arts) and even New York-style break dancing. Jaipongan dance/music is a rather

recent derivation of a more traditional Sundanese form called Ketuktilu, in which a group of professional female dancers (sometimes prostitutes) dance for male spectators. The newer form involves males and females dancing alone and together, although in lengthy performances Jaipongan songs are usually interspersed with the older Ketuktilu style.

Other Sundanese dance forms include Longser, Joker and Ogel. Longser and Joker are couples dances which involve the passing of a sash between the couples. Ogel is an extremely difficult form that features very slow dance movements. Traditional Ogel is in danger of dying out, because few younger performers are patient enough to endure the many years of training required to master the subtle movements.

Wayang Although the wayang golek puppet play can be seen elsewhere in Java, it is traditionally associated with West Java and the Sundanese prefer it to the shadow play. First used in north-coast towns for Muslim propaganda, this type of puppet play was Islamic and a popular, robust parody of the stylised aristocratic wayang kulit play. In the early 19th century a Sundanese prince of Sumedang had a set of wooden puppets made to correspond exactly to the wayang kulit puppets of the Javanese courts. With these he was able to perform the Hindu epics with the traditional splendour of his rivals, but at the same time preserve his regional identity by using puppets long associated with anti-Javanese art. In West Java the stories are still usually based on the Mahabharata and Ramayana legends and the puppets are larger and more vivid than those found in Central Java.

Sundanese Food

Long-standing connections with Sumatra have probably made a significant contribution to West Java's regional cuisine. Padang restaurants abound, particularly in the north-west of the province, but in Bandung you'll find a local variation of Padang food. There is the same emphasis on meat but, while the Sumatrans go for the really hot stuff, Sundanese food is spicy rather than chilli hot. Popular dishes include: *pepes usus*, chicken steamed in bamboo leaf; steamed goldfish; fish flavoured with *laos*, a spice rather like ginger; and spiced buffalo meat similar to Sumatran rendang. There is often a plate of *petei* (huge broad beans), tempe, salad and sambal. *Soto Bandung* is a soup made from tripe – it's another Sundanese speciality of Bandung. In Cirebon, the local speciality is *nasi lengko*, rice with bean sprouts, tahu, tempe, fried onion, cucumber and peanut sauce.

Things to Buy

In Bandung you can can buy wayang golek puppets and Sundanese musical instruments, including the bamboo angklung. Cirebon is famous for its batik, which you'll find in shops and markets in Cirebon and in the villages of Trusmi and Indramayu where the batik is made. Tasikmalaya is a centre for woven bamboo crafts, colourful umbrellas and batik. In Bandung and Cirebon it's easy to find cassette tapes of kecapi-suling, degung, tarling and Jaipongan music.

JAKARTA TO MERAK

Although most people just head straight through from Jakarta to Merak on their way to (or from) Sumatra, there are a couple of places of interest between the two centres and, along this route, you can also branch off and head for the west coast. The west coast's greatest attractions are undoubtedly the Krakatau Islands and Ujung Kulon – both of which require some effort to get to – but the beaches are worth considering if you're feeling in need of a break from the noise and hassle of Jakarta. These places can also be reached using Jakarta as a base.

The Jakarta to Merak road runs through a flat coastal area which is slated for industrial development. It's one of the busiest in Java, with a great deal of traffic of all types. Getting out of Jakarta from Kalideres used to be agonisingly slow but a 'superhighway' has cut down on travel time a bit.

Serang

This town, 90 km west of Jakarta, is important mainly for its crossroads function. From here you can turn off to Banten, 10 km north of the town on the coast, or turn south and take the inland route via Pandeglang to Labuhan and Carita Beach on the west coast, which in turn is the jumping off point for Krakatau and Ujung Kulon. An interesting alternative route to Carita is to continue on from Serang to Cilegon and take a colt from there along the coastal road.

Serang is a convenient base from which to visit Banten but only very basic accommodation is available and there's no real need to stay here. If you take an early morning bus from Jakarta and a late afternoon bus back (or on to the west coast) you're going to have all the time in the world to fit in a trip to explore Banten's ruins. The bus between Jakarta and Serang takes roughly two hours.

Places to Stay Along Jalan A Yani, which runs from the Ciceri bus station to the town square, there's a collection of rather drab and dismal shacks masquerading as hotels – OK for a night but not much longer. Near the bus station there's the *Hotel Abadi* (☎ 81641) with rooms costing from 7000 rp, and further down is the similarly priced *Penginapan Buyis*. The latter is run by friendly people and it's clean enough but bathrooms consist of a toilet, tap and heavy-duty garbage can. Still further down, near the square, the *Hotel Serang* is another possibility.

Banten

Due north of Serang, on the coast, are the few fragments of the great maritime capital of the Banten sultanate where the Dutch and English first landed on Java to secure trade and struggle for economic supremacy. Banten reached its peak during the reign of Sultan Agung (1651-83) but he unwisely clashed with rising Dutch power in Batavia. In 1680 Agung declared war on Batavia but, before he could make a move, internal conflict within the royal house led to Dutch intervention on behalf of the ambitious crown prince. Agung fled from Banten but finally surrendered in 1683 and his defeat marked the real beginning of Dutch territorial expansion in Java. Not only was Banten's independence at an end but their English East India Company rivals were driven out, which effectively destroyed British interests in Java.

The Dutch maintained trading interests in Banten for a time but they did a good job of demolishing the place in the 19th century. At some point too this coastline silted up and Banten became a ghost town, a small dusty fishing village which is really all that Banten is today.

The chief landmark of a prosperous era is

the 16th-century Mesjid Agung mosque which dominates the village, and this is perhaps the most interesting part of a visit to Banten. It's a good example of early Hindu-Islamic architecture, but the mosque's great white lighthouse of a minaret was reputedly designed by a Chinese Muslim and it's quite unlike any other in Java. A narrow staircase spirals up through the thick walls of the minaret to two high balconies, from the top you have a fine view of the coastline.

The mosque also has a small archaeological museum with a very modest collection of old clay pipes and weapons including a few of the long, iron, chained spikes which the 'Debus players' are famous for. Banten has long been a centre for practitioners of the Debus tradition which is supposed to have come from India. These are Islamic ascetics who reputedly engage in masochistic activities such as plunging sharp weapons into their bodies (without drawing blood!), and are able to control pain and fear by the strength of their faith. It's said that in Banten this was originally part of the training of the invincible special soldiers to the court.

Directly across from the mosque is the large grass-covered site of Hasanuddin's fortified palace, the Surosowan, which was wrecked in the bloody civil war during the reign of Sultan Agung and rebuilt, only to be razed to the ground by the Dutch in 1832.

Other points of interest around the mosque include the massive ruins of Fort Speelwijk to the north-west, which now overlook an expanse of sand-silt marsh, although at one time it stood on the sea's edge. The fort was built by the Dutch in 1682 and finally abandoned by Governor-General Daendels at the beginning of the 19th century. Opposite the entrance to the fort is a Chinese temple, dating from the 18th century, which is still in use. Back along the road to Serang are the huge crumbling walls and archways of the Kaibon palace and near it is the tomb of Maulana Yusuf, who died in 1580.

Pulau Dua Bird Sanctuary Off the coast at Banten, Pulau Dua is one of Indonesia's major bird sanctuaries. The island has a large resident population – mainly herons, storks and cormorants – but peak time is between March and July when great numbers of migratory birds (an estimated 50,000) flock here for the breeding season. At low tide the island may be accessible by land now that the mudflats between it and the mainland have silted up; otherwise it's a half-hour boat ride from the Karanghantu harbour in Banten. A PHPA guard is stationed on the island and there's a watchtower and guesthouse but if you are planning to stay bring both food and water. For more information you could try the PHPA office in Bogor.

Getting There & Away Colts depart from the Pasar Lama bus stand (a bemo ride from the Ciceri bus station) in Serang. The fare is 600 rp and they will drop you right by the mosque.

Cilegon

Cilegon, 20 km north-west of Serang, is almost 100% industrial and dominated by the vast Krakatau steel plant. This giant enterprise was begun in the early 1960s with Russian aid, partially dismantled when the Russians were expelled after the 1965 coup, and has now been resurrected with foreign aid and backing from Pertamina.

MERAK

Right on the north-western tip of Java, 140 km from Jakarta, Merak is the terminus for ferries shuttling to and from Panjang and Bakauheni on the southern end of Sumatra. It's of little interest otherwise – just an arrival and departure point – and most people shoot straight through.

Places to Stay

If you do have a reason to stay you could try the *Hotel Anda* – singles/doubles with fan and mandi at 10,000/12,500 rp – or the *Hotel Robinson* next door. They're standard, clean losmen and both are on Jalan Florida (Pulorida), just across the railway line opposite the bus station. The bus station cafeteria is pretty good.

For those determined to pay more, there's

the modern *Merak Beach Hotel* (☎ 367808 ext 164) several km out of town on the road to Cilegon. It has small air-con units on the beach, a bar and restaurant; singles/doubles cost from 40,000/52,000 rp. The hotel is also known as the Ramayana.

Getting There & Away

The bus station and the railway station in Merak are right on the docks and only a hundred metres or so apart.

Bus A bus from Jakarta (Kalideres) to Merak takes about three hours and costs 2000 rp. There are plenty of them, operating almost every ten minutes from 3 am to midnight.

Train From Jakarta, trains for Merak depart from the Tanah Abang railway station at 6 am and 5 pm. The fare is 1550 rp 3rd class-only and the trip takes about four hours. The day train is faster and links up with the daytime ferry service to Strengsem (Panjang). Going the other way, trains depart Merak at 6.30 am and 4.30 pm.

Ferry The ferry to Strengsem leaves at 11 am and 11 pm from the dock near the train station and takes four to six hours. It costs from 1500 rp in 3rd class to 4150 rp in 1st class. Ferries to Bakauheni depart every hour from the dock near the bus station and the trip takes 1½ hours; it's 900 rp in 3rd class and 2000 rp in 1st class.

The Merak to Bakauheni crossing is becoming one of the busiest waterways in Indonesia as more people are encouraged by better roads including the Trans-Sumatran Highway. One disadvantage of this progress is that there can be enormous traffic jams during the holiday seasons, although passenger cars and buses are usually given priority over goods trucks.

DOWN THE WEST COAST

At Cilegon the road branches south to Anyer and runs close to the sea all the way to Labuhan along a flat green coastal strip bordered by long stretches of white-sand beach. Here there are masses of coconut palms and banana trees and, along the roadside, piles of old white coral which the villagers collect to make building lime. The area is fairly sparsely populated with small fishing settlements and coconut ports. This is perhaps simply because the land isn't suitable for intensive rice agriculture but it's also said that survivors of the Krakatau eruption, and succeeding generations, believed it to be a place of ill omen and never returned.

From the coast, particularly around Carita, you'll often see a mass of lights strung out across the sea at night. They're the night fishermen, fishing for shrimp, prawns and lobster from platforms called *bagang* – small bamboo huts on stilts firmly embedded in the sea bottom way out from the shore.

Anyer

The Anyer beach, 15 km south of Cilegon, is an up-market resort principally frequented by the expatriate community working at the Cilegon steel plant. The most interesting story about Anyer is that this was once the biggest Dutch port in Selat Sunda before being totally destroyed by tidal waves generated by Krakatau. One Dutch freighter is said to have been pushed 100 km inland by the tidal waves. The Anyer lighthouse was built by the Dutch at the instigation of Queen Wilhelmina in 1885 after the disaster.

From here you can hire a boat, for about 35,000 rp return, to make the 1½ hour trip to explore the deserted island of Sangiang. Surrounded by coral reef, it is seven square km of jungle, mangrove and monkeys. Parts of the island are inhospitably swampy and mosquito-ridden (so be prepared) but on the east coast there are small coves with coloured coral and shells washed up on the shore where you could possibly camp. The water is fine for swimming and snorkelling but be careful of the tides. To the south of the island are the remains of Japanese fortifications built to control the narrow strait between Java and Sumatra during WW II.

Places to Stay The *Anyer Beach Hotel* (☎ Jakarta 510322), part of Pertamina's hotel chain, is a modern motel complex with individual beachfront cottages – all with air-con, bathroom and hot and cold running water – costing from 149,000 rp (plus tax & service). The resort has a restaurant and bar, swimming pool and bowling alley.

A new luxury hotel, the posh *Mambruk Beach Resort* has just opened, with a poolside bar, three restaurants and comfortable air-con rooms ranging in price from 122,000 rp standard to 343,000 rp deluxe.

Karang Bolong

There's another good beach here, six km south of Anyer and 30 km north of Labuhan, where a huge stand of rock forms a natural archway from the land to the sea.

LABUHAN

Aside from the coastal road from Anyer, Labuhan can also be reached from Jakarta by taking the more direct inland route through Serang and Pandeglang. The port of Labuhan is really only important as a junction town and this is where you'll find the PHPA office for the Ujung Kulon National Park. Otherwise it's a dreary, dirty little place, where the beach is pretty much the local toilet. Worse still, female travellers report being hassled here.

Ujung Kulon Permits

If you're planning a trip to Ujung Kulon National park (for more information see the Ujong Kulon section later in this chapter) you must first get a permit and make reservations for accommodation at the Labuhan PHPA office, which is about two km from the centre of town on the road to Carita. They have maps of the reserve and the PHPA staff will also arrange boat transport to the Ujung Kulon peninsula. The office is open from 7 am to 2 pm Monday to Thursday, to 11 am on Friday and until noon on Saturday. It's closed on Sunday.

Places to Stay & Eat

You can stay at the very basic *Hotel Citra Ayu* for 5500/9000 rp for singles/doubles with a shared toilet, and 11,000 rp with private bath, or at the *Hotel Caringin* where rooms cost 12,000 rp with bath, but with a pleasant hotel so close by at Carita there's not much point in doing so.

CARITA BEACH

There's a German-run beach resort at Carita, seven km north of Labuhan. It has a good white-sand beach and swimming and, about five minutes out by boat, good snorkelling on the reef. Masks, surfboards and windsurfers can be hired from the hotel, although most of the equipment is in poor condition.

This is a popular base for visits to the Krakatau Islands and the Ujung Kulon National Park – if you're interested in either, ask to see the hotel's free video documentary about the 1883 eruption and its effects on the west coast. Around Carita there are plenty of opportunities to go wandering along the beach or inland. About two km from Carita across the rice paddies see the village of Sindanglaut ('end of the sea') where the giant tsunami of 1883 ended. The Curug Gendang waterfall is a six-km hike through the hills and jungle.

Places to Stay

The *Carita Krakatau Beach Hotel* has simple 'Badui-style' wooden cottages strung out along the beach, a few hostel rooms and a restaurant/bar on a pleasant shaded verandah. It's a very easy-going, friendly place and the hostel rooms are good value – basic but clean with big comfortable beds and towels provided. Rooms in the hostel across the road from the beach cost 10,000 rp or 16,000 rp with bath during the week, 22,000 rp on weekends. On the beachfront, spacious rooms with mandi cost 70,000 rp during the week, 120,000 rp on weekends. There are also a few more expensive beachfront cottages. Although cheaper economy rooms are said to exist, they are rarely available. If you're coming from Jakarta you can get a Krakatau newsletter from the tourist office that will get you a 25% discount on your first night (10% on weekends). During the low season you may be able to negotiate lower prices. One budget alternative to the Carita

Beach Hotel, about one km away from the resort, is *Losman Gogana*, offering what some travellers called clean, basic rooms for 9000 rp.

North of the Carita Krakatau Beach Hotel, *Desiana Cottages* (☎ Jakarta 593316) has clean, comfortable bungalows with kitchens and dining rooms, starting at 65,000 rp on weekdays (85,000 rp on weekends). A two-bedroom bungalow with two double beds costs 95,000 rp on weekdays (120,000 rp on weekends).

Across the road and north a bit is the *Wisma Wira Carita* (☎ Jakarta 341240). It also has large, clean rooms for 50,000 rp during the week and 75,000 rp on weekends. Nearby, the *Narida Beach Inn* has wooden bungalows (doubles) at 47,000 rp.

Places to Eat

The restaurant at the *Carita Krakatau Beach Hotel* is outdoors and serves both Indonesian and Western food. Prices are reasonable but not cheap – the fish of the day with rice is 7000 rp and a small beer is 2800 rp – but portions are large and the food is pretty good. Noodles/fried rice cost 4200/5100 rp. The *Desiana* and the *Wisma Wira Carita* both have restaurants but few people seem to eat at either of these hotels. The latter restaurant is the cheaper, with fried rice at 3700 rp and a small beer at 2500 rp.

If you're on a tight budget, head south to the warungs close by on the main road. The one nearest to Carita Krakatau Beach Hotel has good nasi goreng and mie kuah for 950 rp and the local people are delighted to have visitors. There are also a number of local children who tour the beach selling pineapples and bananas and you can always buy basic foods in Labuhan.

The massage women who frequent the beach in front of the Carita Krakatau Beach Hotel will also deliver home-cooked Indonesian meals to guests upon request.

Getting There & Away

Buses depart hourly from the Kalideres station in Jakarta for Labuhan. The trip, through Serang and Pandeglang, takes about three to four hours on a winding road and costs 2500 rp. (Some travellers claim bus drivers tried to rip them off, asking as much as 5000 rp.) Other travellers said they had to bargain for their fare. From the Labuhan bus station, walk about 100 yards and flag down a colt which for 300 rp will take you to the Carita Beach minibus stand, where you can catch another colt to the hotel for 600 rp. More expensively, a becak will take you directly from the bus station to the Carita Beach minibus stand for 3000 rp (where you can either catch a colt to the hotel for 600 rp or, after some hard bargaining, have the becak take you straight from the bus station to the Carita Beach Hotel for 10,000 rp). The Carita Beach Hotel is affiliated with the Menteng Hotel (☎ 330846) in Jakarta, Jalan Gondangdia Lama 28, which operates a transport service on Friday afternoons for 30,000 rp.

Buses from Merak go to Carita via Cilegon in about 2½ hours and cost 1400 rp. You can also take buses from Merak to Bogor for 1000 rp and to Bandung for 1800 rp, departing at 7.45, 11.20 am and 3.15 pm.

These often fill up, so get to the bus terminal early.

KRAKATAU

The legendary Krakatau lies only 50 km from the West Java coast. Today only a small part of the original volcano remains but when Krakatau blew itself apart in 1883, in one of the world's greatest and most catastrophic eruptions, the effects were recorded far beyond Selat Sunda and it achieved instant and lasting infamy.

For centuries Krakatau had been a familiar nautical landmark for much of the world's maritime traffic which was funnelled through the narrow Selat Sunda. The volcano had been dormant since 1680 and was widely regarded as extinct but from May through to early August in 1883 passing ships reported moderate activity. By 26 August Krakatau was raging and the explosions became more and more violent. At 10 am on 27 August Krakatau erupted with the biggest bang ever recorded on earth. On the island of Rodriguez, more than 4600 km to the south-west, a police chief reported hearing the booming of 'heavy guns from

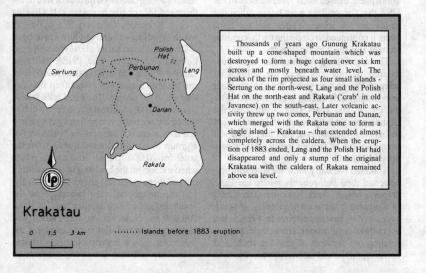

Thousands of years ago Gunung Krakatau built up a cone-shaped mountain which was destroyed to form a huge caldera over six km across and mostly beneath water level. The peaks of the rim projected as four small islands - Sertung on the north-west, Lang and the Polish Hat on the north-east and Rakata ('crab' in old Javanese) on the south-east. Later volcanic activity threw up two cones, Perbunan and Danan, which merged with the Rakata cone to form a single island – Krakatau – that extended almost completely across the caldera. When the eruption of 1883 ended, Lang and the Polish Hat had disappeared and only a stump of the original Krakatau with the caldera of Rakata remained above sea level.

Krakatau

0   1.5   3 km

········ Islands before 1883 eruption

eastward'; in Alice Springs, 3500 km to the south-east, residents also reported hearing strange explosions from the north-west.

With its cataclysmic explosions, Krakatau sent up a record column of ash 80 km high and threw into the air nearly 20 cubic km of rock. Ash fell on Singapore 840 km to the north and on ships as far as 6000 km away; darkness covered Selat Sunda Straits from 10 am on the 27th until dawn the next day. Far more destructive were the great ocean waves triggered by the collapse of Krakatau's cones into its empty belly. Giant tsunamis more than 40 metres high swept over the nearby shores of Java and Sumatra, and the sea wave's passage was recorded far from Krakatau, reaching Aden in 12 hours over a distance 'travelled by a good steamer in 12 days'. Measurable wave effects were even said to have reached the English Channel. Coastal Java and Sumatra were devastated: 165 villages were destroyed and more than 36,000 people were killed.

The following day a telegram sent to Singapore from Batavia (160 km east of Krakatau) reported odd details such as 'fish dizzy and caught with glee by natives'! Three months later the dust thrown into the atmosphere caused such vivid sunsets in the USA that fire engines were being called out to quench the apparent fires, and for three years it continued to circle the earth, creating strange and spectacular sunsets.

The astonishing return of life to the devastated islands has been the subject of scientific study ever since. Not a single plant was found on Krakatau a few months after the event; 100 years later – although the islands are virtually bereft of fauna except for snakes, insects, rats, bats and birds – it seems almost as though the vegetation was never disturbed.

Krakatau basically blew itself to smithereens and died but, roughly where the 1883 eruption began, Anak Krakatau (the 'Child of Krakatau') has been vigorously growing ever since its first appearance in 1928. It has a restless and uncertain temperament, sending out showers of glowing rocks and belching smoke and ashes, but boats can land on the east side and it is possible to climb right up the cinder cones to the caldera. The hike is best made in the early morning when it's cool, which means an overnight trip.

A Guide to Krakatau, by zoologist I W B Thornton, has detailed maps and information and is available at the Carita Krakatau Beach Hotel or from the Krakatau Foundation, PO Box 4507, Jakarta 10001.

Organised Tours

A couple of tour agencies in Jakarta which do pinisi (Makassar-style schooner) tours of Ujung Kulon National Park, including visits to the islands of Krakatau, are: Kalpataru Club (☎ 336545), Kartika Plaza Hotel and Krakatau Ujung Kulon Tours & Travel (☎ 320251), Wisata International Hotel.

Getting There & Away

The islands of Krakatau are about 50 km from the nearest point on Java and getting out there can be a real hassle – during the rainy season there can be strong ocean currents and during July and August there are sometimes strong south-east winds. So the best times to visit are April-June and September-October. When weather conditions are fine it's a long one-day trip, four or five hours there and four or five hours back, but having visited Krakatau we'd say it's definitely worth the effort – *if* you can hire a safe boat.

It's possible to charter a boat yourself from Labuhan or Carita. The PHPA office in Labuhan or the Carita Krakatau Beach Hotel can arrange a boat for 300,000 rp that can take up to 20 people. The hotel tells you in advance that if your boat has to return due to inclement weather, you will not get a refund and they mean it. I encountered members of a group that had chartered a boat from the hotel for 20,000 rp each who had to return when a storm hit the boat as it was just setting out and were given no refund. Alternatively, you can haggle with the fishermen on the beach and get a much smaller boat for about 200,000 rp. However, be forewarned that many of these smaller boats used by the fishermen have a history of engine trouble when they get into the strong currents of

Selat Sunda. It's not unusual for a four-hour trip to turn into two or three days drifting at sea. While researching the previous edition, writer Joe Cummings spent the night on such a boat in high swells along with ten other travellers, and reports that it was a dire situation. In 1986, two foreigners and their Indonesian crew drifted for nearly three weeks before washing up at Bengkulu, Sumatra. If you do decide to take one of the fishing boats, be sure to take along a food reserve, some water and warm clothes in case you go adrift.

UJUNG KULON NATIONAL PARK

Covering about 420 sq km, the Ujung Kulon National Park is on the remote south-western tip of Java, cut off from the rest of the island by a narrow marshy isthmus. Getting there usually involves a long boat ride from the port of Labuhan, roughly midway along the west coast. The best time for visiting Ujung Kulon is the dry season (April to August) when the sea is generally calm and the reserve is not so boggy. Another option is to go by land from Labuhan to Taman Jaya. In Taman Jaya you can hire a guide for a two-day walk down the peninsula.

The main park area is on the peninsula but the park also includes the nearby island of Panaitan and the smaller offshore islands of Peucang and Handeuleum. Much of the peninsula is dense lowland rainforest and a mixture of scrub, grassy plains, swamps, pandanus palms and long stretches of sandy beach on the west and south coasts. Walking trails loop round Gunung Payung on the western tip, along the south coast and north to the park headquarters at Taman Jaya.

Ujung Kulon is best known as the last refuge on Java for the once plentiful one-horned rhinoceros. The shy Javan rhino, however, is an extremely rare sight (there are only about 55 in the park at the time of writing) and you are far more likely to come across less exotic animals such as banteng (wild cattle), wild pigs, otters, squirrels, leaf monkeys and gibbons. There are about 300 blue panthers living in the forest, but these too are a rare sight. Green turtles nest in some

Green turtle

of the bays and Ujung Kulon also has a wide variety of birdlife. On Gili Peucang, rusa deer, long-tailed macaques and big monitor lizards are common, and there is good snorkelling around coral reefs.

Secure your permit for this park, as well as making guide and accommodation arrangements, with the PHPA office in Labuhan. There are a couple of bungalows on Gili Peucang and Gili Handeuleum. Most people base themselves at Peucang – 10 minutes and 6500 rp by boat from the far western tip – and make trips to the mainland from there. If you want to visit the peninsula you must hire a PHPA guide for 10,000 rp a day plus 7500 rp per meal – which the guide will cook. Plus 2700 rp for insurance – in case they have to transport your injured or lifeless body out of the park, according to the PHPA. Two Australian visitors reported making a four-day hike from Peucang along the south coast trail to Karangranjang and walking out of the reserve to the PHPA headquarters at Taman Jaya (about 45 km in total); they also suggested walking around the reserve from Taman Jaya or establishing a base for walks at the Karangranjang PHPA office, which is right on the beach. They didn't spot any rhinos!

Places to Stay

On Gili Handeuleum there is a PHPA guesthouse and another two on Gili Peucang where most visitors stay. Again, make your arrangements with the PHPA office in Labuhan. Each bungalow on Gili Peucang sleeps thirty people and small rooms cost 10,500 rp, larger rooms 14,000 rp. A cook and bedding are provided but you must bring your own food, unless you have made provisions for this in Labuhan. The bungalow on Handeuleum sleeps a maximum of ten. Bring your own food.

Within the park on the peninsula you can camp but there are also huts at regular intervals along the trails. They're basically a roof over your head but along the south coast trail hikers have found a 'good roof' at Citadahan and a good PHPA hut on the beach at Karangranjang. You need to provide bedding and food for yourselves and the PHPA guide, but he cooks. The best place to buy provisions is Labuhan; Taman Jaya is more expensive.

Getting There & Away

You must first get a permit from the PHPA office at Labuhan, so this fishing port on the west coast, about four hours from Jakarta, is the usual jumping-off point for park visits. From Labuhan you can charter the PHPA government boat for around 300,000 rp return to Gili Peucang or Taman Jaya on the mainland; or you can hire a local fishing boat for about half that but you'll have to bargain hard. As with boat rides to Krakatau, try to make sure you hire a seaworthy boat. The boat ride to Peucang takes between six and nine hours depending on the weather.

A cheaper alternative is to take a colt for 2900 rp from Labuhan south to Sumur. From Sumur it's possible to get a ride on a motorbike to Taman Jaya for around 6500 rp. In Taman Jaya you can hire a PHPA guide (10,000 rp per day) for the 45-km walk across the peninsula, or hire a local boat to

Peucang for about 50,000 to 75,000 rp one way. You might also be able to take a colt from Labuhan to Panimbang, the main coconut port on the west coast, charter a local boat to Peucang (37,000 rp one way) and then walk out through the reserve.

BOGOR

Bogor, 60 km south of Jakarta, is most famous for its botanical gardens. In the days before independence, however, this was probably the most important Dutch hill station, midway between the mountains and the heat-ridden plains. Governor- General van Imhoff is credited with its discovery in 1745. He built a large country estate which he named 'Buitenzorg' ('Without a Care') but it was not until 1811 that it was first used as a country residence by Sir Stamford Raffles, during the British interregnum, and not until many years later that Bogor became the semiofficial capital.

Raffles judged it as 'a romantic little village' but Bogor has grown and, other than the gardens, its beauty has faded somewhat. Nevertheless, Bogor has become an important centre for scientific research, including botany, agronomy and forestry. Although the town itself has become more or less a suburb of Jakarta, it makes a good base for nearby mountain walks. Many people visit the gardens from Jakarta or stop off on their way to Bandung and points further east, but Bogor could also be used as a Jakarta base since it only takes 30-45 minutes (depending upon traffic) by bus between the two. From Bogor you can continue east to Bandung via the Puncak Pass or turn south to Pelabuhanratu on the coast.

Though Bogor stands at a height of only 290 metres it's appreciably cooler than Jakarta, but visitors in the wet season should bear in mind the town's nickname: the 'City of Rain'. Bogor has probably the highest annual rainfall in Java and is credited with a record 322 thunderstorms a year.

Orientation & Information

The bus station south of town is about 10 minutes' walk from the botanical gardens entrance. Many of Bogor's losmen and hotels are near the railway station, roughly two km from the bus station.

From the tourist office on the west side of the gardens, at Jalan Ir H Juanda 38, a rough map of the town is available. The office is open from 8 am to 2 pm Monday to Thursday, from 8 am to 6 pm (closed 11 am to 2 pm) on Friday and from 8 am to 1 pm on Saturday. At No 9 on the same street, next to the garden gates, is the headquarters of the PHPA – the official body for administration of all of Indonesia's wildlife reserves and national parks.

The Bogor Regency Tourist Office at Jalan Veteran 2 also has information on things to do in and around Bogor, especially hiking. If you're interested in caving, see Suwesta Wignyakuta at Esta Sports Equipment (☎ (0251) 21050), at the Muria Plaza shopping centre near the railway station. You can also write in advance to Dr Ko at the Federation of Indonesian Speleological Activities (FINSPAC), PO Box 55, Bogor. Dr Ko can arrange speleological expeditions in the area as well as treks along the Buena Vista Trail outside Bogor.

Kebun Raya (Botanical Gardens)

At the heart of Bogor are the huge botanical gardens, known as the Kebun Raya, covering an area of 100 hectares. The gardens were the inspiration of Governor-General Raffles but they were originally laid out by Professor Reinhardt and assistants from Kew Gardens, and officially opened in 1817. It was from these gardens that various colonial cash crops such as tea, cassava, tobacco and cinchona were developed by early Dutch researchers during the so-called Forced Cultivation Period in the 19th century.

The gardens contain streams and lotus ponds and more than 15,000 species of trees and plants; these include 400 types of magnificent palms and the world's largest flower, the *Rafflesia*, which blooms in October. The garden's orchid houses are reputed to contain more than 3000 orchid varieties but unfortunately appear to be closed for the present. Some mutter that visitors have been pinching precious orchid cuttings. Close to the main entrance of the gardens is a small monument in memory of Olivia Raffles who died in 1814 and was buried in Batavia.

The gardens are open between 8 am and 4 pm and although they tend to be very crowded on Sundays, on other days they are very peaceful and a fine place to escape from the hassles and crowds of Jakarta. The entrance fee is 1000 rp during the week and 650 rp on Sundays and holidays.

Zoological Museum

Adjacent to the botanical gardens entrance is a good zoological museum, with a skeleton of a blue whale and other interesting exhibits and a large library of rare botanical books. It is open from 8 am to 2 pm daily except Friday when it closes at 11 am. The entrance fee is 300 rp.

Presidential Palace

In the north-west corner of the botanical gardens, the summer palace of the president was formerly the official residence of the Dutch governors-general from 1870 to 1942. The present huge mansion is not 'Buitenzorg' though; this was destroyed by an earthquake and a new palace was built on the site a few years later in 1856. In colonial days, deer were raised in the parklands to provide meat for banquets. The Dutch elite would come up from the pesthole of Batavia and many huge, glamorous parties were held there. Following independence, the palace was a much favoured retreat for Sukarno, although Suharto has ignored it.

Today the building contains Sukarno's huge art collection of 219 paintings and 156 sculptures (which is reputed to lay great emphasis on the female figure) but the palace is not normally open to the public. The Hotel Salak, opposite the palace, arranges tours for groups of 10 people or you can write directly to the Head of Protocol at the Istana Negara, Jalan Veteran, Jakarta. You need to give at least a week's notice. Through the gates you can see herds of white-spotted deer roaming on the immaculate lawns.

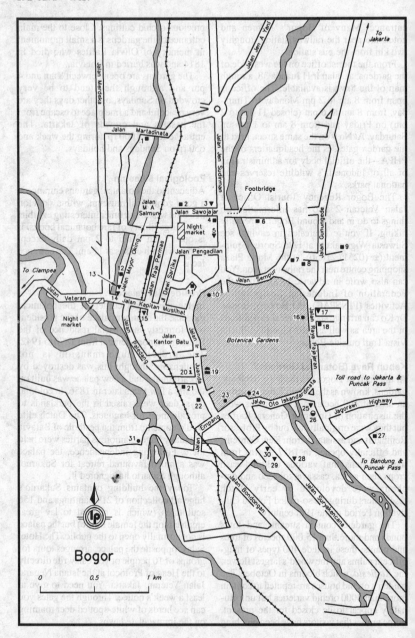

To Jakarta

Jalan Jen A Yeni

Jalan Jen Sudirman

Jalan Martadinata

1

Jalan Merdeka

Footbridge

Jalan MA Salmun

2   3 ▼

Jalan Sawojajar

4

Night market

5

Jalan Pengadilan

6

Jalan Gunungede

7   8 ▼

9 ■

Jalan Sempur

Jalan Raya Pedati

13

12

Jalan Mayor Oking

Jalan Raya Permas

J Dewi Sartika

11

10

Botanical Gardens

16 ▼   17 ▼

18

To Ciampea

Jalan Veteran

14

Jalan Kapitan Muslihat

15 ▼

Jalan Kantor Batu

Jalan Padang

Jalan Ir H Juanda

Night market

Toll road to Jakarta & Puncak Pass

20 ℹ 19

Jagorawi Highway

21

22

23   24

Jalan Oto Iskandardinata

25

26

27 ■

31 ●

Jalan Empang

To Bandung & Puncak Pass

Jalan Raya Pajajaran

30 ▼   28 ▼

29

LP

Bogor

0   0.5   1 km

Jalan Bondongan

Jalan Suryakencana

■ PLACES TO STAY

1	Wisma Mirah
2	Wisma Teladan
4	Elsana Transit Hotel
6	Wisma Karunia
7	Sempur Kencana Guesthouse
8	Hotel Pangrango
9	Bogor Inn
11	Hotel Salak
12	Abu Pensione
18	Wisma Permata
21	Homestay Puri Bali & Pensione Firman
22	Wisma Ramayana
27	Wisma Duta

▼ PLACES TO EAT

3	Bogor Permai Coffee House
5	Lautan Restaurant
13	Food Court
14	Singapore Bakery
15	Hidangan Trio Masakan Padang & Hidangang Puti Bungsu
17	Pizza Hut
25	Kentucky Fried Chicken
28	Adem Ayem Restaurant
29	Dunia Baru Restaurant
30	No 99 Restaurant

OTHER

10	Presidential Palace
16	Orchid House
19	Post Office
20	Visitor Information Centre
23	Zoological Museum
24	Botanical Gardens Entrance
26	Bus Station
31	Gong Foundry

Other Attractions

South of the gardens, on Jalan Batu Tulis and almost opposite the former home of ex-president Sukarno, the 'Batu Tulis' is a small shrine with a stone inscribed by a priest of the region in 1533. A small donation is expected and you have to remove your shoes before entering the shrine. It's said that Sukarno chose this spot for his home because he believed the stone to be a source of mystical power.

One of the few remaining gongsmiths in West Java is Pak Sukarna's at Jalan Pancasan 17. Here you can order gongs and other gamelan instruments and see them being made in the workshop. The gong foundry is a short walk south from the garden gates down Jalan Empang and west across the river. It consists of two buildings facing each other on both sides of the street; on one, a sign reads 'Gong Factory', on the other, 'Gong Home'. On Jalan Kantor Batu, near the tourist office, the Java carpet works of P P Dobbe & Son make wool rugs in natural colours, and attractive floor and doormats out of coconut fibre and sisal.

Places to Stay – bottom end

The *Abu Pensione* (**☎** 322893) is one of the new travellers' standbys, at Jalan Mayor Oking 7, near the train station. It's a friendly, family-run guesthouse with dorm beds at 4000 rp. Clean, comfortable private rooms are 12,000 rp with shared bath, 25,000 to 35,000 rp with a river view and attached bath. All room rates (but not the dorm) include a large breakfast of toast with Mama's delicious homemade pineapple jam, eggs, cheese and coffee or tea. Other tasty, reasonably priced meals are available and there's a pleasant garden terrace that overlooks the river. The effervescent owner, Abu, is a good source of information on do-it-yourself tours around Bogor. Abu also organises tours. The guesthouse provides laundry service, wraps and mails packages, and has an in-house travel agency run by Abu's daughter, Selfiah. To get there from the bus terminal, take a No 3 Daihatsu costing 200 rp and get off at the Muria Plaza shopping centre at the intersection of Jalan Mayor Oking and and Jalan Kapitan Muslihat. Another recommended place is *Homestay Puri Bali* at Jalan Paledang 30, not far from the Kebun Raya. Rooms start at

7000 rp and doubles with private bath range from 16,000 to 20,000 rp. The tariff includes a large breakfast. The similar *Pensione Firman* next door at No 48 offers dorms for 5000 rp, rooms with shared bath at 10,000 rp, and doubles with shared bath for 17,500 to 25,000 rp.

Near the main gates for the botanical gardens at Jalan Ir H Juanda 44 is *Wisma Ramayana*, where rooms range from 14,000 with shared bath to 26,000 rp for quite nice doubles with fan and private bath. Breakfast is included in the tariff and a laundry service is offered. Also near the gardens and not far from the bus station, but a trifle hard to find (ask a local) is the tranquil *Wisma Duta* (☎ 328494) on Jalan Baranangsiang II, Kav 7. The guesthouse's quite decent rooms cost 13,500 to 36,000 rp including breakfast.

Places to Stay – middle

Two more guesthouses, across the river and north of the botanical gardens, are a little out of the way but quiet. *Wisma Karunia* (☎ 323411), Jalan Sempur 34- 37, is a large private home with clean well-kept rooms starting at 13,000 rp for a double with shared bath and rooms with private bath at 21,000 to 28000 rp. There is also a large dorm which costs 7000 rp per bed. *Sempur Kencana* (☎ 328347) at Jalan Sempur 6 is similar and also has a restaurant. Doubles here are 13,000, 16,000 and 21,000 rp. They also have a large double with attached bath for 28,000 rp and a family room with verandah for 43,000 rp. To get to Jalan Sempur from the railway terminal, take a No 7 Daihatsu, or from the bus terminal, a No 8 or 9.

At Jalan Sawojajar 36, the *Elsana Transit Hotel* has doubles with attached bath costing from 23,000 rp including breakfast and tax. It's nothing special, but the staff are friendly and the rooms fairly well kept. On the same street, the *Wisma Teladan* at Jalan Sawojajar 3A offers similar rooms and prices.

Places to Stay – top end

The *Bogor Inn* (☎ 328134) at Jalan Kumbang 12 is run by very nice people and includes a small pool. Rooms with fan cost 20,000 to 40,000 rp and those with air-con run for 30,000 to 50,000 rp, including breakfast.

Wisma Permata (☎ 323402) at Jalan Raya Pajajaran 35 has a pool and a restaurant. It has a few small, fan-cooled rooms for 24,000 to 35,000 rp. Air-con rooms with TV cost 50,000 to 65,000 rp.

The extremely pleasant *Hotel Pangrango* (☎ 328670) at Jalan Pangrango 23 has a pool and air-con rooms with TV ranging in price from 34,000 to 70,000 rp, including breakfast.

The *Hotel Salak* at Jalan Ir H Juanda 8 opposite the palace, is a big colonial hotel with enormous rooms from 26,000 rp without bathroom, from 44,000 rp with bathroom, or 64,000 to 82,000 rp with air-con. It could be quite a nice place to stay if it weren't run-down, decaying and damp. Hordes of lackeys do nothing for the standards in this all but deserted hotel.

Places to Eat

Many of the recommended guesthouses serve food. For good, basic Indonesian fare and Western breakfasts at modest price in a pleasant open-air setting, dine at *Abu Pensione* at Jalan Mayor Oking 28, whether or not you are staying there.

The *Puja Sera Muria* is an open-air hawkers' centre on Jalan Mayor Oking between the Muria Plaza shopping centre and Abu Pensione. It is a good clean place with an assortment of Indonesian and Chinese stalls. The *kwetiaw* (a rice-noodle combo dish) here is particularly good, and ice drinks and beer are available. One of the better little eateries here is the *Es Teler KK*, serving inexpensive lunches. Cheaper food stalls appear at night along Jalan Dewi Sartika and during the day you'll find plenty of food stalls and good fruit at Pasar Bogor, the market close to the garden gates. Behind the bus station is another good area for cheap *warung* food.

Within the Muria Plaza shopping centre, on the corner of Jalan Mayor Oking and Jalan Veteran, you'll find good pastries for breakfast at the *Singapore Bakery* and decent, inexpensive fare next door at the *Food Court*.

Also in the vicinity of the railway station and Muria Plaza on Jalan Kapitan Muslihat are two cheap Padang restaurants: the *Hidangan Trio Masakan Padang* and the *Hidangan Puti Bungsu*. Good Sundanese cuisine is served at *Bunga Seruni* at Jalan Perintis Kemerdekaan 7.

The *Bogor Permai Coffee House*, at Jalan Jenderal Sudirman 20 near Jalan Sawojajar, is a large, semi-modern restaurant and bakery complex offering Chinese and Western fare, including steaks. There is also a supermarket here. The nearby *Lautan Restaurant* at No 15 serves largely Chinese cuisine.

More good and moderately priced Chinese food recommended by locals is found a considerable hike south of the gardens at the upper end of Jalan Siliwangi, the continuation of Jalan Suryakencana. Among these are *No 99* and the nearby *Dunia Baru*, located on the right just after the street's name change, and roughly 100 metres further up on the left just past the petrol station, the excellent *Adem Ayem*.

Bogor also has a *Kentucky Fried Chicken* south of the garden near the bus terminal. On the east side of the garden, you will find a *Pizza Hut*.

Getting There & Away

Bus Buses depart every 10 minutes or so from the Cililitan bus station in Jakarta. Take a Jalan Tol bus which goes via the toll expressway and is a fair bit faster (30-45 minutes) and only marginally more expensive at 800 rp than the buses which go via Cibinong. If you're heading west from Bogor there are buses straight through to Merak, via Jakarta and Serang, for around 1700 rp (four hours). You can also travel by bus between Labuhan on the west coast and Bogor, changing buses in Pandeglang. With the exception of weekends when they are banned from the Puncak Pass and must go the long route via Sukabami, buses run frequently between Bogor and Bandung via the

Puncak Pass. The fare is 1900 rp and the weekday trip takes three hours.

Colts also depart from the bus station for Cibadak, the turn-off point for Pelabuhanratu. Colts to villages around Bogor, including Ciampea, depart from the stand near the railway station.

Train Trains operate to and from Jakarta (Gambir station) at least every hour between 7.20 am and 6.30 pm – OK for day trips but the bus is faster. Avoid the crowded commuter trains in the early morning and late afternoon at all costs. The trip takes about 1½ hours and the fare is 500 rp on 3rd class-only. Faster and more comfortable are the direct *Pakuan* trains which run twice a day non-stop to Jakarta's Gambir station for 1200 rp. Three daily trains operate between Bogor and Sukabumi; they depart Bogor at 6.30 am, 11.30 am and 4.30 pm, and take about two hours. There is no direct railway link to Bandung.

Getting Around

There are lots and lots of bemos for a fixed fare of 200 rp around town for three-wheelers and 250 rp for four-wheelers. They run between the bus station and the main bemo/colt stand near the train station. There are plenty of becaks too, but they're banned from the main street, Jalan Ir H Juanda.

AROUND BOGOR
Purnawarman Stone (Batu Tulis)

From the village of Ciampea, which is about 18 km north-west of Bogor, you can take a colt to the village of Batu Tulis, where sits a huge black boulder on which King Purnawarman inscribed his name and footstep around 450 AD. His inscription, in the Palawa script of South India, reads: 'This is the footstep of King Purnawarman of Tarumanegara kingdom, the great conqueror of the world.'

Another stone inscription of the Taruma kingdom – the Prasati Tugu – can be seen in the National Museum in Jakarta. It refers to the digging of an 11-km-long canal in the

Jakarta area during the reign of Purnawarman – which may have been the first of many efforts to solve Jakarta's flooding problem! The canal was dug by Brahmans in only 21 days and for their labours they were rewarded with 1000 cows. The Ciampea boulder has been raised from its original place, embedded in the shallow water of Sungai Ciaruteun. The inscription on the stone is still remarkably clear after more than 1500 years.

Other Attractions

In Ciampea, you can see one of the last remaining Chinese gamelan ensembles at the home of Lu Liang Beng. He needs two to three days' advance notice to arrange a performance and can be contacted through Abu Pensione in Bogor. Ciampea can be reached from Bogor by a 500 rp, 20-minute Daihatsu ride.

Several travellers have recommended hiking in the Lokapurna area near Bogor. To get there, take a colt (500 rp) to Cibadak, then another to Pasar Jumbat (800 rp). From Pasar Jumbat it's a 5-km walk to Lokapurna, about 1½ hours. Most people spend the night in Lokapurna so they can get in a full day's hiking the next day. From Lokapurna, you can hike either to the local hot springs (air panas), to the volcano crater of Kawa Ratu or, if you're feeling fit, all the way to Pelabuhanratu on the south coast.

Another traveller recommends trekking in the pretty Sungai Ciapus Valley. To get there, charter a Diahatsu to Ciapus and walk one km up a road called Proyek Aneka Usaha Pertanian on the lower slopes of Gunung Salak, past the president's farm. From here you can rock hop into Gunung Salak's gorge or bath in cooling mountain springs.

Places to Stay

In Lokapurna, you can stay at *Haji's* for 5000 rp per night. The *Kopo Hostel* at Cisarua, just outside Bogor, is good value at 4000 rp a bed. See the Bogor to Bandung section for more information.

PELABUHANRATU

A small fishing town 90 km south of Bogor and roughly 150 km south-west of Bandung, Pelabuhanratu is a popular local seaside resort. Though quiet during the week, it can be crowded at weekends and holidays and – unless you camp out – accommodation is fairly expensive. This is mainly a place for hiking – there are magnificent rocky cliffs along West Java's deserted southern coastline, and deep river gorges and caves. There's also a fine beach but the crashing surf can be treacherous. One or two people reportedly are drowned every year in spite of the warning signs which went up after the Bulgarian Ambassador disappeared here some years ago.

Swimming off most of Java's south coast is dangerous. If you want to go into the realms of legend, Pelabuhanratu ('Harbour of the Queen') actually witnessed the creation of Nyai Lara Kidul, the malevolent Goddess who takes fishermen and swimmers off to her watery kingdom. Locals will tell you not to wear green on the beach or in the water (it's her colour), and in the Samudra Hotel a room is always kept unoccupied for offerings to the Queen of the South Seas. The beach is also the scene for an annual Sea Festival in April during which the fishermen sacrifice a buffalo, giving the head to the sea and scattering flowers on the water.

Five km or so west of the Samudra Beach Hotel, at Pantai Karang Hawu, is a towering cliff with caves, rocks and pools which were created by a large lava flow that pushed over the beach. According to legend, it was from the rocks of Karang Hawu that Nyai Lara Kidul leapt into the mighty ocean to regain her lost beauty and never returned. Farther west, near the fishing village of Cisolok, are hot springs. Cikotok, about 30 km from the Samudra, is the site of Java's most important gold and silver mines.

Places to Stay – bottom end

Along the four km between Pelabuhanratu's odoriferous fish market and the big Samudra Beach Hotel, there's a camping place and a

umber of beach bungalows to rent but rates
or the latter are in the 15,000 rp range.

The *Bayu Armta* (☎ Pelabuhanratu 31 or
Bandung 50882) has basic but comfortable
bungalows perched on the edge of a cliff.
Doubles and triples cost between 18,000 rp
and 32,000 rp. Also known as 'Hoffman's'
after the owner) or the 'Fish Restaurant',
his is a popular place but its attached
seafood restaurant is overrated and a trifle
pricey. The proprietor also runs the *Buana
Ayu* where bungalows with sea views and
ans run for 26,000 to 65,000 rp.

Places to Stay – top end

A few km west of town, the *Samudra Beach
Hotel* (☎ Pelabuhanratu 23) is a modern
high-rise with several restaurants and a good
swimming pool. Rooms rates are high and
standards may not be as good as they once
were; air-con singles/doubles cost from
98,000/128,000 rp and suites from 235,000
p, plus 15.5% tax and service.

The *Pondok Dewata* (☎ Pelabuhanratu 22
or Bandung 772426) has cottages (all air-
con) from 52,000 to 115,000 rp, a restaurant
and swimming pool. The *Karang Sari* on the
right past Pondok Dewata has fan cooled
cottages for 25,000 rp and air-con bungalows
costing 52,000 to 95,000 rp.

Getting There & Away

By road or rail from Bogor the route cuts
south over the pass between Gunung Salak
and Pangrango through valleys and hillsides
of rubber, coconut, cocoa and tea plantations
and terraced rice fields. You can take a colt
or the train from Bogor as far as Cibadak or
Sukabumi (20 km further east) and then
another colt south to the coast. You can also
hike here in one day from Lokapurna, a
village near Cibadak. See Things to See &
Do in the Around Bogor section for details
on how to get to Lokapurna.

From Bandung it's about 4½ hours by bus
or 1900 rp. From Labuhan you can take
various buses through the towns of Saketi
and Malimping for seven hours and a total of
2400 rp – it's a little-travelled and very
scenic route .

BOGOR TO BANDUNG
Puncak Pass

If you take the bus from Bogor to Bandung
you cross over this beautiful 1500-metre-
high pass on a narrow, winding mountain
road which passes through small resort
towns and tea plantations. At high altitudes
it's cool and often misty but in the early
mornings the views across the valleys can be
superb. There are some good hikes in this
area, especially from Tugu and Cisarua on
the Bogor side of the pass or Cibodas and
Cipanas on the other side. You can get up to
the towns on the pass by taking a colt or any
Bandung bus from Bogor.

Cisarua

Ten km from Bogor on the slopes of the
Puncak, there are good walks to picnic spots
and waterfalls around this small town. On the
way up to the Puncak summit you can stop
at the huge Gunung Mas tea plantation for a
free tour of the tea factory. Then walk on
through the plantation to Telaga Warna, a
small 'lake of many colours' just below the
top of the pass which reflects red, yellow or
green with changing daylight. Cut back to
the main road nearby and you can flag down
a bus or colt as they pass by the Rindu Alam
Restaurant.

Places to Stay The *Kopo Hostel* (☎ (0251)
4296) is at Jalan Raya Puncak 557 in
Cisarua. Its several bungalows offer a total
of 17 rooms and three dormitories in a garden
setting. It's excellent value with dorm beds
at 4000 rp and rooms from 14,000 rp with
blankets provided. There are discounts available for IYH cardholders. Coffee, cold
drinks and meals are available. They also
have maps of walks and information on
places of interest in the area. The hostel is
open from 7 am to 10 pm and from Bogor
it's about 45 minutes by bus or colt (500 rp).
Ask for the Cisarua petrol station (*pompa
bensin Cisarua*) and you'll find the hostel
right next door.

The *Chalet Bali International* in Cisarua
is affiliated with the infamous Bali International in Jakarta and has dorm beds at 5500

rp, and singles/doubles at 14,000/17,500 rp. The Kopo Hostel is far more pleasant.

In Cibulan, the next town on towards the Puncak, the *Hotel Cibulan* is a fairly run-down old-world Dutch hotel but a friendly place. Rooms with a mandi cost from around 10,000 rp and include free admission to the swimming pool opposite. Rates are more expensive on weekends when people from Jakarta flock up here to escape the heat.

Along the main road, in the various towns, there are numerous satay places and restaurants. The Puncak is an excellent place for fruit which is sold along the roadside – pineapples, melons, durian and delicious mangosteens (in season around November, December).

Cibodas

At Cibodas, just over the Puncak Pass, there is a beautiful high-altitude extension of the Bogor botanical gardens surrounded by thick tropical jungle on the slopes of the twin volcanoes Gunung Gede and Gunung Pangrango. These 80 hectare gardens were originally planted in 1860. The gardens are five km off the main road from Bogor to Bandung and only a short distance from Cipanas.

Places to Stay A truly tranquil place to lodge is right within the gardens themselves at the *Cibodas Botanical Gardens Guest-house*. You certainly can't beat the surrounding ambience and a pleasant room here costs 12,000 per person. Food is also served, at 3000 rp for breakfast and 6000 rp for other meals. You can book reservations for the guesthouse at the Bogor botanical gardens or when the Cibodas gardens are open to the public.

The modern *Pondok Pemuda Cibodas* near the Cibodas PHPA office has dorm beds at 6000 rp and doubles at 11,000 rp. It's a friendly comfortable place in a superb location, but by putting small windows under the eaves they've successfully managed to block out the lovely view! In the village, 500 metres down the hill, you can stay with Muhamed Saleh Abdullah (also known as Freddy) for around 3000 rp. There's cheap food at the warungs near the gardens and in the village.

Gunung Gede

The Cibodas gardens are also the start of the climb to the 2958-metre peak of volcanically active Gunung Gede. From the top of Gede on a clear day you can see Jakarta, Cirebon and even to Pelabuhanratu on the south coast – well, Raffles reported he could! To make the climb you must first get a permit for 500 rp from the PHPA office just outside the garden entrance. You can purchase an inexpensive route map here and get useful information on the Gede-Pangrango National Park at the same time. The office is open from 8 am to 3 pm Monday to Thursday, to 11.30 am on Friday and until 2 pm on Saturday. It is closed on Sunday and holidays.

Along the trail there are beautiful waterfalls such as Cibeureum Falls (one hour) and another where the falls drop deep into a steaming gorge (another hour). It's a 10-km hike right to the top, which takes six to 12 hours there and back so you should start as early as possible and take warm clothes (night temperatures can drop to 5 °C). There is also a steeper trail to the top of Gunung Pangrango (3019 metres) which requires an extra one to two hours. Dense fog is common on the mountain so take extra care when on the steeper trails – hikers have been known to walk off into unseen gorges during foggy conditions. The best time to make the hike is from May to October. Gede is only marginally less rainy than Bogor and the climb isn't recommended during the rainy season. An alternative approach is to climb Gede from the south and take the trail from the PHPA office at Selabintana, seven km north of Sukabumi.

Cipanas

At Cipanas, five km beyond the Cibodas turn-off, there is another seldom-used summer presidential palace. Built in 1750, it is an elegant country house in beautiful gardens but, like the Bogor palace, it is not normally open to the public. In the centre of town, the Roda Restaurant is a popular lunch stop. There's good food and from the terrace at the back of the restaurant you have a fine view of the valleys around the Puncak. From Cipanas, Bandung is about two hours away by bus.

BANDUNG

With its population of 1,700,000, Bandung is the capital of West Java and Indonesia's third largest city. Despite its size, it is a fairly unhurried provincial place and lacks the often suffocating overcrowding of Jakarta and Surabaya. At 750 metres above sea level and with a cool and comfortable climate, it's the city to which people from all over Indonesia, and from abroad, go to look for work and higher education. The majority of the population are the native Sundanese of West Java, who not only have a reputation as extroverted, easy-going people compared with the extremely refined Javanese, but also as zealous guardians of their own ancient culture. In contrast, the city itself is relatively new.

Bandung was originally established in the late 19th century as a Dutch garrison town of some 90,000 Sundanese, Chinese and Europeans. It rapidly acquired importance as a commercial and educational centre, renowned in particular for its Institute of Technology. Up until 1962 there was speculation – and hope – that it was to become the capital of the nation, but Bandung's chief claim to fame has been that it was the site for the Afro-Asian conference in 1955. On the industrial front, Bandung has maintained some of its European-created production centres, and its major concerns include textiles, an aircraft factory, tea and food processing and one of the world's largest quinine factories.

Although in the past Bandung has been described as the 'Paris of Java', due to its many fine parks and gardens, much of the city's former glamour has faded. As far as its general appearance goes, what exists today is a mish-mash of dilapidated colonial and modern buildings. One exception is the Savoy Homann Hotel, a superb example of Art-Deco architecture.

Bandung is an excellent place to visit if you're interested in Sundanese culture; otherwise its main attractions lie in the beautiful countryside around the city. To the north and south there's a wild tangle of high volcanic peaks, including the famous Tangkuban Prahu volcano, and several huge tea plantations. There are some fine walks in the area – one of the best is the river walk from the village of Maribaya to Dago Hill on the outskirts of Bandung.

Orientation

Bandung sprawls out over the northern foothills of a huge plateau surrounded by high mountain ridges. The city is divided into two parts by the railway line which cuts roughly through the centre. The main part of the city lies south of the railway line and is very compact. Bandung's main road, Jalan Asia Afrika, runs through it and the main focal point is the city square (alun-alun) which is only about 700 metres from the train station. Along Jalan Asia Afrika are the tourist offices, the post office and most of the banks, airline offices, restaurants and top-range hotels. On the south side of the square the Parahyangan Plaza is a modern shopping complex with bakeries, snack bars and a variety of retail outlets. Jalan Braga, on the north side, is the ritzy central shopping area with several useful bookshops, plenty of souvenir shops and cafes.

The budget hotel area in Bandung lies on either side of the railway station. Across the railway tracks to the north is the residential area studded with tree-lined streets and parks, and bordered on the northernmost edge by the hills of Dago.

Bandung's Kebun Kelapa bus station, on Jalan Dewi Sartika, is centrally located just south of the city square. If you're arriving from anywhere west of Bandung, you'll come into this station. Cicaheum bus station, way out on the east side of town, is the arrival point for buses from the east. The airport is to the north-west of the city.

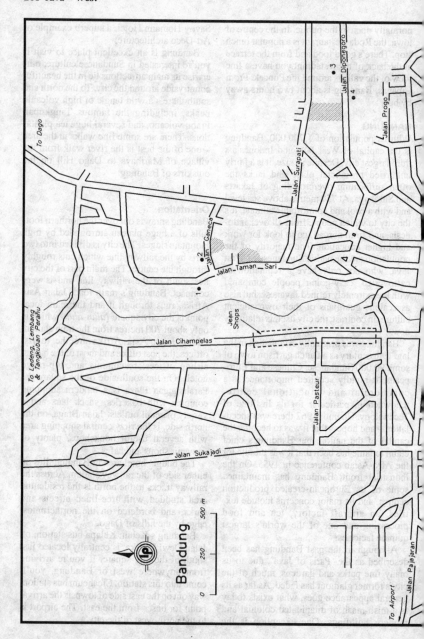

Bandung

0   250   500 m

To Dago

To Ledeng, Lembang
& Tangkuban Perahu

Jalan Cihampelas

Jean
Shops

Jalan Sukajadi

Jalan Pasteur

Jalan Ganeca

Jalan Taman — Sari

Jalan Surapati

Jalan Diponegoro

Jalan Progo

Jalan Pajajaran

To Airport

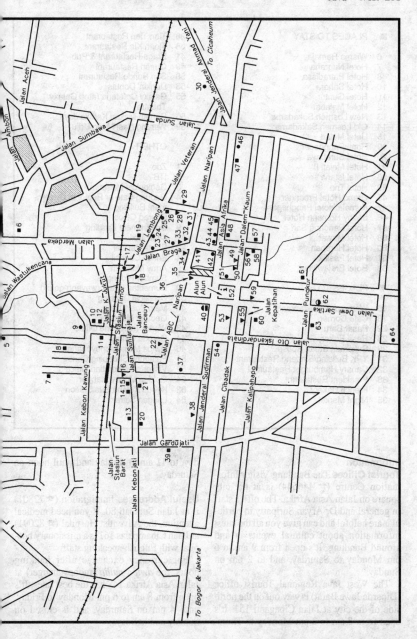

■ PLACES TO STAY

6	Wisma Remaja
7	Hotel Nugraha
8	Hotel Patradissa
10	Hotel Sahara
11	Hotel Guntur
12	Hotel Malabar
13	New Losmen Sakadarna
14	Old Losmen Sakadarna
15	Hotel Melati
19	Hotel Panghegar
20	Hotel Surabaya
21	Hotel Melati II
26	Hotel Istana
39	Hotel Trio
45	Grand Hotel Preanger
47	Kumala Hotel Panghegar
48	Savoy Homann Hotel
57	Hotel Pangang Sari
58	Hotel Mawar
60	Hotel Harapan
61	Hotel Pasifik
63	Hotel Brajawijaya

▼ PLACES TO EAT

16	Warungs & Restaurants
18	Cafe Corner
22	Pasar Baru
28	Rasa Bakery
29	Sukarasa Steak House
31	YPK Building/Sindang Restaurant
32	Canary Hamburger Restaurant
33	President Restaurant
34	French Bakery
35	Night Market
36	Tien Tien Restaurant
38	Tjoen Kie Restaurant
41	Braga Restaurant & Pub
49	Queen Restaurant
50	Sari Bundo Restaurant
53	Dunkin' Donuts
55	Galaxy Cafeteria (atop Galaxy Theatre)
56	Rumah Makan Kartika Jaya
59	Warung Nasi Mang Udju

OTHER

1	Zoo
2	ITB
3	Geological Museum
4	Gedung Sate or Regional Government Building
5	Bouraq Office
9	Government Building
17	4848 Taxi
23	Braga Permai
24	British Council
25	Army Museum
27	Sumber Hidangan
30	Rumentan Siang (wayang golek)
37	Classical Dancing
40	Main Post Office
42	Gedung Merdeka
43	Wartel Telephone Office
44	Garuda Office
46	Dwipa Mulia Moneychanger
51	Palaguna Shopping Centre
52	Visitor's Information Office
54	Golden Moneychanger
62	Kebun Kelaba Bus Station
64	Langen Setra

Information

Tourist Offices The Bandung Visitor Information Centre (☎ 446644) is at the city square on Jalan Asia Afrika. The office staff in general and Dr Aryan Suripatty in particular are helpful and can give you all the latest information about cultural events in and around Bandung. It's open from 9 am to 6 pm Monday to Saturday, and to 2 pm on Sunday.

The West Java Regional Tourist office (Diparda Jawa Barat) is way out on the north side of the city at Jalan Cipaganti 151. It's open from 8 am to 2 pm Monday to Thursday, to 11 am on Friday and until noon on Saturday.

Useful Addresses Immigration (☎ 72801) is at Jalan Surapati 80. If you need medical attention, the Adventist Hospital (☎ 82091) at Jalan Cihampelas 161 is a missionary hospital with English-speaking staff.

For currency exchange after banking hours, the *dwipa mulia* (moneychanger) at Jalan Asia Afrika 148 has the best rates. It's open from 8 am to 6 pm Monday to Friday, until 4 pm on Saturday, and is closed on Sunday and holidays.

The post office, at the corner of Jalan Banceuy and Jalan Asia Afrika, is open 24 hours a day.

Geological Museum

North across the railway tracks, at Jalan Diponegoro 57, the museum and the office of the Geological Survey of Indonesia are housed in the massive old headquarters of the Dutch Geological Service. There are some interesting exhibits such as relief maps, volcano models and an array of fossils, including one of the skull of a *Pithecanthropus erectus*, the famous pre-historic Java man. You can also buy topographical and geological maps of all places in Indonesia from the museum's publications department. It's open daily from 8 am to noon; entrance is free. From the train station you can take a colt bound for 'Terminal Gang Tilil' and get off at the Gedung Sate, about 50 metres from the museum.

Freedom Building (Gedung Merdeka)

If you're interested in learning more about the Afro-Asian conference, visit the Freedom Building on Asia-Afrika and see the film of the meeting between Sukarno, Chou En-Lai, Ho Chi Minh, Nasser and other Third-World leaders of the '50s. The Freedom Building itself dates from 1879 and was originally the 'Concordia Societeit', a meeting hall of Dutch associations. Entrance is free; it's open from 8 am to 1 pm and is closed on Monday and Saturday.

Other Museums

The West Java Cultural Museum, to the south-west of the city on Jalan Ottista, is open daily from 8 am to noon. The Army Museum, at Jalan Lembong 38, is devoted to the history and exploits of the West Java Siliwangi division (based in Bandung). The museum is full of grim and explicit photographs of the Darul Islam (Islamic State) rebellion of 1948-62, which was centred largely around Bandung. It seems to be a popular place to take schoolchildren for an excursion.

Institute of Technology/ITB

North of town on Jalan Ganeca is the Bandung Institute of Technology, constructed at the beginning of the century. The university has large grounds and gardens and the main campus complex is notable for its Minangkabau style of architecture. You can get there by taking a Dago Honda from the railway station terminus.

Opened in 1920, the ITB was the first Dutch-founded university open to Indonesians. It was here that Sukarno studied civil engineering (1920-25) and helped to found the Bandung Study Club, members of which formed a political party which grew as the PNI (Indonesian Nationalist Party) with independence as its goal. The institute's students have maintained their reputation for outspokenness and political activism and in 1978 they published the *White Book of the 1978 Students Struggle* against alleged corruption in high places. It was banned in Indonesia but later published in the USA. The ITB is the foremost scientific university in the country but it's also reputed to have one of the best fine arts schools, and its art gallery can be visited. Across from the main gate is a useful canteen in the *asrama mahasiswa* (student dorm complex) where many of the students congregate.

Zoo

A few minutes' walk from the ITB, Bandung's zoo on Jalan Taman Sari has Komodo dragons, a wide variety of Indonesian birdlife and lots of open park space. It's open daily from 9 am to 5 pm and admission costs 500 rp.

Dago

At the end of Jalan Merdeka, Jalan Haji Juanda climbs up to Dago Hill to the north, overlooking the city. Although the once famous Dago Tea House which offered commanding views is now closed, the bluff still affords some lovely vistas and is a fine place for catching the sunset.

Dago itself is an expensive residential suburb with some elegant Sundanese-style restaurants. It's a pleasant tree-shaded area to walk around. Just behind the former tea-house is the Dago waterfall, and about 2½ km to the north is a huge cliff in which the Gua Pakar Cave was hacked out by the Japanese to store ammunition in during the war. The latter is the start (or the end) of the walk between Maribaya and Dago along Sungai Cikapundung (see the Around Bandung section for more information).

Jeans

No discussion of Bandung's sights would be complete without mention of its famous jeans street, Jalan Cihampelas, in the more affluent northern side of town. Celebrating its standing as a major textile centre, stores with brightly painted humungous plaster statues of King Kong and other legendary monsters compete with one another for teenage Indonesian customers. This is the ultimate in kitsch and has to be seen to be believed. Incidentally, the jeans sell for about 25,000 rp.

Performances

The wayang golek puppet performances held every other Saturday night at Rumentang Siang on Jalan Ahmad Yani are worth seeing. They cost 1500 rp and are presented between 9 pm and 4 am. It's a lively performance punctuated by exploding fireworks – just to make sure you keep awake – and ends in time for you to catch an early morning train out! Check with the tourist office to determine whether the wayang is performed the weekend you are in town. If not, you can catch a scaled down exhibition every Saturday night from 8 to 10 pm at the Sindeng Reret Restaurant, Jalan Naripan 7. It's free for the price of a meal.

You can see Sundanese dance every Wednesday and Saturday at 7.30 pm at the Hotel Panghegar – admission is free with the hotel's expensive dinners, or a staggering 15,000 rp plus the cost of an obligatory drink. Langen Setra is a Jaipongan dance club that features Ketuktilu and Jaipongan every evening from 9 pm to 2 am. Entry is a steep (for Indonesia) 5000 rp, but it's the real thing. If you join the performers for a dance,

1000 rp is added to your bill for each song. There's a bit of ambiguity in the air as to whether the dancers are for hire after hours, but this is in keeping with the original spirit of Jaipongan's progenitor, Kutuktilu, which is traditionally danced by prostitutes. The club is in the Purwa Setra building on Gang Tegalega off Jalan Oto Iskandardinata, about 700 metres south of Kebun Kelapa bus station.

The ASTI-Bandung (or Kokar-Konservatori Karawitan), also in the southern part of the city at Jalan Buah Batu 212, is a school for traditional Sundanese arts – music, dancing and pencak silat (the art of self defence). It is open to visitors every morning, from 8 am to 1 pm, except Sunday. You can get there by bemo from Kebun Kelapa bus station. Take one going to the Buah Batu bus terminal for 250 rp.

Pak Ujo's Bamboo Workshop (*Saung Angklung*) on Jalan Padasuka has angklung performances some afternoons at 3.30 pm but it's expensive at 5000 rp and reportedly rather tailored to Western tastes. To get there, take a Damri city bus towards Cicaheum and ask for 'Saung Angklung' or 'Pak Ujo'. Some drivers may only know the stop called 'Padasuka' – ask directions from there.

Some of the large hotels, including the Hotel Panghegar and the Grand Hotel Preanger on Jalan Asia Afrika, also have programmes of Sundanese music and dancing.

Finally, when strolling down Jalan Braga, keep an eye out for local celebrity Braga Stone, a blind kecapi player. He sometimes plays on the sidewalk when not touring with the Sundanese pop music group 'Rollies'.

Day Trips

At the Visitor Information Centre, either the knowledgeable Dr Aryan Suripatty or Makmun Rustina will organise day trips to Papandayan volcano near Garut for a minimum of four people at 45,000 rp per person including breakfast. They also lead trips to Cibuni Hot Springs, renowned as a meditation spot, for 25,000 rp per person with breakfast.

Ram fights

On the second and fourth Sunday mornings of the month, noisy traditional ram-butting fights (known as *adu dombak*) are held at Cilimus near Ledeng to the north of the city. To the sound of drums, gongs and hand clapping, two rams keep charging at each other with a head-on clash of horns until one of them gets knocked out. If a ram gets dizzy they tweak his testicles and send him back into combat until he's had enough! This sport has been popular in West Java for so long that most villages have their own ram-fight societies and there are organised tournaments to encourage farmers to rear a stronger breed of ram. At village level it's just good fun; at district and provincial level there's wild betting.

Places to Stay – bottom end

Near the railway station and the centre of town on Jalan Kebonjati are two economical guest houses with similar names. The original *Losmen Sakadarna* (☎ 439897) at No 50/7B is a small, quiet place with an upstairs balcony and basic rooms from 5000/8000 rp. When there is sufficient demand, the hotel runs a minibus at 1 pm to Pangandaran for 5500 rp and the affable proprietor Yeddi also runs a tour costing 60,000 rp for six people to scenic attractions outside Bandung. This includes the Cankuong Temple, Papandayan Crater, Naga Village, and Cipanas Hot Springs.

Further down at Jalan Kebonjati 34 is the newer and more spacious *Sakadarna International Travellers Homestay & Restaurant*, run by the outgoing Rusty Muchfree and his Dutch wife Marjo. On the bottom floor is a good restaurant with a full selection of breakfasts – tea or coffee with toast and jam is only 600 rp; other breakfasts start at 2150 rp. On the roof is a pleasant terrace and the whole place is well kept and clean. Dorm beds are 4000 rp, rooms cost 7000/8000 rp for singles/doubles.

The *Hotel Surabaya* (☎ 444133), near the Sakadarnas at Jalan Kebonjati 71, is a rambling old colonial building with grubby singles/doubles at 5500/11,000 rp. Not recommended unless it's the only thing available. Just north over the railway pass is the *Hotel Malabar* at Jalan Kebun Jukut 3. Small, dingy singles cost 8500 rp including free tea in the morning, or better doubles/triples cost 10,000/13,500 rp. The lobby is set up as an information centre of sorts, with maps, train schedules, and so on. It's fairly clean, if a little dark.

The *Wisma Remaja*, in a lively government youth activities centre at Jalan Merdeka 64, is cheap and popular but sometimes rather crowded. Dormitory beds cost 3500 rp, singles/doubles 9000/17,500 rp and there is a small, reasonably priced cafe. It's about a 20-minute walk from the train station or take a Dago minibus and ask for the youth centre, Gelanggang Generasi Muda Bandung.

Right in the centre of town, the *Hotel Mawar* (☎ 51934) at Jalan Pangarang 14 is a short walk from the Kebun Kelapa bus station. Very few Westerners stay here but it's quiet and friendly, if not the cleanest place in town, and has something of a garden. The rooms are 8500/14,000 rp including coffee in the morning. The *Pangarang Sari Hotel* (☎ 444205) nearby at No 3 has slightly better rooms with mandi at singles/doubles 15,000/25,000 rp including the usual jam sandwich and coffee breakfast.

Places to Stay – middle

Round the corner from the Malabar, the *Hotel Sahara* (☎ 444684) at Jalan Oto Iskandardinata 3 has clean, simple rooms around a courtyard, with singles/doubles at 10,000/15,000 rp with shared mandi, and 25,000/34,000 rp with private bath and TV. The tariff includes breakfast. A short *ankutan* (the name for bemos in Bandung) ride from the railway station is the recently renovated *Hotel Nugraha* (☎ 436146) at Jalan H Mesri 11, off Jalan Kebon Kawung. Surrounding a garden with rattan and bamboo furniture are clean rooms that range between 18,000 and 38,000 rp including breakfast. The friendly staff and good service make it good value. A block from the Nugraha is *Hotel Patridassa* (☎ 56680) at Jalan H Moch Iskat 8, in a new building with pleasant singles/doubles costing 20,000/30,500 rp.

The *Hotel Guntur* (☎ 443763) at Jalan Oto Iskandardinata 20, just north of the railway line and near the Malabar, is a very comfortable mid-range hotel. Singles/doubles with hot water, telephone and TV cost 27,709 rp including a substantial breakfast.

Near the Kebun Kelapa bus terminal are three more hotels in this range. Best of the three is *Hotel Harapan* (☎ 444212) at Jalan Kepatihan 14-16. Room rates for singles/doubles are in the 16,350/27,500 rp range, the facilities are nice (hot water during certain morning and evening hours) and it is generally very well maintained. *Hotel Braja Wijaya* (☎ 443693), just west of the bus terminal at Jalan Pungkur 28, is a passable Indonesian-style place where doubles start at 23,500 rp including a bread and coffee breakfast. The *Hotel Pasifik* (☎ 56027), to the east of the terminal on the other side of Jalan Pungkur, is in the same price range with doubles starting at 22,000 rp, but a bit nicer with quiet, fairly clean rooms, some of which are carpeted.

Straddling the bottom and middle categories are two places with mid-range prices but bottom-end facilities. *Hotel Melati II* (☎ 446409) on Jalan Kebonjati near the two Sakadarna hotels, has just adequate singles/doubles for 21,000/32,500 rp. Its older sister, *Hotel Melati I* starts at 12,000/14,000 rp but is noisy and poorly kept.

Places to Stay – top end

The *Savoy Homann Hotel* (☎ 432244) is conveniently central at Jalan Asia Afrika 112. Once 'the' hotel of Bandung, it is still a stylish old Art-Deco building with spacious rooms off a small courtyard garden. Air-con singles/doubles with bathroom cost 88,000/122,000 rp (plus 21% tax and service charge) or there are 'deluxe' rooms available at 243,000 rp. The hotel has a comfortable coffee lounge and restaurant.

The *Hotel Panghegar* (☎ 445141) at Jalan Merdeka 2 is believed by some locals to be Bandung's top hotel. Rooms cost from 142,000/372,000 rp and the hotel has all the modern facilities.

The *Sheraton Inn* (☎ 210303) at Jalan Juanda 390 is a typical Sheraton with all the modern amenities, such as a swimming pool, gym and satellite TV. Standard rooms run at 177,000 to 196,000 rp here.

Built in 1928, the recently renovated *Grand Preanger* (☎ 430682) at Jalan Asia Afrika 140 has all you would want in a luxury hotel with colonial architecture and a tariff to match. Rooms start at 235,000 rp.

A fairly new hotel is the modern *Kumala Panghegar* (☎ 51242) at Jalan Asia Afrika 140. Rooms, all air-con, start at 67,000 rp and the hotel has a bar and restaurant.

The *Hotel Trio* (☎ 615055) at Jalan Gardujati 55-61 is a very clean, unpretentious, centrally located hotel frequented by Chinese businesspeople with rooms in the 78,000/118,000 rp range.

Places to Eat

Bandung has some excellent food venues. In the railway station area, the restaurant at *Sakadarna International Travellers Homestay* at Jalan Kebonjati 34 is popular, even among travellers who aren't staying there, for its reasonably priced (but not cheap) Dutch and Indonesian meals and Western- style breakfasts. Directly in front of the railway station, in the area where the bemos stop between the station and Jalan Kebonjati, is a selection of good night warungs and restaurants. Popular places include *Rumah Makan Hadori Satay House, Rumah Makan Gahaya Minang, Sugema Satay* and *Warung Gizi*. There is also an alley of inexpensive warungs between the Sahara and Malabar Hotels off Jalan Oto Iskandardinata. Where Jalan Kebonjati becomes Jalan Suniaraja at No 99 (as you head towards Iskandardinata), the *Roti Lux* bakery serves up some scrumptious pastries. For even fancier baked goods, visit the *French Bakery* at Jalan Braga 29.

Restaurants in the centre of town can be fairly expensive but there is a good, lively night market on Jalan Cikapundung Barat, directly across Asia Afrika from the Visitor

Information Centre. There are stalls for all kinds of food, from soto and satay to gado-gado and seafood, and probably the number one *martabak manis* in Java. One traveller has recommended trying *roti bakar* – a whole loaf sliced horizontally and spread with peanut butter and condensed milk! Well, he reported it to be 'delicious and filling'. For the cheapest warung food try those up near the river where the becak men eat.

At the *Simpang Raya*, beside the central square to one side of the Tourist Information Centre, you'll find excellent Padang food and have a view of the square. For modestly priced Padang food, eat at *Sari Bundo*, Jalan Dalem Kaum 75. The fare here is preferable to the Padang served nearby at No 84, *Rumah Makan Kartika Jaya*.

On the ground floor of the Palaguna shopping centre on the east side of the square is the *Istana Peters* ice-cream parlour, which features interesting flavours like durian, jackfruit and zurzat for 850 rp. Upstairs there are other fast food type places – *Home Bakery*, *Hero Fast Food* and *California Fried Chicken*. Nearby on Jalan Dalem Kaum, there's even a *Dunkin' Donuts* (750 rp each) with what looks like a thousand varieties of doughnuts.

The *Galaxy Cafeteria* on the top floor of the Galaxy Theatre complex on Jalan Kepatihan has probably the cheapest beer in central Bandung. A large bottle of Bintang is only 2200 rp. The Chinese and Indonesian food on the menu is also cheap, and most nights there is live pop music – nothing spectacular but it's free. Out by the Kebun Kelapa bus terminal on Jalan Dewi Sartika is a popular outdoor restaurant called *Taman Parahyangan* where a large bottle of beer is 2100 rp, draught beer 1850 rp.

Bandung also has a number of excellent Chinese restaurants including the popular *Queen* at Jalan Dalem Kaum 53A, a block south of the Savoy Homann. The Cantonese *Tjoen Kie* at Jalan Jenderal Sudirman 62 is as good and slightly cheaper; most dishes are around the 5000 rp mark. At Jalan Merdeka 17 the *Rumah Makan Vanda Sari* has good,

though pricey, Chinese food. The *President Restaurant* near the railway tracks at Jalan Braga 106 also has tasty Chinese fare.

On Jalan Braga there's a string of fancy coffee shops and bakeries where you can indulge yourself in a sort of east-west food fantasy. The centrepiece of this quasi-European avenue is the *Braga Permai* sidewalk cafe at No 74. Most meals are in the 6000 to 11,000 rp range, with simpler dishes like nasi goreng 4000 to 6000 rp, sandwiches at 2200 to 3000 rp, plus a variety of cakes and ice creams at 1500 to 3000 rp. Skip the mediocre *Braga Coffee Shop* in front of the Braga Hotel. Across the road at No 17 is the *Braga Restaurant and Pub*, a shiny place with reasonable Indian, Indonesian and light Western meals. On the corner of Jalan Braga and Jalan ABC/Naripan is the *Canary Bakery*, and a little further along are the *Sumber Hidangan* bakery and the *French Bakery*, good places for a snack or light meal – try croissants, Danish pastries or chicken curry puffs.

If you're looking for a minor splurge you could try the restaurant in the *Savoy Homann*; they do a rijstaffel for 14,000 rp.

Sundanese Restaurants Bandung is one of the few places where you can try traditional Sundanese food. The *Warung Nasi Mang Udju* on Jalan Dewi Sartika just south of the square is a simple place, but the food is excellent and you can eat well for about 3500 rp. Try the chicken steamed in bamboo leaf and fish with ginger. The owners speak little English but you simply help yourself from the various dishes on the table and pay for what you eat.

Sakadarna International Travellers Homestay & Restaurant does a modest set dinner in the Sundanese style for 4100 rp. Other well-known and moderately priced Sundanese restaurants are the *Babakan Siliwangi* on Jalan Siliwangi (near the zoo), and the *Ponyo* on Jalan Prof Eykman. For a real treat, take a taxi to the Dago area in the north of the city to the lovely *Penineungan Endah* Sundanese restaurant. Here, each party has its own individual tearoom in which to dine, surrounded by Japanese-style gardens bounded by tranquil brooks. From the waters which surround your teahouse, sizeable goldfish are freshly netted to serve as the Sundanese delicacy *ikan mas*. Delicious!

Things to Buy
Wayang golek puppets, both new and old, are good buys. In the centre of town, down a small alley behind Jalan Pangarang 22, there's a small 'cottage industry' run by Pak Ruhiyat at No 78/17B where you can buy puppets and masks and see them being carved. It's an interesting place to visit and the puppets are really very fine, with a range of sizes, and prices from 25,000 to 75,000 rp. A full set of wayang golek puppets consists of 81 characters, enough for performances of both the *Ramayana* and the *Mahabharata*. The asking price for a full set is six million rp. Pak Ruhiyat's son, Maman Permana, speaks good English.

The Cupu Manik puppet factory is on Gang Haji Umar, off Jalan Kebon Kewung just north of the train station. On Jalan Arjuna, about one km from the railway station, there is a daily antique market. Jalan Braga is a good shopping street for crafts and antiques. Traditional Sundanese musical instruments can be bought at Pak Ujo's Workshop or the Toko Musik at Gang Suniaraja 3, off Jalan ABC.

A stroll down Jalan Braga for a look at the fancy furniture and fashion boutiques is worthwhile if only to gain an insight into the upper-class Indonesian consumer consciousness. The Leather Palace at No 113 is known for its custom-made coats, purses and shoes.

Getting There & Away
Air The domestic airline offices are all centrally located on or near Jalan Asia Afrika but if you want to compare prices and make bookings/reservations you could try the Vista Express Travel Agent in the Savoy Homann Hotel. Mandala Airlines does not operate flights out of Bandung.

Merpati flights to and from Bandung include Jakarta (nine flights daily), Batam,

Denpasar, Palembang, Semarang, Surabaya and Ujung Pandang. The Garuda/Merpati office (☎ 51497) is at Jalan Asia Afrika 73, opposite the Savoy Homann Hotel. It's open from 8 am to 2 pm Monday to Thursday, to 11 am on Friday and until 1 pm on Saturday; it's closed on Sunday.

Bouraq flies to Jakarta, Yogya, Surabaya, Denpasar, Banjarmasin and Balikpapan. The Bouraq office (☎ 437896) is at Jalan Cihampelas 27. It's open from 8 am to 4 pm Monday to Friday, and to 2 pm at the weekend.

Bus Buses depart from the Cililitan station in Jakarta every 10 minutes or so for the 4½ hour trip to Bandung, via Bogor and the Puncak Pass. The fare is 2600 rp. Bandung has two bus stations. Go to Kebun Kelapa bus station if you're travelling west or south to places like Bogor, Jakarta, Sukabumi and Pelabuhanratu. If you're heading east, the Cicaheum bus station's services include those to Cirebon, Banjar and Yogya.

The following information will give you an idea of fares and travel time. Buses run from Bandung to Bogor for 1900 rp (3½ hours), Sukabumi 1450 rp (three hours), Pelabuhanratu for 1900 rp (four hours), Banjar for 2500 rp (five hours), Merak for 4100 rp (eight hours) and Cirebon for 1900 rp (3½ hours).

To reach Pangandaran by bus, you must change in Banjar for another two-hour ride. The fare totals 4500 rp. When there are enough customers, Losmen Sakadarna runs a minibus at 1 pm to Pangandaran, which costs 5500 rp.

Public buses to Yogya cost from 8450 rp and take about 12 hours. There are also daily night buses to Yogya run by private bus companies. Bandung Cepat has buses that go the northern route via Semarang; they leave Jalan Doktor Cipto 5 at 7 pm, arriving in Yogya at 6 pm. Yogya Cepat buses take the southern route via Banjar, leaving from Jalan Sunda 4 at 5 pm, arriving at 4 am the following morning. Kramat Jati also has a night bus which departs from Jalan Cihampelas 10 – ring them (☎ 51402) for times. The fares are

11,500 rp for non-air-con buses, or 15,500 rp for air-con.

Train There are nine daily *Parahyangan* trains between Jakarta and Bandung. From Gambir, Jakarta, trains depart at 5.39 am, 9.33 am, 11.33 am, 1.33 pm, 3.33 pm, 4.50 pm, 6.55 pm, 10.40 pm, and 11.40 pm. Going the other way trains depart Bandung at 5 am, 6 am, 9 am, 11 am, 1 pm, 3 pm, 5 pm, 6.20 pm, and 7.30 pm. Fares are 7500 rp in 3rd class, 10,000 rp in 2nd class, 15,000 rp in 1st and it's a comfortable, hassle-free train for the 3-hour trip. Though the train avoids the hills around the Puncak, it cuts east of the huge dam and lake at Jatiluhur, and the views are quite spectacular at times along this route.

There are three daily trains to Yogya. The all-3rd-class *Cepat Siang* departs at 7.40 am, takes 9½ hours and costs 4000 rp, or there's the faster *Ekspress Siang* at 5.35 am – 7000 rp *bisnis* class, 4400 rp 3rd class and 10,000 rp 2nd class. The *Mutiara Selatan* is a night express train that leaves Bandung at 5.40 pm and arrives in Yogya at 1.21 am. Second class costs 14,000 rp, 1st class 23,000. The same trains continue on to Solo for the same fare, except for the *Cepat Siang* which terminates in Yogya. In the reverse direction the *Cepat Siang* leaves Yogya at 8.10 am, the *Express Siang* at 11.27 am, and the *Mutiara Selatan* at 11.37 pm.

Taxi Apart from the regular buses there are also door-to-door taxi services between Jakarta and Bandung for 12,000 rp through *4848* on Jalan Kramat Raya in Jakarta (you can also get off in Bogor on this run for 11,000 rp). In Bandung the 4848 Taxi office (☎ 43470) is located near the railway station. They also have taxis from Bandung to Pangandaran at 7 am and 2 pm (6000 to 7500 rp), Cirebon (5000 rp), and to Semarang (9500 rp).

Getting Around

To/From the Airport Bandung's Husein Sastranegara airport is four km north-west of town, about half an hour away and 6000 rp by taxi.

Bus Bandung has a fairly good city bus service using Indian Tata buses which charge a fixed 200 rp fare, or 250 rp if they are express buses. The most useful service is city bus No 1 to the Cicaheum bus station, which operates between 7 am and about 9 pm. It runs from the west of town right down Asia Afrika and along Jalan Jenderal A Yani to Cicaheum in the east. The Kebun Kelapa bus station is centrally located on Jalan Dewi Sartika, about 10 minutes' walk south of the city square.

Bemo, Becak & Taxi Downtown bemos (ankutans), Hondas and Daihatsus charge a fixed 250 rp fare. For destinations north (including Dago, Lembang and Tangkuban Prahu) they depart from the terminal outside the railway station. Ankutan No 5 runs between the railway station and Kebun Kelapa bus terminal. As in other cities the becaks are being relegated to the back streets and are no longer seen in great numbers. Taxis can usually be found near the city square on Jalan Asia Afrika; these are metered at about the same rates as in Jakarta and Surabaya.

AROUND BANDUNG
Lembang

On the road to Tangkuban Prahu, 16 km north of Bandung, Lembang is a good place to stop for lunch or a snack. It is renowned for its market and on Jalan Raya Lembang, the main Bandung road, you'll find excellent fruit and cheap avocados at the Pasar Buah Buahan. Along the same street there are a number of good, cheap restaurants. At the market and on the road up to the crater there are stalls selling delicious hot corn on the cob for 100 rp.

Lembang's planetarium – the Bosscha Astronomical Observatory – can be visited on special request. You have to contact the Director of the Department of Astronomy at ITB, Jalan Ganeca 10.

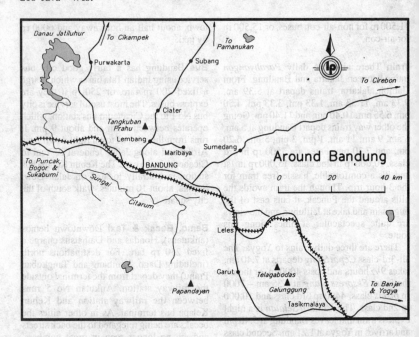

Around Bandung

Places to Stay The *Grand Hotel* (☎ 82393), just down the road from the market at Jalan Raya Lembang 288, is an old-fashioned and comfortable place with beautiful gardens, a swimming pool and tennis courts, as well as a pleasant bar and mediocre restaurant. The Grand is not cheap. Its newly renovated standard rooms cost 75,000 rp, although there are some economy rooms with shared bath for 45,000 rp.

Tangkuban Prahu

The 'overturned prahu' volcano crater stands 30 km north of Bandung. Years ago the centre of Tangkuban Prahu collapsed under the weight of built-up ash and, instead of the usual conical volcano shape, it has a flat elongated summit with a huge caldera more than seven km across. There is, of course, a legend to explain this phenomenon. It tells of an estranged young prince who returned home and unwittingly fell in love with his own mother. When the Queen discovered the terrible truth of her lover's identity she challenged him to build a dam and a huge boat during a single night before she would agree to marry him. Seeing that the young man was about to complete this impossible task, she called on the gods to bring the sun up early and as the cocks began to crow the boat builder turned his nearly completed boat over in a fit of anger. Tangkuban Prahu still simmers and bubbles, sending up noxious sulphurous fumes. Its last serious eruption was in 1969.

Tangkuban Prahu is the only volcano in Java easily accessible by car, so it's very much a tourist attraction. Up at the crater there are carparks and warungs, and you'll find that foreigners are as much a photographic attraction for snap-happy Indonesian tourists as the volcano itself! There used to be an unnerving bevy of enterprising locals hustling postcards, souvenirs and other junk. Recently, the government moved this parade of peddlers to a lower carpark and has built a helpful information centre at the top. And while the scene is still more commercial than most other Javanese volcanoes, there are plenty of opportunities to walk away from this bedlam of activity. For a start the main crater is divided into two parts. Ignoring the obnoxious guides, you can walk away from the carpark around the rim of the first for almost 20 minutes before the second is fully visible. From the top you can also head off across country towards Ciater. .

Getting There & Away At 1830 metres, Tangkuban Prahu can be quite cool and around noon the mist starts to roll in through the trees so try to go early. From Bandung's minibus station, take a Subang colt (1000 rp) via Lembang to the park entrance, where there is a 500 rp admission charge. At weekends there's a minibus up to the main crater – other days you'll have to hitch or walk. It's four km by road but there is a more interesting, little-used shortcut through the jungle. There's no need for a guide; start up the road and take the first turning on the right. The path leads through the jungle to the Kawah Domas crater, an active open area of bubbling hot geysers, and another steep path with steps cut up to the main crater.

An alternative is to get dropped off at Bukit Jayagiri, just outside Lembang, and from there you can walk up through the forest to the crater (about eight km).

Ciater Hot Springs
Eight km beyond Tangkuban Prahu, Ciater is a pretty little place in the middle of huge tea and clove estates, and there are good walks in the area. Opposite the turn-off to Ciater is the Ciater tea factory (*paberik teh Ciater*). At the end of the road through the village you'll come across the Ciater Hot Springs Resort. Although quite commercialised, the pools are probably the best of all the hot springs around Bandung and if you've been climbing around the volcano on a cool, rainy day there's no better way to get warm. There is a 750 rp admission into the resort area and it costs another 600 rp to use

the pool. You can walk to Ciater – about 12 km across country – from the main crater of Tangkuban Prahu, or flag down a colt (300 rp) at the entrance point.

Maribaya Hot Springs
Maribaya, five km east of Lembang, has a thermal spa, landscaped gardens and a thundering waterfall. It's another tourist spot, crowded on Sundays, but worth visiting. You can extend your Tangkuban Prahu trip by walking from the bottom end of the gardens down through a brilliant, deep and wooded river gorge all the way to Dago. There's a good track and if you allow about two to three hours for the walk (six km) you can be at a Dago vantage point for sunset. From there it's only a short trip by colt back into Bandung.

Danau Jatiluhur & Dam
This artificial lake, 70 km north of Bandung in the hills near Purwakarta, is a popular resort for swimming, boating and waterskiing. The tourist blurb certainly raves about the giant Jatiluhur Dam which stretches 1200 metres across, is 100 metres high, and has created a lake some 80 ha in surface area! It's part of a hydroelectric generating system supplying Jakarta and West Java and also provides irrigation water for a large area of the province. Jatiluhur is also the site of the country's ITT earth satellite station, opened in 1969. The village was built by the French for their staff when they were building the dam. Purwakarta is the access point either from Jakarta (125 km by rail or road) and from Bandung (by road).

BANDUNG TO PANGANDARAN
Heading south-east from Bandung, the road passes through a scenic and fertile stretch of hilly countryside and volcanic peaks. This is the Bandung-Yogya road as far as Banjar; the Bandung to Yogya railway line passes through Tasikmalaya and Banjar, but not Garut. The district is known as Priangan.

Garut
Fifty-seven km south-east of Bandung,

Garut is a small Sundanese town and a centre for orange and tobacco growing. From Garut you can visit the hot springs (air panas) at Tarogong, five km north of town. Near Leles, about 10 km further north, is the site of one of the few stone Hindu temples found in West Java. Dating from the 8th century, some of its stones were found to have been carved into tombstones for a nearby Islamic cemetery. What little remains of the temple lies on the edge of Danau Cangkuang.

To the east, Gunung Telagabodas (2201 metres) has a bubbling bright-green crater lake alive with sulphur. Off to the southwest, you can climb Gunung Papandayan (2622 metres) for magnificent views of the area. One of the most active and spectacular of Java's volcanoes, Papandayan has only existed since 1772 when a large piece of the mountain exploded sideways in a catastrophe that killed more than 3000 people.

Garut is famed for its *dodol* – a confectionery made of coconut milk, palm sugar and sticky rice rolled into a long brown tube shape. At the bus station hawkers selling tubes of sweet dodol besiege the passing buses and it's sold at many shops around town. The 'Picnic' brand is said to be the best quality.

Places to Stay The *Hotel Nasional*, at Jalan Kenanga 19, is neither very cheap nor reportedly very friendly. You could try the *Hotel Mulia* at No 17 on the same street, where rooms cost around 7500 rp.

At Tarogong, the choices are better: the *Bratayuda* has rooms from 10,000 rp; the *Sari Panas* and *Tarumanegara* are both in the 20,000 to 32,000 rp range.

Tasikmalaya

Sixty km east of Garut, this small town is a centre for rattan crafts. Palm leaf and bamboo are used to make floormats, baskets, trays, straw hats and paper umbrellas. For cheaper rattan, visit the village of Rajapolah, 12 km north of town, where many of the weavers work. Tasikmalaya also has a small batik industry.

Gunung Galunggung, 17 km to the north-west, is a volcano which exploded dramatically only a few years ago in 1982. You can get there from Tasikmalaya by motorcycle for 1000 rp.

Places to Stay Two inexpensive places to stay are the centrally located *Hotel Tugu* at Jalan Selakaso 2 and *Hotel Kencana* at Jalan Yudanegara 17 close to the mosque. Adequate rooms at these hotels run between 10,000 and 20,000 rp.

Banjar

Banjar, 42 km east of Tasikmalaya, is the junction point where the Pangandaran road branches from the Bandung to Yogya road and rail route. There are banks in Banjar where you can change money before continuing on to Pangandaran, where there are no money changing facilities. See the Getting There & Away section for Pangandaran for details of transport to and from Banjar. If you arrive in Banjar by train it is only five minutes' walk to the bus station. There are good warungs at both stations.

PANGANDARAN

Pangandaran is one of Java's finest beaches but take great care when swimming, especially at the west beach: the undertows here are dangerous even though a coral reef cuts the surf and reduces their impact. The Pangandaran Nature Reserve is part of this small fishing town, and the focus for travellers; it lies along the narrow isthmus of a peninsula with broad white-sand beaches that sweep back along the mainland. The large jungle headland of the peninsula teems with wild buffalo, barking deer and monkeys. Secluded, tree-fringed beaches are to be found nearly all the way around the headland, though the best beaches for swimming and snorkelling are on the west side. As if all this isn't enough, at Pangandaran it's possible to enjoy the unique experience of seeing the sun set and the moon rise over the ocean simultaneously at full moon. And every evening, at dusk, you'll see a mass of fruit bats flying west across the setting sun.

With so much going for it, it's hardly

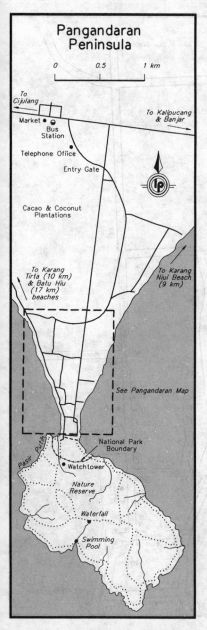

Pangandaran Peninsula

0   0.5   1 km

To Cijulang

Market ●
Bus Station

Telephone Office

Entry Gate

Cacao & Coconut Plantations

To Karang Tirta (10 km) & Batu Hiu (17 km) beaches

To Kalipucang & Banjar

To Karang Niui Beach (9 km)

See Pangandaran Map

National Park Boundary

Pasir Putih

● Watchtower

Nature Reserve

Waterfall

Swimming Pool

surprising that Pangandaran is a popular local resort. It can be crowded at weekends but during holidays – Christmas and after Ramadan in particular – there can be a floating population of literally thousands on the beaches. At any other time this is an idyllic place to take a break from travelling; the people are exceptionally friendly, there are plenty of cheap places to stay and excellent seafood is available. The locals live mostly by fishing, many of them rowing their boats out to sea from the east beach where you'll nearly always find whole families working together to pull in the nets.

If lazing around the beaches and trekking through the jungle reserve of Pangandaran begins to pall, you can head off east or west to other quieter beaches nearby. About a five-km walk along the west beach there are buffalo at Karang Tirta pond. Further west, surf pounds the beaches at Batu Hui (17 km by colt) and there's also a beach at the fishing village of Batu Keras (40 km). Heading east, about seven km, there is another one at Lembah Putri.

Information

You will find a tourist information booth around the corner from Cafe Sympathy on Jalan Jagalautan. The maps given out here are so-so. Guides may be hired here for jungle walks in the nature reserve at 7500 rp a day. Mail may be sent to you care of post restante at the Pagandaran Post Office. There is a Bank Rakyat Indonesia on Jalan Kidang Pananjung north of its intersection with Jalan Talanca. After banking hours, if you're desperate, the Cilacap Restaurant may change US-dollar travellers' cheques, but below the going rate. Electricity comes on between 6 pm and 6 am, though blackouts are pretty common when it's raining hard.

There's a 500 rp admission charge for the beach area, and another 500 rp for the reserve. Maps of the reserve are available from the PHPA office just inside the east gate.

Places to Stay – bottom end

Most of Pangandaran's cheap hotels are

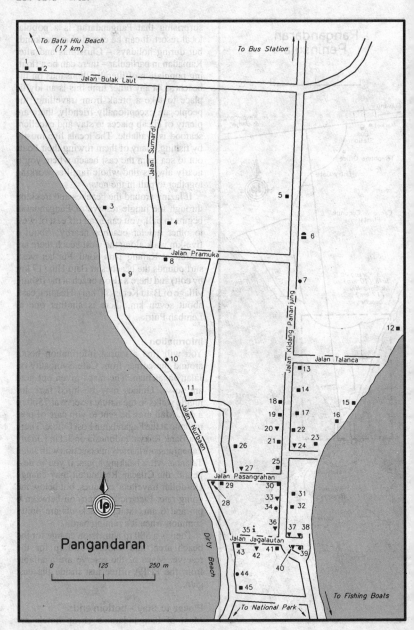

To Batu Hiu Beach
(17 km)

To Bus Station

Jalan Bulak Laut

Jalan Sumardi

To Fishing Boats

Jalan Pramuka

Jalan Kidang Pananjung

Jalan Talanca

Jalan Nurbaen

Jalan Pasangrahan

Jalan Jagalautan

Pangandaran

Dirty Beach

0   125   250 m

To National Park

■ PLACES TO STAY

1	Pondok Wisata Bulak Laut
2	Pondok Wisata Sari
3	Pondok Perconotohan
4	Hotel Bahtera Jaya
5	Penginapan Bahagia
8	Anggia Motel
11	Hotel Bumi Nusanatra
12	Hotel Bumi Pananjung
13	Penginapan Pantai Indah
14	Hotel Pamordian
15	Pantai Indah Timur
16	Losmen Panorama
17	Losmen Srihana
18	HotelFlamboyan
19	Pantai Indah Bahrat
21	Hotel Samudra
22	Sunrise Homestay
23	Penginapan Adem Ayam
25	Penginapan Damai
26	Losmen Mini II
29	Pondok Pelangi
30	Penginapan Rawamangun
31	Penginapan Setia Famili
32	Losmen Mini I
41	Laut Biru

43	Hotel Mangkabumi
45	Pangandaran Beach Hotel

▼ PLACES TO EAT

20	Rumah Makan Budi Jaya
24	Cilacap Restaurant
27	Rumah Makan Sari Harum
28	Rumah Makan Nanjung
33	Ayem Goreng & Bakar Restaurant
36	Sympathy Cafe
37	Inti-Laut Restaurant
38	Lonely Planet Restaurant
40	Warungs
42	Rumah Makan Mambo

OTHER

6	Post Office
7	Bank Rakyat Indonesia
9	Souvenir Market
10	Star Meridian Disco
34	Books for Sale
35	Tourist Office & Guide Service
39	Fish Auction
44	Aquarium

along the main street but they're all squeezed in between the beaches on either side, so no matter where you stay you can hear the sea. A number of them are particularly popular with travellers but they are all good and friendly places, which makes it difficult to recommend one more than another. It's worth having a look around if you're planning to stay for more than a few days; many people do stay, regardless of previous intentions.

At the far north end of the west beach, *Pondok Wisata Bulak Laut* on Jalan Pamugaran has attractive bungalows surrounded by pretty Sundanese gardens. Bungalows with fans cost 17,500 to 20,000 rp and air-con cottages cost 25,000 rp. Breakfast is included. Each bungalow has a living room, open-air bathroom and bedroom with a large double bed. Next door at similar prices are the bungalows of *Pondok Wisata Sari*, with a Chinese restaurant on the premises.

On Jalan Kidang Pananjung, the main road, is the basic but friendly *Laut Biru* where doubles with attached mandi cost 12,500. The hotel has a large sitting room where you can help yourself to tea and coffee.

Losmen Mini II, between the main road and the west beach, has its own garden and is also good value. Singles/doubles here cost 5000/7000 rp and a room with a private bath and fan costs 9000 rp. Free tea and coffee are always available. All the above places are particularly good for information – travel, free (well, sometimes) guided walks in the jungle, etc – and they'll often organise barbecue fish suppers.

Losmen Mini I is on the main street, in a small courtyard of palm trees. It has basic singles/doubles with private mandi at 6000/7500 rp including breakfast. The somewhat dirty and dilapidated *Adem Ayam*, close to the east beach and near the Cilacap Restaurant, has a few rooms at 6000 rp including breakfast, plus better ones at 11,000 rp. If you stay here, try to get an upstairs room on the balcony with a good view over the sea. The nearby *Losmen Panorama* is right on the beach and has 15,000 rp rooms overlooking the sea. There are cheaper rooms here without a private mandi and view, ranging from 8000 to 12,500 rp.

On Jalan Sumardi, not far from the Anggia Motel, is *Hotel Bahtera Jaya*, run by a Dutch woman named Willy. Spartan rooms are 9500 rp with a fan and breakfast.

Slightly more expensive places include the *Anggia Motel* at Jalan Pramuka 15, which has standard doubles at 25,000 rp and air-con rooms at 35,000 rp as well as expensive sizeable bungalows for 100,000 rp.

On Jalan Kidang Pananjung, the *Hotel Samudra* has a pleasant courtyard with a terrace (and hammock!), and offers good rooms, albeit a bit expensive for some budget travellers at 25,000 rp and 50,000 rp for air-con.

Places to Stay – top end

The Sunrise Homestay at Jalan Kidang Pananjung 175 on the east beach is a clean, pleasant place with, at the time of writing, the only swimming pool in town. Attractive, sizeable rooms range from 25,000 to 35,000 rp for a double with a fan, 45,000 to 52,500 rp for a room with air-con. For budget travellers considering a minor splurge, this is *the* place!

Across the street from the Sunrise is the new *Pantai Indah Barut* which, along with its plush new cousin on the east beach *Pantai Indah Timur*, offers attractive air-con rooms with TV and refrigerator at 60,000 rp for a standard double and 150,000 rp for cottages. Despite the name similarity, don't confuse these upscale digs with the spartan *Penginapan Pantai Indah* on the main street.

There are a number of bungalows and rather flash hotels along the west beachfront but most are poorly maintained and overpriced. The *Pondok Pelangi* (☎ Bandung 81531), opposite the turn-off for Mini I, has comfortable bungalows in an attractive garden, each with a mandi, living room and

small terrace. A bungalow with kitchen facilities costs 35,000 rp for two rooms and 45,000 rp for three rooms. Bungalows without kitchens cost 30,000 rp.

The pricey *Hotel Bumi Pananjung* (☎ Bandung 84963) is right on the east beach behind the post office. The hotel has large airy rooms, some with a bathroom and a balcony, costing 35,000 to 50,000 rp for doubles and 60,000 to 80,000 rp (plus 20% tax and service) for triples. Air-con rooms range from 40,000 to 90,000 rp. Rates include a continental buffet breakfast and afternoon tea. It's an impressive Tyrolean-style chalet of timber and thatch with the bedrooms off a gallery surrounding a large, central sitting area. The owner has obviously been strongly influenced by his visits to Germany!

On the west beach is the equally imposing *Bumi Nusantara*, although the architectural style is more Indonesian, as are the prices. Doubles here begin at 25,000 rp. Or there's the *Pangandaran Beach Hotel* on the west beach near the park entrance. Simple rooms are overpriced at 35,000 to 40,000 rp with private bath. On the northern sector of the west beach, the government-run *Pondok Perconotohan* has air-con cottages from 40,000 to 60,000 rp. For tranquility's sake, choose one back from the road.

Places to Eat

Almost all the restaurants and warungs along the main street cater to Western tastes – Western-style breakfasts (toast, jam, omelettes, porridge, etc), seafood (shrimps, lobster, and fish sometimes with chips), pancakes and a variety of fruit juices and fruit salads. If fresh fish isn't on the menu (fish is generally fried crisp so that it will keep, but it's good) they'll usually cook fresh seafood for you if you order it or buy it yourself at the fish market. There are, of course, plenty of Indonesian dishes too and for as little as 700 rp you can get a big plateful of nasi campur.

They're nearly all good and prices are much the same – eg a breakfast of omelette, toast, tea/coffee is around 1100 rp, prawns or lobster around 5000 rp, noodle soup 950 rp. Popular places to try include the group of small, warmly lit warungs opposite the Laut Biru Hotel. The *Sympathy Cafe* is usually packed out because its prices are so reasonable; it serves excellent fruit salads, gado-gado (only 750 rp) and a variety of grilled fish. But what your pocketbook saves, your stomach may pay for as sanitation here is less than adequate. More expensive but worth it, the *Cilacap Restaurant* at Jalan Kidang Pananjung 187 probably has the most extensive menu in town; they always have fresh fish and the food is excellent. Savory prawns with garlic for 4000 rp and their banana pancakes are enough to feed a family. At night they make good mixed fruit juices.

At the end of Jalan Pasangrahan on the west beach is *Rumah Makan Nanjung* with a pleasant open-air dining area and good food, including excellent barbecued fish for around 4500 rp. Right on the west beachfront there are many late-night warungs which catch the sea breezes. You can get good coffee, pisang goreng and snacks away from the crowds.

Across the street from the Sympathy Cafe, the *Inti-Laut* restaurant serves grilled fish and Indonesian fare. It's quite popular with Indonesians on holiday. Heading east from the Inti-Laut, you will find the *Lonely Planet* restaurant! I wish I could say that the fish and Chinese food served here was out of this world, but it's not bad and, given the eatery's name, at least the prices are budget.

In addition to the restaurants, there are a number of local women who do the rounds of the hotels selling fruit, and there's a good market on the main road in town. A decent loaf of brown bread and croissants can be bought from the Bumi Pananjung Hotel. Be careful if you're buying seafood at the fish market. Naturally they'll sell you anything you are willing to buy and it hasn't always just been caught. To make sure fish is really fresh an easy check is to look at the gills, which should be a good red colour, not brown; the eyes should be bright. Tuna and shark are plentiful.

Beer is usually cold and cheap; Orang Tua, probably the most popular drink locally, is cheaper. This is basically a jamu (all-purpose medicine) but with a strong alcoholic content and, according to the label, will transform the most decrepit old man into Mr Universe. Mixed with coca cola it's not bad at all. There's also a special brand for women called Kancur, which is supposed to taste a bit like advocaat.

Getting There & Away

Pangandaran lies more or less half-way between Bandung and Yogya or Dieng. Banjar is the turn-off point on the Bandung to Yogya rail and road route. If you're coming from Central Java, an alternative to taking the train and bus all the way is to head for Cilacap and make the very nice backwater trip by boat from there to Kalipucang, 17 km north of Pangandaran. See the Boat section below for details. Note that it can save travelling time to slot in a visit to Dieng between Yogya and Pangandaran.

Bus – to/from Jakarta From Cililitan station in Jakarta, you can bus non-stop to Pangandaran on Patas buses, which leave at 8 and 9 am, as well as 8 and 9 pm. It takes 8 hours and the fare is 5000 rp.

Bus – to/from Banjar If the departure times of the direct bus from Jakarta to Pangandaran are inconvenient, you can catch a bus from Cililitan station in Jakarta directly to Banjar (via Bogor and Bandung). The fare is 4700 rp. Buses depart every hour until about 11 pm. If you're travelling straight through to Banjar, it's a good idea to take a night bus; they're less crowded and faster (eight to nine hours), but watch your gear on this night run. Bandung to Banjar by bus takes about five hours and costs 2500 rp. When there is sufficent demand, Bandung's Losmen Sakadarna runs a minibus at 1 pm direct to Pangandaran for 5500 rp. Yogya to Banjar takes about nine hours and costs 3650 rp; buses depart every hour until 11 pm. There are also buses from Tasikmalaya (three hours) and Clamis (2½ hours).

Train From Bandung or Yogya you can also approach Banjar by rail – about a five-hour trip from Bandung or six to eight hours from Yogya.

The final stretch from Banjar to Pangandaran, by bus or colt, takes two hours and costs 2000 rp. The colts along this stretch are about the most unscrupulous in Java when it comes to overcharging. Last colts/buses leave around 8 to 9 pm. From the bus stop on the main road you can walk a couple of km or take a becak to the tourist area of Pangandaran.

Taxi The 4848 intercity taxi company in Bandung has a direct minibus service between Bandung and Pangandaran for 6000 to 7000 rp (depending upon where it is booked) that leaves every day at 6 am and 3 pm, assuming there are five passengers, arriving in Pangandaran six to seven hours later.

Boat The boat ride from Cilacap to Kalipucang is one of the highlights of a trip to Pangandaran. It takes you across the lagoons of Segara Anakan – a stretch of inland sea sheltered by the long island of Nusa Kambangan to the south. You'll pass mangrove swamps and a few fishermen in dugout canoes, and the boat calls at small fishing villages along the way – clusters of small thatched houses on the water's edge, perched high on stilts off the mud banks. This is the most easy-going trip you can make in Java and it feels an eon away from any of the hassles that Indonesian buses and trains can turn up! The ferry is a small boat – perhaps 10 metres – but there is usually plenty of room and baggage is no problem.

Note that whether you are embarking from Yogya or Pangandaran, you can save a lot of hassle connecting with buses and getting to and from the ferry by booking a bus-ferry-bus combination ticket with a travel agency in either town. The cost of the total ticket is 13,500 rp and is well worth it, as private buses and minibuses connect directly with the ferry. In Yogya, a recommended agency

which sells this ticket is Kresna Travel at No 4 and No 26 on Jalan Prawirotaman.

To Kalipucang Boats depart daily from Sleko Harbour (Pelabuhan Lomanis) in Cilacap at 7, 8 am, noon and 1 pm. The trip takes roughly four hours and costs 1000 rp.

Once you've got to Kalipucang, it's a 500-metre walk to the main road and a 1000 rp, 45-minute ride by bus or colt to Pangandaran.

To Cilacap From Kalipucang, boats depart at 7.30 and 8.30 am, and at 10.30 and 12.30 am, although the latter arrive too late for direct connections to Yogya by bus.

Getting Around
Whenever a bus – especially an express minibus – arrives in Pangandaran with foreigners on it, the local becak drivers assault it in a screaming horde, trying to grab your bags to put in their becaks. There's no need to be alarmed, but keep an eye on your gear; if you don't want a becak, calmly remove your stuff from it and walk on. On the other hand, it's over a km from the bus stop to the beach so you may need one. The drivers will ask outrageous rates but you shouldn't have to pay more than 600 rp maximum. Some will go for less, but that means you go to their choice of hotels so they get a commission. You can always walk to another hotel. Note that one of the advantages of booking a bus-ferry ticket through a travel agency in Yogya is that a minibus will take you from the ferry right to the hotel of your choice, thereby avoiding the becak hussle.

You can rent bicycles from Toha, opposite the Rumah Makan Mambo, for 3500 rp per day. They also organise jungle walking tours. It's easy to get lost in the reserve, so a guide is a good idea. Government-certified guides may be hired at the Tourist Information booth around the corner from the Sympathy Cafe. Their going rate is 7500 per day. If you wish to charter a boat at Pagandaran, be wary, as travellers have had hair-raising experiences aboard small, unseaworthy craft.

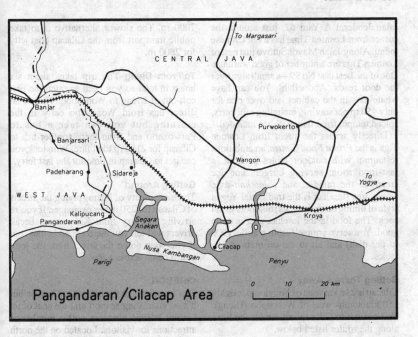

Pangandaran/Cilacap Area

At Hotel Bahtera Jaya on Jalan Sumardi there's a small travel agency that sells bus tickets, rents bicycles and motorcycles, and also does tours to Nusa Kambangan three times a week for 16,000 rp per person.

CILACAP

Cilacap is actually in Central Java but for convenience it's included here. The only natural harbour on Java's south coast for ocean-going vessels, Cilacap is a fairly big town in a growing industrial area. The only reason travellers would come here is to make the backwater trip to Kalipucang for Pangandaran. Boats depart from the Sleko boat jetty, which is a becak or 250 rp-bemo ride from the bus station or centre of town.

Places to Stay & Eat

If you get into Cilacap in the afternoon, you'll have to stay there overnight as there's no connecting ferry for Kalipucang after 1 pm. *Losmen Tiga*, at Jalan Mayor Sutoyo 61,

is a clean, comfortable and friendly place with singles/doubles at 5000/6500 rp – good value if you don't mind being in the centre of town. If you arrive by bus, it can drop you off at the hotel on its way through town to the bus station. Around the corner on Jalan Anggrek is *Losmen Anggrek* with slightly larger rooms for 6000/7500 rp, 10,000/12,500 rp with fan, or 15,000 rp for 'VIP' rooms.

You can also try the *Losmen Akhmad* where rooms cost 7500 rp or the *Losmen Bahagia* which has rooms with a small mandi at 5000 rp. They're basic and there are lots of mosquitoes, but they're OK for the night. They're both on Jalan Sudirman, a short distance from the Sleko boat jetty.

At the top end is the *Hotel Wijaya Kusuma* (☎ 22871), Jalan Jenderal A Yani 12A, on Cilacap's main downtown street. All rooms have air-con, hot water and color TV; rates start at 90,000 rp.

The *Restaurant Perapatan (Sien Hieng)* at

Jalan Jenderal A Yani 62, just around the corner from Losmen Tiga, has a fair Chinese menu. Along Jalan Mayor Sutoyo just east of Losmen Tiga are a number of good warungs. One of the best is at No 99 – a small sign over the door reads 'Abdoellah'. You can have whatever's in the cabinet laid over rice for only 450 rp per serving, including tofu curry, spiced tempe, fried fish, with tea included.

Directly across the street from Losmen Tiga is the *Prima Food Centre*, an ambitious restaurant with outdoor tables in front, a fast-food room serving burgers and ice cream in the middle, and a *lesehan*-style eating area (lesehan is the traditional Yogya style of dining on straw mats) outdoors in the back. The food in the lesehan area is quite good. You serve yourself from a buffet (900 rp per dish) and sit to eat on mats at low tables.

Getting There & Away

Cilacap is 216 km west of Yogya and roughly 150 km south-west of Wonosobo (Dieng). You can get to Cilacap in time for the ferry along the routes listed below.

To/From Yogya From Yogya you can take the early morning train at 7 am to Kroya for 2650 rp (four to six hours) – and from there take a colt for the one-hour ride to Cilacap. The bus from Yogya to Cilacap costs 2800 rp and takes about five hours, though you may have to change buses en route at Purworejo. In other words, if you don't get an early enough start, you will most likely spend the night in Cilacap. Alternatively, there are also direct private buses from Kresna Travel at No 4 and No 26 Jalan Prawirotaman in Yogya: their minibus departs direct from your hotel at 7 am, costs 7000 rp and drops you at the boat jetty at around noon in time for the last ferry.

Going the other way, to opt for convenience, the early ferries from Kalipucang link up with a door-to-door private minibus service from Cilacap to Yogya. You can arrange for this direct link by purchasing your ticket at a travel agency in Pangandaran. The trip takes six hours and costs

7000 rp. The slower alternative is to take public transport from the Cilacap boat jetty for 2800 rp.

To/From Dieng The trip takes about six hours in total so you need to catch the first colt out of Dieng to Wonosobo. There's no direct bus from Wonosobo early in the morning but you can take a bus to Purwokerto and from there another bus to Cilacap for 2150 rp total fare. With luck you can get to Cilacap in time for the last ferry.

Getting Around

There are plenty of bemos plying the streets of Cilacap for 250 rp per passenger. If you're arriving by ferry from Kalipucang, becak drivers will tell you there are no bemos, but if you walk down the street from the jetty you'll come across a few.

CIREBON

Few people make the trip out to Cirebon but it's an interesting seaport and the seat of an ancient Islamic kingdom with a number of attractions for visitors. Located on the north coast, right on the border with Central Java, the city's history has been influenced by both the Javanese and Sundanese with a bit of Chinese culture thrown in for good measure. A multi-ethnic city, many of the people speak a local dialect blending Sundanese and Javanese, and it has been suggested that the name Cirebon comes from 'Charuban' which is Javanese for 'mixture'.

Cirebon was one of the independent sultanates founded by Sunan Gunungjati of Demak in the early 16th century. Later the powerful kingdoms of Banten and Mataram fought over Cirebon, which declared allegiance to Sultan Agung of Mataram but was finally ceded to the Dutch in 1677. By a further treaty of 1705 Cirebon became a Dutch protectorate, jointly administered by three sultans whose courts at that time rivalled those of Central Java in opulence and splendour. During the Dutch 'culture' system period a flourishing trade in colonial crops attracted many Chinese entrepreneurs, and the Chinese influence can still be seen in

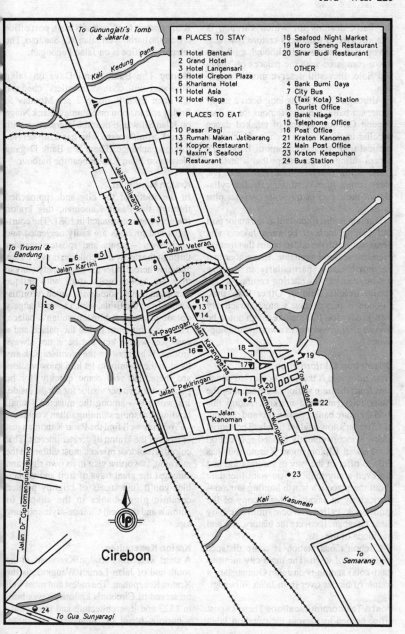

■ PLACES TO STAY

1 Hotel Bentani
2 Grand Hotel
3 Hotel Langensari
5 Hotel Cirebon Plaza
6 Kharisma Hotel
11 Hotel Asia
12 Hotel Niaga

▼ PLACES TO EAT

10 Pasar Pagi
13 Rumah Makan Jatibarang
14 Kopyor Restaurant
17 Maxim's Seafood
   Restaurant

18 Seafood Night Market
19 Moro Seneng Restaurant
20 Sinar Budi Restaurant

OTHER

4 Bank Bumi Daya
7 City Bus
  (Taxi Kota) Station
8 Tourist Office
9 Bank Niaga
15 Telephone Office
16 Post Office
21 Kraton Kanoman
22 Main Post Office
23 Kraton Kesepuhan
24 Bus Station

Cirebon

the batik designs for which Cirebon is famous. Two of Cirebon's kratons (palaces) are open to visitors and, although a bit run-down compared with the palaces of Yogya and Solo, they still deserve more recognition.

Although Cirebon has long been a major centre for batik, it is also famous for its Tari Topeng Cirebon, a type of masked dance peculiar to the Cirebon area, and tarling, a musical tradition reminiscent of Bandung's kecapi-suling music, except that it features guitar, suling (bamboo flute) and voice. The name comes from combining the last syllables of these two instruments (gui- tar plus su-ling).

Cirebon is also important as the major port and fishing harbour between Jakarta and Semarang, with the added bonus that there is excellent seafood available. Remember that the north coast, particularly in the dry season, can be a sweltering contrast to the cooler heights inland. Other than that, Cirebon is one of Java's most attractively well-kept cities. It is small enough not to be overwhelming and makes a worthwhile stopover.

Orientation & Information

Jalan Siliwangi is the main boulevard which runs from the train station to the canal by the Pasar Pagi (morning market). Along this road there are banks, restaurants and the bulk of Cirebon's low-budget hotels. The tourist office is inconveniently located way out on No 1 Jalan Ciptomangan Kusmo, but has little to offer in the way of information and not even a city map! If you want literature about the place it's worth hunting around – particularly in Jakarta – for a copy of the guidebook called *Cerbon*, published by Sinar Harapan. It covers the history, arts and traditions of the city.

Cirebon's bus station is some distance south-west of town. The main city minibus (taxi-kota) station is on Jalan Gunungsari, a couple of blocks over from Jalan Siliwangi.

Post & Telecommunications There's a post office branch just across the canal on Jalan Karanggetas, but Cirebon's main post office is near the harbour on Jalan Yos Sudarso. The telephone office is on Jalan Pagongan.

Money The Bank Bumi Daya on Jalan Siliwangi will change travellers' cheques; it's open from 8 am to 2 pm Monday to Friday and to noon on Saturday. Bank Niaga on Jalan Siliwangi near the intersection with Jalan Kartini/Veteran, also has a full-service foreign exchange. There is a Bank Dagang Negara on Jalan Kantor near the harbour.

Kraton Kanoman

In the south of the city and approached through the Pasar Kanoman, this kraton (palace) was constructed in 1681. The courtyards and grounds are sadly neglected and overgrown – goats and roosters wander through the decay and children now fly kites and play here. Under the huge shady banyan trees are broken walls stuck with antique European plates, some with Dutch reformist scenes from the Bible, which seem strangely out of place in a Muslim sultan's palace. There is a museum inside the palace and a caretaker with a key but he is not always around. If he's not on the premises, ask any local in the vicinity to let him know visitors are there. He will come quickly, for he pockets 1000 rp per visitor for a look inside. It's worth it – among the museum's small holdings are some stunning sultan's chariots.

You may well find the Pasar Kanoman just in front of the kraton of greater interest. This colourful outdoor market, most vibrant in the morning, is worth a visit in its own right and amongst the great trays of fruit and vegetables you'll find stacks of brightly painted ceramic piggy-banks in the shapes of animals and the local Cirebon-style spinning top.

Kraton Kesepuhan

A short walk from Kraton Kanoman, at the south end of Jalan Lemah Wungkuk, is the Kraton Kesepuhan. The oldest and most well preserved of Cirebon's kratons, it was built in 1527 and its architecture and interior are a curious blend of Sundanese, Javanese,

Islamic, Chinese and Dutch styles. Although this is the home of the Sultan of Kesepuhan, part of the building is open to visitors. Inside the palace is a cool pavilion with white-washed walls dotted with blue-and-white Delft tiles, a marble floor and a ceiling hung with glittering French chandeliers.

The museum outside the kraton has an interesting, if somewhat run-down, collection of wayang puppets, kris, cannon, Portuguese armour and ancient royal clothes. But the *pièce de résistance* of the Sultan's collection is a 17th-century gilded coach with the trunk of an elephant (Hindu), the body and 'head of a dragon (Chinese-Buddhist) and wings (Islamic)! In the courtyard office you'll find a caretaker who will unlock doors and show you around for a 5000 rp admission charge, a camera fee of 1000 rp and a 1000 to 2000 rp contribution for his guide service.

On the west side of the playing field, the Mesjid Agung with its tiered roof is one of the oldest mosques in Java, and is similar in style to the Mesjid Agung in Banten.

Every Sunday from 10 am to 2 pm in the courtyard there are gamelan and Tari Topeng performances in the traditional Cirebon style.

Kraton Kecirebonan

More of a mansion than a palace, Kraton Kecirebonan was built in 1839 and is occupied by members of the current royal family. Visitors are not usually admitted but the house is worth a quick look for its exterior architecture, a blend of Dutch and Indonesian styles.

Gua Sunyaragi

About four km south-west of town, a not-to-be-missed attraction is this bizarre ruined 'cave' (gua) – a sort of grotto of rocks, red brick and plaster honeycombed with secret chambers, tiny doors and staircases leading nowhere. It was originally a water palace for a Sultan of Cirebon in the early 18th century and owes its present strange shape to the efforts of a Chinese architect who had a go at it in 1852.

Sunan Gunungjati Tomb

In the royal cemetery, five km north of Cirebon, is the tomb of Sunan Gunungjati, who died in 1570. The most revered of Cirebon's kings, Gunungjati was also one of the nine walis who spread Islam throughout Java and his tomb is still one of the holiest places in the country. Although pilgrims are allowed to worship at the doorway, the inner tomb is closed to all but members of the royal family who visit on Fridays.

Other Attractions

Cirebon's harbour is always an interesting place to wander around to see the sailing schooners and freighters unload their wares, but it seems that photography is prohibited for 'security reasons'. Along the port area there are several old Dutch East Indies warehouses which were used at a time when opium, tobacco and sugar were shipped out from Cirebon.

Places to Stay – bottom end

There are a number of inexpensive hotels very close to the train station and along Jalan Siliwangi between the train station and the canal. Walking east from the station towards Jalan Siliwangi, the *Palapa Hotel* on the left looks rather grey and dreary but is OK inside. Rooms with a fan are 7500 rp with a private bathroom; triples are 10,000 rp. On the corner of the same street, at Jalan Siliwangi 66, the *Hotel Famili* has adequate rooms starting at 7000 rp for a single without bath, or 10,000/12,000 rp for doubles\triples.

Further south down Jalan Siliwangi is a string of slightly more expensive motel-type hotels beginning with *Hotel Slamet* at No 66, where standard rooms are 10,000 rp with attached bath. For 30,000 rp you can get similar rooms with air-con. Next at No 77 is the *Hotel Cordova*, which is slightly better value, with doubles without bath for 8000 rp, or 25,000 rp with bath and air-con. Across from the Grand Hotel is *Hotel Langensari* at No 117, a clean place with friendly staff where rooms are 8000 rp without bath, or 14,000 rp with bath. The nearby *Hotel Priangan* at No 108 is fairly new and clean, with doubles/triples with attached bath for 14,000/18,000 rp. They also have more expensive air-con rooms with hot water.

For atmosphere in this price range, you can't beat *Hotel Asia* (☎ 2183) at Jalan Kalibaru Selatan 15, alongside the quiet tree-lined canal near the Pasar Pagi. It's about a 15-minute walk or 500 rp by becak from the train station. This is a fine old Dutch-Indonesian inn with a terraced courtyard where you can sit and have breakfast; it's very well kept and the staff are friendly. Rooms range from 8000 to 16,000 rp, including breakfast (coffee and jam sandwiches) and a big pot of evening tea. There are also more expensive rooms with private mandi and/or fan.

South along Jalan Siliwangi you can give the *Hotel Baru* at No 163 a miss – it's damp and dingy and the mosquito nets are remarkably grubby. Further down there's a cluster of hotels between the railway tracks and the Pasar Pagi, including the *Hotel Islam* at Jalan Siliwangi 116, which is nearly as bad as the Baru. The *Hotel Damai* (☎ 3045) at No 130 is reasonable at 7000 rp without bath, or 10,000 rp with bath. Better value is the *Losmen Semarang* next door at No 132; large, fairly clean rooms here are 7000/ 11,000 rp.

Places to Stay – top end

The *Grand Hotel Cirebon* (☎ 2014/5) at Jalan Siliwangi 98, next to the town square, is a pleasantly old-fashioned place with large rooms and a big front verandah. Newly renovated, its prices have risen accordingly: air-con singles with TV begin at 42,000 rp including breakfast and a variety of larger rooms start at 50,000 rp, rising to 105,000 rp for a 'VIP' suite. Chauffeurs (no less) can have a room for 15,000 rp. The hotel has a restaurant, coffee shop, as well as a bar (open until midnight) and a disco frequented by ladies of the evening.

The new luxury-challenger to the Grand in Cirebon is the *Hotel Bentani* (☎ 23246) at Jalan Siliwangi 69. Air-con doubles with TV cost 59,000 rp and suites run 113,000 rp.

Hotel Niaga (☎ 6018), Jalan Kalibaru

Selatan 47, is a newer hotel that is very good value in this price range. Near the older Hotel Asia, it has clean, carpeted single and double rooms with air-con, TV, telephone and hot water for 35,000/50,000 rp.

The modern *Cirebon Plaza* (☎ 2061) at Jalan R A Kartini 54 has carpeted air-con rooms with TV, hot water and so on, from 42,000 (including breakfast) to 50,000 rp for VIPs. Chauffeurs' rooms here cost 12,000 rp. The hotel has a restaurant and coffee shop.

Next door at Jalan R A Kartini 48 is the newer and flashier *Kharisma Hotel* (☎ 2795) with well-appointed rooms at 36,050/50,000 rp. The hotel's satellite dish receives TV broadcasts from Thailand, Malaysia and the US as well as Jakarta, and the water system is solar-heated – it's a very high-tech establishment and it takes Visa and MasterCard.

At Jalan R A Kartini 27 is the *Hotel Aurora* (☎ 4541) with reasonably priced air-con rooms for 16,000/25,000 rp with TV and hot water. *Hotel Sidodadi* (☎ 2830) at Jalan Siliwangi No 74 offers economy fan-cooled rooms from 19,000 rp and air-con rooms for 30,000 to 56,000 rp.

Overpriced for its motel-like quarters, the Pertimina-owned *Patrajasa* (☎ 29402) at Jalan Tuparev 11 charges 68,000 rp for an air-con room with TV, or 180,000 rp for a suite.

Places to Eat

Apart from Cirebon's fine seafood, a local speciality to try is nasi lengko, a delicious rice dish with bean sprouts, tahu, tempe, fried onion, cucumber and peanut sauce. One good place for nasi lengko as well as other local and standard Indonesian dishes is *Rumah Makan Jatibarang* on the corner of Jalan Karanggetas and Jalan Kalibaru Selatan. Just south a few doors is the popular *Kopyor Restaurant* at Jalan Karanggetas 9. It's clean and reasonably priced with meals ranging from 2450 to 5000 rp. They also have a nice selection of kerupuk – *kerupuk rambak*, made from dried buffalo skin, *kerupuk bodin*, from sweet potatoes, and others. For decent Chinese food, try the *Hong Kong Restaurant* at No 20 nearby.

At the central market, or Pasar Pagi, you'll find a great array of delicious fruits and plenty of food stalls and warungs which stay open till evening. Further along Jalan Karanggetas there are a number of good bakeries where you can also buy ice cream; the *Toko Cermin* at No 22 is a small grocery store with bread, pastries, ice cream and various canned goods. The *Toko Famili*, near the Pasar Pagi, at Jalan Siliwangi 96 is good for all kinds of kerupuk and other baked snacks.

Most of the seafood restaurants are along Jalan Bahagia, towards the junction with Jalan Pasuketan. Of the many along this street, one of the best known is *Maxim's* at No 45-47, which specialises in Chinese, shrimp and crab dishes – 3700 rp for fresh shrimps or 4600 rp for shrimps fried with delicious oyster sauce.

Cirebon also has a good Chinese seafood night market. Surprisingly, the prices here are similar to those in the restaurants – a meal of grilled fish, rice and tea for two costs about 7000 rp, but there's plenty of it and it's delicious. The market sets up every evening in the small square at the south end of Jalan Bahagia.

In this same area the *Sinar Budi* restaurant at Jalan Pasuketan 15 has excellent, if slightly expensive, Padang food and good ice juices for around 1200 rp.

Near the harbour, the *Moro Seneng Restaurant* is down a small lane at the corner of Jalan Pasuketan and Yos Sudarso. It's worth trying; the menu includes seafood, it's clean and cheap (dishes start at around 1000 rp) and you can choose to eat inside or out. It's open from 9 am to 10 pm.

Things to Buy

Cirebon is well known for its distinctive batik which shows a strong Chinese influence in its designs, including the classic 'cloud and rock' motif, birds and sometimes the white lion of Cirebon royalty. Traditional colours are rich reds and tones of blue.

In town a number of shops along Jalan Karanggetas sell batiks from Cirebon, Pekalongan and Solo. Most of them claim to have set prices and start at about 8000 rp for a sarong. *Batik Purnama* on Jalan Karanggetas has a good selection although you'll have to bargain in Bahasa Indonesia. Another place to try is Pasar Balong on Jalan Pekiringan.

There are several cassette shops along Jalan Pasuketan and Jalan Pekiringan where you can buy tapes of tarling and other Cirebon music. One of the better ones is Toko Wijaya at Jalan Pasuketan 57, where you can have 'mie & music', since they also serve noodles.

Getting There & Away

The road and rail route to Cirebon from Jakarta (259 km) follows the flat north coast but it's more interesting to travel up from Bandung (127 km). The trip is by bus only but on a road which covers much more scenic hilly country.

Bus The Cirebon bus station is a 15-minute, 200 rp minibus trip to the south-west part of town. Buses between Jakarta and Cirebon take about five hours and cost 3850 rp. Bandung to Cirebon takes about 3½ hours and costs 1900 rp. Semarang (245 km) is about five hours away; from 3200 rp by public bus to 11,500 rp by air-con night bus. Yogya (365 km) is about six to seven hours by bus, from 5100 rp.

For shared taxis from Cirebon, the ACC Kopyor 4848 office (☎ 4343) is conveniently located in town at Jalan Karanggetas 7, next door to the Kopyor Restaurant. Their minibuses operate to Bandung (7500 rp), Semarang (7500 rp) and Yogya (9000 rp).

Train Cirebon is on both the main northern Jakarta-Semarang-Surabaya railway line and the southern Jakarta-Yogya-Surabaya line, so there are frequent day and evening trains. There are seven daily departures from the Gambir station in Jakarta and trains also depart from Kota and Pasar Senen. Fares vary widely from 6000 rp in 3rd-class-only to 28,000 rp for a 1st-class seat on the *Bima Express*; the trip takes around 3½ hours.

Getting Around

Cirebon's city minibus (taxi kota) service operates from the taxi kota station on Jalan Gunungsari, a couple of blocks west of Jalan Siliwangi. They're labelled G7, GG, etc and charge a fixed 200 rp fare around town – some even offer 'full music'! The most useful buses are: G7 to the kratons, G4 or GP to Trusmi, G9 or G10 to Gua Sunyaragi and GG to the Sunan Gunungjati Tomb. City buses, however, have been banned along Jalan Siliwangi between the train station and the Jalan Kartini junction near the mayor's residence so you'll have to take a becak or walk.

There are plenty of becaks ringing through the streets of Cirebon – if they didn't leave Jakarta for Bandung, they surely must have come here. A becak from the train station to Pasar Pagi costs around 500 rp.

Trusmi

Some of Cirebon's finest batik is made in the village of Trusmi, five km west of town. You can get there by taking the G4 city bus from Gunungsari station to Plered. Then, from the main road, walk down a cobbled country lane of whitewashed cottages. At the end of the lane, Ibu Masina's is probably the biggest studio where you can see batik tulis being made. Her showroom has a wide range of colours and designs from 9000 rp, or from 25,000 rp for the finer pieces. It's also worth wandering through the lanes to see the work in progress at the many small home workshops in Trusmi and the adjacent village of Kalitengah. Prices are no lower than those in the shops in Cirebon, but there is a wider selection of textiles to choose from and it's an interesting place to visit besides the workshops.

Indramayu

Some say the 'very best' Cirebon batik comes from the small workshops of Pamuan village near Indramayu, 30 km north along the coast. The patterns of the batik are more involved and some of the batik tulis is still coloured with traditional vegetable dyes. For the finest pieces you can expect to pay between 50,000 and 75,000 rp. Bargain hard for the best price. You can get there by taking a colt to Indramayu, and from the colt station it's about a 1½ km walk, or a 450 rp becak ride, to the village of Pamuan.

Central Java

Central Java has a population of about 29 million, an area of 34,503 sq km and Semarang as its capital. It's at the heart of Java and is the most 'Indonesian' part of Indonesia. This was the centre of Java's first great 'Indianised' civilisation and much of the island's early culture. Later, the rise of Islam created powerful sultanates centred around the kratons or courts of Surakarta (Solo) and Yogyakarta. Although the north coast was the early Muslims' first foothold on Java, further inland the new faith was gradually infused with strong Hindu-Buddhist influences and even older indigenous beliefs. The old Javanese traditions and arts, cultivated by the royal courts, are at their most vigorous here. The years of Dutch rule made little impact and even though the Indonesian revolution stripped the sultans of their political powers, the influence of kraton culture still lingers in the minds of many Javanese.

Within the province, the 'special territory' of Yogyakarta forms an enclave shaped like a triangle with its base on the south coast and its apex at the volcano, Gunung Merapi. Although the capital of Central Java is Semarang, the cities of Yogya and Solo (formerly Surakarta) are the emotional and cultural centres, having both been capitals of Javanese kingdoms and, frequently, rival cities. Most of Central Java's main attractions are in, or close to, these two cities and include the magnificent Borobudur and Prambanan temples. There are also earlier temples in Central Java, particularly the ancient shrines of Dieng, and the province also has some fine hill resorts like Kaliurang.

Despite its population pressure, Central

Java is a relaxed, easy-going state. The enclave of Yogyakarta in particular remains one of Indonesia's most important tourist destinations and for the traveller it offers excellent value. Accommodation prices are generally lower than elsewhere and standards are often higher; food is also good and low-priced.

History

Central Java has been a great religious centre for both Hindus and Buddhists. Under the Sailendra and Old Mataram kings, the Hindu-Javanese culture flourished between the 8th and 10th centuries AD and it was during this time that Java's most magnificent religious monuments were built. The province has also been the major centre for the political intrigues and cultural activities of the Islamic states of old Java, and it was here too that some of the most significant historical events took place.

The renaissance of Central Java's political ascendancy began in the late 16th century with the disintegration of the Hindu Majapahit empire. Strong maritime Muslim states arose in the north but in the south the most powerful of the later Javanese dynasties had started to develop. According to the legend, the founder of this second Mataram empire sought the support of Nyai Lara Kidul, the Goddess of the South Seas, who was to become the special protector of the House of Mataram and is still very much a part of court and local traditions.

From its capital at Kota Gede, near Yogya, the Mataram empire eventually dominated Central and East Java and Madura. It reached its peak under Sultan Agung, one of the classic warrior figures of Java's history. Agung also sent missions further afield to Palembang, Banjarmasin and Makassar. The only permanent defeats of his career were his failure to take Dutch Batavia and the sultanate of Banten in the west. Sultan Agung was the greatest conqueror in Indonesia, probably since Majapahit times. He not only had military ability but he relied upon a cult of mystical glory and wealth about him to attract loyalty. His tomb is at Imogiri near Yogya and is still revered as a holy place.

Following Agung's death in 1646 the empire rapidly began to disintegrate and was ultimately to fall to growing Dutch power. Amangkurat I followed Sultan Agung and devoted his reign to destroying all those he suspected of opposing him. In 1647 he moved to a new palace at Plered, not far from the old court. He constructed a more permanent palace, built of brick rather than wood, but also ensured its downfall by alienating his subjects through his tyrannical policies. He soon had to cope with revolts on all sides, which eventually led to the start of Dutch intervention in Javanese affairs. Rebellion broke out in 1675 and Plered fell to a predatory raid by Prince Trunojoyo of Madura, who then withdrew to Kediri, taking the Mataram treasury with him.

After Amangkurat's death in 1677, his son and successor made an alliance with the Dutch and began his reign from a new capital at Kartosuro, near present-day Solo. In 1678, Dutch and Javanese troops destroyed Trunojoyo's stronghold at Kediri, and the Mataram treasury was plundered by the victors, although some of it was later restored. The Dutch Captain Francois Tack is remembered for being presumptuous enough to sell a piece of royal regalia to Amangkurat II, who was later unwilling to pay up and finally repaid Tack for his effrontery by having him killed at court in 1686.

The Mataram rulers of the 18th century were a uniformly hopeless lot, and intrigues and animosities at court erupted into what became known as the First and Second Javanese Wars of Succession. Later, the repercussions of the Batavian Chinese massacre in 1740 spilled into Central Java and the fighting lasted almost 17 years. Pakubuwono II unwisely joined those Chinese who escaped slaughter in their siege of Dutch headquarters along the north coast, but was forced to retreat. Madurese intervention on behalf of the Dutch added to the confusion and in 1742 the court of Mataram was once again conquered by Madurese troops. The struggle was finally resolved by

JAVA SEA

Indramayu

Cirebon

Jatiwangi

Gunung Ciremay
3078 m ▲

Danau
Darma

Danau
Melahayu

▲ *Gunung*
Sawal
1784 m Ciamis

Tasikmalaya   Banjar

W E S T
J A V A

Pangandaran

Cilacap

Pemalang

Tegal   Pekalongan

Brebes   Batang

Waleri   Kaliwur

Danau
Cacaban

Dieng Plateau
Gunung
Perahu (Prau)
2565 m ▲

C E N T R A L

Bumiayu

▲ *Gunung Slamet*
3418 m

J A V A   *Gunung Sundoro*
3135 m ▲

Temanggun

Wonosobo   ▲ *Gunung Sumbin*
3371 m

Magelang

Purwokerto

Kroya   Kebumen   Purworejo

I N D I A N   O C E A N

Central Java

0   40   80 km

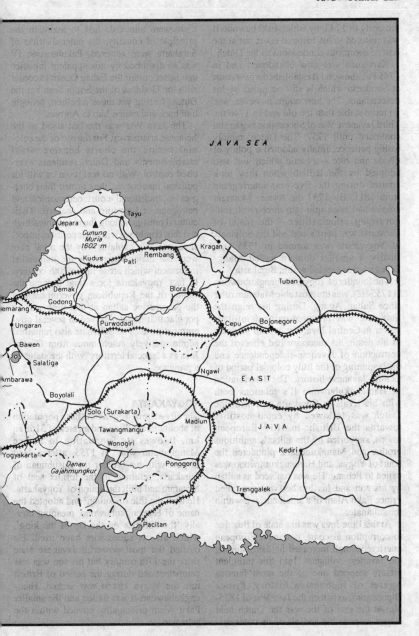

J A V A   S E A

Jepara

Gunung
Muria
1602 m

Tayu

Kudus

Rembang

Kragan

Pati

emarang

Demak

Godong

Blora

Tuban

Ungaran

Purwodadi

Cepu

Bojonegoro

Bawen

Salatiga

Yogyakarta

Ambarawa

Boyolali

Ngawi

E A S T

Solo (Surakarta)

Madiun

J A V A

Tawangmangu

Wonogiri

Kediri

Danau
Gajahmungkur

Ponorogo

Trenggalek

Pacitan

the treaty of 1743, by which Pakubuwono II was restored to his battered court but at the cost of enormous concessions to the Dutch.

Kartosuro was now abandoned and in 1745 Pakubuwono II established a new court at Surakarta which is still occupied by his descendants. The new court, however, was no more stable than the old and in 1746 the Third Javanese War of Succession began and continued until 1757. The Dutch, rapidly losing patience, finally adopted a policy of divide and rule – a tactic which was also adopted by the British when they took control during the five-year interregnum from 1811. By 1757 the former Mataram empire had been split into three rival, self-governing principalities – the realm of Surakarta was partitioned and the Sultanate of Yogyakarta was formed in 1755 and, finally, a smaller domain called Mang-kunegara was created within Surakarta.

The founder of Yogya, Hamengkubuwono I (1755-92), was the most able Mataram ruler since Sultan Agung. During his reign the Sultanate was the predominant military power in Central Java. Yet, within 40 years of his death, his successor had effected the destruction of Javanese independence and the beginning of the truly colonial period of Central Javanese history. The deterioration of Hamengkubuwono II's relations both with his rivals in Surakarta and with the Dutch was followed by equal hostility towards the British. In 1812 European troops, supported by the sultan's ambitious brother and Mangkunegara, plundered the court of Yogya, and Hamengkubuwono was exiled to Penang. He was replaced as sultan by his son and his brother was appointed Prince Paku Alam of a small enclave within the sultanate.

At this time Java was in a state of flux due to corruption at court, continual European interference and increased hardship among the Javanese villagers. Into this turbulent picture stepped one of the most famous figures of Indonesian history, Prince Diponegoro, to launch the Java War of 1825-30. At the end of the war the Dutch held Yogya responsible and all of its outer dis-tricts were annexed. Just to maintain the principle of equality, the outer districts of Surakarta were annexed. Pakubuwono IV was so disturbed by this apparent injustice that he set out for the Indian Ocean to confer with the Goddess of the South Seas but the Dutch, fearing yet more rebellion, brought him back and exiled him to Ambon.

The Java War was the last stand of the Javanese aristocracy. For the rest of the colonial period the courts became ritual establishments and Dutch residents exercised control. With no real room or will for political manouevre, they turned their energies to traditional court ceremonies and patronage of literature and the arts. Their cultural prestige among the masses was high and this, combined with their political impotence, possibly explains why the royal elite were not major targets for the nationalist movement which arose in the 20th century. In fact Yogyakarta for a time became the capital of the Republican government and the progressive sultan at that time was so popular that he later served in several government posts. The Sultanate also remained administratively autonomous from Central Java as a 'special territory' with the status of a province.

YOGYAKARTA

The city-state of Yogyakarta has a population of about three million and an area of 3169 sq km. It owes its foundation to Prince Mangkubumi who, in 1755, after a land dispute with his brother the Susuhunan of Surakarta, returned to the former seat of Mataram and built the kraton of Yogyakarta. He took the title of 'sultan' and adopted the name of Hamengkubuwono, meaning literally 'the universe on the lap of the king', which all his successors have used. He created the most powerful Javanese state since the 17th century but his son was less competent and during the period of British rule the Yogya kraton was sacked, Hamengkubuwono II was exiled and the smaller Paku Alam principality created within the sultanate.

For the Javanese, Yogya has always been a symbol of resistance to colonial rule. The heart of Prince Diponegoro's Java War (1825-30) was in the Yogya area. More recently, Yogya was again the centre of revolutionary forces and became the capital of the Republic from 1946 until independence was achieved in 1949. As the Dutch took control of other Javanese cities, part of the kraton was turned over to the new Gajah Mada University which opened in 1946. Thus, as one of the sultan's advisers observed, in Yogya 'the Revolution could not possibly smash the palace doors, because they were already wide open'.

When the Dutch occupied Yogya in 1948, the patriotic sultan locked himself in the kraton, which became the major link between the city and the guerillas who retreated to the countryside. The Dutch did not dare move against the sultan for fear of arousing the anger of millions of Javanese who looked upon him almost as a god. The sultan let rebels, including Suharto, use the palace as their headquarters and as a result of this support Yogya has continued as a semi-autonomous territory with the status of sultanate. Under Suharto's government, Sultan Hamengkubuwono IX was Indonesia's vice president until he stepped down in March 1978. The sultan passed away in October 1988 and in March 1989 Prince Bangkubumi, the eldest of 16 sons, was installed as Sultan Hamengkubuwono X. The coronation involved great pomp and ceremony and included a procession of dwarfs and albinos. The new sultan is a member of the National Assembly and, like his father, is intent on preserving the traditions of Yogya.

Today Yogya is one of the foremost cultural centres of Java and the sultan's walled palace remains the hub of traditional life. The sultan lived here until his death and, during the three special Garebeg festivals held each year, he led Java's most colourful and grand processions. Palace guards and retainers in traditional court dress and large floats of flower-bedecked *gunungans* (mountains) of rice all make their way to the mosque west of the kraton to the sound of prayer and the inevitable music of gamelan. These are ceremonies not to be missed if you're anywhere in the area at the time.

Traditional Javanese performing arts can also be seen in various places around Yogya. It is also a major craft centre and one of the best places to shop in Indonesia. Yogya is particularly well known for its fine batik and there are numerous batik workshops selling an incredible range of items, including batik paintings. The contemporary arts are also flourishing; Yogya has given its name to an important school of modern painting, perhaps best personified by the well-known Indonesian impressionist Affandi.

Just south of the city lies Kota Gede, the first capital of Mataram and today a major silverwork centre. The hilltop royal cemetery of Imogiri and the tomb of the famous Sultan Agung are also close by. To the northeast are the ruins of Prambanan; to the north-west is massive and magnificent Borobudur. Once a city of bicycles and pedestrians, Yogya has grown enormously but the pace is still slower than that of other large Indonesian cities. It's one of the most popular cities for travellers in Indonesia and it's easy to see why – apart from its many attractions, Yogya is interesting, friendly and easy-going, with an excellent range of economical hotels and restaurants.

Orientation & Information

The old, walled kraton of Yogya is situated in the south of the city while the newer parts have spread to the north. Jalan Malioboro, in the centre of the city, is the main street linking the old and new parts of Yogya and the busy main shopping centre. The tourist office is here, as are numerous restaurants and one long colourful bazaar of bookshops, souvenir shops and sidewalk stalls. Most of the hotels and restaurants frequented by travellers on a tight budget are located just off Malioboro around the railway station. The bus station is some distance south-east from the centre of town.

Yogya's tourist attractions are concentrated mainly in the kraton area of the old

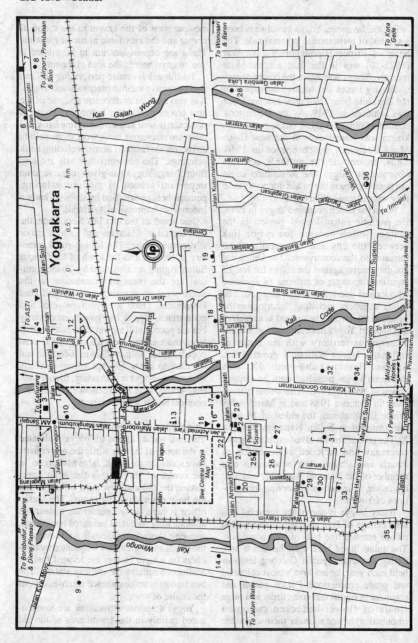

Yogyakarta

PLACES TO STAY		16	Museum Bekas Benteng Vredeburg
		17	Senopati Shopping Centre & Colt Station
3	Hotel Santika	18	Paku Alam Kraton
7	Ambarrukmo Palace Hotel	19	Batik Research Centre
		20	Nitour
▼ PLACES TO EAT		21	Sono-Budoyo Museum
		22	Post Office
5	Holland Bakery	23	Taxi Stand
15	Pasar Beringharjo	24	Wartel Telephone Office
		25	Mesjid Besar
OTHER		26	Museum Kareta Kraton
		27	Yogya Kraton
1	Bus Stop For Borobudur	28	Zoo
2	Monument	29	Pasar Ngasem Bird Market
4	Army Museum	30	Taman Sari (Water Castle)
6	Affandi Museum	31	Sasono Hinggil
8	Yogyakarta Craft Centre	32	THR (People's Amusement Park)
9	Monument Diponegoro	33	Batik Galleries
10	Garuda Airways	34	Dalem Pujokusuman Theatre
11	Gramedia Bookshop	35	Agastya
12	Telephone Exchange Office	36	Bus Station
13	Tourist Information Office		
14	ISI (Institute of Arts)		

city. In the north is the Diponegoro Museum, the Gajah Mada University and, on the east bank of the river, the Yogyakarta Craft Centre and Yogya's best hotel, the Ambarrukmo Palace. The Adisucipto Airport is a few km further east of the Ambarrukmo, on the road to Solo.

Note that although Yogyakarta is now spelt with a 'Y' (not Jogjakarta) it's still pronounced with a 'J'. In the 'new' Indonesian spelling system devised in the '60s, the letter 'Y' was chosen to represent what is a 'J' sound in English. Asking for Yogya with an English pronunciation will get you blank stares.

Yogya is notorious for pickpockets and thieves, so take care. Be particularly wary around the poste restante counter of the post office.

Tourist Office The Tourist Information Office (☎ 2812) is at Jalan Malioboro 16 and is open from 8 am to 9 pm Monday to Saturday. Useful, detailed maps of the city are available, and they can give you all the latest information on cultural performances in and

around Yogya. They also have reference maps of city bus routes and lists of train times pinned to various noticeboards.

Money The Bank Negara Indonesia, at the junction of Jalan Malioboro and Jalan Senopati, has a quick and efficient foreign exchange counter. It's open from 8 am to 4 pm Monday to Thursday, from 8 to 11 am and 2 to 4 pm on Friday, and from 8 am to 1 pm on Saturday.

Post & Telecommunications The main post office, with its efficient poste restante, is on Jalan Senopati and is open from 8 am to 8 pm Monday to Thursday, from 8 am to 5 pm on Saturday, and from 8 to 11 am and 2 to 8 pm on Friday. The telephone office is at Jalan Yos Sudarso 9 and is open from 7 am to midnight for both domestic and international calls. Alternatively, there are a number of Wartels open 24 hours which, in addition to domestic and international calls will send faxes, telegrams and telexes. Among the handiest Wartels are those at Jalan Pasar Kembang 37 near the budget Sosro hotels,

Jalan Suryatmatjan near Jalan Marlioboro and Jalan Parangtritis near the middle-range Prawirotaman accommodation places.

Other The immigration office is on Jalan Adisucipto, a short distance from the Ambarrukmo Palace Hotel. It's open from 7.30 am to 2 pm Monday to Thursday, from 7.30 to 11 am on Friday, and from 7.30 am to 12.30 pm on Saturday.

You can use the swimming pool at the Mutiara Hotel or the Ambarrukmo Palace Hotel (9 am to 6 pm) for 2500 rp a day.

Yogya Kraton

In the heart of the old city the huge palace of the sultans of Yogya is effectively the centre of a small walled-city within a city. Over 25,000 people live within the greater kraton compound, which contains its own market, shops, batik and silver cottage industries, schools and mosques. A large section of it is still used by the Gajah Mada medical faculty and until fairly recently (from 1949 to 1973) university students attended lectures in the northern courtyards of the palace.

The innermost group of buildings, where the current sultan still lives, were built between 1755 and 1756, although extensions were made over almost 40 years during the long reign of Hamengkubuwono I. European-style touches to the interior were added much later by the sultans of the 1920s, but structurally this is one of the finest examples of Javanese palace architecture, providing a series of luxurious halls, and spacious courtyards and pavilions. The sense of tradition holds strong in Yogya, and the palace is attended by very dignified and elderly retainers who still wear traditional Javanese dress.

The centre of the kraton is the fabulous reception hall known as the Bangsal Kencana or Golden Pavilion, with its intricately decorated roof and great columns of carved teak. A large part of the kraton is used as a museum and holds an extensive collection including gifts from European monarchs and gilt copies of the sacred *pusaka* (the heirlooms of the royal family), gamelan

instruments, royal carriages and a huge bottle-shaped wooden alarm gong. One of the most interesting rooms contains the royal family tree, old photographs of grand mass weddings and portraits of the former sultans of Yogya.

Other points of interest within the kraton palace include the small European bandstand with stained-glass images of musical instruments. In another part of the kraton there are 'male' and 'female' entrances indicated by giant-sized 'he' and 'she' dragons, although they look pretty much alike!

Outside the kraton, in the centre of the northern square, you'll see two sacred *waringin* or banyan trees where, in the days of feudal Java, white-robed petitioners would patiently sit, hoping to catch the eye of the king. Entrance to the kraton is from the west gate. It's open from 7 am to 1 pm daily, except Friday when it closes at noon. It is closed on national and kraton holidays. Admission is 1000 rp, which includes an excellent guided tour, although some people have reported that there is a tendency to rush visitors through. Booklets about the palace and excellent postcards of the old sultans are on sale inside. On Monday and Wednesday you can see gamelan playing at the pavilion from 10.30 am to noon, and classical dancing on Sunday mornings.

Taman Sari

Just west of the kraton is the Taman Sari or Fragrant Garden. Better known in Yogya as the Water Castle, this was once a splendid pleasure park of palaces, pools and waterways for the sultan and his entourage. The architect of this elaborate retreat built between 1758 and 1765 was Portuguese, from Batavia, and the story goes that the sultan had him executed to keep his hidden pleasure rooms secret. They were damaged first by Diponegoro's Java War, and an earthquake in 1865 helped finish the job. Today most of the Water Castle has tumbled down amidst dusty alleys, small houses and batik galleries, but it's an interesting place of eerie ruins with underground passages and a large mosque at a cool subterranean level which is worth seeking out. There are often students around who will help out with a guided tour (though some will spirit you afterwards to a batik gallery – you are not obligated to buy).

Of the remaining fragments, the bathing pools have been restored – not terribly well perhaps, but they give an impression of the ornate architecture and the scale on which things were built here. It was no doubt intended as a cool place for the sultan and ladies of the harem to relax in the days when it was surrounded by gardens, and from the tower overlooking the pools the sultan was able to witness what was going on below. Eating the round and pale-brown fruit of the *kepal* trees growing near the pool is supposed to do wonders for body odour! Entrance to this site costs 300 rp and it's open from 9 am to 4 pm daily.

On the edge of the site, the Pasar Ngasem is a colourful bird market crowded with hundreds of budgies, orioles, roosters and singing turtle-doves in ornamental cages. This is a breeding ground, though, for big red ants (the eggs are sold for bird feed) so beware – they have a mean bite!

Other Palaces

The smaller Paku Alam kraton, on Jalan Sultan Agung, is also open to visitors and gamelan concerts are held there about every fifth Sunday. The Ambarrukmo palace, in the grounds of the Ambarrukmo Palace Hotel, was built in the 1890s as a country house for Hamengkubuwono VII. The pavilion has recently been restored and is another good example of Javanese palace architecture.

Sono-Budoyo Museum

On the north side of the main square in front of the kraton, the museum is housed in an attractive building constructed in traditional Javanese style. It contains a first-rate collection of Javanese, Madurese and Balinese arts including wayang kulit puppets from China and Bali, a beautiful statue of the monkey god Hanuman as well as exhibits from the Yogya royal family. Nothing is labelled in English but the museum's keeper speaks English and may be around to give you a

tour. It's open from 8 am to 1.30 pm Monday to Thursday, to 10.30 am on Friday, and to 11.30 am on weekends. Entrance is 300 rp.

Sasmitaluka Jenderal Sudirman

The memorial house on Jalan B Harun was the home of General Sudirman, the Commander of the Revolutionary forces whose portrait decorates the older series of Indonesian paper currency. Wasted by tuberculosis, Sudirman reputedly often led his forces from a litter. He died shortly after the siege of Yogya in 1948. The house is open every morning except Monday.

Monumen Diponegoro

This museum was built to honour the Indonesian hero, Prince Diponegoro, leader of the bloody but futile rebellion of 1825-30. The eldest son of Sultan Hamengkubuwono III, Diponegoro had become thoroughly fed up with the corruption of court life and decided to dedicate himself to more spiritual matters. He is supposed to have received a sign from Nyai Lara Kidul that he was destined to be the man of action to oust the Dutch from Java and, as a religious mystic of royal blood, Diponegoro was an ideal Javanese leader. The bitter five-year war was finally resolved when Diponegoro was cunningly tricked into discussing truce negotiations, captured at Magelang and exiled to Manado on the island of Sulawesi. He was later taken to better quarters in Makassar, where he died in 1855. His grave there is now a shrine.

Most of the prince's belongings and sacred pusaka are kept in this reconstruction of his Yogya residence, which was burned and destroyed by the Dutch in 1825. There's still a hole in the wall which Diponegoro is supposed to have shattered with his bare fists so that he and his supporters could escape. The museum is open from 7.30 am to 4 pm daily.

To get to Monumen Diponegoro, about four km from the centre of town, take a No 2 bus heading north along Jalan Mataram.

Taking a No 1 bus will get you back to Jalan Malioboro.

Other Museums

The Museum Biologi at Jalan Sultan Agung 22 has a collection of stuffed animals and plants from the whole archipelago. It's open daily at 8 am, closing at 1 pm Monday to Thursday, at 11 am on Friday and at noon on weekends. Admission is 150 rp. The Museum Perjuangan, in the southern part of the city on Jalan Kol Sugiyono, has a small and rather poor collection of photographs documenting the Indonesian Revolution. The large Army Museum, on the corner of Jalan Jenderal Sudirman and Simanjuntak, displays more documents, home-made weapons, uniforms and medical equipment from the revolution years. Records also trace Suharto's rise in the ranks of Yogya's Diponegoro Division.

Across from the post office at the end of Jalan Jen A Yani, you will find the Museum Bekas Benteng Vredeburg built within an old Dutch fort. Here you will find exhibits on Yogya's history and its role in the war for independence. The museum is open from 8.30 am to 1.30 pm Tuesday to Thursday, to 11 am on Friday and to noon on weekends. Admission is 300 rp. Between the kraton entrance and the Sono-Budoyo Museum on the palace square, the Museum Kareta Kraton holds some opulent chariots of the former sultans. It's open from 8 am to 4 pm daily and admission is 300 rp.

Performances

All the traditional Javanese arts have their place in Yogya. Classical dancing and gamelan rehearsals in the kraton have already been mentioned. Check with the tourist office to find out what else is going on while you are in town. Wayang kulit can be seen at several places around Yogya on virtually every night of the week. Most of the centres offer shortened versions for visitors but at Sasono Hinggil, in the south palace square, there are marathon all-night performances every second Saturday from 9 pm to 5 am. Tickets cost around 4000 rp for the

better seats. This performance and most others are viewed from the dalang's side of the screen, but if you want to see the 'shadow-play' there are one-hour shows held outdoors at the Yogyajarkata Craft Centre on Jalan Adisucipto near the Ambarrukmo Hotel about 7 km from Yoga. Shows begin at 9.30 pm on Monday, Wednesday and Saturday, and tickets cost 2250 rp. The Arjuna Plaza Hotel, Jalan Mangkubumi 48, also has two-hour wayang kulit shows on Tuesday at 7 pm for 4000 rp. You can catch abbreviated wayang kulit during the day, except Saturday, at the Agastya Art Institute, Jalan Gedong Kiwo MD III/237, where dalang are trained. Admission is 3200 rp and the two-hour show begins at 3 pm.

Wayang golek plays are also performed frequently. The Nitour performance, from 11 am to 1 pm every day except Sunday, has a useful handout explaining the history of the wayang and the *Ramayana* story. Performances are held at Jalan Ahmad Dahlan 71, and tickets cost 2400 rp. On Saturday there are wayang golek performances at the Agastya Art Institute from 3 to 5 pm for 2550 rp, and at the Arjuna Plaza Hotel at Jalan Mangkubumi 44 from 7 to 9 pm for 2800 rp. You can also see wayang practice sessions at Agastya daily between 3 and 5 pm. There are alos performances at Hanoman's Forest Restaurant. For more information, see Jalan Prawirotaman, in the Places to Eat section.

There are evening performances of wayang orang or the 'Ramayana ballet' at theatres and hotels in the city from Monday to Friday. Those at the THR Sasono Suko, or People's Park Theatre on Jalan Katamso are excellent; they are performed nightly from 8 to 10 pm and admission is 5000 rp. Another fine troupe performs at Dalem Pujokusuman at Jalan Katamso 45 on Monday, Wednesday and Friday evenings from 8 to 10 pm for 6000 rp. On Monday, Wednesday and Saturday evenings there are Ramayana ballet performances for 4500 rp at the old palace pavilion of the Ambarrukmo Hotel; on Tuesday and Thursday evenings they're put on at the hotel's Borobudur Restaurant and are free with dinner. As this schedule is somewhat erratic, it is best to check with the hotel (☎ 88488). Arjuna Plaza Hotel has Ramayana performances from 8 to 10 pm every Thursday night for 4000 rp.

Schools The KONRI (Conservatory of Classical Dance) on Jalan Agus Salim near the kraton, and the ISI (Indonesia Institute of Arts) on Jalan Colombo in north Yogya are both open to visitors from 8 am to 2 pm, Monday to Saturday. Bagong Kussudiarja, one of Indonesia's leading dance choreographers, has a school at Jalan Singosaren 9 (off Jalan Wates) where modern and classical dance practice sessions can be seen daily except Friday, from 4 to 6 pm. Kussudiarja's main studio is at Padepokan, five km from Yogya, where he runs six-month courses for foreign students.

Ramayana Ballet – Prambanan The Ramayana Ballet held at the outdoor theatre in Prambanan, 17 km east of Yogya, is Java's most spectacular dance-drama. Performances are held on the four successive full-moon nights each month of the dry season, from May to October, and you should make time to see a performance if you're here then. The origins of this contemporary version of the *Ramayana* epic go back to the traditional wayang wong of classical Javanese theatre but far greater emphasis is given to the dancing. With the magnificent floodlit Shiva temple as a backdrop, more than 100 dancers and gamelan musicians take part in a spectacle of monkey armies, giants on stilts, clashing battles and acrobatics. It's a somewhat abbreviated version of the *Ramayana*, which unfolds over the four nights – the second in the series is the most spectacular, when all the leading characters perform before being killed off in this or later episodes.

Performances last from 7 to 9 pm. Tickets sold through the Tourist Information Office, Nitour at Jalan Ahmad Dahlan 71 and other travel agents in Yogya include transport to the theatre direct from your hotel, but it's

cheaper (albeit less convenient) to make your own way to Prambanan. If you do the latter, it is probably wise to be at the theatre to buy tickets about two hours early. At the box office, ticket prices range from 1800 to 8000 rp, depending on how close they are to the stage. There are no truly bad seats in the amphitheatre. The same dance troupe performs in less elaborate fashion indoors at Prambanan's Trimurti covered theatre at 7.30 pm every Tuesday, Wednesday and Thursday.

Batik
For a first-hand introduction to batik, the best place to visit would have to be the government-run Balai Penelitian Kerajinan dan Batik (Batik & Handicraft Research Centre) at Jalan Kusumanegara 2. They have an excellent display of batik found throughout Java plus some unusual batik from other islands, and they'll give you a detailed guided tour of the processes involved in producing both hand-painted and cap-printed

Ramayana ballet dancer

(stamped) batik. Some of the batik made there is for sale.

Shops & Workshops Batik in the markets is cheaper than in the stores, but you need to be careful about quality and be prepared to bargain. If you don't know much about batik, a good place to start looking is the Terang Bulan shop (just before the market as you head south on Jalan Malioboro) which will give you an idea of what you should be paying. There are all kinds of materials and batik lengths (cap and tulis) at fixed, reasonable prices and the quality is reliable. Locally made lurik homespun is always the cheapest. Other shops in town include Ramayana Batik on Jalan Ahmad Dahlan, specialising in Yogya-style batik, and the more expensive Batik Keris (Jalan Mangkubumi) and Danar Hadi showrooms (Jalan Solo), with Solo-style work. Most of the batik workshops and several large showrooms are along Jalan Tirtodipuran and Jalan Prawirotaman to the south of the kraton.

Galleries Many of Yogya's better known artists produce batik paintings as well as paintings in oils. Batik paintings generally start at around 8000 rp but oil paintings are very much more expensive. There are a great number of galleries exhibiting work of varying prices, so look around before you buy.

Top of the scale is probably Amri Yahya's gallery at Jalan Gampingan 67. His dynamic modern batiks range in price from 185,000 rp to over two million rp and there are some quite stunning abstract oil paintings on display – nice to look at even if you can't afford them. Amri Yahya also sells clothing of original modern design. The gallery is open Tuesday to Sunday from 9 am to 5 pm.

Almost next door to Amri Yahya's is Yogya's ISI (Institute of Arts), which you can visit in the mornings, from Monday to Saturday. Carry on up Jalan Wates (the extension of Jalan Ahmad Dahlan) and you'll come to other galleries with more reasonable prices. Kussudiarja is a student of art as well as dance and his Yogya dance

studio off Jalan Wates has a large display of batik and oil paintings.

Kuswadji's, in the north square near the kraton, is another good place for top-quality classical and contemporary batik art. Tulus Warsito has a superb gallery with a contemporary orientation nearby on Jalan Nyai Dahlan. Bambang Utoro has a gallery to the east of town off Jalan Kusumanegara, the continuation of Jalan Senopati.

Affandi, Indonesia's internationally best known artist, lives in an unusual tree-house about 6 km from the centre of town overlooking the river on Jalan Solo and close to the Ambarrukmo Palace Hotel. On the grounds Affandi keeps a museum of his own impressionist works, and paintings by his daughter Kartika and other artists. It's open from 9 am to 4 pm and there's now an entry fee of 300 rp. An interesting film about the artist – *Hungry to Paint: Profile of the Indonesian Painter Affandi* – has had occasional showings in Jakarta and is worth looking out for.

The Taman Sari (Water Castle) is the site of most of the cheaper batik galleries. Some of the batik is quite interesting; lots of it is very poor quality and boringly repetitive in theme – endless birds and butterflies and soaring moons over rice paddies, which is fine if you like that sort of thing but you still need to be prepared to hunt around and be selective if you're buying here. Some batik artists only bother to draw the outline and then have teams of women fill in the intricate details, which certainly enables them to churn out pictures in great numbers! On the positive side in this area, the Astuti Batik Gallery has some good quality surrealist and landscape work.

Beware of the teams of touts who follow you around taking you to galleries – Yogya is positively crawling with would-be batik salesmen and they'll inevitably rake off a commission at your expense. Many of the touts have taken to pretending that they are guides who will escort you around the water palace without fee – simply out of friendship. If you go along with them, you are in no way obligated to visit or purchase batiks from the

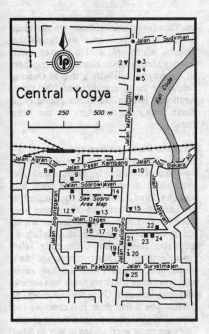

Central Yogya

0   250   500 m

galleries, to which they will ultimately steer you.

Batik Courses If you want to have a go at batik yourself there are lots of batik courses and classes in Yogya. Many of the teachers are just self-proclaimed 'experts' out to make some easy rupiah, so before investing time and money it's a good idea to ask around among other travellers who may have just completed a course. There are any number of batik courses in the budget accommodation Sosro area, ranging from 10,000 rp for a single day of instruction to 25,000 rp for three days.

The Intensive Batik Course of Hadjir Digdodarmojo seems to have a generally high approval rating, although some people have also reported it to be rather mechanical and dull. There are three or five-day courses from 2 to 6 pm daily. It's on the left of the main entrance to the Water Castle at Taman Kp 3/177.

The Batik Research Centre has recommended Tulus Warsito at Jalan Tirtodipuran 19A. He offers various courses including one-day beginners' classes for 15,000 rp and three-day courses for 42,000 rp. A one-week course, covering the four basic methods of using batik as an art medium, costs 85,000 rp. It covers theory and practice with chemical dyes and waxing, as does a ten-day course costing 140,000 rp. Wiko Djoan is a young artist who offers a similar variety of curricula and tuition at his batik workshop, at Jalan Wates 31.

The most thorough course with the best facilities is likely to be at the Batik Research Centre, which offers a comprehensive one-month course (limited to three students at a time) for 500,000 rp per person, including dyeing, waxing and processing.

Curios & Other Crafts

Jalan Malioboro is the main antique/curio shop area. There are also a handful of places near the Ambarrukmo Palace Hotel, and you can find an interesting variety of antiques at the Jul Shop, Jalan Mangkubumi 29. Toko Tan Jam An on the same street is a silver jewellery shop but if you're visiting Kota Gede you'll find cheaper silver there.

Most of the leather workshops are in the kraton area. Yogya's leatherwork can be excellent value for money but the quality is not always high on closer inspection, so look for thick leather, and strong stitching and buckles. Kusuman on Jalan Kauman is one good place for leather. Good quality wayang puppets are made at the Mulyo Suhardjo workshop on Jalan Taman Sari and also sold at the Sono-Budoyo museum shop.

Brightly painted children's moneyboxes in the shapes of elephants, roosters and garudas are sold around Yogya, particularly in the bird-market area near Taman Sari. At Kasongan, the potters' village a few km south-west of Yogya, you can see pots being made.

Along Jalan Malioboro, a few vendors create rubber stamps for around 3200 rp apiece. Choose from among the designs in their sample books or have them create an original from your own design. They can usually have the finished stamp for you in 24 hours or less.

Organised Tours

There are various tours from Yogya to the Borobudur and Dieng Plateau temples and around the sights of Yogya. Several travel agencies and hotels can arrange them, including Kresna Travel, run by Antol, a most helpful fellow, with two offices on Jalan Prawiromatan at No 4 and No 26; and Jaya Tour and the Hotel Asia-Afrika in the Sosro area. The going low price for a day tour to Borobudur and Dieng is 12,000 rp, including admission to the temple sites and less-than-filling snacks. There are also tours run solely to Prambanan and Borobudur temples, which will enable you to climb Gunung Merapi for the sunrise, and transport all the way to Bali with a stop at Gunung Bromo for the sunrise en route. The aforementioned Kresna Travel has gotten good marks from other travellers for the latter tours.

Places to Stay – bottom end

Yogya offers a superb choice of places to stay. Most of the cheap hotels are in the Sosro area, which is bordered on the north and south by Jalan Pasar Kembang, parallel to and immediately south of the railway line, Jalan Sosrowijayan, a block further south, and on the east and west by Jalan Malioboro and Jalan Jogonegara. Connecting Jalan Pasar Kembang and Sosrowijayan and just a couple of doors down from the main street of Yogya (Jalan Malioboro) are two narrow alleyways known as Gang Sosrowijayan I & II. Here you'll find more real cheapies and some of Yogya's most popular eating places. There are more good places to stay in other small gangs in this area.

Jalan Pasar Kembang At the end of Jalan Pasar Kembang it changes names to Jalan Agran Lor and at No 79 you'll find the spotlessly clean and highly efficient *Hotel Kota*. Although the general consensus is that it's a well-run and pleasant place, some people find it a bit over-officious and even too security conscious. They now require a hefty deposit of 20,000 rp per person and 'full', some travellers report, may simply mean that the owner doesn't like the look of you! Singles/doubles cost 6000/10,000 rp and larger rooms cost from 12,000 rp. There are comfortable open lounges and the only real drawback to its corner location is that the front rooms can be rather noisy. It also closes its doors from 11.30 pm to 5.30 am.

Back along Jalan Pasar Kembang towards Malioboro is a whole string of cheap hotels including the *Mataram* at No 61 with rooms (private mandi and toilet) at 7500 rp. At No 59 is the *Nusantara* at 7500 rp ('swarming

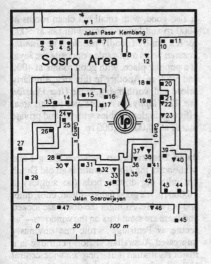

with cockroaches', reported one traveller, 'and not your small rubbish either – the twitching five cm jobs'). Then there are the similarly priced *Dua-Satu* and *Losmen Shinta*, which don't always take foreigners. A cut above these at No 49 is the *Hotel Mendut* (☎ 66721) with a range of decent-looking rooms starting at 27,000 rp for a double with fan and private mandi, 35,000 rp for an air-con room and 63,000 for a larger deluxe double with TV.

The *Hotel Asia-Africa* (or 'A-A') (☎ 4489) at No 25 has a variety of rooms from economy singles/doubles at 12,5000/15,000 rp to more expensive rooms with private mandi at 17,500/25,000 rp and air-con rooms for 25,000/30,000 rp. It's a good place and there's a garden at the back. The nearby *Guesthouse Asia-Africa II* owned by the same people is cheaper but not as nice.

■ PLACES TO STAY

2	Hotel Mendut
3	Losmen Shinta
4	Hotel Cendana
6	Batik Palace Hotel
7	Hotel Asia-Afrika
8	Hotel Ratna
10	Kencana Hotel
11	Guest House Asia-Afrika II
13	Losmen Setia
14	Losmen Gandhi 2
15	Hotel Bagus
16	Supriyanto Inn
17	Losmen Setia Kawan
18	Losmen Sastrowihadi
19	Losmen Beta
20	Losmen Lucy
21	Losmen Bu Purwo
25	Losmen Betty
26	Utar Pension Inn
27	Hotel Selekta
28	Jaya Losmen
29	Losmen Wisma Wijaya
31	Gandhi Losmen
32	Losmen Atiep
34	Dewi Homestay
35	Losmen Happy Inn
39	Lima Losmen
41	Hotel Jogja
42	Hotel Rama
43	Hotel Kartika
44	Hotel Aziatic
45	Hotel Indonesia
47	Wisma Gambira

▼ PLACES TO EAT

1	Mama's
9	Restaurant & Pub Cappucino
12	Cheap Warungs
22	Old Superman's Restaurant
23	Bu Sis Restaurant
24	Anna's Restaurant
30	Heru Jaya Restaurant & Losmen
33	Lovina Coffee Shop
36	Eko Restaurant
37	Superman 3 Restaurant
38	New Superman's Restaurant
40	French Grill Restaurant
46	Ris Restaurant & Bakery

OTHER

5	Wartel Telephone Office

At No 17A *Hotel Ratna* (☎ 86851) has basic rooms from 9000/11,000 rp, or 16,000 rp with private mandi and toilet. It's set back from the road and is relatively quiet.

Gang Sosrowijayan I This small connecting alley has some very cheap places but make sure your room is secure. Yogya is notorious for theft, including the straight-from-your-room variety. None of the following hotels offers private mandis with their rooms – it's shared bath only. The popular *Losmen Beta* is small, noisy and fairly commercial, with singles/doubles at 3000/5000 rp. Nearby on or just off Gang I are *Losmen Sastrowihadi*, only 3000/4500 rp, *Losmen Bu Purwo* with bed-size rooms for 2500/3200 rp and the slightly nicer *Losmen Lucy*, at 5000/6500 rp.

A bit further along the gang are the *Hotel Rama* with 4000/5000 rp rooms and the *Hotel Jogja* with better rooms for 7500 rp. The *Lima Losmen* is on a tiny alley perpendicular to Gang I towards Malioboro, with cheap OK rooms at 2500/4000 rp. The coffee shop next door is not particularly good. On a parallel alley is *Dewi Homestay*, where fair-sized rooms without bath are 5000 rp, or 9000 rp with attached bath.

Gang Sosrowijayan II In the next major alley to the west, the modern *Hotel Bagus* is clean and quiet; it's good value and very popular. It's built around a central courtyard and run by a veritable classroom of children. Singles/doubles with fan cost 4000/4500 rp, two beds run at 5500 rp, and a big room costs 6000 rp. There's free tea three times a day. The *Losmen Setia*, down an alley off Gang II (to the right coming from the train station), is a friendly, quiet place with spartan rooms at 4000 rp. Rooms on the roof for 5000 rp are cooler (they have windows) and are a bit more private than other rooms. Down another little alley to the left is the *Losmen Setia Kawan*, which is nothing special, for 4000/4500 rp. A better place for the same rates is at the end of the next alley off Gang II. The *Supriyanto Inn* is clean, airy and well-run at 4000/5000 rp. The *Jaya Losmen*

is also good, with small but clean rooms at 4000 rp and larger rooms with fan at 5000 rp. It's run by friendly people. The *Gandhi Losmen*, in its own garden opposite the Jaya, is a popular place, with good rooms at 4000 and 5000 rp. Another in this area, similarly priced and worth trying, is the *Utar Pension Inn*. The *Happy Inn* is quite nice for this area, offering singles/doubles with fan and private mandi at 14,000/16,000 rp.

Jalan Sosrowijayan Between Gang I and Malioboro, the *Hotel Aziatic* is an old Dutch inn with big double beds (no singles) at 10,000 rp. It's good value – clean, cool, quiet and very safe. At night the doors are locked and there are stout bars on the windows – 'as secure as Pentridge' wrote one obviously impressed Australian visitor. Pentridge is a major Australian jail! There's a wide central hallway where you can sit and chat, and a good restaurant in the back.

Across the road, the *Hotel Indonesia* has a nice courtyard, basic rooms for 4000/5000 rp and better rooms with mandis at 8000/10,000 rp. Further west on Jalan Sosrowijayan on the same side of the street is *Wisma Gambira*, with fair rooms overpriced at 12,500 rp with attached mandi. Across the street and down a short alley at Jalan Sosrowijayan 1/192, the friendly *Losmen Wisma Wijaya* has plain but clean singles/doubles at 4000/5000 rp including a small breakfast. The people who run it are reportedly 'very friendly and informative'.

New and the class of the neighbourhood at Jalan Sosrowijian 49 is *Hotel Oryza* (☎ 2605). This modern structure has pleasant rooms with shared mandi for 12,500 rp and rooms with private bath starting at 20,000 rp. Across the street at No 76 and also new is *Hotel Karunia*, whose unusual design is the product of its architect-owner. Quite nice rooms start at 8000 rp for a double with shared mandi and rooms with private bath start at 10,000 rp – a pretty good deal.

Other Across Malioboro, Jalan Sosrokusuman DN I is a quiet street alongside the

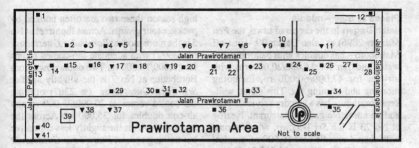

■ PLACES TO STAY

1	Hotel Sri Timur
2	Borobudur Guesthouse
4	Sriwijaya Guesthouse
10	Perwita Sari Guesthouse
12	Vagabond Youth Hostel
13	Warung Java Timur
14	Wisma Gajah Guesthouse
15	Airlangga Guesthouse
16	Putra Jaya Guesthouse
18	Wisma Indah
20	Sumaryo Guesthouse
21	Duta Guesthouse
22	Rose Guesthouse
24	Wisma Pari Kesit
25	Prayogo Guesthouse
26	Galunggung Guesthouse
27	Kirana Guesthouse
28	Sartika Homestay
29	Delta Homestay
30	Muria Guesthouse
31	Metro Guesthouse
32	Metro Guesthouse
33	Agung Guesthouse
34	Palupi Guesthouse
35	Post Card Guesthouse
36	Makuta Guesthouse
40	Sunarko Guesthouse

▼ PLACES TO EAT

5	Hanoman's Forest Pub Restaurant
6	Griya Bujana Restaurant
7	Putri Restaurant
8	Simco Restaurant
9	French Grill Restaurant
11	Galunggung Restaurant & Pub
17	Palm House Restaurant
19	Le Beng Beng Restaurant
37	Nini Restaurant
38	Bamboo House Restaurant
39	Morning Market
41	Slomoth Restaurant

OTHER

3	Mario Gallery
23	Prawirotaman International Bookshop

Helen Restaurant. The *Hotel Puri* at No 22 is an attractive place built around a small courtyard. It's well kept and very quiet. Singles/doubles start at 5000/7500 rp, 6000/7500 rp with fan and there's free tea or coffee in the mornings and evenings. At No 16 the nearby *Wisma Hasta Wisata* is similarly priced but not quite so nice. In the same range is The *Prambanan Guesthouse* at No 18-20. Near the end of Jalan Sosrokusuman toward Jalan Mataram, *Hotel Zamrud* (☎ 2446) at No 47 is the best on this street;

rooms start at 10,000 rp for a single including breakfast and cost 17,000 rp for a double with fan and shower.

One place for the shoestring budget traveller in the Jalan Prawirotaman area (see Places to Stay – middle) is the *Vagabond Youth Hostel* (☎ 71207), at Jalan Prawirotaman MGIII/589. Dorm beds here cost 5000 rp, singles cost 6500 to 10,000 rp and doubles 12,500 to 15,000 rp. If you show a YHA or student card, you may get a discount.

Places to Stay – middle

Jalan Dagen In the centre of town, the *Peti Mas* (☎ 2896) at Jalan Dagen 39 – just off Malioboro – has doubles with bathroom, hot water and fan for 16,000/20,000 rp, with air-con for 47,000/60,000 rp, including morning and evening tea. This clean, well-kept guesthouse has a laundry service, a pool and an attractive garden restaurant. Nearby at No 23 is the *Sri Wibowo*, where rooms with shared mandis cost 19,500 rp, singles/doubles with mandis run 24,500/30,000 rp, and air-con rooms cost 35,500 rp. The *Blue Safir* at No 34-36 has a similar range of rooms and prices. There are others: the *Lilik Guesthouse*, similar to the Peti Mas, and two slightly cheaper places, *Wisma Nendra* and *Sweet Home Hotel*.

Jalan Prawirotaman There are a number of good middle-range places south of the kraton and well away from the centre of town in the area of Jalan Prawirotaman. Most of them are converted houses that are spacious, airy, quiet and have central garden areas. An information desk at the railway station has details on some of them. They often send touts to intercept travellers at the station and you get a free becak ride there – if you don't like the place you only have to say no. Becaks into town from this area cost about 1500 rp, a price virtually comparable with the metered taxi fare. The cheapest way here from Marlioboro is to take the blue or white No 14 bus for 200 rp. Returning to Prawirotaman, catch the orange No 2 bus on Jalan Mataram.

Starting from the west end of Jalan Prawirotaman, at Jalan Parangtritis are a couple of semi-flash places with swimming pools – *Wisma Gajah Guesthouse* (☎ 5037) at No 4 and *Airlangga Guesthouse* (☎ 63344) at No 6-8. The Wisma Gadja has singles/doubles with fan for 25,000/30,000 rp and air-con for 35,000/40,000 rp. The all air-con Airlangga has singles/doubles for 40,000/45,000 rp. Note that Airlangga also has a nightclub where the music continues until midnight, a possible nuisance for those who hope to bed down earlier. During the

high season these two are often booked by package tour groups. Across the street at No 5 is the more modest *Borobudur Guesthouse* (☎ 63977) with adequate fan-cooled rooms for 12,000/18,500 rp. Two doors down from Borobudur at No 7 is the slightly spiffier *Sriwijaya Guesthouse* (☎ 2387) offering fan-cooled rooms at 20,000/25,000 rp and air-con doubles for 35,000 rp. Across the street at No 4A is the slightly less expensive but nothing special *Putra Jaya Guesthouse* where rooms with fan cost 15,000 rp.

Towards the middle of Jalan Prawirotaman are *Wisma Indah Guesthouse* (☎ 88021) at No 12, the *Sumaryo Guesthouse* (☎ 2852) at No 18A, and the *Duta Guesthouse* (☎ 5219) at No 20. The Wisma Indah is the least distinguished of the three, offering singles/doubles at 15,000/20,000 rp and air-con for 35,000/40,000 rp. Sumaryo is one of the nicest guesthouses in the entire area, with a pool, excellent service and a substantial breakfast at 25,000/30,000 rp for singles/doubles and 40,000 rp for air-con. The popular Duta (☎ 5219) has decent rooms in a nice price range, starting with economy singles/doubles at 8000/12,000 with shared mandi, standard singles/doubles at 16,000/20,000 rp, larger rooms at 36,000 rp and air-con rooms starting at 34,000/40,000 rp. The tariff includes breakfast and, when you consider that the Duta has a swimming pool, the lower-priced rooms are a particularly good deal. Unsurprisingly, it's often full.

Next to the Duta at No 22 is the ever-popular *Rose Guesthouse* (☎ 87991), which has singles/doubles for 20,000/25,000 rp and air-con rooms from 35,000 rp. Across the road and east a bit at No 23 is the *Perwita Sari Guesthouse* (☎ 5592), one of the cheapest on the street, with a few singles/doubles at 10,000/15,000 rp without bath, or 15,000/20,000 rp with bath.

At the east end of Jalan Prawirotaman are three more places: *Prayogo Guesthouse* (☎ 3715) at No 26, *Galunggung Guesthouse* (☎ 2715) at No 28, and *Kirana Guesthouse* (☎ 3200) at No 30. Starting at 12,000 rp, rooms at Prayogo are overpriced for what you get. The Galunggung is slightly better at

14,000 rp with a fan and 30,000 rp with air-con; it has a large swimming pool across the street. The Kirana is quite nice; pleasant doubles cost 32,000 rp including breakfast, or 43,000 rp with air-con.

Near the end of the street, the *Sartika Homestay* (☎ 87399) at No 44A came highly recommended by its lodgers as friendly and good-value accommodation. Without the glitz of some of its neighbours, this guesthouse offers clean rooms for 12,500 to 18,000 rp.

The next street south is Jalan Prawirotaman II, where the Pasar Pagi (morning market) is located. This street is somewhat quieter than Jalan Prawirotaman I. The *Metro* (☎ 5004) at No 71, often filled with Europeans, is the most popular and has a garden area and pool; pleasant rooms with breakfast and hot water range from 8000/10000 rp for singles/doubles with shared mandi, or 18,000/22,000 rp with private bath, to 35,000/40,000 for air-con rooms. The Metro has friendly staff and provides laundry, postal and telephone service, and a travel agency. *Agung Guesthouse* (☎ 5512) at No 68 is also popular. It has a pretty garden, pool and rooms with private baths ranging from economy singles/doubles at 10,000/12,500 rp, or standard rooms at 15,000/17,500 rp, to air-con doubles at 30,000 rp.

The following offer generally cheaper, though adequate, lodging. Near the Metro, the *Muria* (☎ 87211) at MGIII/600 is a friendly place where simple singles/doubles with attached mandi cost 12,500/15,000 rp. The *Makuta* (☎ 71004) at No 72 has basic but OK rooms with private bath starting from 7000/10,000 rp for singles/doubles. The *Palupi Guesthouse* (☎ 3823) located toward the east end of the street and the *Merapi* at No 599 are bare, basic but acceptable lodges. The Merapi has some cheap rooms with shared mandi starting at 10,000 rp and rooms with private bath costing 12,000/16,500 rp. The Merapi has singles/doubles with private mandi at 15,000/20,000 rp. Another budget lodge in the vicinity is the *Post Card Guesthouse* at the east end of the street, well run

by the Metro. Spartan but clean singles/doubles with shared mandi cost 8000/16,000 rp and a few with private bath run to 12,500/25,000 rp.

Toward the west end of the street, the *Delta Homestay* (☎ 55135) at No 597A is an efficiently run glitzier inn owned by the Duta Guest House. Here, you can enjoy a pool and pleasant singles/doubles for 16,000/20,000 rp and air-con doubles for 27,000 rp.

Around the corner from the west end of Jalan Prawirotaman at Jalan Parangtritis 73 is *Sunarko Guesthouse* (☎ 2047), a cosy little place with fan-cooled rooms and private bath starting at 10,000 rp. It lacks the glamour of some places on Jalan Prawirotaman, but the staff try hard to please.

Other Near the train station, the *Batik Palace Hotel* (☎ 2149) at Jalan Pasar Kembang 29 is a small, friendly hotel with a nice garden. Air-con singles/doubles (with bathroom, shower and hot water) are 32,500/39,450 rp and deluxe rooms 54,000 rp. The tariff includes breakfast and afternoon tea. A delightful newer branch of the Batik Palace (☎ 2229) at Jalan Mangkubumi 46 has singles/doubles at 49,000/59,000 rp and a swimming pool. Both hotels have a bar and restaurant. At the same price as the Batik Palace, next door at Jalan Mangkubumi 48, the Arjuna Plaza (☎ 3063) has comfortable air-con rooms and comparable facilities.

Places to Stay – top end
Yogya's most prestigious hotel is the grand *Ambarrukmo Palace Hotel* (☎ 88488), Jalan Adisucipto, which contains the old Ambarrukmo Palace in its grounds. There are singles/doubles beginning at 137,000/157,000 rp and more expensive suites. The hotel has restaurants, a coffee shop, bar, good shopping arcade, swimming pool and tennis courts.

The *Mutiara Hotel* (☎ 4531) is centrally located at Jalan Malioboro 18 near the Tourist Information Centre. The old part of the hotel has air-con singles/doubles from 59,000 to 88,000 rp (plus 20% tax and service) and more expensive suites. The new hotel next door is brighter and more expensive, with rooms from 122,000 to 275,000 rp for an executive suite. It also has a swimming pool, restaurant, bar, laundry and free airport transport.

The big Dutch-built *Garuda Hotel* (☎ 2113) at Jalan Malioboro 60 is a superb old building that has recently undergone renovations under the new ownership of the Nitour Group. It now has a swimming pool, shopping arcade and other features. Standard singles/doubles are 108,000/130,000 rp and suites start at 225,000 rp.

Places to Eat

Sosro Area There is as wide a variety of eating places as there are hotels in Yogya. Two of them have earned a permanent niche in the travellers' bottleneck department – everybody seems to pay a visit to either *Mama's* or the original *Superman's* (the first of three restaurants owned by the same family). They both serve Western-style breakfasts (eggs, porridge, french toast, yoghurt, etc) and snacks as well as Indonesian dishes. They have big helpings, the food is generally good and prices are low. If there's a catch to either of these places, it's that they're overwhelmed by Westerners and the only local people in sight are the Yogya trendies wasting time at Superman's.

You'll find the original Superman's on Gang Sosrowijayan I. It's very popular at breakfast time, there's good music and it's a relaxed place to while away a rainy afternoon. Some people say *New Superman's*, a bit further down Gang I, is better. A more expensive *Superman III*, also known as *Restaurant Mariko*, signifying the Japanese fare on the menu, has recently opened. On Jalan Pasar Kembang, beside the railway line, there are a whole host of good warungs but Mama's is definitely number one. You'll find great gado-gado here. Evening is when it comes into full swing and it's always crowded. The *Pandito Alam* on Jalan Pasar Kembang near Hotel Ratna has fair Padang food.

For delicious spicy food it would be hard to beat the two small warungs just up from Superman's at the station end of Gang I. They are just a couple of tables and benches along the wall, but the food is superb and there's a terrific selection of vegetarian dishes as well as excellent rendang; a large nasi campur with tea costs around 550 rp.

Also on Gang I, *Bu Sis Steakhouse* is a small and popular restaurant specialising in – what else – steak. Nearby, *Anna's* is also quite reasonable. Although the restaurant could use a little better ventilation, it has a Balinese cook and an interesting and varied menu, including fruit and cheese jaffles for 400 rp, *kefir* (yoghurt drink) and *arak* (fiery distilled rice brandy). Another well patronised restaurant near Gang I is the modestly priced *N & N. Eko Restaurant*, down the alley that runs next to Superman III, serves steak and fries for a remarkable 3100 rp. Also in this cul de sac is the *Lovina Coffee Shop*, with an outdoor eating area. It is popular with local people and has principally been recommended for its good music and atmosphere; the food is unexceptional but filling. On Jalan Sosrowijayan, the most popular budget eatery is the *Bladok Coffee House* at No 76. Good Indonesian fare and excellent desserts are served here at reasonable prices.

Jalan Malioboro Along this boulevard there are a number of places to try. Many of them cater to Western tastes, and there's often *Time* and other magazines available for you to catch up on world events while you're eating.

The *Shinta* at No 57 has some of the best iced juice in Indonesia. Ditto the *Columbo* at No 25. Further down and not far from Malioboro, the *New Happy* at Jalan Jen A Yani 95, as Yani intersects Jalan Gandekan, serves the usual fare at cheap prices.

On the corner of Jalan Malioboro and Perwakilan, the *Legian* is a roof-garden restaurant overlooking the main street. It has Western food and ice creams – it's slightly expensive but fairly quiet and free from petrol and diesel fumes, and a good place for a minor splurge. Try the excellent frogs' legs.

Around the corner from the tourist office,

in a small cul-de-sac, are three small warungs. One is the *Pak Wongso*, serving good cheap food, including good satay for 1000 rp and *tahu telur* (tofu omelette) for 850 rp.

Jalan Malioboro is also a good area for night food stalls serving Yogya's specialities, such as *nasi gudeg* (rice with jackfruit in coconut milk) and *ayam goreng* (fried chicken). At about 9 pm, when the souvenir vendors pack up, a lesehan area comes alive along the north end of Malioboro and stays open till early morning. Here young Indonesians sit around strumming guitars and playing chess into the wee hours. You take a seat on the mats spread over the pavements; a meal of nasi gudeg plus a glass of hot orange juice costs only 700 to 800 rp. A large bottle of tepid beer is around 2200 rp. The quality really varies from vendor to vendor, so have a look at the food first. There is also a nightly lesehan area within the kraton walls near the two big banyan trees.

North across the railway line, on Jalan Mangkubumi there are some excellent Padang restaurants including the *Sinar Budi* at No 41, which make a change from all the pseudo-Western travellers' delights found elsewhere in Yogya. The *Tip Top* at Jalan Mangkubumi 28 is good for cakes and delicious ice cream – from tutti frutti and lychee to durian for 400 rp. On Jalan Jenderal Sudirman the *Holland Bakery* and *Chitty 2 Bang 2* (Chitty Chitty Bang Bang) are next to the President movie theatre – their ice cream and cakes are reputed to be better.

At Jalan Mangkubumi 105, opposite the Garuda office, the *Malioboro* is a friendly place with an extensive menu of Western, Chinese and Indonesian food. Attached is the *Zangrandi Ice Cream Palace*, one of Java's best ice-cream places. Both are open from 7.30 am to 3 pm, and from 5 to 10 pm.

Jalan Prawirotaman There are several medium-priced restaurants along this street, but they mostly seem to specialise in slow service and mediocre food for tourists. Fortunately, there are some exceptions to this. The best restaurant on the street is

Hanoman's Forest Restaurant, featuring moderately priced Indonesian and Western cuisine, along with classical Javanese dance, wayang golek or wayang kulit shows each night. There is a 2000 rp cover charge for each performance and, given the quality, it's well worth attending. If you are not staying on Prawirotaman, the tourist office can tell you what is being performed at the restaurant that week. The *Griya Bujana* is not bad either and is very clean. For savoury soy chicken and some good fish dishes, dine at the *Palm House*. Other restaurants filled nightly with patrons, but not up to the quality of those noted above, are *Le Beng Beng*, *Prambanan* and *Galunggung*.

The primary budget recommendation in this area is *Tante Lies*, also known as *Warung Java Timur* at the Jalan Parangtritis intersection. They serve excellent satay, *nasi pecel*, *soto ayam* and other Central and East Javanese dishes at very reasonable prices.

Other For a major splurge, the *Floating Restaurant* at the Ambarrukmo Palace is worth considering for a 12,500 rp Indonesian buffet meal. The hotel bar is very smart, with cocktails at 6000 rp and free peanuts.

Also not cheap, but not outrageously priced, the *Pesta Perak* at Jalan Mataram 8, with its delightful garden ambience serves excellent Indonesian lunch and dinner buffets. For good steaks worth the price, those not watching their rupiah for every meal might try the *Gita Buana* at Jalan Diponegoro.

Note that most non-hotel restaurants in Java that are frequented by travellers (Indonesian as well as foreign) follow the custom of handing you a menu with a notepad to write your order on.

Things to Buy
Batik is one of Yogya's major attractions but other popular buys in Yogya include leather, wayang puppets, silver and antiques. And like any good travellers' centre there are plenty of cheap, cotton Bali-style clothes. Jalan Malioboro is one great long colourful bazaar of souvenir shops and stalls and

Malioboro's labyrinthine market, Pasar Beringharjo, is always worth a browse. Elsewhere you can visit galleries and workshops and see the crafts being done. There's a fair selection of regional crafts at the government-promoted Yogyakarta Craft Centre, opposite the Ambarrukmo Palace on Jalan Adisucipto. It's a fixed-price place but it will give you an idea of prices and quality even if you buy elsewhere. They have some interesting items which you may not see in the shops.

We've had letters from a number of travellers who were pressured into buying batik 'today, because tomorrow we are taking our best batik to Singapore as part of an ASEAN-sponsored exhibition' – don't fall for it.

Getting There & Away

Air Flights to outer islands, and Garuda international flights, are generally routed through Jakarta or Denpasar.

The Garuda/Merpati office (☎ 4400) is at Jalan Mangkubumi 56, near Jalan Diponegoro. It's open from 7 am to 4 pm Monday to Friday, from 7 am to 1 pm on Saturday, and from 9 am to noon on Sunday. After office hours you can ring 3034 for information.

Direct flights on Merpati/Garuda include those to Bima, Denpasar, Mataram, Surabaya and Waingapu. By changing flights, there are same-day connections to Ambon, Bajawa, Balikpapan, Bandarlampung, Banjarmasin, Ende, Kendari, Palu, Ruteng, Samarinda, Tarakan, Rantepao and Ujung Pandang.

Bouraq flies direct to Bandung and Banjarmasin daily. Other flights to Balikpapan, Samarinda, Tarakan and Palu are routed through Banjarmasin, and the daily flight to Jakarta goes through Bandung. The Bouraq office (☎ 2143) at Jalan Mataram 60 is open daily from 8 am to 5 pm.

Bus Yogya's new bus station is four km south-east of the city centre. Buses operate regularly from here to all the towns in the immediate area: Prambanan 400 rp (550 rp minibus); Parangtritis 500 rp; Muntilan (for Borobudur) 400 rp, then a change of buses and 300 rp more to Borobudur; Magelang 650 rp; Kaliurang 550 rp (750 rp minibus); Solo 1000 rp (2500 by minibus); Purworejo 950 rp; Ambarawa 1050 rp (2½ hours); Semarang 2200 rp (3½ hours). The bus to Parangtritis can also be caught along Jalan Sisingamangaraja going south near Jalan Prawirotaman. You can catch the Muntilan bus going north along Jalan Magelang near the Yogyakarta Monument. For Kaliurang buses, you should head east on Jalan Kaliurang (which extends east from Jalan Diponegoro).

Buses to Surabaya depart at 8 am, 11 am, 3 pm and 6 pm; they cost 5650 rp and take about eight hours. Note that colts to/from Solo can be waved down as they run up Jalan Mataram, a block over from Malioboro. There is a door-to-door minibus service to Solo from SAA (☎ 3238), Jalan Diponegoro 9A, for 2500 rp. The non-stop trip takes 1½ to two hours.

The bus company offices are mainly along Jalan Mangkubumi but it's less hassle to simply check fares and departures with the ticket agents along Jalan Sosrowijayan, near the Hotel Aziatic. They sell tickets for the various bus companies and in some cases run their own services too. On Jalan Prawirotaman, the two offices of Kresna Travel at No 4 and 26 are recommended. Fares from Yogya include Jakarta from 15,000 rp (21,000 rp air-con); Bandung from 15,500 rp with air-con (11,500 rp without); Surabaya 15,000 rp with air-con; Probolinggo 17,500 rp (24,000 rp air-con); Denpasar from 18,000 rp (25,000 rp air-con). Early morning buses from Jalan Sosrowijayan to Cilacap (for the ferry to Pangandaran) cost from 7000 rp.

Train There is only one station in Yogya and it's right in the centre of town. See the introductory Getting Around Java section for details of Jakarta-Yogya and Surabaya-Yogya travel. Solo is on the main Yoga-Surabaya rail route, only about an hour out of Yogya. Three daily trains operate on the Bandung-Banjar-Yogya route. Fares from

Bandung to Yogya are 4000 rp for 3rd class on the *Cepat Siang,* 10,000 rp for second class, 4,400 rp for third on the *Express Siang,* and 23,000 rp for 1st class on the *Mutiara Selatan* night express. The trip takes eight to 10 hours.

Getting Around

To/From the Airport A taxi to Yogya's airport, 10 km to the north-east, is a standard 7500 rp. To go by taxi into town costs 6000 rp, but if you stroll out to the main road, only 200 metres from the terminal, you can get any Solo colt or bus coming by for about 400 rp into Yogya (Yogya's to your left). From Yogya you can catch a colt bound for Solo from Jalan Mataram.

Bus Yogya's city buses – known as *bis kotas* – are bright orange minibuses operating on eight set routes around the city until 6 pm for a flat 250 rp fare. They work circular routes – a No 2 bus from the bus station will drop you on Jalan Mataram a block from Jalan Malioboro but the No 1 bus from Jalan Malioboro takes a more direct route to the bus station. The bus for Borobudur runs along Jalan Magelang to the north of the city and a No 5 bus will drop you at the bus stop there. There are route maps for reference in the information centre.

Becak & Andong Becaks cost around 500 rp a km in general and there are plenty of them. If you're touring the batik galleries, for example, it's probably cheapest to negotiate a round trip or an all-in daily rate. The becak drivers on Jalan Prawirotaman belong to a street union and the standard one-way price to Jalan Malioboro is 1500 rp (though they'll ask for more). Note that metered taxis cost about the same, so unless you have bargained for a round trip on a becak – usually 2000 rp – you may be better served by taking a taxi. There are also horse-drawn andongs around town.

Bicycle If you don't want to walk or be pedalled around, Yogya is traffic-free enough for you to comfortably pedal your-self. Pushbikes can be rented from the Hotel Aziatic and a couple of hotels along Gang I for 1500 to 2000 rp a day. If you lose a bike or it gets stolen, it could cost you around 150,000 rp, so take care – theft is big business in Yogya. Along Jalan Pasar Kembang you can hire motorcycles for around 11,000 rp a day.

Colt Colts leave from the bus station next to the shopping centre on Jalan Senopati for sites around Yogya, including Imogiri 350 rp, Parangtritis 600 rp, Kaliurang 750 rp and Prambanan 550 rp.

AROUND YOGYA
Kota Gede

Kota Gede has been famous since the 1930s as the centre of Yogya's silver industry, but this quiet old town was the first capital of the Mataram kingdom founded by Panembahan Senopati in 1582. Senopati is buried in the small mossy graveyard of an old mosque near the town's central market. The sacred tomb is open only on Monday and Thursday mornings from 10 am to noon, and on Friday from 1 to 3 pm. Visitors must wear conservative dress, which basically means hiring a sarong. On other days there is little to see here but a murky mandi, a few goldfish and an ancient three-legged yellow turtle said to be 100 years old and to possess magical powers!

The main street of town is lined with busy silver workshops where you're free to wander round and watch the silversmiths at work. Most of the shops have similar stock, including hand-beaten bowls, boxes, fine filigree and modern jewellery. Tom's Silver (☎ 3070) on Jalan Ngeksiganda is one of the largest and best-known workshops for high-quality silver. The HS800-925, a bit cheaper than Tom's, has some attractive modern jewellery. You can pick up small filigree pieces here for as little as 3000 rp; a better quality ring might cost 8000 to 12,000 rp.

It's only five km to Kota Gede from Yogya – you can take a bis kota (city bus) No 1 or becak or quite easily cycle out there and back

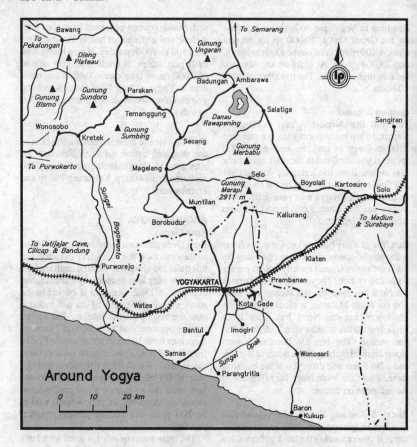

Around Yogya

0   10   20 km

in half a day. The road is pretty flat all the way.

Imogiri

Perched on a hilltop 20 km south of Yogya, Imogiri was built by Sultan Agung in 1645 to serve as his own mausoleum. Imogiri has since been the burial ground for almost all his successors and for prominent members of the royal family, and it is still a holy place. The cemetery contains three major court-yards – in the central courtyard are the tombs of Sultan Agung and succeeding Mataram kings, to the left are the tombs of the Susu-

hunans of Solo and to the right those of the sultans of Yogya. It's an impressive complex, reached by an equally impressive flight of 345 steps, but there are plenty of shady trees on the way up! From the top of the stairway there's a walkway circling the whole complex and leading to the real summit of the hill. Here you have a superb view over Yogya to Gunung Merapi.

The point of major interest for pilgrims is the tomb of Sultan Agung, a king credited with having supernatural powers who has been worshipped as a mystical source of guidance. Legend relates that shortly before

Diponegoro's rebellion, the prince's servant was sent to the tomb of Sultan Agung to wait for a sign. This duly appeared in the form of a huge bloodstain on the curtain covering the entrance. The tomb is only open from 10 am to 1 pm on Monday and from 1.30 to 4 pm on Friday, but there is no objection to visitors attending the praying and chanting sessions then. You have to sign the visitors' books and there is a 300 rp entrance charge to the site. For another 200 rp you can hire the traditional Javanese court dress – *kain* and *kebayan* for women and sarong for men – and enter the tomb. You must leave your shoes in the changing room and no cameras or bags are allowed in the graveyard – the attendants will guard them for you. Once in the tomb you're expected to kneel twice by the stone sarcophagus as tomb attendants recite prayers and distribute roses and incense to be placed on the coffin. You must pay exactly 500 rp for these materials each time you kneel. The heavy aroma of rose and incense lends an especially mystic atmosphere to the proceedings.

You can get there by colt from Yogya for 350 rp. The colt stand in the village is only about 500 metres from the base of the hill. Drinks and snacks are available around the stairway to the cemetery.

Parangtritis

Twenty-seven km south of Yogya, Parangtritis has rough surf and a long sweep of shifting, black sand dunes backed by high, jagged cliffs. It's a place of superstition and, like so many places along the south coast, a centre for the worship of Nyai Lara Kidul, the Queen of the South Seas. Legend has it that Senopati, the 16th-century Mataram ruler, took her as his wife and thus established the strong tie between the goddess and the royal house of Mataram. Their sacred rendezvous spot is at Parangkusumo, one km down the beach, where the sultans of Yogya still send offerings every year at Labuhan to appease this consort of kings.

In spite of the fact that the currents and undertows are reputed to be dangerous, several travellers have written to say that swimming is quite possible. Perhaps it's seasonal. You can swim very safely, though, in freshwater pools *(pemandian)* at the base of the hill near the village, where spring water spills out through high bamboo pipes from the hilltop. The village promenade of warungs and souvenir stalls is nothing to rave about, but this is a quiet, simple place if you want to get away for a while – just avoid weekends and holidays when buses are crowded and the beach is swamped by mobs from Yogya. Parangtritis has 'lovely sand dunes and terrible magic mushrooms,' reported one traveller.

There are trails along the hills above the sea to the west of Parangtritis. A couple of km from town is a cave used for meditation and, some say, witchcraft. A narrow trail leads down the cliff face to the cave opening, where a 'caretaker' usually sits. Branches of the cave extend deep into the hillside where would-be mystics sit in contemplation, sometimes for days on end.

Places to Stay Plenty of more or less similar hotels line the main street/promenade down to the beach. Rooms rent for around 4000 rp but facilities are limited (generally there's no electricity) and sometimes a bit unhealthy. *Penginapan Parang Endong*, just beyond the village, is probably the best cheapie. Rooms at 4000 rp are simple (you sleep on mats in some), but clean enough and it has a well-kept freshwater swimming pool.

The *Losmen Widodo* has OK rooms for 10,000 rp and 17,500 rp, including breakfast. Its garden courtyard is quite pleasant, bathrooms are clean, and the restaurant's not bad. Nearby is the similar *Agung Hotel & Garden Restaurant* with rooms ranging from 10,000 to 20,0000 rp including breakfast.

Food is cheap in the warungs along the promenade.

Getting There & Away From Yogya it's 600 rp from the main bus station or by colt from the station on Jalan Senopati; it's a bumpy one-hour trip over one of the worst roads in Java! At one time buses went only as far as Kreteg and you had to take a ferry across the river, followed by a long walk or dokar ride to the beach – this may still be the case in the wet season. The last bus back from Parangtritis leaves at around 6 pm.

If you're staying in the Jalan Prawirotaman area in Yogya, you can catch the Parangtritis bus (Jatayu line) going south on Jalan Sisingamangaraja, at the east end of Prawirotaman.

Other Beaches

Parangtritis is the best known of the southern beaches. Further afield are the relatively isolated beaches of Baron and Kukup. Baron, inside a sheltered cove with somewhat safer swimming, is 60 km south-east of Yogya via Wonosari; Kukup is a white-sand beach one km east of Baron. Samas is only 25 km south of Yogya but is said to be less attractive than any of the other beaches. There's hot black sand, violent surf and several warungs.

Kaliurang & Gunung Merapi

Kaliurang, 25 km north of Yogya, is the nearest hill resort to the city . It stands at 900 metres on the slopes of volcanically active Gunung Merapi. Pick a clear, cloudless day during the week when it's quiet and this is a great place to escape from the heat of the plains. There are good bushwalks, waterfalls, two chilly swimming pools and superb views of the smoking, fire-spewing mountain.

Merapi, the 'Fire Mountain', is one of Indonesia's most destructive volcanoes and there are times when the summit is off limits because of dangerous sulphurous fumes. It's a safer and easier climb from Selo, to the north of Merapi (see Around Solo), but many people do climb from Kaliurang. The summit, which often cuts through cloud, is 2911 metres high and the climb from Kaliurang is generally considered the most difficult climb in Central Java.

The time needed for the trek can range from 8 to 16 hours there and back, depending upon what shape you are in – it's by no means an easy stroll. The trail up the mountain begins at the car park where colts from Yogya stop. It's a one-hour walk to the obser-

vatory (1260 metres), from where you can watch Merapi when it's in action; some trekkers stop here too. From Kaliurang to the crater takes about four hours; all the way to the summit from Kaliurang takes about six hours. Again, it will take decidedly longer if the most exercise you have had of late is getting up from the dinner table. Moreover, it is necessary to begin your ascent shortly after midnight so that you can reach the summit during the few early morning hours when the volcano is free of clouds and mist. Do register (300 rp) for your own safety and sign out upon your return.

Should you decide to go for the top, it's a good idea to talk to the owner of the *Vogel* hotel, Christian Awuy, who is friendly, knows the mountain and will advise you on how to get up there and down again. He has maps and keeps a log book written up by travellers who've made the great assault. It makes interesting reading and, depending on your level of confidence, will either discourage you from making the climb or convince you to go for it.

Every evening but Saturday (when ascents should be avoided, as too many locals climb, sending dangerous small rocks falling onto those beneath them), Christian Awuy holds a briefing at 7 pm on Gunung Merapi and the best routes to the top. He supplies a free map and schedule of approximate times to reach particular locales on the way up. The talk is free and open to everyone.

Places to Stay & Eat There are a few excellent places to stay in Kaliurang. *Vogel* is the former residence of a Yogya prince and has dorm beds for 4000 rp and rooms starting at 6500 rp. At the back there's a two-storey bungalow with views of Merapi where rooms are 9500 rp and up. The food here is quite good and they even have fresh milk. A number of travellers have written to recommend this place. 'We were dining in candlelight while the rain poured down (as it does every afternoon)', reported one visitor, 'when the staff put on a crackling Bing Crosby record from the '40s – we briefly floated out of Indonesia!'.

Christian Awuy has opened the new *Christian Hostel* nearby in Kaliurang's former town hall, where independence negotiations between the Dutch and the Indonesians were once held. This large hostel has dorm beds for 4000 rp and very nice rooms for 6500/11,000 rp. If you have a IYHF membership card, you can get the 11,000 rp rooms for 8500 rp. The Christian Hostel has a great bar and restaurant with a nice view, and a large lounge area with dozens of maps, travel guides, novels, newspapers and 'word of mouth' travel logs.

There are nearly a dozen other places to stay in Kaliurang, including Christian Awuy's new venture, the *Hotel Merapi*, a particularly good deal as decent rooms with mandi start at 6000 rp. Alternatively, there's the fair *Hotel Muria* where rooms are 6000 rp. *Losmen Merapi* has adequate rooms at 5000 rp and better rooms for 7500 rp. Other hotels worth trying are *Lestari, Garuda Ngalayang, Corner, Bumi Putra, Gadjah Mada* and *Senoreno*, all with rooms for about 6000 rp.

Vogel and Christian Hostel have the most varied menus in Kaliurang, but if you want to get out into the village a bit, try *Restaurant Puas* or *Restaurant Joyo*. The local speciality is *gemblong*, small rounds of pounded sticky rice that are eaten with *tempe bacem*, sweetened soybean cakes.

PRAMBANAN

On the road to Solo, 17 km east of Yogya, the temples at Prambanan village are the cream of what remains of Java's period of Hindu cultural development. Not only do these temples form the largest Hindu temple complex in Java, but the wealth of sculptural detail on the great Shiva Temple makes it easily the most outstanding example of Hindu art. As intriguing as the beauty and scale of the Prambanan temples is the fact that this huge complex dedicated to the Hindu god Shiva stands amidst a number of Buddhist temple groups scattered across the Prambanan Plain. And the greatest Buddhist monument of all, Borobudur, lies only 40 km away.

All the temples in the Prambanan area were built between the 8th and 10th centuries AD. Though the origins of the Central Javanese powers during this time are hazy, historians have suggested that two dynasties were established then – the Buddhist Sailendras in the south and the Hindu Sanjayas of Old Mataram in the north. Possibly by the second half of the 9th century these two dynasties were united by the marriage of Rakai Pikatan of Hindu Mataram and the Buddhist Sailendra Princess Pramodhavardhani. This may explain why a number of temples, including the Prambanan Temple and the smaller Plaosan group, reveal Shivaite and Buddhist elements in architecture and sculpture. On the other hand, you find this mixture to some degree in India and Nepal, too, so it's hardly a novel idea.

Following this two-century burst of creativity, the Prambanan Plain was abandoned when the Hindu-Javanese kings moved to East Java. In the middle of the 16th century there is said to have been a great earthquake which toppled many of the temples and, in the centuries that followed, their destruction was accelerated by greedy treasure hunters

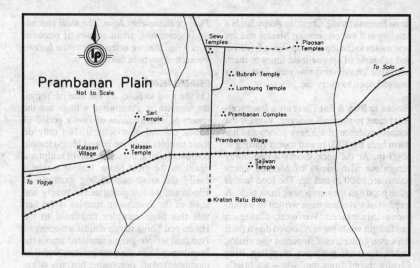

Prambanan Plain
Not to Scale

Sewu Temples

Plaosan Temples

Bubrah Temple

Lumbung Temple

To Solo

Prambanan Complex

Sari Temple

Prambanan Village

Kalasan Village

Kalasan Temple

Sajiwan Temple

To Yogya

Kraton Ratu Boko

and local people searching for building material. Most of the restoration work of this century has gone into the preservation of Prambanan. Of the outlying temple sites, some are just decayed fragments. Perhaps half a dozen are of real interest.

Orientation & Information

The Prambanan temples *(candi)* can be visited using either Yogya or Solo as a base. The largest of the temples is locally called Candi Loro Jonggrang, or Slender Virgin, and sometimes the entire complex is referred to by this name. Prambanan village is tiny and has little in the way of accommodation facilities (one passable spartan hotel). On its northern boundary is the temple complex and the outdoor theatre where the *Ramayana* ballet is performed on full-moon nights (see Yogya). The temple enclosure is open daily from 6 am to 6 pm. Entry costs 500 rp and there is a 250 rp fee for cameras.

At the temple complex you can buy a copy of *A Short Guide to the Prambanan Complex*, published by the Archaeological Service of Indonesia. It's quite good value and also covers a number of the other temple sites on Prambanan Plain.

Most of the outlying temples are spread out within a five-km radius of Prambanan village. You'll need at least half a day to see them on foot, or you can hire a horsecart by the hour in Prambanan. As with any of Java's major tourist attractions, the best time to visit Prambanan is early morning or late in the day when it's quiet. Very few people visit the other sites and the walk through the fields can be as much of a pleasure as the temples themselves.

Prambanan Temple Complex

The huge Prambanan Complex was constructed in about the middle of the 9th century – around 50 years later than Borobudur – but remarkably little is known about its early history. It's thought that it was built by Rakai Pikatan to commemorate the return of a Hindu dynasty to sole power in Java. Some have even suggested it was intended as a counterpart to Borobudur, but more likely it was a counterpart to Candi Sewu, a Buddhist complex three km away.

Prambanan has been in ruins for years and although efforts were made in 1885 to clear the site, it was not until 1937 that reconstruction was first attempted. Of the original group the outer compound contains the remains of 244 temples, two of which have been repaired. Eight minor and eight main temples stand in the highest central courtyard. The largest of these, the Shiva temple, has been restored; a few others are still shrouded in scaffolding.

Shiva Mahadeva The temple dedicated to Shiva is not only the largest of the temples, it is also artistically and architecturally the most perfect. The main spire soars 47 metres high and the temple is lavishly carved. The 'medallions' which decorate its base have the characteristic 'Prambanan motif' – small lions in niches flanked by 'trees of heaven' (or *kalpaturas*) and a menagerie of stylised half-human and half-bird heavenly beings *(kinnaras)*. The vibrant scenes carved onto the inner wall of the gallery encircling the temple are from the *Ramayana* – they tell how Lord Rama's wife, Sita, is abducted and how Hanuman the monkey god, and Sugriwa his white monkey general, eventually find and release her. To follow the story, ascend the main eastern stairway and go around the temple clockwise. The reliefs break off at the point where the monkey army builds a bridge to the island of Lanka; the end of the tale is found on the smaller Brahma Temple.

In the main chamber at the top of the eastern stairway, the four-armed statue of Shiva the Destroyer is notable for the fact that this mightiest of Hindu gods stands on a huge lotus pedestal, a symbol of Buddhism. In the southern cell is the pot-bellied and bearded Agastya, an incarnation of Shiva as divine teacher; in the western cell is a superb image of the elephant-headed Ganesha, Shiva's son. In the northern cell, Durga, Shiva's consort, can be seen killing the demon buffalo. Some people believe that the Durga image is actually an image of Loro Jonggrang, the 'Slender Virgin' who, legend has it, was turned to stone by a giant she refused to marry. She is still the object of pilgrimage for many who believe in her and the name of the cursed princess is often used for the temple group.

Brahma & Vishnu Temples These two smaller temples flank the large Shiva Temple. The Brahma Temple to the south, carved with the final scenes of the *Ramayana*, has a four-headed statue of Brahma, the god of creation. Reliefs on the Vishnu Temple to the north tell the story of Lord Krishna, a hero of the *Mahabharata* epic. Inside is a four-armed image of Vishnu the Preserver.

Nandi Temple This small shrine, facing the Shiva Temple, houses one of Prambanan's finest sculptures – a huge, powerful figure of the bull, Nandi, the vehicle of Shiva. '

The shrines to the north and south of Nandi may once have contained Brahma's vehicle, the swan, and Vishnu's sun-bird, the garuda.

Northern Group
Of the northern group of temples, the Sewu and Plaosan temples are the most interesting and they are within three km of Prambanan. To start, take the road behind Prambanan and follow signs pointing towards the Lumbung Temple.

Sewu Temples The 'Thousand Temples', dating from around 850 AD, originally consisted of a large central Buddhist temple surrounded by four rings of 240 smaller 'guard' temples. Outside the compound stood four sanctuaries at the points of the compass, of which the Bubrah Temple is the southern one.

All but a few of the minor temples are in various stages of collapse, a great jumble of stone blocks littering the field. Only the shell of the main temple remains but this is interesting for the unusual finely carved niches around the inner gallery, with shapes resembling those found in the Middle East. Once these would have held bronze statues but plundering of the temple went on for many years – some of the statues were melted down and others disappeared into museums and private possession.

Plaosan Temples One or two km east of

Sewu, you walk across rice paddies and sugar cane fields to this temple group. Believed to have been built at about the same time as the Prambanan temple group by Rakai Pikatan and his Buddhist queen, the Plaosan temples combine both Hindu and Buddhist religious symbols and carvings. Of the original three main temples, once linked by a multitude of small shrines and solid stupas, one has been reconstructed and is notable for its unusual three-part design. It is a two-storey, six-room structure with an imitation storey above and a tiered roof of stupas rising to a single larger one in the centre. Inside the temple are impressive stone Bodhisattvas on either side of an empty lotus pedestal within the various cells and intricately carved *kala* (dragon) heads above the many windows. The Buddhas that once sat on the lotus pedestals are now in the National Museum in Jakarta.

Southern Group

Sajiwan Temple Not far from the village of Sajiwan, about 1½ km south-east of Prambanan, is this very ruined Buddhist temple. Around the base are carvings from the Jataka (episodes from the Buddha's various lives).

Kraton Ratu Boko A steep rocky path (opposite the 'Yogya 18 km' signpost) leads up to the main site, two km south of Prambanan village on a small plateau in the Gunung Kidul hills. Ratu Boko, the 'Palace of the Eternal Lord', is believed to have been a huge Hindu palace complex dating from the 9th century. Although little remains apart from a large gateway and a series of bathing places, it is worth the walk. The view from this site across the Prambanan plains is magnificent. On a smaller plateau a few hundred metres further south is a large platform of waterspouts and staircases and, below, a group of pools which are still used by the local villagers.

Western Group

There are three temples in this group between Yogya and Prambanan, two of them

close to Kalasan village on the main Yogya road. Kalasan and Prambanan villages are three km apart, so it is probably easiest to take a colt or bus to cover this stretch.

Kalasan Temple Standing 50 metres off the main road near Kalasan village, this temple is one of the oldest Buddhist temples on the Prambanan Plain. A Sanskrit inscription of 778 AD refers to a temple dedicated to the female Bodhisattva, Tara, though the existing structure appears to have been built around the original one some years later. It has been partially restored during this century and has some fine detailed carvings on its southern side where a huge, ornate kala head glowers over the doorway. At one time it was completely covered in coloured shining stucco, and traces of the hard, stone-like 'diamond plaster' that provided a base for paintwork can still be seen. The bat-infested inner chamber of Kalasan once sheltered a huge bronze image of Buddha or Tara.

Sari Temple About 200 metres north of Kalasan Temple, in the middle of coconut and banana groves, the Sari Temple has the three-part design of the larger Plaosan Temple but is probably slightly older. Some students believe that its 2nd floor may have served as a dormitory for the Buddhist priests who took care of the Kalasan Temple. The sculptured reliefs around the exterior are similar to those of Kalasan but in much better condition.

Sambisari Temple A country lane runs to this isolated temple, about 2½ km north of the '10.2 km Yogya' post on the main road. Sambisari is a Shiva temple and possibly the latest temple at Prambanan to be put up by the Mataram rulers. It was only discovered by a farmer in 1966. Excavated from under ancient layers of protective volcanic ash and dust, it lies almost six metres below the surface of the surrounding fields and is remarkable for its perfectly preserved state. It has some fine decorations and in the niches

Top: Borobudur, Java (JC)
Bottom: Relief, Borobudur, Java (LH)

Top: Sultan's Palace, Yogyakarta, Java (JL)
Bottom: Dalang (puppet master) with shadow puppets, Yogyakarta, Java (AS)

you can see the stone images of Durga, Ganesh and Agastya.

Places to Stay Opposite the entrance to the temple is the basic *Ny Muharti Losmen and Restaurant*, where nondescript rooms range in price from 8500 to 11,000 rp.

Getting There & Away

From Yogya it takes only half an hour by road and costs 400 rp by bus (bound for Solo) from the main bus station, or you can catch a Solo colt along Jalan Mataram. Buses from Solo take 1½ hours and cost 600 rp. Prambanan is one of the best places in Java to get to by bicycle as there's a special cycle roadway all the way from Yogyakarta.

BOROBUDUR

From the plain of Kedu, 42 km north-west of Yogya, a small hill rises up out of a pattern of palm trees and fields of rice and sugar cane. It's topped by one of the greatest Buddhist relics of South-East Asia – up there with Cambodia's Angkor Wat and Burma's Pagan – and it ranks as one of Indonesia's most famous attractions. Rulers of the Sailendra dynasty built the colossal pyramid of Borobudur sometime between 750 and 850 AD. Very little else is known about Borobudur's early history but the Sailendras must have recruited a huge workforce, for some 60,000 cubic metres of stone had to be hewn, transported and carved during its construction. According to tradition, the main architect was Gunadharma, whose face can

be seen in the jagged ridge of the Menoreh mountain range in the background. The name Borobudur is possibly derived from the Sanskrit words 'Vihara Buddha Uhr', which means the 'Buddhist monastery on the hill'.

With the decline of Buddhism and the shift of power to East Java, Borobudur was abandoned soon after completion, and for centuries lay forgotten, buried under layers of volcanic ash. It was only in 1815, when Raffles governed Java, that the site was cleared and the sheer magnitude of the builders' imagination and technical skill was revealed. Early in the 20th century the Dutch began to tackle the restoration of Borobudur but over the years the supporting hill had become waterlogged and the whole immense stone mass started to subside at a variety of angles. A mammoth US$21 million restoration project, begun in 1973, is now complete.

However, restoration of the mighty temple suffered a setback in 1984 at the hands of both humans and nature – the huge central stupa was damaged when struck by lightning and nine of the smaller stupas were badly damaged by bombs thought to have been planted by Muslim extremists. Not that humans haven't damaged it in the past – in 1896 the Dutch colonial government presented eight cartloads of sculpture to the visiting King of Siam.

Although they are easily forgotten, standing as they do in the shadow of the great Borobudur, two smaller structures form a significant part of the complex. The Mendut and Pawon temples, built at about the same

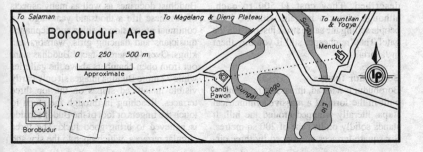

time as Borobudur, are aligned east-west and are thought to have been places for purification before entering the main sanctuary.

Orientation & Information

The village of Borobudur consists of little more than a crowd of becaks and a handful of warungs and souvenir stalls clustered around the bus station. A park has been built around the monument and there are now several places to stay in the village. There is also a new bus station at the base of the hill.

The temple site is open from 6.15 am to 5.15 pm and admission is 550 rp, with an additional 500 rp charge for photography. On weekends it can be crowded and noisy, which isn't going to do anything for your appreciation of this contemplative sanctuary – the finest time to see Borobudur and capture something of the spirit of the place would be at dawn or sunset. The first busloads of package tourists usually start arriving at around 10 am. If you're stopping off at Borobudur en route to somewhere else, you can leave your bags in the hut at the entrance to Borobudur, where they'll be looked after for a small fee.

At the entrance to the site are a number of useful books on sale about Borobudur and the Mendut Temple. *Glimpses of Borobudur* and *Chandi Mendut* are small booklets published by the Archaeological Service of Indonesia for 3000 rp each. *Borobudur* by Yazir Marzuki and Toeti Heraty, and another version by Jurgen Wickert, can also be worthwhile investments. The former has good illustrations which help in the identification of the symbolic Buddhas that are described. They cost 11,500 rp each, although you can bargain with the local people selling the same stock just outside the gate! They're cheaper still if you buy them in Jakarta.

Borobudur Temple

Borobudur is a broad, impassive monument, built in the form of a massive symmetrical stupa, literally wrapped around the hill. It stands solidly on its base of 200 sq metres. Six square terraces are topped by three circular ones, with four stairways leading up through finely carved gateways to the top. The paintwork is long gone but it's thought that the grey stone of Borobudur was at one time washed with white or golden yellow to catch the sun. Viewed from the air, the whole thing looks like a giant three-dimensional tantric mandala. It has been suggested, in fact, that the Buddhist community that once supported Borobudur were early Vajrayana or Tantric Buddhists who used it as a walk-through mandala.

The entire monument was conceived as a Buddhist vision of the cosmos in stone, starting in the everyday world and spiralling up to nirvana – eternal nothingness, the Buddhist idea of heaven. Below the base of the monument is a series of reliefs representing a world dominated by passion and desire, where the good are rewarded by reincarnation as some higher form of life and the evil are punished by a lowlier reincarnation. Strangely, these carvings were covered with stone, possibly to hide them from view, but they are partly visible on the south side. The latest theory is that these covering stones may have been added to keep the base from collapsing.

Starting at the main eastern gateway, go clockwise (as one should around all Buddhist monuments) around the galleries of the stupa. Although Borobudur is impressive for its sheer bulk, it is the close-up sculptural detail which is quite astounding. The pilgrim's walk is about five km long. It takes you along narrow corridors past nearly 1500 richly decorated relief panels in which the sculptors have carved a virtual textbook of Buddhist doctrines as well as many aspects of Javanese life a thousand years ago – a continual procession of ships and elephants, musicians and dancing girls, warriors and kings. Over 400 serene-faced Buddhas stare out from open chambers above the galleries while 72 more Buddha images sit only partly visible in latticed stupas on the top three terraces. Reaching in through the stupa to touch the fingers or foot of the Buddha inside is believed to bring good luck. The three circular terraces, which open to the sky and

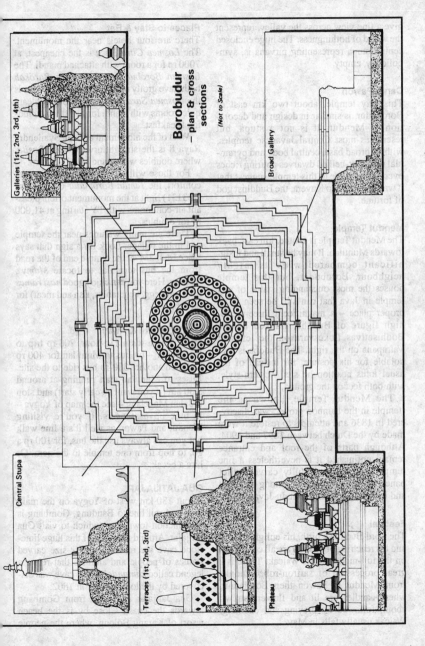

Galleries (1st, 2nd, 3rd, 4th)

Borobudur
– plan & cross sections

(Not to Scale)

Broad Gallery

Central Stupa

Terraces (1st, 2nd, 3rd)

Plateau

give a fine view across the valley, represent the world of nothingness. The huge enclosed central stupa representing nirvana is, symbolically, empty.

Candi Pawon

This tiny temple, about two km east of Borobudur, is similar in design and decoration to Mendut. It is not a stupa, but resembles most Central Javanese temples, with its broad base, central body and pyramidal roof. Pot-bellied dwarves pouring riches over the entrance to this temple suggest that it was dedicated to Kuvera, the Buddhist god of fortune.

Mendut Temple

The Mendut Temple is another km east, back towards Muntilan. It may be small and insignificant compared with its mighty neighbour, Borobudur, but this temple houses the most outstanding statue of any temple in Java that can still be seen in its proper place – a magnificent three-metre-high figure of Buddha, flanked by the Bodhisattvas Lokesvara on the left and Vairapana on the right. The Buddha is also notable for his posture, for instead of the usual lotus position he sits Western-style, with both feet on the ground.

The Mendut Temple, known as the 'temple in the bamboo grove', was discovered in 1836 and attempts to restore it were made by the Dutch between 1897 and 1904. Although parts of the roof and entrance remain unfinished it is nevertheless a fine temple and the gracefully carved relief panels on its outer walls are among the finest and largest examples of Hindu-Javanese art.

Festival

The Lord Buddha's birth, his enlightenment and his reaching of nirvana are all celebrated on the full-moon day of Waicak. There is a great procession of saffron-robed monks from Mendut to Pawon then Borobudur, where candles are lit and flowers strewn about, followed by praying and chanting. Waicak usually falls in May.

Places to Stay & Eat

There are four hotels near the monument. The *Losmen Citra Rasa* is the cheapest, at 7000 rp for a room with attached mandi. The *Losmen Borobudur* and *Losmen Barokah* both have grotty rooms for 8500 rp. Better is the *Losmen Saraswati*, which offers clean, quiet rooms with mandi for 11,500 rp including breakfast.

West of the monument at Jalan Syailendra Raya 8 is the straightforward *Villa Rosita*, where doubles with mandi are 11,500 rp.

For those willing to spend more for real comfort, the *Taman Borobudur Guesthouse* (☎ 3131) right at the monument offers pleasant air-con rooms with TV starting at 41,000 rp for doubles.

There are many warungs near the temple and in the village. Look for a sign that says 'Rice Stall 2M' at the temple end of the road from the bus terminal to locate *Mamy's* warung. Here you can enjoy good *nasi rames* (rice with egg, vegetables, fish and meat) for 600 rp.

Getting There & Away

From Yogya it's a 1½-hour, 700-rp trip to Borobudur – by bus to Muntilan for 400 rp and then another 300-rp bus ride to the site. Buses to Muntilan start running at around 5.30 am (if you want an early start) and stop at Jalan Magelang – see the map of Yogya – to pick up passengers. If you're visiting Mendut and Pawon as well it's a fine walk but you can always use the bus, for 100 rp a go, to hop from one temple to the next. Or hire a becak.

GUA JATIJAJAR

About 130 km west of Yogya on the main road and rail line to Bandung, Gombang is the junction town from which to visit Gua Jatijajar. Around the sides of this huge limestone cave are remarkable life-size carved statues of people and animals that relate a legend called *kamandaka*. The cave was discovered by the local people in 1802.

Gua Jatijajar is 20 km from Gombang towards the coast. Close by is the beach resort of Karang Bolong, where the people make a living collecting the nests of sea swallows from the steep cliff faces above the surf. The nests are collected every three months and sold to Chinese restaurants at home and abroad.

MAGELANG

Magelang was formerly a Dutch military garrison and it was here that the Javanese hero, Prince Diponegoro, was tricked into captivity in 1829. In the house where he was captured is a small museum of Diponegoro items, although the main collection is in Yogya.

Magelang is 42 km north of Yogya, on the main road to Semarang. Shortly before the town is Gunung Tidar, which legend credits as the 'Nail of Java', a mountain planted there by the gods to stop Java from shaking.

WONOSOBO

Some people who come to visit the Dieng Plateau use Wonosobo as a base. At 900 metres, in the hills of the central mountain range, Wonosobo has a good climate. It's a fairly typical country town with a busy market, quiet streets, a few horse carts and dilapidated buses. For most of the year it's not a particularly interesting place, but on national holidays it comes alive as people from the surrounding villages gather there for festivities held in the main square. If you're here on any of these days you might see the Kuda Kepang dance from nearby Temanggung, or the local Lengger dance in which men dress as women and wear masks. Virtually the whole town turns out to watch or take part.

Information

If you want detailed information about the Dieng Plateau, visit the Dieng Restaurant on Jalan Kawadenan. The owner, Mr Agus, used to be a guide for Dieng and has quite useful duplicated handout maps of the area, and plenty of stories and legends to tell. His wife has a very large photograph album!

There is also an official tourist office at Jalan Pemuda 2, where you can get a map of the Dieng Plateau area.

Places to Stay – bottom end

The *Hotel Jawa Tengah* (☎ 202), on Jalan A Yani next to the market and colt station for Dieng, is probably the most pleasant hotel in town for the price. Formerly the old Railway Guesthouse, it has small, clean rooms at 6000/8000 rp for singles/doubles. Larger rooms for three or four people cost 10,000 rp. The staff are helpful and there's hot water in the shared mandi. Rates include a small breakfast, as do those of all the hotels mentioned below.

Losmen Petra is also good value, with small singles at 4500 rp and larger rooms with attached mandi from 8000 rp. It's at Jalan A Yani 81, between the bus station and the Jawa Tengah. The *Losmen Famili* (☎ 396) at Jalan Sumbing 6 is clean and comfortable, with singles/doubles at 4500/7500 rp and larger rooms for three or four. The TV in the lobby could be an attraction or a drawback, depending on your taste. Also on Jalan Sumbing at No 10 is *Losmen*

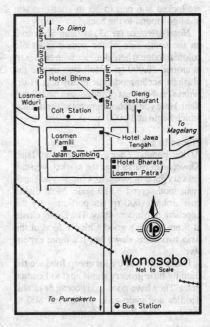

Wonosobo
Not to Scale

Sindoro. It has the same rates as the Losmen Famili and is fairly clean and comfortable-looking, but it also has a lobby TV.

At Jalan Tanggung 21 is *Losmen Pendawa Lima*, an adequate little place with singles for 5000 rp without mandi and 7500 rp with. Doubles/triples are 9500/11,500 rp with bath. The *Losmen Widuri* on the same street, opposite the colt station, costs 4500/6000 rp for small, dark rooms and hard beds – not recommended.

Places to Stay – top end

The *Hotel Bharata* (☎ 522), Jalan A Yani 72, has clean, good-sized rooms starting at 9,000 rp without bath, or 21,000/30,000 rp with a hot-water shower and breakfast included.

The Chinese-owned and operated *Losmen Nirwana* (☎ 66) at Jalan Tanggung 18 is clean, secure, quiet and friendly. A nicely decorated standard room costs 25,000 rp with hot shower and Western toilet, and includes a substantial breakfast of toast, juice, eggs, cheese and fruit. The main gates are locked at 6 pm; to get in after that you must go around to the back.

Hotel Merdeka (☎ 53) at Jalan Sindoro 2 on the south side of the square is an old colonial lodge where doubles with bath start at around 20,000 rp. A full step up and the plushest accommodation in town is *Hotel Bhima* (☎ 44), west of the square on Jalan A Yani. Here you get hot showers with doubles, which begin at 32,000 rp.

Places to Eat

At the popular *Dieng Restaurant* at Jalan Kawedanan No 29 near the market, you can get very good Indonesian, Chinese and European food served buffet-style. Most dishes cost around 1000 rp per portion – try the excellent mushroom satay. The Dieng closes at 9 pm. There's good Chinese food at the *Asia* two doors down but it's more expensive.

Other places to try for cheap food are the friendly little grocery shops next to Losmen Petra. They have good nasi goreng or rames, noodles and gado-gado for around 800 to 1000 rp. The *Rumah Makan Klenyer* has

Indonesian dishes, while the *A-A* has mostly Chinese fare. They close around 10 pm.

There is also a night market across from the Widuri and Pendawa Lima hotels in the colt station area.

Getting There & Away

To/From Yogya From Yogya take a bus or colt to Magelang (700 rp, 40 minutes) and from there another colt to Wonosobo. The fare from Magelang is 950 rp by day, 1200 rp by night and the last colt leaves at 7 pm. Allow plenty of time for this stretch because none of the colts will leave until they're packed to the gunwales – the actual road time is about two hours but it may take at least an hour longer.

It is possible to see Borobudur on the way from Yogya to Wonosobo but you need to start out early to complete the trip by night, particularly if you plan to continue on to Dieng the same day. Yogya-Muntilan-Borobudur (700 rp) takes 1½ hours. Borobudur-Magelang-Wonosobo (1200 rp) takes three hours. Maybe.

Rahayu Travel on Jalan A Yani in Wonosobo has a minibus service to Yogya at 8, 10 am, noon, 2 and 4 pm for 3200 rp per person.

If you're heading south to Yogya, take a bus to Secang to get back on the main bus route.

To/From Semarang There are several buses daily to Semarang (via Secang and Ambarawa) for 1850 rp and the journey takes about four hours. If you miss these, there are frequent buses and colts to Secang, which puts you back on the main Semarang to Yogya bus route.

To/From Cilacap There are buses to Cilacap at 8.55 and 11.15 am daily. The journey takes five hours and costs 2100 rp. If you're heading for Pangandaran in West Java note that these buses are not early enough to connect with the ferries from Cilacap. However, there is a much faster minibus going non-stop to Cilacap at 7 am and 2 pm for 10,000 rp; the earlier minibus arrives in time for the ferry to Kalipucang. These minibuses can be arranged by any Wonosobo hotel.

Alternatively, you can travel between Wonosobo and Cilacap via Purwokerto – the first bus leaves at 5.30 am and if you catch it, you will arrive in time for the ferry. There are buses every half hour until late. From Wonosobo to Purwokerto takes three hours and costs 1050 rp; Purwokerto to Cilacap takes about three hours and costs 1000 rp.

To/From Dieng Frequent colts leave from the Wonosobo market in the centre of town between 6 am and 6pm. The fare is 800 rp to Dieng and drivers sometimes ask 1000 rp for the return to Wonosobo. It takes 1½ hours uphill and one hour downhill.

Getting Around

Buses to Wonosobo turn down Jalan A Yani (past the Losmen Petra) to the bus station. For any of the hotels or the Dieng colt station in the centre of town, tell the driver where you want to get off – otherwise you'll have to walk about a km back up the hill. Horsecarts from the bus station to the centre cost 700 rp, but if you arrive by colt you'll be dropped in the centre of town anyway.

DIENG PLATEAU

On the magnificent heights of the Dieng Plateau are some of the oldest Hindu temples in Java. The name 'Dieng' comes either from 'Di-Hyang', which means 'Abode of the Heaven' in Indonesian, or from 'Adi-Aeng', which is Javanese for 'Beautiful-Amazing'. It is thought that this was once the site of a flourishing temple-city of priests. The temples, built between the 8th and 12th centuries, were dedicated to the Hindu god Shiva, yet the stone stairways for visiting pilgrims (which years ago led up to the sanctuary from the north and the south) were known as the Stairs of Buddha.

With the mysterious depopulation of Central Java, this site, like Borobudur, was abandoned and forgotten. When people returned to Dieng around 1830 they found the holy city buried and overgrown. At that time the ruins of 400 temples were reputedly still standing, but in the years that followed, most were destroyed by local people in their quest for building material. The eight remaining temples are characteristic of early Central Javanese architecture – stark in appearance, simple, squat and box-like in structure. Although they're Shiva temples, in more recent times the villagers have named each of them after the heros of the *Mahabharata* epic.

The Dieng temples are set in a strange and beautiful landscape within the huge, marshy caldera of a volcano that collapsed long ago. Steep, rugged mountainsides, cool mineral lakes and the volcanic inferno of steaming craters surround it. One of the best parts of Dieng is the journey there along a narrow, winding and very steep mountain road that follows the swift Sungai Serayu and passes through terraced slopes of vegetable and tobacco crops. The village of Dieng lies on the north side of the plateau and there is an unobtrusive, if rather odd, mushroom factory nearby. Dieng's thermal powers are also being tapped to provide electricity for the area and there is a geothermal plant already in operation not far from the Sikidang crater. The whole region is very obviously volatile – in 1984 there was an earthquake at Kawah Sileri and you could feel the tremor at the Bu Jono Losmen.

It is quite possible to see all the temples in one day on foot but the superb 'natural' sights around Dieng are scattered over a large area. Although accommodation in Dieng is limited, the plateau has a magical quality about it. In the early morning light the village houses, lacking chimneys, literally steam blue smoke through their walls. If you plan to stay overnight in Wonosobo instead, you need to be at Dieng early, before the mist sets in around noon. At 2000 metres, Dieng alternates between sunshine and rain, and is one of the few places in Indonesia where there can be morning frost on the ground – the Dieng people call it *bun upas*, or 'poison dew'. Nights can be as cold as an English winter (as low as 4°C) so you will need warm clothing.

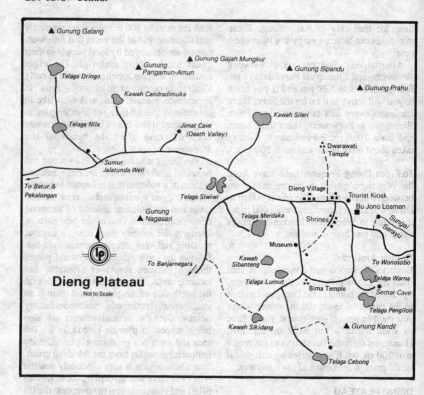

Dieng Plateau
Not to Scale

Gunung Galang
Telaga Dringo
Gunung Pangamun-Amun
Gunung Gajah Mungkur
Gunung Sipandu
Gunung Prahu
Kawah Candradimuka
Telaga Nila
Jimat Cave (Death Valley)
Kawah Sileri
Dwarawati Temple
Sumur Jalatunda Well
To Batur & Pekalongan
Dieng Village
Tourist Kiosk
Bu Jono Losmen
Telaga Siwiwi
Gunung Nagasari
Telaga Merdaka
Shrines
Sungai Serayu
Museum
To Banjarnegara
Kawah Sibanteng
Telaga Lumut
Bima Temple
To Wonosobo
Telaga Warna
Semar Cave
Telaga Pengilon
Kawah Sikidang
Gunung Kendil
Telaga Cebong

The five main temples are clustered together on the central plain. Raised walkways link the temples as most of this land is waterlogged, but you can see the remains of ancient underground tunnels which once drained the marshy flatlands. The outlying structures are the Bima Temple, which is probably unique in Java, with its strange sculpted heads like so many spectators looking out of windows, and the Dwarawati Temple on the northern hills with the ruined Parekesit Temple nearby. At the source of the Serayu, the Spring of Youth was once a holy spring, although the villagers now use it for more mundane activities such as washing and drinking.

Any number of long walks to quiet, lonely places can be made around Dieng – to the highest village in Java if you're feeling energetic. Close at hand is the beautiful Telaga Warna (the Many-Coloured Lake) and the holy cave of Semar, which for years has been used for meditation. Suharto is said to visit the cave occasionally when things get tough; in 1974 he was reportedly accompanied by the then Australian Prime Minister, Gough Whitlam, when the latter made an unofficial visit to Indonesia. The cave itself is empty and pitch black but the entrance is marked by a huge rock resembling the clown-god Semar. Just south past the Bima Temple, Kawah Sikidang with its steaming vents and frantically bubbling mud ponds is a spectacular place to see at sunset.

Warning: There are no guard rails to keep

you from slipping off the sometimes muddy trails into the scalding hot waters. Exercise caution here.

Information
At the entrance to the plateau, next to the Bu Jono Losmen, is a kiosk which sells tickets for Dieng for 400 rp (though not everyone buys one) and very vague sketch maps of the area for 200 rp. The tourist office almost next door has similar maps for free, as well as a few leaflets. It's open from 7 am to 6 pm, and on Friday it closes from noon to 1 pm.

On the south side of the plateau is a small site museum containing Hindu statues, including the rather famous image of Shiva sitting astride the shoulders of a seated Nandi (Shiva's bull mount). The museum is often locked but there's usually someone around who can open it upon request.

Places to Stay & Eat
Of Dieng's spartan hotels, *Losmen Asri* seems to draw the most budget travellers, with singles for 5000 to 7500 rp and doubles for 6000 to 7500 rp. The *Bu Jono Losmen* is not bad, with small rooms at 4500 to 7500 rp for singles and 6000 to 7500 rp for doubles. Blankets and perishingly cold mandi water (so you can forget about washing) are provided. You'll find plenty of flies but no mosquitoes. There's a small restaurant at the front and a balcony with a fine view over the plateau. One traveller commented that Mr Soedijono who runs the place is 'a neat old guy who plays lots of cassettes and speaks interesting English'. The *Hotel Dieng Plateau*, beside the tourist office, has about the same rates but is not as well kept; singles and doubles cost 4500 rp, or 7500 rp including blankets.

The food at Bu Jono's is OK – for 3500 rp you get a set three meals a day. Down the road towards the mushroom factory, the *Rumah Makan Bima Lukar* is cheaper; the tiny *Warung Sederhana* is cheaper still, with good meals of spicy nasi goreng or noodles. It's a very homely place; you're just about eating in their living room. Although *Losmen Gunung Mas* with its unkempt rooms is not

recommended for lodging, some travellers report that the food served at its cafe is pretty decent and cheap.

Getting There & Away
Dieng is 26 km from Wonosobo, which is the usual access point. Minibuses cost 800 rp there, up to 1000 rp back and the trip takes around an hour. There is also a road between Batur, to the west of Dieng, and Pekalongan on the north coast. If you're feeling fit you can walk out of Dieng and take a colt from Batur to the coast. The bus trip takes about four hours (downhill most of the way but the road surface is broken on long stretches and hair-raisingly steep in places – hence the long journey). Start early from Dieng and you can be in Pekalongan by the afternoon.

You can take buses and colts to Dieng from Yogya for around 2500 rp, including a stop at Borobudur, provided you leave sufficiently early to make all the connections this venture requires: Yogya to Muntilan, Muntilan to Borobudur, Borobudur to Magelang, Magelang to Wonosobo, Wonosobo to Dieng. To save all this hassle, you can take a day tour out of Yogya that includes a stop at Borobudur for 12,000 rp. Kresna Travel at Nos 4 and 26, Jalan Prawirotaman, and other Yogya agencies can arrange this. The round trip means a great deal of the day spent in the bus and a minimum spent at the sites. But although some travellers complain about the long drive and some are disappointed by the temples at Dieng, most visitors agree that the scenery en route is magnificent.

AROUND DIENG
Banjarnegara, 55 km south-west of Dieng, is a centre for ceramic crafts. The Tirta Teja is a fine swimming pool at Paweden Karangbokar, 15 km north of Banjarnegara.

AMBARAWA
At the junction where the Bandungan road branches from the Yogya to Semarang road, this small market town is the site of the Ambarawa Railway Station Museum (Museum Kereta Api Ambarawa). At the old Ambarawa depot, 25 steam locomotives

built between 1891 and 1928 are on show, including a 1902 cog locomotive still in working order. Most of the engines were made in Germany and assembled in Holland. The museum is run by a volunteer guide, Mr Rubiya, who is quite delightful, has remarkably few teeth and talks a riddle of gauges, statistics and dates!

Years ago Ambarawa was an important connecting rail link, providing a special cog railway locomotive which forged its way through the central mountain range. Until 1977 the Semarang-Ambarawa-Magelang line was fully operational. The service closed partly as a result of faster, cheaper road transport and partly because of the destructive activities of Merapi – but it's still possible to charter a train for the 18-km trip from Ambarawa to Bedono on the old cog railway. Indonesian groups do this quite frequently – the railway needs at least one day's notice, but a week's notice is better. The train can take up to 80 passengers for a total cost of 350,000 rp, which works out to a little more than 4375 rp per person! The round-trip journey takes a day and includes a picnic lunch. This special charter trip can be booked through major railway stations such as Yogya or Semarang, in Ambarawa, or through the Central Java Exploitation Office (Exploitasi Jawa Tengah) (☎ 24500), PJKA, Jalan Thamrin 3, Semarang.

Getting There & Around

The public bus from Semarang to Ambarawa (40 km, 550 rp) takes about one hour; Yogya to Ambarawa (90 km, 1050 rp) via Magelang takes 2½ hours. If you're coming from Solo, you may have to change buses at Salatiga or Bawen.

You can get around Ambarawa by horse and cart; they quote around 500 rp from the bus station to Pasar Projo or the Railway Museum.

GEDUNG SONGO TEMPLES

The site of these nine small Hindu temples is probably the most beautiful of all the temple locations in Java. The temples are scattered along the tops of the foothills around Gunung Ungaran, among ravines and gushing hot sulphur springs, and the clouds sweep down the mountains like an ethereal apparition appearing suddenly out of the shifting mists. This 1000-metre perch gives one of the most spectacular views in Java – across the shimmering Danau Rawa Pening to the smouldering Gunung Merbabu and Gunung Merapi.

'Gedung Songo' means 'nine buildings' in Javanese. Built in the 9th century AD and devoted to Shiva and Vishnu, most of the temples are in good condition, but the fifth is in the most complete state of reconstruction. The site is approached from Bandungan, 15 km from Ambarawa, which in turn is on the main Yogya to Semarang road. The temples are about six km from Bandungan and a further three km off the main road. A well-trodden path links the temples and it could take three to six hours to visit all of them on foot – or you can go on horseback. Bandungan and Gedung Songo are very popular with domestic tourists, so if you want peace and solitude try to avoid the weekends.

Places to Stay

The small town of Bandungan, at 980 metres, is a popular hill resort for people from Semarang so there's quite a range of accommodation here. The *Losmen Riani I* has rooms with small mandi for 7500 rp and, reportedly, it's 'nice but can be noisy'. The *Wisma Kereta Api*, run by the Central Java Railways, has quite comfortable bungalows for 7500 to 13,000 rp and is very popular locally. In its grounds is a good public swimming pool you can use for 400 rp a day. The modern *Madya Hill View Inn* has rooms with mandi costing from 9500 rp, including tea and coffee. The hotel has friendly staff and comfortable rooms but it's had problems in the past with invasions of cockroaches. By now they may have done something about it. Blankets and piped muzak are provided and there is hot water in the mornings.

There are a number of other places along the road to the Gedung Songo temples, including the pleasant *Losmen Pojok Sari* with rooms at 9000 rp. The *Rawa Pening Hotel* (☎ 134), about one km out of town, is at the more expensive end of the scale; rooms with attached mandi cost 24,000 rp and there are also cottages which can accommodate six people for 45,000 rp. The *Rawa Pening* is a lovely old colonial-style wood bungalow with a front terrace, fine gardens, tennis courts and a restaurant. This is also *the* place to stay for that fantastic view from the temple site but, as you might imagine, it is often full at weekends. Cheaper cottages can be found next door at the *Bumi Wisata*, where you can get a bungalow that sleeps six for the modest cost of 22,000 rp, and smaller cottages where two can stay for as little as 11,000 rp. For fine views from your verandah at the luxurious end of Bandungan's scale, *Amanda Cottages* (☎ 145) provides comfortable doubles for 32,000 rp and luxurious suites for 100,000 rp.

Near the junction where the road to Gedung Songo turns off from Bandungan's main street there's an excellent roadside market with fruit and vegetables. In the same area are several cheap eating places. At around 7 am, a flower market gathers here briefly before dispersing to outlying towns and villages.

Getting There & Away

To get to the Gedung Songo temples, get a colt from Pasar Projo (two or three km from the bus station) for the half-hour trip to Bandungan. Once there, catch a colt from the bustling marketplace to the temples.

SOLO (Surakarta or Sala)

On the Yogya to Surabaya road, 65 km north-west of Yogya, the old royal city of Solo lies on the west bank of one of Java's most important rivers – the Bengawan Solo. Formerly known as Surakarta, its founding in 1745 has a mystical past. Following the sacking of the Mataram court at Kartasura in 1742 the Susuhunan, Pakubuwono II, decided to look for a more auspicious site. The transfer of the capital had something to do with voices from the cosmic world – according to legend the king was told to go to the village of Solo because 'it is the place decreed by Allah and it will become a great and prosperous city'.

By the end of the 18th century Solo had already reached the peak of its political importance and the realm of Mataram had crumbled, split by internal conflict into three rival courts, of which Yogya was one. From then on the ruler of Surakarta and the subsidiary prince of Mangkunegara remained loyal to the Dutch, even at the time of Diponegoro's Java War. During the revolution they fumbled opportunities to play a positive role and with the tide of democracy in the 1940s, the kratons of Solo became mere symbols of ancient Javanese feudalism and aristocracy.

Although Solo's economy once thrived on great sugar, coffee and tobacco estates, smaller businesses such as textile mills have since taken their place – Solo is an excellent source of high quality batik. Solo also competes with Yogya as a centre for Javanese culture, attracting many students and scholars to its academies of music and dance. With its tradition of religious tolerance, Solo has more recently become a major centre of Kebatinan schools, which are popular with Westerners interested in spiritualism and meditation.

Solo has two kratons, one even larger and more venerable than Yogya's. It's quite possible to make a day-trip to Solo from Yogya but the place is worth far more than a day, particularly if you visit the ancient archaeological site of Sangiran and the mysterious Sukuh Temple, just outside the city.

Orientation & Information

The oldest part of the city is centred around the Kraton Surakarta to the east where the Pasar Klewer, the main batik market, is also located. Kraton Mangkunegara is the centre of Solo. Once you're away from these tranquil palaces Solo can be as busy as any other Javanese city, but it is less congested than its younger sister city, Yogya, and not overwhelmed by tourists. It is perhaps the least Westernised of Java's cities and there are

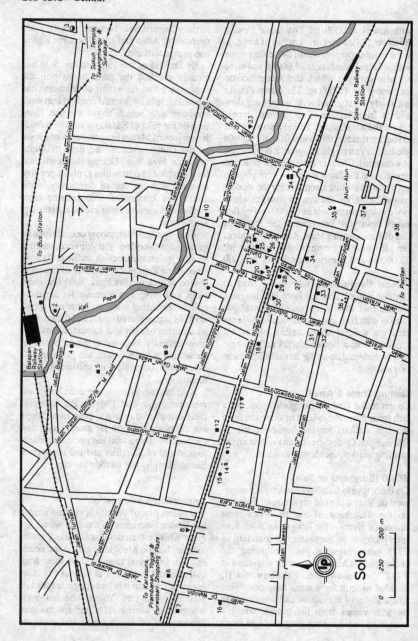

To Sukuh Temple,
Tawangmangu &
Surabaya

To Suhu Temple,
Tawangmangu &
Surabaya

Jalan Urip Sumoharjo

Solo Kota Railway
Station

Jalan Monginsidi

Jalan Tambaksegaran

Alun-Alun

Jalan Sugiopranoto

Jalan Sutowijoyo

10

24

35

37

38

To Pacitan

Jalan Imam Bonjol

Jalan Setyowidan

Jalan Setyowidan

22
25
26
34

21
20
19
7
29 28
27

Dahlan

Jalan Teuku Umar

Jalan Kos Sudarso

Jalan Pasaredi

11

Kali Pepe

1

2

Jalan Balapan

4

5

Balapan
Railway
Station

To Bus Station

33

30

Jalan Gatot Subroto

Jalan Slamet Riyadi

31

32

To Kraton

9

Jalan Gajah Mada

Jalan Ronggowarsito

18

Jalan Pasar Nongko/R/R – M Said

Jalan Dr Supomo

Jalan Hasanuddin

Jalan Honggowongso

17

12

13

Jalan Dr Radjiman

14
15

Jalan Bayang kara

Jalan Turisari

8

Jalan Yosodipuro

To Kartasura, Yoga &
Prambanan, Yogya &
Purwosari Shopping Plaza

Jalan Dr Muwardi

6

7

16

Jalan Dr Wahidin

Jalan Lawean

Solo

0   250   500 m

PLACES TO STAY		19	American Bakery
		20	Jalan Teuku Umar Night Market
1	Hotel Yayakarta	21	Warung Baru
4	Hotel Agung	23	Pasar Gede
5	Hotel Kondang Asri	26	Superman's Restaurant
6	Solo Inn	27	Kasuma Sari Restaurant
7	Hotel Putri Ayu	30	New Holland Bakery
9	Sahid Solo Hotel		
10	Kusuma Sahid Prince Hotel & Garuda Office		OTHER
12	Hotel Dana	2	RRI Radio Station
16	Ramayana Guesthouse	3	Bus Stop
18	Hotel Cakra	11	Kraton Mangkunegara
22	Losmen Nirwana	13	Radya Pustaka Museum
25	Hotel Central	14	Tourist Office
28	Hotel Kota	15	Sriwedari Amusement Park
33	Westerners (Pak Mawardi's Homestay)	24	Post Office
		29	Wartel Telephone Office
34	Westerners II	31	Singosaren Plaza
		32	Taxi Stand
▼ PLACES TO EAT		35	Mosque
		36	Vihara Rahayu Chinese Temple
8	Adem Ayam Restaurant	37	Pasar Klewer
17	Cipta Rosa Restaurant	38	Kraton Surakarta

corners with narrow walled streets and a strong village-like atmosphere.

Jalan Slamet Riyadi, the broad tree-lined avenue running east-west through the centre of Solo, is the main thoroughfare. Here the city's double-decker buses run their sedate course. You will also find the tourist office at one end and most of the banks at the east end, near Kraton Surakarta. Solo's Balapan railway station is in the northern part of the city, about two km from the centre, and the main bus station is just north again. Most hotels, restaurants and craft shops are in the area between Jalan Slamet Riyadi and the railway station. The Adi Sumarmo Airport is eight km north-west of the city centre.

Tourist Office The Solo Tourist Office (☎ 6508) at Jalan Slamet Riyadi 275 is one of the best you'll find in the country. They have a useful *Solo Guide Map* and information on cultural events in town and places to visit in the area, including free booklets on Candi Sukuh and Sangiran. It's also worth having a rummage through their bookcase of general leaflets, where they keep a good stock of information on the whole country. The office is open from 8 am to 5 pm; it's closed on Sunday.

Post & Telecommunications The main post office and poste restante on Jalan Jenderal Sudirman are open from 8 am to 1 pm Monday to Thursday and on Saturday; they close at 11 am on Friday. The post office is rarely crowded and is very efficient. The telephone office for international calls is across the street from the post office.

Other You can use the swimming pool at the Kusuma Sahid Prince Hotel for 2000 rp a day. If you're interested in making a day tour of the city and/or surrounding sites by bicycle, travellers have highly recommended those run by Warung Baru, just off Jalan Slamet Riyadi at Jalan Ahmad Dahlan No 23. On the city tour, you will see batik weaving, gamelan making, tofu, arak and rice-cracker processing. (For further details, see the Around Solo section.) Kabul at the Westerners also runs bike tours, including gamelan, wayang kulit, batik, weaving and food processing factories.

Bengawan Solo

The Bengawan Solo, flowing right through the city, is the longest river in Java. From its source in the south near the East Java border to its mouth on the Java Sea near Selat Madura, the river was a vital navigable link between the rice-growing heart of Central Java and the coastal trading ports. At one time, extravagant royal barges made the long journey, although the last of them was retired from service towards the end of the 19th century. Today the Solo is shallow and muddy for most of its length, although a project was started a few years ago to rehabilitate it and provide dams for water conservation. South of Solo, you can cross this river on a regular poled ferry.

Kraton Surakarta

In 1745, Pakubuwono II moved from Kartasura to Kraton Surakarta in a day-long procession which transplanted everything belonging to the king, including the royal banyan trees and the sacred Nyai Setomo cannon (the twin of Si Jagur in old Jakarta), which now sits in the northern palace pavilion. Ornate European-style decorations were later added by Pakubuwono X, the wealthiest of Surakarta's rulers, from 1893 to 1939.

The kraton museum/art gallery is one of the better museums in Java and has English-speaking guides. Exhibits include fine silver and bronze Hindu-Javanese figures, and three magnificent Dutch carriages which have been used for weddings. The oldest, named Kiyai Grudo, was used by the Susuhunan for his stately entry into the new capital. The giant pop-eyed figurehead with hairy whiskers graced the royal barge which once navigated the Solo.

A heavy carved doorway leads through from the museum to the Susuhunan's apartments and there is a cool inner courtyard of shady trees. You have to remove your shoes before entering and no cameras are allowed there. The large Pagelaran pavilion, or audience hall, is noted for its richly gilded columns, marble statues and beautiful stained-glass screen. The tower to one side of the courtyard was built in 1782 and here the king once communed with the Goddess of the South Seas.

Kraton Surakarta is open from Monday to Thursday and Saturday from 9 am to 2 pm; on Sunday it's open from 9 am to 3 pm; it's closed on Friday. Admission is 1000 rp (less for students), and there is a 1000 rp fee for still cameras, or 5000 rp for video cameras.

Performing Arts Academy (ASKI)

The Sasono Mulyo building near the kraton is used by the Akademi Seni Karawiton Indonesia (Indonesian Academy of Performing Arts) for dance and gamelan practice sessions, which can be seen here every afternoon, except Sunday, between 2 and 4 pm. The academy is based in the Pagelaran building by the kraton, but part of the school has moved to Kentingan, north-east of Solo.

Kraton Mangkunegara

In the centre of the city, Kraton Mangkunegara, dating back to 1757, is the palace of the second ruling house of Solo. It was founded after a bitter struggle against the Susuhunan of Surakarta, launched by Raden Mas Said, a member of the Surakarta aristocracy, and an ancestor of Tien Suharto. The Prince and Princess of Mangkunegara still live at the back of the palace.

The centre of the palace compound is the pavilion, bordered on its northern side by the *dalam*, or main ceremonial hall, which forms the palace museum. The pavilion has been added to over the centuries and is probably the largest ever constructed in the country. Its high rounded ceiling was painted in 1937 and is intricately decorated with a central flame surrounded by figures of the Javanese zodiac, each in its own mystical colour. In Javanese philosophy yellow signifies a preventative against sleepiness, blue against disease, black against hunger, green against desire, white against lust, rose against fear, red against evil and purple against wicked thoughts! On the south-west side of the pavilion is one of the kraton's oldest sets of gamelan known as 'Kyai Kanyut Mesem', which translates as 'Drifting in Smiles'.

The museum here is a real delight. Most of the exhibits are from the personal collection of Mangkunegara VII. Amongst the items are gold-plated dresses for the royal Srimpi and Bedoyo dances, jewellery and a few oddities including huge Buddhist rings and a gold genital cover for a queen. There's also a magnificent collection of masks from various areas in Indonesia, a series of royal portraits and a library collection of classical literary works by the Mangkunegara princes.

The palace is open daily from 9 am to 2 pm, except Sunday when it closes at 1 pm; entry is 750 rp (less for students). On Wednesday mornings there are dance practice sessions at the pavilion from 10 am and on Saturday mornings there is gamelan. Wayang kulit puppets, most of them made by the kraton's dalang, can be bought at the shop inside the palace. Prices are fixed but the puppets are generally of very fine quality and reasonably priced. You'll also find a few beautiful, though expensive, *wayang beber* scrolls.

Radya Pustaka Museum

This small museum, next to the tourist office on Jalan Slamet Riyadi, has good displays of gamelan instruments, jewelled kris, wayang puppets from Thailand and Indonesia, a small collection of wayang beber scrolls and another hairy muppet figurehead from a royal barge. On Tuesday, Wednesday and Thursday it's open from 8 am to noon; on Friday, Saturday and Sunday it's open from 8 to 11 am, and is closed on Monday. Entrance is 300 rp.

Meditation

In Solo there are a number of contemporary mystical groups, of different philosophies and religions, teaching the practice of Kebatinan, which has been recognised as one of the official religions of Indonesia. (See the Religion section in the Facts for the Visitor chapter for more information.) A few schools in Solo have large followings of Westerners

and most gatherings are generally held informally at private homes.

The Majapahit Pancasila, founded by Hardjanta Pradjapangarsa, is a school for studying Hinduism which is popular among Westerners. Hardjanta gives lectures in English and the Kundalini yoga method of meditation is practised by his pupils. He lives in a shophouse on Jalan Sidikoro, a lane behind Kraton Surakarta, and you can visit for short or long-term study. Pak Suwondo, on Gang 1 Jalan Kratonan, teaches the traditional theory and practice of Javanese meditation. Or you can simply drop by for the evening group meditation sessions at the home of Ananda Suyono, a Javanese 'New Age' eclectic, who lives at Jalan Ronggowarsito 60.

Performances

Wayang orang performances of the *Ramayana* can be seen at the Sriwedari Amusement Park, Jalan Slamet Riyadi, from 8 to 11 pm Monday to Saturday and every Sunday morning. The Sriwedari theatre boasts one of the most famous wayang orang troupes in Java but it's had mixed reports from travellers – some say that 'the costumes are stunning', others that it's 'a washout, nobody seems to go'. Still, the seats are cheap – 500 rp for the cheapest, 800 rp for quite good ones. It's a small, pleasant park and, if you want to just wander around and eat at the cheap warungs, the entrance fee is 150 rp. On some Saturday nights there may be wayang kulit instead of wayang orang.

At the Kusuma Sahid Prince Hotel, gamelan performances are held in the lobby every evening from 6 pm and there are also wayang orang dance-drama shows.

Various cultural performances are also held at the local broadcasting station of Radio Republik Indonesia (RRI). The RRI performances (which are very popular and often excellent) can be a laugh a minute. Note all the action going on in the broadcasting/lighting room right on stage – the technicians have a habit of leaving the curtains open, blissfully unaware of their audience. Or perhaps this is the modern equivalent of watching the dalang behind the screen in wayang kulit! The station has wayang kulit shows on the third Saturday night of every month from 9 pm to around 4 am; on the first Tuesday evening of the month there is wayang orang from 9 pm to midnight.

The tourist office has details of other cultural events around Solo. Wayang kulit shows are occasionally performed by the famous dalang, Anom Suroto, at Jalan Notodiningran 100 – you can count on a show there every Malam Rabu Legi, a certain Tuesday evening occurring regularly in the Javanese calendar. Anom also occasionally performs at the Sriwedari Amusement Park.

Other Attractions

The Balekambang Sports Centre on Jalan Jenderal Ahmad on the north-west edge of town has a public swimming pool and a roller disco. There is a government-sanctioned and regulated red-light district along Jalan Prof Dr Supomo.

Places to Stay – bottom end

There are two main areas for cheap hotels in Solo: in the centre of town within one block's walk of Jalan Slamet Riyadi; or along Jalan R M Said (Pasar Nongko), about five minutes from the train station, which in turn is close to the bus station.

You're unlikely to find better value in Solo than the popular *Pak Mawardi's Homestay* (☎ 33106) at Kemlayan Kidul 11, a small alley between Jalan Gatot Subroto and Jalan Yos Sudarso, parallel to Jalan Secoyudan. The alley's west entrance is opposite the Singosaren Plaza on Jalan Gatot Subroto. The house is tucked away in a kampung, which makes it wonderfully quiet, but also difficult to find! If you're lost, try asking for the 'Westerners', its other name, although people will only know what you're talking about if you're in the immediate vicinity.

Pak Mawardi's rooms are clean and airy, and set in a pleasant courtyard with tables and chairs. The family who run the place are friendly and helpful without being overpowering. Rooms cost 5500/7000 rp for singles/doubles, and extra beds cost 1000 rp. There are a couple of spacious 'private rooms' (not adjoining others) for 10,000 rp. You can help yourself to free tea and cold drinking water from the kitchen; coffee and soft drinks are also available. A good breakfast (egg, toast, fruit salad and coffee) costs 2000 rp. They also rent bicycles for 1500 rp a day. It's easily one of the best budget hotels in Java, about 1000 rp by becak from the train station.

If the homestay is full, the owners can book you at their similarly priced *Westerners II* which is adequate, albeit not quite as nice. It's OK to stay there for a night until a room opens at the primary homestay.

Hotel Kota (☎ 32841), Jalan Slamet Riyadi 125, still seems to be reasonably popular despite higher prices and reports of a slide in standards. It's a double-storey place built around a large open courtyard. Rooms cost from 8500 rp, or from 11,000 rp with mandi.

Close by on Jalan Ahmad Dahlan there are a number of places in the same price range, including the open and airy *Hotel Central* at No 32. It's a fairly clean and pleasant place in the old 'grand' style with some fine Art-Deco woodwork. Rooms cost 6000 to 7500 rp (shared bath only) and you get coffee in the morning and tea in the afternoon. Street rooms can be a bit noisy but you have a great view of the town, the sunset and Gunung Merapi. On this same street you'll also find the lesser *Islam, Moro Seneng* and *Hotel Keprabon*. The *Losmen Timur*, down a small alley alongside the Hotel Central at Keprabon 2/5, has been popular with budget travellers probably because of the price. Singles cost 5000 rp but it's pretty dismal; fine if you don't mind dingy, not-so-clean rooms, although the staff are friendly enough. Further down the alley you will find similar prices and conditions at *Losmen Srigati*.

At Jalan Imam Bonjol 52, a block over, the *Hotel Mawar Melati* (☎ 36434) has adequate rooms from 8000 rp including tea twice a day; rooms with bathroom and fan start at 11,500 rp. Another popular inexpensive place in this area is *Mama's Homestay*, in a little alley off Jalan Yos Sudarso. Singles/doubles with shared mandi cost 5000/7000 rp, including reputedly huge breakfasts.

Near the railway station are several places on Jalan Pasar Nongko (R M Said). The *Wismantara* at No 53 has rooms for 7500 to 10,000 rp around a somewhat gloomy court-yard. The *Kondang Asri* at No 86 has singles at 6000 rp with friendly people, good music (even if it is too loud sometimes) and free tea (sometimes).

The *Hotel Putri Sari* (☎ 46995) at Jalan Slamet Riyadi 382 is good value at the high bottom end; doubles cost 10,000 rp without bath, 20,000 rp with bath, or 25,000 rp for a 'deluxe' room with TV, fan, soap and towels.

If you are exhausted after your journey and want to lodge within walking distance of the train station, there are two possibilities. Right next to the station is *Hotel Jayakarta* (☎ 32813) at Jalan Monginsidi 106, where pleasant rooms with mandi and fan cost 15,000 rp or 19,000 rp, and air-con doubles 25,000 rp. The hotel has a bare basic older wing where doubles with mandi cost about 7500 rp. For those watching their rupiah, the *Agung* (☎ 33034) at Jalan Gajah Mada 119 has adequate doubles with mandi for 7500 rp.

For unique lodgings recommended by several long-term visitors, consider the former prince's mansion converted into an attractive homestay – the *Joyokusuman*. It's a pretty fair walk from the centre of town, south of the kraton, just off Jalan Gajahan at RT9/I No 16. The rooms, which are adequate, are not the reason to stay here. Rather, the tranquil grounds graced by colourful birds and luxuriant foliage make you feel like a sultan residing in your palace. And considering the ambience, you can't beat the price. Doubles with shared mandi cost 7000 rp and rooms with private mandi 8000 rp. You may get a further price break if you rent by the week or month.

Places to Stay – middle

Many of the hotels in this bracket are strung out along or just off Jalan Slamet Riyadi, west of the town centre. Becaks from the bus terminal or railway station to this area should cost about 1000 rp. Several readers have recommended the well- maintained *Hotel Putri Ayu* (☎ 36154), Jalan Slamet Riyadi 331, where all the rooms have their own mandis. Rooms with fan, single or double, cost 15,000 rp including breakfast, or 22,000 to 24,000 rp with air-con.

The *Ramayana Guesthouse* (☎ 32814), also in this part of town at Jalan Dr Wahidin 15, is an attractive house with a guest wing around a garden. It has a choice of large comfortable rooms with fan or air-con, all with their own mandi. Rooms here start at 17,500 rp with fan and range from 29,000 to 50,000 rp with air-con. Rates include break-fast, afternoon snack and tea. There's a restaurant and the staff are friendly.

Conveniently located across the street from the tourist office and museums is the recently refurbished *Hotel Dana* (☎ 33891), Jalan Slamet Riyadi 286. The clean and peaceful grounds surround a spacious, tiled floor lobby in the main building; a unique wood-and-hide chandelier hangs from a high ceiling supported by gracefully carved wooden columns. Behind the main building, well off the street, is the guest building which features sitting areas both inside and outside the rooms. Note that the outdoor sitting rooms can turn into a liability should you have noisy neighbours. Rates are 12,000 rp without bath, or 22,000 rp with bath and fan. There are also air-con rooms for 33,500 rp, or 48,000 rp for larger 'deluxe' rooms.

Another good mid-range hotel is the newish *Wisata Indah* (☎ 43753), Jalan Slamet Riyadi 173. Rooms here are clean, nicely decorated, and feature comfortable beds for 25,000 rp with attached shower and breakfast, or 35,000 rp with air-con.

Places to Stay – top end

The *Kusuma Sahid Prince Hotel* (☎ 46356), Jalan Sugiyopranoto 22, has been designed around a former Solonese palace. It's a grand place set in beautiful grounds with a swimming pool. Other facilities include a coffee shop serving Indonesian and Western meals, a bar, shopping arcade, Javanese herb shop, and massage and laundry services! In the lobby, guests are serenaded by a gamelan. Singles/doubles range from 49,000/59,000 rp to 125,000/137,000 rp, bungalows start at 176,000 rp, and there are three 'royal' suites with rates 'upon request'.

The *Hotel Cakra* (☎ 45847), centrally located at Jalan Slamet Riyadi 171, has a variety of air-con rooms and cottages. Singles/doubles range from 51,000/59,000 rp to 88,000/100,000 rp including breakfast; cottages start at 107,000 rp.

Places to Eat

There are countless warungs and restaurants in Solo, including several serving excellent Chinese food. For the cheapest food listen for the weird and distinctive sounds which are the trademarks of the roaming street hawkers. The bread seller sings (or screeches) a high-pitched 'tee'; 'ding ding ding' is the bakso seller; 'tic toc' is mie; a wooden buffalo bell advertises satay; a shrieking kettle-on-the-boil sound is the *kue putu*. Kue putu are coconut cakes, which are pushed into small bamboo tubes to cook over a steam box and then served hot, sprinkled with coconut and sugar.

Jalan Ahmad Dahlan has a number of well patronised budget travellers' eateries. Without question, the most popular is *Warung Baru* at No 23, and deservedly so. Here you will find the most delicious freshly baked bread in Indonesia. Try the famous black bread, along with substantial breakfasts and delicious Indonesian and Western fare at most reasonable prices. The warung has become a meeting place for travellers to dine while exchanging information and also runs some recommended bike tours of Solo and environs (see Around Solo for details). Warung Baru's ebullient proprietor, Suntari Haryono, presides over the spectacle, maintaining a sense of contagious good humour no matter how rushed she may be. Sunny Suntari is one of the folks who make international travel so wonderful. May she never change!

Across the street is another good cafe, *Yant Favourite* at No 22, known for its excellent *nasi liwet* (a delicious Solonese speciality of rice with spiced chicken and creamy coconut sauce) and good breakfasts. Also in the vicinity are *Rumah Makan Laris* and *Warung Makan Sari Rejeki*, both small, clean places with inexpensive Chinese and Indonesian food.

In the past, one of the best eating places in Solo was the night market along Jalan Teuku Umar. But by government decree a few years ago, the market was moved to the tourist office/museum Sriwedari Park area west of

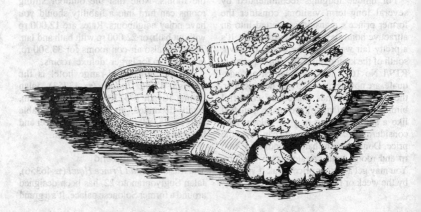

the town's centre. Relocated to such a distance from Solo's centre, many of the warungs went bankrupt and some of the survivors moved back to their old haunt on Jalan Teuku Umar.

So, while old Solo hands may be disappointed that the old epicurean night market is not what it once was, the food stalls near the tourist area and along Jalan Teuku Umar still afford an inexpensive taste of local specialities. Among these are *susu segar* or fresh milk, also known as *minuman sehat* (healthy drink) – hot or cold milk with optional egg and honey – and a wide assortment of tasty snacks. Some of the warungs also serve nasi gudeg from Yogya, and also nasi liwet for 600 rp. Yet another local food speciality to try is *srabi* – small coconut/rice puddings served up on a light crispy pancake with banana, chocolate or jackfruit on top – best eaten when they're piping hot. Another good night market is Pasar Lagi. Jalan Yos Sudarso is the street for satay warungs. Pasar Gede near the intersection of Jalan Urip Sumoharjo and Jalan Sugiopranoto has lots of cheap fruit.

For those willing to spend more in a restaurant for excellent Soloese specialities served in a pleasant ambience, walk half a block west of Sriwedari to the *Pringgondani* at Jalan Bhayangkara 77. Here you can dine seated on casual yet comfortable furniture, or local-style on a bamboo floor. The savoury *ayam bakar* (roast chikcen) is not to be missed. Considerably cheaper nearby, around the corner from the Radjapustaka Museum on Jalan Musium, the tiny *Rumah Makan Denai* offers a budget potpourri of good Padang food.

The *New Holland Restaurant & Bakery*, near the Hotel Kota at Jalan Slamet Riyadi 135, is clean and quiet, and a good place for breakfast or a break from Indonesian food. Downstairs is the coffee shop and bakery with delicious savoury martabak rolls for 550 rp, good coffee, cold drinks and ice cream. The restaurant upstairs has Western food, including good – albeit somewhat expensive – hamburgers, as well as a varied Indonesian menu. Across the street and

further down from the New Holland is the *American Bakery*, which some long-term visitors say has the best pastries in town. Further west on Jalan Slamet Riyadi, next door to the Hotel Dana at No 232, is the clean and reasonably priced *Restaurant Dani Sari Rosa*. Open from 6 am till midnight, it has all the standard rice and noodle dishes, plus good *ayam goreng*. The *Restaurant Rosana*, next to the Hotel Wisata Indah at No 173, has a good, inexpensive Indonesian buffet with clearly marked prices.

A number of decent Chinese places along Jalan Slamet Riyadi include the *Jakarta* close to the centre, the *Cipta Rosa* at 245, the *Orient* further out at 397 and the *Adem Ayam* at 342. For cheap, filling, good Chinese fare, the unpretentious Cipta Rosa is your best bet. The Adem Ayam is split into two restaurants, one serving Chinese food and the other Javanese – locals often recommend the Adem Ayam but a few travellers have found it disappointing.

The *Centrum* at Jalan Yos Sudarso 180 offers very good Chinese food. It's a small restaurant with a pleasant atmosphere and an enormously varied menu, and you really get your money's worth. It's very popular and always busy, so to be sure of a meal it's best to go early; the doors are usually closed at around 8 pm.

The *Taman Sari* at Jalan Gatot Subroto 63 has good helpings of noodles and excellent ice juices. On the same street, look out for the *Bu Mari* warung, which has miniature chairs around a low table on the sidewalk – great nasi gudeg and chicken curry with rice and sambal for only 1250 rp.

Along Jalan Diponegoro, near the entrance to Pasar Triwindu, there's a row of warungs for cheap meals, snacks and iced fruit juices. The *Rumah Makan Hijau* has good gado-gado and *soto Madura*.

The *Malibu Restaurant*, next to the Hotel Kota on Jalan Slamet Riyadi, serves delicious ayam bakar as well as various rice and noodle dishes at fairly reasonable prices in an indoor-outdoor pub atmosphere. A large bottle of cold beer costs 2300 rp, further discounted by 15% between 1 and 6 pm. You can get not-so-cheap Western food in air-conditioned comfort at the *Sasmaya Pub & Restaurant* on Jalan Dr Rajiman, or the *Dynasty Pub & Restaurant* on Jalan Honggowongso.

Heading toward the western end of Jalan Slamet Riyadi, the Purwosari shopping plaza has a number of good restaurants. On the south side of Jalan Slamet Riyadi here, locals recommend the *Sari Restaurant* as one of the best purveyors of Solonese specialities. Just beyond the plaza on the north side of Slamet Riyadi is *Tio Ciu*, known for its seafood hotplates. Nearby is *Ojo Gelo*, offering tasty ayam bakar and other Indonesian fare.

Things to Buy

Solo is a batik centre rivalling Yogya but with a totally individual style. Many people find it better value than Yogya for batik and other crafts and curios, quite possibly because it attracts far fewer tourists.

Batik At Pasar Klewer, a two-storey 'hanging market' near the Susuhunan's palace, there are hundreds of stalls selling traditional fabrics, mainly batik and *lurik*. Bargaining is obligatory here and if you're buying used 'cap' (stamp) batik, look it over carefully for holes!

For more sophisticated work, there are numerous shops around town – most of them are marked on the Solo guide map. Batik Semar on Jalan Said is one good place for modern cotton and beautiful silk batiks. In the mornings (weekdays only) you can see the batik being made. The Danar Hadi showroom on Jalan Slamet Riyadi has a good range of batik fabrics and ready-made clothes, and attractive tie-dyed cottons for around 7500 rp. Another major batik exporter whose showroom has a diversity of good quality batiks at fixed prices is Batik Keris on Yos Sudarso.

You can take batik courses in Solo but most people do this in Yogya, where courses tend to be cheaper.

Curios Pasar Triwindu on Jalan Diponegoro is Solo's flea market. All kinds of bric-a-brac plus a few genuine antiques are sold here – old buttons and buckles, china dogs and fine porcelain, puppets, batik tulis pens, oil lamps, bottles and bell jars – but if you're looking for bargains you have to sift carefully through the rubbish and be prepared to bargain hard. Old batik 'cap' stamps are worth looking out for – they tend to be much cheaper here than in Yogya (about 4500 to 8000 rp) but check that they're not damaged.

Toko Bedoyo Srimpi, Jalan Ronggowarsito 116, is the place for dancers' costumes and theatrical supplies, where you'll find all those gold gilt headdresses, painted armbands and so on that you've always wanted. They also sell masks and wayang kulit puppets.

Jalan Secoyudan is the goldsmiths' street. On Sundays and holidays in particular, there's sometimes an early morning market for handmade toys from villages around Solo in front of the Rudya Pustaka Museum.

Getting There & Away

Air At the time of writing, only Garuda and Merpati fly to and from Solo (although Sempati may soon initiate a service between Jakarta and Solo). In addition there are flights to Balikpapan, Banjarmasin, Denpasar, Kupang and Surabaya (54,000 rp).

The Garuda/Merpati office (☎ 6846) is in the Kusuma Sahid Prince Hotel, Jalan Slamet Riyadi 113, and is open from 7 am to 3 pm Monday to Friday, from 7 am to 1 pm on Saturday and from 9 am to noon on Sunday and holidays.

Bus The main bus station (Gilingan) is about three km north of the centre of town, 1000 rp by becak. Travelling to or from the west – Semarang, Prambanan and Yogya for example – you can save a few rupiah by taking the city double-decker (200 rp) to the bus station west of town at Kartasura.

Going west, there are frequent buses to Prambanan for 600 rp (1½ hours) and Yogya for 1000 rp (two hours). Papsa Kasatriyan operates a door-to-door minibus service to Yogya for 2500 rp from their office opposite the Batik Keris shop. Some other minibus companies run to Yogya from their station near the kraton just opposite the batik market. Various travel agencies can arrange for you to be picked up at your hotel.

Going north, buses include those to Boyolali for 500 rp (one hour), Salatiga for 750 rp (1½ hours) and Semarang for 1450 rp (2½ hours).

Going east, buses include those to Wonogiri for 500 rp (one hour) – this is the bus to take if you're heading for Pacitan beach in East Java. There are also buses to Blitar for 4100 rp (six hours) and Surabaya for around 4600 rp (six hours). To Malang, buses leave frequently in the morning between 7 and 9 am; the trip takes about nine hours and the fare is 5100 rp.

Night Bus Many of the night bus companies for Malang and Surabaya are along Jalan Urip Sumoharjo. Agung Express operate night buses to Malang and Surabaya for 8000 rp including a meal. Most buses depart between 9.30 and 10.30 pm. Rosalie Indah minibuses have five daily departures to both Malang and Surabaya for 12,500 rp. If you are headed for Bali, Cakrawala has non air-con coaches for 19,000 rp and air-con buses, both departing daily at 5 pm.

The long haul from Solo to Bandung takes 12 hours, so you're really best off opting for a night express train. But if you wish to take a bus, both Muncul and Bandung Express offer 4 pm departure air-con services on this route for 15,000 rp. Muncul and Appolo also operate air-con night buses to Jakarta for 17,000 rp, departing at 4 pm. Should you wish to go directly to Bogor, the aptly named *Bogor Express* leaves Solo at 3 pm and costs 17,000 rp.

Train From the Balapan railway station, it's around 1000 rp by becak into the centre. Solo is on the main Jakarta-Yogya-Surabaya train route so there are frequent day trains, as well as night trains. The most comfortable way to get to Jakarta is to take the fast *Bima Express*, which departs Solo at 8 pm, arriving at Jakarta Kota at 7 am and costing 44,000 rp

for a 1st-class seat or 49,000 with a sleeping berth. Coming the other way, the train leaves Jakarta Kota at 4 pm and arrives in Solo at about 2 am.

Trains from Solo to Surabaya take five hours, with fares ranging from 4200 rp in the 3rd-class-only *GBM Selatan* to 44,000 rp in a 1st-class sleeper on the *Bima Express*.

From Bandung there are two trains daily to Solo: the *Express Siang* at about 5.30 am (4400 rp for 3rd class; 10,000 rp for 2nd class) and the *Mutiara Selatan* at 5.30 pm (14,000 rp for 2nd class; 23,000 rp for 1st class). From Solo, these trains depart at 10 am and 10 pm, arriving in Bandung at 10 pm and 7.30 am respectively.

Yogya is only an hour and 20 minutes away on the *Express Siang* and costs 3800 rp in 3rd class, or 6200 rp in 2nd class.

Getting Around

There are plenty of becaks all over town and there are taxis, but they're unmetered. A taxi to or from the Adi Sumarmo Airport eight km west of town costs 9000 rp. A taxi from the Yogya airport all the way to Solo or vice versa is 30,000 rp. *Hayumas Setia Travel Service* (☎ 0271) at Jalan Sugiopranoto 22 arranges these taxis in Solo.

There's a useful double-decker city bus service with a flat 200 rp fare. The bus runs from Kartasura in the west, along Jalan Slamet Riyadi and Jalan Jenderal Sudirman to Palur in the east. Bicycles can be hired from Pak Mawardi's Homestay (the Westerners) for 2000 rp a day.

The main colt stand is on the opposite side to Pasar Klewer, for destinations south of Solo, including Gua Tabuhan and Pacitan (see the East Java section). The taxi stand is on Jalan Kratonan in the same area.

AROUND SOLO
Organised Tours

Warung Baru at Jalan Ahmad Dahlan No 23 runs bike tours of Solo and of sites outside the city limits. These tours are reasonably priced and have earned the praise of numerous travellers. For 6500 rp one full-day tour

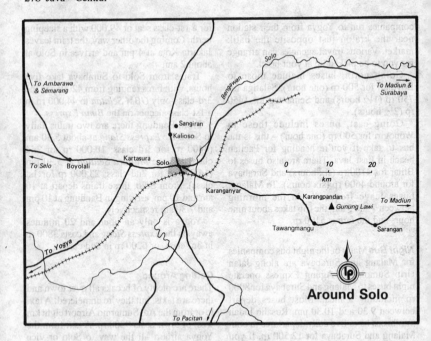

Around Solo

takes you through beautiful countryside to see batik weaving, gamelan making, and tofu, arak and rice-cracker processing. Among its other itineraries, Warung Baru has a good walking tour to the Sukuh and Centho temples as well as the waterfall at Tawangmangu for 9000 rp.

Sangiran
Fifteen km north of Solo, Sangiran is an important archaeological excavation site, where the fossil skull of prehistoric 'Java Man' *(Pithecanthropus erectus)* was unearthed by a Dutch professor in 1936. There is a small site museum with a couple of skulls, various pig and hippopotamus teeth and fossil exhibits including some amazing 'mammoth' bones and tusks. Archaeologists are still finding things in the area and if you wander up the road past the museum a bit and have a look in some of the exposed banks you may find shells or fossil bones and crabs.

The museum is open daily, except Sunday, from 9 am to 4 pm. Admission is 500 rp. At the museum you can buy a copy of the booklet *Sangiran* for 800 rp, but booklets are available for free at the Solo tourist office. To get there, take a bus or colt from the Solo bus station. It will drop you at Kalioso and from there you have to walk about three km to the museum.

Sukuh Temple
One of Java's most mysterious and striking temples, the Sukuh Temple stands 900 metres high on the slopes of Gunung Lawu, 36 km east of Solo. In form it is a large truncated pyramid of rough-hewn stone with a curious Inca look and, while the sculpture is carved in the 'wayang style' found particularly in East Java, the figures are crude, squat and distorted. The temple is hardly as wildly erotic as it is sometimes made out to be but there are fairly explicit and humorous

representations of a stone penis or two and the elements of a fertility cult are quite plain.

Built in the 15th century during the declining years of the Majapahit, Sukuh seems to have nothing whatsoever to do with other Javanese Hindu and Buddhist temples, and the origins of its builders and strange sculptural style remain a mystery. It is the most recent Hindu-Buddhist temple in the region, yet it seems to mark a reappearance of the pre-Hindu animism and magic that existed 1500 years before. It's a quiet, isolated place (although the ubiquitous visitors' book may make a brief appearance!) with a strange and potent atmosphere.

At the gateway before the temple is a large stone lingam and yoni. Flowers are still often scattered over it and there's a story that the symbol was used mainly by villagers to determine whether a wife had been faithful or a wife-to-be was still a virgin. The woman had to wear a sarong and stride across the lingam – if the sarong tore, her infidelity was proven. Other interesting cult objects stand further in amongst the trees, including a tall-standing monument depicting Bima, the *Mahabharata* warrior hero, with Narada, the messenger of the gods, in a stylised womb followed by Bima dropping through at his birth. In the top courtyard three enormous flat-backed turtles stand like sacrificial altars.

From the site the views are superb, to the west and north across terrace fields and mountains. About a one-hour climb beyond Sukuh is the less interesting Ceta Temple (1470 metres). Built at about the same time, this temple is similarly terraced and carved with Bima figures but is in poor condition.

Getting There & Away From Solo, take the city double-decker to Tertomoyo, then a bus bound for Tawangmangu as far as Karangpandan for 400 rp. From Karangpandan catch a minibus to Sukuh for 300 rp. The trip takes about 1½ hours in total. On market days the minibus stops right beside the temple but most days it's a couple of km hike uphill from the bus stop to the site. There is a 250 rp admission charge to the site.

Tawangmangu

Trekkers can make an interesting 2½-hour walk from Sukuh Temple along a well-worn cobbled path to Tawangmangu, a pretty hill resort on the other side of Gunung Lawu. Or you can get there by bus from Solo via Karangpandan, which is just as fine a trip along a switchback road through magnificent tightly terraced hills. At Tawangmangu is Grojogan Sewu, a 100-metre high waterfall and favourite playground for monkeys. It's reached by a long flight of steps down a hillside from the village and you can swim in the very chilly pool at the bottom. Nobody else uses it.

An interesting alternative to backtracking to Solo is to take a colt to Sarangan, 15 km from Tawangmangu on the mountain road to Madiun, a picturesque hill town with hotels clustered at the edge of a crater lake.

Places to Stay In Tawangmangu, the *Pak Amat Losmen* is quite pleasant and has its own garden. The rooms, from 8500 rp, are individual little houses with mandi and verandah. The *Losmen Pondok Garuda* has a choice of rooms with and without mandi from 8500 rp. There's a mosque right next door. The place has a fine location and the front rooms opening onto the garden offer a superb view over the valley. About one km up from the bus station, the *Hotel Lawu* at Jalan Lawu 20 has double rooms with TV from 22,000 to 29,000 rp. If you want to camp at the top of Tawangmangu, you can pitch a tent at *Camping Tawangmangu Baru* for 3400 rp with your own equipment or 6200 rp with a tent provided.

For good Indonesian dishes, eat at *Sapto Argo* on Jalan Raya Lawu. Continue down Jalan Raya Lawu and you may dine in the tranquil ambience of *Lesehan Pondok Indah* while seated crosslegged on bamboo mats overlooking the rice paddies. For cheaper fare, there's good food in the warungs further up the hill.

Gunung Merapi

On the northern slopes of volatile Gunung Merapi, 50 km from Solo, it is roughly a four-hour trek from Selo to the summit of the volcano (2911 metres) – and this is a safer and easier climb than the one from Kaliurang to the south. (For more information, see the Around Yogya section.) However, you shouldn't try to hike around the side of the peak from Selo to see the crater, as this is a very dangerous climb. From the Kaliurang side you can hike to both crater and summit if you're in good shape. Guides can be hired at either of the two hotels in Selo for 4000 rp per person, with a minimum of four people.

Places to Stay The Agung Guesthouse of Yogya has a branch in Selo called *Agung Merapi*, where dorm beds cost 5000 rp, rooms 8500 rp. About 150 metres east is a small unmarked hotel where beds are 3000 rp per person or 4000 rp with a nasi goreng breakfast. Also in Selo, some people bed down in the central market in sleeping bags – you need to leave Selo at 3 am to make the summit by dawn. In Yogya, the Kartika Travel Agency at Jalan Sosrowijayan 10 arranges guided treks to the summit of Gunung Merapi, including transport, food, accommodation in Selo and a guide.

Getting There & Away From Solo, take a Semarang bus to Boyolali and from there a colt to Selo. If you want food for the climb it's worth stocking up at Boyolali, which is also the milk centre of Java.

SEMARANG

The north coast port of Semarang, which is the capital city of the province of Central Java, is a strong contrast to the royal cities of Solo and Yogyakarta. Under the Dutch it became a busy trading and administrative centre, and great numbers of Chinese traders joined the Muslim entrepreneurs of the north coast. Even in the depressed 1950s, great wealth flowed through the city, with sugar and other agricultural produce going out, and industrial raw materials and finished goods coming in.

Today, Semarang is the only port open to large ships on the central coast. Deep-water berthing facilities were recently completed,

so ocean-going vessels no longer have to anchor out in the mouth of Sungai Kali Baru.

More a commercial centre than a city for tourists, Semarang's main point of interest is the famous Chinese Gedung Batu Temple. This little-visited city can also be a good starting point for trips along the north coast or south to the central mountains. It can be a pleasant place to stop in for a night or two, for it seems less crowded and more relaxed than its large size and population (just over one million) would indicate.

Orientation & Information

Semarang is split into two parts. 'Old' Semarang is on the coastal plain, sandwiched between the two Banjir canals, while the new town has spread away to the southern hills of Candi. An important 'hub' in the old town is the Pasar Johar on the roundabout at the top of Jalan Pemuda. In this area you'll find the main Tawang railway station, the taxi and colt stations, the main post office and the telephone office. Three main roads – Jalan Pemuda, Jalan Imam Bonjol and Jalan Gajah Mada – radiate out from the roundabout to the southern boundary of the old town. The airport is off to the west of the city. The Gedung Batu Temple is on the western outskirts of the city across the Banjir Canal 'Barat'.

Candi is the wealthy residential area of Semarang where many of the more expensive hotels are located. From these hills there is an excellent view over the city.

Tourist Offices The Semarang City Tourist Office is in the the Wisma Pancasila building on Simpang Lima, the town square. There is another Semarang tourist office in the old amusement park, Tegal Wareng, at Jalan Sriwijaya 29. Both are open from 8 am to 2 pm Monday to Thursday, to 11 am on Friday and to 1 pm on Saturday.

There's also a good Central Java Tourist Office, Kantor Dinas Pariwisata, at Jalan Pemuda 171. Although information is not always on display, lots of maps and brochures on the province, including a regional *Calendar of Events*, are available if you ask

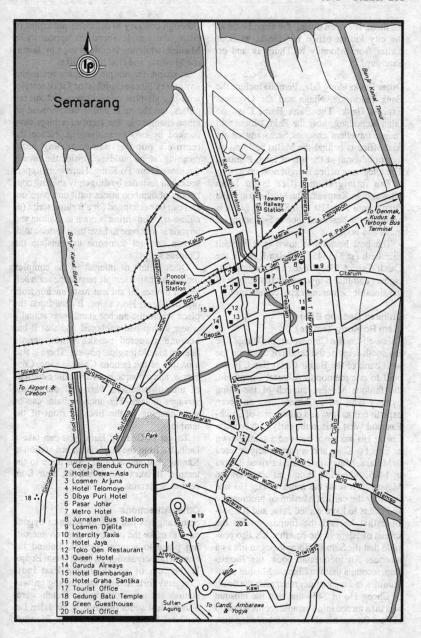

Semarang

1 Gereja Blenduk Church
2 Hotel Oewa-Asia
3 Losmen Arjuna
4 Hotel Telomoyo
5 Dibya Puri Hotel
6 Pasar Johar
7 Metro Hotel
8 Jurnatan Bus Station
9 Losmen Djelita
10 Intercity Taxis
11 Hotel Jaya
12 Toko Oen Restaurant
13 Queen Hotel
14 Garuda Airways
15 Hotel Blambangan
16 Hotel Graha Santika
17 Tourist Office
18 Gedung Batu Temple
19 Green Guesthouse
20 Tourist Office

for them. It's open during the same hours as the city tourist office but closes an hour earlier from Monday to Thursday and on Saturday.

Other Banks along Jalan Pemuda include the Bank Indonesia, Niaga and the Overseas Express Bank. The Bank Bumi Daya on Jalan Kepodang, near the Pelni office, will change travellers' cheques. Semarang's main post office is behind the Metro building on the roundabout at the top of Jalan Pemuda. The telephone office is right next door.

The immigration office is on Jalan Siliwangi in Krapyak. The Merbabu at Jalan Pandanaran 108-110, near Simpang Lima, is probably the best bookshop in Semarang for maps and books.

The best hospital in town is R S Saint Elizabeth (☎ 315345) on Jalan Kawi in the Candi district. They're used to treating foreigners and this is always the first choice of the sizeable Semarang expat community.

Chinese Gedung Batu (Sam Po Kong Temple)

This well-known Chinese temple stands five km south-west of the centre of town, on the west bank of the Banjir Canal Barat. It was built to commemorate Admiral Cheng Ho, the famous Muslim eunuch of the Ming dynasty who led a Chinese fleet on seven expeditions to Java and other parts of South-East and West Asia in the early 15th century. Cheng Ho has since become a saint known as Sam Po Kong and is particularly revered in Melaka, Malaysia. He first arrived in Java in 1405, when the Hindu influence of the Majapahit was on the wane. Cheng Ho was possibly the earliest Muslim of prominence and status to have visited Java, and it's possible that he laid the foundation for the spread of Islam in the country. It's also possible that the Sam Po Temple began life as a mosque. An Indonesian book, the *Tuanko Rao*, recounts that the Chinese Muslim communities in Java disintegrated after the death of Cheng Ho in 1434 and that the mosque was then turned into a temple for the worship of Sam Po and his aides. It's interesting that,

although contrary to orthodox principles of Islam, the temple attendants appear to be Muslim, while the temple is used by Javanese Muslims and Buddhists alike.

In shape, the temple complex resembles any other Chinese Buddhist or Taoist temple, with pagoda-type curved eaves and tall red pillars, but the main hall is built around an inner chamber in the form of a huge cave flanked by two great dragons. Hence the temple's popular name, *gedung batu,* meaning 'stone building'. Inside the cave is the idol of Sam Po Kong. Here worshippers seek their fortunes by diligently shaking containers of bamboo sticks until one pops out and can be exchanged for a fortune script (or *chiam-si)*. The shrine is open to visitors and anyone is welcome to have their fortune told, if you can get someone to translate the Chinese script.

Other points of interest in the complex include a smaller temple next to the main hall which houses an ancient rusty anchor from one of Cheng Ho's ships. It's said that the place where the anchor stands was actually where a ship had anchored and that it has become a sacred pusaka which people believe to hold magical powers. There is also a picture of the famous Chinese sage, Confucius, and a plaque honouring the hundreds of unknown sailors who died during the voyages to Java. The anchor chains can be seen hanging in the trees in front of the temple.

To get to Gedung Batu, you can take a Daihatsu from the city's Baru bus station to Karang Ayu and another from there to the temple. It takes about half an hour from central Semarang.

Other Attractions

Semarang has just enough relics of bygone days to make the old town quite an interesting place to wander around. Behind the Poncol railway station on Jalan Imam Bonjol is the ruin of an old Dutch East India Company fort. Around the Tawang railway station are numerous bulky Dutch warehouses. Just south of Tawang, on Jalan Let Jenderal Suprapto, is the **Gereja Blenduk**

Church, built by the Dutch in 1753 and still functioning. It has a huge copper-clad dome and inside there is a baroque organ which is now little more than a facade, as a modern organ was installed some years ago.

For a complete change you could plunge into the narrow streets of Semarang's old Chinatown, south of the Christian church, and seek out the brightly painted Tay Kak Sie Temple. This Chinese temple complex dates from 1772 and is on Gang Lombok, a small alley off Jalan Pekojan.

Around the Simpang Lima square are more modern buildings, including the large two-storey Mesjid Baiturrakhman (mosque). The Tuga Muda, at the southern end of Jalan Pemuda, is a candle-shaped monument commemorating Semarang's five-day battle against the Japanese in October 1945. Nearby is an impressive European-style building, formerly Dutch offices and later headquarters of the Japanese forces, known to the Javanese as Lawang Sewu – '1000 doors'.

Semarang is known for its two large jamu (herbal medicine) manufacturers – Jamu Jago and Jamu Nyonya Meneer. By phoning Budi Satyo (☎ 285533) you can visit the Jamu Jago factory on Jalan Setia Budi. You'll come across their jamus all over Java – their adverts use a squad of dwarves! Jamu Nyonya Meneer (☎ 285732) has a jamu museum that's open Monday to Friday from 10 am to 3.30 pm. It's at their factory at Jalan Raya Kaligawe Km 4 (about 45 minutes from the centre of town on a Kudus-bound bus). They will also give tours of their factory upon request. One traveller reported trying a *jamu sekhot* which, according to the packet, 'increases health and vitality in men, curing impotence and bringing you to a happy family'. Unfortunately, the traveller went on to say, 'it didn't help and tasted like shit'!

Every evening there are wayang orang performances at the long-established Ngesti Pandowo Theatre at Jalan Pemuda 116. Performances start at 7 pm and tickets cost 700 to 1500 rp for the best seats. The *Sobokarta Folk Theatre* at Jalan Cipto 31-33,

north of the market, has wayang kulit performances every Saturday night from 8 to 11 pm for about 1000 rp. Radio Republik Indonesia on Jalan A Yani puts on wayang kulit shows at least once a month.

The Semarang Harbour is worth a look to see the pinisi and other traditional ocean-going vessels, but no photography is allowed. Or you could take a city bus out to Candi and have a drink at the Sky Garden Hotel or the even higher Gombel Indah Restaurant. From here you have a fine view over the city, and the hazy silhouettes of huge merchant ships can be seen anchored out at sea. To get there take a city bus down Jalan Pemuda bound for Jatingaleh and ask for Bukit Gombel, which is just past the Sky Garden.

Organised Tours

If you're interested in organising a group journey on the old cog railway from Ambarawa (40 km from Semarang), it can be arranged with the Central Java Tourism Office (Exploitasi Jawa Tengah) (☎ 24500), PJKA, Jalan Thamrin 3, Semarang.

Festivals

Semarang's Dugderan Festival marks the beginning of the Muslim fasting month. Its highlight is the great bazaar in front of the city's Grand Mosque in the Pasar Johar area and at Pasar Ya'ik where street vendors gather for several days and nights and a special talisman in the form of a rhinoceros with a duck's egg on its back is sold. The festival's name is taken from the sound of the big mosque drum being beaten combined with the der-r-r of firecrackers. It ends when the drum is beaten to announce the start of the fast, next dawn.

The Jaran Sam Po, held in July, is one of the biggest annual Chinese ceremonies in Java, during which a colourful procession, including brightly decorated horses and a 'Liong' Chinese dragon, makes its way from the Tay Kak Sie Temple to Gedung Batu. Nowadays, barred from marching in large numbers, the Chinese do not do the entire route on foot, so trucks and cars are used until the last 50 metres or so to Gedung Batu.

The Semarang Fair is held throughout August on Jalan Sriwijaya near the old zoo every evening after 5 pm. Exhibits from around Central Java, food stalls and various forms of entertainment are featured.

Places to Stay – bottom end

The cheaper hotels in Semarang don't have a great reputation – many say they're full to avoid taking in foreigners and, when you can get a room, conditions are not the best. Most places are in the centre of town near Pasar Johar and the old bus terminal, now a shopping centre. The *Losmen Jaya* at Jalan M T Haryono 85-87 has adequate rooms with fan from 7000 rp including breakfast, to 9500 rp with mandi. The *Losmen Agung*, in the same area at Jalan Petolongan 32-34, is a colonial relic with doubles at 5000 rp. It's had mixed reports – some think the reasonably clean rooms are good value, but one traveller has written that it is 'appalling, rat-infested, dirty and noisy'!

A slightly better hotel in this area is the *Djelita* at Jalan M T Haryono 34-38, with fairly clean economy singles for 7500 rp as well as more expensive rooms with bath and fan for 17,000 rp. There are some air-con rooms in the newer section for 23,000 rp. The *Nendra Yakti* (☎ 22538) at Gang Pinggir 68 in the heart of Chinatown is also worth considering, as quite decent doubles with mandi cost 14,000 rp, and rooms with air-con cost 25,000 rp.

Perhaps the best hotel for those watching their budget in these parts is the *Hotel Blambangan* (☎ 21649), well located at Jalan Pemuda 23. You can stay in a clean dorm here for 5500 rp a bed or in a small but decent double for 12,000 rp. Triples here cost 18,500 rp.

Other cheap hotels are scattered along or just off Jalan Imam Bonjol. This road is very busy with traffic so try and get a room away from the street. Ten minutes' or so walk from the Tawang railway station (500 rp by becak), there's the *Losmen Singapore* at Jalan Imam Bonjol 12, which has good

singles/doubles at 6000/8500 rp including breakfast. The *Hotel Oewa-Asia* (☎ 22547), near the Singapore at Jalan Kol Sugiono 12, spans the lower-to-middle bracket. This is an old colonial hotel so you can expect creaky floors and antiquated plumbing but it's comfortable and reasonably well maintained. Simple, clean rooms cost 9500 rp including breakfast. Rooms with fan and mandi start at 12,000 rp and there are also air-con rooms in a modern extension for 19,000 rp. It's in a good central location, near Pasar Johar and the post office, and the friendly staff do their utmost to please.

Further down near the Poncol railway station, the *Losmen Arjuna* at No 51 is fairly comfortable and friendly; rooms at 9000 rp include breakfast. *Losmen Rahayu* (☎ 22532) at No 35 has rooms with fan at 8500 rp including breakfast. Rooms with mandi cost 10,000 rp and there are some air-con rooms for 27,000 rp.

Much further out on Imam Bonjol at No 144 is the *Bali* (☎ 21974), which has clean if somewhat overpriced rooms starting at 16,500 rp with an exhaust fan, and air-con rooms for about twice that. Becak drivers may want to steer you to the Bali so they can claim an outrageous fare. Better value is *Green Guesthouse* (☎ 312787) at Jalan Kesambi 7 in the tranquil hilly Candi district a considerable distance from the centre. Clean air-con singles/doubles cost 18,500/24,500 rp including breakfast. This is a favourite temporary quarters for expats moving in or out of Semarang. For a really good deal in Candi, stay at the *Continental* (☎ 311969) at Jalan Dr Wahidin 195, where pleasant doubles with mandi cost 21,000 rp.

Places to Stay – middle

At an excellent central location, the *Telomoyo* (☎ 20926) at Jalan Gajah Mada 138 is patronised by many foreigners. Pleasant doubles with balconies start at 43,000 rp. Also in the centre of town, the *Dibya Puri* (☎ 27821) at Jalan Pemuda 11 is a nice rambling old hotel that has perhaps seen better days but still has some colonial atmosphere. Some rooms are air-con and all rooms have a private bathroom with a shower, hot water and a terrace. Singles/doubles cost 31,000 to 42,000 rp including breakfast and afternoon tea. There are a few economy rooms for about 20,000 rp. The hotel has its own garden, restaurant, bar and laundry service.

The *Queen Hotel* (☎ 27063) is at Jalan Gajah Mada 44-52 and is also central. It's a motel kind of place, well run and fully air-con; rooms with a private bathroom cost from 42,000 rp including breakfast and afternoon tea.

Once the top hotel in Semarang, the *Metro Grand Park Hotel* (☎ 27371) at Jalan H A Salim 2 is right in the middle of town. Standard singles/doubles cost 80,000/88,500 rp, deluxe 110,500/120,000 rp, plus 21% tax and service. The Metro has a discotheque, small supermarket, supper club, coffee shop and bar.

There are also a number of upper-notch hotels on the hills of Candi, including the *Candi Baru* (☎ 315272) at Jalan Rinjani 21, with air-con doubles beginning at 40,000 rp and the *Srondol Indah* (☎ 318180) at Jalan Setia Budi 221, with decent air-con doubles a bargain at 34,000 rp.

Places to Stay – top end

The top luxury hotel in Semarang is the *Graha Santika* (☎ 318850) at Jalan Pandanaran 116-120. Among the amenities are a pool, restaurant, gym and satellite TV. Fully air-con doubles here start at 147,000 rp and suites cost 352,000 rp.

The *Patra Jasa* (☎ 31441) at Jalan Sisingamangaraja 31441 in Candi offers a fine view of Semarang, bowling alleys, a pool and golf. Lovely air-con doubles begin at 142,000 rp and suites with whirlpool baths 196,000 rp.

Places to Eat

The *Toko Oen*, Jalan Pemuda 52, is not to be missed. It's a large, old-fashioned tea room where white tablecloths, basket chairs and ancient waiters in white jackets and *peci* (black caps) are all part of the genteel colonial atmosphere. It has an Indonesian, Chinese and European menu, good food if

slightly expensive (from 2700 rp) and a great selection of ice creams.

Near Toko Oen, on Jalan Pemuda, the *Sari Medan* serves superlative Padang food.

Along Jalan Gajah Mada are a number of Chinese restaurants, including the reasonably priced *Gajah Mada* at No 43 with good Chinese and seafood. On Sunday mornings they do a inexpensive 'breakfast a la Hongkong' dim sum. Gang Lombok, off Jalan Pekojan in Chinatown, is another good area for Chinese restaurants although reconstruction has meant that many, like the well-known *Hap Kie* or the *Soen*, have relocated to the Jalan Gajah Mada area. Near the Tay Kak Sie Temple at Gang Lombok No 23-25, you'll find *Kit Wan Kie*, one of the best Chinese places in Semarang; it's ugly but air-conditioned and the food is good. Close by at Gang Lombok No 11 is another good Chinese restaurant famous for its Indonesian spring roll lumpias, *Loempia Semarang*. The restaurant has another branch on Jalan Gajah Mada next to the Gajah Mada Apotik.

The *Timlo Solo*, Jalan A Yani 182, has good, inexpensive Javanese food. Try the *lontong timlo* or *nasi timlo*. *Istana Sate Sriwijaya*, Jalan Sriwijaya 20, has some of the best satay in town.

For a splurge, the fairly expensive *Rumah Makan Istana*, Jalan M T Haryono 836, has a good variety of European, Japanese, Chinese and Indonesian dishes, plus burgers and ice cream. In the evenings they sometimes have live music. *Ritzeky Pub* on Jalan Sinabung Buntu, is an expat hangout, especially on Friday nights, which is 'Darts Night'. It's open 'eight til late' Tuesday to Saturday.

At night you'll find dozens of food stalls around Pasar Ya'ik, Semarang's best speciality market, which assembles every evening from 5 to 8 pm near the Pasar Johar day market.

Things to Buy

Pasar Johar on Jalan A Salim near the Metro Hotel is Semarang's most intriguing night market. You can find a little bit of almost everything from food to hardware to clothing and it's worth an hour or so of wandering around. For fresh vegetables, live seafood, and other foodstuffs, the Pasar Cina, also called Pasar Gang Baru, is good. It's a morning market at its best before 7 am, in the small Chinese quarter. Jalan Pemuda is a good area for craft and antique shops. On Jalan Widoharjo, east of the bus station, the Pandjang Art & Gift Shop has a good display of Javanese crafts including silver, Jepara wood carvings and wayang puppets.

Getting There & Away

Air Garuda/Merpati (☎ 20178) is at Jalan Gajah Mada 11. It's open from 8 am to 4 pm Monday to Friday, from 8 am to 1 pm on Saturday and from 9 am to noon on Sunday. Merpati has direct flights between Semarang and Balikpapan, Bandung, Banjarmasin, Denpasar, Jakarta (105,000 rp, nine flights per day), Ketapang, Palangkaraya, Pangkalanbun and Surabaya (64,000 rp). With connecting flights there is a same-day service to Ambon, Bandarlampung, Banda Aceh, Batam, Bengkulu and Ujung Pandang.

Bouraq (☎ 23065) at Jalan Gajah Mada 61A is open daily from 8 am to 4 pm. They have daily direct flights from Semarang to Jakarta (105,000 rp) and Banjarmasin (154,700 rp).

Mandala (☎ 285319) at Jalan Pemuda 40 is open daily 8 am to 4 pm with daily direct flights to Jakarta (94,200 rp).

Both Garuda/Merpati and Mandala provide free transport between Semarang and the airport.

Bus Semarang's Jurnatan bus station on Jalan Let Jen Haryono is fairly close to the Tawang railway station, a conveniently central location. Most ticket-agent offices for night and express buses may be found near the bus station on Jalan Haryono. For express minibuses go to the old bus terminal area, on the corner of Jalan H A Salim and Jalan M T Haryono near Pasar Johar.

Going south, there are frequent services to Yogya for 2200 rp by public bus (3½ hours) or 3350 rp by express minibus, and Solo

1450 rp (2½ hours) or 2100 rp by air-con Patas (express) bus. Buses to Wonosobo for Dieng leave early in the morning and cost 1850 rp (four hours).

Going east, Kudus via Demak costs 650 rp (one hour). Night buses to Surabaya start at 9100 rp (5700 rp public bus) and take eight hours.

Going west, Pekalongan costs 1500 rp (about three hours) and Cirebon 3200 rp (six hours). Taxi 4848 express minibuses between Cirebon and Semarang cost 7500 rp; there are three per day from Rajawali Express (☎ 288812), Jalan Dr Cipto 96 in Semarang. Fares to Jakarta start at 6800 rp by public bus or around 17,000 rp by private express bus, but it's a long nine-hour haul and buses arrive at ungodly hours at the remote Pulo Gadung station. You're better off taking the train.

Train Semarang is on the main Jakarta-Cirebon-Surabaya train route and there are frequent services operating to and from these cities. Tawang is the main railway station in Semarang.

Trains between Jakarta and Semarang take about seven hours and cost from 5000 rp on the 3rd-class-only *Cepat* to 44,000 rp on the 1st-class-only *Mutiara Utara*. Third-class fares are 2550 rp on the *Cepat* between Semarang and Cirebon, and 4500 rp on the *GBM Utara* between Semarang and Surabaya. Oddly enough, fares on the Semarang-Cirebon and Semarang-Surabaya legs of the *Mutiara Utara* are exactly the same as those from Jakarta to Semarang – 44,000 rp.

Trains between Semarang and Pekalongan take four hours (same as the bus) and cost only 1100 rp for 3rd class.

Boat The Pelni Office (☎ 20488) is at Jalan Tantular 25, near the Tawang railway station. It's open from 8 am to 4 pm Monday to Friday and to 1 pm on Saturday. Jakarta and Surabaya are the usual ports for catching ships to the outer islands but there is one biweekly passenger ship, Pelni's *Kelimutu*, which originates in Semarang and sails to

Banjarmasin, Padang Bai, Lembar, Ujung Pandang, Bima, Waingapu, Ende and Kupang. There are also occasional cargo boats from Semarang to Banjarmasin which take passengers for around 25,000 rp – enquire in the harbour area.

Getting Around

To/From the Airport Ahmad Yani Airport is eight km to the west of town and 6000 rp by taxi. Transport can easily be arranged through the Dibya Puri and Metro Hotels or by calling Taxi 515 (☎ 312515) or Indra Kelana Taxi (☎ 22590).

Local Transport Semarang has becaks, taxis and a big city bus service, supplemented by orange Daihatsu minivans. City buses charge a fixed 200 rp fare and depart from the main Jurnatan bus station. The most useful service is the bus that runs south along Jalan Pemuda to Jalan Dr Sutomo and Jalan Sultan Agung to Candi. Daihatsus cost 200 rp and start out from Baru bus station – on Jalan H A Salim, behind the Pasar Johar – and operate to Karangayu, Tegal Wareng and Candi.

A becak from Tawang railway station or the bus station to the Oewa Asia Hotel will cost about 500 rp. You shouldn't pay more than 800 rp for any becak ride in town, though the drivers here will ask much more, especially at night. Becaks aren't allowed along Jalan Pemuda or Jalan Gajah Mada.

There are a limited number of taxis around town, used mostly by guests of large hotels like the Metro. They are unmetered, so bargaining is usually required.

AROUND SEMARANG

The people of north-east Central Java are noted for their extreme orthodoxy. During the 15th and 16th centuries this area was the home of nine shrewd, capable Muslims who have been immortalised as the wali songo, or nine saints, to whom the establishment of Islam in Java is credited. With the exception of Suan Gunungjati in Cirebon, the tombs of the walis all lie between Semarang and Surabaya and are important pilgrimage points

for devout Muslims. A number of these places lie on the road to Surabaya and can also be visited using Semarang as a base.

Kudus lies roughly on the border of land which is the product of gradual soil erosion and is known as the Gunung Muria Peninsula – at the beginning of the colonial era it was an island. In this region there are many houses of purely local design, often with interesting scroll-shaped decorations along the roof tops.

Demak

Twenty five km east of Semarang on the road to Surabaya, Demak was once the capital of the first Islamic state on Java and the most important state during the early 16th century. At the time this was a good seaport but silting of the coast has now left Demak several km inland. Ancient Javanese chronicles traditionally picture Demak as Majapahit's direct successor and even suggest that Raden Patah, the first 'Sultan' of Demak and the Muslim hero who defeated the Majapahit empire, was of Chinese origin. Named Jin Bun, he may have been the son of Majapahit's last king by a Chinese princess, Putri Cina, who had been sent away from court before her son was born. In 1474 Jin Bun is supposed to have visited Cheng Ho's mosque in Semarang only to find that it had been converted into a temple for idol worship. Three years later he led a 1000-strong Islamic army against the Hindu Majapahits and vowed that, if his revolt was successful, he would make the non-Muslim Chinese conform to Islamic rule in Demak.

The Mesjid Agung mosque dominates the village of Demak and is one of Indonesia's most important places of pilgrimage for Muslims. It's so holy that seven pilgrimages to it are said to be the equivalent of a pilgrimage to Mecca. It is the earliest mosque known on Java, founded jointly by the wali songo in 1478, and it combines Javanese-Hindu and Islamic elements in its architecture. Constructed entirely of wood, it has four main pillars, called the *soko guru*, in the central hall. The pillars are said to have been made by four of the saints – one of them, erected by Sunan Kalijagga, is made of chips of wood glued together. This early mosque has been deteriorating over the centuries but it's still much in use and is now being restored.

The mausoleum of Sunan Kalijagga is at Kadilangu, two km south of Demak.

PEKALONGAN

On the road and rail route between Semarang (100 km away) and Cirebon, Pekalongan is another major centre for batik and is often called Kota Batik or Batik City. It's a small town which few travellers visit so it's surprising how rapidly street peddlers descend upon you, casually waving batik from the doorways of hotels and restaurants. There are also a number of shops along Jalan Hayam Wuruk in the centre of town. B L Pekalongan, perhaps the best shop, and the most expensive, is at Jalan Mansyur 87. Others include the Kencana Souvenir Shop at Gang Podosugih I No 3, Jalan Mansyur.

There are batiks in Pekalongan which you won't easily find elsewhere in Java and if you're really interested you can visit the batik village of Kedungwuni, nine km south of town. At Oey Soe Tjoen's small workshop here, intricate and colourful batik tulis is still produced. Some experts say these are among the highest quality you will find. You can see it being made every day of the week except Friday.

Pekalongan also has a batik museum, near the fruit market on Jalan Pasar Ratu. It's open from 9 am to 1.30 pm and closed on Sundays.

In late August or early September, on Kliwon Friday of the Javanese calendar, Sedekah Laut is celebrated at Wonokerto Kulon on the coast. Miniature boats laden with offerings of buffalo heads, flowers, cookies and farm implements are floated into the sea. There are also cultural performances and boat-racing.

Places to Stay

Directly opposite the train station on Jalan

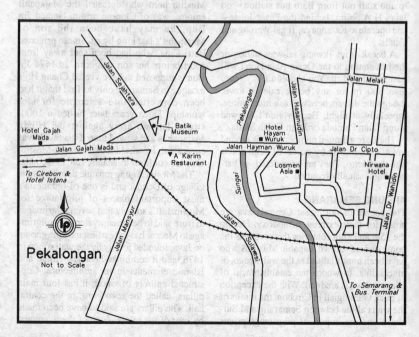

Pekalongan
Not to Scale

Top: Rice fields, Java (TO)
Left: Javanese woman (PS)
Right: Candi Bima, Dieng Plateau, Java (JC)

Top: Gunung Batur – dormant but not extinct, Bali (JL)
Bottom: Cloth stall in Tenganan, Bali (PW)

Gajah Mada there are three budget hotels. The best of the three is probably the *Hotel Gajah Mada* (☎ 41185) at No 11A, which has basic but clean rooms with mandi at 7500 rp. The *Losmen Ramayana*, behind the Ramayana 'Billyard Room' at Jalan Gajah Mada 9 and *Losmen Damai* at No 7 are similarly priced.

The *Hotel Istana* (☎ 61581) is near the train station at Jalan Gajah Mada 23. Singles/doubles with fan cost from 22,500/28,500 rp and there are more expensive rooms with air-con ranging from 36,000 to 81,000 rp. Rates include breakfast, and there's a swimming pool. In the centre of town, Pekalongan's best budget-to-moderate bet is the *Hotel Hayam Wuruk* (☎ 41823) at Jalan Hayam Wuruk 152-158. Here you will find a variety of decent rooms ranging in price from 16,000 to 20,000 rp for singles, and from 21,000 to 25,000 rp for doubles including breakfast. The *Nirwana Hotel* (☎ 41691), Jalan Dr Wahidin 11, is similar in price to the Istana and also has a pool; standard air-con singles/doubles cost 36,000/44,000 rp including breakfast and afternoon tea.

Places to Eat

Rumah Makan Saiyo, near the train station, has reasonable Padang food. The *Buana Restaurant*, at Jalan Mansyur 5, is a moderately priced seafood restaurant. Coming into town from the railway station, one of the first restaurants you will see signposted on Jalan Gajah Mada (there is no number) is *A Karim*. It may look like a hole-in-the-wall, but the satay served here is superlative. The *Purimas Bakery* on Jalan Hayam Wuruk has unusual decor – mirrors, pink doilies and plastic greenery – loud music, a cheap restaurant, bakery and good ice-cream sodas. At the *Pekalongan Remaja*, Jalan Dr Cipto 20, good and reasonably cheap Chinese food is available. The *Es Teler 77* at No 66 has a selection of cold ice juices and a cool shady garden. There are mangoes and avocados at the Pasar Ratu and plenty of food stalls in this area at night.

Getting There & Away

Pekalongan is on the main Jakarta-Semarang-Surabaya road and rail route. There is also a road linking Pekalongan and the Dieng Plateau.

Pekalongan's bus station is a fair distance east of the centre of town, 300 rp by colt or 700 rp by becak. If you're arriving by bus from Cirebon you can get dropped off on the way through town. Similarly, you can catch a bus to Semarang or Cirebon from outside the Hotel Gajah Mada. From Cirebon to Pekalongan takes about four hours and costs 2300 rp. The bus from Semarang takes about three hours and costs 1500 rp.

Getting Around

Colts to villages around Pekalongan depart from the stand behind the Pertamina petrol station on Jalan Hayam Wuruk, near the train station.

TEGAL

Halfway between Pekalongan and Cirebon, this north coast town is a centre for ochreware pottery. The best place to buy pottery and local handicrafts is at roadside stalls about 10 km south of Tegal.

KUDUS

Fifty-five km north-east of Semarang, Kudus was founded by the Muslim saint, Sunan Kudus. It was something of an Islamic holy city and, like Demak, is still an important place of pilgrimage. Its name comes from the Arabic *al-Quds*, which means 'holy', and it is the only place in Java that has permanently acquired an Arabic name. The people of Kudus are noted for their extreme orthodoxy and the old part of the town is strongly Muslim in feeling. Yet, strangely, some old Hindu customs prevail and there is still a tradition that cows may not be slaughtered within the town. History and religion aside, Kudus is a prosperous town and a major centre of Java's *kretek* (clove cigarette) industry.

Old Town

West of the river on the road to Jepara,

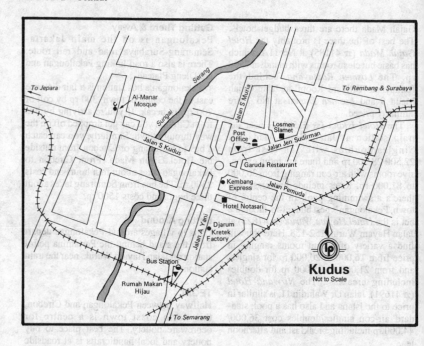

Kauman, the oldest part of town, can be an interesting place to wander around. Its streets are narrow and winding, stark white and almost Middle-Eastern in atmosphere, crowded with little boys in sarong and topi and women in full orthodox Muslim dress. Some of the buildings are colourful adat (traditional) houses with ornately carved wooden fronts.

In the centre of the old town, the Al-Manar (or Al-Aqsa) Mosque was constructed in 1549 by Sunan Kudus. The mosque is notable for its name, which is like that of the mosque of Jerusalem and, like so many of Java's early mosques, it displays elements of Islamic and Hindu-Javanese design such as the Old Javanese carved split doorways. In fact it was probably built on the site of a Hindu-Javanese temple and is particularly famous for its tall red-brick minaret or *menara*, which may have originally been the watchtower of that temple. Leaving your

shoes at the bottom, you can climb up the wooden ladder inside the tower; from the top there is a fine view over the town.

In the courtyards behind the mosque is the imposing tomb of Sunan Kudus, which is now a shrine. His mausoleum of finely carved stone is hung with a curtain of lace. The narrow doorway, draped with heavy gold-embroidered curtains, leads through to an inner chamber and the grave.

Kretek Factories

One of those distinctive 'aromas' of Indonesia is the sweet spicy smell, almost like incense, of clove- flavoured cigarettes. The kretek was invented in Kudus by a man who claimed they relieved his asthma. Today the addiction to kretek is almost nationwide. So high is the consumption of cloves for smoking that Indonesia, traditionally a supplier of cloves in world markets, has become a substantial net importer from centres like Zanzibar and Madagascar.

In Kudus more than 100 businesses account for roughly a quarter of Indonesia's annual production of kretek. Although in the last few years modern tools and methods have been brought to various economic enterprises, there has been official protection of labour-intensive techniques in the kretek industry. Huge numbers of people are employed, mostly young women who hand-roll cigarettes on simple wooden forms. The process is quite interesting to see. The most convenient business to visit is the Chinese-owned Djarum company which started in 1952 and is now the biggest producer in Kudus. Their head office is a rather incongruous modern block on Jalan A Yani. Factory tours are free.

...1000 women were employed in one large room, full of the clacking noise of the wooden rolling machines. The women work in pairs with one rolling the cigarettes and the other snipping ends. They work an eight to 10-hour day: one roller gets 350 rp per 1000 cigarettes; 500 rp per 1000 after the first batch of 3000 cigarettes. Maximum production was cited as 6000 to 8000 cigarettes. The tobacco is grown locally but the cloves come all the way from Madagascar.

Places to Stay

The *Hotel Notasari* (☎ 21245), Jalan Kepodang 12, is within reasonable walking distance of the bus station. Comfortable rooms with mandi start at 26,000 rp including breakfast (coffee, bread and eggs or nasi goreng); air- con rooms start at double that price. It's well kept, there's a swimming pool, quiet courtyard and restaurant and the staff are friendly.

The central *Losmen Slamet*, Jalan Jenderal Sudirman 63, has spartan rooms at 9050 rp. It's just OK – some rooms are better than others. *Air Mancur* (☎ 22514) at Jalan Pemuda 70 is preferable, with decent doubles with mandi for 14,000 rp. The *Hotel Duta Wisata* (☎ 22694) is at Jalan Barongan 194, north of town. It's a bit out of the way but it's a nice place, in a quiet residential area, with rooms from 12,000 rp including breakfast (coffee, bread and eggs). A becak

from this area into the centre of town costs about 600 rp.

Places to Eat

Local specialities to try include *soto Kudus*, chicken soup, and *jenang Kudus*, which is a sweet made of glutinous rice, brown sugar and coconut. The *Rumah Makan Hijau*, near the bus station at Jalan A Yani 1, is cheap and good for Indonesian food and super-cool fruit juices. It's closed on Fridays. There are also night food stalls at the Pasar Bitingan near the bus station.

The *Hotel Notasari* restaurant is reasonably priced for the big helpings you get. The *Garuda* at Jalan Jenderal Sudirman 1 has Indonesian, Chinese and Western food.

Getting There & Away

Kudus is on the main Semarang to Surabaya road. From Semarang to Kudus is 55 km, a one-hour bus trip costing 650 rp. Surabaya is 286 km away. Kembang Express (☎ 282) at Jalan A Yani 90 has night express buses to Surabaya and Jakarta. Public buses to Solo cost 2550 rp and the trip takes two hours.

Colts to villages around Kudus depart from the bus station and include Jepara (650 rp), Rembang (950 rp) and Mantingan (1100 rp).

AROUND KUDUS
Mayong

Raden Ajeng Kartini (1879-1904) was born in Mayong, 12 km north-west of Kudus on the road to Jepara. She was the daughter of the Regent of Jepara and was allowed, against Indonesian custom, to attend the Dutch school in Jepara along with her brothers. As a result of her education, Kartini questioned both the burden of Javanese etiquette and the polygamy permitted under Islamic law. In letters to Dutch friends she criticised colonial behaviour and vocalised an 'ever growing longing for freedom and independence, a longing to stand alone'.

Kartini married the Regent of Remban, himself a supporter of progressive social policies, and they opened a school in Remang for the daughters of regents. In 1904 Kartini died shortly after the birth of her son. Perhaps the first modern Indonesian writer, Kartini's letters were published in 1911 in the original Dutch, entitled *Through Darkness to Light*; the English edition is available in a Norton paperback.

At Mayong there is a monument to Kartini. Jepara and Rembang are other important places where ceremonies are held on 21 April to celebrate Kartini Day.

Jepara

Jepara, only 35 km north-west of Kudus, is famed as the centre for the best traditional woodcarvers in Java. Intricately carved wooden chests, tables, wall panels, jewellery boxes, picture frames and the like are most often carved from teak. They usually follow a similar pattern to the ornate floral designs of batik, although wall panels often depict scenes from Javanese legends. Fine chess sets are sometimes carved out of ebony. The road into Jepara passes workshops stacked high with furniture, so you get a fair idea of places to visit as you arrive. Tirto Samodro, eight km from town, is a white-sand beach.

Jepara is a small, peaceful country town but it has a colourful history. An important port in the 16th century, it had both English and Dutch factories by the early 1600s and was involved in a violent dispute between the VOC and Sultan Agung of Mataram. After some of the Dutch reputedly compared Agung to a dog and relieved themselves on Jepara's mosque, hostilities finally erupted in 1618 when the Gujarati who governed Jepara for Agung attacked the VOC trading post. The Dutch retaliated by burning Javanese ships and much of the town. In 1619 Jan Pieterszoon Coen paused on his way to the conquest of Batavia to burn Jepara yet again and with it the English East India Company's post. The VOC headquarters for the central north coast was then established at Jepara.

Places to Stay The *Meno Jaya Inn* (☎ 143) at Jalan Diponegoro 40B, the top choice in Jepara, has pleasant rooms for 7000 to 14,500 rp. It's friendly and the owner, Mr Teopilus Hadiprasetya, speaks good English.

He runs a woodcarving shop at the front of the hotel and without a doubt he'll proudly show you the 'thank you' letter from Prince Charles and Lady Di for a carved plaque he sent them as a wedding present!

Other places include the *Hotel Terminal* right by the bus station, where rooms with fan cost from 6000 rp, with air-con 21,000 rp. The hotel has a pleasant garden but, given its location, it can be a bit noisy. The *Losmen Asia* at Jalan Kartini 32 has rooms for 6000 to 7500 rp.

Rembang

Pantai Kartini is a good beach for swimming at Rembang, a small fishing town 59 km east of Kudus. The Kartini Museum is in the Rembang Regency Office building.

Mantingan

The memorial tomb of Kartini stands in the grounds of the old mosque at Mantingan, 20 km south of Rembang on the road to Blora and 80 km from Jepara.

The tomb of Ratu Kalinyamat is also here. Kalinyamat was the great warrior-queen of Jepara who twice laid siege to Portugal's Melaka stronghold in the latter part of the 16th century. Neither campaign was successful but she scared the Portuguese witless. The mosque was restored some years ago and the tomb has some interesting Hindustyle embellishments, particularly medallions.

East Java

The province of East Java, or Jawa Timur, officially includes the island of Madura off the north-west coast. Including Madura it has a total population of 29.2 million and an area of 47,922 sq km. The majority of its population are Javanese, but many Madurese farmers and fishermen live in East Java. They are familiar faces, particularly around Surabaya, the capital of the province. In the Bromo area is a small population of Hindu Tenggerese.

Geographically, much of the province is flatter than the rest of Java. In the north-west is lowland with deltas along the rivers Brantas and Bengawan Solo, and km upon km of rice-growing plain. But the rest of East Java is mountainous and hilly, containing the huge Bromo-Tengger massif and Java's highest mountain (Gunung Semeru, 3680 metres). This region offers a raw, natural beauty and magnificent scenery.

Major attractions for the visitor include the magnificent Gunung Bromo, still one of Java's most active volcanoes. Then there's a host of other mountains, pleasant walks and fine hill towns like Malang. In the north-east corner of the province there is also the important Baluran National Park, the most accessible of Java's wildlife reserves. Finally, although East Java is closely related culturally to Central Java, the Madurese are best known for their rugged sport called *kerapan sapi*, the famous bull races which take place on the island during August and September.

History

East Java's hazy past comes into focus with its political and cultural ascendancy in the 10th century AD, and the reign of Airlangga. Before claiming the throne in 1019 AD, Airlangga had spent many years as a hermit, devoting time to accumulating wisdom through fasting and meditation. Significantly, it was during his reign that the ancient Hindu poem of Arjuna's temptation, the *Arjuna Wiwaha*, was first translated into Old Javanese and it is still one of the most popular of the wayang stories. Under Airlangga's government, eastern Java became united and powerful but shortly before his death he divided his kingdom between his two sons, creating Janggala, east of Sungai Brantas, and Kediri to the west. A third kingdom, Singosari, joined in the struggle for the ascendancy.

In 1049 the Kediri dynasty rose to power and continued its rule through to 1222. Kediri is best remembered today for the famous prophecy attributed to its soothsayer King Joyoboyo, who predicted that the 'white buffalo' (the Dutch) would come to rule Java until supplanted by the 'yellow chicken' (the Japanese) who would remain for only the lifetime of the maize plant, after which the Ratu Adil, the Just Prince, would take power and usher in a golden age. This prophecy was revived during the Japanese occupation of the Dutch East Indies in WW II and sustained Indonesian hopes during the hard years that followed.

In 1222 the Singosari kingdom came to power and gradually superseded Kediri under the leadership of the usurper, Ken Angrok. Angrok was a violent man who took the throne by murdering the former ruler of Singosari and then marrying his wife. Legend relates that Ken Angrok first tried out his murder weapon on its maker, who then cursed it with his dying breath, predicting that seven kings would die by the sword. The curse was fulfilled – the rule of Singosari lasted a mere 70 years, but under its kings the Javanese culture nevertheless flourished. East Java inherited some of its most striking temples from that era and the Singosaris also pioneered a new sculptural style that owed little or nothing to original Indian traditions. Shivaism and Buddhism also evolved into a new religion called Shiva-Buddhism, which even today has many followers in Java and Bali.

Kertanagara (1262-92) was the last of the Singosari kings and a skilful diplomat who sought alliance with other Indonesian rulers in the face of the threat from another great power. In 1292 the Mongol ruler, Kublai Khan, demanded that homage be paid to China. Kertanagara, however, foolishly humiliated the Great Khan by having the nose and ears of the Mongol envoy cut off and sent back to China. This effrontery precipitated the launching of a Mongol invasion of Java but by the time they arrived Kertanagara had already been killed in a civil war. The new king, Wijaya, defeated the Mongols but the barbaric invasion left such a bitter taste that for nearly a hundred years relations between China and Java remained at a standstill.

Wijaya was also the founder of the

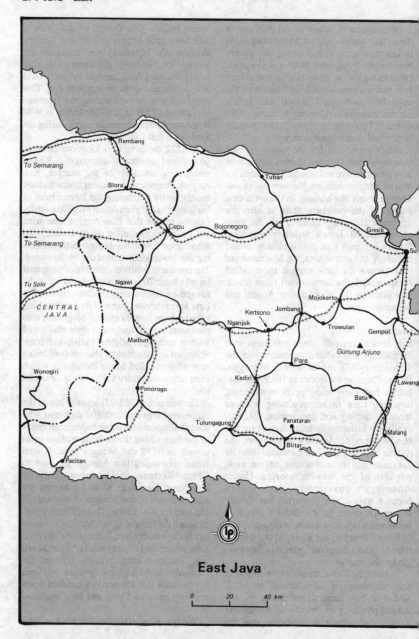

To Semarang

To Semarang

To Solo

CENTRAL JAVA

Rembang

Blora

Cepu

Ngawi

Madiun

Wonogiri

Ponorogo

Pacitan

Tuban

Bojonegoro

Gresik

Su

Mojokerto

Kertsono   Jombang

Nganjuk   Trowulan

Gunung Arjuno

Pare

Kediri

Tulungagung   Panataran

Blitar

Trowulan

Gempol

Lawang

Batu

Malang

East Java

0   20   40 km

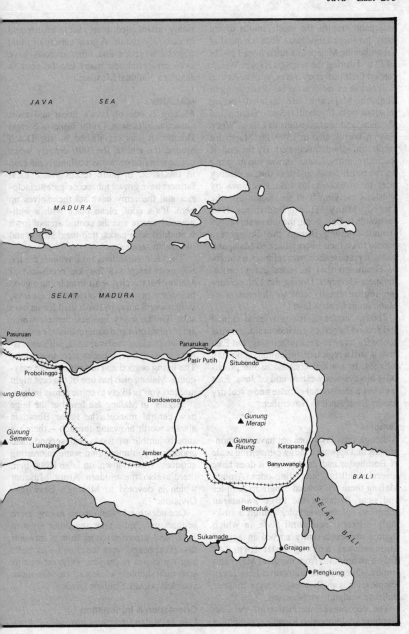

JAVA   SEA

MADURA

SELAT   MADURA

Pasuruan

Panarukan

Pasir Putih   Situbondo

Probolinggo

Bondowoso

ung Bromo

Gunung
Merapi

Gunung
Semeru

Gunung
Raung   Ketapang

Lumajang

Jember

Banyuwangi

BALI

Benculuk

SELAT

BALI

Sukamade

Grajagan

Plengkung

Majapahit empire, the most famous of the early Javanese kingdoms. With a capital at Trowulan the Majapahits ruled from 1294 to 1478 and during the reign of Hayam Wuruk carried their power overseas, with raids into Bali and an expedition against Palembang in Sumatra. Majapahit also claimed trading relations with Cambodia, Siam, Burma and Vietnam, and sent missions to China. When Hayam Wuruk died in 1389, the Majapahit empire rapidly disintegrated. By the end of the 15th century, Islamic power was growing on the north coast, and less than a century later there were raids into East Java by Muslims carrying both the Koran and the sword. Many Hindu-Buddhists fled eastwards to Bali, but in the mountain ranges around Gunung Bromo the Tenggerese people trace their history back to Majapahit and still practise their own religion, a variety of Hinduism that includes many proto-Javanese elements. During the 17th century the region finally fell to the rulers of Mataram in Central Java.

Today, Surabaya, the provincial capital and second largest city in Indonesia, is a vital centre for trade and manufacturing, but East Java is still a region of agriculture and small villages. In marked contrast to the practically-always-wet western end of Java, East Java has a monsoonal climate and a real dry season from April to November.

Temples

Although East Java does not have any monuments that approach the awe-inspiring scale of Borobudur and Prambanan, it does have several small but interesting ones. Around Malang there are several Singosari temples and near Blitar is the large Panataran complex. All these temples exhibit a strikingly different sculptural style in which figures are exuberantly carved in a two-dimensional wayang kulit form. At Trowulan are ruins from the great Majapahit empire. Overall, the innovative East Javan temple style is an obvious prototype for later Balinese sculpture/architecture.

The decorative imagination of the East Javanese sculptors also found expression in richly ornamented items cast in bronze and more costly metals. A great variety of ritual objects, weapons and other utensils have been preserved and many can be seen in Jakarta's National Museum.

MALANG

Malang is one of Java's finest and most attractive hill towns. On the banks of Sungai Brantas, it was established by the Dutch around the end of the 18th century when coffee was first grown as a colonial cash crop in this area. In more recent years, local farmers have grown tobacco; cigarette factories and the army have set themselves up here. It's a cool, clean place with a well-planned square and the central area of town is studded with parks, tree-lined streets and old Dutch architecture.

The main attractions for travellers are the Singosari temples a few km north-east of Malang but the city, apart from being a good base for many points of interest in East Java, is also worth a day or two's visit for its own sake. Unlike many Javanese towns, which are planned on a grid pattern, this one sweeps and winds along the river bank, with surprising views and quiet backwaters to explore. The living is good and the atmosphere easygoing. Malang also has one of the best night markets you're likely to come across in Java.

'Sights' in Malang are few, but the huge new central market, the Pasar Besar, is always worth browsing through – there's a superb jumble of foods and second-hand goods and you might find some interesting antiques. West of town, on Jalan Besar Ijen, there's also the modern Army Museum which is devoted to Malang's Brawijaya Division.

One negative: Malang seems to have more beggars per capita than any other town in Java. And a recent report from a traveller says pickpockets work the crowd-trick here: a group closes in on you, someone bumps your right shoulder while someone else picks your left pocket. Strollers beware!

Orientation & Information

Life in Malang revolves around the town

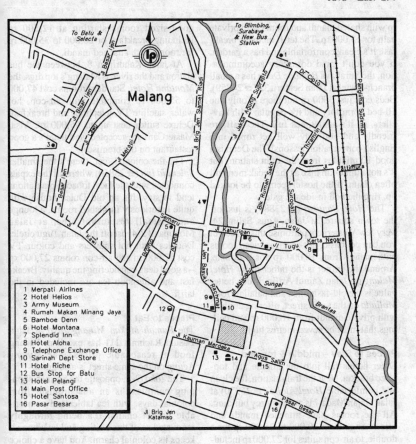

Malang

1 Merpati Airlines
2 Hotel Helios
3 Army Museum
4 Rumah Makan Minang Jaya
5 Bamboe Denn
6 Hotel Montana
7 Splendid Inn
8 Hotel Aloha
9 Telephone Exchange Office
10 Sarinah Dept Store
11 Hotel Riche
12 Bus Stop for Batu
13 Hotel Pelangi
14 Main Post Office
15 Hotel Santosa
16 Pasar Besar

square and the busy streets of Agus Salim and Pasar Besar near the central market. Here are the main shopping areas, restaurants, cinemas, the main post office and many of Malang's hotels. The square in particular is a very popular area in the evenings, when families and students promenade, buskers perform before riveted crowds, and long queues form outside the cinemas. North-west of the square along Jalan Basuki Rachmat you'll find banks, the telephone office, restaurants and a few interesting souvenir shops. For maps and books try the

Riang Bookshop on Jalan Basuki Rachmat near the square, or Toko Atlas further north.

The tourist office at Jalan Tugu 1 has a few brochures; Tanjung Permai Travel, Jalan Basuki Rachmat 41, is very helpful if you need information.

Although the train station is a short distance east across the river, the new bus station is in the far northern sector of the city.

Places to Stay – bottom end
The *Hotel Helios* (☎ 62741) at Jalan Pattimura 37 has doubles for 7000 to 9500

rp with shared mandi and rooms with private bath for 15,000 rp. The tariff includes breakfast. It's clean, comfortable and has a garden. If you don't mind dormitory accommodation, the Surabaya *Bamboe Denn* has a small branch-hostel at Jalan Semeru 35 (☎ 24859). Beds cost just 3000 rp but there is only one 10-bed dormitory and it's popular with travellers, so it's sometimes full. The staff are friendly and you may well get roped into English conversation lessons! The Denn is a good 10 minutes from the train station, but it's not a three-km hike as the becak men will often claim. If the hostel seems to be locked up, ring the bell inside the gate.

The *Hotel Santosa* (☎ 23889) is just off the town square, at Jalan Agus Salim 24. Very few Westerners patronise this place but you can get basic, not-so-clean clean rooms with mandi from 18,000 rp for a double. Around the corner is the rather noisy *Hotel Malang* on Jalan Zainul Arifin. Much better value is the old-fashioned and palatial *Hotel Malinda* on the same street, offering doubles with private mandi from 18,000 rp and ceilings that must be seven metres high!

Places to Stay – middle & top end

Other hotels fall into the middle and top-price bracket. Near the train station, the clean and comfortable *Hotel Aloha* (☎ 26950) at Jalan Gajah Mada 7 is a two-storey building. All the rooms have attached mandi and prices range from 20,000 to 25,000 rp for a double, to air-con suites for 27,000 rp including breakfast. All rooms have hot water. Right on the town square, the *Hotel Pelangi* (☎ 27456), Jalan Merdeka, is also good. It's a large, pleasant old Dutch hotel with spacious rooms – all with bathroom, showers and hot and cold running water. Doubles range in price from excellent-value economy rooms for 12,500 rp to standard rooms for 30,000 rp. Air-con rooms range from 40,000 to 58,000 rp. The hotel has a restaurant, bar and laundry service.

Also on the town square, near the Sarinah department store and Toko Oen restaurant, is *Hotel Riche* (☎ 24560) at Jalan Basuki Rachmat 1. It's a rambling old place with good-sized rooms starting at 12,500 rp including breakfast, or 20,000 to 35,000 rp for rooms with attached mandi.

At Jalan Kahuripan 8, between the bus station and the river, is Malang's top digs, the *Montana Hotel*. Standard rooms cost 47,000 to 55,000 rp complete with air-con, hot water, satellite TV, telephone and breakfast. Deluxe suites cost up to 95,000 rp. Visa/MasterCard are accepted, and there's a good restaurant on the premises.

For the colonial feel, there's the smaller *Splendid Inn* (☎ 23860) where all the expats connected with the local tobacco plantations tend to stay. It's an old Dutch house with quite luxuriously furnished rooms, a lounge and a small restaurant area, at Jalan Mohopahit 2-4 just off the Jalan Tugu circle. Doubles with hot showers and colour TV cost 22,000 rp and air-con rooms 27,000 rp – a good deal, considering the quality. Breakfast and afternoon tea are included in the tariff.

Places to Eat

The *Rumah Makan Minang Jaya* at Jalan Basuki Rachmat 111 has excellent Padang food at reasonable prices. The *Minang Agung* on the same street is also good.

The *Toko Oen*, opposite the Sarinah shopping complex, is an anachronism from colonial days, with tea tables and comfortable basket chairs. It's being throughly renovated as of this writing and let's hope it keeps its colonial charm. You have a choice of two menus here: the more expensive Toko Oen menu and a cheaper one from the *Cafeteria Aneka Rasa* next door. They have Chinese and Western dishes plus good Indonesian food and delicious home-made ice cream. Most meals are in the 2500 to 5000 rp bracket but there are mie/nasi goreng and soto ayam for 1200 rp. This is one of the most relaxing places for a meal and a good place for breakfast; it's open from 8.30 am to 9 pm every day except Monday.

The *Splendid Inn* has set Western and Indonesian meals for 5000 rp; they also have a bar and lounge area where you can order liquor as well as cold beer. The *Hotel*

Montana also has similar fare and prices. Next to the Montana, the *Melati Pavilion* restaurant serves continental cuisine at upscale prices. For a splurge, locals recommend taking a taxi out to the *Ambassador Restaurant* on Jalan Kawiatas for fine European fare.

On Jalan Pasar Besar, the *Depot Pangsit Mie Gadjah Mada* is popular and serves good bowls full of cheap wonton and noodles. At the Pasar Besar, open until 8 pm, you'll find warung food and good fruit – mangoes, apples and cheap avocados (100 rp).

In Malang Plaza, on Jalan Agus Salim, are a couple of modern food centres, including a *Kentucky Fried Chicken* and a supermarket.

Finally, there's the *Pasar Senggol* night market – a bustling crowd of hawkers and warmly lit warungs strung out along Jalan Majapahit and across the Sungai Brantas. The *Warung Sederhana* here has excellent gado-gado for 550 rp and *tahu telur*, a bean-curd omelette with bean sprouts, cucumber and peanut sauce.

Getting There & Away

Malang can be approached from a number of directions. The back route between Yogya and Banyuwangi takes you through some beautiful countryside. For an interesting trip, you could take a train from Solo to Jombang, then colts south to Blimbing, Kandangan, Batu and finally Malang.

Air The airport in Malang closed in 1985 and as of this writing has not yet been reopened, although it is said service will be reinstated in the future.

Bus Service includes frequent buses to and from Surabaya for 1450 rp (2½ hours), Probolinggo 1400 rp (two hours), Banyuwangi for around 5100 rp (nine hours via Probolinggo and Jember), Blitar 1400 rp (two hours) and Kediri 2450 rp (three hours, with the last bus at 3.45 pm). Buses to Yogyakarta cost 5900 rp and take all day. Some fares by colt include Blitar 1500 rp and Purwodadi/

Lawang 800 rp (half an hour); Pasuruan 800 rp and Surabaya 1600 rp. Express minibuses to Surabaya cost 6800 rp and can be arranged by any hotel.

Night Bus For Bali, Bali Indah at Jalan Pattimura 11A runs a bus that leaves at 6 pm and arrives in Denpasar at 3 am, for around 15,800 rp. There's also Pemudi Express at Jalan Basuki Rachmat 1 near the town square, next door to Hotel Riche. Their bus to Bali departs at 7 pm and the fare is 15,800 rp. This same company has express buses to Yogya (15,000 rp) Solo (12,500 rp), Banyuwangi (13,000 rp) and Bandung (28,500 rp). Rosalie Indah and several other agents along Jalan Agus Salim across from Malang Plaza shopping complex run express buses to Yogya (15,000 rp), Probolinggo (4700 rp) and Surabaya (6100 rp).

Train There are nine services daily between Malang and Surabaya. The trip takes about three hours and the fare is 1400 rp in 3rd class. Trains also run between Malang and Blitar for 1200 rp in 3rd-class-only. There are six trains to Blitar daily between 7 am and 6 pm.

Trains from points west such as Solo and Yogya are 3rd-class-only and very slow. Bus is a much better choice on these routes.

Getting Around

Around Malang there are becaks and bemos. The biggest bemo station is on Jalan Pasar Besar, in front of the market, and they run around town for a fixed fare of 200 rp. A becak for the considerable haul between the bus station and the town square will cost around 1000 rp. Apart from that, the best way to see Malang is to walk.

Local Colts A bemo ride north of town, Blimbing is the focal point for colts to the temples around Malang. Other colt stations are at the Pattimura bus station, on Jalan Julius Usman and Jalan Halmahera.

AROUND MALANG
Singosari Temples

A good day trip is a rough circle north from Blimbing colt station in Malang to Candi Singosari, backtracking to Blimbing for a colt east to the Jago Temple at Tumpang, and from there south-east to the Kidal Temple. Finally, you can circle back south to Malang via Tajinan. All you need is a pocketful of change for a total fare of about 2500 rp.

Singosari Right in Singosari village, 12 km north of Malang, this temple stands 500 metres off the main Malang to Surabaya road. One of the last monuments erected by the Singosari dynasty, it was built around 1300 AD in honour of Hindu and Buddhist priests who died with King Kertanagara in the bloody war against the Kingdom of Kediri. The main structure of the temple was completed but, for some reason, the sculptors never finished their task. Only the top

part has any ornamentation and the kala heads have been left strangely stark, with smooth bulging cheeks and pop eyes. Of the statues that once inhabited the temple's chambers, only Agastya the Shivaite teacher remains – the others disappeared long ago to museums in The Netherlands.

About 200 metres beyond the temple are two enormous figures of *dwarapalas* (believed to be guardians against evil spirits) wearing clusters of skulls and twisted serpents. These may have been part of the original gates to the headquarters of the Singosari kingdom. There is a 400 rp entry fee to the temple area, plus another 300 rp fee to view the dwarapalas.

Tumpang Along a small road near the market in Tumpang (18 km from Malang), the Jago (or Jajaghu) Temple was built in 1268 AD and is thought to be a memorial to another Singosari king, Vishnuvardhana.

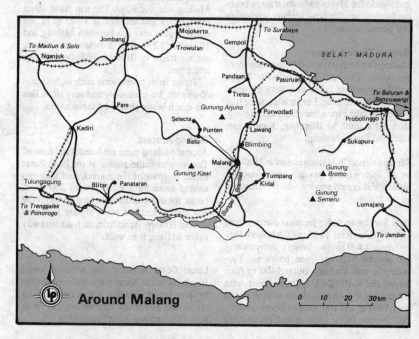

Around Malang

The temple is in fairly poor condition but it still has some interesting decorative carving – in the two-dimensional wayang kulit style typical of East Java – which tells tales from the *Jataka* and the *Mahabharata*. The caretaker describes it as a Buddhist temple, but scattered around the garden are Javanese-Hindu statues including a six-armed death-dealing goddess and a lingam, the symbol of Shiva's virility and male potency.

Kidal The Kidal Temple, a small gem and perhaps the finest example of East Javanese art, is 24 km east of Malang. Built around 1260 AD to honour King Anushapati of Singosari, it is tapering and slender, with pictures of the garuda on three sides, bold, glowering kala heads and medallions of the *haruna* and garuda symbols. Two *kala makara* (dragons) guard the steps – like those at the kraton steps in Yogya, one is male and the other female.

Batu & Selecta

If you feel like a day or two's outing, take a bus to Batu, a small hill town on the slopes of Gunung Arjuno, 15 km north-west of Malang. In Batu there's a good night market on Jalan Agus Salim near the town square. Three km from Batu there are well-known hot springs at Songgoriti.

Selecta, smaller still, is only five km further up the mountain from Batu. From this hill resort there are superb views over the surrounding volcanoes. There are good walks and you can visit the tiny mountain village of Sumber Brantas, high above Selecta at the source of the Sungai Brantas. The Senkaling Pemandian swimming pool has a superb setting in landscaped gardens and is worth the trip from Malang. A swim costs 900 rp and there is a fine terrace restaurant overlooking the pool. The pool is open daily from 6 am to 6 pm.

Places to Stay There are a few basic budget hotels in Batu such as the *Perdana* and the *Losmen Kawi* on Jalan Panglima Sudirman, both friendly places with rooms from 8500 rp. On the same street, the *Asida* offers

greater comfort as well as TV and pool for 25,000 rp.

In Selecta there are a couple of upper-notch hotels, such as the *Hotel Selecta*, where rooms with a bathroom start at 19,000 rp (including free use of the swimming pool). Larger, more expensive rooms cost 30,000 rp. In Punten, halfway between Batu and Selecta, the *Palem Punten* has rooms at 10,000 rp. Other places include the similarly priced *Losmen Garuda* and the *Losmen Mustikasari*.

Wendit

This is another hill resort, nine km east of Malang, with a pool, forests and a troupe of monkeys. At the end of Ramadan, Wendit is the site of a festival called Lebaran Kupatan. The celebrations last 11 days, and on the seventh day thousands of people jump into the pool in the belief that they will be blessed with eternal youth.

Gunung Kawi

Near the village of Wonosari on Gunung Kawi, 40 km west of Malang, is the tomb of a great Muslim sage, Mbah Jugo, who died in 1871. It has, surprisingly, become a Mecca for non-Muslim Chinese and attracts a regular stream of pilgrims who attend daily prayer sessions at 6, 11 am and 7 pm. Inside the sanctified property is a warning sign forbidding 'painting, writing on walls, use of radio or tape recorders, photographs – and *explosives*'.

Lawang

At Lawang, a hill town 18 km from Malang on the road to Surabaya, you can visit the *Hotel Niagara*. Dating from the turn of the century, this grand five-storey Art-Nouveau mansion was designed by a Brazilian architect for a wealthy Chinese gentleman but the family sold their inheritance in the early 1960s. There is lots of beautiful old furniture, some of it quite unusual, painted wall tiles, terrazzo floors and stained-glass lights. From the rooftop there is a magnificent view of Gunung Arjuno. The hotel even has a story about three ghosts who haunt one of the rooms.

The inmates of the Sumber Porong Mental Institution in Lawang give free musical performances every Wednesday and Saturday morning at 9 am.

Purwodadi

A few km north of Lawang, the Kebun Raya Purwodadi are big dry-climate botanical gardens with a high waterfall.

PANATARAN

The Hindu temples at Panataran are the largest remaining Majapahit sanctuaries and perhaps the finest examples of East Javanese architecture and sculpture. Construction began around 1200 AD during the Singosari dynasty but the temple complex took some 250 years to complete. Most of the important surviving structures date from the great years of the Majapahit during the 1300s. The arrangement of the three gradually rising courtyards and the beautiful detailed reliefs and sculptures of Panataran are similar to those of many temples in Bali.

Around the base of the first level platform, which would once have been a meeting place, the comic-strip carvings tell the story of a test between the fat meat-eating Bubukshah and the thin vegetarian Gagang Aking.

Farther on is the small Dated Temple, so called because of the date 1291 (1369 AD) carved over the entrance. On the next level are colossal serpents snaking endlessly around the Naga Temple which once housed valuable sacred objects.

At the rear stands the Mother Temple – or at least part of it, for the top of the temple has been reconstructed alongside its three-tiered base. Followed anticlockwise, panels around the base depict stories from the *Ramayana*, with Hanuman's secret mission to Rawana's palace on Sri Lanka to find Sita, a drama of battles, flames and giants, Hanuman flying across the trees and monkeys building bridges across the seas. The more realistic people of the Krishna stories on the second tier of the base show an interesting transition

from almost two-dimensional representation to three-dimensional figures.

Nearby is a small royal mandi with a frieze of lizards, bulls and dragons around its walls.

Getting There & Away

Panataran is 10 km from Blitar, which is the most convenient place to use as a base. It is possible to see the Panataran temples comfortably in a day from Malang – and possibly from Surabaya – so long as you're prepared to hire a motorbike or dokar in Blitar to take you there and back. Colts from Blitar generally only run as far as Nglegok village, three km short of Panataran. You could also hire a minibus from any of Malang's hotels to Panataran and back – figure on about 60,000 rp for the day.

BLITAR

Blitar is the usual base from which to visit Panataran. It's quite a pleasant country town to stay in overnight, and is also of interest as the site of President Sukarno's grave.

There are no official moneychangers in Blitar but, if you're in a pinch, the Hotel Sri Lestari will change travellers' cheques at below the Bank Indonesia's rate.

Makam Bung Karno (Sentul)

At Sentul, a few km outside Blitar on the road to Panataran, an elaborate monument now covers the spot where former President Sukarno was buried in 1970. Sukarno is looked on by many as the 'father of his country', although he was only reinstated as a national hero in 1978 by the present regime. The leader of Indonesia from 1949 to 1965, he had been worshipped by the people (almost as a god) but by 1970 he was little more than a figurehead, suspected of having had ties with the attempted Communist coup of 1965 and discarded by the army. His last two years were spent under house arrest, in isolation in Bogor and Jakarta.

Sukarno was given a state funeral but, despite family requests that he be buried at his home in Bogor, the hero of Indonesian independence was buried as far as possible from Jakarta in an unmarked grave next to his mother in Blitar. It was only in 1978 that the lavish million-dollar monument was built over the grave and opened to Indonesian pilgrims.

Places to Stay

Blitar is a small compact town and there are a few hotels within 10 minutes' walk of the bus station. The *Hotel Sri Lestari* (☎ 81766), Jalan Merdeka 173, is definitely the best of them. It's a well-kept colonial house and you can get rooms for 6000 rp facing a pretty garden and pond (plus an orchestra of frogs that can make enough noise to waken the dead!). In the main building, standard rooms cost 8500 to 11,500 rp, larger rooms for three or four people cost 15,000 rp and doubles with attached mandi cost 21,000 rp. There are also more expensive rooms with hot and cold running water. In spite of vocal frogs the hotel is excellent value. All room rates include breakfast; there is also a bar and good tasty meals are available in the family kitchen (nasi rawon or nasi campur for 1150 rp). The woman who runs the place is friendly and can arrange transport to Panataran (car or motorcycle) for reasonable fees.

The *Penginapan Aman*, Jalan Merdeka 130, has rooms for 5000 to 8500 rp. There's also the *Penginapan Harjuna*, in a small lane off Jalan Anggrek, which in turn runs off Jalan Merdeka. Rooms cost a rock-bottom 3500 rp. It's adequate, but we're loath to recommend it – somehow we didn't feel welcome in this area. There are a couple of other budget hotels on this lane which won't take foreigners.

Places to Eat

Overall, the *Hotel Sri Lestari* kitchen is your best bet in Blitar, but *Rumah Makan Jaya* and *Ramayana*, both on Jalan Merdeka, are worth trying for Chinese food.

Getting There & Away

From Malang to Blitar is 80 km and it takes about two hours by bus for 1400 rp. There are also several trains daily between Malang and Blitar. From Surabaya to Blitar, via

Malang, it's about four hours by bus, for 2800 rp.

From Solo to Blitar is 370 km. Four early morning buses from Blitar to Solo, via Kediri, depart on the hour between 5 and 8 am and take about six hours. The fare is 4100 rp. The Timbul Jaya Company also have two express minibus services from Solo for 6500 rp leaving the bus station at 8 and 9 am. Even with a stop for lunch, this trip takes only five hours (they drive fast enough to scare you witless) and the minibus drops you right in the centre of town, so it can be a useful service.

If you're not staying at the Sri Lestari Hotel, you can hire a motorcycle (with rider) near the bus station. It's likely to cost 3000 rp for the round trip to Panataran and you can stop off en route at Sentul. Dokars also hang about near the bus and train stations and they're another possibility. Alternatively you can take a colt (or an antique '47 Dodge – there are a few of them around) from the bus station as far as Nglegok village for 750 rp. Panataran is another three km along the main road; it's probably simplest to walk. Colts occasionally go all the way to Panataran, but they don't make the return trip very often.

PACITAN

On the south coast near the provincial border, Pacitan is a quiet beach, one of the finest in East Java. The village of Pacitan is three km from a large bay enclosed by the rocky outcrops of rugged cliffs. The beach here is beautiful and deserted apart from a few outriggers, but the best place to swim is at small, secluded cove on the south-western side of the bay. Up on a hill above the cove is a *pasanggrahan* (a kind of lodge) and a public swimming pool. On the road out there from Pacitan (seven km) is a strangely misplaced classical Greek temple, inscribed with the words *Gegaan maar niet vergeten*, 'Gone but not forgotten'. About five km beyond the pasanggrahan is a picnic spot from where you have probably the best view of the coastline.

Other beaches accessible from Pacitan are Watu Karung (22 km) and Latiroco Lorok

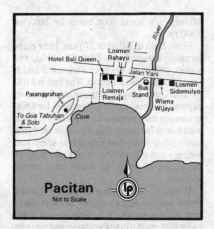

Pacitan
Not to Scale

(41 km). Just beyond Punung village, 30 km east of Pacitan, the Gua Tabuhan or (Musical Cave) is a huge limestone cavern said to have been a refuge for the 19th-century guerilla leader Prince Diponegoro. Here you can listen to an excellent 'orchestral' performance, played by striking rocks against stalactites, each in perfect pitch and echoing pure gamelan melodies. You have to hire a guide and a lamp (for about 800 rp) and the concert lasts about 10 minutes; it's 2500 rp for six tunes. Bargaining is obligatory! This is also agate country and there are lots of people at the cave selling very reasonably priced polished stones and rings.

Places to Stay & Eat

There are a number of budget hotels in Pacitan strung out along Jalan Yani, the main street between the bus station and the road to the beach. One traveller has recommended the *Losmen Remaja* on Jalan Yani, which costs 4000/5000 rp. Other places to stay include the *Losmen Sidomulyo* and *Wisma Wijaya* near the bus station, and the cheaper *Rahayu*. The prices of these places range from 4000 to 6000 rp. The *Hotel Bali Queen* is more upmarket, with doubles at 12,000 rp.

For food, there are plenty of warungs, especially around the bus stand. The *Depot Makan Pujabar*, a block behind Jalan Yani,

has excellent food: gado-gado for 650 rp, nasi campur and fish for 750 rp, nasi goreng for 800 rp and fruit juices for 400 rp. There's good music and maps of the area here.

If you want to stay near the sea at the pasanggrahan, ask at the kabupaten office in Pacitan. The cottage has only two bedrooms and is often full, particularly on weekends. There are warungs nearby, or you could take your own food.

Getting There & Around

Pacitan can be approached from Solo, via Wonogiri, or from Ponorogo, which is just south of Madiun. From Solo it is almost a four-hour bus journey and the fare is 1750 rp. From Pacitan to Ponorogo takes about four hours and the fare is 1400 rp; from Ponorogo to Surabaya, via Madiun, is a five-hour bus journey for 2200 rp. Or you might head from Ponorogo or Madiun to Blitar and Malang. Buses to Solo pass the junction point where the road from Pacitan meets the final short track to the beach, so you can use these buses if you don't want to walk or take a becak.

MADIUN

North of Ponorogo, on the Solo to Surabaya road, is a group of cheap hotels clustered on the Surabaya side of town. The *Hotel Madiun* and *Hotel Sarangan* are similarly priced from 10,000 rp; the *Hotel Matahari* is a little cheaper. In the top-end range, the *Hotel Indah* has rooms for 35,000 to 60,000 rp.

SURABAYA

The capital of East Java, the industrial city of Surabaya has a population of just over two million, making it second only to Jakarta in size and economic importance within Indonesia. Its distinction is that it is the main base for the Indonesian navy and for centuries has been one of Java's most important trading ports. Surabaya is a city on the move, yet signs of poverty are always in sight and the narrow streets in some parts of the city, crowded with warehouses, bullock carts and jostling becaks, contrast strongly with the modern buildings and shopping centres making an appearance on the city skyline. For most people this is just a short stop between Central Java and Bali or you also might be visiting Madura. For some travellers, this is also an important focal point for shipping to Kalimantan and Sulawesi, but otherwise it's a hot and dusty, crowded city with precious little to see. People who do find Surabaya interesting – and to be fair, quite a few people do – generally enjoy the real Indonesian atmosphere of the place.

Orientation & Information

Surabaya is spread over a considerable area but the tourist office and most of the restaurants and banks are all on, or very near, Jalan Pemuda, which runs through the centre of the city from Gubeng railway station to the Tunjungan Plaza shopping centre. Most of the budget hotels are also in this area, although few of them can really be recommended as good places to stay.

Tanjung Perak Harbour is several km north of Jalan Pemuda. The main bus station, Bungurasih, and Surabaya's zoo are several km south. Surabaya has two other main railway stations aside from Gubeng – the Kota railway station to the north of Jalan Pemuda and Pasar Turi to the north-west.

Warning: There have been a couple of reports from people who have been befriended in Surabaya, have then been given drugged coffee and woken up later to find their valuables gone. Take care.

Tourist Office The East Java Regional Tourist Office is at Jalan Pemuda 118. Although the staff have a few maps, some information on places to visit in the province and a regional calendar of events, they are rather limited in providing practical information about the city itself, let alone nearby destinations like Madura. The office is open from 7 am to 2 pm Monday to Thursday, to 11 am on Friday and to 1 pm on Saturday.

Money The Bank Niaga on Jalan Tunjungan will change US and Australian travellers'

cheques. The Bank BNI on Jalan Pemuda also has moneychanging facilities. You may also convert your currency and cheques to rupiah at Empress Moneychanger on Jalan Taman Nasution where it intersects with Jalan Jen Sudirman.

Post & Telecommunications A branch post office on Jalan Pemuda, roughly opposite the Mitra cinema, is open from 8 am to 2 pm Monday to Thursday, to 11 am on Friday, and to noon on Saturday. Surabaya's main post office and poste restante, on Jalan Kebon Rojo, is a good half-hour walk from Jalan Pemuda so you will need to take a bemo or city bus to get there. The telephone office is just off Jalan Pemuda beyond its intersection with Jalan Basuki Rakhmad.

Immigration The immigration office (☎ 45496) is at Jalan Jenderal S Parman 58A. It's a half-hour ride from Jalan Pemuda on an 'Aloha' bus (300 rp).

Surabaya Zoo

On Jalan Diponegoro, near the Joyoboyo bus station, the Surabaya Zoo (kebun binatang) is reputed to be the largest zoo in South-East Asia. It specialises in nocturnal animals, exotic birds and fish. The animals look just as bored as they do in any other zoo, but the park is quite well laid-out, with large open enclosures, a great collection of pelicans and lively otters, and a couple of rather dazed-looking Komodo dragons.

The zoo is open from 7 am to 6 pm. Entry costs 1000 rp and another 400 rp for the aquarium (which is worth it) or the nocturama. This park is popular with local people and outside there are warungs and a permanent gaggle of vendors selling drinks, and peanuts for the monkeys. The zoo is about an hour's walk from Jalan Pemuda, or a short ride on city bus No 2 or bemo V, from Jalan Panglima Sudirman.

MPU Tantular Museum

Across the road from the zoo, this small archaeological museum is open from 8 am to 1 pm Tuesday to Thursday, to 10 am on

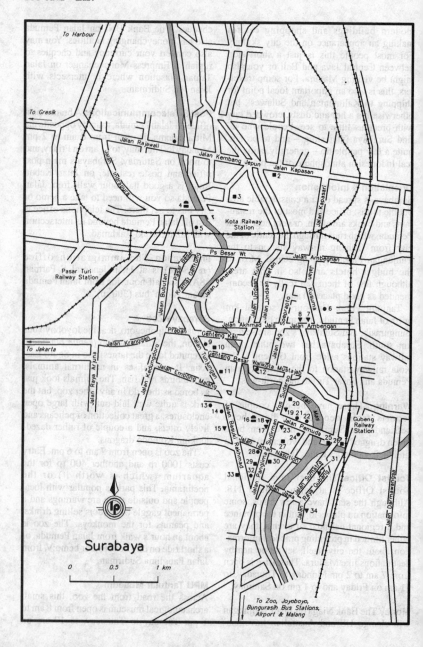

To Harbour

To Gresik

Jalan Rajawali

Jalan Kembang Jepun

Jalan Kapasan

Jalan Indrapura

Jalan Kapasari

1

2

3

4

5

Kota Railway
Station

Pasar Turi
Railway Station

Ps Besar Wt

Jalan Ambengan

Pasar Besar

Jalan Kranggan

Jalan Gemblongan

Jalan Pasar Besar

Jalan Bubutan

Jalan Pieneleh

Jalan Undaan Kulon

Jalan Undaan Wetan

Jalan Kusuma

Jalan Raya Arjuna

Jalan Kedungdoro

Jalan Embong Malang

Jalan Tun Nungan

Jalan Akhmad Jais

Genteng Kali

Genteng Besar

Walikota Mustajab

Jalan Ag Soeprapto

Jalan Ambengan

Praban

6

8 7

9

10

11

12

To Jakarta

13

14

15

16 18

17

19 21 22

20

23

24

25 26

27

28

29

30

31

32

33

34

Jalan Basuki Rachmad

Jalan Taman Nasution

Jalan Yos Sudarso

Kali Mas

Jalan Pemuda

Jalan Panglima Sudirman

Jalan Sumatra

Jalan Jawa

Jalan Raya Gubeng

Jalan Darmawangsa

Gubeng
Railway
Station

Surabaya

0   0.5   1 km

To Zoo, Joyoboyo,
Bungurasih Bus Stations,
Airport & Malang

■ PLACES TO STAY		19	Zangrandia Ice Cream
		23	Granada Modern Bakery
2	Losmen Ganefo	31	Bon Cafe & Steakhouse
3	Hotel Merdeka	34	Chez Rose Restaurant
10	Hotel Paviljoen		
11	Majapahit Hotel	OTHER	
12	Bamboe Denn Transito Inn		
20	Garden & Garden	1	Jembatan Merah
	Palace Hotels		Colt Station
25	Hotel Gubeng	4	Main Post Office
26	Sahid Surabaya Hotel	5	Pelni Ticketing
27	Hotel Remaja	6	THR Amusement Park
29	Elmi Hotel	9	Garuda Office
30	Tanjung Hotel	13	Telephone Office
33	Hyatt Bumi	14	Tunjungan Plaza
			Shopping Centre
▼ PLACES TO EAT		16	Post Office
		21	Bank Ekspor Impor
7	Soto Ambengan	22	Surabaya Delta Plaza
8	Cafe Venezua	24	East Java Regional
15	Kentucky Fried Chicken		Tourist Office
	& Swensen's Ice Cream	28	Empress Moneychanger
17	Antika Restaurant	32	Bouraq & Thai Offices
18	Canadaa Bakery		

Friday, to noon on Saturday and 2 pm on Sunday. It's closed on Monday.

Taman Hiburan Rakyat

On the east side of town, but close to the centre, the THR (People's Amusement Park) is Surabaya's amusement centre after dark. The Taman Remaja (Children's Park) (1000 rp entrance), on one side, features carnival rides and sometimes live pop bands. The THR on the other side (250 rp entrance) has a couple of theatres showing nightly performances (from 8 pm) of wayang orang and *srimulat* (East Javanese comedy). There are plenty of cheap warungs, but it's all a bit sad and gloomy – nobody seems to bother going anymore. The sidewalks outside are more lively, with a bizarre collection of street hawkers and some excellent snacks.

East Java Ballet Festival, Pandaan

The East Java ballet festival takes place on the first and third Saturday nights from May until October at the Candra Wilwatikta amphitheatre in Pandaan, 40 km south on the road to Tretes.

The festival season includes performances of a one-night version of the *Ramayana* but a large part of the programme consists of dances based on East Java's indigenous tales. It takes about one hour to get to Pandaan; you travel by bus from Joyoboyo (650 rp) and then by colt (300 rp) to the theatre.

Other Attractions

One of the most interesting places in Surabaya to wander round is the harbour. It's both busy and decrepit, filled with a variety of vessels, from brightly painted schooners to ageing warships and small craft shuttling back and forth to the island of Madura. On Jalan Pemuda, across from the governor's residence, is the statue of Joko Dolog which dates from 1289 and commemorates King Kertanagara of Singosari. It's known as the 'fat boy'. When you've had enough of Surabaya's heat and dust, you can cool off in the Garden Hotel swimming pool, or try the Simpang Lima pool.

There is a French Cultural Centre (☎ 68639) at the French Consulate, at Jalan Darmokali 10-12, and a Goethe Institute

(☎ 40368) at Jalan Taman Ade Irma Suryani Nasution 15.

Organised Tours

If you have to hang around for a while – waiting for a ship to Sulawesi, for example – the Bamboe Denn Transito Inn offers a morning walking tour of the city.

Places to Stay – bottom end

If you're staying in this busy port town – and many people do at least overnight here between Yogya and Bali – there's really only one very cheap place. The *Bamboe Denn Transito Inn* (☎ 40333) when on Jalan Pemuda became a Surabaya institution, always packed out with travellers. Old Indonesian hands should note that it has moved to Jalan Ketabang Kali 6A, a 20-minute walk from Gubeng railway station. From the station, go along Jalan Pemuda, turn right into Jalan Yos Sudarso (an extension of Jalan Panglima Sudirman) and then, after the bridge, turn left (near the house of the naval commander-in-chief) into Jalan Ketabang Kali. Singles/doubles with shared mandi cost 4000/6500 rp and dorm beds cost 3000 rp. It's clean and friendly and you can get lots of travel information (everything you ever wanted to know about Bromo and more!). There's a dining room and a cafeteria which is open 24 hours. Safe-keeping facilities and comfortable sitting rooms are also provided. Bring a padlock for the dorm's lockers.

The Denn is close to bus routes, a supermarket and a bank. You may well get roped into a little English conversation with Indonesian students at the language school, which also runs from this youth hostel. If becak drivers haven't heard of the Denn, ask for the Transito.

Other cheap hotels in the Gubeng railway station area tend to be fairly dismal. The *Hotel Gubeng* at Jalan Sumatra 18, only 100 metres from Gubeng station, is good but not too cheap. Rooms with fan cost 17,000 rp including breakfast. *Hotel Kayoon* on Jalan Kayoon is dirty and none too quiet; at 10,000 rp per room this should be a last choice.

If you go past the Bamboe Denn and cross the river to Jalan Genteng Besar 94-98, you will find the colonial relic *Hotel Paviljoen* where basic rooms range between 14,000 rp for small and 28,000 rp for larger doubles, a pretty good deal for budget accommodation in Surabaya.

There are a few hotels close to the Kota railway station, a considerable distance north of the centre, but some of the cheaper places in this area won't take foreigners as they then have to fill in forms for the police, which is a nuisance (this is true of a number of towns in Java). *Losmen Ganefo* (☎ 311169) at Jalan Kapasan 169-171, a sizeable older hotel where large, clean but quite basic rooms with shared mandi start at 15,000 rp. Doubles with bath start at 21,500 rp. You can also get air-con rooms here for 27,500 rp.

Places to Stay – middle & top end

Conveniently located and an excellent middle-range deal in expensive Surabaya is *Hotel Remaja* (☎ 41359) on quiet little Jalan Embong Kenongo 12 not far from Jalan Pemuda. Pleasant all air-con singles cost 36,000 to 44,000 rp and doubles 38,000 to 46,000 rp.

Also well located is the *Tanjung Hotel* (☎ 44031) at Jalan Panglima Sudirman 43-45. Although dear by Indonesian standards for a middle-range hotel, its prices are reasonable for Surabaya. Air-con rooms with satellite TV, hot-water showers and telephone start at 60,500 to 69,000 rp for singles and 71,500 to 80,000 rp for doubles, including 21% tax and breakfast. Bigger rooms start at 81,000 rp and range up to 105,500 rp for suites. There are also a couple of economy rooms with fan at 36,500 rp for singles and 42,500 rp for doubles.

At the modern *Elmi Hotel* (☎ 471571), Jalan Panglima Sudirman 42-44, singles/doubles cost from 105,000 rp. It has a restaurant, bar, disco, fitness centre and and the biggest hotel swimming pool in the city, but it's a bit sterile. By contrast, at Jalan Tunjungan 65, the older *Majapahit Hotel* has charm and a surprisingly fine garden; it was designed in 1910 by the Dutch architect

Sarkies. Singles/doubles cost from 98,000 rp and substantial suites cost 225,000 rp.

The *Garden Hotel* (☎ 470001) is central at Jalan Pemuda 21. It has three restaurants (one on the rooftop overlooking the city – with a choice of Chinese, Indonesian and Western food), banking and travel facilities, swimming pool and sauna. All the rooms have air-con, with bathroom and hot water, and start at 148,000 rp. These rates include an all-you- can-eat buffet breakfast including mie/nasi goreng, omelettes, pancakes, croissants, fruit and juices/coffee/tea. Just behind the Garden Hotel and attached by an interior hall, the 250-room *Garden Palace Hotel* (☎ 479250) at Jalan Yos Sudarso 11 is one of Surabaya's top tourist-class hotels. Luxurious rooms start at 196,000 rp. There are three restaurants and a pub with live jazz music; the Cathay Pacific Airlines office is here.

On the outskirts of the city on the road to the airport, the modern *Hotel Mirama* (☎ 69501), Jalan Raya Darmo 68-76, is convenient for passengers in transit. Rooms here (all with air-con) start at 137,000 rp and there's a swimming pool.

Note that all hotels in this category have a 21% service charge and government tax on top of the room charge.

Places to Eat

Food here seems painfully expensive compared with that in Bali or Yogya but it can be quite good.

The *Granada Modern Bakery* on the corner of Jalan Pemuda and Jalan Panglima Sudirman is a good place for breakfast buns and cakes. Just around the corner on Jalan Yos Sudarso, you can have an expensive ice cream at the *Zangrandi Ice Cream Palace* and watch the wealthy Surabayans roll up in their Mercedes and Volvos. Or try the *Garden Restaurant* at Jalan Pemuda 3 for delicious Turin Italian ice cream for only 700 rp.

At the Surabaya Delta Plaza there are two Pizza Huts (check out the squid pizza), a Dairy Queen, a Church's Texas Fried Chicken, a Japanese fast-food place and

several bakeries. There is also a food centre serving moderately priced Chinese and Indonesian dishes (near the Pizza Hut on the ground floor) and a Hero supermarket.

Another place for fast food is the *Tunjungan Plaza Shopping Centre* on Jalan Basuki Rakhmad near its intersection with Jalan Pemuda. Here you will find a *Kentucky Fried Chicken* and a *Swenson's Ice Cream* as well as a host of restaurants on the 6th floor, like the *Singapore Self-Serve Steamboat* and the *Mie Kembang Jepun*. The 7th floor has the Indonesian *Tirtomoyo* and the Cantonese BBQ *New Fajar*.

For really cheap eating you can go to the stalls around Gubeng station, near the THR or off Jalan Tunjungan. There is a good hawkers' centre open at night near the flower market on Jalan Kayoon and on Jalan Pandegiling.

The *Chez Rose* at the start of Jalan Raya Gubeng is a good place for a splurge if you want a break from Indonesian food. They do a great lunchtime buffet – the eat-all-you-can and lie-down-to-recover variety. A litte further down Jalan Raya Gubeng at No 44-46, the *Bon Cafe and Steakhouse* serves up great steaks and chops for 7000 to 8000 rp, as well as savory ice cream specialities such as peach melba and banana splits for 2000 rp.

For the best Padang food in town, spend a bit more at *Antika* at Jalan Yos Sudarso No 3 – it's worth it. Next door is the excellent *Canadaa Bakery*.

Locals recommend two eateries on Jalan Ambengan. At No 16 *Cafe Venezia Steakhouse* is said to rank with the best in Surabaya. And if you wish to try a soup known throughout the island for its preparation here, enjoy the lemon grass, coriander Madurese chicken soup served at *Soto Ambengan* at No 3A.

Entertainment

Surabayans are big on discos. Popular places include the *Top Ten* in Tunjungan Plaza, *Blue Sixteen Bar & Nightclub* at Jalan Pemuda 10, and *Tifa*, on the ground floor of the Hyatt Bumi on Jalan Basuki Rakhmad.

Things to Buy

Surabaya has no particular crafts of its own, but the city is a good hunting ground for antiques. At the junction of Jalan Basuki Rakhmad and Jalan Urip Sumoharjo, there are a number of small shops where you'll find good quality antiques – with prices to match. The Sampurna at No 144 has an interesting collection. Surabaya also has something of a reputation as a free port, but it's nothing like Singapore. Tunjungan shopping centre is a hunting ground for electrical goods and cheap music cassettes. The new Surabaya Delta Plaza shopping centre on Jalan Pemuda is very flash and Indonesians claim it's the largest shopping centre in South-East Asia (a title also claimed by the Subang Jaya shopping complex outside Kuala Lumpur, Malaysia). For batik, you will find good quality at Batik Keris, at Jalan Tunjungan 12.

Getting There & Away

Air Surabaya is an important hub for domestic flights. Garuda/Merpati flights depart from Surabaya to most major Indonesian centres. Some important connections include Jakarta (Garuda 166,600 rp, 14 flights daily); Denpasar (Merpati 83,750 rp, five daily); Palembang (Garuda 242,150 rp, five daily); Banjarmasin (Merpati 133,250 rp, three daily); and Ujung Pandang (Merpati 188,250 rp, four daily). The Garuda/Merpati office (☎ 470640), at Jalan Tunjungan 29, is open from 7.30 am to 4 pm Monday to Friday, to 1 pm on Saturday and from 9 am to noon on Sunday.

Bouraq, Mandala, and Sempati all have cheaper domestic fares than Garuda/Merpati, but because only Garuda/Merpati and Sempati are allowed to operate jets (to stifle competition), other airlines' flights generally take a bit longer.

Bouraq operate flights from Surabaya to Jakarta (166,600 rp), Bandung (131,600 rp), Denpasar (83,750 rp), Banjarmasin (132,700 rp) and Balikpapan (197,600 rp). Bouraq (☎ 42383) at Jalan Panglima Sudirman 70 is open from 7 am to 9 pm daily.

Mandala operate flights to Jakarta

(166,600 rp), Ujung Pandang (172,400 rp), Ambon (332,500 rp) and Manado (341,700 rp). Mandala (☎ 66861) at Jalan Raya Darmo 109 is open from 8 am to 4 pm Monday to Friday, to 1 pm on Saturday and from 9 am to noon on Sunday.

Bus Most buses operate from Surabaya's main Bungurasih bus station, which is on the southern edge of the city quite a distance from the city's centre and west of the airport. Damri buses run between the bus station and the centre for 250 rp and a taxi costs 7000 rp. If you're heading for the north coast, buses and colts depart from the Jembatan Merah station, which is north of Kota railway station.

Going east, there are frequent buses to Probolinggo 1500 rp (2½ hours). Buses to Banyuwangi cost 4200 rp (10 hours) via Situbondo or 4600 rp via Jember (11 hours). There are also buses to Jember (2500 rp), Pasir Putih (2450 rp) and Situbondo (2900 rp).

Going south, buses to Pandaan cost 800 rp. From Pandaan you have to continue by colt (400 rp) to Tretes. There are frequent buses to Malang, via Purwodadi and Lawang, for 1450 rp (2½ hours). Hotels in Surabaya can also arrange express minibuses to Malang for 6800 rp.

Going west, there are frequent buses to Trowulan, via Mojokerto for 800 rp (1½ hours), to Solo via Madiun for 4600 rp (6½ hours), and to Yogya for 5150 rp (eight hours). Buses depart between 6 and 9 am.

Going north, buses and colts (from Jembatan Merah) include Gresik for 400 rp, Tuban for 2050 rp, Kudus for 4950 rp and Semarang for 5700 rp.

Madura Buses depart every hour to major towns on Madura. From Surabaya to Kamal is 950 rp (one hour); to Pamekasan 2550 rp (two/three hours) and to Sumenep 3700 rp (four hours). Fares include the ferry. To simply get to the ferry, take a city bus or K bemo to the harbour.

Night Bus Most night buses depart from the

main Bungarasih bus terminal between 5 and 9 pm. Bali Indah is about the cheapest and fares include a snack and stopover meal. To Denpasar their fare is 22,000 rp and the trip takes around 16 hours. The best night bus service to Denpasar is reputed to be Jawa Indah, who charge 28,000 rp for the 'deluxe bus' trip. Elteha has also been recommended for night buses to Denpasar (24,700 to 26,000 rp depending on the bus); their offices are at the Bungarasih bus station (open from 8 am to 5 pm). For convenience, travel agencies in and around the city's centre sell tickets on the various night bus services.

To Solo, Yogya, Kudus or Semarang, night bus fares are around 10,000 rp. It's a long 859 km trip to Jakarta by bus – for 29,950 rp regular air-con or up to 40,000 rp deluxe – but you're really better off taking the train.

Train Surabaya has three main train stations. Gubeng station has trains to Jakarta via Solo and Yogyakarta, plus trains east to Banyuwangi and south to Malang and Blitar. Pasar Turi railway station handles services to Jakarta via Semarang. Note that some trains arriving at Gubeng continue on to Kota. Gubeng is much more convenient to the Bamboe Denn Inn and other central places than either Kota or Pasar Turi.

See the introductory Getting Around section for Java for details on travelling by rail between Jakarta and Surabaya, and between Yogyakarta and Surabaya. Apart from services to the main cities, there are several trains operating from Surabaya to Malang. There are nine services daily by the *Tumapel* train between Kota or Gubeng station and Malang; the first departs Gubeng at about 7.30 am and the last departs at about 6.30 pm. The trip takes two to three hours each way and the fare is 1400 rp in 3rd-class-only. Some of these trains continue on from Malang to Blitar, a five-hour trip costing 2600 rp.

Mutiara Timur trains depart from Gubeng station at 10 am and 10 pm for Banyuwangi and the ferry to Bali. The trip takes seven

hours to Banyuwangi. The fare is 4400 rp in 3rd class and 6200 rp in 2nd. Through to Denpasar, the trip takes 15 hours; the fare is 6400 rp in 3rd class and 8200 rp in 2nd, including the ferry to Bali and a bus to Denpasar. At Gubeng station, they may claim they can't sell 2nd-class tickets to Banyuwangi – if this is the case, simply purchase a 3rd-class ticket and once you're on the train take a 2nd-class seat and pay the conductor the difference. But check the information board in the terminal first to make sure that the train you're taking has 2nd-class cars.

Boat Surabaya is a travellers' centre for ships to Kalimantan and Sulawesi in particular; Pelni operates regular services to both these islands and to Sumatra. Tickets for both passenger services and Pelni cargo ships must be bought at the Pelni ticketing office (☎ 21041, 21694) at Jalan Pahlawan 20. Catch a Bemo M on Jalan Pemuda near the Warung Kosgoro. The office is open from 9 am to 1.30 pm Monday to Friday and from 8 am to 1 pm on Saturday. Tickets can be bought up to 10 days before departure. The front ticket counter can be hopelessly chaotic. If you can't get through to the surly staff in front, go around to the office at the back where the staff are more helpful.

Pelni Liners Surabaya is served by the Pelni liners *Kerinci, Rinjani, Kambuna, Tidar, Umsini* and *Kelimutu*. The complete timetable for these ships can be found in the Getting Around chapter.

Fares (in rp) from Surabaya are the same for all six ships, except for the *Kelimutu*, which has no *kelas* (class) III or IV. (See the table on the next page.)

Cargo Ship There are at least 15 cargo ships a day from Surabaya to the outer islands. For fares and departure dates, you really have to get down to the harbour and ask around at the shipping company offices. For information about Pelni cargo ships see Mr Rifai or Captain Abu at the Tanjung Perak office (☎ 293347). For information about non-

Pelni ships, go to the ground floor of the harbour master's office at Kalimas Baru 194, Tanjung Perak. Each morning they get a list of every ship leaving that day and some, if already confirmed, for the following day.

For Banjarmasin, try P T Sumber Kalimas Agung on Jalan Kalimas Baru; the *KM Eska* sails every week and the journey takes about 18 hours for around 25,000 rp. PT Meratus Shipping Co (☎ 293096) at Jalan Alun-Alun, Tanjung Perak has a weekly cargo ship *(KM Meratus)* to Ujung Pandang.

Pinisi In the nearby port town of Gresik, you may be able to hitch a ride on a pinisi, the traditional Makassar schooner (also sometimes called Bugis – actually these boats are built in East Java and South Kalimantan as well as in Sulawesi, home of the Bugis), with a little persistence. Strictly speaking, pinisi crews transporting cargo are forbidden to take passengers to other islands, but money rules the day here.

PT Wisata Bahari Mas Permai (☎ 291633) does 'East Java Pinisi Traditional Cruises' at reasonable (for cruises) rates. They have a 10-day cruise to Madura, Bali and Lombok for 1,862,000 rp per person, a 17-day cruise to Bali, Lombok, Sumbawa, Komodo, and Flores for 2,744,000 rp and a 31-day cruise to Bali, Sumbawa, Komodo, Flores, Solor, Alor, Wetar, Tanimbar, Banda, Ambon, Bau-Bau, and Ujung Pandang for 4,802,000 rp. Rates include transport to and from and accommodation on the pinisi, three meals a

day and guided tours; all cruises end with a night in a mountain resort in Trawas, near Mojokerto. The 17-day cruise includes air transport between Ende and Surabaya and the 31-day cruise includes passage on Pelni's *Rinjani* from Ambon to Surabaya. Wisata Bahari is at Jalan Tanjung Priok 11, Blok H, Tanjung Perak, not far from the harbour. A minimum of 15 people are needed for a confirmed departure.

Getting Around

To/From the Airport The cheapest transport between the city's centre and the airport are public buses which, unfortunately, run infrequently. They cost 2000 rp. A taxi to or from the Juanda airport (15 km) costs 9000 rp.

Local Transport The taxis, becaks and hordes of bemos around town are useful for local transport. To get to Bungurasih bus terminal from the centre, take a Damri bus for 250 rp.

Surabaya also has big city buses which charge a fixed 200 rp fare and basically run north-south. Useful buses include the No 1 bus from Jalan Basuki Rakhmad to Tanjung Perak harbour, and the No 2 bus from Jalan Panglima Sudirman to the zoo.

Becaks aren't allowed on the main streets of Surabaya, but in neighbourhoods where they are, expect to pay about 400 rp per km.

Most taxis in Surabaya run on meters with similar rates to Jakarta's: 800 rp for flagfall, 40 rp each quarter kilometre.

Kelas:	I	II	III	IV	Ekonomi
Ambon	195,300	144,300	104,800	79,800	51,600
Balikpapan	177,800	87,800	64,800	51,800	33,600
Banjarmasin	82,300	64,800	–	–	25,100
Belawan	220,300	160,800	117,800	91,300	61,600
Bitung	248,800	182,300	132,800	104,300	66,100
Ende	187,800	137,300	–	–	53,600
Padangbai	49,300	36,300	–	–	16,100
Tarakan	154,800	119,800	87,300	68,800	48,600
Tanjung Priok	67,300	51,800	33,800	29,300	20,600
Ujung Pandang	96,300	71,300	52,800	41,800	26,300

Bemos are labelled A, B or K etc and they run all over town for a fixed 300 rp fare. The biggest bemo stations are Wonokromo station and Jembatan Merah station.

AROUND SURABAYA
Gresik

On the road to Semarang, 25 km from Semarang, this port was once a major centre for international trade and a major centre of Islam in the 15th century. Close by, at Giri, is the tomb of the first Sunan Giri, who is regarded as one of the greatest of the nine wali songo. He was the founder of a line of spiritual lords of Giri which lasted until it was overwhelmed by Mataram in 1680. According to some traditions, Sunan Giri played a leading role in the conquest of Majapahit and ruled Java for 40 days after its fall – to rid the country of pre-Islamic influences.

Gresik has a colourful pinisi harbour that is probably the last fully traditional one in Java – everything is carried on board by hand and there are no fixed departure schedules.

Tretes

This hill town, standing at 800 metres on the slopes of gunungs Arjuno and Welirang, is renowned for its cool climate and beautiful views. Tretes also has an intriguing reputation as a red-light district. If you have to kill time in Surabaya, it can be a pleasant enough place to escape to but there's not a great deal to do. The Katek Boko and Putuh Truno waterfalls are nearby and there are a number of interesting walks around the town, including the trek to the Lalilijiwo Plateau and Gunung Arjuno (3339 metres).

Tretes is 55 km south of Surabaya. On the way you pass through Pandaan, the site for the East Java Ballet Festival which takes place over the dry season (see the Surabaya section). The Jawi Temple here is an early 14th-century Hindu temple, basically a Shivaite structure, although some time later a Buddhist stupa was added on top. The remains of other old temples are scattered over the slopes of Gunung Penanggunan to the west. The Belahan bathing place on Pen-

anggunan, perhaps a 10-km hike from Tretes, was the home of the Airlangga-as-Vishnu statue now in the Mojokerto Museum.

Places to Stay & Eat If you're planning to stay here, the best bet is to look for a room in a private home. Take a cottage if you plan to stay long – there are plenty available if you ask around. Prigen, a bit lower down, is cheaper than Tretes. Typical of hotel accommodation is the *Tanjung Plaza* (☎ 81102) at Jalan Wilis 7, with rooms starting at 68,000 rp and suites for 125,000 rp. *Tretes Bungalow Park & Motel* is one of the cheapest places, with rooms from 12,000 rp including breakfast. For bare basic budget rooms, *Wisma Semeru Indah* at Jalan Semeru 7 has doubles for 10,000 rp.

There are some good, reasonably priced places to eat around the fruit market and shopping centre, near the police station.

PULAU MADURA

Madura is a large and rugged island, about 160 km long by 30 km wide, and separated from Surabaya on the East Java coast by a narrow channel. It is especially famous for its bull races, the kerapan sapi, but also has a few interesting historical sites, some fine beaches and beautiful scenery. The place is almost completely undiscovered by tourists.

The people of Madura are familiar faces in East Java, particularly in Surabaya where many have gone to look for work. Since independence, Madura has been governed as part of the province of East Java but the island has had a long tradition of involvement with its larger neighbour and with the Dutch. The Dutch were not interested in the island itself, which was initially of little economic importance, but rather in the crucial role the Madurese played in Javanese dynastic politics.

The southern side of the island, facing Java, is shallow beach and cultivated lowland, while the northern coast alternates between rocky cliffs and beaches of great rolling sand dunes, the best of which is at Salopeng. At the extreme east is tidal marsh

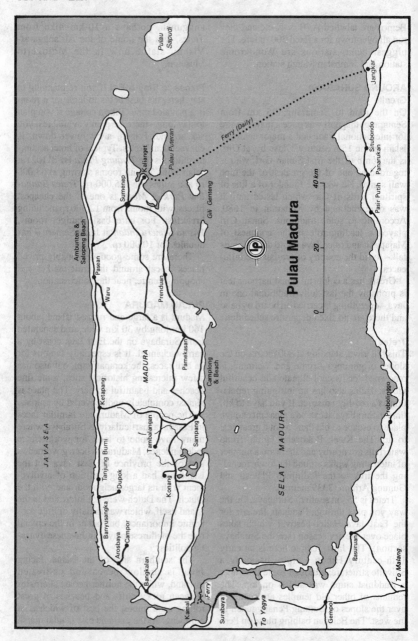

and vast tracts of salt around Kalianget. The interior of this flat and somewhat arid island is riddled with limestone slopes and is either rocky or sandy, so agriculture is limited. There are goat farms, tobacco estates, some orchards and extensive stands of coconut palms but the main industry of Madura would have to be cattle, followed by salt and fishing.

History

In 1624 the island was conquered by Sultan Agung of Mataram and its government united under one Madurese princely line, the Cakraningrats. Until the middle of the 18th century the Cakraningrat family fiercely opposed Central Javanese rule and harassed Mataram, often conquering large parts of the kingdom. Prince Raden Trunojoyo even managed to carry off the royal treasury of Mataram in 1677, which was restored only after the Dutch intervened and stormed Trunojoyo's stronghold at Kediri. In 1705 the Dutch secured control of the eastern half of Madura following the conflict of the First Javanese War of Succession between Amangkurat III and his uncle, Pangeran Puger. Dutch recognition of Puger was largely influenced by Cakraningrat II, the lord of West Madura. He probably supported Puger's claims simply because he hoped a new war in Central Java would give the Madurese a chance to interfere but, while Amangkurat was arrested and exiled to Ceylon, Puger took the title of Pakubuwono I and concluded a treaty with the Dutch which, along with large concessions in Java, granted them East Madura.

The Cakraningrats fared little better by agreeing to help the Dutch put down the rebellion in Central Java that broke out after the Chinese massacre in 1740. Although Cakraningrat IV attempted to contest the issue, a treaty was eventually signed in 1743 in which Pakubuwono II ceded full sovereignty of Madura to the Dutch. Cakraningrat fled to Banjarmasin and took refuge on an English ship but was robbed, betrayed by the Sultan and finally captured by the Dutch and exiled to the Cape of Good Hope. Under the Dutch, Madura continued as four states, each with its own *bupati*, or lord mayor. Madura was initially important as a major source of colonial troops but in the second half of the 19th century it acquired greater economic value as the main supplier of salt to Dutch-governed areas of the archipelago, where salt was a profitable monopoly of the colonial government.

Kerapan Sapi (Bull Races)

As the Madurese tell it, the tradition of bull races began long ago when plough teams raced each other across the arid fields; this pastime was encouraged by an early king of Sumenep, Panembahan Sumolo. Today, when stud bull breeding is big business in Madura, the kerapan sapi are as much an incentive for the Madurese to breed good stock as simply a popular form of entertainment and sport. Only bulls of a certain standard can be entered for important races and the Madurese keep their young bulls in superb condition, dosing them with an assortment of medicinal herbs, honey, beer and raw eggs.

Traditional races are put on annually between mid-August and October in bull-racing stadiums all over Madura. The first races in August are small village events, then in late August and September contests are held at district and regency level, until the cream of bulls fight it out for the big prize at the grand final in Pamekasan, the island's capital.

This is, of course, the biggest and most colourful festival. As many as 100 bulls, wearing fancy halters and yokes of gilt, ribbons and flowers, are paraded through town and around the open field of the stadium to a loud fanfare of drums, flutes and gongs. For each race two pairs of bulls, stripped of their finery, are matched against each other with their 'jockeys' perched behind on wooden sleds. Gamelan is played to excite the bulls and then, after being given a generous tot of arak, they're released and charge flat out down the track – just as often plunging right into the seething crowds of spectators! The race is over in a flash – the best time recorded so far is nine seconds over the 100 metres, which is faster than the human world track record. After the elimination heats the victorious bulls are proudly trotted home to be used at stud.

The regency centres where major bull-racing events are held are Bangkalan, Pamekasan and Sumenep. The *East Java Calendar of Events* available at times (no guarantee) from the tourist office in Surabaya may have a general schedule for the main races, but you are best off just chancing a visit to major Maduran cities during the season and inquiring whether, when and where the races are being held. (It's maddening that this information is not readily available in Surabaya and perhaps by the time you read this, the tourist office will finally have it on hand.) For the grand final, entry to the stadium costs only 500 rp or, if you want a seat, you can pay 2000 to 3800 rp. PT Orient Express Tours (☎ 43315, Surabaya) has operated a tourist bus to the Madura Grand Final in September from Surabaya during times when they believe they have enough patrons. The bus collects from major hotels and the day trip costs around 40,000 rp per person.

Things to Do

To see something of the island, it's interesting to take a colt from Pamekasan inland through tobacco country to Waru, another to Pasean, then along the north coast to the beach at Salopeng and back down to Sumenep. Taking the south coast road from Pamekasan, there is a colourful market at Prenduan with everything from fruit, batik and bright children's toys to painted bird cages, goats and the village barber.

Getting There & Away

From Surabaya, ferries sail to Kamal, the port town on the western tip of Madura, from where you can catch colts to other towns on the island. It's a half-hour trip by ferry and they cost just 400 rp, operating about every 10 minutes until late at night. Buses go directly from Surabaya's main bus station station via the ferry as far as Pamekasan,

Sumenep and Kalianget, but if you're already based in the centre of town it's just as easy, and probably quicker, to take a city bus or K bemo to the ferry terminus at Tanjung Perak, take the ferry across to Kamal, and then take local buses around the island.

Another possibility, if you're coming from Bali, say, is to take a ferry from Jangkar (near Situbondo) to Kalianget on the eastern tip of Madura. This trip takes about four hours and a ferry departs daily from Jangkar at 1.30 pm, except Thursday when it departs at 3.20 pm and Friday at noon. To Jangkar, the ferry departs from Kalianget at 7.30 am. Tickets are 2550 rp.

Pintu Laut Express, across from the Wijaya I, Sumenep, operates a daily collect-and-drop minibus service between Sumenep and Surabaya for 6000 rp. It departs Sumenep at 4 am to catch the 7 am ferry from Kamal. Any of the hotels in Sumenep should be able to make arrangements for the minibus service.

Getting Around

Becaks exist in the main towns and colts go just about everywhere on the island. From Kamal to Bangkalan takes half an hour; from Kamal to Pamekasan is a two to three-hour ride by bus. Allow plenty of time if you're travelling along the north coast; the roads are rough and colts only run short distances between the villages. There are hardly any private cars on the island but then this is a place where you're more than likely to get offered a ride on a motorcycle – or even a bicycle!

Bangkalan

This is the next town north of Kamal along the coast and one of the primary locations for the annual bull races. There is also a small museum of Madurese history and culture in a building on the grounds of the Bupati's home. The Museum Cakraningrat is open from 8 am to 2 pm Monday to Saturday, except Friday when it closes at 11 am.

Places to Stay There are a few possibilities.

Central at the alun-alun on Jalan Veteran, the *Wisma Pemda* has all of two rooms with shared mandi, a six-bed room for 16,000 rp and a room with nine beds for 25,000 rp. The *Losmen Purnama* at Jalan Kartini 19 may be cheap, with basic rooms starting at 8000 rp, but you are not likely to get much sleep as it doubles as a brothel. Nearby are several small restaurants – the *Citra Rasa* is decent. For good Chinese food, try the *Mirasa Restaurant* at Jalan Trunojoyo 75A near the police station.

The rather new *Cakra Ningrat Hotel* (☎ 388) at Jalan Kahaji Muhammed Cholil 113, on the main road through Bangkalan, has air-con singles/doubles with TV and hot water for 40,000/52,000 rp, or fan-cooled economy rooms for 16,500/22,000 rp. The furnishings are traditional Madurese – very elegant.

Air Mata

Near Arosbaya, 27 km north of Kamal, the tombs of the Cakraningrat royalty are at the Air Mata cemetery, which is superbly situated on the edge of a small ravine overlooking a river valley. The ornately carved gunungan headstone on the grave of Ratu Ibu, consort of Cakraningrat I, is the most impressive and is on the highest terrace. The turn-off to Air Mata is shortly before Arosbaya and from the coast road it's a four-km walk inland. *Air mata* means 'tears'.

Tanjung Bumi

The village of Tanjung Bumi is on the north-west coast of Madura, about 60 km from Kamal. Although primarily a fishing village, it's also the island headquarters for the manufacture of traditional Madurese batik and Madurese prahus. On the outskirts is what may be Madura's most beautiful beach, Pantai Siring Kemuning.

Places to Stay There's no official place to stay in either Air Mata or Tanjung Bumi, but you can camp on the beach near Tanjung Bumi with the permission of the kepala desa.

Pamekasan

On the southern side of the island, 100 km east of Kamal, the capital of Madura is a quiet and pleasant enough town, although during August and September each year it comes alive with the festivities of the Kerapan Sapi Grand Final. From this town you can visit a natural fire resource, known locally as Api Alam. Legend tells that the fire comes from the mouth of a giant that was sentenced by the gods to spew fire for an eternity.

Camplong (15 km west of the town) is the nearest beach to Pamekasan and is safe for swimming, although the Pertamina storage tanks nearby do nothing for its visual appeal. However, it is a breezy oasis from the interior of Madura, which can be quite hot. Strung out along this coastline are small fishing villages where twin-outrigger dugout canoes are used and the prahus carry huge, triangular striped sails. The local people are friendly but travellers are a rare sight, so you can expect to be the centre of interested mobs of children, if not the whole village!

Places to Stay & Eat In the centre of town, 300 rp by becak from the bus station, the *Hotel Garuda* (☎ 81589) at Jalan Masigit 1 has doubles with shared mandi at 6000 rp and with private bath for 10,000 rp. Around the corner and better but more expensive than the Garuda, the *Hotel Trunojoyo* (☎ 81181), down a small alley off Jalan Trunojoyo, is clean and quiet. Rooms cost from 16,000 rp including breakfast; rooms with air-con cost 38,000 rp. *Losmen Bahagia*, further up Jalan Trunojoyo, is basic and less than immaculate, but cheap, and the family who run it are friendly. Singles/doubles cost 5500/7000 rp including breakfast.

The *Hotel Purnama* (☎ 81375) is conveniently near the bus terminal at Jalan Ponorogo 10A. It's clean and friendly; the regular rooms have attached mandi and are good value at 11,000 rp. Air-con rooms have nothing going for them except air conditioning, so they're a bit overpriced at 40,000 rp.

The Garuda and Trunojoyo hotels both have attached restaurants. The small restaurant next to Losmen Bahagia serves cheap and tasty Chinese food. Also on Jalan Trunojoyo, the *Tolomoyo* has basic Indonesian fare. On the traffic circle in the middle of town is the clean, green *Lezat* with outdoor tables arranged cafe-style. They have good food, including local specialties like *soto Madura*.

Sumenep

At the eastern end of the island, Sumenep is Madura's most interesting town. It is centred around the kraton, mosque and markets; many of the attractive old houses are examples of typical Madurese architecture, constructed with an unlikely frontage of thick, white Roman-style columns under overhanging red-tiled roofs.

Orientation Near the main square of this small, quiet, easy-going town are a few budget hotels and restaurants, along with the post office (there are no banks with moneychanging facilities). The main bus station is on the southern edge of town and buses to Surabaya via Pamekasan and Kamal operate from here. The bus stand for colts to the north coast is near the Giling bull-race stadium on the northern side. Sumenep is reputed to breed champion bulls, and on most Saturday mornings practice bull races can be seen at the stadium.

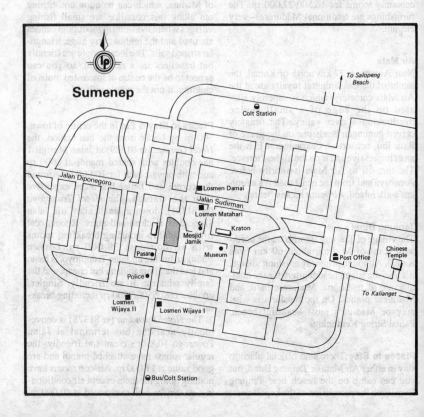

Sumenep

Things to See The **kraton** and its *taman sari* (pleasure garden) are worth visiting. It was built in the 18th century by Panembahan Sumolo, son of Queen Raden Ayu Tirtonegoro and her spouse, Bendoro Saud, who was a commoner but a descendant of Muslim scholars. The architect is thought to have been the grandson of one of the first Chinese to settle in Sumenep after the Chinese massacre in Batavia. The kraton is occupied by the present bupati of Sumenep but part of the building is a small museum with an interesting collection of royal possessions including Madurese furniture, stone sculptures and *binggels*, the heavy silver anklets worn by Madurese women. Opposite the kraton, the royal carriage house contains the throne of Queen Tirtonegoro and a superb Chinese-style bed reputedly 300 years old.

Sumenep's 18th century **Mesjid Jamik** (mosque) is notable for its three-tiered Meru-style roof, Chinese porcelain tiles and ceramics. Sumenep also has a **Chinese temple.**

The tombs of the royal family are at the **Asta Tinggi cemetery**, which looks out over the town from a peaceful hilltop one km away. The main royal tombs are interesting and decorated with carved and painted panels, two depicting dragons said to represent the colonial invasion of Sumenep. One of the small pavilions in the outer courtyard still bears the mark of an assassin's sword from an unsuccessful attempt to murder Bendoro Saud.

Around Sumenep

Salopeng, near the village of Ambunten 20 km north-west of Sumenep, has a beautiful beach with strong waves, rolling sand dunes and coconut groves. Here you may see men fishing in the shallower water with large cantilevered hand nets which are rarely seen elsewhere in Java.

Lombeng beach, 30 km north-east of Sumenep, is said to be even more beautiful and remote. You can get out there by colt from Sumenep but there's no road all the way

to the village. The local people ride their bicycles along the sands.

Places to Stay & Eat The *Syafari Jaya* (☎ 21989) is a sizeable hotel where doubles with shared mandi cost 8000 rp, or 10,000 with mandi. Air-con costs 18,000 rp here. *Losmen Wijaya I* and *Wijaya II* (☎ 21532), near the main bus station, are clean and well-run and have small restaurants. Doubles with common mandi start at 8000 rp including morning coffee and there are more expensive rooms with private mandi and air-con for 25,000 rp. Alternatively there's the *Losmen Damai* where rooms cost 6500 rp, or the similarly priced *Losmen Matahari*. Both are on Jalan Sudirman. Both could be cleaner.

Decent restaurants to try around town include the *Mawar* at Jalan Diponegoro 105 for Chinese fare and *Rumah Makan 17 Agustus* at Jalan Sudirman 34, serving both budget Chinese and Indonesian. There are good day and night markets in the area around the mosque.

TROWULAN

Trowulan was once the capital of the largest Hindu empire in Indonesian history. Founded by a Singosari prince, Wijaya, in 1294 it reached the height of its power under Hayam Wuruk (1350-89), who was guided by his powerful prime minister, Gajah Mada. During his time Majapahit claimed control over, or at least received tribute from, most of today's Indonesia and even parts of the Malay peninsula. The capital was a grand affair, the kraton forming a miniature city within the city and surrounded by great fortified walls and watchtowers.

Its wealth was based both on the fertile rice-growing plains of Java and on control of the spice trade. The religion was a hybrid of Hinduism with Shiva, Vishnu and Brahma being worshipped, although, as in the earlier Javanese kingdoms, Buddhism was also prominent. It seems Muslims too were tolerated and Koranic burial inscriptions, found on the site, suggest that there were Javanese Muslims within the royal court even in the

14th century when this Hindu-Buddhist state was at the height of its glory. The empire came to a sudden end in 1478 when the city fell to the north coast power of Demak and the Majapahit elite fled to Bali, thus opening up Java for conquest by the Muslims.

The Majapahit ruins are scattered over a large area – along the winding lanes of the small village of Trowulan and across great fields planted out with tobacco and other crops. Some of the ruins are superb in their shattered grandeur and this is a fine place to simply walk around and explore. It's possible to get round the sites in one day on foot if you start early, but hiring a becak makes life a lot easier.

On the main road from Surabaya to Solo, the Trowulan Museum houses some superb examples of sculpture collected locally. There's also a large table-top map here of the sites in the area. Some of the most interesting sites include the Kolam Segaran (a vast

Majapahit swimming pool); the gateway of Bajang Ratu with its strikingly sculptured kala heads; the Tikus Temple (the Queen's bath) and the recently restored Siti Inggil Temple with the impressive tomb of Wijaya (people still come to meditate here and in the early evening it has quite a strange spiritual atmosphere). The Pendopo Agung is an open-air pavilion recently built by the Indonesian Army. Two km south of the pavilion, the Troloyo cemetery is the site of the oldest Muslim graves found on Java, the earliest being from 1376 AD.

Information

The Trowulan Museum is open from 7 am to 2 pm Tuesday to Thursday, to 11 am Friday, to 12.30 pm Saturday and to 2 pm on Sunday. It's closed on Monday. If you're en route to somewhere else, you can leave your gear safely at the museum office. Entry is 250 rp. There is nowhere to stay in Trowulan but you

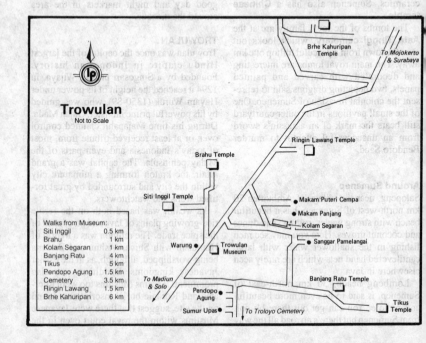

Trowulan
Not to Scale

Brhe Kahuripan Temple

To Mojokerto & Surabaya

Ringin Lawang Temple

Brahu Temple

Siti Inggil Temple

Makam Puteri Cempa

Makam Panjang

Kolam Segaran

Warung

Trowulan Museum

Sanggar Pamelangai

Banjang Ratu Temple

To Madiun & Solo

Pendopo Agung

Tikus Temple

Sumur Upas

To Troloyo Cemetery

Walks from Museum:	
Siti Inggil	0.5 km
Brahu	1 km
Kolam Segaran	1 km
Banjang Ratu	4 km
Tikus	5 km
Pendopo Agung	1.5 km
Cemetery	3.5 km
Ringin Lawang	1.5 km
Brhe Kahuripan	6 km

can get a cheap meal at the restaurant opposite the museum.

Getting There & Away

Trowulan is 60 km west of Surabaya, which is the place many people use as a base, and only 10 km from Mojokerto which is an alternative if you want to stay near the ruins. From the Bungurasih bus station in Surabaya it's a one-hour trip, via Mojokerto, to Trowulan and buses will drop you right in front of the museum. The bus fare is 800 rp. At the museum it's quite easy to hire a becak to get you around the sites – perhaps 7000 rp for a four-hour round trip – but you have to bargain hard.

When you're leaving Trowulan there's no problem flagging a bus down on the road from Surabaya to Solo. There are scores of buses going in either direction and from Trowulan it's 1400 rp on to Madiun towards Solo. If you're heading east to Probolinggo or south to Malang, you can take a bus or colt as far as Gempol and continue on from there by public bus, which is cheaper. For Malang, an interesting alternative to backtracking through Mojokerto to Gempol is to travel by colt via Jombang and the hill town of Batu.

MOJOKERTO

Like Surabaya, Mojokerto can be a useful base from which to visit the Majapahit ruins at Trowulan. On the banks of Sungai Brantas, this is quite an attractive town with an old quarter of winding alleys, canals and old houses from the Dutch era. Mojokerto also has a small archaeological museum of its own, with various Majapahit stone carvings and a splendid statue of Kediri's King Airlangga-as-Vishnu astride a huge Garuda. The Museum Purbakala is in the centre of town on Jalan A Yani, and open the same hours and days as the Trowulan museum.

Places to Stay

Opposite the bus station, the *Hotel Nagamas* has singles/doubles with mandi at 5700/7500 rp including breakfast, and more expensive rooms with fan and hot water.

The *Wisma Tenera* is on Jalan Hos Cokroaminoto, roughly halfway between the bus station and the centre of town. There are good singles/doubles here at 10,000 rp including breakfast, or with mandi at 13,500 rp. Most of the other hotels are in the centre of town, about 3½ km from the bus station, so you would definitely need to take a becak. They include *Losmen Merdeka*, Jalan Pamuji 73, with rooms at 10,500 rp including breakfast. The old *Penginapan Barat* is along a quiet canal on Jalan Kradenan, just off Jalan Majapahit. It has reasonable rooms at 5500/7500 rp, plenty of mosquitoes and goldfish in the mandi – well, what more could you ask for?

Places to Eat

One of the best places to eat in Mojokerto is the *Depot Murni* at Jalan Majapahit 72. It's run by very friendly people and they serve excellent Indonesian food; most meals cost around 1500 rp. There are also plenty of warungs at night around the market, Pasar Kliwon, on the same street. The *Rumah Makan Surya* next to the alun-alun has also had good reports.

Getting There & Away

Buses along the road from Surabaya to Madiun all pass through Mojokerto. If you stop off here for the night en route to Trowulan, you can pick up a colt going that way from the road running parallel to Jalan Majapahit (behind Pasar Kliwon) in the centre of town rather than heading back out to the bus station. The fare between Surabaya and Mojokerto is 700 rp.

PROBOLINGGO

Probolinggo is basically important as the transport centre for people visiting Gunung Bromo. There's nothing special about it, although it can be a useful mid-point on the Surabaya to Banyuwangi coastal road. The last colt to Gunung Bromo leaves around 7 pm, after which you'll have to charter a colt for about 20,000 rp or stay overnight in Probolinggo. The main post office and most of the banks and government buildings are on Jalan Suroyo.

Places to Stay

There are hotels and some cheap restaurants along the main street, Jalan P Sudirman, all within a 10-minute walk west of the bus station. The *Hotel Bromo Permai II* (☎ 41256), opposite the bus station, is a source of copious but not always reliable information on Bromo and transport for Bali. It's a sister location of the Bromo Permai I up at the Gunung Bromo crater in Cemoro Lawang and together these two hotels would like to get all the rupiah you spend between Probolinggo and the crater. The hotel itself is comfortable enough and a reasonably priced place to stay; single/doubles with share mandi cost 3500/5200 rp, doubles with fan and mandi range from 6160 to 8000 rp, and air-con doubles/triples cost 12,320/16,600 rp.

At the west end of Jalan P Sudirman at the crossroads with Jalan Suroyo you'll find the imposing *Hotel Victoria* (☎ 21461). It has adequate singles/doubles ranging from 7000 to 15,000 rp, or 15,000/17,500 with mandi and fan. Singles/doubles with air-con start at 22,000/25,000 rp. Tea on arrival and breakfast are included.

The *Hotel Kemayoran*, almost opposite the Victoria, is cheap but cheerless and grubby. *Hotel Ratna* (21597) further up at No 94 is a good place. Economy rooms cost 6000 and 7000 rp including breakfast; doubles with mandi and fan range from 15,000 to 22,5000 rp. There are also air-con rooms at 25,000 and 30,000 rp.

On Jalan Suroyo at No 16, just around the corner from Jalan P Sudirman, you'll find perhaps Probolinggo's most pleasant place to stay, the *Hotel Tampiarto Plaza* (☎ 21280). Small economy rooms with shared mandi cost 5750 rp. Single/doubles with mandi are 10,000/15,000 rp. Rooms with air-con range in price from 20,000 to 34,500 rp for a deluxe double with TV.

Places to Eat

The *Warung Sudi Mampir*, near the bus station at No 206-208, has good meals for around 1000 to 1500 rp. The nearby *King Restaurant* has mostly Chinese and seafood;

it's slightly pricey but good. *Restaurant Malang*, Jalan P Sudirman 104 near the Hotel Victoria, is also a bit expensive but there's a wide range of items on the menu and the food is good – most meals cost around 1500 to 3000 rp. For ice cream and iced juice try the *Sumber Hidup* garden cafe near the Hotel Ratna – they also have good satay. You'll find plenty of small restaurants and 'depots' at the night market around Pasar Gotong Royong near the colt station.

Getting There & Away

Bus Probolinggo is a 1500-rp bus ride from the Bungurasih bus station in Surabaya. There are several departures an hour and the trip takes about 2½ hours. Malang is only two hours away by bus and the fare is about 1400 rp.

Coming from Bali it's 10,000 rp (12,500 rp for an air-con bus) to Probolinggo from Denpasar; an evening bus departing around 7.30 to 8.30 pm will get you there at about 4 am. The bus from Banyuwangi via Situbondo costs 3100 rp and takes about five hours.

To Denpasar, a night bus leaves Probolinggo every hour between 6 and 11 pm. It takes eight hours and the fare is 18,500 rp. To Yogya, night buses start running at 11 pm; it's an eight-hour ride, with prices ranging from 17,000 to 24,000 rp. Cheap, slow daytime buses cost 9000 rp.

To/From Gunung Bromo The colt station in Probolinggo is only 300 metres or so west of the bus station (away from the railway line). There are frequent colts between 7 am and 7 pm from Probolinggo as far as Ngadisari via Sukapura. The fare is 1750 rp and the trip to Ngadisari takes 1½ to two hours uphill (less on the way down). From Probolinggo to Ngadisari is 45 km; from Ngadisari to Bromo is three steep km on foot. Jeep bemos do the short run from Ngadisari to Cemoro Lawang (the village at the edge of the crater) for 1000 rp per person.

Don't believe the staff at Hotel Bromo Permai II in Probolinggo if they tell you their private colt is the only one going to Bromo

– it costs twice as much as the public colts. And it stops for passengers along the way, just like the public colts! They may also tell you their colt goes all the way to Cemoro Lawang (which would save you the steep walk or 1000 rp); this is also a lie.

Train The train station is about three km from the bus station; two km if you cut along the railway tracks. From Surabaya to Probolinggo (two trains a day) the fare is 4400 rp in 2nd class, 2800 rp in 3rd class; from Probolinggo to Banyuwangi (two trains a day) the fare is the same but it's quicker to take a bus. A train to Yogya (one train per day departing at 7.30 am) is 4400 rp in 3rd class but it's a long, slow trip.

GUNUNG BROMO

This powerful volcano is one of the most spectacular sights in Java. Bromo rises up in a desolate landscape – a vast sea of lava sand that stretches 10 km across, surrounded by craggy peaks – and has a strange end-of-the-world feeling, particularly at sunrise. Like Gunung Batur on Bali, Bromo is a crater within a crater – one of four mountains that have emerged within the caldera of the ancient Tengger volcano. Legend has it that the great Tengger crater was dug out with just half a coconut shell by an ogre smitten with love for a princess. When the king saw that the ogre might fulfil the task he had set, which was to be completed in a single night, he ordered his servants to pound rice and the cocks started to crow, thinking dawn had broken. The coconut that the ogre flung away became Gunung Batok, and the trench became the Sand Sea – and the ogre died of exhaustion.

If you read any of the literature turned out by the Indonesian Tourist Office, you'll probably come across some delightful Indonesian-English turns of phrase. Here's a lyrical example:

Bromo should be the choice for only there, on the crater rim with the sea of sand stretching below as far as the eyes can see on one's left and the ghostly grumble mixed with dense lumps of smoke crumple up from the inner pitfall on one's right, and on the height of 2,383 metres above sea level would one see how lustrous the aurora of the sun, in mixing colours of white, pale yellow, yellowish red turning red appears from behind the hills quite in front, to brighten the atmosphere to daylight, does one feel oneself to be like one grain of small green pea amidst a vessel of sand – you'll be aware of the Greatness of the Creator of men!

Bromo is also a centre for the Tenggerese farmers who cultivate market vegetables on the steep mountain slopes and are found only on the high ranges of the Tengger-Semeru massif. The history of these people can be traced back to the rule of the Hindu-Majapahit empire, when followers of Brahma worshipped on the volcanic mountain of Bromo ('Bromo' is in fact the Javanese pronunciation of 'Brahma'). Each year, in January or February, Bromo is the site for the Kesada (Kesodo) festival, with a colourful procession of Tenggerese who come to throw offerings into the crater at sunrise to pacify the god of the volcano.

Probolinggo Approach

Most people turn off at Probolinggo, north of Bromo, and plan to be on the rim of the crater for sunrise. From Probolinggo you have to get up the mountain to Ngadisari, sign the visitor's book at the police office and pay your 1050 rp. (If you're planning a day trip, note that the police aren't prepared to look after bags.) You can stay in Ngadisari, take a shared jeep bemo for 1000 rp or climb the last steep three km on foot to the hotels at Cemoro Lawang on the rim of the Tengger crater.

From Cemoro Lawang it's another three km down the crater wall and across the Sand Sea to Bromo. Sunrise is at about 5 am, so if you're staying in Ngadisari you'll have to leave at around 3 am, from Cemoro Lawang at 4 am. There's no real need for a guide or horses, although if you want to ride across to Bromo it costs 7500 to 10,000 rp – bargain hard – return from Ngadisari. (Some travellers who were not in the best shape report that they were glad they hired horses.) It's cold and windy in the early morning so you'll need warm gear, and take a torch (flashlight) – the descent on the path to the Sand Sea can be a bit dodgy in the dark. Once you're on the sand, white-painted rocks mark the trail straight across to Bromo (about half-way across they fork right to the Penanjakan viewpoint) and by the time you've crossed the plain and started to climb up Bromo (246 steps, one traveller reported) it should be fairly light. The view from the top, of the sun sailing up over the outer crater, and that first glimpse into the steaming depths of Bromo, is fantastic.

From Cemoro Lawang, trekkers can take an interesting walk across the Sand Sea to Ngadas (eight km) on the southern rim of the Tengger crater. Along the road from Ngadas you can eventually flag down a colt to Malang, via Gubug Klakah and Tumpang. It entails at least six or seven hours of walking, so you'd need to start early in order to get to Malang by evening.

Ngadas Approach

If you want to avoid the Probolinggo to Gunung Bromo shakedown, you can trek into the Tengger crater from Ngadas to the south-west of Gunung Bromo. This is definitely a trek for those willing and able to rough it a bit. The reward is spectacular mountain scenery and not having to deal with the Bromo hustlers until after you've experienced Bromo.

You can start this route from either Malang or Surabaya – either way you must get to Blimbing, just north of Malang. From Blimbing it's a short bemo ride east to Tumpang; in Tumpang get another bemo to the town of Gubug Klakah. From Gubug Klakah it's a full-day 13-km walk to the village of Ngadas which is two km south-west of the crater rim – you may be able to catch a ride along the way and shorten the journey. You can spend the night with the villagers of Ngadas and explore Gunung Bromo and the Tengger crater the next day. It's about a three-hour walk (eight km) across the crater to Cemoro Lawang, where you can get a bemo down to Probolinggo – or do the entire route in reverse.

The PHPA office in Ngadas has good information and maps of the Bromo-Semeru area.

From Gubug Klakah you also have the option of trekking to Gunung Semeru, the tallest mountain in Java. See the Nature Reserves in East Java section later in this chapter.

Whichever route you take, the ideal time to visit Bromo to be sure of a blood-red sunrise is during the dry season, April to November. In the wet season the dawn and the clouds are likely to arrive simultaneously so an early rise may not be worth the effort – you might as well stroll across later when it's warmer. At any time of year it's cold on these mountains; from June to September night temperatures can get down to around 2 to 5°C; from October to May, minimums range from 10 to 15°C.

This is such a fascinating area, both for interesting local people and beauteous topography, that it is hard to understand why travellers rush off after they have seen sunrise at the volcano.

Places to Stay

In Ngadisari, you will find a pleasant, albeit basic, budget lodge called *Yoschi's* at Jalan Wonokerto 1. This friendly inn offers doubles with shared mandi for 6000 rp and cottages for 15,000 to 20,000 rp. It also serves food. If you find Yoschi's full, there are plenty of villagers who will offer you a room for the night, although the quality varies a lot and security is usually minimal. Prices vary from around 3500 rp – less for really basic rooms (kapok beds) and much more if you arrive too late to hunt around. There are a couple of warungs and a small restaurant near the police office.

Up at Cemoro Lawang, right on the rim of the Tengger crater, the *Hotel Bromo Permai* is a pleasant place to stay before you embark upon your ascent of the volcano. The hotel has a restaurant in the moderate price range, a bar and evening entertainment by quite a good singer who doubles as the hotel administrator. It's also an excellent place for a hardy breakfast before your sunrise trek.

Rooms range from basic to deluxe and breakfast is included in the tariff. A dorm bed costs 3500 rp (slightly less with a YHA card), rooms with shared mandi cost 10,000 to 15,000 rp and doubles with a private toilet range from 29,500 to 40,000 rp. There are also luxury suites with TV for 61,500 rp.

There are a couple of budget alternatives to the Bromo Permai. As you head down the road toward the village beneath the hotel, you will see the cheap and popular *Losmen Lava*. Single/doubles with shared mandi cost 5000/7000 rp with breakfast included. There is also a large room for 10,000 rp. Basic, inexpensive meals are served. The owner plans to add a dorm. In Lawang Sair village below Cemoro Lawang, another inn for those minding their rupiah is the home of *Mbuk Artini*, who provides lodging and food at prices similar to those of Losmen Lava.

It's hard to understand why anyone would stay at the plush new *Grand Bromo Hotel* (☎ 711802), a full nine km from the crater – jeeps to Cemoro Lawang can be chartered here for a mere 50,000 rp! But for those who want the details, there are dorm rooms here (probably for Indonesian teenagers on holiday, as what budget lodger would stay this far from the volcano?) for 10,000 rp a bed, doubles with TV start at 78,000 rp and luxury cottages cost 196,000 rp. It is said that the Suharto family has invested in this dubious enterprise.

Getting There & Away

Probolinggo, 42 km away, is the departure point for colts as far as Ngadisari. The trip takes 1½ hours and the fare is 1750 rp. For Ngadas, catch a bemo from Blimbing to Tumpang, then another to Gubug Klakah – this should take two hours at most and the total fare is 850 rp. From Gubug Klakah it's walk or hitch.

PASIR PUTIH

Roughly halfway between Probolinggo and Banyuwangi, on the north coast road, this is East Java's most popular seaside resort, but its name (*pasir putih* means 'white sand') is a misnomer – the sand is more grey-black

than white! There are lots of picturesque outrigger boats, swimming and boats to hire but – compared with Lovina Beach only a few hours away on Bali – it's really no big deal. It's a useful stopover point, but go during the week if you want the beach to yourself. Pasir Putih is mobbed on weekends by sun'n'sand worshippers from Surabaya.

Places to Stay

There are a number of hotels, restaurants, fruit and souvenir stalls all jammed in between the highway and the beach. The *Pasir Putih Inn* (☎ Situbondo 22 ext 2) has its own garden and is probably the nicest of them although, at 11,000 rp, their rooms (with mandi) are somewhat overpriced. The more expensive rooms from 16,500 rp are good and have a terrace. There are also suites for 32,000 rp.

Also quite pleasant, the *Hotel Sidho Muncul* (☎ Situbondo 22 ext 3) has clean, airy rooms on the beachfront for 11,000 rp, and larger air-con rooms with verandahs overlooking the water for 45,000 rp. *Hotel Bhayangkara Beach* is the cheapest of all, with rooms facing the highway: some small and stuffy ones cost 7500 rp; better rooms (with mandi) facing the beach start at 10,000 rp. Also decent is the *Mutiara Beach Hotel*, which has rooms with mandi for 10,000 rp, and the *Oriental Palapa* where rooms with private mandi cost but 8500 rp.

SITUBONDO

Only a short distance on the Banyuwangi side of Pasir Putih, Situbondo is a reasonably large town with several places to stay. The *Hotel Asia*, near the bus station, is on the main road and is quite pleasant. The *Losmen Asita* is near the railway station or there's the *Hotel Situbondo*.

KALIKLATAK

At Kaliklatak, 20 km north of Banyuwangi, you can go on tours of large coffee, cocoa, rubber, and clove plantations for 7000 rp. Accommodation is available at the *Wisata Irdjen Guesthouse* (☎ 323 in Kaliklatak, 41896 in Banyuwangi), but at 58,000 rp it is expensive. Note that tours and accommodation must be booked in advance – many travel agencies in Bali as well as Surabaya can make the arrangements, or call Wisata Irdjen directly.

BANYUWANGI

Although there are no particular attractions to drag you there, schedules or just the urge to be somewhere different might take you to Banyuwangi, the ferry departure point for Bali. The ferry terminus for Bali is actually a few km north of town, at Ketapang.

The old Banyuwangi railway station has been closed down and replaced by a new one in Ketapang, just a couple of hundred metres from the ferry terminus. This means more people will probably be travelling straight through without stopping in Banyuwangi. If you choose to spend a night or two here, you'll find the town fairly pleasant, if not particularly attractive.

Banyuwangi has its own music/dance style that has been likened to Sundanese Jaipongan. Called Gandrung Banyuwangi, it can be seen at weddings and during holiday periods. In the nearby villages of Bakungan and Oleh Sari you can see the Seblang, a trance dance performed in propitiation of certain spirits by female dukuns, who pass the gift of trance from mother to daughter. On Satu Suro, the first day of the Javanese calendar, a ceremony called Petik Laut is performed at the seaside in Muncar to give thanks to the sea spirits for good harvests.

Orientation & Information

There are three bus stations in Banyuwangi, the main one being Blambangan to the north of town on the road to Ketapang. Blambangan and Ketapang are quite some distance from each other so you will need to take a bemo from one to the other.

There's a tourist office in the LCM Ferry Building in Ketapang, from where ferries ply to Bali. In Banyuwangi, the tourist office is on the town square at Jalan Diponegoro 2. At either office, a map of Banyuwangi with a leaflet on places of interest in the area is available if you ask for it; the staff have little

else but they speak English and are very helpful. The office is open from 7 am to 2 pm Monday to Thursday, to noon on Friday and to 1 pm on Saturday. Opposite the Banyuwangi Tourist Office you'll find the post office and telephone office. Next to these offices in the grounds of a school there's another tourist information centre, open from 3 to 9 pm, run by an enterprising junior guide. There's a bank nearby on Jalan Dr Sutomo.

Wildlife Parks/Nature Reserves If you're coming from Bali and planning a visit to Baluran National Park (37 km from Banyuwangi) or the Ijen Plateau (about 18 km from Banyuwangi) you can get information from the Baluran National Park Office (☎ 41119) at Jalan A Yani 108, Banyuwangi (☎ 41119). There is a PHPA office at the entrance to Baluran in the village of Wonorejo, but you can book accommodation in advance through the main Banyuwangi office if you want to be sure of a bed for the night. A rough map of Baluran is available here and the staff are very helpful. The office is open from 7 am to 2 pm Monday to Thursday, to 11 am on Friday, to 1 pm on Saturday and to 2 pm on Sunday.

To get to Baluran National Park from Banyuwangi, take a bus to Wonorejo and ask the driver to let you off in Baluran. At the park's office, ask an official to arrange for an *ojek* (motorcycle becak) to take you to the park for 3000 rp a person. It costs 13,000 rp to charter a bemo.

Places to Stay – bottom end

The *Hotel Baru* (☎ 21369), Jalan Pattimura 82-84, is one of Banyuwangi's most popular places to stay for budget travellers. It's clean, well run and friendly, and there are big airy rooms. Singles/doubles cost 6000/7000 rp including breakfast; rooms with mandi and fan start at 7500/11,000 rp. Nearby, there's also the similarly priced *Hotel Berlin Barat* (☎ 21323) on Jalan Letjen Haryono. *Hotel Slamet*, next to the old railway station at Ka'am Wahid Hasyim 96, charges 7500 for a double with fan and 15,000 rp for air-con.

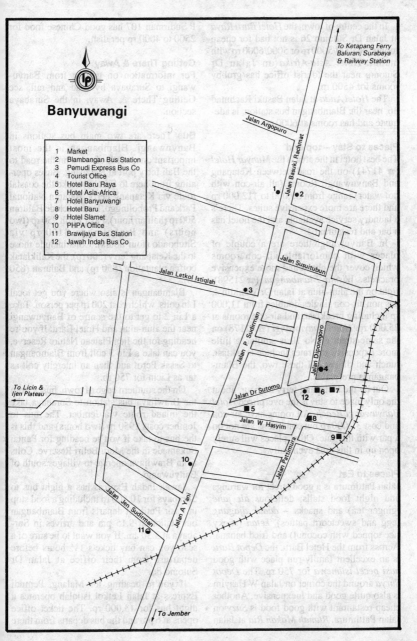

Banyuwangi

1 Market
2 Blambangan Bus Station
3 Pemudi Express Bus Co
4 Tourist Office
5 Hotel Baru Raya
6 Hotel Asia-Africa
7 Hotel Banyuwangi
8 Hotel Baru
9 Hotel Slamet
10 PHPA Office
11 Brawijaya Bus Station
12 Jawah Indah Bus Co

Jalan Argopuro

Jalan Basuki Rachmat

Jalan Susuitubun

Jalan Letkol Istiqlah

Jalan P Sudirman

Jalan Diponegoro

Jalan Dr Sutomo

Jalan W Hasyim

Jalan Pattimura

Jalan Jen Sudirman

Jalan A Yani

To Ketapang Ferry
Baluran, Surabaya
& Railway Station

To Licin &
Ijen Plateau

To Jember

In the centre of town, the *Hotel Baru Raya* at Jalan Dr Sutomo 26 is not bad for cheap rooms, at 4000/5000 rp or 5000/6000 rp with mandi. *Hotel Asia-Afrika* on Jalan Dr Sutomo near the tourist office has grubby rooms for 4500 rp.

The *Hotel Anda* at Jalan Basuki Rachmad 36, near the Blambangan bus station, is adequate and has rooms at 6000 rp.

Places to Stay – top end

The best hotel in the area is the *Manyar Hotel* (☎ 41741) on the road between Ketapang and Banyuwangi. Rooms (all air-con with hot water) range from 39,000 to 112,000 rp and there are more expensive suites. There's a laundry service available and the hotel has a bar and restaurant.

In Banyuwangi there are a couple of places with comfortable air-con rooms which cover the cheap and more expensive brackets. *Wisma Blambangan* (☎ 21598), right on the alun-alun at Jalan Dr Wahidin 4, has non air-con singles/doubles from 11,000 rp including breakfast, and air-con rooms at 25,000 rp. *Hotel Banyuwangi* (☎ 41178) on the same street at No 10 is similar, a little more expensive but rates include breakfast, lunch and dinner. Of these two, the Blambangan is preferable.

Out by the Ketapang ferry harbour, about the only place to stay is the overpriced *Hotel Banyuwangi Beach*. All rooms have air-con and cost 31,000 rp but conditions are not on a par with this rate. Other places will surely open up in this area eventually.

Places to Eat

Jalan Pattimura is a good street for warungs and night food stalls; delicious *air jahe* (ginger tea) and snacks – *dadak djagung* (egg and sweetcorn patties), *ketan* (sticky rice topped with coconut) and fried banana. Across from the Hotel Baru, the *Depot Baru* is an excellent family-run place with good *nasi pecel istimewa* for 750 rp. The *Depot Surya* around the corner on Jalan W Hasyim is also quite good and inexpensive. Another cheap restaurant with good food is *Suzy* on Jalan Pattimura. *Rumah Makan Ria* at Jalan

P Sudirman 107 has good Chinese food for 2500 to 4000 rp per dish.

Getting There & Away

For information on getting from Banyuwangi to Surabaya by road and rail, see Getting There & Away, in the Surabaya section.

Bus There are two main bus stations in Banyuwangi. Blambangan is the most important one, north of town on the road to the Bali ferry port at Ketapang. Buses operating from here to Surabaya take the coastal route via Ketapang Ferry, Baluran National Park and Probolinggo. Fares include Baluran 500 rp (half an hour), Pasir Putih 950 rp (two hours) and Probolinggo 3100 rp via Situbondo (four hours). Colts include those to the Ketapang ferry (500 rp), the Kaliklatak coffee plantation (850 rp) and Baluran (850 rp).

Blambangan is also where you get local Lin colts, which cost 200 rp per person. Take a Lin 2 to get to the centre of Banyuwangi near the alun-alun and Hotel Baru. If you're heading for the Ijen Plateau Nature Reserve, you can take a Lin 3 colt from Blambangan to Sasak Perot and then an intercity colt as far as Licin for 750 rp.

On the southern edge of town, buses from the Brawijaya bus station to Surabaya take the inland route via Jember. The bus to Jember costs 1950 rp (two hours) and this is the bus to take if you're heading for Pantai Sukamade in the Meru Betiri Reserve. Colts from Brawijaya operate to villages south of Banyuwangi.

Jawah Indah Express has a night bus to Surabaya for 10,500 rp including a food stop in Pasir Putih. It departs from Blambangan bus station at 9.15 pm and arrives in Surabaya at 3.30 am. If you want to be sure of a seat, you can buy tickets 1½ hours before departure from their office at Jalan Dr Sutomo 86.

If you're heading for Malang, Pemudi Express at Jalan Letkol Istiqlah operates a night bus for 13,000 rp. The ticket office opens at 6 pm and the bus departs from there at 10 pm, arriving in Malang at the crack of dawn.

Ferry Ferries from Ketapang, eight km north of town, depart every hour round the clock for Gilimanuk on Bali. You can book from Surabaya right through to Denpasar, including the ferry. See the Bali chapter for more details.

Getting Around

Banyuwangi has a squadron of bemos running between the various colt and bus stations; they're marked Lin 1, 2, 3 and charge a fixed 200 rp fare around town.

Useful bemos include: Lin 1 between Ketapang Ferry and the Blambangan and Brawijaya bus stations; Lin 2 between Blambangan (past the train station) and Brawijaya bus station; Lin 3 between Blambangan (past the tourist office) and Sasak Perot, where you get colts to Licin and then on to the Ijen Plateau.

NATURE RESERVES IN EAST JAVA

Baluran National Park, on the extreme north-eastern tip of the province, is the most accessible of Java's large wildlife sanctuaries, the other being the relatively more remote Ujung Kulon National Park in West Java. Six areas in East Java have also been designated 'nature reserves' – three on the south coast and the others in the volcanic mountain regions inland. The latter three areas offer limited wildlife but magnificent scenery and are likely to appeal to those interested in trekking.

Guesthouse accommodation is available at Baluran but facilities in the nature reserves are basic if they exist at all. In some cases you need to be relatively self-sufficient and equipped with provisions and, sometimes, cold-weather gear.

Baluran National Park

On the north-east corner of Java, Baluran National Park covers an area of 250 sq km. The parklands surround the solitary hump of Gunung Baluran (1247 metres) and contain a mixture of monsoon forest and, on the north side, surprisingly extensive dry savannah grassland threaded by stony-bedded streams. The main attractions are the herds of feral water buffalo, banteng (wild cattle), rusa deer, muncaks (barking deer), monkeys, and the wild pigs, leopards and civet cats that live in the upland forest. Birds include the green junglefowl, peacocks, bee-eaters, kingfishers and owls.

It's possible to make arrangements with the PHPA staff at the park entrance for a jeep to take you to some of the more remote parts of the savannah, but you will have to negotiate a price. Even around Bekol, where the main guesthouse is located, you can see deer and water buffalo, usually in the early morning or late afternoon, so you should stay here for the night. Banteng are sighted less often – they come down to the savannah only in the dry season and are being displaced by the large numbers of buffalo, which apparently breed more efficiently.

The main service area for Baluran is the village of Wonorejo, on the main coast road between Surabaya and Banyuwangi, where food supplies can be bought – the PHPA office is just inside the park entrance. Baluran is open daily from 7 am to 5 pm and, if you're not staying overnight, baggage can be left safely at the PHPA office.

Baluran can be visited at any time of the year but the best time is the dry season, between June and November. The best time of day is in the very early morning or late evening.

Places to Stay Accommodation is available at two places. The *Bekol Guesthouse*, 12 km into the park, sleeps up to 10 people at 4000 rp per person; there's a mandi and kitchen but you must take your own provisions. It is in the middle of the savannah and a watchtower and water reservoir are nearby. *Bama Guesthouse* is three km east of Bekol on the beach. Bookings for both can be made in advance at the PHPA office in Banyuwangi but you're more than likely to have the place to yourself. If you arrive at Baluran after dark there is a free camping area at the entrance

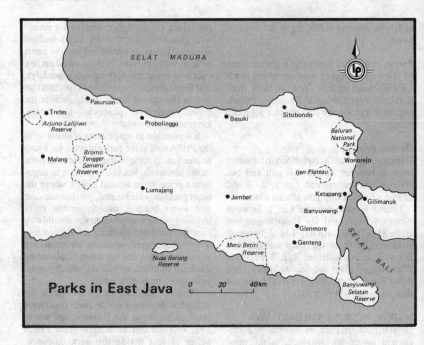

SELAT MADURA

• Pasuruan

• Tretes
Arjuno-Lalijiwo
Reserve

• Probolinggo

• Besuki

• Situbondo

Baluran
National
Park

• Malang

Bromo
Tengger
Semeru
Reserve

• Wonorejo

Ijen Plateau

• Lumajang

• Ketapang

• Gilimanuk

• Jember

• Banyuwangi

• Glenmore

• Genteng

Meru Betiri
Reserve

Nusa Barung
Reserve

SELAT BALI

Parks in East Java   0   20   40 km

Banyuwangi
Selatan
Reserve

and a small guesthouse (also free) available for a temporary stay.

Getting There & Away Surabaya to Banyuwangi buses, taking the coast road via Probolinggo, will stop at Wonorejo if there's anyone getting off. If you're leaving the park, buses are easily flagged down. From Banyuwangi (or Ketapang ferry, if you're coming from Bali) it's only a half-hour journey on the Wonorejo bus, which costs 500 rp. Ask the driver to let you off at the park and at the entrance ask an official to arrange an ojek to take you into the park for 3000 rp per person. Alternatively, you can charter a bemo for about 13,000 rp. Coming from the west, Baluran is 3½ hours from Probolinggo/Gunung Bromo and the bus costs 1900 rp.

Ijen Plateau

The Ijen Plateau, part of a reserve area which stretches north-east to Baluran, was at one time a huge active crater complex 134 sq km in area. Today Ijen is dormant, not dead, and the landscape is dominated by the volcanic cones of Ijen (2400 metres) and Merapi (2800 metres) on the north-eastern edge of the plateau and Raung (3332 metres) on the south-west corner. Coffee plantations cover much of the western part of the plateau, where there are a few settlements.

This is not an outstanding area for wildlife, but the Ijen crater has a magnificent turquoise sulphur lake and this high region is completely unspoilt. The Ijen crater lake is almost surrounded by sheer walls but the north-west face has crumbled and it may be possible to climb down to the 'safety-valve' dam which was built here to regulate the flow of water into the Banyu Pahit, the 'Bitter River'. There are a few people in this area: sulphur is being extracted from the lake and a vulcanology post at Ungkup-Ungkup, on the south side of the crater, is staffed year-round.

The best time to make the hike is in the dry season between April and October. Note that night temperatures at high altitudes can drop to around 10 to 16°C.

Places to Stay A Forestry Office Guesthouse is available at the village of Jampit. At Ungkup-Ungkup, a former resthouse provides shelter but little else; it's run-down and there are no facilities. The sulphur quarry workers may cook for you, but you must take provisions. There's also a government plantation lodge at Blawan charging 49,000 rp for room and board – the room may be booked in the town of Jember through Mr Wahab at Jalan Gajah Mada 249.

Getting There & Away You can approach the Ijen Crater from Banyuwangi by bus to Jambu (19 km) and then on foot to Ungkup-Ungkup (five to six hours) and the crater rim (one hour). There are sometimes colts to Sodong, but you can't count upon this. Some travellers are lucky enough to hitch a ride with one of the sulphur trucks. The crater can also be reached from Bondowoso or Wonosari to the west, by bus from either point to Jampit via Gempol. The trek across the plateau between Jampit and Ungkup-Ungkup takes about five hours.

Banyuwangi Selatan Reserve

Also known as Blambangan, this reserve occupies the whole of the remote Purwo peninsula at the south-eastern tip of Java. This is perhaps the last area in Indonesia where the fast-dwindling species of Indonesian wild dog *(ajak,* a subspecies of the Indian dhole) still exists in any numbers. The reserve is also noted for its turtle-nesting beaches which, sadly, are often raided by Balinese turtle hunters. There are jungle fowl, leaf monkeys, muncaks, rusa deer, leopards and wild pigs.

Surfers from Bali have 'discovered' Teluk Grajagan and there is a small surfing camp at Plengkung which apparently has official permission to build bamboo bungalows – actually tree-houses. Facilities are likely to be limited though, and you should take your own provisions. You can book ahead at travel agencies in Surabaya (Orient Express) or Bali (Bhayangkara Travel).

Getting There & Away You can get to Blambangan by bus from Banyuwangi to Benculuk; colt from Benculuk to Grajagan, and then by fishing boat across the Grajagan Bay (2½ hours) to Plengkung.

Meru Betiri Reserve

Covering 500 sq km, the Meru Betiri Reserve is on the south coast just south of the Jember district. The major attraction here is the protected Sukamade 'Turtle Beach', a three-km sand strip where five species of turtle come ashore to lay their eggs. In the mountain forests there are wild pigs, muncaks, squirrels, civets jungle cats and some leopards; the silvered-leaf monkey and long-tailed macaque are common. Meru Betiri is also known as the home of the almost extinct Javan tiger *(hariman macam jawa)* but you'd be very lucky to see one. An intensive study in 1978 revealed that there were between three and five tigers; in 1981 a 'fairly reliable' sighting was reported. The reserve contains pockets of rainforest and the area is unusually wet for much of the year. The best time to visit is the dry season, from April to October.

Places to Stay There are two possibilities at Sukamade village. The *Wisma Sukamade* has rooms at 7500 rp; accommodation is also available at the *Sukamade Baru Estate* (about 30 beds), a large plantation of coffee, rubber and coconut palms – it may be possible to hire a jeep and driver here. There is also a *PHPA Guesthouse* at Rajegwesin village, about two hours from Sukamade beach, which sleeps four to six people with food available by arrangement.

Getting There & Away Sukamade can be reached by bus from Genteng or Glenmore, both on the Jember to Banyuwangi road for 400 rp. From Genteng to Sukamade is 70 km (about three hours); From Glenmore to Sukamade is 100 km and the best access point if you're coming from the west. If you can't catch a bus in Genteng, take a bemo to Pesanggaran for 450 rp and try to hitch to Sukamade by truck.

Gunung Semeru

Part of the huge Bromo-Tengger massif, Gunung Semeru is the highest mountain in Java at 3680 metres. Also known as Mahameru, the Great Mountain, it has been looked on by Hindus since time immemorial as the most sacred mountain of all and father of Gunung Agung on Bali.

The trek to the peak commences from Rano Pani, a small village on a lake at 2200 metres, accessible by bus and colt from Malang via Tumpang, Gubug Klakah and Ngadas. It's also possible to cross the Tengger Sand Sea from Gunung Bromo (12 km) and then ascend to Rano Pani (another 12 km). From Rano Pani the path trails up through open grasslands and woods, across the 2800 metre pass of Gunung Ayek-Ayek, and drops steeply to the beautiful Rano Kumbolo crater lake (2400 metres). From Rano Pani to Kumbolo is about 10 km. To the top of Semeru and back it's a hard day's

climb and you need to be well equipped and prepared for camping overnight. At Rano Pani there is a small PHPA resthouse – free but no bedding or food provided. The best time to make the climb is May to October.

Gunung Arjuno-Lalijiwo Reserve

This reserve includes the dormant volcano Arjuno (3339 metres), the semi-active Gunung Welirang (3156 metres) and the Lalijiwo Plateau on the north slopes of Arjuno. From the hill resort of Tretes, 55 km south of Surabaya, there is a track used by people collecting sulphur which leads to the summit of Arjuno. It's a stiff four-hour climb from Tretes to the plateau and another two hours to the saddle between the mountains. To the summit and back would be a long day's climb. Arjuno has meadows and, on the higher slopes, forests where deer and wild pigs are common. There are hotels in Tretes (but they're expensive – see the Around Surabaya section). On the Laliliwijo Plateau, there's a shelter used by the sulphur gatherers but you would have to take camping gear and food – water is no problem.

Bali

For many Westerners, Bali doesn't extend beyond the tourist leaflet: idyllic tropical beaches, lush green forests and happy islanders who work and play in childlike innocence. This vision of paradise has been turned into a commodity for the tens of thousands of Western tourists who flood into Bali's tourist areas every year, and see little of Bali beyond their hotel.

For most Balinese, the tourist trade is a peripheral thing; away from the southern beaches you can still find Bali's soul, towards the mountains where it has always been. It is there you'll find dense tropical jungles, rice paddies tripping down hillsides like giant steps, and holy mountains reaching up through the clouds. And it's there you'll discover the extraordinary resilience of the Balinese people and their culture.

HISTORY

There is no trace of the Stone Age in Bali although it's certain that the island was already populated before the Bronze Age commenced there about 300 BC. Nor is much known of Bali during the period when Indian traders brought Hinduism to the Indonesian archipelago. The earliest records found in Bali, stone inscriptions, date from around the 9th century AD and by that time Bali had already developed many similarities to the island you find today. Rice was grown with the help of a complex irrigation system probably very like that employed now. The Balinese had also already begun to develop the cultural and artistic activities which have made the island so interesting to visitors right down to the present day.

Hindu Influence

Hindu Java began to spread its influence into Bali during the reign of King Airlangga from 1019 to 1042. At the age of 16, when his uncle lost the throne, Airlangga fled into the forests of western Java. He gradually gained support, won back the kingdom once ruled by his uncle and went on to become one of Java's greatest kings. Airlangga's mother had moved to Bali and remarried shortly after his birth, so when he gained the throne there was an immediate link between Java and Bali. At this time the courtly Javanese language known as Kawi came into use amongst the royalty of Bali, and the rock-cut memorials seen at Gunung Kawi near Tampaksiring are a clear architectural link between Bali and 11th-century Java.

After Airlangga's death Bali retained its semi-independent state until Kertanagara became king of the Singasari dynasty in Java two centuries later. Kertanagara conquered Bali in 1284 but his greatest power lasted only eight years until he was murdered and his kingdom collapsed. However, the great

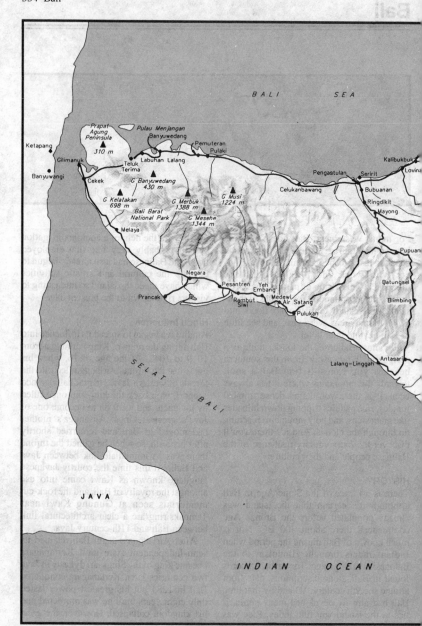

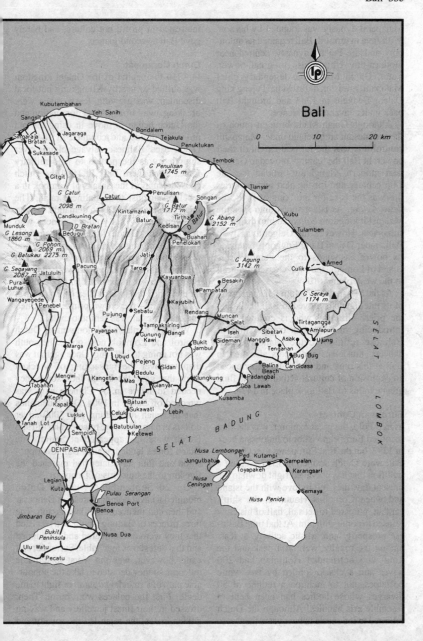

Bali

0   10   20 km

Majapahit dynasty was founded by his son. With Java in turmoil, Bali regained its autonomy and the Pejeng dynasty, centred near modern-day Ubud, rose to great power. Later, Gajah Mada, the legendary chief Majapahit minister, defeated the Pejeng king Dalem Bedaulu in 1343 and brought Bali back under Javanese influence.

Although Gajah Mada brought much of the Indonesian archipelago under Majapahit control this was the furthest extent of their power. In Bali the 'capital' moved to Gelgel, near modern Klungkung, around the late 14th century and for the next two centuries this was the base for the 'king of Bali', the *dewa Agung*. As Islam spread into Java the Majapahit kingdom collapsed into disputing sultanates. However, the Gelgel dynasty in Bali, under Dalem Batur Enggong, extended its power eastwards to the neighbouring island of Lombok and even crossed the strait to the western end of Java.

As the Majapahit kingdom fell apart many of its intelligentsia moved to Bali, including the priest Nirartha, who is credited with introducing many of the complexities of Balinese religion to the island. Artists, dancers, musicians and actors also fled to Bali at this time and the island experienced an explosion of cultural activities. The final great exodus to Bali took place in 1478.

European Contact

Marco Polo, the great explorer, was the first recorded European visitor to Indonesia back in 1292, but the first Europeans to set foot on Bali were Dutch seamen in 1597. Setting a tradition that has prevailed right down to the present day, they fell in love with the island and when Cornelius Houtman, the ship's captain, prepared to set sail, half of his crew refused to come with him. At that time Balinese prosperity and artistic activity, at least among the royalty, were at a peak and the king who befriended Houtman had 200 wives and a chariot pulled by two white buffaloes, not to mention a retinue of 50 dwarves whose bodies had been bent to resemble kris handles! Although the Dutch returned to Indonesia in later years they were interested in profit, not culture, and barely gave Bali a second glance.

Dutch Conquest

In 1710 the capital of the Gelgel kingdom was shifted to nearby Klungkung but local discontent was growing, lesser rulers were breaking away from Gelgel domination and the Dutch began to move in using the old policy of divide and conquer. In 1846 the Dutch used Balinese salvage claims over shipwrecks as the pretext to land military forces in northern Bali. In 1894 the Dutch chose to support the Sasaks of Lombok in a rebellion against their Balinese rajah. The rajah capitulated to Dutch demands, only to be overruled by his younger princes who defeated the Dutch forces in a surprise attack. Dutch anger was raised, a larger and more heavily armed force was despatched and the Balinese on Lombok were overrun. Balinese power in Lombok finally came to an end with the loss of their stronghold at Cakranegara – the crown prince was killed and the old rajah was sent into exile.

With the north of Bali long under Dutch control and Lombok now gone, the south was not going to last long. Once again it was disputes over the ransacking of wrecked ships that gave the Dutch the excuse they needed to move in. A Chinese ship was wrecked off Sanur in 1904, Dutch demands that the rajah of Badung pay 3000 silver dollars in damages were rejected and in 1906 Dutch warships appeared at Sanur. The Dutch forces landed against Balinese opposition and four days later had marched the five km to the outskirts of Denpasar.

On 20 September 1906 the Dutch mounted a naval bombardment on Denpasar and then commenced their final assault. The three princes of Badung (south Bali) realised that they were outnumbered and outgunned and that defeat was inevitable. Surrender and exile, however, was the worst imaginable outcome so they decided to take the honourable path of a suicidal *puputan* or fight to the death. First the palaces were burnt. Then, dressed in their finest jewellery and waving golden krises, the rajah led the royalty and priests out to face the modern weapons of the Dutch.

The Dutch begged the Balinese to surrender rather than make their hopeless stand but their pleas went unheard and wave after wave of the Balinese nobility marched forward to their death. In all, nearly 4000 Balinese died in defence of the two Denpasar palaces. Later, the Dutch marched east towards Tabanan, taking the rajah of Tabanan prisoner, but he committed suicide rather than face the disgrace of exile.

The kingdoms of Karangasem and Gianyar had already capitulated to the Dutch and were allowed to retain some of their powers, but other kingdoms were defeated and their rulers exiled. Finally, the rajah of Klungkung followed the lead of Badung and once more the Dutch faced a puputan. With this last obstacle disposed of, all of Bali was now under Dutch control and part of the Dutch East Indies. Fortunately, the Dutch government was not totally onerous and the common people noticed little difference between rule by the Dutch and rule by the rajahs. Some far-sighted Dutch officials encouraged Balinese artistic aspirations which, together with a new found international interest, sparked off an artistic revival. Dutch rule over Bali was short-lived, however, as Indonesia fell to the Japanese in WW II.

Independence

On 17 August 1945, just after the end of WW II, the Indonesian leader Sukarno proclaimed the nation's independence, but it took four years to convince the Dutch that they were not going to get their great colony back. In a virtual repeat of the puputan nearly half a century earlier, a Balinese resistance group was wiped out in the battle of Marga on 20 November 1946, and it was not until 1949 that the Dutch finally recognised Indonesia's independence. The Denpasar airport, Ngurah Rai, was named after the leader of the Balinese forces at Marga.

Bali has undergone three great convulsions in the years since independence. The huge eruption of Gunung Agung in 1963 killed thousands, devastated vast areas of the island and forced many Balinese to accept transmigration to other parts of Indonesia. Only two years later, in the wake of the attempted Communist coup, Bali became the scene of some of the bloodiest anti-Communist killings in Indonesia, perhaps inflamed by some mystical desire to purge the land of evil, but equally likely from motives of revenge. The killings were probably no more brutal than elsewhere in Indonesia, but they certainly conflicted with the stereotyped image of the gentle Balinese.

While the Balinese may have survived Dutch control, Japanese occupation, an anti-Communist bloodbath and intermittent lava flows, the question now is whether they'll survive the tourist boom which started in the 1970s. Although tourism has certainly brought economic benefits to Bali, it seems sometimes to threaten the survival of the remarkable culture which makes the island so interesting. But the offerings of food, flowers and incense which are reverently placed outside every home and business every morning, even in tourist ghettos like Kuta, testify to the amazing resilience of Balinese culture.

THE BALINESE

Something like 2½ million people are crammed onto this tiny island. The Balinese have their own clearly defined social strata resembling the Indian Hindu caste system, although there are no untouchables. Nor is there an intricate division of labour based on caste and, except for the Brahmana priesthood, a particular title does not entail an exclusive right to a given occupation.

They do, however, speak a language which reflects their caste; it's a tiered system where the choice of words is governed by the social relationship between the two people having a conversation. Low Balinese is used between intimates, between equals and when talking to inferiors. Middle Balinese is used when speaking about superiors, or when addressing superiors or strangers, mainly when one wishes to be very polite but doesn't want to emphasise caste differences. High

Balinese is used when talking to superiors. Although it sounds remarkably complex, the difference between each of the languages is only in the words used. High Balinese includes its own additional vocabulary of about 600 words, essentially connected with the person and bodily actions.

Balinese Society

Balinese society is an intensely communal one; the organisation of villages, the cultivation of farmlands and even the creative arts are communal efforts – a person belongs to their family, clan, caste and the village as a whole. Religion permeates all aspects of life so each stage of existence is marked by ceremonies and rituals. In fact the first ceremony of life takes place at the third month of pregnancy, when a series of offerings is made at home and at the village river or spring to ensure the wellbeing of the baby. When the child reaches puberty its teeth are filed to produce an aesthetically pleasing

straight line – crooked fangs are, after all, reminiscent of the ghastly grimaces of witches and demons. These days, the filing is more ceremonial than orthodontic.

Balinese women are not cloistered away and social life in Bali is relatively free and easy, although the roles of the sexes are fairly well delineated, with certain tasks handled by women and others reserved for men. For instance, the running of the household is very much the women's task, while artistic work is almost totally a male preserve.

Balinese society is held together by a sense of collective responsibility. The notion of spiritual uncleanliness (sebel) is one of the central pillars of Balinese religion; contact with death, menstruation, physical deformity, sexual intercourse, insanity and sexual perversion can all be sources of spiritual uncleanliness under certain circumstances. To enter a temple during menstruation, for instance, is a kind of irreverence, an insult to the gods, and their displeasure falls not just

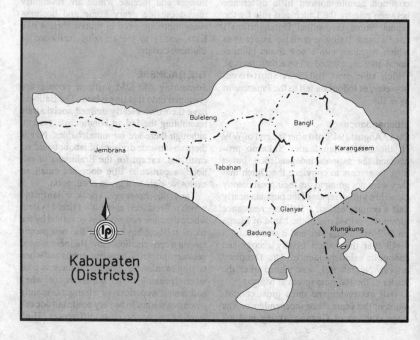

Kabupaten
(Districts)

on the transgressor, but on the community as a whole. This collective responsibility produces considerable pressure on the individual to conform to traditional values and customs.

Village Organisation

One of the important elements of village government is the *subak*. Each individual rice field is known as a *sawah* and each farmer who owns even one sawah must be a member of the local *subak*. The rice paddies must have a steady supply of water and it is the job of the subak to ensure that the water supply gets to everybody. It's said that the head of the local subak will often be the farmer whose rice paddies are at the bottom of the hill, for he will make quite certain that the water gets all the way down to his fields, passing through everybody else's on the way!

Each village is subdivided into *banjars*, which all adults join when they marry. It is the banjar which organises village festivals, marriage ceremonies and even cremations. Throughout the island you'll see the open-sided meeting places known as *bale banjars* – they're nearly as common a sight as temples. Gamelan orchestras are organised at the banjar level and a glance in a bale banjar at any time might reveal a gamelan practice, a meeting going on, food for a feast being prepared, even a group of men simply getting their roosters together to raise their anger in preparation for the next round of cockfights.

Households

Despite the strong communal nature of Balinese society, their traditional houses are designed to divide the family from the outside world. Traditional houses (many of which can be seen in Ubud) are surrounded by a high wall and the compound is usually entered through a gateway backed by a small wall known as the *aling aling*. It serves a practical and a spiritual purpose – both preventing passers-by from seeing in and stopping evil spirits from entering. Evil spirits cannot easily turn corners so the aling

aling stops them from scooting straight in through the gate. Inside there will be a family temple in one corner, a garden and a separate small building (bale) for each household function: cooking, sleeping, washing and the toilet.

ECONOMY

Bali's economy is basically agrarian. The vast majority of Balinese are peasants working in the fields. Coffee, copra and cattle are major agricultural exports, while most of the rice grown goes to feed the island's own teeming population. Unlike most island people, the Balinese are not great seafarers and actually shun the sea, believing it to be the abode of demons and evil spirits. This is reflected in the very small size of the Balinese fishing industry, although there are many fishing villages and fish provides a useful part of the Balinese diet. The people also keep domestic animals: cows are kept to plough the fields, pigs to clean up refuse and to be spit-roasted at feasts, chickens and ducks for food, cocks as fighting birds, monkeys to ward off evil spirits. Apart from the many mongrels you usually see in Bali, some dogs are kept as pets.

Rice, grown on wet paddies, is the staple food of the Balinese and at least two crops are grown per year. Because the rice terraces are often situated high above the rivers and streams, the water has to be tapped at a considerable distance upstream and conveyed to the fields through a system of dams, sluices, canals, tunnels and aqueducts.

The process of rice growing starts with the bare, dry and harvested fields. The remaining rice stalks are burnt off and the field is then liberally soaked, then repeatedly ploughed. Nowadays this may be done with a Japanese cultivator, but more often it will still be done with two bullocks or cows pulling a wooden plough. Once the field is reduced to the required muddy consistency, a small corner is walled off and the seedling rice is planted. The rice is grown to a reasonable size then dug up and replanted, shoot by shoot, in the larger field. Once this is done, the walls of the fields have to be kept in working order and the fields have to be weeded, but otherwise there is little work until the harvest. Planting the rice is strictly a male occupation, but everybody takes part in harvesting it.

GEOGRAPHY

Bali is a tiny, extremely fertile and dramatically mountainous island just 8° south of the equator. It is only 140 km by 80 km, with an area of 5620 sq km. Bali's central mountain chain, which runs east-west the whole length of the island, includes several peaks over 2000 metres and many active volcanoes, including the 'mother' mountain Gunung Agung (3142 metres). Bali's volcanic nature has contributed to its exceptional fertility and the high mountains provide the dependable rainfall which irrigates the island's complex and beautiful rice terraces.

South and north of the central range are Bali's fertile agricultural lands. The southern region is a wide, gently sloping area where most of Bali's abundant crops of rice are grown. The northern coastal strip is narrower, rising more rapidly into the foothills. Here the main export crops of coffee and copra are produced, along with some rice, vegetables and cattle. Bali also has arid areas; the lightly populated western mountain region, the eastern and north-eastern slopes of Gunung Agung, the Bukit Peninsula in the south and the island of Nusa Penida get little rain and have only limited agriculture. Selat Bali, between Bali and Java, is only 60 metres deep at its narrowest point while, to the east, Selat Lombok is one of the deepest stretches of water in the archipelago.

RELIGION

The Balinese are nominally Hindus but Balinese Hinduism is half a world away from that of India. When the Majapahits evacuated to Bali they took with them their religion and its rituals as well as their art, literature, music and culture. The Balinese already had strong religious beliefs and an active cultural life and the new influences were simply overlaid on existing practices – hence the peculiar Balinese interpretation of Hinduism.

The Balinese worship the same gods as the Hindus of India – the trinity of Brahma, Shiva and Vishnu – but they also have a supreme god, Sanghyang Widhi. Unlike the case in India, the trinity is always alluded to, never seen – a vacant shrine or empty throne tells all. Nor is Sanghyang Widi often worshipped, though villagers may pray to him when they have settled new land and are about about to build a new village; his image appears at the top of many temple shrines and on magic amulets. Other Hindu gods such as Ganesh, Shiva's elephant-headed son, may occasionally appear, but a great many purely Balinese gods, spirits and entities have far more everyday reality.

The Balinese believe that spirits are everywhere, an indication that animism is the basis of much of their religion. Good spirits dwell in the mountains and bring prosperity to the people, while giants and demons lurk beneath the sea and bad spirits haunt the woods and desolate beaches. The people live between these two opposites and their rituals strive to maintain this middle ground. Offerings are carefully put out every morning to pay homage to the good spirits and nonchalantly placed on the ground to placate the bad ones. You can't get away from religion in Bali – there are temples in every village, shrines in every field and offerings made at every corner. Although it enforces a high degree of conformity it is not a fatalistic religion – the bad spirits can be placated or driven out and if you follow the rules, you won't offend the gods and the good spirits.

Funerals

Religion in Bali has two overwhelming features – it's absolutely everywhere and it's good fun. Even a funeral is an amazing, colourful, noisy and exciting event – a stark contrast to the solemn ceremony practised in the West.

A Balinese funeral is a happy occasion, as it represents the destruction of the body and the release of the soul so that it can be united with the supreme god. The body is carried to the cremation ground in a high multi-tiered tower made of bamboo, paper, string, tinsel, silk, cloth, mirrors, flowers and anything else bright and colourful. Carried on the shoulders of a group of men, the tower represents the cosmos and the base, in the shape of a turtle entwined by two snakes, symbolises the foundation of the world. On the base is an open platform where the body is placed – in the space between heaven and earth. The size of the group carrying the body and the number of tiers on the tower varies according to the caste of the deceased.

On the way to the cremation ground the tower is shaken and run around in circles to disorientate the spirit of the deceased so that it cannot find its way home. A gamelan sprints along behind, providing a suitably exciting musical accompaniment and almost trampling the camera-toting tourists. At the cremation ground the body is transferred to a funeral sarcophagus and the whole lot – funeral tower, sarcophagus and body – goes up in flames. The eldest son does his duty by poking through the ashes to ensure there are no bits of body left unburnt. Finally, the colourful procession heads to the sea (or a nearby river if the sea is too far away) to scatter the ashes.

Temples

The number of temples in Bali is simply astonishing. They're everywhere, in fact, because every village has several and every home has at least a simple house-temple. There are actually more temples than homes. The word for temple in Bali is *pura*, which is a Sanskrit word literally meaning a space surrounded by a wall. Like a traditional Balinese home, a temple is walled in – so the shrines you see in rice fields or next to sacred old trees are not real temples.

You'll find simple shrines or thrones in all sorts of unusual places, often overlooking crossroads, intersections or even just dangerous curves in the road. They're there to protect passers-by or perhaps to give the gods a ringside view of the accidents. As in so much of Balinese religion the temples, although nominally Hindu, owe much to the pre-Majapahit era, with temples aligned towards the mountains *(kaja)*, the sea *(kelod)* or the sunrise *(kangin)*.

There are three basic temple types which

almost every village will have. The most important is the *pura puseh* or 'temple of origin' which is dedicated to the village founders and is located at the kaja end of the village. In the middle of the village is the *pura desa* for the spirits which protect the village community in its day-to-day life. At the kelod end of the village is the *pura dalem* or temple of the dead. The graveyard is also located here and the temple will often include representations of Durga, the terrible incarnation of Shiva's wife. The destructive powers of Shiva are also honoured here.

Apart from these three basic temple types, others include the temples dedicated to the spirits of irrigated agriculture. Families worship their ancestors in family temples, clans in clan temples and the whole village in the pura puseh. Certain special temples in Bali are of such importance that they are deemed to be owned by the whole island rather than by individual villages. These 'world sanctuaries' include Pura Besakih on the slopes of Gunung Agung.

Architecture Balinese temples usually consist of a series of courtyards entered from the sea side. In a large temple the outer gateway will generally be a *candi bentar*, modelled on the old Hindu temples of Java. These gateways resemble a tower cut in halves and moved apart, hence the name 'split gate'. The first courtyard is used for less important ceremonies, preparing food, holding meetings and will have a number of open-sided shelters. There will also be a *kulkul* (alarm drum) tower in this outer courtyard and perhaps a banyan or frangipani tree.

The innermost and holiest courtyard (small temples may have just two courts) is entered by another candi-like gateway. A passage through the middle of it symbolises the holy mountain through which you must pass to enter the inner court. This gateway will be flanked by statues of guardian figures or by small protective shrines.

In the inner court there will usually be two rows of shrines, the most important on the mountain side and the lesser on the sunrise side. These shrines vary in number and design from temple to temple, although there are detailed rules to cover all of them. In the major temples the shrines will include multi-roofed pagodas known as *meru*. The word comes from Mahameru, the Hindu holy mountain. The number of roofs are, apart from some rare exceptions, always odd and the holiest meru will have 11 roofs. The meru are roofed with long-lasting black sugar-palm. The inner court may also contain simple little thrones for local and less important gods to use.

Behaviour There are a couple of rules for visiting temples. Except on rare occasions anyone can enter, anytime; there's nothing like the attitude found in some temples in India where non-Hindus are firmly barred from entry. Nor do you have to go barefoot as in many Buddhist shrines, but you are expected to be politely dressed. You should always wear a temple scarf – a sash tied loosely around your waist. Many of the larger, more touristed temples rent them out for 50 or 100 rp. You can also buy one yourself for 500 rp or less. You'll soon recoup the cost if you visit a few temples and it's a nice thing to have when visiting temples where sashes are not available for rent.

Priests should be shown respect, particularly at festivals. They're the most important people and should, therefore, be on the highest plane. Don't put yourself higher than them by climbing up on a wall to take photographs. There will usually be a sign outside temple entrances asking you to be well dressed, to wear a temple scarf, be respectful and also requesting that women not enter the temple during their periods. Once upon a time the little lakeside temple at Bedugul had the quaintest 'no entry' sign in Bali, saying simply that 'It is forbidden to enter women during menstruation'.

Nearly every temple (or other site of interest to tourists) will levy an entry charge or ask for a donation from foreigners – any non-Balinese is a foreigner. Usually this is around 100 rp – occasionally less, occasionally more. If there is no fixed charge and a donation is requested, 100 rp is sufficient.

Ignore the donation book figures indicating that people have paid thousands – zeros are easy to add on afterwards.

Festivals For much of the year Balinese temples are deserted, empty spaces. But on holy days, the deities and ancestral spirits descend from heaven to visit their devotees and the temples come alive with days of frenetic activity and nights of drama and dance. Temple festivals come at least once a Balinese year of 210 days. Because most villages have at least three temples, you're assured of at least five or six annual festivals in every village. The full moon periods around the end of September to beginning of October or early to mid-April are often times of important festivals. One such festival is the Galungan, which takes place throughout the island. During this 10-day period all the gods, including the supreme deity, Sanghyang Widi, come down to earth for the festivities.

Temple festivals are as much a social occasion as a religious one. Cockfights (where two cocks fight with sharp barbs attached to their legs) are a regular part of temple ceremonies: a combination of excitement, sport and gambling. They also provide a blood sacrifice to dissuade evil spirits from interfering with the religious ceremonies that follow. While the men slaughter their prized pets, the women bring beautifully arranged offerings of foods, fruit and flowers artistically piled in huge pyramids, which they carry on their heads to the temple. Outside, warungs offer food for sale, stalls are set up to sell toys, trinkets and batik and there are sideshows with card games, gambling, buskers, mystic healers, music and dancing, while the gamelan orchestra plays on in the outer courtyard.

Inside, the *pemangkus* (temple priests) suggest to the gods that they should come down and enjoy the goings on. The small thrones in the temple shrines are symbolic seats for the gods to occupy during festivals, although sometimes small images called *pratimas* are placed in the thrones to represent them. At some festivals the images and thrones of the deities are taken out of the temple and ceremonially carried down to the sea (or to a suitable expanse of water) for a ceremonial bath. Inside the temple the proceedings take on a more formal, mystical tone as the pemangkus continue to chant their songs of praise before shrines clouded by smoking incense. The women dance the stately pendet, in itself an offering to the gods through the beauty of their motions.

During the course of these rituals it's quite common for people to fall into a trance – during this time they're believed to be possessed by a deity. The trance is taken as a religious experience, a form of communication with the gods and spirits, and certain men and women in every village – like the head pemangku – serve the deities as established trance mediums. Through such a medium a request is made to the gods, or advice is given. If a person goes into a trance and speaks during the ceremony it is taken as a good sign, a divine indication to the people that their prayers and offerings have been accepted. When the message is passed on to the priest the person in trance is woken with prayers and sprinklings of holy water.

As dawn approaches, the entertainment and ceremonies wind down and the women dance a final pendet, a farewell to the deities. The pemangkus politely suggest to the gods that it's time they made their way back to heaven, and the people make their own weary way back to their homes.

ARTS & CRAFTS

The Balinese have no words for 'art' and 'artist' because traditionally, art has never been regarded as something to be treasured for its own sake. Prior to the tourist invasion art was just something you did – you painted or carved as a part of everyday life and what you produced went into temples or palaces or was used for festivals. Although respected, the painter or carver was not considered a member of some special elite; there was no cult of the artist as there is in the West, the artists' work was not signed and there were no galleries or craft shops. 'Crafts' were produced for a specific purpose or function;

they were made today, deteriorated tomorrow, wore out the next day and were thrown away the day after.

It's a different story today, with hundreds, even thousands, of galleries and craft shops in every possible crevice a tourist might trip into. You can't turn around without falling over another technicolour garuda statue, and in the galleries there are so many paintings that the walls can't accommodate them all and they're stacked in piles on the floor. Although much of Balinese art is churned out quickly for people who want a cheap souvenir, buried beneath the reproductions of reproductions there's still quite a lot of beautiful work to be found – if you dig deep enough.

Of course not all works of art are ephemeral, or aimed at the tourist trade. An example is the sacred kris, a knife which is thought to contain great spiritual force and thus require great care in handling, use and even in making. The wayang kulit shadow puppet figures cut from buffalo hide are also magical items since the plays enact the eternal battle between good and evil. The Balinese weave a variety of complex fabrics for ceremonial and other important uses, including songket cloth (silk cloth with gold or silver threads woven into it). Even more impressive is the 'double ikat' cloth in which the pattern is dyed onto the lengthwise and crosswise threads before the threads are woven together – this cloth is produced only in Tenganan.

It's the everyday, disposable crafts which are probably most surprising in Bali. Even the simplest activities are carried out with care, precision and artistic flair. Just glance at those little offering trays thrown down on the ground for the demons every morning – each one a throwaway work of art. Look at the temple offerings, the artistically stacked pyramids of fruit or other beautifully decorated foods. Look for the *lamaks*, long woven palm-leaf strips used as decorations, the stylised female figures known as *cili*, and the intricately carved coconut-shell wall-hangings. At funerals you'll be amazed at the care and energy that goes into constructing huge funeral towers and exotic sarcophagi, all of which go up in flames.

Architecture & Sculpture

Of all the Balinese arts it's said that architecture and sculpture have been the least affected by Western influence and the tourist boom – nobody's taking temples home and your average stone statue doesn't roll up and stuff in your bag too easily. Architecture and sculpture are inextricably bound together – you don't just put up a temple gateway, you carve every square cm of it and put a diminishing series of demon faces above it as protection. Even then it's not finished without a couple of stone statues to act as guardians.

Like the other arts, sculpture and architecture have traditionally served the religious life of Bali. Balinese houses, though often attractive places, have never been lavished with the architectural attention that is given to temples and palaces, although some of the new tourist hotels (like the Nusa Dua Beach Hotel) are making use of traditional styles.

It's the temples that are the showcase of Balinese sculpture and architecture. They are designed to set rules and formulas, with sculpture serving as an adjunct, a finishing touch to these design guidelines. In small or less important temples, the sculpture may be limited or even non-existent, while in other temples – particularly some of the exuberantly detailed temples of north Bali – the sculpture may be almost overwhelming in its detail and intricacy.

Door guardians, of legendary figures like Arjuna or other protectors, flank the steps to the gateway. Similar figures are also often seen at both ends of bridges. Above the main entrance to a temple, a kala's monstrous face often peers out, sometimes a number of times – its hands reach out beside its head to catch any evil spirits foolish enough to try to sneak in. The ancient swastika symbol indicates good fortune and prosperity. Other carved panels may show scenes of sensuous love-making, and nowadays even bicycles, automobile breakdowns, beer parties or aeroplanes. The front of a pura dalem (temple of the dead) will often feature images of the rangda (witch) and sculptured panels may show the horrors that await evil-doers in the after-life.

Painting

The art form probably most influenced both by Western ideas and demand is painting. Prior to the arrival of a number of Western artists after WW I, painting was – like other Balinese art – primarily for temple and palace decoration. The influence of these artists not only expanded it beyond these limited horizons, it also introduced new subject matters and, perhaps most important of all, gave the artists new materials to work with. Until these new arrivals, Balinese painting was strictly limited to three basic kinds: *langse*, *iders-iders* and calendars. Langse are large rectangular hangings used as decoration or curtains in palaces or temples. Iders-iders are scroll paintings hung along the eaves of temples. The calendars were usually astrological, showing auspicious days of each month.

Most of the paintings were narratives with mythological themes, illustrating stories from Hindu epics and literature – rather like a cartoon strip with a series of panels each telling a segment of the story. These paintings were always executed in the wayang style, the flat two-dimensional style imitative of the wayang kulit shows, the figures invariably shown in three-quarters view. Even the colours artists could use were strictly limited to a set list of shades (red, blue, brown, yellow and a light ochre for flesh).

In these narratives the same characters appeared in several different scenes, each depicting an episode from the story. The individual scenes were usually bordered by mountains, flames or ornamental walls. The deities, princes and heroes were identified by their opulent clothing, jewellery, elaborate head-dresses and their graceful postures and gestures; and the devils and giants by their bulging eyes, canine teeth, bulbous noses and bulky bodies. Klungkung is still a centre for the traditional wayang style of painting

and the painted ceiling of the Hall of Justice in Klungkung is a fine example. Astrological calendars also remain a popular subject.

Under the influence of Walter Spies and Rudolf Bonnet, who settled in Bali in the 1930s, Balinese artists started painting single scenes instead of narrative tales, and using scenes from everyday life rather than romantic legends as their themes. More importantly, they started painting pictures purely as pictures – not as something to cover a space in a palace or temple. The idea of a painting being something you could do by itself (and for which there might be a market!) was wholly new.

In one way, however, the style remained unchanged – Balinese paintings are packed full; every spare millimetre is filled in. A Balinese forest is branches and leaves reaching out to fill every tiny space and inhabited by a whole zoo of creatures. Idyllic rural scenes or energetic festival scenes were the order of the day for many of the new artists. Others painted engagingly stylised animals and fish. You can see fine examples of these new styles at the Puri Lukisan museum and the Museum Neka in Ubud – and of course you can find them in all the galleries and art shops.

This new artistic enthusiasm was interrupted by WW II and by the political turmoil of the 1950s and 1960s. The new styles degenerated into stale copies of the few original spirits. In Ubud, however, another new style grew up – with particular encouragement from the Dutch painter Aries Smit. His 'young artists', as they were known (they weren't necessarily young), picked up where those of the 1930s had left off, painting Balinese rural scenes in brilliant technicolour.

Woodcarving

Like painting, woodcarving is no longer done simply for decoration or other symbolic purposes in temples and palaces, but is now created for its own sake. It was originally used for functional objects such as carved doors or columns, figures with a protective or symbolic nature like garudas or demons, or minor functional carvings like decorative bottle-stoppers. As with Balinese painting, it was the same demand from outside which inspired new subjects and styles and some of the same Western artists who provided the stimulus.

As with the new painting styles, Ubud was a centre for the revolution in woodcarving. Some carvers started producing highly stylised and elongated figures, leaving the wood in its natural state rather than painting it, as was the traditional practice. Others carved delightful animal figures, some totally realistic and others wonderful caricatures, while other artists carved whole tree trunks into ghostly, intertwined 'totem poles' or curiously exaggerated and distorted figures.

MUSIC, DANCE & DRAMA

Music, dance and drama are all closely related in Bali – in fact, drama and dance are synonymous. While some dances are more drama and less dance, and others more dance and less drama, they can basically all be lumped in together. Just like the painter or the sculptor, a dancer is almost always an ordinary person who dances in the evening or in their spare time. You learn dancing by doing it and long hours may be spent practising, usually by carefully following the movements of an expert.

There's little of the soaring leaps of Western ballet or the smooth flowing movements often found in Western dance. Balinese dance tends to be precise, jerky, shifting and jumpy. In fact, it's remarkably like the Balinese gamelan music which accompanies most dances, with its abrupt shifts of tempo, its dramatic changes between silence and crashing noise. There's also virtually no contact in Balinese dancing, with each dancer moving completely independently. To the expert, every movement of wrist, hand and fingers is important. Even facial expressions are carefully choreographed to convey the character of the dance.

There are dances where the story is as important as the dancing, like the Kechak. And dances like the Barong where the forces of magic, both good and evil, clash. Nor is Balinese dance a static activity. Old dances fade out and new dances or new developments of old dances still take place. The Oleg Tambulilingan, for example, was developed in the 1950s as a solo female dance, but later a male part was added and the dance now mimics the flirtations of two *tambulilingan* or bumblebees.

The Balinese like a blend of seriousness and slapstick and their dances show this. Basically, the dances are straightforward ripping yarns – like vaudeville shows where you cheer on the goodies and cringe back from the stage when the baddies appear. Some dances have a comic element, with clowns who counter-balance the staid, noble characters. The clowns often have to put across the story to the audience, since the noble characters may use the classical Javanese Kawi language while the clowns (usually servants of the noble characters) converse in everyday Balinese.

It's not hard to find dances – they're taking place all the time, all over the island and are usually open to anyone. Dances are a regular part of almost every temple festival and Bali has no shortage of these. There are also dances virtually every night at all the tourist centres; admission is usually costs from 1000 to 3000 rp for foreigners. Many of the shows put on for tourists offer a smorgasbord of Balinese dances with a little Topeng, a taste of Legong and some Baris to round it off. If you see one disappointing performance of a particular dance, look around for another venue, as the quality and the level of drama varies. Some of the more common dances are:

Kechak Probably the best known of the many Balinese dances, the Kechak is also unusual because it doesn't have a gamelan accompaniment. Instead, the background is provided by a chanting 'choir' of men who provide the 'chak-a-chak-a-chak' noise which distinguishes the dance. Originally this chanting group was known as the Kechak and they were part of a Sanghyang trance dance. Then in the 1930s the modern Kechak developed in Bona, a village near Gianyar, where the dance is still held regularly.

The Kechak tells the tale of the *Ramayana* (see the

Java chapter for a rundown of the story) and the quest of Prince Rama to rescue his wife Sita after she had been kidnapped by Rawana, the King of Lanka. Rama is accompanied to Lanka by Sugriwa, the king of the monkeys, with his monkey army. Throughout the Kechak dance the circle of men, all bare-chested and wearing checked cloth around their waists, provide a non-stop accompaniment, rising to a crescendo as they play the monkey army and fight it out with Rawana and his cronies. The chanting is accompanied by the movements of the 'monkey army' whose members sway back and forth, raise their hands in unison, flutter their fingers and lean left and right, all with an eerily exciting co-ordination.

Barong & Rangda

Like the Kechak, the Barong & Rangda or kris dance is a battle between good and evil. Barongs can take various forms but in this dance it takes the form of the Barong Keket, the most holy of the Barongs. The Barong Keket is a strange creature – half shaggy dog, half lion – and is played by two men in much the same way as a circus clown-horse. Its opponent is the rangda, or witch.

The barong personifies good and protects the village from the rangda, but is also a mischievious and fun-loving creature. It flounces into the temple court-yard, snaps its jaws at the gamelan, dances around and enjoys the acclaim of its supporters – a group of men with krises. Then the rangda makes her appearance, her long tongue lolling, her pendulous breasts wobbling, human entrails draped around her neck, fangs protruding from her mouth and sabre-like fingernails clawing the air.

Now the barong is no longer the clown, but the protector. The two duel with their magical powers and the barong's supporters draw their krises and rush in to attack the witch. The rangda puts them in a trance and the men try to stab themselves, but the barong also has great magical powers and casts a spell which stops the krises from harming the men. This is the most dramatic part of the dance – as the gamelan rings crazily the men rush back and forth, waving their krises around, all but foaming at the mouth, sometimes even rolling on the ground in a desperate attempt to stab themselves. Finally, the rangda retires defeated – good has won again. Good must always triumph over evil on Bali, and no matter how many times the spectators have seen the performance or how well they know the outcome, the battle itself remains all-important.

The end of the dance still leaves a large group of entranced Barong supporters to be brought back to the real world. This is usually done by sprinkling them with holy water, sanctified by dipping the Barong's beard in it. Performing the Barong and Rangda dance – with all that powerful magic – is an operation not to be taken lightly. Extensive ceremonies must be gone through to begin with, a temple priest must be on hand

to end the dancers' trance, and at the end a chicken has to be sacrificed to propitiate the evil spirits.

Legong

This is the most graceful of dances and, to sophisticated Balinese connoisseurs of dancing, the one of most interest. A Legong, as a Legong dancer is always known, is a girl, often as young as eight or nine years and rarely older than her early teens. Such importance is attached to the dance that even in old age a classic dancer will be remembered as a 'great Legong' even though her brief period of fame may have been 50 years ago.

There are various forms of the Legong but the Legong Kraton, or Legong of the palace, is the one most usually performed. Peliatan's famous dance troupe, which visitors to Ubud often get a chance to see, is particularly noted for its Legong. A performance involves just three dancers – the two Legongs and their 'attendant' known as the *condong*. The Legongs are identically dressed in tightly bound gold brocade. So tightly are they encased that it's something of a mystery how they manage to move with such agility and speed. Their faces are elaborately made up, their eyebrows plucked and repainted and their hair decorated with frangipanis.

It's a very stylised and symbolic dance – if you didn't know the story it would be impossible to tell what was going on. The dance relates how a king takes a maiden, Rangkesari, captive. When Rangkesari's brother comes to release her he begs the king to let

Legong dancer

her free rather than go to war. The king refuses and on his way to the battle meets a bird bringing ill omens. He ignores the bird and continues on to meet Rangkesari's brother, who kills him. The dance, however, only relates the lead-up to the battle and ends with the bird's appearance. When the king leaves the stage he is going to the battle that will end in his death.

The dance starts with the condong dancing an introduction. The condong departs as the Legongs come on. The Legongs dance solo, in close identical formation, and even in mirror image when they dance a nose-to-nose love scene. They relate the king's sad departure from his queen, Rangkesari's request that he release her and the king's departure for the battle. Finally, the condong reappears with tiny golden wings as the bird of ill fortune and the dance comes to an end.

Baris The warrior dance known as the Baris is a male equivalent of the Legong in which femininity and grace give way to the energetic, warlike martial spirit. The solo Baris dancer has to convey the thoughts and emotions of a warrior preparing for action and then meeting an enemy in battle. The dancer must show his changing moods not only through his dancing, but also through facial expression. Chivalry, pride, anger, prowess and, finally, regret, all have to be there. It's said that the Baris is one of the most complex of the Balinese dances, requiring a dancer of great energy, skill and ability.

Ramayana The *Ramayana* is a familiar tale in Bali but the dance is a relatively recent addition to the Balinese repertoire. It tells much the same story of Rama and Sita as told in the Kechak but without the monkey ensemble and with a normal gamelan orchestra accompaniment. It's also embellished with many improvisations and comic additions. Rawana may be played as a classic bad guy, the monkey god Hanuman can be a comic clown, and camera-wielding tourists amongst the spectators may come in for some imitative ribbing.

Kebyar This is a male solo dance like the Baris, but with greater emphasis on the performer's individual abilities. Development of the modern Kebyar is credited in large part to the famous pre-war dancer Mario. There are various forms of the dance including the seated Kebyar Duduk where the 'dance' is done from the seated position and movements of the hands, arms and torso plus, of course, facial expressions, are all important. In the Kebyar Trompong the dancer actually joins the gamelan and plays an instrument called the trompong while still dancing.

Janger Both Covarrubias and Powell, in their between-the-wars books on Bali, comment on this strange new, almost un-Balinese, dance which appeared in the 1920s and '30s. Today it is part of the standard repertoire and no longer looks so unusual. It has similarities to several other dances including the Sanghyang, where the relaxed chanting of the women is contrasted with the violent chak-a-chak-a-chak of the men. In the Janger dance, formations of 12 young women and 12 young men do a sitting dance where the gentle swaying and chanting of the women is contrasted with the violently choreographed movements and loud shouts of the men.

Topeng The word Topeng means 'pressed against the face', as with a mask. In this mask dance, the dancers have to imitate the character their mask indicates they are playing. The Topeng Tua, for example, is a classic solo dance where the mask is that of an old man and requires the performer to dance like a creaky old gentleman. In other dances there may be a small troupe who dance various characters and types. A full collection of Topeng masks may number 30 or 40.

Another mask dance is the Jauk, but this is strictly a solo performance. The dancer plays an evil demon, his mask an eerie face with bulging eyes, fixed smile and long, wavering fingernails. Mask dances require great expertise because the character's thoughts and meanings cannot be conveyed through the dancer's facial expressions, so the character of the unpleasant, frenetic, fast-moving demon has to be conveyed entirely through the dance.

Pendet This is an everyday dance of the temples, a small procedure gone through before making temple offerings which doesn't require arduous training and practice. You may often see the Pendet being danced by women bringing offerings to a temple for a festival, but it is also sometimes danced as an introduction and a closing for other dance performances.

Sanghyang Dances The Sanghyang trance dances originally developed as a means of driving out evil spirits from a village. The Sanghyang is a divine spirit which temporarily inhabits an entranced dancer.

The Sanghyang Dedari is performed by two girls who dance a dream-like version of the Legong. The dancers are said to be untrained in the intricate pattern of the dance and, furthermore, they dance in perfect harmony but with their eyes firmly shut. A female choir and a male Kechak choir provide a background chant but when the chant stops the dancers slump to the ground in a faint. Two women bring them round and at the finish a priest blesses them with holy water and brings them out of the trance. The modern Kechak dance developed from the Sanghyan.

In the Sanghyang Jaran a boy in a trance dances round and through a fire of coconut husks riding a coconut-palm hobby horse – it's labelled the 'fire dance' for the benefit of tourists. Once again the priest must be on hand to break the trance at the close of the dance.

The Gamelan

As in Sumatra and Java, Balinese music is based around the gamelan orchestra – for more details see the Java chapter. The whole gamelan orchestra is known as a gong – an old fashioned gong gede or a more modern gong kebyar. There are even more ancient forms of the gamelan such as the gong selunding, still occasionally played in Bali Aga villages like Tenganan.

Though the instruments used are much the same, Balinese gamelan, on the other hand, is very different from the form you'll hear in Java. The Yogyakarta style, for example, is the most reserved, formal and probably the gentlest and most 'refined' of gamelans. Balinese gamelan often sounds like everyone going for it full pelt. Perhaps a more telling point is that Javanese gamelan music is rarely heard except at special performances, whereas in Bali you seem to hear gamelans playing all the time everywhere you go.

BOOKS & BOOKSHOPS

There are a number of older books on Bali, but the most interesting is Island of Bali (Oxford Paperback) by Mexican artist Miguel Covarrubias. First published in 1937, it is still available as an Oxford in Asia paperback. Despite the tourist boom, much of Bali is still exactly as Covarrubias describes it. Although it's fairly expensive (25,000 to 30,000 rp in Bali) it's a good investment, as few people have come to grips with the island as well as Covarrubias.

Colin McPhee's A House in Bali is a lyrical account of a musician's lengthy stay in Bali to study gamelan music. The Last Paradise by Hickman Powell and A Tale from Bali by Vicki Baum also date from that heady period in the 1930s when so many Westerners 'discovered' Bali. All three are available as Oxford Paperbacks. K'Tut Tantri's Revolt in Paradise (available in an Indonesian paperback) again starts in the '30s but this Western woman who took a Balinese name remained in Indonesia through the war and during part of the subsequent struggle for independence from the Dutch.

Our Hotel in Bali by Louis G Koke (January Books) tells of the original Kuta Beach Hotel which was established by Americans Robert and Louis Koke during the '30s and run by them until WW II spread to the Pacific. Although the book was written during the war it was not published until 1987. From the same publisher comes New Zealander Hugh Mabbett's The Balinese, an interesting collection of anecdotes, observations and impressions, and In Praise of Kuta, a sympathetic account of that much maligned beach resort.

For a rundown on Balinese arts and culture look for the huge and expensive The Art & Culture of Bali by Urs Ramseyer (Oxford University Press). From the same publisher comes Dance & Drama In Bali by Beryl de Zoete and Walter Spies. Originally published back in 1938, this book draws from Walter Spies' deep appreciation and understanding of Bali's arts and culture. An economical and handy introduction to Balinese painting is Different Styles of Painting in Bali published by the Neka Gallery in Ubud – it covers the various schools of painting and also has short biographies of well known artists, including many of the foreign artists who have worked in Bali. Balinese Paintings by A A M Djelantik (Oxford University Press) is a concise and handy overview of the field.

The Krishna Bookshop on the Legian Rd in Kuta and the Family Bookshop on Jalan Tanjung Sari in Sanur have a wide selection of English-language books, particularly on Indonesia. You will also find small but interesting collections of books on Bali and Indonesia at the Bali Foto Centre in Kuta, Murni's Warung in Ubud and the Neka Gallery in Ubud. There are numerous second-hand bookshops around Kuta, Legian and Sanur which might have the odd interesting book on Bali.

GETTING THERE & AWAY

Bali has direct international flights from a number of countries, and frequent domestic flights to Java in the west, the island of Lombok in the east, and to many other parts of Indonesia. There are also regular ferries to/from Java and Lombok, which carry vehicles as well as passengers, and a hydrofoil service between Bali and Lombok.

Air

Bali's airport is referred to as Denpasar, although in fact it is a few km to the south, just beyond Kuta Beach. Officially the airport is named Ngurah Rai, after a hero of the struggle for independence from the Dutch.

The airport has a hotel-booking counter, although it covers only the more expensive places. There's also a tourist information counter with some useful brochures and helpful staff, a left-luggage room and a fairly quick and efficient moneychanging desk. If you come in on an uncrowded or obscure international flight, you're likely to find it all closed up!

On departure there's a duty-free shop and a row of souvenir shops at the airport – they only accept foreign currency. The departure lounge cafeteria takes rupiah, but it's much more expensive than the shop outside. You can change excess rupiah back into hard currency at the bank counter by the check-in desks. There's an 11,000-rp departure tax on international flights. Domestic flights have a departure tax of about 3500 rp, but it's usually included in your ticket price.

International The number of direct international flights to Bali has increased in recent years. Garuda and Qantas fly between Denpasar and Australia. Garuda and Air New Zealand have direct fights to/from Auckland. Garuda has an interesting route between Los Angeles and Denpasar via Honolulu and Biak. Other airlines now flying directly to Denpasar include Singapore Airlines and Thai International. See the introductory Getting There & Away chapter of this book for more details.

If you're flying out of Bali, reconfirm your bookings at least 72 hours before departure. Most travel agents in the main tourist areas can do this, but make sure you get the piece of computer printout that shows you are actually confirmed on the flight. There are Garuda offices in Denpasar, Kuta and Sanur, and most of the other airlines have offices in the Hotel Bali Beach in Sanur.

Domestic Garuda/Merpati and Bouraq have flights between Denpasar and other Indonesian airports. Merpati is now combined with Garuda, and there are offices in Kuta and Sanur and Denpasar. The Bouraq office is in Denpasar. There are direct flights on Garuda/Merpati to: Ambon (294,000 rp), Bandung, Biak (474,000 rp), Bima (125,000 rp), Dilli, Jakarta, Jayapura (579,000 rp), Kupang (201,000 rp), Mataram (42,000 rp), Maumere (181,000 rp), Ruteng, Semarang, Solo, Sumbawa Besar (82,000 rp), Surabaya, Timika, Ujung Pandang (140,000 rp), Waingapu (168,000 rp) and Yogyakarta. There are also same-day connections to Bajawa, Balikpapan, Bandarlampung, Ende, Kendari, Labuhanbajo, Palu, Rantepao and Waikabubak (Tambolaka).

Bus & Boat

You can get bus tickets from Java to Bali which include the short ferry trip across the Selat Bali, and sometimes a meal at a rest stop along the way. Generally you have to book a day in advance and air-con and non-air-con buses are available. Typical fares to Denpasar from Surabaya are 16,000 to 19,000 rp, from Yogyakarta 25,000 to 32,000 rp. You're assigned a seat number when booking so make your own choice from the seating chart. The night buses now make the Denpasar to Surabaya trip so quickly that an early evening departure is liable to arrive at an absurdly early, pre-dawn hour.

The usual route from Denpasar includes departing from Suci bus station, going west to Gilimanuk, then by ferry to Ketapang, then bus again to Surabaya or beyond. It's also possible to do it in stages – take a local bus to Gilimanuk, take the ferry across, then another bus on the Java side. The straight-through buses will drop you in Probolinggo if you want to climb Gunung Bromo. Denpasar is the usual arrival/departure point, but you can buy tickets from agents at Kuta Beach, and some of the more tourist-oriented bus services, such as Perama, will pick up from Kuta or even Sanur.

There's also a bus service between Java and Singaraja, on Bali's north coast; Singaraja to Surabaya costs from 16,000 rp.

Bus, Boat & Train

There are bus and ferry services connecting with trains at Banyuwangi in Java; tickets are available from the railways office in Denpasar or from agents in Kuta. Combined tickets include the bus to Gilimanuk, the ferry crossing to Java, another bus from Ketapang to the station in Banyuwangi and the train from there.

Boat

To/From Java A ferry shuttles back and forth across the narrow strait from Gilimanuk on the Bali side to Ketapang, the port for Banyuwangi on the Java side. The 15-minute ferry crossing costs 2000 rp per adult, about 1000 rp for a bicycle, 3000 rp for a motorbike and 25,000 rp for a car, depending on the size. Ketapang is several km from Banyuwangi but there are regular buses between the port and town and most bus services depart directly from the ferry terminal.

To/From Lombok There are at least two ferries a day between Padangbai (Bali) and Lembar (Lombok) and up to four services at busy times such as Ramadan. Scheduled departure times from Padangbai are 8 and 11 am, 2 and 5 pm, and from Lembar at 8 and 10 am, 2 and 5 pm. The schedules vary, so check first. *Ekonomi* costs around 4000 rp, 1st class 5700 rp. You can take a bicycle (600 rp), motorbike (4300 rp) or car (49,000 rp for a Suzuki Jimny).

For 1st-class passengers there's an air-conditioned cabin with aircraft-type seats, a snack bar and video entertainment. Ekonomi passengers sit on bench seats or wherever they can find a spot. It can be a long and uncomfortable trip in either class, and very hot outside the 1st-class cabin. Food and drinks are available on board or from the numerous hawkers who hang around the wharf until the ferry leaves. The trip takes at least four hours, sometimes up to seven; the afternoon ferries seem to be slower than the morning ones.

To/From Nusa Tengara Bali's main shipping harbour is Benoa Harbour, just south of Denpasar. There's a Pelni office (☎ 204387) at Jalan Pelabuhan, Benoa. The luxurious Pelni ship *Kelimutu* stops in Lembar on Lombok, not in Bali. See the Getting Around chapter for the complete timetable.

Hydrofoil

A hydrofoil service now operates between Bali's Benoa Port and Lembar Harbour on Lombok. Scheduled departure times from Benoa are 8.45 am and 3.30 pm, and from Lembar 10.45 am and 3.30 pm. The trip takes about two hours and costs 35,000 rp to Lombok, 32,000 rp the other way. The service is run by the Nawala company which has offices in Denpasar (☎ 2031339) at Jalan Iman Bonjol 234 and Mataram (☎ 2021655) at Jalan Langko 11A. Tickets can also be bought at Manu Madi Tours (☎ 2088901) in Sanur and at Benoa Port and Lembar Harbour. Perama also sell hydrofoil tickets with bus connections to/from Benoa and Lembar. Although not much cheaper than flying, the hydrofoil is a fun trip and is certainly much quicker, more comfortable and more convenient than the ferry.

GETTING AROUND

Bali is a small island with good roads and regular, inexpensive public transport. Once you've got out of the southern Bali traffic tangle, the roads are remarkably uncrowded. Traffic is heavy from Denpasar south to Kuta and Sanur, east about as far as Klungkung and west as far as Tabanan. Over the rest of the island it's no trouble at all and mostly it's very light. If you've got your own vehicle it's easy to find your way around – roads are well signposted and maps are readily available. Off the main routes, most roads are surfaced, but often very potholed.

To/From the Airport

The Ngurah Rai Airport is just south of Kuta Beach. Outside is a taxi counter where you pay for your taxi in advance. Fares from the airport are:

Kuta Beach (to Jalan Bakung Sari)	4500 rp
Kuta-Legian (to Jalan Padma)	6000 rp
Legian (beyond Jalan Padma)	9000 rp
Denpasar	9000 rp
Sanur	12,000 rp
Nusa Dua	12,000 rp
Oberoi Hotel (beyond Legian)	10,000 rp
Ubud	34,000 rp

You can, however, start walking towards the gate, in which case the taxi drivers will descend upon you independently and they can be negotiated down to slightly lower rates! The even more impecunious should keep walking all the way to the airport gate, a couple of hundred metres from the international terminal, where they'll find the bemo stop. The truly impecunious (and lightly laden) can walk straight up the road into Kuta, although it's a more pleasant stroll along the beach.

Bemo

Denpasar is the transport hub of Bali and has several bus/bemo stations for the various destinations – see the Denpasar section for details. Unfortunately, travel in southern Bali often requires you to travel via one or more of the Denpasar stations, and this can make for an inconvenient and time-consuming trip.

Bemos in Bali follow the usual rules applying to the rest of Indonesia, but beware of the *harga turis* or special tourist price, which is becoming far too prevalent. On many of the public transport routes the vehicle may be a bus or a minibus, but they operate the same way as the older, three-wheeled bemos.

You can charter a whole bemo for a trip,

which may be more convenient, and between a few people not much more expensive than the standard fare. You can also charter bemos by the day: the cost is similar to renting a car (from 35,000 to 45,000 rp per day) but includes a driver and petrol.

Beware of pickpockets on bemos – on common tourist routes like Denpasar to Kuta Beach they've become notorious. While someone engages you in a friendly conversation, an accomplice cleans you out, often using a painting, parcel or similar cover to hide the activity. Sometimes half the bemo will be in on the game, so the odds will really be stacked against you.

Tourist Bus

As well as the public buses and bemos, there are a growing number of shuttle bus services between various tourist centres such as Kuta, Sanur, Candidasa, Kintamani and Lovina – look for the advertisements outside tour and travel agencies. There are also connections to the ports of Gilimanuk, Padangbai and Benoa, and you can book through-tickets to destinations on Java, Lombok and Sumbawa. The Perama company seems to have the most comprehensive service, but there are others. They are more expensive than the bemos, but much quicker and more convenient.

Motorcycle

Motorcycles are a favourite way of getting around Bali but also a controversial one. Bali is no place to learn how to ride a motorcycle – every year a number of visitors go home in boxes.

Motorcycles for hire in Bali are almost all between 90 and 125 cc, with 100 cc the usual size. You really don't need anything bigger – the distances are short and the roads are rarely suitable for going very fast. Anyway, what's the hurry? Rental charges vary with the bike, the period of hire, and demand. The longer the hire period the lower the rate; the bigger or newer the bike the higher the rate. Typically you can expect to pay from around 8000 to 12,000 rp a day, but rates are always lower for longer periods.

Most bikes are rented out by individual owners, probably to raise money to help pay for the bike. There are a few places around Kuta which seem to specialise in bike hire, but generally it's just travel agents, restaurants, losmen or shops with a sign saying 'motorcycle for hire'. You can ask around but guys will often approach you along Jalan Legian near bemo corner. Kuta and Sanur are the main bike-hire places but you'll have no trouble finding a motorcycle to rent in Ubud, Candidasa or Lovina. Check the bike over before riding off – there are some poorly maintained, rotten old clunkers around.

There's a scattering of petrol stations around Bali but they often seem to be out of petrol, out of electricity or out on a holiday. In that case look for the little roadside fuel shops where you fill up with a plastic jug and a funnel. They often have a hand-painted sign saying 'Premium'.

Licences If you've got an international driving permit *endorsed for motorcycles* you've got no problems. If you haven't then you've got to get a local licence, which is easy but time-consuming. Your bike owner will take you to Denpasar, where you'll probably find 50 or so other bike renters lined up for their licence. You're fingerprinted, photographed, given a written test (to which you are told the answers in advance) and then comes the hard part. After a friendly send-off from the police examiner, who wishes you luck and dispenses the cheerful news that if you fail you can always try again, off you go. Ride once round a circle clockwise, once round anti-clockwise, do a slalom through a row of tin cans, don't put your feet down and don't fall off or bump into anything. Eventually everyone passes and is judged fit to be unleashed on Bali's roads. It costs 25,000 rp and the whole process takes about four hours.

Registration & Insurance Apart from your licence you must also carry the bike's registration paper with you – make sure the bike's owner gives it to you before you ride off. Insurance is a bit of a mystery in Bali – some

renters seem to insist on it, others don't. The agents obviously make money from the insurance too because it's usually quite expensive. Read the small print on your own travel insurance policy – you may find you're only covered if you have a proper motorcycle licence, not a Balinese one.

Car
You can also rent cars in Bali. They're usually small Suzuki jeeps or open VW safari vehicles, but these days you may find anything from regular cars to bemo-style minibuses. Typical costs are around 35,000 to 45,000 rp a day including insurance and unlimited km. It's substantially cheaper by the week. As with motorcycles, just look around for 'car for rent' signs. An alternative to hiring a car is to hire a bemo by the day.

Bicycle
In the main tourist areas it is quite easy to rent a pushbike by the hour or the day, and it's a good way to get around locally. A bike in reasonable condition costs about 3000 rp per day, but many of them are in less than reasonable condition. Rates by the week or longer are, of course, cheaper. Proper 10-speed bicycles are becoming more common in Bali, and there even some mountain bikes around.

Touring the whole island by bicycle has become quite popular in recent years. If you want to try it, it's probably best to bring your own bike with you; airlines will generally carry a bike as part of your 20 kg baggage allowance. Otherwise be prepared to spend some time looking for a good machine to rent, and/or some effort making it suitable for long-distance touring. Good brakes, seat, tyres and a lock are essential; bells, lights and luggage racks are desirable.

At first glance, Bali with its high mountains, narrow bumpy roads, tropical heat and frequent rain showers does not seem like a place for a bicycle tour. But with some short bemo trips to scale the central mountains you can accomplish a beautiful, 200-km circle trip of Bali, level or downhill almost the whole way. Although the roads are narrow, once you're out of the congested southern region traffic is relatively light. The bumpy roads are no great problem if you invest in a good, padded seat. Since a large part of the trip is level or downhill, the tropical heat problem literally turns into a breeze and the many roadside foodstalls make it remarkably easy to duck out of a passing shower.

Bicycles are used extensively by the Balinese and even the smallest village has some semblance of a bike shop. Some shops will allow you to borrow tools to work on your own bike. If you're not used to working on bicycles ask them to repair it for you. Labour charges are very low for tyre puncture repairs in particular. The best shops for extensive repairs are in Denpasar.

A 200-km Bicycle Tour This route is designed to take in the greatest number of points of interest with the minimum use of motorised transport and the maximum amount of level or downhill roads. For convenience the tour is divided into six days of actual riding in a clockwise direction, which takes advantage of evening stops where there are convenient losmen.

Day 1 – Kuta to Bedugul (53 km) The first 37 km is by bicycle, the rest by bemo. Estimated riding time seven hours. On a good bicycle the uphill section is quite manageable.

Day 2 – Bedugul to Singaraja (21 km) Estimated riding time three hours, downhill most of the way.

Day 3 – Singaraja to Penelokan (44 km) The 24 km up to Penulisan is a long hard slog, so don't try it unless you've got a good bike, you're very fit and you have lots of drinking water. The first 10 km and the final 10 km are fine.

Day 4 – Penelokan to Klungkung (31 km excluding Besakih) Estimated riding time four hours.

Day 5 – Klungkung to Denpasar (31 km) Estimated riding time six hours. This road has heavy traffic.

Day 6 – Denpasar to Kuta If you go via Sanur and Benoa this is a 24-km ride and estimated riding time is five hours. Again there are some stretches of heavy traffic on this run.

Tours

Tours can be a good way of seeing a lot of things in a short time. Numerous day and evening excursions operate out of Kuta –

look along Jalan Legian and Jalan Pantai Kuta near bemo corner for the travel agents who organise them. An excursion to Bona village to see the Kechak dance, the Sanghyang Dedari and the Sanghyang Jaran (Fire) dance is a pretty nifty way of spending an evening. Other tours vary in quality; some are nothing more than shop-crawls, carting you from one warehouse to another, so check the itinerary carefully!

Denpasar

The capital of Bali, with a population of around 250,000, Denpasar has been the focus of much of the growth and wealth in Bali over the last 15 or 20 years. It now has all the bustle, noise and confusion associated with the fast-growing cities of Asia. It also has an interesting museum, an arts centre and lots of shops. Denpasar means 'next to the market', and the main market (called Pasar Badung) is said to be the biggest and busiest in Bali. The city, sometimes referred to as Badung, is the capital of the Badung District which incorporates most of the tourist areas of southern Bali and the Bukit Peninsula.

Those who have visited Bali over a number of years will tell you that Denpasar was a pleasant, quiet little town 15 years ago. It still has the tree-lined streets and some pleasant gardens, but today the traffic, noise and pollution make it a difficult place to enjoy. Most tourists and travellers find it more comfortable and convenient to stay at Kuta, Legian or Sanur, and only venture into Denpasar for the few bits of bureaucratic business which cannot be done elsewhere. If you're one of those who feel that Bali is overcrowded with tourists, you'll find that tourists are vastly outnumbered in Denpasar – it mightn't be a tropical paradise, but it's as much a part of 'the real Bali' as the rice paddies and temples.

Orientation & Information

The main street of Denpasar, Jalan Gajah Mada becomes Jalan Surapati in the centre,

Jalan Hayam Wuruk in the east, and Jalan Sanur before turning south then east and heading towards Sanur. This name-changing is common for Denpasar streets, and is one source of confusion. Another problem is the proliferation of one-way traffic restrictions, sometimes for only part of a street's length, which often change and are rarely marked on maps. For example, sections of Gajah Mada and Surapati are one-way only, from west to east, but there's a short section near the Jalan Veteran intersection where they're two-way. Despite, or perhaps because of, these control measures, the traffic jams can still be intense. Parking can also be difficult, so avoid driving – take taxis or bemos, or walk.

In contrast to the rest of Denpasar, the Renon area, south-east of the town centre, is laid out on a grand scale, with wide streets, large car parks and big landscaped blocks of land. This is the area of government offices, many of which are impressive structures, built with lavish budgets in modern Balinese style. If you come here to collect mail or visit the immigration office you can have a look around. It's reminiscent of Canberra or Brasilia or the embassy district of New Delhi – a place to visit in a chauffeured limousine.

Tourist Office The Badung District Tourist Office is on Jalan Surapati 7, just past the roundabout and across the road from the Bali Museum. A useful calendar of festivals and events in Bali, and a pretty good map, are available. The office is open Monday to Thursday from 7 am to 2 pm, Friday from 7 to 11 am and Saturday from 7 am to 12.30 pm. The Bali government tourist office is in the Renon area, but doesn't provide information.

Money All the major Indonesian banks have their main Bali offices in Denpasar, principally along Jalan Gajah Mada. The Bank Ekspor-Impor Indonesia, which is a block to the south, is probably the best for transfers from overseas.

Post The main Denpasar post office, with a poste restante service, is in the Renon area.

It's a long way from the nearest bemo station, and a real nuisance if you have come into town only to pick up your mail. Avoid getting mail sent to you here – the offices in Kuta or Ubud are much more convenient.

Telecommunications Permuntel has an office at Jalan Teuku Umar 6, near the intersection with Diponegoro.

Foreign Consulates & Consular Agents

Australia
    Jalan Raya Sanur 146, Tanjung Bungkak, PO Box 243 Denpasar (☎ 35092, 35093)
Finland
    See Sweden
France
    PT Muria Manca Buana, Jalan Sekar Waru, Sanur 3 (☎ 88090, 88639)
Germany
    Jalan Pantai Karang 17, Batujimbar, Sanur, PO Box 100 Denpasar (☎ 88535)
Italy
    Jalan Padang Galak, Sanar, PO Box 158 Denpasar (☎ 88777, 88327)
Japan
    Jalan Mohamad Yamin 9, Renon, Denpasar (☎ 24203, 31308)
Netherlands
    Jalan Raya Imam Bonjol 599, Kuta (☎ 51094, 58371)
Sweden
    Segara Village Hotel, Jalan Segara, Sanur, PO Box 91 Denpasar (☎ 88407, 88022)
Switzerland
    Swiss Restaurant, Jalan Legian, Kuta (☎ 51735)
USA
    Consular agent only, Jalan Segara, Sanur

Immigration The immigration office or kantor imigrasi (☎ 2027828) is at Jalan Panjaitan 4, in the Renon area, just around the corner from the main post office. It's open Monday to Thursday from 7 am to 2 pm, Friday from 7 to 11 am and Saturday from 7 am to 12.30 pm. If you have to apply for changes to your visa, get there on a Sanglah-bound bemo and make sure you're neatly dressed.

National Parks Office The PHPA has an office south of Denpasar but doesn't have much information of value to tourists. (If you're planning to visit the Bali Barat

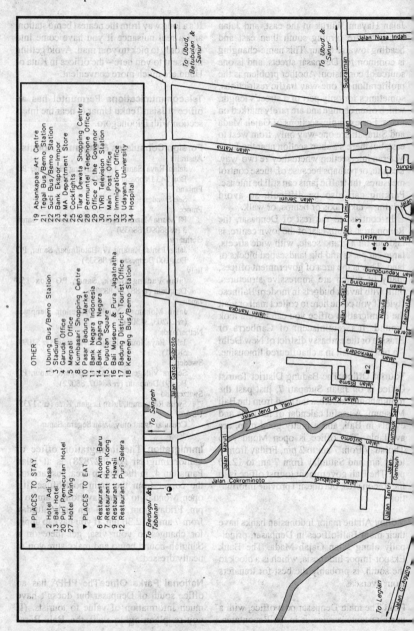

■ PLACES TO STAY

2 Hotel Adi Yasa
13 Bali Hotel
20 Puri Pemecutan Hotel
27 Hotel Viking

▼ PLACES TO EAT

6 Restaurant Atoom Baru
7 Restaurant Hong Kong
9 Restaurant Hawaii
12 Restaurant Puri Selera

OTHER

1 Ubung Bus/Bemo Station
3 Stadium
4 Garuda Office
5 Merpati Office
8 Kumbasari Shopping Centre
10 Pasar Badung Market
11 Bank Negara Indonesia
14 Bank Dagang Negara
15 Puputan Square
16 Bali Museum & Pura Jagatnatha
17 Badung District Tourist Office
18 Kereneng Bus/Bemo Station
19 Abiankapas Art Centre
21 Tegal Bus/Bemo Station
22 Suci Bus/Bemo Station
23 Bank Ekspor–Impor
24 MA Department Store
25 Cockfights
26 Tiara Dewata Shopping Centre
28 Permutel Telephone Office
29 Office of the Governor
30 TVRI Television Station
31 Main Post Office
32 Immigration Office
33 Udayana University
34 Hospital

To Ubud & Sanur
Jalan Nusa Indah
Jalan Supratman
To Ubud, Batubulan & Sanur
Jalan Katua
Jalan Gunupati
Jalan Senur
Jalan Patimura
Jalan Melati
Jalan Kenduing
Jalan Belimbing
Jalan Yudistira
Jalan Nakula
Jalan Rambutan
Jalan Nangka
Jalan Sumerta
Jalan Merkdara
Jalan Biswa
Jalan Kartini
Jalan Jend A Yani
Jalan Gatot Subroto
To Sangeh
Jalan Kumbuk Sahadewa
Jalan Sutomo
Jalan Maruti
Jalan Tantri
Jalan Gambuh
Jalan Satrhpud
Jalan Cokrominoto
To Bedugul & Tabanan
To Legian
Jalan G. Agung

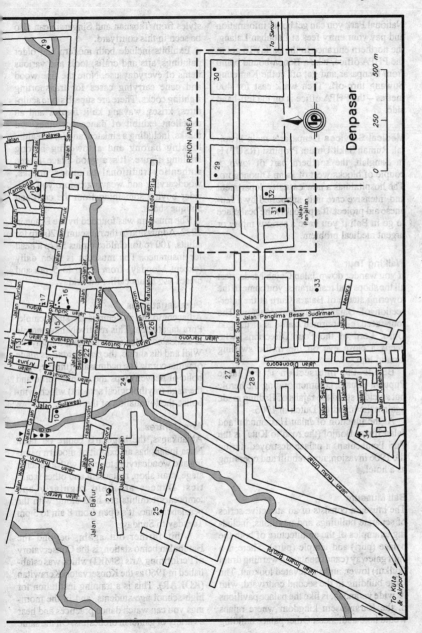

National Park you can get better information and pay your entry fees at Labuhan Lalang, the northern entrance to the park.) To get to the PHPA office, take a Benoa-bound bemo from Denpasar and get off at the Kampung Suwang turn-off. Then walk east for 400 metres – the PHPA office is on the left-hand side.

Medical Services Denpasar's main hospital, Rumah Sakit Umum Propinsi (RSUP) is in Sanglah, the southern part of town, a couple of blocks west of Jalan Diponegoro. The hospital has a new casualty department and intensive care unit, supported by a Japanese aid project. It's probably the best place to go in Bali if you have a serious injury or urgent medical problem.

Walking Tour

If you wander down Jalan Gajah Mada, past all the shops and restaurants, you come to the towering statue of Batara Guru at the intersection of Gajah Mada and Veteran. The four-faced, eight-armed statue is of the god Guru, Lord of the Four Directions, who keeps a close eye on the traffic swirling around him.

Beside the intersection is the large Puputan Square, commemorating the heroic but suicidal stand the rajahs of Badung made against the invading Dutch in 1906.

At the junction of Jalan Hasannudin and Jalan Imam Bonjol (the road to Kuta) is the Puri Pemecutan, a palace destroyed during the 1906 invasion, now rebuilt and operating as a hotel.

Bali Museum

The museum consists of an attractive series of separate buildings and pavilions, including examples of the architecture of both the palace (puri) and temple (pura). There is a split gateway (candi bentar), a warning drum (kulkul) tower, and an elevated lookout. The large building in the second courtyard, with its wide verandah, is like the palace pavilions of the Karangasem kingdom where rajahs would hold audiences. Other palace building styles from Tabanan and Singaraja can also be seen in this courtyard.

Exhibits include both modern and older paintings, arts and crafts, tools and various items of everyday use. Note the fine wood and cane carrying cases for transporting fighting cocks. There are superb stone sculptures, krises, wayang kulit figures and an excellent exhibit of dance costumes and masks, including a sinister rangda, a healthy looking barong and a towering barong landung figure. It's a good place to see authentic, traditional paintings, masks, woodcarving and weaving before you consider buying something from the craft and antique shops.

The museum was founded by the Dutch in 1932. Admission to the museum is 200 rp for adults, 100 rp for children, plus 50 rp a head for insurance. The museum is open daily (except Monday) from 8 am to 5 pm and closes 1½ hours earlier on Friday.

Pura Jagatnatha

Adjacent to the museum is the state temple, Pura Jagatnatha. This relatively new temple is dedicated to the supreme god, Sanghyang Widi and his shrine, the *padmasana*, is made of white coral. The padmasana (throne, symbolic of heaven) tops the cosmic turtle and the naga (mythological serpent) which symbolise the foundation of the world.

Arts Centres

Abiankapas, the large arts centre on Jalan Nusa Indah, has an exhibit of modern painting and woodcarving together with a dancing stage, craft shop, restaurant and other facilities. Dances are held regularly and temporary exhibits are held along with the permanent one. It's open from 8 am to 5 pm Tuesday to Sunday.

A bit further out again, beyond the Batubulan bemo station, is the Conservatory of Performing Arts (SMKI) which was established in 1960 as the Konservatori Kerawitan (KOKAR). This is a training institution for high-school age students, and in the mornings you can watch dance practices and hear a variety of gamelan orchestras. On the same site is Sekolah Tinggi Seni Indonesia (STSI), formerly called the Academy of Indonesian Dance (ASTI), which runs more advanced courses. Here you may also see dance practices. Both groups hold public performances at Abiankapas, particularly during the summer arts festival in June and July.

Places to Stay

Most people who stay in Denpasar are Indonesian visitors, principally on business. The noise, confusion and pollution is simply too much for most tourists. Once upon a time Denpasar was the *only* place to stay, and people made day trips to the beaches at Sanur or Kuta. Now Sanur and Kuta are far more comfortable environments, and people who want to visit more than just beaches in Bali head up to Ubud. There are plenty of places to stay in Denpasar, however, and you won't be bothered by a surfeit of tourists.

Places to Stay – bottom end *Adi Yasa* (☎ 2022679), at Jalan Nakula 11, was once one of the most popular travellers' hotels in Bali. The rooms are arranged around a garden, and it's a pleasant, well kept and friendly place, even if it's no longer a travellers' mecca. Rooms cost 8000 rp with shared mandi, 12,000 rp with private bathroom, breakfast included. There are several other cheap losmen around, but most travellers on a tight budget head for Kuta, a short bemo ride away.

Places to Stay – middle There are a number of mid-range places on or near Jalan Diponegoro, the main road on the south side of town. The *Hotel Viking* (☎ 2026460), at No 120, has economy rooms from 12,500 rp for singles and air-con rooms up to 50,000 rp. (Even quite small hotels catering for Indonesians often have a wide range of rooms, facilities and prices. If the first room you're offered is too expensive or too grotty, it's always worth asking for something else.)

Further south on the eastern side of Diponegoro is the *Hotel Rai*, a middling to expensive place catering mainly for business travellers. There are some similar places in the small streets behind the Rai, and these may be a bit quieter. Other hotels in the southern part of Diponegoro include the *Queen* and the *Oka*. The popular Hotel Denpasar at Diponegoro 103 has been demolished, but may rise again.

The *Puri Pemecutan Hotel* is in the rebuilt palace at the junction of Jalan Hasannudin and Jalan Imam Bonjol (the road to Kuta), near the Tegal bemo station. Singles/doubles in A-class rooms, with air-con, phone, TV and private bathroom, cost 40,000/50,000 rp; B-class rooms cost 25,000/30,000 rp; C-class rooms cost 12,500/15,000 rp, so you should be able to find something to suit your budget.

Places to Stay – top end There are no luxury hotels of Sanur standard in Denpasar, but the three-star *Bali Hotel* (☎ 2025681/5), at Jalan Veteran 3, is only a notch down from that level. It's a pleasantly old-fashioned place dating from the Dutch days. You wouldn't call it a masterpiece of colonial architecture, but there are some nice Art-Deco details (look at the light fittings in the dining room and the leadlight windows in the lobby) and the place has a sense of history. Singles/doubles start at about 84,000/94,000 rp including breakfast; rooms with air-con cost an extra 10,000 rp. A suite costs 141,000 rp. Some of the rooms are actually on the other side of Jalan Veteran, so you'll have to walk across the road to use the dining room, bar and swimming pool. If you want to sample the atmosphere without paying for a room, just come for the rijstaffel dinner.

Places to Eat

The eating places in Denpasar cater for local people and Indonesian visitors rather than for Western tourists. A number of restaurants along and near Jalan Gajah Mada are operated by and for the Chinese community, and many of them serve very good Chinese food.

The *Restaurant Atoom Baru*, at Gajah Mada 98, is a typical Asian (as opposed to Western) Chinese restaurant. It's big, spartan and has an interesting menu with lots of seafood, and dishes such as beef balls soup (1500 rp) and pig's bladder with mushrooms (5500 rp). Other main courses cost from 3000 to 7000 rp. Across the road is the *Restaurant Hong Kong*, with Chinese and Indonesian food and cafeteria-style self-service or a menu. It's a bit classier, with tablecloths and air-conditioning, and a bit pricier. The *Restaurant Hawaii*, around the corner in the Kumbasari shopping centre, has an oriental set menu for 5000 rp and a European set menu for 6500 rp. Further down Gajah Mada is the relatively expensive *Restaurant Puri Selera* which does excellent Chinese food.

At Jalan Kartini 34, just off Gajah Mada, the *Depot Mie Nusa Indah* is a reasonably priced and friendly Indonesian restaurant. There are also several Padang food restaurants along Gajah Mada.

You'll find excellent and cheap food at the market stalls by the Suci bus station and at the other markets, especially in the evenings. A number of rumah makans down Jalan Teuku Umar serve real Balinese food, as well as the standard Indonesian fare.

The *Bali Hotel* on Jalan Veteran is decorated in Dutch East Indies colonial style. You can get a rijstaffel in the old-fashioned dining room for 7000 rp and the service is friendly and efficient.

Entertainment

Dances in and around Denpasar are mainly for tourists – there are regular performances at the Abiankapas arts centre, and a Barong & Rangda dance every morning at the SMKI or STSI schools in nearby Batubulan. Wayang kulit performances can be seen a couple of times a week at the Puri Pemecutan. Cockfights used to be held regularly near the Tegal bemo station; officially they're banned, but in practice they probably continue as before.

There are a number of cinemas *(bioskop)* in Denpasar. US movies are popular, particularly 'action movies', along with kung fu titles from Hong Kong, the occasional Indian epic and some Indonesian productions.

Movies are usually in the original language, subtitled in Bahasa Indonesia. They are advertised in the papers, and also with garish posters on which your favourite actor may be unrecognisable.

For Western-style bars, discos and nightclubs you'll have to go to Kuta or Sanur. You'll find the younger, more affluent denizens of Denpasar congregating around the shopping centres in the evening, and later around their local bioskop. There are always students keen to practise their English, and you might meet some around the Udayana University campus near the southern end of Jalan Panglima Besar Sudirman.

Things to Buy

Denpasar has no particular crafts of its own, but there are numerous 'factories' around town churning out mass-produced handicrafts. There are also many shops selling crafts from Bali and from other Indonesian islands.

Countless craft shops line Jalan Gajah Mada, the main shopping street of Denpasar. The main market, the three-storeyed building of Pasar Badung, is a bit to the south, near the east bank of the river. Kumbasari is another market/shopping centre, on the opposite side of the river from Pasar Badung.

There are now two Western-style shopping centres in Denpasar – quite a recent innovation for Bali. The MA department store in Jalan Diponegoro, and the Tiara Dewata shopping centre on Jalan MJ Sutoyo are both very popular with affluent Balinese, and are good places to pick up clothing, fashion goods and toys.

At Tohpati, about six km north-east of town just beyond the Sanur to Batubulan road intersection, is the government handicraft and arts centre, Sanggraha Kriya Asta (☎ 2022942). This large shop has an excellent collection of most types of Balinese arts and crafts. Prices are fixed, and most of the items are of good quality so it's a good place to look around to get an idea of what's available, what sort of quality to expect and at what prices. The best of the work here is really superb, and worth a trip just to see.

Prices for these pieces can be well over 1,000,000 rp. Don't be too alarmed – that's about US$520, and not unreasonable for something that may have taken a trained and talented person several months to make. It's open Monday to Friday from 8.30 am to 5 pm, and on Saturday from 8.30 am to 4.30 pm; it's closed on Sunday. If you telephone they'll send a minibus to collect you from Denpasar, Kuta, Legian or Sanur.

Getting There & Away

Denpasar is the focus of road transport in Bali – here you'll find buses and minibuses bound for all corners of the island. There are also buses for Java, boat tickets, train tickets and the Garuda/Merpati and Bouraq airline offices.

See the Getting There & Away section at the beginning of this chapter for details of transport between Bali, Lombok, Java and the other Indonesian islands.

Air It's not necessary to come into Denpasar to arrange booking, ticketing or reconfirmation of flights. Most of the travel agencies in Kuta, Sanur, Ubud or other tourist areas can provide these services.

The Garuda office, at Jalan Melati 61, was closed for major renovations in 1991. Merpati (☎ 2035556/7), next door at Jalan Melati 57, may be able to help with Garuda arrangements as it's now a subsidiary of Garuda, though it would probably be better to find a Garuda agency in one of the tourist areas. Merpati's hours are Monday to Friday from 7 am to 4 pm, Saturday from 7 am to 1 pm and Sunday from 9 am to 1 pm. Merpati has flights to Lombok and the other islands of Nusa Tenggara.

Bouraq (☎ 2023564, 22252) at Jalan Kamboja 45D, has similar fares to Merpati and flies to Java and Nusa Tenggara.

Bus The usual route for land travel between Bali and Java is the Denpasar to Surabaya day or night bus. There are a number of bus companies doing this run, and they're found mainly around the Suci bus station or along Jalan Hasannudin. If you're staying in Kuta, however, there's no need to trek into Denpasar for tickets as there are numerous agencies at Kuta. Tickets through to Lombok are also available, combining bus and either the ferry from Padangbai or the hydrofoil from Benoa.

Bemo For travel within Bali, Denpasar has five stations for bemos and/or buses, so in many cases you'll have to transfer from one station to another if you're making a trip through Denpasar. Kereneng used to be the station for northern and eastern Bali, but it became so congested that bemos and buses for these destinations now operate from the new station at Batubulan, about six km north-east of town. If, for example, you were travelling from Kuta to Ubud you'd get a bemo from Kuta to the Tegal bemo station in Denpasar (400 rp), transfer to the Kereneng station (500 rp), transfer again to Batubulan (500 rp), then take a bemo from there to Ubud (500 rp). (You might be able to get directly from Tegal to Batubulan, but this doesn't seem to be a regular service yet.) Squadrons of three-wheeled mini-bemos shuttle back and forth between the various stations and also to various points in town, though they are progressively being replaced with more conventional, four-wheeled minibuses. The Jalan Thamrin end of Jalan Gajah Mada, for example, is a stop for the transfer bemos. You'll find transfer bemos lined up for various destinations at each of the stations.

Fares vary from around 300 to 500 rp between the stations. You can also charter bemos or little three-wheelers (cheaper of course) from the various stations. You could, for example, arrive from Surabaya at Ubung or Suci stations and charter a mini-bemo straight to Kuta rather than bothering with transferring to Tegal station and then taking a bemo to Kuta. Between a few people it might even be cheaper.

Further afield, fares vary with the type of bus you take. The smaller minibuses are more expensive than the larger old buses. The stations and some of their destinations and fares are:

Tegal South of the centre on the road to Kuta, this is the station for south Bali and the Bukit Peninsula.

Destination	Fare (rp)
Kuta	400
Legian	500
Airport	500
Nusa Dua	1000
Sanur (blue bemo)	500
Ulu Watu (before 10 am)	1500
Ubung	400
Suci station	300
Kereneng station	500
Batubulan station	500

Ubung North of the centre on the Gilimanuk road, this is the station for the north and west of Bali. To get to Tanah Lot take a bemo to Kediri, and another one from there. To get to the Lovina beaches, take a bemo to Singaraja, and another one from there.

Destination	Fare (rp)
Kediri	800
Mengwi	900
Negara	3000
Gilimanuk	3500
Bedugul	1700
Singaraja	2500
Tegal station	500
Kereneng station	500
Batubulan station	500

Ubung is also the main station for buses to Surabaya, Yogyakarta and other destinations in Java.

Destination	Fare (rp)
Surabaya	19,000
Yogyakarta	25,000
air-con	32,000
Jakarta	48,000

Kereneng East of the centre, off the Ubud road, this is now just an urban transfer station.

Destination	Fare (rp)
Tegal station	500
Ubung station	500
Suci station	500
Batubulan station	500

Batubulan This is the new station for the east and central area of Bali.

Destination	Fare (rp)
Ubud	700
Gianyar	700
Tampaksiring	900

Klungkung	1000
Bangli	1000
Padangbai	1500
Candidasa	1500
Amlapura	2500
Kintamani	1700
Tegal station	500

Suci South of the centre, this station is mainly just the bemo stop for Benoa (700 rp) but the offices of many of the Surabaya bus lines and shipping line agencies are also here. Benoa bemos also leave from the Sanglah market.

Train There are no railways in Bali but there is a railway office where you can get tickets to Surabaya or other centres in Java. This includes a bus ride to Gilimanuk and the ferry across to Banyuwangi in Java from where you take the train.

Boat The usual boat route out of Bali (not counting the short Bali to Java ferry which is included in bus-ticket prices) is the ferry from Padangbai to Lombok. Usually you get tickets for one of the daily ferries at Padangbai, but some agencies now sell inclusive bus-ferry-bus tickets through to destinations in Lombok. Tickets for the Benoa to Lombok hydrofoil are sold by agencies on a similar basis. Pelni and other shipping agencies are at the Suci bus station if you wish to inquire about boat transport further afield.

Getting Around

Three-wheeled mini-bemos shuttle back and forth between the various Denpasar bus stations and Jalan Gajah Mada. The set fares are around 500 rp. You can also charter these tiny bemos (they'll even buzz you out to Kuta Beach) or you can find taxis. Agree about all prices before getting on board because there are no meters.

Despite the traffic, dokars (horse-drawn carts) are still very popular around Denpasar; again, agree on prices before departing. Note that dokars are not permitted on Jalan Gajah Mada and may also be barred from some other streets with heavy vehicle traffic.

South Bali

The southern part of Bali, south of the capital Denpasar, is the tourist end of the island. The overwhelming mass of visitors to Bali is concentrated down here. All the higher-priced package tour hotels are found in this area and many visitors only get out on day trips. Some never leave it at all.

The Balinese have always looked towards the mountains and away from the sea – even their temples are aligned in the kaja direction (towards the mountains) and away from the inauspicious kelod direction (towards the sea). So Sanur and Kuta, being fishing villages, were not notable places prior to the arrival of mass tourism. Today they're Bali's major international resorts, but they're artificial enclaves, not really part of Bali at all. Of course the residents have made the most of their new-found opportunities, particularly in Kuta where an enormous number of small, locally run losmen and restaurants have sprung up, though many of the Balinese who work at Kuta and Sanur are from other parts of the island. The Indonesian government is determined that the rest of Bali

South Bali

should remain as unspoilt as possible, so all future large-scale development will be confined to this southern region, particularly the newer tourist enclave at Nusa Dua.

The southern region, and Singaraja in the north, have been most influenced by the world outside Bali. Even some of Bali's earliest legends relate to this area. The first European to make a mark in the south was Mads Lange, a Danish copra trader who set up at Kuta about 1830. Lange had some success in persuading local rajahs to unite against the Dutch encroachments from the north but he also made enemies and was later poisoned and buried at Kuta. The Dutch takeover of the south finally took place at Sanur in 1906. The Balinese fell back all the way from Sanur to Denpasar and there the three princes of the kingdom of Badung made a suicidal last stand, a puputan in which the old kingdoms of the south were wiped out. When the Japanese left Indonesia after WW II the Dutch again returned to Bali at Sanur.

Sanur was an early home for visiting Western artists and is still an artistic centre, famed for its gamelan orchestras. The courtly Arja opera and wayang kulit are also popular at Sanur, and a positive mania for flying gigantic kites has swept the region.

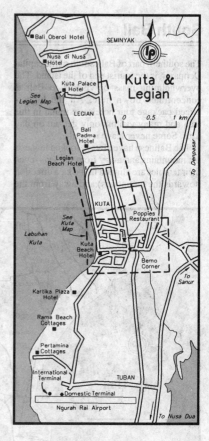

An unfortunate side effect of the building explosion in the south has been massive destruction of the coral reefs. Coral makes an excellent building material, both ground down to make lime and cut as whole building blocks. The blocks are very attractive and, since the coral grows a little after it has been removed from the water, it actually locks itself together. But as more and more coral is removed there will be fewer and fewer fish and the unprotected beaches can quickly disappear. Some prime offenders, where you can see whole stretches of coral reef literally turned into walls, include the Bali Hyatt at Sanur, the Bali Oberoi at Legian and Poppies Cottages at Kuta.

KUTA & LEGIAN
Kuta is the budget beach in Bali. It's only a couple of km from the airport and for many people it's their first and only taste of the island. Kuta may be good fun and quite a scene but Bali it most certainly is not. If you want to get any taste of the real Bali you have

to abandon the beaches and get up into the hills, where the tourist impact is not so great and where Bali's 'soul' has always been.

Still, most visitors will hit Kuta to start with so it might as well be enjoyed. Basically, Kuta Beach is a strip of pleasant palm-backed beach with some fine surf (and tricky undercurrents that take away a few swimmers every year) plus the most spectacular sunsets you could ask for.

Behind the beach, a network of narrow roads and alleys (known as gangs) runs back to the most amazing hodgepodge of big hotels, little hotels (losmen), restaurants, bars, food stalls (warungs) and shops. There are hundreds of different places to stay at Kuta and Legian and still more are being opened. Kuta is a totally self-contained scene and, with so many places to work your way through, it's hardly surprising that so many people get stuck there semi-permanently.

Although the original Kuta Beach Hotel was operating in the 1930s (its modern namesake opened in 1959) Kuta only really began to develop as a resort in the late '60s. At first, most people made day trips there from Denpasar but gradually more hotels opened and, in the early '70s, Kuta was an extremely pleasant place to stay, with its relaxed losmen, pretty gardens, friendly places to eat and delightfully laid-back atmosphere. Then travellers began to abandon Denpasar as the traffic there became intolerable and Kuta started to grow rapidly. Legian, the next beach village north, sprang up as an alternative to Kuta in the mid-70s. At first it was a totally separate development but Kuta sprawled north towards Legian and Legian spread back towards Kuta until today you can't tell where one ends and the other begins. Kuta and Legian are now just the names for different sections of one long, continuous beach.

Unhappily, all this rampant development, almost all of it unplanned, has taken its toll. Old hands who first visited Bali in the late '60s or early '70s will find Kuta a rather sad and seedy place. Fortunately, new arrivals, and even old hands who avoid making too many comparisons, may still find it just fine – for a short stay.

Orientation & Information

An important Kuta landmark is 'Bemo Corner', the intersection of Jalan Pantai Kuta (Kuta Beach Rd) and Jalan Legian (Legian Rd). Other important roads are Jalan Bakung Sari, running parallel to Jalan Pantai Kuta and, in Legian, Jalan Melasti and Jalan Padma. Smaller lanes or alleys, really too small for cars although they do squeeze down some of them, are known as gangs. The best known is Poppies Gang.

You can visit Bali and never have to leave Kuta. There are hotels, restaurants, travel agencies, banks, moneychangers, a post office, doctors, markets, motorbike and car rental places; in fact, you name it and Kuta has it.

Tourist Office The large building on the corner of Jalan Bakung Sari and the airport road has tourist information counters for Bali and several other regions in Indonesia. The Bali counter has some brochures and copies of a Bali tourist newspaper.

Money There are now several banks around Kuta but for most people the numerous moneychangers are faster, more efficient, open longer and offer equal rates of exchange. The only reason to use a bank is for some complicated money transfer or other bank-like activity.

A number of the moneychangers have safety deposit boxes where you can leave airline tickets or other valuables and not have to worry about them during your stay in Bali.

Post There's a post office near the cinema and night market, off the airport road. It's small, efficient and has a sort-it-yourself poste restante service. The post office is open Monday to Saturday from 8 am and closes at 11 am on Friday and at 2 pm on the other days of the week. There's also a postal agency on Jalan Legian, about half a km along from Bemo Corner. If you want mail sent there have it addressed to 'Kuta Postal Agent, Jalan Legian, Kuta'. These Kuta post offices and the one in Ubud are much more convenient than the main Denpasar post office. The tourist office on the corner of the airport road and Jalan Bakung Sari also has a small post office counter, which is open longer than the main post office and is more convenient.

Telephone There are wartels (private telephone offices) on Jalan Legian and on Jalan Bakung Sari in Kuta (see map). You cannot yet dial international calls yourself nor are there the card phones which are becoming increasingly common in Indonesia. You can,

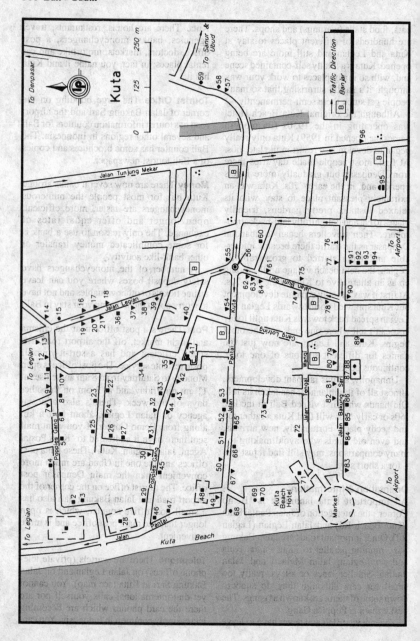

■ PLACES TO STAY

1	Sahid Bali Seaside Hotel
2	Puri Beach Inn
3	Indah Beach Hotel
4	The Bounty Hotel
5	Poppies Cottages II
6	Palm Garden Homestay
8	Barong Cottages
11	Taman Sari Cottages
22	Puri Ayodia Inn
23	Sari Bali Bungalows
24	Suji Bungalows
25	Sorga Cottages
26	Mimpi Bungalows
27	Berlian Inn
28	Kuta Seaview Cottages
29	Kuta Puri Bungalows
33	Mutiara Bungalows
34	Kempu Taman Ayu
36	Viking Beach Inn
41	Poppies Cottages I
43	La Walon Bungalows
45	Cempeka
46	Sari Yasa Samudra Bungalows
47	Aneka Beach Bungalows
48	Yasa Samudra Bungalows
51	Kodja Beach Inn
52	Bali Summer Hotel
53	Budi Beach Inn
60	Anom Dewi Youth Hostel
65	Suci Bungalows
66	Yulia Beach Inn
70	Kuta Beach Hotel
71	Kuta Cottages
72	Asana Santhi (Willy) Homestay
73	Ida Beach Inn
84	Ramayana Seaside Cottages
85	Kuta Beach Club
86	Agung Beach Bungalows
89	Flora Beach Hotel
92	Bamboo Inn
93	Zet Inn
94	Jesen's Inn II

▼ PLACES TO EAT

7	Bali Corner Restaurant
9	Twice Pub Restaurant
10	Tubes Bar
12	Batu Bulong Restaurant
13	SC (Sari Club)
14	George & Dragon

16	Burger King
17	Peanuts Disco, Koala Blu Pub & Other Bars
18	Indah Sari Seafood
19	SC Restaurant
20	Twice Bar
21	Mini Restaurant
30	Tree House Restaurant
31	Warung Transformer
32	Nusa Indah Bar
35	TJs
37	Prawita Garden Restaurant
38	Aleang's
40	Poppies
42	Fat Yogi's Restaurant
44	Kempu Cafe
49	Made's Juice Shop
50	Melasti Restaurant
54	Made's Warung
55	Quick Snack Bar
57	Kentucky Fried Chicken
61	Casablanca Bar
62	Dayu II
63	Wayan's Tavern
64	Bali Indah
67	Green House Restaurant
74	Bagus Pub
75	Serrina Japanese Restaurant
77	Gantino Baru Padang Restaurant
78	The Pub
79	Bali Blessing Restaurant
80	Bali Bagus Restaurant
81	Nagasari Restaurant
82	Dayu I
83	Rama Bridge Restaurant
90	Gemini Chinese Restaurant
91	Kuta Plaza Restaurant
96	Night Market

OTHER

15	Kuta Postal Agency
39	Perama
56	Bemo Corner
58	Supermarket
59	Petrol Station
68	Kuta Lifesaving Club
69	Garuda Office
76	Tourist Information Office
87	Supermarket
88	Wartel Telephone Office
95	Post Office

however, make international calls quite quickly if you pay in cash. Reverse-charge calls are much more time-consuming. A Home Country Direct phone where one button gets you through to your home country operator can be found outside the airport's international terminal. There are card phones in several locations including the domestic departure lounge. There's also a Permuntel phone office across the car park from the terminals.

Bookshops If you develop a real interest in Kuta read Hugh Mabbett's *In Praise of Kuta* (January Books, Wellington, New Zealand, 1987). It's widely available in Bali and recounts Kuta's early history and its frenetic modern development. There are fascinating accounts of Kuta's local entrepreneurs, the development of surfing and what happens to visitors who get caught with drugs.

Kuta and Legian have lots of little bookshops selling new and second-hand books. The best place to look for English-language books (new ones) is the Krishna Bookshop on Jalan Legian.

Dangers & Annoyances If you have something stolen in Kuta you can almost certainly put it down to your own carelessness. Theft, though increasing, is still not an enormous problem and when visitors do lose things it is usually from unlocked hotel rooms or from the beach. Always lock your room, even at night. Valuable items should be checked with reception or, if not needed, left in a security box. Going into the water and leaving valuables unwatched on the beach is simply asking for trouble.

Some years ago Kuta had a number of muggings but the problem was handled with quite amazing efficiency and in a very traditional fashion. The local banjars organised vigilante patrols and anybody they came across who wasn't a tourist or a local Balinese had to have a damn good reason for being there. Thefts in the dark gangs stopped dead and there has been no repeat performance.

The efficient Kuta Lifesaving Club is modelled on the Australian system and guards patrol areas at Kuta and Legian. The surf at Kuta can be tricky and there are drownings every year, many of them visitors from other Asian countries who are not good swimmers. In 1980, before the lifesaving club began, there were 18 deaths; since then, the number has varied from five to 13 a year.

Kuta Beach is much more likely to cost you money than your life, however. The whole beach is now fenced off and admission is charged. Also, there are usually more sellers on the beach than swimmers – you're constantly pressed to buy anything from a cold drink to a massage or a hair-beading job. What can cost you a whole lot more money is to leave things on the sand while you're in the water. Believe it or not, this is how a lot of people lose their passports each year!

Places to Stay
Kuta and Legian have hundreds of places to stay, and more are still being built. Apart from central Kuta and around Jalan Padma and Jalan Melasti in Legian, the area is, surprisingly, far from crowded. Even in the central area you only have to walk a couple of steps back from the main street to find palm trees and open fields.

Kuta has numerous mid-range and top-end hotels, many of them catering to international package-tour visitors, but there are also a great many cheap and attractive places to stay. Standards have risen over the years and although you can still find a few of the old rock-bottom places, even cheaper losmen have bathrooms these days.

Beware of throwaway words like 'beach', 'seaview', 'cottage' and 'inn' when it comes to Kuta hotel names. Places with 'beach' in their name may not be anywhere near the beach, and a featureless three-storeyed hotel block may rejoice in the name 'cottage'. The honourable line about building nothing taller than a palm tree also seems to be going out the window, unless there are plans to grow some awfully tall palm trees. Note that any hotel north of Jalan Pantai Kuta in Kuta and south of Jalan Melasti in Legian is separated from the beach by the coast road, even if the hotel is described as being on the beach front.

Places to Stay – bottom end Once upon a time even the cheapest Kuta losmen was an attractive and relaxed place built around a lush and well-kept garden. Today many places have obviously been thrown together as quickly and cheaply as possible to try and turn over maximum rupiah with minimum effort.

What to look for in a losmen? You can start with that well-known advice from real estate agents – location, location, location. Many places are close to busy roads where the traffic noise and exhaust fumes can make you think you're in the centre of some busy Western city. There are also places so isolated that getting to a restaurant is a major trek. Where do you want to be – close to the action or away in the peace and quiet? It's often possible to find a good combination of both factors – a place far enough off the main roads to be quiet but close enough so that getting to the shops and restaurants is no problem.

Then look at what the rooms are like and how pleasant and generally well kept the losmen is. For those interested in experiencing Balinese culture, look for a losmen which is fairly small and as much like a traditional Balinese home as possible. That is, enclosed by an outer wall and built around a central courtyard and garden. The courtyard should be an attractive and peaceful place to sit around and read or talk. It should also be clean and well kept. Many cheaper losmen still offer breakfast, even if it's only a couple of bananas and a cup of tea. It's a pleasant little extra that disappears as you move up the price scale.

With so many places to choose from it's quite easy to wander from place to place until you find one that suits. If it's late, you're not in a wandering mood or you've hit one of those rare occasions when everything seems to be full, you can be certain someone will ask 'Do you want a room?' – you'll have no trouble finding a place. The main secret to losmen hunting is to remember that there are lots more of them – if you don't like your first choice it's very easy to move somewhere else.

You can still find basic losmen for around 10,000 rp a double although Kuta is not as good value as other parts of Bali. The bottom end extends up to about 30,000 rp; above that is middle range. As you move up the price scale you get private bathrooms, Western-style toilets, better furnishings and a generally less spartan atmosphere. The prices are likely to be higher closer to central Kuta than they would be further out.

Because these places are so similar in what they offer, specific recommendations are almost unnecessary. The 17 places that follow offer a wide variety of standards at an equally wide variety of locations, from the centre of busy Kuta to the outer reaches of Legian. The location key number on the Kuta or Legian map is indicated after the name:

Anom Dewi Youth Hostel (Kuta No 60) Right in the thick of things in central Kuta, this YHA associated losmen offers standard rooms at 10,000 and 12,000 rp.

Baleka Beach Inn (Legian No 12) At the northern end of Legian this place has rooms for 12,000 to 25,000 rp and a swimming pool.

Bamboo Inn (Kuta No 92) This traditional little losmen in central Kuta is some distance from the beach but close to the restaurants and bars. Good rooms cost 10,000 to 15,000 rp including breakfast.

Berlian Inn (Kuta No 27) A good central location just off Poppies Gang and rooms at 15,000 to 25,000 rp make this place good value.

Budi Beach Inn (Kuta No 53) This old-style losmen is in a busy location on Jalan Pantai Kuta and has rooms for 10,000 to 20,000 rp for singles and for 12,000 to 25,000 rp for doubles.

Jesen's Inn II (Kuta No 94; ☎ 2052647) This inn, a pleasant little two-storeyed block with a garden, is close to the centre of Kuta yet in a reasonably quiet location. It's some distance from the beach but good value at 10,000 to 15,000 rp.

Kempu Taman Ayu (Kuta No 34) Just around the corner from TJ's and Poppies, this long-running and friendly little place has fairly standard rooms at 9000 to 12,000 rp.

La Walon Bungalows (Kuta No 43) On Poppies Gang, handy for the beach and the Kuta 'scene', La Walon has pleasant little rooms with verandah and open-air bathrooms. It's good value at 20,000 rp for a double including breakfast.

Legian Beach Bungalows (Legian No 34) Right in the centre of Legian on busy Jalan Padma, these bungalows cost 19,600 to 29,500 rp for singles and 23,500 to 35,000 rp for doubles.

Palm Garden Homestay (Kuta No 6) This is a neat and clean place in a quiet location and the rooms are good value at 15,000 to 20,000 rp.

Puri Ayodia Inn (Kuta No 22) This small and very standard losmen is in a quiet but convenient location and has rooms for just 10,000 rp.

Sari Yasai Beach Inn (Legian No 7) On Jalan Purana Bagus Taruna, at the northern end of Legian, this small losmen has rooms at 12,000 rp.

Sinar Beach Cottages (Legian No 16) Towards the northern end of Legian, this pleasant little place has a garden and singles/doubles at 15,000/17,000 rp.

Sinar Indah (Legian No 22) Also at the midpoint between Jalan Padma in central Legian and Jalan Purana Bagus Taruna at the northern end of Legian, this standard-style losmen has rooms at 8000 to 20,000 rp plus bigger rooms with kitchen facilities.

Sorga Cottages (Kuta No 25) There's a pool, the location is quiet and rooms cost 12,500 to 21,000 rp with fan, or 21,000 to 31,500 rp with air-con.

Three Sisters (Legian No 37) One of Legian's original losmen still offers straightforward rooms at low prices and a very central location. Rooms cost 12,000 rp.

Yulia Beach Inn (Kuta No 66) This standard small hotel on Kuta Beach Rd has been going for years. Rooms cost 19,500 to 43,000 rp for singles, 23,500 to 49,000 rp for doubles.

Places to Stay – middle There are a great many mid-range hotels, which at Kuta means something like 29,000 to 117,500 rp. A tax and service charge (15½%) is usually added as well. Most of these places cater to visitors on one or two-week package tours and many of them are utterly featureless and dull. They seem to have a checklist of amenities which must be supplied and so long as these 'essentials' (like air-conditioning and a swimming pool) are in place, nothing else matters. Balinese style is unlikely to make an appearance, and monotonous rectangular blocks or places with the maximum number of rooms crammed into the minimum space are all too familiar.

As usual, there are exceptions. The following list includes 12 mid-range places, all with swimming pools unless otherwise noted, which are either good value or offer some style:

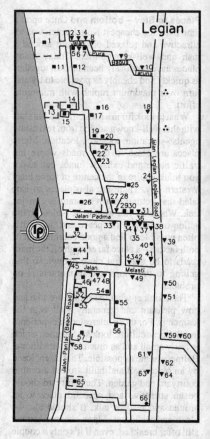

Asana Santhi (Willy) Homestay (Kuta No 72) Right in the heart of Kuta and not far from the beach, this attractive small hotel is surprisingly relaxed for its central location. The well-kept rooms have interesting furnishings and art and there's a good central swimming pool. Air-con rooms cost 60,000 to 88,000 rp.

Bali Niksoma Inn (Legian No 13) Right on the beach near the northern end of Legian this smaller hotel has two-storeyed units in relatively spacious grounds with rooms at 39,000 to 117,500 rp.

Bali Sari Homestay (Legian No 23) On the northern side of Legian this smaller hotel is a short walk from the beach and has attractively designed rooms, some with a touch of eccentricity. Rooms cost 78,000/88,000 rp for singles/doubles.

■ PLACES TO STAY

1 Kuta Palace Hotel
5 Orchid Garden Cottages
7 Sari Yasai Beach Inn
11 Mabisa Beach Inn
12 Baleka Beach Inn
13 Bali Niksoma Inn
14 Bali Coconut Hotel
15 Maharta Beach Inn
16 Sinar Beach Cottages
17 Adika Sari Bungalows
19 Bhvana Beach Cottages
20 Abdi Beach Inn
21 Surya Dewata Beach Cottages
22 Sinar Indah
23 Bali Sari Homestay
25 Sri Ratu Cottages
26 Bali Padma Hotel
27 Garden View Cottages
29 Legian Village Hotel
30 Puspasari Hotel
32 Bali Mandira Cottages
34 Legian Beach Bungalows
37 Three Sisters
44 Legian Beach Hotel
46 Bali Intan Cottages
52 Kul Kul Hotel
53 Bruna Beach Inn
54 Camplung Mas
55 Legian Mas Beach Inn
56 Sayang Beach Lodging
57 Kuta Jaya Cottage
65 Bali Anggrek Hotel

▼ PLACES TO EAT

2 Topi Koki Restaurant

3 Swiss Restaurant
4 Arak Bar
6 Sawasdee Thai Restaurant
8 Rum Jungle Road
9 Bamboo Palace Restaurant
10 Benny's Cafe
18 Restaurant Glory
24 Warung Kopi
28 Legian Snacks
31 Restaurant Happy
33 Padma Club Restaurant
35 Rama Garden Restaurant
36 Norman Garden Restaurant
38 MS Restaurant
39 Ned's Place
41 Do Drop Inn
42 Gosha Restaurant
43 Bali Waltzing Matilda Too
45 Karang Mas Restaurant
47 Restaurant Puri Bali Indah
48 Legian Garden Restaurant
49 Orchid Garden Restaurant
50 Manhattan Restaurant & Bar
51 Made's Restaurant
58 Southern Cross Restaurant
59 Yanies
60 Il Pirata
61 The Bounty
62 Depot Viva
63 Za's Bakery & Restaurant
64 Mama's German Restaurant

OTHER

40 Wartel Telephone Office
66 Krishna Bookshop

Bruna Beach Inn (Legian No 53) This simple and straightforward place has a good central location near the beach. The rooms are nothing special but they're cheap at 23,500 to 49,000 rp for singles and 33,000 to 59,000 rp for doubles.

Kuta Cottages (Kuta No 71, ☎ 2051101) Close to the beach, near the end of Jalan Bakung Sari, this older hotel is reasonably priced at 35,000 to 49,000 rp for singles and 43,000 to 59,000 rp for doubles.

Kuta Seaview Cottages (Kuta No 28, ☎ 2051961) By the beach, but separated from it by the road, the rooms are definitely not cottages and most don't have any view of the sea. Yet despite the cramped site and three-storeyed block, prices are good value at 49,000/59,000 rp for singles/doubles.

Legian Beach Hotel (Legian No 44, ☎ 2051711) PO Box 308, Denpasar. On the beach at Jalan Melasti in the heart of Legian, this large hotel has a wide variety of rooms, most of them in three-storeyed blocks, with singles for 68,500 to 147,000 rp, doubles at 78,000 to 157,000 rp.

Mimpi Bungalows (Kuta No 26) This small hotel is good value in a pleasant location with a nice little pool. Rooms cost 29,000 to 68,500 rp.

Mutiara Bungalows (Kuta No 33) Conveniently located on Poppies Gang, the Mutiara is also excellent value with a spacious, lush garden and straightforward if slightly tatty fan-cooled rooms with verandah at 33,000 rp.

Nusa di Nusa (Kuta & Legian, ☎ 2051414) PO Box 191, Denpasar. Well north of Legian in Seminyak and right on the beach, you get isolation and a better stretch of beach in exchange for the distance from restaurants, entertainment and shopping. Very pleasant rooms cost 49,000 to 59,000 rp for singles, 59,000 to 68,500 rp for doubles. There are also family 'bungalows' for 147,000 rp, and houses with two or three bedrooms and a kitchen for 294,000 rp.

Poppies Cottages I (Kuta No 41) Still setting the standard for what a good Bali hotel should be, Poppies has an exotically lush garden with cleverly designed and beautifully built rooms. It's right in the centre of things on Poppies Gang and has a swimming pool every bit as stunning as the overall design. At 100,000/110,000 rp for singles/doubles it's right at the top of the mid-range category.

Poppies Cottages II (Kuta No 5) The earlier Poppies is not quite as stunning in its design or setting, nor is it quite as central. There is no pool but it's cheaper at 45,000/55,000 rp.

Places to Stay – top end Although Kuta isn't like Nusa Dua or Sanur where most (if not all) the hotels are strictly at the top end of the price range, there are still some places in this category. These include some of Kuta's larger hotels, one of which, the Bali Oberoi, is a contender for the top of the 'best hotels in Bali' ranking.

All of the hotels in this bracket have air-conditioning, swimming pools and other mod cons. There is a 15½% tax and service charge on top of the quoted prices. Eight of the more popular or more interesting places in this category include:

Bali Intan Cottages (Legian No 46, ☎ 2051770) PO 1002, Denpasar. On Jalan Melasti, close to the beach in Legian, this very standard large hotel has rooms in two-storeyed blocks plus cottages with singles at 127,000 to 147,000 rp, doubles at 137,000 to 157,000 rp.

Bali Oberoi Hotel (Kuta & Legian, ☎ 2051061) PO Box 351, Denpasar. Situated right on the beach at Seminyak, way up beyond Legian, the Bali Oberoi is isolated and decidedly deluxe, with beautiful individual bungalows and even some villa rooms with their own private swimming pools. The regular rooms are 294,000 to 470,000 rp while the villa rooms start at around 588,000 rp.

Bali Padma Hotel (Legian No 26, ☎ 2052111) PO Box 1107 TBB, Legian. This big 400-room hotel is on the beach on Jalan Padma in the middle of Legian. Rooms are in two or three-storeyed blocks or in six-room units and cost from 196,000 to 235,000 rp for singles, 215,000 to 255,000 rp for doubles.

Kartika Plaza Hotel (Kuta & Legian, ☎ 2051067) PO Box 84, Denpasar. Right on the beach, just south of central Kuta, this larger hotel has rooms at 157,000/167,000 rp.

Kul Kul Hotel (Legian No 52, ☎ 2052520) PO Box 97, Denpasar. Separated from the beach by the road just south of Jalan Melasti in Legian, this big hotel has two- and three-storeyed blocks plus bungalows in relatively spacious grounds. Rooms cost from 163,000 rp.

Kuta Beach Hotel (Kuta No 70, ☎ 2051361) PO Box 393, Denpasar. The original Kuta hotel is close to the site of its prewar predecessor of the same name. Unfortunately there's no sense of history here and the rooms are somewhat dull and tired. The location is very central at the beach end of Jalan Pantai Kuta and you can walk right out on to the beach but, with singles/doubles from 139,000/157,000 rp up to 176,000/220,000 rp, it's not great value.

Kuta Palace Hotel (Kuta & Legian, ☎ 2051433) PO Box 244, Denpasar. At the northern end of Legian, this big hotel is right on the beach and has a pleasant pool and garden. Singles cost from 127,000 to 147,000 rp, doubles from 147,000 to 166,000 rp.

Pertamina Cottages (Kuta & Legian, ☎ 2023061) PO Box 121, Denpasar. On the beach at the airport end of Kuta this large deluxe hotel has rooms at 210,000 to 220,000 rp.

Places to Eat

There are countless places to eat around Kuta and Legian, ranging from tiny hawker's carts to fancy restaurants, cheap warungs to bars and pubs, steakhouses to juice bars. Like so much else about Kuta there's not much which is truly Indonesian or Balinese – you could stay in Kuta for a month, eat in a different place for every meal and never have to confront so much as a humble nasi goreng. In Kuta the cuisine is pseudo-Western from top to bottom and always seems to be going through some transient craze, whether a spate of Mexican restaurants or the discovery of pizzas.

Prices in Kuta's fancier restaurants are no longer rock bottom either. If you want to eat cheaply try places like *Depot Viva* on Jalan Legian, the food carts which cater to local workers or the night market near the post office. Many of the fancier places have Australian wine for around 3500 rp a glass.

Around Kuta Places may come and go but *Poppies* has been one of the most popular restaurants ever since it opened in the early '70s. The food is very basic – you're not going to get any culinary surprises but nor are you going to get any awful shocks. It's on Poppies Gang, close to the heart of things, with a beautiful garden, attentive service and most main courses cost from around 6000 to 9000 rp.

A few steps beyond Poppies is *TJ's*, the place in Kuta for Mexican food. Again, the ambience is cranked up high and while Mexico may be a long way from Bali the food is surprisingly good. In this deservedly popular restaurant, main courses cost 5000 to 8000 rp.

Further down Poppies Gang towards the beach there are several popular places for light meals. *Fat Yogi's* turns out pretty good pizzas from a genuine wood-fired pizza oven and their croissants aren't bad at breakfast time either. Further down the gang there's *Warung Transformer* and the pleasant *Tree House Restaurant*, a good place for an excellent and economical breakfast.

On Jalan Pantai Kuta (Kuta Beach Rd), quite close to Poppies, is *Made's Warung*. Like Poppies, this simple open-fronted place has been going since the early '70s and is probably the best place in Kuta for people-watching, both visitors and the local glitterati. The food is getting a touch expensive these days but there's always somebody unusual to watch from first thing in the morning until late at night. Bali has lots of Made's so *Made's Juice Shop*, at the beach end of the road, is no relation although it's also popular.

Jalan Buni Sari, which connects Jalan Pantai Kuta with Jalan Bakung Sari, has some more long-term survivors including the *Bali Indah, Wayan's Tavern* and *Dayu II*. These three turn out standard dishes at reasonable prices. Further along this short street there are some popular pubs including *The Pub* – the original Kuta pub, though not in its original location. See the Entertainment section for more details.

On Jalan Bakung Sari the *Gemini Restaurant* is a popular choice for Chinese dishes. Across the road is the *Gantino Baru*, a nasi Padang specialist. Down Jalan Bakung Sari towards the beach there are several restaurants including *Dayu I* and the supermarket which has many Western-style goods.

Along Jalan Legian There are lots of possibilities down Jalan Legian. Most of the time the road is an almost continuous traffic jam and a table near the road can mean you have to shout to be heard. Right on Bemo Corner is the *Quick Snack Bar*, a good place for a snack or breakfast (the yoghurt is particularly good). A little further along is *Aleangs*, another popular snack bar with good yoghurt, cakes and ice cream, plus lots of traffic noise.

Continue north towards Legian and you reach the *Mini Restaurant*, which is not very 'mini' at all. It's a big, open, busy place serving simple food at low prices. Across the road is Kuta's disco and bar centre, with the extremely popular Koala Blu pub and Peanuts disco. In the same vicinity there are several Western fast-food outlets. Slightly hidden off the eastern side of Jalan Legian is *George & Dragon*, reputed to have the best Indian curries in Bali. On the other side of the road is the *LG Club*, a big, bright restaurant where you choose your seafood at the front and it's cooked in the frenetic open kitchen area to one side.

Continue north along Jalan Legian to *Depot Viva* (see the Legian map). It's an open-roofed place with surprisingly good Indonesian and Chinese food despite the restaurant's bare and grubby appearance. The prices are pleasantly low too, which accounts for its steady popularity. Across the road is the *The Bounty*, notable for its amazing ship-stern architecture, and then *Za's Bakery & Restaurant* which is not only a good spot for breakfast but also has a menu featuring everything from pasta to curries.

Just off Jalan Legian is *Yanies*, which has

excellent burgers for 3500 to 6000 rp. A little further along this same road is *Il Pirata*, noted for its very good pizzas at 5000 to 7000 rp and for its late opening hours.

Return to Jalan Legian and you'll soon be in the heart of Legian, with numerous restaurants on Jalan Melasti, Jalan Padma and the other Legian streets. Further along Jalan Legian you'll come to the ever popular *Do Drop Inn* and *Restaurant Glory*.

Around Legian Jalan Melasti has several good restaurants, including the big *Orchid Garden Restaurant*, the *Legian Garden Restaurant* and the *Restaurant Puri Bali Indah* with excellent Chinese food. Jalan Padma also has restaurants but some of the most interesting places in Legian are further north on Jalan Purana Bagus Taruna, the somewhat twisting road leading to the big Kuta Palace Hotel. Right by the hotel entrance is the *Topi Koki Restaurant* which has a pretty good go at la cuisine Franaise. The menu features main courses at 7000 to 10,000 rp, wine by the glass at 4500 rp; a meal complete with pre-dinner drinks, starter, main course, dessert and coffee could reach 50,000 rp for two. Not bad for pretty authentic French food.

A little further back from the beach is the *Swiss Restaurant*, which is popular with homesick Deutschlanders; main courses cost 5000 to 10,000 rp and Indonesian dishes a bit less. Other restaurants along this street include the *Sawasdee Thai Restaurant*, *Yudi Pizza* and, closer to Jalan Legian, the big and very popular *Bamboo Palace Restaurant* and the small, but also popular, *Benny's Cafe*.

Entertainment

Nightspots are scattered around Kuta and Legian, many along Jalan Legian. Discos go through strange fads – five nights a week you need a crowbar to clear a space on the dance floor but come back three months later and there's not a body in sight. One year you can't even find enough space to park your motorbike outside – come back next year and there's enough room to dump an elephant. So

if the places listed here turn out to be ever so dull and dreary – don't blame us.

Some of the wilder drunken excesses of Kuta have been cleaned up. The pub crawls, where bus loads of increasingly noisy and drunken revellers were hauled from one venue to another, have been cut back considerably. Plus many pubs and discos have been closed down and others concentrated into a sort of 'combat zone' on Jalan Legian. There everybody can get as drunk as they like without bothering other people.

The centrepiece of the Jalan Legian entertainment complex is the large *Peanuts* disco – it's rather like an Australian barnyard-pub venue, which might explain its popularity. Admission is usually around 5000 rp and this includes a couple of drinks. There's a series of open bars flanking the entrance road into Peanuts. These places kick off earlier than the main disco, and continue even after it's in full swing. For some reason *Koala Blu* has been the firm favourite for some time and Koala Blu T-shirts seem to pop up all over Asia. After midnight it's quite a scene, with music blasting out from every bar, hordes of people, mostly upright but some decidedly horizontal, and out in the parking lot lines of bemos and dokars waiting to haul the semi-conscious back to their hotels.

There are other places. If you're in pursuit of this sort of activity you'll soon hear about them.

Bars & Pubs You can make a fairly clean division between the bars you go to for a drink and the ones you go to for entertainment, music and pick-ups. It's generally immediately clear which category they fall into. The *Casablanca* on Jalan Buni Sari is definitely in the noise and activity category; ideal if you can handle beer-drinking contests, cheese and vegemite sandwich eating contests, women's arm wrestling contests and other scenes of Australian depravity. Also on Jalan Buni Sari is the *Pub Bagus* and *The Pub*, one of Kuta's original bars. The Pub is still a popular place for a beer without the associated noise and confusion.

Down Poppies Gang the *Nusa Indah Bar* is a straightforward and pleasant little open-air place with about the cheapest beer prices around. Head further north to Poppies Gang II and just off Jalan Legian is *Tubes Bar*, with video movies every night and a giant concrete wave complete with an embedded surfboard where you can stand for heroic surfing snapshots! Continue a little further up Jalan Legian to the *Sari Club* (SC for short), a big, noisy, crowded, open-air bar. There are numerous other bars of all sorts along Jalan Legian.

Things to Buy

Parts of Kuta are now almost door-to-door shops and over the years these have become steadily more sophisticated. Of course there are still many simple stalls as well, and many of these cheaper shops are now crowded together in 'art markets' like the one at the beach end of Jalan Bakung Sari. With so many things to buy around Kuta it's very easy to be stampeded into buying things you don't really want during the first few days of your stay. In fact, there are so many people trying to sell to you that you need real endur-

ance not to succumb. Unless you want to end up with lots of things you can definitely do without, get an overall impression before you consider buying anything and shop around before you do buy. Some items of interest follow.

Crafts If it's made anywhere in Bali then 10 to one you can find it on sale at Kuta. Of course, Kuta isn't really the centre for any of Bali's notable crafts but the Kuta shops have arts and crafts from almost every part of the island, from woodcarvings to paintings to textiles and just about everything else in between.

Clothing Clothes, on the other hand, are a Kuta speciality and Kuta has become the centre for Bali's energetic rag trade. Countless boutiques for men and women display the sort of Balinese interpretations of the latest styles which now find their way all over the world. You may never need to wear a sports coat or leather boots in Bali but you can certainly find plenty of them on sale and at competitive prices. You'll probably see the same items later on in shops from Berkeley to Double Bay at 10 times the cost.

Other Items The pirate cassette business was run out of town a few years ago but it's bounced back with 100% legal tapes which still considerably undercut anything you'd buy in the West. There are lots of tape shops around Kuta with a wide range of all the latest hits.

One thing there is no harm in paying for as soon as you arrive is a massage. Kuta has countless masseurs operating along the beach or coming around to the hotels – for just a few thousand rp, they'll quickly prove you have dozens of muscles you never knew existed.

Getting There & Away

Air See the Getting There & Away chapter for details of flying to or from Bali. Kuta has lots of travel agencies but if you're looking for onward tickets, Bali is no place for cheap bargains. If you're looking for a discounted deal to a faraway place, wait until you get to Singapore.

If you already have tickets and need to reconfirm, there's a small Garuda office (☎ 2024764) in the Kuta Beach Hotel at the beach end of Jalan Pantai Kuta. The office sometimes gets hopelessly crowded so it's a good idea to arrive before opening time or during the lunch break and be at the head of the queue. It's open Monday to Friday from 7.30 am to 4 pm, Saturday and Sunday from 9 am to 1 pm.

There's a Qantas office and another Garuda office at the Hotel Bali Beach in Sanur. The myriad Kuta travel agencies will offer to make reconfirmations for you but there's a charge and some agencies are said to be less than scrupulous about actually reconfirming.

Bemo From Kuta there are buses to other places in Bali and direct to Java although the cheaper 'public' buses generally depart from the Denpasar bus stations. Fares from Kuta include Surabaya from 19,000 rp, Yogyakarta from around 29,000 rp and Jakarta for 48,000 rp.

You can get a regular public bemo from just beyond Bemo Corner into Denpasar for 400 rp, but anywhere else you're almost certainly going to have to charter. Kuta bemo jockeys bargain hard but they're good humoured about it and once you've agreed on a price they usually stick to it. Note that there is no direct bemo public service to Sanur. By public bemo you have to go into Denpasar, change bus stations and take another bemo out.

Tourist Bus Perama, on Jalan Legian, operates regular tourist shuttle buses direct from Kuta to the other main tourist centres in Bali. These services save you having to get to the appropriate bus station and find the bus you want and, since they don't make frequent intermediate stops they're much faster. Services include Sanur and Ubud for 4000 rp, Padangbai and Candidasa for 7500 rp, Kintamani for 7000 rp and Lovina for 10,000

rp. Perama also operates bus-ferry-bus services to Lombok. You can travel directly to Mataram or Senggigi Beach for 13,000 rp or to Bangsal, from where the boats cross to the Gili Islands, for 15,000 rp.

Getting Around
To/From the Airport Ngurah Rai Airport is so close to Kuta you could actually walk if you were in the mood. The official taxi fare is 4500 rp from the airport to any place south of Jalan Bakung Sari (the southern part of Kuta), 6000 rp for anywhere north of Bakung Sari but south of Jalan Padma (central Kuta right up to the centre of Legian), 9000 rp north of Jalan Padma (the northern part of Legian) and 10,000 rp to the Oberoi Hotel (way north of Legian in Seminyak).

From Kuta to the airport you can generally bargain with bemo or taxi drivers to get these fares without too much effort but you will have to work hard to get lower fares. Theoretically, you could get to the airport from Kuta by regular public bemo for just a few hundred rp. Just try to do it! The Perama bus service to the airport costs 3500 rp.

Bemo & Taxi There are plenty of taxis around Kuta Beach (any car is a taxi) and even larger numbers of bemos (minibuses). Constant offers of 'transport' follow any pedestrian. None of the vehicles is metered so you have to negotiate the fare before you get on board. You should be able to get from the middle of Kuta to the middle of Legian for around 3000 rp.

Rental There are countless bicycle, motorbike and car rental places around Kuta. By the day you can rent a bike for about 3000 rp, a motorbike for around 8000 to 12,000 rp or a car for around 35,000 to 40,000 rp including insurance and unlimited km.

Tours There are countless tours organised from Kuta which can be booked through the many travel agencies. Tours further afield – to places like Lombok, Komodo or Sulawesi – are also offered. Agencies also rent cars, motorbikes and bicycles, sell bus and train tickets to Java and perform other travel agency services.

SANUR

Sanur is the up-market alternative to Kuta for those coming to Bali for sea, sand and sun. The resort of Nusa Dua is intended to be an up-market alternative to Sanur. Sanur is principally a locale for Hyatts, Sheratons and the like and, although it does have some more reasonably priced accommodation, prices are not down to the lower Kuta levels.

Sanur has a pleasant beach sheltered by a reef. At low tide it's very shallow, and you have to pick your way out over rocks and coral through knee-deep water. The Indonesians, both locals and 'domestic tourists', think it's ideal and you'll find many of them paddling here on Sundays and holidays, particularly at the northern end of the beach. At high tide the swimming is fine, and there is an array of water sports on offer – windsurfing, snorkelling, water-skiing, parasailing, paddle boards etc – all for a price. For surfers there is a good right-hand break on the reef, which works best in the wet season, from November to April.

What Sanur doesn't have, thankfully, is the noise, confusion and pollution of Kuta. You're not in constant danger of being mown down by motorbike maniacs, the traffic isn't horrendous and you're not constantly badgered to buy things – badgered yes, but not constantly.

Orientation

Sanur stretches for about three km along an east-facing coastline, with the landscaped grounds and restaurants of expensive hotels fronting right onto the beach. The conspicuous, '60s style Hotel Bali Beach is at the northern end of the strip, and the newer Surya Beach Hotel, invisible behind its walls and gardens, is at the southern end. West of these hotels the main drag, Jalan Danau Tamblingan (formerly Jalan Tanjung Sari), runs parallel to the beach, with the hotel entrances on one side and wall-to-wall tourist shops and restaurants down the other side. To the west of this road are some small streets and lanes, then the main Sanur bypass road, Jalan Baja Letkol Ngurah Rai, which runs south then west to Kuta and the airport, and north towards Ubud.

Information

Sanur has travel agencies, moneychangers and other facilities just like Kuta. Most of them are along Jalan Danau Tamblingan.

Post & Telecommunications Sanur's post office is on the southern side of Jalan Segara, a hundred metres or so west of the bypass road. If you're an American Express customer you can have your mail sent to their office, c/o PT Pacto Ltd, PO Box 52, Sanur (☎ 2088449), which is in the Hotel Bali Beach. Of course, you can also have mail addressed to the large hotels.

There's no Permuntel telephone office in Sanur – it's probably assumed that everyone who wants to make international phone calls can do so from their hotel room. There's a Home Country Direct phone next to the Malaysian Airlines office in the Hotel Bali Beach. You can make reverse-charge (collect) calls or pay with your credit card; it's very easy to use.

Foreign Embassies The US consular agency is on Jalan Segara, 80 metres west of the Segara Village Hotel. There is a small sign next to the driveway. A number of other consulates and consular agencies are in Sanur, or not far away in the Renon area of Denpasar. For details, see Consulates & Consular Agencies in the Denpasar section.

Museum Le Mayeur

Sanur was one of the places in Bali favoured by Western artists during their prewar discovery of the island. It was a quiet fishing village at that time but few traces of the Sanur of 50 years ago remain. The exception is the former home of the Belgian artist Le Mayeur, who lived here from 1932 to 1958. It must have been a delightful place then, a peaceful and elegant home right by the

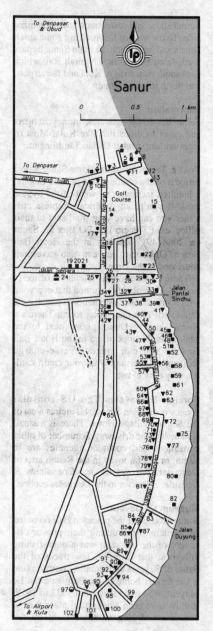

beach. Today it's squeezed between the Hotel Bali Beach and the Diwangkara Beach Hotel but it's still maintained by his widow, Ni Polok, who was once a renowned Legong dancer.

The home displays paintings and drawings by Le Mayeur but unfortunately many of them are yellowed, dirty and badly lit. They are nevertheless interesting impressionist-style paintings from his travels in Africa, India, Italy, France and the South Pacific. The more recent works, from the

98 Santrian Bali Beach Bungalows	73 Number One Club
100 Semawang Beach Inn	74 Penjor Restaurant
101 Hotel Sanur Beach	77 New Seoul Korean Restaurant
102 Surya Beach Hotel	78 Kulkul Restaurant
	79 Melanie Restaurant
▼ PLACES TO EAT	81 Restaurant Telaga Naga
	84 Paon Restaurant
2 Bali Raja restaurant	86 Legong Restaurant
3 Si Pino Restaurant	87 Whitesands Bar & Restaurant
10 Oasis & Borobudur Restaurants	88 Oka's Bar Restaurant
11 Bali	89 Bali Pub & Restaurant
16 Steak House	91 Rumah Makan Wayan
17 Kentucky Fried Chicken &	92 Kesumasari
Swensens Ice Cream	93 Norman's Bar
18 Lenny's Restaurant	94 Alita Garden Restaurant
23 Swiss Restaurant	95 Balita Restaurant
25 Warung Mini	96 Sanur Kuring Restaurant &
27 The Corner Restaurant	Karaoke
31 Warungs	99 Trattoria da Marco
32 Carlo Restaurant	
34 Merry Bar & Restaurant	OTHER
37 Queen Bali Restaurant	
40 Bali Moon Restaurant	7 Boats to Nusa Lembongan
41 Mango Bar & Restaurant	13 Museum Le Mayeur
42 Aga Restaurant	14 Police Station
43 Swastika I Restaurant	16 Supermarket
44 Sindhu Corner Restaurant	24 Post Office
47 Raoul's & Dragon Restaurant	26 Apotik & Moneychanger
50 Kuri Putih Restaurant	28 US Consular Agency
54 Sita Restaurant	30 Sanur Beach Market
55 Ratu's Pizza	35 Night Market
57 Arena Restaurant	56 Sanur Foto Centre
60 Mina Garden Restaurant & Yamcha	65 Petrol Station
Restaurant	67 Temptation
62 Laghawa Grill	71 Handicraft Market
64 Warung Aditya	83 Supermarket
68 Swastika II Restaurant	85 Double U Shopping Centre
70 Umasari Restaurant	90 Wisma Bahari Art Gallery
72 Blue Diamond Restaurant	97 Bemo Stop

1950s, are in much better condition, with the vibrant colours of Bali and the scenes of daily life which later became popular with Balinese artists. All the works have titles, descriptions, dates etc in both Indonesian and English. The museum is also an interesting example of architecture in its own right. Notice the beautifully carved window shutters which recount the story of Rama and Sita from the *Ramayana*.

Admission is 200 rp (children 100 rp) and it's open from 8 am to 2 pm on Sunday, Tuesday, Wednesday and Thursday, from 8 to 11 am on Friday and from 8 am to noon on Saturday. It's closed on Monday.

Other Attractions

Just wandering around Sanur, along the beach or through the rice paddies, is an interesting activity in itself. The rice farmers of Sanur are said to grow some of the finest rice in Bali. The beach at Sanur is always full of interesting sights such as the colourful outriggers known as *jukungs* ready to take you for a quick trip out to the reef. At low tide you can walk across the sand and coral to this sheltering reef. Villagers collect coral here to make lime for building.

Beyond the Hotel Sanur Beach, at Belanjong, there's a stone pillar with an inscription recounting military victories of over 1000 years ago. Tanjung Sari, with its coral pyramid, was once a lonely temple by the beach.

Places to Stay

There are no rock-bottom Kuta-style places in Sanur although there are a few cheapies. There's also a handful of mid-range places, a few of which are as good value as equivalent places at Kuta. Principally, however, Sanur is a high-price resort, the place for 'international standard' hotels where the majority of Bali's package tours go, and where prices don't include the 15½ to 21½% service charge. The prices quoted in the following sections don't include this additional charge.

Note also that the prices given in the top-end section are the quoted walk-in rates, but hardly anyone just walks in to these places. It may actually be cheaper to book ahead through a travel agency, especially as part of a package.

Places to Stay – bottom end

The cheapest places are away from the beach at the northern end of town. On Jalan Segara, west of the main road, there are three lower priced places side by side – the *Hotel Sanur-Indah*, closest to Denpasar, is the most basic and the cheapest at about 12,000/12,500 rp for singles/doubles. In the middle, the *Hotel Taman Sari* has doubles from 15,000 rp with fan to 45,000 rp with hot water and air-con. The *Hotel Rani* has rooms from 12,500/15,000 rp for singles/doubles, and some with air-con and hot water for about 40,000 rp.

You might also find a cheap room at *Made Pub & Homestay*, on the west side of Jalan Danau Toba almost opposite the Gazebo Beach Hotel. There are some small rooms downstairs from 15,000 rp for singles, and some bigger rooms upstairs for 30,000 rp a double.

Places to Stay – middle

At the north end of Sanur Beach the *Ananda Hotel* (☎ 208827) is behind the restaurant of the same name, right by the beach. It's neat and clean and rooms with fan and cold water cost 25,000/30,000 rp for singles/doubles.

Watering Hole Homestay, (☎ 2088289) on Jalan Hang Tuah (the Sanur to Denpasar road) opposite the Hotel Bali Beach entrance, has clean, pleasant rooms at 20,000/25,000 rp. It's a friendly, well-run place with good food and a bar. On Hang Tuah, on the other side of the bypass road, the *Hotel Bali Continental* has singles and doubles with air-con, TV and hot water for 50,000 rp.

The *Kalpataru Homestay & Restaurant* (☎ 2088457), on the west side of Jalan Danau Toba, is a pleasant place with a garden and swimming pool. It's clean and good value at 20,000/25,000 rp for budget rooms, 25,000/30,000 rp for better rooms, and 40,000/45,000 rp for rooms with air-con.

A little further south, on a sideroad which runs towards the beach between some government buildings, is the *Werdha Pura*. It's a government-run 'beach cottage prototype', with the kind of service that will make you believe in private enterprise, but it's cheap enough at 25,000/50,000 rp for singles/doubles and 60,000 rp for family rooms.

The more expensive mid-range places tend to add on about 15% for tax and service. Starting again from the northern end of town, the *Sanur Village Club* (one of the Bali Sanur Bungalows group), on Jalan Hang Tuah, costs 68,500/78,000 rp with air-con but is not in a good location. The *Bali Eka Beach Inn* (☎ 2088939) is on a small road off the northern side of Jalan Hang Tuah. It's clean and characterless, and costs 68,500/78,000 rp. *Alit's Beach Bungalows* are also on Hang Tuah, a bit closer to the beach, costing 72,500/78,000 rp with air-con and hot water. On Jalan Pantai Sindhu, two streets further south, and right on the beach, is the *Baruna*

Beach Inn with a great location and only seven rooms at 55,000/59,000 rp including breakfast, tax and air-con. Rooms cost a few dollars extra in the high season. On the other side of the road, a bit further from the beach, the *Queen Bali Hotel* (☎ 2088054) has standard rooms at 49,000/59,000 rp and bungalows at 59,000/68,500; extra beds are 15,000 rp. The price includes tax, breakfast, air-con and hot water. There's a bar and disco.

Continuing along Jalan Danau Tamblingan you'll find the *Laghawa Beach Inn* (☎ 2088494, 87919) on the beach side of the road, with air-con singles/doubles for 68,500/78,000 rp and air-con triples for 88,000 rp. Fan-cooled rooms are 20,000 rp less and all prices include tax and continental breakfast. An extra bed costs 13,000 rp. The inn has an attractive garden setting, restaurant and bar and looks like quite good value for Sanur. On the other side of the road, with identical prices, the *Swastika Bungalows* has comfortable rooms, pretty gardens and two swimming pools. A few metres further south is the *Hotel Ramayana* (☎ 2088429) with rooms at 45,000 rp for singles or doubles, excluding tax and breakfast.

At the southern end of town, on a small road between the big hotels, the *Semawang Beach Inn* is close to the beach and offers good facilities and breakfast for 53,000 rp (air-con) and 39,000 rp (fan) for singles or doubles.

Places to Stay – top end Sanur's first 'big' hotel and still one of the biggest is the massive *Hotel Bali Beach* (☎ 2088511; PO Box 275, Denpasar). Dating from the Sukarno era of the mid-60s, today it's very out of place in Bali – a Miami Beach-style rectangular block squarely facing the beach. It's got all the usual facilities from bars, restaurants and a nightclub to swimming pools, tennis courts and even an adjacent golf course. The pool-side snack bar here is quite reasonably priced. Air-con rooms cost from 180,000 to over 233,000 rp and there are suites for 268,000 to 701,000 rp, some with

kitchenettes. Adjoining the hotel to the south is the newer cottage section.

Almost all the more expensive hotels are on the beach front. Immediately north of the Bali Beach and adjacent to the Museum Le Mayeur is the partially secluded *Diwangkara Beach Hotel* (☎ 2088577, 88591; PO Box 120, Denpasar). Air-con rooms cost from 88,000 to 108,000 rp.

Going south from the Hotel Bali Beach you come first to the *Segara Village Hotel* (☎ 2088407/8, fax 87242). It's a more expensive place with motel-style rooms and two-storeyed cottages for 98,000 to 343,000 rp. The hotel is in a pleasant landscaped area with swimming pools and a children's playground. The *Sindhu Beach Hotel* (☎ 2088351/2), right on the beach, has 50 air-con rooms for 108,000 to 157,000 rp. The *La Taverna Bali Hotel* (☎ 2088497; PO Box 40, Denpasar), also right on the beach, has air-con rooms for 118,000 to 137,000 rp. There's also the smaller *Gazebo Beach Hotel* here with air-con cottages set in a lush garden.

Sanur has several places to stay in the Bali Sanur Bungalows group. Heading south, you come first to the *Irama* then to the *Respati*, both priced at 78,000/88,000 rp for single/doubles. Further south is the *Besakih* and to the *Peneeda View* bungalows, which are more expensive at 98,000/117,000. Breakfast, tax and service are extra.

In between the Irama and the Besakih is the *Tandjung Sari Hotel* (☎ 2088441) with air-con rooms for 156,000 to 196,000 rp. Some of the bungalows in this pleasantly relaxed and fairly expensive place are interesting two-storeyed buildings.

Then it's the *Bali Hyatt* (☎ 2088271/7; PO Box 392, Denpasar), one of the biggest hotels in Sanur and an interesting contrast with the Hotel Bali Beach built 10 years earlier. The lesson had been learnt in the '60s and a regulation was passed that no hotel could be 'taller than a palm tree'. The Hyatt, with its sloping balconies overflowing with tropical vegetation, blends in remarkably well. Look for the interesting pottery tiles used as decorations on various walls. Air-con rooms start at 185,000 rp. Sanur's flashiest and most popular disco is also here.

Further south is the big *Hotel Sanur Beach* (☎ 2088011, fax 87566), where air-con rooms cost 195,000 to 234,000 rp and suites and bungalows 341,000 to 1,660,000 rp.

The *Santrian Bali Beach Bungalows* (☎ 2088184, 89133; fax 88185) have air-con rooms for 117,000 to 157,000 rp, plus two swimming pools and tennis courts. The newer *Sativa Sanur Cottages* (☎ 2087881, fax 87276) are a bit off the beach, but attractively arranged around a swimming pool and gardens. Air-con rooms cost 115,640 to 186,000 rp.

Places to Eat

All the top-end hotels have their own restaurants, snack bars, coffee bars and bars of course – generally with top-end prices too! The food at Sanur is basically Western-style – there's even a place for homesick pasta lovers – *Trattoria da Marco* down at the southern end of the beach road. There's the *New Seoul Korean Restaurant* halfway down Jalan Danau Tamblingan on the beach side, and a *Japanese Restaurant* a bit further north. The *Swiss Restaurant*, on Jalan Segara just south of the Hotel Bali Beach, is very plush, with thick carpet and a grand piano. Fondue is 31,000 rp for two, and other Swiss dishes 10,000 to 20,000 rp. There's a *Kentucky Ayam Goreng* and *Swensen's Ice Cream* next to the supermarket, on the bypass road opposite the golf course.

There are a number of quite reasonably priced places, very much in the Kuta restaurant mould. You'll find plenty of them down the main street, mostly on the western side. Just south of the Hotel Bali Beach is the slightly more expensive beach-front *Sanur Beach Market*. Agung and Sue's *Watering Hole*, opposite the Hotel Bali Beach entrance, has good food at affordable prices.

For seafood, *Lenny's* and the *Kulkul Restaurant* are worth trying. *Carlo Restaurant*, on Jalan Pantai Sindhu, is reasonably priced and has good food. *Kesumasari*, on the beach south of the Bali Hyatt, has good and commendably fresh food. If you continue to the southern end of the Sanur hotel strip, beyond the Hyatt, there are a number of inexpensive small restaurants and bars.

For cheaper eats try the rumah makans on the bypass road, but the cheapest, and possibly the tastiest, food is from the food carts and stalls at the northern end of the beach, close to where boats leave for Nusa Lembongan.

Things to Buy

Like Kuta, Sanur has many shops, selling everything from T-shirts to fluoro-print beachwear, as well as a range of handicrafts from Bali and other Indonesian islands. The Sanur Beach market, just south of the Hotel Bali Beach, has a variety of stalls so you can shop around. There are plenty of other shops down the main street, as well as two small market areas, each with a cluster of shops. Temptation, near the Hotel Ramayana, has a curious collection of 'artyfacts', including an 'Egyptian mummy'. There are a few other art and antique shops, some with very interesting stock. The sellers are not afraid to ask for a high 'first price', so shop around for some idea of quality and price before you consider parting with your money.

The supermarket on the bypass road is a good place for those small odds and ends that you might need but don't know what to ask for. There's another supermarket at the southern end of town near the Bali Hyatt. There's also a traditional market between the bypass road and Jalan Danau Toba near the northern end of the main street. It caters a bit for tourists, but still sells fresh vegetables, dried fish, pungent spices, plastic buckets and other household goods that the local people need for themselves.

Getting There & Away

Air For those wanting to reconfirm pre-booked flights or buy onward tickets, there's a Qantas office (☎ 2088331/2/3) at the Hotel Bali Beach; it's open Monday to Friday from 8.30 am to 4.30 pm, Saturday from 8.30 am to 12.30 pm. You will also find a Garuda office here (☎ 2088511) which is open Monday to Friday from 7.30 am to 4.30 pm and on Saturday from 9 am to 1 pm. The KLM office is open Monday to Friday from 8 am to 4.30 pm, Saturday 8 am to 1 pm. The Continental Airlines agency is open Monday to Friday from 8 am to 4 pm, Saturday 8 am to noon. Singapore Airlines, Cathay Pacific, Thai International and Malaysian Airlines agencies are also in the Hotel Bali Beach and keep similar hours.

Bemo Two different bemos operate between Sanur and Denpasar. Coming from Sanur, the blue ones go past Kereneng station, across town to Tegal station (the Kuta station) and then back to Kereneng. The green bemos *sometimes* take this route around town but usually just go straight to Kereneng station. The fare is 500 rp.

To get from Kuta to Sanur you have to go into Denpasar and then out again. You get one bemo from Kuta into the Tegal bemo station, then get a blue bemo to Sanur via Kereneng. If you get a green bemo at Tegal, it will stop at Kereneng and you'll have to get a third one out to Sanur. It's much faster and, between a few people, not that much more expensive to charter a bemo for a Kuta to Sanur trip, for around 10,000 rp.

Boat Boats to Nusa Lembongan leave from the northern end of the beach, in front of the Ananda Hotel & Restaurant. Unless the boat captains' price-fixing cartel has collapsed, it costs 15,000 rp (including your surfboard) to get to the island.

Getting Around

To/From the Airport The taxi fare from the airport to Sanur is 12,000 rp, while in the other direction (from Sanur to the airport) the fare is between 8000 and 10,000 rp. A new 'super highway', Jalan Baja Lektol Ngurah Rai, runs from Nusa Dua in the south, past the airport and Kuta to Sanur and Denpasar. It makes transport along this route quite fast.

Bemo Small bemos shuttle up and down the beach road in Sanur at a cost of 200 rp. Make it clear that you want to take a public bemo, not charter it. Know where you want to go

and accept that the driver may take a circuitous route to put down or pick up other passengers. There is a bemo stop at the southern end of town near where the main street rejoins the bypass road, and another stop at the northern end of town outside the entrance to the Hotel Bali Beach.

Rental There are numerous places around Sanur renting cars, motorbikes and bicycles, for about 40,000 rp, 10,000 rp and 3000 rp a day respectively. Tunas Tours & Travel, in the Hotel Bali Beach Arcade, rents mountain bikes for about 15,500 rp a day and also organises bicycle tours of Bali.

PULAU SERANGAN

Very close to the shore, south of Sanur and close to the mouth of Benoa Harbour, is Pulau Serangan (Turtle Island). At low tide you can actually walk across to the island. Turtles are captured and fattened here in pens before being sold for village feasts. (See Sea Turtles, in the Facts for the Visitor chapter, for more information on the problems associated with the increasing slaughter of these turtles.)

The island has an important temple, Pura Sakenan, noted for its unusual shrines (candi). Twice a year major temple festivals are held here, attracting great crowds of devotees. The giant puppet figures used in the Barong Landung dance are brought across to the island for these festivals.

Day trips to Serangan have become popular with the travel agencies at Kuta and Sanur, but Serangan has a very strong tourist-trap air and is not terribly popular with visitors. You're constantly hassled to spend, spend, spend. In fact, you get pounced on as soon as the prahu beaches and you're followed, cajoled, pleaded with and abused until you leave.

One traveller who actually enjoyed Serangan said that the southern end of the island was less 'developed' and had nice beaches. The problem is to negotiate a return trip which gives you enough time to walk the length of the island, enjoy the beach, and then walk back. If you want to try this, a boat from Benoa village to the south of Serangan may be a better option, though still quite expensive.

Getting There & Away

Like Kuta, Serangan has been affected by tourism – badly. It's not a place to waste time or money on but if you do decide to take a look you can either get there on an organised tour or charter a prahu yourself. If you decide to charter a boat, the starting price may be around 25,000 rp, but for a boat big enough for about six people, you should be able to negotiate the price down to around 10,000 rp. Allow about 20 minutes each way for the trip, and an hour to look around the island. Charters are available from Suwang, a small mangrove inlet near a rubbish dump. Pulau Serangan is hard work from start to finish.

JIMBARAN BAY

Just beyond the airport, south of Kuta, Jimbaran Bay is a superb crescent of white sand and blue sea. Jimbaran is basically a fishing village with, until recently, minimal tourist development.

Places to Stay

Jimbaran is being developed as a small, up-market resort area. Fortunately, there are now a couple of places where budget travellers can stay within walking distance of the beautiful bay. There is a basic losmen, the *Puri Bambu Bungalows*, on the western side of Jalan Ulu Watu. Further south, at Jalan Ulu Watu 28A, is *Puri Indra Prasta*. These bungalows have a restaurant, bar and swimming pool, and clean comfortable rooms from 20,000 to 25,000 rp for singles or doubles, including breakfast.

The first of the 1st-class hotels here, the *Pansea Puri Bali* (☎ 2052227, fax 52220), has a full range of facilities and services, including two bars, two restaurants (one on the beach) and about 40 air-con bungalows and rooms. Depending on the season, these cost from 215,000 to 303,000 rp for singles or doubles, dinner and breakfast included. A bit to the north, the *Keraton Bali Cottages*, opened in 1991, are a really fine example of

Balinese hotel architecture, beautifully decorated and tastefully landscaped, and somewhat cheaper at 108,000 to 156,000 rp depending on the room and the season.

Further south you'll find the site of the large *Hotel Intercontinental Bali*, due to be opened in 1993. South of the village area, on a small road off to the west of Jalan Ulu Watu, is the *Jimbaran Beach Club* (☎ 2080361). It's a bit isolated, and attracts mainly package-tour groups. Walk-in rates are from 69,000 to 88,000 rp for singles or doubles.

Places to Eat

The big hotels all have their own restaurants. You can eat in them even if you're not staying at the hotel, but you can expect to pay at least 20,000 rp for lunch or dinner. There are some warungs in the main street, and you'll find cheap food in the market on market days.

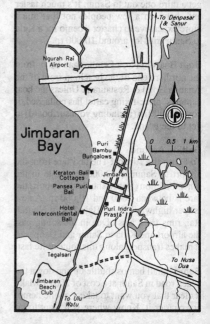

BENOA PORT

The wide but shallow bay east of the airport runway, Benoa Harbour (Labuhan Benoa), is one of Bali's main ports. It's also the main harbour for visiting yachts and there's nearly always a few overseas vessels moored here.

Benoa is actually in two parts. Benoa Port is on the northern side, with a two-km long causeway connecting it to the main Kuta to Sanur road. It consists of little more than a wharf and a variety of port offices. Benoa village is on the point on the southern side of the bay.

Hydrofoil

The Nawala hydrofoil service to Lombok arrives and departs from Benoa Port. If you've booked your hydrofoil ticket through an agent such as Perama, the deal should include transport between the port and where you're staying. If not, a public bemo from Denpasar will cost around 500 rp from Suci bemo station, or 1000 rp from Tegal station. A chartered bemo direct to Kuta will cost around 4000 rp per person. Hydrofoils leave Benoa Port at 8.45 am and 3.30 pm, take about two hours to reach Lombok's Lembar Harbour, and cost 35,000 rp. From Lembar the hydrofoils leave at 10.45 am and 3.30 pm, take about the same time but cost only 32,000 rp. Initial demand for the service was low, and prices may eventually be lowered.

Bali Hai

The *Bali Hai* is a luxury tourist excursion boat that operates from Benoa Port. Its sightseeing, diving and surfing trips to various locations around Bali and the offshore islands are well promoted in the main tourist areas. One popular trip is for well-heeled surfers, who pay 115,000 rp to anchor offshore and paddle *in* to the reef breaks off Nusa Lembongan.

BENOA VILLAGE

To get to Benoa village, on the southern side of the bay, you have to take the highway to Nusa Dua and then the smaller road along the coast from there. Boats also shuttle back and forth between Benoa Harbour and Benoa village. There's an interesting Chinese temple in Benoa.

The village of Benoa has become much cleaner and more affluent in recent years and it's something of an activities centre for Nusa Dua. If you want to go windsurfing, parasailing, scuba diving or indulge in various other water sports, this is the place.

Places to Stay & Eat

The few places to stay are near the beach front on the road which heads south to Nusa Dua. They're all within a stone's throw of each other, so you won't have any trouble finding them. The cheapest place is the *Homestay Asa*, a bit off the road, which has clean, comfortable singles and doubles from 17,000 rp – good value for the area. The *Rasa Dua* has nice upstairs rooms for 30,000 rp and downstairs rooms for 20,000 rp. *Chez Agung Pension/Homestay* is now managed by the *Sorga Nusa Dua* next door (☎ 2071604, fax 71143). Prices for singles/doubles are 59,000/68,500 rp for standard rooms and 78,000/88,000 rp for deluxe rooms. Rooms at the Sorga Nusa Dua cost 98,000 to 147,000 rp, with air-con and hot water.

There are several restaurants in Benoa, like the *Dalang Sea View Restaurant*, the *Entari Restaurant*, the *Jeladi Suta Restaurant* or the *Rai Seafood Restaurant*. They're mostly on the beach front opposite the hotels, and they tend to be expensive by Bali's usual standards. You should be able to find a rumah makan in the village for cheaper food.

NUSA DUA

Nusa Dua, literally 'two islands', is Bali's top-end beach resort – a luxury tourist enclave, planned to ensure that the mistakes of Kuta would not be repeated! The two islands are actually small raised headlands, connected to the mainland by sand spits. Nusa Dua is south of Kuta and Sanur, on the eastern side of the sparsely populated Bukit Peninsula.

The beach here is very pleasant and there is often good surf. This is really a place for people who want to get away from Bali.

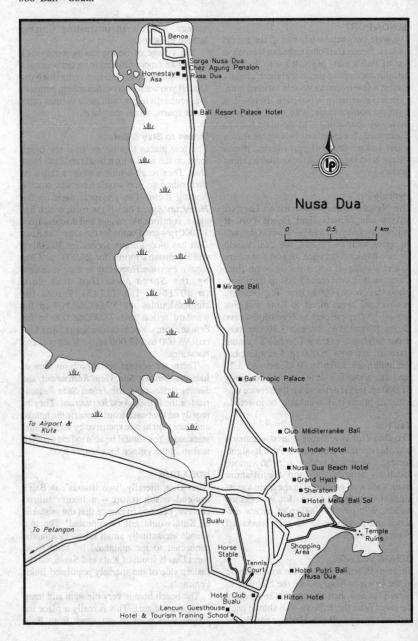

Benoa

Sorga Nusa Dua
Chez Agung Pension
Homestay ■ Rasa Dua
Asa

■ Bali Resort Palace Hotel

Nusa Dua

0   0.5   1 km

■ Mirage Bali

■ Bali Tropic Palace

To Airport &
Kuta

■ Club Méditerranée Bali

■ Nusa Indah Hotel

■ Nusa Dua Beach Hotel

■ Grand Hyatt
■ Sheraton
■ Hotel Melia Bali Sol

Nusa Dua

To Petangon

Bualu

Temple
Ruins

Shopping
Area

Horse
Stable

Tennis
Court

■ Hotel Putri Bali
Nusa Dua

Hotel Club
Bualu
Lancun Guesthouse
Hotel & Tourism Training School ■

■ Hilton Hotel

There are no independent developments permitted within the compound so you have a km or so to walk if you want to get even so much as a Coke at less than international hotel prices, or if you want to get a bemo to the rest of Bali.

Places to Stay & Eat

The Nusa Dua hotels all have swimming pools, a variety of restaurants and bars, entertainment and sports facilities and various other international hotel mod cons.

Starting at the northern end of the beach, the *Bali Resort Palace Hotel* is the first you'll come across. It has about 200 rooms from 156,000 to 313,000 rp, and a full range of facilities and restaurants. The next one south is the *Mirage Bali*, with 100 expensive rooms. South again is the *Bali Tropic Palace*, then the *Club Méditerranée Bali*, which is strictly a package-tour operation.

Next is the smaller *Nusa Indah Hotel*, then the *Nusa Dua Beach Hotel* (☎ 2071210) which is huge (450 rooms) with all the luxuries you could expect and prices from around 235,000 to 313,000 rp for standard rooms, plus 15½% service and tax. It's attractively designed using Balinese architecture and statuary, but how seriously can you take a hotel that promotes itself as being the place where Ronald Reagan stayed when he came to Bali?

South of the Nusa Dua Beach Hotel is the new, 750-room *Grand Hyatt Nusa Dua*. Built on a massive budget, it is pressing for the title of one of the best hotels in Bali. Next is another international name, the *Nusa Dua Sheraton*, then the 500-room *Hotel Melia Bali Sol* (☎ 2071510) with regular rooms for 152,000 to 176,000 rp and suites at 270,000 rp.

The shopping area near the Bali Sol has a variety of shops and restaurants. South of this is the *Hotel Putri Bali Nusa Dua* (☎ 2071020, 71420) which has 425 rooms, plus suites, cottages and so on. South again is the Nusa Dua *Hilton*, and just inland from there, the smaller *Hotel Club Bualu* (☎ 2071310). There are just 50 rooms at this hotel, costing 135,000 to 220,000 rp.

Next to the Club Bualu is the closest you will come to budget accommodation in Nusa Dua. The *Lancun Guesthouse* (☎ 2071983, 71985) is run by the Hotel & Tourism Training School, and has rooms for about 49,000 rp a double, with bathroom and air-con. If it's empty you might be able to negotiate a cheaper rate, and the service could be anything from overattentive to nonexistent.

The hotels offer a large number of restaurants but there's no choice apart from the hotels, since it's a long walk to get out of the resort area. If you can make it to Bualu village, just to the west, you can find the places where the hotel staff eat, which should offer better value for money. There are some other eating places in the shopping area but you can't just stroll outside to other restaurants, as you can at Sanur.

Getting There & Away

The taxi fare from the airport is 12,000 rp. A bemo from Denpasar costs around 700 rp from Suci bemo station (1000 rp from Tegal station) to Bualu village, just outside the Nusa Dua compound. From there to the hotels is about a km. The bemo service operates on demand but there's usually one every hour, and more when the hotel staff are finishing their shifts – many people commute from Denpasar to Nusa Dua. There's a hotel bus service to Kuta for about 6000 rp return, or to Sanur or Denpasar for 10,000 rp return. You can easily charter a whole bemo between Kuta and Nusa Dua for around 8000 rp, but avoid being pressured into chartering a bemo by yourself if you're happy to wait for the public one.

ULU WATU

The southern peninsula is known as Bukit (*bukit* means 'hill' in Indonesian), but was known to the Dutch as Tafelhoek (Table Point). The road south from Kuta goes around the end of the airport runway, and the main route goes south then east to Nusa Dua. A couple of turn-offs to the west will take you to Jimbaran village, whose main road, Jalan Ulu Watu, continues right down to the end of the peninsula at Ulu Watu. The road is now sealed for the whole distance. At times the road climbs quite high, reaching 200 metres, and there are fine views back over the airport, Kuta and southern Bali. When you see the Ugly Boys 'restaurant' on the left side near the top of a rise, you'll know you're getting close to the surf. The place is littered with surfboards (hire one for 10,000 to 15,000 rp per day if you know how to handle big waves) and Dexter here can give you some information about conditions.

Along the road you'll notice numerous limestone quarries where large blocks of stone are cut by hand. Many of the buildings in southern Bali are constructed from such blocks. Further inland there are some industrial developments, making preformed concrete products from the local limestone cement. This is a dry, sparsely inhabited area – a contrast to the lush, rice-growing country which seems to commence immediately north of the airport.

Pura Luhur Ulu Watu

The temple of Pura Luhur Ulu Watu perches at the south-western tip of the peninsula, where sheer cliffs drop precipitously into the clear blue sea – the temple hangs right over the edge! You enter through an unusual arched gateway flanked by statues of Ganesh; there's a resident horde of monkeys in the compound. Ulu Watu is one of several important temples to the spirits of the sea to be found along the southern coast of Bali. Other temples include Tanah Lot and Rambut Siwi.

Ulu Watu, along with the other well-known temples of the south – Pura Sakenan on Pulau Serangan, Pura Petitenget at Krobokan and the temple at Tanah Lot – is associated with Nirartha, the Javanese priest credited with introducing many of the elements of the Balinese religion to the island. Nirartha retreated to Ulu Watu for his final days.

Surfing

Ulu Watu has another claim to fame. It's

Bali's surfing Mecca, made famous through several classic surfing films. It's a popular locale for the surfers who flock to Bali from all over the world, but particularly from Australia. At a dip in the road, just before the Ulu Watu car park, a sign indicates the way to the Suluban Surf Beach (Pantai Suluban). There will be a crowd of guys on motorbikes here, waiting to taxi you down towards the beach. It's two km down a narrow footpath – OK for motorbikes but nothing more. Take care on a motorbike – the path is narrow, some of the corners are blind and there have been some nasty accidents. From a motorbike park at the end of the track, continue on foot another 250 metres, down to the small gorge which gives access to the surf. There are half a dozen warungs on the northern side of the gorge, perched on a cliff with great views of the various surf breaks. All the serious surfers bring their own boards, but you can hire one here for about 5000 rp an hour. You can also get wax, ding repair stuff and a massage, depending on what you need most.

Places to Stay & Eat

The warungs around the cliff tops offer basic Indonesian food (nasi and mie) and Western fare (jaffles and pancakes) to the keen surfers who flock here. Food prices are reasonable, but it seems cruel to charge surfers 4000 rp for a large beer! The warungs are not really places to stay, but surfers are sometimes able to crash here to get an early start on the morning waves. One tiny losmen, the *Gobleg Inn*, is off the motorbike track to the surf. Run by Wayan Wena, it has only four rooms and asks 15,000 rp per person, including breakfast. The *Bali Cliffs Resort Hotel* is an expensive place, off to the south of the Ulu Watu road overlooking the Indian Ocean.

There are a few places to eat along the road into Ulu Watu. There's the *Ugly Boys* restaurant with basic food and normally priced beer, and the *Warung Indra* opposite – one letter from a hungry surfer raved on about their food for three pages! Further on is the *Corner Pub* and a place to buy petrol.

Denpasar to Ubud

The road from Denpasar via Batubulan, Celuk, Sukawati, Batuan and Mas is the main tourist shopping route of Bali but there are also alternative, quieter routes between the two towns.

The construction of a new central bus and bemo station at Batubulan, east of Denpasar, has radically changed the transport system in the south. To get to Ubud from the beach resorts you first take a bemo to Batubulan. Bemos run directly from Sanur but from Kuta you must take one bemo to Tegal station and another to Batubulan station. The bemo fare from Batubulan to Ubud is about 700 rp and bemos shuttle back and forth so regularly it's no problem jumping on and off along the way. If you want to take a more obscure back route it's easier if you have your own transport.

The official taxi fare between the airport and Ubud is 34,000 rp. You can also charter a bemo between Ubud and Kuta or Sanur for around 20,000 rp.

From the southern beach centres to Ubud there are a couple of alternatives to the regular Batubulan, Celuk, Sukawati and Mas route. Both routes continue directly north from Batubulan. Indeed, the signpost at the junction points to Ubud via this route, rather than the usual main route. Three km from the junction, you fork right at Belaluwan and enter Ubud through Pengosekan and Padangtegal.

If you take the left fork at Belaluwan (which really means continuing on the main road through Belaluwan rather than turning right on to a minor road) the road continues north through Sayan and you can then turn back down to Ubud at Kedewatan and enter the town through Campuan. The road via Sayan is very narrow at times and oncoming vehicles must stop and try to squeeze by each other.

BATUBULAN

Soon after leaving Denpasar the road is lined

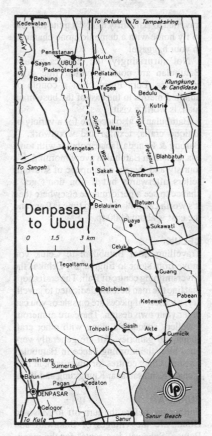

with outlets for Batubulan's main craft – stone sculpture. Batubulan means 'moon stone'. Stone carvers continue along the road to Tegaltamu, where the main road to Ubud does a sharp right turn while the back-road route continues straight on. Batubulan is where the temple gate guardians – seen all over Bali – come from. You'll also find them guarding bridges or making more mundane appearances in restaurants and hotels. The sculpting is often done by quite young boys and you're welcome to watch them chipping away at big blocks of stone. The stone they use is surprisingly soft and light, so if you've travelled to Bali fairly light it's quite feasible to fly home with a demonic stone character in your baggage!

Not surprisingly, the temples around Batubulan are noted for their fine stone sculptures. Pura Puseh, just a couple of hundred metres to the east of the busy main road, is worth a visit.

Batubulan is also a centre for a variety of antique crafts, textiles and woodwork. A Barong & Rangda dance, popular with tourists, is held in Batubulan every morning. It's touristy and there's a stampede of souvenir sellers afterwards but if you don't get a chance to see a performance elsewhere then it's worth catching. Starting time is 9 am and the cost is about 6000 rp.

CELUK

Travelling from Batubulan to Celuk you move from stone to filigree, for Celuk is the silversmithing centre of Bali. The craft shops that line the road here are dedicated to jewellery; a variety of pieces are on sale or you can order your own design. There are numerous jewellery specialists along with other craft shops and galleries. All are generally very busy after the morning dance in Batubulan finishes. Other centres for silverwork in Bali include Kamasan near Klungkung and Kuta.

SUKAWATI

Further on, before the turn-off to Mas and Ubud, are the villages of Sukawati and Batuan. Sukawati is a centre for the manufacture of those noisy wind chimes you hear all over the island and also specialises in temple umbrellas and *lontar* (palm) baskets, dyed with intricate patterns. Sukawati, a bustling market town with a morning fruit and vegetable market, also has a busy art and craft centre (the Pasar Seni). It's just across from the produce market and sells semifinished artwork to craft shops who do the final finishing themselves.

The old palace is behind the produce market, and the town has a long tradition of dance and wayang kulit shadow puppet performance. The small village of Puaya, about a km west from the main road, specialises in

making high-quality leather shadow puppets and masks.

There's an alternative but little-used route via the coast, bypassing Batubulan and Celuk and rejoining the main road to Ubud just before Sukawati. It passes through the coastal village of Gumicik (which has a good beach) and, just back from the coast, the village of Ketewel. A road branches off from Ketewel to the beach at Pabean, a site for religious purification ceremonies. Just north of Ketewel, before the main road, is Guang, another small woodcarving centre.

BATUAN

Batuan is a noted painting centre which came under the influence of Bonnet, Spies and the Pita Maha artists' cooperative at an early stage. Batuan painters produced dynamic black-ink drawings, good examples of which can be seen in Ubud's Puri Lukisan Museum. The big Batuan galleries have the usual range of work on display but some original work still comes from this village.

Today the distinct Batuan style of painting is noted for its inclusion of some very modern elements. Sea scenes are likely to include the odd windsurfer, while tourists with video cameras or riding motorbikes pop up in the otherwise traditional Balinese scenery. Batuan is a centre for carved wooden relief panels and screens, and is also noted for its traditional dance classes.

MAS

Mas means 'gold' but it's woodcarving, particularly mask carving, which is the craft here. The great Majapahit priest Nirartha once lived here and Pura Taman Pule is said to be built on the site of his home. During the three-day Kuningan festival, a Wayang Wong performance (an older version of the Ramayana ballet) is put on in the temple's courtyard.

The road through Mas is almost solidly lined with craft shops and you are welcome to drop in and see the carvers at work, and inspect the myriad items for sale. The price tags in dollars indicate that most business is done with the tour bus hordes but there are plenty of smaller carving operations in the small lanes off the busy main road. Many of these places virtually mass-produce carvings which are then sold to the numerous craft shops. The bigger and more successful craft outlets are often lavishly decorated with fine woodcarvings. The renowned artist Ida Bagus Tilem, whose father was also a noted woodcarver, has a particularly fine gallery. Mas sprawls virtually the whole five km length of road from the Sakah turn-off to Teges.

If you want to stay in Mas, *Taman Harum* has elegant individual bungalows, some of them two-storeyed with balconies overlooking the rice paddies, and there's a swimming pool.

From Mas you can follow the main road the last few km into Ubud or take back-road routes and approach the town through Pengosekan, Padangtegal or even the Monkey Forest.

BLAHBATUH

Although the most direct route to Ubud is to turn off the main road at Sakah and head north through Mas, you can continue on a few km to the turn-off to Blahbatuh and go via Kutri and Bedulu before turning off again for Ubud. In Blahbatuh the Pura Gaduh has a metre-high stone head said to be a portrait

of Kebo Iwa, the legendary strongman and minister to the last king of the Bedulu kingdom (see Bedulu and Gunung Kawi in the Around Ubud section later in this chapter). Gajah Mada, the Majapahit strongman, realised that he could not conquer Bedulu, Bali's strongest kingdom, while Kebo Iwa was there so he lured him away to Java (with promises of women and song) and had him killed.

The stone head is thought to be very old, possibly predating Javanese influence in . Bali, but the temple is a reconstruction of an earlier temple destroyed in the great earthquake of 1917.

About a km west of Blahbatuh on Sungai Petanu is the Tegenungan Waterfall (also known as Srog Srogan) at Belang Singa village. There's a signpost to 'Air Terjun Tegenungan' from the village of Kemenuh on the main road, *(air terjun* means waterfall).

KUTRI

Just beyond Blahbatuh on the western side of the road is Pura Kedarman (also known as Pura Bukit Dharma). If you climb Bukit Dharma nearby, you'll find a hill-top shrine with a stone statue of the eight-armed goddess, Durga. The statue, in the act of killing a demon-possessed water buffalo, is thought to date from the 11th century and shows strong Indian influences.

Another theory is that the image is of Airlangga's mother Mahendradatta, who married King Udayana, Bali's 10th-century ruler. When her son succeeded to the throne she hatched a bitter plot against him and unleashed evil spirits *(leyaks)* upon his kingdom. She was eventually defeated but this incident eventually led to the legend of the rangda, a widow-witch and ruler of evil spirits. The temple at the base of the hill has images of Durga and the body of a barong can be seen in the *bale barong* (literally 'barong building'); the sacred head is kept elsewhere.

From the hill-top lookout you can see down to Sanur on the coast or out to Nusa Lembongan and Nusa Penida. Just beyond

Kutri is a T-junction where you turn west to Bedulu and Ubud or east to Klungkung. The road east crosses a series of deep gorges, the bridges rising high above the valleys.

Ubud

In the hills north of Denpasar, Ubud is the calm and peaceful cultural centre of Bali. It has undergone tremendous development in the past few years but, unlike Kuta, hasn't been ruined by it. Ubud has managed to stay relaxed and beautiful, a place where the evenings are quiet and you can really tell you're in Bali. It's worth remembering that electricity arrived in Ubud only in the mid-70s, and telephones in the late-80s. There's an amazing amount to do in and around Ubud so don't plan to do it in a day. You need at least a few days to appreciate it properly. Ubud is one of those places where days can quickly become weeks and weeks become months.

Orientation

The once small village of Ubud has expanded to encompass its neighbours – Campuan, Penestanan, Padangtegal, Peliatan and Pengosekan are all part of what we see as Ubud today. The crossroads, where the bemos stop, marks the centre of town. On the north (kaja) side is the Ubud Palace, on the south (kelod) side is the market. Monkey Forest Rd, beside the market, runs south to, of course, the Monkey Forest and Ubud's pura dalem (temple of the dead).

Continuing through Ubud, the road drops steeply down to the ravine at Campuan where you find Murni's Warung on one side of the suspension bridge, artist Antonio Blanco's house on the other and the Campuan Hotel on the site of Walter Spies' prewar home. From there the road bends north past many craft shops and galleries. Penestanan, famous for its painters, is just west of Campuan. Further west again is Sayan, where musician Colin McPhee lived in the '30s.

Entering Ubud from Denpasar, the road passes through Peliatan before reaching the junction on Ubud's east side.

Information

Ubud is just high enough to be noticeably cooler than the coast. It's also noticeably wetter.

Tourist Office Ubud has a very friendly and helpful tourist office *(bina wisata)* on the main street. Ubud's survival has been largely due to local efforts. The Ubud tourist office is a local venture, not a government one. It was set up in an effort to defend the village from the tourist onslaught – not by opposing tourism but by providing a service aimed at informing and generating a respect amongst visitors for Balinese culture and customs. The UK-based magazine *New Internationalist* recounted some of the problems that faced the village:

The locals cursed the tourists, for they disturbed ceremonies and dressed impolitely. Guidebooks had told their readers about the family events, airlines had promoted Bali with all its glamorous ceremonies, photographers had made public exhibitions out of private occasions. All of this without asking permission. Foreigners were attracted. They came to Ubud full of expectations. They entered any private house as though the religious ceremonies there were tourist attractions. Conflict after conflict developed, anger mounted.

Boards were put on the gates or walls to warn tourists that the ceremony inside was a private event: 'No Tourist, Please', 'For Guest Only', 'This is a Religious Event', 'Entrance is Forbidden', 'Only for the Family Members'. It was really ugly to see religious offerings and decorations at a compound entrance disturbed by these emergency boards written in a foreign language. Tempers rose further when a group of tourists was ordered to leave a temple because they were disturbing the praying parishioners. The tourists blamed their guide for not informing them. The guide accused the locals of being unfriendly and uncooperative. The villagers chased the guide away.

In 1981, with the problems of the village so acute, a move was made to revive Ubud's former beauty by extensive tree-planting. Then the tourist office was established and its publications even included an English-language newspaper, probably the first such paper to be produced by a village in Indonesia. In many ways the offices have been very successful, although it takes time for the message to get through – an article in the now defunct Australian newspaper, the *National Times*, summed up the problem:

Some greenhorn visitors frequently think the tourist is a king who can do no wrong, possessing an unlimited right to see anything he or she wants to see and to grab as much as possible with as little expense as possible. 'Do you sell tickets for a wedding tour?' 'I want to see a cremation today.' 'Can you give me a good price?' 'How much do you charge to see a tooth-filing ceremony?' ...I know the Balinese do not cry. But I do. I cry when visitors think that Bali is a huge open stage on which any local activity is exhibited to collect money...

Post The town has a pleasant little post office with a poste restante service – the letters sit in a box on the counter and you sort through them yourself. Have your mail addressed to Kantor Pos, Ubud, Bali, Indonesia. You can also get stamps at a couple of places around town, identified by a 'postal services' sign.

Telephone Telephone services in Bali in general and Ubud in particular have improved dramatically in the past few years. Many hotels and losmen now have telephones and you can make international direct-dial calls from Ubud. There's a telephone office on the main street, between the market and the post office turn-off.

Bookshops The excellent Ubud Bookshop is on the main road right next to Ary's Warung in central Ubud. You'll also find a small but excellent selection of books in Murni's Warung and the Museum Neka. The Bookshop is a book exchange on the Monkey Forest Rd.

Other There's the usual selection of bicycle and motorbike hire places and a number of shops selling most items you might require. Ubud even has banks now but they're not as fast as the numerous moneychangers and they do not offer as good an exchange rate.

Ubud's colourful produce market operates every third day. It starts early in the morning but pretty much winds up by lunch time. The main road in the centre becomes one way on market day so, if you're coming in from Denpasar, you have to make a loop around the market and come up the Monkey Forest Rd .

Museums & Galleries

Ubud has two interesting museums, numerous galleries with art for sale, and a number of artists' homes which you can visit to view their work.

Puri Lukisan Museum On the main street of Ubud the Puri Lukisan (Palace of Fine Arts) was established in the mid-50s and displays fine examples of all schools of Balinese art. It was in Ubud that the modern Balinese art movement started, where artists first began to abandon purely religious and court scenes for scenes of everyday life. Rudolf Bonnet, who played such an important role in this change, helped establish the museum's permanent collection in 1973. It's a relatively small museum and has some excellent art.

You enter the museum by crossing a river gully beside the road and can wander from building to building through beautiful gardens with pools, statues and fountains.

In the late '80s the buildings and the gardens were beginning to look rather tired, worn and in need of rejuvenation. Fortunately, a new building has been opened and the permanent collection is now better housed, although the humid weather is still taking its toll on these important works. This gallery, along with the Museum Neka, is worth looking around before you make any decisions about buying art in Ubud.

The museum is open from 8 am to 4 pm daily and admission is 500 rp. There are exhibitions of art for sale in other buildings in the gardens and in a separate display just outside the main garden.

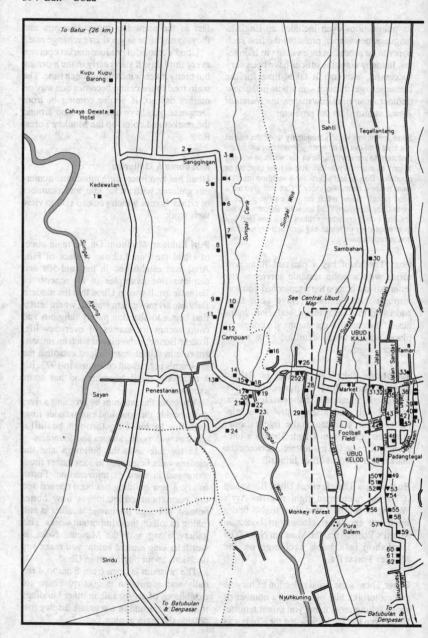

To Batur (26 km)

Kupu Kupu
Barong

Cahaya Dewata
Hotel

Kedewatan

Sahti

Tegallantang

2
Sanggingan
3

4

5

6

7

8

Sungai Cerik

Sungai Wos

Sambahan

30

9   10

11

12
Campuan

See Central Ubud
Map

Sungai Ayung

Sungai

Sayan

Penestanan

13

14
15
17
20
21   22
23

18
19

24

16

26
2527
28

29

UBUD
KAJA

Jalan Suweta

Jalan Sandat

Taman

33

Market

3132

36

Jalan

39
40
421
45
41

43

44

46

Monkey
Football   Forest   47
Field   Road   48

UBUD
KELOD

Padangtegal

49

50   53
51   54
52

55
58

Sindu

Sungai Wos

Monkey Forest

Pura
Dalem

56

57

59

60
61
62

Nyuhkuning

To Batubulan
& Denpasar

To Batubulan
& Denpasar

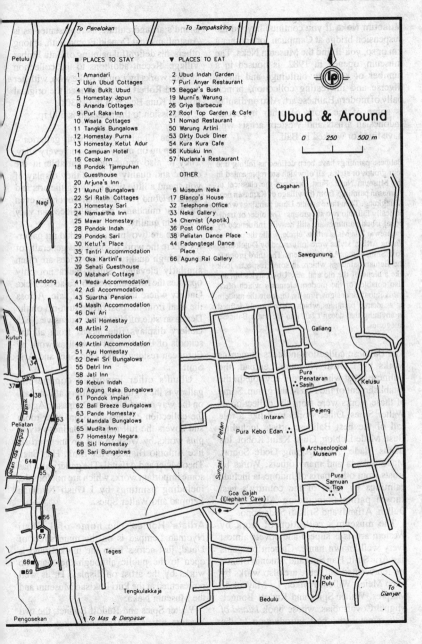

To Penelokan   To Tampaksiring

Ubud & Around

0   250   500 m

■ PLACES TO STAY

1 Amandari
3 Ulun Ubud Cottages
4 Villa Bukit Ubud
5 Homestay Jepun
8 Ananda Cottages
9 Puri Raka Inn
10 Wisata Cottages
11 Tangkis Bungalows
12 Homestay Purna
13 Homestay Ketut Adur
14 Campuan Hotel
16 Cecak Inn
18 Pondok Tjampuhan
   Guesthouse
20 Arjuna's Inn
21 Munut Bungalows
22 Sri Ratih Cottages
23 Homestay Sari
24 Namaartha Inn
25 Mawar Homestay
28 Pondok Indah
29 Pondok Sari
30 Ketut's Place
35 Tantri Accommodation
37 Oka Kartini's
39 Sehati Guesthouse
40 Matahari Cottage
41 Weda Accommodation
42 Adi Accommodation
43 Suartha Pension
45 Masih Accommodation
46 Dwi Ari
47 Jati Homestay
48 Artini 2
   Accommodation
49 Artini Accommodation
51 Ayu Homestay
52 Dewi Sri Bungalows
55 Detri Inn
58 Jati Inn
59 Kebun Indah
60 Agung Raka Bungalows
61 Pondok Impian
62 Bali Breeze Bungalows
63 Pande Homestay
64 Mandala Bungalows
65 Mudita Inn
67 Homestay Negara
68 Siti Homestay
69 Sari Bungalows

▼ PLACES TO EAT

2 Ubud Indah Garden
7 Puri Anyar Restaurant
15 Beggar's Bush
19 Murni's Warung
26 Griya Barbecue
27 Roof Top Garden & Cafe
31 Nomad Restaurant
50 Warung Artini
53 Dirty Duck Diner
54 Kura Kura Cafe
56 Kubuku Inn
57 Nuriana's Restaurant

OTHER

6 Museum Neka
17 Blanco's House
32 Telephone Office
33 Neka Gallery
34 Chemist (Apotik)
36 Post Office
38 Peliatan Dance Place
44 Padangtegal Dance
   Place
66 Agung Rai Gallery

Petulu

Nagi

Andong

Kutuh

Raya

Mantik

Peliatan

Jalan Ida Bagus

Teges

Tengkulakkaja

Pengosekan

To Mas & Denpasar

Cagahan

Sawegunung

Galiang

Pura
Penataran
Sasih

Kelusu

Pejeng

Intaran

Pura Kebo Edan

Archaeological
Museum

Sungai Petan

Goa Gajah
(Elephant Cave)

Pura
Samuan
Tiga

Bedulu

Yeh
Pulu

To
Gianyar

Museum Neka If you continue beyond the suspension bridge at Campuan for another a km or so, you'll find the Museum Neka. The museum, opened in 1982, is housed in a number of separate buildings and has a diverse and interesting collection, principally of modern Balinese art. Also on display is some of the work of other important Indonesian artists and Western artists who have lived or worked in Bali.

Balinese paintings have been defined as falling into four groups or styles, all of which are represented in the Museum Neka. First there are the classical or Kamasan paintings from the village of Kamasan near Klungkung. Then there are the Ubud paintings which basically fall into two subgroups. The older or traditional Ubud paintings are still heavily influenced by the prewar Pita Maha artists' circle, while the postwar Young Artists' styles were influenced by Dutch artist Arie Smit, still an Ubud resident. The third group is the Batuan paintings which, in some respects, look like a blend of the old and new Ubud styles but are also notable for the modern elements which often sneak into their designs. Finally, there are the modern or 'academic' paintings, which can be loosely defined as anything that doesn't fall into the main Balinese categories.

The Balinese collection includes numerous works by I Gusti Nyoman Lempad, the Balinese artist who played a key role in the establishment of the Pita Maha group. Some of these works were from the collection of Walter Spies. Other works read like a role call of the best Balinese artists including Gusti Made Deblog, Gusti Ketut Kobot, Ida Bagus Made, Anak Agung Gede Sobrat, Made Sukada and many others. Works by artists from other parts of Indonesia include paintings by most of the country's best known painters, including Abdul Aziz, Dullah, Affandi and Srihadi Sudarsono.

The museum's collection of work by Western artists is superb and covers almost every well-known name. Current residents like Arie Smit, Han Snel and Antonio Blanco are represented but there are also works by Theo Meier, Willem Hofker, Le Mayeur de Merpres, Walter Spies and Rudolf Bonnet. Miguel Covarrubias, whose book *Island of Bali* remains the best introduction to the island's art and culture, is represented as is Australian artist Donald Friend with, among others, his delightful painting of Batu Jimbar Village. Recent additions to the collection include works by Louise Koke who, with her husband Robert Koke, founded the original hotel at Kuta Beach in the 1930s.

Admission to the museum is 500 rp.

Galleries Ubud is dotted with galleries – they pop up on every street and every alley. They're also enormously variable in the choice and quality of items they display. If you spend a little time studying the arts and crafts in Ubud you'll soon discover that even the most mundane 'me too' piece can vary widely in quality.

There are two 'must see' Ubud art galleries where the work displayed is generally of a very high quality and the prices are often similarly elevated. Suteja Neka not only operates the Museum Neka but also the Neka Gallery where the work is for sale. Across the road from the post office turn-off on the Denpasar side of Ubud, the extensive Neka Gallery displays fine pieces from all the schools of Balinese art as well as work by European residents like Han Snel and Arie Smit.

Ubud's other important commercial gallery is the Agung Rai Gallery at Peliatan, on the way out of Ubud to Denpasar. Again, the collection extends for room after room and covers the full range of Balinese styles plus works by Western and Javanese artists like Antonio Blanco, Arie Smit, Han Snel, Theo Meier and Affandi. The gallery also has some important works which are not for sale, including paintings by I Gusti Nyoman Lempad and Walter Spies.

Artists' Homes The home of I Gusti Nyoman Lempad is on the main street of Ubud, just across from the market, and is open to the public although there are no works by the artist on display. He is well represented at the Puri Lukisan Museum and the Museum Neka.

Walter Spies and Rudolf Bonnet, the two Western artists who played a key role in changing the course of Balinese art from a purely decorative skill, both lived for some time at Campuan, near the suspension bridge. Spies' home is now one of the rooms at the Campuan Hotel and can be inspected if it is not in use; you can even stay there if you book well ahead.

These original visiting artists have been followed by a steady stream of Western dreamers, right down to the present day. Just beside the Campuan suspension bridge, across the river from Murni's Warung, the driveway leads up to Filipino-born artist Antonio Blanco's superbly theatrical house. Entry to the beautiful house and gallery is 500 rp. Blanco's speciality is erotic art and illustrated poetry, though for Blanco, playing the part of the artist is probably just as important as painting.

Arie Smit and Han Snel are other well-known Western artists currently residing in Ubud. In the 1960s Smit sparked the Young Artists' school of painting in Penestanan, just west of Campuan. Han Snel's work is exhibited in a private collection at his restaurant and hotel, just off the main road through Ubud.

Adjoining Villages

The growth of Ubud has engulfed a number of nearby villages, though these have still managed to retain their distinct identities.

Peliatan Just over a km south-east of central Ubud, en route to Denpasar, Peliatan is the dance centre of Ubud and its dance troupe has performed overseas on many occasions. Many long-term visitors stay here to study Balinese or Indonesian dance. There are numerous craft shops and galleries in Peliatan and a variety of places to stay. The village can be a cheaper and quieter alternative to staying in Ubud itself.

Campuan Continuing through Ubud to the west, the road dives down to the deep gorge at Campuan, crossing Sungai Wos on a newer road bridge and a picturesque old suspension bridge. Right by the river is Murni's Warung (see the Places to Eat

section in this chapter), and overlooking the river from the other side is the Hotel Campuan (sometimes spelt Tjampuhan, in the old Dutch manner). This was the site of artist Walter Spies' home (now one of the hotel's rooms) and the centre for the Western circle of the '30s. Visitors can use the hotel's pool for a fee. Across the road from the hotel and across the river from Murni's Warung is the home and gallery of artist Antonio Blanco (see the earlier Artists' Homes section).

The word *campuan* means 'where two rivers meet' and at the confluence of the Wos and Cerik rivers, far below the bridges, is the Pura Gunung Labuh, a temple thought to date back as far as 1000 years. From beside the temple a walking track leads away to the north along the ridge between the rivers.

Penestanan The road bends sharply as it crosses the river at Campuan and then runs north, parallel to the river. If you take the steep uphill road which bends away from the main road you reach Penestanan, centre for the Young Artists' movement instigated by Arie Smit in the 1960s. There are more galleries, many of them specialising in paintings of the Young Artists' style, and numerous losmen around Penestanan. The road winds through the small village and rice paddies, past a small patch of forest and eventually meets the road through Sayan and Kedewatan.

Sayan & Kedewatan West of Penestanan is Sayan, site for Colin McPhee's home in the '30s, so amusingly described in McPhee's *A House in Bali*. North of Sayan is Kedewatan, another small village where the road turns off past Museum Neka and back into Ubud via Campuan. Just west of the villages and the main road is the Yeh Ayung. The deep gorge of this swift-flowing river is now the site for the homes of a number of modern-day McPhees and for several up-market hotels, including one of the most expensive places you can stay in Bali.

Walks

Ubud is a place for leisurely strolls – wanders through the rice paddies, lazy rambles through the forests, walks to surrounding villages. There are lots of interesting walks in the area, including one to Ubud's famous Monkey Forest.

Around Town There's plenty to see simply wandering around the centre of Ubud. Look around the market in the early morning, it's across the road from the old palace in the centre of town and operates every third day. Or sip a coffee in the *Lotus Cafe* and gaze across the lotus-filled pond a little further up the road.

When you're wandering the streets of Ubud, look for the little black signs by each gateway. They detail the name, occupation and other vital details of the occupant, like the number of children; LK stands for laki (boy), PR for prempuan (girl) and JML for jumlah (total). In one early morning stroll the biggest I saw were $8 + 6 = 14$ and $7 + 8 = 15$! Few families seem to have fewer than five or six children.

Tony Wheeler

Monkey Forest Just wander down the Monkey Forest Rd from the centre of Ubud and you'll arrive in a small but dense forest. It's inhabited by a handsome band of monkeys ever ready for passing tourists who just might have peanuts available for a handout. Peanut vendors are usually waiting to provide monkey sustenance but be warned, the monkeys have become far too used to visitors and can put on ferocious displays of temperament if you don't come through with the goods, and quick. If you're not planning on feeding them don't give any hint that you might have something interesting in a pocket or a bag. Although the forest is a regular thoroughfare you'll be asked for a donation (500 rp is more than sufficient) at the start of the forest.

Ubud's interesting old pura dalem (temple of the dead) is in the forest, for this is the inauspicious, kelod side of town. Look for the rangda figures devouring children at the entrance to the inner temple. You can walk to Peliatan from Ubud via the Monkey Forest, which is more interesting and quieter than following the main road.

Turning right down the track immediately after the Monkey Forest Hideway will take you to a pool, down the gorge on the left.

Nearby Villages Popular strolls to neighbouring villages include one to Peliatan, with its famous dance troupe, and to Penestanan, the 'village of young artists'. You can walk north from Penestanan and rejoin the main road near the Museum Neka, or walk south and cross the river to the Monkey Forest. If you continue through the Monkey Forest from Ubud you'll come to the small village of Nyuhkuning, which is noted for its woodcarving. Or follow the road down to Pengosekan, south of Peliatan, another village with many painters.

Petulu In the late afternoon each day you can enjoy the spectacular sight of thousands of herons arriving home in Petulu. They nest in the trees along the road through the village and make a spectacular sight as they fly in and commence squabbling over the prime perching places.

Some recent road works have made it possible to visit the village as a pleasant round-trip walk or bicycle ride of about 10 km. From Ubud take the road beside the cinema and bemo stop (Jalan Suwatu) and walk straight north. It's surprising how quickly you get out of glitzy Ubud and into relatively unchanged countryside. Although people hail you in English, older women are often bare-breasted and the dogs definitely don't like foreigners.

The road continues through the village of Tunjungan, which seems to be totally devoted to the carving of garudas. Half a dozen shops by the roadside offer them in all sizes from a few cm high to giant two-metre garudas which probably weigh a ton. Shortly after Tunjungan there's a well signposted right turn to Petulu. It's about seven km from Ubud; there are roadside markers every km to help you gauge your progress.

Walk quickly under the trees if the herons are already roosting – copious droppings on the road will indicate whether it's wise not to hang around. Donations are requested at the other end of the village. About a km past the village is the Tegallantang to Ubud road, from where it's a couple of km back to the centre of Ubud. A number of woodcarving outlets and an umbrella shop mark the Petulu turn-off if you're coming up from Ubud on this road.

Pejeng If you take the road east out of Ubud and continue straight on past the T-junction, there's a wonderful trail that leads through typical Balinese country to the superb gorge of Sungai Petanu that runs by the Goa Gajah (Elephant Cave). Following the trail beyond the river eventually brings you out at Pejeng, a very fine walk. You can visit the important temples at Pejeng (see the Ubud & Around map) and make your way back to Ubud via Yeh Pulu and Goa Gajah, or continue up the road to Tampaksiring.

Other Walks Take the trail up beside the river on the Ubud side of Murni's Warung to the beautiful hill at Campuan. Or walk down to the lovely Yeh Ayung in the villages of Kedewatan or Sayan.

Places to Stay

Even in the mid-70s, when the tourist boom had definitely arrived down on the coast, Ubud had only a handful of accommodation possibilities. The construction boom that reached here in the '80s, however, is still continuing and today Ubud not only has a great many budget hotels but also a wide choice of mid-range and expensive places. Fortunately, Ubud still does not have any of the big mass-tourism hotels found at Sanur or Nusa Dua but there are some very luxurious small hotels.

You'll find places fairly widely scattered around Ubud – they are along the main road and on the roads leading off it. In particular the Monkey Forest Rd has become a real accommodation centre, with places all the way down to the forest.

There are also lots of places in surrounding villages like Peliatan and Penestanan or simply scattered around the rice paddies. Several of the new top-end establishments are perched on the edge of the spectacular Yeh Ayung Gorge, at Kedewatan and Sayan, a few km out of Ubud. If you're staying in one of the budget-priced 'remote' losmen – and they can be very relaxing, peaceful places to stay – it's probably wise to have a torch (flashlight) with you if you want to avoid falling into a rice paddy on some starry, starry night.

Since Ubud is full of artists and dancers you can often find a losmen run by someone involved with the arts – this will enable you to pick up some of the guidelines for appreciating Balinese art. At most cheaper and mid-range places, breakfast is included in the price.

Places to Stay – bottom end Ubud has a huge choice of places to stay and, since they tend to congregate, you can easily look at several before making a choice. What follows is just a sample; there are many other excellent places apart from those mentioned. These days prices tend to vary with demand but you can often find cheaper doubles with toilet and mandi for 10,000 rp or less. In the off-season you can still find a double for 6000 rp.

Ubud There are lots of places in the bottom-end price bracket off the main road and down the Monkey Forest Rd. The small lanes and alleys between the football field and the market have much of Ubud's cheaper accommodation. There's nothing to choose between these numerous losmen. Just wander down the narrow lanes, have a look in a few, compare the prices and facilities and make your choice. Prices depend on the demand at the time but you should be able to find doubles with breakfast at 10,000 rp or less.

Close to the top of Monkey Forest Rd, near the market, is one of Ubud's really long runners – *Canderi's* (or Candri's or Tjanderi's depending which sign or spelling style you choose). It's a fairly straightforward losmen-style place with singles for

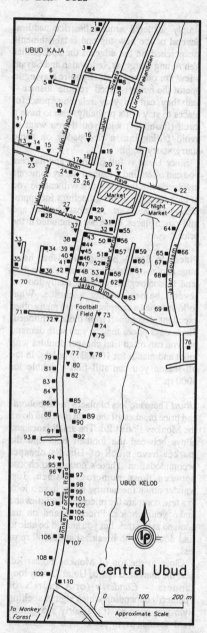

■ **PLACES TO STAY**

1   Kajeng Homestay
2   Gusti's Garden Bungalow
3   Lecuk Inn
4   Arjana Accommodation
5   Siti Bungalows
7   Shanti's Homestay
8   Hotel Ubud
9   Suci Inn
10 Roja's Homestay
12 Mumbul Inn
14 Puri Saraswati
20 Sudharsana Bungalows
27 Suarsena House
29 Happy Inn
30 Canderi's Losmen & Warung
31 Yuni's House
32 Hibiscus Bungalows
34 Oka Wati's Sunset Bungalows
35 Igna 2 Accommodation
36 Sari Nadi Accommodation
38 Alit's House
39 Puri Muwa Bungalows
41 Dewa House
42 Igna Accommodation
43 Pandawa Homestay
44 Gayatri Accommodation
46 Badra Accommodation
48 Ibu Rai Bungalows
50 Gandra House
51 Sudartha House
52 Seroni Bungalows
53 Mertha House
54 Surawan House
55 Widiana's House Bungalows
56 Sania's House
57 Wija House
58 Ning's House
59 Sayong's House

8000 to 10,000 rp and doubles for 15,000 rp. Canderi's has been going almost as long as travellers have been staying in Ubud.

Other places along the Monkey Forest Rd include *Warsi's House* and *Karyawan Accommodation*, both simple, friendly and quite typical losmen-style places. The very clean and well-kept *Frog Pond Inn* is becoming surrounded by encroaching development but there's still a sign at the entrance suggesting that if there's nobody around you can select a vacant room and make yourself at

60	Dewi Putra House
61	Raka House
62	Devi House
63	Esty's House
64	Wayan Karya Homestay
65	Wena Homestay
66	Shana Homestay
67	Nirvana Pension
68	Agung's Cottages
69	Yoga Pension
71	Bendi's Accommodation
74	Wahyu Bungalows
76	Ramasita Pension
79	Accommodation Kerta
81	Karyawan Accommodation
82	Frog Pond Inn
83	Ubud Village Hotel
85	Puri Garden Bungalow
87	Adi Cottages
88	Pertiwi Bungalows
89	Rice Paddy Bungalows
90	Sri Bungalows
91	Villa Rasa Sayang
92	Nani House (Karsi Homestay)
93	Jati 3 Bungalows & Putih Accommodation
95	Jaya Accommodation
97	Ibunda Inn
98	Ubud Bungalows
99	Warsi's House
100	Dewi Ayu Accommodation
103	Ubud Tenau Bungalows
104	Fibra Inn
105	Ubud Inn
106	Lempung Accommodation
108	Pande Permai Bungalows
109	Monkey Forest Hideaway
110	Hotel Champlung Sari

▼ PLACES TO EAT

6	Han Snel's Garden Restaurant
13	Mumbul's Cafe
15	Lotus Cafe
16	Coconut's Cafe
21	Restaurant Puri Pusaka
23	Menara Restaurant
24	Ary's Warung
28	Satri's Warung
33	Oka Wati's Warung
37	Ayu's Kitchen
45	Enny's Restaurant
47	Restaurant Dennis
49	Lilies Restaurant
70	Beji's Cafe
72	Bendi's Restaurant
73	Harry Chew's Restoran
75	Ubud Dancer Restaurant
77	Ibu Rai Restaurant
78	Cafe Bali
80	Dian Restaurant
84	Coco Restaurant
86	Cafe Wayan
94	Jaya Cafe
96	Yudit Restaurant & Bakery
101	Warsa's Cafe
102	Ubud Restaurant
107	Fruit Bat Restaurant

OTHER

11	Museum Puri Lukisan
17	Cinema
18	Bemo Stop
19	Palace & Hotel Puri Saren Agung
22	IGusti Nyoman Lempad's home
25	Ubud Bookshop
26	Tourist Office (Bina Wisata)
40	Bookshop

home. Singles/doubles including breakfast cost 7000/10,000 rp.

Further down, *Ibunda's Inn* is a pleasant place with rooms at 15,000 rp or 25,000 rp with hot water. There are many other places along the road but right at the bottom, almost in the forest, is the secluded and pleasant *Monkey Forest Hideaway* (☎ 200361-95354). Doubles cost around 20,000 rp and some of the rooms, with their balconies overlooking the forest, are quite romantic.

On Jalan Suwata, *Suci Inn* is across from the banyan tree. Simple rooms with bathroom cost 8000 rp in the front, 10,000 rp in the back area. The rooms all have small verandahs looking out on the central garden and it's a friendly, relaxed place, pleasantly quiet yet very central. Next door to the Suci Inn is the *Hotel Ubud* one of Ubud's oldest places; for many years it was called the 'Hotel Oboed', the Dutch spelling indicating its age.

If you continue walking along Jalan Suwata for another 10 minutes you'll come to a small group of places to stay, the best known of which is *Ketut's Place* (☎ 200361-95304). See the Ubud & Around map. The rooms are in a family compound and cost 10,000/15,000 rp for singles/doubles in the front and 25,000 rp (35,000 rp with hot water) for the individual cottages at the back. There's a pleasant garden in this comfortable and friendly place where Ketut Suartana puts on his regular Balinese feasts – see the Places to Eat section for more information.

There are many other places worth investigating in central Ubud. *Roja's Homestay*, off Jalan Kajang, is close to other low-priced losmen. The *Mumbul Inn* (☎ 200361-95364) is near the Puri Lukisan Museum on the main road and has simple, spartan rooms at 10,000/20,000 rp for singles/doubles. More losmen can be found down towards Murni's Warung at Campuan or around the post office.

Around Ubud There are lots of places around Ubud, either in neighbouring villages or just out in the rice paddies. Cross the suspension bridge by Murni's, for example, and take the steep path uphill by Blanco's house. There you'll find a pretty little group of homestays including the attractive *Arjuna's Inn*, run by the artist's daughter. There are more further up in the rice paddies around Penestanan, like the nicely situated *Namaartha Inn*.

You'll find several places out of Ubud on the Peliatan road, like the *Mudita Inn* with its shady garden. At the junction where the road bends sharp left to Denpasar you'll see a sign for the *Sari Bungalows*, just 100 metres or so off the road. It's a pleasantly quiet location and good value with singles at 3500 to 5000 rp and doubles from 6000 rp, all including a 'big breakfast'. Nearby is the *Siti Homestay* with a beautiful garden and charming owners.

Take the back road from Peliatan to Ubud and you'll pass the *Bali Breeze* and the pleasant *Jati Inn* which has two-storeyed rooms with great views across the rice paddies. There's been a lot of recent construction

along this road and into Ubud through Padangtegal.

Places to Stay – middle Accommodation places costing around 20,000 to 30,000 rp are becoming more common and are almost always equipped with a swimming pool. Where the Campuan Hotel's prewar pool was once the only one in Ubud, there are now a great many pools dotted amongst the rice paddies. For most mid-range hotels, service, tax and breakfast are usually included in the price.

Ubud The Monkey Forest Rd has a number of these newer mid-range places, although some of them are very dull and featureless. Near the top of the Monkey Forest Rd and off to the right you'll find *Oka Wati's Sunset Bungalows* (☎ 200361-95063), a very pleasant and clean place right on the rice paddies. Prices range from 39,000/49,000 to 78,000/98,000 rp for singles/doubles. There's a swimming pool and a restaurant presided over by Oka Wati, a familiar face to visitors to Ubud since the early '70s.

A little further down, the *Ubud Village Hotel* (☎ 200361-95069) is one of the few new places built with some imagination and taste. The pleasantly decorated rooms, each with a separate garden entrance, cost 59,000/68,500 rp. There's a swimming pool with swim-up bar and other luxuries.

Also on Monkey Forest Rd and almost at the forest, the *Ubud Inn* (☎ 200361-95188) is one of the longer established places on this road. It has a variety of bungalows and rooms dotted around a spacious garden area with a swimming pool. Rooms cost 49,000/59,000 rp with fan, 59,000/78,000 rp with air-con and there are some two-storeyed family rooms at 88,000 rp. The brick rooms have carved wood and thatched roofs and they're quite cool, each with a private bathroom. The upstairs verandah on the two-storeyed rooms is ideal for gazing out over the rapidly disappearing rice paddies. Next door the, *Fibra Inn* has rooms at 49,000/59,000 rp, and a swimming pool.

The newer Monkey Forest Rd hotels are

not always so interesting. *Pertiwi Bungalows* (☎ 200361-95236) has comfortable rooms and a swimming pool but there's nothing very special about it. Nightly costs are 59,000/68,500 rp or 68,500/78,000 rp but service, tax and breakfast are all extra.

There are a number of places along the main road through Ubud but one of the nicest has to be artist Han Snel's *Siti Bungalows*, hidden away behind the Lotus Cafe. Some of the very pleasant individual cottages are perched right on the edge of the river gorge, looking across to the Puri Lukisan Museum on the other side. There are seven rooms, the nightly cost is 78,000 rp and it's pleasantly quiet, back off the main road, yet close to the town centre.

Along the main road, several of the places to stay are associated with the old palaces of Ubud. The pleasant and well-kept *Puri Saraswati*, near the palace of that name, has rooms at 29,000/39,000 rp and 59,000/68,500 rp. The *Hotel Puri Saren Agung*, near the bemo stop in the centre of Ubud, is part of the home of the late head of Ubud's royal family. The bungalows each have a private courtyard and displays of Balinese antiques.

Around Ubud On the main road but at the Peliatan end of Ubud is *Oka Kartini's*, another long-term survivor now with a swimming pool and other mod cons.

Close to the river junction in Campuan is *Murni's House*, run from Murni's Warung. There are apartments with verandahs for 78,000 rp and also complete six-roomed houses for 156,000 rp. Right across the river from the warung, squeezed between the river and Blanco's house, is the *Pondok Tjampuhan Guesthouse*, with doubles at 45,000 rp. Many other mid-range places with pools have popped up recently, including the *Baliubud Cottages* just beyond Campuan in Penestanan and the *Dewi Sri Bungalows* down towards the Monkey Forest by the back route in Padangtegal.

Some distance out of town, opposite and a little before the Museum Neka, the relaxed and pretty *Ananda Cottages* has rooms at 59,000/88,000 rp or two-storeyed family

rooms for 186,000 rp; prices include breakfast.

Places to Stay – top end Just up beyond the suspension bridge the long-established *Hotel Campuan* (or Tjampuhan if you prefer the old spelling) is beautifully situated overlooking the river confluence and Pura Gunung Labuh. The rooms are individual bungalows in a wonderful garden and cost 88,000 rp. The hotel is built on the site of artist Walter Spies' 1930s home and his small house is now one of the rooms. He was also responsible for the pool although it has been refurbished in the hotel's recent major renovation.

From the Campuan Hotel, the road out of Ubud passes the Neka Gallery, about a km further on, and just beyond the gallery is the turn-off to the *Ulun Ubud Cottages* (☎ 200361-95024). The bungalows are beautifully draped down the hillside overlooking the Sungai Cerik and rooms cost 78,000/107,000 to 117,000/166,000 rp for singles/doubles. There are also larger, two-bedroom family bungalows at 215,000 rp. Rates include breakfast, taxes and service and there's a restaurant, bar and swimming pool.

Beyond Ulun Ubud Cottages, near the Kedewatan junction, is Ubud's most luxurious hotel, the *Amandari* (☎ 200361-95333). Standard rooms cost 392,000 to 588,000 rp a night but if this doesn't seem good enough there are 'pool deluxe' rooms at 980,000 rp a night or you can even have a room with your own private swimming pool at 1,176,000 rp a night. Service (10%) and tax (5½%) are extra. The 27 beautifully decorated rooms are huge and have superb views over the rice paddies or down to the Yeh Ayung. The hotel's large swimming pool seems to drop over the edge right down to the river. The Amandari is close to where prewar visitor Colin McPhee built the home he wrote about in *A House in Bali*.

If you head north from the Kedewatan junction you soon come to *Cahaya Dewata* (☎ 200361-95495), which overlooks the same magnificent river gorge. Rooms cost

78,000/88,000 rp for singles/doubles or 117,000 rp for suites, plus service and tax. A little further along, about 800 metres north of the junction, is *Kupu Kupu Barong* (☎ 2095470/8/9). Clinging precariously to the steep sides of the Yeh Ayung Gorge, each of the beautiful two-storeyed bungalows has a bedroom and living room and costs 382,000 or 441,000 rp a night. Six of the 17 bungalows have two bedrooms, some of them have open-air spa baths. Tax and service charges are extra and children under 12 years of age are not welcome. The view from the pool and restaurant is also superb.

Back in Ubud, the *Hotel Champlung Sari 2* (☎ 200361-95418, 95473, 95349) overlooks the Monkey Forest. Singles/doubles cost from 98,000/117,000 to 137,000/176,000 rp and there's a swimming pool, restaurant, bar and all other mod cons. Despite these luxuries, the place is featureless and dull – a sad indication that Ubud has been targeted for an injection of mass tourism.

Places to Eat

Ubud's numerous restaurants probably offer the best, most interesting and, if you search them out, most authentically Indonesian and Balinese food on the island. This is not to say you can't get excellent Western food if you want, simply that nasi campur (steamed rice mixed with a bit of everything) will also feature on the menu.

Monkey Forest Rd Start with the best by wandering down Monkey Forest Rd to *Cafe Wayan*, which many Ubud regulars claim has the best food in town. There's a room in the front and a surprising number of tables in the open air at the back. At 2900 rp the nasi campur is terrific, the curry ayam (curried chicken) at 5250 rp is superb. Western dishes like spaghetti at 4500 rp also feature. Desserts include the famed coconut pie, or you could even risk 'death by chocolate', a definite case of chocolate cake overkill.

The Monkey Forest Rd has several other interesting eating possibilities including, a little further down towards the forest, the popular and long-running *Ubud Restaurant* which also features some authentic local dishes. Or try the *Yudit Restaurant & Bakery* which has pretty good pizzas for 5000 rp and good bread, rolls and other baked goods. *Oka Wati's*, one of Ubud's long-term institutions and still a pleasant, friendly and economical place to eat, has no surprises on the menu but you can get a good mee goreng (fried noodles) and excellent pancakes.

There are a number of low-priced eating places along the market end of Monkey Forest Rd. *Canderi's Losmen and Warung* is another real institution. Travellers from the early '70s will remember when this was one of the very few places to eat in Ubud, back in the days when Ubud didn't even have electricity. *Lilies Restaurant* and *Restaurant Dennis* are other popular small places up at this end of the road, or try *Bendi's* across from the football field or *Harry Chew's Restoran* near the northern side of the field.

Jalan Raya The main road through town also offers plenty of interesting dining possibilities including the popular and dirt-cheap night market (Pasar Malam) which sets up at dusk beside the main market area. Just beyond the Pasar Malam is the *Nomad Restaurant*, notable as one of the few places open really late at night, although these days everything in Ubud seems to be open a bit later.

Right in the centre of town, the *Lotus Cafe* is a relaxed place for a light lunch or a snack any time. Compared with other places in Ubud it's definitely rather pricey but that doesn't seem to scare many people away; the Lotus is still the place to see and be seen in Ubud. Even a humble nasi campur is around 5000 rp at the Lotus, most main courses are 5000 to 7000 rp, a slice of cheesecake will set you back 3000 rp and even an ice juice is 2000 rp. The Lotus is closed on Monday.

Across the road, *Ary's Warung* is just as glossy as the Lotus but somewhat cheaper – a nasi campur costs 2700 rp. Or continue a few steps beyond the Lotus on the same side of the road to *Mumbul's Cafe*, a small place with friendly service and excellent food. There's even a children's menu.

One of Ubud's real dining pleasures is *Han Snel's Garden Restaurant* off the main road and more or less directly behind the Lotus Cafe. The food is good, the quantities copious, the setting beautiful (frogs croak in the background) and the service impeccable. Main courses are generally 6000 to 7500 rp and desserts 2000 to 3000 rp. It's closed on Sunday.

Continue down the main road towards Campuan to find the *Menara Restaurant* opposite the Lotus, the *Rumah Makan Cacik* which is popular even with local people, the *Griya Barbecue* for barbecued food and the *Roof Top Garden & Cafe* with good views from its elevated position.

Ubud has something of a reputation as an international jet-setters' hangout and if they aren't at the Lotus then Murni's is where you're likely to find them. *Murni's Warung*, beside the Campuan suspension bridge, offers excellent food in a beautiful setting. The satay is served in a personal charcoal holder for 3900 rp, the nasi campur for 3400 rp is fantastic and you can get an excellent hamburger for the same price. To top it all the cakes are simply superb. Murni's also has some interesting arts and crafts on sale and a small but very good selection of books on Bali. It's closed on Wednesday.

Other interesting places to try include the *Puri Pusaka*, opposite the market with a lengthy menu of Indonesian and Balinese specialities. Above the suspension bridge and across the river from Murni's, *Beggar's Bush* has a pleasant bar with draught Bintang beer. It's the local Hash House Harriers meeting point. There are also places along the road to Peliatan and, of course, countless warungs scattered everywhere.

Entertainment

Entertainment in Ubud means watching Balinese dances so head down to Kuta if you want discos and Western music. If you're in the right place at the right time you can still catch dances put on for temple ceremonies and an essentially local audience, but even the strictly tourist dances are generally put on with a high degree of skill and commitment. Indeed, the competition between the various Ubud dance troupes is so intense these days that local connoisseurs even whisper the unthinkable – that the Peliatan troupe is no longer necessarily the best!

Entry is usually 5000 rp, and this includes transport to performances further out from central Ubud, particularly at Bona village, 12 km away. You can buy tickets at the performance place but it's hard to escape the attentions of commissioned ticket sellers around Ubud market and down Monkey Forest Rd. Ubud's bina wisata (tourist office) has information on current performance nights but the following list gives a good idea of the possibilities:

Sunday
    Kechak dance – Padangtegal, Ubud
    Kechak and Sanghyang dances – Bona
    Ladies' orchestra & dance – Peliatan
Monday
    Legong – Puri Saren, Ubud
    Kechak and Sanghyang dances – Bona
    Ramayana ballet – Pura Dalem, Ubud
Tuesday
    Mahabharata dance – Teges
    Ramayana ballet – Puri Saren, Ubud
Wednesday
    Wayang kulit play – Oka Kartini, Ubud
    Kechak and Sanghyang dances – Bona
    Sunda Upabunda – Puri Saren, Ubud
    Legong – Banjar Tengah, Peliatan
Thursday
    Gabor – Puri Saren, Ubud
Friday
    Barong & Rangda – Puri Saren, Ubud
    Kechak and Sanghyang dances – Bona
    Legong dance – Peliatan
Saturday
    Legong dance – Puri Saren, Ubud
    Legong dance – Pura Dalem, Puri Ubud

For descriptions of these dances, see the Music, Dance & Drama section earlier in this chapter.

Things to Buy

Ubud has a wide variety of shops and art galleries. It's also worth investigating smaller places or places further out from the centre. As in other places in Bali, so much is completely standard that it's a great pleasure when you find something really different. Murni's, down by the river, always seems to have something unusual – pretty cushion covers, carved and painted mirror frames, strange pottery.

Small shops by the market and along Monkey Forest Rd often have good wood-carvings, particularly masks. M Nama, on the Peliatan corner, also has lots of interesting woodcarvings. There are some other good woodcarving places along the road from here to Goa Gajah. At Goa Gajah is a host of stalls selling leatherwork. You'll find good places for paintings along the main road through Ubud or beyond the suspension bridge towards the Museum Neka. The main problem with Ubud is that there are so many places, it's difficult to find items that rise above the 'average'.

Getting There & Away

Bemos leave from the stop beside the cinema building in the middle of town. To get to Denpasar or the southern tourist centres you first take a bemo to Denpasar's Batubulan bus/bemo station for about 700 rp. From there bemos run to places all over Bali. There are direct bemos between Batubulan and Sanur but for Kuta you have to take a bemo from the Batubulan station to the Tegal station on the Kuta side of Denpasar for 500 rp and another bemo from there.

If you're staying in Ubud and have gone to Denpasar or Kuta for the day remember that bemo services tail off rapidly after about 4 pm. If you miss the last bemo you'll either have to stay overnight or charter a bemo.

A chartered bemo is the Balinese equivalent of a taxi and you will get regular offers of 'transport' from bemo operators. A typical charter fare to Kuta or the airport is about 20,000 rp, while the official taxi fare from the airport to Ubud is 34,000 rp.

If tangling with bemos, either public or chartered, doesn't appeal you can take one of the tourist shuttle buses which operate to a fixed schedule directly between Ubud and other tourist centres. There are plenty of signs around Ubud announcing departure times and ticket sales. Fares to Sanur, Kuta or the airport are 3000 rp; to Padangbai, Candidasa or Kintamani 6000 rp and to Singaraja and Lovina Beach 10,000 rp.

Getting Around

To get to places around Ubud you can generally count on paying 200 to 350 rp by bemo. Count on about 30 rp a km with a 200 rp minimum. Many places in Ubud rent mountain bikes at 3000 rp a day, or 2500 rp a day for longer-term rental. Places hiring out cars and motorbikes are equally plentiful.

Numerous tours (day trips or longer) also operate from Ubud. A day tour typically costs 10,000 to 15,000 rp.

Around Ubud

The Pejeng region around Ubud encompasses many of the most ancient monuments and relics in Bali, some of them well known and very much on the beaten track, others relatively unknown and little visited. Most of them are found along the route from Ubud via Goa Gajah and Bedulu then up the road towards Gunung Batur via Gunung Kawi and Tampaksiring. Some of these sites are heavily overrun by the tourist hordes, but others are just far enough off the beaten track to leave the crowds behind.

Getting Around

You can reach most of the places around Ubud by bemo and on foot. If you're planning to see a lot of them it's a good idea to start at Tampaksiring (14 km from Ubud), then any walking you have to do is back downhill. It's only two km from Tirta Empul at Tampaksiring to Gunung Kawi – you can follow the path beside the river.

From Gunung Kawi you can take bemos back down to Pejeng, Bedulu, Goa Gajah and on to Ubud. Pejeng to the Bedulu turn-off is only about a km and from there it's a half km or so to Yeh Pulu and a similar distance to Goa Gajah. Alternatively, from

Pejeng you can cut across directly to Ubud, a pleasant walk with fine views. See Walks, in the Ubud section, for more details.

If you have your own transport you can make a loop trip by turning north from the T-junction just east of Ubud (ie away from Peliatan) and following the road north to the fork just beyond Tegalalang. From there take

the right fork to Kedisan where you turn east to Tampaksiring. You can then return from Tampaksiring by the regular road through Pejeng.

GOA GAJAH

Only a short distance beyond Peliatan, on the road to Pejeng and Gianyar, a car park on the

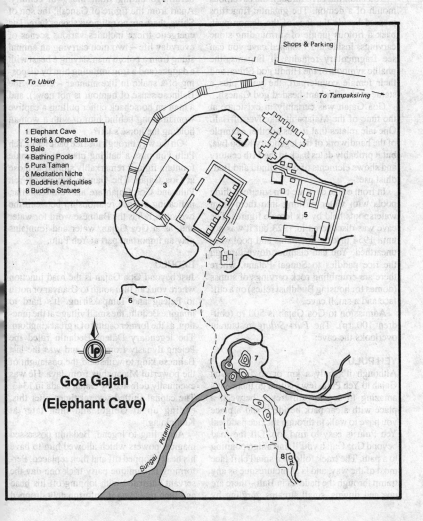

Legend

1 Elephant Cave
2 Hariti & Other Statues
3 Bale
4 Bathing Pools
5 Pura Taman
6 Meditation Niche
7 Buddhist Antiquities
8 Buddha Statues

Shops & Parking

To Ubud

To Tampaksiring

Goa Gajah
(Elephant Cave)

Sungai Petanu

northern side of the road marks the site of Goa Gajah (Elephant Cave). The cave is carved into a rock face, reached by a flight of steps down from the other side of the road. There were never any elephants in Bali; the cave probably takes its name from nearby Sungai Petanu, which at one time was known as Elephant River.

You enter the cave through the cavernous mouth of a demon. The gigantic fingertips pressed beside the face of the demon push back a riotous jungle of surrounding stone carvings. Inside the T-shaped cave you can see fragmentary remains of lingams, the phallic symbols of the Hindu god Shiva, and their female counterpart, the yoni, plus a statue of the elephant-headed god Ganesh.

Goa Gajah was certainly in existence at the time of the Majapahit takeover of Bali. One tale relates that it was another example of the handiwork of the legendary Kebo Iwa, but it probably dates back to the 11th century and shows elements of both Hindu and Buddhist use.

In front of the cave are two square bathing pools with water gushing into them from waterspouts held by six female figures. The cave was discovered in 1923 but it was not until 1954 that the fountains and pool were unearthed. You can clamber down through the rice paddies to Sungai Petanu, where there are crumbling rock carvings of stupas (domes for housing Buddhist relics) on a cliff face and a small cave.

Admission to Goa Gajah is 500 rp (children 100 rp). The *Puri Suling* restaurant overlooks the cave.

YEH PULU

Although it's only a km or so from Goa Gajah to Yeh Pulu, few visitors go there – it's amazing to see the difference between a place with a car park beside it and a place you have to walk to through the rice paddies! Yeh Pulu is easy to find too. Off the road beyond Goa Gajah you'll find a sign pointing to a path. The track follows a small cliff face most of the way, and is as picturesque as any tramp through the paddies in Bali – there are ups and downs, small streams gurgling by

and Heath Robinson bamboo contraptions channelling water across gullies from one series of paddies to another.

Eventually, a small gateway leads to the ancient rock carvings at Yeh Pulu. Only excavated in 1925 these are some of the oldest relics in Bali. The carved cliff face is about 25 metres long and is believed to be a hermitage dating from the 14th century. Apart from the figure of Ganesh, the son of Shiva, there are no religious scenes here. The energetic frieze includes various scenes of everyday life – two men carrying an animal slung from a pole, a man slaying a beast with a dagger (and a frog imitating him by disposing of a snake in like manner – clearly the Balinese sense of humour is not new!), and a man on horseback either pulling a captive woman along behind him or with a woman holding the horse's tail?

On the way through the rice paddies to Yeh Pulu you pass a bathing place with female fountain figures remarkably similar to those at Goa Gajah. The Ganesh figures of Yeh Pulu and Goa Gajah are also quite similar, indicating a close relationship between the two sites. *Yeh* is the Balinese word for water and, as at Goa Gajah, water and fountains play an important part at Yeh Pulu.

BEDULU

Just beyond Goa Gajah is the road junction where you can turn south to Gianyar or north to Pejeng and Tampaksiring. It's hard to imagine Bedulu, the small village at the junction, as the former capital of a great kingdom. The legendary Dalem Bedaulu ruled the Pejeng dynasty from here and was the last Balinese king to withstand the onslaught of the powerful Majapahits from Java. He was eventually defeated by Gajah Mada in 1343. The capital shifted several times after this, ending up at Gelgel and then later at Klungkung.

According to legend, Bedaulu possessed magical powers which allowed him to have his head chopped off and then replaced. Performing this unique party trick one day the servant entrusted with lopping off his head and then replacing it unfortunately dropped it in a river and, to his horror, watched it float away. Looking around in panic for a replacement he grabbed a pig, cut off its head and popped it upon the king's shoulders. Thereafter the king was forced to sit on a high throne and forbade his subjects to look up at him; Bedaulu means 'he who changed heads'.

AROUND BEDULU

There are several interesting sites around Bedulu and up the road towards Pejeng.

Pura Samuan Tiga

The Pura Samuan Tiga (Temple of the Meeting of the Three) is about 100 metres east of the Bedulu junction. Follow the sign to the government rest house to find this important 11th-century temple. The annual Odalan festival takes place here on the full moon of the 10th month of the lunar calendar, rather than on the shorter 210-day Balinese calendar. Throngs of Balinese flock to the huge temple courtyard from all over the island.

Bedulu Arkeologi Gedong Arca

The Bedulu Archaeological Museum (Bedulu Arkeologi Gedong Arca) is about two km north of Bedulu and includes a collection of pre-Hindu artefacts including stone sarcophagi from the time before cremations were practised in Bali. It's a rather dry and dusty museum, probably more of interest to serious students of archaeology. It's open from 8 am to 2 pm on Monday and Thursday and from 8 am to 1 pm on other days, except Sunday when it is closed.

PEJENG

Continuing up the road to Tampaksiring you soon come to Pejeng and its famous temples. Like Bedulu this was once the capital of the Pejeng kingdom and an important seat of power, which fell to the Majapahit invaders in 1343.

Pura Kebo Edan

The Crazy Buffalo Temple (Pura Kebo Edan) with its nearly four-metre-high statue

of Bima, endowed with six penises, is on the western side of the road as you come in to Pejeng. There's considerable conjecture over what this fearsome image is all about. The dead body that the image tramples upon appears to relate to the Hindu Shiva cult but it may also have Tantric Buddhist overtones. Other figures flank the main one and male and female buffaloes lie before it. It's said that dukans (witch doctors) gather here on certain nights.

Pura Pusering Jagat

The large Navel of the World Temple (Pura Pusering Jagat) is said to be the centre of the old Pejeng kingdom. Dating from 1329, this temple is also said to be visited by dukans during the full moon and by young couples who pray at the stone lingam and yoni (Hindu genital symbols).

Pura Penataran Sasih

In the centre of Pejeng, Pura Penataran Sasih was once the state temple of the Pejeng kingdom. In the inner courtyard, high up in a pavilion where you really cannot see it very well, is the huge bronze drum known as the 'Moon of Pejeng'. It is believed to be more than 1000 years older than the kingdom of Pejeng itself, a relic from the Bronze Age in Indonesia. The hourglass-shaped drum is more than three metres long, the largest single-piece cast drum in the world.

A Balinese legend relates how the drum came to earth as a fallen moon, landing in a tree and shining so brightly that it prevented a band of thieves from going about their unlawful purpose. One of the thieves decided to put the light out by urinating on it but the moon exploded, killed the foolhardy thief and fell to earth as a drum – with a crack across its base as a result of the fall.

TAMPAKSIRING

Continuing up the road to Tampaksiring you pass through pleasant paddy fields along the steady upward climb which continues all the way to the rim of the crater at Penelokan. Tampaksiring is a small town with a large and important temple and the most impressive ancient monument in Bali.

Gunung Kawi

On the southern outskirts of Tampaksiring, a sign points off the road to the right to Gunung Kawi. From the end of the access road a steep stone stairway leads down to the river, at one point making a cutting through an embankment of solid rock. There, in the bottom of this lush green valley with beautiful rice terraces climbing up the hillsides, is one of Bali's oldest, and certainly largest, ancient monuments.

Gunung Kawi consists of 10 rock-cut candi, memorials cut out of the rock face in imitation of actual monuments – in a similar fashion to the great rock-cut temples of Ajanta and Ellora in India. Each candi is believed to be a memorial to a member of the 11th-century Balinese royalty but little is known for certain. They stand in seven-metre-high sheltered niches cut into the sheer cliff face. There are four on the west side of the river, which you come to first. To reach the five on the eastern side, you have to cross the river on a bridge. A solitary candi stands further down the valley to the south; this is reached by a trek through the rice paddies.

Legends relate that the whole group of memorials was carved out of the rock face in one hard-working night by the mighty fingernails of Kebo Iwa. It's uncertain who the real builders were but they may date from the Udayana dynasty of the 10th and 11th centuries. It's said that the five monuments on the eastern bank are to King Udayana, Queen Mahendradatta (see the Kutri section in this chapter), their son Airlangga and his brothers Anak Wungsu and Marakata. While Airlangga ruled eastern Java, Anak Wungsu ruled Bali. The four monuments on the western side are, by this theory, to Anak Wungsu's chief concubines. Another theory is that the whole complex is dedicated to Anak Wungsu, his wives, concubines and, in the case of the remote 10th candi, to a royal minister.

Each of the sets of memorials has a group of monks' cells associated with it, including one on the eastern side with perhaps Bali's one and only 'No shoes, sandals, boots may be worn' sign. There are other groups of candi and monks' cells in the area of Bali encompassed by the ancient Pejeng kingdom, but none so grand as these.

Entry to Gunung Kawi is 500 rp. It's another two km to the Tirta Empul temple at Tampaksiring.

Tirta Empul

After Tampaksiring, the road branches. The left fork runs up to the grand palace once used by Sukarno, while the right fork leads to the temple at Tirta Empul and continues up to Penelokan. You can look back along the valley and see Gunung Kawi from this road, just before you turn into Tirta Empul. The holy springs at Tirta Empul are believed to have magical powers, so the temple here is an important one.

Each year an inscribed stone is brought from a nearby village to be ceremonially washed in the spring. The inscription on the stone has been deciphered and indicates that the springs were founded in 962 AD. The actual springs bubble up into a large, crystal-clear tank within the temple and gush out through waterspouts into a bathing pool. According to legend, the springs were created by the god Indra who pierced the earth to tap the 'elixir of immortality' or *amerta*. Despite its antiquity, the temple is glossy and gleamingly new – it was totally restored in the late '60s.

The springs of Tirta Empul are a source of Sungai Pakerisan, which rushes by Gunung Kawi only a km or so away. Between Tirta Empul and Gunung Kawi is the temple of Pura Mengening where you can see a free-standing candi similar in design to those of Gunung Kawi. There is a spring at this temple which also feeds into the Pakerisan. Overlooking Tirta Empul is the Sukarno Palace, a grandiose structure built in 1954 on the site of a Dutch resthouse. Sukarno, whose mother was Balinese, frequently visited the island. It's said he used a telescope to spy on women bathing at the Tirta Empul pool below.

The car park outside Tirta Empul is surrounded by the familiar unholy confusion of souvenir and craft shops. Chess sets and bone carving are popular crafts here. There is an admission charge to Tirta Empul and you have to wear a temple scarf. It's a good idea to come early in the morning or late in the afternoon to avoid the tour-bus hordes.

Places to Stay & Eat

Tampaksiring is an easy day trip from Ubud or even Bangli, but it's also possible to stay here. In the village itself there's the small *Homestay Gusti* and the *Homestay Tampaksiring*. Both charge about 4000/5000 rp for singles/doubles.

Apart from the usual selection of warungs there's also the expensive *Tampaksiring Restaurant* for tourist groups; it's some distance below the village.

UBUD TO BATUR

The usual road from Ubud to Batur is through Tampaksiring but there are other lesser roads up the gentle mountain slope. If you head east out of Ubud and turn away from Peliatan, towards Petulu at the junction, this road will bring you out on the crater rim just beyond Penelokan towards Batur. It's a sealed road all the way except for a few km near the top where it's cobbled and fairly rough. Along this road you'll see a number of woodcarvers producing beautiful painted birds, frogs, garudas and tropical fruit. Tegalalang and the nearby village of Jati, just off the road, are noted woodcarving centres. Further up, other specialists carve stools and there are a couple of places where whole tree trunks are carved into whimsical figures.

Another route from Ubud to Batur can be followed by taking the road through Campuan and Sanggingan and then turning up the hill, instead of down towards Denpasar, at Kedewatan. On this route you pass through Payangan, the only place in Bali where lychees are grown. It's possible to get bemos some distance up the road on both these routes but finding public transport

at the top can be difficult. The roads, once quite rough, are not bad now.

Of course you could walk up to Batur from Ubud too. If you take the path from near the temple down by the Campuan suspension bridge and follow it steadily uphill you'll pass unspoilt villages like Bangkiang Sidem, Keliki and Sebali. Just walking through is pleasant and from Sebali you can cut across to Tegalalang and get a bemo back to Ubud. And if you keep walking? Well, it's 30 km to Batur, uphill all the way.

East Bali

The eastern end of Bali is dominated by mighty Gunung Agung, the 'navel of the world' and Bali's 'mother mountain'. Towering at 3142 metres, Agung has not always been a kind mother – witness the disastrous 1963 eruption. Today Agung is again a quiet but dominating mountain and the mother temple Pura Besakih, perched high on the slopes of the volcano, attracts a steady stream of devotees...and tourists.

The east has a number of places of great interest. Here you'll find Klungkung, the former capital of one of Bali's great kingdoms. From Klungkung the road runs close to the coast past interesting fishing villages like Kusamba, past the bat-infested cave temple of Goa Lawah, the beautiful port of Padangbai, the turn-off to the pretty little Bali Aga village of Tenganan and the popular beach centre of Candidasa, before finally reaching Amlapura, another former capital.

At Amlapura you can about-turn and retrace your route or take an alternative route higher up the slopes of Agung to Rendang. From Rendang you can turn north to Besakih, south to Klungkung or continue west on a pretty but lesser-used route to Bangli. As a third alternative you can continue right around the coast from Amlapura to Singaraja in the north. See the North Bali chapter for more details on this lightly populated coastal route.

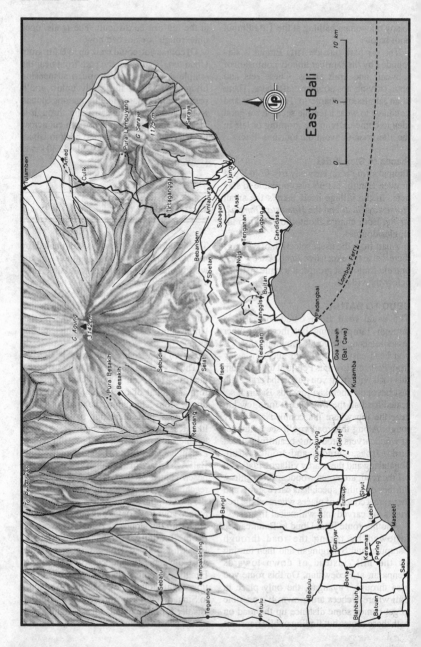

East Bali

The 1963 Eruption

The most disastrous volcanic eruption in Bali this century took place in 1963 when Agung blew its top in no uncertain manner and at a time of considerable prophetic importance: 8 March 1963 was the culmination of Eka Desa Rudra, the greatest of all Balinese sacrifices and an event which only takes place every 100 years on the Balinese calendar. At the time of the eruption, it had been more than 100 Balinese years (115 years on the lunar calendar) since the last Eka Desa Rudra. Naturally, the temple at Besakih was a focal point for the festival but Agung was already acting strangely as preparations were made in late February. Agung had been dormant since 1843 but by the time the sacrifices commenced, the mountain was belching smoke and ash, glowing and rumbling ominously.

On 17 March 1963 it exploded in a catastrophic eruption that killed more than 1000 people and destroyed entire villages. Streams of lava and hot volcanic mud poured right down to the sea at several places, completely covering roads and isolating the eastern end of the island for some time. The entire island was covered in ash and crops were wiped out everywhere. The torrential rainfall that followed the eruptions compounded the damage as boiling hot ash and boulders known as *lahar* were swept down the mountain side, wreaking havoc on many villages like Subagan, just outside Amlapura and Selat, further along the road towards Rendang. The whole of Bali suffered a drastic food shortage and many Balinese, whose rice land was completely ruined, had to be resettled in Sulawesi.

Although Besakih is high on the slopes of Agung, only about six km from the crater, it suffered little damage from the eruption. Volcanic dust and gravel flattened timber and bamboo buildings around the temple complex but the stone structures came through unscathed. The inhabitants of the villages of Sorga and Lebih, also high up on Agung's slopes, were all but wiped out. Most of the people killed at the time of the eruption were burnt and suffocated by searing clouds of hot gas that rushed down the volcano's slopes. Agung erupted again on 16 May, with serious loss of life, although not on the same scale as the March eruption.

The Balinese take signs and portents seriously – that such a terrible event should happen as they were making a most important sacrifice to the gods not taken lightly. The interrupted series of sacrifices finally resumed 16 years later in 1979.

Getting There & Away

Buses to eastern Bali generally depart from the Batubulan station in Denpasar. Fares include: Gianyar (700 rp), Klungkung (1000 rp), Padangbai (1500 rp), Amlapura (2500 rp) and Bangli (1000 rp). To get to Besakih take a bus to Klungkung and then a bemo from there for 600 rp.

Klungkung to Amlapura costs about 900 rp, then from Amlapura to Singaraja buses cost 2500 rp. From Culik, a little beyond Tirtagangga, to Kubutambahan, costs 1800 rp and takes about 3½ hours. Local bemos run from Amlapura to Tirtagangga.

To reach the centres in eastern Bali from Ubud you can take a bemo either to Gianyar or to Batubulan, the main bus/bemo station just outside Denpasar.

GIANYAR

Gianyar is the administrative centre of the Gianyar District, which also includes Ubud but is of minimal interest in its own right. On the main road from Denpasar, and still in the heavy traffic region of southern Bali, the town has a number of small textile factories on the Denpasar side. You're welcome to drop in, see the materials being woven and even make a purchase. It takes about six hours to weave a complete sarong. At the height of the tourist season the regular arrival of buses and free-spending visitors can push prices up to higher levels than in Denpasar.

In the centre of town, across from the large open space known as the alun alun, the old palace is little changed from the time the Dutch arrived in the south and the old kingdoms lost their power. The Gianyar royal family saved their palace by capitulating to the Dutch, rather than making a heroic last stand like the other Balinese kingdoms. Despite its relatively original appearance, the palace, dating from 1771, was destroyed in a conflict with the neighbouring kingdom of Klungkung in the mid-1880s and was rebuilt, only to be severely damaged again in the 1917 earthquake. Nevertheless, it's a fine example of traditional palace architecture, surrounded by high brick walls. The royal family of Gianyar still live in the palace, so without a formal invitation you can do no more than look in through the gates.

Gianyar's warungs are noted for their fine roast piglet, babi guling. Eat early though, as the warungs are usually cleaned out by late morning.

BONA

The village of Bona, on the back road between Gianyar and Blahbatuh, is credited with being the modern home of the Kechak dance. Kechak and other dances are held here every week and are easy to get to from Ubud. Tickets (including transport) from Ubud cost around 5000 rp.

Bona is also a basket-weaving centre and many other articles are also woven from lontar (palm leaves). Nearby Belega, en route to Blahbatuh, is a centre for bamboo work.

LEBIH & THE COAST

South of Gianyar the coast is fringed by black-sand beaches and small coastal villages like Lebih. The Sungai Pakerisan, which starts up in the hills at Tampaksiring, reaches the sea near Lebih. Here, and at other coastal villages south of Gianyar, funeral ceremonies reach their conclusion when the ashes are consigned to the sea. Ritual purification ceremonies for temple artefacts are also held on these beaches.

Further west is Masceti, where the Pura Masceti is one of Bali's nine directional temples. On the beach the local villagers have recently erected a huge and somewhat horrific 'swan' (chicken?) in an attempt to create a tourist attraction! Masceti is reached via Bona, Keramas and Pering. Further west

again is Saba, another small coastal village. One of the best beaches along this stretch of coast is found to the east of Lebih at Siyut, reached via Tulikup.

SIDAN

Continuing east from Gianyar you come to the turn-off to Bangli at Sidan, just a few km out of town. Follow this road for about a km until you reach a sharp bend. Here you'll find the Sidan Pura Dalem, a good example of a temple of the dead. Note the sculptures of Durga with children by the gate, and the separate enclosure in one corner of the temple – this is dedicated to Merajapati, the guardian spirit of the dead. If you continue up the Bangli road there's another interesting pura dalem at Penunggekan, just before you reach Bangli. See the Bangli section for more details.

KLUNGKUNG

Klungkung was once the centre of Bali's most important kingdom and a great artistic and cultural focal point. The Gelgel dynasty, the most powerful kingdom in Bali at that time, held power for about 300 years, until the arrival of the Dutch. It was here that the Klungkung school of painting was developed. This style, where subjects were painted in side profile (like wayang kulit figures), is still used today, but most of the paintings are produced in Kamasan, a few km outside Klungkung.

Klungkung is a major public transport junction – from here you can find buses to Besakih or further east to Padangbai, Candidasa and Amlapura. Modern Klungkung is a dusty, busy market town with pony-drawn carts (dokars) providing an exotic touch. The bus and bemo station is a major gathering point, particularly at night when a busy night market (Pasar Malam) operates there.

Kertha Gosa

The Kertha Gosa (Hall of Justice) stands beside the road as you reach the centre of town from Denpasar. It's in the grounds of the Taman Gili, the remains of the palace of the Dewa Agungs. Entrance costs 500 rp (children half-price). The Kertha Gosa, an open pavilion surrounded by a moat, is a superb example of Klungkung architecture; the roof is completely painted inside with fine paintings in the Klungkung style. The paintings, done on asbestos sheeting, were installed in the 1940s, replacing the cloth paintings which had deteriorated. Further repainting and restoration took place in the '60s and '80s but the style of the paintings appears to have been fairly consistent. Virtually the only record of the earlier paintings was a photograph of the ceiling taken by Walter Spies in the '30s. Given Bali's humid climate there is, of course, rapid deterioration and already the current paintings are looking very second-hand.

This was effectively the 'supreme court' of the Klungkung kingdom, where disputes and cases which could not be settled at the village level were eventually brought. The defendant, standing before the three priests who acted as judges *(kerthas)*, could gaze up at the ceiling and see wrongdoers being tortured by demons and the innocent enjoying the pleasures of Balinese heaven.

The capital of the kingdom was shifted to Klungkung from nearby Gelgel in the early 1700s and the Kertha Gosa was probably constructed around the end of that century. The building was damaged in 1908 and rebuilt in 1920, under the Dutch, to deal with questions of traditional law (adat). Colonial law was handled by the Dutch.

Bale Kambang

Adjoining the Kertha Gosa in the Taman Gili is the beautiful Bale Kambang (Floating Pavilion). Its ceiling is painted in Klungkung style, having been repainted in 1945. Around the Kertha Gosa and the Bale Kambang note the statues of top-hatted European figures, an amusing departure from the normal statues of entrance guardians. Admission to the

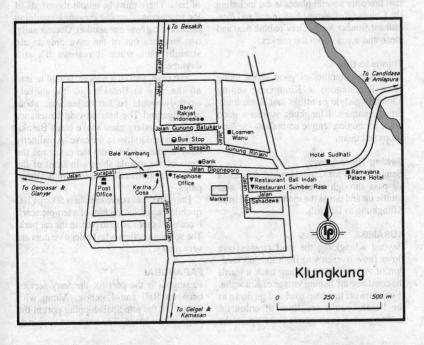

Klungkung

0   250   500 m

palace and Kertha Gosa is 500 rp (children 200 rp).

Places to Stay & Eat

Few travellers stay overnight in Klungkung as it's only 40 km from Denpasar, even less from Ubud and, in the other direction, only another 16 km to Padangbai or 25 km to Candidasa. If you do want to stop for the night there are a couple of possibilities, the nicest of which is the *Ramayana Palace Hotel* on the Candidasa side of town. It's a pleasant place and set far enough back from the busy main road to be quiet. There's a restaurant and the fairly spartan rooms cost 8000/12,000 rp for singles/doubles.

Less attractive alternatives include the *Losmen Wisnu* near the bus station in the centre. The upstairs rooms are much brighter than those downstairs. The very basic *Hotel Sudihati* is between the town centre and the Ramayana Palace Hotel.

Apart from the Ramayana Palace's restaurant there are several places to eat including the Chinese *Restaurant Bali Indah* and *Restaurant Sumber Rasa*. They're both neat and clean and across from the market.

Things to Buy

There are a number of good shops along Jalan Diponegoro in Klungkung selling Klungkung-style paintings and some interesting antiques. Klungkung is also a good place for buying temple umbrellas – several shops sell them.

Getting There & Away

Bemos bound for Candidasa and Amlapura all pass through Klungkung. Bemos also shuttle up and down the mountain road from Klungkung to Besakih.

KUSAMBA

Beyond Klungkung the road crosses lava flows (now overgrown) from the '63 eruption of Agung before turning back towards the coast and the fishing village of Kusamba. If you turn off the main road and go down to the beach, you'll see lines of colourful fishing prahus (outriggers) lined up on the beach. Fishing is normally done at night and the 'eyes' on the front of the boats help navigation through the darkness. You can charter a boat out to Nusa Penida, clearly visible opposite Kusamba. Regular supply trips are made to the island; you could try to get on one of these cargo prahus. The crossing takes several hours.

Just beyond Kusamba you can see the thatched roofs of salt-panning huts along the beach. Saltwater-saturated sand from the beach is dried out around these huts and then further processed inside the huts. You can see the same process being carried out beside the Kuta to Sanur road. Although salt processed by machine is cheaper, connoisseurs still demand real sea salt.

GOA LAWAH

Beyond Kusamba the road continues close to the coast and after a few km reaches the Goa Lawah (Bat Cave). The cave in the cliff face here is packed, crammed, jammed full of bats. There must be untold thousands of the squeaking, flapping creatures, tumbling and crawling over one another. Occasionally, one launches out of the cave only to zip straight back when it realises it's still daytime.

The cave, part of a temple, is said to lead all the way to Besakih but it's unlikely anybody would be too enthusiastic about investigating! The bats provide sustenance for the legendary giant snake Naga Basuki, which is said to live in the cave. A distinctly batty aroma exudes from the cave, and the roofs of the temple shrines in front of the cave are also liberally coated with bat droppings.

Entry to the bat cave temple is 500 rp (100 rp children) including hire of a temple scarf. It costs another 150 rp to park in the car park. The souvenir sellers who besiege visitors are very pushy.

PADANGBAI

Padangbai is the port for the ferry service between Bali and Lombok. Along with Benoa it's the principal shipping port in the south of the island. The town is a couple of

Top: Barong Dance, Bali (TW)
Bottom: Legong Dance, Bali (LH)

Top: Snorkelling at the reef off Lovina Beach, Bali (TW)
Bottom: A Buddha and other statuary at Kapal, the 'garden gnome centre of Bali' (TW)

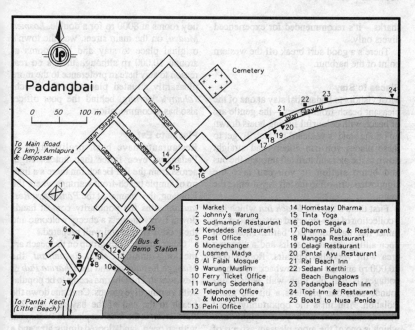

Padangbai

0   50   100 m

Cemetery

To Main Road
(2 km), Amlapura
& Denpasar

To Pantai Kecil
(Little Beach)

Bus &
Bemo Station

Pier

1 Market	14 Homestay Dharma
2 Johnny's Warung	15 Tinta Yoga
3 Sudimampir Restaurant	16 Depot Segara
4 Kendedes Restaurant	17 Dharma Pub & Restaurant
5 Post Office	18 Mangga Restaurant
6 Moneychanger	19 Celagi Restaurant
7 Losmen Madya	20 Pantai Ayu Restaurant
8 Al Falah Mosque	21 Rai Beach Inn
9 Warung Muslim	22 Sedani Kerthi
10 Ferry Ticket Office	Beach Bungalows
11 Warung Sederhana	23 Padangbai Beach Inn
12 Telephone Office	24 Topi Inn & Restaurant
& Moneychanger	25 Boats to Nusa Penida
13 Pelni Office	

km off the main road, a scruffy little place on a perfect little bay, one of the very few sheltered harbours in Bali. It's very picturesque, with a long sweep of sand where colourful outrigger fishing boats are drawn up on the beach. Like some other coastal towns there's a large Muslim population.

Padangbai can be an interesting place to spend a day or so if you don't want to simply arrive in the morning and depart straight for Lombok. If you walk around to the right from the wharf and follow the trail up the hill, you'll eventually come to the idyllic Pantai Kecil (Little Beach) on the exposed coast outside the bay. Out on the northern corner of the bay is the temple of Pura Silayukti, where Empu Kuturan, who introduced the caste system to Bali in the 11th century, is said to have lived.

Cruise ships visiting Bali use Padangbai but have to anchor offshore outside the harbour as only small ships can actually enter the bay. When the cruise ships are in,

Padangbai is temporarily transformed into a cacophonous souvenir market, with sellers flocking in from all over the island.

Information

There are no banks or moneychangers in Padangbai so, whether you plan to stay or continue to Lombok, make sure you've changed enough money before you arrive. Otherwise you may have to backtrack to Klungkung to the nearest bank or continue to Candidasa to find a moneychanger. Johnny, at Johnny's Warung, will sometimes change US or Australian dollars (cash, not travellers' cheques) into rupiah at a discount.

Diving & Surfing

There's some excellent diving on the coral reefs around Pulau Kambing, off Padangbai. Gili Toapekong, which has a series of coral heads at the top of a sheer drop-off, is perhaps the best site. The currents here are strong and unpredictable and there are also sharks – it's recommended for experienced divers only.

There's a good surf break off the western point of the harbour.

Places to Stay

Most visitors to Padangbai stay at one of the pleasant beach-front places – the gentle arc of beach with colourful fishing boats drawn up on the sand is postcard perfect. To get to these places you can either head straight down to the pier and turn left through the bus and bemo station or you can take the signposted turn-off to the left as you enter the town.

First there's the *Rai Beach Inn* which has a collection of two-storeyed cottages looking rather like traditional rice barns. There's an open sitting area downstairs and a sleeping area with verandah upstairs. Rooms cost 20,000 rp and the only drawback with these cottages is that the high wall which surrounds each one provides a bit too much isolation. You miss the opportunity to sit outside and chat with your neighbours, which is one of the more pleasant aspects of staying in a traditional losmen. The inn also has straightforward single-storeyed rooms with bathroom at 15,000 rp.

Next along the beach is the *Sedani Kerthi Beach Bungalows* with simple rooms at 8000 rp and also double-storeyed thatched cottages very similar in style to the Rai Beach Inn. The third place in the central beach-front cluster is the *Padangbai Beach Inn* where rooms are 6000/8000 rp for singles/doubles. The rooms are straight out of the standard losmen design book but, as they all face the sea, they're the best situated rooms in Padangbai.

If you continue along the beach right to the end of the bay, you'll find the *Topi Inn & Restaurant*. It's a new addition to the Padangbai beach scene with rooms upstairs at 7000/10,000 rp for singles/doubles.

The beach-front places keep most visitors to Padangbai happy but there are several other alternatives. Back towards the main street of town the *Homestay Dharma* is a plain family compound with very neat and tidy rooms at 8000 rp for a double. *Losmen Madya*, on the main street, was the town's original place to stay and has rooms at around 10,000 rp although there's no real reason to stay here in preference to the more pleasantly situated places on the beach. *Johnny's Warung*, behind the post office, also has accommodation.

Places to Eat

Restaurants have been proliferating in Padangbai even faster than hotels. Right across from the Rai Beach Inn there's a line-up of simple beach-front warungs where Ibu Komang, the 'mama' of the *Pantai Ayu Restaurant* wins the popularity contest hands down. Everyone gets a cheery welcome and the food is simple and well prepared.

Other places in this group on the beach are the long-running *Celagi Restaurant*, the *Mangga Restaurant* and the *Dharma Pub & Restaurant*. The Dharma seems to be popular with visiting dive groups. Continue down the beach to the end of the bay and the *Topi Restaurant* is the fanciest place in Padangbai with an open, sand-floored dining area and a colourful menu featuring fish dishes plus the Indonesian regulars.

Along the main street there are a host of small Indonesian restaurants including the *Warung Muslim* in front of the mosque. Round by the post office there's *Kendedes Restaurant*, the *Sudimampir Restaurant* and *Johnny's Warung*.

Getting There & Away

See the Getting There & Away chapter for information on the ferry service between Padangbai and Lombok. The ticket office is down by the pier. Buses meet the ferries and go straight to Denpasar.

On the beach just east of the pier car park you'll find the twin-engined fibreglass boats that run across the strait to Nusa Penida (3000 rp).

There are also connections from Padangbai right through to Surabaya and Yogyakarta in Java. Padangbai is a couple of km off the main Klungkung to Amlapura road, 54 km from Denpasar.

BALINA BEACH (BUITAN)

It's 11 km from the Padangbai main road turn-off to Candidasa and between the two is Balina Beach, the tourist name bestowed on the village of Buitan. The original resort development here was intended to be the major scuba-diving centre for Bali. The resort has diving equipment for hire and organises snorkelling and diving trips all around Bali including Nusa Penida and the northern coast. The development is unusual in its association with the nearby village of Manggis; villagers from Manggis also manage the handicraft centre near the beach.

Diving

Diving trips from the Hotel Balina Beach, including transport and a full tank, range from 59,000 to 78,000 rp on the trips closer to Balina, from 98,000 rp for Nusa Penida and from 117,000 rp to Pulau Menjangan on the northern coast. You can also go on the same trips to snorkel, for a lower cost. Snorkelling trips start from 20,000 rp.

Places to Stay

Balina Beach Bungalows (☎ 200361-88451) has rooms at a host of prices from as low as 29,000/35,000 rp for singles/doubles and up to 78,000/88,000 rp for fancier rooms or 107,000 rp for a large family unit. All prices include breakfast but the 15½% service and tax charges are extra. This is a quite large and attractive development and the beach here is reasonably good.

Directly opposite the Balina Beach Bungalows is *Puri Buitan* (☎ 200361-87182), a new development with fan-cooled rooms at 59,000/68,500 rp plus tax and service.

If you walk east along the beach for 200 metres, you'll find *Cangrin Beach Homestay* and *Sunrise Homestay*, which have standard losmen doubles for about 20,000 rp.

TENGANAN

From Padangbai the road moves inland through a beautiful stretch of scenery: while clambering up the hills you can catch glimpses of fine beaches back on the coast. At the turn-off to Tenganan a little posse of motorbike riders waits by the junction, ready to ferry you up to Tenganan. There's also a walking path to Tenganan from Candidasa but the trail is sometimes hard to follow.

Tenganan is a Bali Aga village, a centre of the original Balinese prior to the Majapahit arrival. Unlike the other well-known Bali Aga centre, Trunyan, this is a reasonably friendly place and also much more interesting. Tenganan is a walled village and consists basically of two rows of identical houses stretching up the gentle slope of the hill. The houses face each other across a grassy central area where the village's public buildings are located. The Bali Aga are reputed to be exceptionally conservative and resistant to change but even here the modern age has not been totally held at bay. A small forest of television aerials sprouts from those oh-so-traditional houses! The most striking feature of Tenganan, however, is its exceptional neatness, the hills behind providing a beautiful backdrop.

Tenganan is full of unusual customs, festivals and practices. Double ikat cloth known as *gringsing* is still woven here – the pattern to be produced is dyed on the individual threads, both warp (lengthwise) and weft (crosswise), before the cloth is woven. This is the only place in Indonesia where the double ikat technique is practised. All other ikat produced in the archipelago is single ikat, where only the warp or weft, never both, is dyed. Double ikat cloth is only produced in small quantities and at great expense, so don't come here expecting to find a bargain piece to purchase.

A magical cloth known as *kamben gringsing* is also woven here – a person wearing it is said to be protected against black magic! A peculiar, old-fashioned version of the gamelan known as the gamelan selunding is still played here and girls dance an equally ancient dance known as the Rejang.

At the annual Usaba Sambah festival, held around June or July, men fight with their fists wrapped in sharp-edged pandanus leaves – similar events occur on the island of Sumba, far to the east in Nusa Tenggara. At this same festival, small, hand-powered Ferris wheels are brought out and the village girls are ceremonially twirled round. There are other Bali Aga villages in the vicinity including Asak where an even more ancient instrument is played – the *gamelan gambang*.

In recent years, festivals have often been cancelled in Tenganan because the village's population has been in steep decline. If a villager marries outside the Tenganan circle he or she loses their Bali Aga status. With such a small population pool and declining fertility, this village and its unique culture may eventually be wiped out.

If you walk right up through the village to the road off to the right you'll see a sign pointing to the home of I Made Muditadnana, who produces lontar books – the traditional Balinese palm-leaf books. He's a friendly man and well worth visiting but if you're thinking of buying one of his books check the prices at the village handicraft shops first!

CANDIDASA

Candidasa has had a remarkably rapid rise to fame but, like Kuta 10 years earlier, is now hopelessly overbuilt and rapidly becoming unattractive and squalid. This decline is not helped by the condition of the beach, which has been all but washed away since hotel construction got into high gear.

The road reaches the sea just beyond the turn-off to Tenganan, about 13 km before Amlapura, and runs close to the coast through the small village of Candidasa. The proliferation of hotels has now spread back to well beyond the Tenganan turn-off and hotel signs start appearing a couple of km before Candidasa itself. In 1983 Candidasa was just a quiet little fishing village. Two years later a dozen losmen and half a dozen restaurants had sprung up and suddenly it was *the* new beach place in Bali. Now it's shoulder to shoulder development and suffering all the Kuta-style problems.

Beyond Candidasa the road spirals up to the Pura Gamang Pass (*gamang* means 'to get dizzy'), from where there are fine views down to the coast.

Information

Candidasa has the full complement of shops, moneychangers, travel agencies, bicycle, motorbike and car rental outlets, film developers and other facilities. There are a couple of bookshops and book exchanges and a number of postal agencies where you can buy stamps, and mail cards and letters.

Things to See & Do

Even with the tide out Candidasa's beach is nothing special:

Even the tourist brochures admit that Candidasa's beach disappears at high tide. If they wanted to be scrupulously honest they could add that even at low tide there isn't much of it. So how did a beach resort end up without a beach? The answer lies a few hundred metres offshore where the Candidasa reef used to be. Building all of Candidasa's hotels required large amounts of cement. An essential ingredient of cement is lime, and coral is a convenient source of limestone. So the Candidasa reef was ripped out, ground down and burnt to make the lime for the cement used to build the hotels. Without the protection of the reef the sea soon washed the beach away. A series of remarkably ugly T-shaped piers have been built to try to conserve what little beach is left, but don't come to Candidasa in search of a beach – there really isn't one.

Candidasa's temple is on the hillside across from the lagoon at the northern end of the village strip. The fishing village just beyond the lagoon has colourful fishing prahus drawn up on the beach. In the early morning you can watch them coasting in after a night's fishing. The owners regularly canvas visitors for snorkelling trips to the reef and the nearby islets.

If you follow the beach from Candidasa towards Amlapura you'll find a trail climbing up over the headland with fine views over the rocky islets off the coast. From the headland you'll notice that although the islets look as if they're in a straight line, they're actually made up of one cluster of smaller ones plus the solitary larger island off to the east. The diving around these islands is good.

Looking inland, there's no sign at all of the village below or the road – just an unbroken sweep of palm trees. On a clear day, Agung rises majestically behind the range of coastal hills. Around the headland there's a long sweep of wide, exposed, black-sand beach.

Places to Stay

When places first popped up at Candidasa they were almost all out of the standard losmen mould – simple rooms with bathrooms and a small verandah area out front. Now mass tourism has arrived and there are a number of larger and more luxurious places with air-conditioning, swimming pools and the other accoutrements of the modern travel industry. A number of smaller, more exclusive hostelries have also popped up but shoestring travellers needn't worry, for there are still plenty of low-cost places to choose from. Accommodation now extends from before the Tenganan turn-off right through the tourist part of the village to the original fishing village, hidden in the palm trees where the road turns away from the coast. Basic doubles can be found from less than 10,000 rp but, like Kuta or Ubud, there are so many places to choose from that the best advice is simply to wander around and have a look at a few rooms.

Places to Stay – bottom end Look into a few places before making a decision about where to stay. Starting at the Denpasar side don't confuse the *Candidasa Beach Bungalows* with the larger, mid-range *Candidasa Beach Bungalows II* in the centre of the village strip. At the original, the rooms are pleasant if a little tightly packed together. Next to it is the cheaper *Homestay Geringsing*. The *Wiratha's Bungalows* has simple but well kept singles/doubles with private mandi for 8000/10,000 and 11,000/13,000 rp. The more expensive 20,000/22,000 rp rooms are not worth the extra money. Rooms at the *Puri Bali* are simple, clean and good value.

Continuing along the road there's the *Pandan Losmen* and the popular but rock-bottom *Homestay Lilaberata*. The *Pondok Bamboo Seaside Cottages* is a fancier place with singles/doubles at 26,000/32,000 rp and

a beach-front restaurant. *Puri Amarta Beach Inn* has regular losmen-style rooms at 6000 rp plus larger ones at 10,000 rp. At the *Homestay Natia* next door, smaller rooms are 6000 rp although there are a couple of larger rooms on the sea front at 18,000 rp.

Homestay Ida, close to the lagoon, definitely doesn't fit the usual pattern, with pleasantly airy bamboo cottages dotted around a grassy coconut plantation. Smaller rooms are 20,000 rp, the larger rooms with mezzanine level 40,000 rp, all including breakfast. Fortunately the owners don't seem intent on cramming more rooms onto the spacious site.

Next door is the *Homestay Kelapa Mas* which is also well kept and a little more spacious than most. The rooms facing the seafront are particularly nicely situated. Prices start from 10,000 rp for the smallest rooms and continue upwards to 30,000 rp.

Beyond the Kelapa Mas is the lagoon and there are plenty of small losmen further along the beach. These include *Dewi Bungalows, Rama Bungalows* and the *Sindhu Brata Homestay*, three fairly standard losmen right beside the lagoon. Further along the beach the *Puri Oka* offers standard rooms at 25,000 rp and there's a swimming pool. Right at the end of the beach the *Bunga Putri (Princess Flower) Homestay* is picturesquely situated, looking back down the coast.

Places to Stay – top end More expensive places are a relatively recent addition to the Candidasa scene. Coming from Denpasar, *Candi Beach Cottages* is a couple of km before the Candidasa village. It runs a bus to the village twice a day for its guests. Singles/doubles cost from 117,000/137,000 to 156,000/176,000 rp plus 15½% tax and service, depending on the room and the season. It's a pleasant new hotel with air-con rooms, pool, tennis courts and full facilities. The distance from Candidasa itself means the beach is a bit better here.

About one km from the centre are the *Rama Ocean View Bungalows* (☎ 200361-51864/5) with similar facilities and style at 117,000 to 127,000 rp plus tax and service.

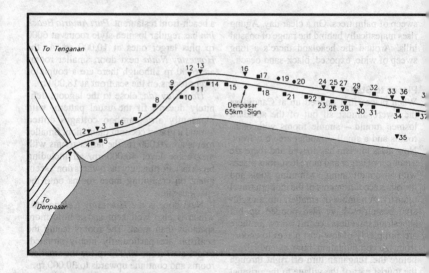

	PLACES TO STAY		
4	Bali Samudra Indah Hotel	32	Homestay Sasra Bahu
5	Homestay Catra	34	Pondok Bamboo Seaside Cottages
6	Saputra Beach Inn	37	Puri Amarta Beach Inn
7	Bambu Garden Bungalows & Restaurant	39	Natia Homestay
		40	Cantiloka Beach Inn
8	Homestay Sri Artha	42	Homestay Ida
10	Candidasa Beach Bungalows	43	Homestay Kelapa Mas
11	Homestay Geringsing	46	Dewi Bungalows
14	Homestay Segara Wangi	47	Rama Bungalows
15	Homestay Ayodya	48	Sindhu Brata Homestay
17	The Watergarden (Taman Air)	49	Pandawa Homestay
18	Puri Bali	54	Srikandi Bungalows
21	Wiratha's Bungalows	55	Barong Beach Inn
22	Pandan Losmen & Restaurant	56	Ramayana Beach Inn
23	Candidasa Beach Bungalows II	57	Nani Beach Inn
26	Homestay Lilaberata	58	Genggong Cottages
31	Agung Bungalows	59	Puri Oka
		60	Puri Pudok Bungalows
		61	Asoka Beach Bungalows

Nirwana Cottages, immediately before the Rama Ocean View, is a smaller resort with 12 very comfortable individual cottages at 69,000 rp and 88,000 rp, a swimming pool and a restaurant.

Continuing towards the centre, the *Bali Samudra Indah Hotel* (☎ 200361-23358, 31246) is right beside the Tenganan turn-off at the start of the Candidasa village. This is a rather featureless place aimed squarely at the package-tour market. The hotel's amusing brochure claims that each room's 'comprehensive facilities' include 'hot and cold running water, telephone, discotique!' It goes on to announce that the large swimming pool has a 'sunken bar.' Rooms are

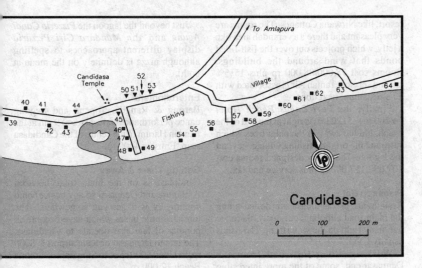

Candidasa Temple
To Amlapura
Village
Fishing
Candidasa

0   100   200 m

62	Sekar Orchid Bungalows
63	Puri Bagus Beach Hotel
64	Bunga Putri Homestay
▼	**PLACES TO EAT**
1	Restaurant Agung
2	Restaurant Flamboyant
3	Molly's Garden Cafe
9	Arie's Restaurant
12	Candidasa Restaurant
13	The Coffee Shop
16	TJ's Restaurant
24	Camplung Restaurant
25	Tunjung Restaurant
27	Restaurant Chandra
28	Restaurant Sumber Rasa
29	Hawaii Restaurant

30	Tirtanadi (The TN) Restaurant
33	Sanjaya Beer Garden
35	Pondok Bamboo Restaurant
36	Kubu Bali Restaurant
38	Murni's Cafe
41	Legend Rock Cafe
44	Warung Rasmini
45	Kusuma Restaurant
50	Raja's Restaurant
51	Pizzeria Candi Agung
52	Ngandi Restaurant
53	Mandara Giri Pizzaria

OTHER

| 19 | Bookshop |
| 20 | Pandun Harum |

29,000/39,000 rp, 49,000/59,000 rp or 68,500/78,000 rp for singles/doubles including breakfast; service and tax are extra.

Right in the centre of Candidasa, the *Candidasa Beach Bungalows II* takes considerable liberty with the word 'bungalow': it's a three-storeyed hotel which gives the distinct impression that the maximum number of rooms has been crammed into the minimum amount of space. Singles are 55,000 rp and doubles 64,000 to 78,000 rp. Breakfast is included but service and tax are extra.

On the side of the road away from the beach *The Watergarden* or *Taman Air* (☎ 200361-35540) is a smaller, low-key resort, like Nirwana Cottages. The rooms are very pleasant and there's a verandah area like a jetty, which projects out over the fish-filled ponds that wind around the buildings. Rooms cost 78,000/88,000 rp plus 15½% tax and service. Taman Air is associated with TJ's restaurant next door.

Finally, the *Puri Bagus Beach Hotel* (☎ 200361- 51223/6) is right at the end of the beach, hidden away in the palm trees which surround the original fishing village, beyond the lagoon. The nicely designed rooms cost 107,000/117,000 rp plus service and tax.

Places to Eat

Restaurants in Candidasa are dotted along the main road although, curiously, there are not many right on the waterfront. The fish is usually good.

Working along the road from the Denpasar end, some of the more interesting places include *The Coffee Shop*, a quietly relaxed place for lunch or a snack. There's a choice of teas at 500 to 700 rp, wine by the glass for 3500 rp and a range of fresh salad baguettes for 5500 rp.

TJ's Restaurant is related to the popular TJ's in Kuta and certainly looks similar, but the only Mexican dish on the menu here is guacamole. The fish is good at 3750 rp, there's an excellent nasi campur for 3500 rp and from 6.30 to 9.30 pm the 'jukung salad bar' is open.

The *Camplung Restaurant, Restaurant Sumber Rasa* and the *Hawaii Restaurant* are all long-term survivors at Candidasa. Straightforward and reasonably priced Indonesian food is the order of the day at the Hawaii. The *Puri Amarta*, another place which has been around since Candidasa's early development as a tourist destination, has quite good food in its roadside restaurant.

On the beach side of the road, *Tirtanadi (The TN) Restaurant* is a cheerful place with a long cocktail list. On the other side of the road is the *Kubu Bali Restaurant*, a big place built around a pond with a bright and busy open kitchen area out front where Indonesian/Chinese dishes are turned out with great energy and panache.

Just beyond the lagoon the *Pizzeria Candi Agung* and the *Mandara Giri Pizzaria* display different approaches to spelling although pizza is definitely on the menu at both!

Entertainment

Barong & Rangda, Topeng and Legong dance performances take place at 9 pm at the Pandan Harum in the centre of the Candidasa strip. Entry is 4000 rp.

Getting There & Away

Candidasa is on the main route between Amlapura and Denpasar so any bus or bemo coming by will get you somewhere! The tourist shuttle buses which have become so popular of late also operate to Candidasa. The fare to Denpasar or Kuta airport is 8000 rp, to Ubud 6000 rp or to Singaraja or Lovina Beach 12,000 rp.

AMLAPURA

Amlapura is the main town in the eastern end of Bali and the capital of the Karangasem District. At Amlapura the main road turns north and then bends west to follow the coast to Singaraja and the north coast. From Ujung, south of Amlapura, there's now a smaller road which follows the coast around Gunung Seraya before rejoining the main road at Culik.

The Karangasem kingdom broke away from the Gelgel kingdom in the late 17th century and 100 years later had become the most powerful kingdom in Bali. Amlapura used to be known as Karangasem, the same as the district, but it was changed after the '63 eruption of Agung in an attempt to get rid of any influences which might provoke a similar eruption!

Information

Amlapura is the smallest of the district capitals, a sleepy place which doesn't seem to have fully woken up from its period of enforced isolation after the '63 eruption of Agung cut the roads to the west of the island. There are banks in Amlapura but it's probably easier to change money in Candidasa.

The Palaces

Amlapura's three palaces are decaying reminders of Karangasem's period as a kingdom. They date from the late 19th and early 20th centuries but only one of the palaces is open for general inspection. You can study the Puri Gede and Puri Kertasura from the outside but special arrangements must be made for an internal inspection.

Admission to Puri Agung (also known as Puri Kanginan) costs 200 rp. There's an impressive three-tiered entry gate and beautiful sculptured panels on the outside of the main building. After you pass through the entry courtyard a left turn takes you to the Bale London, so called because of the British royal crest on the furniture. The decrepit building is not open to the public, as a solitary elderly member of the old royal family still lives there.

A right turn from the entrance leads to the main palace courtyard. The main building is known as Maskerdam, after Amsterdam in The Netherlands, because it was the Karangasem kingdom's acquiescence to Dutch rule which allowed it to hang on long after the demise of the other Balinese kingdoms. This may be your best opportunity to view a Balinese palace but it's certainly not impressive. A number of old photographs and paintings of the royal family are displayed on the verandah. You can buy an explanation sheet at the palace entry desk.

Inside you can see into several rooms including the royal bedroom and a living room with furniture which was a gift from the Dutch royal family. On the other side of this main courtyard is the Balai Kambang, surrounded by a pond like the similar but better preserved Bale Kambang in the palace grounds at Klungkung. The Balai Pemandesan was used for royal tooth-filing and cremation ceremonies, while the Balai Lunjuk was used for other religious ceremonies.

There are other courtyards around the

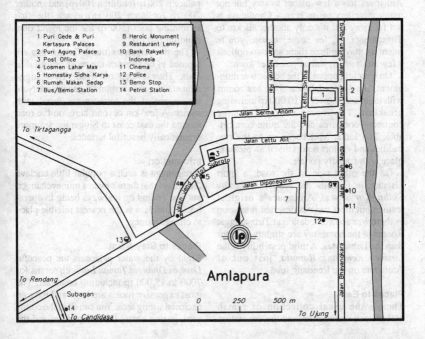

1 Puri Gede & Puri Kertasura Palaces
2 Puri Agung Palace
3 Post Office
4 Losmen Lahar Mas
5 Homestay Sidha Karya
6 Rumah Makan Sedap
7 Bus/Bemo Station
8 Heroic Monument
9 Restaurant Lenny
10 Bank Rakyat Indonesia
11 Cinema
12 Police
13 Bemo Stop
14 Petrol Station

To Tirtagangga
To Rendang
To Candidasa
To Ujung

Jalan Sultan Agung
Jalan Nurah Rai
Jalan Lettu Sintha
Jalan Lettu Umar
Jalan Serma Anom
Jalan Letkol Mada
Jalan Lettu Alit
Jalan Gajah Mada
Jalan Diponegoro
Jalan Gatot Subroto
Jalan Bhayangkara

Subagan

Amlapura

0   250   500 m

main one. It's said that about 150 members of the old family and their servants still live in this slowly deteriorating relic of a now-forgotten era of Balinese history.

Ujung Water Palace

A few km beyond Amlapura, on the road down to the sea, is the Ujung Water Palace, an extensive, picturesque and crumbling complex. It has been deteriorating for some time but a great deal more damage has been done to it since the mid-70s, principally by an earthquake in 1979. The last king of Karangasem, Anak Agung Anglurah, was obsessed with moats, pools, canals and fountains and he completed this grand palace in 1921. You can wander around the pleasant park, admire the view from the pavilion higher up the hill above the rice paddies or continue a little further down the road to the fishing village on the coast.

Places to Stay

Amlapura has a few places to stay but not many travellers pause here – Candidasa is not far away and it's only another six km to Tirtagangga. If, for some reason, you're intent on staying here there are two options a few steps apart, just as you enter town.

On your left, opposite the heroic war monument, the *Losmen Lahar Mas* has rooms with toilet and shower at 10,000 rp including breakfast. The rooms surround a large common-room area and are quite comfortable. The Lahar Mas backs on to the rice paddies and visitors report that it's a pleasant place with friendly people.

On the other side of the road, a short distance in towards the centre, *Homestay Sidha Karya* was Amlapura's original losmen but most visitors deserted it as soon as there was accommodation at Tirtagangga. Rooms at the homestay are slightly cheaper than the Lahar Mas. A third possibility is the *Losmen Kembang Ramaja*, just out of Amlapura on the Rendang road.

Places to Eat

There's the usual collection of rumah makans and warungs around the bus station plus the *Restaurant Lenny* and the *Rumah Makan Sedap* on Jalan Gajah Mada. Amlapura tends to shut down early so don't leave your evening meal until too late.

Getting There & Away

Although Amlapura is the 'end of the road' for bus services from Denpasar, there are buses from here to Singaraja and the north coast.

TIRTAGANGGA

Amlapura's water-loving rajah, having constructed his masterpiece at Ujung, later had another go at Tirtagangga. This water palace, built around 1947, was damaged in the 1963 eruption of Agung and during the political events that wracked Indonesia around the same time. Nevertheless, it's still a place of beauty and solitude and a reminder of the power the Balinese rajahs once had. The palace has a swimming pool as well as the ornamental ponds. Entrance to the water palace is 200 rp (children 100 rp) and another 700 rp (children 200 rp) to use the fine swimming pool (500 rp for the lower one, children 100 rp).

The rice terraces around Tirtagangga are reputed to be some of the most beautiful in Bali. They sweep out from Tirtagangga almost like a sea surrounding an island. Note how some of the terraces are faced with stones. A few km beyond here, on the road around the east coast to Singaraja, are more dramatically beautiful terraces.

Information

Tirtagangga is such a popular little enclave these days that there's even a moneychanger, but don't count on it always being in operation. Candidasa is the nearest reliable place to change money.

Places to Stay & Eat

Right by the water palace is the peaceful *Losmen Dhangin Taman Inn* with rooms for 7000 to 15,000 rp including breakfast. The most expensive rooms are large and have an enclosed sitting area. You can sit in the courtyard, gazing across the rice paddies and the water palace while doves coo in the background. The losmen owner here is very amusing and the food is not bad, although the warung nearest the losmen also does excellent food. This was the original Tirtagangga losmen.

Within the palace compound the *Tirta Ayu Homestay* has pleasant individual bungalows at 20,000 rp including admission to the water palace swimming pools. The restaurant has a superb outlook over the palace pools.

Alternatively, you can continue 300 metres beyond the water palace and climb the steep steps to the *Kusuma Jaya Inn*. The 'Homestay on the Hill' has a fine view over the rice paddies and rooms at 8000 to 15,000 rp including breakfast and dinner. Lunch is also available and the owners have information about local walks.

Across the road from the palace the *Rijasa Homestay* is a small and simple place with extremely neat and clean rooms at 5000/7000, 6000/8000 and 10,000/15,000 rp, all including breakfast and tea. A few steps back towards Amlapura the *Taman Sari Inn* has rooms at 7000 and 8000 rp but looks rather derelict.

Getting There & Away

Tirtagangga is about five or six km from the Amlapura turn-off on the main road that runs around the eastern end of Bali. Bemos from Amlapura cost 250 rp. Buses continue on the main road to Singaraja.

TIRTAGANGGA TO TULAMBEN

Soon after leaving Tirtagangga, the road starts to climb. Look for the sign to Pura Lempuyang, one of Bali's nine 'directional temples'. From the turn-off, there is a steep and winding road for eight km which stops just short of the temple. Lempuyang is perched on a hilltop at 768 metres.

Further on, the main road climbs over a small range of hills and passes by some of the most spectacular rice terraces in Bali. They're the last rice paddies for some distance, however, for this part of Bali is relatively dry and barren.

The road gets back down towards sea level at Culik and thereafter follows the coast, though rarely right beside it. There's a good beach near Culik but the main feature of this route is the superb view of Gunung Agung. On this stretch of coast, Bali's mightiest mountain descends to meet the sea, its slopes beckoning climbers. The road crosses a great number of dry riverbeds, most of them too wide to be easily bridged and, in the dry season at least, showing no sign of water. They're probably similar to many rivers in Australia, running briefly during the heavy rains of the wet season but remaining dry for the rest of the year.

TULAMBEN

The small village of Tulamben has the only places to stay around the east coast. The beach here is composed of pebbles rather than sand but the water is clear and the snorkelling good. In June and July there's good windsurfing but Tulamben's prime attraction is the huge WW II wreck of a US cargo ship.

The recently constructed losmen at Tulamben make this an interesting place to pause on your way around the barren east coast.

The Wreck of the Liberty

On 11 January 1942 the armed US cargo ship USAT *Liberty* was torpedoed by a Japanese submarine about 15 km south-west of Lombok. It was taken in tow by the destroyers HMNS *Van Ghent* and USS *Paul Jones* with the intention of beaching it on the coast of Bali and retrieving its cargo of raw rubber and railway parts. When its condition looked perilous the crew were evacuated and, although it was successfully beached, the rapid spread of the war through Indonesia prevented the cargo from being saved.

Built in 1915, the *Liberty* sat on the beach at Tulamben, a prominent east coast landmark, until 1963 when the violent eruption of Gunung Agung toppled it beneath the surface. Or at least that's one version of the story. Another relates that it sank some distance offshore and the lava flow from the eruption extended the shoreline almost out to the sunken vessel. Whatever the course of events it lies just 40 or 50 metres offshore, almost parallel to the beach with its bow only a couple of metres below the surface.

It's within easy reach of snorkellers although scuba divers, who make frequent trips from Candidasa,

Balina Beach and other diving centres, get the best views of this very impressive wreck. The bow is in quite good shape, the midships region is badly mangled and the stern is intact. Snorkellers can easily swim around the bow which is heavily encrusted with coral and a haven for colourful fish. The ship is more than 100 metres long – this is a *big* wreck – and as you follow it back, it soon disappears into the depths. Scuba dives are generally made at depths of 10 to 30 metres.

To find the wreck, walk about 100 metres north of the Gandu Mayu Bungalows, the northernmost beach losmen, to the small white building by the beach. It's liberally plastered with dive-shop stickers and when there's a dive group on the wreck you'll see Balinese girls shuttling back and forth from the losmen car park toting air tanks elegantly balanced on their heads. Swim straight out from the white building and you'll suddenly see this huge wreck rearing up from the depths.

Places to Stay & Eat

Until the late '80s there was no place to stay on the east coast from Tirtagangga to Yeh Sanih. Now the original losmen constructed here has been joined by two more.

Paradise Palm Beach Bungalows, the village's first accommodation place, is a cheerful little losmen right on the beach. Singles/doubles cost 10,000/15,000 rp with breakfast. The rooms are neat, clean and well kept, with bamboo chairs and a table on the verandahs. The garden is lovely and, at night, there is electricity.

Alternatives are the *Bali Timur Bunga-lows* at 10,000 rp, just on the Amlapura side, and the *Gandu Maya Bungalows* at 12,000 rp, on the other side. Because the Gandu Maya is closest to the wreck, dive trips usually stop there.

TULAMBEN TO YEH SANIH

Beyond Tulamben the road continues to skirt the slopes of Agung, with frequent evidence of lava flows from the '63 eruption. Beyond Agung, Gunung Abang and then the outer crater of Gunung Batur also slope down to the sea. Shortly before Yeh Sanih there's a famous (but not very interesting) horse bath at Tejakula. You can turn inland to the interesting village of Sembiran just before Yeh Sanih.

AMLAPURA TO RENDANG

The Amlapura to Rendang road branches off from the Amlapura to Denpasar road just a km or two out of Amlapura. The road gradually climbs up into the foothills of Gunung Agung, running through some pretty countryside. It's a quieter, less-travelled route than the Amlapura to Denpasar road, which is very busy between Klungkung and Denpasar. At Rendang you meet the Klungkung to Besakih road close to the junction for the very pretty minor road across to Bangli.

The road runs through Bebandem (which has a busy market every three days), Sibetan and Selat before reaching Rendang. Sibetan and Rendang are both well known for the salaks grown there. If you've not tried this delicious fruit with its curious 'snakeskin' covering then this may be the time to do so. It's worth diverting a km or so at Putung to enjoy the fantastic view down to the coast. Only here do you realise just how high up you have climbed.

Shortly before Selat you can take a road that runs south-west through Iseh and Sideman and meets the Amlapura to Klungkung road. The German artist Walter Spies lived in Iseh for some time from 1932. Later, the Swiss painter Theo Meier, nearly as famous as Spies for his influence on Balinese art, lived in the same house.

Although the route from Amlapura to Rendang is fine with your own transport it can be time-consuming by bemo, requiring frequent changes and lots of waiting. Taking the busier coastal route to Gianyar is much faster.

Places to Stay

Three km along the Rendang (or Bebandem) road from the junction as you leave Amlapura, *Homestay Lila* is a very pretty little place in the rice paddies. It's quiet and well away from everything, an ideal place to relax. The individual bungalows have bathrooms and a verandah out front, but no electricity. Singles/doubles cost 6000/10,000 rp including breakfast – there's nowhere else to eat in the area but the homestay also prepares other meals. It's a half-hour walk from the homestay to Bukit Kusambi.

Further along towards Rendang, 11 km beyond Bebandem, you can turn off the road a km or so to the superbly situated *Putung Bungalows*. On the edge of a ridge, the bungalows overlook the coast far, far below. You can see large ships anchored off Padangbai and across to Nusa Penida. There are two-storeyed bungalows, with a bathroom and small sitting area downstairs and also 'losmen-class' rooms. Prices start at 20,000 rp. Putung Bungalows also has a restaurant.

BANGLI

Half-way up the slope to Penelokan the town of Bangli, once the capital of a kingdom, is said to have the best climate in Bali. It also has a very fine temple and quite a pleasant place to stay. Bangli is a convenient place from which to visit Besakih, and makes a good base for exploring the area. However, there's one catch in Bangli – the dogs are even worse than in Ubud.

Pura Kehen

At the top end of the town, Pura Kehen, the state temple of the Bangli kingdom, is terraced up the hillside. A great flight of steps leads up to the temple entrance and the first courtyard, with its huge banyan tree, has colourful Chinese porcelain plates set into the walls as decoration. Unfortunately most of them are now damaged. The inner courtyard has an 11-roofed meru (Balinese shrine) and a shrine with thrones for the three figures of the Hindu trinity – Brahma, Shiva and Vishnu. This is one of the finest temples in Bali. There's a large arts centre just round the corner from the Pura Kehen.

Bukit Demulih

Three km from Bangli, along the Tampaksiring road, is Bukit Demulih, a hill just off the south side of the road. If you can't find the sign pointing to it, ask local children to direct you. You can make the short climb to the top where there's a small temple and good views back over Bangli, or you can walk along the

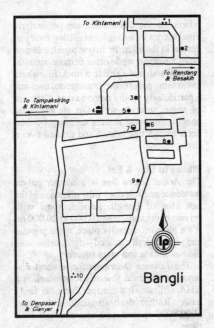

1	Pura Kehen
2	Arts Centre
3	Losmen Dharmaputra
4	Post Office
5	Cinema
6	Artha Sastra Inn
7	Bus Stop
8	Market
9	Telephone Office
10	Pura Dalem Penunggekan

ridge line to a viewpoint where all of southern Bali spreads out below. You can see the long sweep of Sanur Beach with the Hotel Bali Beach, a minuscule rectangular box, far away.

Pura Dalem Penunggekan

Just below Bangli, beside the road to Gianyar, there's an interesting temple of the dead, the Pura Dalem Penunggekan. The reliefs on the front illustrate particularly vivid scenes of wrongdoers getting their just deserts in the afterlife. In one panel, a demon rapes a woman while other demons simultaneously stab and castrate a man. Elsewhere in the same panel demons gouge out eyes and a particularly toothy demon takes a bite out of some ne'er-do-well. On an adjoining panel unfortunate sinners are hung by their heels from a tree branch and roasted over a fire.

Places to Stay & Eat

The *Artha Sastra Inn* is a former palace residence and still run by the grandson of the last king of Bangli. Rooms, some with private bathrooms, cost 10,000 to 20,000 rp. It's a pleasant, friendly place, quite popular and very centrally located – right across from the bus station and main square.

The *Losmen Dharmaputra*, a short distance up the road towards Kintamani, is a YHA affiliate. It's cheaper but also fairly basic. Rather drab singles/doubles cost 6000/8000 rp and you can also get food there.

Bangli has a good night market (Pasar Malam) in the square opposite the Artha Sastra and there are some great warungs but they all close early.

BESAKIH

Perched nearly 1000 metres up the side of Gunung Agung is Bali's most important temple, Pura Besakih. In all, it comprises about 30 separate temples in seven terraces up the hill, all within one enormous complex. The temple was probably first constructed more than 1000 years ago; 500 years later, it became the state temple of the powerful Gelgel and Klungkung kingdoms. Today, it's the 'mother temple' of all Bali – every district in Bali has its own shrine or temple at Besakih and just about every Balinese god you care to name is also honoured there. Apart from its size and majestic location, Besakih is also probably the best kept temple you'll see on the island. This is not a temple simply built and then left to slowly decay.

As well as being the Balinese mother temple, Besakih is also the 'mother' of Balinese financial efforts. You pay to park, pay to enter, pay to rent a scarf and then brave the usual large collection of souvenir sellers. And, after all that, it's quite possible you'll find the inner courtyards are all closed to visitors!

The temple is definitely impressive, but you do not need a guide to see it. So if someone latches on to you and begins to tell you about the temple, let them know quickly whether you want their services. Without a firm no, they'll continue being a guide and expect to be paid at the end; whatever you pay them, however, is certainly not going to be enough – they have no qualms about asking for more.

Places to Stay

About five km below Besakih the *Arca Valley Inn* has rooms and a restaurant. It's prettily situated in a valley by a bend in the road. This is a good place to stay if you want to climb Gunung Agung from Besakih and want an early start. There is also a losmen close to the temple entrance.

Getting There & Away

The usual route to Besakih is by bus or bemo to Klungkung, from where there are regular bemos up the hill to the temple for 750 rp.

If you have your own wheels, take the left fork about a km before the temple, ignoring the 'No Entry' sign. This fork brings you to a car park close to the entrance. The right fork ends about half a km from the temple, leaving you with a long walk up the entrance road or a little hassling with the motorbike gang who'll offer to ferry you up there. The first price is usually 1000 rp. You can't take your own bike up the entrance road.

The 'guardhouse' on the right fork is a bit of a scam as well. Here they'll try and get you to sign a visitor's book where you'll find that lots of previous foreign guests have dispensed little donations – like 50,000 rp! Taking the left fork not only brings you out closer to the temple, it also bypasses the souvenir sellers and 'donation' collectors.

GUNUNG AGUNG

You can climb 3142-metre-high Gunung Agung, Bali's highest and most revered mountain, from the village of Sorga or from Pura Besakih. To get to Sorga, turn off the Amlapura to Rendang road at Selat and follow the road up the slopes of the mountain to Sebudi and finally Sorga. This area was devastated by the 1963 eruption. From Sorga the road ends and the walking begins, first to the temple of Pasar Agung and then to the holy spring of Tirta Mas. From the spring it takes about two hours to reach the summit. You can either make an early start from Sorga and climb all the way to the top in one go or start late in the afternoon and camp at Tirta Mas. The spring is just below the tree line and a good base for an early ascent the next morning.

If you want to climb Gunung Agung from Besakih you must leave no later than 6.30 am. Start earlier if you want to reach the top before cloud obscures the view. From either starting point it's a pretty tough climb of about five hours. It's easy to get lost on the lower trails so it's worth hiring a guide. They're available in Sorga or at Besakih. The cost could be anything from 15,000 to 30,000 rp depending on the size of your party, plus a few thousand rp as a tip. Take plenty of food and water, an umbrella, waterproof clothing, a warm woollen sweater and a torch (flashlight) with extra batteries – just in case you don't get back down by nightfall.

South-West Bali

Most of the places regularly visited in south-west Bali, like Sangeh or Tanah Lot, are easy day trips from Denpasar. The rest of the west tends to be a region travellers zip through on their way to or from Java. In the latter half of the last century this was an area of warring kingdoms, but with the Dutch takeover, the princes' lands were redistributed among the general population. With this bounty of rich agricultural land the region around Tabanan quickly became one of the wealthiest parts of Bali.

Further west, two spectacular roads head inland across the central mountains to the north coast. Even further west, the rugged hills are sparsely populated and the agricultural potential is limited by the low rainfall. Much of the area is a virtual wilderness and is part of the Bali Barat National Park (see the North Bali section for details). There are periodic rumours of the continued existence of the Balinese tiger, but no evidence to support them.

Along the southern coast are long stretches of wide black-sand beach and rolling surf. Here the main road runs close to the coast but never actually on it, so you rarely catch a glimpse of the sea. Countless tracks run south of the main road, usually to fishing villages which rarely see a tourist despite being so close to a main transport route.

Getting There & Away

Public buses to western Bali generally leave from the Ubung station in Denpasar. Costs are around 3500 rp to Gilimanuk, 3000 rp to Negara and 900 rp to Mengwi.

SEMPIDI, LUKLUK & KAPAL

Kapal is the garden gnome and temple curlicue centre of Bali. If you're building a new temple and need a balustrade for a stairway, a capping for a wall, a curlicue for the top of a roof, or any of the other countless standard architectural motifs then the numerous shops which line the road through Kapal will probably have what you need. Or if you want some garden ornamentation, from a comic book deer to a brightly painted Buddha then again you've come to the right place.

Lukluk's pura dalem (temple of the dead) and Sempidi's three pura desa (temples of the spirits) are all worth inspecting but Kapal's Pura Sadat is the most important temple in the area. Although it was restored after WW II (it was damaged in an earthquake earlier this century), the Sadat is a very ancient temple, possibly dating back to the 12th century.

TANAH LOT

The spectacularly placed Tanah Lot is possibly the best known and most photographed temple in Bali. It's almost certainly the most visited – the tourist crowds here are phenomenal, the gauntlet of souvenir hawkers to be run is appalling and the commercial hype is terrible. Signs direct you to the best place to photograph the sunset, and the faithful line up, cameras poised, ready to capture the hallowed moment.

It's easy to see why Tanah Lot is such an attraction – its setting is fantastic. The temple is perched on a little rocky islet, connected to the shore at low tide but cut off as the tide rolls in. It looks superb whether delicately lit by the dawn light or starkly outlined at sunset.

It's also an important temple – one of the venerated sea temples respected in similar fashion to the great mountain temples. Like Pura Luhur Ulu Watu, at the southern end of the island, Tanah Lot is closely associated with the legendary priest Nirartha. It's said that Nirartha passed by here and, impressed with the tiny island's superb setting, suggested to local villagers that this would be a good place to construct a temple. There's a small charge to enter the temple.

Getting There & Away

Tanah Lot is reached by turning off the Denpasar to Gilimanuk road at Kediri and taking the road straight down to the coast. From Denpasar you'll have to take a bemo from Ubung to Kediri (600 rp) then another to the coast (about 250 rp). There is no regular service out of Tanah Lot and, after sunset, when all the visitors have disappeared, you may find the car park empty. Your only options may be to charter a bemo or walk. If you have your own wheels, leave early to miss the tourist jam.

MENGWI

The huge state temple of Pura Taman Ayun, surrounded by a wide moat, was the main temple of the kingdom which ruled from Mengwi until 1891. The kingdom split from the Gelgel dynasty, centred near Klungkung in eastern Bali. The temple was built in 1634 and extensively renovated in 1937. It's a very large, spacious temple and the elegant moat gives it a very fine appearance. The first

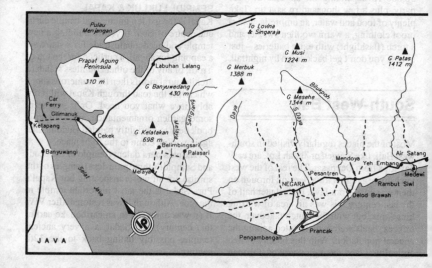

courtyard is a large, open grassy expanse and the inner courtyard has a multitude of merus (multi-tiered shrines).

In a beautiful setting across the moat from the temple is a rather lost-looking arts centre. Built in the early '70s it became an almost instant white elephant and today is beginning to take on the ageless look of all Balinese architecture. There's also a small museum. The *Water Palace Restaurant* overlooking the moat is not a bad place for lunch.

BLAYU

In Blayu, a small village between Mengwi and Marga, traditional songket sarongs are woven with intricate gold threads. These are for ceremonial use only, not for everyday wear.

MARGA

Near Mengwi stands a peculiar memorial to Lt Colonel I Gusti Ngurah Rai who, in 1946, led his men in a futile defence against a larger and better armed Dutch force. The Dutch, trying to recover Bali after the departure of the Japanese, had called in air support but the Balinese refused to surrender. The outcome

was similar to the puputans of 40 years before; all 94 of Ngurah Rai's men were killed. Denpasar's airport is named in his memory.

SANGEH

About 20 km north of Denpasar, near the village of Sangeh, stands the monkey forest of Bukit Sari. It is featured, so the Balinese say, in the *Ramayana*. To kill the evil Rawana, king of Lanka, Hanuman had to crush him between two halves of Mahameru, the holy mountain. Rawana, who could not be destroyed on the earth or in the air, would thus be squeezed between the two. On his way to performing this task, Hanuman dropped a piece of the mountain near Sangeh, complete with a band of monkeys. Of course, this sort of legend isn't unique – Hanuman dropped chunks of landscape all over the place!

There's a unique grove of nutmeg trees in the monkey forest and a temple, Pura Bukit Sari, with an interesting old garuda statue. Plus, of course, there are lots of monkeys. They're very worldly monkeys, well aware of what the visiting tourists have probably

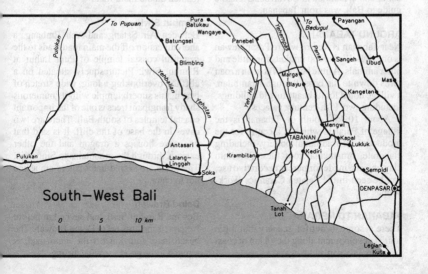

South–West Bali

0   5   10 km

bought from the local vendors – peanuts! Take care, for the monkeys will jump all over you if you've got a pocketful of peanuts and don't dispense them fast enough. The Sangeh monkeys have also been known to steal tourists' hats, sunglasses and even, as they run away, their thongs! A new variation on this mischief has been created by some local people, who reclaim the items from the monkeys and then charge a ransom for their return.

There are also plenty of Balinese clamouring to sell you anything from a sarong to a carved wooden flute. This place is geared to tourists.

Getting There & Away

You can reach Sangeh by bemos which run direct from Denpasar but there is also a road across from Mengwi and from Ubud.

TABANAN

Tabanan is in the heart of the rice belt of southern Bali, the most fertile and prosperous rice-growing area on the island. It's also a great centre for dancing and gamelan playing. Mario, the renowned dancer of the prewar period, who perfected the Kebyar dance and is featured in Covarrubias' classic guide to Bali, was from Tabanan.

AROUND TABANAN

Near Tabanan is Kediri, where Pasar Hewan is one of Bali's busiest markets for cattle and other animals. A little beyond Tabanan a road turns down to the coast through Krambitan, a village noted for its beautiful old buildings, including two 17th-century palaces.

About 10 km south of Tabanan is the village of Pejaten, which is a centre for the production of traditional pottery, including elaborate, ornamental roof tiles. Porcelain clay objects, made for purely decorative use, can be seen in the Pejaten Ceramics Workshop.

TABANAN TO NEGARA

There's some beautiful scenery but little tourist development along the 74 km of coast between Tabanan and Negara.

Lalang-Linggah

The *Balian Beach Club* overlooks Yeh Balian (Balian River) and is surrounded by coconut plantations. There are bunk beds for 6000 rp plus bungalows at 8000/10,000 rp or a pavilion for 25,000 rp. To get to Lalang-Linggah from Denpasar, take any Negara or Gilimanuk bus and ask the driver to stop at the 49.6 km post.

Medewi

About 30 km from Soka, and 25 km before Negara, a large but faded sign announces the side-road south to 'Medewi Surfing Point'. The turn-off is just west of Pulukan village. Medewi is noted for its *long* left-hand wave – if you catch one of these on a good day you should bring a packed lunch.

Places to Stay There are now two places to stay near the beach. The *Hotel Nirwana*, on the west side of the road, has rooms for 15,000 to 20,000 rp. The restaurant has standard fare for slightly higher than standard prices. The *Medewi Beach Cottages* on the other side of the road are new, luxurious and cost 45,000/65,000 rp for singles/doubles. For bottom-end accommodation, there's a losmen on the main road.

Rambut Siwi

Between Air Satang and Yeh Embang, a short diversion off the main road leads to the beautiful coastal temple of Pura Luhur at Rambut Siwi. Picturesquely situated on a cliff top overlooking a long, wide stretch of beach, this superb temple with its numerous shady frangipani trees is one of the important coastal temples of south Bali. There are two caves in the base of the cliff. It is said that one cave houses a dragon and the other extends through the mountains to Singaraja. The caves are sacred and visitors are asked not to enter.

Delod Brawah

Beyond Rambut Siwi, and seven km before Negara, is the turn-off to Delod Brawah. The beach here, four km off the main road, is reputed to be good for windsurfing.

NEGARA

Negara, the capital of the Jembrana District, comes alive each year when the bullock races take place between July and October. These normally docile creatures charge down a two-km stretch of road pulling tiny chariots. Riders often stand on top of the chariots, forcing the bullocks on. The winner, however, is not necessarily first past the post. Style also plays a part and points are awarded for the most elegant runner!

Places to Stay & Eat

Hotel Ana, on Jalan Ngurah Rai, the main street through town, is a standard losmen with rooms at around 3000, 5000 and 7000 rp. Nearby is the *Hotel & Restaurant Wirapada* (☎ 2041161), at Jalan Ngurah Rai 107, which costs 12,500 rp including breakfast or 18,500 rp for a room with a shower. The Wirapada serves good food, as does the *Rumah Makan Puas*, a little further east on the same street.

The Denpasar to Gilimanuk road, which bypasses the town centre, has several possibilities. *Hotel Ijo Gading*, at Jalan Nakula 5, is clean and friendly and has singles/doubles for 7500 to 10,000 rp. The *Losmen & Rumah Makan Taman Sari*, at Jalan Nakula 18, has rooms from 6000 rp.

GILIMANUK

At the far western end of the island, Gilimanuk is the terminus for ferries which shuttle back and forth across the narrow strait to Java. There's a bus station and a market on the main street about a km from the ferry port. Most travellers buy combined bus and ferry tickets and don't need to stop in Gilimanuk. There's little of interest here for the traveller anyway, as it's just an arrival and departure point.

Gilimanuk is off the main road. About a km on the Denpasar side from the junction is a curious pagoda-like structure with a spiral stairway around the outside. In the same area, Cekek is supposed to be the headquarters and information office for the Bali Barat National Park. Although there's an impressive visitors' centre with a large carpark and a children's playground, it seems to be locked up and deserted. If you want

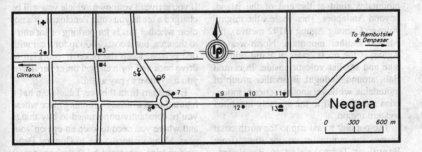

1 Hospital	8 Bank
2 Telephone	9 Hotel Ana
3 Losmen & Rumah Makan Taman Sari	10 Hotel & Restaurant Wirapada
4 Hotel Ijo Gading	11 Rumah Makan Puas
5 Mosque	12 Petrol Station
6 Bus station	13 Post Office
7 Market	

information about the park, go to the office at Labuhan Lalang, further north, which is the most interesting part of the park anyway.

For more information about the park, or the route from Gilimanuk to the north coast, see the North Bali section.

Places to Stay

Most people simply zip straight through Gilimanuk, but if you do have a reason to stay, there are several places along Jalan Raya, the main road into the port. Within a km or so of the ferry port you'll find *Homestay Gili Sari, Homestay Surya* and *Lestari Homestay*.

Central Mountains

Bali has lots of mountains, as you'll quickly realise from a glance at one of the three-dimensional terrain models so common in Balinese hotels. Most are volcanoes, some dormant, some definitely active. The mountains divide the gentle sweep of fertile rice land to the south from the narrower strip to the north. In east Bali is a small clump of mountains right at the end of the island, beyond Amlapura. Then there's the mighty volcano Gunung Agung (3142 metres), the island's mother mountain. North-west of Agung is the great crater of Batur with its lake and smaller volcano inside. In central Bali, around Bedugul, is another group of mountains, while yet another series of mountains stretches off to the sparsely inhabited western region.

The popular round trip to the north coast crosses the mountains on one route (from Bangli or Tampaksiring to Penelokan, Kintamani and Gunung Batur), and returns on another (from Singaraja on the coast back through Lake Bratan and Bedugul to Denpasar), thus covering most of the mountain region.

It's often said that the Balinese look away from the sea (the home of demons and monsters) and towards the mountains (the abode of the gods). But although they may look towards the mountains, the Balinese don't actually live on them. The true Balinese heartland is the gentle, fertile land rising up to the mountains. The mountain villages tend to be strange, often chilly and cloudy places.

PENELOKAN

The roads up to Batur from Bangli and from Tampaksiring meet just before reaching the crater rim at Penelokan, a spectacular place. The road runs along the narrow rim of the crater, with superb views across to Gunung Batur and down to Lake Batur at the bottom of the crater. Penelokan appropriately means 'place to look'. At the far end of the crater road, at Penulisan, you can look back into the crater or turn the other way and see Bali's northern coastline spread out at your feet, far below.

At Penelokan, where a sideroad runs down into the crater to Kedisan, the views are stunning. Penelokan is a popular place to stay, but those intending to tour the lake or climb the mountain might find it more convenient to stay at Kedisan or Tirta, at the bottom of the crater.

Information

If you arrive in your own vehicle you will be charged a fee as you enter Penelokan. It's not clear whether this is for parking or for entry to the area, but it costs 1000 rp for a car with one person. Keep the ticket if you plan to drive back and forth around the crater rim or you may have to pay again.

Even apart from this fee, Penelokan has a reputation as a money-grubbing place where you're constantly importuned to buy things and where you need to keep an eye on your gear. Many visitors come to Gunung Batur on day trips organised by their (expensive) hotels, stopping for lunch at Penelokan. Hence the selling style of the hawkers, who have trained themselves to make their pitch and close the deal quickly. The only thing sure to discourage them is the arrival of a bus-load of tourists more affluent than yourself.

It can get surprisingly chilly up here so come prepared. Clouds often roll in over the crater, sometimes getting hung up along the rim and making all the crater rim towns cold and miserable places to be.

Places to Stay

There are several places to stay in Penelokan, a couple teetering right on the edge of the crater. Apart from the views, these are just basic losmen with basic prices, though prices will change depending on what the owners reckon the market will bear.

If you arrive from the south, the first place in Penelokan is the *Caldera Batur*, which has a great view and may even rent rooms, if you can find any staff. A little further along, the *Lakeview Restaurant & Homestay* (☎ 2032023), which clings to the crater rim, has economy rooms for 15,000 rp and more comfortable bungalow-style rooms with bathroom for 29,000 rp. The economy rooms are impossibly small – if the beds weren't so tiny and narrow they wouldn't be able to get two in a room. Ah, but the view, the view...!

Continuing past the road down into the crater, you come to *Losmen & Restaurant Gunawan*. Again, the view is terrific, the economy rooms are tiny at 10,000 rp and the better, bungalow-style rooms cost from 15,000 rp.

Places to Eat

Along the road between Penelokan and Kintamani you'll find a crowd of restaurants which are geared to bus-loads of tour groups. All the restaurants have fine views and all prepare buffet-style lunches at international tourist prices. The restaurants, from Penelokan to Kintamani, include the *Lakeview, Batur Garden, Gunawan, Puri Selera, Puri Aninditha* and the *Kintamani Restaurant*. Lunch costs from around 10,000 rp if you order from the menu. Of course there are also cheap warungs along the main road like the *Warung Makan Ani Asih* or the *Warung Makan Sederhana*.

Getting There & Away

To get to Penelokan from Denpasar, you can either get a Kintamani-bound bemo from Batubulan station (1700 rp), which will pass through Penelokan, or you can take one of the more frequent bemos to Gianyar (700 rp) or Bangli (1000 rp) first and then another from there up the mountain. To get to Penelokan from Ubud, go first to Gianyar. Bemos shuttle back and forth fairly regularly between Penelokan and Kintamani (300 rp) and less frequently down to the lakeside at Kedisan (500 rp).

The two main routes up the mountains to Penelokan (through Gianyar and Tampaksiring) meet just before you get to Penelokan. There are, however, lesser roads which are being improved and are OK for motorbikes and the standard Suzuki rental cars, but have very little public transport. (See Ubud to Batur, in the Ubud & Around section, for details.) You could, for example, follow the road which starts out around the crater rim then drops down to Rendang, joining the Rendang to Besakih road at Menanga. If the weather's clear you'll have fine views of Gunung Agung along this route.

Most of the rivers and streams in this area run from north to south, and most of the roads run between them. The few east to west roads tend to be very rough with lots of creek crossings and plenty of opportunities to get lost. Consequently, the country west of Batur, though not remote, is seldom visited.

Getting Around

From Penelokan you can hike around the crater rim to Gunung Abang (2152 metres), the high point of the outer rim. You could also continue hiking, in an anticlockwise direction, all the way round to Penulisan and take a bemo back to your starting point.

BATUR & KINTAMANI

The village of Batur used to be down in the crater. A violent eruption of the volcano in 1917 killed thousands of people and destroyed more than 60,000 homes and 2000 temples. Although the village was wiped out, the lava flow stopped at the entrance to the villagers' temple. Taking this as a good omen, they rebuilt their village, only to have Batur erupt again in 1926. This time the lava flow covered all but the loftiest temple shrine. Fortunately, the Dutch administration had anticipated the eruption and evacuated the village, partly by force, so very few lives were lost. The village was relocated up on the crater rim, and the surviving shrine was also moved up and placed in the new temple, Pura Ulun Danu. Construction on the new temple commenced in 1927. Gunung Batur is the second most important mountain in Bali – only Agung outranks it – so the temple here, one of the island's nine directional temples, is of considerable importance.

The villages of Batur and Kintamani now virtually run together – it's impossible to tell where one ends and the other begins. Kintamani is basically one main street spread out along the rim of the crater. Although often cold and grey, it is a major centre for growing oranges and you'll often see them on sale. Kintamani is famed for its large and colourful market, held every three days. Like most markets throughout Bali it starts and ends early – by 11 am it's all over. The high rainfall and cool climate up here make this a very productive fruit and vegetable growing area. Kintamani is also a contender for the hard-fought title of 'miserable howling dog capital of Bali'.

Places to Stay & Eat

There are a number of losmen along the main street of this volcano-rim town, but most are pretty drab and don't have the spectacular setting of the places at Penelokan. The only reason to stay here is to do a trek down the outer rim and into the crater itself.

Starting from the Penelokan end of town is *Losmen Superman's*, on the left side of the road, where cheap rooms with bathroom cost 4000 rp.

Further north, on the same side of the road, is the *Hotel Miranda*. Singles/doubles here cost 5000 to 6000 rp, the most expensive with bathrooms. It's a bit better than the general run of Kintamani accommodation and has good food and an open fire at night. Made Senter, who runs it, is very friendly and informative and also acts as a guide for treks into the crater and around Gunung Batur.

Continuing along the road for a few hundred metres you come to *Losmen Sasaka*. It appears to be new, even modern, but a closer look reveals that the washbasin has no taps, the toilet has to be flushed with a bucket and the hot-water tap is mostly for decoration. The rooms cost 15,000 rp.

Further along again, a sign points off the road to the *Puri Astini Inn* – it says 200 metres, but the distance is probably more like four times that, down quite a rough track. The original rooms in Astini 1 have a minimal bathroom, no view and cost 12,000 to 20,000 rp including breakfast. The four new rooms in Astini 2 are better and have great views if the weather is clear, but cost a little more. The inn is a bit hard to get to unless you've got your own wheels, but it's a convenient spot from which to start a trek into the crater, and Putu Arya here is a trekking guide.

Getting There & Away

From Denpasar (Batubulan station) a bemo to Kintamani is about 1700 rp, though there are more frequent bemos from Gianyar or Bangli. Buses run between Kintamani and Singaraja on the north coast for 1800 rp.

For lesser-used routes from Ubud to Penelokan, see the Around Ubud section in this chapter.

PENULISAN

The road continues along the crater rim beyond Kintamani, climbing gradually. If you come up from the south, sometimes you'll find yourself ascending through the clouds around Penelokan and Kintamani, then coming out above them as you approach Penulisan. If it's clear, there are more fine views down over the crater, this time looking across the land to the north of Gunung Batur. Sometimes you can even see as far as Gunung Rinjani on Lombok.

At a bend in the road at Penulisan, a steep flight of steps leads to Bali's highest temple, Pura Tegeh Koripan, at 1745 metres. Inside the highest courtyard are rows of old statues and fragments of sculptures in the open bales (buildings). Some of the sculptures date back as far as the 11th century. The views from this hilltop temple are superb: facing north you can see down over the rice terraces clear to the Singaraja coast.

Towering over the temple, however, notice the shrine to a new and powerful god – Bali's television repeater mast!

GUNUNG BATUR & LAKE BATUR

The views from the crater at Penelokan, Batur, Kintamani and Penulisan may be superb, but the most exciting activities are to descend into the massive outer crater, take a boat across the crater lake and/or to climb the dormant Gunung Batur volcano.

A hairpin-bend road winds its way down from Penelokan to Kedisan on the shore of the lake. From Kedisan you can take a boat across the surprisingly large and very deep lake to Trunyan, the Bali Aga village on the eastern side. To get to the hot springs at Tirta, take a boat or the quaint little road which winds around the lakeside from Kedisan, over many turns and switchbacks, through the lava field. The road continues to Songan, under the north-eastern rim of the crater, and a sideroad goes around to the north side of Gunung Batur until it is stopped by a huge 'flow' of solidified black lava. You can climb to the summit of Gunung Batur in just a few hours from either Kedisan or Tirta, or make longer treks over and around the central volcano and up the crater rim.

Kedisan

Places to Stay Coming into Kedisan from Penelokan you reach a T-intersection. Turning left towards Tirta you come first to the *Segara Bungalows*, where basic singles/doubles cost from 6000/8000 rp and more comfortable rooms with hot water cost 12,000/20,000 rp, including breakfast. A bit further on is the *Surya Homestay & Restaurant* with rooms for 8000 to 12,000 rp. The cheapest rooms are not fancy, but definitely OK. Turning right as you come into town will bring you to the *Segara Homestay*, which has similar prices (and the same owner) as the Segara Bungalows.

Getting Around Getting across the lake from Kedisan was once one of Bali's great rip-offs. After negotiating a sky-high price, your boat operator would then want to renegotiate halfway across. Meanwhile, your motorbike was being stripped back at Kedisan. It got so bad that the government took over and set prices. The boats leave from a jetty near the middle of Kedisan, where there is a boat office, a fenced car park and the usual assortment of rumah makans and warungs. Your car or motorbike will be safe here!

The set prices are expensive, however. The listed price for a boat for a round trip stopping at Trunyan, the cemetery and the air panas (hot springs) at Tirta, then returning to Kedisan is posted at 32,500 rp, plus 500 rp per person for entrance to the cemetery and 75 rp insurance. The first boat leaves at 8 am and the last at 4 pm; the later departures won't leave much time for sightseeing.

If you want to do it on the cheap don't consider the alternative of hiring a dugout canoe and paddling yourself – the lake is much bigger than it looks from the shore and it can quickly get very choppy if a wind blows up. A better alternative is to walk. The road continues from Kedisan to Buahan and from there you just follow the good footpath around the lakeside to Trunyan, an easy hour or two's walk. From Trunyan you should be able to negotiate a cheaper boat to the cemetery and hot springs.

Buahan

A little further around the lake is Buahan, a small place with market gardens right down to the lake shore. *Baruna Cottages* is a very peaceful and pleasant place to stay. It's new, clean and has a restaurant; singles/doubles with mandi cost 5000/8000 rp. You can walk around the lake shore from here to Trunyan in about 1½ hours.

Trunyan

The village of Trunyan, on the shore of Lake Batur, is squeezed between the lake and the outer crater rim. This is a Bali Aga village, inhabited by descendants of the original

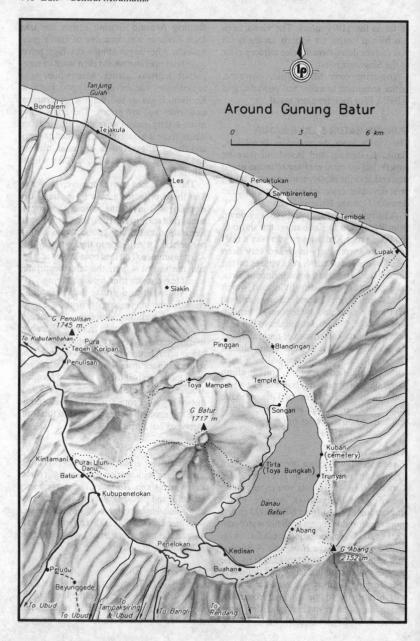

Around Gunung Batur

0   3   6 km

Bondalem
Tanjung
Gulah
Tejakula

Les
Penuktukan
Sambirenteng
Tembok
Lupak

Siakin

G Penulisan
1745 m
To Kubutambahan
Pura
Tegeh Koripan
Penulisan

Pinggan
Blandingan

Temple

Toya Mampeh

G Batur
1717 m
Songan

Kuban
(cemetery)

Kintamani
Pura Ulun
Danu
Batur
Tirta
(Toya Bungkah)
Trunyan

Kubupenelokan

Danau
Batur

Penelokan
Abang

Kedisan
G Abang
2152 m

Peludu
Buahan

Beyunggede
To Ubud
To Ubud
To
Tampaksiring
& Ubud
To Bangli
To
Rendang

Balinese, the people who predate the Majapahit arrival. Unlike the other well-known Bali Aga village, Tenganan, this is not an interesting and friendly place. It's famous for its four-metre high statue of the village's guardian spirit, Ratu Gede Pancering Jagat, but you're unlikely to be allowed to see it. About all you do get to do at Trunyan is sign the visitors' book, make a donation and be told you can't visit the temple.

Kuban

A little beyond Trunyan, and accessible only by the lake (there's no path) is the village cemetery. The people of Trunyan do not cremate or bury their dead – they lie them out in bamboo cages to decompose. Despite their reticence in the village they're quite happy for you to visit the cemetery. Unless you're a serious anthropologist, this is a tourist trap for those with morbid tastes.

Tirta (Toyah Bungkah)

Directly across the lake from Trunyan is the small settlement of Tirta, also known as Toyah Bungkah, with its famous hot springs – *tirta* and *toyah* both mean 'holy water'. The hot springs (air panas) bubble out in a couple of spots and are used to feed a bathing pool before flowing out into the lake. For 500 rp you can join half the village for a hot bath – women on one side, men on the other, soap and shampoo under the shower heads where the water flows out. The water is soothingly hot, ideal for aching muscles after a volcano climb.

Many travellers now stay in Tirta rather than Penelokan. It's more convenient if you want to climb Gunung Batur in the early morning, places to stay are a bit cheaper and you don't get hassled as much.

Places to Stay There are quite a few places to stay in Tirta, and more are being built. If there are empty rooms all over town and the asking price seems a bit high, you may be able to negotiate.

Under the Volcano Homestay in the village has rooms at 5000/8000 rp for basic singles/doubles; better rooms cost up to 15,000 rp. It's quite a pleasant place with a popular restaurant. *Awangga Bungalows*, at the other end of the village near the lake, advertises itself as the 'cheapest', with simple rooms from 5000 rp including breakfast. The nearby *Losmen Tirta Yatra* and *Setana Boga Guesthouse* are right by the lake. Other cheap places include the *Walina Losmen* from 6000 rp and the *Amerta Homestay & Restaurant*, near the hot springs, which has singles/doubles at 6000/8000 rp.

The small and basic *Siki Inn* has rooms from 8000 rp, and also offers a tourist shuttle-bus service to other parts of Bali. (The list of destinations and fares is in the restaurant.) *Kardi's Mountain View Losmen*, at 8000 rp for room only, is back from the lake, on the far side of the village. *Alina* has rooms at 8000 rp and comfortable bungalows at 15,000/20,000 rp; the amazing bathrooms have been done out to resemble fairy grottos! *Nyoman Pangus Homestay & Restaurant*, on the right as you come in from Kedisan, is clean and friendly with rooms at 10,000 to 15,000 rp.

The *Balai Seni Toyabungkah* (Toya Bungkah Arts Centre), up the hill on the western side of the village, is a pleasant place with rooms at 15,000 rp and bungalows at 25,000 rp, definitely a cut above the other small losmen. There's an excellent library there. The three *Putu Bungalows* behind Nyoman Mawa's restaurant are new, and the only rooms with Bali-style decorations. Doubles cost 25,000 rp, and you'll have to ask around to find someone to take your money and let you in.

Places to Eat Fresh fish from the lake is the local speciality, usually barbecued with onion and garlic. The fish are tiny but tasty, and you get three or four for a meal. There are a number of warungs and restaurants, mostly with similar menus and prices. *Nyoman Pangus Restaurant* (it used to be called a warung) does a good version of the barbecued fish. It has an interesting visitors' book with some very critical reviews of Lonely Planet guidebooks! On the other side of the road, the *Under the Volcano* restaurant has good, cheap food, as does the restaurant at *Alina* at the other end of town. The arts centre restaurant has a slightly higher standard at correspondingly higher prices.

Climbing Gunung Batur

Soaring up in the centre of the huge outer crater is the cone of Gunung Batur (1717 metres). It has erupted on several occasions this century, most recently in 1963 and 1974. There are several routes up, and some interesting walks around the summit. You can take one route up and another one down, then get a bemo back to your starting point. A bemo from Kedisan to Tirta will cost about 300 rp. You should start very early in the morning, before mist and cloud obscure the view. Ideally you should get to the top for sunrise – it's a magnificent sight.

You will be hassled by people offering to guide you up the mountain, sometimes asking outrageous prices. A few of the losmen also offer guides. If you have a reasonable sense of direction, and it's not totally dark when you start climbing, you won't need a guide for the usual routes up and down. About 5000 rp would be a fair price for guiding you up one of these routes and back. If you want to explore the crater, or take an unusual route up the mountain, then you may need a guide with more expertise than the kids who hassle you in town. The best source of information is Jero Wijaya, who can be found at Awangga Bungalows. He has some useful hand-drawn maps showing the whole crater area, with a variety of treks on Gunung Batur, up to the outer rim and beyond to the east coast. His knowledge of the history and geology of the area is way ahead of some of the local amateur guides, who can do little more than show you the path.

The most straightforward route is probably from Tirta. Walk out of town on the road to Kedisan and turn right at one of the signs pointing to Gunung Batur. There are quite a few paths at first, but just go uphill, tending south-west. After half an hour or so you'll be on a ridge with quite a well-defined track; keep going up. It gets pretty steep towards the top, and it can be hard walking over the loose volcanic sand – climbing up three steps and sliding back two. It takes about two hours to get to the top.

There are several refreshment stops along the way, and people with ice buckets full of cold drinks. It'll cost you more than 2000 rp for a small coke, but it's been carried a long way. The warung at the top has tea (500 rp), coffee (700 rp), jaffles (2000 rp) and a brilliant view (free).

At the summit it's possible to walk right around the rim of the volcanic cone, or descend into the cone from the southern edge. Wisps of steam issuing from cracks in the rock, and the surprising warmth of the ground, indicate that things are still happening down below. Some people bring eggs and cook them for breakfast in the steaming fissures – they take about seven minutes.

Other popular routes are from Kedisan or from Purajati, the ruined village on the Kedisan to Tirta road. These routes are well used and should be easy to follow across the lava flows to the west of Gunung Batur, then up to the smaller cone, created by the most recent eruption. Another possibility is to ascend from Kintamani, first descending the outer crater rim and then climbing the inner cone. For an interesting round trip, you can climb Gunung Batur from Tirta, follow the rim around to the other side, then descend on the regular route back to Kedisan. Climbing up, spending a reasonable time on the top and then strolling back down can all be done in four or five hours.

Songan

The road continues from Tirta around the lake to Songan, quite a large village which extends to the edge of the outer crater. Not many tourists come this far, but there's one place to stay, the *Restttt Inn Homestay & Restaurant* (that's how they spell it), on the left side of the road past the main part of the village, which looks quite OK and costs 12,000 rp for a room with a mandi.

From the temple at the crater edge you can climb to the top of the crater rim in just 15 minutes and from there you can see the east coast, only about five km away. It's an easy downhill stroll to the coast road at Lupak but, unless you want to walk back, remember to take your stuff with you – there's no direct public transport back to Tirta.

LAKE BRATAN AREA

The serenely calm Lake Bratan is on the most direct road from Denpasar to Singaraja. This route to the north coast is quicker than the one via Kintamani, but a good round trip would be to go one way via Kintamani, stopping at Gunung Batur, and back the other way via Bedugul and the Lake Bratan area. Approaching Bedugul from the south, you gradually leave the rice terraces behind and ascend into the cool, damp mountain country. There are several places to stay near the lake, and Bedugul can be an excellent base for walking trips around the other lakes and surrounding hills. There is also an interesting temple, botanical gardens, an excellent golf course and a variety of activities on Lake Bratan itself.

Taman Rekreasi Bedugul

The Bedugul Leisure Park (Taman Rekreasi Bedugul) is at the southern end of the lake. It's along the first road to the right as you come in to Bedugul from the south, and it costs 200 rp to get into the lakeside area. Along the waterfront are restaurants, souvenir shops, a hotel, and facilities for a number of water activities. You can hire a canoe and paddle across to the temple, or hire a motorboat (17,500 rp for half an hour, maximum four people) for a trip around the lake. Waterskiing and parasailing are also available.

It's possible to hire a prahu for 5000 rp an hour (but we got the same rate for a half day) and paddle across Lake Bratan from the lakeside just below the Lila Graha to some caves which the Japanese used during WW II. You can also walk there in about an hour. From there a very well-marked path ascends to the top of Gunung Catur. It takes about two hours for the climb up and an hour back down. The final bit is steep and you should take some water but it is well worth the effort. There is an old temple on the summit with lots of monkeys.

Anne Whybourne & Peter Clarke, Australia

Pura Ulu Danau

At Candikuning, on the shores of the lake a few km north of Bedugul, is the Hindu/Buddhist temple of Ulu Danau. It's very picturesque, with a large banyan tree at the entrance, attractive gardens and one courtyard isolated on a tiny island in the lake. The temple, founded in the 17th century, is dedicated to Dewi Danau, the goddess of the waters. It is the focus of ceremonies and pilgrimages to ensure the supply of water. Ulu Danau has classical Hindu thatched-roof merus and an adjoining Buddhist stupa. Admission is 200 rp (children 100 rp).

Botanical Gardens

Between Bedugul and Candikuning is the market of Bukit Mungsu, noted for its wild orchids. From the intersection, conspicuously marked with a large, phallic sculpture of a sweet corn cob, a road leads west up to the entrance of the Kebun Raya Eka Karya (kebun raya is Indonesian for 'botanical gardens'). The gardens were established in 1959 as a branch of the national botanical gardens at Bogor, near Jakarta. They cover more than 120 hectares on the lower slopes of Gunung Pohon, and have an extensive collection of trees and some 500 species of orchid in the Lila Graha. It's a very peaceful place, cool and shady with very few visitors. Unfortunately there is almost nothing in the way of visitor information, and the gardens are not as attractively laid out or as well established as those at Bogor or Cibodas in Java – so, if you've seen those two superb gardens you may be disappointed.

Around the Lakes

North of Candikuning, the road descends past the Bali Handara Kosaido Country Club, with its beautifully situated, world-class golf course. Green fees are 82,000 rp for 18 holes, and you can hire a half-set of clubs for 17,500 rp.

If you continue to Danau Buyan, there's a fine walk around the southern side of Buyan, then over the saddle to the adjoining, smaller Danau Tamblingan. From there you can walk uphill, then west to the village of Munduk

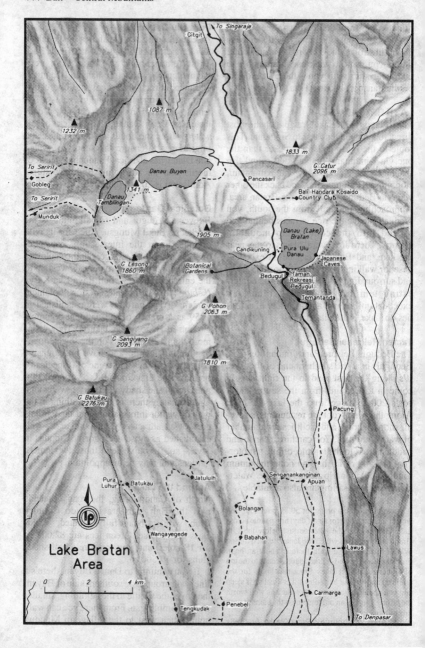

To Singaraja
Gitgit

1087 m

1232 m

1833 m

G Catur
2096 m

To Seririt
Gobleg

Danau Buyan

Pancasari

Bali Handara Kosaido
Country Club

To Seririt

Danau
Tamblingan

1341 m

Munduk

1905 m

Danau (Lake)
Bratan

Candikuning

Pura Ulu
Danau

Japanese
Caves

G Lesong
1860 m

Botanical
Gardens

Bedugul

Taman
Rekreasi
Bedugul

Temantanda

G Pohon
2063 m

G Sangiyang
2093 m

1810 m

G Batukau
2276 m

Pacung

Pura
Luhur

Batukau

Jatuluih

Senganankanginan

Apuan

Bolangan

Wangayegede

Babahan

Lawus

Lake Bratan
Area

0   2   4 km

Tengkudak

Penebel

Carmarga

To Denpasar

(about two to three hours) and then take the road around the northern side of the lakes back to Bedugul. Alternatively, you can follow the road west from Munduk, and then north, descending through picturesque villages to Seririt on the north coast.

Heading north from the Lake Bratan area, on the scenic main road, you come to the coastal town of Singaraja, about 30 km away (see the North Bali section). On the way there's a beautiful waterfall west of the road just past Gitgit village, about 10 km north of Bedugul. To get there, find the 'air terjun' sign, then walk for about a km through rice fields and jungle. It's a great place for a swim or a picnic, and entry costs 200 rp.

Places to Stay & Eat

There are several places to stay along the road and around the lake. In the Taman Rekreasi Bedugul, at the southern end of the lake, you'll find the *Bedugul Hotel & Restaurant* (☎ 2026593) with lakeside rooms at 21,500 and 25,000 rp, and bungalows from 39,500 rp. On the main road just by the turn-off is the *Hadi Raharjo*, a fairly basic losmen with rooms at 10,000 rp.

Continuing north, the road climbs up the hillside to the *Bukit Mungsu Indah Hotel* turn-off. 'Deluxe' rooms cost 39,000 to 45,000 rp, and 'executive' rooms from 53,000 to 84,000 rp. Prices include breakfast, TV, hot water, a fireplace and a great view, but tax is extra. On the road up to the botanical gardens (turn left at the giant sweet corn) you'll find the unprepossessing *Losmen Mawa Indah* which asks 10,000 rp for singles and doubles, but may lower prices if you negotiate.

The main road turns right and drops down towards the lake, passing the turn-off up a steep driveway to the *Lila Graha*, with rooms and bungalows from 25,000/30,000 rp for singles/doubles. It is well located, clean and comfortable, and the accommodation incorporates an old Dutch resthouse. On the other side of the road right by the lake is the *Hotel Ashram*, with rooms from 15,000 to 40,000 rp.

Top-end accommodation is at the *Bali Handara Country Club*, north of Candikuning, where a 'standard cottage' costs 96,000 rp, and an 'executive suite' 686,000 rp, plus 15½% tax and service. Meals here cost from 23,500 rp, but the view from the bar might be worth the price of a drink.

In Candikuning you'll find the *Restaurant Pelangi*, *Rumah Makan Mini Bali* and others in the same area. The eating places at the Taman Rekreasi are OK, but a bit expensive.

Getting There & Away

Bedugul is on the main north-south road, and so is easy to get to from either Denpasar or Singaraja. It costs 1700 rp from Denpasar's Ubung bus station, and about the same from the western bus station in Singaraja. The road is sealed all the way and signposted, so it's easy to follow if you have your own transport.

GUNUNG BATUKAU

West of the Mengwi to Bedugul and Singaraja road rises 2276-metre Gunung Batukau, the 'coconut-shell mountain'. This is the third of Bali's three major mountains and the holy peak of the western end of the island.

Pura Luhur

Pura Luhur, on the slopes of Batukau, was the state temple when Tabanan was an independent kingdom. The temple has a seven-roofed meru to Maha Dewa, the mountain's guardian spirit, as well as shrines for the three mountain lakes: Bratan, Tamblingan and Buyan.

There are several routes to Pura Luhur but none of them are particularly high-class roads – it's a remote temple. You can reach it by following the road up to Penebel from Tabanan. Or turn off the Mengwi to Bedugul road at Baturiti near the 'Denpasar 40 km' sign and follow the convoluted route to Penebel. Wangayagede, the nearest village to the temple, is surrounded by forest and is often damp and misty.

Jatuluih

Also perched on the slopes of Gunung

Batukau, but closer to Bedugul and the Mengwi to Bedugul road, is the small village of Jatuluih, whose name means 'truly marvellous'. The view truly is – it takes in a huge chunk of southern Bali.

ROUTES THROUGH PUPUAN

The two most popular routes between the south and north coast are the roads via Kintamani or Bedugul, but there are two other routes over the mountains. Both branch north from the Denpasar to Gilimanuk road, one from Pulukan and the other from Antosari, and meet at Pupuan before dropping down to Seririt, west of Singaraja. They're interesting and little-used alternatives to the regular routes.

The Pulukan to Pupuan road climbs steeply up from the coast, providing fine views back down to the sea. The route runs through spice-growing country and you'll often see spices laid out on mats by the road to dry – the smell of cloves rises up to meet you. At one point, the narrow and winding road actually runs right through an enormous banyan tree which bridges the road. Further on, the road spirals down to Pupuan through some of Bali's most beautiful rice terraces.

The road from Antosari starts through rice paddies, climbs into the spice-growing country, then descends through the coffee-growing areas to Pupuan.

If you continue another 12 km or so towards the north coast you reach Mayong, where you can turn east to Munduk and on to Danau Tamblingan and Danau Buyan. The road is rough but passable, and offers fine views of the mountains, lakes and out to the northern coast.

North Bali

North Bali, the district of Buleleng, makes an interesting contrast with the south of the

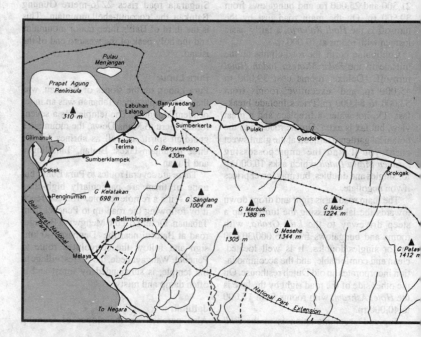

island. It's separated from the south by the central mountains – a short distance, but it keeps many of the tourist hordes at bay. There's a string of popular coastal beaches west of Singaraja, but these are nothing like the first-class tourist ghettos of Sanur or Nusa Dua. There's also a good variety of places to stay and eat, but nothing like the hassle and confusion of Kuta, and nowhere near the expense of Sanur. Many travellers arriving from Java go straight from Gilimanuk to the north coast, rather than taking the south-coast road which would leave them in Denpasar or, horror of horrors, Kuta Beach. Apart from the peaceful beaches, there are a number of other features worth visiting.

History

The north coast has been subject to European influence for longer than the south. Although the Dutch had established full control of northern Bali by 1849, it was not until the beginning of this century that their power extended to the south. Having first encountered Balinese troops in Java in the 18th century, the Dutch were the main purchasers of Balinese slaves, many of whom served in the Dutch East India Company armies. Although the Netherlands did not become directly involved with the island's internal affairs, as it had in Java, in 1816 it made several unsuccessful attempts to persuade the Balinese to accept Dutch authority. Various Balinese kings continued to provide the Dutch with soldiers but, in the 1840s, disputes over the looting (salvaging?) of shipwrecks, together with fears that other European powers might establish themselves in Bali, prompted the Dutch to make treaties with several of the Balinese rajahs. The treaties proved ineffective, the plundering continued and in 1844 disputes arose with the rajah of Buleleng over the ratification of agreements.

In 1845 the rajahs of Buleleng and

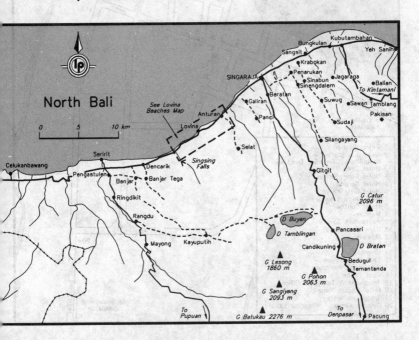

Karangasem formed an alliance, possibly to conquer other Balinese states or, equally possibly, to resist the Dutch. In any case, the Dutch attacked Buleleng and Karangasem in 1846, 1848 and 1849, seizing control of the north in the third attempt. The western district of Jembrana came under Dutch control in 1853 and the rajah of Gianyar surrendered his territory in 1900, but it was not until 1906 that the south was finally subdued. The last confrontation was in 1908, when Klungkung rebelled – unsuccessfully.

From the time of their first northern conquests, the Dutch interfered increasingly in Balinese affairs. It was here that Balinese women first covered their breasts – on orders from the Dutch to 'protect the morals of Dutch soldiers'.

SINGARAJA

Singaraja was the centre of Dutch power in Bali and remained the administrative centre for the islands of Nusa Tenggara (Bali through to Timor) until 1953. It is one of the few places in Bali where there are visible reminders of the Dutch period, but there are also Chinese and Muslim influences from Singaraja's time as a centre of

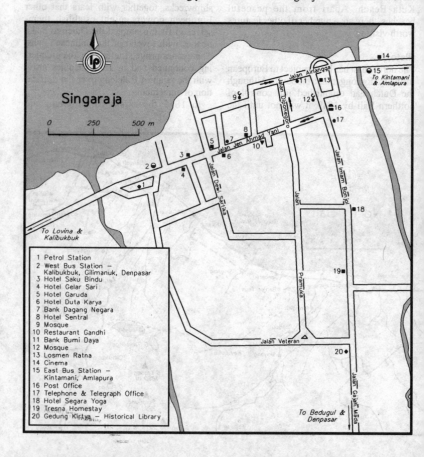

Singaraja

0   250   500 m

To Lovina & Kalibukbuk

To Kintamani & Amlapura

To Kintamani & Amlapura

To Bedugul & Denpasar

1 Petrol Station
2 West Bus Station –
   Kalibukbuk, Gilimanuk, Denpasar
3 Hotel Saku Bindu
4 Hotel Gelar Sari
5 Hotel Garuda
6 Hotel Duta Karya
7 Bank Dagang Negara
8 Hotel Sentral
9 Mosque
10 Restaurant Gandhi
11 Bank Bumi Daya
12 Mosque
13 Losmen Ratna
14 Cinema
15 East Bus Station –
   Kintamani, Amlapura
16 Post Office
17 Telephone & Telegraph Office
18 Hotel Segara Yoga
19 Tresna Homestay
20 Gedung Kirtya – Historical Library

Top: Early morning in Ubud, Bali (JL)
Bottom: Lembongan beach, Bali (JL)

Top Left: Rice paddy terraces near Tirtagangga, Bali (TW)
Top Right: Drive-through banyan tree, Pupuan, Bali (JL)
Bottom Left: Small rice paddy shrine, Bali (TW)
Bottom Right: Planting rice shoots, near Pulukan, Bali (TW)

administration and trade. With a population of around 50,000 Singaraja is a busy town, but orderly, even quiet compared with Denpasar. Dokars (horse-drawn two-wheeled carts) are still a common means of transport on the pleasant tree-lined streets, and there are some interesting Dutch colonial houses. The 'suburb' of Beratan, south of Singaraja, is the silverwork centre of northern Bali.

For years the port of Singaraja was the usual arrival point for visitors to Bali – it's where all the prewar travel books started. Singaraja is hardly used as a harbour now, due to its lack of protection from bad weather. Shipping for the north coast generally uses the new port at Celukanbawang, and visiting cruise ships anchor at Padangbai in the south. Singaraja has a conspicuous monument on its waterfront, with a statue pointing to an unseen enemy out to sea. It commemorates a freedom fighter who was killed here by gunfire from a Dutch warship early in the struggle for independence.

Singaraja is still a major educational and cultural centre. Apart from two university campuses there is the Gedung Kirtya Historical Library, with a magnificent collection of around 3000 old Balinese manuscripts inscribed on lontar (palm). These lontar books include literary, mythological, historical and religious works. Even older written works, in the form of inscribed metal plates called *prasastis*, are kept here. You're welcome to visit, but you'll find this a place for scholars rather than tourists.

Places to Stay

There are plenty of places to stay and eat in Singaraja but few people bother – the attractions of the beaches, only 10 km away, are too great. It's a pity because Singaraja is not a bad place to stay for a day or so – at least there are not too many tourists.

As in Denpasar, most of the hotels are principally used by local business travellers. You'll find a string of hotels along Jalan Jen Ahmad Yani, starting in the east with the *Hotel Sentral*, where basic singles/doubles

cost 6500/9000 rp or 20,000/25,000 rp with air-con. The *Hotel Garuda* (☎ 2041191), further west at No 76, has rooms from 7500 to 12,500 rp including breakfast, while the *Hotel Duta Karya*, across the road, costs 7500/10,000 rp for singles/doubles, or 35,000 rp with air-con. Further west again, and handy to the bus station, are the *Hotel Saku Bindu* and the *Hotel Gelar Sari*.

On Jalan Imam Bonjol, the street that continues south to Bedugul and Denpasar, you'll find the *Hotel Segara Yoga*, with clean, fan-cooled rooms from 8000/12,000 rp. Further south this street becomes Jalan Gajah Mada, with the *Tresna Homestay* (☎ 2021816) on the western side. It's cheap, with very basic rooms at 3000 rp and better rooms at 5000/ 8000 rp for singles/doubles. The proprietors are very friendly and interesting, and the place is filled with an amazing collection of antiques and old junk, some of it for sale.

Places to Eat

There are plenty of places to eat in Singaraja, including a batch of places in the small Mumbul market on Jalan Jen Ahmad Yani. You'll find the popular *Restaurant Gandhi* here, with a good Chinese menu and glossy, clean surroundings. Across the road is the *Restaurant Segar II*, where a good Chinese meal will run to about 5000 rp. There are also a few restaurants along Jalan Imam Bonjol, and some warungs near the two bus stations.

Getting There & Away

Singaraja is the north coast's main transportation centre and there are bus stations on the eastern and western sides of town. From the western station, minibuses to Denpasar (Ubung station) via Bedugul leave about every half hour from 6 am to 4 pm and cost around 2500 rp. Buses to Lovina cost 400 rp and to Gilimanuk, 2500 rp (about two hours). From the eastern station, minibuses to Kintamani are 1800 rp, and to Amlapura (via the coast road) about 2500 rp. On many routes there are also full-sized buses which are typically more crowded, less frequent, and about 500 rp cheaper.

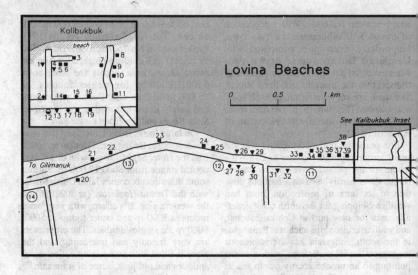

Lovina Beaches

0   0.5   1 km

See Kalibukbuk Inset

To Gilimanuk

Kolibukbuk
beach

■ PLACES TO STAY

3	Nirwana Cottages & Restaurant	24	Parma Beach Homestay
5	Susila Beach Inn 2	25	Aditya Bungalows & Restaurant
6	Angsoka Cottages & Restaurant	33	Puri Tasik Madu
7	Astina Cottages	34	Mangalla Homestay & Restaurant
8	Rini Hotel	35	Susila Beach Inn
9	Puri Bali Bungalows	36	Purnama Homestay
10	Rambutan Cottages & Restaurant	37	Permata Cottages
11	Ayodya Accommodation	39	Arjuna Homestay
14	Chono Beach Cottages	41	Kali Bukbuk Beach Inn
16	New Srikandi Hotel, Bar & Restaurant	42	Yudhistira Inn
18	Wisata Jaya Homestay	43	Banyualit Beach Inn
19	Khie Khie Hotel & Restaurant	44	Mas Bungalows
20	Ayu Pondok Wisita	45	Janur's Dive Inn
21	Krisna Beach Inn	46	Adi Homestay
22	Samudra Cottages	47	Lila Cita
23	Toto Pub	48	Celuk Agung Cottages

There are also direct buses to Surabaya (Java). You'll find a number of ticket offices near the junction of Jalan Jen Ahmad Yani and Jalan Diponegoro, but you can also arrange tickets from the Lovina Beach places. There are no direct buses to Yogyakarta but it is possible to arrange to connect with a direct Denpasar to Yogyakarta bus in Gilimanuk.

LOVINA

West of Singaraja is a string of coastal villages – Pemaron, Tukad Mungga, Anturan, Lovina, Kalibukbuk and Bunut Panggang – which have become popular beach resorts collectively known as Lovina. They developed much later and more slowly than Sanur and Kuta and, by comparison, the area is relaxed and unhassled. The shops, bars and

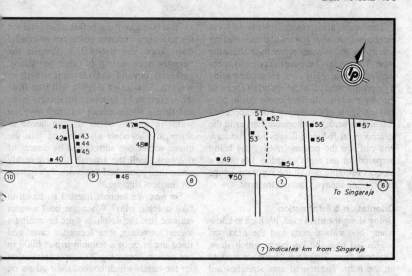

7 indicates km from Singaraja

49	Hotel Perama & Postal Agency	29	Marta's Warung
51	Simon's Seaside Cottages	31	Superman Restaurant
52	Homestay Agung & Restaurant	32	Singa Pizza Restaurant
53	Mandhara Cottages	38	Bali Ayu Restaurant
54	Bali Taman Beach Hotel	50	Harmoni Restaurant
55	Jati Reef Bungalows		
56	Permai Beach Bungalows		OTHER
57	Baruna Beach Cottages		
		2	Beny Tantra's Shop
▼	PLACES TO EAT	12	Bus Stop
		15	Tourist Office & Police Station
1	Bali Bintang Restaurant	17	Moneychanger
4	Kakatua Bar & Restaurant	27	Spice Dive
13	Badai Restaurant	30	Mosque
26	Johni's Restaurant	40	Radio Mast
28	Restaurant Adi Rama		

other tourist facilities don't dominate the place as they do at Sanur and, to an even greater extent, Kuta. The local hustle is 'You want to see the dolphins?', but apart from that you are not endlessly harassed to buy things, have a massage, or do anything more than simply laze on the beach. It's a popular stop for those who have come overland through Java and beyond, and want to take it

easy for a few days. It's a good place to meet travellers, as there's quite an active social scene.

The beaches here are black volcanic sand, not the white stuff you find in the south. It doesn't look as appealing but it's perfectly clean and fine to walk along. Nor is there any surf – a reef keeps it almost flat calm most of the time.

The beach also provides plenty of local entertainment, with goats and ducks making a morning and evening promenade along the sand. The sunsets here are every bit as spectacular as those at Kuta and are accompanied by a programme of 'local' entertainment: as the sky reddens, the bats come out to play and the lights of the fishing boats appear as bright dots across the horizon. Earlier in the afternoon, at fishing villages like Anturan, you can see the prahus (outriggers) being prepared for the night's fishing. It's quite a process bringing out all the kerosene lamps and rigging them up around the boat.

Orientation & Information

Going along the main road, it's hard to know where one village ends and the next one begins, so note the km posts which show distances from Singaraja. These are marked on the map. The tourist area stretches out over seven or eight km, but the main focus is at Kalibukbuk, about 10½ km from Singaraja. This is where you'll find the tourist office and the police station, which share the same premises. The tourist office is open Monday to Thursday from 7 am to 2 pm, Friday from 7 to 11 am, and Saturday from 7 am to 12.30 pm. If you need information outside these times the police may be able to help.

There are a couple of good bookshops on the other side of the road, beside the Badai Restaurant. Opposite the Badai you'll find Beny Tantra's T-shirt shop. It's not cheap, but it's worth a look because his designs are so good, brilliant in fact. He'll also make them to order.

There's no post office at Lovina, but you can buy stamps and post letters at the Hotel Perama. Local and long-distance telephone calls can be made at Aditya Bungalows – just ask at the front desk.

Dolphins

From the moment you set foot in Lovina you'll be inundated with offers to see the dolphins; to the extent that you might feel like refusing on principle. In fact it's quite an experience, and not to be missed.

You take a boat out before dawn, and see the sun burst over the volcanoes of central Bali. Then you notice that, despite the ungodly hour, dozens of other boats have gathered beyond the reef and lie there waiting. Suddenly a dolphin will leap from the waves, to be followed by several more and then a whole school, vaulting over the water in pursuit of an unseen horde of shrimps. The boats all turn and join the chase, sometimes surrounded by dozens of dolphins, until the animals unaccountably cease their sport, and the boats wait quietly for the next sighting.

So why are tourists hassled so much to take dolphin trips? When the boat owners realised that the dolphins were becoming a tourist attraction, they formed a cartel and fixed the price of a dolphin trip at 8000 rp per person, including 2000 rp commission for the hotels which booked their guests on a trip. Then some freelancers started selling dolphin trips on their friends' boats, and claiming the 2000 rp commission for themselves. A new 'service' industry was born. Flogging dolphin trips to tourists must seem better than, for example, working as a labourer, who might be paid only 2000 rp for a day's hard work. Unfortunately, as you will notice, competition between the touts is now so intense as to be a public nuisance, and the touts can be almost hostile towards tourists who book dolphin trips through a hotel instead of with them. Lovina has lost its reputation as a place where tourists don't get hassled.

Diving

Generally, the water is very clear and the reef is terrific for snorkelling. It's not the best coral you'll find but it's certainly not bad and getting out to it is very easy. In many places you can simply swim out from the beach. Elsewhere you can get a prahu to take you out to the reef, and the skipper should know where the best coral is. All the hotels seem to have their own boat, or access to one, but plenty of touts on the beach will offer you snorkelling trips, usually just after you have declined an invitation to see the dolphins. It costs about 4000 rp per person for an hour, including the use of mask, snorkel and fins. Out on the reef the water is calm, clear and relatively shallow, and even beginner swimmers can have a good look around with the boat's outrigger to hang on to for security. It's great for kids.

For those with a scuba qualification, there's also a diving operation here. Spice Dive, in humble premises on the south side of the main road near Johni's restaurant, runs trips out to Lovina reef (from 88,000 rp), to the wreck at Tulamben (107,000 rp) and to the island of Pulau Menjangan in the Bali Barat National Park (117,000 rp). Menjangan offers probably the best diving in Bali, but transport costs make it an expensive dive with operators from anywhere else in Bali. From Lovina, a trip to Menjangan is good value if you can arrange a group of around six people. If you're interested, talk to Imanuel or Nancy at Spice Dive – they're friendly and very informative.

Places to Stay

There are now so many places to stay along the Lovina Beach strip that it's impossible to list them all, or to keep the list up to date. For most of the year it's easy to find a place to stay, but because these are strung out over several km it may be hard to get to a particular place in the peak periods. The first hotel is north of the main road just after the six km marker, and the last is nearly 14 km from Singaraja. Places are usually clustered in groups on one of the sideroads to the beach, then there might be nothing for half a km or so.

During peak times (mid-July to the end of August and mid-December to mid-January) accommodation can be tight and prices somewhat higher. At other times prices may be more negotiable, particularly if there are a lot of empty rooms around. Generally the cheapest places are away from the beach, some on the south side of the main road. Upstairs rooms are cooler and a bit more expensive, especially if they have a view. There's a 5% tax on accommodation.

Singaraja to Anturan Starting from the Singaraja end, the first place is the slightly higher priced *Baruna Beach Cottages*, with individual cottages and rooms in a larger two-storeyed block. All have bathrooms, and prices range from 78,000 rp with fan, and from 102,000 rp with air-con, including breakfast. There's a swimming pool, and a bar/restaurant on the beach. You can also rent windsurfers (12,000 rp per hour) and other water-sports equipment.

On the next side-road, the *Jati Reef Bungalows*, in the rice paddies close to the beach, look a bit like concrete bunkers. The comfortable double rooms have private, open-air bathrooms for around 15,000 rp. Further inland are the new *Permai Beach Cottages* where basic rooms cost from 10,000 rp and rooms with hot water and air-con cost from 30,000 rp. The reef off the beach here is reputed to be the best along the Singaraja to Lovina coastal strip.

Fronting onto the main road, but extending all the way down to the beach, is the new and expensive *Bali Taman Beach Hotel* (☎ 2041125). Standard singles/doubles cost 29,000/39,000 rp and air-con rooms cost an extra 49,000 rp.

Anturan Continuing along the road, you come to the turn-off to the little fishing village of Anturan, where there are three places to stay, and lots of local colour. *Mandhara Cottages* is a neat little complex where singles/doubles with bathroom cost 8000/10,000 rp including breakfast. Walking east along the beach for about 100 metres will bring you to *Simon's Seaside Cottages*, an old establishment which has been completely rebuilt and where comfortable rooms cost 39,000 rp. There's actually a little track leading from the main road directly to Simon's, but it's hard to spot. Next door to Simon's is the neat and clean *Homestay Agung*, with rooms for 7000 to 10,000 rp – the more expensive rooms are interesting two-storeyed places, with bedroom upstairs and bathroom downstairs. The food at Agung can be quite good.

Anturan to Kalibukbuk Continuing west from Anturan you pass the *Hotel Perama* (☎ 2021161) on the main road, with rooms for 10,000 rp and a good restaurant. This is also the office for the Perama bus company, and a good source of information for tours. The next turn-off goes down to the *Lila Cita*, right on the beach front. It's simple, but the owners are friendly and welcoming and it's a popular place. Singles/doubles cost 8000/ 10,000 rp, or 15,000/20,000 rp with private mandi, and the sea is just outside your window. On the way there you'll pass the *Celuk Agung Cottages*, with rooms from 27,000 rp, or 50,000 rp with air-con. The complex has satellite TV, tennis courts and a pool.

Back on the main road, on the side away from the beach, is the *Adi Homestay*, with rooms from 6000 rp including breakfast.

The next sideroad down to the beach has quite a few places to stay. The pleasant *Kali Bukbuk Beach Inn* has rooms for 15,000 to 30,000 rp. On the other side, back a bit from the beach, is the similarly priced *Banyualit Beach Inn*. Other places here include *Yudhistra, Mas Bungalows* and *Janur's Dive Inn*.

Kalibukbuk A little beyond the 10-km marker is the 'centre' of Lovina – the village of Kalibukbuk. Here you'll find *Ayodya Accommodation*, a traditional place in a big old Balinese house. It's clean, friendly and extremely well run. Rooms cost from 4000 to 8000 rp and are bare and functional, but you sit outside and take your meals there. It's very pleasant in the evening, with the bamboo gamelan tinkling in the background, although the traffic noise can be annoying.

Follow the track beside Ayodya down towards the beach and you'll come to the delightful *Rambutan Cottages*. The beautifully finished rooms cost 15,000 rp downstairs and 20,000 rp upstairs, 5000 rp more in peak seasons. Next along are the *Puri Bali Bungalows* where singles/doubles cost 8000/10,000 rp, good value for this location. Closest to the beach is the superclean and well-run *Rini Hotel*. Rooms cost

15,000 to 30,000 rp and there's a good restaurant. Families and children are welcome. Opposite Rini are the *Astina Cottages*, in a pretty garden setting, with a variety of rooms and bungalows for 7000 to 10,000 rp; prices are a bit higher in the peak season.

Along the main road west of Ayodya, among the bars, restaurants and other facilities, you'll find the *Khie Khie Hotel & Restaurant*. It has a pool and rooms for 12,500 to 15,000 rp. A bit further along is the small *Wisata Jaya Homestay*, one of the cheapest around, with basic but satisfactory rooms for 5000 rp. On the other side of the road is the *New Srikandi Hotel Bar & Restaurant*, with singles/doubles at 5000/7000 rp. Further along, *Chono Beach Cottages* has rooms for 10,000 to 17,000 rp.

The next turn-off, just beyond the 11-km marker, takes you down a driveway to *Nirwana Cottages* (☎ 2041288). This is the biggest development at Lovina, with a large slab of beach-front property extending to the back of Astina Cottages. It's a great location, and the restaurant overlooking the beach is one of the best places to enjoy the sunset. Double rooms cost from 11,000 to 19,000 rp, and delightful, double-storeyed Bali-style cottages from 34,000 rp – ideal for families. Prices are higher in peak season. Some people think the rooms and the restaurant are overpriced, but it's a well-run place and the location is unbeatable.

Right behind Nirwana are the *Angsoka Cottages*, a small (but expanding) place with simple rooms from 6000 rp – excellent value for money. The newer rooms cost more: up to 50,000 rp for a bungalow with air-con. If you want to stay in Kalibukbuk, it's worth asking at Angsoka; there should be something to suit your budget. The small *Susila Beach Inn 2*, beside the Angsoka, is a straightforward losmen with cheap rooms from about 6000 rp.

Back on the main road there's a string of cheaper places with prices from about 5000 rp. These include the *Arjuna Homestay*, the *Permata Cottages, Purnama Homestay* and *Susila Beach Inn*, which are all grouped together on the northern side the road. Some of the places here extend through to the beach, so you can get away from the road noise. Further along is the slightly more expensive *Mangalla Homestay*, then the *Puri Tasik Madu*.

Beyond Kalibukbuk Further along is the top-end *Aditya Bungalows & Restaurant*, with beach frontage, pool, shops and a variety of rooms with TV, phone, fridge etc. Some of the rooms are right on the beach and costs range from 25,000 to 78,000 rp. Next, there's the friendly *Parma Beach Homestay*, with cottages from 5000 rp, set in a garden extending down to the beach. The *Toto Pub* is another bottom-end place with a top location; it's at the end of town but right on the beach. Very basic rooms are 7000 rp for a double. The *Samudra Cottages* have a secluded location even further along the road, but are expensive at about 30,000 rp for rooms with air-con. The *Krisna Beach Inn* is the next one out, with rooms from 5000 rp, and there are more places extending further west.

Places to Eat
Most of the places to stay along the beach strip also have restaurants and snack bars, and you're generally welcome to visit other losmen for a meal, even if you're not staying there. Many of the restaurants are also bars, depending on the time of night, and you can stop at any of them just for a drink. With all these places, plus a handful of warungs, there are dozens of places to eat. Some of them are listed here, but you'll do well just looking around and eating anywhere that takes your fancy.

Starting from the Singaraja end, the small *Homestay Agung* has a good reputation for its food, and people from other losmen often drop in. On the main road nearby there's the *Harmoni Restaurant* which has great fresh fish and other seafood dishes.

At Kalibukbuk village the *Khie Khie Restaurant* has a good seafood menu, and a bit further along is the popular *Badai Restaurant*. It has a relaxed, friendly feel and is a convivial meeting place for travellers in the evening. The food is pretty good too, with some excellent 'order a day in advance' dishes like fish curry, duck, or Hidangan Jawa (like a rijstaffel). The Badai also has a useful bulletin board.

The restaurant at *Nirwana*, overlooking the beach, is pricey but popular. It's worth at least one visit for a drink at sunset. On the road down to Nirwana there's also the *Bali Bintang Restaurant* on one side and the *Kakatua Bar & Restaurant* on the other. The Bintang is good, relatively cheap and happy to tackle food not featured on the menu. The Kakatua (Cockatoo) also offers good meals in a very convivial atmosphere.

Further along is *Singa Pizza Restaurant*, the *Superman Restaurant*, *Marta's Warung* and then *Johni's Restaurant*. All these places are popular, and their menus and prices are similar so it's impossible to single out individual places. There are also some small warungs in this area which serve tasty food at good prices, even if the surroundings are not quite as salubrious.

Entertainment
Some of the hotel restaurants have special nights with an Indonesian buffet meal and Balinese dancing. At about 3500 rp for entertainment and all you can eat, this can be very good value. *Rambutan* does a good one on Wednesdays and Sundays. *Aditya*, the *New Srikandi* and *Angsoka* also have buffet nights which are well advertised by leaflets that circulate around the beach and the bars.

There is something of a social scene in Lovina – it could even be described as a romantic place. On the beach and in the bars you can meet young people from all over the world, including quite a few Indonesians.

Warning: Balinese guys can be very charming and are not averse to accepting gifts from foreign girlfriends. There's nothing wrong with this, but a few of these guys are con artists who are mainly interested in the girl's money. The routine often involves taking a new girlfriend to see 'his' village – usually it's not the guy's own village but the girl doesn't know that. She may be shocked by the poor circumstances of her new lover, particularly when she hears about his sick mother who can't pay for an operation, the brother who needs money for his education or the important religious ceremony that they can't afford. If the girl does not give him money on some such pretext, the guy may well try to steal it from her. After he has her money the guy dumps the girl, often in a very hurtful fashion, to clear the way for another unsuspecting tourist. Of course most guys are OK, and no doubt there have been thousands of delightful holiday romances in Bali, but don't let the romantic atmosphere cloud your better judgement.

Getting There & Away

To get to Lovina from the south of Bali you first have to get to Singaraja, then take a bemo out from there. The regular bemo fare from Singaraja to the middle of Lovina's beach strip is 400 rp. See the Singaraja section for details.

There are direct public buses between Surabaya (Java) and Singaraja, but if you're coming in from Surabaya you can get off along the beaches rather than have to backtrack from Singaraja. If you're heading west you can flag down a bus or bemo in the main drag and save going into Singaraja then back out. Drivers will probably stop anywhere, but the main stop is around the Badai Restaurant; you can buy bus/bemo tickets near here as well.

The Perama bus company's office (☎ 2021161) and bus stop is at the Perama Hotel in Anturan, about eight km from Singaraja. Perama's tourist shuttle buses are more expensive than regular public transport, but are often worth the extra for the sake of convenience. Fares are 10,000 rp to Kuta or Ubud, 12,000 rp to Candidasa or Padangbai, 16,000 rp to Lombok, 16,000 rp to Surabaya and 25,000 rp to Yogyakarta.

WEST OF SINGARAJA

There are numerous places of interest along the north coast, both west and east of Singaraja. The road west of Singaraja follows the coast through Lovina then cuts through the Bali Barat National Park to join the south coast road near Gilimanuk, the port for ferries to Java. There are several places along this road, or near to it, which are worth a visit.

Waterfalls

At the village of Labuhan Haji, five km from the middle of the Lovina beach strip, there's a sign to Singsing Air Terjun (Daybreak Waterfall). About one km from the main road there's a warung on the left and a car park on the right – you may be asked to pay 100 rp for parking. Walk past the warung and along the path for about 200 metres to the lower falls. The waterfall is not huge, dropping about 12 metres into a deep pool which is good for a swim. The water isn't crystal clear either, but it's much cooler than the sea and very refreshing. Local kids will leap from a tree high up on the hill into the deep water – for a fee or just for fun.

You can clamber further up the hillside to the second waterfall (Singsing Dua), which is slightly bigger and has a mud bath that is supposedly good for the skin. This one also cascades into a deep pool in which you can swim. It's a pretty setting and makes a nice day trip from Lovina. The falls are more spectacular in the wet season.

Banjar

Buddhist Monastery Bali's only Buddhist monastery (*wihara*) is about half a km beyond the village of Banjar Tega, which is about three km up a steep track from the main coast road. It is vaguely Buddhist-looking, with colourful decoration, a bright orange roof and statues of Buddha, but overall it's very Balinese, with the same decorative carvings and door guardians. It's quite a handsome structure, in a commanding location with views down the valley and across the paddy fields to the sea. The road continues past the monastery, winding further up into the hills.

Hot Springs The hot springs (*air panas*) are only a short distance west of the monastery if you cut across from Banjar Tega, rather than return to the main road. From the monastery, go back down to Banjar Tega and turn left in the centre of the village. The small road runs west for a km or so to the village of Banjar. From there it's only a short distance uphill before you see the 'air panas one km' sign on the left. Follow the road to the car park where you'll be shown a place to park. Buy your ticket from the little office (400 rp, children 200 rp) and cross the bridge to the baths. There are changing rooms under the restaurant, on the right side.

Eight carved stone nagas (mythological serpents) spew water from a natural hot spring into the first bath, which then overflows (via the mouths of five more nagas), into a second, larger pool. In a third pool, water pours from three-metre-high spouts to give you a pummelling massage. The water is slightly sulphurous and pleasantly hot, so you might enjoy it more in the morning or the evening than in the heat of the day. You must wear a swimsuit and you shouldn't use soap in the pools, but you can do so under an adjacent outdoor shower.

The whole area is beautifully landscaped with lush tropical plants. The restaurant, a striking example of modern Balinese architecture, is not too expensive and has good Indonesian food.

Getting There & Away The monastery and hot springs are both signposted from the main road. If you don't have your own transport, it's probably easiest to go to the hot springs first. Heading west from Singaraja, continue beyond the turn-off to Banjar Tega to the Banjar turn-off (around the 18 km marker) where there are guys on motorbikes who will take you up to the air panas for 1000 rp or so. From the springs you can walk across to the monastery and back down to the main road.

Seririt
Seririt is little more than a junction town for the roads that run south over the mountains to Pulukan or Bajera, on the way to Denpasar. The road running west along the coast towards Gilimanuk is quite good. In parts it is quite scenic, even spectacular, and it's certainly not overrun with tourists.

Seririt has a petrol station and a reasonable selection of shops. If you need to stay there, the *Hotel Singarasari*, near the bus and bemo stop, has singles/doubles for 5000/7000 rp, or 17,000/20,000 rp with air-con. There are places to eat in the market area, just north of the bemo stop.

Celukanbawang
Celukanbawang, the main port for northern Bali, has a large wharf. Bugis schooners, the magnificent sailing ships which take their name from the seafaring Bugis people of Sulawesi, sometimes anchor here. There's also a small beach – so it's very picturesque. The *Hotel Drupadi Indah*, a combination losmen, cinema, bar and restaurant, is the only place to stay.

Pulaki
Pulaki is famous for its Pura Pulaki, a coastal temple which was completely rebuilt in the early '80s. The temple has a large troop of monkeys. Pulaki itself seems to be entirely devoted to grape growing and the whole village is almost roofed over with grapevines. For some reason grape growing has become popular at several locations on the north coast in recent years. A local wine is made which tastes a little like sweet sherry – mixed with lemonade it's drinkable, sort of. The grapes are also exported as dried fruit. One km past Pulaki are the Pemuteran hot springs, a few hundred metres off the road.

BALI BARAT NATIONAL PARK
The Bali Barat (West Bali) National Park covers nearly 20,000 hectares of the western tip of Bali. In addition, 50,000 hectares are protected in the national park extension, as well as nearly 7000 hectares of coral reef and coastal waters. On an island as small and densely populated as Bali, this represents a major commitment to nature conservation. The management of the area is to be integrated with a conservation and environment plan for all of Bali. Information and facilities

for visitors are quite limited, but this may improve as the area becomes better known.

The main north coast road connects with Gilimanuk through the national park, and you don't have to pay any entrance fees just to drive through. If you want to visit any places of interest (they're called 'visitor objects'), then you have to pay separately for each one.

Banyuwedang Hot Springs

Coming from the north coast, this is the first 'visitor object' you will encounter. There is a Balinese temple here and, according to one brochure, the hot springs will 'strengthen the endurance of your body against the attack of skin disease'. Entrance costs 450 rp, including 50 rp insurance; 250 rp for children.

Labuhan Lalang & Pulau Menjangan

Labuhan Lalang is the place to get a boat to Pulau Menjangan (Deer Island), an unspoilt and uninhabited island reputed to offer the best diving in Bali. The office at the entrance has some information and a good relief model of the national park. They also sell the 400 rp ticket to enter the foreshore area. There's a jetty for the boats to Menjangan, a warung with the usual sort of menu, and a pleasant white-sand beach 200 metres to the east. There are coral formations close to the shore which are good for snorkelling and, since this area of Bali is sparsely populated and now protected in the national park, the variety of fish and coral is amazing.

Excursions from Labuhan Lalang to Pulau Menjangan start at 35,000 rp, including the half-hour boat trip, three hours on or around the island, and the return trip. If you want to stay longer, each additional hour costs about 5000 rp. Both snorkelling and scuba diving are excellent around the island, with superb unspoiled coral, caves, lots of tropical fish and a spectacular drop-off. Boats usually visit the same areas, where fixed moorings have been installed to prevent the coral being damaged by anchors. Diving is usually best in the early morning, when the water is clearest. Diving trips to the island can be arranged by various dive operators in Bali, but it's a

long way to come for a day trip from the south. The closest dive operation is Spice Dive at Lovina Beach. There is a short nature trail on the island, and most trips allow some time to walk around and look at the flora and fauna, particularly the wild deer after which the island is named.

Teluk Terima

Teluk means bay or inlet, but Teluk Terima refers more generally to an area just west of Labuhan Lalang. The 'visitor object' here (400 rp admission) is Jayaprana's grave, a 10-minute walk up some stone stairs from the south side of the road. The foster son of a 17th-century king, Jayaprana, planned to marry Leyonsari, a beautiful girl of humble origins. The king, however, also fell in love with Leyonsari and had Jayaprana killed. In a dream, Leyonsari learned the truth of Jayaprana's death, and killed herself rather than marry the king. This Romeo and Juliet story is a common theme in Balinese folklore, and the grave is regarded as sacred even though the ill-fated couple were not deities. From the site, there's a fine view to the north and, according to a national park pamphlet, '...you will feel another pleasure which you can't get in another place'.

Jungle Treks

Three-hour guided treks around the Teluk Terima area can be arranged through the national park office at Labuhan Lalang. The treks cost about 5000 rp, and the best times to go are in the early morning and around dusk. The peninsula north of the Terima to Gilimanuk road, Prapat Agung, is within the park, and a 25-km walking track skirts the coast. There are no facilities and it's a hot walk, so take plenty of liquids.

Places to Stay

At Labuhan Lalang there are some basic bungalows on the foreshore area near the boat jetty. Both singles and doubles cost 7500 rp, but there are only a few of them so they may be full – ask at the warung. A little further west at Teluk Terima, *PT Margarana Accommodation* is just off the road at the 13 km marker before Gilimanuk. It has a small restaurant and clean rooms with showers for 15,000 rp.

Getting There & Away

The road east follows the coast to Lovina and Singaraja. The road west goes to Cekek, where there is a T-intersection – if you turn right, it's a couple of km to Gilimanuk, while turning left will take you to Negara (see the South-West Bali section) and Denpasar. You should be able to flag down public transport in either direction.

EAST OF SINGARAJA

There are a number of places of interest close to the coast road between Singaraja and the turn-off to Kintamani, including some of northern Bali's best known temples. The north-coast sandstone used in temple construction is very soft and easily carved, allowing local sculptors to give free rein to their imaginations. You'll find some delightfully whimsical scenes carved into a number of the temples here. Overall, the exuberant, even baroque, style of the north makes temples in the south appear almost restrained in contrast.

Although the basic architecture of the temples is similar in both regions, there are some important differences. The inner courtyard of southern temples usually houses a number of multi-roofed shrines (merus) together with other structures, whereas in the north, everything is grouped on a single pedestal. On the pedestal you'll usually find 'houses' for the deities to use on their earthly visits and also for storing important religious relics. Also, there will probably be a padmasana or throne for the sun god.

At Kubutambahan there is a turn-off to the south which takes you up to Penulisan and Kintamani, or you can continue east to the lovely spring-fed pools at Yeh Sanih. From there the road continues right around the east coast to Amlapura – see the East Bali section for details.

Sangsit

At Sangsit, only a few km beyond Singaraja,

you'll find an excellent example of the colourful architectural style of northern Bali. Sangsit's Pura Beji is a subak temple, dedicated to the spirits that look after irrigated rice fields. It's about half a km off the main road towards the coast. The sculptured panels along the front wall set the tone with their demons and amazing nagas.

The temple is just the same on the inside, with a variety of sculptures covering every available space. Like many other northern temples the inner courtyard is spacious and grassy, shaded by a frangipani tree.

If you continue beyond Sangsit to Bung kulan, you'll find another fine temple with an interesting kulkul (warning drum).

Jagaraga

The village of Jagaraga, a few km off the main road, has an interesting pura dalem. The small and otherwise unprepossessing temple has delightful sculptured panels along its front wall, both inside and out. On the outer wall look for a vintage car driving sedately past, a steamer at sea and even an aerial dogfight between early aircraft. Jagaraga is also famous for its legong troupe, said to be the best in northern Bali.

It was the capture of the local rajah's stronghold at Jagaraga that marked the arrival of Dutch power in Bali in 1849. A few km past Jagaraga, along the right-hand side as you head inland, look for another small temple with ornate carvings of a whole variety of fish and fisherpeople.

Sawan

Several km further inland, Sawan is a centre for the manufacture of gamelan gongs and complete gamelan instruments. You can see the gongs being cast and the intricately carved gamelan frames being made. It's very much a local cottage industry and, as the craft workers don't get many visitors, they're usually pleased to see you and show you around.

Kubutambahan

Only a km or so beyond the Kintamani turn-off at Kubutambahan is the Pura Maduwe

Temple guardian, Kubutambahan

Karang. Like Pura Beji at Sangsit, the temple is dedicated to agricultural spirits, but this one looks after unirrigated land. The temple is usually kept locked but if you ask at the shop opposite, you may get the key.

This is one of the best temples in northern Bali and is particularly noted for its sculptured panels, including the famous bicycle panel depicting a gentleman riding a bicycle with flower petals for wheels. It's on the base of the main plinth in the inner enclosure, but there are other panels worth inspecting in this peaceful and pleasant temple.

Yeh Sanih

About 15 km east of Singaraja, Yeh Sanih (also called Air Sanih) is a popular local spot where freshwater springs are channelled into some very pleasant swimming pools before flowing into the sea. Yeh Sanih is right by the sea and the area with the pools is attractively laid out with pleasant gardens, a restaurant and a couple of places to stay. It's well worth a visit and admission to the springs and pool costs 150 rp (children 100 rp). On the hill overlooking the springs is the Pura Taman Manik Mas temple.

Places to Stay & Eat There are a couple of places to stay near the springs. In fact, the *Bungalow Puri Sanih* is actually in the springs complex. It has a very pretty garden and doubles cost 10,000 to 20,000 rp – the most expensive rooms are little two-storeyed bungalows. Just beyond the springs, *Yeh Sanih Seaside Cottages* has pleasant rooms at 25,000/30,000 rp for singles/doubles.

The Puri Sanih also has a restaurant overlooking the springs and the gardens. There are a number of warungs across the road from the springs, and a restaurant up on the hillside which you reach by climbing some steep stairs.

Nusa Penida

Nusa Penida, an administrative region within the Klungkung district, comprises three islands – Nusa Penida itself, the smaller Nusa Lembongan to the north-west, and tiny Nusa Ceningan between them. Nusa Lembongan attracts many visitors for its surf, seclusion and snorkelling. The island of Nusa Penida is right off the tourist track and has few facilities for visitors, while Nusa Ceningan is virtually uninhabited.

Economic resources are limited on Nusa Penida. It has been a poor region for many years and there has been some transmigration from here to other parts of Indonesia. Thin soils and a lack of water do not permit the cultivation of rice, but other crops are grown, some for export to mainland Bali. Fishing is another source of food, and some sardines and lobster are also sold to Bali. The cultivation of seaweed is a recent development but now quite well established, and the underwater fences on which it is grown can be seen off many of the beaches. After harvesting, the seaweed is spread out on the beach to dry, then exported to Japan and Europe, where it is used as a thickening agent in processed foods and cosmetics.

NUSA LEMBONGAN

Most visitors to Nusa Lembongan come for

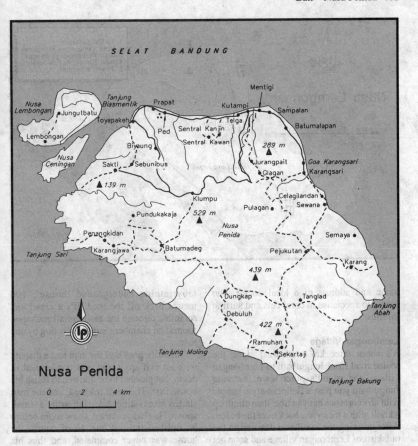

SELAT   BANDUNG

Nusa Lembongan
Jungutbatu
Lembongan
Tanjung Biasmentik
Prapat
Toyapakeh
Ped
Biyaung
Nusa Ceningan
Sakti
Sebunibus
▲ 139 m
Mentigi
Kutampi
Telga
Sentral Kanjin
Sentral Kawan
Sampalan
Batumalapan
▲ 289 m
Jurangpait
Glagan
Goa Karangsari
Karangsari
Klumpu
Pundukakaja
▲ 529 m
Nusa
Penida
Celagilandan
Pulagan
Sewana
Penangkidan
Karangjawa
Batumadeg
Tanjung Sari
Pejukutan
Semaya
Karang
▲ 439 m
Dungkap
Tanglad
Tanjung Abah
Debuluh
▲ 422 m
Tanjung Moling
Ramuhan
Sekartaji
Tanjung Bakung

Nusa Penida

0   2   4 km

the surf that breaks on the coral reef offshore, and stay around the beach at Jungutbatu. The reef protects the beach, a perfect crescent of white sand with clear blue water, and there are superb views across the strait to Gunung Agung on mainland Bali. There's also good snorkelling on the reef, with some spots accessible from the beach. To reach other snorkelling spots you need to charter a boat, which costs about 5000 rp per hour. Apart from the attractions of the beach, the coral and the surf, there's not much else to do.

There's no jetty – the boats usually beach at the village of Jungutbatu and you have to jump off into the shallows. Your boat captain might be able to leave you at the eastern end of the beach where most of the bungalows are, but otherwise you'll have to walk a km to reach them.

Apart from the few basic bungalows and restaurants there are virtually no tourist facilities. There's no post office and the bank doesn't change travellers' cheques. The notice board at the Main Ski restaurant advertises excursions and day trips to various locations around the three islands, as well as the cost of bicycle and motorbike hire. The restaurant owners also know the

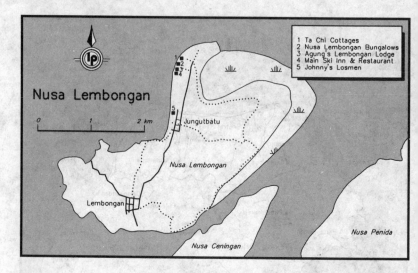

1 Ta Chi Cottages
2 Nusa Lembongan Bungalows
3 Agung's Lembongan Lodge
4 Main Ski Inn & Restaurant
5 Johnny's Losmen

Nusa Lembongan

0   1   2 km

Jungutbatu

Nusa Lembongan

Lembongan

Nusa Penida

Nusa Ceningan

name and address of a local doctor who seems to specialise in coral cuts and surfing injuries.

Lembongan Village

It's about three km south-west along the sealed road from Jungutbatu to Lembongan village, the island's other town. Leaving Jungutbatu you pass a Balinese-style temple with an enormous banyan tree, then climb up a knoll with a nice view back over the beach. After crossing the knoll you descend to the outskirts of Lembongan village and soon get the feeling that tourists are a rarity here. The people aren't hostile, but neither do they display the welcoming smiles that greet you elsewhere in Bali. It's an antiquated, vaguely spooky place. Following the road downhill brings you to the lagoon which separates Nusa Lembongan from Nusa Ceningan. It's possible to continue right around the island, following the rough track which eventually comes back to Jungutbatu.

The Underground House As you enter Lembongan you'll pass a warung on the right with a couple of pool tables. For 1000 rp the kids here will offer to take you through the labyrinthine underground 'house', 100 metres back off the road. It's a crawl and scramble through the many small passages, rooms and chambers, supposedly dug by one man.

The story goes that the man lost a dispute with an evil spirit and was condemned to death, but pleaded to be allowed to finish his house first. The spirit relented, and the man started excavating his cave with a small spoon. He always started a new room before he finished the last one, so of course the house was never completed, and thus his death sentence was postponed indefinitely.

The kids provide a candle but it would be a good idea to bring your own torch (flashlight). Be very careful as there are big holes in unexpected places. On your way back to the road, have a look down the well and see from how far down the villagers must draw their water.

Surfing

There are three main breaks on the reef. Off the beach where the bungalows are is Shipwreck, a right-hand break named for the remains of a wreck which is clearly visible from the shore. West of this is Lacerations, which breaks over shallow coral, and further west again is Playground. You can paddle out to Shipwreck, but for the other two it's better to hire a boat. Prices are negotiable depending on time and numbers, but it's about 2500 to 3000 rp to be taken out and back, with an hour's surfing in between. Strangely, the surf can be crowded even when the island isn't, as charter boats often bring groups of surfers for day trips from the mainland.

Places to Stay & Eat
In the village, *Johnny's Losmen* was the first place on Lembongan to accommodate visitors. It's basic but quite OK, and cheap at 3000/4000 rp for singles/doubles, although not many people stay here. These days most of the accommodation is further along the beach to the north-east, and that's where most of the visitors go.

Heading in that direction you'll pass some miscellaneous bungalows (which may get a name and a restaurant soon), before you get to the conspicuous *Main Ski Inn & Restaurant*. The two-storeyed restaurant, right on the beach, is a little more expensive than some of the others, but serves good food and has a great view. Binoculars are provided so you can watch the surf while you're waiting for lunch. Upstairs rooms are 10,000/12,000 rp for singles/doubles, rooms downstairs are 8000/10,000 rp.

Agung's Lembongan Lodge has double rooms from 5000 rp, and a restaurant with cheap but tasty food. Next to that is the *Nusa Lembongan Restaurant & Bungalows*. Finally, there's *Ta Chi* with rooms from 10,000 to 12,000 rp and reputedly the best cook on the island.

Getting There & Away
From Sanur Boats leave from the northern end of Sanur Beach, in front of the Ananda Hotel. The boat captains – that's what they're called – have fixed the tourist price to Lembongan at 15,000 rp. The strait between Bali and the Nusa Penida islands is very deep and huge swells develop during the day, so the boats leave before 8.30 am. You may get wet with spray, so be prepared. The trip takes at least 1½ hours, more if conditions are unfavourable. The return trip is a bit cheaper at about 12,000 rp.

From Kuta Some agencies in Kuta sell a ticket through to Lembongan via Sanur for 15,000 rp. This is pretty good value as it gets you, in effect, free transport to Sanur.

From Kusamba Most boats from Kusamba go to Toyapakeh on Nusa Penida, but sometimes they go to Jungutbatu on Lembongan. Although it might be a bit cheaper to go to Lembongan than Penida, you may have to wait a long time for the boat to fill up before it leaves.

From Nusa Penida There are boats which take the local people between Jungutbatu and Toyapakeh on Nusa Penida, particularly on market days. You'll have to ask around to find when they leave, and discuss the price. The public boats will be chock full of people, produce and livestock. A charter boat will run to about 25,000 rp, which would be OK between six or eight people.

Getting Around
The island is fairly small and you can easily walk around it in a few hours. You can also hire a motorbike or get a lift on the back of one.

NUSA PENIDA
Clearly visible from Sanur, Padangbai, Candidasa or anywhere else along Bali's south-east coast, the hilly island of Nusa Penida has a population of around 40,000 and was once used as a place of banishment for criminals and other undesirables from the kingdom of Klungkung. Nusa Penida is also the legendary home of Jero Gede Macaling, the demon who inspired the Barong Landung dance. Many Balinese believe the island to be a place of enchantment and evil power *(angker)*. Paradoxically, this is an attraction – although foreigners rarely visit, thousands of Balinese come every year for religious

observances aimed at placating the evil spirits.

The island has a number of interesting temples dedicated to Jero Gede Macaling, including Pura Ped near Toyapakeh and Pura Batukuning near Sewana. There is also a huge limestone cave, Goa Karangsari, on the coast about four km from Sampalan. The mountain village of Tanglad in the south-east, with its throne for the sun god, Surya, is also interesting.

The north coast has white-sand beaches and views over the water to the volcanoes on Bali. This coastal strip, with the two main towns of Toyapakeh and Sampalan, is moist and fertile, almost lush. The south coast has limestone cliffs dropping straight down to the sea – a spectacular sight if you're coming that way by boat. The interior is a hilly, rugged landscape, not barren but with sparse-looking crops and vegetation and unsalubrious villages. Rainfall is limited here, and there are large square concrete tanks called *cabangs* in which water is stored for the dry season. The hillsides are terraced, but they are not like the wet rice paddies of Bali. The terraces are supported with stone walls and the crops include sweet potatoes, cassava, corn and soybeans, but not rice, which is brought in from the mainland.

The population is predominantly Hindu, but the culture is distinct from that of Bali. The language is an old form of Balinese no longer heard on the mainland, and there are also local types of dance, architecture and craft, including a unique type of red ikat weaving. The people have had little contact with foreign visitors and the children are more likely to stare than shout 'hello mister'. They are not unfriendly, just bemused. Many people do not speak Indonesian and almost no-one speaks English.

Sampalan

There's nothing inspiring about Sampalan, but it's pleasant enough, with a market, warungs, schools and shops strung out along the coast road. The market area, where the bemos congregate, is on the northern side of the road, by definition almost in the middle of the town. Buyuk Harbour, where the boats leave for Padangbai, is a few hundred metres west of the market. The town's only losmen is opposite the police station, a few hundred metres in the opposite direction.

Goa Karangsari

If you follow the coast road south-east from Sampalan for about six km, you'll see the cave entrance up the hill on the right side of the road, just before the village of Karangsari. You might have to ask for directions. The entrance is a small cleft in the rocks, but the cave is quite large, extending for over 200 metres into the hillside. Many small bats live in the cave – they're noisy but harmless. During the Galungan festival there is a torch-lit procession into the cave, followed by ceremonies at a temple by the lake in one of the large chambers. If you want to do more than put your head in the entrance, bring a good torch.

Toyapakeh

If you come by boat from Nusa Lembongan you'll probably be dropped on, or just off, the beach at Toyapakeh. It's a pretty town with lots of shady trees. The beach has clean white sand, clear blue water, a neat line of prahus and Bali's Gunung Agung as a backdrop. Step up from the beach and you're at the roadhead, where there will be bemos to take you to Ped or Sampalan. Few travellers stay here, but if you want to, you'll find the *Losmen Terang* on your right, which has rooms for about 5000 rp.

Pura Dalem Penetaran Ped

This important temple is near the beach at the village of Ped, a few km east of Toyapakeh. It houses a shrine for Jero Gede Macaling, the source of power for the practitioners of black magic, and it's a place of pilgrimage for those seeking protection from sickness and evil. The temple structure is crude, even ugly, which gives it an appropriately sinister ambience.

Getting There & Away

The strait between Nusa Penida and southern

Bali is very deep and subject to heavy swells – hence the big surf on the reefs around Nusa Penida. If there is a strong tide running, the boats may have to wait. You may also have to wait a while for a boat to fill up, unless you are prepared to pay extra for a charter.

From Padangbai Fast, twin-engined fibreglass boats now operate between Padangbai and Nusa Penida. The boats are about eight or 10 metres long and look pretty seaworthy, and some are well-supplied with life jackets, which is unusual for small Indonesian craft, as well as reassuring. The trip takes less than an hour and costs 3000 rp. It's an exciting ride as the boat bounces across the water beneath the looming volcano of Agung. At Padangbai, the boats land on the beach just east of the car park for the Bali to Lombok ferry. On Nusa Penida, the boats land at the beach at Buyuk Harbour, just west of Sampalan, but some may also go to Toyapakeh.

From Kusamba Prahus carry produce and supplies between Nusa Penida and Kusamba, which is the closest port to Klungkung, the district capital. The boats leave when they're full, weather and waves

permitting, and cost about 2500 rp one way. They are slower than the boats from Padangbai, and may be heavily loaded (overloaded?) with provisions.

From Nusa Lembongan The boats that carry local people between the islands usually land at Toyapakeh. Ask around the beach-front area to find when the the next boat is leaving, and discuss the price. You may have to wait quite a while, or charter a boat.

Getting Around
There are regular bemos on the sealed road between Toyapakeh and Sampalan, on to Sewana and up to Klumpu, but beyond these areas the roads are rough or nonexistent and transport is uncertain. If you want to charter a bemo, try to find Wayan Patra, from Banjar Sentral Kanjin in Ped. He knows Nusa Penida well, and speaks English. You may be able to get someone to take you on the back of a motorbike, although this can be a high-risk form of transport. You could also try bringing a bicycle from the mainland, but remember Nusa Penida is hilly. If you really want to explore the island, you'll probably have to walk.

Sumatra

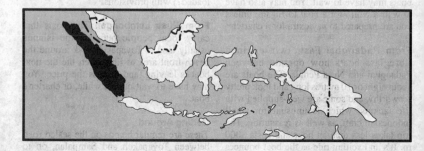

Indonesia's 'new frontier', Sumatra has an extraordinary wealth of natural resources, people and cultures. Compared to Java it is relatively underpopulated and underdeveloped, but during Dutch rule this island provided the world with an enormous quantity of everything from oil and rubber to pepper and coffee. With its seemingly inexhaustible resources Sumatra continues to prop up the Indonesian economy today. Its oil wells and rubber plantations are set against a background of people which could drive an ethnologist delirious. These range from former Batak head-hunters and cannibals, to matrilineal Muslim Minangkabau and the almost-fundamentalist Islamic Acehnese. The diversity of cultures on this island may well be unmatched in the archipelago.

That's not the only attraction. There is also wild jungle country in the south, the peculiar architecture of the Minangkabau and Batak people, orang-utan and elusive Sumatran tigers lurking in the forests, massive rivers like muddy facsimiles of the Amazon, perfect cone-shaped volcanoes, and the Bukit Barisan or 'marching mountains', which do just that right down to the west coast.

HISTORY
The reasons for the remarkable diversity of cultures on Sumatra and its outlying islands are numerous, but certainly the geography and the way this has influenced contacts between its inhabitants as well as those with foreigners has been of great importance. Sumatra's northern tip faces the west, while much of the island's eastern shore borders the Straits of Melaka – a natural gateway to the South China Sea through which ships make their way from India to Java and China.

Trade, controlled initially by Hindu merchants, favoured the development of coastal Hindu city-states. The kingdom of Srivijaya which arose in the second half of the 7th century with its capital on or near the site of modern day Palembang was the most famous, and one of the most important in South-East Asia. Unlike the more insular Javanese kingdoms of the time, Srivijaya always looked outwards towards the sea and trading routes, but since it built no huge monuments like Prambanan or Borobudur there are few traces left of its existence today.

With foreign trade came other developments. Buddhism, court-centred Brahmanism and other new religions were introduced as well as new political ideas which transformed the coastal chiefdoms and filtered into the tribal societies of the mountainous interior. Later on, Arab, Portuguese and Dutch influences (particularly Islam and Christianity) were introduced.

Sumatra

0   100   200 km

Pulau We

Banda Aceh   Bireuen
    Sigli   Lhokseumawe
Meureudi

Calang   Takengon

Meulaboh

Gunung Leuser   Medan   Belawan
National Park   Bukit Lawang
        Berastagi

Pulau   Siantar
Simeuleu   Parapat   Labuhanbilik

            Lake   Rantauprapat
            Toba

        Sibolga   Dumai

Pulau   Gunung
Nias   Sitoli   Tanahbatu   Selatpanjang

    Hilisimaetano   Teluk Dalam   Natal   Pakanbaru
                Bonjol

equator — *equator*

        Bukittinggi
        Padangpanjang

    Padang   Solok   Sungaidareh
        Gunung   Muaratebo
Pulau   *Kerinci*
Siberut   ▲ Muaratembesi   Jambi

    Sungaipenuh   Bangko   Gresik
Mentawai   Sarolangun

Islands   Palembang

        Lubuklinggau   Perabumlih
    Bengkulu

A huge globe by the roadside north
of Bukittinggi marks the equator.
Spend 5 minutes hopping back
and forth across the line and you'll
be able to say, 'The equator? Oh,
I've crossed it dozens of times.'

        Danau   Martapura
        Ranau   Kotabumi
                    Bandarlampung
            Krui   (Tanjungkarang)

                    Bakauheni
            SELAT SUNDA   Merak   JAVA

MALAYSIA

Pulau
Penang

SINGAPORE

Pulau Bintan
    Tanjung Pinang
        Riau Archipelago
Pulau
Batam

        Dabo
    Pulau Singkep

                Pulau
                Bangka
            Muntok   Pangkalpinang
                Tanjung Pandan

                Pulau
                Belitung

Geographically, the narrow western coastal strip rising steeply to the rugged Bukit Barisan with its series of lakes set in fertile volcanic plateaus (from Lake Toba in the north to Ranau in the south) favoured the development of a chain of very distinct cultures. Intensive agriculture coupled with fishing supported sizeable groups of tribal people strong enough to resist conversion to cultural ideas coming up from the lowlands. The outlying islands of Nias, Mentawai, and Enggano also resisted foreign culture until quite recent times because of their remote location.

Srivijaya's control of the Straits of Melaka continued for seven centuries before it was ended by a Javanese Majapahit attack in 1377. It is said that a Srivijayan prince, Parameswara, fled to the Malay Peninsula, made his way to a tiny port-settlement called Melaka and proceeded to develop it into a major international port, shifting the centre of power in the region from Sumatra to the Malay Peninsula.

About the same time, but for obscure reasons, Islam became an important force in Sumatra. Islamic communities are known to have existed in northern Sumatra since at least the 13th century (Marco Polo mentions finding Muslims here when he visited Sumatra in 1292 on his way home from China). After the decline of Srivijaya many Islamic trading kingdoms operated on Sumatra, although none enjoyed the wide-reaching power that Srivijaya had possessed. By the early 16th century, most of the kings of the Sumatran coastal states from Aceh at the far north to Palembang in the south were Muslim. South of Palembang and around the tip of Sumatra and up the west coast most of the kingdoms were not Muslim, nor had Islam been able to win many converts in the interior inhabited by numerous tribal people who continued to follow their old beliefs and customs.

When the Dutch arrived they found this cultural stew much more difficult to digest than they appear to have initially expected, and some of the most protracted fighting of the colonial era followed. The Dutch wanted Sumatra for several reasons: it was rich in spices (mainly pepper) and other valuable products such as tin, it occupied a strategic position and was the subject of intense colonial rivalry with the British. The United East India Company or VOC (Vereenigde Oost-Indische Compagnie) had been active for a long time in Sumatra, but after its demise and the short period of British rule in Indonesia during the Napoleonic Wars, the Dutch had to rebuild their influence virtually from nothing.

Palembang suffered its first attack from the Dutch in 1818, but was not finally subdued until 1849. Dutch involvement with Jambi began anew in 1833 but it was not until 1907 that guerrilla resistance in the interior was stifled. In the west coast Minangkabau districts, Dutch expansionism clashed head on with the first major Islamic revival movement of Indonesia – known as the Padri movement because its leaders had made their pilgrimage to Mecca via the Acehnese port of Pedir. A civil war erupted between the Islamic reformists and the supporters of traditional or adat law. Sensing the opportunity, the Dutch backed the latter entering the Padri War in 1821, but it was not until 1838 that they subdued all the Minangkabau territories.

To establish their authority over the island of Nias the Dutch needed three military expeditions – in 1847, 1855 and 1863. A treaty with the British in 1824 resulted in those interlopers clearing out of their settlement at Bengkulu in return for the Dutch leaving Melaka and their settlements in India. Treaties and alliances brought other areas of Sumatra under Dutch rule, and a war with the Bataks in 1872 ended in victory for the Dutch, although the Batak resistance was not wiped out until 1895.

The war with the Acehnese, however, was the bloodiest in Sumatra and probably in the whole archipelago. The last of the Acehnese sultans, Tuanku Muhamat Dawot, surrendered to the Dutch in 1903 after a war of more than 30 years – but even then unrest continued and the Dutch were forced to keep a military government in the area until 1918. It is certainly significant that the Dutch did not try to return to Aceh after WW II. From 1945 until Indonesian independence in 1949, Aceh was ruled chiefly by Daud Beureueh, the leader of an Islamic modernist movement. The region was in rebellion from 1953 until 1961 when it became a province of Indonesia. Even today it retains a sort of semi-autonomous status within the republic.

GEOGRAPHY

Stretching nearly 2000 km from end to end, Sumatra is one of the largest islands in the world. For most of its length the Bukit Barisan form a backbone down the island, dropping steeply to the sea on the west coast but sloping gently down on the east. This eastern region is a low-lying swampland, much of it bordering on the shallow Straits of Melaka and comprising a third of the island. It's poorly drained (much of it covered in mangrove swamps) and traversed by wide, meandering rivers.

The river towns of the eastern side of the island include Jambi and Pakanbaru, but the main population is concentrated along the highlands closer to the mountains and towards the west side of the island. Many of the peaks are around 2500 metres high but some are over 3000 metres. The mountains include nearly 100 volcanoes, 15 of them still active.

Off the west coast are a string of islands geologically older than the rest of Sumatra. They are isolated not only geographically but also culturally as the people living here have developed quite separately from those on Sumatra and still follow some ancient customs.

FLORA & FAUNA

Large areas of the Sumatran rainforest have been cleared for agricultural use, but great stretches of jungle remain where orang-utan and elephants can still be seen. One place where orang-utan may be found is the Bukit Lawang sanctuary in northern Sumatra.

Almost as famous as the orang-utans is Sumatra's amazing flower, the *Rafflesia*, named after Sir Stamford Raffles, founder of Singapore, who was also a noted botanist. The Rafflesia has orange petals spreading up to a metre in diameter.

ECONOMY

Both the Dutch and the Indonesian governments have sought to exploit the enormous economic potential of Sumatra. Since the 1860s, the existence of oil deposits in Sumatra was known to the Dutch and by the end of the 1880s it was being drilled in commercially viable quantities. By 1930 about 85% of the total oil output of Indonesia was being produced by just one company – Royal Dutch Shell. As early as 1864 the first rubber plantations were established in West Java and eastern Sumatra and by 1930 Indonesia was producing nearly half the world's rubber supply.

Sumatra continues to be Indonesia's most important island in terms of exports which include oil, natural gas, tin, rubber, palm oil, tea, coffee, tobacco and lumber. Although the most agriculturally productive areas of Sumatra are in the highlands, one exception is the region around Medan. Here the coastal plains are better drained and the soil is richer than further south. This plain is very densely

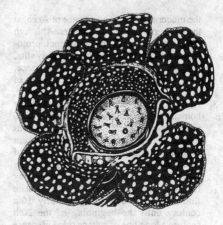

Rafflesia

populated and was being exploited by Dutch and British plantation owners a century ago. Today tobacco, tea, coffee, oil palms and rubber are all grown here, and the rubber plantations are very obvious to any visitor passing through.

Even more important than these cash crops are the oil fields found along the east coast. Palembang, Jambi, Medan and, in particular, Pakanbaru are all oil towns. Indonesia is still a major oil exporter and three-quarters of its oil production comes from this region of Sumatra.

PEOPLE

Sumatra is the second most populous island of the archipelago, although its population density is minuscule compared to that of Bali or Java. It's also a major target of the transmigration programme. The 30 million people of the island are some of the most fascinating in the archipelago and can be divided into about 10 major groups of which the best known are the Niassans of the island of Nias off the west coast of Sumatra, the Minangkabau, the Islamic Acehnese, and the Christian Bataks.

Acehnese

The Acehnese are the native inhabitants of

the modern Indonesian province of Aceh, at the northernmost end of Sumatra. Although these people range from distinct proto-Malay types to those who are relatively slim, tall and almost Caucasian in appearance, racially they are a product of centuries of mixing with Bataks, Indians, Javanese, Arabs, Chinese, and Niassan slaves. Their homeland has been inhabited for some 1500 years. As early as 500 AD, Chinese sources refer to a kingdom which existed in northern Sumatra within the present boundaries of Aceh, but which was apparently ruled by Buddhists of Indian extraction. Certainly by the 14th century, a strongly Islamic state flourished here and from the early 16th century until the beginning of the 20th century a long line of sultans ruled. Because of its geographical position Aceh was heavily engaged in foreign trade for more than 1000 years, particularly with the Malay Peninsula, China and India, although essentially the Acehnese have always been an agricultural society with rice as the main crop.

Bataks

The Bataks inhabit an interior plateau of north-central Sumatra, surrounded by mountain peaks and centred on Lake Toba. There is cultural, linguistic and physical evidence of early Hindu contact (such as their Indian-derived script, either incised on bamboo or written on bark leaves and bound in book form). In the past century there has been widespread conversion to Christianity as well as substantial conversion to Islam.

Despite these influences and being surrounded on all sides by Islamic peoples, the Batak lived a way of life which developed largely in isolation. Their bloody feuds and guerrilla attacks on each other's villages gained them an apparently well-earned reputation for ferocity. They also practised ritual cannibalism in which a token piece of flesh – of a slain enemy or of one judged guilty of a major violation of adat – was eaten. The heads and hands of war captives were sometimes preserved as trophies.

According to Batak tradition all Bataks are descendants of Si Radja Batak, a hero-ancestor of supernatural parentage born on a holy mountain next to Lake Toba. Through him the Batak received their sacred adat laws.

A long period of relative isolation was ended in the 19th century, first by the spread of Islam from the Minangkabau in the north and later, beginning about 1860, by the rapid spread of Protestant Christianity through the efforts of missionaries. Western education furthered by missionaries and the Dutch colonial government gained ground rapidly, particularly amongst the Toba Bataks (those living around Lake Toba).

Minangkabau

The Minangkabau are Muslims whose traditional homeland is the highlands of west-central Sumatra from where they have spread out into all of western Sumatra and parts of other Sumatran provinces. They are also called *orang padang* (Padang people) after their provincial capital. Not much is known about the Minangkabau before the arrival of the Dutch, although archaeological remains of human settlement in the area date at least as far back as the 12th century. Portuguese records suggest there was a lively trade between western Sumatra and Melaka, and that the Minangkabau were bringing pepper to both eastern and western Sumatran ports as early as the beginning of the 17th century.

Acehnese suzerainty in the early 17th century led to increased Islamic influence which culminated in the Padri War of 1803 to 1837. That resulted in the entry of the Dutch into the highlands in support of the adat rulers. Dutch forts in time became towns and many Minangkabaus came to live urban lives and develop as an educated class of Indonesians. Many were active in the Indonesian independence movement – Mohammad Hatta, vice-president under Sukarno for a time, was the most famous of these.

Niassans

The Niassans, the native people of the large

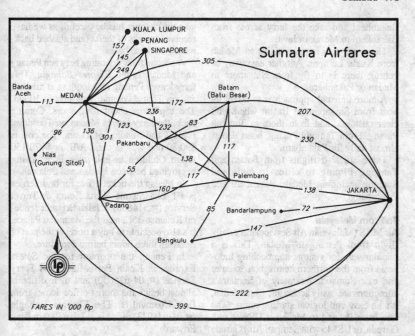

Sumatra Airfares

FARES IN '000 Rp

island of Nias off the west coast of Sumatra, have long captured the imagination of ethnologists and anthropologists with their monumental use of stone and wood, and their complex social and religious organisation. The importance of head-hunting and human sacrifice in days gone by, as well as their physical features, suggest a mixed descent with some relationship to the Bataks of Sumatra, the Naga people of the Indian province Assam, and even the aboriginal people of Taiwan.

Other Peoples
Along the east coast and particularly in the scattered islands of the Riau Archipelago are the nomadic *orang laut* (sea people or sea gypsies). Also seafarers, but more settled, are the coastal Malays who gave their name to the common language of modern Malaysia and Indonesia.

ACCOMMODATION
Prices listed in this chapter are charged during the high season in July and August. Outside this time prices are lower and fluctuate. In most losmen it's almost always possible to bargain over the price of your room or bed, and of course the longer you stay the less you can pay per day. Some of the more expensive hotels offer discounts to attract more customers. These can be worth checking out.

In most establishments an additional bed in a room costs an extra 25%.

GETTING THERE & AWAY
You can approach Sumatra from a number of directions and by a number of means. The most conventional route is to fly from Penang to Medan (or take the ship from Penang to Belawan, the port of Medan), travel through the island by bus, then either take the ship from Padang to Jakarta or continue right down through Palembang to

Bakauheni and take the ferry across from Bakauheni to Merak in Java.

There are also regular flights to Medan from Kuala Lumpur. Another easy way of getting there is to fly from Singapore to Medan or Pakanbaru.

A more unusual approach is to travel by boat from Singapore to Batam where you clear customs, and from there to Tanjung Pinang. From Tanjung Pinang, boats depart almost daily for Pakanbaru.

There are also flights from Batam and Tanjung Pinang to cities in mainland Sumatra including Medan, Pakanbaru and Palembang.

To/From Malaysia
Air MAS (Malaysian Air Service) has a daily flight from Penang to Medan. This is a popular way for visitors approaching Indonesia from the northern hemisphere to enter and exit Sumatra. As many of Sumatra's attractions are easily accessible from Medan, it's an easy and logical starting point. (The fare from Penang to Medan is US$60 with Garuda, or US$45 with Sempati Air.) Garuda and MAS have daily flights from Kuala Lumpur to Medan for US$79. There is also an irregular charter service between Pakanbaru and Melaka.

Sea There are catamarans, ferries and ships operating between Sumatra and Malaysia.

To/From Penang The high-speed catamaran *Selesa Express* operates between Penang and the Medan port of Belawan. It operates on Tuesdays and Fridays, leaving Penang at 8 am and on the return journey leaving Belawan at 2 pm for the six-hour journey. The one-way fare is M$90 in economy class, and M$100 in 1st class. From Belawan the cost is 76,000 rp and 96,000 rp respectively.

There's an extra charge of 4000 rp for a tourist bus from Medan to Belawan, or a taxi costs 10,000 rp. It's possible to take the public bus from Medan to Belawan which costs 600 rp plus 200 rp port entrance charge, but in the other direction you are charged M$5 regardless of which bus you take. If you

take the cheaper bus be careful, as we have received reports of thefts (and slashed backpacks) on these buses.

A second ferry operating between Penang and Medan is the *Ekspres Bahagia*. This ferry leaves Penang on Mondays at midday, and on Thursdays and Saturdays at 10 am. The trip takes about four hours. Coming back, the ferry leaves Medan on Tuesdays, Fridays and Sundays at 11 am. The cost is $90/80 one way in class A/B, or $170/150 return. Children are half-price. Free transfer is provided between Medan and Belawan.

In Medan the ticket office for both ferries is PT Eka Sukma Wista Tours & Travel Service (☎ 514888) at Jalan Brigadir Jenderal Katamso 35C, near the Maimoon Palace. It's also possible to buy a ticket at the port of Belawan three hours before departure.

In Penang the operator for the Selesa Express is Kuala Perlis-Langkawi Ferry Service (☎ 04-625630) and their office is almost beside the tourist office across from Fort Cornwallis. The Ekspres Bahagia (☎ 04-631943) office is at Jalan Pasara King Edward.

To/From Melaka & Kuala Lumpur There's a daily ferry from Melaka to Dumai. From Dumai you can take a bus to Pakanbaru and Bukittinggi. The ferry crossing takes around 3½ hours and the fare is M$80 plus M$9 for port tax. It's also possible to take a ferry from Dumai to Pulau Batam, and continue on to Singapore. Unfortunately, Dumai is not a recognised 'no visa' entry or exit point to Indonesia, although some visitors have managed to leave this way without a proper visa. Arriving or departing, however, you must have an Indonesian visa. Occasionally there are ships between Port Kelang, the port of Kuala Lumpur, and Dumai.

To/From Singapore
Air Garuda has a number of flights from Singapore to several cities in Sumatra. These include daily flights to Medan for US$127, Padang, and Palembang, and four days a week to Pakanbaru.

Pakanbaru itself is not much of a draw

card, but Bukittinggi, one of Sumatra's most appealing hill towns, is easily accessible from Pakanbaru and the bus trip between the two is quite beautiful.

Sea There are regular hydrofoils between Singapore to the islands of Batam and Bintan in the Riau Archipelago, just off mainland Sumatra. From Tanjung Pinang, the chief centre on Pulau Bintan, you can catch a ferry to Pakanbaru.

Hydrofoils to Batam and Bintan islands depart from Singapore's Finger Pier (☎ 3360528) on Prince Edward Rd. There are several ways of taking the first step from Singapore. The longest and cheapest route is to take the ferry from Singapore to Sekupang on Pulau Batam, where you go through Indonesian immigration. The fare is S$18 (20,200 rp from Sekupang). From there you take a bus for 600 rp or taxi to Nagoya. From Nagoya there are shared taxis to Kabil for 2000 rp, where regular ferries depart for Tanjung Uban on the west coast of Bintan Island and cost 3000 rp. From Tanjung Uban there are regular buses for 3000 rp and taxis to Tanjung Pinang. The total cost of this route is 28,700 rp taking around six hours.

A faster alternative is to take a direct hydrofoil from Singapore to Tanjung Pinang, via Sekupang. It costs S$45 and 31,500 to 50,000 rp in reverse direction. There are two morning and one afternoon departures, taking about 2½ hours for the trip.

It's also possible to take a direct boat from Pakanbaru to Pulau Batam three times a week. It takes 15 hours and costs 27,500 rp for deck class and 32,500 rp for a cabin. Another way from Pakanbaru to Batam and Singapore is via Selatpanjang, on either a slow or a fast boat. First from Pakanbaru to Selatpanjang you can either take a daily boat that costs 9000 rp deck class or 13,500 rp in a cabin taking 16 hours, or a faster one costing 15,000 rp and taking three hours. From Selatpanjang there is a boat to Batam – also for 15,000 rp and it takes three hours. From Batam there is always a connecting boat to Singapore. In Pakanbaru the tickets

for the faster boat are available only at the port.

To/From Tanjung Pinang There are usually three ferries a week from Tanjung Pinang to Pakanbaru. The trip takes at least 39 hours. Fares are 15,900 rp for deck class and 20,900 rp for a cabin.

The ferries are typical Indonesian boats with cramped conditions and abysmal food, but it's a great journey upriver. It's a good idea to take food and drink with you since two meals of boiled rice garnished with a bit of dry salted fish and a dollop of chilli sauce washed down with lukewarm, brackish water is all your ticket includes. All is not lost if you forget or don't have the time to stock up because the boat stops at various river villages along the way and flotillas of sales people circle around hawking soft drinks, peanuts and fruit.

Travel in Sumatra can often be a memorable experience, and far more amusing in retrospect than it is at the time. The ferry ride between Pakanbaru and Tanjung Pinang is a bit like the novel *Heart of Darkness*. If you've seen the movie *Apocalypse Now* and recall the journey upriver in search of Kurtz you'll have a good idea of what it's like – but at least no one's shooting at you. The trip takes you across the Straits of Melaka, through a vast malarial swamp via the wide, brown and greasy Siak River lined with grotesquely twisted mangroves, and past small villages and logging camps lit by fireflies and kerosene lamps.

There are a few things you should know about the boat. Firstly, a 'cabin' does not constitute a private room with a lockable door and a bed. It's a wooden platform constructed on stilts about a metre from the deck. Each cabin is indicated by a number at one end and is separated from the next by painted lines on either side, or perhaps low wooden dividers. However, if you get a cabin you should consider yourself lucky as the rest of the passengers have to squeeze themselves into a foetal position to find enough space on the deck to sleep. With a bit of nimble footwork, you can avoid stepping on bunches of bananas, bags of pineapples, packets of nuts, baskets of beans or other fruit and vegetables that are festooned along the top of the boat, or on a prone body.

The din of the boat's engine is deafening but it seems like the hush of a monastery once the music begins – your ears will take days to adjust. To add to the discomfort, they seem to have a very limited selection of tapes to play. But whatever the decibel level and however dubious their taste in music, at 5 o'clock the faithful – usually women – turn to Mecca and chant their prayers.

The two toilets at the prow of the boat are occupied for the entire trip so you must be prepared to spend hours balanced precariously with legs crossed waiting your turn. Though cramped and grotty, they're not as sordid as many toilets you'll be forced to use in Sumatra as their design is a simple, but effective, hole in the planks and you can see straight down to the river below. Watch where you put your feet as some people's aim is well off the mark.

The musky smell of clove cigarettes eventually becomes heavy and cloying and when it rains it will be your turn to pray. Pray that the wooden shutters or canvas blinds, the main protection from the elements, have not rotted away entirely and that they can be yanked across or let down. Otherwise you can add sodden bedding to your discomfort. Lastly, you will have to accept that you are likely to be the only Westerner on board and will be harried with the usual 'What is your name? Where are you from? Where are you going? Can I practise my English?' questions until you are heartily sick of it.

There are other ways of reaching mainland Sumatra from the Riau Islands. Garuda have a number of flights from Batu Besar (on Pulau Batam) including daily flights to Pakanbaru. Merpati and two small airlines called SMAC and Sempati have flights from Tanjung Pinang to various destinations, including Pakanbaru. For more details see the Riau Archipelago section in this chapter.

To/From Java

Air Garuda and Merpati have flights from Jakarta to all sorts of places in Sumatra including Banda Aceh, Bengkulu, Jambi, Medan, Padang, Palembang and Pakanbaru.

Sea There are several options for travel by sea between Java and Sumatra.

Pelni Ships Pelni has four ships which operate between Jakarta and various ports in Sumatra. The most popular ship with foreigners is Pelni's *Kerinci* which runs between Sibolga, Padang and Tanjung Priok, the port of Jakarta. The *Kerinci* is modern with air-con, hot-water showers and a variety of accommodation to choose from. The other three ships are the *Kambuna, Lawit* and *Rinjani*. For all these ships, see the Getting Around chapter for the complete timetable.

Merak – Bakauheni Ferry Ferries shuttle across the narrow Selat Sunda between Merak at the western end of Java and Bakauheni at the eastern end of Sumatra. In Merak, the ferries depart from the dock near the railway station at roughly 1½ hour intervals, 24 hours a day. The trip costs from 1100 rp for economy class and up to 2200 rp for 1st class, taking about 1½ hours. If you travel by bus between Jakarta and destinations in Sumatra, the price of the ferry is included in your ticket.

You can get to Merak from Jakarta by train or bus. Buses depart frequently (about every 10 minutes) from the Kalideres Bus Station, cost 2700 rp and take three hours. Trains leave from Tanah Abang Railway Station and the morning train is faster.

To get to Bakauheni from the Sumatran side you need to get a bus from Bandarlampung. If you arrived by train from Palembang or Lubuklinggau, you'll end up at Bandarlampung's railway station in Tanjungkarang. From here take an opelet (also known as a Colt) to Rajabasa Bus Station in Bandarlampung for 200 rp. Buses depart regularly from Rajabasa to Bakauheni costing 2000 rp and taking two hours. A bus from anywhere in Sumatra will drop you off at Rajabasa.

GETTING AROUND

To explore Sumatra for the first time and see some of its out-of-the-way attractions you need three things: time (all of the two-month visa), the patience of Job, and the endurance of a marathon runner. If you really want to get off the beaten track you could easily outstay your Indonesian welcome. If you take the well-worn travellers' trail – Medan, Berastagi, Bukit Lawang, Parapat, Lake Toba, Pulau Nias, Bukittinggi, Padang and then on to Java – you need about a month to do it quickly and more time to have a reasonably decent look around.

To get some satisfaction from travelling in Sumatra, it's worth taking time out to think about what you're hoping to do or see. If you're especially interested in the culture, history or people of the region then you've got problems.

If you don't speak Indonesian huge areas of Sumatra will effectively be closed to you. If you fall into the tourist trench, you tend to end up spending most of your time with other Westerners and your trip will be self-defeating. Often your impressions of the island and people will be filtered through touts or other people who attach themselves to the tourist trade.

These problems are not so different from some other parts of Indonesia, but they seem to be much more acute in Sumatra. This is probably because of the sheer number of Westerners travelling along a fairly defined trail. The northern part of the island is no longer the adventure it has often been made out to be.

Climatic Considerations
Sumatra is a large island – 1760 km long, around 450 km at its widest point, 288,000 sq km in area – and you can get around by bus, aircraft and ferry in some of the more isolated areas. Apart from distance it's also important to take weather into account.

The equator splits Sumatra into neat halves and the monsoons in the north and south occur at different times of the year. North of the equator the wet season starts in October and can go through to April and the dry season lasts from May until September. The exception is the area around Banda Aceh and the We island group in the extreme part of north Sumatra. Here the wet season is from June to October. However, travel is not a problem during this time. In the south the rains start in October but the worst months are between December and February.

Travel along the Trans-Sumatran Highway is not greatly affected during the wet season, but it's very difficult to get around the rest of Sumatra and takes a lot longer. Occasionally transport stops functioning altogether. You should aim to visit during the dry season, sometime between May and September.

Air
Of course it's possible to fly around Sumatra and save a lot of time. The Garuda/Merpati cartel flies to all the main centres of out-of-the-way spots. You should also check what Mandala has to offer since they often fly the same routes as Garuda and Merpati but on different days, at different times and for cheaper prices. Sempati and SMAC cover some routes that Garuda/Merpati do but are cheaper, and they also fly to even remoter destinations that the larger airlines don't fly to. Since most of the interesting attractions are in northern Sumatra, many people skip the southern half and fly from Jakarta to Padang. For airfares around Sumatra and to adjacent areas, see the Domestic Airfares chart.

Bus
The most popular and economical method of travel is by bus. Wherever you go in Sumatra the roads take you through country full of contrasts and changing moods – exotic, lush, romantic, wild, poetic and ugly. Between Palembang and Padang the road (just a dirt track until a few years ago) cuts through magnificent jungle. At that time, when the road wasn't completely impassable, passengers and driver spent most of the trip winching the bus out of wheel-high muddy bogs.

Things have looked up since the bad old days – or good old days – of the '60s and early '70s when enterprising visitors started coming to Sumatra. Today most of the roads are sealed and the Trans-Sumatran Highway has made a huge improvement to speed and pleasure. Minibuses and modern Mercedes buses have been introduced, although it's unlikely that Mercedes ever imagined their vehicles could contain so many seats!

As on the Sumatran buses of days gone by, the seats are usually hard and far too small for average-size Westerners. The drivers are still madmen sustained and kept awake by prodigious quantities of fiery Padang food. Rivers are still muddy, wide, and winding, and still too many bridges get washed away. You can still get stranded for hours or even days on end in the middle of nowhere if you travel during heavy rains. Travel is slow and arduous but you rarely have to get out and push. But if you want to experience some hard travelling, do Tapaktuan to Sidikalang: several river crossings, km after km of pot-holed unsurfaced road, virgin jungle, little villages. It's wild and remote and takes eight or more hours to travel 230 km.

The truth is that if you travel in the dry season and confine yourself to the main tourist route in the north and along the Trans-Sumatran Highway you won't have these problems. Outside these areas you should not expect to be able to cover the entire island by bus if you're pressed for time. Avoid seats at the rear of the bus where the bouncing is multiplied.

Bus Trekking Through Sumatra

Every traveller who has travelled extensively throughout Sumatra has their own share of bus horror stories, but nowadays travellers who stick to the Sumatran Highway are bound to miss out on this experience.

My journey commenced in the tiny village of Gudang, which consists of eight wooden houses packed tightly together and is the last stop before a 30-km stretch of deserted road through mountainous jungle before the next village of Ise Ise. I was aiming to get to Takengon, a further 66 km.

The road for the first few kilometres up the mountain was newly sealed, but after that it became a pot-holed nightmare. The passengers were often forced to walk alongside the opelet, because of the danger of the vehicle flipping over when going through one of the deeper potholes and rolling over the edge of the mountain.

I was admiring the jungle, which I had plenty of time for as we could not have been averaging more than 20 km/hour, when suddenly the opelet seemed to lift, then stopped. As usual, everyone got out. The first thing that was visible was a 30-cm gap at the mid-top section of the opelet, where the driver's cabin and the rear section of the vehicle meet. I checked out the undercarriage of the opelet and found a hairline fracture from one end to the other – the vehicle had almost split in half!

As we prepared to walk the remaining four km to the village of Ise Ise, Acehnese ingenuity came to the rescue; three men jumped up and down on top of the vehicle until the two halves became level again. Then they tied the two halves together with rope! Passengers and luggage were squashed into the centre of the vehicle, and off we went.

It took another 2½ hours to cover the 24 km to

Uwak, which was the driver's home village, leaving us 46 km short of Takengon, our destination. Night was approaching and the opelet driver refused to take his vehicle any further – and who could blame him?

The next day we took the regular Ise Ise to Takengon minibus, which took four hours. The entire journey, 96 km, had taken 26 hours.

Bus fares can vary greatly from one bus company to another – for example, the Medan to Jakarta route can cost 35,000 rp with ALS, while another bus company may charge 45,000 rp for the same trip, also with a non air-con bus and exactly the same service. The following will give you an idea of what particular sections of roads are like in Sumatra:

Java to Palembang You can take an air-con bus straight from Jakarta to Palembang (30,000 rp), Jambi (28,150 rp) or Padang (49,100 rp) crossing the Selat Sunda between Java and Sumatra by ferry. Jakarta to Palembang takes about 20 hours by bus and there are frequent departures. ANS is one of the best of the various Sumatran bus companies.

An alternative to the bus is the train, which involves taking the ferry from Merak to Bakauheni, and the bus to Rajabasa, and catching an opelet to the railway station in Tanjungkarang (both are in the city of Bandarlampung).

Palembang to Padang The trip from Palembang to Padang takes about 24 hours if the going is easy. It takes jam karet, or rubber time, during the wet season. Fares are around 17,500 rp or 20,000 rp with air-con. The section of road between Padang and Lubuklinggau (at the end of the railway line northwards) runs along the eastern side of the mountains and is now one of the best and most scenic in Sumatra.

Bengkulu to Lubuklinggau The Bengkulu-Lubuklinggau road is fairly good but slow going. It's surfaced but has some potholes.

Padang/Bukittinggi to Parapat Most

people make one or more stops on this sector, either at Bukittinggi and/or Sibolga. The roads are paved and travel is now much more reliable than it was several years ago. It can still be difficult in the wet season if bridges or sections of the road get washed out. From Bukittinggi to Parapat there is a special tourist minibus which makes the trip in 12 to 13 hours, and costs 20,000 rp.

Padang to Bukittinggi The Padang-Bukittinggi road is excellent and travelling this scenic sector is no trouble at all.

Parapat to Medan Buses between Parapat, which is the departure point for Samosir Island and Lake Toba, and Medan operate very frequently and take about four hours. Buses also operate frequently between Medan and Berastagi and take two hours. The trip on from Berastagi to Parapat involves changes at Kabanjahe and Pematang Siantar, and usually takes all day.

Medan to Banda Aceh The Medan-Banda Aceh road is a good surfaced road. The bus trip takes about 14 hours, mainly because of prolonged stops along the way. There are frequent departures in either direction.

Train

There only two regular train services in Sumatra. The more useful one is between Tanjungkarang (Bandarlampung), and Palembang as well as to Lubuklinggau in the south. The second one runs between Medan, Tanjungbalai and Rantauprapat.

Boat

Sumatra's rivers are also major transport routes which team with a motley but colourful collection of multifarious, multi-purpose vessels – rowing boats, speedboats, outriggers, ferries, junks and large cargo vessels. Boats are usually available for hire and will take you almost anywhere it's possible to go.

If you want a break from travelling by bus then catching a boat is a good way of seeing another side of Sumatra. There are also some places in Sumatra which you can't get to any other way – islands which don't have an airstrip, or river villages not connected by road.

Palembang and Jambi are important towns for river transport. There are also boats out to neighbouring islands. These include the ferries from Sibolga to Nias, from Padang to Siberut, from Banda Aceh to Pulau We, from Tanjung Pinang to Pakanbaru and those which link the islands of the Riau Archipelago. There is limited coastal shipping, like that between Padang and Bengkulu.

Local Transport

The usual Indonesian forms of transport (bemos, opelets, becaks and dokars) are available for getting around towns and cities in Sumatra. The base rate for a bemo is still 150 rp and the minimum fare by becak is 300 rp. The more modern *ojeks* (motorcycle-becaks) cost 500 rp minimum; the three-wheel bicycle type is less. Dokars also have a minimum 500 rp fare.

Hang back and watch what the locals pay if you are not certain of the fare, can't understand what they are telling you or just don't want to be ripped off. Also ask other travellers the correct price.

Lampung

Lampung was made a province in 1964. The provincial capital Bandarlampung is really two cities – Tanjungkarang and the port of Telukbetung – and looks across the Selat Sunda to Krakatau and Java.

When Krakatau erupted in 1883, Telukbetung and Tanjungkarang were blanketed in ash and thousands of houses and hectares of crops were destroyed. Most of Lampung is very flat and its highest mountains – Gunung Pesagi, Tanggamas, Seminung, Sekincau and Raya – are all dormant volcanoes.

Historically, the Lampungese forged close cultural and trading links with West Java soon after they began exporting their black pepper crops to Banten. However by 1684, the Dutch East India Company had acquired a monopoly on Lampung pepper and after the fall of the kingdom of Banten in 1808 the Lampungese found themselves subjects of the Dutch.

The cultural links with Java became even closer when the Dutch instituted transmigration schemes between the two regions in an effort to find a solution to Java's overpopulation. The Javanese brought with them the gamelan and wayang. They also successfully introduced sawah rice cultivation and other innovative agricultural techniques to Lampung. Coffee, cloves and rubber are also grown as cash crops.

BAKAUHENI

Bakauheni is the major ferry terminal on Sumatra's southern tip, and a major exit and entry point between Java and Sumatra. There is no point staying here. Most people who arrive here catch a bus to Bandarlampung for a bus or train connection to other parts of Sumatra, or the ferry across the Selat Sunda to Merak, in Java.

The ferry crosses the Selat Sunda between Bakauheni and Merak at roughly 1½ hour intervals in both directions, 24 hours a day. The 1½-hour trip costs from 1100 rp in economy to 2200 rp in 1st class. There is a local bus between Bakauheni and the Rajabasa Bus Station in Bandarlampung. The buses meet the ferry, cost 1400 rp and take two hours.

BANDARLAMPUNG

There are some beaches in the vicinity of this town. Most people come here to take the train or the bus onward to other parts of Sumatra. In the northern part of Bandarlampung is the town of Tanjungkarang from where the trains depart to Palembang and Lubuklinggau. Buses depart from the Rajabasa Bus Station.

Places to Stay

Most people only stay overnight in Tan-
jungkarang if they miss their train. In front of the railway station is Jalan Kota Raja where there is a string of not so cheap and very basic hotels. One place to try is *Losmen Gunungsari* at No 21, where singles and doubles cost 12,000 rp. Further away is *Garden Hotel* (☎ 55512) on Jalan Kartini 72, where rooms with fan and mandi cost from 13,000 rp.

Getting There & Away

Bus From Rajabasa Bus Station in Bandarlampung you can travel by bus to Palembang and all other major destinations. Buses go all the way to Bukittinggi or even Medan although most people will prefer to travel sector by sector. ANS is probably the best of the various Sumatran bus companies. If you take the bus to Jakarta or another destination in Java from here, the boat fare between Bakauheni and Merak is included in the cost of the bus ticket.

There are frequent opelets between the Tanjungkarang railway station and Rajabasa bus station. They cost 200 rp.

Be careful here, as fare rip-offs by opelet drivers from Rajabasa are common. It's advisable to approach the police for assistance in finding the right opelet and they'll make certain you pay the correct fare.

Train Passenger trains only operate in south Sumatra, and a small section around Medan. It's possible to take a train from Tanjungkarang to Palembang, and continue to Jambi or Pulau Bangka; or to Lubuklinggau and catch a bus from there to Bengkulu or Padang.

Trains run twice a day between Tanjungkarang and Palembang and the trip takes about 10 hours. The better of the two trains on this route is the night train *Kamalam Express* which departs at 9 pm. First class seats cost 11,000 rp. There is usually enough room to stretch out on both seats. The day train is the *KA Ekspress Siang* which departs at 9 am. Seats in 2nd/1st class cost 3500/5000 rp.

South Sumatra

The province of South Sumatra stretches from Lubuklinggau in the Barisan foothills in the west to the islands of Bangka and Belitung in the east. All roads, rivers and the railway lead to Palembang, the provincial capital.

PALEMBANG

The word Palembang literally means 'the gold out of the ground', but tin is also mined in this city. Built along Sungai Musi and only 80 km upstream from the sea, Palembang was forced into the 20th century rather abruptly because of its strategic position. When Sumatra's oil fields were discovered and opened early in the century, Palembang quickly became the main export outlet for south Sumatra. Over a third of Indonesia's total revenue comes from this province.

Today Palembang, the second largest city in Sumatra with 650,000 inhabitants, is a heavily industrialised city and a rather dull place to visit.

History

A thousand years ago, Palembang was the centre of the highly developed civilisation of Srivijaya. When the Chinese scholar I Tsing was in Palembang in 672 he recorded that a thousand monks, scholars and pilgrims were studying and translating Sanskrit. Few relics from this period remain – no sculpture, monuments or architecture of note – nor is there much of interest from the early 18th century when Palembang was an Islamic kingdom. Most of the buildings of the latter era were destroyed in battles with the Dutch, the last of which occurred in 1811.

Orientation & Information

Coming into Palembang from the south you pass plantations of rubber, coffee, pepper and pineapples. In complete contrast are the smokestacks of the Sunggai Gerong refinery and the petrochemical complex at Plaju,

which give the landscape a spuriously futuristic look, particularly at night.

The city is split in half by the Musi River and sprawls along both banks. The two halves are connected by the Ampera Bridge, only built in the mid '60s. A hodgepodge of wooden houses on stilts crowd both banks, but the south side known as Seberang Ulu is where the majority of people live. The 'better half', Seberang Ilir, is on the north bank where you'll find most of the government offices, shops, hotels and the wealthy residential districts. Jalan Jenderal Sudirman is the main street of Palembang, running right on to the bridge.

Be careful, especially at night, as many locals will warn you of the possibility of theft and/or stabbings.

Tourist Office The tourist office (☎ 28450) is at the Museum Sultan Machmud Badaruddin II. You can also get a lot of information and maps from the South Sumatra Regional Government Tourist Office (☎ 24981) at Jalan Bay Salim 200.

Money The Bank Bumi Daya is on the corner of Jalan Iskandar & Kol Atmo. The Bank Ekspor Impor is on Jalan Rustam Effendy. Dhrama Perdana at Jalan Kol Atmo 446 is a moneychanger.

Post The post office is close to the river and the Mesjid Agung (Grand Mosque).

Museums

There are two museums in Palembang. The **Museum Budaya Sultan Machmud Badaruddin II** is in the city centre, near the Musi River and Ampera Bridge. There are three rooms where you can see traditional Palembangese decor, and a number of ancient Hindu statues.

The other museum is about five km from the centre of Palembang, in the subdistrict of Telang Kelapa of Musi Banyu Asin district. To get there take one of many buses departing to the area along Jalan Jenderal Sudirman. The museum building reflects Palembang traditional architecture with a

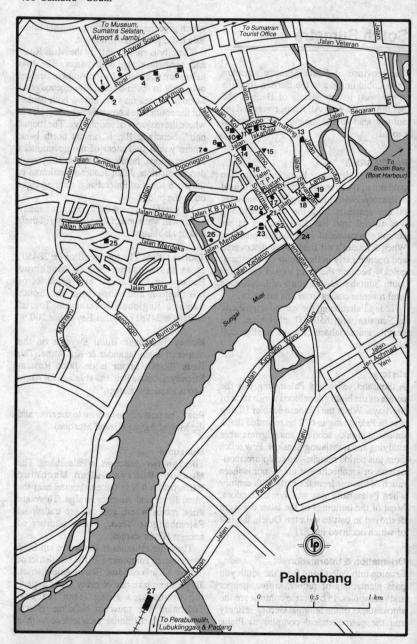

To Museum,
Sumatra Selatan,
Airport & Jambi

To Sumatran
Tourist Office

Jalan Veteran

To
Boom Baru
(Boat Harbour)

Sungai Musi

Palembang

0   0.5   1 km

To Perabumulih,
Lubuklinggau & Padang

number of halls and rooms. There are exhibits of ethnographic materials, natural and cultural history. The cultural and historical exhibits are the most interesting with around 2000 artefacts.

Close by is the impressive **Lima House**, a model of a traditional Palembang house which is fully furnished.

Markets

Next to the Ampera Bridge on the other side of the museum is the **Pasar 16 Ilir**, Palembang's frenetic and fascinating market. The main part is housed in an old building built by the Dutch. The colourful market is full of food, household goods and clothing. The smaller **Pasar Kuto** is also interesting.

Other Attractions

With permission from the commander, it's possible to visit the late 18th century **Dutch fort** which is still used by the army today. Sections of the outside walls still stand. There's also the **Mesjid Agung** (Grand Mosque) built by Sultan Machmud Badarudd in the 18th century, or you can while away an hour or two observing the frenetic river life.

Places to Stay – bottom end

Cheap hotels in Palembang are nothing to write home about. At Jalan Sudirman 45 E, close to the intersection with Jalan Letkol Iskandar, the *Hotel Asiana* is bare and basic with rooms at 6000/9000 rp. It's reasonably clean and not as noisy as it might be because it's high up.

Two other similarly styled and priced hotels are *Penginapan Riau* (☎ 22011) at Jalan Dempo 409 C, and *Hotel Segaran* at Jalan Segaran 207C. The numbers of Jalan Segaran follow no discernible pattern.

Back on the main road, at Jalan Jenderal Sudirman 38, *Hotel Sintera* has very variable rooms. The cheaper tiny, gloomy and noisy rooms at the front are 12,000/15,000 rp, the better and larger doubles are 22,000 rp or 27,500 rp with air-con. Breakfast is included.

Places to Stay – middle

There are numerous middle-range hotels. The *Hotel Sriwidjaja* (☎ 24193) at Jalan Letkol Iskandar 31/488, close to the junction with Jalan Jenderal Sudirman, has rooms at 13,000/14,465 rp with fan and from 25,410/36,905 rp with air-con. The price includes breakfast.

The *Hotel Nusantara* (☎ 23306) at Jalan

■	PLACES TO STAY		11	French Bakery
			15	Bonanza Fried Chicken
5	Hotel Sandjaja			
6	Sari Hotel &			OTHER
	Rumah Makan Sari Bundo			
8	Hotel Asiana		1	Telephone Office
9	King's Hotel		2	Garuda / Merpati Office
12	Penginapan Riau		3	Governor's Office
13	Hotel Segaran		4	Bank Rakyat Indonesia
14	Hotel Nusantara &		7	ANS Bus Office
	Hotel Sriwidjaja		10	Bank Bumi Daya
16	Hotel Sintera		17	Bank Ekspor Impor
18	Losmen Jakarta		20	Grand Mosque
19	Hotel Surabaya		21	Ampera Opelet Station
25	Hotel Swarna Dwipa		22	Museum Sultan Machmud
				Badaruddin II & Tourist Office
▼	PLACES TO EAT		23	Post Office
			24	Pasar 16 Ilir (Market)
6	Sari Hotel & Rumah Makan		26	Dutch Fort
	Sari Bundo		27	Kerapati Railway Station

Letkol Iskandar 17, in the little alley off the main road next to JM Plaza, has rooms at 14,000/25,000 rp with fan/air-con, including breakfast.

The *Sari Hotel* at Jalan Jenderal Sudirman 1301, on the corner with Jalan Kapt A Rivai, has singles/doubles from 17,000/24,200 rp, all including breakfast. *Hotel Surabaya* (☎ 26874) at Jalan Sayangan 669 has clean rooms from 17,500 to 30,000 rp with fan/air-con.

Places to Stay – top end

King's Hotel (☎ 310033) is at Jalan Kol Atmo 623, a fine upmarket place. All rooms have air-con and the usual amenities with prices starting from 62,800 to 242,300 rp plus tax. The similarly priced *Hotel Swarna Dwipa* (☎ 313322) at Jalan Tasik 2 is some distance west of the centre.

Places to Eat

A Palembang speciality is *pempek*, which is floured fish, grilled or fried, garnished with a hot pepper and sweet & sour sauce. This can be found at many street stalls.

At night Jalan Sajangan, parallel to Jalan Jenderal Sudirman, is crowded with some excellent Chinese food stands and satay places. Aound the corner on Jalan Rustam Effendy, there are fruit stalls and stands selling pisang goreng (fried bananas) and other snacks.

On Jalan Iskandar, near Jalan Jenderal Sudirman, there is a cluster of places including *Yohan Bakery & Fried Chicken* and the *Warna Warni* ice cream parlour next door. There are a number of bakeries along Jalan Jenderal Sudirman which also do mie (noodle) dishes and other simple meals, or try the *French Bakery* at Jalan Kol Atmo 481B, opposite King's Hotel.

Nasi Padang restaurants can be found all over town. The *Rumah Makan Sari Bundo* on the corner of Sudirman and Jalan Kapitan Rivai is good, but more expensive. Finally *Bonanza Fried Chicken* is Palembang's closest approach to a Western fast food joint. It's at Jalan Kol Atmo 425, upstairs in the 'Yuppies Centre'!

Getting There & Away

Few Westerners stop in Palembang as it's off the Trans-Sumatran Highway. You can skip past it on the direct Jakarta to Padang buses, or fly or take one of the direct Jakarta to Padang or Medan ships.

Air Merpati (Garuda) (☎ 21604) is on Jalan Kapten A Rivai. Bouraq (☎ 20410) is at Jalan Dr Sutomo 11.

Merpati operates flights between Palembang and Bandung, Bandarlampung, Batam, Bengkulu, Dumai, Jakarta (138,000 rp), Jambi, Medan, Padang, Pangkalpinang, Pakanbaru, Rengat and Tanjungpandan.

Bus The bus company ANS is at Jalan Iskandar 903 C just off Jalan Jenderal Sudirman. Other bus companies are in the same area and there is a bus station at Km 5. There are frequent departures for Jakarta. The 20-hour trip costs 22,500 rp or 30,000 rp with air-con. ANS have a daily bus to Padang, which takes 24 hours and costs 17,500 rp or 20,000 rp with air-con. There are also buses from Palembang to Jambi, costing 6000 rp.

Train The Kertapati Railway Station is on the south side of the river, eight km from the town centre. See the Bandarlampung section for details.

Boat It's possible to travel from Palembang to Pulau Bangka and back by jetfoil for 20,000 rp. The trip takes about 2½ hours, leaving Palembang at 1.30 pm from Bom Baru. The boat has air-con and is enclosed, so it's not possible to go on deck.

Getting Around

To/From the Airport Sultan Badaruddin II Airport is 12 km north of town and a taxi costs a standard 10,000 rp from the airport. The road runs right by the front of the terminal and you can get into town on a opelet for 350 rp.

Local Transport Opelets around town cost a standard 150 rp. Most routes start or finish at Ampera Station, the opelet stop opposite the Mesjid Agung (Grand Mosque). Take a Kertapati opelet for the railway station for 200 rp, or a Km 5 opelet for the Jambi buses and the nearby museum.

AROUND PALEMBANG

Take an opelet from Ampera Station across the Musi, then catch an opelet to Kayuagung for 2000 rp. Kayuagung is a small village on the banks of the Komering, where the women in the Kedaton district make superb pottery using a unique method. The pots, mostly cooking and household utensils like jugs and rice dishes, are fired under a kiln of brushwood in the open air.

The arts building has pictures of local life that include a bride and groom in traditional costume, pencak silat fighting, flora and fauna and the battle against the Dutch. Gold and red Palembang cabinets are still made in this village which is also known for its sago cakes and krupuks.

Once a year, usually on August 17 Proclamation Day, a *jalur* race is held by the people of Rantau Kuantan in the district of Inderagiri Hulu. A jalur is a canoe 25 to 30 metres long, a metre wide, and rowed by 40 to 60 men – it's a bit like a Chinese dragon boat.

DANAU RANAU

This is a beautiful mountain lake in the Bukit Barissan of South Sumatra. It is a good place to relax in the cool climate or hike in the surrounding mountains. It's possible to climb Gunung Seminung (1881 metres) that dominates the lake region. Bandingagung is the main town on the north side of the lake, where there are few places to stay. There are also some quieter hotels on the west side of the lake, south of Simpangsukarama.

Getting There & Away From Bandarlampung take the train to Martapura, and then a bus to the lake, or take the bus all the way.

PASEMAH HIGHLANDS

The most important group of megalithic monuments remaining at their original site is concentrated at Tegurwangi, near Lahat on the Pasemah Plateau. There are two distinct styles of sculpture. The older, more primitive style features figures squatting with hands on knees or arms folded over chests; the second is more sophisticated and has single statues as well as groups.

The sculptures in this group are dynamic, powerful and passionate studies of men, women, children and animals. They include several sculptures of men riding buffaloes or elephants, groups of people standing next to elephants and buffaloes, two men battling with a snake, a man struggling with an elephant lying on its back, and a couple of tigers – one guarding the head of a human between its paws. The sculptures have expressive facial features and are thought to date from the late Bronze Age. Their makers have used the natural curve of the rocks to create a three-dimensional effect, though all the sculptures are in bas-relief.

A couple of stone graves at Tanjungara, also in the Pasemah Highlands, contain fragments of paintings in broad bands of black, yellow, red, white and grey on the inner walls, in the same style as the sculptures. Two are scenes of a warrior and a buffalo, the third is a man with an elephant.

In the village of Karang Dalum, about 15 km from Lahat on the road to Pagaralam, is an incantation stone. Ask the villagers where it is. About four km along the same road is the Tanjung Serai complex.

About 12 km from the main road, just past the village of Tinggi Hari (in the Kecamatan Pulau Pinang area, not the Pagaralem District, where there is a village of the same name), is the Sinjar Bulam megalith complex.

The megaliths around Pagaralam are accessible by bus. You'll find them near the villages of Pajar Bulam, Tanjung Aro and Belumai. Ask the locals in the area where they are – they might not know where the megaliths are, but they'll know where the various villages are. Note that if you are staying at Lahat, the last bus leaves Pagaralam at 4 pm.

Many of the megaliths can be explored

using the towns of Lahat and/or Pagaralam as a base. Buses go directly from Palembang to Pagaralam (six to seven hours), stopping at Lahat (4½ to 5½ hours). Both towns have several moderately priced hotels and losmen, with a limited number of economy-class rooms. Lahat hotels, all on Jalan Jayor Ruslam III, include the *Losmen Simpang* (5500 rp per room), the *Simpang Baru Wisma* (65000 rp), the *Nusantara Hotel* and the *Presido Hotel* (up to 46,000 rp).

PULAU BANGKA

The island is off the eastern coast of southern Sumatra. Its name is taken from the word 'wangka', meaning tin, and of course there is a tin mining company on the island. There are only small pockets of natural forest left on the island, the attraction of the island are its beaches, but unless you're staying in one of the more expensive beach resorts they can be difficult to get to due to a lack of public transport.

Pangkalpinang

This is the capital city of the island. It is an important business and transportation centre. There is a large colourful market in the centre of town. On the way to the airport at the edge of the town there is a large cemetery divided into Muslim, Buddhist and Christian sections with many extravagant looking graves. There are supposedly around 100,000 people buried here, while the population of Pangkalpinang is around 40,000. Pantai Pasir Padi is the closest beach to the town, 2.4 km away, and there is no regular transport to it.

Orientation & Information Pangkalpinang is a fairly small town with most banks, travel agents and the post office along Jalan Jenderal Sudirman. The post office is the only place not centrally located, it is at the edge of town, along the way to Sungailiat. The banks, like BNI 1946, and travel agents, like Duta Bangka Sarana are in the area where Jalan Jenderal Sudirman and Jalan Masjid Jami meet. From here just down Jalan N

Pegadaian you can also get to the bus station and the market.

Places to Stay A cheap and friendly place to stay is *Penginapan Srikandi* (☎ 22991) at Jalan Masjid Jami 42, where rooms cost 5000 rp, or 7500 rp with mandi and fan. Opposite at No 43 is the *Bukitshofa Hotel* (☎ 21062), a clean new place with a balcony, where rooms with mandi cost 9900/16,490 rp.

There are plenty of mid-range hotels. The best value is the *Menumbing Hotel* (☎ 22991) at Jalan Gereja 5, where rooms cost from 15,000/20,000 to 75,000 rp, plus tax, including bath, air-con and TV. The hotel has a restaurant and a nice pool. If you are not staying in the hotel a swim costs 2200 rp.

Places to Eat The island is well known for its small but fiery chillies. There are plenty of places to eat Indonesian and Chinese food along Jalan Jenderal Sudirman and in the market area. For Padang-style food try *Sari Bundo* at Jalan Jenderal Sudirman 77. On the same street at No 3 is *Tirta Garden*, a good but expensive seafood restaurant.

Mentok

Mentok is a port for the boats to and from Palembang. There is no other reason to come here. If you need a place to stay, near the harbour is *Losmen Mentok* at Jalan Jenderal A Yani 42, where very basic rooms will cost you 3500 rp.

Around Bankga

There are many nice beaches on the island. The best are just north of Sungailiat. Pantai Paraitenggiri is four km from Sungailiat, but unfortunately spoiled by the Parai Beach Hotel. The deserted Pantai Matras is a couple of km further up the coast. About seven km from Sungailiat is the Pemali Air Manis (hot springs). There are several pools there to bathe in and the entry fee is 600 rp. There is no public transport to the hot springs.

Places to Stay Close to the town of Belinyu, at a deserted beach, is the luxurious hotel

Remodong Cottages (☎ 0717-21573). The cottages start from 45,000 rp plus tax. The *Parai Beach Hotel* (telex 27697) is also at a deserted beach, 4 km from Sungailiat. Cottages cost from 110,000 rp, plus tax.

Getting There & Away
Air Merpati has daily flights from Pangkalpinang to Jakarta and Palembang. Deraya Air has two flights a week to Pulau Singkep (73,179 rp) and Tanjung Pinang (98,500 rp).

Boat There is a daily jetfoil to and from Palembang and Mentok on Bangka, leaving Palembang at 8.30 am and Mentok at 1.30 pm. The 2½-hour journey costs 20,000 rp. For this price you get a snack and air-conditioning that will almost freeze you to death. Because the boat is fully enclosed and it's not possible to go out on the deck, you see much of the scenery through small grotty windows.

The Pelni liner *Lawit* stops at Mentok on its fortnightly journey between Medan and Jakarta, and costs from 18,000 rp. Refer to the Getting Around chapter for the complete timetable.

Getting Around
To/From the Airport Opelets run from the airport to Pangkalpinang and cost 200, or a taxi is 3000 rp.

Local Transport There is regular transport between major towns, but most opelets stop running around mid-afternoon. The fare from Pangkalpinang to Sungailiat is 500 rp, and to Muntok is 2500 rp (taking 4 hours). Taxi charges are about 5000 rp per hour.

Jambi

Jambi Province is on the east coast of Sumatra, facing the Straits of Melaka. Jambi was made a province in 1957 and now has a population of 1½ million.

Because of its geographical situation Jambi has long been a melting pot for different ethnic groups. The main groups living in Jambi today are Chinese, Arabs, Japanese, Malaysians, Pakistanis, Javanese, Minangkabaus, Sudanese, Bataks and the earliest inhabitants of Jambi, the Kubus, who were among the first wave of Malays to migrate to Sumatra, predating the Bataks.

Almost 85% of the existing Kubus, originally nomadic forest dwellers, now live in one area in the jungle fringing Jambi, but they were once scattered far and wide. Only a few of them managed to find sanctuary in the rainforest. Government resettlement programmes enforced to combat overpopulation in Java have subjected the people to diseases like measles and tuberculosis, which have decimated their numbers.

Historically, Jambi was a dependency of Java's Majapahit empire from 1294 to 1520 before coming under the sway of the Minangkabaus of West Sumatra. In 1616, the Dutch East India Company opened an office in Jambi and the Dutch quickly formed a successful alliance with Sultan Muhammad Nakhruddin to protect their ships and cargoes from pirates.

The Dutch negotiated a trade monopoly with Nakhruddin and successive sultans. The predominant export was pepper, which was grown in such abundance in Jambi that it could provide Melaka, Johore, Pattani and Gris with most of their supplies and China with a large percentage of its pepper stocks. In 1901, the Dutch moved their headquarters to Palembang and from then on were not able to retain effective control in Jambi.

JAMBI
Jambi, capital of the province of the same name, is on the banks of Sumatra's longest river, the Batanghari, about 155 km from the coast.

Orientation & Information
Jambi is spread over a wide area. The centre of the city with most of the banks, hotels, shops and restaurants spreads out from the harbour along Jalan Sultan Taha up to

Rawasari Opelet Station between the streets of Jalan Dr Sutomo and Husni Thamrin.

Tourist Office The Dinas Parawisata (☎ 25330) is a fair way out of town in Kota Bharu on Jalan Basuk. Catch an opelet there from Rawasari, costing 150 rp.

Post There is a post office at Jalan Sultan Thana 9.

Museum Negeri Jambi
The museum is on the corner of Jalan Urip Sumoharjo and Jalan Prof Dr Sri Sudewi. It has a small but interesting collection of costumes, handicrafts and tools from the province. It's open daily from 9 am to 4 pm. Admission is 200 rp.

Muara Jambi Temples
This is a group of seven most important and impressive temples 25 km from Jambi. They can easily be visited in one day. The easiest way to see them is by boat – on Sunday there are public boats for 5000 rp for a return trip, otherwise it costs 25,000 rp to charter a boat.

Kubu People
The Kubu or Anak Dalam as they are also referred to can be visited from the town of Limbur which is not far from Bangko (on the Trans-Sumatran Highway). The Kubu live in the jungle in their natural environment. If you want to see them you need to get in touch with the head of the village who comes to Limbur once a week. There are direct buses to Limbur from Bangko or Jambi.

Places to Stay
The cheaper places are generally drab and unpleasant. The more expensive places show some improvement in quality for the extra cost. *Hotel Merpati Inn* (☎ 24861) at Jalan Y Leimena 71, has stuffy and very basic rooms with mandi for 5000 rp, and airier rooms with windows for 6000 rp. The *Penginapan Sumatera* on Jalan R A Kartini is a rock bottom, survival-only place where rooms cost 7000 rp.

A reasonable place, where rooms start

from 22,500 rp, plus tax, is the *Hotel Marisa* (☎ 23533) at Jalan Kol Abun Jami 12. An international-class hotel is *Harisman* (☎ 24677) at Jalan Prof Dr Mohd Yamin. Rooms here cost 30,000 to 90,000 rp.

Places to Eat
Of course you'll be eating Padang food. Try the restaurants on Jalan Wahidin and Jalan Thamrin. One of the better places is *Restaurant Safari* at Jalan Veteran 29. There are also plenty of stalls selling slices of chilled fruit.

Getting There & Away
Air Garuda/Merpati fly to Jambi regularly, connecting directly with Jakarta (122,000 rp) and to other centres via Palembang. There are same-day air connections between Jambi and Balikpapan, Bandung, Bandarlampung, Denpasar, Palembang, Pangkalpinang, Semarang, Solo, Surabaya and Yogyakarta.

Bus Like Palembang, the Trans-Sumatran Highway does not run through Jambi. There are buses from Palembang to Jambi (6000 rp), and from Jambi you can continue on to Padang or Sungaipenuh (7000 rp).

Boat A boat plies the route to Tanjung Pinang and back twice a week.

Getting Around
Rawasari is the main opelet station in the centre of the town at Jalan Kenuming where all opelets commence and end their journey. The standard fare is 150 rp. The terminal for buses to Padang and Sungaipenuh is Simpang Kawat, a few km from the city centre.

KERINCI
Kerinci is a mountain-valley accessible by bus from either Jambi or Padang – the road from Padang is more beautiful and also much better. It's a rich, green area with two very dominating features: Gunung Kerinci, at 3800 metres the highest mountain in Indonesia outside Irian Jaya, and Danau Kerinci, at the other end of the valley.

Sungaipenuh is the largest town with some 200 small villages in the area. Its matrilineal social structure is similar to that found in West Sumatra.

Things to See

In Sungaipenuh there is a large, pagoda-style **Mesjid Agung** which is said to be over 400 years old. It has large carved beams and old Dutch tiles, but you need permission to go inside. **Sungai Tutung** is nationally renowned for its basket weaving. It's easy to find a cheap guide for day-trips from Sungaipenuh.

There are stone carvings which have not been carefully investigated all over the area, the most well known being at **Batu Gong**. Locals have a legend of a great kingdom here long ago. The carvings are very different from those of the Majapahit or Srivijaya areas.

Tours around the lake are good to start from either **Jujun** or **Keluru** (20 km from Sungaipenuh and half a km apart). About 40 km out of Sungaipenuh on the way to Gunung Kerinci, there is a tea plantation called **Kayu Aro**. There are hot springs nearby where it's too hot to swim in the main pool, but you can get a private room with a hot mandi. The village of Pelompek is 51 km from Sungaipenuh, and a starting point for visiting **Danau Tujuh** and **Letter 'W' Waterfall**.

To climb **Gunung Kerinci**, first a permit *(surat ijin)* is required from the PHPA office at the Visitor Information Centre at Jalan Arga Selebar Daun 11, in Sungaipenuh. It's a tough two-day climb for which you need to bring food, a water bottle (water is scarce on the mountain), a tent and a sleeping bag, as it is cold (down to 2°C at night). A guide is not necessary as there is only one well-marked trail. The climb starts from the village of **Kersik Tuo** where it is possible to stay at the PHPA office. From here it's an eight-hour walk to Pandok II, from where it's a further four hours to the top. It is recommended to be at the top by 8 am before the mist closes in.

Places to Stay & Eat

In Sungaipenuh the *Mata Hari Losmen* is cheap and the owner provides plenty of information. Rooms cost from 3000 to 12,000 rp. *Hotel Yani* on Jalan Muradi has clean rooms from 7000 to 19,000 rp. A restaurant with good and cheap Padang food is the *Minang Soto*. There are a few places to eat in the bus station/market area. Try the speciality of the region, *dending batokok*, which is strips of beef smoked and grilled over a fire.

Getting There & Around

The bus station is in the market area at Jalan Prof M Yamin. The Habeco bus company tries to overcharge on their fares. The bus to Padang takes 10 hours and costs 4000 rp. It's better to take the bus going along the coast than through the mountains, as it's faster and more scenic. Buses to Bangko (on the Trans-Sumatran Highway) cost 4000 rp, while those to Bengkulu cost 9000 rp, and to Kersik Tuo 1500 rp.

Dokars cost 150 to 200 rp per ride around Sungaipenuh.

Bengkulu

A rather isolated province, particularly during the rainy season when land transport often breaks down completely, Bengkulu (Bencoolen) has particular historical significance for the Indonesians, Dutch and the British.

The British moved into Bengkulu in 1685, three years after they had been kicked out of Banten in Java. From the word go things did not go well for them as disease and outbreaks of malaria decimated the British colony. Pepper was an obvious natural resource to exploit. The first factory was started by Ralph Ord who didn't survive long enough to enjoy success as he was poisoned in 1687.

Involvement in internal Sumatran wars, corruption within the colony, and the destruction of British settlements by the French fleet in 1760 all took their toll. When

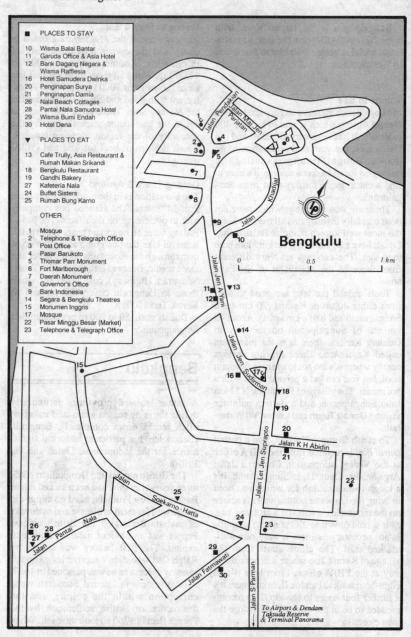

PLACES TO STAY

10 Wisma Balai Bantar
11 Garuda Office & Asia Hotel
12 Bank Dagang Negara &
    Wisma Rafflesia
16 Hotel Samudera Dwinka
20 Penginapan Surya
21 Penginapan Damia
26 Nala Beach Cottages
28 Pantai Nala Samudra Hotel
29 Wisma Bumi Endah
30 Hotel Dena

PLACES TO EAT

13 Cafe Trully, Asia Restaurant &
    Rumah Makan Srikandi
18 Bengkulu Restaurant
19 Gandhi Bakery
27 Kafeteria Nala
24 Buffet Sisters
25 Rumah Bung Karno

OTHER

1   Mosque
2   Telephone & Telegraph Office
3   Post Office
4   Pasar Barukoto
5   Thomar Parr Monument
6   Fort Marlborough
7   Daerah Monument
8   Governor's Office
9   Bank Indonesia
14 Segara & Bengkulu Theatres
15 Monumen Inggris
17 Mosque
22 Pasar Minggu Besar (Market)
23 Telephone & Telegraph Office

Bengkulu

0   0.5   1 km

To Airport & Dendam
Taksuda Reserve
& Terminal Panorama

Sir Stamford Raffles arrived in 1818 the colony was still not a going concern.

Bengkulu became a separate province from South Sumatra in 1968. It covers an area of 17,858 sq km and is split into the city of Bengkulu (with a population of 55,000), North Bengkulu, South Bengkulu and the mountainous Rejang Lebong.

BENGKULU

Bengkulu was Raffles' foot in the door to Indonesia, but this British attempt to displace the Dutch was half-hearted and never very successful. The British established themselves here in 1685 and Raffles arrived in 1818. In 1824, Bengkulu was traded for Melaka on the Malay coast and the British and Dutch now stared at each other across the Straits of Melaka. There are still some reminders of the British presence in Bengkulu but overall the town is of very little interest and, like Palembang and Jambi, getting there requires a detour from the Trans-Sumatran Highway.

Raffles was anxious to establish a British trading base in Sumatra. His Benteng Malioboro (Fort Marlborough) is still there. In the short time he was there, Raffles made the pepper market profitable and started cash crops in coffee, nutmeg and sugar cane.

Orientation & Information

Although Bengkulu is right by the sea it only really touches it near Benteng Malioboro. Otherwise the town is set back from the coast. Jalan Suprapto and the nearby Pasar Minggu Besar are the modern town centre, separated from the old town area around the fort by the long, straight Jalan Jenderal Ahmad Yani. The coast is surprisingly quiet and rural only a km or so from the centre.

Fort Marlborough

Raffles' fort, Benteng Malioboro, was built between 1714 and 1719. It was restored in 1983 and reopened to the public in 1984 after a long period of use by the army. There are a few small and uninteresting exhibits about the restoration, together with a pile of

cannon-balls and a couple of old British gravestones. Admission is 200 rp.

Bengkulu has a few other British reminders, including the **Thomas Parr monument** in front of the Pasar Barukoto and a couple of 'Monumen Inggris'. The one near the beach is to Captain Robert Hamilton who died in 1793, 'in command of the troops'.

Sukarno's House

Sukarno was exiled to Bengkulu by the Dutch from 1938 until the Japanese arrived here in 1941. At his house you can see a few faded photos, a wardrobe and even Bung's trusty bicycle, which like any real Indonesian bicycle has brakes that don't work. His house is closed on Mondays, open other days from 8 am to 2 pm, except on Fridays when it closes at 11 am and on Saturdays when it closes at noon.

Other Attractions

The Bengkulu beach **Pantai Panjang** is long, grey, wide, featureless and decidedly unattractive. The **Bengkulu Museum Negeri** is south of the centre at Jalan Pembangunan P D Harapan and is open the same hours as the Rumah Bung Karno. **Dendam Taksuda** is a reserve area four km south of the town.

Places to Stay – bottom end

As in other towns in south Sumatra, the cheap hotels are no great bargains.

Penginapan Damia (☎ 32912) at Jalan Abidin 18 is a rock-bottom place where rooms with mandi cost 6500 rp. Two other survival places at similar prices are *Penginapan Surya* (☎ 31341) at Jalan Abidin 26 and *Wisma Rafflesia* (☎ 31650) at Jalan Jenderal Ahmad Yani 924.

Wisma Bumi Endah (☎ 31665) at Jalan Fatmawati 29 is much better and still conveniently close to the centre. It's quiet, quite pleasant and rooms are small but clean. Single/double rooms cost 10,000/15,000 rp or 20,000 rp with air-con.

Places to Stay – middle

There are a number of middle-range hotels,

some of them quite pleasant. *Nala Beach Cottages* (☎ 31855) at Jalan Pantai Nala 133 is right by the beach, below the expensive Pantai Nala Samudra Hotel. The individual cottages are good value at 25,000 rp. It's quiet and relaxed here and more than a km from the centre.

Wisma Balai Buntar (☎ 31254) is at Jalan Khadijal 122, near the fort. Rooms at this quiet and pleasant guest house are 22,000 to 25,500 rp. Close to the centre at Jalan Sudirman 245, *Hotel Samudera Dwinka* (☎ 31604) is big, clean and well kept. Rooms are 20,000 rp with fan, 34,000 rp with air-con.

Places to Stay – top end
Pantai Nala Samudra Hotel at Jalan Burniat 217 is more than a km from the centre and a top-class establishment.

Places to Eat
There are a number of restaurants along Jalan Suprapto in the centre including the neat little *Buffet Sisters* with the usual mie and nasi menu. You can try the *Gandhi Bakery* with its amazing selection of ice creams.

Half way along Jalan Jenderal Ahmad Yani, between the centre and the fort, there is a small cluster of restaurants opposite the Garuda office and Hotel Asia. They include *Cafe Trully*, the seafood specialist *Asia Restaurant* and the *Rumah Makan Srikandi*.

Overlooking the beach, at the corner right next to the Nala Beach Cottages and the Pantai Nala Samudra Hotel, the *Kafeteria Nala* is a good place for a cold beer. You can look out to sea and wonder what brought you to Bengkulu in the first place!

Getting There & Away
Air Garuda (☎ 21416) is at Jalan Ahmad Yani 922B. There are direct flights with Merpati to Jakarta (147,000 rp) and Palembang (85,000 rp). By changing planes, you can get same-day connections to Bandarlampung, Denpasar, Semarang, Surabaya and Yogyakarta.

Bus Terminal Panorama, the long distance

bus station, is several km south of the centre (150 rp by opelet). Buses run to Lubuklinggau, the junction town 110 km away on the Trans-Sumatran Highway, for 4000 rp. Other fares include Curup (half way to Lubuklinggau) for 2000 rp, Palembang for 8500 rp and Padang for 14,500 rp. Long distance bus operators also have offices in the town centre, like Bengkulu Indah at Jalan Suprapto 5.

Boat The harbour below Benteng Malioboro is just for small boats and fishing boats; the main harbour is 15 or so km south, beyond the airport. Sometimes you can get ships going to Padang.

Getting Around
To/From the Airport The airport is 14 km south of town and the standard taxi fare is 8000 rp. You can walk 100 metres out to the road from where you should be able to get a bemo or bus into Bengkulu.

Local Transport There are countless tiny mikrolets shuttling around town at a standard fare of 150 rp. These operate out as far as eight km, but make sure any vehicle that picks you up from there doesn't decide it's a chartered taxi.

PULAU ENGGANO
Pulau Enggano was isolated for so long and so little was known about it that only about one hundred years ago some Sumatrans believed it was inhabited entirely by women. Apparently, these women managed to procreate miraculously through the kind auspices of the wind or by eating certain fruit.

Enggano is a tiny island of just 680 sq km, about 100 km off the coast of Bengkulu. It's featured on a map of Asia drawn in 1593 and the name, Enggano, is Portuguese for deceit or disappointment, which suggests that the Portuguese were the first Europeans to discover it. It wasn't until three years later that Dutch navigators record coming across it.

The original inhabitants are believed to be native Sumatrans who fled from the mainland when the Malays migrated there. The present day inhabitants live by cultivating rice, coffee, pepper, cloves and copra. Wild pigs, cattle and buffalo are abundant.

There are five villages on the island, including Banjar Sari on the north coast, Meok on the west, Kaana and Kahayupin in the east and Malakoni, the harbour. The island is relatively flat (the highest point is Bua Bua which rises to 250 metres) and the coastline's swampy. It's worth visiting if you are a keen anthropologist and/or a real adventurer with plenty of time.

Getting There & Around

The only way to get to Enggano is by boat from Bengkulu (a very irregular service) which docks at Malakoni. The villages are connected by tracks originally made by the Japanese and not very well-maintained since. Once you're there, the only way of getting around is to walk.

West Sumatra

The province of West Sumatra is like a vast and magnificent nature reserve, dominated by volcanoes, with jungles, waterfalls, canyons and lakes. This is the homeland of the Minangkabau, one of Indonesia's most interesting and influential ethnic groups who make up 95% of the province's population of 3½ million.

Padang is the province capital, the other major cities are Payakumbuh, Bukittinggi, Padangpanjang, Solok and Sawahlunto. There are four large lakes in West Sumatra – Singkarak near Solok, Maninjau near Bukittinggi, and Diatas and Dibawah east of Padang.

The fascinating Mentawai Archipelago also falls into the province of West Sumatra. Only recently emerged from the stone age, the inhabitants of these islands are quite different from the people of mainland Sumatra.

The economy, although predominantly based on agriculture (coffee, rice, coconuts and cattle), is strengthened by industries like coal mining.

History

Legend has granted the Minangkabau descent from none other than that tyrannical Macedonian, Alexander the Great. It is said that the original Minangkabau ancestors arrived in Sumatra under the leadership of King Maharjo Dirajo, the youngest son of Alexander, more commonly known in Indonesia as Iskandar Zulkarnair. It is said that the new immigrants settled in the Padangpanjang region, and gradually spread out over western Sumatra.

History suggests that, in fact, the Minangkabau arrived in Indonesia some time between 1000 and 2000 BC. The early Malayu kingdom, which later extended to include what is now West Sumatra, was established by Hindu colonists by the seventh century and became a power in the 12th century following the demise of the Srivijaya empire. It is thought to have been founded by a prince of the Javanese Majapahit empire, and was listed as a dependent of Java in the year 1365. At its zenith, between the 14th and 15th centuries, it stretched right across central Sumatra and included Padang, Jambi, Bengkulu and other cities.

In the 14th century, Islam began to penetrate the area with small Muslim states ruled by sultans. They gradually pushed the Minangkabau kingdom further and further inland until by the early 17th century, when the Europeans arrived, it had all but disintegrated. At that time it consisted of little more than a few small-time rajas ruling over minuscule village-states headed by a Palembang-based ruler who was effectively a figurehead.

It continued to survive in this form until the early 19th century when the Padri rebellion erupted, instigated by a group of Muslim fanatics known as the 'men of Pedir'. It was called the Padri rebellion because the Muslim hajis who started it returned to Sumatra via Pedir after their pilgrimage to

West Sumatra

0   30   60 km

Approximate Scale

Mecca. Determined to force the Minang people to follow the strict Mohammedan law to the letter, the Padri resorted to killing and enslaving anyone who resisted them. The Minangkabau leaders were not prepared to relinquish their power without a fight and defended their rights to follow the traditional system of matriarchy, indulge in gambling and drinking, and practise other pre-Islamic customs.

The bitter struggle lasted from 1820 to 1837 but, backed by the Dutch army and non-Muslim Bataks, the adat leaders finally overcame the Padri strongholds. Today a curious mix of traditional beliefs and Islam is practised in West Sumatra.

Flora & Fauna

Tigers, rhinoceroses, sun bears, elephants, and various species of monkey and deer are all native to West Sumatra. Of particular interest in the Mentawai Islands is a rare species of black and yellow monkey, the *siamang kerdil*, usually called *simpai mentawai* by the locals. Their numbers are small and they are strictly protected. There is also diverse birdlife.

The Rafflesia grows in West Sumatra.

– a ruse which came as a surprise to both the bull and the onlookers. The calf, which appeared helpless, charged straight for the bull and began to press its nose along the bull's belly searching for milk. Soon after the bull let out a bellow of pain and took to its heels with blood pouring from its stomach and the calf in hot pursuit. When the bull finally dropped dead, the people of West Sumatra were heard to shout, 'minangkabau, minangkabau!' which literally means 'the buffalo wins, the buffalo wins!'

It seems that the owners of the calf separated it from its mother several days before the fight. Half-starved and with sharp metal spears attached to its horns, they sent the calf into the arena. Believing the Javanese bull to be its mother the calf rushed to assuage its hunger and ripped the belly of the bull to shreds.

Some specimens measure as much as a metre across and weigh over seven kg. The flower of the Rafflesia is a gaudy red and white and it gives off a putrid smell which attracts numerous flies and insects. It blooms every year between August and November and can be seen in the small village of Palupuh, 16 km north of Bukittinggi. This province is also famous for its many species of orchids.

People

For centuries, the West Sumatrans have built their houses with roofs shaped like buffalo horns and called themselves and their land Minangkabau. They have a long literary tradition which includes many popular and imaginative legends about their origins. There are several theories on the derivation of the name Minangkabau, but the West Sumatrans prefer a colourful 'David & Goliath' version that also demonstrates their shrewd diplomacy and wit:

About 600 years ago one of the kings of Java, who had ambitions of taking over West Sumatra, made the mistake of sending a messenger to advise the people of his intentions and ordering them to surrender. The West Sumatrans, being neither gullible nor stupid, were not prepared to give up without a fight. So as a way of avoiding bloodshed they proposed a bullfight between a Javanese and a Sumatran bull.

When the time came the West Sumatrans dispatched a tiny calf to fight the enormous Javanese bull

A far more prosaic explanation is that it is a combination of two words *minanga*, a river in that region, and *kerbau*, meaning buffalo. Or that it comes from the archaic expression *pinang kabhu* meaning original home, Minangkabau being the cradle of the Malay civilisation.

The Minangkabaus are known by their compatriots as the 'gypsies of Indonesia'; they are adaptable, intelligent people and one of the most economically successful ethnic groups in the country. Though staunchly Muslim, the Minangkabau society is still matriarchal and matrilineal. According to Minangkabau adat, a man does not gain possession of a woman by marriage, nor does a woman a man. Men have no rights over their wives other than to expect them to remain faithful. The eldest living female is the matriarch and has the most power in the household, which can number as many as 70 people descended from one ancestral mother, under the same roof. She is deferred to in all matters of family politics.

Every Minangkabau belongs to his or her mother's clan. At the lowest level of the clan is the *sapariouk* which consists of those matri-related kin who eat together. These include the mother, grandchildren and son-in-law. The name comes from the word *periouk* which means rice pot. A number of genealogically related sapariouk make up a lineage or *sapayuang*. The word *payung* means umbrella. Children born of a female member of the lineage will, by right of birth, be members of that lineage. Ancestral property, although worked collectively, is passed down this female line, rather than down the male line.

All progeny from a marriage are regarded as part of the mother's family group and the father has no say in family affairs. The most important male member of the household is the mother's eldest brother, who replaces the father in being responsible for the children's education and offers them economic advice as they grow older. He also discusses and advises them on their prospective marriages.

Arts & Crafts

West Sumatra has a reputation for exquisite, hand-loomed songket cloth and fine embroidery. The development of textile art in West Sumatra was influenced by various countries, but the strongest impact came from Muslim traders when Islam became powerful in the region. One of the many commodities introduced to Sumatra by Muslim traders following the fall of the Hindu Majapahit empire and the emergence of the kingdom of Mataram was the high quality gold and silver threads interwoven through songket cloth.

Today, synthetic substitutes have replaced real silver and gold, but the designs – usually elaborate floral motifs and geometric patterns – are purely Islamic in inspiration. One of the most popular designs, used in both weaving and embroidery, incorporates stylised flowers and mountains in an ornate pattern known as *gunung batuah* or 'magic mountain'.

There are various weaving centres in West Sumatra, but the main one is at Silungkang, a small village on the Agam Plateau near the coal mining town of Sawahlunto, which specialises in vividly coloured silk songket sarongs and scarves. Often the weavings take up to three months to complete. An easily accessible centre is Pandai Sikat, near Padangpanjang on the main road between Padang and Bukittinggi. Pandai Sikat is also known for its intricate and decorative woodcarvings.

Another highly developed art form found in West Sumatra is silverwork. Silversmiths are particularly skilled in creating filigree jewellery as fine as spider webs. Koto Gadang near Bukittinggi is the place to go if you're interested.

Dance & Music

The Minangs perform various dances, including the tari payung or umbrella dance which is a welcome dance about a young man's love for his girlfriend. The tari lilin or candle dance is performed by a group of young girls who manage by some miracle of physical coordination to rhythmically juggle and balance china saucers which have lighted candles attached to them and simultaneously click castanets.

Randai & Pencak Silat The most popular of the Minang dances is the Randai, a unique dance-drama performed at weddings, harvest festivals and other celebrations. The steps and movements for the randai developed from the pencak silat, a self-defence dance with various styles. The dance is learnt by every Minang boy at the stage when they are considered too old to remain in their mother's house and too young to move into another woman's.

It is the custom for Minang youths to spend some time in a *surau* (prayer house) where they are taught, among other things, how to look after themselves. This includes learning the pencak silat. The style of pencak silat most often performed is the Mudo, a mock battle which leads the two protagonists to the brink of violence before it is concluded. It is a dramatic dance involving skilled technique, fancy footwork and deliberate pauses which follow each movement and serve to heighten the tension.

The most aggressive and dangerous style of pencak silat originated in the Painan district of West Sumatra. The steps for the Harimau-Silat imitate a tiger stalking and killing its prey. With their bodies as close to the ground as possible, the two fighters circle around menacingly, springing at each other from time to time.

The randai combines the movements of pencak silat with literature, sport, song and drama. Every village in West Sumatra has at least one randai group of 20 performers. Both the female and male roles are played by men wearing traditional *gelambuk* trousers and black dress. The traditional version tells the story of a woman so wilful and wicked that she is driven out of her village before she brings complete disaster on the community. The drama, backed by gamelan music, starts when the actors stand up. Keeping the formation of the circle and adhering faithfully to the pencak silat movements, they begin to sing and dance. Each new scene is indicated when the actors sit down and the characters who have leading roles move to the centre of the circle and begin their performance. The seated actors fulfil three separate functions: they are a living set, they respond to the action centre-stage, and are a prose chorus.

The percussion instruments used to accompany most of the dances are similar to those of the Javanese gamelan and are collectively called the *telempong* in West Sumatra. Two other instruments frequently played are the *puput* and *salung*, both primitive kinds of flute which are usually made out of bamboo, reed or rice stalks.

Activities

Horse Racing Horse racing is held at Padang, Padangpanjang, Bukittinggi, Payakumbuh and Batu Sangkar throughout the year. It's a vivid, noisy spectacle, nothing like the horse racing of Western countries. The horses are ridden bareback and the jockeys are dressed in the traditional costume of the region or village they come from. The aim is to gain prestige for the district where the horse is bred and raised.

Bullfights Bullfighting, known locally as *adu sapi*, is a popular entertainment, unique to West Sumatra. Bullfights are held regularly at the villages Koto Baru and Air Agnat, between Padang and Bukittinggi. They're held every Saturday afternoon at around 5 pm at Koto Baru, which is closer to Bukittinggi, or every Tuesday from 4 pm at Air Agnat.

The afternoon usually kicks off with a meeting of the village elders who discuss matters of communal interest. This is occasionally followed by a demonstration of pencak silat and then the bullfight. West Sumatran bullfighting has no resemblance to the Spanish kind – there is no bloodshed (unless by accident) and the bulls, often water buffaloes or *kerbau*, don't get hurt. The original intention was to help develop cattle breeding in the region, but of no less importance is the fact that it gives the men an opportunity to get together to have a good time and to try to make some easy money betting.

Two bulls of roughly the same size and weight are let loose to chase each other round an open field with their owners or attendants goading them on. Once the fight starts it continues until the losing bull tires and runs out of the ring pursued by the winner. Part of the battle is concerned with the animals' strength in pushing each other with locked horns, while another aspect is their skill in breaking away from each other.

The fun for foreigners is in watching the locals make their bets and in seeing them crowd into the ring to urge their favourite on. Occasionally, they get too close for comfort to the tip of the bulls' horns and have to run like crazy with the bulls hot on their heels.

It's an interesting insight into local culture, and well worth going to see. If you want a good vantage spot, far enough away from the stampeding participants to be safe but close to the action, get there early.

Catch a bus or a bemo from Bukittinggi to Koto Baru for 200 rp. Give yourself time to check out the Tuesday market which has a small, but good selection of embroidered scarves and sarongs interwoven with gold threads. Follow the crowd down the steps (there are lots of them and they are quite daunting on the way back) and along a path through an exquisite terraced rice paddies until you arrive at the arena.

Other Activities Kite flying is a popular

pastime among adults and children. West Sumatrans make huge, colourful kites and many villages hold competitions throughout the year to see whose kite can fly the highest.

In the village of Limbuku, Payakumbuh (the only place in Sumatra where it occurs) they hold a novel duck race with ducks trained to fly a course! It is customary for the young village girls to attend the race dressed in traditional costume with the idea of attracting a suitor.

Festivals
Tabut At the historic seaside town of Pariaman, 36 km north of Padang, the colourful Islamic festival of Tabut is held once a year. It is celebrated in the month of Muharam (the first month of the Islamic lunar calendar) to honour Mohammed's grandchildren, Hassan and Hussein, who were killed in the Kerbala War defending the Muslim faith. Central to the festival is the *bouraq*, a winged horse-like creature with the head of a woman, which is believed to have descended to earth to collect the souls of the dead heroes and take them to heaven.

All the nearby villages construct effigies of bouraqs which they paint in vibrant reds, blues, greens and yellows and adorn with gold necklaces and other paraphernalia. The effigies are carried through the streets with much merriment, dancing and music and are finally tossed into the sea. Spectators and participants then dive into the water themselves and grab whatever remains of the bouraqs, the most valued memento being the gold necklace. When two bouraqs cross paths during the procession a mock fight ensues. Each group praises its own bouraq, belittling and insulting the other at the same time. So popular has this festival become, that people come from all over Indonesia to witness or take part in it. Admission to the area is by donation.

Other West Sumatran towns also celebrate Tabut, but usually on public holidays, such as Independence Day or Hero Day.

PADANG
Padang is a flat, sprawling city (the name means plain) which looks out across the Indian Ocean and has the Bukit Barisan as a backdrop. It is not only the capital of West Sumatra, but also the biggest seaport along the west coast, Sumatra's third largest city and the province's centre of business and government. For travellers from Java the port of Teluk Bayur is a major entry and exit point for Sumatra.

Although not particularly inspiring itself, Padang has some fine palm-fringed beaches nearby, the mountains a few hours away and the unique Mentawai Archipelago for the adventurous to explore. The road between Padang and Solok takes you through some of the most picturesque scenery in Sumatra, past exquisite examples of high-peaked Minangkabau houses and lush green carpets of terraced rice paddies. The final descent into Padang from Solok offers spectacular sweeping views along the coastline.

Orientation & Information
Padang is easy to find your way around and the central area is quite compact. Jalan Mohammed Yamin, from the bus station corner at Jalan Pemuda to Jalan Azizcham, is the main street of town. The main bus station and opelet station are both centrally located across from the market. We've received several letters from women travellers complaining that they were harassed in this town.

Tourist Office The Dinas Parawisata (tourist office) (☎ 28231) is at Jalan Khatib Sulaiman and is open from 8 am to 2 pm Monday to Thursday and Saturday, and from 8 to 11 am on Friday. It's a fair way out of the city centre. Take an opelet going up Jalan Sudirman and tell them where you're going, or look for a 269 mikrolet at the opelet station. The staff are very helpful and several can speak fairly good English. Make sure you make the effort to go to the tourist office if you plan to visit the Mentawai Archipelago. They have lots of information on the islands.

Money Bank Negara Indonesia 46 at Jalan Dobi 1 changes foreign cash and travellers' cheques. Moneychangers include C V Eka Jasa Utama at Jalan Niaga 241 and several others are in the market.

Post & Telephone The post office is at Jalan Azizchan 7, near the junction with Jalan Mohammed Yamin. The Perumtel telephone office is at Jalan Veteran 47.

Other If you need a good hospital you can try the privatly owned Ruman Sakit on Jalan Yos Sudarso.

Things to See

Padang itself does not have much to offer apart from Padang food, although in the harbour you can see the rusting remains of Dutch ships, sunk by the Japanese during WW II.

In the centre of town just down the road from the bus station is the **Adityawarman Museum** on Jalan Diponegoro, built in the Minangkabau tradition with two rice barns out the front. It has a small but excellent collection of antiques and other objects of historical and cultural interest from all over West Sumatra, and a particularly good textile room. The museum is open daily except Monday, from 9 am to 6 pm. Admission is 200 rp.

Next to the museum is the **Taman Budata** (Cultural Centre) where local, regional, national, traditional and modern music and dances are performed regularly. They also hold poetry readings, stage plays and exhibitions of paintings and carvings.

Festivals

Every year on 17 August, Padang holds a carnival and a huge and colourful boat race on the Sungai Batanghari to commemorate Independence Day. On 5 October the Islamic festival of Tabut commemorates the deaths of Mohammed's grandsons Hassan and Hussein.

Places to Stay – bottom end

Hotel Old Tiga Tiga (☎ 22633) is opposite the bus station at Jalan Pemuda 31. It's still a pretty bare and basic place with clean rooms at 6000 rp per person. In front there are some newer rooms with attached bathroom at 18,000/25,000 rp with fan/air-con. At No 27 is *Cendrawasih* (☎ 22894) with rooms from 6000/10,000 rp.

Hotel Benyamin (☎ 22324) is 100 metres down the lane next to Hotel Femina at Jalan Azizchan 15. The clean and airy rooms on the top floors are better than the dark and dingy rooms on the ground floor. They cost from 5500/11,000 rp.

The *Hotel Sriwijaya* (☎ 23577) at Jalan Alanglawas has clean singles/doubles from 6000/8000 rp. The rooms are simple but each has a little porch area. It's a quiet, small street, although not far from the centre.

Places to Stay – middle

The *Hang Tuah Hotel* (☎ 26556) is a modern hotel at Jalan Pemuda 1, right at the corner with Jalan Yamin. Rooms with a bathroom cost 11,000 to 15,000 rp with fan, 19,500 to 23,500 rp with air-con, plus tax. There's a second *Tiga Tiga* (☎ 22173) further out at Jalan Veteran 33; rooms in this newer hotel are from 15,000/20,000 rp.

Hotel Padang (☎ 22563), at Jalan Azizcham 28, has a large garden area and a variety of rooms starting from simple doubles with fan at 12,500 rp. Better rooms with a bathroom and a pleasant little porch out the front are 20,000 rp with fan, 40,000 rp with air-con.

Places to Stay – top end

The *Muara Hotel* (☎ 25600) at Jalan Gereja 34 is Padang's number one establishment, complete with swimming pool and rooms at 49,000 to 75,000 rp, plus tax.

Pangeran's Beach Hotel (☎ 31333), at Jalan Ir Juanda 79, is on the outskirts of Padang and on the road towards the airport. It's on the beach complete with a swimming pool, and rooms cost from 86,850 rp, plus tax.

Places to Eat

West Sumatra is renowned for its hot, spicy food known throughout Indonesia as Padang or Minang cooking. Basic ingredients are

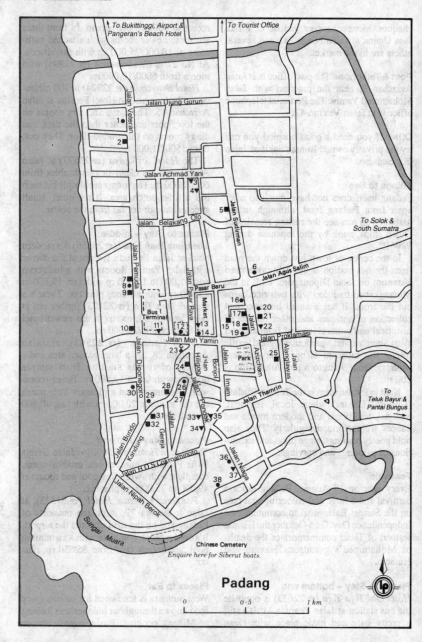

↑ To Bukittinggi, Airport &
Pangeran's Beach Hotel

↑ To Tourist Office

Jalan Veteran

Jalan Ujung Gurun

Jalan Achmad Yani

Jalan Belakang Olo

Jalan Sudirman

To Solok &
South Sumatra

Jalan Pemuda

Jalan Agus Salim

Jalan Pasar Baru

Jalan Pasar Raya

Market

Bus
Terminal

Jalan Moh Yamin

Jalan Diponegoro

Jalan Proklamasi

Jalan Alanglawas

Jalan

Park

Jalan Azizchan

Jalan Bonjol

Jalan Imam

Jalan Hiligoo

Jalan Thamrin

To
Teluk Bayur &
Pantai Bungus

Jalan Pondok

Jalan Gereja

Jalan Kandung

Jalan Bundo

Jalan H Cokroaminoto

Jalan Niaga

Jalan Nipah Berok

Sungai Muara

Chinese Cemetery
Enquire here for Siberut boats.

Padang

0   0.5   1 km

beef, mutton, fish, eggs and vegetables with lots of fiery red chillies tempered with turmeric and thick coconut milk. The most famous of the Padang dishes is rendang, chunks of beef or water buffalo cooked for days in coconut milk until the sauce is sludgy thick and the meat is black. In some places rendang is so hot you'd swear you'd received third degree burns to the throat – at least temporarily. Be cautious! Other dishes include eggs dusted in red chillies *(telor balado)*, fish *(ikan balado)* and a mutton stew *(gulai kambing)*.

There are no menus in a Padang restaurant. Dishes are placed on the table in small bowls – sometimes there could be as many as 10 different kinds of food to sample – with a big bowl of plain rice. You are not obliged to try them all and you only pay for what you eat. Specialties of the restaurant are often displayed in the front window so you can take a look at what you're going to eat before entering and go somewhere else if you don't like what you see. Don't be overly concerned about the odd fly cruising around the food on

display, you'll starve if you try to find a restaurant without flies. Fresh fruit, usually pineapple and bananas, is offered for dessert.

Some of the well-known Padang food specialists include the *Roda Baru*, upstairs at Jalan Pasar Raya 6, in the market buildings. And *Simpang Raya* at Jalan Azizcham 24, opposite the post office. *Pagi Sore* (Morning Evening) is down towards the end of Jalan Pondok at No 143.

There are also some Chinese-Indonesian restaurants, particularly along Jalan Pondok and Jalan Niaga. *Restaurant Octavia* at Jalan Pondok 137 is a simple little place with the standard nasi goreng, mie goreng menu. Across the road is *Chan's* at No 94 with live music at night, and the *Ri & Ri* at No 86A.

Towards the end of Jalan Niaga is the *Aromey Bakery* with good baked goods. Or try the *Restoran Kubang* at Jalan Mohammed Yamin 138 near the bus station. They really turn out the martabaks here and it's a busy scene with tables set up across the pavement and lots of obviously satisfied customers. There are also several big restaurants like the *Taman Sari* and *Tanpa Nama* along Jalan Ahmad Yani north of the centre.

Getting There & Away

Air Garuda/Merpati and Mandala have flights to and from Padang. You can arrive in Indonesia at Padang since Garuda connects it with Singapore.

Merpati (☎ 32010) is at Jalan Sudirman 2. Garuda/Merpati has flights from Padang to many other parts of Indonesia, including Bandarlampung, Batam, Jakarta (222,000 rp), Medan, Palembang and Pakanbaru.

Mandala (☎ 21979) is at Jalan Pemuda 29A. Mandala has daily flights from Padang to Jakarta. Merpati has a flight once a week from Padang to Pulau Siberut.

Bus The Padang bus station is conveniently central and there are frequent departures for buses north and south.

There are frequent buses to Bukittinggi. The PTNPM bus is a good one to take and it leaves by the side of the Hang Tuah Hotel. The trip costs 1300 rp and takes about 2½ hours along a good road with wonderful scenery. If you arrive in Padang by air there's no need to go into town as the main road with buses bound for Bukittinggi is only 100 metres from the airport terminal.

From the city bus station there are buses to: Jambi (7500 rp, 12 hours), Palembang (18,100, or 21,500 rp with air-con, 24 hours), Pakanbaru (5100 rp), Parapat (10,000 rp), and Jakarta (19,100, or 49,100 rp with air-con).

You can also take long-distance taxis from Padang. Check with Natrabu at Jalan Pemuda 29B.

Train The railway line from Padang to Bukittinggi used to be quite an attraction for railway enthusiasts, but now it's only used as far as Padangpanjang and only for freight trains. You can see some old steam engines permanently parked at Padang Panjang. The line beyond here is spectacular, crossing and recrossing the road, but derelict and overgrown. Tourist groups often charter a train.

Boat The Pelni ship *Kerinci* operates a regular Jakarta-Padang-Sibolga service, twice a month. Jakarta to Padang takes about 27 hours and costs from 40,200 to 132,700 rp. The Pelni office (☎ 22109) is on Jalan Tanjung Priok, Teluk Bayur.

There are occasional ships from Padang to Bengkulu and Pulau Nias and a regular shipping service from Padang to Pulau Siberut.

Getting Around

To/From the Airport Padang's Tabing Airport is nine km north of the centre on the Bukittinggi road. The standard taxi fare into town is 8000 rp, but you can walk 100 metres out to the road and catch an opelet for 150 rp, or head straight north to Bukittinggi.

Local Transport There are numerous opelets and mikrolets around town. Their station is Pasar Raya at Jalan Mohammed Yamin. The standard fare is 150 rp. Dokars are also numerous in town and cost 750 rp. There's a taxi stand beside the market building on the corner of Jalan Mohammed Yamin.

AROUND PADANG
Air Manis

Four km south of Padang is the fishing village Air Manis, which literally means 'sweet water'. To get there take a bemo to Muaro, then hire a *prahu* across the river and walk up to the Chinese cemetery which overlooks the town. A one-km walk will take you to the village of Air Manis. There at low tide you can wade out to a small island or take a sampan to a larger one. According to local mythology, the rock at the end of the beach is all that remains of Malin Kundang (a man who was transformed into stone when he rejected his mother after making a fortune) and his boat.

Climb the hill beyond Air Manis for a good view of the port of Teluk Bayur. You can walk to Teluk Bayur, take a look around the harbour and from there get an opelet for 300 rp into the city centre. In the village you can stay at cheerful Papa Chili-Chili's, and yes, his food is hot! It costs 3000 rp per person plus food.

Beaches

Taman Nirwana is not a bad beach 12 km south of Padang. Bungus, 22 km south of Padang, was a nice palm-fringed beach until they built a timber mill there. Pasir Putih is a good beach 24 km from Padang where you can stay at Losmen Tin Tin at a cost of 5000 rp per double. Opelets run between Pasir Putih and Padang all day – they cost 400 rp.

Islands

There are four islands: Pisang Besar, Sikoai, Padang and Bintangur (all within easy reach of Padang and not too expensive to get to) where you can indulge in the life of a lotus-eater. All four offer good skin-diving and snorkelling opportunities, lots of fish and coconut palms. Although it's not difficult to catch your own dinner, take food with you. There are camping grounds on each island and fresh water is available.

The closest island is Pulau Pisang Besar (Big Banana Island), which is only 15 minutes from Muara river harbour. Hire a sampan with an outboard motor from there. The others are between one and two hours from Teluk Bayur. You can arrange to be dropped off and picked up at a stipulated time a few days later. Ask the harbour master who to approach to take you out to whichever island you choose. It's best to organise a few people to go on this trip. A sampan to carry up to eight passengers with reasonable comfort will cost about 30,000 rp to charter.

Contact the Tourist Information Centre in Padang for more information if you are interested in staying on one of these islands.

PADANG TO BUKITTINGGI

The 90-km drive north from Padang to Bukittinggi is lyrically beautiful with its pastiche of rice paddies, Minangkabau houses, glimpses of the sea and views of the towering Singgalang and Merapi volcanoes – each almost 3000 metres high. (Merapi last erupted in 1926.) Along this route is the Lembah Anai Nature Reserve, renowned for its waterfalls, wild orchids and the giant Rafflesia flowers. Danau Singkarak, which is bigger than Danau Maninjau and with fewer tourists, is nearby.

PADANGPANJANG

Padangpanjang is the main town that the Padang to Bukittinggi road passes through. It's interesting for its conservatorium of Minangkabau culture, dance and music – the ASKI. This is the best place to get accurate information on live dance and theatre performances. It has a fine collection of musical instruments which includes Minangkabau and Javanese gamelan outfits. There are also excellent costume displays, which are particularly interesting for the bridal jewellery and ornaments like the headdress, necklace and the deceptively light bracelet called *galang-gadang*.

Places to Stay

If you need a place to stay try *Hotel Makmur* (☎ 140), at Jalan K H A Dahlan 34, where a room per person is 3500 rp.

Getting There & Away

Padangpanjang is a good afternoon or morning trip from either Padang or Bukittinggi. There are regular buses between Bukittinggi, Padang and Padangpanjang. Passenger trains no longer run between Padang and Bukittinggi but there is still an ancient steam train that hauls coal up and down the line. Try hitching; a good short trip can be made between Koto Baru and Padangpanjang.

BUKITTINGGI

This cool, easy-going mountain town (about 900 metres above sea level) is one of the most popular tourist destinations in Sumatra. It's often called Kota Jam Gadang, the Big Ben Town, because of the clock tower that overlooks the large market square. Bukittinggi is known locally as Tri Arga, after the three majestic mountains that encircle it – Merapi, Singgalang and Sago. A Dutch stronghold during the Padri rebellion (1821-37), Bukittinggi is today the cultural

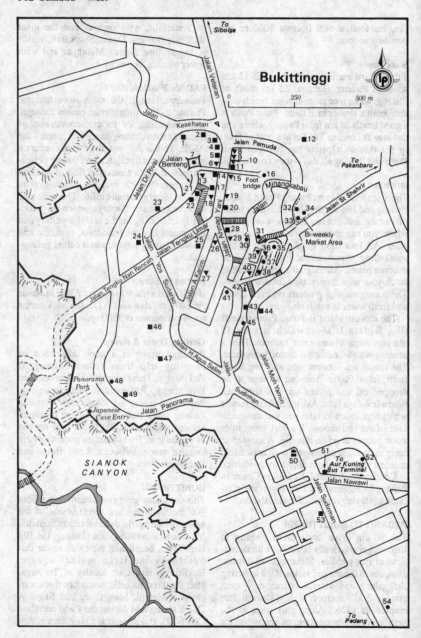

Bukittinggi

0   250   500 m

and educational centre of the Minangkabau people.

Orientation & Information

The centre of town is compact and the rusty iron roofs make it look remarkably like hill station towns in India. Like them the different levels of streets connected by steps make it initially a bit confusing. Jalan Yamin is also known as Jalan Perintis Kemerdekan.

Tourist Office The tourist office is beside the market car park, overlooked by the clock tower. They have a few leaflets, maps and brochures on West Sumatra and they are open from Monday to Thursday from 8 am to 2 pm, Friday from 8 to 11 am, and Saturday from 8 am to 12.30 pm.

Money There's a Bank Negara Indonesia in the Pasar Atas (market) building. You can also change money at the Toko Eka on Jalan Minangkabau, in the central market.

Post & Telecommunications The post office is on Jalan Jenderal Sudirman 75. A small branch is next to the tourist office. The 24-hour telephone office is at Jalan Ahmad Yani, next to the Grand Hotel.

Travel Agencies You'll easily find travel agents who charge 4000 rp to take people to see the bullfight, even though a round trip by opelet, including the entry fee only costs 1500 rp. Also, don't go on trips to Pulau Siberut with locals from Bukittinggi as they usually are ignorant of the island's culture

■ PLACES TO STAY	
1	Hotel Denai
2	Lima's Hotel
3	Sri Kandi Hotel
4	Murni's Hotel
5	Nirwana Hotel
11	Singgalang Hotel
12	Tropic Hotel
14	Hotel Yany
17	Grand Hotel & 24-hour Telephone Office
20	Tigo Balai Hotel
21	Benteng Hotel
22	Suwarni Guesthouse
23	Mountain View Guesthouse
24	Wisma Bukittinggi
25	Surya Hotel
28	Gangga Hotel
43	Hotel Jogja
44	Hotel Antokan
46	Gallery Hotel
47	Sumatera Hotel
49	Minang Hotel
51	Dymen's Hotel
53	Bagindo Hotel

▼ PLACES TO EAT	
6	The Coffee House
8	Rendezvous Coffee Shop
9	Three Tables Coffee House
10	Mexican Coffee Shop
13	Famili Restaurant
15	Bukittinggi Coffee Shop
18	Jazz & Blues Coffee Shop
19	Golden Leaf Restaurant
26	Singgalang Coffee Shop
27	ASEAN Restaurant
29	Mona Lisa Restaurant
36	Roda Group Restaurant
39	Simpang Raya Restaurant
40	Simpang Raya Restaurant

OTHER	
7	Fort de Kock
16	Zoo & Museum
30	Mosque
31	Gloria Cinema
32	Roda Barn
33	Pasar Bawar (Market)
34	Bemo & Opelet Station
35	Pasar Wisata
37	Pasar Atas
38	Bank Negara Indonesia
41	Clocktower
42	Tourist Office & Small Post Office
45	Medan Nan Balituduang (Saliguri Dance Group)
48	Military Museum
50	Post Office
52	Telephone Office
54	Police

and language, which means you'll miss out on a unique experience.

Market

Bukittinggi's large and colourful market is crammed with stalls of fruit and vegetables, clothing and crafts. Market days are Wednesdays and Saturdays.

Museum & Zoo

On a hill-top site right in the centre of town is Taman Bundokanduag, a museum and zoo. The museum, which was built in 1934 by the Dutch 'Controleur' of the district, is a superb example of Minangkabau architecture with its two rice barns (added in 1956) out the front. It is the oldest museum in the province and has a good collection of Minangkabau historical and cultural exhibits. The zoo is disgusting – the best thing you could do for its inmates would be to shoot them, or get the warders to stay in the cells. All visitors are required to pay the 600 rp entry fee to the zoo to see the museum, where another fee of 200 rp is charged.

Fort de Kock

Except for the defence moat and a few cannons, not much remains of Bukittinggi's old Fort de Kock, built during the Padri Wars (1821-1837) by the Dutch. It provides fine views over the town and surrounding countryside from its hill-top position. The entry fee is 200 rp.

Panorama Park & Japanese Caves

Panorama Park, on the southern edge of the town, overlooks the deep Sianok Canyon that cuts right into Bukittinggi. From the park you can enter the extensive grid of caves which the Japanese tunnelled out during WW II. Many of the tunnels look out from the cliff faces over the canyon. Entry to the Japanese Caves (Lobang Jepang) is 250 rp. At the entrance there's a bas-relief showing the Japanese herding the helpless Indonesians inside.

Military Museum

Next to the Minang Hotel and overlooking Panorama Park is the Military Museum, which mainly houses a collection of faded photographs from the independence war against the Dutch. Of particular interest are photos of the bodies of the five Indonesian generals murdered at the time of the supposed Communist-led attempted coup of 1965, plus war souvenirs and photos from Indonesia's war against the Fretilin guerrillas in East Timor. The entry fee is a donation.

Organised Tours

It's easy to get tours of the area. Ask around in the coffee shops, restaurants and hotels along Jalan Ahmad Yani. They organise tours of the local area, usually on Tuesdays and Saturdays when the bullfighting takes place. A great deal depends on the guide you get. There are a few good guides who are informative and knowledgeable, but others can only provide some basic translation.

If you take these tours for what they really are – a quick way of getting a glimpse of a lot of places – and then go back for a better look at the places you found interesting, they're worthwhile. Sometimes they take you to places like blacksmithing homesteads and sugar cane crushing works that you wouldn't have known existed unless someone showed you. Recently there have also been tours on Sunday to see a pig hunt, for 29,000 rp.

Places to Stay – bottom end

Bukittinggi's cheap hotels are a pretty plain, dull and charmless lot although they're certainly cheap. Most of them are concentrated along Jalan Ahmad Yani, right in the centre of town. *Murni's* at No 115 has plain but clean singles/doubles at 3500/5000 rp and a nice sitting area upstairs. The similarly priced *Nirwana's* (☎ 21292) is right next door at No 113. The *Singgalang Hotel* (☎ 21576) at No 130 is also plain and basic with rooms at 5000 rp.

The *Tigo Balai Hotel* (☎ 21824), at Jalan Ahmad Yani 100, is a rock-bottom rabbit warren with musty rooms for 3500 rp. It's the same story with *Hotel Yany* (☎ 22740) at Jalan Ahmad Yani 101 which seems to be an old colonial building gone to rack and ruin. Shabby, box-like rooms are 3000 rp per person.

The *Grand Hotel* (☎ 2133) at Jalan Ahmad Yani 99 is a fairly clean, agreeable and quiet hotel. It has some dingy ground-floor rooms for 5000 rp, but there are some better upstairs rooms for 10,000 rp.

Wisma Bukittinggi (☎ 22900) at Jalan Yos Sudarso 1A has single and double rooms from 6000 to 7000 rp. The quiet *Suwarni's* at Jalan Benteng 2B has dorm beds or rooms at 7000 or 8000 rp.

Places to Stay – middle

On the way up to Fort de Kock is the *Mountain View Guesthouse* (☎ 21621) at Jalan Yos Sudarso 3. It is a pleasant place with rooms at 15,000 rp with mandi.

There are few new hotels in town that are reasonable. The *Tropic Hotel* at Jalan Pemuda 20, is actually off the street in a little lane down the hill. The hotel is visible from Jalan Pemuda. There are small rooms for 5000/9000 rp and large clean ones with mandi for 10,000/15,000 rp.

Two other hotels are on top of the hill off the Jalan H Agus Salim. *Sumatera Hotel* (☎ 21309) is at Jalan Dr Setia Budhi 16E, and is a quiet place with a friendly manager. Rooms cost from 5000/8000 rp to 15,000/17,500 rp. Close by is *Gallery Hotel* at Jalan H Agus Salim 25, where rooms are from 5000/7500 rp to 27,000/30,000 rp, and dorms are 3500 rp.

Places to Stay – top end

Hotel Jogja (☎ 21142) is directly below the market and clock tower at Jalan Mohammed Yamin 17. There are straightforward rooms upstairs for 7500/13,000 rp (poor value for two people) and downstairs rooms with mandi from 15,000/20,000 rp and deluxe rooms for 25,000/30,000 rp.

The *Benteng Hotel* (☎ 21115) at Jalan Benteng 1 (the road leading up to what remains of the old fort), has good views of the town. It has nice rooms from 18,000/ 20,000 to 50,000 rp, plus tax.

Lima's Hotel (☎ 22641, 22763) at Jalan

Kesehatan 34 has rooms at 17,500 rp or with bathroom at 27,500 rp and 40,000 rp, plus tax. It's modern, but the rooms are rather cramped.

A very fine place is *Dymen's Hotel* (☎ 21015) at Jalan Nawawi 3. It has rooms from 50,000 rp, plus tax.

The *Hotel Denai* (☎ 21524) at Jalan Dr Rivai 26 has rooms from 52,670 rp, plus tax. It's a very commodious hotel, with very comfortable rooms as well as several cottages in traditional Minangkabau style.

Places to Eat

In amongst the cheap hotels along Jalan Ahmad Yani are many very popular restaurants with menus which feature all those familiar travellers' specials from fruit salad to banana pancakes. The *Coffee House* at No 103 is small and has a pleasant outdoor area overlooking the street. The *Three Tables Coffee House* at No 142 is a bit bigger (there are more than three tables) and equally popular. Next door are two identical places the *Mexican* and *Rendezvous*. Near the Grand Hotel are two more places – the *Bukittinggi* and *Jazz & Blues*.

Further down at Jalan Ahmad Yani 58 is the *Mona Lisa*, a tiny place with a good Chinese-influenced menu. Just off that street, at Jalan Tengku Umar, is the popular *Canyon Coffee House* that also provides tourist information.

Padang food is important in Bukittinggi and the *Roda Group Restaurant* in the Pasar Atas market building has good food. Directly across from it is *Kedai Kopi Sianok* where you can sample the local sweet *sarikaya* (custard on top of bread or rice), which tastes better than it sounds.

In the Pasar Wisata building (right next to the Pasar Atas building) there are more restaurants and warungs, including a branch of the *Simpang Raya* nasi Padang restaurants at each end of the block. Up on the Fort de Kock hill, right at the top of the road, the *Famili Restaurant* also does pretty good Padang food.

A number of places in Bukittinggi, including the Western-oriented coffee houses, do the local speciality *dadhi campur*, a tasty mixture of oats, coconut, avocado, banana, molasses and buffalo yoghurt.

Things to Buy

Bukittinggi is one of the more pleasing parts of Indonesia to accumulate handicrafts and souvenirs which are for the most part attractive and in good taste. There are a number of antique, souvenir and curio shops around. Try Kerajinan at Jalan Ahmad Yani 44, and Aladdin at Jalan Jenderal Ahmad Yani 14. There are more around the market area.

Some interesting Minangkabau artefacts are *salapah panjang*, or long boxes, which are brass boxes used for storing lime and tobacco. *Salapah padusi* are silver boxes used for storing betel nut and lime (although, of course, the silver is not always real).

Another form of Minangkabau weaving, though one you're probably not likely to find any examples of, uses a technique called 'needle weaving'. In this process, certain threads of the cloth are removed and the remaining ones stitched together to form patterns. These patterns may include identifiable motifs such as people, crabs, insects, dogs or horses. Traditionally, such cloth is used to cover the *carano* – a brass sireh stand with receptacles for betel nut, tobacco, lime – which is used for ceremonial occasions.

Songket cloth is distinguished by the silver and gold threads which are woven into the fabric. Although it would be possible to get cloth with genuine silver and gold thread, all the stuff you commonly see for sale around Bukittinggi uses imitation silver and gold thread imported from India. However, even cloth using imitation thread is moderately expensive because of the amount of time and work involved in weaving it.

Songket cloth is made in the Tanah Datar region in the villages of Pandai Sikat and Tanjung Sungayang. Also worth trying is Sungayang, near Batu Sangkar. Pandai Sikat is easy to get to from Bukittinggi. Take a bemo for 200 rp from the main bus station and get off at the Pandai Sikat turnoff (half an hour down the road towards Padang-

Panjang). From there it's half an hour's walk to the village. Pandai Sikat has many workshops making songket cloth and the finely carved furniture for which this village is also known.

In the region of Lima Puluh Kota, near the border with Riau Province, traditional weaving is done in several villages. Commercial weaving is done in Kubang, 13 km from the town of Payakumbuh. Ceremonial cloth is produced at Silungkang. Other weaving villages in this area include Balai Cacang, Koto Nan Ampek, and Muaro.

The Minangkabau are also noted for their fine embroidery work. Villages which specialise in this are Koto Gadang, Ampek Angkek, Naras, Lubuk Begalung, Kota Nan Ampek and Sunguyang.

Getting There & Away

Bus The Air Kuning Bus Station is some distance from the town centre but you can get there easily on the local opelets.

Padang is only about 2½ hours south of Bukittinggi. The road north to Sibolga and Parapat has improved considerably over the years; regular buses make the trip to Parapat in 15 hours, although heavy rain can still cause big problems.

A special tourist bus operates several times a week to Parapat, and stops at the equator and the hot springs. It costs 20,000 rp and takes 12 to 13 hours. The tourist buses can be booked at the numerous travel agents and coffee houses. However, travel agents and coffee houses can charge up to 40% more for bus tickets. They also overcharge for the Padang to Jakarta boat and are reluctant to book berths.

It is advisable to buy your bus tickets at the bus station. ANS (☎ 21679) have an office at the bus station.

Typical bus fares from Bukittinggi are: Sibolga 7000 rp, Parapat 11,000 rp, Medan 12,500 rp (or 17,500 rp with an air-con bus), Padang 1300 rp, Pakanbaru 4000 rp, Jakarta 23,000 rp (or 49,000 rp with an air-con bus).

Train The old steam trains on this route no longer carry passengers. However, railway enthusiasts may be able to organise a ride on the freight trains.

Getting Around

The main bemo, dokar and opelet station is in the middle of town. From here you catch one of these to the Air Kuning Bus Station (Bukittinggi's main station just on the outskirts of town). Opelets around town cost a flat 150 rp, and dokars are 500 to 750 rp.

AROUND BUKITTINGGI

Koto Gadang

There is a path through the Sianok Canyon to the other side and on to the village of Koto Gadang. There are two different ways to go. The longer way is along the river bed. Turn left at the bottom of the road just before the canyon and the asphalt bridge, and keep going. The shorter way, taking 1½ hours, follows the same route as the longer walk until you reach the river in the canyon. Here you cross on the bamboo bridge and go up the steps. No guide is necessary for either walk. There have been a few reports of travellers being harassed while walking through the canyon, and some lone female travellers being chased by local men.

Koto Gadang is noted for its silverwork, which, though exquisite, is limited in range. It is about 10 km south-west of Bukittinggi.

Pandai Sikat

There are several other villages around Bukittinggi which are still producing traditional crafts. One of the more interesting is Pandai Sikat, 13 km south of Bukittinggi, a centre for weaving and wood carving.

Ngalau Kamanga

Ngalau Kamanga, 15 km north-east of Bukittinggi, was the scene of active resistance against the Dutch in the 19th and early 20th centuries. The story goes that the villagers used a 1500-metre-long local cave as a hide-out from the Dutch, conducting effective guerrilla attacks in the surrounding country from this base. The cave is dripping with stalactites and stalagmites and has a small, clear lake.

Around Bukittinggi

Koto Baru

Bullfights are held every Saturday afternoon around 5 pm in the village of Koto Baru. Entry fee is 500 rp. The fight is known as adu sapi and involves two water buffaloes of roughly the same size and weight locking horns under the watchful eyes of their respective owners. Most of the fun is in watching the locals make their bets. Once the fight starts it continues until one of the bulls breaks away and runs out of the ring – which usually results in two bulls chasing each other around and the onlookers running in every direction. Opelets run to Koto Baru regularly and cost 350 rp.

Air Angat

The village Air Angat is near Koto Baru. Bullfights are held here on Tuesday afternoons around 4 pm.

Batu Sangkar

About 45 km south-east of Bukittinggi, off the Padangpanjang-Solok road, is the village of Batu Sangkar. Turn off the road towards the village of Pagaruyang (four km distance) and you'll see many Minangkabau houses.

Along the roadside are stone tablets inscribed in Sanskrit.

Rafflesia Sanctuary

There is a Rafflesia sanctuary about 15 km north of Batu Sangkar; a sign at the village of Batang Palupuh indicates the path. The Rafflesia blooms between August and December. Further north on the way to Sibolga, a large globe stands in a rice paddy beside the road, indicating the position of the equator. Up this way there's horse racing on Sundays, definitely not the Grand National or the Melbourne Cup, but lots of fun.

Gunung Merapi

Gunung Merapi can be climbed, but it is an active volcano and therefore occasionally it's off limits to climbers. Most people climb at night. The path is clear and no guide is necessary. The tourist office in Bukittinggi will tell you the mountain is off limits, but will offer their services as guides! To get there take a bus towards Padangpanjang and get off at the Koto Baru turnoff. From Koto Baru it's a one-hour climb to the forestry station (which is a hut minus the walls) and then another four hours to the top.

Harau Valley

To get to the Harau Valley, first take a bus to Payakumbuh. Then take a bemo across town to the market. From here you get another bemo to Harau Valley or to Sari Lamak (from here it's a five-km walk to the valley). The valley is more of a canyon, with a waterfall cascading down one side. On Sundays it's very crowded with Indonesian day-trippers, although this may be the only day you can get transport the whole way out there. You can walk to Harau village which is three km up the valley.

Other Attractions

Other attractions include **Sungai Tarab** where you can see coffee mills worked by waterwheel. **Pagaruyang** has a reconstruction of a massive Minangkabau king's house. Nearby is **Lima Kaum** where there are a number of stones carved with ancient San-

skrit writing. The village of **Balimbing** is noted for its fine Minangkabau traditional houses. On Wednesday and Saturday mornings there are displays of traditional Minangkabau self-defence at **Ujung Bukit**.

DANAU MANINJAU

About 30 km south-west of Bukittinggi is Lawang Top and directly below it, Danau Maninjau. The final descent to the lake involves covering 12 km with four-score hairpin bends, while enjoying great views of the lake and the surrounding area. The lake is 17 km long, eight km wide and 480 metres deep at its broadest points.

Danau Maninjau is warmer than Toba and is an extremely beautiful crater lake. It's good for swimming and boating. Hire a dugout canoe or an inflated tractor tube from some of the guest houses. There are several nice walks around the lake area that are popular. Most are through the jungle like the Sakura Hill Track. From Sakura Hill it's a short walk to the Lawang Top where there is a small restaurant. From both points there are excellent views of the lake and the surrounding area. The fewer people in your group the more wildlife you'll see. Of course, as in most places in Sumatra, there are hot springs about 500 metres from the town of Maninjau, and further on there is a waterfall.

Orientation & Information

Most people arrive here from Bukittinggi. The bus stop is at the T-intersection where the Bukittinggi road meets the main street of Maninjau, near the Guemala Coffee Shop. If you are facing the lake the street straight ahead has the post, telephone and police offices. At the end of the street on the edge of the lake is the expensive Maninjau Indas Hotel. Still facing the lake from the Guemala Coffee Shop on the left is Jalan H Udin Rahmani where the market, some restaurants and guest houses are. On your right are more guest houses, most of which are built on the lake's edge.

Beware of the 'horse hair hat' scam, when locals will try to persuade travellers that the hat is unique and worth 20,000 rp, while in actual fact it is only worth 5000 rp.

Places to Stay

There are 13 guesthouses and two hotels in Maninjau. Many of the guesthouses are very similar and basic, but not all are positioned on the banks of the lake. Most people wash in the lake, but each guest house also has a mandi.

The bulk of the guesthouses are on the right hand side of the T-intersection. The first guest house is the *Muaro Pysang*, followed by the small but clean *Della Villa*. Further on the edge of the lake is the friendly *Beach Guesthouse* where the owners provide plenty of information, and rent canoes. A bed in the teak house is 3000 rp, and bungalows cost 6000 rp.

About half a km further is *Hotel Pasir Panjang Permai* (☎ 22), an expensive place that provides TV, and a bath with hot and cold water. All the rooms look out over the lake where you can also go for a swim. Rooms cost from 35,000/45,000 rp. Almost next door is the basic *Abang*, followed by the popular *Palentha* where rooms on the lake cost 4000/5000 rp.

Maninjau Indas Hotel (☎ 18) is near the T-intersection. Their basic rooms start at 20,000 rp but aren't good value; their better rooms cost from 30,000 rp.

There are three guest houses and several restaurants on the right hand side of the T-intersection. The *Amai Cheap* (☎ 54) is an old colonial Dutch house with a nice balcony, and a friendly and helpful owner. Large and clean rooms cost 3000/4000 rp and 5000 rp. Nearby is *Srikandi Home Stay* with similarly priced rooms. Further down is *Pillie* where rooms are 4000/6000 rp. Past the mosque is the cheap *Nuaroindah* where a bed costs 2000 rp.

Places to Eat

Most guest houses can provide some basic meals like mie or nasi goreng. There are several restaurants in Maninjau but *The Three Tables Coffee House* and *Srikandi* restaurant in the guest house of the same name,

stand out above the rest as far as the food is concerned. They both have the usual travel menus, but are much better value than the similar places in Bukittinggi.

Getting There & Around

You can take a bus there direct from Bukittinggi for 700 rp, taking about half an hour. Or get off at Matur, climb to Lawang Top for the view and then walk down to the lake, which takes a couple of hours if you're fit and much longer if you're not. In Maninjau there are plenty of places that rent mountain bikes and motorbikes.

The Mentawai Islands

Not far off the west coast of mainland Sumatra, in the Indian Ocean, are the islands of the Mentawai Archipelago. The four islands in the group – Siberut, Sipora, Utara and Selatau – are almost entirely surrounded by coral reefs. The largest is Siberut. Over 30,000 people live on the islands, the majority of them on Siberut. The closest major port is Padang's Teluk Bayur, which is only 150 km away from Siberut.

History

Very little is known about the origins of the Mentawaians but it is assumed that they emigrated from Sumatra to Nias and made their way to Siberut from there. They remained isolated and undisturbed by other cultures until late in the 19th century when the Dutch permitted Protestant missionaries to attempt to convert them to Christianity.

There are several references to the islands before the 19th century. In 1621, it appears that Siberut was the only island inhabited. The Mentawaians are also mentioned in a scientific paper presented in 1799 by the Englishman John Crisp. Sir Stamford Raffles appears to have been particularly impressed by the Mentawaians and their culture. In one of the many reports he wrote urging the British government to compete

Mentawai Islands

0   20   40 km

with the Dutch in colonising Indonesia he says:

Formerly, I intended to write a book to prove that the Niassans were the most contented people on earth. Now I have to acknowledge the fact that the people of the Mentawai Islands are even more admirable and probably much less spoiled than we.

In 1864 the Mentawai Archipelago was nominally made a Dutch colony, but it was not until 1901, at the time of the Russo-Japanese war, that the Dutch placed a garrison on the islands to prevent another foreign power using them as a naval base.

Economy

Agriculture Taros and bananas are the staple crops of both the Pagai islands and Sipora, while on Siberut sago is also cultivated. Traditionally, the women own the taro fields and are responsible for planting and maintaining them. The taros are planted under water in loose, marshy earth and it takes a year before they can be eaten. The banana plantations belong to the men – some are worked by one or two families, others by an entire *uma* (communal house). The Mentawaians also grow cassava, sweet potatoes and other crops. Their diet is supplemented by hunting and fishing.

People

Although the distance between mainland Sumatra and the Mentawai Islands is not great – strong winds, unpredictable seas and coral reefs made navigation to the islands difficult in earlier centuries. The result was that the inhabitants of the Mentawaians had very little contact with the outside world and remained one of the purest indigenous Indonesian societies until early in the 20th century when the missionaries arrived. They had their own language, their own adat and their own religion. They were skilled in boat building, but had not developed any kind of handicraft nor cultivated rice.

Physically, the Mentawaians are slim and agile. Traditional clothing consists of a loin cloth made from the bark of the breadfruit

Banana palm

tree for men and a bark skirt for women. They sharpen their teeth and decorate themselves with tattoos which cover part of their faces and most of their bodies and wear bands of red-coloured rattan, beads and imported brass rings on their arms, fingers and toes. Both men and women often thread flowers through their long hair. The government has banned tattoos, sharpened teeth and long hair, and although the ban has not been enforced it's rare to see people looking like this, especially in the more accessible villages.

Culture

Villages are built along river banks and consist of one or more communal houses (uma) surrounded by single-storey family houses *(lalep)*. A number of families (between five and 10) live in the same building. Bachelors and widows have their own living quarters, known as *rusuk*, which are identical to the family longhouse except that they have no altar. Traditionally all the houses stand on wooden piles and are designed without windows.

Although it is essentially a patriarchal society, it is organised on egalitarian princi-

ples. There are no inherited titles or positions, and no subordinate roles. It is the uma, not the village itself, which becomes the pivot of social, political and religious life in Mentawai society. It is here that discussions affecting the community take place. Everyone – men, women and children – are present at meetings, but the prominent men make most of the major decisions, including choosing a *rimata* (the person who leads religious affairs and is the community's spokesperson to the outside world), building an uma, clearing forests, or laying out a banana plantation.

On such occasions the people of the uma carry out a religious festival known as *punen*. This usually involves ritual sacrifices of both pigs and chickens and, depending on the importance of the occasion, can last for months on end and sometimes years. All kinds of everyday jobs and activities become taboo; work in the fields is stopped and strangers are denied access to the uma – its isolation being marked by a cordon of palm leaves and flowers.

Religion

Indigenous Religion The native Sibulungan religion was a form of animism, involving the worship of nature spirits and a belief in the existence of ghosts as well as the soul. The chief nature spirits are those in the sky, sea, jungle and earth. There are also two river spirits: Ina Oinan (mother of rivers) is beneficent while Kameinan (father's sister) is regarded as being evil. Apart from these nature spirits all inanimate objects have spirits or kina which give them life. There is no hierarchy among the spirits, although the sky spirits are considered the most influential, nor do they have any particular gender, but like human beings there's a mixture of men, women and children.

As with all religions in Indonesia, the worship of the soul is of the utmost importance, being vital to good health and longevity. The soul is believed to depart the body at various times during life before its ultimate escape at death. Sickness, for example, is the result of the temporary absence of the soul from the body, while dreams also signify that the soul is on 'vacation'. When the soul leaves the body at death it is transformed into a ghost (sanitu). Mentawaians try to avoid these ghosts, whom they suspect of malevolently attempting to rob the living of their souls. To protect themselves from such an awful fate, they place fetish sticks at every entrance to the village. This tactic is considered foolproof, provided no-one has committed a ritual sin or broken a taboo.

Introduction of Other Religions Apart from taking a few minor precautions to protect the Mentawai Islands from being taken over by any other imperialist nations, the Dutch showed very little interest in them. It was the missionaries who had the most influence on the people, creating fundamental changes in their culture.

The first permanent mission was set up in 1901 in Pagai Utara by a German missionary, August Lett. Eight years later, Lett was murdered by the local people but the mission survived and by 1916 there had been 11 baptisms recorded. There are now more than 80 Protestant churches throughout the islands. Over half the population claims to be Protestant, 16% to be Catholic, 13% Muslim, while the rest have no official religion.

It was over 50 years after the advent of the Protestant missionaries that the Catholics moved into the islands to vie for converts. They opened a mission in south Siberut which combined a church, a school and a clinic. Free medicines and clothes were given to any islander who became a Catholic and by 1969 there were almost 3000 converts.

The Islamic influence began to make inroads once government officials were regularly appointed from Padang during the Dutch era. To complicate religious matters further, the eclectic Baha'i faith was introduced in 1955.

SIBERUT
In the past only a few adventurous foreigners

visited Siberut, but it's now becoming increasingly popular as people seek out areas relatively untouched by tourism. Although Siberut is being promoted as a tourist destination, the deluge is not likely to happen overnight. There is no public transport, only one hotel and a handful of restaurants. However, the government's resettlement policy and the activities of timber felling companies have already created enormous changes in the living conditions of the local people and in the flora and fauna.

Information
Try to minimise your impact on the local culture and lifestyle. Remember the introduction of money and foreign goods takes the people away from their traditional way of life, so don't give anything to the locals just because they ask you to. Most already think that many white people are rich fools as they seem to part with anything asked of them.

Climate Heavy rains occur in April and May, and October and November, but at any time of the year you can expect heavy rains on Siberut. The treks usually include plenty of mud slogging, river crossings and battles with indigenous insects, so it's definitely not a casual hiking experience. The seas can get very rough between May and July, and getting to and around the island can be dangerous at this time.

Money & Costs Take plenty of cash as there are no banks on the island and you cannot change foreign cash or travellers' cheques there. In Muarasiberut cash is the everyday currency, but in most other villages the people may prefer food, tobacco and tools. The biggest expense on the island is the cost of getting around.

A visit to an off-the-beaten-track village, including the boat fare to the island, fees for the local guide, accommodation, food and presents for the villagers cost about 250,000 rp for two people for a three-week visit. You can buy most supplies in Muarasiberut and

Muarasikabaluan, but they are much cheaper if bought in Padang.

Presents should not be given to just anyone, even though you will be constantly asked for them. It is best to refuse all requests, except for cigarettes. Only give presents to people who helped you when you leave the village.

What to Bring You need to bring food supplies – rice and sugar – a stock of cigarettes and other goods like pens, exercise books, tools and medicines for presents and bartering. In addition, a smaller backpack is recommended as it's easier to carry in the jungle and transport in the sampans. Other essential items are a mosquito net, insect repellent, torch and strong plastic bags. If you bring medicine to give as presents make certain that it is nothing the locals can harm themselves with through incorrect use.

Photography It is best to get familiar with people before photographing them. You will not be well received in a village if you enter it while taking photos. In particular, elderly people dislike cameras and are afraid of flashes. At most ceremonies the islanders ask for money to have their photo taken, otherwise they rarely do.

Health Chloroquine-resistant malaria is a common problem and many locals die from it every year. There are plenty of snakes around, but they are not likely to be a problem. The rivers are used for washing and as running toilets, and thus are a source of disease. Never drink water unless it has been boiled or purified.

Dangers & Annoyances Theft can be a problem but normally only of small items left lying around.

Things to See
Despite recent changes to the island, about two-thirds of the island is still covered with tropical rainforest. It's also surrounded by magnificent coral reefs teeming with fish. The two main towns on Siberut are **Muarasikabaluan** in the north and **Muarasiberut** at the southern tip of the east coast. There is no public transport on the island so you either have to walk between the villages, or hire and catch public boats to take you along the coast.

Of the four villages accessible by foot from Muarasiberut, **Sakelot** (one km away) is the most interesting because it is the oldest and has retained its traditional houses. The others are new – part of the government's resettlement policy of moving the people out of the jungle and setting them up in villages along the coastal strip.

One of the quickest and easiest villages to get to is **Tiap**, which takes two hours by boat along a narrow branch of jungle river. A more adventurous, but still comparatively easy trip is to **Rokdok**. The people live in small, traditional houses and someone has taught the village children to sing Silent Night in Bahasa Indonesian to travellers – a rather eerie experience. It takes between five and six hours there and back by boat.

Two more remote villages are **Sakudai** and **Madobak**. The journey to Sakudai takes two days – one day by boat and the other trekking through the jungle. The trip to Madobak takes six hours by boat.

Organised Tours
Many people take the easy option, which is to join an organised tour to the island. These can be booked in Bukittinggi at several travel agencies, or in Padang, and last roughly seven to 10 days. The charge is around 200,000 rp per person, but you may have to pay more because of the extra expenses once you're on the island. The problem with these treks is that the trekking guides are not Mentawai islanders. They are Sumatrans who are not liked by the Mentawais and that will create a barrier between you and the locals. Often, they themselves have to hire a local guide to get to the more remote areas of the island as they don't know the area or the language. The best guides are local people, who speak the language, know the customs which they respect and can explain, and bring enough food for the entire trip.

Places to Stay & Eat

The only losmen on Siberut is in Muarasiberut. A bed here costs 6000 rp. You can stay at missionary buildings, schools or with private families but don't expect any comforts. Accommodation is usually on the floor. You should never pay for accommodation in the villages as it is not the custom. It is better to give tobacco or a book as a present. (This has changed in the more touristy places where money is expected.)

There are only a few small restaurants in Muarasiberut and Muarasikabaluan. In the villages it is a custom to eat for free, but of course a donation is expected. Of course in the more touristy places you might be asked for money. The situation is totally different if you are on a tour.

Getting There & Away

Air Enquire at Merpati in Padang about flights from Padang to Pulau Siberut, but tickets usually have to be booked at the airport. There is usually one flight per week for about 50,000 rp.

Boat Three boats leave Padang once a week to Siberut and other islands, a distance of approximately 150 km. The boats usually leave from Teluk Bayur (the port of Padang) or Muara Padang. You can buy the tickets from PT Rusco Lines office (**☎** 21941) at Jalan BT Arau 31, Teluk Bayur. The fare is 7000 rp deck class, and 10,500 rp in a cabin per person. The boats normally depart at 7 am for the 12-hour trip to Muarasiberut and Muarasikabaluan. Check with the tourist office in Padang for information.

Other options include chartering private boats from Padang or Nias. Small boats are available for charter but are not advised as the sea and winds are rough and unpredictable in this region – the journey is not only likely to be uncomfortable, but could also be dangerous. If you only intend chartering the boat one way, you will have to pay the return passage if it goes back empty.

Getting Around

Speed boats are the way to travel around the coast, but these are not always safe and regularly capsize, often with a loss of life. A seven to eight-hour journey from Muarasikabaluan costs 20,000 rp. The river transport is more expensive, and you need to bargain hard.

Riau

Riau consists of four mainland districts – Kampar, Bengkalis, Upper Indragiri and Lower Indragiri – stretching along the eastern seaboard of Sumatra and its myriad islands. The capital of this rich province dripping in oil, tin and bauxite is Pakanbaru, but the islands have their own capital at Tanjung Pinang.

It was not until 1958 that Riau was separated from West Sumatra and became a province in its own right. Its history has all the right ingredients for a best-selling blockbuster: the high seas, pirates, violence, the conflict of nations, greed and romance.

Only a small percentage of mainland Riau's rainforest has been cleared for oil development; most of the country is still covered in thick jungle and mangrove swamps. Several animistic and nomadic tribes (including the Sakai, Kubu and Jambisals) still live in the jungle, mostly around Dumai where the Pertamina refinery has been established.

History

Before air travel, the quickest route between India and China was through the Straits of Melaka (Selat Melaka) which gave eastern Sumatra strategic importance and subjected it to diverse cultural influences. The first people known to have migrated to its shores were hunter-gatherers who arrived between 600 and 2000 BC and left hardly anything behind except their dead and piles of shells.

After the 16th century, Riau became the centre of the Malay civilisation which managed to cling on to it until the 18th century, despite constant attacks from pirates and the opportunistic Portuguese, Dutch and

English. The Portuguese and Dutch struggled for control over the strait with the Dutch eventually gaining the upper hand.

Mainland Riau (then known as Siak) finally became a Dutch colony in 1745 when the Sultan of Johore surrendered his claim to the Dutch East India Company. The Dutch were more interested in ridding the seas of pirates so their fleet could trade without losses and danger than in governing or developing the region, so they left Riau alone.

Information

Health Mosquitoes are rife in these islands and chloroquine-resistant malaria has been reported.

Visas Sekupang, on Pulau Batam, and Tanjung Pinang, on Pulau Bintan, are the immigration points to and from Singapore. A visa and a return ticket are not required to enter or leave Indonesia through these ports. If you get asked for a return ticket, you can always buy a ferry ticket back to Singapore.

PAKANBARU

Pakanbaru, the capital of Riau Province, lies 160 km upstream on Sungai Siak. A sprawling city built with oil money, its sleazy port area contrasts sharply with the galaxy of public buildings at the other end of town. In fact, the further away from the port you go the better Pakanbaru gets. If you came in from the other end it's rather like arriving in a Sumatran version of Canberra or Brazilia. Yet, take two steps off the main street and you're almost back in the jungle again.

For most visitors, Pakanbaru is really just a transit town on the way to or from Singapore via Tanjung Pinang and Batam. Most visitors find this town unpleasant as many of the locals and agents try to overcharge travellers when buying tickets. If you stay a bit longer you might find that Pakanbaru is not that bad a place and that the people can be friendly.

Oil was discovered in this area by US engineers just before WW II, but it was the Japanese who drilled the first well at Rumbai. The main fields, not far from Pakanbaru, are connected by pipeline to refineries at Dumai because ocean-going tankers cannot enter the heavily silted Sungai Siak.

Rumbai, just north of Pakanbaru, is the base for Caltex Pacific Indonesia, jointly owned by Standard Oil of California and Texaco. A resort-like complex with manicured lawns, it's a world away from downtown Pakanbaru. If you go to Rumbai, it's worth checking with the Caltex public relations office to see whether you can get hold of a visitor's pass which will allow you to use the club facilities.

Pakanbaru is surrounded by a wilderness of dense rainforest and mangrove swamps. The nearby jungle is crisscrossed by pipelines and dotted with oil wells. The creatures lurking in the jungle include the hairy Sumatran rhinoceros, tigers, bears, tapirs and elephants (the latter occasionally storm through villages). Some of these animals can be seen early in the morning along the roads.

Orientation & Information

The main street of Pakanbaru is Jalan Jenderal Sudirman. Practically everything in the way of banks, hotels and offices is spread out along it or on adjoining streets. The port of Pakanbaru is on Sungai Siak, at the end of Jalan Saleh Abbas. Some boats also leave from the wharf at the end of Jalan Jenderal Sudirman. The main bus station is at the other end of town on Jalan Nangka, and the airport is further out in the same direction.

Tourist Office There is no tourist office as such, but the local government department in the Governor's Office on Jalan Gajah Mada 200 is responsible for handling tourism in Riau Province.

Money The Bank Negara Indonesia 1946 is at Jalan Jenderal Sudirman 119. The Bank Rakyat Indonesia is at No 268. You cannot change money at the airport. The Kirana moneychanger at Jalan Cokroaminoto 17, near the corner with Jalan Jenderal Sudirman, will change US, Malay and Singapore

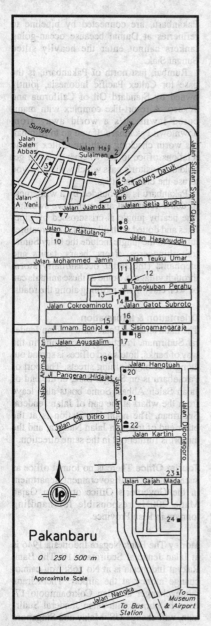

Pakanbaru

0   250   500 m

Approximate Scale

To Bus Station

To Museum & Airport

■ PLACES TO STAY

4   Penginapan Nirmala & Rina
6   Afri Hotel
10 Hotel Sri Indrayani
13 Hotel Rauda
14 Hotel Anom
17 Hotel Tutenja Atas
18 Hotel Dharma Utama
24 Riau Hotel

▼ PLACES TO EAT

7   Jumbo Seafood Restaurant
11 New Holland Bakery
12 Bima Sahti Corner

OTHER

1   Port
2   Some boats depart from here
3   CV Effi
5   SMAC
8   Telegram & Telex Office
9   Bank Negara Indonesia
15 Market
16 Sempati Air Agent
19 Bank Rakyat Indonesia
20 Telephone Office
21 Merpati (Garuda)
22 Post Office
23 Tourist Office

cash, but will only change US dollar travellers' cheques.

Post & Telecommunications The telephone office is at Jalan Jenderal Sudirman 199. The telegram and telex office is at No 117. The post office is also on the same street, near the corner with Jalan Kartini.

Riau Province Museum

The new Riau Province Museum has a historical and cultural display. It is a fair way out of town on the way to the airport along Jalan Jenderal Sudirman. It is open from Monday to Saturday from 8 am to 2 pm.

Places to Stay – bottom end

There are few cheap places worth mentioning. Popular with travellers is *Tommy's Place* at Gang Nantongga, off Jalan Nangka. It is a clean and friendly place, where the owner provides plenty of travel information. Dormitory beds cost 2500 rp, and a double with a fan is 5000 rp. It's not an easy place to find. From the bus station turn right. Walk down to Gang Nantongga, which is the second lane on your right, and ask the locals for Tommy's. They all know it and will point you in the right direction.

In a convenient location opposite the bus station is *Penginapan Linda* (☎ 22375) on Jalan Nangka 133-135. It's basic with musty, noisy rooms from 7500 rp.

If you're departing by boat there are a couple of run-down, depressing hotels near the port. These include the *Penginapan Nirmala* on Jalan M Yatin, a few minutes walk from the port. The Nirmala has accommodation reminiscent of the type so prominently depicted in *Midnight Express*. Rooms are around 6000 rp per person. A slightly better but more expensive place is *Penginapan Rina* next door.

In the centre of town the cheapest place is *Hotel Tutenja Atas* (☎ 22985) at Jalan Sisingamangaraja 4, near the corner with Jalan Jenderal Sudirman. They have basic, noisy and musty rooms with mandi costing 7000/8000 rp. Almost next door, at No 10, is the more depressing and similarly priced *Hotel Dharma Utama* (☎ 22171).

Places to Stay – middle
The *Hotel Anom* on Jalan Gatot Subroto, near the corner with Jalan Jenderal Sudirman, has rooms from 16,500/18,000 rp with private bathroom and 22,500 rp with air-con. The rooms are set around a courtyard and it's a reasonably pleasant place. The cheaper rooms are better value.

The *Rauda Hotel* on Jalan Tangkuban Perahu, near the corner with Jalan Jenderal Sudirman, has overpriced rooms with fan from 25,000/30,000 rp.

The *Riau Hotel* (☎ 22986) at Jalan Diponegoro 26 has rooms from 18,000 rp. It's a fine, quiet hotel in the government area of town.

Places to Stay – top end
One of the most central and friendly hotels is the *Hotel Sri Indrayani* (☎ 31870) on Jalan Dr S Ratulangi. Their rooms start from 35,000 rp, plus tax.

The flashiest and most expensive hotel is the *Mutiara Panghegar Hotel* (☎ 23102) on Jalan Jos Sudarso 12A, before the bridge across the Siak. They have rooms from 114,950 to 296,450 rp. If you're not staying there it's possible to use the swimming pool for 3500 rp. The cheaper *Indrapura Hotel* (☎ 25229) on Jalan Dr Sutomo 86 only charges 2500 rp for a swim.

Places to Eat
There are innumerable cheap places to eat along Jalan Jenderal Sudirman, particularly around the market in the evening. Try the satay, mertabak or Chinese food at *Bima Sahti Corner* on Jalan Tengkuban Perahu, opposite Rauda Hotel. For something different the *New Holland Bakery* at Jalan Jenderal Sudirman 153 has a fine selection of cakes, pastries, hamburgers and ice cream. The fresh fruit juices are excellent, especially the mango.

Getting There & Away
Air Merpati (☎ 33575) is at Jalan Jenderal Sudirman 207. SMAC (☎ 21421) is at Jalan Jenderal Sudirman 25.

Merpati/Garuda has daily flights from Pakanbaru to Banda Aceh, Batam, Jakarta (230,000 rp), Medan, Padang, Palembang, Semarang, Surabaya, Tanjung Pinang and Singapore. SMAC has daily flights from Pakanbaru to Pulau Batam. Sempati Air has daily flights to Tanjung Pinang, which are more reliable and cheaper (98,400 rp) than Merpati's. It's possible to buy Sempati Air tickets from the PT Kotapiring agent on Jalan Sisingamangaraja 3.

Bus Few people hang around in Pakanbaru. Most people take a boat to Tanjung Pinang the day they arrive or get a bus to Bukittinggi. There are daily buses to Bukittinggi. The trip takes four to six hours

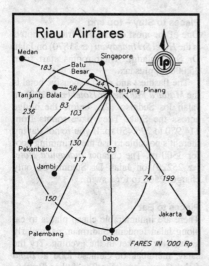

Riau Airfares

Medan
Singapore
183   Batu
       Besar
Tanjung Balai   58   44   Tanjung Pinang
236   83   103
       130
Pakanbaru   117   83
Jambi
       74   199
150
                    Jakarta
Palembang   Dabo   FARES IN '000 Rp

and the fare is 3500 rp. There are daily buses to other major cities in Sumatra.

Boat Buy tickets for the ferry to Tanjung Pinang from the boat companies in the harbour or from CV Effi (☎ 25730) at Jalan Saleh Abbas 4, which leads to the entrance to the harbour. There are boats to Tanjung Pinang and to Batam three days a week. There is also a fast way of getting to Batam, via Selatpanjang. For more details see the Getting There & Away section at the beginning of this chapter.

Watch the Selat Abadi agent, who may overcharge and whose information is unreliable.

Getting Around
To/From the Airport The airport is 12 km from town. A taxi costs 8500 rp. Hotels like Anom provide taxi vouchers, otherwise it's possible to catch a bemo for 200 rp to the turn-off from the main road to the airport. From here it's a one-km walk.

AROUND PAKANBARU
Taluk Kuantan
Every year there are jalur races (Pacu Jalur) held in this town around the middle to end of

August. The jalur is a long canoe made from a single trunk with a capacity to carry 40 to 60 people. The race is preceded and followed by many other cultural activities all unique to the region.

Taluk Kuantan is south of Pakanbaru, and connected by daily buses that cost 3000 rp and take about three hours.

DUMAI
On the coast 158 km from Pakanbaru, Dumai is the port for the ferry service to Melaka in Malaysia and the islands of Riau Archipelago. Dumai is strictly a one-street town and once you arrive the only thing to do is to catch the ferry to Melaka or Riau or the bus to Pakanbaru. Remember that Dumai is not a free visa entry/exit point and that you need a visa to leave or arrive here.

Places to Stay
If you need a place to stay try the City Hotel (☎ 21550) on Jalan Jenderal Sudirman. Clean rooms with fan are 7000/8000 rp and with air-con 20,000 rp.

Getting There & Away
Dumai is a port of call for the large Pelni liner *Lawit*. The port is two to three hours from the bus terminal; a becak costs 1000 rp. See the Getting Around chapter for the complete timetable.

RIAU ARCHIPELAGO
Scattered across the South China Sea like confetti are the islands of the Riau Archipelago. There are more than 3000 islands (many uninhabited) curving south-east from Sumatra to Kalimantan and north to Malaysia, dotted over 170,000 sq km of sea.

The islands can be divided roughly into two groups: one bunched closely to the coast of Sumatra, the second nearer to Singapore and the administrative district of Riau (Kabupaten Kepulauan Riau). The main islands in the first group consist of Bengkalis, Rupat, Padang, Tebingtinggi, Rangsang, Lalang, Mendol, Penyalai, Serapung, Muda, Kijang, Pucung and Katemun. The second can be broken down

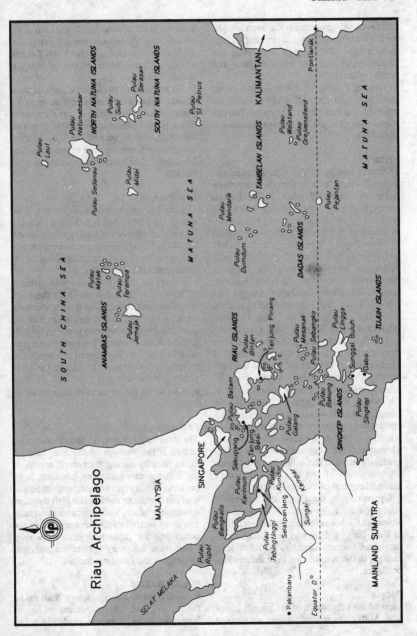

into seven sub-groups: the Karimun islands, the Riau islands (after which the archipelago is named), the Lingga-Singkep, the Tambelan, Anambas, North Natuna and South Natuna groups.

Tanjung Pinang on Pulau Bintan is the main centre in the archipelago. There are regular boats there from Singapore. You can island hop through the archipelago, but it takes time.

History

The early history of the Riau Archipelago suggests a wave of migration from southern India. Around 1000 AD, Pulau Bintan emerged as a separate kingdom which was enlarged by a propitious marriage to the son of a king of Palembang. A capital was built in Temasik (now Singapore) and the principality was renamed Bintan Temasik Singapura. By 1500, the kingdom of Melaka had conquered the Riau islands of Kundur, Jemaja, Bunguran, Tambelan, Lingga and Bintan. Later still, the archipelago came under the control of Raja Hang Tuah for whom a street in Tanjung Pinang is named.

The Portuguese held power in Riau for a brief period following their conquest of Melaka. From 1530 to the end of the 18th century the archipelago was the pivot of Malay civilisation with the main centres at Penyenget and Lingga. In 1685, Sultan Mahmud Syah II was coerced into signing a cooperative agreement with the Dutch, which greatly diminished his authority. Throughout the next centuries, the Dutch gradually reduced the authority of the rajas. On the death of the raja in 1784, they assumed control of the archipelago.

Opposition to the Dutch did not really re-emerge until the early 1900s when the Rusydiah Club was formed by the last Sultan of Riau-Lingga. This was ostensibly a cultural and literary organisation, but later assisted in the struggle for Indonesian independence.

People

Most of the inhabitants of the islands are of pure Malay origins, but there are several indigenous groups like the Orang Laut of the Natuna islands, the Akit tribes of Bengkalis, the Mantang peoples of Penuba and Kelumu islands and the Baruk people of Sunggai Buluh, Singkep.

Bintan has the largest population of these islands, comprising various ethnic groups – Malay, Batak, Minangkabau and a comparatively large Chinese community. It is also physically the biggest of the Riau islands, being three times the area of neighbouring Singapore. The population is about 90% Islamic.

Architecture

The traditional architecture of the Riau islands is called *rumah lipat kijang*, meaning 'hairpin', derived from the shape of the roof. The style is undergoing a revival at present and most new public buildings are being constructed in this manner.

Houses are usually adorned with carvings of flowers, birds and bees. Often there are wings on each corner, said to symbolise the capacity to adapt. Four pillars have much the same meaning: the capacity to live in the four corners of the universe. The flowers are supposed to convey a message of prosperity and happiness from owner to visitor, the birds symbolise the one true God and the bees symbolise the desire for mutual understanding.

Festivals

The main local celebration in the Riau Archipelago is the Festival of the Sea, held on Pulau Sarasan during the second month of the Islamic calendar. The islanders hang packets of sticky rice on trees near the beach, then cut logs from the forest which they cart down to the beach, load into canoes and drop into deep water to appease the gods of the ocean and for protection from drowning. Apart from this, they uphold the principal festivals of the Islamic calendar.

PULAU BATAM

Squashed between Singapore and Pulau Bintan is Pulau Batam. Almost as big as Singapore itself, Batam is gradually being

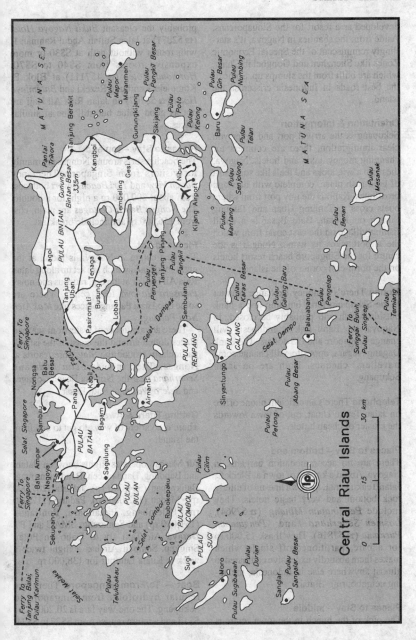

Central Riau Islands

developed as a resort for the Singaporeans. Aside from the shanties in Nagoya, it's startlingly reminiscent of the Special Economic Zones like Shenzhen and Gongbei in China, which are built from the stumps up. Some of the best roads in Indonesia crisscross the island.

Orientation & Information

Sekupang is the arrival port and, after you clear immigration, there are counters for changing money, taxis and hotels. Nagoya, the main town, looks and feels like some sort of gold-rush place, complete with bars and prostitutes. Kabil is the tiny port from where boats cross to Tanjung Uban and Tanjung Pinang on Bintan. Batu Besar is a small fishing village on the east coast from which the airport takes its name. Nongsa is the centre for the Singapore beach resort hotels on the north-east corner of the island.

Money There's a money exchange counter at the Sekupang ferry building and a bank outside which will probably be closed. In Nagoya, the Bank Rakyat Indonesia will change Singapore and US dollars. The Bank Dagang Negara, opposite, will change some travellers' cheques. Both are on Jalan Sekupang.

Telephone There's an efficient phone office on Jalan Teuku Umar, out of town towards the cluster of cheap hotels.

Places to Stay – bottom end

There are no accommodation bargains in Nagoya. About a km out of town at Block C, Jalan Teuku Umar, there's a line-up of utterly rock bottom and very basic hotels. They include *Penginapan Minang* (☎ 57964), *Losmen Sederhana* and *Penginapan Purnama* (☎ 57816). They'll ask 15,000 rp for a bare, partitioned-off single which makes them absurdly expensive compared to almost anywhere else in Indonesia, including neighbouring Bintan.

Places to Stay – middle

The pick of the bunch in the town centre is probably the pleasant *Bukit Nagoya Hotel* (☎ 52871) at Jalan Sultan Abdul Rahman 1, with rooms without bath at S$30 or more expensive rooms from S$40 to S$70. *Horisona Hotel* (☎ 457111) at Blok E, Kompleks Lumbung Rezeki and *Batamjaya Hotel* (☎ 58707) on Jalan Raja Ali Haji are not as good value but still fine at similar prices.

Places to Stay – top end

The beach resorts around Nongsa are mainly for visitors from Singapore. The fancy *Batam View* and *Turi Beach Resort* both cost from about 200,000 rp a night for a double. The *Nongsa Beach Cottages* are plain, cost from 156,000 rp and include breakfast.

Places to Eat

The best eating in Nagoya is found at the night food stalls which are set up along Jalan Raja Ali Haji or at the big, raucous and noisy *Pujasera Nagoya* food centre. There are some good nasi Padang places like *Mak Ateh Nasi Padang*.

There are a number of waterfront seafood places dotted around the coast of the island, particularly around the Singapore resorts at Nongsa. They include *Setia Budi* and *Sederhana* near the Nongsa Beach Cottages and *Selera Wisata* at Batu Besar.

Getting There & Away

There is a variety of ways to get to and from the island.

Air Merpati operates flights between Batam and Bandung, Banda Aceh, Bandarlampung, Balikpapan (304,000 rp), Jakarta (207,000 rp), Medan (172,000 rp), Padang (117,000 rp), Palembang, Pakanbaru, Pontianak (151,000 rp) and Semarang. SMAC and PT Deraya Air Taxi fly to Dabo on Pulau Singkep. Sempati Air has a flight twice a week to Kuala Lumpur for 138,000 rp.

Boat – To/From Singapore There are regular hydrofoils from Singapore to Sekupang. The one-way fare is 20,200 rp, or S$18 and a return ranges from S$27 to S$34.

The trip takes less than half an hour. In Singapore the ferries to Batam depart from Finger Pier. There are about a dozen companies servicing the route. Don't believe claims that their boat is 'the next departure' until it's independently verified! Avoid Auto Batam who are particularly bad at keeping to schedules.

Boat – To/From Pulau Bintan From Kabil, on the other side of the island, there are regular ferries to Tanjung Uban on Pulau Bintan, from where you can get buses and taxis to Tanjung Pinang. The ferry crossing takes 45 minutes and costs 3000 rp. From Tanjung Uban, there is a bus to Tanjung Pinang that takes two hours and costs 3000 rp. Shared taxis, when available, cost 5000 rp per person. .

There are also several morning services from Kabil to Tanjung Pinang. The fastest taking only 30 minutes (12,500 rp), the medium-speed boats taking 75 minutes (8800 rp) and the slow boats taking three to four hours (5000 rp).

It probably makes more sense to take the ferry-bus combination via Tanjung Uban. It's slightly cheaper, slightly faster and a lot more comfortable.

Boat – To/From Elsewhere in Indonesia There is a ferry service between Tanjung Balai (on Pulau Karimun) and Batu Ampar (on Pulau Batam). There are daily departures in both directions six days a week. The ticket office is at the ferry terminal in Batu Ampar.

There are also boats to/from Selatpanjang (on Pulau Tebingtinggi) that take three hours and cost 15,000 rp.

Getting Around
Transport options for travel around Batam are fairly limited.

To/From the Airport The airport is at Batu Besar and it's a scruffy and stuffy little place. From Nagoya to the airport costs 4000 rp by taxi. Don't believe cards showing 'official' fares.

Local Transport Although difficult to find, there is a bus service from Sekupang to Nagoya for 600 rp. Otherwise the only transport around Batam is taxi and you have to bargain hard. Between Sekupang and Nagoya or between Nagoya and Kabil, you should be able to get a shared taxi at around 1500 to 2000 rp per person, otherwise pay 5000 rp for the whole taxi. Again, don't believe 'official' fares.

There is a taxi counter and a moneychanger in the Sekupang Ferry Terminal. The large hotels also have taxi counters, or you can hail a taxi on the street.

PULAU BINTAN
Bintan, like Batam, is a rough island. Apart from some large rubber plantations it appears largely uncultivated, and what small farms there are seem to support barely more than subsistence agriculture. On the other hand, there are some fine opportunities for diving and snorkelling most of the year except from November to March when the monsoon is blowing.

Tanjung Pinang
Tanjung Pinang is the biggest town on Bintan and in the archipelago. This is where most visitors stay, although the majority of people only hang around for 24 hours or so waiting for boat connections. Tanjung Pinang is a good base for exploring other islands in the group and has a few interesting sights of its own. There is a constant stream of boats and sampans sailing between the islands and upriver. There's an old section of the town that juts out over the sea on stilts.

The town is famous for its two red-light villages – Batu Duabelas and Batu Enambelas – no prizes for guessing that they are respectively 12 (duabelas) km and 16 (enambelas) km out of town.

Information There is no tourist office but PT Info Travel, one of the shipping agents at the main wharf, is used to dealing with visitors and has all the shipping information.

Money The town is not a good place to

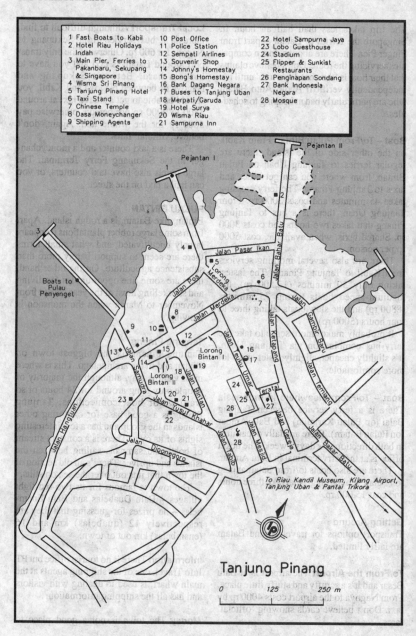

1 Fast Boats to Kabil
2 Hotel Riau Holidays Indah
3 Main Pier, Ferries to Pakanbaru, Sekupang & Singapore
4 Wisma Sri Pinang
5 Tanjung Pinang Hotel
6 Taxi Stand
7 Chinese Temple
8 Dasa Moneychanger
9 Shipping Agents
10 Post Office
11 Police Station
12 Sempati Airlines
13 Souvenir Shop
14 Johnny's Homestay
15 Bong's Homestay
16 Bank Dagang Negara
17 Buses to Tanjung Uban
18 Merpati/Garuda
19 Hotel Surya
20 Wisma Riau
21 Sampurna Inn
22 Hotel Sampurna Jaya
23 Lobo Guesthouse
24 Stadium
25 Flipper & Sunkist Restaurants
26 Penginapan Sondang
27 Bank Indonesia Negara
28 Mosque

Pejantan I

Pejantan II

Jalan Pasar Ikan

Lorong Merdeka

Jalan Bahar Batu

Boats to Pulau Penyenget

Jalan Pos

Jalan Merdeka

Jalan Gambir Baru

Jalan Ketapang

Jalan Samudra

Lorong Bintan I

Jalan Teuku Umar

Lorong Bintan II

Jalan Bintan

Jalan Teratai

Jalan Hangtuah

Jalan Yusuf Khahar

Jalan Tabib

Jalan Mesjid

Jalan Gaee

Jalan Bakar Batu

Jalan Diponegoro

To Riau Kandil Museum, Kijang Airport, Tanjung Uban & Pantai Trikora

Tanjung Pinang

0   125   250 m

change money, the banks are either choosy about what currencies they accept or offer bad rates. The Bank Dagang Negara on Jalan Teuku Umar, changes foreign cash and travellers' cheques – for which it requires that you show the original purchase receipt. The PT Dasa Moneychanger rates are not that good.

Post The post office is on Jalan Merdeka, not far from the harbour.

Riau Kandil Museum A short distance from the city centre by bemo or *ojek* (motorbike) is the Riau Kandil Museum which has a mish-mash treasure-trove of artefacts from the days of the Sultanates and the Dutch, including old guns, ceramics, charts, antique brassware and other memorabilia. Follow Jalan Ketapang out of town to the museum. It's on the right-hand side just past the junction of Jalan Bakar Batu (an extension of Jalan Ketapang) and Jalan Kemboja.

Other Attractions Tanjung Pinang is a good place to stroll around. For a peaceful hour or two, wander down to the old harbour of Pejantan II. There is a Chinese temple in town and another, across the harbour by sampan, in Senggarang.

Organised Tours There are a couple of tour operators in Tanjung Pinang. Try PT Riau Holidays in the Hotel Riau Holidays Indah.

Places to Stay – bottom end At the end of Lorong Bintan II, which runs off Jalan Bintan in the centre of town, is the very popular *Bong's Homestay* at No 20. A bed costs 3000 rp, includes breakfast and the friendly Mr and Mrs Bong make this a great place to stay. Next door, at No 22, *Johnny's Homestay* is a good overflow. Another similar establishment is *Lobo Guesthouse* at 8 Jalan Diponegoro. Dorms cost 4000 rp and rooms are 6000/10,000 rp, including breakfast.

On Jalan Yusuf Khafar the *Penginapan Sondang* is very bare and basic, and costs 10,000 to 12,500 rp.

Places to Stay – middle The *Hotel Surya* on Jalan Bintan is basic but in pretty good condition. Rooms are from 11,500/15,000 rp or 17,500 rp with bath.

The *Tanjung Pinang Hotel* (☎ 21236) on Jalan Pos has spartan rooms from 11,000 rp with fan. Rooms with bathrooms start from 22,000 rp. It's location right in the centre of town will probably make it quite noisy.

The *Sampurna Inn* on Jalan Yusuf Kahar is a simple but modern hotel, where rooms with fan and bathroom cost from 15,000 rp or from 25,000 to 45,000 rp with air-con.

The *Wisma Riau* (☎ 21023) on Jalan Yusuf Kahar has rooms from 20,000/24,000 rp with private bathroom. It's very clean and comfortable.

Places to Stay – top end The *Hotel Sampurna Jaya* (☎ 21555) at Jalan Yusuf Khahar 15 is probably the best of the up-market hotels. Rooms start from 135,000/156,000 rp.

Pretty much the same, but slightly more unusual, is the *Riau Holidays Indah* (☎ 21812) built on pylons over the water near a long pier. Rooms are very comfortable with bathrooms (including bathtubs), carpet and television. Prices start from 69,000/92,000 rp.

Places to Eat The town has a superb night market with a variety of delicious food available – particularly Indonesian, Chinese and seafood dishes. A meal typically costs 1800 to 2500 rp. The market sets up in the bus/taxi station on Jalan Teuku Umar. More nighttime food stalls can be found at the Jalan Pos and Lorong Merdeka intersection.

During the day, there are several pleasant cafes with outdoor eating areas in front of the stadium (Kaca Puri) on Jalan Teuku Umar. Try *Flipper* or *Sunkist*.

Getting There & Away Tanjung Pinang is the major transport hub in the Riau Archipelago.

Air Bintan's airport is much smaller than

Batam's, there are fewer flights and they operate with smaller aircraft.

Garuda and Merpati are in the same building on Jalan Bintan. SMAC is at Jalan A Yani (Batu 5) – five km away from the city centre. Sempati Air Transport (☎ 21042) is at Jalan Bintan 9.

Garuda/Merpati flies from Tanjung Pinang to Batam, Jakarta, Pakanbaru, Singkep and other destinations. SMAC has flights from Tanjung Pinang to Pakanbaru, Singapore, Pulau Singkep and Jambi.

Sempati is usually cheaper than the other airlines. It has flights from Tanjung Pinang to Jakarta, Pakanbaru and Palembang.

Bus Buses to Tanjung Uban leave from the bus station on Jalan Teuku Umar. There are frequent departures throughout the day and the trip takes two hours. There are also shared taxis on this route.

Boat – Local The best way, and often the only way to get to most places is to island hop or travel upriver by boat.

Boats – including rowboats, sampans, ferries and medium sized ships – of varying degrees of speed and comfort operate around the islands.

Ferries to Kabil on Pulau Batam leave from Tanjung Uban which is two hours by bus or taxi from Tanjung Pinang. There are regular departures throughout the day. The crossing takes half an hour and costs 3000 rp. There are also direct ferries (departing in the morning) from Kabil to Tanjung Pinang, the fastest taking 30 minutes and costing 12,500 rp, and the slowest taking up to four hours and costing 5000 rp.

There are ferries at least two days a week from Tanjung Pinang to Tanjung Balai. You can buy tickets from PT Ayodhia on Jalan Pelabuhan in Tanjung Balai, and from PT Netra at the port in Tanjung Pinang. The fare is 16,500 rp.

Boat – Pelni Ships Pelni (☎ 21513) is at Jalan A Yani (Batu 5), which is five km from the Tanjung Pinang harbour. Pelni's *Lawit* leaves once every two weeks from the port

of Kijang (the port at the south-eastern corner of Pulau Bintan) for Dumai, Belawan (the port of Medan) and Tanjung Priok (the port of Jakarta). The fares from Tanjung Pinang to Tanjung Priok are 34,500/134,000 rp in Economy/1st class. The fares to Belawan are 34,500/129,500 rp in Economy/1st class. See the Getting Around chapter for the complete timetable of the *Lawit*.

Pelni ships to the eastern Riau Islands leave about once every 10 days, and do a 10-day round-trip out of Tanjung Pinang stopping off at various ports.

To get to Kijang take a shared taxi from Jalan Merdeka in Tanjung Pinang. It's a half-hour ride and the fare is 1500 rp per person.

Boat – To/From Batam & Singapore From Tanjung Pinang there are boats to Singapore via Sekupang on Pulau Batam. Several companies run the boats and there are several departures daily for both Sekupang and Singapore.

In Tanjung Pinang there are ticket offices on Jalan Pos and Jalan Merdeka that sell boat tickets. In Singapore, the hydrofoils depart from Finger Pier. Tickets can be bought at the offices here.

For more details about boats to/from Singapore see the Getting There & Away section at the beginning of this chapter.

Boat – To/From Pakanbaru Tickets in Tanjung Pinang are sold on the quay. See also To/From Singapore and To/From Tanjung Pinang in the Getting There & Away section at the beginning of this chapter.

Boat – To/From Pulau Singkep See the Singkep section.

Getting Around There are a number of options for getting around the island.

To/From the Airport Kijang airport is on the south-eastern tip of Pulau Bintan about 17 km from Tanjung Pinang. A shared taxi will cost you 5000 rp and to charter one about 25,000 rp.

Local Transport Buses to other parts of Bintan, including Tanjung Uban for the cheap boat to Kabil, operate from the bus and taxi station on Jalan Teuku Umar. The Tanjung Uban bus costs 3000 rp and takes two hours. The Kijang bus costs 1100 rp.

Public motorbikes, known as ojeks, are the favourite form of local transport. You can recognise them by their riders' yellow construction worker helmets. Around town a ride costs about 250 rp. There are also some local opelets around town, they also cost from 250 rp.

You can rent motorbikes from PT Info Travel on the main wharf for 25,000 rp a day.

Around Tanjung Pinang

You can charter a sampan from Tanjung Pinang to take you up the Sunggai Ular (Snake River) through the mangroves to see the Chinese Temple with its arrestingly gory murals of the trials and tortures of hell. Nearby you can see the ruins of old Sea Dayak villages.

Pulau Penyenget

This tiny island, less than 2½ sq km in area (you could walk around it in an hour or two), was once the capital of the Riau rajas. It is believed to have been given to the ruling raja as a wedding present in 1805. The Riau rajas moved house from Daik (on Pulau Lingga) to Penyenget around 1900. A bit of fossicking around the jungle reveals ruins, graveyards and other reminders of the past all over the island.

Penyenget, incidentally, is said to take its name from a certain type of bee which was in the habit of stinging pirates whenever they landed on the island. History does not record if this interesting line of defence ever kept the pirates from coming back.

Things to See The island is a charming place, with a very different feel to neighbouring Bintan and Tanjung Pinang.

The map shows the locations of the various tombs and monuments, many of them dilapidated or in ruins. Most of the village houses are by the shore, but the ruins

of the **old palace** of Raja Ali and the **tombs** and **graveyards** of Raja Jaafar and Raja Ali are further inland. All the main sites are sign-posted. A poster in the local mosque depicts the lineage of the former rulers, but for the most part the names of the long dead rajas are as meaningless to outsiders as those of ancient Hittite kings.

A particularly impressive site is the sulphur-coloured **mosque** with its forest of domes (13 of them), pillars and minarets – a bit like an Islamic version of the Disneyland Castle. Within the mosque is a library which contains hundreds of tomes on history, culture, law, languages and religions, including hand-written and illustrated copies of the Koran. There is a 500 rp charge. You won't be allowed into the mosque if you're wearing shorts or a short skirt – even though the caretaker might be wearing a short sarong that reaches half way between his waist and knees.

Getting There & Away Motorboats depart from halfway along the main pier at Tanjung Pinang and the cost is 500 rp per person each way. There are always boats going there, so there's no need to charter.

AROUND PULAU BINTAN
Beaches

There are several beautiful white-sand beaches lapped by sapphire seas here. They are relatively untouched apart from the inevitable overlay of bottles and other drift plastic. The best of them are Berakit, Teluk Dalam and Trikora, but they're on the east coast and there's no public transport there. Pantai Trikora is a fine 30-km-long strip of white sand along the east coast.

The beaches are a bit overrated overall, but if you come on a quiet day you probably won't be disappointed. Huge egrets take-off from boulders by the shore and glide across the water. Snorkelling is fine most of the year, except during the November to March monsoon period.

Mapor and several other small palm-covered islands with white sand beaches can be seen from Pantai Berakit.

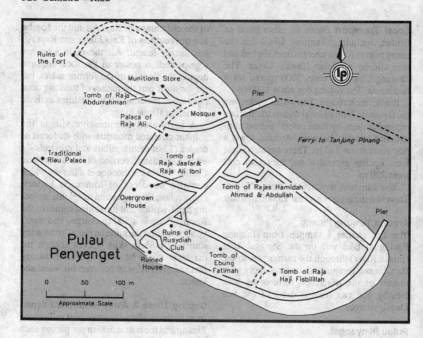

Pulau Penyenget

Ruins of
the Fort

Munitions Store

Tomb of Raja
Abdurrahman

Palaca of
Raja Ali

Mosque

Pier

Ferry to Tanjung Pinang

Traditional
Riau Palace

Tomb of
Raja Jaafar &
Raja Ali Ibni

Tomb of Rajas Hamidah
Ahmad & Abdullah

Overgrown
House

Pier

Ruins of
Rusydiah
Club

Ruined
House

Tomb of
Ebung
Fatimah

Tomb of Raja
Haji Fisbilillah

0   50   100 m

Approximate Scale

Places to Stay *Yasin's Guesthouse*, at the Km 46 marker, has simple wooden huts with a bed, mosquito nets, verandah and not much else. It's situated on a beach cum trash heap and costs 15,000 rp per day including three meals. At the Km 38 marker, the flashier *Trikora Country Club* has singles from S$50 to S$70 and doubles from S$60 to S$80.

Getting There & Away The main beach stretch is 40 to 50 km from Tanjung Pinang. Getting there costs 4000 rp per person by shared taxi, which mainly operate in the morning. It's also possible to charter a taxi or an ojek to get to the beaches.

Gunung Bintan Besar
You can climb Gunung Bintan Besar (348 metres) in about two hours. It's a fair way out of Tanjung Pinang by road or boat.

Pantai Dwi Kora
About a 20-minute drive from Tanjung

Uban, on the west coast of Bintan, is a beach called Pantai Dwi Kora. It's a long strip of white, palm-fringed sand facing Pulau Batam, and a fine place for a swim with clear, calm sea – although it's very crowded on weekends.

Pulau Bayan
Just off Tanjung Pinang is a lump of rock called Pulau Bayan. Once a dry dock and repair yard, it has now been cleared of scrap metal to make way for the construction of a massive boating marina with hotel, swimming pool, helipad and other facilities for wealthy Singaporeans (all within sight of the Indonesian shanties).

Nearby Islands
You can make excursions to other islands like Pulau Mapor or Pulau Terkulai, where the lighthouse keeper lives in solitary splendour and to get there you have to charter a boat.

PULAU SINGKEP

Well to the south of Pulau Bintan, Pulau Singkep is the third largest island in the archipelago. It is the headquarters of the Riau Tin and Timah mining companies. It has a large Chinese population. Few outsiders visit here, although it's a handy stopover point on the Singapore, Tanjung Pinang, Singkep, Pangkalpinang, Palembang run and has most of the services of a much larger place.

Dabo

The main town, Dabo, is shaded by lush trees and gardens and is clustered around a central

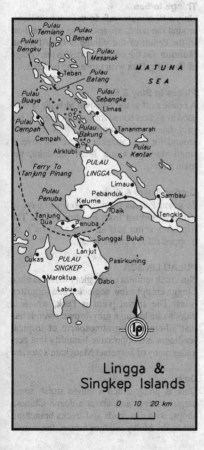

Lingga & Singkep Islands

0   10   20 km

park. Nearby, on the road to Sunggai Buluh, a big mosque dominates the skyline. Dabo is set in the middle of a huge, half-moon beach of white sand, which is perhaps as big as Bali's Kuta Beach.

Information Bank Dagang Negara on Jalan Penuba will change cash and travellers' cheques. The post office is on Jalan Pahlawan. The telephone office is about three km out of town on the road to Sunggai Buluh.

Things to See The fish and vegetable markets near the harbour are interesting to wander around and are among the best places in town to buy fresh, cheap food. Jalan Pasar Lamar is a good browsing and shopping area.

Places to Stay There are a couple of places to stay in Dabo. The *Penginapan Sri Indah* at Jalan Perusalaan 10 costs 13,500 rp with private bathroom. It's a very simple but clean and agreeable hotel.

The *Penginapan Garupa Singkep* on Jalan Pasar Lama is similar, with rooms from 6500/8500 rp, and rooms from 15,000/17,000 rp with air-con and private bathroom.

The salubrious *Wisma Singkep* is a fine hotel situated in a quiet spot above the town. Rooms are 30,000/60,000 rp.

Places to Eat Eat at the markets behind Penginapan Sri Indah or try any of the warungs on Jalan Pasar Lama and Jalan Merdeka. Eating places pop up all over the place at night.

Getting There & Away You can get to Singkep by air or sea.

Air SMAC (☎ 73) is on Jalan Pemandian. They have flights from Singkep to Tanjung Pinang and Singapore (two days a week), and Pakanbaru (four days a week). Deraya Air Taxi has two return flights a week from Tanjung Pinang and Pangalpinang on Pulau Bangka to Singkep. Sempati Air has flights from Singkep to Batam and back at the

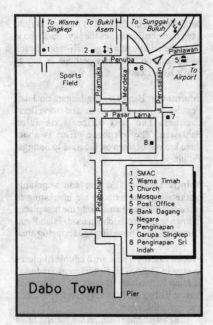

To Wisma Singkep
To Bukit Asem
To Sunggai Buluh
Jl Penuba
Pahlawan
To Airport
Sports Field
Jl Pasar Lama
Pramuka
Merdeka
Perusalaan
Jl Pelabuhan

1 SMAC
2 Wisma Timah
3 Church
4 Mosque
5 Post Office
6 Bank Dagang Negara
7 Penginapan Garupa Singkep
8 Penginapan Sri Indah

Dabo Town

Pier

lowest price, 74,000 rp. Merpati also has flights to Singkep from Tanjung Pinang.

The airport is five km from Dabo, on Jalan Pahlawan.

Boat Daily boats depart from Dabo to Daik, on Pulau Lingga. Departure time depends on the tide and it's a three-hour trip. The fare is 1000 rp. The 'ferries' are just small motorboats and it's definitely not a trip to contemplate in rough weather.

There are ferries on Monday to Saturday departing from Tanjung Pinang at 9 am for Sunggai Buluh on Pulau Singkep, and returning the same day at 3 pm. The fare is 17,500 rp, taking four hours for the one-way trip. The ferry docks at Sunggai Buluh, where you take a bus to Dabo on the other side of the island. This takes two hours and costs 3000 rp.

A regular ferry between Singkep and Jambi, departs once a week. Several shops in Dabo act as ticket agents.

There are regular boats between Singkep and Pulau Bangka run by Riau Tin. You have to register first at the Riau Tin office. There are departures two days a week and the boat pulls into Belinyu on Pulau Bangka.

PULAU PENUBA

Penuba is an idyllic place to relax and the people are friendly. It's fine for doing nothing but swimming, walking and reading. The main settlement on this island is the village of the same name, which is tucked into a small bay on the south-east coast.

Things to See

Only a 10-minute walk from Penuba village, around the point, are several sandy beaches. In the centre of the village is the **Attaqwa Mosque**. On the northern coast is the village of **Tanjung Dua** with more fine beaches.

Places to Stay & Eat

A house next to the Attaqwa Mosque is now used as a guest house for foreign visitors. It's very basic, and rooms are 4000 rp. Ask around for the caretaker. There are several small warungs along Jalan Merdeka, the main street.

Getting There & Away

To get to Penuba from Singkep you have to rent a motorboat from Sunggai Buluh. The trip takes about half an hour and you'll be dropped off at Penuba village.

PULAU LINGGA

Not much remains of the glory that was once Lingga except a few neglected and forgotten ruins. The arrival point is Daik, which is hidden one km up a grey-brown river. It has that all-enveloping atmosphere of tropical seediness and oppressive humidity that pervades many of Somerset Maugham's stories.

Daik

Daik is pretty much a single street, some cargo wharves and about a dozen Chinese shops, with dirt roads and tracks branching out to the Malay villages around the island.

You must report to the police as soon as you arrive.

Things to See The main site of historical interest is the ruin of the **old palace** of Raja Suleiman, the last raja of Lingga-Riau. To one side of the palace are the foundation stones of a building which is said to have been the living quarters of the raja's extensive harem. Otherwise there's not much left of the palace; a few staircases, the foundations of the floor, pavilions and halls. In the jungle you find overgrown bathing pools and squat toilets. The ruins are a two-hour walk from Daik, but you'll need someone to guide you through the maze of overgrown forest paths. Along the same trail is the **tomb** of Raja Muhammed Jusuf, who reigned from 1859-99.

A half-hour walk from Daik is the **Makam Bukit Cenckeh** (Cenckeh Hill Cemetery). Situated here are the graves of Raja Abdul Rakhman (who ruled from 1812-1831) and Raja Muhammad (who ruled from 1832-1841). Like the palace, there is not much left of the tombs, which are slowly crumbling into rubble.

On the outskirts of Daik is the **Mesjid Sultan Lingga**, in the grounds of which is the **tomb** of Raja Makmud I, who ruled in the early 19th century.

Inland is **Gunung Daik**, its three peaks looking like a crown. It's possible to scale the two outer peaks but the central one is said to have never been climbed because it's too steep and too dangerous. If you've got some equipment you can walk across the island camping along the way, but get explicit directions before you start out. There are a number of Malay villages on the island (look at the map in the police station in Daik) and it would be possible to walk to them, although you would need quite a lot of time.

Places to Stay & Eat There is one hotel in Daik, on the main street just near the ferry dock. It's simple but clean, and rooms are 6500 rp. There are a few small warungs on the main street, but there's not much variation in the food.

Getting There & Away There are daily boats from Daik to Dabo on Pulau Singkep. The fare is 1500 rp and the trip takes three hours. There are occasional boats direct between Tanjung Pinang and Daik. You might be able to get a ride on a cargo boat from Pakanbaru or Jambi.

Getting Around You have to walk to most places as there are only two vehicles in use, one of them a truck of 1945 vintage.

PULAU KARIMUN

The main centre is the port of Tanjung Balai. There is a regular ferry service between Tanjung Pinang and Karimun. SMAC flies from Karimun to Dabo on Pulau Singkep, and to Pakanbaru.

PULAU GALANG

You need an official permit (yellow ticket) to go to this island, which is where Indonesia puts its Vietnamese and Cambodian boat people. There's a US sub-consul based on the island and a number of Western expatriates.

THE EASTERN ISLANDS

These islands are right off the beaten track and difficult to get to. But this could change in the next few years since Pulau Natuna is being exploited for its oil deposits. A road now links Bangurun Timor on the east coast to Bunguran Barat on the west coast. There is talk of Ranai (Bunguran Timor) being converted to an international airport.

The population of the island is fairly small, although there's also an extensive transmigration programme on the Sungai Ulu 3with settlers from Java growing cash crops like peanuts and green peas.

The islands are noted for fine basketweave cloth and various kinds of traditional dance. One particularly idiosyncratic local dance is a kind of *Thousand & One Arabian Nights* saga, incorporating episodes from Riau-Lingga history. Dancers from Pulau Sedanau often perform at the national dance contest held in Jakarta each year.

North Sumatra

The province of North Sumatra covers an area of 70,787 sq km, stretching from Aceh in the north to West Sumatra in the south and from the Indian Ocean in the west to Selat Melaka in the east. It has a population of over eight million and is divided into 11 kabupaten (regencies) and six kotamadya (municipalities).

There are five main ethnic groups in North Sumatra: the Coastal Malays who live along Selat Melaka ; the Karonese, Simalungun, Dairi and Toba Batak groups in the highlands around Lake Toba and Pulau Samosir; the Pesisirs (Central Tapanuli) along the Indian Ocean coastline; the Mandailings and Angkolas (South Tapanuli) in the south and the people from Pulau Nias. These ethnic groups all have their own dialects, religious beliefs and traditional customs, arts and cultures, which in turn are overlaid by the dominant influences of Islam and the national language, Bahasa Indonesia.

North Sumatra produces more than 30% of Indonesia's exports and handles about 60% of them. Fine tobacco is grown around Medan and oil, palm-oil, tea, and rubber are also produced in large quantities and exported from the port of Belawan, about 26 km from Medan.

MEDAN
Medan is the capital of North Sumatra and the third largest city in Indonesia. The city has had a chequered history and has witnessed various wars. From the end of the 16th century through to the early 17th century it was a battlefield in the power struggle between the two kingdoms of Aceh and Deli and during the 19th century it was involved in the Sunggal War against the Dutch.

The name is said to derive from the Portuguese word 'medina', dating its first use in Sumatra from the beginning of the 16th century. In Indonesian the word 'medan' literally means field, battlefield or arena and it

was on the fertile swamp at the junction of the Deli and Babura rivers, near the present Jalan Putri Hijau, that the original village of Medan Putri was founded in 1590 by Raja Guru Patimpus.

Medan remained a small village until well into the 19th century. In 1823, when a British government official John Anderson visited the place it had 200 inhabitants. Only after the arrival of the Dutch did it start to grow. It became a Dutch plantation centre soon after an enterprising Dutchman named Nienhuys successfully started growing tobacco in 1865. In 1886 the Dutch made it the capital of North Sumatra. But by 1910 it was still a fairly small place with only 17,500 residents. At the end of Dutch rule in 1942 the population was around 80,000, and today it's well over a million.

Medan is a multi-racial melting pot which includes large communities of Europeans, Chinese, Indians, Arabians, Javanese and various Sumatran ethnic groups like the Minangkabau and the Batak. Solid Dutch buildings inspire images of bloated bureaucrats and fat European burghers from the colonial era, while jerry-built lean-tos house large families. Mixed in with the people are antique shops, some impressive palaces, mosques and museums, and the remnants of the old Dutch planter aristocracy.

The city is quite polluted, especially by the becaks belching their noxious fumes through the streets, and does not have much to offer the traveller, so it's mostly used as an entry and exit point. It's actually not a bad city, but some travellers find it hard to handle the more aggressive locals.

Orientation & Information
Tourist Office The Dinas Pariwisata Sumatera (☎ 511101) is at Jalan Ahmad Yani 107, next to the Bank Dagang Negara. It's open from Monday to Thursday from 8 am to 3 pm, Friday from 8 am to noon and Saturday from 8 am to 2 pm. There is also an information centre at the arrival terminal at Polonia International Airport, which has a map of the city, a few brochures and not much else.

Money There are a number of banks in Medan, particularly along Jalan Pemuda, Jalan Jenderal Ahmad Yani and Jalan Balai Kota, which is really one continuous street. Bank Negara Indonesia on Jalan Soekarno-Hatta normally has the best rates. There is also a branch of the Bank Rakyat Indonesia in the lobby of the Hotel Danau Toba, where you can change cash and travellers' cheques, outside banking hours even if you're not staying at the hotel.

Post & Telecommunications The post office, an old Dutch building, is on the main square in the middle of town. International phone calls can be made from PT Indosat at Jalan Ngalenko at the Jalan Thamrin junction.

Foreign Embassies There are consulates for West Germany, UK, the USA and various other countries in Medan.

Things to See

The level of activity that makes Medan such an interesting place also makes it overwhelming and a difficult place to spend a long time in. Its population and stark contrasts make it one of those places where you can step out onto the street and always find something new.

The main European buildings are scattered along Jalan Balai Kota and include the buildings now used as the Bank Indonesia and the post office – both fine examples of colonial architecture. Breaking up the skyline are modern edifices like the **Deli Dharma Shopping Complex**, three floors of glittering neon-lit shopping arcades straight out of Singapore and a nightly hangout for Medan's gays.

The **Parisada Hindu Dharma** temple is on the corner of Jalan Teuku Umar and Jalan H Zainul Arifin. Cultural performances are put on at **Taman Budaya** on Jalan Perintis Kemerdekaan, near PT Indosat. The tourist office has a list of what's on. The amusement park or Taman Ria is on Jalan Binjai and is the site for the **Medan Fair** around August.

A bemo ride further along Jalan Sisingamangaraja is Medan's zoo, the **Taman** Margasawata. There's a **crocodile farm** in Medan as well.

Belawan is the port for Medan, through which most of the area's exports flow. It's 28 km from the city.

The Hash House Harriers

Another reminder of the colonial days still going strong is Medan's Hash House Harriers. The Harriers originated in Malaysia in the 1930s, although the game has its real origins in British public schools. The name is supposed to come from an eating house in Kuala Lumpur then referred to as the 'Hash House'. The English would run after work on Monday afternoons – partly for amusement, partly for sport and partly to baffle the locals.

The general idea is that a bunch of mad dogs and Englishmen (the runners or 'hounds') chase a trail laid out by an imaginary 'hare'. When the trail comes to a dead-end the runners shout 'checking' and then fan out to try and pick up the trail again. When this is done, cries of 'On! On!' rally the hounds, who continue the 'chase'.

The Medan Hash House Harriers usually run on Mondays at 5 pm. For instructions on when and where to meet, collect the Hash Sheet at Lyn's Bar at Jalan Ahmad Yani 98 (next to the Tip Top Restaurant). There's a fee of about 4000 rp for men and 3000 rp for women, and all are welcome.

Mesjid Raya & Istana Maimoon

The Great Mosque is on Jalan Sisingamangaraja while the Maimoon Palace is nearby on Jalan Katamso. The large and neglected mosque dates from 1906 and the palace from 1888. They were both built by the Sultan of Deli.

Museums

The new **Museum of North Sumatra** (☎ 716792), at Jalan H M Joni 51, is open Tuesday to Sunday from 8 am to 5 pm and costs 200 rp. It is a good and quite extensive cultural and historical museum of the North Sumatra Province. Most exhibits are well marked, and there are well-informed

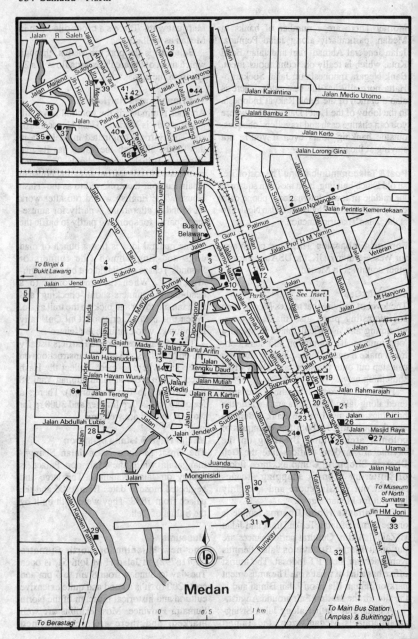

Medan

English-speaking guides who will happily answer any questions.

Diagonally opposite the Hotel Danau Toba International on Jalan H Zainul Arifin 8, the **Bukit Barisan Military Museum** has a small collection of weapons, photos and memorabilia from WW II, the War of Independence and the Sumatra Rebellion of 1958.

Places to Stay – bottom end

The *Sigura Gura* at Jalan Suprapto 2K is rather dull and dismal, although for Medan it's good value with dorm beds for 2500 rp and rooms for 6000 rp.

The *Losmen Irama*, in a little alley at Jalan Palang Merah 1125, by the junction of Jalan Listrik and very close to the big Hotel Danau Toba International. It's a convenient and well-kept place with dorm beds for 2500 rp and rooms for 3500/5000 rp, some of which are box like.

The *Penginapan Tapian Nabaru* (☎ 512155) is at Jalan Hang Tuah 6, right by the river. This is a quiet place with dorm beds at 2500 rp and rooms at 5000 rp per person.

Wisma Sibayak is at Jalan Pattimura 627, several km from the city centre on the road towards Berastagi. It's associated with Wisma Sibayak in Berastagi and has dorm beds at 2000 rp, rooms at 5000 rp.

Other cheap places in town include the *Hotel Rion* at Jalan Palang Merah 5b, near the railway lines. Also try the *Hotel Melati* (☎ 516021) at Jalan Masjid Raya 6, close to the bus station on Jalan Sisingamangaraja. It's a larger hotel with rooms at 7500, 17,500 and 20,500 rp. Or there's *Wisma Juli* (☎ 323104), off Jalan S M Raja at Gang Pagaruyung 79B, where there are plenty of good and clean rooms with fans for 5000/10,000 rp.

Krishen's Yoghurt House (☎ 516864), at Jalan Kediri 96 was formally the infamous Jacky's. He renamed himself and the place because of his bad reputation for harassing Western women and for selling overpriced tickets. Lately, we have received letters from many travellers complaining that Krishen is still overcharging them for tickets, and that transport arranged by him fails to show up.

Places to Stay – middle

There are a string of middle and upper-range hotels along Jalan Sisingamangaraja. The *Hotel Sumatera* (☎ 24973) at Jalan Sisingamangaraja 35 has rooms from 20,000 rp with mandi and fan, and from 26,000 rp with air-con, including breakfast.

The *Hotel Garuda* (☎ 22775) at Jalan Sisingamangaraja 27 has clean rooms from 20,000 rp without bathroom, and 30,000 rp with bathroom. It has been recently renovated, but the rooms facing the street are noisy.

The *Hotel Dhaksina* (☎ 324561) on Jalan Singamangaraja has rooms from 22,000 rp with bathroom and fan, and up to 48,000 rp with bathroom, air-con and television. It's a clean and bright place.

Places to Stay – top end

There are many up-market hotels in Medan. Not to be confused with the Hotel Garuda is the *Hotel Garuda Plaza* (☎ 326255) at Jalan Sisingamangaraja 188. It is a fine hotel with rooms from 90,000 rp, plus tax.

In the middle of town is the high-rise *Hotel Dharma Deli* (☎ 327011) at Jalan Balai Kota, next to the Deli Dharma Shopping Complex. Rooms start from 50,000/70,000 rp plus tax and service charges.

The *Hotel Danau Toba* (☎ 327000) at Jalan Imam Bonjol 17 is a huge edifice in the middle of town with rooms from 139,400 rp.

A few other fine hotels to try are the *Polonia Hotel* (☎ 325300) at Jalan Jenderal Sudirman 14; or *Hotel Dirga Surya* (☎ 321555) at Jalan Imam Bonjol 6; and *Hotel Tiara Medan* (☎ 516000) at Jalan Cut Mutiah.

Places to Eat

During the day Jalan Semarang is just a dirty back alley but come nightfall it's jam-packed with food stalls which set up along the street across Jalan Bogor between Jalan Pandu and Jalan Bandung. Jalan Semarang is the third block beyond the railway line. It's got great Chinese food.

Kampung Keling on Jalan H Zainul Arifin is an area with lots of small *gangs* (lanes) and numerous warungs specialising in different kinds of food – Chinese, Indian, Indonesian and European.

The *Tip Top Restaurant* at Jalan Ahmad Yani 92 has consistently good food at reasonably cheap prices, and is very popular with travellers. They also do baked goods and ice cream. A few doors down at No 98 is *Lyn's Restaurant*, a gathering place for Medan business people and expatriates, with a predominantly Western menu. The *France Modern Bakery* is at No 24 C Jalan Pemuda.

There are several Padang restaurants near the junction of Jalan Sisingamangaraja with Jalan Pandu. Or try the *Rumah Makan Famili* at Salan Sisingamangaraja 21B or the *Rumah Makan Gembira* by the railway line.

A good and cheap Indian restaurant is *G's Koh I Noor* at Jalan Mesjid 21. It is a family-run place with good curries and biriyanis. They also provide travel information. *Medan Bakers*, just beyond the Hindu temple at Jalan H Zainul Arifin 150, has excellent baked goods.

If you're hanging out for some junk food there is *Kentucky Fried Chicken* on the corner of Jalan IR Juandu and Brigjend Katamso. *Pizza Hut* is on the corner of jalans Multatuli and Let Jenderal Suprapto.

Things to Buy

Medan has a number of interesting arts and crafts shops, particularly along Jalan Ahmad Yani. Try Toko Asli at No 62, Toko Rufino at No 64 and Toko Bali Arts at No 68. There is a good selection of antique weaving, Dutch pottery, carvings and other pieces in all of these shops. Other good ones include Rufino at Jalan Ahmad Yani 64 which has a wide range of artefacts from Nias and northern Sumatra. The Toko Buku Deli at Jalan Ahmad Yani 48 has many books on Indonesia in English.

Getting There & Away

Medan is the major travel centre in Sumatra

and an important arrival or departure point for overseas.

Air There are international flights from Medan to Singapore, Kuala Lumpur and Penang. For details see the Getting There & Away section at the start of the Sumatra chapter. Sempati Air have the cheapest fare from Medan to Penang for 88,000 rp.

Airport tax for international departures is 10,000 rp.

MAS (☎ 519333) is in the Hotel Danau Toba International at Jalan Imam Bonjol 17. Garuda have two offices, one is in the Hotel Tiara Medan (☎ 25702) and the second office is in the Hotel Dharma Deli (☎ 516400), opposite the post office. Singapore Airlines (☎ 51811) is in the Polonia Hotel on Jalan Jenderal Sudirman. Merpati (☎ 514102) is at Jalan Brigjen Jenderal Katamso 41J. Mandala (☎ 513309) is at Jalan Katamso 37 E. SMAC (☎ 516617) is at Jalan Imam Bonjol 59.

Merpati/Garuda has the most domestic flights from Medan. In Sumatra these include daily flights to Bandarlampung, Banda Aceh, Batu Besar (Pulau Batam), Padang, Pakanbaru and Palembang. There are also daily flights to Jakarta (304,000 rp). Mandala has daily flights from Medan to Jakarta. SMAC has daily flights from Medan to Gunung Sitoli on Pulau Nias.

Bus Medan is the major crossroads for bus travel in North Sumatra. See the relevant sections for more detailed information.

Parapat is the number one destination from Medan and buses depart very regularly. The trip takes about four hours and costs 3000 rp. Touts may besiege you for this bus but you can safely ignore them. The buses depart along Jalan Sisingamangaraja.

There is a new main bus station, Amplas, in South Medan on Jalan Pertahanan, off Jalan S M Raja. A yellow opelet costs 250 rp to and from the centre of Medan. All the old bus stations around Medan still operate buses to various destinations. See the map for locations. The trip to Berastagi takes less than two hours and costs 1000 rp. Other fares

include Bukittinggi 12,500 rp or 17,500 rp with air-con, Padang at 14,000 rp or 18,000 rp with air-con and Banda Aceh for 20,000 rp or 22,275 rp with air-con.

Boat See the introductory Sumatra Getting There & Away section for information on the ferry service between Penang and Medan. The Medan agent for the high-speed catamaran *Selesa Ekspres* is Eka Sukma Wisata Tour at Jalan Brigjen Jenderal Katamso 35C. Pelni ships connect Medan with Jakarta and on to other ports in Indonesia.

The Pelni liner *Lawit* operates a service from port to port along the Sumatran east coast, stopping in Medan's port of Belawan. See the Getting Around chapter for the *Lawit's* timetable. The Pelni office in Medan is at Jalan Sugiono, a block back from Jalan Pemuda and close to the tourist office.

Train The train from Medan runs twice a day to Tanjungbalai and Pematangsiantar in North Sumatra, costing 2500 rp one way or 5000 rp return.

Taxi There are several long-distance taxi operators in Medan. Inda Taxi (☎ 510036) is at Jalan Brigjen Jenderal Katamso 60, near the Merpati office and the Penang ferry office. They have taxis to Parapat for 9500 rp, to Sibolga for 12,000 rp and to Pakanbaru for 25,500 rp. Another taxi company is Surya at Jalan Sisingamangaraja 107, and there are many other taxi companies in the area.

Getting Around
To/From the Airport The standard taxi fares from the airport depend on your destination in the city, but count on around 2000 rp in a taxi with a meter. Becaks are not allowed right into the airport area, so you have to walk the last couple of hundred metres. However, if you walk out of the terminal, becak drivers will instantly materialise. The fare into town is around 500 to 1000 rp.

The domestic terminal has a restaurant, snack bar, magazine stand and is much better than the international terminal. There's a tourist office outside the international terminal.

Local Transport There are plenty of opelets around town at a standard 200 rp. Medan also has plenty of motorised and human-powered becaks. Fares are from 500 to 1000 rp for most destinations around town by motorised becak, but you need to bargain.

You can get out to the port of Belawan for 250 rp by opelet. There is also a Damri Patas bus from Medan Plaza to Belawan that costs 600 rp per person, and an opelet from there to the harbour is 250 rp. Or you can charter a bemo for 2000 rp, take a tourist bus for 4000 rp, and catch a taxi for around 15,000 rp one way.

BINJEI

Binjei is on the road to Bukit Lawang from Medan, and it's necessary to change bemos here going either way. If you get stuck here it's possible to stay at Cafe de Malioboro Garden at Jalan Ksatria 1.

BUKIT LAWANG

Eighty km from Medan at Bukit Lawang is the Orang-utan Rehabilitation Station where these fascinating creatures are retrained to survive in the wild after a period of captivity. Apart from the attraction of the apes, the country around here is wild and enchanting with dense jungle and clear, fast-flowing rivers. There is a large rubber plantation on the edge of the reserve and it may be possible to visit the rubber processing plant.

Recently tube rafting has become very popular. Some guest houses and stalls on the way to the orang-utan rehabilitation centre rent them out for about 1000 rp. Be sure to ask about the water level first, as tubing can be very dangerous when the river is swollen by rains.

The Orang-utans

The reserve is bordered by the Bohorok River, and the PHPA have set up a viewing point over the river half an hour's walk uphill into the jungle. You need a permit to visit the reserve. These are available from the PHPA

office in Bukit Lawang. The permit is valid for three days and costs 3000 rp. The orang-utan feeding times are in the morning from 8 to 9 am and in the afternoon from 3 to 4 pm. These are posted in the PHPA office. These are the only times you're allowed to visit the reserve, other than with a guide and an organised trek. Beware as there are official and unofficial park rangers who might try to charge you each time you enter the park. When viewing the orang-utans, please don't touch or feed them. Remember you are there as an observer.

As for the orang-utans themselves, you are likely to see about half a dozen during each feeding session. A wooden platform has been built in the jungle and the Indonesian PHPA staff feed the orang-utans milk and bananas. The animals live off this until they have learnt to fend for themselves in the wild, and then wander off on their own accord. Once in the jungle they tear up tree bark, break open hard nuts and grind up tough vegetation with their large jaws and teeth. They mostly eat fruit, but also leaves and the shoots of plants, insects, eggs and small mammals.

Despite their remarkably human expressions, of all the great apes the orang-utan is considered to be the most distantly related to humans. In contrast to the smaller monkeys, the orang-utan is actually quite a lumbering creature, moving far slower and with less agility than, say, the gibbons. Unlike the gorilla, the orang-utan spends most of its time in the trees, only occasionally walking on the ground. They have very long arms, and use their heavy weight to sway trees back and forth until they can reach the next.

The name *orang hutan* is Malay for 'person of the forest'. Stories were told of how the orang-utan would carry off pretty girls. Others told of how the orang-utan could speak, but refused to do so because it did not want to be made to work. The orang-utan lives solely in Sumatra and Borneo, although fossilised remains have been found in China and Java.

The orang-utan has a long life-span but tends to breed slowly. Females reach sexual maturity at about the age of ten years. They have few young that don't leave their mothers completely until they are about seven to 10 years old. The females remain fertile until about the age of 30, and on average have only one baby every six years. The orang-utan tends to be quite a solitary creature.

Apart from Bukit Lawang and the Gunung Leuser National Park, orang-utans can also be found in Tanjung Puting and Kutai national parks and the Gunung Palung and Bukit Raja reserves in Kalimantan, and in neighbouring Sarawak and Sabah.

Orientation & Information

The Orang-utan Rehabilitation Station is part of the Taman Nasional Gunung Leuser (Gunung Leuser National Park). Bukit Lawang is the name of the settlement on the edge of the reserve, where the tourist camp and PHPA camp are situated. The small township near Bukit Lawang is called Bohorok, and you pass through it on your way up from Medan.

Next to the PHPA office is the WWF International Visitor Centre. It has plenty of information and displays on orang-utans and the fauna and flora of the national park area. They try to educate foreign visitors and locals alike on conservation of nature. Each night there is a good film about orang-utans at 8 pm, free of charge, that all visitors to the rehabilitation centre should see. Try to avoid seeing the orang-utans on Sunday as too many people come to see them.

Places to Stay & Eat

Those expecting accommodation in the wilds of Bukit Lawang will be disappointed or relieved, depending on your point of view. The tourist trade is now catered for by a row of nine bungalows and several restaurants resembling a slap-up, low-budget Club Med Resort.

The *Wisma Leuser Sibayak*, complete with bungalows, restaurant and concrete giraffes, is by the river on the edge of the reserve. Lodging is fairly expensive for what you get. Dorms cost 3000 rp, rooms start from 5000 rp, and bungalows on the river are

10,000 rp. This place is overrun with travellers, but the management is still friendly, although we have reeived complaints from travellers about the standards of service and cleanliness here.

A few minutes' walk downstream is the *Wisma Bukit Lawang Cottages* – basically a very similar place, but with dorms for 2000 rp, and rooms that start from 3000 rp. This place is further away from the centre of Bukit Lawang and therefore is quiet. It has nice, new bungalows on the river's edge for 10,000 rp.

The other places to stay are all spread along the river bank up to the rehabilitation centre. They have basic smaller bungalows which are cheaper than the two above mentioned establishments. Their prices vary from 1500 to 6000 rp. These are *Yusman, Wisma Bukit Lawang Indah, Selayang Indah, Queen Paradise, Jungle* and *Bohorok River*.

The food in the guesthouses is the usual travellers' fare at slightly higher prices, so don't expect too much, although the Sibyak does toss together the biggest fruit salads you have probably ever laid eyes on. There are a few warungs on the other side of the river which cater to the Indonesian tourist trade – the Sunday deluge is amazing to behold.

Getting There & Away

It takes two steps to get from Medan to Bukit Lawang on a very badly potholed road. First you take a bus from Jalan Sei Wempa in Medan to Binjei. The fare is 300 rp and the trip takes about 45 minutes. The bus will drop you off on the street in Binjei where you catch an opelet to Bukit Lawang. This costs 1750 rp and takes two to three hours. You should allow five hours to get from Medan to Bukit Lawang.

SIBOLGA

Sibolga is a little port north of Bukittinggi, where the road turns inland to Parapat and Lake Toba. The descent into Sibolga, approaching from Parapat, is very beautiful, particularly at sunset. The harbour itself is attractive and there are some good beaches nearby. It's not an unpleasant place, but is mainly a jumping-off point for Nias or an overnight stop between Bukittinggi and Parapat.

Orientation & Information

The main streets in the centre of town are Jalan Suprapto, Jalan Diponegoro and Jalan S Raja. There are two harbours. One is at the end of Jalan Horas. The other is at Jalan Pelabuhan. The centre of town is about midway between these two harbours, both only a short becak ride away.

The post office is at Jalan Dr Sutomo 40.

Beaches

Pantai Pandan is a pleasant beach and part of the village of the same name. There is a good restaurant there, the Ramayana, that has great inexpensive seafood. A few hundred metres further from Sibolga is Pantai Kalangan which is isolated but has a 250 rp entry fee. Both beaches get very crowded with locals on the weekend, but are great for a short visit while you're waiting for a boat or a bus from Sibolga. Opelets run to and from Sibolga to both beaches all day for 250 and 300 rp respectively.

Places to Stay

The only sore point regarding Sibolga is a lack of decent hotels. Most are drab, gloomy and depressing. Many hotels are on Jalan Suprapto, Jalan Horas and Jalan Diponegoro.

One the best hotels in town is the *Hidap Baru* (☎ 21957) at Jalan Suprapto 123. This is a clean, quiet, modern hotel. Simple rooms start from 8000 rp. Rooms with bathroom and air-con start from 22,000 rp.

Also try the reasonable *Hotel Indah Sari* (☎ 21208) at Jalan A Yani 29 which has basic rooms from 7000 rp, and air-con rooms with bathrooms from 15,000 rp. At No 20 *Hotel Mutiara Indah* (☎ 21681) has basic rooms for 5,000 rp, and clean and airy rooms with mandi from 10,000 rp. In the north end of town is the *Hotel Tapian- Nauli* (☎ 21116), at Jalan Let Jen S Parman 5, which has nice

rooms with balcony and bathroom starting at 18,000 rp.

Among many other cheap places with depressing rooms the *Losmen Subur*, at Jalan Diponegoro 19, and the *Hotel Sudi Mampir*, at Jalan Mesjid 100, have rooms for around 2000 rp.

There are a number of cheap hotels and losmen along Jalan Horas near the port where boats to Nias depart from. Try the *Hotel Karya Samudra* at 134 where rooms cost from 5000 rp. Probably the best of the bunch is *Losmen Bando Kanduang* (☎ 21149) which has simple rooms for 5000 rp.

Places to Eat

As in most places in Sumatra, there are plenty of places to eat Padang or Chinese food. You can try Padang food at the *Berita* on Jalan Suprapto 102, almost opposite the Hotel Hidap Baru. A good, but more expensive Chinese restaurant is *Teluk Indah* on Jalan A Yani 63.

Getting There & Away

Bus The main bus station is on Jalan Sutoyo, but a number of bus companies have their own offices and terminals around town.

Makmur and Bintang Udara bus companies on Jalan Sutoyo have buses to Parapat and Medan, departing in the morning or the evening only. ALS on Jalan Sutoyo 30 have buses to Bukittinggi and Jakarta, as does KMS at Jalan A Yani 66 and they also have buses to Padang. PO Terang at Jalan Diponegoro 50 has buses to Padang and Bukittinggi.

Typical fares and journey times from Sibolga are: Parapat 4000 rp (four hours), Bukittinggi 7000 rp (12 hours), and Medan 6000 rp (eight hours).

Boat The Pelni liner *Kerinci* departs Sibolga once every two weeks for Padang, Tanjung Priok, Surabaya and beyond. See the Getting Around chapter for the timetable. Pelni (☎ 22291) is at Jalan Patuan Anggi.

From Sibolga you can take a ferry to Teluk Dalam or Gunung Sitoli on the island of

Nias. See the Getting There & Away information in the Nias section for more details.

Getting Around

Becaks cost 300 rp for most distances in town. Of course when you arrive in town at the bus station they try to charge you many times this amount.

Karo Batak Highlands

The Karo Bataks inhabit a portion of north Sumatra covering some 5000 sq km immediately to the north of Lake Toba. The town of Berastagi is the main centre of the area. The Karo Bataks are bounded by coastal Malays in the east, the Simalungun Bataks to the south, and other ethnic groups to the west. Only Lake Toba prevents any direct contact between the homelands of the Karo Batak and the Toba Bataks.

The Karo are just one of several Batak groups in northern Sumatra, grouped together because of their similar culture and languages.

History

Not much is known about the pre-colonial history of the Karo Bataks, or for that matter of the other Batak people. Although there is an indigenous Batak script it was never used to record events, and for the most part it seems to have been used only by priests and *dukuns* in divination and to record magic spells.

Batak stories suggest that the Bataks came from somewhere to the east of Sumatra, perhaps from India. The cultivation of wet field rice, the type of houses, chess, cotton and even the type of spinning wheel used by the Bataks has been put down to Indian influence. Indian writing as well as Hindu religious ideas are also supposed to have had a strong influence on the Batak. Much of this may have come to an end as Islam began to take hold in Sumatra.

However, the Karo Batak for the most part never adopted Islam themselves. They were constantly at odds with the Islamic Acehnese to the north, who several times tried to conquer them and convert them to Islam. The Karo were possibly able to resist because they could never be finally defeated in battle. The Karo were never organised as a single political entity and had no centralised authority. If one Karo group was defeated, the enemy always had the next group to contend with.

Interestingly enough, despite long years of resistance to the Acehnese, when the Dutch arrived on the scene the Karo were easily subdued. Poorly armed, the Karo put up little show of resistance against the Dutch, who established control of this part of northern Sumatra in 1906. The Karo now came under centralised colonial control. Slavery was abolished, inter-village warfare was stopped, and Christianity began to take root. Kabanjahe developed as the centre of Dutch administration of the region, until the Japanese invasion and occupation in WW II.

Today the Karo Batak highlands are known primarily in Indonesia as a rich source of fruit and vegetables, much of it sent down to Medan and other cities of eastern Sumatra, or exported to Penang and Singapore. The area is also an important tourist area, rivalling Lake Toba in popularity. In the area around Berastagi you can find many interesting villages with high roofed traditional houses, very different from those built by the Toba Bataks, where it is still possible to see traditional marriage, funeral and other ceremonies. Berastagi is also close to some of north Sumatra's mighty volcanoes, some of which can be climbed.

BERASTAGI (BRASTAGI)

Centre of the Karo Batak people, Berastagi is a hill town some 1300 metres above sea level and 70 km along the back road from Medan to Lake Toba.

Orientation & Information

Berastagi is essentially a one-street town spread along Jalan Veteran. Wisma Sibayak and the Ginsata Hotel are both good information sources. In the middle of Jalan

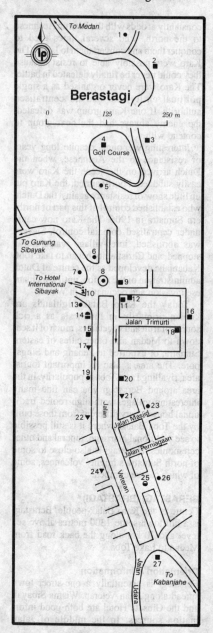

To Medan

Berastagi

0   125   250 m

To Gunung
Sibayak

To Hotel
International
Sibayak

Golf Course

Jalan Trimurti

Jalan Masjid

Jalan Perniagaan

Veteran

Jalan Udara

To
Kabanjahe

■ PLACES TO STAY

2   Rose Garden Hotel
3   Rudang Hotel
4   Hotel Bukit Kubu
9   Ginsata Hotel
11 Losmen Timur
12 Hotel Anda
15 Torong Inn
16 Losmen Trimurty
18 Merpati Inn
20 Losmen Sibayak Guesthouse
27 Wisma Sibayak

▼ PLACES TO EAT

17 Asia Restaurant
21 Rumah Makan Terang
22 Eropah Restaurant
24 Restaurant Ora et Labora

OTHER

1   Peceren Traditional Longhouse
5   Power Station
6   Petrol Station
7   Fruit Market
8   Memorial
10 Tourist Office
13 Telephone Office
14 Post Office
19 Public Health Centre
23 Ria Cinema
25 Bus & Opelet Station
26 Market

Veteran, near the tourist office, is a travel agent called Rafflesia Tourist Information. However, many travellers have complained that they have been overcharged and given incorrect information by them.

Tourist Office The newly built tourist office is between the post office and the fruit market, but was not in operation at the time of research.

Money It's best to change money before arriving here. The Wisma Sibayak will change US dollar travellers' cheques, as well as cash for various foreign currencies at a bad rate. The Bank BNI 1946 on Jalan Sakti in

Kabanjahe, near Berastagi, has better rates. Even better rates are available at one of the large hotels like the Hotel Bukit Kuba or Hotel International Sibayak in Berastagi.

Post The post office is on Jalan Veteran.

Things to See

Dominating the main street of Berastagi is the cone-shaped volcano Gunung Sibayak. Although it's not visible from most of Berastagi because of the buildings, you can see it from the fruit market/post office area of the town, on the walk to Lingga or from the bus heading down to Kabanjahe. Although Berastagi has some interesting markets, the main attractions are the villages and volcanoes in the surrounding area.

Jungle Trekking

The great Sumatran jungle trekking scene is probably the most comical product of the island's mass tourist trade. While there are a few good guides around, the usual thing seems to be for little bands of foreigners to lumber off into the wilds in the company of self-appointed escorts who speak minimal English, can't knock together two facts about a jungle (or if they can, can't explain them) and get lost anyway.

Those people who are really hoping to see the elusive Sumatran tigers, woolly rhino or even a couple of wild orang-utans, would be better off teaming up with David Attenborough the next time he wanders through. Or try the local zoo. Failing that, there are always the locals who actually make their living in the jungle. But contacting them would require a different approach to travel – plus more time, money and effort than most people care to put into it.

On the other hand, if you don't expect too much, then by most accounts the wild and unruly expeditions seem to be fun. Gather together a few hardy Swedes, a couple of lunatic-fringe Australians, stir gently with some wacky Indonesians, add water (usually in the form of great tropical downpours) and you wind up with Tarzan's Sumatran Adventure. The guest books in the Wisma Sibayak at Berastagi are a fine source of comment and opinions regarding the various jungle jaunts around Berastagi and Bukit Lawang.

Places to Stay – bottom end

Berastagi has a very popular travellers' centre and some other good back ups. *Wisma Sibayak* at Jalan Udara 1, the Kabanjahe end of the main street, has dorm beds at 2500 rp and rooms at 5000 rp per person, all with shared toilet facilities. It's packed with travellers and has a very popular restaurant. A lot of people seem to make lengthy stays here and their guest books are packed with useful and amusing information about sightseeing, festivals, transport, walks, climbs and other things to do in the area. The owner, Mr Pelawi, is a fund of local information. As they get quite full, their back-up place is *Losmen Sibayak Guesthouse* at Jalan Veteran, where singles/doubles are 3500/4000 rp.

At the other end of the main street at Jalan Veteran 79 is the *Ginsata Hotel*. It is clean and quite OK, with rooms including mandi for 6000 rp and a nasi Padang restaurant downstairs. The manager, Mr Ginting, is helpful and informative.

There are a number of alternatives, including the modern *Torong Inn* at Jalan Veteran 128 with basic dorms at 3000 rp and similar rooms at 5000 rp. Much better rooms including mandi cost 7500 rp. Just off the main road at Jalan Trimurti 4 is the new *Merpati Inn* with clean rooms from 3000 rp and larger ones including mandi at 7500 rp.

Places to Stay – middle

There are a few mid-range and expensive hotels on the northern outskirts of the town. The *Hotel Bukit Kubu* (☎ 20832) at Jalan Sempurna has rooms from 25,000/30,000 rp, including breakfast but plus tax. This is a fine, chalet-style hotel in the middle of a manicured golf-course – there are even a few tennis courts thrown in.

The *Rudang Hotel* (☎ 20921), at Jalan Piceren, has bungalow accommodation from 31,500/37,000 rp, plus tax. It's set in a valley with a large restaurant overlooking a big swimming pool.

Places to Stay – top end

The *Rose Garden Hotel* (☎ 529078) at Jalan Piceren has rooms from 48,000 rp, including breakfast. It's a great place, decorated in a pseudo-Spanish hacienda style with two and three storey buildings built around a central courtyard and swimming pool.

Hotel International Sibayak (☎ 20928) at Jalan Merdeka is just outside Berastagi on the road to Bukit Gundaling. It's a modern international hotel offering all the facilities usually provided by such an establishment, including a large swimming pool. Rooms cost from 82,000 rp up to 215,000 rp plus tax.

Places to Eat

Restaurants are stretched out like beads on a string along Jalan Veteran, Berastagi's main street. A good Padang food restaurant is the *Rumah Makan Muslimin* at Jalan Veteran 128, just around the corner from the cinema. This place has a great selection of meat (including chicken heads), fish and vegie dishes at remarkably cheap prices. Another good place is the *Ginsata Hotel*.

Other restaurants include the simple Chinese *Rumah Makan Terang* at No 369 with straightforward but tasty food. Across the street is the equally bright and cheerful *Eropah Restaurant* at 48G. The *Asia Restaurant* at Nos 9 and 10 is a bigger, more expensive Chinese place. The food is deservedly popular at the *Wisma Sibayak*.

You can buy your own food from the fruit and vegetable market off Jalan Veteran or try the local market further up the road. At night try the delicious cakes made from rice flour, palm sugar and coconut and steamed in bamboo cylinders. Buy them at the stall outside the cinema for 100 rp.

The only places in Indonesia where the sweet *marquisa*, a type of passionfruit, grows are Berastagi and Sulawesi. In Berastagi it's used to make a cool drink which is very popular locally.

Things to Buy

There are a number of interesting antique and souvenir shops along Jalan Veteran. Crispo Antiques has particularly interesting items.

Getting There & Away

Bus Berastagi's bus station is on Jalan Veteran. There are frequent buses from Berastagi to Medan. The trip takes two hours and costs 1000 rp. There are also frequent buses from Berastagi to Kabanjahe, 12 km away, costing 200 rp.

To get to Parapat from Berastagi, first take a bus to Kabanjahe for 200 rp. From Kabanjahe, take another bus to Pematang Siantar for 1400 rp. From Pematang Siantar, take a bus to Parapat for 600 rp. From Parapat you can catch the ferry to Samosir Island on Lake Toba. It's a rough ride between Pematang Siantar and Kabanjahe and takes three to four hours.

Berastagi is the jumping-off point for visiting Kutacane and the Gunung Leuser National Park. For details, see the section on Kutacane, in the Aceh Province section.

AROUND BERASTAGI

Gunung Sibayak

From Berastagi you can climb Gunung Sibayak, a 2094-metre-high volcano, and have a soak in the hot springs (500 rp) on the way back. Wear good walking boots because the path is wet and slippery all year round and start early because the walk takes all day. Bring food and water.

The guest books at Wisma Sibayak have a lot of useful information about making this climb and various other walks in the area. The walk takes about six hours there and back and you should be able to get a map at the Ginsata or the Wisma Sibayak. Avoid going on weekends as there are hordes of Medan weekenders on the mountain.

Gunung Sinabung

Taking the bus from Berastagi to Kabanjahe you'll spot the cone-shaped Gunung Sinabung. It's also possible to climb this volcano – six hours up and fours hours back

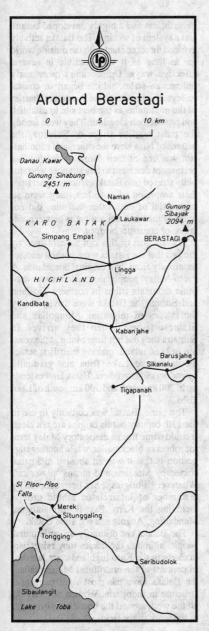

Around Berastagi

0   5   10 km

Danau Kawar
Gunung Sinabung
2451 m
Naman
Gunung Sibayak
2094 m
K A R O   B A T A K
Laukawar
Simpang Empat
BERASTAGI
Lingga
H I G H L A N D
Kandibata
Kaban jahe
Barusjahe
Sikanalu
Tigapanah
Si Piso-Piso
Falls
Merek
Situnggaling
Tongging
Seribudolok
Sibaulangit
Lake   Toba

down. The trek starts from the village of Mardingding. The trail to the top of the mountain starts near the village; you take the same one down again. The views from the top are very impressive as Gunung Sinabung is some 2450 metres high. Take food and water with you, and a torch, just in case you end up walking back down in the dark.

Si Piso-Piso Waterfalls

The impressive Si Piso-Piso waterfalls are near the northern end of Lake Toba. They're 24 km from Kabanjahe and only about 300 metres from the main road.

Kampung Peceren

This cluster of traditional houses is on the outskirts of Berastagi and has almost been absorbed by the town. The village comprises of half a dozen traditional houses – all occupied, except one.

Lingga

If you're interested in architecture, visit the village of Lingga 16 km south of Berastagi. Lingga is an interesting, if rather run-down Karo Batak village with many traditional houses – some in a very poor state of repair.

The design of these houses with their horn-shaped roofs has remained unchanged for centuries. Most of the ones in Lingga are reputed to be well over 250 years old and not a single nail was used in their construction. Whether the houses are really that old is not known.

There's a 200 rp entry fee into the village. The people, especially the women, do not like being photographed.

To get to Lingga by bus, first go by bus from Berastagi to Kabanjahe for 200 rp. Then take a bemo to the junction of Jalan Kapten Bangsi Sembiring, Jalan Kapten Pala Bangun and Jalan Veteran, where you catch another bemo to Lingga for 150 rp.

Cingkes

Cingkes is a Karo Batak village in the Simalungun Batak region, about 22 km from Berastagi. You have to take a round-a-bout way to get there.

The village has about two dozen traditional houses, most in a good state of preservation, as well as a spirit house or *tambak law burawan*. From Cingkes you can head back to Berastagi via the Si Piso-Piso Falls.

To get to Cingkes on public bemos you first have to go from Berastagi to Kabanjahe, then Kabanjahe to Situnggulung, Situnggulung to Seribudolok, and Seribudolok to Cingkes. You would be better off chartering a bemo from Kabanjahe. If you have a particular interest in Karo Batak architecture it is worth visiting this village.

Barusjahe

Barusjahe has a number of impressive traditional houses and rice barns, but their dilapidated condition suggests that this form of architecture is gradually dying out. There are several uninhabited houses as you come into Barusjahe, and another cluster of inhabited houses at the other end of the village. Two km from Barusjahe is the village of Sukajulu, which has one remaining traditional house, also in poor condition.

Buses to Barusjahe depart from the bus station in Kabanjahe. The trip takes half an hour to cover the 20 km and costs 500 rp. It stops off at Sukajulu.

Lake Toba Region

The Bataks, who live around Parapat, Lake Toba and in the Karo highlands, are one of North Sumatra's most interesting ethnic groups. Kabanjahe, Lingga and Berastagi are the centres of the Karo Batak lands. Pulau Samosir is in the middle of Lake Toba, and Parapat, on the shores of the lake, is the main jumping-off point for the island.

History

In 1783 Marsden astonished the 'civilised' world with his account of a cannibalistic kingdom in the interior of Sumatra, which nevertheless had a highly developed culture and a system of writing. The Bataks actively avoided direct contact with the outside world for as long as it was possible in several effective ways. Unlike most other early Indonesian states, which began in coastal valleys, the Bataks chose the natural barrier of the mountains as the best site to establish and protect their kingdom. They were among the most warlike tribes of Sumatra, the natives of Nias were the other, and cannibalism was one of their forms of defence – a permanent deterrent to any stranger who stupidly strayed into Batak territory. Apart from their suspicion of outsiders, they were so mistrustful of each other that they did not build or maintain natural paths between villages, or construct bridges.

Perhaps part of this can be explained by the fact that the Bataks were pushed unceremoniously from their original homelands. A Proto-Malay people descended from neolithic mountain tribes in northern Thailand and Burma, the Bataks were driven out by the hordes of migrating Mongolian and Siamese tribes. When they arrived in Sumatra they did not linger long at the coast but trekked inland, making their first settlements around Lake Toba and gradually spreading out from there. Batak land extends up to 200 km north and 300 km south of Lake Toba.

The name 'Batak' was certainly in use in the 17th century but its origins are not clear. It could come from a derogatory Malay term for robber or blackmailer, while another suggestion is that it was an abusive nickname coined by Muslims and means 'pig-eater'. Whatever its origins it has been adopted by a number of interrelated ethnic groups including the Karo, Pakpak, Simalungun, Mandailing, Angola and the Toba Batak.

The Bataks are primarily an agricultural people, although the horses they raise, particularly in the Karo highlands, are famous. In contrast to the matrilineal Minangkabau, the Bataks have the most rigid patrilineal structure in Indonesia. Women not only do all the work around the house but also much of the work in the fields.

Arts & Crafts

Traditionally the Bataks are skilled metalworkers and woodcarvers; other materials they use are shells, bark, bone and horns. They decorate their work with fertility symbols, magic signs and animals.

One particularly idiosyncratic form of art developed by the Toba Bataks is the magic augury book called *pustaha*. These books comprise the most significant part of their written history. Usually carved out of bark or bamboo, they are important religious records which explain the established verbal rituals and responses of priests and mourners. Other books, inscribed on bone or bamboo and ornately decorated at each end, document Batak myths.

Music is as important to the Bataks as it is to most societies, but traditionally it was played at religious ceremonies, rather than for everyday pleasure. Today they are famous for their powerful and emotive hymn singing. Most of their musical instruments are similar to those found elsewhere in Indonesia – cloth-covered copper gongs in varying sizes struck with wooden hammers, a small two-stringed violin which makes a pure but harsh sound, and a kind of reedy clarinet.

Porhalaan are divining calendars – of 12 months of 30 days each – engraved on a cylinder of bamboo. They are used to determine auspicious days on which to embark on certain activities such as marriage or the planting of the fields.

Architecture

Traditional Batak houses are built on stilts a metre to two metres from the ground. They are made of wood and roofed with sugar palm fibre or, more often these days, rusting corrugated iron. The roof has a concave, saddleback bend, and each end rises in a sharp point which, from certain angles, look like the buffalo horns they are invariably decorated with. The gables are usually extravagantly embellished with mosaics and carvings of serpents, spirals, lizards and monster heads complete with bulbous eyes.

The space under the main structure is used for rearing domestic animals like cows, pigs and goats. The living quarters, or middle section, is large and open with no internal walls and is often inhabited by up to a dozen families. This area is usually sectioned off by rattan mats which are let down at night to provide partial privacy. It is dark and gloomy, the only opening being a door approached by a wooden ladder.

A traditional village is made up of a number of such houses, similar to the villages of the Toraja people of central Sulawesi. A traditional Toba village or *huta* was always surrounded by a moat and bamboo trees to protect the villagers from enemy attack. The villages had only one gateway because of this. The houses in the village are lined up to the left and right of the king's house. In front of the houses is a line of rice barns, used for storing the harvest. Even today, walking around Samosir, you can still see how the villages were designed with defence in mind.

Culture

Traditional Lifestyle A purely Batak tradition is the *sigalegale* puppet dance, once performed at funeral ceremonies but now more often a part of wedding ceremonies. The puppet, carved from the wood of a banyan tree, is a life-size likeness of a Batak youth. It is dressed in the traditional costume of red turban, loose shirt and blue sarong. A red *ulos* (a piece of rectangular cloth traditionally used to wrap round babies or around the bride and groom to bless them with fertility, unity and harmony) is draped from the shoulders.

One story of the origin of the sigalegale puppet concerns a loving but childless couple who lived on Pulau Samosir. Bereft and lonely after the death of her husband, the wife made a wooden image of him. Whenever she felt intensely lonely she hired a dalang to make the puppet dance and a dukun to communicate with the soul of her husband through the puppet.

The other story goes that there was once a king who had only one child, a son. When his son passed away the king was grieved because he now had no successor. In memory of his dead son the king ordered a wooden statue to be made in his likeness, and when he went to see it for the first time invited his people to take part in a dance feast.

The sigalegale stand up on long, wooden boxes, through which ropes are threaded and operated like pulleys to manipulate the jointed limbs of the puppet. This enables the operator to make the sigalegale dance to gamelan music accompanied by flute and drums. In some super-skilled performances the sigalegale weeps or smokes a cigarette. Its tongue can be made to poke out, and its eyelids to blink. The sigalegale is remarkably similar in appearance to the *tau tau* statues of Tanatoraja in central Sulawesi, although the tau tau do not move.

Whatever, the sigalegale soon became part of Batak culture and was used at funeral ceremonies to revive the souls of the dead and to communicate with them. Personal possessions of the deceased were used to decorate the puppet and the dukun would invite the deceased's soul to enter the wooden puppet as it danced on top of the grave. At the end of the dance, the villagers would hurl spears and arrows at the puppet while the dukun performed a ceremony to drive away evil spirits. A few days later the dukun would return to perform another ceremony, sometimes lasting 24 hours, to chase away evil spirits again.

Religion & Mythology

Squeezed between two Islamic strongholds, the Acehnese to the north and the Minangkabau to the west, the Bataks were traditionally repressed or ignored. They were virtually isolated until the mid-19th century when Christian missionaries moved in.

Today the northernmost Batak groups are animists, Toba Bataks are Protestant and those further south Muslim, but most Bataks practise a complex mixture of traditional animist belief and ritual combined with aspects of Hinduism, Christianity and Islam. This combination is split into three main divisions: cosmology, *tondi* or concept of the soul, and ancestor and spirit worship.

The Bataks regard the banyan as the tree of life and relate a creation legend of their omnipotent god Ompung:

One day Ompung leant casually against a huge banyan tree and dislodged a decayed bough that plummeted into the sea. From this branch came the fish and all the living creatures of the oceans. Not long afterwards, another bough dropped to the ground and from this issued crickets, caterpillars, centipedes, scorpions and insects. A third branch broke into large chunks which were transformed into tigers, deer, boars, monkeys, birds and all the animals of the jungle. The fourth branch which scattered over the plains became horses, buffalo, goats, pigs and all the domestic animals. Human beings appeared from the eggs produced by a pair of newly-created birds, born at the height of a violent earthquake.

The tondi is described as the spirit, the soul, or a person's individuality. It is believed to develop before the child is born. It exists near the body and from time to time takes its leave, which causes illness. It is essential for Bataks to make sacrifices to their tondi to keep it in good humour.

PARAPAT

Almost sliding into the crater of Lake Toba is Parapat, a pleasure spot of the Medan wealthy set. The main centre in the area, Parapat is described glowingly in local tourist literature as the 'most beautiful mountain and lake resort in Indonesia' although, in fact, it's quite ordinary. For travellers it's mainly a jumping-off point for Pulau Samosir. Most travellers head straight to the island nine km away, unless they arrive after dark or at an inconvenient time to catch a boat.

Orientation & Information

Parapat is essentially in two parts: the line of restaurants and shops up on the Trans-Sumatran Highway, which buses bound to or from Medan or Bukittinggi pass by; and the part down by the lakeside from where ferries to Pulau Samosir depart. It's about one km between these two areas. Just where Jalan Pulau Samosir turns off from the Trans-Sumatran Highway there's a small tourist office with some limited information about Parapat and the lake.

Money The Sejahtera Bank Umum at Jalan Pulau Samosir changes travellers' cheques and currencies at reasonable rates.

Post The post office is at Jalan Sisingamangaraja.

Travel Agencies Parapat travel agents are notorious for bungling bus bookings, neglecting to make flight reservations from Medan (after you've paid) and other problems. Many agents also greatly overcharge for tickets, so make sure you know your fares before buying one.

Andilo Travel, with a main office at the main bus station and a smaller one by the ferry dock, generally seem to be quite good and will also change money (at 5% less than the bank rate). Bolok Silau is another agency by the dock, and operate a weekly tourist bus between Parapat and Berastagi.

Things to See
Look in at the expensive Parapat Hotel, where they sometimes put on performances of Batak singing or other local culture for tour groups.

Labuhan Garaga The village of Labuhan Garaga, 25 km from Parapat, is well worth a visit if you are interested in buying Batak blankets *(kain kulos)*. The colour and patterns vary a bit from tribe to tribe but the majority of weavings have vertical stripes on a background of ink blue with rust red and white the predominant colours. They're not cheap, but they are attractive and practical buys. The price range is from 30,000 to 70,000 rp or more for good quality cloth.

Organised Tours
There are various agencies operating tours of the surrounding area. Try PT Dolok Silau at the ferry dock. They have a tourist coach once or twice a week which includes tours to coffee, tea, ginger, clove and cinnamon farms, as well as other places of interest.

Festival
The week-long Danau Toba Festival is held every year in June. Canoe races are a highlight of the festival but there are also Batak cultural performances.

Places to Stay – bottom end
Parapat has plenty of places to stay, some of them quite pleasant, but the places on Pulau Samosir are such a bargain that Parapat ends up looking more expensive. You've got a choice of either staying up on the main road which is handy for buses but rather noisy, or down by the lake which is handy for the Samosir ferry. The expensive hotels, popular with weekend visitors from Medan or local holiday-makers, are mainly along the road from the Trans-Sumatran Highway to the ferry dock.

At the main bus station on the outskirts of the town along the Trans-Sumatran Highway is *Youth Hostel Melati*, where basic rooms cost 7000 rp. Next door is *Andilo Travel* with a restaurant, and they have a losmen behind their travel agency with rooms at 5000/7500 rp. Andilo also have a similar place at the Samosir Ferry Dock.

At Jalan Sisingamangaraja 84, directly opposite the lakeside turn-off, is the small and rather basic *Sudi Mampir* with rooms at 3000 rp. Continue further along and at No 109 the *Singgalang Hotel* has spacious and clean rooms at 5000 rp per person.

Down at the lakeside there are several places along Jalan Haranggaol, including the *Pago Pago Inn* close to the harbour at No 50. It's airy, has clean but simple rooms with shared toilet facilities at 5000 rp per person and there are fine views across the lake. Just down from it at No 47, the *Hotel Soioh Jaya* is also a modern place, but some of the rooms are just little boxes, even windowless, at 7500 rp. Better rooms with mandi are 15,500 and 17,500 rp.

Go right down to the ferry dock at the end of the road, turn the corner and *Wisma Gurning* is by the lakeside. It is a simple place with twin rooms including mandi for 10,000 rp.

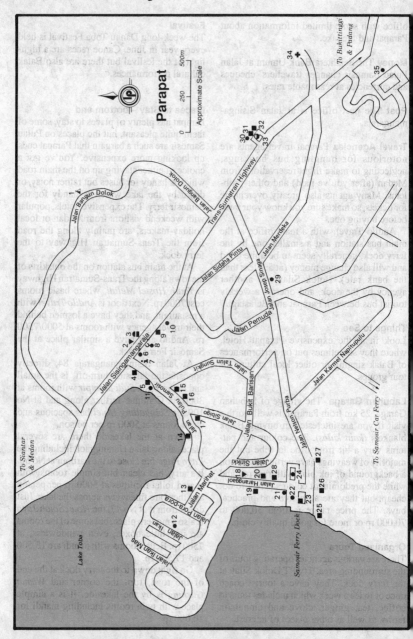

Parapat

Approximate Scale

0   250   500m

■ PLACES TO STAY		▼ PLACES TO EAT	
1	Camping Ground	2	Restaurant Asia & Losmen Sudi
2	Restaurant Asia & Losmen		Mampir
	Mampir	18	Hong Kong & Bali Restaurant
4	Wisma Danau Toba		
5	Toba Hotel		OTHER
9	Singgalang Hotel & Restaurant		
13	Hotel Parapat	3	Post Office
14	Hotel Tarabunga	6	Police Station
15	Hotel Atsari	7	Tourist Office
16	Hotel Danau Toba International	8	Mosque
17	Hotel Tarabunga Sibolga	10	PT Dolok Silau
19	Pago Pago Inn	11	Sejahtera Bank Umum
20	Riris Inn	12	Souvenir Shops
23	Andilo Travel & Losmen	21	Bolok Silau Travel Agency
25	Wisma Gurning	22	Market & Bus Station Area
26	Danau Toba Cottage	24	Market
27	Marina Inn	29	Telephone Office
28	Hotel Soloh Jaya	30	Health Centre
31	Andilo Travel & Losmen	33	Bus Terminal
32	Youth Hostel Melati	34	Hospital
		35	Golf Course

Places to Stay – middle

The *Hotel Atsari* at Jalan Pulau Samosir has rooms from 27,500/32,500 rp. The *Wisma Danau Toba* (☎ 41302) at Jalan Pulau Samosir 3/6 (not to be confused with the Hotel Danau Toba) has rooms from 24,000/33,000 rp plus tax.

The *Riris Inn* (☎ 41392) at Jalan Haranggaol 39, is a modern place with straightforward, well-kept rooms with mandis from 15,000 to 25,000 rp.

Places to Stay – top end

The *Hotel Parapat* (☎ 41012 at Jalan Marihat 1 is a good up-market hotel with rooms from 85,000 rp. It's a very salubrious hotel on a spacious block of land overlooking the lake.

The *Hotel Danua Toba International* (☎ 41583) at Jalan Pulau Samosir 17 has rooms from 65,000/75,500 rp. Despite it's rather mundane appearance, it's actually quite a comfortable place.

The *Hotel Tarabunga* (☎ 41700) at Jalan Pulau Samosir 20, has comfortable rooms

from 35,000/40,000 rp. There is a restaurant overlooking the lake. The similarly named *Hotel Tarabunga Sibolga* (☎ 41800) has rooms from 38,000/45,000 rp but it's a rather cavernous and sterile building.

Places to Eat

There are many cheap restaurants down towards the lake along Jalan Haranggaol, including some good Padang places. Try the side-by-side *Restaurant Hong Kong* at Nos 9 and 11 and the *Restaurant Bali* at No 13. They have very similar Chinese menus which are not cheap, but chicken with lychees at the Bali for 4500 rp is delicious. Padang and Chinese restaurants can also be found along Jalan Sisingamangaraja, as you come into Parapat from Medan.

Things to Buy

Parapat is also a good place to get Batak handicrafts like lime containers, leather, batik or woodcarvings. There is a weekend market in the harbour area.

Getting There & Away

Bus Buses to or from Medan run very regularly and cost 3500 rp or 7500 rp with air-con. The trip takes about four hours. If you want to travel via Berastagi you have to change buses at Siantar and Kabanjahe and it takes quite a time. See the Berastagi section for details and for information on the weekly tourist bus. It is cheaper to buy tickets as you change buses, rather than buy the overpriced through ticket that the travel agents try to sell you.

Buses to Bukittinggi take about 15 hours (although it can take much longer) and cost 11,000 rp or 15,000 rp with air-con. There's a weekly tourist minibus which costs 20,000 rp and is supposed to make the trip in 12 or 13 hours. Usually these are OK, but we have received several complaints that the air-con doesn't always work and that the journey takes two to four hours longer than advertised.

Typical bus fares from Parapat are: Berastagi 2200 rp, Medan 3000 rp, Sibolga 4000 rp, Bukittinggi 11,000 rp, Padang 10,100 rp, Pakanbaru 12,500 rp, Palembang 25,000 rp, and Jakarta 35,000 rp or 65,000 rp with air-con.

ANS bus company prices are very high, but it doesn't provide better service or buses than most other bus companies. A few travel agents in town charge very similar high prices so be careful.

Boat See the Lake Toba section for details of ferries to Pulau Samosir.

Getting Around

Opelets around Parapat, including from the main road down to the harbour, cost 200 rp.

LAKE TOBA & PULAU SAMOSIR

Lake Toba is dead centre in North Sumatra, 176 km south of Medan. It's high (800 metres above sea level), big (over 1700 sq km) and deep (up to 450 metres). The largest lake in South-East Asia, it is completely surrounded by steep mountains and ridges and sandy, pine-sheltered beaches.

The lake is, in fact, a volcanic depression now filled with water. The last volcanic eruptions are said to have occurred some 30,000 to 75,000 years ago. Pulau Samosir, in the middle of Lake Toba, is covered in lake sediment which indicates that at one time it was also submerged.

As the legendary birthplace of the mountain-dwelling Bataks, it is the centre of Batak culture and has several villages of historical interest. Tomok, Ambarita and Simanindo are the main ones. Christian tombs and the boat-shaped stone graves of Batak animists are scattered around the fields. Behind the narrow lakeside strip there's a high plateau.

Pulau Samosir is much more commercial than it was 10 or 15 years ago. What you get out of the place depends on what you're interested in doing here. Most foreigners stay in Tuk Tuk where there is nothing to see but it's a good place to relax. Anyone with an interest in the Toba Batak will gain more satisfaction from scrambling over the mountain ridge to the villages on the other side of the island.

Orientation & Information

The villages of Tomok, Tuk Tuk and Ambarita are the main tourist centres. Tuk Tuk and Ambarita have most of the accommodation, while Tomok and Ambarita are noted for their handicrafts and souvenir markets. From Tomok or Ambarita it is possible to trek over the mountains to the other side of the island. There are many villages along this route, and a number of settlements on the west coast of the island. The largest settlement is the township of Pangururan on the west coast.

Post The post office is in Ambarita. Several shops in Tuk Tuk sell stamps and have postboxes and lists of rates for overseas mail.

Money Change your money before you get to Lake Toba; exchange rates in Parapat are reasonable but on Samosir are poor. The Bank Rakyat Indonesia is in Ambarita. At the moment it doesn't change money, but the post office does.

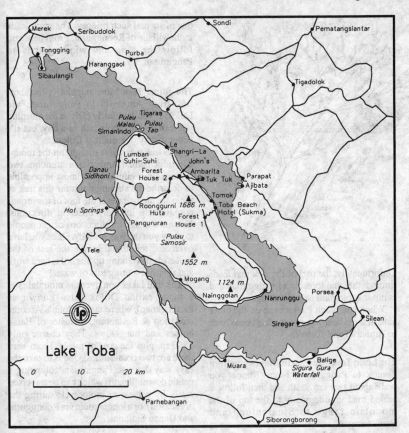

Lake Toba

0   10   20 km

Trekking

There are two main routes you can take to trek from the Tuk Tuk/Tomok/Ambarita area to the other side of the island. These are the Long Trek and the Short Trek.

Either way, you don't need to take much with you, but rain gear may make life more comfortable. The Samosir Bataks are hospitable people and although there are no warungs you can buy cups of coffee at villages along the way and reasonably priced meals can be arranged. All you have to do is ask and someone will volunteer to accom-modate you, offer you coffee or prepare you a meal. The going rate for overnight accom-modation is about 2000 rp.

If you are interested in ornithology there are many different kinds of birds to observe along the way. The flora is also varied with lots of coffee, cinnamon and clove trees as well as a carnivorous plant known as a monkey cup, which grows profusely on vines and devours insects.

Neither walk takes you through jungle or rainforest. In fact, most of Samosir is either pine forest, rubber trees or mixed scrub.

Clove

Unfortunately, the part of the trek that leads through the pine forest is a logging road and is not that pleasant to walk along.

When you reach Pangururan on the other side of the island you can catch a bemo back to Ambarita and Tomok.

The Long Trek The long trek takes you from Tomok to Pangururan. From Tomok you walk about two km south and then follow a sealed road up diagonally to the top of the mountain range to Sigarantung and Parmonangan.

After about 13 km you come to what is now a derelict building with a radio tower, called Forest House One (or Pasanggrahan to the locals). The house is reportedly very basic with a 'filthy mandi' although the people here will put you up for the night (for about 2000 rp) and cook food for you. This place is not safe for women travelling alone.

From Forest House One you walk along a muddy, dirt road 15 km to Forest House Two, that is used by logging trucks. Forest House Two is a ruin, although it's OK to shelter in. There's also a Batak village nearby.

Shortly after Forest House Two the track forks. Take the right fork, which soon afterwards crosses a bridge with a roof over it –

one of several such bridges. The track leads to the village of Roonggurni. From here you follow the long and winding road to Pangururan.

The Short Trek More popular is the short trek from Ambarita to Pangururan, via Dolok. If you start fairly early in the morning you can do the whole trek in a day, but it's better to stay overnight at Dolok.

This trek takes you straight up the mountain ridge behind Ambarita, a strenuous two to three-hour climb. It is almost impossible to describe the starting point for this trek as there are many trails at the foot of the mountain running in many different directions. You have to ask for directions or get people to show you the way initially. Once you have overcome this initial hurdle the rest of the trail is clear. Walking up this hill is hard work and *very* hot – bring lots of water!

The trail takes you over the mountains to a place called Dolok (also known as Partungkoan), where there's John's Accommodation & Restaurant, a cluster of Batak houses and bungalows. They charge only 1500 rp, plus the cost of meals. From here there are two possibilities. One is to take the easy way down to Pangururan, following a gentle downhill path (which can be traversed easily by vehicle or motorcycle during the dry season), or a longer route via Roonggurni and Danau Sidihoni.

Places to Stay

Samosir is a great place to rest up if you've just suffered the rigours of long days travelling on Sumatran buses from Padang or further south. Or to prepare yourself for that trip if you've only just arrived from Medan! Although it's no longer the traffic-free island it once was, Samosir is certainly easy-going and carefree enough to suit most people. This is not a place for frenetic activity, unless you define walking that way.

The standard cheaper losmen cost around 3000/5000 rp for singles/doubles, often in wooden batak-style buildings with private mandi (although overall they're pretty simple and basic). Some places have dorms. You can still find some very basic places at 2000 rp a single and 3000 or 4000 rp a double but these are extremely spartan.

Above these basic cheapies are the better-equipped rooms, sometimes in batak-style houses, typically around 7500 rp and usually with a verandah. There are so many places to stay the best advice is to wander around until you find something that suits. If you looking for quiet and isolated places there are a few to choose from. Nearly all of them are right by the lake.

Places to Eat

Once upon a time dining at Samosir was quite an occasion. 'Smorgasbords' were laid out for everybody at the place you stayed and these communal dinners were a nightly highlight of a Samosir stay. These days the food is much like any other travellers' centre and there are no real surprises, although most places still run a book for each guest with each banana pancake or fruit salad added to a list which can stretch to a surprising length over a week or two. There are few independent eating places, most are connected with the places to stay.

Getting There & Away

Boat There is always a host of colourful boats at the Parapat harbourside but most of them are tour boats. The ferry is simpler.

To/From Tuk Tuk Ferries operate between Parapat and Samosir from 7 am to 7.30 pm at one or two hour intervals. Treat departure times with caution and double check them. The trip over costs 800 rp and takes about half an hour if the weather is reasonable. It drops people off at Carolina's and the village centre of Tuk Tuk.

On your return journey the ferries will pick up passengers from various points on the Tuk Tuk Peninsula – ask the locals for location pick up points. They pull into the main ferry dock in Parapat, where buses are usually waiting to gather up passengers for Medan, Sibolga and other destinations. The

return fare is 500 rp, unless it's market day when it is 800 rp.

To/From Tomok There's also a car ferry which runs from Ajibata (about two km from Parapat) to Tomok every one or two hours between 7 am and 9.30 pm. The passenger fare is 500 rp.

To/From Ambarita Direct ferries to Ambarita leave Parapat every one or two hours for 800 rp.

Bus See the Parapat section for information on bus travel to and from Lake Toba. If you want to be certain of your booking and getting a fair price book any tickets in Parapat, not on the island.

To/From Berastagi There is a daily bus service from Pangururan to Berastagi via Sidikalang, but the road is very poor. A better but not a regular way to get to/from the island is via Haranggaol, a market town at the northern tip of the lake.

Every Monday there is a 7 am ferry from Ambarita to Haranggaol that costs 1000 rp and meets a bus to Berastagi that costs 1500 rp. The trip takes 2½ hours. On Thursday a ferry leaves Simanindo at 9 am and meets a bus to Berastagi.

From Sidikalang, it's also possible to get buses to Kutacane or Tapaktuan.

Getting Around

Local Transport It is possible to take irregular bemos from Pangururan to Ambarita (1500 rp) and Tomok (1800 rp). A road circles the entire island.

There are now some opelets irregularly running between Tomok and Ambarita, and continuing to Simanindo less frequently. There is no specific time schedule but services are more frequent in the morning.

Don't count on finding any public transport after 3 pm. Even at the best of times you can wait a long time between minibuses. It's a pleasant one-hour, five-km stroll from Tomok to Tuk Tuk. Apart from one's legs there's no regular public transport around or to Tuk Tuk.

You can rent motorcycles in Tuk Tuk for 20,000 rp a day, which is expensive compared to elsewhere in Indonesia. Bicycles can also be hired.

AROUND PULAU SAMOSIR
Tuk Tuk

Tuk Tuk is a tourist resort on the bulb-shaped peninsula on the east coast. This is where most foreigners stay, although there's nothing to see here. However, if you're recovering from your 19th nervous breakdown it's a great place to relax. On the other hand, it's fair to say that the peninsula is chronically overrated as a tourist attraction. Take Tuk Tuk for what it is – a quiet foreigner's enclave – and you'll probably have a pleasant enough time there, but don't expect to do much more than swim, swap travellers tales or gaze pensively across the

water from the verandah of your hotel or restaurant.

Lately we have received complaints that some of the locals are not as friendly anymore and are now concerned with only making money. There are quite often problems over rented motorbikes that have breakdowns, and the owner wants the renter to pay for the fault. Also, watch your gear as there have been some thefts even from Batak houses.

Places to Stay & Eat There are now some larger hotels popping up on Samosir, appealing to wealthy North Sumatrans or package tourists from Singapore.

Carolina's is still the longest running and most popular up-market place. They have a wide variety of rooms starting from the simplest ones at 10,000 through to 45,000 rp for the deluxe rooms with bathroom and balcony overlooking the lake. There's a restaurant, bar and even a diving board into the lake.

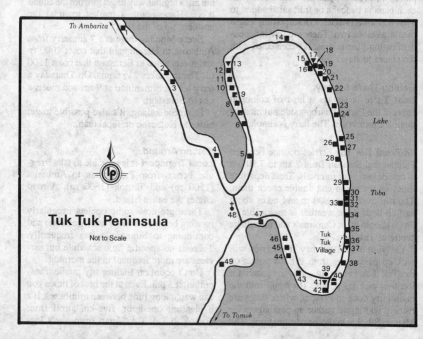

Tuk Tuk Peninsula
Not to Scale

The famous *Pepy* has a couple of 3000 rp rooms with the restaurant, close to Carolina. Continuing round the peninsula from Carolina you come to the big *Silintong Hotel* with rooms at 29,000 rp up to 78,000 rp. Then there's *Bernard's* and *Matahari's* which are two of the longest-running places on Samosir. Bernard's has rooms and bungalows for 10,000 rp. Matahari's has cheaper rooms for 6000 rp or for 7000 rp with bathroom. Others in this area include *Marraon*, *Romlan* and *Pos*.

After this cluster of places at Tuk Tuk there are more scattered along the road. The *Ambaroba Resort Hotel* is a three-star place under construction at the time of writing. Further on is *Endy's* with Batak houses at 3500 rp. Then there's a gap before coming to several modern places like *Samosir* where rooms cost 5000 rp per person, and there are several restaurants in the area. Past a longer

gap is the *Toledo Inn*, a big package-tour hotel with rooms at 50,000/55,000 rp. After another gap there's a tightly packed cluster of places. These include *Abadi's*, *Tony's*, *Kuridin's* and the very basic *Antonius*, all with rooms from 2000 to 3000 rp.

Continue on towards Ambarita and a trail descends down from the road past *Christina's*, *Miss Nina* and *Mas* to *Tuktuk Timbul* by the lakeside. This quiet and isolated place has simple rooms for 4000 rp and nicer rooms for 6000 rp. It's a fine place if you want to get away from it all.

Most places to stay also provide food and some owners can get nasty if you don't eat at the place you're staying. One of the old establishments is the famous *Pepy's Restaurant*. Back in the early days the Samosir smorgasbord reached its heights when Pepy was the power in the kitchen at *Bernard's*. Today her restaurant, just outside Carolina's, still turns out good food. *Carolina's* restaurant is still good and popular. There is occasionally live folk music at *Bernard's* restaurant but the food is unappetising, expensive and the portions are small.

Tomok

The village of Tomok is on the southern coast of Samosir. There are many examples of traditional Batak houses in Tomok and also fine old graves and tombs – carved stone sarcophagi with grotesque three-horned heads and bulging eyes. These creatures are called *singa* and their faces also decorate the facades of Toba Batak houses, at either end of the two big beams which support the main house structure.

If you follow the road away from the lake front and the souvenir stalls in the village you will come to the grave of King Sidabatu. This powerful Batak animist king not only had his own image carved on his tombstone but also that of his Muslim military commander and bodyguard, Tengku Mohammed Syed, and that of the woman he is said to have loved for many years without fulfilment, Anteng Melila Senega.

One of Tomok's traditional houses is now being used as a museum by the descendants of a Batak king said to have ruled Tomok 500 years ago.

Places to Stay & Eat Although few people stay at Tomok these days, there are plenty of restaurants and warungs for day-trippers. If you really want to stay there's *Mongoloi's* and a few other straightforward places like the *Tomok Shoganda Penginapan*.

A traveller's place is *Roy's Accommodation & Restaurant.* Roy is friendly and provides plenty of information about the island. His restaurant is in the middle of the town on the main street. The accommodation is on the edge of town and the basic rooms cost 3000/5000 rp. Ask about staying in a batak house.

Ambarita

A few km beyond Tuk Tuk is Ambarita, a pretty village. Like Tuk Tuk it's undergone

something of a development boom but it's still nowhere near as popular a place to stay as Tuk Tuk. Ambarita has several well-preserved reminders of its gory past. The most important of them is a group of stone chairs and a table, known as the cannibal king's dinner table. It was here that village meetings were held, disputes settled, war declared and wrongdoers tried and judged. It is said that serious offenders were led to a further group of stone furniture in an adjoining courtyard, where they had to kneel down and rest their head on a stone chopping block. Then, watched by a crowd of village men, they were dispatched from this world by the swift application of axe to neck. The villagers revel in telling you how the bodies were carved up and consumed bit by bit, but it's probably just a story for the tourists.

Places to Stay & Eat For those who really want to get away from it all *Gordon's* is a couple of km beyond Ambarita on the way to Simanindo. Most travellers who stay there like it, although we have had a number of complaints about it and their meals in the past. Rooms cost between 3000 to 7500 rp. A few hundred metres from it, is the Gordon family's other place, *Barbara's*, with unfriendly staff. On the other side of Gordon's is the flashy *Sopotoba* with rooms at 45,000/50,000 rp, including breakfast plus tax, and surrounded by lots of barbed wire.

A really isolated and friendly place is the popular *Le Shangri-la*. It's six km from Ambarita and you can get there by opelet for 300 rp. These run irregularly but are more frequent in the afternoons. Don't trust the locals when they tell you that there are no opelets as they want you to take their overpriced motorbikes. Dorms cost 2000 rp and bungalows are 4000/5000 rp.

Simanindo

About 16 km from Ambarita on the northern tip of the island is the village of Simanindo. Simanindo has a fine old adat house that has been meticulously restored and now functions as a museum. It was formerly the home of a Batak king, Raja Simalungun, and his 14 wives. Originally the roof was decorated with 10 buffalo horns which represented the 10 generations of the dynasty. Simalungun was the last in a line of 13 kings and according to one story he was assassinated because he collaborated with the Japanese. Other people say the last king died a natural death.

The museum has a very small collection of brass cooking utensils, spears, krises, weapons, Dutch and Chinese crockery, sculptures and other Batak carvings. Batak dances are performed at the museum daily (at least during the tourist season) starting at 10.30 am, including a performance using a sigalegale. The performance lasts two hours and costs 3000 rp.

Pangururan

Pangururan is the main settlement on the island, and is 16 km beyond Simanindo on the west coast. Stop off at the village of Lumban Suhi-Suhi if you are interested in seeing hand-weaving.

Places to Stay & Eat A good and cheap place to stay is *Mr Barat Accommodation* where rooms cost 3500 rp. Another good but more expensive place to stay is the *Hotel Wisata Samosir* (☎ 50) at Jalan Kejaksaan 42, on the west coast of Pulau Samosir. This clean hotel has rooms from 16,000 rp, and dorm beds for 5000 rp per person.

Things to Buy Day-to-day artefacts include wooden cylinders used to store lime, and old gunpowder flasks and bullet-holders made from buffalo horn. The *topeng* is a wooden mask used in funerary dances, designed to assure the deceased that their descendants will continue to serve them. *Silaon na bolon* are small wooden ancestral figures (usually in male/female pairs) revered as protection against evil. Most motifs on Batak artefacts have some meaning. For example, the land lizard (which Batak farmers often encounter when clearing forest for cultivation) represents the earth spirit and is therefore a symbol of fertility.

Toba Batak musical instruments include the *grantung*, consisting of several pieces of non-resonating slats of wood strung out on a harness, and hit with sticks – like a xylophone.

Both the Toba Batak and the Karo Batak employed *datu* – sorcerers or witch doctors. Pustaha are magic books made of accordion-folded bark leaves and wooden covers, which contain the datu's magic formulae written in Batak script. The *tunggal panaluan* is a magic wand which was used by the datu to predict the future and protect the village.

A Karo Batak variation on this is the *tungkot malehat* which is a magic wand characterised by a carved figure on the top end sitting on a horse which has the head of a *singa*. A singa is a mythical underworld figure which is half buffalo and half snake and which has the power to drive away evil spirits.

Porhalaans, the bamboo divining calendars, are commonly sold around Tomok, Tuk Tuk and Ambarita. There is a great deal of badly produced carving and handicrafts around Tuk Tuk and Ambarita. One person who produces much better wood-carving than almost everything else you'll see is Marlen Manik who has a coffee and cake shop on the road from Tuk Tuk to Ambarita.

Nias

Off the west coast of Sumatra, along the same latitude as Sibolga, is the large island of Nias. The island is very rugged, consisting mainly of rolling hills and thick tropical jungle.

It is said that the first Niassans were six people, some of whom were descended from the gods. Like other people of Sumatra and various parts of Indonesia, the Niassans made use of stone to produce monumental works of art.

Head-hunting and human sacrifice once played a part in their culture, as it did in the culture of the Bataks and the Torajas.

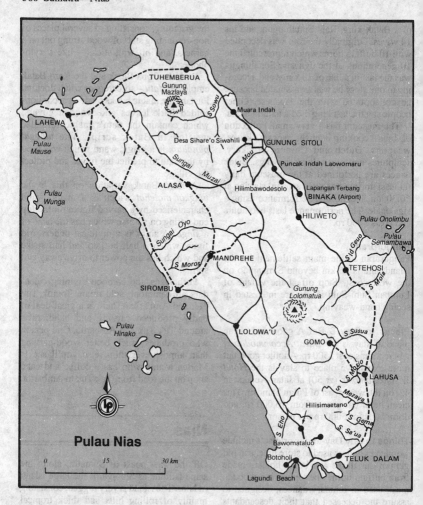

Pulau Nias

Because of this and other cultural connections, the Niassans are thought to be related to the Bataks of Sumatra, the Naga of Assam in India, the aborigines of Taiwan, and various Dayak groups in Kalimantan.

The Niassans developed a life based mainly on agriculture and pig raising. Hunting and fishing, despite the thick jungle and the proximity of many villages to the coast, was only of secondary importance. The Niassans relied on the cultivation of yams, rice, maize and taro. Pigs were both a source of food and of wealth and prestige; the more pigs you had the greater your status in the village. Gold and copper work, as well as wood carving, were important village industries.

The indigenous religion was thought to

have been a combination of animism and ancestor worship, together with some Hindu influences. Christianisation of the island did not really get under way until the 1850s, and during the first decades of the 20th century had become tied up with a number of indigenous messianic movements. Islam only gained some converts around the coast and in townships like Gunung Sitoli.

Villages were presided over by a village chief, heading a council of elders. Beneath the aristocratic upper caste were the common people, and below them the slaves (often used as trade merchandise). Sometimes villages would band together in federations, which were often perpetually at war with other federations. Prior to the Dutch conquest, inter-village warfare was fast and furious, usually spurred on by the desire for revenge, slaves, or human heads. Heads were needed when a new village was built and during the burial ceremony of the chief. In central Nias heads were reportedly a prerequisite for marriage. Today you can still see samples of the weapons used in these feuds: vests of buffalo hide or crocodile skin; helmets of metal, leather or plaited rattan; spears, swords and shields.

The recorded history of Nias only begins in the last years of the 18th century and the first years of the 19th century, when people like the Englishman Stamford Raffles began to send back reports about the island, and when the Dutch military and German missionaries began to make forays into it. Yet it was not until 1914 that the island came under complete Dutch control.

Orientation & Information
The southern part of the island is interesting for its traditional villages, unique customs and fine beaches. Roads around Nias are bad but the most interesting places in the south are fairly close together, connected by roads and jungle tracks.

Teluk Dalam is the port and main town in the south. Gunung Sitoli is the main town in the north and the only place on the island where you can cash travellers' cheques, even then at a poor rate.

Health Chloroquine-resistant malaria has been reported in Nias, so take precautions.

Getting There & Away
You can reach Nias either by boat from Sibolga or by air from Medan.

Air SMAC has daily flights from Medan to Gunung Sitoli, costing 96,000 rp.

Boat There are regular ferries from Sibolga to Gunung Sitoli and Teluk Dalam. Most of the places of interest are in the south, so Teluk Dalam is the better destination to head for.

In Sibolga, buy the tickets to Gunung Sitoli and Teluk Dalam at the shipping office of P T Simeulue at Jalan Pelabuhan 2 near the old harbour. The office is open until 8 pm, but if space is available it's sometimes possible to buy a ticket on the boat. The boats leave from the new harbour at the other end of town where it's not possible to purchase boat tickets.

Getting Around
The island is a sadly neglected part of Indonesia. The only road of any consequence connects Teluk Dalam and Gunung Sitoli.

To/From the Airport The airport is 20 km from the town and it's 3500 rp per person into town by SMAC taxi.

Local Transport Motorised transport is very poor and many villages are only accessible by foot. To get around you can rent bicycles, catch some trucks and buses or walk. The locals will give you pillion rides on their motorbikes for a price.

You may be able to catch a small boat from Gunung Sitoli to Teluk Dalam, but this could involve hanging around for several days before one departs.

GUNUNG SITOLI
This is the main town of Nias in the northern part of the island. It's a fairly innocuous little place with a certain seedy, tropical charm to it. Most people who arrive on the island will

1	Mosque
2	Bank Rakyat
3	Tourist Office
4	Hotel Wisata
5	Tennis Courts
6	Telephone Office
7	Post Office
8	Pelni & Ticket Office
	for Sibolga Ferry
9	Hotel Gomo
10	Nasionac Restaurant
11	Bank Negara Indonesia
12	Chinese Temple
13	Penginapan Banuada
14	Market
15	Hotel Beringin

dollar travellers' cheques at a very bad rate. The only other place to change money is with a moneychanger in Teluk Dalam at an equally bad rate.

Post The post office is on Jalan Gomo.

Things to See

There are several nice walks near the town. The village of **Hilimbawodesolo** is about 14 km from Gunung Sitoli, and there are some traditional houses uphill from the road. You get there by a bemo, and you might have to walk the two km from the crossroad to the village. There are other traditional houses on the road between the airport and Gunung Sitoli.

Places to Stay & Eat

The cheap places to stay are very cheap but also very depressing. They include *Hotel Beringin* at Jalan Beringin where rooms cost 4000 rp, *Penginapan Banuada* at Jalan Jenderal A Yani and *Losmen Hidayat (Bata)* at Jalan Diponegoro 131, near the bus station, where rooms cost around 1000 to 1500 rp.

One of the best places to stay is *Wisma Soliga* which is on the main road 4 km out of town. It's clean, spacious and they serve up big Chinese meals. Rooms start from 10,000

come through Gunung Sitoli as the only airport is nearby and daily boats from Sibolga arrive here.

Orientation & Information

The port is a few km north of town, and the bus station is on the main road in the southern part of town past the bridge.

Tourist Office The tourist office (Dinas Pariwisata) (☎ 21545) is at Jalan Sukarno 6.

Money The Bank Negara Indonesia on Jalan Pattimura, will change US and Australian rp, and they can organise all kinds of tickets and transport.

In the centre of town is the *Hotel Gomo* (☎ 21926) at Jalan Sirao 8. There are some very dreary rooms on the bottom floors but the rooms on the higher floors are good. Rooms start from 7500 rp, or from 15,000 rp with TV, bathroom and air-con.

There are two newer hotels in town. *Hotel Wisata* (☎ 21858), at Jalan Sirao 2, has nice clean rooms from 7500 rp, and rooms including fan and mandi are 10,000 rp. The *Hawaii Hotel* at Jalan Jend A Yani has rooms from 7500 rp. If you stay here beware of the young manager, Ryland (regardless of your gender).

There are a few warungs serving Padang or Chinese style food. *Nasionac* at Jalan Sirao is worth trying for Padang food.

Getting There & Away

To/From Sibolga Depending on the weather, there are daily boats (except Sunday) between Sibolga and Gunung Sitoli. They depart around 8 to 10 pm. The fare is 7500 rp in deck class and 11,500 rp in a four berth cabin. The overnight trip can take seven hours on the faster *KM Sumber Usaka*.

To/From Teluk Dalam There are daily buses between Gunung Sitoli and Teluk Dalam. Normally two or three buses depart anytime between 8 am and 10 pm. The fare is 5000 rp. Buses from Gunung Sitoli leave from the terminal on Jalan Diponegoro, and also meet the boats at the port.

The trip between Gunung Sitoli and Teluk Dalam takes about six hours, but that depends on the condition of the road. The road is surfaced for the first half, but deteriorates badly after that. It's amazing the route is not lined by overturned buses and shattered surfboards! Transport is OK in the dry season, but during the wet the roads turn to mud and the flimsy bridges are washed away, in which case buses often form a shuttle service. One bus goes as far as it can, then passengers pile out and clamber over (or

under) the obstacle and board another bus on the other side.

On the other hand, when one bus tries to make it the whole way this is what (according to one reader) can happen:

> The road is...appalling...we hit a section of mud holes which on a conservative estimate would have been one metre deep. Charged in at full speed relying on momentum to get us through – this was not always successful and all Western passengers were seconded to dig and push the thing out...so 4000 rp, a broken window, cut feet, a wrecked set of clothes and 11 hours later we got to Teluk Dalam (we also sat for an extra three hours on the bus before it left while they worked on the engine!). Met one couple who took 18 hours! Chartered bus back to Lagundi and collapsed!

Buses from Gunung Sitoli usually stop at a cross road between Teluk Dalam and Lagundi Beach, where there are locals on motorbikes waiting to take travellers on the six km trip to Lagundi for 1000 rp. To get the buses to Gunung Sitoli it's better to go to Teluk Dalam, as they are full by the time they reach the crossroad.

GOMO

In the vicinity of this village are the most famous of the menhirs that are spread around this island. This is not an easy place to get to, so unless you are interested in archaeology you might want to think twice about going there. The best way to get there is from Teluk Dalam on a motorbike along a goat trek. It's a two-day round trip and the asking price is 50,000 rp, so bargain hard.

TELUK DALAM

Teluk Dalam is a nondescript township in the south of Nias. Set on a pretty, palm-fringed bay this is the jumping-off point for Lagundi Beach, about 12 km away. There are also regular boats from Teluk Dalam to Sibolga.

Information

Money The only place to change money here is at U D Emerita, Jalan Jenderal A Yani 4 at a very bad rate.

Post & Telecommunications The post

office is in front of the harbour, and the telephone office Perumtel is at Jalan Pancasila 1A.

Places to Stay

The only budget hotel in Teluk Dalam for a while has been the *Wisma Jamburae* by the harbour. It's a very simple and clean place with rooms at 7500 rp. The more expensive *Hotel Ampera* at Jalan Pasar has clean rooms with mandi for 15,000 rp.

Getting There & Away

To/From Sibolga There is a regular boat between Sibolga and Teluk Dalam. It usually departs three times per week, leaving Sibolga on Monday, Wednesday and Friday, returning the next day. It's a cargo boat with a few cabins available. The fare is 8000 rp in deck class, which is just a space on the floor of the boat around the engine. A bed in one of the four berth cabins costs 13,000 rp and the trip takes about 10 hours.

In Teluk Dalam you can buy tickets at the Sibolga Nauli office on Jalan Ahmad Yani, near the harbour, or from hotel owners in Lagundi Beach. Leaving Teluk Dalam, the boat arrives in Sibolga too late to catch the morning buses north to Medan and Parapat, so you have to wait for the evening buses.

Boats also depart every two weeks from Teluk Bayur, the port of Padang. The trip takes about two days, so it's much less arduous to go by land from Padang to Sibolga and take a boat from there.

To/From Lagundi From Teluk Dalam you catch a truck or a bemo the last dozen km to Pantai Lagundi (Lagundi Beach) for 500 rp. This stretch of road is surfaced as far as the village of Botohili. Or hire a motorcyclist to take you for 2000 rp.

LAGUNDI BEACH

Lagundi Beach is a perfect horseshoe bay 12 km from Teluk Dalam. This is Indonesia's surfing Mecca, the destination for a steady stream of surfing enthusiasts. For those not into surfing it is also an idyllic place to swim

and bask in the sun. From the direction of Teluk Dalam, the nearer side of the creek to the town is the swimming beach, and the other side is the surfing beach with plenty of coral instead of sand on the beach.

The far end of the peninsula is still untouched by development, and for the most part the wood and thatch losmen blend in sympathetically with the shoreline. Only in a few places have too many palm trees been cut down to make way for the losmen, and this may be a sad portent of things to come, as more people head for the island.

Places to Stay & Eat

There are many losmen, most of which are clustered together in several groups at the far end of the horseshoe bay where the waves roll in across the reef. Most cost 500 to 2000 rp per person for a room, or 2000 to 4000 rp for a bungalow.

All the losmen provide food from menus which are almost exactly the same: omelettes, mie goreng, fried rice and vegetables, gado gado, pancakes, chips and so on. People also catch fish and lobster out on the reef, then sell them on the beach – you can buy your dinner straight from the ocean and get your losmen to cook it for you. Some hotel owners expect their lodgers to eat there and if you don't they can get nasty. To be fair to the hotel owners one has to consider the fact that they make more money from the food than from the lodging.

It would be pointless, and maybe a bit unfair, to mention any one losmen in particular. They are all pretty much the same, with wooden and bamboo huts of varying size built on stilts by the shore.

Near the centre of the horseshoe are two more established losmen, the *Dedi* and the *Yanti*. The owner of the Yanti, Mr Milyar, is friendly, helpful and speaks good English. He also acts as a guide and knows a lot about the area. Rooms are 1000 rp per person. Two other places that are popular and worth trying are *Magdalena* and *Risky*. Between them is the less friendly *Aman Inn*.

The white-washed concrete *Fanayama* (behind the Yanti) is a government-run place.

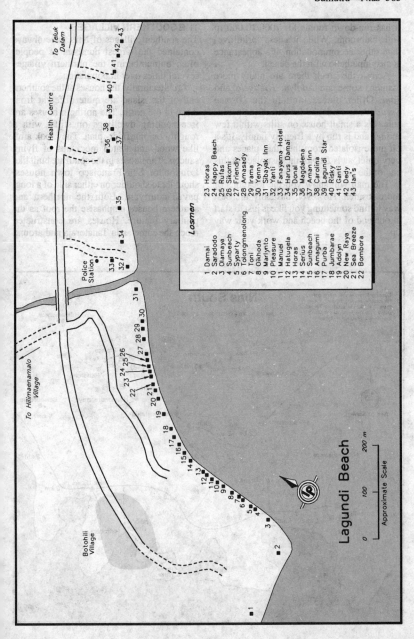

To Teluk Dalam

● Health Centre

To Hilimaenamalo Village

Police Station

To Hilimaenamalo Village

Botohili Village

Lagundi Beach

Approximate Scale

0   100   200 m

Losmen

1   Damai
2   Saradodo
3   Olamaya
4   Sunbeach
5   Sparty
6   Tolongmenolong
7   Toni
8   Oikhoda
9   Marlynto
10 Pleasure
11 Manuel
12 Hatugela
13 Horas
14 Serius
15 Sunbeach
16 Amagumi
17 Purba
18 Jumbarae
19 Adolyn
20 New Raya
21 Sea Breeze
22 Bombora
23 Horas
24 Happy Beach
25 Rufas
26 Sikomi
27 Friendly
28 Amasady
29 Irama
30 Yenny
31 Sibayak Inn
32 Yanti
33 Fanayema Hotel
34 Harus Damai
35 Donal
36 Magdalena
37 Aman Inn
38 Carolina
39 Lagundi Star
40 Risky
41 Ganti
42 Dedy
43 Ian's

It has run-down rooms for 7000/10,000 rp with bathroom. While it's less 'primitive' than other accommodation, it's appearance is unsympathetic with the beach.

Across the creek there are many more losmen, some are *Adolyn*, *Hatugela* and *Toni*. Other places include the *Losmen Saradodo* towards the far end of the peninsula. It's a small house on stilts with a few rooms, and is run by a friendly family. It's a bit more isolated from the other places and very quiet, as is *Damai* the last place at this end of the beach.

The map will show you the locations of more losmen. However, basically the best way to find something you like is just to start at one end of the beach and work your way up.

THE SOUTHERN VILLAGES

The southern villages of Nias have always contained the largest numbers of people, often outnumbering the northern villages several times over in population.

Architecturally, the houses at the southern end of the island are quite different from those in the north. The northern houses are free-standing dwellings on stilts, with a roughly oblong floor-plan. They look a bit like wood and thatch mock-ups of flying saucers. The houses in the south are built like London or San Francisco town houses, shoulder to shoulder on either side of a long, paved courtyard. Both the northern and southern houses emphasise the roof as the primary feature. Houses are constructed much the same as in Tanatoraja and around

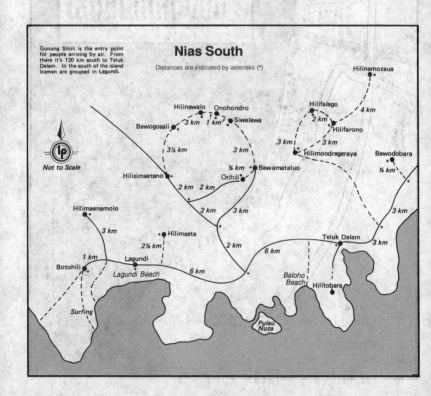

Gunung Sitoli is the entry point for people arriving by air. From there it's 120 km south to Teluk Dalam. In the south of the island losmen are grouped in Lagundi.

Nias South

Distances are indicated by asterisks (*)

Not to Scale

Lake Toba, with pylons and cross-beams slotted together without the use of bindings or nails.

Southern villages were built on high ground with defence in mind. Often stone walls were built around the village. Stone was used to pave the area between the two rows of houses, the bathing pools and staircases. Benches, chairs and memorials were made out of carved stone.

Getting There & Away

Several south Nias villages, such as Botohili and Hilimaeta, are an easy walk from Lagundi Beach. Bawamataluo is only 14 km from Lagundi, but the winding road is mostly uphill. It's a tedious walk, so it's much better to pay someone to take you there on the back of their motorcycle for about 2000 rp. Occasionally trucks take passengers to some villages, but others are only accessible on foot.

Bawamataluo (Sunhill)

At Bawamataluo you can see high-roofed traditional houses. The village is impressive if only for its size – it's virtually a small town. The focus of interest is the reconstructed 'palace' of the former king, a monumental structure supported by huge pylons made from whole tree trunks. In the paved area between the houses are stone tables where, it is said, dead bodies were once left to decay.

Traditional war dances may be performed at festival time (or at shows staged for tourists) by young, unmarried males, who decorate themselves with feathers. Stone-jumping is also performed. Once a form of war training, the jumpers had to leap over a two-metre-high heap of stones surmounted by pointed sticks. These days the sticks are left off.

Bawamataluo is now very touristy and prices for statues or for watching the stone-jumping really are exorbitant by anyone's standards. They ask anywhere between 15,000 to 75,000 rp for a jump. Many of the villagers will pose for photographs and then demand money for doing it – and sometimes get quite aggressive if you don't pay up.

Orihili

From Bawamataluo a stone staircase and trail leads downhill to the village of Orihili. From Bawamataluo you can see the rooftops of Orihili in a clearing in the trees.

Hilisimaetano

This larger, newer village is 16 km from Teluk Dalam and has around 140 traditional houses. Stone-jumping is performed here most Saturdays.

Botohili

This is a smaller village on the hillside above the peninsula of Lagundi Beach. It has two rows of traditional houses, with a number of new houses breaking up the skyline. The remains of the original entrance way, stone chairs and paving can still be seen.

Hilimaeta

This village is similar to Botohili. The stone-jumping pylon can still be seen and there are a number of stone monuments, including benches and a four legged stone table. In the middle of the paved area stands a two-metre-high stone penis. A long pathway of stone steps leads uphill to the village.

Hilimaenamolo

This is a small village. It's in particularly poor condition with much of the paving ripped up and many stone monuments either collapsed or dismantled.

Aceh

I am the mighty ruler of the Regions below the wind, who holds sway over the land of Aceh and over the land of Sumatra and over all the lands tributary to Aceh, which stretch from the sunrise to the sunset.

This extract from a letter sent by the Sultan of Aceh to Queen Elizabeth I of England in 1585 marked the beginning of a trade agreement between Aceh and England that lasted until the 19th century. It also shows the extent of Aceh's sphere of influence as a trading nation, its sense of independence and its autonomy at that time.

Years before Melaka fell to the Portuguese, Aceh was Melaka's chief competitor for trade. Rivalry between them was intensified by religious hostility as Aceh was one of the earliest centres of Islam in the archipelago. Religious differences and the harsh Portuguese rule spurred many traders of different nationalities – Islamic scholars, Egyptians and Arabians, craftspeople from India and goldsmiths from China – into abandoning Melaka and setting themselves up in Aceh.

The influx of traders and immigrants contributed to Aceh's wealth and influence. Aceh's main exports were pepper and gold; others were ivory, tin, tortoise-shell, camphor, aloe-wood, sandalwood and spices. The city of Greater Aceh was also important as a centre of Islamic learning and as a gateway for Indonesian Muslims making the pilgrimage to Mecca.

Aceh is also interesting because, despite its early and strong allegiance to Islam, there have been four women rulers (although it is possible that real power lay with a council of 12 men). However, such a state of 'grace' could not last and in 1699 a legal recommendation from Mecca condemned rule by women as contrary to Islamic practice. The fourth woman ruler was deposed and replaced by a government headed by religious leaders.

Although Aceh's power began to decline towards the end of the 17th century it was able to remain independent for a long time. Singapore and Aceh were active trading partners with the help of the long-standing secret treaty with Britain. All that came to an end in 1871 when the Dutch negotiated a new treaty with the British in which England withdrew all objections to the possibility of a Dutch occupation of Aceh. The Acehnese tried to counteract this blow by negotiating with both the Italian and US consuls in Singapore. The draft of an US-Acehnese treaty of friendship was sent to Washington. The Dutch, however, forestalled further attempts by declaring war on Aceh in 1873.

The first Dutch expeditionary force of 7000 retreated when its commander, General Kohler, was killed. A new army contingent, twice as large, succeeded in taking the capital, the central mosque and the sultan's palace, but the war went on for 35 years before the last of the sultans, Tuanku Muhamat Dawot, surrendered. Even then no Dutch area was safe from sabotage or guerrilla attack from the Acehnese until the Dutch surrendered to Japan in 1942.

The Japanese were welcomed at first but resistance soon sprang up when local institutions were not respected. During this period the Islamic Party, which had been formed in 1939 under the leadership of Daud Beureuh, gained increasing support. In 1951 the central government dissolved the Province of Aceh and incorporated its territory into the Province of North Sumatra under a governor in Medan. The dissatisfaction of the people was so widespread that Daud Beureuh proclaimed Aceh an Islamic Republic in September 1953. This state lasted until 1961 when the military and religious leaders had a falling out.

The central government resolved the conflict by giving Aceh provincial status again. The military yielded to this decision because it felt its objective had been achieved and the religious leaders, without the support of the military, were forced to surrender. Jakarta later granted special status to the province in the areas of religion, culture and education and in 1967 Aceh was given the title of Special Territory.

People & Religion

The Acehnese comprise the majority of people in this province. Others are the Gayo and Alas in the mountains, the Minangkabau along the west coast, the Kluet in the south and Javanese and Chinese throughout. Aceh is the most staunchly Muslim part of Sumatra and Christians and Buddhists comprise only a small percentage of the population.

Nevertheless, animism is also part of the everyday fabric of Acehnese life. There is a prevailing popular belief in the existence of spirits who dwell in old trees, wells, rocks and stones. Ghosts and evil spirits are said to be particularly malicious around dusk when they can wreak havoc on all those they come in contact with. Dukuns are still called in to help solve grievances, cure illnesses and cast spells on enemies.

Offerings and rituals are still observed at significant times of the agricultural year, such as harvest time, and dreams and omens are interpreted. In some parts of Sumatra pilgrimages are made to the tombs of Acehnese scholars and religious leaders.

Arts & Crafts

Music & Dance Every region in Aceh has its local dances but there are three that are popular throughout the province – the *seudati*, *meusakat* and *ranub lam puan*.

Typical Acehnese instruments include a three-stringed zither (called an *arbab*) made of wood from the jackfruit tree with strings of bamboo, rattan or horsetail hair; bamboo flutes *(buloh merindu, bangsi, tritit* and *soeling)*; and gongs and tambourines *(rapai)*. The tambourines are made of goatskin, while the gongs are usually brass (sometimes dried goatskin) and are struck with padded wooden hammers. They come in three sizes: *gong, canang* and *mongmong*.

Seudati The Seudati is a quick-tempoed dance which involves a complicated pattern of forward, sideward and backward leaps. The songs are led by a dancer (called the *syech)* and two narrators *(aneuk syahi)*, and no instruments are used. The rhythm is accentuated by the variation in the movements of the dancers, who also heighten the tension by snapping their fingers and beating their chests. The pace is hotted up even more when contests are held between performing groups.

The traditional Seudati has five parts: the *salaam* (greeting), *likok* (special movements), *kisah* (story), *dhiek* (poetry) and *syahi* (songs). Recently this dance has been used to disseminate information on govern-

ment policy and to urge people to become better Muslims.

Meusakat The Meusakat, or dance of the thousand hands, originated in the region of Meulaboh and is performed by a group of 13 young girls. It consists of a series of precise hand, head, shoulder and torso movements. Traditionally, the dance was performed to glorify Allah or to offer prayers, but today, like the seudati, it is often used to get across a government message on development policy.

Like the seudati, instruments are not used. The songs are led by a girl positioned in the middle of a row of kneeling performers.

Ranub Lam Puan The Ranub Lam Puan is a modern adaptation of various traditional dances from throughout Aceh. It is performed to welcome guests and to convey hospitality, which is symbolised in the offering of betel nut or snacks by the dancers.

The *seurene kalee*, a single-reed woodwind, provides the haunting musical accompaniment.

Weapons Metallurgy was learned early from Arab and Persian traders and, because of Aceh's continued involvement in wars, weapon-making became a highly developed skill. Acehnese daggers and swords comprise three parts: blade, handle and sheath. The blade can have both edges sharpened or just one, and can be straight, concave or convex. The handles of weapons are usually of buffalo horn, wood or bone, and carved in the form of a crocodile's mouth, a horse's hoof or a duck's tail and embellished with gold or silver. The sheaths are made of rattan, silver or wood and fastened with bands of a mixture of gold, brass and copper called *sousa*.

The best example of this art form is the *rencong*, a dagger which has a convex iron, damascened blade with one sharpened edge. Less well-known Acehnese weapons are the *siwah* (knife) and *pedang* (a pointed sword).

Jewellery While there is a long tradition,

stemming from the early days of the sultanate, of fine craftsmanship in gold and silver jewellery, there is almost no antique jewellery to be found in Aceh today. Most of it was sold to raise money for the war against the Dutch.

Excellent gold and silver jewellery is still produced but there is not much variation in design.

Weaving & Embroidery Despite its long history and high reputation Acehnese weaving is rapidly disappearing.

On the other hand, embroidery is a very vital art form. Areas around Sigli, Meulaboh and Banda Aceh are renowned for embroidery using gold-coloured metallic thread (*soedjoe*) on tapestry, cushions, fans and wall hangings. The main motifs are flowers, foliage and geometric designs and the finished work is also decorated with mirrors, golden. pailletes, sequins and beads in an effect known as *blet blot*.

One type of embroidery which is not doing so well is *mendjot beboengo*. This kind of hand embroidery originated in the region of Takengon around Gayo and Alas and was done by men only. Stylised motifs of geometric flowers in red, white, yellow and green thread were embroidered on a black background.

Other Crafts Various domestic items are made from coconut husks, tree bark, water buffalo horns, palm leaves and clay. These include spoons, baskets, mats, earthenware pots and dishes.

BANDA ACEH

Banda Aceh, the capital of Aceh, is a large, sprawling city at the northern tip of Sumatra. A city of contrast, it's an odd mix of faded grandeur and economic prosperity. Money is being poured into prestigious buildings and development programmes and the appearance of the city is changing rapidly.

As a result of their history of extensive and mixed immigration, the Acehnese are a curious racial blend of Indonesian, Arab,

Tamil, Chinese, and hill tribe. Some of the tallest people in Indonesia live here.

Unlike Medan, Banda Aceh is a relaxed city and the Acehnese tend on the whole to leave you alone. Foreign prejudices about Aceh being the stronghold of the Sumatran Muslim 'heavies' are more in the imagination of the beholders than they are in those of the believers.

Orientation & Information

The city centre is marked by an imposing five-domed mosque and clustered around it are markets, bus stations and some hotels. The Sungai Krueng Aceh divides the city in two. On the other side of the river from the mosque is Jalan Ahmad Yani, which has several hotels. Pelni (☎ 23976) is at Jalan Cut Meutia 51.

Tourist Office The tourist office (☎ 21377) is at Jalan Nyak Arief 92.

Money Bank Negara Indonesia 1946 on Jalan Merduati has good rates for travellers' cheques and cash. The Bank Rakyat Indonesia on Jalan Cut Meutia, will change only US dollar travellers' cheques.

Post & Telephone The main post office is on Jalan Teukuh Angkasah, one block from Simpang Tiga. Long distance telephone calls can be made from Permuntel at Jalan Nyak Arief 13.

Pasar Aceh

The central meat and fish market on Jalan Sisingamangaraja is one of the most striking and lively in Sumatra. At the rear, by the river, you can see the boats off-loading their cargo of shark, tuna and tubs of prawns. Nearby, running off Jalan S M Yamin, is 'Banana Street', an alley full of banana stalls. Opposite is a bundle of huts where two dozen workers shell and pulverise coconuts, grating the flesh with noisy machines. Not only is this a good place for picking through the meat and vegies, it's also a great place for people watching.

Sultanates

Of the old Acehnese Sultanates there is not a great deal left. Just a few peculiar buildings, a gateway, a couple of white-washed tombs attest to a once powerful royal house.

Hash House Harriers

For those wishing to forgo the imperial days for a reminder of the colonial days, travelling joggers will be pleased to know that the Banda Aceh Hash House Harriers have a run every second Friday afternoon.

Cultural Centre

For those with a more spiritual bent, behind the Governor of Aceh's official residence, Pendopo, is a new complex built in 1981 for the National Koran Reading Competition. Two modern buildings surround an open-air performance centre where dances and theatre are staged on special occasions.

Mesjid Raya Baiturrahman

With its stark white walls and liquorice-black domes, this imposing building rises up in the centre of Banda Aceh. The first section of the mosque was kindly built by the Dutch in 1879 as a conciliatory gesture towards the warring Acehnese after the original one had been burnt down. Two more domes – one on either side of the first – were added by the Dutch in 1936 and another two in 1957 by the Indonesian government. Ask the keeper to let you climb the staircase to one of the minarets so you can get a view of the city.

Gunongan

For a contrast in architectural styles go and see the Gunongan on Jalan Teuku Umar, near the clock tower. This 'stately pleasure dome' was built by Sultan Iskandar Muda (who reigned 1607-36) as a gift for his wife, a Malayan princess, and was intended as a private playground and bathing place. Its three storeys are each meant to resemble an open leaf or flower. The building itself is a series of frosty peaks with narrow stairways and a walkway leading to hummocks which were supposed to represent the hills of her native land.

Basically, it looks like the concoction of a confectioner given carte blanche to create a pop art wedding cake. Whether it actually cheered her up is anyone's guess since it doesn't conjure up much feeling nowadays.

Directly across from the Gunongan is a low vaulted-gate in the traditional Pintu Aceh style, which gave access to the sultan's palace and was supposed to have been used by royalty only.

Dutch Cemetery (Kerkhof)

Close to the Gunongan is the last resting place for more than two thousand Dutch and Indonesian soldiers who died fighting the Acehnese. The entrance is about 250 metres from the clock tower on the road to Uleh-leh. Tablets implanted in the walls by the entrance gate are inscribed with the names of the dead soldiers – many of whom include native Dutch, Eurasians, Javanese and Ambonese.

Museum

Banda Aceh has a large museum at Jalan Aloudin Mahmudsyah 12, with three floors of exhibits of weapons, household furnishings, ceremonial costumes, everyday clothing, gold jewellery and books.

In the same compound is the Rumah Aceh – a fine example of traditional Acehnese architecture, built without nails and held together with cord or pegs. It contains more Acehnese artefacts and war memorabilia. In front of the Rumah Aceh is a large cast-iron bell, said to have been given to the Acehnese by a Chinese Emperor centuries ago.

They are both open Tuesday to Sunday from 8.30 am to 6 pm, and cost 200 rp.

Uleh-leh

Five km west of Banda Aceh is the old port of Uleh-leh where you can while away a few interesting hours watching the traders come in from outer islands. There are some attractive villages around Uleh-leh and a not so attractive black-sand beach, stripped of its trees, and complete with sharks and other dangers. In colonial times the Dutch fenced

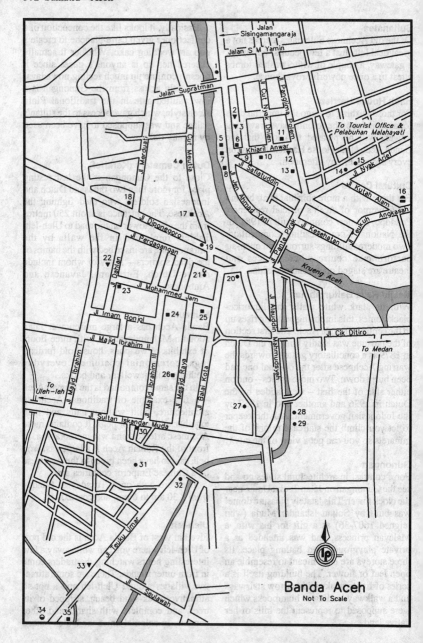

Banda Aceh
Not To Scale

part of it off with metal netting and came up here for a dip.

Beaches

Against a backdrop of mountains is the beach of **Lhok Nga**, base for a large expatriate community who work for the company Semen Andalas Indonesia. Lhok Nga is only about 16 km out of Banda Aceh along the East Coast road near the mosque. Its beach is inconsequential and the rocky coast seems far too rough for swimming. It's mainly set up as a weekend picnic spot for the Acehnese, with lots of warungs and shorn grass. Bemos from Jalan Diponegoro in Banda Aceh are 700 rp.

About 15 km along the road to Krueng Raya is **Ujung Bate**, a black-sand beach rimmed with pines and overlooking the Selat Melaka. It is said that Ujung Bate is haunted by ghosts, whether it is or not it is a good beach to walk along and collect shells. Pulau We is visible from here.

Lampu'uk is a beautiful white-sand beach on the Indian Ocean. Take the road to Meulaboh and turn left after passing the golf course and left again when you reach the sea.

It is not advisable to wear a bikini, or to walk along beaches in Aceh dressed only in a swimsuit. Most local women swim fully clothed.

Places to Stay – bottom end

A decent bottom-end hotel is the *Losmen International* (☎ 21834) on Jalan Ahmad Yani, opposite the night market. There are small rooms for 5000 rp, and larger rooms with bathroom for 7000 rp. It's very basic but reasonably clean, and rooms at the rear are quiet. Across the road is a very similar *Losmen Pacific*.

Better than the Losmen International is the *Wisma Lading* (☎ 21359) at Jalan Cut Meutia 9. Rooms start from 5000 rp, and there are more expensive rooms with fan for 6000 rp and with air-con for 10,000 rp. All rooms have a private bathroom.

The *Hotel Sri Budaya* (☎ 21751), on Jalan Prof A Majid Ibrahim III 5E, has rooms for 8000 rp, rooms with fan and private bathroom for 10,000 rp and with air-con from 22,000 rp. It's an old Dutch house with spartan but clean and well-kept rooms.

A couple of other places are *Losmen Aceh*

■ PLACES TO STAY		33	Toko Setia Baru Bakery
5	Losmen Internasional		**OTHER**
6	Losmen Pacific		
7	Wisma Prapat	1	Pasar Aceh (Market)
8	Hotel Medan	4	Bank Rakyat Indonesia
10	Losmen Palembang	9	Night Market
11	Losmen Aceh Barat	14	Telephone Office
13	Sultan Hotel	15	Telegram Office
17	Wisma Lading	16	Post Office
23	Losmen Yusri	18	Bank Negara Indonesia 1945
24	Hotel Sri Budaya	19	Opelet Station
25	Losmen Aceh	20	Bemo Station
26	Kuala Tripa Hotel	21	Mesjid Raya Baiturrahman (Mosque)
35	Hotel Rasa Sayung Ayu & Garuda	27	Tomb of Kandang XII
		28	Aceh Museum
▼ PLACES TO EAT		29	Tomb of Sultan Iskander Muda
		30	Entry to Cemetery
2	Restoran Happy	31	Dutch Cemetery (Kherkof)
3	Restoran Tropicana	32	Gunongan
12	Satyva Modern Bakery	34	Bus Station
22	Toko Muara Bakery		

Barat (☎ 23250) on Jalan Kharil Anwar 16 (not to be confused with the Losmen Aceh which is opposite the big mosque), and *Losmen Palembang* (☎ 22044) on Jalan Kharil Anwar.

Places to Stay – middle

The *Hotel Medan* (☎ 22636) on Jalan Ahmad Yani, has basic but agreeable rooms for 13,500 rp with private bathroom, and from 22,000 rp with air-con. The *Wisma Prapat* (☎ 22159) on Jalan Ahmad Yani is similar to the Hotel Medan. It has rooms for 13,500 rp, and for 20,000 rp with air-con.

The *Losmen Aceh* (☎ 21354) on Jalan Mohammed Jam is opposite the big mosque in the centre of town. Rooms are from 4000 rp and 12,100 rp with air-con. The hotel appears to have once been an old Dutch villa and it has a certain dilapidated charm.

Places to Stay – top end

The *Sultan Hotel* (☎ 23582) is in a quiet location on an alley leading off Jalan Panglima Polem. Rooms are from 35,000 to 75,000 rp and have three-quarter size beds, carpet, television, and air-con.

The *Hotel Rasa Sayang Aya* (☎ 21983), diagonally opposite the Seutia Bus Station on Jalan Teuku Umar is a bit far out of town. It's very well kept and the rooms have big double beds, carpet and TV, from 25,000 rp.

The *Kuala Tripa Hotel* (☎ 21455) at Jalan Mesjid Raya 24 is similar to the Rasa Sayang, and although it is centrally located the rooms are much more expensive, starting from 78,000 rp. It also has a basement swimming pool.

Places to Eat

Jalan Ahmad Yani is a good place to start looking for food. There are many moderately priced Padang-style places along this street, and along nearby Jalan Cut Nyak Dien and Jalan Panglima. For seafood and kindergarten decor, try the *Restoran Happy* at Jalan Ahmad Yani 74-76. At present they have Karaoke so it is very noisy in the evenings. Close by is *Restoran Tropicana* at Nos 90-92. *Aroma* at Jalan Cut Nyak Dien has good Chinese food.

The night market at the corner of Jalan Ahmad Yani and Jalan Kharil Anwar is a good place for cheap food, and has a lively atmosphere.

Like other Sumatran cities there are also many bakeries around the middle of town, try *Satyva Modern Bakery* at Kharil Anwar 3, *Toko Muara* at Jalan K H A Dahlan 17, and *Toko Setia Baru* across from the Pasar Setui on Jalan Teuku Umar.

Things to Buy

There are several markets in Banda Aceh with a colourful jumble of laden stalls of different foodstuffs. In the large city block area beside the mosque is the vast Pasar Aceh, which is good for buying fresh fruit and vegetables, household goods or utilitarian handicrafts (on the Jalan Diponengoro side).

Most of the jewellery shops are in a row along Jalan Perdagangan. Goldsmiths can produce any design you like provided they have something to copy from. If you are interested in antiques there are several shops worth browsing around. Toko Daud on Jalan Perdagangan has a good selection of Acehnese weapons, including traditional knives and swords.

The shop at Jalan Perdagangan 115 specialises in Acehnese antiques, but also has a good selection of old Dutch and Chinese porcelain. The owner has a private collection at his house (not for sale) which you might be able to arrange to see.

Another possible source of souvenirs are the *tukang* (skilled labourers or artisans) who occasionally drop by hotels. They're a bit like travelling souvenir shops with their bundles of artefacts, however, their stuff is often of fine quality.

Close to the police station on Jalan Cut Meutia is a small government shop called Pusat Promosi Industri Kecil. It has a limited selection of handicrafts on display.

Opposite the mosque there's a bookshop which sells English books.

Getting There & Away

Air Garuda (☎ 21983) is in the Hotel Rasa Sayang Aya on Jalan Teuku Umar, at the southern edge of town.

Garuda/Merpati has daily direct flights from Banda Aceh to Jakarta (398,700 rp). There are also five flights weekly to Medan, allowing same-day connections with Singapore, Batam, and Pakanbaru.

Bus The main bus station is the Terminal Bus Seuti on Jalan Teuku Umar at the southern end of town. Several companies have daily buses to Medan. They cost around 19,000 rp or 30,000 rp for air-con and take about 12 to 14 hours. The road is surfaced all the way, but because sections may get washed out in the wet season the journey will take longer then expected. The buses to Bireuen cost 5000 rp or 8000 rp for air-con.

You can also get buses from Banda Aceh to Meulaboh (five hours along a sealed road that costs 6000 rp) and from Meulaboh continue on to Tapaktuan, Sidikalang, and than either Lake Toba or Medan via Berastagi completing a loop around northern Sumatra.

Bemos to Ulee Lheu, Lhok Nga and Pelabuhan Malahayati leave from Jalan Diponegoro, near the big mosque. Fares to Ulee Lheu are 400 rp, Lhok Nga 750 rp, and Pelabuhan Malahayati 1200 rp.

Getting Around

Bemos are a common mode of transport around town and cost 200 rp. There are also motorised becaks from 400 rp; you must bargain hard before you accept a ride.

PULAU WE

North of Banda Aceh, accessible by ferry, is the port of Sabang on Pulau We. This spectacular island is at the western end of the Indonesian archipelago. It has some nice palm-fringed beaches with coral reefs, rocky coves, a rugged jungle covered hilly interior with great hillside lookouts.

The best time to visit the island is between October and May as the wet season on this northern tip of Aceh is at the opposite time to the rest of Sumatra.

Things to See

This is lotus-eating territory. There is not much to do except to lie around basking on a beach and there are plenty of beaches to stretch out on. Ten minutes from Sabang is **Pantai Paradiso**, a white-sand beach shaded by coconut palms. Not much further away is **Pantai Kasih** and about 30 minutes from town is **Pantai Sumur Tiga**, popular as a picnic place.

Less than two km from town is a serene freshwater lake called **Danau Anak Laut**. From the nearby hills it is possible to see the port and the whole of Sabang Bay.

Gunung Merapi is 17 km from town. This semi-active volcano holds boiling water in its cauldron, and occasionally emits smoke.

Unfortunately, a lot of the coral around the Pulau We is dead, but the fish are still very colourful. An hour away by boat is densely forested **Pulau Rubiah**, surrounded by coral beaches and reefs, including the **Sea Garden** – a famous and popular place known for the spectacular fish and coral. It is a favourite snorkelling and diving spot.

Adjacent to the Sea Garden is the **Iboih Forest**, a nature reserve with plenty of native animals in the jungle. The reserve also has **coastal caves** that can be explored by boat.

SABANG

During the Dutch rule the port of Sabang was a major coal and water depot, but after WW II as diesel ships became prominent Sabang stopped being a refuelling centre. During the seventies it was a duty free port, but when this status was eliminated in 1986 Sabang once again became a sleepy fishing town.

Information

The post office is at Jalan Perdagangan. The telephone office is at Jalan T Hamzah.

If you plan to do some diving or snorkelling the Stingray Dive Center at Losmen Pulau Jaya has reasonable equipment. Malaria has been reported on the island.

Places to Stay

There are several cheap places to stay in

Sabang that cater to travellers. *Losmen Pulau Jaya* (☎ 21344), at Jalan T Umar 17, is a good clean place with basic rooms from 2500 rp per person. Rooms with fan and mandi are 10,000 rp, and with air-con 15,000 rp. The front rooms are noisy but the rear ones are quiet. The common mandi have peepholes in the doors. They have several bungalows at a deserted beach, Tupiang Gapang, for 5000 rp plus meals. The losmen provides transport to the beach for 500 rp.

The *Losmen Irma* (☎ 21235) is on the same street at No 3, and has rooms at similar but slightly lower prices, but there are no air-con rooms. Their front rooms also get some street noise. They have bungalows on two different beaches: Balik Gunung (closed from June to September because of high winds) and Iboih. The cost is 1500 rp with no mattress or 2000 rp with one per person.

Tucked away in a quiet side lane down Jalan Perdagangan is *Holiday Losmen* with rooms at 6000/10,000 rp and air-con rooms for 25,000 rp. Mr Amin, a guide who operates from the hotel, can organise hiking, snorkelling and diving trips as can the staff from Pulau Jaya and Irma Losmen.

Two other cheap losmen are *Raja Wali* and *Sabang Merauke*.

Places to Eat

There are numerous coffee places around town, especially on Jalan Perdagangan. One of the best is *Riezky Restaurant* at Jalan T Umar 5, with good seafood, Chinese and Indonesian meals. *Café Ban* has a travellers type of menu at higher prices.

Getting There & Away

Boats from Banda Aceh to Balohan on Pulau We leave every afternoon at 3 pm (returning at 9 am the next morning) from Pelabuhan Malahayati, which is a port of Krueng Raya, 35 km from Banda Aceh. The voyage takes two hours and costs 3400 rp in deck class or 5400 rp in 1st class. There are regular bemos throughout the day leaving to the port from Jalan Diponegoro in Banda Aceh. The bus trip takes 45 minutes and costs 1200 rp. It's also possible to fly to Sabang from Banda Aceh.

Getting Around

Sabang is 12 km from the harbour of Balohan. Opelets and taxis run between the two localities, and cost 1000 rp per person. The taxi station is on Jalan Perdgangan. Ask about renting motorcycles and boats. The hire of taxis and boats is around 50,000 rp per day, but bargain hard for a better price. The island is good for walking and cycling, but it's better to bring your own bicycle.

PULAU BERAS

It's possible to hire a boat for a day and go out to Pulau Beras or several other islands off the coast of Banda Aceh when the sea and weather are calm. Fishing boats can be rented by the day at Uleh-leh. You may have to get permission from the harbour master before you set off.

Pulau Beras is lightly populated but most of the other islands are uninhabited. If you like snorkelling there are some good spots around these islands, so take equipment with you. You will also need food, drink, insect repellent and, if possible, life jackets.

BANDA ACEH TO SIDIKALANG

Along this coast there is beautiful scenery with contrasts of wild seas, jungle and rocky shorelines. To get down the west coast it used to be a long, dusty, bumpy ride riddled with potholes. The road is now good down to Tapaktuan but the stretch between Tapaktuan and Sidikalang is still rough. From Sidikalang there is a good road to Medan.

Calang

Calang is roughly half way between Banda Aceh and Meulaboh. About 15 km from Calang is a village called **Lhok Geulumpang**, where it's possible to stay at Dieter's Farm, a place on the beach that we have had some mixed reports about. The bus from Banda Aceh takes 5 hours and costs 4000 rp, while to Meulaboh it's 3000 rp.

Top: Becak drivers, Palembang, Sumatra (RN)
Left: Pantai Matras, Pulau Bangka, Sumatra (RN)
Right: Samosir ferry, Parapat, Sumatra (TW)

Left: Mesjid Raya Baiturrahman, Banda Aceh, Sumatra (RN)
Right: Museum, Padang, Sumatra (RN)
Bottom: Water lilies, Lake Toba, Sumatra (RN)

Meulaboh

Almost 250 km from Banda Aceh on the south-western coast is the small, sleepy town of Meulaboh. It's a departure point for Pulau Simeulue but it is also a surfing Mecca. Lhok Bubon, an excellent and safe beach, is 16 km back towards Banda Aceh. The beaches closer to Meulaboh are considered dangerous because of strong, unpredictable currents. Take extreme care if you are swimming at any of them. In the meantime, watch out for the monument honouring Teuku Umar, hero of the Acehnese resistance – it's shaped like a traditional Acehnese hat (*kupiah meukeutop*).

There are a number of unspoiled and tranquil villages nearby which are worth exploring. Articles of clothing and other items embroidered in the traditional style are for sale in some of these villages. Tutut, the site of an old gold mine which was in operation until 1945, is 60 km north of Meulaboh along a dirt track.

Places to Stay In Meulaboh stay at either the *Mustika* on Jalan Nasional or the *Mutiara*. They're basic but clean.

Getting There & Away Meulaboh is a five-hour trip by road from Banda Aceh, and costs 6000 rp or 9500 rp for air-con. Merpati flies from Banda Aceh to Meulaboh.

Simeulue

Off the west coast of Aceh is the isolated island of Simeulue, known for its clove and coconut plantations. It's a long, hard haul to get there but it could be worth the effort. The island is said to be restful and the people friendly and helpful. There are very few shops on Simeulue and no luxuries but there is plenty of fruit, coffee, rice, noodles and fish to eat.

Getting There & Away From Meulaboh it's a sardine-packed boat trip to Sinabang on Simeulue. Merpati flies from Meulaboh to Sinabang.

Tapaktuan

This quiet place is about half way between Meulaboh and Sidikalang.

Places to Stay A good, but not cheap place, to stay is *Hotel Panorama* on the seafront where a room costs 10,000 rp. A cheaper, basic place on the main street is the *Losmen Jambu* costing 5000 rp for a room.

Getting There & Away The road between Meulaboh and Tapaktuan is good. It takes five hours and costs 4000 rp.

From Tapaktuan to Sidikalang the road is being repaired and isn't in good condition. It's a rough trip through virgin jungle and little villages in a very wild and remote area, involving some river crossings and a road which in parts can be many km of great crater-size potholes. The trip takes eight hours or more depending on the weather and costs 4500 rp.

The trip to Bukittinggi takes about 12 hours and costs 7000 rp.

BANDA ACEH TO MEDAN

There are several interesting villages on this road if you want to take it easy and stop off along the way.

Saree

Saree is about 1½ hours from Banda Aceh. It's not as pretty as Sigli but the climate is refreshingly cool and the surrounding area attractive.

You can climb the nearby Gunung Seulawah (1000 metres) but it's best to go with a guide – perhaps ask the local police. It takes up to six hours to climb to the top and another three hours to descend at a fairly brisk pace. Take a sweater or jacket as it's cold at the top.

One of Sumatra's last elephant herds lives around Seulawah for part of the year. You may also come across monkeys, deer and tropical birds. Corn, sweet potatoes and a local variety of almonds grow in abundance in this region and are usually available at the market.

Sigli

About three hours from Banda Aceh, Sigli is the source of many traditional regional handicrafts. Gold embroidered cloth and other articles are available from Kampung Garot, eight km from Sigli. Pots and ceramics are available from Kampung Klibeit. It's also the centre for a major irrigation project and has a factory which produces pre-stressed concrete units for bridges.

Places to Stay You can stay here at *Losmen Paris* (☎ 21521) near the bus station on Jalan Melati 1. There are a variety of rooms costing from 5000 to 19,000 rp. There is also the air-con *Hotel Riza*.

Places to Eat Sigli is well known for its curries. Try them at one of the many coffee houses or the local Chinese restaurants.

Getting There & Away The bus from Banda Aceh to Sigli costs 2600 rp or 4000 rp air-con.

KUTACANE & GUNUNG LEUSER NATIONAL PARK

Kutacane is in a valley surrounded by the Gunung Leuser National Park, in the south of Aceh Province. The area is predominantly Muslim, although there's a large Christian Batak minority. Few foreigners came this way until a few years ago, when the area started to become more popular because of the jungle trekking possibilities offered by the Gunung Leuser National Park.

This park carves out a sizeable chunk of northern Sumatra, and also includes the Orang-utan Rehabilitation Centre at Bukit Lawang, Pakembang which is noted for its birds, and Aras Napal which has elephants. The Leuser is, in fact, one of the largest national parks in the world encompassing about 800,000 hectares of virgin rainforest. It is spread across both the province of Aceh and northern Sumatra, cut almost in half by the Alas river valley which is a prime agricultural region. The park contains many species of animals, including orang-utan,

gibbons, monkeys, elephants, tigers and the elusive Sumatran rhinoceros.

The departure point for the park is the town of Kutacane. The town itself has nothing really to offer, although it's set in the middle of a picturesque valley. However, from Kutacane there is transport to Pulau Latong and Lawe Gurah which are tourist areas of the Gunung Leuser National Park.

Information

Permits To enter the Leuser National Park you need a permit. You get this from the PHPA (National Parks) office in Tanah Merah, about 15 minutes by bemo from Kutacane. Permits are obtained from the Departmen Kehutanan Taman Nasional Gunung Leuser. The permit costs 1000 rp, and you need to provide three photocopies of your passport. It's also possible to get the permit from a house with a Tourist Information sign on it next door to the post office, near the bus station in Kutacane.

Things to See

Tigers, rhinos and elephants lure many people to the park, but your chances of seeing them appear fairly slim. People report seeing the tracks of rhinos and big cats, and occasionally hear growling tigers, but actual sightings seem to be few and very far between. Since there are very few animals (perhaps 300 elephants, 500 tigers and 100 rhinos) in a very large area, there's no guarantee that you will get to see them. Areas where there are concentrations of these animals are deeper inside the park, and you have to walk for several days to get there. At Ketambe there is a research station and the whole area is closed to tourists.

Long Walks

Most of the trails are difficult and some involve walking in rivers. Sometimes it's hard to find the starting point and some seem to end up in the middle of nowhere. Longer walks should be undertaken with the help of guides. Guides can be hired in Kutacane or the PHPA office. There is no set charge although it's usually around 10,000 rp per

Around Gunung Leuser National Park

day. The guides will construct shelters at night, cook food, carry baggage, cut through the trails (or what's left of them) and, if possible, show you the wildlife.

One possibility is to trek up to the Lawe Mamas, one of the major tributaries of Sungai Alas that forms the central valley of southern Aceh Province. The Mamas is a wild, raging river with white-water rapids which enters the Alas about 15 km north of Kutacane, near the village of Tanjung Muda. For such a trek you will have to hire a PHPA guide (no fixed fee) and they should be able to outfit you with the necessary trekking

gear, such as proper tents and sleeping bags (it gets quite cool in the evenings). Gibbons, hornbills, butterflies and the tracks of the elusive rhinos and big cats are all thrown in.

It's also possible to walk to Gunung Leuser, which could possibly be a round-trip of two weeks or more. The fist step is to take a bus to Kuta Panjang, then walk to the village of Panosan. The trek starts from Panosan. Or you can start from the village of Agusang, near Kungke.

The trek to Gunung Bendahara is a ten to 14-day round-trip starting from the village of Aunan near Laklak.

The trek to Gunung Kapi is a one-week round-trip starting from the village of Marpunga. The area around Marpunga is supposed to offer the best chance of seeing wild elephants.

The trek to Gunung Simpali is a one-week round-trip starting from the village of Engkran and following the valley of the Lawe Mamas. Rhinos live in this area.

Rafting

It is possible to raft Sungai Alas in an inflatable rubber boat. An expedition would normally take four to five days. You start from a point north of Ketambe and finish down river in Gelombang where the river reaches the lowland areas before entering the sea. Crocodiles inhabit the lower reaches of the river.

From Gelombang there are buses to Medan, Lake Toba and Berastagi. For more details try contacting Sobek Expeditions, c/o Pacto Travel Agency, Jalan Palah Merah 29F, Medan.

Places to Stay

There are a few uninspiring places to stay in Kutacane. Nearly all the accommodation is in the same area, on Jalan Besar, near the bus station.

Wisma Renggali on Jalan Besar has terrible rooms from 2000 rp. Their 4000 and 7500 rp rooms are OK. On the same street is *Wisma Rindualam* with not so clean rooms. Dorms cost 2500 rp, rooms start from 5000 rp and with fan are from 8500 rp. They provide plenty of travel information, but I found some of their information on getting to Takengon incorrect.

The *Hotel Bru Dihe* is more expensive, and is on a road which runs parallel to Jalan Besar. To get there turn left from the bus station, walk to Jalan Mesjid, turn right into it and then left into Jalan Cut Nyak Dien. It's on your right past the mosque. Rooms start from 12,500 rp with fan and bathroom, and 20,000 rp with air-con. Opposite is *Wisma Sari Alga*, which has dark and smelly rooms downstairs, but bearable rooms upstairs for 3000 rp.

Places to Eat

There are plenty of places to eat along Jalan Besar, especially in the bus station area. A little stall, *Sapo Bawan*, opposite the bus station has good nasi or mie goreng. If you're after Padang food *Anita*, opposite Wisma Renggali, is worth a try.

Getting There & Away

To get to Kutacane and the Gunung Leuser National Park from Berastagi, first take a bus to Kabanjahe. There are buses every ten minutes or so, and the trip takes about 20 minutes and costs 200 rp. Coming from Lake Toba you have to take a bus from Parapat to Pematang Siantar, and another from there to Kabanjahe.

From Kabanjahe, take a bus to Kutacane. The bus departs Kabanjahe from the Garuda terminal and not the main bus station – these are about 200 metres apart. The trip takes five to seven hours and the fare is 3200 rp. There are also direct buses between Medan and Kutacane. The road winds its way over the mountains with fine views of Gunung Sinabang, valleys occupied by the Karo Batak people, and the Alas river valley. The winding road allows the drivers to use their favourite toy – the air horn. Every bend, shack and village is an excuse for a triple or quadruple blast.

From Kutacane take a minibus for 200 rp to the PHPA office in nearby Tanah Merah to get a permit for the park.

BLANGKEJEREN TO TAKENGON

Further north of Kutacane, on the road to Takengon, is Blangkejeren. The opelet takes four hours and costs 3500 rp. From Blangkejeren it's a 30-km walk to the village of Gudang, via the village of Rikit Gaib (otherwise known as Koneng), or a 2000 rp opelet ride. From Gudang it's about a 30-km walk through beautiful, mountainous jungle to the village of Ise Ise. From Ise Ise it's a 20-km walk to Uwak via Lumut. From Lumut or Uwak you can catch an opelet to Takengon, that takes four hours and costs 3000 rp.

It's possible to bus it the whole way from

Gudang to Uwak, but the frequency of the opelets depends on the will of Allah. If you are planning to bus it, then it's better to wait one or two days in Blangkejeren for an opelet to depart, as further down the road they might be too full to pick you up. The fare to Takengon costs 13,000 rp, the trip taking around 10 hours. From Takengon you can carry on by bus to Bireuen which is on the Medan to Banda Aceh highway.

Places to Stay & Eat

You can buy food and coffee in the villages along the way, and most people will put you up for the night for a small price.

In Blangkejeren, it's possible to stay at *Penginapan Juli* which is run by a friendly family. It costs 2500 rp per person. They can also organise a viewing of Gayo dancing – a local traditional dance. There have been some reports of women being observed while having a wash in the mandi, so be careful.

Penginapan Mardhatillah has nice clean rooms for 3000 rp, but is next to a mosque so you may be woken by the muezzin calling the faithful to prayer.

There are a few places to eat, but one of the best is an unnamed Chinese place opposite the police station.

TANGSE

Tangse is in a cool valley in the mountains about seven hours from Banda Aceh. It is considered by many people to grow the best rice in Aceh. There are lots of good walks around here through picturesque rice paddies and forest.

Places to Stay

Tangse is also the site of a Save the Children aid project and it's possible to stay at their guest house by contacting the office.

Getting There & Away

Approaching Tangse from Banda Aceh get off at the 118 km signpost. Tangse is about 70 km along a road branching off to the right from here.

TAKENGON

Takengon is a remote town on the banks of Danau Tawar, surrounded by rice paddies and small coffee plantations and overlooked by mountains and forests. The eerie beauty and rather foreboding atmosphere of the area is increased by stories of the elusive tiger and the dreaded cobra being seen. The town itself is rather ordinary, predominantly Muslim and quite large. Danau Tawar is 26 km long, five km wide and 50 metres deep.

Information

The Grand Mosque is in the centre of the town at Jalan Lebe Kadar, along which the post office, police station and many shops and restaurants are. The main bus station and the market are closer to the lake.

Things to See

Visit the village of **Bintang** across the lake by boat. The villages of **Angkup** or **Pondok Baru** are the starting points to the Geuremong and Telong volcanoes which dominate the scenery.

Hire a guide and climb **Gunung Telong** to see the moss forest with its numerous exotic orchids. It's a four to six-hour walk. Or wander up **Gunung Tetek** for a 360-degree view of the countryside and sea, which is a much less energetic climb taking under an hour.

The **Loyang Koro** (Buffalo Caves) are six km from town, a bemo costs 300 rp to get there. The cave is dimly lit but it's possible to see the stalagmites. Bring a torch.

Six km before you get to Takengon is **Bukit Menjagan**, which also has a wonderful view of the area, but the road up is very steep.

Places to Stay

There are plenty of cheap losmen in town, but most are in dismal condition. A good place that attracts many travellers is the *Penginapan Batang Ruan* (☎ 104) at Jalan Mahkamah 5, next to the cinema. They have clean rooms from 5000 rp, but many have peepholes in the walls. A very basic losmen is *Rajailang* at Jalan Lebe Kadar, where rooms cost 3000/4000 rp.

Around the corner from the bus station is the overpriced mid-range hotel *Triarga Inn* (☎ 21073) at Jalan Pasar Inpres, where rooms cost from 10,000 to 40,000 rp, but if they are not full it's possible to bargain for the rooms. They do, however, provide good service for the tourists. *Hotel Danau Laut Tawar* is a basic hotel opposite the Grand Mosque at Jalan Lebe Kadar with 13,000 rp rooms.

The only international class hotel is 2½ km out of town. *Hotel Renggali* (☎ 0643-21144) sits on the edge of the lake and has rooms from 30,000/35,000 rp. Opelets to and from town cost 150 rp.

Places to Eat
There are plenty of the usual Padang and Chinese-style warungs to eat at. For good satays try *Warung Soto Surabaya*.

Things to Buy
This is the place to buy the traditional Gayo/Alas tapestry – made up into embroidered clothes, belts, purses, cushion holders and tapestry. Brightly woven mats can be bought at Isak or at one of the other small villages on the road to Isak.

At the market in Takengon it's sometimes possible to buy highly decorative, engraved pottery called *keunire* which is used in wedding ceremonies.

Getting There & Away
Takengon is about 100 km off the Trans-Sumatran Highway through hills, forests, coffee plantations and rice paddies. Get off at Bireuen, a junction town, and catch a minibus to Takengon from there for 2000 rp. There are also night buses to Banda Aceh (7,300 rp or 11,750 rp for air-con) or Medan (11,250 rp or 18,000 rp for air-con). The infrequent opelets to Blangkejeren cost 13,000 rp.

Nusa Tenggara

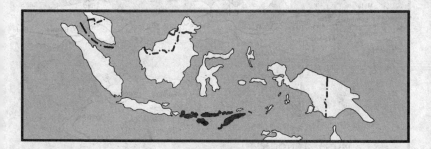

Nusa Tenggara – the name means 'South-East Islands' – is quite different from the rest of Indonesia. As you travel east the climate becomes drier, so people raise corn and sago rather than rice; the flora and fauna are more like parts of Australia than tropical Bali; the people are poorer than elsewhere in Indonesia; and there is a great variety of cultures and religions.

Each island has its own peculiar sights, some of which rival anything seen in Java or Bali. The great stone-slab tombs and traditional villages of Sumba, the intricate ikat weaving of Sumba and Flores, the brilliantly coloured volcanic lakes of Keli Mutu in Flores and the dragons of Komodo must rate as some of the finest attractions of South-East Asia. Though there are few beaches where you can peel off and lie back undisturbed by a crowd of staring locals, there's fine coral off some of the coasts.

Although a steady stream of travellers passes through, there is still nothing like the tourist stampede you find in Bali or Java. The lack of tourists means that your reception will be more natural, but it does create one headache: you will repeatedly be the centre of attention. It's no trouble at all to generate an entourage of over 100 children in a small village, all pre-programmed to yell 'hello mister' repeatedly until either they or you collapse from exhaustion.

Nusa Tenggara is divided into three provinces: West Nusa Tenggara, comprising Lombok and Sumbawa, with its capital at Mataram in Lombok; East Nusa Tenggara, comprising Flores, Sumba, Timor and a number of smaller islands, with the capital at Kupang in Timor; and East Timor with its capital at Dilli.

Only about 2% of the Indonesian population lives in Nusa Tenggara, but there are so many different languages and cultures it's impossible to think of these people as one group. There are several languages on the tiny island of Alor alone, though you won't have any trouble getting by with Bahasa Indonesia anywhere in Nusa Tenggara. Many of the people are now at least nominally Christian; Christians predominate on Flores and Roti, Muslims on Lombok and Sumbawa, and on Timor there's a mixture. But a very strong layer of animism persists, with customs, rituals and festivals from this older tradition still very much a part of life.

Even the wildlife of Nusa Tenggara is different from that of western Indonesia. A 300-metre-deep channel (one of the deepest in the archipelago) runs between Bali and Lombok and extends north between Kalimantan and Sulawesi. The channel marks the 'Wallace Line', named after 19th century naturalist Alfred Russel Wallace, who observed that from Lombok eastwards,

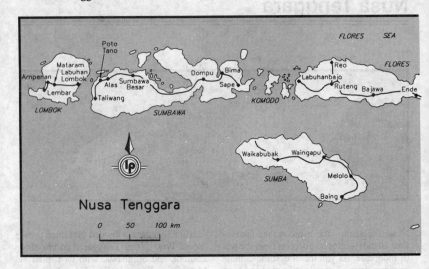

the islands are characterised by more arid country, thorny plants, cockatoos, parrots, lizards and marsupials, while from Bali westwards the vegetation is more tropical and the animals include monkeys and tigers. It's actually not as clear cut as Wallace thought, but Nusa Tenggara is definitely a transition zone between Asian and Australian flora and fauna.

HISTORY

Despite Portuguese interest in the 16th century and Dutch interest from the 17th, Nusa Tenggara was never in the mainstream of colonial activity in Indonesia. Because the area offered few economic temptations, the Dutch largely concentrated on Java, Sumatra and the spice islands of Maluku. In Nusa Tenggara they set up trading posts but didn't find it necessary to exercise much authority. Local rulers and their conflicts, and traditional ways of life including animist religions were largely left to run their own course until around 1840, when the Dutch were spurred into action for a variety of reasons: to protect their ships from pirates; because of disputes (such as those with the Balinese) over the salvaging of shipwrecks;

and to protect their possessions from other powers. As the Europeans scrambled for the last available morsels of territory in Asia and Africa in the last quarter of the 19th century, the Dutch grabbed anything that was left in the archipelago.

Piracy and disputes over shipwrecks motivated the first Dutch assault on Bali in 1846. When the indigenous Sasaks of Lombok rebelled against their Balinese overlords in 1891 and appealed to the Dutch for help, the Dutch took the opportunity to send in a military expedition to finish off the Balinese and take control of Lombok themselves. Flores, further east, was another target. A desire to control the slave trade and disputes over the rights to shipwrecks led to two Dutch expeditions against the island in 1838 and 1846, and a local rebellion in 1907 prompted a complete takeover. The Dutch waited until the early 1900s to subdue the tribespeople in the interior of the Nusa Tenggara islands, and the eastern half of Timor never fell into Dutch hands at all (it remained a Portuguese colony until 1975 when Indonesia invaded and took it over).

After Indonesian independence in the 1940s, Nusa Tenggara remained a remote

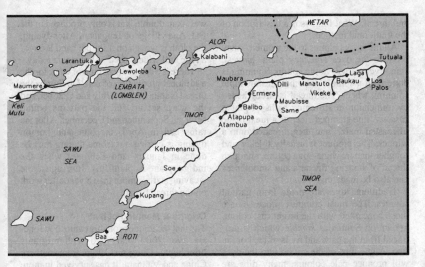

and lonely outpost, kept in order by a handful of Javanese officials and soldiers who considered themselves virtual exiles. The difficulty of the terrain, poor communications and the islands' location on the path to nowhere in particular all helped to deter visitors and maintain this isolation.

IKAT

The Indonesian word ikat, which means to tie or bind, is used as the name for intricately patterned cloth whose threads are tie-dyed by a very painstaking and skilful process *before* they are woven together.

Ikat cloth is made in many scattered regions of the archipelago, from Sumatra to Maluku. Outstanding work comes from the Dayaks of Kalimantan and Sarawak; the people of Tenganan on Bali; the Batak, Lampung and Kroe regions of Sumatra; and the Donggala and Rongkong areas of central Sulawesi, but it's in Nusa Tenggara that this ancient art form thrives most strongly. Ikat garments are still in daily use in many areas, and there's an incredible diversity of colours and patterns, with villages a few km apart sometimes turning out cloths of utterly different appearance. The spectacular ikat of

Sumba and the intricate patterned work of Flores are the best known, but Timor and Lombok and small islands like Roti, Sawu, Ndao and Lembata all have their own varied and high-quality traditions.

Making Ikat

Ikat cloth is nearly always made of cotton, still often handspun, though factory-made cotton thread and even some synthetic threads have come into use. Dyes are traditionally handmade from local plants and minerals, and these give ikat its characteristic earthy brown, red, yellow and orange tones as well as the blue of indigo.

Ikat comes in a variety of shapes and sizes including *selendang* (shawls); sarongs (which may consist of two matching ikat panels sewn together); two-metre-long tubes which can be used as a kind of cloak or rolled down to the waist to resemble a sarong; *selimut* (blankets) which can also serve as cloaks; and four-metre-long pieces (known as *katipa* in Flores or *parilonjong* in Rongkong) used as winding cloths for burial of the dead.

Some aspects of ikat production are changing with the use of manufactured dyes and thread. What follows is a description of the traditional method.

All the work belongs to the women – they produce the dyes and they plant, harvest, spin, dye and weave the cotton. Spinning is done with a spindle or sometimes a simple spinning wheel. The thread is strengthened by immersion in stiffening baths of grated cassava, fine stamped rice, or a meal made of roasted maize, and then threaded onto a winder. The product is usually thicker and rougher than machine-spun cotton, although thread of amazing fineness and smoothness can also be made this way.

Traditional dyes are made from natural sources. The most complex processes are those concerned with the bright rust colour, known on Sumba as *kombu*, which is produced from the bark and roots of the kombu tree. A few dips of the cotton into the dyes will produce pale colours; many dips are needed to obtain the most valued deep colours. Purple or brown can be produced by dyeing the cloth deep blue and then over-dyeing it with kombu.

Each time the threads are dipped in dye, those sections of them that are not due to receive the colour in question are bound together ('ikatted') beforehand with dye-resistant fibre, so that they do not take up the colour. A separate tying-and-dyeing process is carried out for each colour that will appear in the finished cloth – and the sequence of dipping has to consider the effect of over-dyeing. This tying-and-dyeing stage is what makes ikat ikat and it requires great skill, since the dyer has to work out – *before* the threads are woven into cloth – exactly which parts of each thread are to receive each colour in order to give the usually complicated pattern of the final cloth. If the thread is dyed by another process, the product can't be classed as ikat.

The tie-dyeing process may be applied to the warp (lengthwise) threads, in which case the cloth is known as warp ikat; or the weft (crosswise) threads, giving weft ikat; or to both, giving double ikat (gringsing). Nusa Tenggara, Kalimantan and most Sulawesi ikat is warp ikat; Sumatran ikat is mostly weft ikat; double ikat is only produced in the Bali Aga village of Tenganan. After dyeing, the cloth is woven on a simple hand loom of a type still widely used in Indonesia today.

There is a defined schedule of work for the traditional production of ikat. On Sumba the thread is spun between July and October, and the warp set up and the patterns bound between September and December. After the rains end in April, the blue and kombu dyeing is carried out (some dyeing may be done in January and February when the indigo plant is plentiful). In August the weaving starts – more than a year after work on the thread began.

Origins & Meaning of Ikat

The ikat technique probably came to Indonesia over 2000 years ago with migrants bringing the Dongson Culture from southern China and Vietnam. It has survived in more isolated regions that were bypassed by later cultural influences.

Ikat styles vary according to the village and sex of the wearer, and some types of cloth are reserved for special purposes. The spectacular *pua* cloths of Kalimantan serve as wall hangings at rites of passage like marriages and circumcisions; double ikat weavings from Tenganan in Bali are thought to have healing powers and appear at ceremonies all over the island; in parts of Nusa Tenggara high-quality ikat, along with beads or ivory, is part of the 'dowry' that a bride's family must give to the bridegroom's family at a marriage, in return for 'masculine' valuables like gold or livestock. Large collections of such ceremonial cloths are a status symbol. At religious rituals the leaders will sometimes wear ikat garments with potent or significant motifs.

On Sumba, less than 90 years ago only members of the highest clans could own ikat textiles and only they and their personal attendants could make or wear them. Certain motifs were traditionally reserved for noble families (as on Sumba and Roti) or members of a particular tribe or clan (Sawu or among the Atoni of Timor).

In the 20th century, particularly, new

influences have corrupted the meaning of ikat. Commercial trade in ikat, and outside demand for it, which in Sumba began with the Dutch, have turned it into just another product for sale in some areas. Traditional motifs have become mixed up with new ones, some of European origin, and ikat's function in indicating its wearer's role or rank has declined.

Motifs & Patterns

An incredible range of designs is found on ikat across the archipelago, among the most spectacular being the geometric or ancestor-figure motifs of Kalimantan, which are interlinked to form complex overall patterns, and the extraordinary variety of pictorial designs on Sumba. Some experts believe that representations of face-on people, animals and birds, such as are found on Sumba, stem from an artistic tradition even older than the Dongson. The main Dongson influence on patterning was in geometric motifs like diamond and key shapes (which often go together), meanders and spirals. Before European contact, Asian traders also influenced design and the fairly common dragon motif probably came from Chinese porcelain.

A particularly strong influence was cloths known as *patola* from Gujarat in India, which (coincidentally it seems) were made by using the double-ikat process on silk. In the 16th and 17th centuries these became highly prized in Indonesia and one characteristic motif of patola cloths was copied by local ikat weavers. It's still a favourite today – a hexagon framing a sort of four-pronged star which is reminiscent of those nasty critters that bleep around Space Invader screens. On the best patola and geometric ikat, repeated small patterns combine to form larger patterns, and the longer you look at it the more patterns you'll see – rather like a mandala.

More recently, European influence has brought motifs such as the Dutch royal coat of arms on Sikka ikat in Flores, figures of Dutch monarchs in Sumba, floral patterns instead of the old clan symbols of Sawu, and even tourist-oriented motifs like Keli Mutu volcano in Flores or the whales of Lembata.

Judging Ikat

Not so easy! Books on the subject aren't much help when you're confronted with a market trader telling you that yes, this cloth is at least 100 years old and no, it definitely isn't factory thread and yes, of course the dyes are natural. Still, *Textiles of Indonesia* (Indonesian Arts Society, Australia) and *Indonesian Ikats* by Suwati Kartiwa (Penerbit Djambatan, Jakarta) are two well-illustrated, informative and affordable introductions. Taking a look at the process in action is informative too: you can see women weaving in many places, and at the right time of year you may see dye-making, thread-spinning or tie-dyeing.

The best ikat is made from handspun cotton thread, coloured by the traditional tying-and-dyeing process with natural dyes, then woven on a handloom. Factory-spun thread and factory-made dyes can also give pleasing results, but if they don't go through the traditional tie-dyeing process the resulting cloth isn't true ikat.

Mass production techniques include tie-dyeing the same design on to threads for a number of cloths at the same time. These may be woven by hand or machine: they *are* ikat – because the correct hand-dyeing method has been used – but they'll probably

Ikat motif

be inferior quality, often with sloppy outlines to the patterns. Other cloths, however, appear to be either plain machine-woven fabric which has simply been printed with a design resembling those on genuine ikat, or fabric that is machine-woven from thread which has been pre-dyed with appropriate ikat-like colour schemes. Neither of these last two types is genuine ikat, because the proper tie-dyeing method is absent. Cloths made in villages will nearly always be hand-dyed and hand-woven. Machine- produced stuff comes from towns. Here are some tips on distinguishing the traditional product:

Thread Handspun cotton has a less perfect 'twist' to it than factory cotton.

Weave Handwoven cloth, whether made from handspun or factory thread, feels rougher and, when new, stiffer than machine-woven cloth. It will probably have imperfections (perhaps minor) in the weave. On machine-woven cloth you may find specks of colour detached from the motifs that they're supposed to be part of, where the machine hasn't been able to correct for inaccuracies in the dyeing.

Dyes Until you've seen enough ikat to get a feel for whether colours are natural or chemical, you often have to rely on your instincts as to whether they are 'earthy' enough. Sometimes this is obvious, but beware – dye manufacturers are clever at reproducing natural tints. Some cloths contain both natural and artificial dyes.

Dyeing Method The patterns on cloths which have been individually tie-dyed by the authentic method will rarely be perfectly defined, but they're unlikely to have the detached specks of colour that often appear on mass-dyed cloth.

Age Whatever anybody tells you, there are very few antique cloths around. Most of what you'll be offered for sale will be new or newly second-hand. A study made in Sumba in the late 1960s noted that as few as 20 examples could be documented as having

been made in the 19th century. There are several processes to make cloth *look* old.

Buying Ikat

Price depends on the fineness of the materials, techniques and design used in a cloth, the length of time it took to make it (in the best pieces this will amount to maybe four or five months of solid work spaced out over a year or two), its age, and the bargaining powers of you and the seller. You can buy ikat not only in the villages where it's made and in nearby markets, but from shops and merchants in towns in ikat-making regions and further afield in places like Bali and Jakarta. Buying ikat in its home area is on the whole cheaper, but villagers can bargain just as staunchly as shopkeepers (to whom they may have already sold their best stuff anyway) while shopkeepers often have a bigger range and *might* have to offload some stock.

When bargaining, be ready to *wait* – they show you all the crap first but will eventually bring out the better stuff. Hang in there until you finally see something you like. As a foreigner you must expect to pay more than a local: if you see something you really want and can get it for a reasonable price then buy it! You won't get it cheaper anywhere else (you may not even get it anywhere else) and you'd be mad to spend the airfare to Indonesia, tramp all the way to some remote region, then go home empty-handed all for the sake of a few rupiah!

GETTING THERE & AROUND

The good news is that transport in Nusa Tenggara has improved immensely in the last decade. There are now more surfaced roads, more and more regular ferries and buses, and more flights. Previously a lot of travel in Nusa Tenggara was just plain awful – you'd spend days in dreary ports waiting for boats, hour upon hour shaking your bones loose in trucks attempting to travel on roads which resembled minefields. Some of it is still like that, but on the whole if you stick to the main routes you shouldn't have much trouble. The only problems are likely to occur in the rainy season – roughly November to March – but it is shorter and less intense in the eastern and southern parts of the chain. Roads on Flores are often cut by floods or landslides at this time.

Air You can fly direct between Darwin (Australia) and Kupang (Timor) with Merpati, and Kupang is an international gateway (no visa required for most Western nationalities). Merpati has a good network of flights in Nusa Tenggara. Many flights start or finish in Kupang or Bima (Sumbawa), with Ende and Maumere on Flores, Dilli (Timor), Waingapu (Sumba) and Mataram (Lombok) the other busiest airports. Some flights come straight through from Bali or Java, and from Kupang or Maumere you can fly to Ujung Pandang (Sulawesi) and Kalimantan without changing planes. Bouraq also has a number of flights between Bali and Maumere,

Waingapu and Kupang. Garuda flies between Bali and Lombok and Timor.

While it is sometimes possible to get a seat even on the morning of departure, it is wise to book, and essential in the peak August tourist season. The most popular routes are Mataram/Bima/Labuhanbajo and Maumere/Denpasar. If flights from Labuhanbajo or Maumere are full, try Ruteng, which is a less popular departure point. Overbooking sometimes occurs, so make sure your booking has been made when you buy your ticket and always reconfirm.

Boat The Pelni passenger liner *Kelimutu* makes a circuit every two weeks from Semarang in Java to Kupang (Timor) and back, stopping at Banjarmasin (Kalimantan), Surabaya (Java), Lembar (Lombok), Ujung Pandang (Sulawesi), Bima (Sumbawa), Waingapu (Sumba) and Ende (Flores), and once monthly in Dilli (east Timor) – the

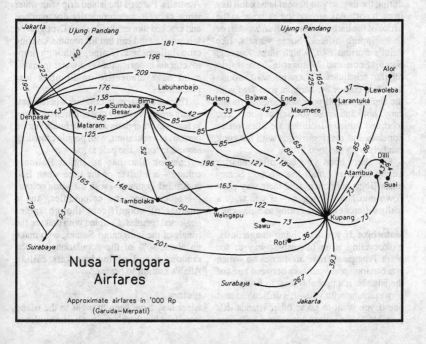

Nusa Tenggara
Airfares

Approximate airfares in '000 Rp
(Garuda–Merpati)

complete schedule is in the Getting Around chapter.

Most of the islands are connected by ferries which are regular, if rarely comfortable – several times daily between Bali and Lombok, and Lombok and Sumbawa; three times a week in each direction between Sumbawa and Flores (stopping at Komodo along the way); four times weekly between Timor and Roti; twice a week between Timor and Flores, and Timor and Alor; and once a week between Timor and Sawu. Small boats chug six times weekly from Flores to the islands of Adonara, Solor and Lembata. There is a small once-weekly boat between Lembata and Alor. Details are provided in the relevant sections.

If you want to do something different you might try finding one of Pelni's other more basic ships, or a freighter working its way through the islands – you can often make quite an interesting trip on the same ship since they usually sail at night and unload during the day, so you have at least a full day in each port. Ask around the harbour, at the office of the harbour master (syahbandar) or the shipping offices. Some vessels, like Pelni's Baruna Eka, which links Kupang, Sawu, Ende and Waingapu, have fairly regular schedules. Otherwise wait around until one comes by, bargain your fare with the captain, unroll your sleeping bag on the cargo hold and make yourself at home. The food and sanitary facilities are often pretty hopeless, but making friends with the cook can help with the food.

For short hops you can often charter sailing boats or small motorboats. Sometimes Bugis schooners find their way right down into Nusa Tenggara – if you want a really different way of getting to Sulawesi!

Motorbike If you like living dangerously, motorcycling is an interesting way to see Nusa Tenggara. There are ferries on which you can transport your bike between most of the islands. It's probably best to bring your own machine with you – it's difficult to rent one if you want to go to other islands. It's possible to find short-term hires in a few

Nusa Tenggara towns. In 1977, when researching the original edition of *South-East Asia on a Shoestring*, Tony and Maureen Wheeler rode a motorcycle from one end of Nusa Tenggara to the other.

Bicycle Bicycles are for rent in and around the main centres of Lombok, but so far they are not a very popular form of transport anywhere in Nusa Tenggara. Long-distance cycling is a possibility on Sumba, where there's a lot of flat terrain, but the idea of trying it out on hilly Flores or Timor requires stamina and a streak of masochism. For serious cycling, you'll need to bring your own bike with you.

Lombok

Lombok has all the lushness of Bali combined with the starkness of outback Australia. Parts of the island drip with water while pockets are chronically dry, parched and cracked like crocodile skin. Droughts on this small island can last for months, causing crop failure and famine, although improvements in agriculture and water management have made life on Lombok less precarious.

There are villages in Lombok where Westerners are such a rarity that children run away in fear – in other parts an *orang bulan* (moon person) is a sensation, with people crowding around to touch the pale skin.

Lombok also has an intact Balinese culture – a leftover of the time when Bali controlled Lombok – with the same colourful processions and ceremonies, and a number of magnificent though rather neglected temples. Coupled with that are the rituals of the indigenous Sasaks, who make up about 80% of the population, and the raucous sound of loudspeakers calling Allah's faithful to prayer.

History
Islam may have been brought to the island from Java but there's really no firm evidence

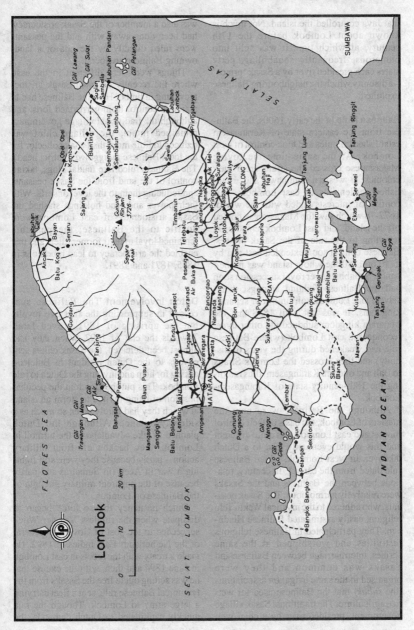

that Java controlled the island. Not much is known about Lombok before the 17th century, at which time it was split into numerous, frequently squabbling, petty states each presided over by a Sasak 'prince' – a disunity which the neighbouring Balinese exploited.

Balinese Rule In the early 1600s, the Balinese from the eastern state of Karangasem established colonies and took control of west Lombok. At the same time the roving Makassarese crossed the straits from their colonies in western Sumbawa and established settlements in east Lombok. This conflict of interests ended with the war of 1677-78 which saw the Makassarese booted off the island, and east Lombok temporarily reverting to the rule of the Sasak princes. Balinese control soon extended east and by 1740 or 1750 the whole island was in their hands. Squabbles over royal succession soon had the Balinese fighting amongst themselves, and Lombok split into four separate kingdoms. It was not until 1838 that the Mataram kingdom subdued the other three, reconquered east Lombok (where Balinese rule had weakened during the years of disunity) and then crossed the Lombok Straits to Bali and overran Karangasem, thus reuniting the 18th-century state of Karangasem-Lombok.

Although the Balinese were now the masters of Lombok, the basis of their control in west and east Lombok was quite different and this would eventually lead to a Dutch takeover. In west Lombok, where Balinese rule dated from the early 17th century, relations between the Balinese and the Sasaks were relatively harmonious. The Sasak peasants, who adhered to the mystical Wektu Telu religion, easily assimilated Balinese Hinduism. They participated in Balinese religious festivities and worshipped at the same shrines, intermarriage between Balinese and Sasaks was common and they were organised in the same irrigation associations (the *subak*) that the Balinese used for wet-rice agriculture. The traditional Sasak village government, presided over by a chief who was also a member of the Sasak aristocracy, had been done away with and the peasants were ruled directly by the raja or a land-owning Balinese aristocrat.

Things were very different in the east, where the recently defeated Sasak aristocracy hung in limbo. Here the Balinese had to maintain control from garrisoned forts, and although the traditional village government remained intact, the village chief was reduced to little more than a tax collector for the local Balinese *punggawa* (district head). The Balinese ruled like feudal kings, taking control of the land from the Sasak peasants and reducing them to the level of serfs. With their power and land holdings slashed the Sasak aristocracy of east Lombok were hostile to the Balinese; the peasants remained loyal to their former rulers and this enabled the aristocracy to lead rebellions in 1855, 1871 and 1891.

Dutch Involvement The Balinese succeeded in suppressing the first two revolts but the uprising of 1891 proved fatal. Towards the end of 1892, when they had almost been defeated, the Sasak chiefs sent envoys to the Dutch resident in Buleleng asking for help and inviting the Dutch to rule Lombok. This put the Dutch in the peculiar position of being invited to storm an island at which they had barely taken so much as a sideways glance. Although the Dutch planned to take advantage of the turmoil in Lombok, they backed off from military action – partly because they were still fighting a war in Aceh (in Sumatra) and partly because of the apparent military strength of the Balinese on Lombok.

Dutch hesitancy to use force began to dissipate when the ruthless Van der Wijck succeeded to the post of Governor-General of the Netherlands East Indies in 1892. He made a treaty with the rebels in east Lombok in June 1894 and then, with the excuse that he was setting out to free the Sasaks from the tyrannical Balinese rule, sent a fleet carrying a large army to Lombok. Though the raja quickly capitulated to Dutch demands, the younger Balinese princes of Lombok over-ruled him and attacked and routed the Dutch.

It was a short-lived victory; the Dutch army dug its heels in at Ampenan and in September reinforcements began arriving from Java. The Dutch counter-attack began, Mataram was overrun and the Balinese stronghold of Cakranegara was bombarded with artillery. The raja eventually surren-dered to the Dutch and the last resistance collapsed when a large group of Balinese, including members of the aristocracy and royal family, were killed in a traditional sui-cidal puputan, by deliberately marching into the fire of the Dutch guns.

Dutch Rule From the time the Dutch had gained control of Lombok, the island became a case study in callous and inept colonial rule. A whole range of new taxes resulted in the impoverishment of the major-ity of peasants and the creation of a new class of Chinese entrepreneurs. The peasants were forced to sell more and more of their rice crops in order to pay the taxes and as a result the amount of rice available for consumption declined by about a quarter from the begin-ning of the century to the 1930s. Famines ravaged the island from 1938 to 1940 and in 1949.

For nearly half a century, by maintaining the goodwill of the Balinese and Sasak aris-tocracy and using a police force that never numbered more than 250, the Dutch were able to maintain their hold on more than 500,000 people! Peasants wouldn't act against them for fear of being evicted from their land and losing what little security they had. Although there were several peasant uprisings against the Dutch, they were never more than localised rebellions, the aristoc-racy never supported them, and the peasants themselves were ill-equipped to lead a wide-spread revolt. Ironically, even after Indonesia attained its independence from the Dutch, Lombok continued to be dominated by its Balinese and Sasak aristocracy.

Post-Colonial Lombok There are few phys-ical reminders of Dutch rule; they built little

apart from the harbour at Ampenan (even then it was too small) and several aqueducts, some of which are still in use, including the one at Narmada. The Balinese can still be found mostly in west Lombok, where they've retained their distinctive Hindu customs; the relics of their occupation and colonisation include their influence on the Sasak's unique Wektu Telu religion. Other leftovers of the Balinese presence include the temples they built at Cakranegara, Narmada, Lingsar and Suranadi, as well as the temple processions and ceremonies still seen on the island today. They hold crema-tion ceremonies identical to those on Bali, and in west Lombok you can see all the traditional Balinese dances, particular favourites being the Legong, the Arja and the Joget Bumbung.

Geography

Lombok is a small island, just 80 km east to west and about the same north to south. Central Lombok, south of Rinjani, is similar to Bali, with rich alluvial plains. The far south and east changes to dry, scrubby, barren hills bearing a striking resemblance to parts of outback Australia. The majority of the population lives, as it always has, in the long narrow corridor of fertile land that stretches between the west coast and the east coast, bounded by the dry, barren areas to the south and the mountainous regions to the north. The central plain is divided into two distinct parts – a smaller, well-watered region along the west coast which is the home of Lombok's Balinese minority and the somewhat less fertile east Lombok, the land of the Sasaks.

Economy

The rice grown on Lombok is noted for its excellent quality but the climate, which is drier than Bali's, can only produce one crop a year. Though rice is the staple crop there are both small and large plantations of coconut palms, coffee, kapok, tobacco and cotton; new crops such as cloves, vanilla and pepper have been introduced. Stock breed-ing on Lombok is only done on a small scale.

Attempts are being made to promote Lombok as a tourist resort – money is being invested in upgrading facilities, particularly hotels and roads, but Bali is far ahead as a popular destination.

Population & People

Lombok has a population of just over two million people, the majority congregated in and around the main centres of Ampenan, Cakranegara, Mataram, Praya and Selong. Almost 80% of them are Sasak, the remainder mainly Balinese. There are also minority populations of Chinese, Javanese, Arabs and Sumbawanese in the east of the island, and Buginese along the coast. There may still be some isolated villages of the Bodha, said to be the aboriginal people of Lombok.

The Sasaks Physically and culturally the Sasaks have much in common with the Javanese, the Balinese and the Sumbawanese; they're Malay people, agriculturalists and animists who practised ancestor and spirit worship, although the majority are now Muslim. Basically hill people, the Sasaks are now spread over central and east Lombok, and are generally much poorer than the Balinese minority. Officially, most Sasaks are Muslims, but in practice they retain many of their ancient animist beliefs.

There are a number of traditional Sasak villages scattered over the island; the easiest to get to that are still completely unspoilt are the villages of Sukarara, Bayan and Senara. Typical Sasak huts are square or rectangular, constructed of wooden frames daubed with lime and covered with grass. Some sit squat on the ground, but generally they rest on stilts and have a high thatched roof. Usually the village is surrounded and protected by a high paling fence and the houses are built in long, straight lines. One of Lombok's most attractive hotels, the Sasaka Beach Cottages on the coast north of Ampenan, was designed in this traditional style.

The Chinese Most of the Chinese living in Lombok today are based in Ampenan or Cakranegara. The Chinese first came to Lombok with the Dutch as a cheap labour force, but the Dutch later fostered them as economic intermediaries between themselves and the Indonesian population. The Chinese soon became a privileged minority and were allowed to set up and develop their own businesses. When the Dutch were ousted from Indonesia in 1949, the Chinese stayed and continued to expand their business interests. Many of those in eastern Lombok, however, were killed in the aftermath of the attempted '65 coup. The massacres were perhaps as much anti-Chinese as anti-Communist.

Culture

Festivals are good times for seeing traditional dances and exhibitions of physical prowess – Lombok has its fair share of both. Unlike Bali, which encourages – in fact hustles – Westerners to go along and see the culture, getting to see any on Lombok depends on word of mouth or pure luck – that is, *if* some of the traditional dances or music are still being performed at all! If you see any of the possibilities listed below write and tell us about it.

Religious Festivals Most of the Wektu Telu religious festivals of Lombok take place at the beginning of the rainy season from October to December or at harvest time from April to May, with celebrations in villages all over the island. Many of these ceremonies and rituals are annual events but do not fall on specific days. Sasak ceremonies are nowhere near as obvious a part of daily life as the ceremonies in Bali – you can't expect to see them as often. Lombok's Muslims celebrae the various events in the Islamic calendar (see the Facts for the Visitor chapter), especially the end of Ramadan.

Dances The Cupak Gerantang is popular all over the island and is usually performed at celebrations and festivals. It probably originated in Java in the 15th century and tells the story of Panji, a romantic hero like Arjuna. The Kayak Sando is another version of a

Panji story but here the dancers wear masks; it's found only in central and east Lombok.

The Gandrung is about love and courtship – gandrung means being in love, or longing. It's a social dance, usually performed by both the young men and women of the village. Everyone stands around in a circle and then, accompanied by a full gamelan orchestra, a young girl dances by herself for a time before choosing a male partner from the audience to join her. It's seen in Narmada in west Lombok, Suangi and Lenek in east Lombok and Praya in central Lombok.

The Oncer is a war dance performed vigorously by men and young boys at festivals in central and east Lombok. The highly skilled and dramatic performance involves the participants playing a variety of musical instruments in time to their movements. The severe black of the costumes is slashed with crimson and gold waist bands, shoulder sashes, socks and caps.

The Rudat is another traditional Sasak dance performed by pairs of men dressed in black caps and jackets and black and white check sarongs. They're backed by singers, tambourines and cylindrical drums called jidur. This dance, its music, lyrics and costume display a combination of Islamic and Sasak influences.

Music The Tandak Gerok is an east Lombok performance which combines dance, theatre and singing to music played on bamboo flutes and the bowed lute called a rebab. Its unique feature is that the vocalists imitate the sound of the gamelan instruments. It's usually performed after harvesting or other hard physical labour, but is also put on at traditional ceremonies. The Genggong involves seven musicians using a simple set of instruments which includes a bamboo flute, a rebab and knockers; they accompany their music with dance movements and stylised hand gestures. The Barong Tengkok is the name given to the procession of musicians who play at weddings or circumcision ceremonies.

Contests If you're inclined to blood sports

you'll find the Sasak fascination with physical prowess, heroic trials of strength and battles fought on a one-to-one basis most appealing – the latter are similar to battles found on Bali and Sumbawa.

The Peresehan is a favourite all over Lombok. Usually held in the late afternoon in the open air, a huge crowd – all men apart from the occasional curious female traveller – gather together to watch two men bash each other with long rattan staves, protecting themselves only with small rectangular shields made from cow or buffalo hide. The staves are ceremoniously handed around the crowd lined up in a large roped-off area, then returned to the referee. The gamelan starts to play and two men, dressed in exquisite clothing including turbans or head scarves and wide sashes at the waist, feign the movements of the contest about to be fought.

Having shown everyone how it is supposed to be done, the men look around the crowd for possible contestants, who are carefully chosen to match each other as closely as possible in height and strength. Skill is another matter altogether. Anyone can be chosen – some perform several times during the afternoon, others refuse to take part at all. No one cares if somebody doesn't want to join in, but it's clearly status-boosting to do so. Having put on the scarves and waist bands, which are supposed to have magical powers of protection, the challengers take off their shirts and shoes, roll up their trousers, pick up their staves and shields and begin to flay at each other.

The battle is usually refereed by one of the two men who select the contestants. If either of the fighters loses his headscarf or waistband the contest is stopped immediately until he puts it back on. It goes for three rounds – often five with more experienced fighters – or until one of the two is bleeding or surrenders. The referee can also declare the contest over if he thinks things are getting out of hand – which they often do. Although the movements are very stylised, unlike Western wrestling matches there's nothing choreographed or rigged about this – both contestants generally come off with great welts all over them. The crowd gets wildly excited and each fighter has his own groupies cheering him on. At the end of each contest the winner is given a T-shirt or sarong and the loser also gets some token prize.

The Lanca is another trial of strength. It originated in Sumbawa and was adopted by the Sasaks who perform it on numerous occasions, particularly when the first rice seedlings are planted. Like the Peresehan it is a contest between two well matched men – this time using their knees as implements of annihilation by striking their opponents with them.

Religion

Islam, Balinese Hinduism and the indigenous Wektu Telu predominate on Lombok. The first two are covered in the introductory Facts about the Country chapter and the Bali chapter. Wektu Telu is unique to Lombok and is thought to have originated in the northern village of Bayan.

Wektu Telu In the Sasak language, *wektu* means 'result' and *telu* means 'three'. This probably denotes the complex mixture of Hindu, Islamic and animist influences that make up this religion, and perhaps the concept of a trinity which appears to incorporate not only Allah, Mohammed and Adam, but the sun, moon and stars (representing heaven, earth and water), and the head, body and limbs (representing creativity, sensitivity and control). Wektu Telu also involves rituals and feasts based on village adat (traditional law) except in Wektu Lima villages, where it's been replaced by the more orthodox beliefs and rituals designated by the written laws of Islam. *Lima* means 'five' and refers to the five pillars of Islam which are considered obligatory for the believer to follow.

The Wektu Telus do not observe Ramadan, the month-long period of abstinence so important in the Islamic faith. Their only concession to it is just three days of fasting and prayer. They also do not follow the practice of praying five times a day as laid down by Islamic law and, although their dead are buried with their heads facing Mecca, it is unheard of for a Wektu Telu follower to make a pilgrimage there. The Wektu Telus believe in praying from the heart whenever and wherever they feel like it, so instead of building mosques, all their public buildings are designed with a prayer corner or a small room which faces Mecca. As for eating pork, the Wektu Telus consider everything which comes from Allah to be good.

Burial rituals also vary: the Wektu Telu believe that ancestral spirits affect the living, and rituals are performed at graves as part of a continuing interaction between the living and the dead. Wektu Lima maintains the Islamic concept of an afterlife and the belief that the deceased is destined for either heaven or hell depending on their performance during life. The concept of hell is, however, quite alien to Wektu Telu. In fact the only fundamental tenet of Islam that the Wektu Telu seem to hold to firmly is the belief in Allah and that Mohammed is his prophet.

They regard themselves as Muslims, although they are not officially accepted by orthodox Muslims as such. Relations between the two groups – at least in the early part of this century after the Dutch invasion upset Balinese control – have not always been good. Part of the problem seems to have been that the native administrators appointed by the Dutch were invariably orthodox Muslims, who were intolerant of Wektu Telu beliefs and customs. Just what percentage of the Sasak population at this time was Wektu Telu is debatable, but it seems that the numbers have gradually declined as more young people turn to orthodox Islam. Possibly 30% of the island's total population – or about 600,000 people – now follow Wektu Telu.

Underlying everything is the unwritten code of adat. 'If we do not possess adat we are not more than horses and cows' is a saying on Lombok. Adat is all-pervasive, regulating marriage, kinship obligations, courting, burial rituals, and circumcision ceremonies. As on Bali and Sumbawa, elopement is a traditional form of choosing a spouse – an accepted means of overcoming the law that a woman may not marry a man of lower caste, of eluding the man's competitors for the woman's hand, and of avoiding family friction or an expensive wedding ceremony. Closely related to adat is the Wektu Telu concept of *maliq* – the word which refers to all acts which are considered breaches of adat. The performance of forbidden acts can be punished during a person's lifetime: illness, madness, poverty and death are all thought to be punishments for maliq. The Wektu Lima equivalent is sin, but that's punished in the afterlife.

Balinese customs have affected Wektu Telu. Like the Balinese Hindus, the Wektu Telu have a caste system, another factor which distinguishes them from the orthodox Muslims of Lombok. Traditionally, caste regulates the acquisition of official positions in the village, and particularly marriage – Sasak men can marry women of a lower caste than themselves, but a woman may not marry a man of a lower caste. You are born a Wektu Telu – you cannot become one through conversion, as you can a Muslim. The caste divisions are reflected in the Sasak language, which is closely related to Javanese and Balinese, and has three caste-associated levels of high, middle and low. Sanskrit words appear in the high language – likewise many Arabic words occur in villages which follow Wektu Lima.

Books

The Village Economies of the Sasak of Lombok: A Comparison of Three Indonesian Peasant Communities by Ruth Krulfeld is a fascinating description of a 20-month study of several Lombok villages in 1960 and 1961. Alfons van der Kraan's *Lombok: Conquest, Colonization and Underdevelopment, 1870-1940* (Heinemann, 1980) describes the economic destitution of the island brought about by the Dutch.

Getting There & Away

There is no international airport on Lombok, but it's quite accessible by air and sea from the neighbouring islands. The vast majority of travellers arrive from Bali, less than 100 km away, while those island-hopping from the east reach Lombok from Sumbawa. It's also possible to fly directly to Lombok from Java, Kalimantan and Sulawesi.

Air There are about seven flights a day with Merpati from Denpasar to Mataram, at about 42,000 rp. There's one Merpati flight a day between Mataram and Sumbawa Besar (47,000 rp) and on some days these continue on to Bima. Merpati has regular flights between Mataram and Surabaya (81,900 rp), Yogyakarta (134,500 rp) and Jakarta (192,400 rp). There should be at least one flight per day, but schedules are variable. There are also air connections to Banjarmasin (Kalimantan) and Unjung Pandang (Sulawesi).

Tourist Bus Perama has services running to/from Kuta, Sanur, Ubud, Lovina, Candidasa and Padangbai on Bali and Lembar, Mataram, Senggigi, Bangsal and the Gili Islands on Lombok. For example, a ticket from Ubud through to one of the Gili Islands off the Lombok coast costs 17,500 rp, including the ferry to Lombok and a boat to the island, with all the connections in between. Perama has an office or agency in most of the places mentioned earlier – you usually have to book the day before. Perama also has bus-ferry-bus connections between Lombok and Sumbawa Besar, Dompu and Bima on Sumbawa.

Ferry – to/from Bali There are at least two ferries a day between Padangbai and Lembar, and up to four services at busy times such as Ramadan. Scheduled departure times from Padangbai are 8 and 11 am, 2 and 5 pm, and from Lembar at 8 and 10 am, 2 and 5 pm. The schedules vary, so check first. *Ekonomi* (economy) costs around 4000 rp, 1st class 5700 rp. You can take a bicycle (600 rp), motorbike (4300 rp) or car (49,000 rp for a Suzuki Jimny). It can be a long, hot and uncomfortable trip in either class. Food and drinks are available on board or from the numerous hawkers who hang around the wharf until the ferry leaves. The trip takes at least four hours, sometimes up to seven; the afternoon ferries seem to be slower than the morning ones.

Ferry – to/from Sumbawa Passenger ferries leave Labuhan Lombok (in eastern Lombok) for Poto Tano (Sumbawa) at 8 and 9.30 am, noon, 3 and 5 pm. In the other direction, boats depart Poto Tano at 7 and 8 am, noon, 2 and 5 pm. Departure times may change, depending on demand and goodness knows what other local considerations. The trip takes about 1½ hours and costs around 2500 rp in ekonomi A, 1500 rp in ekonomi B, 500 rp for a bicycle, 3000 rp for a motorbike and 27,000 rp for a car.

Hydrofoil A hydrofoil service now operates between Bali's Benoa Port and Lembar Harbour on Lombok. Scheduled departure times from Benoa are 8.45 am and 3.30 pm, and from Lembar 10.45 am and 3.30 pm. The trip takes about two hours and costs 35,000 rp to Lombok, 32,000 rp the other way. The service is run by the Nawala company which has offices in Denpasar (☎ 2031339) at Jalan Iman Bonjol 234 and Mataram (☎ 2021655) at Jalan Langko 11A. Perama also sell hydrofoil tickets with bus connections to/from Benoa and Lembar. Although not much cheaper than flying, the hydrofoil is a fun trip and is certainly much quicker, more comfortable and more convenient than the ferry. The large Pelni liner MV *Kelimutu* stops at Lembar on its fortnightly cruise between Java, Nusa Tenggara and Sulawesi. See the Getting Around chapter for the complete *Kelimutu* timetable.

Getting Around
Lombok has a fairly extensive road network, although many outlying villages are difficult to get to by public transport. There is a good main road across the middle of the island between Mataram and Labuhan Lombok, and quite good roads to the south of this route. You can get around the whole island

and to many of the more remote locations if you have your own transport.

Public buses and bemos are generally restricted to main routes; away from these, you have to hire a horse-drawn cart (dokar or *cidomo*), get a lift on a motorbike, or walk. If you are exploring these regions under your own steam, bear in mind two things: firstly, food and drinking water are often scarce so it's a good idea to carry your own; secondly, so few Westerners have been in these parts that you may be regarded as a sensation by villagers you come across.

During the wet season many roads are flooded or washed away, and others are impassable because of fallen rocks and rubble, making it impossible to get to many out-of-the-way places. The damage may not be repaired until well into the dry season.

Most public transport stops at 10.30 or 11 pm, often earlier in more isolated areas.

Bemo & Bus There are several bemo stations on Lombok. The main one is at Sweta, a couple of km east of Cakranegara. Here buses, minibuses and bemos depart for various points all over the island. Other stations are at Praya and Kopang, and you may have to go via one or more of these transport hubs to get from one part of Lombok to another.

Public transport fares are fixed by the provincial government, and at Sweta there is a prominently displayed list of fares to most places on the island. This does not stop the bus and bemo boys from trying to take you for a ride, so check the notice board before setting off, or watch what the locals are paying. You may have to pay more if you have a big bag.

If you're pressed for time, and you can get a few people together, hiring a bemo by the day, or even from one village to the next, can be cheap and convenient. A reasonable price to pay for chartering a bemo for the day would be 35,000 to 40,000 rp, depending a bit on how far you want to go.

Motorbike You can rent a motorbike in the main centres of Lombok, but they are not easy to find: you won't see the 'motorbike for hire' signs stuck up all over the place that you see in Bali. You have to ask around, but there are individual owners who rent out their bikes, and a couple of specialist places in Ampenan and Mataram. See that section for details.

Once off the main roads you will find yourself on dirt tracks and in for a rough and potentially dangerous ride, so take care. Petrol can also be a problem. There are petrol (gasolene) stations around the larger towns, but out in the villages it can be difficult to find; it may be advisable to take some with you if you can carry it safely. It's sometimes available from small wayside shops – look out for signs that read *premium*, or *press ban* (literally 'tyre repair').

Car Car hire on Lombok is usually a less formal arrangement than on Bali – basically you arrange to borrow a car from a private owner. See the Ampenan, Mataram, Cakranegara & Sweta section.

Hotels in Ampenan, Mataram or Senggigi can often arrange car or motorbike hire, as can some of the tourist-type shops. There are some 'official' car rental companies in Mataram which have a wider range of vehicles, but these tend to be more expensive.

Bicycle Bicycles are available for hire in main centres of Lombok, but are not generally a popular form of transport around the island, among the locals or with travellers. If you want to explore Lombok by bicycle you'll probably have to bring your own or be prepared to do a lot of maintenance work on one of the rusty old ones you will find there.

AMPENAN, MATARAM, CAKRANEGARA & SWETA

Although officially four separate towns, Ampenan, Mataram, Cakranegara and Sweta actually run together, so it's virtually impossible to tell where one stops and the next starts. Collectively they're the main 'city' on Lombok, but these days many visitors head straight to Senggigi or the Gili

Islands and don't stay in the town at all. You can now change money and arrange airline tickets at Senggigi, and it's within easy commuting distance if you have other business in town. There are some interesting shops and markets, and a few things to see, but once that's out of the way most visitors head off to other places on the island.

Ampenan
Once the main port of Lombok, Ampenan is now not much more than a small fishing harbour. It's a bit run-down and dirty, but it's also full of hustle and bustle and colour and life. The long main road through Ampenan, Mataram and Cakranegara does not actually reach the coast at Ampenan, but fades out just before it gets to the port's beach.

Ampenan has a curious mixture of people. Apart from the Sasaks and Balinese, there is also a small Arab quarter known as Kampung Arab *(kampung* means 'district' or 'quarter'). The Arabs living here are probably descendants of Arab merchants and Sasak women, and are devout Muslims. They marry among themselves, are well educated and relatively affluent. They're also extremely friendly towards foreigners.

Mataram
Mataram is the administrative capital of the province of Nusa Tenggara Barat (West Nusa Tenggara) which comprises the islands of Lombok and Sumbawa. Some of the public buildings, such as the Bank of Indonesia, the new post office and the governor's office and residence, are impressive. There are also some substantial houses around the outskirts of town – these are the homes of Lombok's elite.

Cakranegara
Now the main commercial centre of Lombok, Cakranegara is usually referred to as Cakra. Formerly the capital of Lombok under the Balinese rajahs, Cakra today is a cacophony of bemos and motorbikes and people trying to keep their heads above the exhaust fumes. It has a thriving Chinese

community as well as many Balinese residents – many shops and restaurants in Cakranegara are run or owned by the Chinese. It's also a craft centre and is particularly well known for its basketware and weaving. Check out the bazaar and watch the silver and goldsmiths at work. You may also be able to find some of the idiosyncratic clay animal figures and ceramics produced on Lombok.

Sweta

Seven km from Ampenan and only about 2½ km beyond Cakra is Sweta, the central transport terminal of Lombok. This is where you catch bemos, buses and minibuses to other parts of the island. There are several warungs here, and numerous food, tobacco and drink vendors. Stretching along the eastern side of the terminal is a vast, covered market, the largest on Lombok. If you

wander through its dim alleys you'll see stalls spilling over with coffee beans, eggs, rice, fish, fabrics, crafts, fruit and hardware. There's also a bird market.

Orientation

The 'city' is effectively divided into four functional areas: Ampenan the port, Mataram the administrative centre, Cakranegara the trading centre and Sweta the transport centre. The towns are spread along one main road which starts as Jalan Pabean in Ampenan, quickly becomes Jalan Yos Sudarso, then changes to Jalan Langko, then to Jalan Pejanggik and finishes up in Sweta as Jalan Selaparang. It's a one-way street, running east from the port through Cakranegara. Just as it's difficult to tell where one town merges into the next, it's also difficult to tell where the road changes names. Indeed, it seems that they overlap,

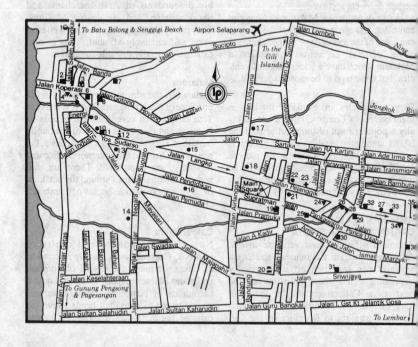

since some places appear to have more than one address.

A second one-way street, Jalan Sriwijaya/ Jalan Majapahit, brings traffic back in the other direction. Bemos run a shuttle service between the bemo stop in Ampenan and the big station in Sweta about seven km away. Getting back and forth is therefore dead easy. You can stay in Ampenan, Mataram or Cakra since there are hotels and restaurants in all three places. Budget travellers tend to head towards Ampenan because it has a little enclave of cheap hotels and places to eat, but Mataram and Cakra are handy to shopping and transport, and the mid-range hotels there are good value.

Mataram has a small commercial 'centre' near the river and a larger shopping area past the Jalan Selaparang/Jalan Hasanuddin intersection. The Cakra market is just east of here, south of the main road. The Mataram government buildings are chiefly found along Jalan Pejanggik. The main square, Lampangan Mataram, is on the south side of Jalan Pejanggik. Art exhibitions, theatre, dance and wayang kulit performances are

■	PLACES TO STAY
2	Losmen Pabean
6	Zahir Hotel
7	Losmen Wisma Triguna
8	Losmen Horas & Latimojong
11	Wisma Melati
19	Hotel Kambodja
25	Losmen Rinjani
29	Mataram Hotel
30	Hotel Granada
31	Puri Indah Hotel
32	Selaparang Hotel
36	Hotel Pusaka
38	Hotel Shanti Puri

▼	PLACES TO EAT
3	Timur Tengah
4	Cirebon & Pabean
24	Garden House Restaurant
28	Rumah Makan Flamboyan
34	Sekawan Depot Es

	OTHER
1	Ampenan Bemo Stop
5	Ampenan Market
9 & 10	Merpati Offices
12	Tourist Office
13	Telephone Office
14	Museum Negeri
15	Bank Negara Indonesia
16	Mataram University
17	Immigration Office
18	Bank Indonesia
20	Main Post Office
21	Governor's House
22	Governor's Office
23	Hospital
26	Bali Ferry Office
27	Perama Office
33	Bank Eskpor-Impor
35	Motorbike Rental
37	Cakra Market
39	Mayura Water Palace
40	Selamat Riady
41	Pura Meru
42	Sweta Bemo/Bus Station
43	Sweta Market

Ampenan, Mataram, Cakranegara & Sweta

held in the square, but you'll only find out about these shows by word of mouth. Alternatively, look for the swarms of police and military personnel that are the most obvious sign of such an occasion.

Information

Tourist Office The main Lombok government tourist office, the Kantor Dinas Pariwisata Daerah (☎ 2021866, 21730), is in Mataram at Jalan Langko 70, on the north side, almost diagonally opposite the telephone office. The people at the tourist office are helpful and reasonably well informed. They have a good pamphlet with tourist information and maps of Lombok, Sumbawa and Ampenan-Mataram-Cakranegara-Sweta. They're not very good maps, but they're the only ones around – every other tourist map seems to have been copied from these.

The Perama office (☎ 2022764, 23368) is at Jalan Pejanggik 66. The staff are very helpful and provide good information, organise shuttle bus connections, change money and arrange day trips around Lombok.

Money There are a number of banks along the main drag, all in large buildings. Most will change travellers' cheques, although it can take some time. The Bank Ekspor-Impor seems to have longer opening hours than other banks: weekdays from 7.30 am to noon and from 1 to 2 pm, Saturdays from 7.30 to 11.30 am. The moneychanger in the Mataram shopping centre (Kompleks APHM), on the south side of Jalan Pejanggik, is efficient, is open longer, and has rates only slightly less than at the banks. You can also change travellers' cheques at the airport and at the Perama office.

Remember that there are only minimal banking facilities elsewhere on the island so make sure you have enough cash with you. On the Gili Islands in particular there is nowhere to change travellers' cheques. In more remote parts of Lombok changing large denominations can be difficult, so don't carry big notes.

Post Mataram's main post office, on Jalan Majapahit (or is it Sriwijaya?), has a poste restante service. It's open from 8 am to 2 pm Monday to Thursday and on Saturday, and from 8 to 11 am on Friday. Mail sent from Lombok goes to Bali first, so it can take some time to get through.

If you want to mail parcels from Lombok you have to get customs clearance before they can be sent. You may need forms CP2 and five copies of form C2 and CP3 from the post office. From most post offices the maximum parcel size is three kg, but you can send 10 kg from the main post office.

Telephone The Permuntel telephone office, at the Ampenan end of Mataram on Jalan Langko, also has telegram and fax services. The international telephone service is very efficient, and you can usually get an overseas call through in minutes. A three-minute call costs around 25,000 rp to Australia, New Zealand or the USA, and 29,000 rp to the UK or Europe.

Immigration Lombok's kantor imigrasi (immigration office) is on Jalan Udayana, the road out to the airport.

Bookshops There are a number of bookshops along the main road through the towns. Toko Buku Titian in Ampenan has some English magazines and maps. The bookshop in Kompleks APHM, the Mataram shopping centre on the south side of Jalan Pejanggik, is also good. The daily *Jakarta Post* usually arrives at 2 pm the day after publication.

Weaving Factories

One of the last weaving factories still operating in Mataram is Selamat Riady, off Jalan Hasanuddin, where women weave delicate gold and silver thread sarongs and exquisite ikats on looms that look like they haven't altered since the Majapahit dynasty. A bemo drops you within a few metres of the factory and you're welcome to wander around. The factory is open from 7.30 am. Rinjani Hand Woven, at Jalan Pejanggik 44-46, beside the

Selaparang Hotel, also has an interesting collection of woven materials.

Pura Segara

This Balinese sea temple is on the beach a few km north of Ampenan. Along the beach you can watch the fishing boats come and go. Nearby are the remnants of a Muslim cemetery and a Chinese cemetery – worth a wander through if you're visiting the temple. You fly right over them on the approach to the airport from Bali.

Museum Negeri

The Museum Negeri Nusa Tenggara Barat is on Jalan Banjar Tilar Negara in Ampenan. With exhibits on the geology, history and culture of Lombok and Sumbawa, it's well worth browsing around if you have a couple of free hours. If you intend buying any antiques or handicrafts have a look at the krises, songket, basketware and masks to give you a starting point for comparison. It's open from 8 am to 2 pm Tuesday to Thursday, from 8 to 11 am Friday, and from 8 am to noon on weekends. Admission is 200 rp, 100 rp for children.

Mayura Water Palace

Just opposite the market, on the main road through Cakra, stands the Mayura Water Palace. It was built in 1744 and was once part of the royal court of the Balinese kingdom in Lombok. The centrepiece is the large artificial lake covered in water lilies. In the centre of the lake is an open-sided hall connected to the shoreline by a raised footpath. This Bale Kambang (Floating Pavilion) was used as both a court of justice and a meeting place for the Hindu lords. There are other shrines and fountains dotted around the surrounding park. Entrances to the walled enclosure of the palace are on the northern and western sides.

Today the Balinese use the palace grounds to graze their livestock and as a place to unleash their fighting cocks and make offerings to the gods. It's a pleasant retreat from Cakra, although less than a century ago it was the site of a bloody clash with the Dutch.

In 1894 the Dutch sent an army to back the Sasaks in a rebellion against their Balinese rajah. The rajah quickly capitulated but the crown prince decided to fight on while the Dutch-backed forces were split between various camps.

The Dutch camp at the Mayura Water Palace was attacked late at night by a combined force of Balinese and Sasaks from the west of Lombok. The camp was surrounded by high walls, and the Balinese and Sasaks took cover behind them as they fired on the exposed army, forcing the Dutch to take shelter in a nearby temple compound. The Balinese also attacked the Dutch camp at Mataram, and soon after the entire Dutch army on Lombok was routed and withdrew to Ampenan where, according to one eyewitness, the soldiers 'were so nervous that they fired madly if so much as a leaf fell off a tree'. The first battles resulted in enormous losses of men and arms for the Dutch.

Although the Balinese had won the battle they had just begun to lose the war. Now they would not only have to continue to fight the eastern Sasaks but also the Dutch, who were quickly supplied with reinforcements from Java. The Dutch attacked Mataram a month after their initial defeat, fighting street to street not only against Balinese and west Sasak soldiers but also the local population. The Balinese crown prince was killed in the battle for the palace and the Balinese retreated to Cakranegara, where they were well armed and where the complex of walls provided good defence against infantry. Cakra was attacked by a combined force of Dutch and eastern Sasaks and, as happened in Mataram, Balinese men, women and children staged repeated suicidal lance attacks, to be cut down by rifle and artillery fire. The rajah and a small group of *punggawas* (commanders) fled to the village of Sasari near the pleasure gardens at Lingsar. A day or two later the rajah surrendered to the Dutch, but even his capture did not lead the Balinese to surrender.

In late November the Dutch attacked Sasari and a large number of Balinese chose the suicidal puputan. With the downfall of the dynasty the local population abandoned its struggle against the Dutch. The conquest of Lombok, thought about for decades, had taken the Dutch barely three months. The old rajah died in exile in Batavia in 1895.

Pura Meru

Directly opposite the water palace and just off the main road is the Pura Meru, the largest Balinese temple on Lombok. It's open every day, and a donation is expected (about 500 rp or 'up to you'). It was built in 1720 under the patronage of the Balinese prince, Anak Agung Made Karang of the Singosari kingdom, as an attempt to unite all the small kingdoms on Lombok. Though now rather neglected-looking, it was built as a symbol of the universe and is dedicated to the Hindu trinity of Brahma, Vishnu and Shiva.

The temple has three separate courtyards. The outer courtyard has a hall housing the wooden drums that are beaten to call believers to festivals and special ceremonies. In the middle court are two buildings with large raised platforms for offerings. The inner court has one large and 33 small shrines, as well as three meru (multi-roofed shrines). Each shrine is looked after by members of the Balinese community. The three meru are in a line: the central one, with 11 tiers, is Shiva's house; the one in the north, with nine tiers, is Vishnu's and the seven-tiered one in the south is Brahma's. A festival is held here each June.

Places to Stay – bottom end

The most popular cheap places to stay are in Ampenan. Although there is plenty of accommodation elsewhere, few travellers bother to go further afield unless they intend to head straight out to Senggigi, just 10 km to the north. It's easy to commute into town from there for business.

Jalan Koperasi branches off Jalan Yos Sudarso in the centre of Ampenan. Only a short stroll from the centre is the *Hotel Zahir* (☎ 2022403) at Jalan Koperasi 12. It's a straightforward place with singles/doubles at 4000/5000 rp, or 5000/6000 rp with bathroom. Prices include breakfast, and tea or coffee throughout the day. The rooms at this popular, convenient and friendly losmen each have a small verandah and face a central courtyard. The owners can arrange motorbike rental for about 7500 rp per day.

Continue along the road to Jalan Koperasi 65 where *Losmen Horas* (☎ 2021695) is very clean and well kept. Singles/doubles with spotless bathrooms cost 4000/6000 rp. Virtually next door is the *Latimojong* at number 64. It's dirt cheap at 1500/2500 rp, but extremely basic and definitely a bottom-end place. Further east is *Losmen Wisma Triguna* (☎ 2021705), which is operated by the same people as the Horas. It's a little over a km from central Ampenan and a quiet,

relaxed place. Spacious rooms opening on to a bright verandah or the garden cost 6000/8000 rp, including breakfast. The people at Horas or Wisma Triguna can help you organise a climb up Gunung Rinjani, and will rent camping equipment and arrange a guide.

Back in the centre of town is *Losmen Pabean* (☎ 2021758) at Jalan Pabean 146, also known as Jalan Yos Sudarso. It's better inside than it looks from the outside. Rooms are 3500/5500 rp for singles/doubles; triples cost 7500 rp.

In Mataram, on the corner of Jalan Supratman and Jalan Arif Rahmat, *Hotel Kambodja* (☎ 2022211) is pleasant and has rooms at 6500/7500 rp.

Hotel Pusaka (☎ 2023119), at Jalan Hasanuddin 23, has doubles from 12,500 to 35,000 rp with air-con. The cheap rooms are pretty basic and the mid-range rooms are quite good at 17,000 rp a double. Close by, at Hasanuddin 17 is the *Losmen Merpati* with rooms at 3000/4000 rp, 5000/6000 rp and 6000/7000 rp. The cheapest rooms are depressingly basic.

Places to Stay – middle

There are quite a few good value, mid-range places in the Mataram-Cakra area. The *Selaparang Hotel* (☎ 2022670), at Jalan Pejanggik 40-42 in Mataram, is close to the Perama office. Air-con rooms cost 35,000/40,000 rp for singles/doubles, and fan-cooled rooms about half this. Across the road at 105 is *Mataram Hotel* (☎ 2023411) with double rooms at 18,000 rp, or rooms with air-con, TV, hot water and other mod cons for up to 35,000 rp. Both these mid-range hotels have pleasant little restaurants. At Jalan Pejanggik 64, just west of the Perama office, is the *Hotel Hertajoga* (☎ 2021775). It's good value, with fan-cooled rooms at 10,000/13,500 rp, and 15,000/18,500 rp with air-con.

Just south of the main drag, at Jalan Maktal 15, is the *Hotel & Restaurant Shanti Puri* (☎ 2022649). Cheap singles/doubles are 5000/6000 rp, and very comfortable rooms cost up to 10,000/12000 rp. It's run by a friendly and helpful Balinese family who can also arrange motorbike and car hire. Also in Mataram, *Wisma Chandra* (☎ 2023979) at Jalan Caturwarga 55, has singles/doubles at 7000/9000 rp, triples at 15,000 rp. Rooms with air-con cost 15,000/17,500/20,000 rp. Prices include breakfast.

Places to Stay – top end

The heavily advertised *Hotel Granada* (☎ 2022275) is a top-end place on Jalan Bung Karno, a little south of the shopping centre in Mataram. There's a swimming pool and all rooms have air-con. The prices include breakfast but not the 10% tax, and start at around 50,000 rp a double. If you want this kind of comfort, the *Puri Indah* (☎ 2027633) on Jalan Sriwijaya also has a restaurant and a pool but is much better value at 15,000/20,000 rp, or 20,000/30,000 rp for air-con singles/doubles.

At the other end of Mataram, almost in Ampenan, the *Wisma Melati* (☎ 202364) is quiet and comfortable, with carpets, air-con, telephone etc. Standard rooms are 26,000/29,000 rp, superior rooms 44,000/52,000 rp for singles/doubles.

Places to Eat

Ampenan has several Indonesian and Chinese restaurants including the very popular *Cirebon*, at Jalan Pabean 113, with a standard Indonesian/Chinese menu and most dishes at 1500 to 2500 rp. Next door at 111 is the *Pabean* with similar food. Closer to the Ampenan bemo stop is the *Rumah Makan Arafat*, at No 64, with good, cheap Indonesian food. Other alternatives are the *Setia* at Jalan Pabean 129, the *Depot Mina* at Jalan Yos Sudarso 102 and the *Timur Tengah* at Jalan Koperasi 22, right across from the Hotel Zahir.

There are a couple of interesting restaurants at the Mataram shopping centre off Jalan Pejanggik, several hundred metres down the road from the governor's residence on the same side. The *Garden House Restaurant* is a pleasant open-air place with inexpensive nasi campur, nasi goreng and other standard meals. There's also a variety of ice cream dishes, plus casatta and tutti frutti! The nearby *Taliwang* offers local dishes. Continue further along the main road towards Cakra and you come to the more expensive *Rumah Makan Flamboyan*, a nice place with seafood and Chinese dishes.

In Cakra the *Sekawan Depot Es* has cold drinks downstairs and a seafood and Chinese restaurant upstairs. Around the corner on Jalan Hasanuddin is the *Rumah Makan Madya*, which serves very good, cheap food in authentic Sasak style. A little further north, the *Rumah Makan Akbar* also looks good. There are a number of other restaurants in this area, a handful of bakeries and, of course, plenty of places to buy food at the market.

Things to Buy

There are a surprising number of antique and handicraft shops in Lombok. Rora Antiques, in Ampenan at Jalan Yos Sudarso 16A, sells some excellent woodcarvings, baskets and traditional Lombok weavings (songket and so on). Renza Antiques, at Jalan Yos Sudarso 92, is also a good place to browse.

Musdah at Dayan Penen, Jalan Sape 16 also has an interesting collection of masks, baskets, krises and carvings for sale in a private residence. Describing how to get to there is virtually impossible but a series of signs leads you from the Hotel Zahir or other accommodation places on Jalan Koperasi.

Another good place to look for handicrafts and other local products is the Sweta market, next to the Sweta bemo station.

Bargaining It's more difficult to bargain in Lombok than it is in Bali. You need to take your time – don't rush or be rushed. Bargaining is a ritual and a pastime as much as a commercial negotiation. It's also harder to make an accurate evaluation of things, particularly antiques. You'll hear a lot of talk about special Lombok prices – these are supposed to be much cheaper than Bali prices – but unless you know what you're doing you can pay as much as, if not more than, than you would in Bali. Be very sure you want to buy before making an offer. Try to get the dealer to put a price on the object before starting to bargain. Always bargain for what you buy, particularly for items like cloth, basketware or antiques. If you manage to get the price down to half the asking price then you're doing very well, although it's more likely that you will end up paying about two-thirds of the starting price or only get a nominal amount knocked off.

Getting There & Away

Air See the Getting There & Away section for details of flights to and from Lombok. There's a Merpati office (☎ 2023762) which can book and reconfirm Garuda flights, at Jalan Yos Sudarso 6 in Ampenan. There's another Merpati office (☎ 2021037) a little closer to the centre of Ampenan at Jalan Yos Sudarso 22, and a third one (☎ 2022670, 23235) at the Selaparang Hotel, Jalan Pejanggik 40-42 in Mataram.

Bus The Sweta bus station is at the inland end of the Ampenan-Mataram-Cakra-Sweta development and is the main bus terminus for the entire island. It's also the eastern terminus for the local bemos which shuttle back and forth between Ampenan at one end and Sweta at the other. There's an office in the middle of the place, with a notice board on which you can check the fare before you're hustled on board one of the vehicles. Some distances and approximate bemo fares from Sweta to other parts of Lombok include:

Destination	Fare (rp)
East (Jurusan Timor)	
Narmada (6 km)	200
Mantang (17 km)	450
Kopang (25 km)	550
Terara (29 km)	800
Sikur (33 km)	800
Masbagik (36 km)	850
Selong (47 km)	1400
Labuhan Lombok (69 km)	2000
South & Central	
(Jurusan Selatan dan Tenggara)	
Kediri (5 km)	500
Gerung (12 km)	500
Lembar (22 km)	1000
Praya (27 km)	700
North (Jurusan Utara)	
Pemenang (31 km)	700
Tanjung (45 km)	800
Gondang (53 km)	1000
Amor-Amor (64 km)	1100
Bayan (79 km)	1600

Boat See the Introductory Getting There & Away section for Lombok, for details of the ferry services to and from Lombok. The ferry docks at Lembar, 22 km south of Ampenan. The Bali ferry office is at Jalan Pejanggik 49 in Mataram.

The office for the Nawala hydrofoil service (☎ 2021655) is at Jalan Langko 11A in Mataram.

Getting Around

To/From the Airport Lombok's Selaparang Airport is only a couple of km from Ampenan, and a taxi there costs about 4500 rp. Alternatively, you can walk out of the airport car park to the main road and take one of the frequent No 7 bemos which run straight to the Ampenan bemo stop for 150 rp. It's not even necessary to go into town from the airport if you want to head out to Senggigi Beach or to the Gili Islands. See those sections for more details.

Local Transport Ampenan-Mataram-Cakra-Sweta is surprisingly sprawling, so don't plan to walk from place to place. Bemos shuttle back and forth along the main route between the Ampenan stop at one end and the Sweta station at the other. The fare is a standard 150 rp regardless of the distance. There are also plenty of dokars to rent for shorter trips around town, although these are not permitted on the main streets.

Chartering a bemo in Lombok is easy. Count on about 35,000 rp a day, or more for a long trip. Check the bemo over carefully as some are in decidedly poor condition. The bemo stop in Ampenan is a good place to charter a bemo.

Motorbike Motorbike rental on Lombok is usually less formal and not as straightforward as it is in Bali, but it's still easy enough to do. At the Cakranegara end of Mataram, go to Jalan Gelantik, off Jalan Selaparang near the junction with Jalan Hasanuddin. The motorbike owners who hang around there have bikes to rent for 8000 to 12,000 rp a day. As usual, the more you pay the better you get and it's wise to check a bike over carefully before saying yes. In fact this is even more important in Lombok because you can be a long way from help should you suffer a breakdown or puncture in a remote area. Some hotels may be able to arrange a motorbike to rent.

Car Car hire is also less formal than on Bali – basically, you arrange to borrow a car from a private owner. They rarely insist on a licence, but may want you to leave a passport for security. There is usually an insurance cover for damage to other people or property, but the car itself is usually uninsured and you drive it at your own risk. It costs from about 35,000 to 50,000 rp per day for a Suzuki Jimny type vehicle, depending on where you get it and how you bargain. If you take it for a few days or a week you should get a discount. Between four people it can be quite a cheap way to get around. Hotels in town or at Senggigi can often arrange car hire. Metro Photo (☎ 2022146) at Jalan Yos Sudarso 79 in Ampenan can arrange pretty cheap rental cars.

There are some 'official' car rental companies, but these tend to be more expensive. Rinjani Rent Car (☎ 2021400), in Mataram opposite the Hotel Granada on Jalan Bung Karno, has Suzuki Jimnys for 50,000 rp per day without insurance. Yoga Rent Car (☎ 2021127), in the Kompleks APHM shopping centre in Mataram, has similar cars for 45,000 rp per day.

Bicycle You can rent bicycles from the Losmen Horas or Wisma Triguna in Ampenan. It costs about 2000 rp a day for an old one, up to twice that for a new one.

GUNUNG PENGSONG

This Balinese temple is built – as the name suggests – on top of a hill. It's nine km south of Mataram and has great views of rice fields, the volcanoes and the sea. Try to get there early in the morning before the clouds envelop Gunung Rinjani, and be ready for a steep climb. Once a year, generally in March or April, a buffalo is taken up and sacrificed to celebrate a good harvest. The Bersih Desa festival also occurs here at harvest time – houses and gardens are cleaned, fences whitewashed, roads and paths repaired. Once part of a ritual to rid the village of evil spirits, it is now held in honour of the rice goddess Dewi Sri. There's no set admission charge, but you will have to pay the caretaker 200 rp or so, especially if you use the car park.

LEMBAR

Lembar, 22 km south of Ampenan, is the main port on Lombok. The ferries and hydrofoils to and from Bali dock here, and there are regular buses and bemos between Lembar and Sweta during the day.

Places to Stay & Eat

There's only one place to stay in Lembar: the *Serumbum Indah*, which has a restaurant and singles/doubles for 12,500/15,000 rp. It's not very convenient, being about two km north of the harbour on the main road, and the owners aren't used to foreign visitors. There's a canteen at the harbour where you can buy snacks and drinks while waiting to catch the ferry.

Getting There & Away

See the Lombok Getting There & Away section for information on the Bali to Lombok ferry and hydrofoil services. You can buy your tickets at the wharf on the day, or from the offices in Mataram.

Regular buses and bemos from Sweta cost 1000 rp during the day. You are dropped off almost directly in front of the Lembar ferry office. If you arrive in Lembar on the afternoon ferry from Bali, buy a bemo ticket on the journey over. Although you'll be paying more than the normal price, you'll have guaranteed transport to Ampenan, Mataram or Cakranegara. Bemo drivers meeting travellers off this ferry often jack up their prices to more than 1000 rp after dark. A minibus from the Zahir Hotel in Ampenan often meets the ferry.

SOUTH-WESTERN PENINSULA

If you approach Lembar by ferry you'll see a hilly and little-developed peninsula on your right. A road from Lembar runs on to this peninsula in Lombok's south-west, but it's pretty rough after Sekotong, and impassable for ordinary cars after Taun. Bangko Bangko is at the end of the track, and from there it's a two or three-km walk to a beach which has great surf but no places to stay or eat. There are a number of picturesque islands off the north coast of the peninsula and one of them, Gili Nanggu, has some tourist bungalows. You can get a boat there from Lembar.

SENGGIGI

On a series of sweeping bays, between seven and 12 km north of Ampenan, Senggigi has become the most popular tourist area on Lombok. These days many travellers head straight for this string of beaches without stopping in Ampenan-Mataram-Cakra-Sweta. Promotional work for the big, expensive Senggigi Beach Hotel has focused much more interest on Senggigi and on Lombok as a whole. There are now a few other fancy places in Senggigi, and the Lombok government is encouraging more four and five-star developments. Fortunately, however, there is still some budget accommodation there.

Senggigi has fine beaches, although they slope very steeply into the water. There's some snorkelling off the point and in the sheltered bay around the headland. There are beautiful sunsets over Selat Lombok and you can enjoy them from the beach or from one of the beach-front restaurants. The nightlife can be pretty active, with home-grown rock bands playing to enthusiastic crowds of locals and visitors.

Information

You can change money or travellers' cheques at the Graha Beach Hotel, in the middle of the Senggigi strip. The staff can also make bookings and confirm flights for Garuda and Merpati. There's a Perama office further north which runs tours and tourist transport and will also provide information and change money. Other facilities include a Permuntel telephone office and some photo-processing places.

Batu Bolong

This temple is on a rocky point which juts into the sea about a km south of Senggigi Beach, eight km north of Ampenan. The rock on which it sits has a natural hole in it which gives the temple its name – batu bolong means literally 'rock with hole'. Being a Balinese temple, it's oriented towards Gunung Agung, Bali's holiest mountain, across Selat Lombok. There's a fantastic view and it's a good place to watch the sunsets. Periodically the local people make offerings here, and legend has it that beautiful virgins were once thrown into the sea from the top of the rock. Locals like to claim that this is why the temple was built and why there are so many sharks in the water near Batu Bolong.

Places to Stay – bottom end

Senggigi is moving up-market. Although there's plenty of mid-range accommodation, and an increasing number of expensive places, there's not that much for shoestring travellers. The most popular travellers' centre at Senggigi is the Pondok Senggigi. It's expanded a bit, but still has some cheaper rooms at 6000/8000 rp for singles/doubles. There's a good restaurant, and rooms with Western-style bathrooms for 15,000/ 18,000 rp. The rooms run off a long verandah with a pleasant garden area in front. Along the other side of the garden are comfortable individual bungalows at 20,000/ 25,000 rp. The Pondok Senggigi sometimes has live music and a lot of people hang around the restaurant area, which isn't separated from the rooms, so security is not great. We've had a report

Top: Catamarans, Pantai Pandan, Sumatra (RN)
Left: Repairing a fishing net, Pantai Pandan, Sumatra (RN)
Right: Danau Tawar, Takengon, Sumatra (RN)

Top: Gunung Rinjani, Lombok, Nusa Tenggara, (JL)
Bottom: Kuta beach, Lombok (JL)

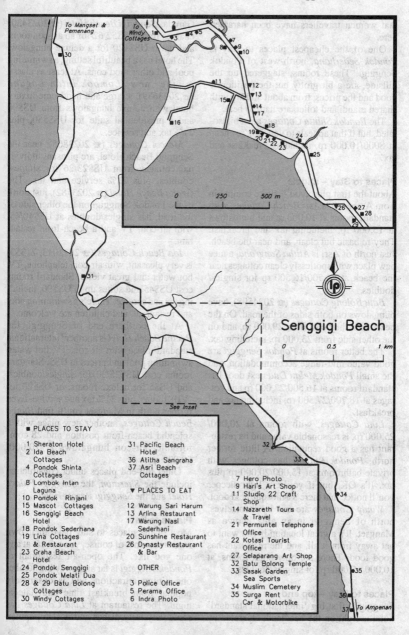

Senggigi Beach

0   250   500 m

0   0.5   1 km

See Inset

To Mangset &
Pemenang

To Windy
Cottages

To Ampenan

■ PLACES TO STAY

1   Sheraton Hotel
2   Ida Beach
    Cottages
4   Pondok Shinta
    Cottages
8   Lombok Intan
    Laguna
10 Pondok Rinjani
15 Mascot Cottages
16 Senggigi Beach
    Hotel
18 Pondok Sederhana
19 Lina Cottages
    & Restaurant
23 Graha Beach
    Hotel
24 Pondok Senggigi
25 Pondok Melati Dua
28 & 29 Batu Bolong
    Cottages
30 Windy Cottages

31 Pacific Beach
    Hotel
36 Atitha Sangraha
37 Asri Beach
    Cottages

▼ PLACES TO EAT

12 Warung Sari Harum
13 Arlina Restaurant
17 Warung Nasi
    Sederhani
20 Sunshine Restaurant
26 Dynasty Restaurant
    & Bar

OTHER

3   Police Office
5   Perama Office
6   Indra Photo
7   Hero Photo
9   Hari's Art Shop
11 Studio 22 Craft
    Shop
14 Nazareth Tours
    & Travel
21 Permuntel Telephone
    Office
22 Kotasi Tourist
    Office
27 Selaparang Art Shop
32 Batu Bolong Temple
33 Sasak Garden
    Sea Sports
34 Muslim Cemetery
35 Surga Rent
    Car & Motorbike

that women travellers have been harassed here.

One of the cheapest places to stay is *Pondok Sederhana*, north-west of Pondok Senggigi. These rooms, staggered up the hillside, are a bit grotty but the position is good and the prices, from about 5000 rp with shared mandi and toilet, are hard to beat.

The *Pondok Shinta Cottages* are a bit isolated, but if that appeals to you they're cheap at 8000/10,000 rp, including breakfast and tax.

Places to Stay – middle

About the first place you'll strike coming in from Ampenan is *Asri Beach Cottages*, with standard rooms at 10,000 rp and bungalows at 15,000 rp, including tax and breakfast. They're basic but clean, and near the beach. Just north of Asri is *Atitha Sangraha*, a nice new place with spotlessly clean cottages near the beach at 14,500/16,500 rp for singles/doubles.

Batu Bolong Cottages (☎ 2024598), have bungalows on both sides of the road. On the beach side they cost from 29,000 rp, and on the other side from 23,000 rp, including tax.

The better rooms at *Pondok Senggigi* are good value mid-range accommodation, and the small *Pondok Melati Dua* next door has standard rooms at 16,500/22,000 rp and cottages at 18,700/27,500 rp, including tax and breakfast.

Lina Cottages, with rooms at 20,000/25,000 rp, is reasonable value and its restaurant has a good reputation. A little further north, *Pondok Rinjani* has cottages with private bathrooms at 15,000/20,000 rp plus tax. It's OK, but if you're a light sleeper you'll notice that there's a mosque next door.

Windy Cottages are out by themselves, north of Senggigi in an area known as Mangset. It's a great location if you want to get away from it all, and the restaurant has good food. There are only eight rooms, at 10,000/15,000 rp for singles/doubles.

Places to Stay – top end

Senggigi's first big 'international standard' hotel is right on the headland. Operated by Garuda, *Senggigi Beach Hotel* (☎ 2023430) charges from US$52/62 for an air-con room and up to US$120 for a deluxe bungalow. The hotel has a beautiful setting, a swimming pool and other mod cons. At least as classy is the new *Lombok Intan Laguna* (☎ 2023659), a large and handsome luxury hotel with deluxe bungalows from US$90 and a presidential suite for US$550, plus 21% tax and service.

Mascot Cottages (☎ 2023865), near the Senggigi Beach Hotel, are pleasant individual cottages from US$23/26 for singles/doubles, plus 21% service and tax. The *Graha Beach Hotel* (☎ 2023782), just north of the Pondok Senggigi on the other side of the road, has singles/doubles at US$40/45, with air-con, TV and a beach-front restaurant.

Ida Beach Cottages (☎ 2021013, 21353) is very pleasant, with air-con, telephone, TV, hot water and great views. Standard rooms cost US$45 and suites up to US$90, including tax and service. There's a swimming pool and restaurant, and children are welcome.

At the northern end of Senggigi, the *Pacific Beach Hotel* is another 'international standard' place with air-con, TV, hot water, swimming pool and prices in US$. Standard rooms cost US$25/30 for singles/doubles; add US$5 for deluxe rooms, or US$20 for 'VIP' rooms, plus 21% tax and service. Even further north in Mangset you'll find *Bunga Beach Cottages*, another new place with a splendid beach-front position and 28 comfortable, air-con bungalows at 70,000/80,000 rp.

Other top-end places under construction include the *Sheraton*, the *Senggigi Palace Hotel* and the *Senggigi Resort Hotel*.

Places to Eat

Most of the places to stay have their own restaurants and, of course, you can eat at any one you like. The open-air restaurant at *Pondok Senggigi* is far and away the number one dining attraction, and is deservedly popular from breakfast time until late at night. The restaurant at *Lina Cottages* has some very tasty dishes and is also popular.

The *Senggigi Beach Hotel* restaurant is noted for its high prices, while the one at the *Graha Beach Hotel* is notable for its slow service.

At the bottom end of the scale, the small *Warung Nasi Sederhani* is mainly for local people, but tourists are quite welcome to enjoy its standard Indonesian food at rock-bottom prices. In the same area, the *Sunshine Restaurant* has a typical tourist menu and good Chinese food. Further north is the *Arlina Restaurant* and the *Warung Sari Harum*, another good-value place.

Coming in from the south you'll pass the *Dynasty Restaurant & Bar* which seems to be poorly patronised. There's a pool table and cheap beer, and Chinese dishes cost from about 3500 rp, which is pretty standard. At the other end of the Senggigi strip, the restaurant at *Windy Cottages* serves good food at reasonable prices in a delightful seaside setting.

Entertainment

There's quite a music scene in this part of Lombok. The local bands do good rock and reggae music with an Indonesian flavour, as well as covers of popular Western numbers. Cassettes of Indonesian bands are available, and you'll probably hear them in bemos and buses. *Pondok Senggigi* and the *Graha Beach Hotel* both have live music on occasions, with both tourists and young locals crowding the dance floor. As the lead singer of one band said, attempting to reach the UK, US, Australian and Indonesian members of his audience, 'It's super mega bloody bagus!'.

Getting There & Away

A public bemo from Ampenan to Senggigi costs about 250 rp. (There's a bemo stop on the coast road just north of Ampenan.) To get to Senggigi from the airport, first get a bemo to Lendang Bajur, just north of the airport on the road to Pemenang. From Lendang Bajur you can catch a bus to Senggigi, making the total fare about 500 rp. A taxi from the airport to Senggigi costs around 7500 rp.

NARMADA

Laid out as a miniature replica of the summit of Gunung Rinjani and its crater lake, Narmada is a hill about 10 km east of Cakra, on the main east-west road crossing Lombok. It takes its name from a sacred river in India and the temple here, Pura Kalasa, is still used. The Balinese Pujawali celebration is held here every year in honour of the god Batara, who dwells on Gunung Rinjani. At the same time the faithful, who have made the trek up the mountain and down to the lake Segara Anak, hold a ritual called *pekelan* in which they dispose of their gold trinkets and artefacts by ceremonially throwing them into the lake.

Narmada was constructed by the king of Mataram in 1805, when he was no longer able to climb Rinjani to make his offerings to the gods. Having set his conscience at rest by placing offerings in the temple, he spent at least some of his time in his pavilion on the hill, lusting after the young girls bathing in the artificial lake.

It's a beautiful place to spend a few hours, although the gardens are neglected. Don't go there on weekends, when it tends to become very crowded. Apart from the lake there are two other pools in the grounds. Admission is 250 rp (125 rp for children) and there's an additional charge to swim in the pool.

Along one side of the pool are the remains of an aqueduct built by the Dutch and still in use. Land tax was tied to the productivity of the land so the Dutch were keenly interested in increasing agricultural output. They did this by extending irrigation systems to increase the area under cultivation. The Balinese had already built extensive irrigation networks, particularly in the west of Lombok.

The construction of roads and bridges was also given high priority, because from both a political and an economic point of view it was in Dutch interests to establish a good communication system. A large number of roads and tracks were constructed which, like the aqueducts, were built and maintained with the unpaid labour of Lombok peasants.

Places to Eat

Right at the Narmada bemo station is the local market, which sells mainly food and clothing and is well worth a look. There are a number of warungs scattered around offering soto ayam (chicken soup) and other dishes.

Getting There & Away

There are frequent bemos from Sweta to Narmada for around 200 rp. When you get off at the bemo station at Narmada, you'll see the gardens directly opposite. If you cross the road and walk 100 metres or so south along the sideroad you'll come to the entrance. There are parking fees for bicycles, motorbikes and cars.

LINGSAR

This large temple complex, just a few km north of Narmada, is said to have been built in 1714. The temple combines the Bali-Hindu and Wektu Telu religions in one complex. Designed in two separate sections and built on two different levels, the Hindu pura in the northern section is higher than the Wektu Telu temple in the southern section.

The Hindu temple has four shrines. On one side is Hyang Tunggal, which looks towards Gunung Agung and is the seat of the gods in Bali. The shrine faces north-west rather than north-east as it would in Bali. On the other side is a shrine devoted to Gunung Rinjani, the seat of the gods in Lombok. Between these two shrines is a double shrine symbolising the union between the two islands. One side of this double shrine is named in honour of the might of Lombok, and the other side is dedicated to a king's daughter, Ayu Nyoman Winton who, according to legend, gave birth to a god.

The Wektu Telu temple is noted for its small enclosed pond devoted to Lord Vishnu. It has a number of holy eels that can be enticed from their hiding places along the water ducts by persistent tapping on the walls and the use of hard-boiled eggs as bait. Apart from their outstanding size, they're rather unprepossessing – like huge swimming slugs. The stalls outside the temple complex sell boiled eggs – expect to pay around 200 rp or so. Next to the eel pond is another enclosure with a kind of large altar or offering place, bedecked in white and

yellow cloth and mirrors. The mirrors are offerings by Chinese business people asking for good luck and success. Many local farmers also come here with offerings, or to feed the holy eels.

On the right as you enter the temple, running almost its entire length and hidden behind a wall, is a women's washing place. It's mainly a series of individual fountains squirting holy water and, once again, there are holy eels here. There's a men's mandi at the back. You can bathe here, but Narmada is probably a better place to swim.

Once a year at the beginning of the rainy season – somewhere between October and December – the Hindus and the Wektu Telus make offerings and pray in their own temples, then come out into the communal compound and pelt each other with *ketupat* – rice wrapped in banana leaves. No-one quite knows what this ceremony is for. Some say it's to bring the rain, others to give thanks for the rain. Be prepared to get attacked with ketupat from both sides if you visit Lingsar at this time!

Getting There & Away

There are frequent bemos from Sweta to Narmada for 200 rp. At Narmada, you can catch another bemo to Lingsar for the same price, and walk the short distance from there to the temple complex. Watch for the school on the main road – it's easy to miss the temple, which is set back off the road behind the school.

There is a large square in front of the temple complex, with a couple of warungs to the right before you enter the main area. There's a small stall closer to the temple where you can buy snacks, and hard-boiled eggs for the holy eels. If the temple is locked ask at one of the warungs for a key.

SURANADI

A few km east of Lingsar, Suranadi has one of the holiest temples on Lombok. This small temple, set in pleasant gardens, is noted for its bubbling, icy cold spring water and restored baths with ornate Balinese carvings. The eels here have also been sanctified. Drop a hard-boiled egg into the water and watch the eels swim out of the conduits for a feed.

You can also swim here so bring your swimsuit. It is polite to ask permission before jumping in.

Hutan Wisata Suranadi

Not far from Suranadi, on the road towards Sesaot, there's a small jungle sanctuary, the Hutan Wisata Suranadi (*hutan* means 'forest' or 'jungle'). There are various types of trees, some with botanical labels, as well as walks of up to 1½ hours. Along the way you can see many types of birds and butterflies as well as some brown monkeys.

Places to Stay & Eat

The *Suranadi Hotel* (☎ 2023686) has rooms at a variety of prices from US$12, and overpriced cottages from about US$30, plus 21% tax and service. It's an old Dutch building, originally an administrative centre, although it's no great example of colonial architecture. There are two swimming pools, tennis courts, a restaurant and a bar. People not staying at the hotel can use the swimming pool for 1000 rp (children 250 rp).

Apart from the restaurant in the hotel, there are also a few warungs in the main street.

SESAOT

About five km from Suranadi, and also worth a visit, is Sesaot, a small quiet market town on the edge of a forest where wood-felling is the main industry. There's regular transport from Suranadi to Sesaot and you can eat at the warung on the main street, which has simple but tasty food.

Go up the main street and turn left over the bridge. There are some nice places for picnics, popular with locals on holidays, and you can swim in the river. The water is very cool and is considered holy as it comes straight from Gunung Rinjani. You can continue up the road about three km to Air Nyet, a small village with more places for swimming and picnics.

CENTRAL LOMBOK

Central Lombok is the name of one of the six administrative districts (kabupaten) of West Nusa Tenggara Province, but here it is used in a more general sense to cover the inland

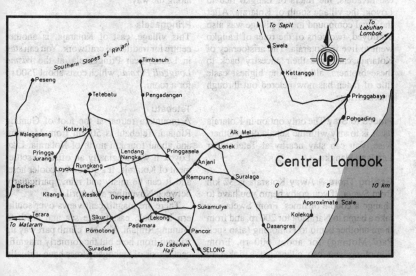

Central Lombok

towns and villages between Gunung Rinjani and the south coast. Most of the places in central Lombok are more or less traditional Sasak settlements, and several of them are known for particular types of local handicrafts. The area on the southern slopes of Gunung Rinjani is well watered and lush, and offers opportunities for scenic walks through the rice fields and the jungle. South of the main east-west road, the country is drier, and some quite large dams have been built to provide irrigation during the dry season.

The villages of Kotaraja and Loyok are noted particularly for basketware and plaited mats, but there are only a couple of places where visitors can buy the stuff. There is some very good quality work, but it seems that most of it is sold directly for export. Exquisitely intricate jewellery, vases, caskets and other decorative objects also come from Kotaraja.

Kotaraja

Kotaraja means 'city of kings', although no kings ruled from here. Apparently, when the Sasak kingdom of Langko, located at Kopang in central Lombok, fell to the Balinese invaders, the rulers of Langko fled to Loyok, the village south of Kotaraja. After the royal compound in that village was also destroyed, two sons of the ruler of Langko went to live in Kotaraja. The aristocracy of Kotaraja can trace their ancestry back to these brothers, although the highest caste title of raden has now petered out through intermarriage.

Places to Stay The only option in Kotaraja itself is to stay with the kepala desa. Otherwise, you can stay nearby at Tetebatu or Lendang Nangka.

Getting There & Away Kotaraja is 32 km from Sweta. If you go by bemo you have to change a couple of times. From Sweta you take a bemo to Narmada for 200 rp, and from there another bemo to Pomotong (also spelt Pao' Motong) for about 600 rp. From Pomotong you can either get a dokar to Kotaraja (400 rp), or wait for one of the infrequent bemos which are a bit cheaper. You might also get a lift on the back of a motorbike. There is a direct bus from Sweta to Pomotong but, as you may have to wait around for a while, it may actually be quicker and easier to take a bemo.

Loyok

Loyok, a tiny village just a few km from Kotaraja, is also noted for its fine handicrafts despite being very much off the trampled track. Most of the craftspeople work from their homes, but the dokar drivers will be able to take you to where the basket weavers work. There's a place in the main street where you can buy some of the excellent basketware.

Getting There & Away To get to Loyok, you can get a bemo from Pomotong to take you as far as the turn-off to the village, and then either walk the rest of the way or get a dokar for 250 rp per person. If you're setting out from Kotaraja for Loyok you've got the same options – either take a dokar or walk. It's a very pretty drive, with traditional thatched Sasak huts and lush rice terraces along the way.

Pringgasela

This village, east of Kotaraja, is another centre for traditional craftwork. You can stay in Lenek, near Pringgasela, at the *Wisma Longgali Permai*, which costs about 7500 rp for a room.

Tetebatu

A mountain retreat at the foot of Gunung Rinjani, Tetebatu is 50 km from Mataram and about four km north of Kotaraja. Like Loyok it was originally an offshoot settlement of Kotaraja. It's quite a bit cooler here, and it can be misty and rainy, particularly between November and April.

There are magnificent views over southern Lombok, east to the sea and north to Gunung Rinjani. You can climb part way up Rinjani from here but the formerly magnificent stands of mahogany trees have virtually disappeared. Other destinations for walks include Jukut Waterfall, six km to the east, and the hutan (forest), four km north-west, where lots of jet-black monkeys will shriek at you.

Places to Stay & Eat The original place to stay is *Wisma Soedjono*, an old colonial house that was once a country retreat for a Dr Soedjono. A number of rooms and bungalows have been added as well as a restaurant and a good-sized swimming pool. In the simplest rooms, prices start at 7500/11,000 rp for singles/doubles, and peak at 25,000/35,000 rp for 'VIP' accommodation. The better rooms have Western-style toilets and showers with hot water, and all prices include tax and continental breakfast. The staff provide good information about walks in the area. The food here is excellent, but costs extra – you can even get a packed lunch if you want to spend the day out walking. In fact, everything here costs extra – even parking a motorbike while you have lunch will cost money.

A cheaper place is *Diwi Enjeni*, on the south side of town. It seems to be stuck out in the rice fields by itself, but has a nice outlook. Bungalows with outside mandi cost 4000/5000 rp for singles/doubles, including breakfast and tax. Bungalows with a private mandi cost about 1500 rp more. There's a restaurant here, and another one, the *Restaurant Alan*, is on the opposite side of the road. There are also two or three warungs in the town.

Getting There & Away Getting to Tetebatu involves a number of changes if you haven't got your own wheels. Take a direct bus from Sweta to Pomotong or, if you can't wait that long, take a bemo to Narmada for 200 rp, and then another to Pomotong for 600 rp. From Pomotong take a bemo (250 rp) or a dokar (400 rp) to Kotaraja, and from there another bemo or dokar to Tetebatu. If you're not in a hurry and you're not carrying too much, you can walk from Pomotong to Tetebatu. It's an easy 2½ to three hours, through attractive country patched with rice fields.

Lendang Nangka

Lendang Nangka is a small village seven km from Tetebatu. Haji Radiah is a local primary school teacher who has been encouraging people to stay in Lendang Nangka, which is a traditional Sasak village with similar surroundings to those of Tetebatu. In and around the village you can see blacksmiths who still make knives, hoes and other tools using indigenous techniques. Jojang, the biggest spring in Lombok, is a few km away or you can walk to a waterfall with beautiful views, or see the black monkeys in a nearby forest.

In August you should be able to see the traditional Sasak form of boxing at Lendang Nangka. It's a violent affair, with leather-covered shields and bamboo poles. Local dances are a possibility at Batu Empas, one km away. At the village of Pringgasela the girls weave Sasak cloths, blankets and sarongs. It's a few km east of Lendang Nangka – take a dokar or walk.

Since Radiah originally wrote to us for the first edition of the *Bali & Lombok* guidebook, his family homestay has become quite popular among travellers who want an experience of typical Lombok village life. He speaks English very well, and is a mine of information on the surrounding countryside and customs. He has a map for local walks and enjoys acting as a guide – he may even drive you around to nearby villages and sights on his motorbike.

Places to Stay Staying with Radiah will cost you about 10,000/14,000 rp for a single/double, including three excellent

meals per day of local Sasak food, and tea or coffee. You will get customary Sasak cake and fruit for breakfast – it's good value and highly recommended. His house is fairly easy to find in Tetebatu (see the map, but everyone knows him), and has 12 bedrooms for guests, each with a bathroom and toilet. If his place is full, he may be able to find accommodation for you in one of the nearby villages – the idea is to avoid a big concentration of visitors in one place.

Getting There & Away Take a bemo from Sweta to Masbagik (42 km, 850 rp) and then take a dokar to Lendang Nangka (about four km, 350 rp). Lendang Nangka is about five km from Pomotong and connected by a surfaced road – take a dokar for 400 rp (500 rp if you have a heavy load).

Rungkang

This small village, less than a km east of Loyok, is known for its pottery, which is made from a local black clay. The pots are often finished with attractive cane work, which is woven all over the outside for decoration and for greater strength. Similar pottery is made in a number of other villages in the area south of the main road.

Sukarara

Twenty-five km south of Mataram, not far off the Kediri to Praya road, is the small village of Sukarara. On the way to this traditional weaving centre are picturesque thatched-roof villages surrounded by rice fields. More unusual are the houses built from local stone found in Sukarara. In this area, watch for Sasak women in their traditional black costume with brightly coloured edgings.

Lombok is renowned for its traditional weaving, the techniques for which have been handed down from mother to daughter for generations. Each piece of cloth is woven on a handloom in established patterns and colours. Some fabrics are woven in as many as four directions and interwoven with gold thread. They can be so complicated that they take one person three months to complete.

Many incorporate flower and animal motifs including buffaloes, dragons, lizards, crocodiles and snakes. Several villages, including Sukarara and Pringgasela, specialise in this craft.

Nearly every house in Sukarara has an old wooden handloom. Along the main street there are half a dozen places with looms set up outside, and displays of sarongs hanging in bright bands. You can stop at one, watch the women weaving and buy direct. One place worth trying is the Taufik Weaving Company on Jalan Tenun. The manager's name is Widasih and he has sarongs, songkets, Sasak belts, tablecloths and numerous other pieces.

Before you go to Sukarara it may be a good idea to check prices in the Selamat Riady weaving factory in Cakranegara, and get some idea of how much to pay and where to start bargaining. There's such a range of quality and size that it's impossible to give a guide to prices, but the best pieces are magnificent and well worth paying for. If you're accompanied to Sukarara it will inevitably cost you more through commissions. Although the village is a regular stop for tour groups, the people are very friendly and if you eat or drink at the warung you'll be surrounded by locals.

Places to Stay Stay with the kepala desa or make a day trip. You could also check with the woman who runs the warung – she sometimes puts people up for the night and has a fine selection of cloth for sale.

Getting There & Away Get a bemo from Sweta towards Praya, and get off at Puyung (about 600 rp). From Puyung you can hire a dokar for about 200 rp to take you the two km to Sukarara.

Penujak

This small village, six km south of Praya, is well known for its traditional *gerabah* pottery made from a local red clay. You'll see the pottery places from the road, and you can watch the pots being made by hand, and fired in traditional kilns. There's a lot worth buying, but the bigger pieces would be hard to carry.

Pots range in size up to a metre high, and there are kitchen vessels of various types, and decorative figurines, usually in the shape of animals. Look for the water containers in a characteristic local design, with a filling hole in the bottom and a drinking spout on the side. They're almost spill-proof, and the clay is slightly porous so some moisture seeps through to the outside, providing natural evaporative cooling. The local industry has formed a partnership with a New Zealand organisation to develop export markets for its products so, hopefully, this distinctive pottery will become more widely known.

Lenang

Just east of the road between Puyung and Praya, Lenang is not really a tourist destination. It is, however, a centre for 'white magic' – Pak Aripin is famous throughout Lombok for healing broken bones, virtually while you wait. Hopefully, you won't need to visit him.

Rembitan (Sade)

The village of Rembitan, also known as Sade, is a slightly sanitised Sasak village where tourists are welcome to look around, with one of the local kids as a guide. It's a few km south of Sengkol and has a population of about 750. You can check the vital statistics of the village on the charts displayed on the porch of the village meeting house. Mesjid Kuno, an old thatched-roof mosque, tops the hill around which the village houses cluster.

The area from Sengkol down to Kuta Beach is a centre of traditional Sasak culture, and there are many relatively unchanged Sasak villages where the people still live in customary houses and engage in indigenous craftwork.

SOUTH LOMBOK

The best known place on the south coast is Lombok's Kuta Beach, a magnificent stretch of sand with impressive hills rising around it. At the moment, it has far fewer tourists

than the better known Kuta Beach in Bali, but there are plans to develop not only Kuta, but a whole stretch of the superb south coast with four and five-star hotels. People flock to Kuta for the annual nyale fishing celebration, usually falling in February or March each year, but otherwise it's very quiet. Stinging seaweed is said to make swimming unpleasant at times, but the south coast has great potential for surfing and windsurfing if you know when and where to go.

East of Kuta is a series of beautiful bays punctuated by headlands. All the beach-front land has been bought by the government for planned tourist resorts. Segar Beach is about two km around the first headland, and you can easily walk there. An enormous rock about four km east of the village offers superb views across the countryside if you climb it early in the morning. The road goes five km east to Tanjung Aan (Cape Aan) where there are two classic beaches with very fine, powdery white sand. You can see the beginnings of the expensive hotels planned for this area. Both the excellent quality of the road and the new hotel developments are said to be related to the political connections of the developers.

The road continues another three km to the fishing village of Gerupak, where there's a market on Tuesday. From there you can get a boat across the bay to Bumgang. Alternatively, turn north just before Tanjung Aan and go to Serneng. Beyond here the road deteriorates, but you can get to Awang with a motorbike or on foot, then continue into south-eastern Lombok.

West of Kuta are more fine beaches at Mawan and Silung Blanak, both known for their surfing possibilities. There are no facilities and no direct roads suitable for ordinary vehicles. You'll have to go into Sengkol first, then out again to the coast.

Kuta Beach

There are no banks or moneychangers in Kuta, so bring enough rupiah to keep you going. There's a market on Sunday and Wednesday.

Once a year a special Sasak celebration is

held in Kuta for the opening of the nyale fishing season. On the 19th day of the 10th month in the Sasak calendar – generally February or March – hundreds of Sasaks gather on the beach. When night falls, fires are built and the young people sit around competing with each other in rhyming couplets called *pantun*. At dawn the next morning, the first nyale are caught, after which it is time for the Sasak teenagers to have fun. In a colourful procession boys and girls put out to sea – in different boats – and chase one another, with lots of noise and laughter.

Places to Stay & Eat The road from the north turns east along the coast, just after the village. Along this beach-front road you'll find most of Kuta's accommodation, which is all of similar price and quality. After the police station you pass *Rambutan*, with rooms at 7500 rp, including tea but not breakfast. The *Wisma Segara Anak* next door has a restaurant, singles/doubles at 6000/8000 rp and bungalows at 8000/10,000 rp including breakfast. Next along, *Pondok Sekar Kuning* (Yellow Flower Cottage), has doubles downstairs for 8000 rp, and upstairs, with a nice view, for 10,000 rp. *Anda Cottages*, next door, is the original place at Kuta. It has some trees and shrubs which make it more pleasant, a good restaurant with Indonesian, Chinese and Western dishes, and rooms for 9000 to 12,500 rp including breakfast.

A bit further along is *New Paradise Bungalows*, with good food and singles/doubles at 8000/10,000 rp, and the *Rinjani Agung Beach Bungalows* with standard rooms at 8000/10,000 rp and 'suit rooms' for 18000/20000 rp including breakfast. The old *Mascot Cottages* may be open again when you get there, or continue to the *Cockatoo Cottages & Restaurant*, the last place along the beach, with a nice restaurant area and rooms for 10,000/15,000 rp, including breakfast.

There are a few cheap, basic homestays in the village, and also the *Losmen Mata Hari*, near the market on the road to Mawan. It has a restaurant and nine small, clean rooms with private shower at 8000/10,000 rp, including breakfast.

There's a big new place at Tanjung Aan, but its opening was apparently delayed by the authorities. It now seems to have been acquired by the government's Lombok Tourist Development Corporation (Pemerintah Pengembangan Parawisata Lombok), and it's anyone's guess when it will open or what it will charge. There's no doubt about the location though – it's magnificent.

Getting There & Away Getting to Kuta by public transport is difficult. It's no trouble getting a bemo to Praya, but beyond there you might have to wait a while for another one to Sengkol (500 rp) and then another down to Kuta (300 rp). Market day in Sengkol is Thursday, so there may be more transport then.

You could also inquire at the Perama office in Mataram – it's only a matter of time before their convenient tourist shuttle bus service is extended to the south coast.

If you have your own transport it's easy – the road is sealed all the way. The final five km to Kuta is a steep and winding descent which suddenly leaves the hills to arrive at the coast.

EAST LOMBOK

Few travellers see any more of the east than the ferry port at Labuhan Lombok, but improvements to the road around the north coast make a round-the-island trip quite feasible. Similarly, the once-remote south eastern peninsula is becoming more accessible, particularly to those with their own transport.

Labuhan Lombok

There are fantastic views of mighty Gunung Rinjani from the east coast port of Labuhan Lombok. Ferries run from here to Sumbawa, the next island to the east. It's a friendly, sleepy little place with a mixed bag of concrete houses, thatched shacks and stilt bungalows. You can climb the hill on the

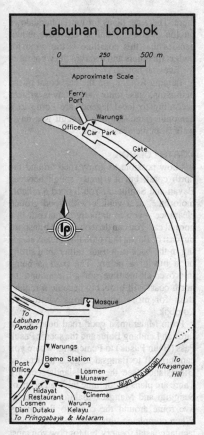

Labuhan Lombok

```
0        250        500 m
     Approximate Scale
```

Ferry Port
Warungs
Office
Car Park
Gate

Mosque

To Labuhan Pandan

Warungs
Bemo Station
Post Office
Losmen Munawar
To Khayangan Hill
Jalan Khayangan
Hidayat Restaurant
Losmen Dian Dutaku
Warung Kelayu
Cinema
To Pringgabaya & Mataram

coming into town, with rooms at 2600/3600 rp for singles/doubles. On Jalan Khayangan, the road that runs round to the ferry port, there's the *Losmen Munawar*, with rooms at 2500/5000 rp; it's pretty basic but quite OK.

There are a couple of warungs around the bemo station, but the menu is restricted and the food is not that good. You can always buy a fish at the market and get it cooked at a warung. The *Hidayat Restaurant*, across the road from the bemo station, is a friendly place. Alternatively there's the fairly clean *Warung Kelayu* right next door.

Getting There & Away There are regular buses and bemos between Labuhan Lombok and Sweta. The 69-km trip costs about 2000 rp and should take a bit less than two hours. If you're zipping straight across Lombok and bound for Bali, you can take a bus via Sweta to Lembar. Other road connections go to Masbagik (1000 rp), Pancordao and Kopang (1500 rp).

Passenger ferries leave Labuhan Lombok for Poto Tano (Sumbawa) at 8, 9.30 am, noon, 3 and 5 pm. In the other direction, boats depart Poto Tano at 7, 8 am, noon, 2 and 5 pm. Departure times may change, depending on demand and goodness knows what other local considerations. The trip takes about 1½ hours and costs around 2500 rp in ekonomi A, 1500 rp in ekonomi B, 500 rp for a bicycle, 3000 rp for a motorbike and 27,000 rp for a car. The boats depart from a new port on the north side of the harbour. It's about two or three km from the port to the town of Labuhan Lombok, on the road which skirts the east side of the bay. It will be too hot to walk, so take a bemo for 250 rp. The ticket office is beside the car park.

There are a couple of food stalls at the port, and one or two warungs serving nasi campur. Men come on board the boat selling fried rice wrapped in banana leaves, and hard-boiled eggs. Take a water bottle with you – it can be a bloody hot trip! The ferries can get very crowded, especially at times such as Ramadan when local people are travelling. Arrive at the dock early to get a seat, or bring

south side of the harbour and watch the boats plying between here and Sumbawa.

If you're just passing through Labuhan Lombok on your way to Sumbawa there's no need to stay overnight. You can catch an early bus from Sweta (5.30 am at the latest) and get to the port in time for the first Sumbawa ferry. The Ampenan losmen are quite used to getting their guests on the road by that time.

Places to Stay & Eat In the village of Labuhan Lombok you can stay at the basic *Losmen Dian Dutaku*, on the main road a hat for sun protection and stretch out on the roof of the ferry.

North of Labuhan Lombok

North of Labuhan Lombok there are some fishing villages where foreigners are still a curiosity. Pulu Lampur, 14 km north, has a black-sand beach and is popular with locals on Sundays and holidays. At Teranset, near Pulu Lampur, you might be able to stay with Pak Moti. He's well known locally and has some rooms for about 10,000/15,000 rp, including three meals.

Labuhan Pandan is another few km to the north. There's not much there, but it's a good place to charter a boat to the offshore islands. You can't stay on them, but the uninhabited islands of Gili Sulat and the Gili Petangan group have lovely white beaches, good coral for snorkelling, and an unspoilt natural environment. It's quite expensive to get a boat out and back, and to wait long enough for you to explore the island. Try to do it with a group, and take drinking water and a picnic lunch. Some of the tour operators in Mataram may run day trips to the islands, but it would be a long day and very expensive. Some new tourist bungalows are being developed near the seashore just south of Labuhan Pandan, and they'll probably cost about 15,000/25,000 rp for singles/doubles with three meals.

South of Labuhan Lombok

On the coast, south of Labuhan Lombok, is Labuhan Haji, formerly a port for those departing on a haji, or pilgrimage to Mecca. There's a beach here, but some people find it a bit dirty. It's accessible from Selong by bemo and dokar. Tanjung Luar is another coastal village a little further south.

Sukaraja, a few km inland, is another slightly sanitised Sasak-style village which tourists are welcome to visit.

The south-eastern peninsula was inaccessible until recently, but a road now extends south from Jerowaru to Ekas, and there are plans to continue it to Serewei. To get to the peninsula, take a bemo to Keruak (1000 rp from Sweta), then perhaps a motorbike from

there. There are plans for tourist bungalows on the peninsula, unless the government decides that this coastline is too good for budget travellers and reserves the whole area for five-star hotels.

Tanjung Ringgit, on the east coast of the peninsula, has some large caves which, according to local legend, are home to a demonic giant. Tanjung Ringgit is a day's walk from the nearest road.

NORTH LOMBOK

It's now possible to go by road around the north coast, but it's pretty rough between Bayan and Sambelia. You'll need a reliable motorbike, or a vehicle with good ground clearance – you're unlikely to make it in a normal car. You can do it on public transport, but east of Bayan that probably means standing in the back of a truck rather than sitting on a bus or a bemo. The road is being improved all the time, and a trip around the north coast will probably become a regular item for more adventurous visitors to Lombok.

From Mataram, a good road heads north through Lendang Bajur and the scenic Pusuk Pass (Baun Pusuk) to Pemenang, where you can turn off to Bangsal to get a boat to the Gili Islands (see the Gili Islands section). There are plans to continue the road north of Senggigi and Mangset, making an alternative route around the coast to Pemenang. When completed, this road will offer spectacular coastal scenery, but for now you must take the inland route through the Pusuk Pass. North of Pemenang, the road runs close to the coast almost as far as Bayan, but there is no tourist development along this stretch – yet.

Sira

Just a few km north of Pemenang, on the coast facing Gili Air, Sira has a wonderful white-sand beach and good snorkelling on the nearby coral reef. There is a proposal to develop a big three-star hotel here but at the moment there's no accommodation, so you'll have to make a day trip. It's a short bemo ride from Pemenang.

Further round the coast, just past Gondang, is Teluk Pandau beach. It's also slated for development, hopefully of a type that budget travellers can afford.

Bayan

Bayan, the birthplace of the Wektu Telu religion, is still an isolated village but the main road now extends to it. Traditional Hindu dances are still performed in Bayan, but getting to see them is a case of stumbling in at the right time, or asking around to find out when they're on. Bayan is also one of the main starting points for the climb up Gunung Rinjani.

Places to Stay & Eat You can stay with the kepala desa for around 5000 rp per person per night, including two meals. There are a couple of warungs in Bayan, one on the road to Senaru just off to the right. You can get fried chicken and rice here for 1500 rp.

Getting There & Away There are several buses daily from Sweta to Bayan, the first leaving at around 9 am. It's a three-hour trip, and you should try to get on an early bus. There may be more frequent buses to intermediate places like Pemenang. Approximate distances and fares from Sweta are: Pemenang (31 km) 700 rp; Tanjung (45 km) 800 rp; Bayan (79 km) 1600 rp.

The north coast road reaches the east coast at Sugian, and connects through Sambelia and Labuhan Pandan to Labuhan Lombok.

Batu Koq

Batu Koq is the usual starting point for a climb up Gunung Rinjani, and the highest village at which you can stay. The local school teacher used to be the person to see for accommodation, food and information, but there are now several homestays in the village, which charge about 5000 rp per person. There are a couple of warungs near where the bus stops and the odd shop where you can buy last minute bits and pieces. Once you get to Batu Koq, numerous children will rush out shouting their 'Hello Misters' and take you to the school teacher.

Make sure you go to the magnificent waterfall near Batu Koq – it can be heard from far away. It's a pleasant hour's walk partly through forest, and partly alongside a water course. Watch for the sleek black monkeys swinging through the trees. Splash around near the waterfall – the water cascades down the mountain slope so fast that it's strong enough to knock the wind out of you.

Getting There & Away From Bayan, you have to walk the four or five km up the road to Batu Koq, or take a truck. The latter is a far better alternative, especially if you arrive in Bayan at around midday when it's hot and dusty. There's not much shade along this road and you'll be carrying a fair amount of junk, as well as three days' worth of food for the walk up Rinjani. Trucks go up and down here with 'regular irregularity'.

Senaru

Perched high in the foothills of Rinjani, about nine km from Bayan, this small traditional village has an air of untainted antiquity. The villagers of Senaru did not encounter Westerners until the 1960s. Until then they lived completely isolated from the rest of the world. You may be able to stay with the schoolmaster or at the warung, but don't expect any privacy in either place.

The village is surrounded by a high wooden paling fence and comprises about 20 thatched wooden huts in straight lines, some on stilts, others low to the ground. On the left, just before you come to the village, is a small coffee plantation. There's a waterfall 2½ km from Senaru. Unless accompanied by a local person it's polite to ask permission before entering Senaru. Nobody in the village speaks English.

Many of the men from this village work in the nearby forests as woodcutters. Part of the ritual of climbing Rinjani is that guides usually stop at Senaru to stock up on betel nut. Young boys in the village thresh rice with long wooden mallets which reverberate with a sound like drums. A large percentage of the population, which is fewer than 500, suffer from goitre due to the lack of iodine in their diet and water.

Getting There & Away It's only a km or so from Batu Koq to Senaru so you can easily walk, or you may be able to get a lift on the back of a motorbike. A truck picks up timber from Senaru regularly – usually on Sundays – so you might be able to get a ride down to Bayan on it.

Sembalun Bumbung & Sembalun Lawang

High up on the eastern slopes of Gunung Rinjani is the cold but beautiful Sembalun valley. The inhabitants of the valley claim descent from the Hindu Javanese, and a relative of one of the Majapahit rulers is said to be buried here. While it seems unlikely that Java ever controlled Lombok directly, similarities in music, dance and language suggest that Lombok may have come under some long-lasting Javanese influence several hundred years ago.

In the valley, five km apart, are the traditional Sasak villages of Sembalun Bumbung and Sembalun Lawang. It's only a 45-minute walk from one village to the other and there are many pleasant walks in the surrounding area. From Sembalun Bumbung there is a steep 1½-hour climb to a saddle with a beautiful panoramic view. After five hours' walk from Sembalun Bumbung, first through rainforest, later through coffee, paw paw, rice and vegetable fields, you'll arrive at a small village close to the village of Sapit. From Sapit, you can take a bemo to Pringgabaya and on to Labuhan Lombok.

Places to Stay In Sembalun Lawang you can stay at a homestay or with the kepala desa for about 5000 rp per person. Accommodation with the kepala desa in Sembalun Bumbung is more basic but probably cheaper.

Getting There & Away From the south, you can get a bemo to Sapit but you'll have to walk from there, unless the road is finished. From Senaru, you can walk around the north-eastern slopes of Rinjani to Sembalun Lawang but you'll have to start early. It's a long way and would take around 12 hours. From Bayan there are sometimes trucks to Sembalun Lawang, or you can walk via Liloan and Sajang, which would take a whole day.

GUNUNG RINJANI

Both the Balinese and the Sasaks revere Rinjani. To the Balinese it is equal to Gunung Agung, a seat of the gods, and many Balinese make a pilgrimage here each year. In a ceremony called pekelan the people throw jewellery into the lake and make offerings to the spirit of the mountain. Some Sasaks make several pilgrimages a year – full moon is the favourite time for paying their respects to the mountain and curing their ailments by bathing in its hot springs.

Rinjani is the highest mountain in Lombok, and the third highest in Indonesia. At 3726 metres it soars above the island and dominates the landscape. Early in the morning it can be seen from anywhere on the island, but by mid-morning on most days the summit is shrouded in cloud. The mountain is actually an active volcano, although its last eruption was in 1901. There's a huge crater containing a large green crescent-shaped lake, Segara Anak, which is about six km across at its widest point. There's a series of natural hot springs on the north-eastern side of the caldera, a testimony to the fact that Rinjani is still geologically active. These springs, known as Kokok Putih, are said to have remarkable healing powers, particularly for skin diseases. The lake is 200 metres below the caldera rim, and in the middle of its curve there's a new cone, Gunung Barujari, only a couple of hundred years old.

Climbing Rinjani

Many people climb up to Rinjani's caldera every year. These are mostly local people making a pilgrimage or seeking the curative powers of the hot springs. Many foreign visitors climb up to the caldera too, though very few people go the extra 1000 or so metres to the very summit of Rinjani. Even the climb to the crater lake is not to be taken lightly. Don't try it during the wet season as the tracks will be slippery and very dangerous, and in any case you would be lucky to see any more than mist and cloud. You need at least three full days to do it, and probably another day to recover. Don't go up during the full moon because it will be very crowded.

There are several routes up Rinjani, but most visitors go from Bayan in the north, ascending via Batu Koq and Senaru and returning the same way. The other main route is from Sembalun Lawang on the eastern side, which is accessible by walking from either Sapit or Bayan. The northern route is more accessible as you can get to Bayan by road. It's an easier climb from the east, but it's also easier to get lost.

Guides & Equipment You can do the trek from Bayan without a guide, but in some places there's a confusion of trails branching off and you could get lost. The other advantage of guides is that they're informative, good company, and also act as porters, cooks and water collectors. When you're doing this walk with a guide make sure you set your own pace – some guides climb Rinjani as often as 20 or 30 times a year and positively gallop up the slopes! A guide will cost about 10,000 to 12,500 rp per day, porters about 8000 rp per day.

It's worthwhile talking to the people at the losmen Wisma Triguna in Ampenan. For about US$80 (!) they will organise the complete trip for you – food, tent, sleeping bag and a guide. But if you don't want to come at that they can tell you how to go about it on your own. They'll explain what food to take, and will rent you a two or three-person tent (12,500 rp for up to five days), a stove (2500 rp) and a sleeping bag (10,000 rp). A sleeping bag and tent are absolutely essential.

Food & Supplies You need to take enough food to last three days – including food for your guide. It's better to buy most of it in Ampenan, Mataram or Cakra as there's more choice available. Take rice, instant noodles,

sugar, coffee, eggs (get a container to carry the eggs in – the Wisma Triguna will lend you one), tea, biscuits or bread, some tins of fish or meat, onions, fruit, and anything else that keeps your engine running.

Bring plenty of matches, a torch (flashlight), a water container and some cigarettes. A guide should provide water and containers for you, but it's a good idea to have your own handy. Even if you don't smoke, the guides really appreciate being given cigarettes. If you have any food left over, leave it at the school.

The Northern Route This is the most popular route taken by visitors, ascending via Batu Koq and Senaru and returning the same way. It takes about four days.

Day 1 Depart Batu Koq at about 8 am for Senaru (altitude 600 metres). From there it's about two hours to the first post, Pos I (920 metres), then another two hours to Pos II (1850 metres), where there is a hut and a water supply. A further two hours brings you to the base camp at Pos III (2100 metres), where there is also water. The climb is relatively easy going through dappled forest, with the quiet broken only by the occasional bird, animal, bell or woodchopper. At base camp pitch the tent, collect wood and water and, if you have enough energy left, climb up to the clearing and watch the sunset. The ground is rock hard at base camp and it's very cold, so bring thick woollen socks, a sweater and a ground sheet with you. If a flock of 30-odd locals arrives unexpectedly out of the gloom, the chances of having the lake and the hot springs to yourself are slim indeed.

Day 2 Set off at about 8 am again, and after approximately two hours you will arrive at Pelawangan I, on the rim of the volcano, at an altitude of 2600 metres. Rinjani is covered in dense forest up to 2000 metres, but at around this height the vegetation changes from thick stands of mahogany and teak trees to the odd stand of pine. As you get closer to the rim the pines become sparser and the soil becomes rubbly and barren. The locals cut down the mahogany and teak trees with axes and then carry the huge logs down the steep slopes, by hand! Monkeys, wild pigs, deer and the occasional snake inhabit the forest. Once you get above the forest and up to the clearing the going is hot as there's not much shade – the land here is harsh and inhospitable – but you have superb views across to Bali and Sumbawa.

From the rim of the crater, it takes up to six hours to get down to Segara Anak and around to the hot springs, though some people will say it takes as little as two. The descent from the rim into the crater is quite dangerous – for most of the way the path down to the lake clings to the side of the cliffs and is narrow and meandering. Watch out for rubble – in certain spots it's very hard to keep your footing. Close to the lake a thick forest sweeps down to the shore. There are several places to camp along this lake, but if you head for the hot springs there are many more alternatives. The track along the lake is also narrow and very slippery – be careful and take it slowly. There are several species of small water bird on the lake, and the lake has been stocked with fish over the last few years.

After setting up camp at the lake, it's time to soak your weary body in the springs and recuperate. It's not as cold here as it is at base camp, but it is damp and misty from the steaming springs. Despite the hundreds of local people around, it can still be an eerie place. Watch your step on the paths – although this is a holy place, some people have few inhibitions or qualms about relieving themselves when and wherever they need to.

Day 3 Once again, departure time is approximately 8 am, and you walk more or less all day, arriving at Batu Koq in the late afternoon. It's a hard walk, between eight and 10 hours.

Day 4 If you get back to Batu Koq late in the afternoon, it's preferable to stay there overnight. Even if you can get a lift down to Bayan by truck, the last bus from there to the Sweta terminal departs around 6 pm and there's a good chance you'll miss it. This means that you'll be stuck in Bayan after a tiring trip with nowhere to stay except with the kepala desa. If you stay overnight at Batu Koq it's still a good idea to leave early in the morning before the sun gets too hot. You may have to walk all the way down to Bayan, but there's a bus to Sweta from there at about 8.30 am and a few others during the day.

The Eastern Route You can climb to the crater of Rinjani directly from either Sembalun Bumbung or Sembalun Lawang, but you must come prepared with sleeping bag, tent, food and other supplies. You can hire a guide in Sembalun Lawang – and you'll probably need one to get through the maze of trails as you climb west from the village. It will take about six hours to get to the village of Pade Belong, and another four hours to get to Pelawangan II on the crater rim at 2400 metres. Near here there's a crude shelter and a trail junction, with one track climbing southwards to the summit of Rinjani and the other heading west, to much more comfortable camp sites near the hot springs or the lake, about four hours away.

Going the other way, you can get from the crater rim down to Sembalun Lawang in about seven hours. It's quite possible to ascend by the northern route and descend by the eastern route, or vice versa, but you'll have to work out how to get yourself, and particularly your guide, back to your starting point.

Other Routes up Rinjani You can climb up to the crater from Torean, a small village just south-east of Bayan. The trail follows Sungai Kokok Putih, the stream that flows from Segara Anak and the hot springs, but it's hard to find; you'll need a guide.

You can also climb the south side of Rinjani, from either Sesaot or Tetebatu. Either route will involve at least one night camping in the jungle, and you may not see any views at all until you get above the tree line. Again, a guide is essential.

To the Very Top The path to the summit branches off the Sembalun Lawang track near Pelawangan II. From the shelter there, allow four hours to reach the summit. Start early in the morning because you have to get to the top within an hour or so of sunrise if you want to see more than mist and cloud.

THE GILI ISLANDS

Off the north-west coast of Lombok are three small, coral-fringed islands – Gili Air, Gili Meno and Gili Trawangan – each with superb, white sandy beaches, clear water, coral reefs, brilliantly coloured fish and the best snorkelling on Lombok. Although known to travellers as the 'Gili Islands', *gili* actually means 'island', so this is not a local name.

The islands have become increasingly popular with visitors, but any development is being carefully monitored and controlled to ensure they retain much of their unspoilt quality. The islanders are all Muslims, and visitors should respect their sensibilities. In particular, topless (for women) or nude sunbathing is offensive to them, although they won't say so directly. Away from the beach, it is polite for both men and women to cover their shoulders and knees.

Although the attractions of sun, sand and sea are common to all three islands, to some extent each has developed an individual character. Unfortunately it is difficult (or expensive) to go directly from one island to another – there are no regular public boats so you have to charter one for yourself. Alternatively, you have to get a public boat back to the mainland, then wait for another boat out to the island you want to go to.

Apart from the hill on Gili Trawangan, all three islands are pancake flat. There are no roads, cars or even motorbikes, so getting around is as easy as walking. Fishing, raising cattle and goats, making palm oil and growing corn, coconuts, tapioca and peanuts are the main economic activities, along with developing tourism.

There are few facilities on these islands, although some of the places to stay have their own electricity generators and there are small shops with a bare minimum of supplies. You can change cash (not travellers' cheques) on Trawangan but there's no other place to change money on the islands, so bring enough rupiah with you.

Places to Stay & Eat

Most places to stay come out of a standard mould – a plain little bungalow on stilts with a small verandah out the front. Inside there will be one or two beds with mosquito nets, and the verandah will probably have a table and a couple of chairs. Mandi and toilet facilities are usually shared. The local tourist corporation has set the price of accommodation at around 10,000/15,000 rp for singles/doubles, including three meals and tea or coffee on call. The food is simple but fresh and healthy. You can live well here and it's certainly cheap!

Getting There & Away

From Ampenan or the airport you can get to one of the islands, and be horizontal on the beach within a couple of hours. The trip involves several stages unless you opt to simply charter a bemo from Ampenan – not a bad move between a group of people.

Usually, the first step in Ampenan is a bemo from the airport or the city to Rembiga for about 200 rp. From Rembiga it's 600 rp for a bus to Pemenang. Alternatively, you may be able to get a bemo from Sweta direct to Pemenang for about 700 rp. The 25-km trip takes one to 1½ hours. It's a scenic journey past many small villages and through lush green forest where you'll see monkeys by the roadside. The road also climbs to the Pusuk Pass, from which you get views down to the north coast. From Pemenang it's a km or so off the main road to the harbour at Bangsal, 200 rp by dokar.

A small information office at Bangsal Harbour has a list of the official fares out to the islands – 700 rp to Gili Air, 900 rp to Gili Meno, 1200 rp to Gili Trawangan. It's a matter of sitting and waiting until there's a full boat load, about 20 people. If you have almost that number waiting, the boat will

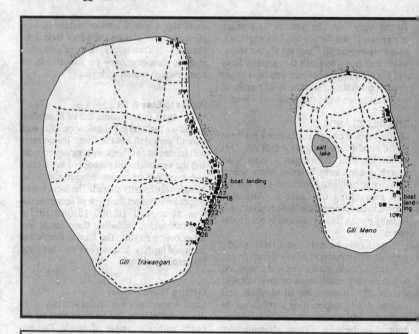

Gili Trawangan

salt lake

Gili Meno

boat landing

boat landing

GILI TRAWANGAN

1 Nusa Tiga Homestay
2 CoralBeach Homestay
3 Pasir Putih II
4 Alex Accommodation
5 Excellent Restaurant
6 Good Heart Homestay
7 Homestay Makmur I
8 Passir Putih I
9 Danau Hijau Bungalows
10 Creative Losmen
11 Melati Losmen
12 Rudy's Cottage Restaurant
13 Dua Sekawan I
14 Pak Majid's Losmen
15 Simple Bungalow
16 Dua Sekawan II
17 Trawangan Beach Cottage & Restaurant
18 Mountain View Cottage & Restaurant, Perama Office
19 Fantasi Bungalows
20 Borobudur Restaurant
21 Holiday Inn Cottages
22 Sandy Beach
23 Paradise Cottages & Restaurant
24 Albatross Diving Adventures
25 Homestay Makmur II
26 Majestic Cottages
27 Rainbow Cottages

leave if you can pay the extra fares between you. As soon as you do this, you'll be amazed at how quickly local people appear from nowhere to fill the boat. It's a good idea to get to Bangsal by 10 am. If you have to hang around that's no problem as it's a pleasant

place to while away some time, and the shaded warungs like the *Parahiangan Coffee House* have good food and coffee.

If you take a Perama minibus from Senggigi, Mataram or elsewhere, it should connect with a boat to the islands; the boat

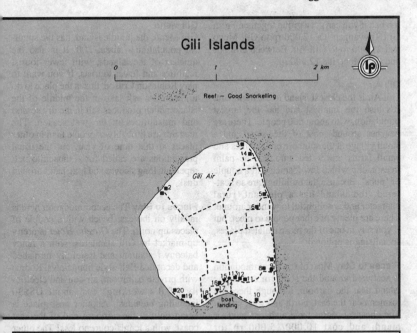

Gili Islands

Reef – Good Snorkelling

Gili Air

boat landing

GILI MENO

1 Good Heart Restaurant
2 Blue Coral Bungalows
3 Pondok Meno
4 New Cottages (Being Built)
5 Janur Indah Cottages
6 Janur Indah Bungalows
7 Matahari Bungalows
8 Malia's Child Bungalows
9 Gazebo Hotel
10 Kontiki Cottage Restaurant

GILI AIR

1 Hink Bungalows
2 Muksin Cottages
3 Hans Bungalows & Restaurant

4 Gusung Indah Bungalows
5 Fantastick Bungalows
6 Gili Air Cottages
7 Gita Gili Sunrise
8 Nusa Tiga Bungalows
9 Gili Beach Inn Bungalows
10 Paradiso Bungalows
11 Sederhana Losmen
12 Bupati's Place Cottages
13 Garden Cottages
14 Village Office
15 Gado Gado Pub
16 Bamboo Cottages
17 Fanta Pub
18 Gili Indah Cottages & Restaurant, Perama Office
19 Sunset Cottages
20 Salabose Cottages

trip will be included in the price of your ticket.

The official prices for chartering a boat are 12,500 rp to Gili Air, 15,000 rp to Gili Meno and 20,000 rp to Gili Trawangan. In practice,

you can usually beat those prices down a bit. The trip out to Gili Trawangan takes about an hour, less to the other islands. If you want to try the other beaches, it's quite expensive to charter boats around the islands but not too bad if you can get a group together. From Gili Trawangan it's 12,000 rp to Gili Meno and 15,000 rp to Gili Air. Between Gili Air and Gili Meno it's 12,500 rp.

Gili Air

Gili Air is the closest island to the mainland. It's also the smallest and has the largest population, with about 600 people. There are beaches around most of the island and a small village at the southern end. Homes and small farms are dotted amongst the palm trees, along with a few losmen and a couple of 'pubs'. Because the buildings are so scattered, the island has a pleasant, rural character and is delightful to wander around. There are plenty of other people to meet, but if you stay in one of the more isolated places, socialising is optional.

Places to Stay Most of the accommodation is scattered around the southern end of the island near the harbour, although there are losmen near the east, north and west coasts. The cheapest rooms have a shared outdoor mandi and cost 10,000/15,000 rp for singles/doubles and 20,000 rp for triples, all with three meals. Rooms are 6000/9000/13,500 rp if you have breakfast only. More expensive rooms with private mandi are 12,500/22,500/26,000 rp with three meals, or 8000/11,000/16,000 rp for breakfast only. This means it costs roughly 4000 rp for lunch and dinner, which is pretty cheap considering the good quality and quantity of the food, although you may prefer the freedom to eat wherever you want.

Gili Indah, one of the bigger places on Gili Air, is where you'll find the Perama office. The office has useful information and you maybe able to change foreign cash. Up north, at the other end of the island, *Hans Bungalows* are well away from everything and have a beautiful view of the beach, but may be more expensive than the standard price. There are about 15 other places to stay, all so similar that it wouldn't be fair to mention any one in particular. Pick one that appeals to you in a location you like, or one that's been recommended on the travellers' grapevine.

Gili Meno

Gili Meno, the middle island, has the smallest population – about 300. It is also the quietest of the islands, with fewer tourist facilities and fewer tourists. If you want to play Robinson Crusoe, this is the place to do it. There's a salt lake in the middle of the island which produces salt in the dry season and mosquitoes in the wet season. The mozzies are probably no worse than in other places at that time of year, but the usual precautions are called for – mosquito net, repellent, long sleeves and long pants around dusk.

Places to Stay The accommodation here is mostly on the east beach with a couple of places up north. The *Gazebo Hotel* is pretty up-market by Gili standards, with a fancy balcony restaurant and tastefully furnished and decorated Bali-style bungalows. Rooms with private bathroom, air-con and electricity (if it's working) cost about US$30 including breakfast. Another posh place is being built at the northern end of the east coast, with a tennis court no less! The other half-dozen places offer standard Gili bungalows, though perhaps a little more spacious, and charge the usual Gili prices – 10,000/15,000 rp for singles/doubles and 20,000 rp for triples with three meals. Rooms with private bathroom cost a bit more, and rooms with breakfast only cost a bit less.

Gili Trawangan

The largest island, with a local population of about 400, Gili Trawangan also has the most visitors and the most facilities, although it is still undeveloped by Western standards. The accommodation and restaurants/bars are all along the east coast beach, and this compact layout gives the island a friendly village atmosphere. Most of the places to stay also serve food, but there are a few convivial restaurants, like the *Excellent* and the *Mountain View*, which are more like bars in the evening. There's usually music and dancing at one of them.

The white-sand beach is the main daytime attraction, and the snorkelling is superb, with beautiful coral and lots of colourful fish. You can rent a mask and snorkel for 2000 rp per day, and fins for the same amount. There's a diving operation here too, Albatross Diving Adventures, though much of the coral in deeper water has been damaged by explosives used for fishing. Fortunately, this destructive fishing method is now banned.

Gili Trawangan also has a hill at its southern end, where you can find traces of two Japanese WW II gun emplacements and enjoy the view across the strait to Bali's Gunung Agung, particularly at sunset. Sunrise over Gunung Rinjani is impressive too. One local described Trawangan's three main attractions as 'sunrise, sunset, sunburn'! It's certainly hot enough, and it can get rather dusty in the dry season.

Places to Stay The accommodation and prices here are even more standardised than those on the other islands. Typical bungalows run to 10,000/ 15,000 rp for singles/ doubles and 20,000 rp for triples. A couple of places, like *Rainbow Cottages*, have private mandis and cost more. Some others don't provide lunch or dinner, so they're a bit cheaper. Pick a place you like the look of (some have prettier gardens), or one recommended by a recent visitor (you can't beat that travellers' grapevine), or go with one of the friendly people who will meet you when the boat comes in. The places in the middle of the beach strip may be a bit better for meeting people, while those at the northern and southern ends of the beach offer more peace and quiet.

Sumbawa

Between Lombok and Flores and separated from them by narrow straits is the rugged land mass of Sumbawa. Larger than Bali and Lombok combined, Sumbawa is a sprawling island of twisted and jutting peninsulas, with a coast fringed by precipitous hills and angular bights, and a mountain line of weathered volcanic stumps stretching along its length.

Sumbawa is the most predominantly Muslim island anywhere east of Java or south of Sulawesi, and few places in Indonesia adhere to Islam in a more orthodox fashion. Christian missionaries never even bothered to try here. The people, particularly in the western half of the island, are curious about foreigners and on the whole pretty friendly – though they're more reserved around Bima in the east. Women travellers find life easier if they cover most of their bodies.

Islam seems to have obliterated much of Sumbawa's indigenous traditions, but it's a scenic island with plenty of scope for exploring off the beaten track. The mountain and coastal regions in the south – not converted to Islam until around the turn of the 20th century – and the Tambora peninsula in the north are rarely visited by outsiders. If you're in the right place at the right time (on holidays and festivals) you might see traditional Sumbawan fighting, a sort of bare-fist boxing called *berempah*. Horse and water buffalo races are held before the rice is planted.

Towards the east end of the island, the narrow Bima Bay cuts deep into the north coast forming one of Indonesia's best natural harbours. It's surrounded by fertile lowlands which reach west into the rich interior Dompu plains.

History

For centuries Sumbawa has been divided between two linguistically – and to some extent ethnically – distinct peoples: the Sumbawanese speakers who probably reached the west of the island from Lombok, and the Bimanese speakers who independently occupied the east and the Tambora peninsula. The squatter, darker-skinned Bimanese are more closely related to the people of Flores, whilst the western Sumbawans are closer to the Sasaks of Lombok. Both their languages have considerable variation in dialect, but the spread of

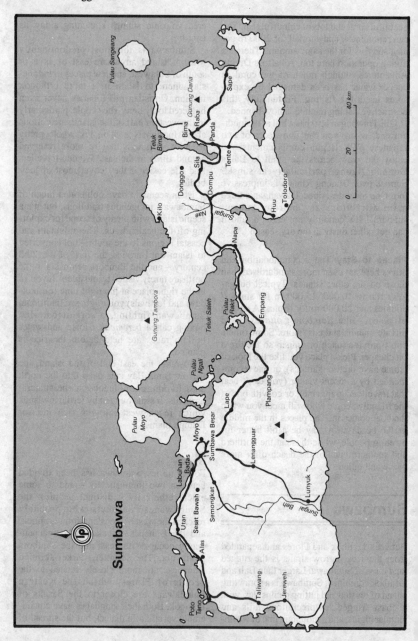

Bahasa Indonesia has made communication easier in the last couple of decades.

Sumbawa, with its rich timber resources in the west, was probably an early trading call for Javanese merchants on the way to or from the spice islands in Maluku. Bima and parts of western Sumbawa are said to have been under the control of the Javanese Majapahit empire, although it's more likely they simply sent tribute.

Along the western coastal lowlands the local population expanded and petty kingdoms developed along the entire length of the island. In eastern Sumbawa the region around Bima Bay, and probably later the Dompu plains, became the leading centres for the Bimanese-speaking population. Before 1600 these were probably animist kingdoms. By that time the domestic horse was being used and irrigated rice agriculture, possibly introduced by Javanese traders, was well established. There appears to have been some intermarriage between the Balinese and western Sumbawanese aristocracy which may have linked the islands from the 15th or 16th centuries. In the early 17th century, the Islamic Makassarese states of southern Sulawesi undertook a military expansion and by 1625, the rulers of Sumbawa had been reduced to Makassarese vassals and had nominally converted to Islam.

Makassar's rise was halted by the Dutch East India Company (VOC) whose forces occupied it in 1669. Soon afterwards treaties were made between the Dutch and the rulers of Sumbawa by which Dutch hegemony in eastern Indonesia was recognised and these rulers were obliged to pay tribute to the Dutch who maintained only a distant supervision of what they considered a politically unstable island with poor commercial possibilities, taking more or less direct control only in the early 1900s.

The western Sumbawans, meanwhile, held nominal control over neighbouring Lombok from the middle of the 17th century till 1750, when the Balinese took it over instead. Then followed 30 years of sporadic warfare between the Sumbawans and the Balinese, including at least one large-scale Balinese invasion of western Sumbawa. It was only through the intervention of the VOC, which was interested in maintaining the status quo, that the Balinese were turned back.

Barely had the wars finished, when Gunung Tambora on Sumbawa exploded in April 1815 killing perhaps 10,000 people with a shower of choking ash and molten debris. Agricultural land was wrecked and livestock and crops wiped out throughout the island. It's estimated that a further 66,000 people, nearly two-thirds of Sumbawa's population, either died of starvation or disease or fled their lands. Some went to other islands, others shifted to higher ground in the interior where less damage had been sustained or the terrain had recovered faster.

By the middle of the 19th century, immigrants from other islands were brought in to help repopulate the blighted coastal regions. The 850,000 people of Sumbawa are therefore a diverse lot – in the coastal regions there are traces of the Javanese, Makassarese, Bugis, Sasak and other groups who migrated to the island.

In 1908 the Dutch government sent administrators and soldiers to Sumbawa Besar and Taliwang to head off the possibility of war between the three separate states that comprised western Sumbawa. This inaugurated a period of far more direct Dutch rule. The sultans kept a fair degree of their power under the Dutch, but after Indonesian independence their titles were abolished; now their descendants hold official power only when they are functionaries of the national government.

Little evidence remains of the Dutch presence and the only traces of the old sultanates are the palaces in the towns of Sumbawa Besar and Bima.

POTO TANO

The port for ferries to and from Lombok is a straggle of stilt houses beside a mangrove-lined bay. It's a few km of dirt track away from Sumbawa's single main road.

Getting There & Away

Bus There's quite a melee when ferries arrive from Lombok as bus conductors try to fill up all the waiting buses quickly. Save a bit of hassle by buying a bus ticket from the guys who come round selling them on the ferry – their prices are the same as you pay on dry land. Fares and journey times are: Taliwang 1000 rp, one hour; Alas 1000 rp, one hour; Sumbawa Besar 2000 rp, 2½ hours; Bima 8000 rp, 10 hours. Buses to Poto Tano from elsewhere on Sumbawa connect with the ferry departures.

Boat Ferries run five times daily between Lombok and Poto Tano. Departures from Poto Tano are at 7 and 8 am, noon, 2 and 5 pm. The crossing takes about 1½ hours. Fares are the same as from Lombok to Poto Tano – see the Lombok introductory Getting There & Away section. You can buy tickets at Poto Tano, or get a combined bus and ferry ticket from Bima or Sumbawa Besar all the way to Lombok, Bali or even Java.

TALIWANG

During the 19th century Taliwang was one of the 'vassal states' of the kingdom of Sumbawa based in Sumbawa Besar. Today it's a sleepy, oversized village, with people who can be friendly and curious almost to the point of being overpowering. It lies close to the west coast of Sumbawa, 30 km south of Poto Tano along a narrow road winding through the hills. By the road into Taliwang, coming from the north, is Danau (lake) Taliwang.

Potobatu, six km from Taliwang, is a local sea resort with many caves, and a decent white-sand beach. Trucks from Taliwang cost 200 rp. Labuhanbalat is a fishing community of just eight houses, seven km from Taliwang – take a truck or dokar there.

Places to Stay & Eat

Taliwang's market is next to the bus station. Behind the market is the lemon-coloured *Losmen Ashar*, with spartan but clean rooms for 1500 rp per person. There's another losmen in front of the cinema in the opposite direction from the bus station, and a tiny rumah makan at the bus station.

Getting There & Away

Direct buses from the ferry at Poto Tano to Taliwang cost 1000 rp. Regular buses between Alas and Taliwang cost 1000 rp for a 1½-hour trip. There are some direct buses from Taliwang to Sumbawa Besar (2500 rp), but if you don't catch one, you can change at Alas.

ALAS

'Alas' is Javanese for 'forest' and may have received its name from Javanese timber traders. It's an ordinary little town on the north coast road between Poto Tano and Sumbawa Besar, with the usual very nosy people.

Labuhan Alas

The little port just off the Sumbawa Besar road about three km east of Alas was, until 1988, the terminal for ferries from Lombok. It's set in a pretty little bay and is not much more than a dock and a few houses. A Sulawesi fishing village clusters offshore on stilts, with television antennae jutting up from its roofs. Dokars (250 rp) run to and from Alas.

Places to Stay & Eat

Losmen Selamat at Jalan Pahlawan 7 in Alas has good clean rooms for 2500 rp per person, or 3000 rp with private mandi. It's a one-minute walk in the Sumbawa Besar direction from the bus/bemo/dokar station. A further 700 metres up the same road the *Losmen Anda* has rooms with small patios round a garden for 3000 rp per person. *Rumah Makan Sebra* beside the bus station serves reasonable food.

Getting There & Away

Buses go to Sumbawa Besar (1500 rp, about 1¾ hours), to Poto Tano (1500 rp, one hour) for the ferries and to Taliwang (2000 rp, 1½ hours).

SUMBAWA BESAR

At one time the name 'Sumbawa' only applied to the western half of the island – the region over which the Sultan of the state of Sumbawa held sway; the eastern half of the island was known as Bima. Almost all that remains of the old western sultanate is the wooden palace in Sumbawa Besar – the showpiece of the town.

Sumbawa Besar is the chief town in the western half of the island; a friendly place of concrete block houses, thatch-roofed and woven-walled stilt bungalows, shacks clinging to hillsides and footpaths of small boulders connecting them with dirt roads. You'll hear 'Hello mister' every five seconds, and the place has quite an 'Asian' feel to it, with dokars rattling round the streets and Muslim men flooding out of the mosques after midday prayer. The town itself has no remarkable attractions except perhaps the old palace, but trips out to villages or Pulau Moyo might prove rewarding.

If you'd like some friendly conversation, you might want to introduce yourself to Mr Muhammad Yusuf at SMA 1 (high school). He's a Florinese who teaches English and is only *too glad* to get conversation practice. However, he also works as a guide, so if he shows you around, establish whether or not you're going to be paying for this service.

Information

There's no tourist office on the entire island of Sumbawa, but if you're going through Lombok on the way, call at the one at Jalan Langko 70 in Ampenan, which deals with Sumbawa as well as Lombok. They have some leaflets and a good relief map of Sumbawa.

Money The Bank Negara Indonesia (☎ 21936) is at Jalan Kartini 10. It's open Monday to Saturday from 7.30 am to 1 pm.

Post For poste restante, go to the main post office which is out past the airport on Jalan Garuda. For stamps, there's also a sub-post office near the town centre on Jalan Yos Sudarso. Both are open Monday to Thursday from 8 am to 2 pm, plus Friday until 11 am and Saturday until 12.30 pm.

PHPA The national parks people (☎ 21358) are in the Direktorat Jenderal Kehutanan office at Jalan Garuda 12. See them about trips to Pulau Moyo. The office is open until 2 pm Monday to Thursday, 11 am Friday and 12 noon Saturday.

Maps There are large maps of Sumbawa in the Hotel Tambora restaurant and the Tirtasari reception.

Sultan's Palace (Dalam Loka)

Back in the early '60s Helen and Frank Schreider passed through Sumbawa Besar in their amphibious jeep, and later described the remnants of this palace in their book *The Drums of Tonkin*:

Sumbawa Besar...had a sultan. A small man with tortoise-shell glasses and a quiet, friendly dignity... his old palace, now deserted except for a few distant relatives, was a long barn-like structure of unpainted wood that seemed on the point of collapsing. Beneath the ramshackle entrance, a rusted cannon from the days of the Dutch East India Company lay half-buried in the ground... Mothers and fathers and naked little children made the palace shake as they followed us up the ramp into a great empty room that was once the audience chamber...Only when the few remaining court costumes, the faded silver brocade kains, the gold-handled krises and the long gold fingernails that were a sign of royalty's exemption from labour were modelled for us did we have any idea of the extravagance of this past era. By government decree, the sultans are no longer in power.

The palace was restored in the early 1980s, but only a few of the original pillars and carved beams remain. Boys will show you round and tell you (in Indonesian) what each room was used for, though there's little in them except a couple of old palanquins. Then they'll ask you to make a donation towards the cost of turning the place into a museum.

New Palace

The imposing building with the bell tower at its gate on Jalan Merdeka is the HQ of the *bupati* (head government official) of west

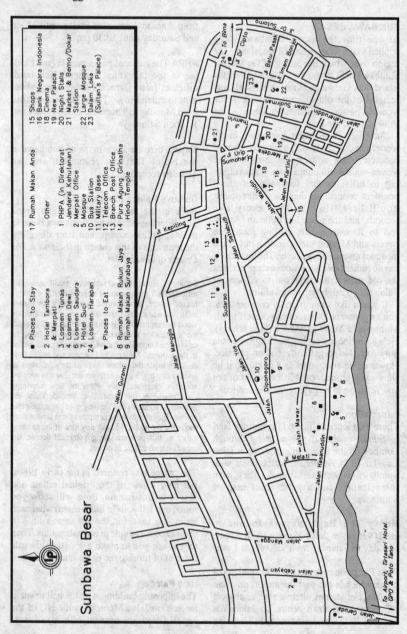

Sumbawa Besar

Places to Stay

2 Hotel Tambora & Merpati
3 Losmen Tunas
4 Losmen Dewi
6 Losmen Saudara
7 Hotel Suci
24 Losmen Harapan

Places to Eat

8 Rumah Makan Rukun Jaya
9 Rumah Makan Surabaya

17 Rumah Makan Anda

Other

1 PHPA (in Direktorat
  Jenderal Kehutanan)
2 Merpati Office
5 Bus Station
10 Telecom Office
12 Military Base
13 Branch Post Office
14 Pura Agung Girinatha
   Hindu Temple
15 Shops
16 Bank Negara Indonesia
18 Cinema
19 New Palace
20 Night Stalls
21 Market & Bemo/Dokar
   Station
22 Large Mosque
23 Dalam Loka
   (Sultan's Palace)

Sumbawa. It's built in imitation of the style of the old sultan's palace – a reminder that the national government now holds the power that was once the sultan's.

Pura Agung Girinatha

This Balinese Hindu temple is on Jalan Yos Sudarso near the corner of Jalan Setiabudi. It's small and usually locked. Next door is a *banjar*, a Balinese community hall.

Places to Stay

Easily the best place in the town itself is the *Hotel Tambora* (☎ 21555), just off Jalan Garuda on Jalan Kebayan II, a 15-minute walk from the bus terminal, or you can take a bemo or dokar. All rooms have attached bath, and the following categories are available: economy, 6050/7900 rp; standard with fan, 12,100/15,150 rp; standard with air-con, 22,700/30,250 rp; VIP, 30,250/38,750 rp; deluxe, 54,450/60,500 rp; and a suite costs 60,500 rp. The hotel has its own restaurant and is helpful to travellers. They can also tell you about Pantai Kencana where they are now building bungalows.

Four hotels are lined up along Jalan Hasanuddin, a five-minute walk from the bus station. All are also in easy range of the 4.30 am wake-up call from the mosque! *Hotel Suci* (☎ 21589) is the best of this group. The clean rooms surround a courtyard and garden which keep out much of the traffic noise. Singles/doubles are 4500/6000 rp or 8800/11,000 rp. All rooms have private bath, and a snack breakfast is included. On the same side of the road the *Losmen Tunas* (☎ 21212) is friendly and reasonably clean at 4500/6000 rp with attached bath.

Losmen Saudara (☎ 21528), opposite the Suci, has lots of traffic noise but a reasonable restaurant. Singles/doubles are 5500/7700 rp with private mandi, 5500/6000 rp without. *Losmen Dewi* (☎ 21170) has a better building layout which holds much of the traffic noise at bay. Rooms with attached mandi and toilet are 5000 rp for singles and doubles.

An alternative is *Losmen Harapan* on Jalan Dr Cipto, the cheapest place in town but often full. Upstairs rooms with shared

bath are 3000 rp per person, and downstairs rooms with attached bath are 3500 per person.

The most attractive hotel of all – if you don't mind a 10-minute bemo ride from town – is *Tirtasari* (☎ 21987), by the beachfront 5½ km west of Sumbawa Besar on the road to Alas. It has a good restaurant and is set in a garden; there's also a swimming pool but don't rely on it containing water. Clean economy rooms with private mandi are 6500 rp single or double; standard rooms for 13,000 rp have verandahs facing the sea and are airy and comfortable with a semi-open-air shower and toilet; there are also VIP rooms for 22,500 rp. In all except economy, a breakfast of egg with toast and coffee is part of the price. Buses from the west can drop you at Tirtasari on the way into Sumbawa Besar.

Places to Eat

The restaurants in the Tambora and Tirtasari hotels are probably the best. The Tambora has excellent food, but for some reason the tea and coffee are awful.

Near the centre of town on Jalan Hasanuddin, *Rumah Makan Rukun Jaya* is a newish, clean place. The older *Rumah Makan Anda* on Jalan Wahidin has a similar menu and prices and stays open to 9 pm. Or there's the friendly, cheap but flyblown *Rumah Makan Surabaya*, a one-minute walk from the bus station, with a menu consisting of nasi everything or gado-gado. Night-time sate stalls set up along Jalan Wahidin, near the corner of Jalan Merdeka.

Getting There & Away

Air Merpati has its office in the Hotel Tambora. There are daily flights to Denpasar (82,000 rp) via Mataram (52,000 rp). There are same day connecting flights to the following destinations: Bandung (264,000 rp), Banjarmasin, Jakarta (280,000 rp), Surabaya (145,000 rp), Ujung Pandang (218,000 rp) and Yogyakarta (186,000 rp).

Bus Sumbawa's single main road runs all the way from Taliwang near the west coast through Sumbawa Besar, Dompu and Bima, to Sape on the east coast. It's surfaced all the way. Fleets of buses, many of them new and comfortable by Nusa Tenggara standards, link all the towns on this road.

The long-distance bus station is on Jalan Diponegoro. Fares, distances and approximate journey times from Sumbawa Besar include:

To	Distance	Fare	Time
Dompu	190 km	5500 rp	5.5 hours
Bima	250 km	6000 rp	7.5 hours
Alas	69 km	2000 rp	1.5 hours
Poto Tano	90 km	2000 rp	2.5 hours

Buses leave for Poto Tano about three hours before the ferry departures. Departures from Poto Tano to Lombok are at 7 and 8 am, noon, 2 and 5 pm. Buses start for Bima hourly from 7 to 10 am, but after that you have to hope for a seat on a bus coming through from the ferries at Poto Tano.

You can buy combined bus and ferry services from Sumbawa Besar through to Lombok or Bali. The Langsung Jaya bus leaving at 9 am daily will have you in Mataram, Lombok, about 5 pm and the same company has a service through to Lembar where you board the Lombok-Bali ferry. Get tickets from Toko Titian Mas (☎ 21686) at Jalan Kartini 89, or Toko Hari Terang (☎ 21403), also on Jalan Kartini. Hotels can tell you of similar services.

Boat Labuhan Sumbawa, about three km west of town on the Alas road, is just a small fishing harbour. Labuhan Badas, seven km further along the same road, is the port of Sumbawa Besar and you *might* be able to pick up a coastal or inter-island craft there. A public bemo from Sumbawa Besar is 200 rp but it's not a very well-trodden route and you may have to charter one for about 3000 rp.

Getting Around
To/From the Airport It's about 300 metres from the airport to the Hotel Tambora, and you can easily walk – turn to your right as

you exit the airport terminal and cross the bridge. Alternatively, take a bemo for 200 rp.

Local Transport Sumbawa Besar is small; you can easily walk around most of it except to a few more distant places like the main post office. Bemos and dokars are 200 rp per person, to just about anywhere around town.

The centrally located long-distance bus station is a 15-minute walk from the Hotel Tambora or the old palace.

The local bemo and dokar station is at the corner of Jalan Setiabudi and Jalan Urip Sumohardjo but you can easily flag them down elsewhere.

For trips to villages etc around Sumbawa Besar, there should be public buses or bemos but alternatively you could charter a bemo; prices are negotiable. The Tirtasari rents motorbikes for 1000 rp an hour or 10,000 rp a day plus petrol.

AROUND SUMBAWA BESAR
Pulau Moyo
Two-thirds of Pulau Moyo, off the coast just north of Sumbawa Besar, is a nature reserve. There are good coral reefs with lots of fish at the southern rim of the island – but watch out for currents and sharks – and a number of villages in the north. Moyo rises to 648 metres and its centre is composed mainly of savannah with stands of forest. The reserve is inhabited by wild domestic cattle, deer, wild pigs and several varieties of birds.

For transport, make arrangements with the PHPA in Sumbawa Besar, which has a good map of Moyo. The PHPA can help you find a ride on a motorbike to Aik Bari on the coast, half an hour north of Sumbawa Besar. From there hire a fishing boat for the three-km crossing to the south coast of the island. You must negotiate your own prices: about 2000 to 5000 rp per person each way for the motorbike, 10,000 rp each way for the boat, including all petrol. There are four PHPA guard posts on Moyo – one at the south end, the others in villages – where you can stay overnight for 2500 rp per person, but take your own food and water. It's about an eight-hour walk from the south to the centre of the island, and about six hours across the middle from east to west.

The PHPA may have a snorkel to lend but don't count on it. You might be able to get a boat independently from Labuhan Sumbawa to Moyo for about 25,000 rp return. The Tirtasari hotel has a boat on which you can do a Moyo day trip for 45,000 rp.

Other Attractions
Look out for 'horse racing' – in reality boys on ponies but still a big local event – around Sumbawa Besar from August to October. Some of the best songket sarongs are made in the village of Poto 12 km east of Sumbawa Besar (500 rp by bus or bemo) and two km from the small town of Moyo. At Semongkat, about 15 km up the road which leads south-west from Sumbawa Besar into the hills, there's an old Dutch swimming pool fed by a mountain river. A stretch of the south coast near Lunyuk, about 60 km from Sumbawa Besar, is said to be a nesting ground for giant turtles. Liang Petang and Liang Bukal are caves near Batu Tering village which locals say are worth a visit. Take a torch. Batu Tering is about 25 km from Sumbawa Besar: you turn off the Bima road after about 10 km. There should be buses to all these places – ask.

CENTRAL SUMBAWA
It's a beautiful ride from Sumbawa Besar to Bima. After Empang you start moving up into the hills through rolling green country, thickly forested, with occasional sprays of palm trees along the shoreline.

Gunung Tambora
Dominating the peninsula which juts north in central Sumbawa is the 2820-metre volcano, Gunung Tambora. It can be climbed from the western side; the huge crater contains a two-coloured lake and there are views as far as Gunung Rinjani on Lombok. The base for ascents is the small logging town of Cilacai, which is eight hours by truck from Dompu, or an hour by speedboat from Sumbawa Besar. Not many people bother since the climb takes three days!

Tambora's peak was obliterated in the explosion of April 1815 (see Sumbawa History), but since then all has been quiet. The eruption wiped out the entire populations of Tambora and Pekat, two small states at the base of the mountain, as well as devastating much of the rest of Sumbawa.

Dompu
The seat of one of Sumbawa's former independent small states, Dompu is now the third-biggest town on the island but if you're travelling between Sumbawa Besar and Bima you don't get to see it: buses detour via the lonely Ginte bus station on a hill two km out of Dompu. From there bemos run into town if you need one. There are a few cheapish losmens in Dompu, which is about two hours (1000 rp) by bus from Bima, 5½ hours (3500 rp) from Sumbawa Besar.

Huu
On the coast south of Dompu, this is where surfers head for on Sumbawa. Special surf camps set up by Australian companies are nearby.

There are now two hotels with cottages and restaurants, and both can be booked at the airport in Bima. The cheaper of the two is *Intan Lestari*, which has rooms for 4000 rp per person with outside bath, or 5000 rp with attached bath.

The other set of cottages is *Mona Lisa*, which can be booked through the Hotel Parewa in Bima. Economy rooms with shared bath are 5000 rp per person, or you can book singles/doubles with attached bath for 10,000/15,000 rp.

Donggo
Buses run to the village of Donggo from Sila on the Dompu to Bima road (500 rp by bus from Dompu or Bima to Sila). You should be able to stay with the kepala desa in Donggo, on the flank of the mountainous west side of Bima Bay. The Dou Donggo ('mountain people') living in these highlands speak an archaic form of the Bima language, and may be descended from the original inhabitants of Sumbawa. Numbering about 20,000

they've adopted Islam and Christianity instead of their traditional animism over the past few decades with varying degrees of enthusiasm; they're being absorbed into Bimanese culture and will probably eventually disappear as a distinct group. The most traditional village is Mbawa where, at least until a few years ago, people still wore distinctive black clothes. A few *uma leme*, traditional houses whose design was intimately connected with the traditional religion, were still standing.

BIMA & RABA

Bima and Raba combined form the major town in the eastern half of Sumbawa. Bima, Sumbawa's chief port, is the main centre; Raba, a few km east, is the departure point for buses east to Sape where you get the ferry to Komodo or Flores.

Bima is one of the most orthodox Muslim areas in Indonesia: girls play volleyball in full headscarves and body-coverings. Compared to the people of western Sumbawa, Bimanese are distinctly cooler to foreigners. They are also very eager to take your money – cheating foreigners seems to be a favourite pastime here.

The Bima region has been known since the 14th century for its sturdy horses, which even then were being exported to Java. Local tradition claims that before the 17th century, when Bima fell to the Makassarese and its ruler was converted to Islam, it had some sort of political control over Timor, Sumba and parts of western Flores.

Today, the former sultan's palace apart, the town is a collection of ramshackle buildings that look like they're either in the middle of being built or in the middle of being demolished. The Jalan Flores night market is worth a wander. President Suharto and Saddam Hussein rub shoulders among the posters on sale there.

Information

Money The Bank Negara Indonesia 1946 on Jalan Sultan Hasanuddin changes foreign cash and travellers' cheques. The bank is open from 7.30 am to 1.30 pm Monday to Friday and from 7.30 am to noon on Saturday. If you're heading east, this is the last place you can change money before Labuhanbajo in Flores.

Post The post office is on Jalan Kampung Salama, in the eastern suburbs past the palace. Approximate opening hours are Monday to Thursday from 8 am to 2 pm, Friday from 8 to 11 am, and Saturday from 8 am to noon.

Sultan's Palace

The former home of Bima's rulers – until they were put out of a job after Indonesian independence – is now partly a museum. The building itself is less impressive than its counterpart at Sumbawa Besar but the exhibits inside – chainmail shirts, sedan chairs, battle flags, weapons, a chart comparing the alphabets of Indonesian languages with our Latin alphabet – hold some interest. The palace had fallen into complete disrepair by the late '50s but has been restored. If you look interested, someone will fetch the old caretaker who'll explain things in Indonesian. He'll show you the royal bedchamber complete with four-poster bed and Koran on the dressing table, and can rattle off the names and dates of all the sultans back to at least the 17th century. There are photos of the tombs of some early Bima rulers which still stand somewhere in the hills outside the town.

Places to Stay

Bima is compact and most hotels are in the middle of town. You often have to bargain a bit to get the right room price.

A good place to start looking is the *Losmen Lila Graha* (☎ 2740), a 10-minute walk from Bima bus station at Jalan Lombok 20. With shared mandi, singles/doubles are 6600/8800 rp; rooms with private mandi and toilet are 11,000/13,200 rp; or try the air-con rooms with hot water showers for 35,750 rp. You get an egg, toast and coffee breakfast.

Just next door is the friendly *Losmen Pelangi* (☎ 2878). It's a bit tattered but not too bad. All rooms are doubles. With shared

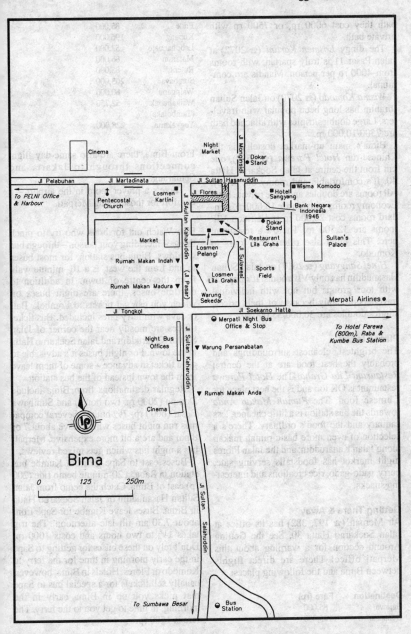

Cinema

Night
Market

Dokar
Stand

Jl Morginsidi

Jl Pelabuhan

Jl Martadinata

Jl Sultan Hasanuddin

To PELNI Office
& Harbour

Pentecostal
Church

Losmen
Kartini

Jl Flores

Hotel
Sangyang

Wisma Komodo

Bank Negara
Indonesia
1946

Jl Sulawesi

Jl Sultan Kaharuddin
(Jl Pasar)

Market

Losmen
Pelangi

Dokar
Stand

Restaurant
Lila Graha

Sultan's
Palace

Rumah Makan Indah ▼

Losmen
Lila Graha

Rumah Makan Madura ▼

Warung
Sekedar

Jl Tongkol

Jl Soekarno Hatta

Merpati Airlines ●

Merpati Night Bus
Office & Stop

To Hotel Parewa
(800m), Raba &
Kumbe Bus Station

Night Bus
Offices

Jl Sultan Kaharuddin

▼ Warung Persanabatan

▼ Rumah Makan Anda

Cinema

Bima

0   125   250m

Jl Sultan Salahuddin

To Sumbawa Besar

Bus
Station

bath they cost 6000 rp, or 7500 rp with private bath.

The dingy *Losmen Kartini* (☎ 2072) at Jalan Pasar 11 is truly spartan, with rooms from 4000 rp per person. Mandis are communal.

Wisma Komodo (☎ 2070) on Jalan Sultan Ibrahim has long been popular with travellers. Large doubles/triples with attached bath are 7500/10,000 rp.

Bima's main up-market hostelry is the Chinese-run *Hotel Parewa* (☎ 2652), one km from the centre at Jalan Soekarno Hatta 40. It's comfortable and roomy but pricey. All rooms are doubles and have private bath. Economy rooms with fan are 15,000 rp, standard rooms cost 20,000 rp and air-con VIP rooms are 32,500 rp. There's a restaurant here. This hotel also offers boat tours to Komodo.

Hotel Sangyang (☎ 2017) on Jalan Sultan Hasanuddin has only VIP rooms. It's popular with tour groups but not with individual travellers, probably because of their prices; singles/doubles are 30,000/35,000 rp.

Places to Eat
The brightest, cleanest surroundings and probably the best food are at the central *Restaurant Lila Graha*. The *Hotel Parewa* restaurant is OK too and is the best place for Chinese food. The *Rumah Makan Anda* towards the bus station is a little cheaper, less sanitary and the food's ordinary. There's a selection of even more basic rumah makan along Jalan Kaharuddin, and the Jalan Flores night market has foodstalls serving sate, curry, gado-gado, rice creations and interesting snacks.

Getting There & Away
Air Merpati (☎ 197, 382) has its office at Jalan Soekarno Hatta 30. See the Getting Around section for a warning about this Merpati office! There are direct flights between Bima and the following places:

Destination	Fare (rp)
Bajawa	85,000
Denpasar	125,000
Ende	85,000
Kupang	196,000
Labuhanbajo	52,000
Mataram	86,000
Ruteng	85,000
Surabaya	203,000
Waingapu	80,000
Waikabubak (Tambolaka)	52,750
Yogyakarta	228,000

From Bima, there are also same-day flight connections through to Jakarta and Semarang.

There's a prayer room in the airport – a comfort for those flying Merpati.

Bus Watch out for brats who try to pinch things – including your person – through bus windows. Bima bus station, for most buses to and from the west, is a 10- minute walk from the centre of town. In addition to daytime buses, there are night buses on which you can get tickets to Lombok, Bali or Java with ferry fares included. Bus ticket offices are mostly near the corner of Jalan Sultan Kaharuddin and Jalan Soekarno Hatta in the town. For night buses it's advisable to get a ticket in advance – some of them leave from the town instead of the bus station.

Regular destinations from Bima include Dompu (2000 rp, two hours) and Sumbawa Besar (6000 rp, 7½ hours). Several companies run night buses which leave about 7 or 8 pm and are a bit more expensive. Merpati has a night bus which gets mixed reviews.

Buses east to Sape go from Kumbe bus station in Raba, a 20-minute bemo ride (200 rp) east of Bima. Catch the bemo from Jalan Sultan Hasanuddin or Jalan Soekarno Hatta in Bima. Buses leave Kumbe for Sape from about 7.30 am till late afternoon. The trip takes 1½ to two hours and costs 1000 rp. Don't rely on these buses for getting to Sape in the early morning in time for the ferry to Komodo or Flores. Hotels in Bima, however, usually sell tickets for a special bus to Sape that picks you up in Bima early in the morning, in time to get you to the ferry. The fare is 1500 rp.

Boat Pelni (☎ 203) is in the port of Bima at Jalan Pelabuhan 103. The *Kelimutu* calls at Bima. See the Getting Around chapter near for the complete *Kelimutu* schedule.

Fares in 1st class/2nd class/economy include: Waingapu (12 hours) 49,300/37,600/16,700 rp; and Ujung Pandang (17 hours) 55,600/42,400/17,700 rp.

There are other irregular ships from Bima to various destinations – ask around the port.

Getting Around

To/From the Airport The ripping off begins with the Merpati office, which will try to sell you a taxi ride to the airport for 10,000 rp. The usual taxi fare is 6500 rp. Not only that, but the Merpati 'taxi' turns out to be a shared bemo, so you'll be paying about eight to 10 times the real price! The airport is 16 km from the centre and the trip by taxi takes about 20 minutes over an excellent road.

Warnings are also in order about the taxi booking desk at the airport. Although they charge the correct fare (6500 rp), they will tell you that you must take a taxi into Bima to catch the bus to Sumbawa Besar. This is not true! Buses heading to Sumbawa Besar stop on the main road about 100 metres in front of the airport terminal.

It is possible to catch a bus at the front of the airport coming from Sumbawa Besar and heading into Bima, but these are not frequent so a taxi may be your best bet.

Local Transport These cost 200 rp per person. The dokar drivers universally try to charge foreigners five times the going rate.

SAPE

Sape is a pleasant little town with amiable people and immense numbers of dokars, which the locals call 'Ben Hurs' because of their faint resemblance to the vehicles made famous by the old movie of that name. These jingling little buggies with their skinny pompommed horses don't look much like Roman chariots, but the drivers obviously think they're Charlton Heston as they race each other along the main street after dark.

If you have to wait for the ferry to Komodo or Flores then it's as well to wait here as in Bima (as long as you aren't run down by an express dokar). The ferry leaves from Pelabuhan Sape which is about three km down the road from Sape.

Information

The PHPA office is a two-minute walk down the road from the Losmen Give, but it can't tell you anything about Komodo. That job belongs to a second PHPA office a further 1½ km down the road towards Pelabuhan Sape, which has some interesting- looking maps and charts but doesn't seem to open till just before the ferry leaves. Go the previous day before 2 pm if you want to talk to the people there.

Places to Stay

Losmen Ratna Sari is cheerful, well lit at night and has a friendly owner who speaks English. Rooms are cheap at 3500 rp per person with shared mandi.

Losmen Friendship is the most upmarket place in town, though they have economy

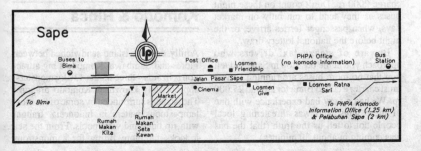

singles at 3500 rp with common bath.
Double rooms with attached bath go for
10,000 rp.

Losmen Give has relatively dingy rooms,
but you can't beat the price at 2500 rp per
person or 6000 rp for a triple. Some travellers
have complained that the owner might try to
put extra people into your room, or up the
price after you've agreed to it.

Places to Eat

If you're not eating at your hotel, two rumah
makan between the market and the bridge
specialise in terrible nasi campur. The area
near the market has a lot of decent warungs
and pushcarts in the evening.

Getting There & Away

Bus Buses always meet ferries arriving at
Pelabuhan Sape, but these are normally
express services from Pelabuhan Sape direct
to Bima, Lombok or Bali, though you may
be able to flag one down in the town. You can
purchase tickets on the boat – indeed, if you
don't want tickets you'll have to fight off the
offers. Some sample fares for express air-con
bus are: Poto Tano, 15,000 rp; Mataram,
22,000 rp; Denpasar, 38,000 rp; Surabaya,
48,000 rp; Malang, 50,000 rp and Jakarta,
70,000 rp. Non air-con is slightly cheaper.

If you don't catch one of these express
services directly from the ferry pier, you
must go to Bima then take another bus from
there. Sape bus station is on the Pelabuhan
Sape side of town but most buses also hang
around a while just past the bridge on the way
out towards Bima. The daytime fare to Bima
is 1000 rp, but the very few night buses
charge 2000 rp. Don't count on these night
buses as they tend to run only on market
days, when passenger ferries arrive, or the
night before the national lottery draw.

Beware of sleazy taxi drivers who
approach you at the bus stop in Sape and tell
you that no more buses are running so you
must charter a taxi to Bima for around 25,000
rp. We had a very bad experience with one
of these guys who was threatening local
people not to tell us the truth (that the bus
was coming in about 30 minutes).

Boat The ferry to Labuhanbajo on Flores
leaves three times a week from Pelabuhan
Sape, the port about three km down the road
from Sape, and calls in at Komodo Island
which is about two-thirds of the way to
Labuhanbajo.

The ferry departs Sape every Monday,
Wednesday and Saturday at 8 am and tickets
should be purchased at the pier about one
hour before departure. The boat returns from
Labuhanbajo every Tueday, Thursday and
Sunday. In both directions, it stops in at
Komodo. Sape to Labuhanbajo and Sape to
Komodo fares are both 8500 rp. Between
Komodo and Labuhanbajo only, it's 2600 rp.
You can take a bicycle from Sape to
Labuhanbajo for 1300 rp, a motorcycle for
5700 rp, a jeep for 50,000 rp, a car for 60,000
rp. The duration of the crossing varies with
tides and weather but allow seven hours from
Sape to Komodo, nine to 10 hours to
Labuhanbajo. You can buy drinks and the
odd light snack on the ferry but it's advisable
to bring a few supplies with you – unless of
course the wind's up, in which case you'll
probably be more concerned with things
coming out of your stomach than with
putting things in it. On the way out from
Pelabuhan Sape, Sangeang Island, a huge
volcano, looms out of the ocean on the left.

Getting Around

A dokar normally carrying five passengers
between Sape and the ferry pier costs 250 rp
per person. Shorter hauls within the city cost
around 150 rp.

Komodo & Rinca

A hilly, desolate island sandwiched between
Flores and Sumbawa, Komodo's big attraction is lizards – three metre, 130 kg monsters,
appropriately known as Komodo dragons.
The island is surrounded by some of the most
tempestuous waters in Indonesia, fraught
with rip tides and whirlpools. From the sea
it looks far more fitting for a monstrous

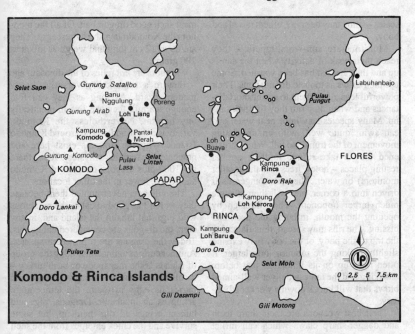

Komodo & Rinca Islands

lizard than for the few hundred people who live in its lone village.

Komodo gets a constant stream of visitors these days, but to understand how far off the beaten track it used to be, read *Zoo Quest for a Dragon* by naturalist-adventurer-TV personality David Attenborough who filmed the dragons in 1956. Dragons also inhabit the nearby islands of Rinca and Padar and coastal west Flores. Some people now prefer to visit Rinca rather than Komodo since it's closer to the Flores coast, has fewer other visitors and dragon-spotting is less organised – if less certain of success.

Komodo Dragons

There were rumours of these awesome creatures long before their existence was confirmed in the West. Fishers and pearl divers working in the area had brought back tales of ferocious lizards with enormous claws, fearsome teeth and fiery yellow tongues. One theory holds that the Chinese dragon is based on the Komodo lizard. The first Dutch expedition to the island was in 1910; two of the dragons were shot and their skins taken to Java, resulting in the first published description.

If you hold one of these monsters down and pin a label on it, what you've got is a monitor lizard. Monitors range from tiny 20 gram things just 20 cm long, to the grand-daddy of them all the Komodo dragon *(Varanus komodoensis)*, known locally as *ora*. All monitors have some things in common – the head is tapered, the ear-openings are visible, the neck is long and slender, the eyes have eyelids and round pupils, and the jaws are powerful. The body is usually massive with four powerful legs, each bearing five clawed toes. The long, thick tail functions as a rudder, and can also be used for grasping and as a potent weapon. The body is covered in small, non-overlapping scales – some may be spiny, others raised and bony.

Monitors are sun-worshippers – they reach their peak of activity when the sun is up and their habitat has been warmed. Some use their claws as tools to dig out dens. Their powerful legs allow them to sprint short distances and when they run they lift their tails up. Many species stay in or near water and can swim quite well, with an undulating movement of the trunk and tail. When threatened they'll take refuge in their normal resting places – holes, trees (for the smaller monitors) or water. They *are* dangerous if driven into a corner, and will then attack a much larger opponent. They threaten by opening the mouth, inflating the neck and hissing. The ribs may spread, thus flattening the top of the body, or the body may expand slightly making the monitor look larger. It often rises up on its hind legs just before attacking and the tail can deliver well-aimed blows that will knock down a weaker adversary.

Their best weapons are their sharp teeth and dagger-sharp claws which can inflict severe wounds. All monitors feed on other animals – small ones on insects, larger ones on frogs and birds, and the Komodo on deer and wild pig which inhabit the island. The Komodo eats rotting carcasses and also hunts, lying in wait beside frequently used tracks and grabbing a leg of a passing victim or knocking it over with a swing of the tail then ripping out its intestines. Once they've caught their prey they don't readily let go! The dragons will also eat their own dead. They can expand their mouth cavity considerably, enabling them to swallow large prey – the Komodo can push practically a whole goat into its throat.

Being such a large reptile the Komodo rarely moves until thoroughly warmed by the sun, though in fact the villagers complain of night-time dragon raids for goats or fish kept under their houses. The dragons *seem* to be absolutely stone deaf – you could fire a cannon three metres from them and they wouldn't bat an eyelid. But they have a very keen sense of smell which makes rotting

meat such good dragon bait. Of all the monitors the Komodo lays the largest eggs. They are up to 12 cm long and weigh as much as 200 grams.

Monitors are *not* relics of the dinosaur age – they're a remarkably versatile, hardy modern lizard. As long as they can find enough warmth they can live in practically any habitat. Nevertheless the Komodo variety is only found on and around Komodo Island. Why the dragons exist here and nowhere else remains a mystery. Today there are 1000-plus dragons on each of Komodo and Rinca, fewer in the other locations.

The villagers never hunted them because they weren't as good to eat as the numerous wild pigs that inhabit the island and, in any case, the dragons are considered dangerous. Today the dragons are a protected species. Another curious animal inhabiting this group of islands is the megapode or bush turkey – it collects a mound of rotting vegetation and buries its eggs in them, the temperature acting as an incubator. Dragons, pigs and human beings all dig them up, but some survive and the chick emerges from the shell fully clawed and feathered and flies away.

Orientation & Information

Komodo The only village is Kampung Komodo, a fishing village in a bay on the east coast. On the same bay a half-hour walk north of the village is Loh Liang, the tourist accommodation camp run by the PHPA – the Indonesian government body responsible for managing nature reserves and national parks. You pay a 1000 rp park entry fee when you arrive on Komodo.

The PHPA warns you not to walk outside the camp without one of their guides, who cost 2500 rp for up to three hours, plus 1000 rp for each extra hour. A lot of emphasis is put on 'danger'. This includes encounters with Komodo dragons that can snap your leg as fast as they'll cut through a goat's throat, or treading on poisonous snakes. Signs around the camp warn you to wear trousers and shoes and to watch for snakes. The PHPA guys will probably get the blame if you have to be shipped home in a crate. Several years ago an elderly European did wander off alone and was never found – Dragons 1, Tourists 0. In any case, many trails around the island are overgrown and you could get lost. No one's likely to stop you if you do head off without a guide – but they're not really expensive, especially between a group, and they're friendly fellows who are full of interesting information if you can speak a bit of Indonesian.

Rinca There's a PHPA tourist camp at Loh Buaya and it's possible to camp in some of the villages. The park entrance fee here is also 1000 rp; PHPA guides are 1000 rp an hour.

Dragon Spotting

Komodo You're likely to see dragons any time of year at Banu Nggulung, a dried up river bed about a half-hour walk from Loh Liang. The beasts get fairly regular feeds here from those tourists who provide them with goats, so they don't need to stray far in search of food. Poreng Valley, 5½ km from Loh Liang, is a second favourite dragon haunt and has a more out-in-the-wild feeling than Banu Nggulung. Elsewhere on the island, the best time to see dragons is from May to September, the driest part of the year, as it's hot and there are more of them out looking for food. From December to February is the wettest season and the dragons don't like rain. Komodo's hot most of the year: take water if you're going further afield than Banu Nggulung.

Unlike days of yore when you had to trek into the interior, string out the bait, hide behind a bush and hope something would happen, these days lizard-hunting at Banu Nggulung is almost like going to the theatre. On the way there you pass a helipad built for President Suharto in 1988. A little 'grandstand' – where presumably the great man sat – overlooks the river bed. A pulley is strung over the river bed for presenting dragons with dead goat, their preferred diet.

The PHPA now feeds the dragons on Wednesdays and Sundays. They will not string up a goat for a fee and will not allow visitors to bring their own goat(s). Take note of the signs warning you to be silent. They're for your sake, not the dragons' – excessive chatter can reduce your alertness.

It's not uncommon to see several dragons, ranging from relatively lively youngsters to lumbering three-metre monsters, clambering over each other to get at the last legs of a goat. The guides may let you go down to the river bed for a close-up look if there aren't too many of you. You need the sun overhead to get good photographs. You definitely need a telephoto lens – don't think you can walk right up to the dragons and have them say 'cheese'.

Rinca There are no established dragon-feeding places on Rinca so spotting them is more a matter of luck and your guide's knowledge. But other wildlife seems to be more abundant than on Komodo – there are monkeys, water buffalo, deer and wild horses.

Around Komodo Island

Kampung Komodo is a half-hour walk from the tourist camp. It's a fishing village of stilt houses, infested with goats, chickens and children – the fishing boats go out with the latter piled high. The inhabitants are all descendants of convicts who were exiled to the island last century by one of the sultans on Sumbawa. You can climb up the hills at the rear of Kampung Komodo or Loh Liang for sweeping views across the islands in the region.

If you go trekking around the island, or climb Gunung Ara (about a six-hour round trip), or go to Poreng Valley, or anywhere else, be warned that this place can be bloody hot! The PHPA guides perform like mountain goats, marching up and down the hilly terrain in the fierce heat. Sights around the island include wild deer and large, poisonous (though not deadly) spiders.

There's good coral just off Pantai Merah east of Loh Liang and the small island of

Pulau Lasa near Kampung Komodo – the PHPA guys say there's little danger from sea snakes or sharks. If you want to snorkel bring your own equipment, although the PHPA may have a snorkel and mask for hire. The PHPA has fixed prices for boat charters from Loh Liang: Kampung Komodo 1000 rp, Pulau Lasa 10,000 rp, Pantai Merah 12,000 rp, both plus Pulau Kalong (which has a large fruit bat colony) 15,000 rp.

Wild pigs are often seen close to the camp or on the beach in front of it early in the morning. The Komodo dragons occasionally wander into the camp, but they normally avoid the kampung because there are too many people. Whales and dolphins are quite common in the seas between Komodo and Flores.

Places to Stay & Eat

The *PHPA camp* at Loh Liang is a collection of large, spacious, clean wooden cabins on stilts. Each cabin has four or five rooms, a sitting area and two mandis (with toilet). You pay 3000 rp per person in a room with two single beds, 8000 rp per couple in a room with a double bed. You can pitch a tent for 500 rp. Electricity, produced by a noisy generator near the camp office, operates from 6 to 10 pm. Once that goes off there's almost total silence.

There's a restaurant at the camp too but the menu is limited to very average nasi goreng or mie goreng at 1500 rp each, plus some expensive drinks including beer and mineral water. Bring other food yourself – the PHPA guys may cook it for you – or try in Kampung Komodo. You should be able to buy fish or eggs there or perhaps get them to kill and cook a chicken. Accommodation at the PHPA camp at Loh Buaya on Rinca Island is similar to Komodo's, at the same prices.

Getting There & Away

Boat – Komodo The ferry between Sape and Labuhanbajo calls in at Komodo and operates every day except Friday. The ferry between Sape, Komodo and Labuhanbajo ferry departs Pelabuhan Sape at 8 am every Monday, Wednesday and Saturday. The Labuhanbajo-Komodo-Sape ferry departs Labuhanbajo at 8 am every Tuesday, Thursday and Sunday.

The ferry costs 8500 rp from Sape or 2600 rp from Labuhanbajo, plus 1000 rp per person for a small boat to transfer you between ferry and shore at Komodo. Tickets can be purchased at the harbour about one hour before departure.

If you don't want to wait for the ferry, you must find another boat to get on or off the island. You can charter a boat for a one-way or return journey. To make things easier, many people opt to charter a boat from Labuhanbajo to Komodo and back. You can fix this through hotels, the PHPA, or by asking around the waterfront. A reliable boat costs about 65,000 rp for a day trip, or 85,000 to 95,000 rp for a two-day trip with an overnight stay; bigger, better and faster boats cost up to 150,000 rp. Additional nights will cost more. Make any agreement with the boat operators very clear, particularly if you might recruit extra passengers. Labuhanbajo to Komodo takes three to four hours in an ordinary boat, which gives you maybe four hours on the island if you're making a day trip – enough to see the dragons and have a swim and a meal. A boat run by the Bajo Beach Hotel in Labuhanbajo takes 10 people and costs 75,000 rp.

Boat charters to Komodo from Pelabuhan Sape on Sumbawa are possible, but more expensive because it's a longer trip.

Boat – Rinca It's only about two hours by motorboat from Labuhanbajo to Loh Buaya, the PHPA camp on Rinca, but the PHPA in Labuhanbajo still asks 60,000 rp per boat for a day trip there, or 75,000 rp for two days and one night. Most other boats will take you for less – the Waecicu Beach Hotel runs day trips for 60,000 rp. If you want to stay at Loh Buaya, make sure you are dropped off at the right place – otherwise you could be faced with a 30-km walk to Loh Buaya.

Other Transport Labuhanbajo has an airport with Merpati flights from Denpasar, Mataram and elsewhere in Nusa Tenggara, you *could* be back in Denpasar 50 hours after leaving it, having visited Komodo in the meantime. There are also a few Komodo tours run from Bali: look around the travel agents there. The prices for these trips decrease the more people there are on the tour.

Flores

One of the biggest, most rugged and most beautiful islands in Nusa Tenggara, Flores also has some of the most interesting cultures, with a strong layer of animism beneath the prevalent Catholicism.

Geographically, a turbulent volcanic past has left Flores with a complicated relief of V-shaped valleys, knife-edged ridges and a collection of active and extinct volcanoes. One of the finest of the latter is the caldera of Keli Mutu in central Flores with its three coloured lakes. There are 14 active volcanoes in Flores – only Java and Sumatra have more. The central mountains slope more gently to the north coast, but along the south coast the spurs of the volcanoes plunge steeply into the sea. The island is part of one of the world's most unstable fracture zones and earthquakes and tremors hit every year. The rugged terrain makes road construction very difficult; although Flores is about 375 km long, its end-to-end road winds, twists, ascends and descends for nearly 700 km, and heavy wet season rains as well as the frequent earthquakes and tremors mean that it has to be repaired year-round.

Difficulties of communication have also contributed to the diversity of Flores' cultures. In some remoter areas you'll find older people who don't speak a word of Bahasa Indonesia and whose parents grew up in purely animist societies.

Physically, the people of the western end of Flores are more 'Malay' whilst the other inhabitants are more Melanesian. The island's 1.4 million population is divided into five main language and cultural groups: from west to east the Manggarai (main town Ruteng), the Ngada (Bajawa), the closely related Ende and Lio peoples (Ende), the Sikkanese (Maumere) and the Lamaholot (Larantuka). Around 85% of the people are Catholic (Muslims tend to congregate in the coastal towns) but, in rural areas particularly, Christianity is welded onto traditional beliefs. Animist rituals still play a big part in the latter, for a variety of occasions ranging from birth, marriage and death to the building of a new house or important points in the agricultural cycle. Even educated, English-speaking Florinese still admit to sacrificing a chicken, pig or buffalo to keep their ancestors happy when rice is planted or a new field opened up. In former times, it seems, it took more than just animal blood to keep the gods and spirits friendly: there are persistent tales of children or virgin girls being sacrificed.

Flores has a thriving ikat-weaving tradition, with almost as many different styles as there are weaving villages, plus the beginnings of a beach spot at Labuhanbajo and some fine snorkelling off some parts of its coast. It has attracted an increasing flow of travellers in recent years, but there's nothing resembling the tourist scene of Bali or even Lombok.

The rainy season (from November to March) is much more intense in western Flores, which receives the brunt of the northwest monsoon and has the highest mountains. Ruteng, near Flores' highest peak, the 2400-metre Renaka, gets an average 3350 mm of rain a year, but Ende has only 1140 mm and Larantuka just 770 mm.

History

Flores owes its name to the Portuguese who named its easternmost cape Cabo das Flores or 'Cape of Flowers'. The island's diverse cultures have enough similarities to suggest that they developed from a common type, differentiated by geographical isolation and the varying influence of outsiders. Long before Europeans arrived in the 16th century,

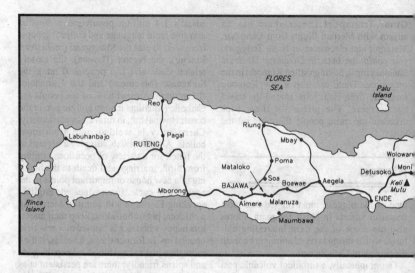

much of at least coastal Flores was firmly in the hands of the Makassarese and Bugis from southern Sulawesi. The Bugis even established their own ports as part of a trading network throughout the archipelago. They brought gold, coarse porcelain, elephant tusks (used as money), a sort of machete known as a *parang*, linen and copperware, and left with rubber, sea cucumber (much of it fished from the bay of Maumere), shark fins, sandalwood, wild cinnamon, coconut oil, cotton and fabric from Ende. Bugis and Makassarese slave raids on the coasts of Flores were a common problem, forcing people to retreat inland.

Fourteenth century Javanese chronicles place Flores (probably rather imaginatively) within the Majapahit realm. In the 15th and 16th centuries most of west and central Flores is thought to have become a colony of the Makassarese kingdom of Gowa in south Sulawesi, while east Flores came under the sway of Ternate in Maluku.

As early as 1512, Flores was sighted by the Portuguese navigator Antonio de Abreu and Europeans had probably landed by 1550. The Portuguese, involved in the lucrative sandalwood trade with Timor, built fortresses on Solor off eastern Flores and at Ende on Flores, and in 1561 Dominican priests established a mission on Solor. From here the Portuguese Dominicans extended their work to eastern Flores, founding over 20 missions by 1575. Despite attacks by pirates, local Islamic rulers and raids from Gowa, the missionaries converted – it is claimed – tens of thousands of Florinese. The fortress at Ende was overrun in 1637 by Muslims and the mission was abandoned, as eventually were all the other missions on southern Flores, but the growth of Christianity continued. Today the church is the centrepiece of almost every village.

In the 17th century the Dutch East India Company (VOC) kicked the Portuguese out of most of their possessions on and near Flores, and concentrated on monopolising the trade in sappan wood (used to make a red dye) and wild cinnamon. The slave trade was also strong; a treaty with Ende outlawed it in 1839 but it was reported to exist into the first years of the 20th century.

Though Ternate and Gowa ceded all their rights on Solor, Flores and east Sumbawa to the Dutch in the 17th century, Flores was too complex and isolated for the Dutch to gain

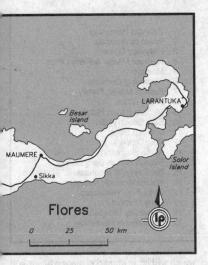

Flores

0   25   50 km

real control. Around 1850 the Dutch bought out Portugal's remaining enclaves in the area including Larantuka, Sikka and Paga on Flores. Dutch Jesuits then took over missionary work on Flores and founded new bases in Maumere and Sikka – still their centres on Flores today.

Even into the first decade of this century, the Dutch were constantly confronted with rebellions and inter-tribal wars. Finally in 1907 a major military campaign brought most of the tribes of central and western Flores under firm control. Missionaries moved into the isolated western hills in the 1920s.

LABUHANBAJO

A little Muslim/Christian fishing town at the extreme western end of Flores, this is the jumping-off point for Komodo, Rinca and Sumbawa. If you've got a few days to while away then Labuhanbajo is a good place to do it. The harbour is littered with outrigger fishing boats. It is also sheltered by several small islands, and this gives the impression that you're standing on the shore of a large lake.

Information

Tourist Office The Kantor Pariwisata is in a ridiculous location about two km south of town and not worth the effort to visit. You can find out more from the PHPA office.

PHPA The PHPA office is a two-minute walk from the Bajo Beach and Mutiara Beach hotels and is open till 2 pm. They're quite helpful with information on Komodo, Rinca and the Labuhanbajo area.

Money The Bank Rakyat Indonesia changes foreign currency and travellers' cheques but the rate is poor.

Things to See & Do

Apart from visiting Komodo or Rinca, you can hire a boat for a snorkelling or diving trip or just to drop you on an uninhabited island in the morning and collect you in the afternoon. Ask at hotels or the waterfront or maybe the PHPA. A half-day trip to Pulau Bidadari, where there's lots of coral and clear water, costs around 20,000 rp. For divers, there's good coral between the islands of Sabolo Besar and Sabolo Kecil.

Pantai Waecicu near Labuhanbajo is that rarity in Nusa Tenggara, an easily accessible beach where (except sometimes at weekends) you can relax without a crowd of curious onlookers. At low tide you can walk there in 1½ hours along the coast from the north end of Labuhanbajo, but it's simpler to take a 20-minute ride in the boat run by the Waecicu hotel. The boat usually leaves from near the pier at about 9 or 10 am, returning in the afternoon. Occasionally, they put on a second boat. The return trip is 2000 rp but is free if you stay at the hotel. The beach at Waecicu is clean and there's reasonable coral off a small island opposite.

Batugosok is another fine beach well worth visiting. Access is by boat which costs 5000 rp for the return trip, but is free if you stay at the hotel there.

Batu Cermin (Mirror Rock) is about four km from the town. It's necessary to charter a bemo to go there and back.

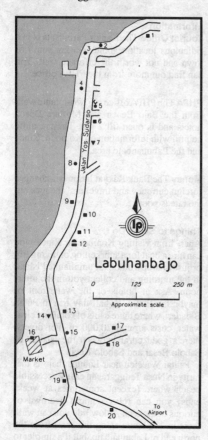

1	Bahagia Homestay
2	Boats to Waecicu
3	Fisheries Office
4	Harbour Master & Ferry Office
5	Mosque
6	Homestay Gembira
7	Rumah Makan Family
8	PHPA Office
9	Mutiara Beach Hotel
10	Bajo Beach Hotel
11	Losmen Sinjai
12	Post Office
13	Asma Homestay
14	Rumah Makan Banyuwangi
15	Bank Rakyat Indonesia
16	Wisma Komodo Makmur
17	Chez Felix Homestay
18	Sony Homestay
19	Homestay Bidadari
20	Oemathonis Homestay

which will be an upmarket place with air-con costing 40,000 rp for a double.

Across the road, *Mutiara Beach Hotel* is similarly well appointed and boasts a sitting area with a fine harbour view. Economy singles/doubles are 3500/7500 rp with shared bath, 5000/10,000 rp with private bath; 1st class costs 8500/15,000 rp. Again, you can and should bargain here.

Outside of these two main hotels, there are a number of small homestays. A personal favourite is *Chez Felix Homestay*, run by a friendly family that speaks good English. Rooms are clean with large windows and there is a pleasant porch area for sitting. With shared bath, singles/doubles are 4000/6000 rp, or 5000/8000 rp with attached bath. Breakfast is included.

Just nearby is *Sony Homestay* with a nice hilltop view. Cost per person is 3000 rp with shared bath and 3500 rp with private bath.

Oemathonis Homestay is on the road leading towards the airport. It's clean and airy. Rooms cost 3500 rp per person.

Bahagia Homestay boasts a nice view of the harbour from the front porch, but sitting here to admire the scenery is a good way to get stared at. Otherwise, it's quiet and clean and costs 3500 rp per person for a room with shared bath.

Places to Stay

You have the option of staying in Labuhanbajo itself, or one of the beach hotels in Batugosok or Waecicu.

In the town, there is the well-appointed *Bajo Beach Hotel* which has a range of very clean rooms costing 5000/8000 rp for singles/doubles with outside bath, or 10,000/ 12,500 rp with attached bath and 15,000/ 17,500 rp for the fancier rooms. You can bargain in this place and it's wise to do so. There's a pleasant open-air sitting and eating area with decent food. The owner has started construction on the *New Bajo Beach Hotel*

Losmen Sinjai is on the main road and is reasonably clean. All rooms are doubles and cost 7000 rp with shared bath and 10,000 rp with private bath.

Asma Homestay is appropriately named – it's a stuffy little box right across the street from the noisy market area. Even the hotel staff stare at you. Singles/doubles with outside bath cost 3000/5000 rp.

Wisma Komodo Makmur is right in the market itself so don't expect much peace and quiet, but it's great if you need to run out and buy bananas in a hurry. It's rather grotty looking but cheap at 2500 rp per person.

Homestay Bidadari is clean enough and costs 4000 rp per person for a room with outside bath.

Homestay Gembira, Jalan Sudarso 28, is convenient if you're a Muslim since it's right next to the mosque, but expect plenty of noise during the five-daily prayer calls. It's a ramshackle little place but is run by a friendly woman.

Waecicu Beach Hotel requires a 20-minute boat ride from Labuhanbajo, but boats normally only go about 9 or 10 am and return in the afternoon. There is usually an extra boat put on to meet incoming ferries and aircraft, or you can fork out the money to charter a boat. Accommodation costs 7500 rp per person which includes three excellent meals. Most of the 20 or so bungalows have attached mandis and toilets. The hotel also does Komodo day trips for 15,000 rp (minimum of five people) as well as Rinca trips.

Batugosok Beach Hotel has a similar arrangement. You must also take a boat to get there and accommodation costs the same as the competition, 7500 rp per person with three meals included. This is an excellent place to stay if you want to be out of the town.

Places to Eat

Labuhanbajo's cheapest meals are at the handful of little rumah makan towards the southern end of town. Choice of food is limited here, and quality variable, but the *Banyuwangi* does a respectable 750-rp *nasi goreng* and the *Ujung Pandang*'s chicken

soup contains recognisable pieces of chicken.

Getting There & Away

Air Merpati has direct flights between Labuhanbajo and Bima for 53,000 rp, Ende for 98,000 rp and Kupang for 164,000 rp. With connecting flights, there is a same-day service to Denpasar (178,000 rp), Jakarta (373,000 rp), Mataram (140,000 rp), Surabaya (257,000 rp) and Yogyakarta (282,000 rp).

The airfield is 2½ km from the town and hotels can arrange a taxi (5000 rp) to get you there. The Merpati office is between Labuhanbajo and the airport, about two km from the town.

Bus & Truck What one Indonesian tourist leaflet charitably calls the 'Trans-Flores Highway' loops and tumbles nearly 700 scenic km from Labuhanbajo to Larantuka at the east end of the island. Though this road has improved over the last few years – more than half of it is paved now – the unsurfaced sections can still rattle the fillings out of your teeth. You should see what our travel notes looked like after trying to write on a moving bus! In the rainy season sections of it become clogged with mud or, worse, are washed away by floods or landslides. The latter event leaves you with the choice between a long muddy walk, trying to get on to a suddenly very popular aeroplane, or resorting to boats – or you could take up long-term residence until the road gets repaired.

In the dry, buses take four hours to Ruteng, in the wet, who knows? Three or four buses leave Labuhanbajo daily around 7 am – a few more depart up till early afternoon, and there's usually an evening bus when the ferry arrives from Sape. The fare to Ruteng is 4000 rp – you can buy advance tickets from hotels or from buses which hang around town displaying signs like *Besok Ke Ruteng*. If you get an advance ticket, the bus will pick you up from your hotel.

Passenger trucks also ply the route to Ruteng. They are less comfortable but still cost the same 4000 rp. If you do find yourself on a truck, it's imperative to get a seat in front of the rear axle; positions behind it are good approximations of ejector seats.

Boat The ferry to Sape (Sumbawa) departs Labuhanbajo at 8 am every Tuesday, Thursday and Sunday. Going the other way, departures from Sape are at 8 am every Monday, Wednesday and Saturday. In both directions, it stops in at Komodo. In Labuhanbajo it docks at the north end of the main street. Get tickets from the harbour master's office *(Direktorat Jenderal Perhubungan Darat)* near the pier one hour before departure.

If there are some really bad hold-ups on the Labuhanbajo-Ruteng road or if you just fancy an unusual route, you can try getting a boat to Reo on the north coast then a bus from Reo to Ruteng. Ask at the harbour master's office or the fisheries office *(Kantor Perikanan)*, both at the north end of Labuhanbajo's main street. Something sails to Reo every few days. The boat fare is negotiable and the voyage takes eight to 10 hours if no stops are made. There are also occasional boats from Labuhanbajo to Maumere or Bima, or even Ende.

REO

Set on an estuary a little distance from the sea, Reo's focal point is the large Catholic church compound in the middle of the town. From the port of Kedindi, five km from Reo, 3000 buffalo per year are shipped to Surabaya. If you want to make a boat trip between Reo and Labuhanbajo, it's probably better to do it from Labuhanbajo than from Reo, so that if you have to wait days for a boat, you do so in a more agreeable place.

Places to Stay & Eat

The *Losmen Telukbayur* at Jalan Mesjit 8 has rooms at 3500 rp per person. The toilets and mandis are Indonesian versions of Australian backyard dunnies and about as clean as you would expect. The top floor rooms are probably best for avoiding the crowds of staring children. This losmen has its own warung.

Better appointed is the *Hotel Nisangnai,*

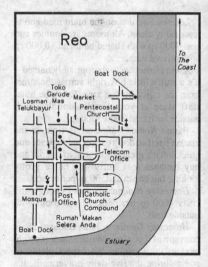

on Jalan Pelabuhan, a little way out of town towards Kedindi, which also costs 3500 rp per person, or 12,500 rp for a double with private bath. *Rumah Makan Selera Anda* is a five-minute walk from the Telukbayur near the Catholic church.

Getting There & Away

There are fairly frequent buses, trucks and bemos (more in the morning than later) between Reo and Ruteng, taking three hours and costing 1500 rp. The whole road is surfaced now. They spend a long time keliling. You may be able to catch one at the dock when the boats from Labuhanbajo pull in.

Look around the river for small boats to Labuhanbajo – these go irregularly and the fare is about 8,000 rp per person. The Bajo Beach Hotel in Labuhanbajo runs boat/snorkelling tours which take in Reo.

RUTENG

A market town and meeting point for the hill-people of western Flores, Ruteng is the heart of the Manggarai country, the region extending to the west coast from a line drawn north from Aimere. The town is surrounded by rice fields on gentle slopes beneath a line of volcanic hills, and is cooler and less humid than the coast – though still hot when the sun shines. Take water if you go hiking.

The Manggarai hill people are everything you'd expect hill-people to be: scruffy, shy, curious. You'll see them in their distinctive black sarongs trailing droopy-stomached black-haired pigs into market, or herding beautiful miniature horses. There are also prolific numbers of Chinese who play their traditional role as the retailers and business-people.

The Manggarai language is unintelligible to the other people on Flores. Makassarese from Sulawesi have mixed with the coastal Manggarai for well over a century and the Bimanese dominated some coastal regions for at least 300 years until early this century, when the Dutch finally took over all of Flores.

Christianity now predominates among the upland Manggarai and Ruteng has several large Christian schools and churches. Traditional animistic practices linger but are less evident than among the Ngada people further east. Traditionally the Manggarai would carry out an annual cycle of ceremonies – some involving buffalo or pig sacrifices – to ask favour from ancestor and nature spirits and the supreme being, Mori. In some villages you can still find the *compang*, a ring of flat stones on which offerings are placed, or you may be shown ritual paraphernalia such as drums which are beaten to accompany sacrifices.

Trials of strength and courage known as *caci* were once a frequent accompaniment to ceremonies. They still take place in Ruteng during the national Independence Day celebrations on 17 August. The two combatants wear wooden masks like up-tilted welders' helmets – one carries a rawhide oval shield and a metre-long whip; the other a short, springy stick and a thick cloth wrapped around his forearm. The two combatants circle each other, loudly proclaiming their own bravery while musicians beat an accompaniment on gongs and wooden drums. The combatant with the whip lashes at his opponent who tries to deflect the blow with his

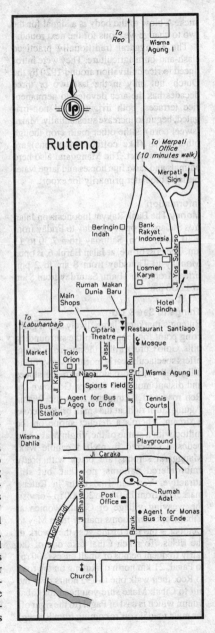

Ruteng

stick. A blow to the body is a signal for the two to change weapons for the next round.

The Manggarai traditionally practised slash-and-burn agriculture. They were introduced to rice cultivation around 1920 by the Dutch, but only in the last two or three decades has the area devoted to permanent rice terraces, both irrigated and non-irrigated, begun to increase substantially. Maize (sweet corn) is the other main crop though other crops (like coffee and onions) are grown for export. The Manggarai also herd animals and raise fine horses and large water buffalo, the latter primarily for export.

Information
Money The Bank Rakyat Indonesia on Jalan Yos Sudarso is open Monday to Friday from 7.30 am to noon, Saturday from 7.30 to 11 am. The post office, at Jalan Baruk 6, is open Monday to Thursday from 8 am to 2 pm, Friday from 8 to 11 am, Saturday from 8 am to 12.30 pm.

Things to See & Do
Ruteng's market is large, lively and a gathering point for people from the surrounding hills. Golo Curu, a hill to the north of Ruteng, offers spectacular early morning views of the hills, valleys, rice paddies, terraced slopes and distant mountain valleys. Go down the Reo road and 10 minutes from the Wisma Agung I turn right at the small bridge across a stream. There's a derelict shrine on the hilltop with a statue of the Virgin Mary on a pedestal covered in melted candle wax. Manggarai sarongs are black with pretty embroidered patterns, not ikat, but still attractive. You can find them in Ruteng market for from 15,000 to 20,000 rp – or visit the weaving village of Cibal. Women at Cibal work their looms mainly from May to October – the rest of the year they work in the fields. To reach Cibal take one of the fairly frequent bemos or small buses (500 rp) to Pagal, 21 km north of Ruteng on the road to Reo, then walk one to 1½ hours over the hill to Cibal. Make sure you head for Cibal Timur, which is east of Pagal (to the right off the main road if you're coming from Ruteng)

– there are other Cibals which are several km in the wrong direction from Pagal.

Places to Stay & Eat
The central *Hotel Sindha* on Jalan Yos Sudarso is the best place in town. The helpful owner also serves up excellent Chinese food. Officially rooms are 8000 rp (shared bath) to 18,000 rp (private bath) for doubles, but bargaining seems to help a little here.

Wisma Dahlia (☎ 377) on Jalan Kartini is also good. Economy rooms with shared mandi are 7500 rp, singles/doubles with private mandi 10,000/12,500 rp and family rooms for 25,000 rp. The better rooms have hot water. There's a Chinese restaurant here too, and you can even get chicken and steak.

Wisma Agung I (☎ 80) at Jalan Wae Cos 10 (the road leading to Reo) gets the thumbs down from travellers. Class I rooms, with private mandi, are 6000/8000 rp; class II rooms, a bit smaller with shared mandis, are 4000/6000 rp. *Wisma Agung II*, behind Toko Agung on Jalan Motang Rua, is more central but darker, mismanaged, and dearer at 10,000/13,000 rp for class I, 6600/8000 for class II.

Losmen Karya near the town centre is cheap though tatty, but it's often 'full'. The owner does not seem to like foreigners, but if you're deemed acceptable, it's 4000 rp per person.

For meals out, try the central *Rumah Makan Dunia Baru*, with good Chinese food, or the *Rumah Makan Beringin* for Padang food. There are a few other places in the town and a handful of warungs at the market, some of which may serve buffalo soup *(soto kerbau)*.

Getting There & Away
Air There are flights most days to/from Bima (85,000 rp) and Kupang (122,000 rp); some of the Bima flights call at Labuanbajo. The Merpati office (☎ 147) is out in the rice paddies, about a 10-minute walk from the centre (see map).

Bus Most buses will drop you at hotels on arrival in Ruteng. Buses to Labuhanbajo

(4000 rp), Bajawa (4000 rp) and Ende (8000 rp) leave in the early morning about 7 am. There are noontime buses to Bajawa and Labuhanbajo. You can buy tickets for the morning buses at the bus station or agents in shops the afternoon before – most hotels will also get them for you, sometimes for a commission. If you have a ticket, buses will pick you up from wherever you want. Then they circle Ruteng's rutted back streets collecting other passengers.

In the dry, it takes about four hours to Labuhanbajo, six hours to Bajawa, 13 hours to Ende. In the wet, you never know. Trucks cover the same routes but at no saving on cost.

Buses, trucks and bemos to Reo leave fairly often until about midday, costing 1500 rp for the 60-km, three-hour journey. Pick them up at the bus station or as they circle the streets.

Getting Around

The airport is a half-hour walk from the town if you don't want to charter a bemo.

BAJAWA

The small hill town of Bajawa, with a population of about 10,000, is the centre of the Ngada people, one of the least modernised groups on Flores. The town is 1100 metres high and surrounded by volcanic hills with the 2245-metre Gunung Inerie to the south predominant. Bajawa is cool, spacious and low-key – an excellent base for trips out to Ngada villages and the surrounding country.

The Ngada

The 60,000 Ngada people inhabit both the upland Bajawa plateau and the slopes around Gunung Inerie stretching down to the south coast. They were subdued by the Dutch in 1907 and Christian missionaries arrived about 1920. Older animistic beliefs remain strong and the religion of many Ngada, to a greater extent than in most of Flores, is a fusion of animism and Christianity.

The most evident symbols of continuing Ngada tradition are the pairs of *ngadhu* and *bhaga*. The ngadhu is a parasol-like structure about three metres high consisting of a carved wooden pole and thatched 'roof', and the bhaga is like a miniature thatch-roofed house. You'll see groups of them standing in most Ngada villages, though in the less traditional ones some of the bhaga have disappeared.

The functions and meanings of ngadhu and bhaga are multiple, but basically they symbolise the continuing presence of ancestors. The ngadhu is 'male' and the bhaga 'female' and each pair is associated with a particular family group within a village. Though the carved trunks of ngadhu often feel like solid stone, their tops are usually dilapidated – some are said to have been built to commemorate people killed in long-past battles over land disputes, and may be over 100 years old. Periodically, on instruction from ancestors in dreams, a pair of ngadhu and bhaga is remade according to a fixed pattern, accompanied by ceremonies which may involve buffalo sacrifices.

The main post of a ngadhu, known as *Sebu*, should come from a tree which is dug up complete with its main root then 'planted' in the appropriate place in the village. Each part of the post has specific designs carved on it on different days: an axe and a cassava on the top part, a dragonhead in the form of a flower in the middle, and a geometric design around the bottom. The three parts are also said to represent the three classes of traditional Ngada society: from top to bottom, the *gae*, *gae kisa* and *hoo*. A crossbeam with two hands holding an arrow and a sword links the top of the pole to the roof. The walls of the bhaga must be cut from seven pieces of wood. Near the ngadhu there's usually a small stone post which is the 'gate-keeper', and the bases of both ngadhu and bhaga are often surrounded by circles of stones, said to symbolise meeting places.

The traditional Ngada village layout – of which there are still a few examples left – is two rows of high-roofed houses on low stilts. These face each other across an open space which contains ngadhu and bhaga and groups of man-high stone slivers surrounding horizontal slabs. The latter, which appear

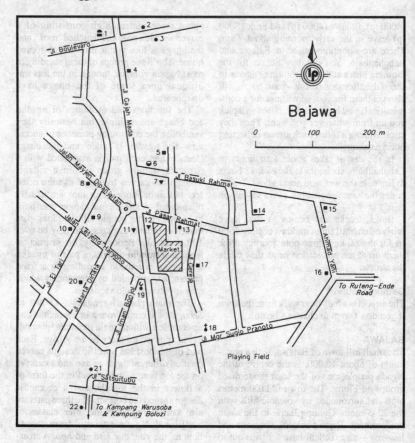

Bajawa

0   100   200 m

Jl Boulevard

Jl Gajah Mada

Jalan Mayen Dipanjaitan

Jl Basuki Rahmat

Jl Pasar Rahmat

Jl Cereja

Jalan Letjend Haryono

Jl El Tari

Jl Marta Dinata

Jl Iman Bonjol

Jl Satsuitubu

Market

Jl Ahmad Yani

To Ruteng–Ende Road

Jl Mgr Sugio Pranoto

Playing Field

To Kampang Warusoba
& Kampung Bolozi

to be graves of important ancestors, have led to some exotic theories about the Ngada's origins.

Traditionally the Ngada believe themselves to have come from Java and they may have settled here three centuries ago. But stone structures which are in varying degrees similar to these 'graves' crop up in other remote parts of Indonesia – among them Nias Island, Sumatra's Batak highlands, parts of Sulawesi, Sumba and Tanimbar – as well as in Malaysia and Laos. The common thread is thought to be the Dongson culture, which arose in southern China and north Vietnam about 2700 years ago then migrated into Indonesia bringing, among other things, the practice of erecting large monumental stones (megaliths). This practice, it's thought, survived only in isolated areas which were not in contact with later cultural changes.

Some writers also claim to have recognised Hindu, Semitic, even Caucasian elements in Ngada culture – and one theory, seeking to explain apparent similarities between Indonesian and Balkan culture, suggests that the Dongson Culture originated in south-east Europe!

1	Post Office
2	Bank Rakyat Indonesia
3	Telecom
4	Hotel Johny
5	Hotel Kencana
6	Bus Station
7	Rumah Makan Siang Malam
8	Hotel Virgo
9	Hotel Kambera
10	Hotel Anggrek
11	Rumah Makan Kasih Bahagia
12	Rumah Makan Wisata
13	Merpati
14	Homestay Sunflower
15	Hotel Korina
16	Hotel Modest Dagalos
17	Hotel Dam
18	Church
19	Mosque
20	Hotel Kembang
21	Cultural Department
22	Ngadhu

What makes the Ngada unusual today is their preservation of animistic beliefs and practices. 'Straight' Christianity has made fewer inroads in the villages than in Bajawa itself. Apart from ngadhu and bhaga and the ancestor worship which goes with them, agricultural fertility rites continue (sometimes involving very gory buffalo sacrifices) as well as ceremonies marking birth, marriage, death or house building. The major annual festival is the six-day *Reba* ceremony at Bena, 19 km from Bajawa, held around late December/early January, which includes dancing, singing, buffalo sacrifices and the wearing of special black ikat costumes. The highest god in traditional Ngada belief is Gae Dewa who unites Dewa Zeta (the heavens) and Nitu Sale (the earth).

Orientation & Information

Bajawa is three km north of the Ruteng-Ende road. It's a small town and everything is within walking distance of the bus station and market. The post office, on Jalan Boulevard, is open Monday to Thursday from 8 am to 2 pm, Friday from 8 to 11 am, Saturday from 8 am to 12.30 pm. The nearby Bank Rakyat Indonesia changes money.

Places to Stay

Hotel Virgo (☎ 61), Jalan Mayjen Dipanjaitan, deserves a plug as one of the better budget places in town. It's new and clean, offering rooms with private bath for 4400 and 5500 rp per person with breakfast thrown in.

Hotel Sunflower (☎ 236) on Jalan H Wuruk is clean, pleasant and has a porch with a good view overlooking the valley. Rooms are 4000 rp per person with attached bath.

Hotel Anggrek (☎ 172) is a congenial place, but beware of rooms near the TV set in the lobby unless you can sleep through an earthquake. Prices are upmarket, with singles/doubles at 10,000/12,000 rp with private bath, or 8,000 rp for a triple with shared bath.

Hotel Kambera (☎ 166), Jalan El Tari 9, has claustrophobic coffin-sized rooms, but the hotel is partially redeemed by the excellent meals served here. Perhaps the management should go into the restaurant business instead. Rooms cost 3300 rp per person with shared bath or 8250 rp per person with private bath.

Hotel Kencana (☎ 155), Jalan Palapa 7, is a bit depressing but OK if you can't find anything else. It's cheap at 5000 rp for a double with attached bath.

Hotel Korina (☎ 162), Jalan Ahmad Yani 81, is one of the better places, helped by the fact that the friendly manager speaks reasonable English. Cheerful, large rooms cost 6000/8000 rp, but all rooms have shared bath only.

Hotel Johny (☎ 79) on Jalan Gajah Mada is bare but has acceptable meals. Rooms go for 3500 rp per person.

Hotel Dam (☎ 45) is a quiet and delightful little place near the church. Rooms feature mosquito nets. Singles go for 3500 rp with outside bath or 6000 rp with attached bath.

Hotel Modest Dagalos on Jalan Ahmad Yani looks much better on the outside than the inside. Small, cave-like rooms go for 3000 rp per person.

The more up-market *Hotel Kembang* (☎ 72) on Jalan Marta Dinata has very clean rooms facing a small garden, at 12,500 rp for a double with private bath and breakfast included.

Places to Eat

Rumah Makan Wisata, near the market, is excellent value. The friendly owner is a gold mine of information about the area, and has some superb photographs of the 1988 eruption of Gunung Api Abulobo.

The friendly *Rumah Makan Kasih Bahagia*, on Jalan Yani almost opposite the bus station, has cold beer and decent food at good prices. *Rumah Makan Siang Malam* on Jalan Basuki Rahmat has Padang food.

Things to Buy

Bajawa market is busy with lots of Ngada women wearing ikat cloth some of which is on sale, both from the Ngada area and further afield. The better local stuff is black with white motifs, often of horses or people. Sarongs are plentiful. There's a ngadhu at the end of Jalan Satsuitubu.

Getting There & Away

Air Merpati has two flights a week each to and from Bima (85,000 rp), Ende (42,000 rp) and Kupang (118,000 rp), with same-day connections possible to Denpasar (209,000 rp), Jakarta (404,000 rp), Mataram (171,000 rp), Surabaya and Yogyakarta. The Merpati office is near the market (see map).

Bus Most buses to/from Ende and Ruteng officially depart at 7 am and noon, but will pick you up at your hotel and then spend an hour keliling through the streets. Buses to both places cost 4000 rp and take almost six hours not counting keliling.

There are buses that do the entire Labuhanbajo-Bajawa trip in one day. This takes about 10 hours and costs 8000 rp.

Small buses and bemos also run from Bajawa to other places on the main road like Mataloko and Boawae in the Ende direction

or Aimere in the Ruteng direction. Regular bus service to Riung should become a reality eventually when the road finally gets sealed, but at the moment it's a long, roundabout haul to reach Riung by truck via Aegela.

The best place to buy bus tickets seems to be Rumah Makan Wisata, but your hotel might be willing to arrange it too.

Getting Around

To/From the Airport The airport is 25 km from town and the only way to get there without chartering a bemo is to take the Merpati bus, which costs 5000 rp.

Bemo You'll have to charter, because there is no regular bemo service around town.

AROUND BAJAWA

Kampung Bolozi

Only a 30 to 45-minute walk along a dirt track from Bajawa, Kampung Bolozi has some ngadhu, a few traditional houses and an old tomb. See the map for directions – if in doubt, ask for Kampung Warusoba which is on the way to Kampung Bolozi.

Langa

There are 10 ngadhu and bhaga and several steep-roofed houses in Langa, seven km from Bajawa. From Bajawa bus station you might find a bemo going all the way, otherwise take one to Watujaji on the main Ruteng-Ende road and walk the remaining four km, or walk the whole way. It's probably a good idea to ask the kepala desa or some other responsible-looking person before taking photos. You might be offered special ceremonial sarongs for sale here. They're worth 100,000 to 150,000 rp depending on the thickness of the material. Locals sometimes exchange a ceremonial sarong for a horse. Three km from Langa is another traditional village, Borado.

Bena

Right underneath the Inerie volcano, 19 km from Bajawa, Bena is one of the most traditional Ngada villages and its stone monuments are a protected site. High thatched houses line up in two rows on a ridge, the space between them filled with ngadhu, bhaga and strange megalithic tomb-like structures. Once, all Ngada villages followed this design. Some of the 'tombs' are said to contain hoards of treasure. The house of the leading family in each part of the village has a little model-house on top of its roof. There's a small Christian shrine on a mound at the top end of the village, showing that Christianity and animism coexist here. Bena is the scene of the important six-day Reba ceremony every December-January.

On arrival, try to chat to the villagers and at least ask before wandering round or taking photos. You may be asked to sign a visitors' book and give up to 5000 rp per person: this seems to be a matter for negotiation. Taking a small gift like cigarettes or betel nut, or offering maybe 500 rp or 1000 rp before you're asked, will probably start you off on a friendlier, less commercial footing. If you want to stay with the kepala desa – which it's possible to do – you could offer to pay 2000 rp or 3000 rp for the accommodation instead of paying the 'visitor's fee'.

In the daytime most of the men and some women are usually out in the fields – only the elderly and a few mothers and ragged children remain in the village, pounding rice or doing other chores. Once you have got past any uneasy money matters, the people will probably be happy to talk.

Bena is 10 km from Langa – occasional vehicles go from Langa to Bena but more often you have to walk. An easier way from Bajawa is to take a bemo to Mangulewa on the Ende road, then walk the 10 km from Mangulewa to Bena – downhill all the way. Occasionally bemos go from Bajawa to Welu, half-way between Mangulewa and Bena. Take water and as much food as you'll need. From Bena you can climb Gunung Inerie in about three or four hours. If it's clear, Sumba and the north coast of Flores will be visible.

Wogo

There are beautiful houses and eight or nine sets of ngadhu and bhaga at Wogo, a 10-minute walk from Mataloko, which is about 20 km from Bajawa on the Ende road. Bemos run from Bajawa to Mataloko. Some non-traditional houses have been built at Wogo but they are not allowed in the original village where the buildings are all traditional. The people are friendly, but you should expect to pay 500 rp to take photos. The English teacher from the mission at Mataloko may be willing to interpret for you.

Boawae

Forty-one km from Bajawa on the road to Ende, Boawae is the centre of the Nage-Keo people related to, but distinct from, the Ngada. Boawae is the source of most of the best Bajawa-area ikat. Buffalo-sacrifice rituals take place here too: the Ladalero museum near Maumere has photos of a bloody killing at Boawae in which the animal was tied to a stake, then the bottom halves of its back legs were chopped off and deep gashes cut in its flanks before it was

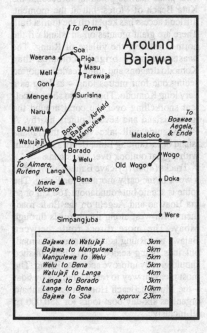

Around Bajawa

To Poma
Soa
Waerana
Piga
Masu
Meli
Tarawaja
Gon
Menge
Surisina
Naru
Bajawa Airfield
Bona
BAJAWA
Mangulewa
Watujaji
Mataloko
To Boawae, Aegela, & Ende
Borado
Welu
Wogo
To Aimere, Ruteng
Langa
Old Wogo
Inerie ▲
Volcano
Bena
Doka
Simpangjuba
Were

Bajawa to Watujaji	3km
Bajawa to Mangulewa	9km
Mangulewa to Welu	5km
Welu to Bena	5km
Watujaji to Langa	4km
Langa to Borado	3km
Langa to Bena	10km
Bajawa to Soa	approx 23km

killed. This apparently is not an uncommon method of ritual buffalo killing in these parts of Flores. A form of boxing called *Etu* is traditionally part of the May to August post-harvest festivities among the Nage-Keo: the boxers wear garments made from tree bark and painted with animal blood, and their gloves may be studded with broken glass!

Soa

About an hour's truck ride north of Bajawa, Soa's attraction is the weekly market which brings in villagers from a very wide area. It starts on Sunday afternoon and seems to go on most of the night and well into Monday. Villagers tramp into Soa with sacks of rice or lone melons perched on their heads. There are also some hot springs *(air panas)* in a river about 1½ km walk from a village six km beyond Soa.

RIUNG

This place has the potential to become the Kuta Beach of Flores, but at the moment, difficult access has kept it off the tourist trail. There are giant iguanas on an island off the north coast near the village of Riung. The beasts are more brightly coloured than Komodo dragons and some readers reported seeing one four metres long – as long as a very long Komodo. There's also some excellent snorkelling over the coral around the iguana island and several others nearby. A PHPA guide will take you to the iguana island or to Tanjung Lima Belay a viewpoint with a great outlook over the islands.

Trucks (4000 rp) leave Bajawa a few times a week in the early morning for Riung. The route is scenic but roundabout 160 km or so via Boawae and Aegela on the Ende road, then north-west along rough roads through Mbay. The more direct route between Bajawa and Riung is a nightmare of a road, but it is being sealed, and when finished should greatly improve access to Riung. The most pleasant way to reach Riung is by boat – the Mutiara Beach Hotel in Labuhanbajo organises six-day boat tours for 250,000 rp all-inclusive.

ENDE

The Endenese are the people gathered in south central Flores in and around the port town of Ende. Like their neighbours, they have a mix of Malay and Melanesian features. The aristocratic families of Ende link their ancestors, through mythical exploits and magical events, with the Hindu Majapahit kingdom of Java. Today most of the 55,000 people living in Ende are Christian, but there are also many Muslims.

It's a drab town running down to a revolting beach, but is surrounded by fine mountain scenery. The perfect cone of Gunung Meja rises almost beside the airport and the larger Gunung Iya occupies a promontory south of Gunung Meja.

Ende is mainly a stopover on the way to or from the attractions of eastern Flores, but trips to some nearby villages may be worthwhile, and you can at least look at some interesting ikat weaving here.

Orientation & Information

Ende is at the neck of a peninsula jutting south into the sea. The port of Ende and most of the shops and offices are on the western side of the neck. Another port, Pelabuhan Ipi, is on the eastern side; north of Pelabuhan Ipi is the airport.

Money The Bank Rakyat Indonesia on Jalan Sudirman is open from 8 am to 12.30 pm Monday to Friday and from 8 am to 11.30 am Saturday.

Post & Telecommunications The main post office, where you must go for poste restante, is out in the north-west of town on Jalan Gajah Mada. It's open Monday to Thursday from 8 am to 2 pm, Friday from 8 to 11 am, and Saturday from 8 am to 1 pm. For stamps, there's a sub-post office a short walk from the centre of town opposite Hotel Dwi Putra. The telecom office is on Jalan Kelimutu, about a 15-minute walk from the waterfront, or take a bemo.

Markets There's a market beside the town bemo station on Jalan Pasar, and lots of shops

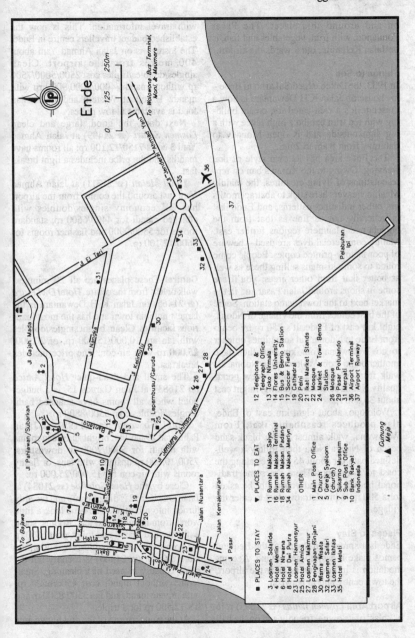

Ende

0 125 250m

To Wolowona Bus Terminal,
Moni & Maumere

To Bajawa

Pelabuhan
Ipi

▲ Gunung
▲ Meja

■ PLACES TO STAY

3   Losmen Solafide
4   Hotel Merlin
6   Hotel Nirwana
8   Hotel Dwi Putra
25 Losmen Hamansyur
25 Hotel Amica
27 Losmen Makmur
28 Penginapan Rinjani
30 Wisma Wisata
33 Losmen Safari
33 Losmen Ikhlas
35 Hotel Melati

▼ PLACES TO EAT

11 Rumah Makan Sayo
16 Rumah Makan Terminal
18 Rumah Makan Padang
34 Rumah Makan Merlyn

OTHER

1   Main Post Office
2   Church
5   Gereja Syaloom
    (church)
7   Sukarno Museum
9   Sub Post Office
10 Bank Rakyat
    Indonesia
12 Telephone &
    Telegraph Office
13 Toko Nirmala
14 Flores University
15 Bus & Bemo Station
17 Soccer Field
19 Cathedral
20 Petni
21 Ikat Market Stands
22 Mosque
24 Market & Town Bemo
    Station
26 Mosque
29 Pasar Potulando
31 Merpati
36 Airport Terminal
37 Airport Runway

on and around this street. The Pasar Potulando, with fruit, vegetables and fish, is on Jalan Kelimutu, out towards the airport.

Things to See

In 1933, the Dutch exiled Sukarno to Ende – his house on Jalan K H Dewantara is now a museum. It's a well-cared for, cream building with red trim behind a high fence with a big sign outside and is open Monday to Saturday from 8 am to 2 pm.

The Ende area has its own style of ikat weaving. Owing to the Koran's ban on representations of living creatures, the mainly Muslim weavers here stick to abstract motifs but rather indistinct patterns, and Ende ikat is generally not as fine as that from the Nggela and Maumere regions further east. Mainly commercial dyes are used – beware of poor factory-printed copies. People come round to some losmens selling these as well as better ikat from other areas; you'll see some in shops around Jalan Pasar and in the market next to the town bemo station. Some of the best comes from the village of Ndona, eight km east of Ende. It's 250 rp by bemo from Ende to Ndona, but sometimes quicker to go Wolowona four km out, then take another bemo from Wolowona to Ndona. Or walk from Wolowona. A large new good-quality Ndona *selendang* (shawl) might cost about 30,000 rp.

Wolotopo, about eight km east of Ende, also produces reasonable ikat. From Wolowona, walk almost to the black-sand beach of Nanga Nesa then follow a well-defined path for about 45 minutes along the coast to Wolotopo. There are some traditional houses here and you might be asked for a 500 rp 'administrative fee' to enter the village.

Places to Stay

Ende is a spread-out town but the frequent bemos make it easy to get around. Accommodation is in three areas: near the airport, the town centre and in between.

Airport Area *Losmen Ikhlas* (☎ 21695) is in a 'khlas' of its own – friendly and on the ball with travel information. This is now the established budget travellers centre in Ende. The losmen is on Jalan Ahmad Yani about 400 metres from the airport. Clean singles/doubles/triples cost 2500/5000/7500 rp without mandi, 4000/7000/9000 rp with mandi. Excellent Western and Indonesian food is available at low prices.

Next door, the good, large and clean *Losmen Safari* (☎ 21499) at Jalan Ahmad Yani 3 costs 7150/12,100 rp; all rooms have mandis and the price includes a light breakfast.

Hotel Melati (☎ 21311) at Jalan Ahmad Yani just around the corner from the airport has OK economy singles/doubles with attached mandi for 4400/6600 rp, standard rooms for 5500/9900 and flashier rooms for 6600/12,100 rp.

Central These places are all 20 minutes' walk or less from the centre. *Hotel Dwi Putra* (☎ 21465) on Jalan K H Dewantara is the largest hotel in town and has the most luxurious facilities. Clean, bright singles/doubles with fan are 10,000/15,000 rp, or 20,000/25,000 rp with air-con. The price includes breakfast.

The small and dead-quiet *Hotel Amica* (☎ 21683), at Jalan Garuda 15, is a budget hotel where all rooms have attached bath. Singles/doubles cost 5500/8800 rp.

Hotel Nirwana (☎ 21199) at Jalan Pahlawan 29 has big, bright and clean rooms with mandi for 5000/7000 rp downstairs, 7500/10,000 rp upstairs with fans, or flashy rooms with air-con for 15,000/25,000 rp.

Close by, the *Hotel Solafide* (☎ 21084) at Jalan One Kore 2 is dingy, damp and recently turned into a brothel. The beds look a little worse from the wear and tear. Rooms, some with attached mandi and toilet, cost 6600 rp for both singles and doubles. Next door, the *Hotel Merlin* (☎ 21465) is friendly but the place is badly in need of a cleaning. Small rooms without mandi cost 4500/6500 rp, with private mandi and fan 5500/8500 rp and it's 12,500 rp for a triple.

At the southern end of the downtown area

is the tattered *Hotel Hamansyur* (☎ 21373), Jalan Loreng Aembonga II. It's depressing-looking but has a courtyard, and rooms are 3500 rp per person.

In Between At Jalan Ahmad Yani 17, *Losmen Makmur* is a Third World nightmare. Its sole redeeming feature is the mosquito netting above the beds. Rooms cost 3000 rp per person. Just next door is the slightly better *Penginapan Rinjani* which also costs 3000 rp per person.

The not-very-busy *Hotel Wisata* (☎ 21368) at Jalan Kelimutu 68 is swish with a lobby and TV lounge but no restaurant. The cheapest uncarpeted rooms are 5500/8500 rp. Carpeted ones with fan, attached mandi and toilet and small verandah are 11,000/15,000 rp, with air-con from 22,500/25,000 rp.

Places to Eat

Around the bus station on Jalan Hatta warungs offer sate, rice, goat soup and vegetables at night. Otherwise it's the usual Chinese places with bare rooms and fierce neon lights – or a few Padang places.

Depot Ende at Jalan Sudirman 6 has good food and a clean kitchen. Its Chinese and Indonesian dishes are reasonable. Try the fresh marquisa juice, in season from August to December.

Right next to the Jalan Hatta bus station, the *Rumah Makan Terminal* has seemingly good food but travellers have been known to get sick after eating here. On Jalan Pasar, the *Rumah Makan Putri Minang* is friendly and has cheap Padang food.

Near the Hotel Nirwana, *Rumah Makan Saiyo* on Jalan Banteng serves Padang food and is clean.

Rumah Makan Merlyn on Jalan Kelimutu, about 300 metres from the airport, looks a decent little place with a longish menu of Chinese and Javanese dishes at low prices. Also in the airport area, over the road from the Hotel Melati, the *Rumah Makan Dewi* has cheap Indonesian food.

Getting There & Away

Air Merpati offers the following flights almost daily:

Destination	Fare (rp)
Bajawa	42,000
Bima	86,000
Denpasar	198,000
Jakarta	393,000
Kupang	86,000
Labuhanbajo	99,000
Mataram	173,000
Ruteng	57,000
Surabaya	266,000
Yogyakarta	302,000

The Merpati (☎ 355) office is on Jalan Nangka, a 15-minute walk from the airport.

Bus Terminal Ende is at the north end of town and easily reachable by bemo. However, most hotels will gladly sell you a ticket and arrange for the bus to pick you up on departure. Buses to Moni depart at 7 and 10 am, and occasionally around noon; trucks run throughout the day on Tuesdays (Moni's market day). Buses to Wolowaru and Maumere depart at 8 am, 4 and 5 pm. If you want an afternoon bus to Moni, you can take the Maumere bus but you have to pay the full fare to Maumere.

Buses to and from the west use the downtown terminal on Jalan Hatta. Buses leave for Bajawa at 7 am and noon. If you're heading to Ruteng or Labuhanbajo, you must spend a night in Bajawa. Distance, fares and journey times are:

Destination	Distance	Fare	Time
Moni	52 km	1500 rp	2.5 hrs
Wolowaru	65 km	2000 rp	3 hrs
Maumere	148 km	4000 rp	6.5 hrs
Bajawa	125 km	4000 rp	5 hrs

Boat There is a ferry to Kupang departing Ende every Wednesday at noon. The *Kelimutu* sails every second Saturday from Ende to Kupang and two days later from Ende to Waingapu, during its fortnightly loop round Nusa Tenggara, Sulawesi, Bali, Kalimantan and Java. It puts in at the port of

Ende in front of the town centre. For the complete *Kelimutu* timetable, see the Getting Around chapter in the front of this book. The Pelni office is a five-minute walk from the pier, on the corner of Jalan Pabean and Jalan Sukarno. Fares to/from Ende (in rp) are:

Destination	1st	2nd	Ekonomi
Banjarmasin	333,000	235,000	80,000
Bima	69,000	48,000	20,000
Dilli	77,000	60,000	21,000
Kupang	45,000	35,000	16,000
Lembar	165,000	120,000	46,000
Padangbai	174,000	127,000	48,000
Semarang	279,000	230,000	101,000
Surabaya	237,000	174,000	65,000
Ujung Pandang	125,000	88,000	36,000
Waingapu	34,000	28,000	13,000

Other boats sail irregularly to these and other destinations – ask at the harbour masters' offices at Ende and Pelabuhan Ipi.

Small boats also chug regularly along the south coast of Flores. Boats to Nggela (55 km east of Ende) depart Pelabuhan Ipi daily except Friday at 7.30 am. You may struggle to pay the same price as the locals. Boats to the west are more likely to leave from Ende harbour.

Getting Around

To/From the Airport You could walk, or just go outside the airport and catch a bemo for 250 rp.

Bemo Bemos run very frequently just about everywhere in the town for a flat fare of 250 rp, even out to Pelabuhan Ipi. You can often get one to where you want simply by hailing the first couple of bemos that pass where you are – most of their routes seem to cover the whole town. If not, you can pick up any bemo from the Jalan Pasar market.

For Pelabuhan Ipi, you might have to change bemos at the corner of Jalan Ahmad Yani and Jalan Ipi. To catch a bemo from the airport, walk 100 metres to the roundabout on Jalan Ahmad Yani.

DETUSOKO & CAMAT

Between the villages of Detusoko and

Camat, 35 km from Ende and 113 km from Maumere, *Wisma Santo Fransiskus* is quiet and peaceful. It's presided over by Sister Maria Graciana who has the distinction of producing a book with 100 recipes for tapioca roots! The nightly price of 3500 rp includes good meals. It's a popular retreat from the towns. Three km from the Wisma is a statue to which the locals pay homage and there are other walks in the area. It should even be possible to walk along foot trails all the way to Keli Mutu.

KELI MUTU

Of all the sights in Nusa Tenggara, the coloured lakes of Keli Mutu are the most fantastic. The three lakes, set in deep craters at a height of 1600 metres near the pine-forested summit of the Keli Mutu volcano (in this region 'Keli' means 'mountain') have a habit of changing colour from time to time. Most recently the largest was a light turquoise, the one next to it olive green and the third black. Only a few years ago the colours were blue, maroon and black, while back in the '30s the colour scheme was similar to today's, and in the '60s the lakes had changed to blue, red-brown and cafe-au-lait.

No one has managed to explain the cause of the colours (except to suppose that different minerals are dissolved in each lake) or why they change. The moonscape effect of the craters gives the whole summit area a distinctly otherworldly atmosphere. There is a story among the local people that the souls of the dead go to these lakes: young people's souls to the warmth of the green lake, old people's to the cold of the milky-turquoise one, and those of thieves and murderers to the black lake. How a soul knows which lake to hop into when the colours keep changing, no one explains!

Keli Mutu has attracted sightseers since Dutch times and today there's a 13½-km road, nearly all paved, up to the lakes from near the village of Moni at the base of the mountain. You even get an occasional busload of tourists up there. A gravelled clearing between two of the lakes was constructed in 1980 for a vice-presidential visit.

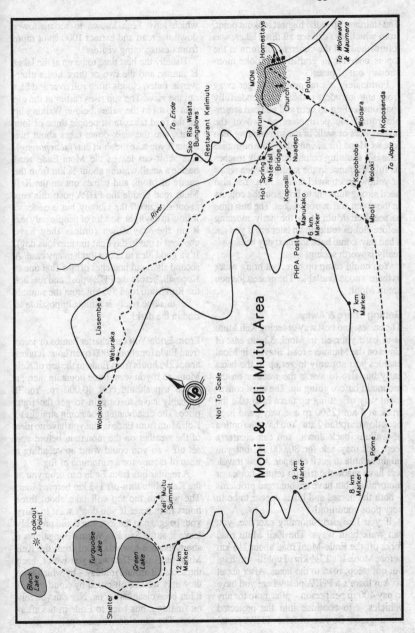

Moni & Keli Mutu Area

Not To Scale

To Ende

To Wolowaru & Maumere

To Japu

Homestays

MONI

Church

Warung

Hot Spring
Waterfall
Bridge

Sao Ria Wisata
Bungalows

Restaurant Kelimutu

Potu

Nuadepi

Koposili

Manukako

PhPA Post

Liasembe

Waturaka

Wolokolo

Keli Mutu Summit

Lookout
Point

Black
Lake

Turquoise
Lake

Green
Lake

Shelter

River

Woloara

Koposenda

Kopobhobe

Woloki

Mboti

Pome

6 km
Marker

7 km
Marker

8 km
Marker

9 km
Marker

12 km
Marker

The staircase up to the highest lookout point, from which you can see all three lakes, was refurbished but the concrete platform at the top is covered in graffiti and looks monstrously out of place.

Fortunately it's no problem to get away from any intruders – there's a wonderfully spacious feeling up here and you can scramble round the perimeters of two of the lake-craters or walk in the surrounding pine forests. Hope for a sunny day – the turquoise lake is a stunning colour but it only reaches its full brilliance in the sunlight when wisps of yellow-green swirl around in it. You also need strong sunlight to bring out the colours in the green and maroon lakes. The best time to see Keli Mutu is in the early morning before clouds settle down later on. If you get a bad day, come back the next day because it really is worth seeing!

You could camp up here, but bring water as there's none available. The nearest losmen are in Moni.

Getting There & Away

The easiest and best way of seeing Keli Mutu is to base yourself in Moni, 52 km east of Ende on the Maumere road. Staying in Moni enables you not only to get up to the lakes early but also to assess the weather on the mountain before going up. The most convenient way of getting up there is to take the truck at 4 am (2500 rp one way), and head back down around 7 am. You have the option of walking back down. You can charter a jeep, but they ask for 30,000 rp, but you might be able to get it cheaper. A few travellers have made the trip on rented horses or motorbikes, but have encountered problems – both the horses and bikes appear to be in very poor condition!

If you like early-morning exercise, you can walk both ways. The Keli Mutu road forks off the Ende-Moni road about 1½ km before Moni. It's 13½ km of uphill-winding, but not steep, road to the lakes. After about six km there's a PHPA post where you have to pay 400 rp per person – plus more for any vehicles – to continue into the protected summit area. Beware of false 'PHPA posts'

which have been known to set up lower down the road and extract 1000 rp or more from unsuspecting visitors!

Usually the best time to be up at the lakes is sunrise and the two or three hours afterwards. Later, clouds often roll over and blot out the view. The sun rises earlier at the top than down in the valley below. Walking up on the road takes most people three or four hours, and the walk down takes about two hours if you take the short cut *(jalan potong)*. The short cut leaves the Moni-Ende road beside a small warung about ¾ km from the centre of Moni, and comes out on the Keli Mutu road beside the PHPA post: this cuts about six km off the journey, but is easier to follow in daylight, so a lot of people only use it on the way down (unless they have checked it out in daylight the previous day). It's a good idea to take a torch in any case. A second short cut branches off the first one at Koposili, before the PHPA post, and reaches the Keli Mutu road 5½ km from the summit – but this one really is almost impossible to find in the dark!

From Ende You can charter bemos or jeeps from Ende for about 5000 rp an hour. It takes about 2½ hours from Ende to the top of Keli Mutu, so if you want three hours up there, a round trip should cost 40,000 rp. You'll probably have to bargain to get the right price. The disadvantage of going straight to Keli Mutu from Ende is that you have no idea of the weather on the mountain before you set off – so you could wind up spending a heap of money for a panorama of fog.

A regular bus from Ende can drop you at the Keli Mutu turn-off 1½ km before Moni. The walk to the top will take about three hours from here. If you don't want to carry your baggage to the top, you could probably leave it at the Sao Ria Wisata Bungalows a short distance towards Moni from the Keli Mutu turn- off. This way, you won't reach the lakes till around midday – by which time they may well be obscured by cloud even if it has been clear earlier on. Nor can you rely on finding a bus back to Ende in the afternoon. The same drawbacks apply to going direct from Maumere, which is even more expensive than from Ende.

MONI (MONE)

This village strung along the Ende-Maumere road at the base of Keli Mutu is in the heart of the Lio region, which extends from just east of Ende to beyond Wolowaru. Lio people speak a dialect of the Ende language and are renowned for their fine ikat weaving, which reaches its height in the coastal village of Nggela. A colourful hill-country market spreads over the playing field in front of Moni's large church every Tuesday morning. People start arriving in Moni on Monday afternoon for the market. The local Moni/Keli Mutu area ikat is quite attractive with bands of blue and rusty-red, but you'll see cloth from the Nggela and Maumere regions too.

In the church an image of Christ stands inside a model rumah adat – a revealing symbol of how Christianity has been fused with traditional beliefs. In the kampung behind the Moni homestays there's a genuine high-thatched rumah adat, still inhabited, with some carved woodwork. You may be asked 500 rp to enter.

Apart from the trek up Keli Mutu, you can do several shorter walks from Moni. From the warung at the beginning of the short cut to Keli Mutu, ¾ km along the Ende road from the middle of Moni, paths lead down to a 10-metre waterfall, with a pool big enough for swimming in, and a couple of hot springs (mandi panas). Locals sometimes use these for washing their clothes and themselves. Another short walk is out past the church to the villages of Potu and Woloara (about 1½ km from Moni). From Woloara you could continue to Jopu, about five km further.

Orientation

The road from Ende winds downhill into Moni, passing the Keli Mutu turn-off and Sao Ria Wisata bungalows about 1½ km before the centre of the village, which focuses on the market and playing field beside the main road. Homestays are across the road from the market; the church and Wisma Kelimutu are behind the playing field.

Places to Stay & Eat

Several new places have opened in Moni and competition between them can be keen. Along the main road, opposite the market, are five very popular and cheap places where beds are rented on a per person basis: *Homestay Daniel* (3000 rp), *Homestay Amina Moe I* (3500 rp), *Homestay Amina Moe II* (4000 rp), *Homestay John* (3000 rp) and *Homestay Friendly* (3000 rp). All have shared bath only and do decent meals if you order in advance. Homestay John has vegetarian food.

Wisma Kelimutu is run by the Catholic church next door and has bigger rooms than the homestays at 5000 rp per person with shared mandi. The accommodation is fine but the food is ordinary. The other option is *Sao Ria Wisata*, a set of small government-owned bungalows with private mandi 1½ km out of Moni close to the Ende road, near the Keli Mutu turn-off. The cost here is 5500 rp per person, but the problem is that it seems to be always full. One other place is *Homestay Nusa Bunga* (3000 rp per person), but it's about one km from the market making it a little inconvenient for the restaurants.

A popular place to eat is *Restaurant Moni-Indah* next to Homestay Daniel. Their food is cheap and good, and they also have two rooms for rent but charge a whopping 9000/11,000 rp for singles/doubles with shared bath. Near to the Moni-Indah is *Restaurant Adriani* which can do frogs on special request. You can also try the small *Wisata Restaurant* about 200 metres away. *Restaurant Kelimutu* is a decent tourist-oriented restaurant 200 metres down the road from Sao Ria Wisata.

Getting There & Away

Moni is 52 km from Ende and 96 km from Maumere. The first bus for Moni usually leaves Ende at 7 am. The fare is 1500 rp for the 2½-hour trip. From Moni to Ende, there is an early morning truck (2500 rp) around 8 am, the same truck which first goes to Keli Mutu. Otherwise, wait for a bus from Maumere at about 11 am. There are also usually others coming through from Wolowaru at about 7 or 8 am. On Tuesday, market day, trucks go to Ende and Wolowaru throughout the day.

From Maumere to Moni, you probably need to take an Ende bus. These start leaving about 7.30 or 8 am. Maumere to Moni costs 2500 rp and takes about four hours including a half-hour break for lunch in Wolowaru, just 13 km before Moni. In the opposite direction, the first buses to Maumere start coming through Moni around 9 or 10 am. Buses through Moni from Ende or Maumere are usually pretty crowded: sometimes you'll have to stand, or you may even have to wait for the next bus. On night buses you will often be required to pay the Maumere-Ende fare (4000 rp) even if you're getting off at Moni. From Moni to Wolowaru costs 250 rp.

Most hotels in Moni can book you a ticket to either Ende or Maumere if you order one day in advance.

WOLOWARU

The village of Wolowaru, straggling along the Maumere road 13 km east of Moni, is a convenient base for visiting the ikat-weaving villages of Jopu, Wolojita and Nggela. The road to these villages branches south from the main road in Wolowaru. Wolowaru itself also has quite a few weavers: people may approach you with ikat to sell, or you may be invited into houses. Otherwise look at the daily market – it winds down about 9 am except on Saturday, the main market day. As you come into Wolowaru from Ende you'll see a group of five traditional houses distinguished by their high sloping roofs.

Places to Stay

The *Losmen Kelimutu*, beside the Rumah Makan Jawa Timur where most buses stop, has helpful staff and decent singles/doubles for 4400/7700 rp with shared mandi and 5500/9900 rp with private mandi. Prices include breakfast.

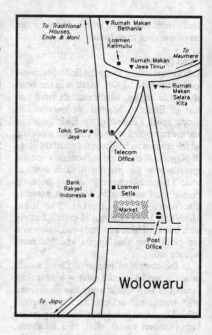

Wolowaru

Losmen Setia, down near the market on Jalan Pasar Wolowaru, is older but still clean. They only have four rooms, two with attached bath (4000 rp per person) and two with shared bath (3000 rp).

Place to Eat

The three rumah makan, the *Jawa Timur*, the *Selara Kita* and the *Bethania* (which is a few hundred metres up the road towards Moni) are all similar with reasonably long menus. Jawa Timur has good bread, and you can buy a loaf to take away.

Getting There & Away

A couple of Wolowaru buses run to and from Maumere and Ende, so you can usually get an early morning departure to and from either place. Leaving Wolowaru it's advisable to book your place the day before. Losmen may fix this for you, or see bus agents such as the Rumah Makan Bethania or the Toko Sinar Jaya. Fares from Wolowaru are: Ende 1500 rp (2½ hours), Maumere from 2500 to 4000 rp (four hours), Moni 500 rp (30 minutes). Otherwise wait around the Rumah Makan Jawa Timur for a bus heading in your direction; you should be able to get one to Maumere or Ende around 10 am to midday – and there may be more at about 7 or 8 pm. As in Moni, it's first come, first served for seats if you're hopping on a bus in mid-route.

NGGELA, WOLOJITA & JOPU

Beautiful ikat sarongs and shawls can be found in these and other small villages between Wolowaru and the south coast.

Though also worth a visit for its fine hilltop position above the coast, the chief attraction of Nggela is its stunning weaving; it's done by hand and still uses many natural dyes and often handspun cotton. This is among the finest weaving in Flores and you'll be able to see women weaving it as

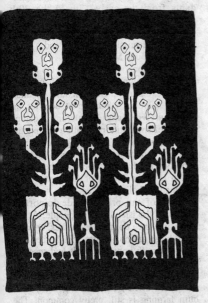

Skull tree – ikat motif

well as the final products. In former times the size, colour and pattern of the ikat shawls of this region indicated the status of the wearer. Patterns range from intricate patola designs to more recent representations of animals, people, ships, and nowadays even Keli Mutu. Nggela ikat has typically black or dark-brown backgrounds with patterns in earthy reds, browns or orange.

You have to bargain hard if you want to buy; for a sarong the starting price might be 100,000 rp, whereas 30,000 or 35,000 rp is more realistic. A selendang (shawl) should cost from around 15,000 to 20,000 rp. As always, watch out for synthetic dyes – though these are a lot less common in Nggela than in many other weaving centres. Nggela ikat is also sold in Ende, Wolowaru and Moni. In the village there are a number of traditional houses as well as a large church and Christian graves. You can stay with the kepala desa or maybe another family for around 4000 rp including a couple of meals.

Wolojita, about 3½ km inland from Nggela, has similar quality weavings but doesn't have Nggela's fine location. At Jopu, a further four km inland and the same distance from Wolowaru, weaving has taken a plunge in the last few years. They no longer seem to use natural dyes, and the designs are not as intricate – once you used to get soft pastel oranges and yellows, but now it's bright yellows with garish red splotches or borders. Still, you might pick up a reasonably good sarong for from 10,000 to 15,000 rp or a poor one for 3000 rp. Old weaving could be worth looking at – there might still be examples of cloth using natural dyes and the patterns may be more intricate. Jopu has a very big church and a market on Thursday.

Getting There & Away

A rough road branches off the Ende-Maumere road at Wolowaru to Jopu (four km), Wolojita (eight km) and Nggela (11½ km). Occasionally a bus or truck goes down it in the morning, but usually you must walk from Wolowaru. It's only two or three km further from Moni, so you could almost as easily start from there. An alternative is the

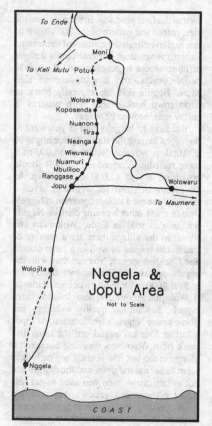

Nggela & Jopu Area

Not to Scale

COAST

small boat which chugs every day except Friday from Pelabuhan Ipi at Ende to Nggela and back. It leaves Pelabuhan Ipi at around 7.30 am and takes about 3½ hours to Nggela if it doesn't make too many stops and isn't too overloaded. The cost is from 1000 rp. Going from Nggela to Ende, the boat usually leaves at about noon. You board or disembark at Nggela by canoe from a rocky cove about 1½ km below the village.

It's an interesting walk from Wolowaru, so long as you avoid the heat of the day. The volcano-studded skyline is beautiful, particularly near Nggela. From Wolowaru it's

about an hour's walk to Jopu, then about an hour from Jopu to Wolojita. From Wolojita to Nggela you can either follow the 'road' or take a short cut (ask for the *jalan potong ke Nggela*). Allow about an hour down to Nggela, a bit more going back uphill. You can easily get from Wolowaru to Nggela and back in a day, even if you have to walk both stretches and allow plenty of time for rests. You might be offered drinks in villages on the way, but take your own too. From Moni, it's a six or seven km walk to Jopu via the villages of Potu and Woloara.

MAUMERE

This seaport of about 40,000 people on the north coast is the main town of the Sikka district which covers the neck of land between central Flores and the Larantuka district in the east. The Sikkanese language is closer to that of Larantuka than to Endenese. The name Sikka is taken from a village in a district on the south coast controlled by Portuguese rulers and their Christian descendants from the early 17th to the 20th centuries. This area has long been one of the chief centres of Catholic activity on Flores with several missions, schools and a large seminary around Maumere.

The missionaries were one of the largest groups of foreigners to establish themselves on Flores: Dutch, German and Spanish priests, some of whom spent decades on Flores surviving Japanese internment camps and an often hostile population during the independence wars. The Portuguese Dominicans were the first to arrive some 400 years ago, then the Jesuits came with the Dutch, and in 1913 the Society of the Divine Word (German Catholics) arrived.

Many of the priests made important studies of the island and its people. At the same time they doubled as medics, encouraged local art and crafts and helped the Florinese with improved tools and seed for their agriculture – as little as two decades ago many Florinese were still tilling the soil with sharpened sticks, and moving slash-and-burn farming is still pretty common. The missions were once real oases and visitors were often dependent on them for transport and, in pre-Bahasa Indonesia days, for their understanding of the local language. Today the European priests are slowly being replaced by Florinese.

To prove that God isn't always White, the interior of Maumere's cathedral on Jalan Slamet Riyadi is adorned with a series of paintings of the crucifixion of a very Indonesian-looking Jesus. A cemetary behind the cathedral is full of tombstones/ monuments to the Western impact on Indonesia. There's a strong ikat-weaving tradition in the Maumere region, and a few interesting trips can be made out of the town. Maumere itself is a rather functional place, though the market is interesting – look for heavy ikat blankets. A shop on Jalan Pasar Baru Timur, beside the market, has the most comprehensive collection of ikat (from Flores and other islands) that you'll find anywhere in Nusa Tenggara except Sumba.

Orientation & Information

Maumere is a rather spread-out town but most of what you're likely to need is within walking distance of the central market – apart from the bus station (1½ km south-

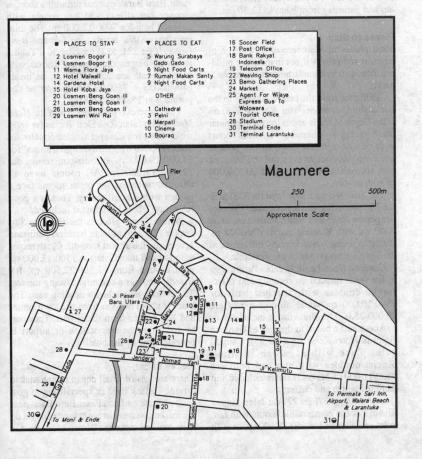

■ PLACES TO STAY	▼ PLACES TO EAT	16 Soccer Field
2 Losmen Bogor I	5 Warung Surabaya	17 Post Office
4 Losmen Bogor II	Gado Gado	18 Bank Rakyat Indonesia
11 Wisma Flora Jaya	6 Night Food Carts	19 Telecom Office
12 Hotel Maiwali	7 Rumah Makan Santy	22 Weaving Shop
14 Gardena Hotel	9 Night Food Carts	23 Bemo Gathering Places
15 Hotel Koba Jaya		24 Market
20 Losmen Beng Goan III	OTHER	25 Agent For Wijaya Express Bus To Wolowara
21 Losmen Beng Goan I	1 Cathedral	27 Tourist Office
26 Losmen Beng Goan II	3 Pelni	28 Stadium
29 Losmen Wini Rai	8 Merpati	30 Terminal Ende
	10 Cinema	31 Terminal Larantuka
	13 Bouraq	

Maumere

0   250   500m

Approximate Scale

west of the centre), the airport (three km east) and a couple of hotels on the way out to them.

Tourist Office The Kantor Dinas Pariwisata is just off Jalan Gajah Mada (see map).

Money The Bank Rakyat Indonesia on Jalan Soekarno Hatta is open from 8 am to noon Monday to Friday, and from 8 to 11 am Saturday.

Post The post office is on Jalan Pos next to the soccer field – hours are Monday to Thursday from 8 am to 2 pm, Friday from 8 to 11 am and Saturday from 8 am to 12.30 pm.

Places to Stay

Most places in Maumere offer a range of comfort and price – if not in the same building then in sister-establishments a short walk away.

A little far from the centre but near to the bus station, *Losmen Wini Rai* (☎ 388) on Jalan Gajah Mada is about the most popular place to stay in Maumere. No-frills rooms with outside bath are 5000 rp per person, while singles/doubles with fan and attached bath are 9000/15,000 rp, and 25,000/30,000 rp with air-con.

The little *Wisma Flora Jaya* (☎ 333) near the Merpati office is very popular. The cost per person for rooms with common mandi is 5000 rp; with attached mandi it's 6000 rp. It's clean, homely and friendly but rooms at the front are noisy. Meals are available.

Gardena Hotel (☎ 489), Jalan Pattirangga 5, has been spruced up recently and offers singles/doubles with attached bath for 7500/10,000 rp, while air-con rooms are 20,000/25,000 rp. Breakfast is included.

About half a block to the east of Gardena Hotel is *Hotel Koba Jaya* (☎ 73), a small, quiet place with a garden in front. Singles/doubles with attached bath are 5500/11,000 rp. No breakfast is included, but there is free tea and coffee.

Losmen Bogor II (☎ 271) at Jalan Slamet Riyadi 1-4 has comfortable rooms with fan, toilet and shower for 6600/8,500 rp, or with shared bath for 4400/6600 rp, including breakfast. It could get a bit hot here since most of the rooms are along a single corridor. Across the road, *Losmen Bogor I* is a brothel, but it's cheaper (excluding special services) at 2750 rp per person.

Losmen Beng Goan I (☎ 41), across the road from the market on Jalan Pasar Baru, is clean enough and relatively quiet. Basic singles/doubles with shared bath are 4500/8000 rp, or with fan, attached mandi and toilet 7000/12,500 rp. Beds have mosquito nets and there's an outdoor sitting area. *Losmen Beng Goan II* (☎ 283), on Jalan Pasar Baru Barat, entered through a shop, is cleaner but airless and has rooms with attached bath for 7000/12,000 rp. The third member of this family, the *Losmen Beng Goan III* (☎ 284, 532) on Jalan K S Tubun, is newer, bigger and cleaner. Rooms with common bath are 3500/6000 rp, an inside bath makes it 7500/12,500 rp and air-con pushes it to 15,000/20,000 rp.

The fanciest place in town is *Hotel Maiwali* on Jalan Raja Don Tomas (☎ 180), which has a few cheaper singles/doubles for 9000/16,800 rp, mid-range rooms for 14,000/19,600 rp and air-con rooms for 22,400/39,200 rp. All rooms have an attached bath, and the better rooms face a garden with a small aviary. There's a good restaurant where breakfast is included.

Another good place is the *Permata Sari Inn* (☎ 171, 249) at Jalan Jenderal Sudirman 1, opposite the airport turn-off. Clean rooms with fan and mandi start at 7500/12,000 rp, with air-con from 17,500/22,500 rp. It's friendly and has a restaurant facing the sea. To get here, take a bemo heading east. The hotel is about two km from the town centre and 800 metres from the airport. Transport to and from the bus station or airport is provided free by the hotel.

Places to Eat

There are lots of small cheap rumah makan serving Padang food or specialising in goat soup and sate on Jalan Pasar Baru Barat near the market. Numerous night food carts set up here too and near the Hotel Maiwali. On

Jalan Pasar Baru nearer the water is the *Warung Surabaya Gado Gado*, specialising in guess what? *Rumah Makan Santy* is spacious and clean with a long menu.

Losmen Bogor I has a reasonable restaurant with a long menu though many dishes are unavailable. The food is tasty and portions large. The restaurant at the *Hotel Maiwali* is very good with a more tourist-oriented menu including burgers, spaghetti, fried prawns, fruit juices and fresh fruit, along with the usual basic Indonesian dishes.

Getting There & Away

Air Maumere is the easiest place on Flores to fly into from other islands, but there are no flights to anywhere else on Flores. Merpati has daily flights to/from Balikpapan (275,000 rp), Denpasar (181,000 rp), Kupang (65,000 rp), Tarakan (409,000 rp) and Ujung Pandang (125,000 rp). With connections you can also go the same day to Jakarta (376,000 rp), Mataram, Palu, Samarinda (319,000 rp), Surabaya (231,000 rp), Semarang (290,000 rp) and Yogyakarta. Merpati (☎ 342) has its office on Jalan Raja Don Tomas.

Bouraq (☎ 165), on Jalan Pasar Baru Timur, has three non-stop flights a week to/from Denpasar (175,000 rp), with same day connections to Jakarta (381,000 rp), Kupang (63,000 rp) and Surabaya (225,000 rp).

Local Transport Long-distance buses leave from the main bus station, Ende, 1½ km from the centre on the Ende road, but hotels can arrange to have the bus come and pick you up. Buses go east to Larantuka (4000 rp, about four hours) and west to Ende (4000 rp, six hours). To Larantuka, they leave about hourly from 8 am to noon and at about 4 and 5 pm. Ende buses start at 7 am, but there's an evening bus at 5 pm. The buses to Larantuka also stop at Larantuka station while keliling around town. There are also usually some morning buses just to Wolowaru (2500 rp). For Moni, take an Ende bus, and you will probably be forced to buy a ticket to Ende even though you want to get off at Moni.

Bemos and small buses leave frequently all through the day to places in the Maumere district like Lela, Sikka, Ladalero and Watublapi. Some go from around the main market but, if you get no joy there ,take one for 200 rp to the main bus station and find another to where you want.

Boat The Pelni office is on Jalan Slamet Riyadi, across the road from the Losmen Bogor. There are no regular passenger craft but you may be able to find something to Reo, Labuhanbajo, Bima, Ujung Pandang or even Surabaya. PT Ujung Tana on Jalan Masjid is an agent for an irregular boat to Ujung Pandang. Also ask around the harbour.

Getting Around

To/From the Airport Maumere's Wai Oti airport is three km out of town, 800 metres off the Maumere-Larantuka road. A taxi to/from town is 3000 rp. Otherwise, it's a long walk from the airport down to the Maumere-Larantuka road to pick up a public bemo (200 rp) into town. Merpati plans to soon start running a shuttle bus for their passengers.

Bemo These cruise the streets regularly and cost 200 rp anyplace within the city.

AROUND MAUMERE
Ladalero & Nita

Many Florinese priests studied at the Roman Catholic seminary in Ladalero, 10 km from Maumere on the Ende road. The chief attraction is the museum run by Father Piet Petu, a Florinese. This has been going for around 20 years, originally with a collection of prehistoric stone implements, but over the past few years Piet Petu has built up a collection of Florinese ikat (some of it for sale) – you'll see examples of design and natural dyes that are either rare or extinct, including softly textured, pastel-coloured old Jopu sarongs. There are also many photo albums showing Florinese rituals and artefacts. All in all, despite its somewhat haphazard layout, the museum is an excellent place to try to piece together the jigsaw of Florinese culture.

It also has an interesting collection of artefacts from elsewhere in Indonesia. Father Petu speaks English and is most helpful, but if he's not there, other attendants speaking varying amounts of English can answer questions. The best way to repay him is to make a donation to the museum! It's closed on Sunday.

Nita, two km beyond Ladalero on the main road, has a Thursday market. There are bemos to Ladalero and Nita from Maumere bus station for 200 rp.

Sikka
On the south coast, 27 km from Maumere, Sikka was one of the earliest Portuguese settlements in Flores dating from the early 17th century; it remained in Portuguese control till the mid-19th century. Its rulers dominated the Maumere region until this century. Today it's interesting mainly as the chief home of the distinctive Sikkanese ikat. A lot of Sikka weaving is predominantly in maroons, blues and browns, and designs have been heavily influenced by the Dutch – you see the Dutch royal coat of arms and

even pairs of baby cherubim probably copied from Dutch porcelain. Prices for the stuff, however, seem to be no lower in the village than in Maumere.

You may be able to stay with the Dutch priest in Sikka. The road to Sikka leaves the Ende road 20 km from Maumere. Take a bemo from Maumere to Sikka – 500 rp, about one hour. About four km before Sikka, Lela is also a Catholic and weaving centre and boasts a large hospital and a few colonial buildings. There's a long, rocky black-sand beach here.

Watublapi
In the hills south-east of Maumere is the large Catholic Mission of Watublapi. From here, you can walk to Ohe and other villages where you can see both coasts of Flores.

Pantai Waiara
Thirteen km east of Maumere, just off the Larantuka road, Waiara is the jumping-off point for the Maumere 'sea gardens'. There's coral inshore here, but in the wet season the water can get so murky you'll hardly see the end of your nose. To get the best out of snorkelling here you may need to rent a boat

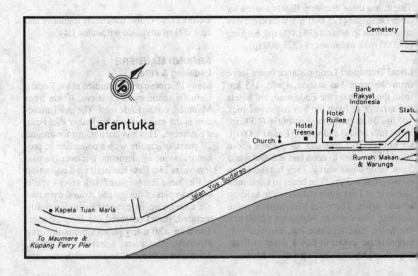

– the coral round the offshore islands of Pulau Besar, Pulau Kambing and Pulau Pemana is supposed to be particularly good.

Two establishments at Waiara provide accommodation, food and equipment for divers and snorkellers. The newer, more luxurious *Sao Wisata* offers a diving package with two dives a day for between 126,750 rp and 224,250 rp per person a day, depending on the room and how many share it. Just to stay there, without the diving, costs from 58,500 to 136,500 rp including meals and transport to/from Maumere airport. The Merpati office in Maumere acts as an agent for Sao Wisata.

The more dilapidated *Sea World Club*, also called *Waiara Cottages*, charges 48,750 rp a day for a bungalow (for one or two people) and breakfast; lunch is 7800 rp per person, dinner 9750 rp. It also has boats and diving and snorkelling gear for hire. Snorkelling gear costs 3000 rp a day. You can eat and take a dip at Sea World's semi-private beach without staying there, if you just want a day out from Maumere though, the beach is nothing special.

Renting a boat alone from one of these establishments would probably cost 30,000

rp or more. Try bargaining – or look for a fisher to take you out (and bargain again). Whoever takes you, make sure they know where the good snorkelling spots are!

Getting There & Away By public transport, take a Talibura bus from Maumere to Waiara (300 rp), or a bemo to Geliting (250 rp) then walk 1½ km along the Larantuka road. A sign points to Sea World Club/Waiara Cottages, which is about 300 metres off the road. The turn-off to Sao Wisata is a further 500 metres along the road towards Larantuka.

LARANTUKA

This little port of about 25,000 people nestles round the base of the Ili Mandiri volcano at the eastern end of Flores, separated by a narrow strait from the islands of Solor and Adonara. Larantuka is the departure point for boats to the Solor Archipelago east of Flores and for a twice-weekly ferry to Kupang.

The Larantuka area has long had closer links with the islands of the Solor Archipelago – Adonara, Solor and Lembata – than with the rest of Flores. It shares a language, Lamaholot, with the islands. The whole area, particularly outside the towns, fascinates

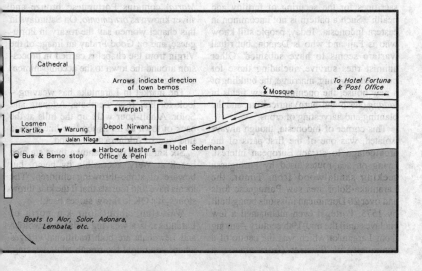

anthropologists because of a complex social and ritual structure which in some parts survives pretty well intact. There's a web of myths about the origins of the Lamaholot people: one version has them descended from the offspring of Watowele, the extremely hairy female god of Ili Mandiri, and a character called Patigolo who was washed ashore, got Watowele drunk, cut her hair (thus simultaneously removing her magic powers and discovering that she was female) and made her pregnant. Alternatively, locals believe their forebears came from *Sina Jawa* ('China Java'), Seram or India – take your pick.

At some stage, probably before the 16th century, the Lamaholot area became divided between two groups known as the Demon and the Paji. The Demon, associated with the 'Raja' of Larantuka, were mainly grouped in east Flores and the western parts of Adonara, Solor and Lembata; the Paji, with allegiance to the 'Raja' of Adonara, were centred in the eastern parts of the three islands. Anthropologists tend to believe that the conflict between the two groups was mainly a ritual affair – as one writer puts it, 'two groups representing the two halves of the universe engaged in regular combat to produce human sacrifices for the securing of fertility and health'. Such a pattern is not uncommon in eastern Indonesia. Today, people still know who is Paji and who is Demon, but ritual warfare seems to have subsided. Other animist rites survive, including those for birth, name-giving, marriage, the building of a new house, the opening of new fields in *ladang* (slash-and-burn) agriculture, and the planting and harvesting of crops.

This corner of Indonesia, though always isolated, was one of the first parts of the archipelago to attract European interest. Lying on sea routes used by Portuguese seeking sandalwood from Timor, the Larantuka-Solor area saw Portuguese forts and over 20 Dominican missions being built by 1575. Portugal even maintained a few enclaves until the mid-19th century – among them Larantuka which was the centre of a community of *Topasses* (from *tupassi*, a south Indian word for 'interpreter'), the descendants of Portuguese men and local women. The Topasses are still a significant group in Larantuka today.

Orientation & Information

Most hotels, ferry pier, shipping offices and the main bus stop are in the compact southern part of town (shown on the map). Further north-east are the homes, mosques and fishing boats of the Muslim population – and the post office, airport and Hotel Fortuna. To the south is the pier for boats to Kupang.

There's some kind of tourist office, Bapparda, at Batuata, near the post office which is on Jalan Pasar, a few km north of the centre, past the main market. Take a bemo from the centre of town opposite the main pier. Hours are Monday to Thursday from 8 am to 2 pm, Friday from 8 to 11 am and Saturday from 8 am to 12.30 pm.

The only place in town to change money is Bank Rakyat Indonesia on Jalan Yos Sudarso.

Things to See

Portuguese-style Catholicism also flourishes in Larantuka. There's a large cathedral, and the smaller Holy Mary Chapel *(Kapela Tuan Maria)* contains Portuguese bronze and silver known as *ornamento*. On Saturdays in this chapel women say the rosary in Portuguese, and on Good Friday an image of the Virgin from the chapel is carried in procession around the town to the accompaniment of songs in Latin.

The market in Larantuka has weaving – look for ikat from Lembata, Adonara and Solor. A half-hour walk up the hills at the back of town as far as the tree line gives a fine view of Adonara and beyond.

Six km north of Larantuka there's a nice beach at Wery, accessible by bemo, but beware of stone-throwing children. The locals have told tourists that if the kids throw stones, it's OK to throw stones back!

Waibalun, about four km north of Larantuka, is a weaving village. Lewoloba and Lewohala are both traditional villages where you might see rumah adat, weaving, or ceremonies of various kinds. People in Larantuka might know about upcoming village festivities. Lewoloba and Lewohala are both near the village of Oka (200 rp by bemo). In Oka, ask the kepala desa for someone to show you the short walk to Lewoloba.

Places to Stay & Eat

The friendly, spotless and spacious *Hotel Rulies* (☎ 198) at Jalan Yos Sudarso 44 is recommended, with rooms at 5500 rp per person. The mandis are outside and meals are available.

Next door, the *Hotel Tresna* (☎ 72) has different levels of accommodation. Economy rooms have outside mandi and cost 6050 rp per person. Standard and VIP rooms cost 9080 rp and 13,200 rp respectively. Some of the rooms look nicer from the outside than they are within. Meals are served here.

Right in the middle of town near the ferry pier is the seedy-looking *Losmen Kartika* (☎ 83), Jalan Jenderal Sudirman 4. The asking price is 3500 rp per person. A similar low standard and the same prices can be found at the *Hotel Sederhana* on Jalan Niaga.

The top place in town is the new *Hotel Fortuna* (☎ 190), two km north-east of town at Jalan Diponegoro 171. All rooms have private bath. Economy singles are 5500 rp while higher-standard rooms are 8250 rp.

There's a clutch of rumah makan/warungs on the right as you go down to the pier.

Getting There & Away

Air Merpati flies from Kupang to Larantuka (81,000 rp), then on to Lewoleba on Lembata and back to Kupang, twice a week. Its office is house No 64, diagonally opposite the cathedral.

Bus Buses to/from Maumere cost 4000 rp and take about four hours. If you're coming in by boat from the Solor archipelago there'll almost certainly be enthusiastic touts ready to arm-wrestle you into waiting buses and whisk you away to Maumere.

Boat The Kupang-Larantuka ferry departs Kupang on Mondays and Thursdays at 3 pm. Going the other way, departures from Larantuka are Mondays and Fridays at 2 pm. You can buy tickets from the office at the pier entrance the same day. The price for the 12-hour voyage is 11,500 rp. There are some seats on board but they get pretty crowded: it's better to find some deck space and rent a sleeping mat on board – the earlier you board the better, since the under-cover deck space fills up pretty fast. Take your own food and drink as there's none available once the ferry has sailed. Departures are from a pier five km south-west of Larantuka which is reachable by taking a yellow-bulb bemo for 200 rp.

Smaller boats to Adonara, Solor and Lembata leave virtually daily from the same pier – see the Solor & Alor archipelagos section. For information on these and other boats out of Larantuka ask around the pier or go to the Pelni and harbour master's offices on Jalan Niaga. Unlikely possibilities occasionally crop up – boats taking Florinese workers to Sabah, cargo ships to Surabaya and Ujung Pandang. The mission ship *Ratu Rosario* is still doing its regular three-week run from Kupang to Surabaya through other ports in Nusa Tenggara, and will take passengers.

Getting Around

To/From the Airport Chartering a bemo to the airport costs 3000 rp per person.

Bemos Bemos run up and down Jalan Niaga and Jalan Pasar and to outlying villages. Catch them from Jalan Niaga opposite the pier. Bemos in town cost 200 rp.

Solor & Alor Archipelagos

A chain of small islands stretches out from the eastern end of Flores: volcanic, mountainous specks separated by swift, narrow

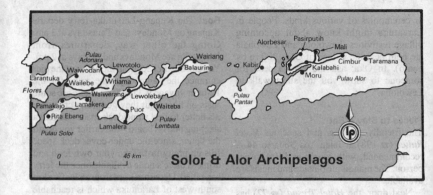

Solor & Alor Archipelagos

straits. Adonara is directly opposite Larantuka; south of Adonara is Solor where the Portuguese first established themselves in the 16th century; further east is Lembata (formerly Lomblen), with the fishing village of Lamalera where whales are still hunted with small boats and harpoons; beyond that are the islands of Pantar and Alor whose people were still head-hunting in the 1950s. The Solor Archipelago – Solor, Adonara and Lembata – has close cultural links with the Larantuka area on Flores and together these people are known as the Lamaholot. Pantar and Alor are the main islands of the Alor Archipelago.

In remote villages, people are extremely poor and not used to Westerners: children and adults will follow you in large excited bunches, and about 20 or 30 of them will gather around the table to watch you eat. They won't follow you into the toilet, but will wait enthusiastically just outside the door for your return. They will follow you right into the house where you're staying, and there is little you can do to prevent this, since your room will not likely have a door. Security can be a problem since there is no way to lock up your luggage. Sleep with your money belt around your waist. Food is generally very poor. If you're looking for a Third World experience, you'll get it. If you can't deal with all this, then limit your stay to the urban centres of Kalabahi and Lewoleba, and

make a few day trips into the surrounding countryside.

One thing you should bring is plenty of money. There is one moneychanger in Kalabahi and that's it for this entire group of islands! Even Lewoleba has no place to change money. Bring a stack of 100, 500, 1000 and 5000 rp notes – people seldom have any change outside of the city.

By way of compensation, the scenery is spectacular, especially on Alor which is the crown jewel of these islands. All the islands, notably Lembata, produce distinctive ikat weaving, and there are some very traditional, almost purely animist villages, despite the spread of Christianity and (less so) Islam.

Kalabahi (Alor) is the main city in these islands, with reliable air and boat connections to Kupang (Timor). Leboleba (Lembata) is the second major city, with small ferries sailing almost every day from Larantuka on Flores and two flights weekly from Kupang. See the sections on these two cities for transport details – the section on Lewoleba has information on the boat connection between Lembata and Alor.

Alor has some bemos. Elsewhere, be prepared to walk – potholes and rocks masquerade as roads and the only motorised transport is maybe one or two trucks per week.

Living conditions are quite comfortable in Kalabahi on Alor Island, and to a lesser extent, in Lewoleba on Lembata Island. However, outside of these two population centres, be prepared for stays in horrific accommodation.

History

European contact was made as early as 1522 when the only remaining ship of Magellan's fleet sailed through the Lembata- Pantar strait. By the middle of the century the Dominican Portuguese friar Antonio Taveira had landed on Solor and set about spreading Catholicism. The Solor mission became the base for extending Christianity to mainland Flores, and a fort was built to protect the converts from Muslim raids. The Portuguese were eventually kicked out of Solor by the Dutch, but until the mid-19th century Portugal held on to Wurek on Adonara and Pamakajo on Solor, while holding claims to Lembata, Pantar and Alor.

SOLOR

Rita-Ebang is the main town on this island. Lohajong towards the east end of the north coast has the ruins of the Portuguese fort. Lamakera on the north-east tip is, like Lamalera on Lembata, a whaling village.

Getting There & Away

From Larantuka there are boats to Pamakajo and Lohajong every morning at about 8 am. From Waiwerang on Adonara boats cross several times a day to Lohajong and Lamakera.

ADONARA

Adonara was known as the 'Island of Murderers' because of a feud between two clans which ran (it is said) for hundreds of years with people in the hills being killed and houses burned year in, year out – very likely a case of ritual conflict between the Demon and Paji groups (see Larantuka). Though such extremes of animism seem to have died out, there are still villages in the hinterland where Christianity has only the loosest of footholds. One traveller reported placing her hands on a sacred rock above one village and being unable to remove them! The chief

settlements are Wailebe on the west coast and Waiwerang on the south. A few bemos link the main villages.

Waiwerang

There's an uninspiring market every Monday and Thursday – follow the streets about 400 metres in the Lembata direction from the pier. *Losmen Taufiq*, run by a stern but friendly Muslim woman, is on the main street a minute's walk from the pier. *Losmen Tresna* is supposedly a little cheaper. A few rumah makan dot the main street and there's another opposite the market.

Getting There & Away

Boats to Waiwerang depart Larantuka every day around 8 or 9 am and noon. The two-hour trip costs 1500 rp. To Wailebe and Waiwodan, further up the west coast) boats usually leave Larantuka about 11 am. At Waiwerang you can pick up boats to Solor any day, to Lewoleba on Lembata most days, to Lamalera on Lembata usually once a week, to Pantar/Alor maybe twice a week.

LEMBATA (LOMBLEN)

Lembata is well known for the whale-hunting village of Lamalera on the south coast. As in the rest of the Lamaholot region, many Lembata inhabitants still use the slash-and-burn method of clearing land – a technique relatively low on labour but high on soil depletion and erosion and which forces the field to lie fallow for several years between crops. Corn, bananas, papayas, and coconuts are grown and most rice is imported.

Lewoleba

Despite Ili Api volcano's smoking ominously in the background, Lewoleba is a relaxed little place and the chief settlement on Lembata. Boats unload you at a pier about a 15-minute walk west of the town – as you exit the pier, turn left. A similar distance from the pier, away from the town, are some fine, empty beaches. Between the pier and town is a Bugis stilt village built out over the sea – some of its people are pearl divers and you can arrange to go out with them on diving trips and/or buy pearls at absurdly low prices. Locals will also take you out to a sandbank off Lewoleba for swimming or snorkelling.

Orientation & Information The centre of Lewoleba is its market place, which comes alive every Monday afternoon and evening with buyers and sellers from around Lembata and other islands. The post office is near the south side of the market and the Merpati agent is in the Losmen Rejeki.

Money The banks do *not* change money, so bring sufficient funds or you'll be sorry!

Places to Stay & Eat The pleasant little *Losmen Rejeki I* is in the centre of town opposite the market. Under the same management is the newer *Losmen Rejeki II* which costs the same price, 5500 rp per person. Mandis are shared but clean. The food's reasonable too – 2000 rp for a big evening meal and you get free tea or coffee three times a day (but only twice a day on the first day). The big problem with this place comes when you pay the bill. They seem to have some trouble with their math, and you're presented with the bill just a few minutes before you have to run to catch your ferry which gives you no time to argue. To avoid hassles, it's better to pay the night before departure and get a receipt.

Alternatively, there's the basic *Losmen Rahmat* at the end of Jalan Aulolon (the street down to the left from the far end of the market as you come from the pier). A bed is 3300 rp per person, and there's no food.

You won't find any restaurants in town, but there are some warungs behind the market.

Getting There & Away – air Merpati flies Kupang-Larantuka-Lewoleba-Kupang twice a week. Kupang to Lewoleba costs 86,000 rp, and Larantuka to Lewoleba is 37,000 rp.

Getting There & Away – boat Boats ply daily both ways between Larantuka and Lewoleba (except from Lewoleba to Larantuka on Monday). They normally leave at 7, cost 3000 rp, and take three to four hours (depending on whether they call at Waiwerang). Beware: our boat left 15 minutes early!

There is a once-weekly boat departing on Saturday at 8 am from Kalabahi (Alor) to Lewoleba. The problem is that this boat first stops and spends the night at Wairiang (Lembata), then spends another night at Balauring on the same island, before finally reaching Lewoleba about noon on Monday. However, spending 2½ days on this boat will at least give you a chance to see two very remote villages, but living conditions here are very harsh (though Wairiang has a satellite dish antenna and one TV!). It might be best to sleep on the deck of the boat, which will be more comfortable than cardboard shacks that pass for 'hotels' in these villages. Bring at least five litres of bottled water, preferably more, and some food with you. The boat returns to Alor on Tuesday, 7 am, and again takes 2½ days because of stops at Balauring and Wairiang. Kalabahi-Lewoleba costs 11,000 rp; Lewoleba-Balauring is 3000 rp; Lewoleba-Wairiang is 4500 rp.

Getting Around Within the town, transport is by foot. Outside of Lewoleba, it's also mostly by foot. There are trucks, but these come into Lewoleba only on Monday for the market and depart on Tuesday morning. The rest of the week sees only a few sporadic trucks delivering freight, but passengers are allowed to ride on the roof! Chartering a truck is possible but quite expensive.

Around Lewoleba

Most of Lembata's finest ikat – recognisable by its burgundy-coloured base and highly detailed patterning – comes from villages on the slopes of Ili Api 15 or 20 km from Lewoleba. Kotagede is one such village – but locals seem reluctant to show, let alone part with, their best work.

Jontona village is near the west side of

Teluk Waienga, the deep inlet in Lembata's north coast. Trucks go there about three times a week – or rent a motor bike in Lewoleba. An hour's walk towards Ili Api from Jontona is the Kampung Lama (old village) with at least 50 traditional houses. These contain many sacred and prized objects including a huge number of elephant tusks, but are occupied by the villagers only for ceremonies such as the *kacang* (bean) festival in late September/early October. You'll probably be able to stay with villagers in Jontona.

Balauring

A very sleepy port on the peninsula jutting off the eastern end of Lembata. Everything here moves slowly, both people and transport. Trucks leave Lewoleba for Balauring once a week, and the 53-km trip takes about four hours over a shocking road. There is a boat at least once a week from Lewoleba to Balauring, sometimes via the village of Lewotolo at the foot of Ili Api. Boats between Kalabahi (Alor) and Leboleba call at Balauring at least once a week.

Lamalera

Like characters out of *Moby Dick*, the people who live in this village on the south coast of Lembata still hunt whales using small boats. There's the added drama of a harpooner who leaps from the boat on to the back of the whale and plunges his harpoon deep into its flesh. The whaling season is limited to those months of the year from about May to October when the seas aren't too rough. Even then, the whales are infrequent and unpredictable, though curiously enough they appear in the wake of south-easterly winds.

It may all sound romantic, but only a few whales a year are caught now, perhaps 20 or 25, since there aren't so many around anymore. Therefore, your chance of actually seeing a whale hunt, or witnessing the bloody business of butchering a whale, is fairly small. Considering just how hard it is to reach this isolated village, it might be a long trek just to see mediocre shacks. On the other hand, some travellers find it worthwhile for the cultural experience.

Lamalera residents certainly hope tourism will increase, because the local economy is on the skids. Declining whale numbers has caused quite a few young men to leave the village to seek work elsewhere. There's a distinct possibility that the whale-hunting skills will eventually be lost.

Most whales caught are sperm whales though occasionally smaller pilot whales are taken. When whales are scarce the villagers harpoon sharks, manta rays and dolphins, which are available all year round. Using nets is alien to these people and fishing rods are used only for sharks.

The whaling boats are made entirely of wood with wooden dowels instead of nails. Each vessel carries a mast and a sail made of palm leaves, but these are lowered during the hunt when the men row furiously to overtake the whale. There's usually a crew of about 15 and as the gap between the boat and the whale narrows, the harpooner takes the three-metre long harpoon, which is attached by a long coil of rope to the frame of the boat, leaps on to the back of the whale and plunges

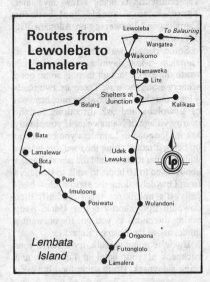

Routes from Lewoleba to Lamalera

Lembata Island

Lewoleba
To Balauring
Wangatea
Waikomo
Namaweka
Lite
Shelters at Junction
Belang
Kalikasa
Bata
Lamalewar
Bota
Udek
Lewuka
Puor
Imuloong
Posiwatu
Wulandoni
Ongaona
Futonglolo
Lamalera

in the harpoon. An injured whale will try to dive, dragging the boat with it, but cannot escape since it has to resurface to breathe.

The whale meat is shared according to traditional dictates. The heads go to two families of original landowners – a custom observed, it is said, since the 15th century. Later settlers from Maluku and Sulawesi were allowed to stay and hunt whales only on condition that the head of each whale be given to the two families. The crew, the boatbuilder, the harpoon maker and the rope keeper all take a share of the catch, with the boat owner and the harpooner being especially rewarded. Most of the whale meat is dried in the sun. The blubber is melted to make fuel for oil lamps. Not all the meat is used in the village – some is traded with the mountain villages for fruit and vegetables.

In Lamalera you may be able to stay with the padre, otherwise ask the kepala desa for somewhere to stay.

Getting There & Away The easiest way to get to Lamalera is on the boat from Lewoleba, which usually leaves each Monday night after the Lewoleba market. The return trip is made a few days later. There's also a weekly boat between Lamalera and Waiwerang on Adonara – its days seem to vary.

Some people walk from Lewoleba to Lamalera – a long dayhike which is often not worth the effort, though there is some good scenery along the way. There are two roads – long and short. For the short one, head out of Lewoleba and ask directions for the nearby village of Namaweke. If you simply ask for the road to Lamalera you could end up being directed along the road that takes a wide circular route around the island. It takes about seven to 10 hours to walk to Lamalera from Lewoleba along the short route – basically it's uphill for the first half, then downhill from shortly before Udek. Keep asking directions as you go. If you want a guide, ask at the Losmen Rejeki.

If you're going to walk, try to leave your backpack at your hotel in Lewoleba and bring a daypack. Bring some food but even

more importantly bring *lots* of water with you – any activity more strenuous than breathing will leave you parched!

Another possibility is to take a truck from Lewoleba to Puor, about three-quarters of the way to Lamalera by the long route. There should be at least one truck a week, then you might be able to hire a horse in Puor or find a motorcycle in Lewoleba. The road consists mostly of stones and potholes.

Getting Around Outside Lewoleba, the roads are in abominable shape and trucks normally only run on Monday (market day) and return to the villages the day after. Nothing moves during the rest of the week. The trucks are frequently overloaded with passengers riding on the roof, dodging tree branches all the way. It is possible to charter boats, but the cost is high.

ALOR & PANTAR

East of the Solor group are the islands of Alor and Pantar. Alor in particular is extremely scenic and has an exotic mix of cultures in a small area. The island is so rugged, and travel there so difficult, that its roughly 100,000 people are divided into some 50 tribes, with about as many different languages. To this day there is still some occasional warfare between tribes. There are seven major language groups on Alor alone, and five on Pantar.

Although the Dutch installed local rajas along the coastal regions after 1908, they had little control over the interior. Apart from infrequent trade with the coastal inhabitants the interior peoples were so little affected by the outside world that in the 1950s they were still taking heads! The mountain villages were hilltop fortresses above valleys so steep that horses were useless and during the rainy season some of the trails became impassable even on foot. They had little contact with each other – except during raids.

When the 20th century came, the warriors put Western imports to good use by twisting wire from telephone or telegraph lines into multi-barbed arrowheads, over the tip of which they pressed a sharpened, dried and hollowed chicken bone. When the arrow hit, the bone would splinter deep inside the wound like some primitive dum-dum bullet.

The coastal populations are predominantly Muslim and today Christianity has made some inroads into the interior, but indigenous animist cultures survive, mainly because travel remains very difficult. Roads are few and boat is a commoner form of transport.

Alor's chief fame in the outside world lies in its mysterious *mokos* – bronze drums (perhaps more accurately 'gongs') about half a metre high and a third of a metre in diameter, tapered in the middle like an hour-glass and with four ear-shaped handles around the circumference. They're closed at the end with a sheet of bronze that sounds like a bongo when thumped with the hand. There are thousands on the island – the Alorese apparently found them buried in the ground and believed them to be gifts from the gods.

Most mokos have decoration similar to that on bronze utensils made in Java in the 13th and 14th century Majapahit era, but others resemble earlier South-East Asian designs and may be connected with the Dongson culture which developed in Vietnam and China around 700 BC and then pushed its influence south into Indonesia. Later mokos even have Dutch or English-influenced decoration.

Theories of the mokos' origins usually suggest they were brought to Alor from further west by Indian, Chinese or Makassarese traders. This fails to explain why old bronze drums found on Java, Bali, Sumatra and Borneo are larger and display finer workcraft than those on Alor – or why the mokos were found in the ground. It's possible that groups of mokos reached Alor at different periods, perhaps with the better examples being bought up earlier on the traders' routes. Maybe the Alorese buried theirs in now-forgotten times, as an offering to spirits at a time of plague, or to hide them during attacks.

Today the mokos have acquired enormous value among the Alorese and men devote great energy and time to amassing collections of them, along with pigs and land. Such wealth is the only avenue to obtaining a bride in traditional Alorese society. The value of a moko depends mainly on its age: the newest, cheapest ones reportedly go for 200,000 rp-plus. In former times, whole villages would sometimes go to war in an attempt to win possession of a prized moko.

Alor was hit by a large earthquake in July, 1991, which killed 28 people, seriously injured another 200 and damaged a lot of roads and buildings. However, repairs are under way and roads should be back to normal (never too good in the first place!) by the time you get there.

Kalabahi & Around

Kalabahi is the chief town on Alor, at the end of a long, narrow and spectacular palm-fringed bay on the west coast. It's a poor place where few people seem to be doing any work at all, but it's the chief city of this archipelago. While Kalabahi itself is not a major drawcard, the nearby indigenous villages and stunning beaches are well worth your time.

Money It's best to bring sufficient funds with you, but it is possible to change money at Ombay, Ltd, one block from the wharf. The local Bank Rakyat Indonesia does *not* change money.

Things to See A very interesting trip is to Takpala, a traditional village 13 km east of Kalabahi. To get there, take a bus (750 rp) from Inpres Market in Kalabahi. From where the bus lets you off, walk two km uphill on the main road to Takpala. Another traditional village is Alor Kecil where there is a good coral reef for snorkelling.

Near the airport at the northernmost point of the island is Mali, an incredibly beautiful white-sand beach. It is possible to rent a boat (1000 rp) for a tour of the area.

Places to Stay & Eat There are three hotels, but most travellers stay at *Hotel Adi Dharma* (☎ 49), Jalan Marta Dinata 12, about 100 metres from the main pier in the centre of

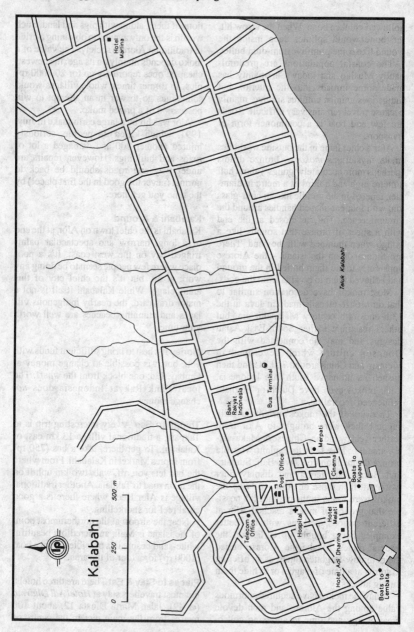

Kalabahi

town. Singles/doubles/triples with outside bath are 5500/9900/13,200 rp, while rooms with attached bath go for 8800/15,400/21,450 rp. The rooms are clean and well maintained, but the prime attraction is the charming owner, Mr Enga, who speaks good English and is a fountain of information.

In case the Adi Dharma is full, you can try the nearby *Hotel Melati* (☎ 73), Jalan Dr Sutomo 1. Rooms with outside bath are 5500 rp per person, while an attached bath makes it 8800 rp per person. Breakfast costs 2000 rp and lunch and dinner are both 3000 rp.

Hotel Marlina (☎ 141) gets relatively few travellers because it's almost three km east of the centre on Jalan El Tari, but you can get there easily by bemo. On the plus side, the standard of accommodation is the best in Alor. Rooms with outside bath are 5500 rp per person, while attached bath pushes it up to 8800 rp per person. Meals cost the same as in the Hotel Melati.

There are some rumah makan near the Inpres bus terminal, but overall, the restaurant situation is dismal. The town closes up at 6 pm, so you'd better eat dinner before this time.

Getting There & Away – air Merpati flies from Kupang to Kalabahi (87,000 rp) and back five days a week.

Getting There & Away – boat The Perum ASDP ferry from Bolok, the port of Kupang, leaves for Kalabahi on Monday at 2 pm, costing 13,900 rp for the 12-hour voyage. The Pelni ship *Elang* calls at Kalabahi every week or two on its circuits round various ports in Timor, Flores and southern Maluku.

From Dilli in East Timor, there is usually one ship per week. The fare is 6500 rp and you can buy tickets from the Pelni office. This ship normally returns by way of Kupang. We took this boat and found that the captain doubles as a priest, leading the passengers in a religious service. Not a bad idea, since faith is needed to keep this old tub afloat.

Most weeks at least one Kalabahi-based boat makes a trip to Lewoleba on Lembata

and back, usually reaching Lewoleba in time for its Monday market and leaving there early on Tuesday morning. They'll stop at one or more of Kabir (Pantar), Wairiang (eastern Lambata), Balauring (also eastern Lembata), Waiwering (Adonara) or Larantuka (Flores) on the round trip. The fare from Lewoleba to Kalabahi is about 11,000 rp. The trip could be done in as little as 12 hours, but normally takes 2½ days because of leisurely stops along the way. Remember to bring sufficient food and water!

Getting Around Kalabahi airport is 28 km from the town. Merpati runs a minibus to greet incoming and departing flights, and the cost is 2500 rp. There are also bemos for 250 rp. There are no taxis or becaks, and transport is only by bemo and bus.

Timor

If you arrive in Timor from Darwin, it will hit you with all the shock of Asia. Kupang, the main city, is very Indonesian, with its buzzing streets and honking horns, and its Third-World smells and sights. Timor's culture, however, seems rather bland compared with that of Sumba or Flores. Away from Kupang, it's little- touristed – a fairly scenic island with a number of destinations that are interesting or agreeable, but not unmissable. New interest was added in 1989 when East Timor, a former Portuguese colony, was opened up to foreign tourists for the first time since Indonesia invaded and took it over in 1975.

Timor's landscape is unique with its spiky lontar palms, rocky soils and central mountains dotted with villages of beehive- shaped huts. The island has some fantastic coastline but no tourist-type beach spots as yet, though you can take trips from Kupang to nearby islands for swimming and snorkelling. East Timor's beaches, which attracted travellers before 1975, are again accessible.

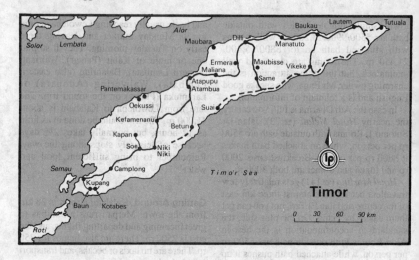

Timor is 60% mountainous; the highest peak, Tata Mai, stands at about 3000 metres. Along the north coast the mountains slope right into the sea. Aggravated by dry winds from northern Australia, the dry season is distinct and results in hunger and water shortages. To remedy the water problem, at least in the west around Soe, there is an intensive programme of small earth-dam building. Maize is the staple crop, but dry rice is also important and some irrigated rice is grown in the river valleys.

Thanks to Merpati's twice-weekly flights between Kupang and Darwin since 1986, and to improved transport in Nusa Tenggara, more travellers are now or from Australia are now passing through Timor. Some Darwinites are also choosing Timor instead of Bali for holidays because it's infinitely less developed and cheaper to reach.

Apart from Kupang, which is probably the most prosperous town in Nusa Tenggara, Timor is poor, especially the eastern half. West Timor has a population of 1.2 million and East Timor about 650,000. Christianity – both Protestant and Catholic – is widespread, though still fairly superficial in some areas: the old animistic cultures have not been completely eradicated. In the hills of the centre and the east, country folk still defer to their traditional chiefs – though major damage seems to have been done to traditional East Timorese society by the Indonesian takeover.

The dark-skinned and lightly built Timorese resemble the Bataks of Sumatra and the Torajans of Sulawesi. About 14 languages are spoken on the island, including both Malay and Papuan types, although Tetum (the language of a people who are thought to have first settled in Timor in the 14th century) is understood in most parts.

History

The Tetum of central Timor are one of the largest ethnic groups on the island. Before the Portuguese and Dutch colonisation they were fragmented into dozens of small states. Skirmishes between them were frequent and head-hunting was a popular activity, although when peace returned the captured heads were kindly returned to the kingdom from which they came.

Another major group, the Atoni, are thought to be the earliest inhabitants of Timor and one theory is that they were pushed westward by the Tetum. The Atoni form the predominant population of west

Timor and like the Tetum were divided into numerous small kingdoms before the arrival of Europeans. It's thought that their traditional political and religious customs were strongly influenced by Hinduism, possibly as a result of visits by Javanese traders, but like the Tetum they held to a strong belief in spirits, including ancestor spirits.

The first Europeans in Timor were the Portuguese, perhaps as early as 1512, the year after they captured Melaka. Like Chinese and western Indonesian traders before them, the Portuguese found the island a plentiful source of sandalwood (prized in Europe for its aroma and the medicinal santalol made from the oil). In the mid-17th century the Dutch occupied Kupang, Timor's best harbour, beginning a long conflict for control of the sandalwood trade. In the mid-18th century the Portuguese withdrew to the eastern half of Timor. The division of the island between the two colonial powers, worked out in agreements between 1859 and 1913, gave Portugal the eastern half plus the enclave of Oekussi on the north coast of the western half, while Holland got the rest of the west. Today's Indonesian province of East Timor has the same boundaries as former Portuguese Timor.

Neither European power penetrated far into the interior until the second decade of this century and the island's political structure was left largely intact, both colonisers ruling through the native kings. Right through to the end of Portuguese rule in East Timor many ostensibly Christian villagers continued to subscribe to animist beliefs. When Indonesia won independence in 1949 the Dutch cleared out of West Timor, but the Portuguese still held East Timor – setting the stage for the tragedy that would take place during the 1970s and '80s.

East Timor (Timor Timur) Until the end of the 19th century, Portuguese authority over their half of the island was never very strong. Their control was often effectively opposed by the *liurai*, the native Timorese rulers, and by the *mestico*, the influential descendants of

Portuguese men and local women. The Dominican missionaries were also involved in revolts or opposition to the government. Eventually a series of rebellions between 1894 and 1912 led to bloody and conclusive 'pacification'.

The colony had been on the decline much earlier as the sandalwood trade fizzled out, and as Portugal fell into a depression after WW I, East Timor drifted into economic torpor. Neglected by Portugal, it was notable only for its modest production of high-quality coffee and as a distant place of exile for opponents of the Portuguese regime. The ordinary Timorese were subsistence farmers using the destructive ladang or slash-and-burn system, with maize (sweet corn) the main crop.

In WW II, though Portugal and her overseas territories were neutral, the Allies assumed that the Japanese would use Timor as a base to attack Australia. Several hundred Australian troops were landed in East Timor and until their evacuation in January 1943 they carried out a guerrilla war which tied down 20,000 Japanese troops, of whom 1500 were killed, on the island. The Australian success was largely due to the support they got from the East Timorese, for whom the cost was phenomenal. The Japanese razed whole villages, seized food supplies and killed Timorese in areas where the Australians were operating. Farms were abandoned in the war zones, resulting in starvation, while other Timorese were killed by Allied bombing. By the end of the war, between 40,000 and 60,000 East Timorese had died.

After the war the Portuguese resumed control. Dilli was rebuilt, the plantations were put back in shape, and the production of livestock and grain increased. Even into the '70s, however, there was little industry, no sign of valuable mineral resources and scant improvement in education.

The turning point came on 25 April 1974 when a military coup in Portugal overthrew the Salazar dictatorship. The new government sought to discard the remnants of the Portuguese empire as quickly as possible.

With the real possibility of East Timor becoming an independent state, three major political groups quickly formed in the colony.

The first was the Timorese Democratic Union. The original memebers of the UDT were mostly officials and small property holders and, although they started out in favour of continued association with Portugal, within a few weeks they were advocating independence.

The second group was known as the association of Timorese Social Democrats. From the start, the ASDT advocated complete independence for East Timor. Later known as Fretilin (Revolutionary Front for an Independent East Timor), it gained the edge over the UDT, perhaps partly because of its more radical social policies.

The third group, known as Apodeti, advocated integration with Indonesia. Its membership probably never exceeded a few hundred, and it probably would not have survived if the Indonesians had not given it financial and moral support, eventually turning it into a front for their own goals.

Indonesian leaders had had their beady eyes on East Timor since the 1940s, though before the '70s they were too involved with separatist rebellions, campaigns in Irian Jaya and Konfrontasi with Malaysia to do much about it. Fretilin, however, was regarded by many of them as communist and there were fears that an independent East Timor might inspire separatism in Indonesia. The Australian government also expressed a preference for integration of East Timor into Indonesia.

In East Timor the rumours flew thick and fast and suspicions grew. On 11 August 1975, the UDT staged a coup in Dilli which led to a brief civil war between it and Fretilin. Military superiority lay from the outset with Fretilin which was supported by 2000 or so Timorese soldiers in the colony – only a few Portuguese soldiers remained. The bulk of the fighting was over by the end of August and the UDT remnants withdrew to Indonesian Timor.

Fretilin proved surprisingly effective in getting things almost back to normal, but by the end of September Indonesia had decided on a takeover. In October Indonesian troops staged trial attacks just within the East Timor border. East Timor and Fretilin now faced Indonesia alone; the Portuguese were certainly not coming back. On 7 December 1975 the Indonesians launched their invasion of East Timor with an assault on Dilli, coincidentally less than 24 hours after US Secretary of State 'Sideshow' Kissinger had left Jakarta.

From the start the invasion met strong resistance from Fretilin troops who quickly proved their worth as guerilla fighters. Though East Timor was officially declared Indonesia's 27th province on 16 July 1976, Fretilin kept up regular attacks on the Indonesians, even on targets very close to Dilli, until at least 1977. But gradually Indonesia's military strength and Fretilin's internal divisions and lack of outside support took their effect. By 1989, Fretilin appeared to have been pushed back to just a few hideouts in the far east of the island. Indonesia was confident enough to open up East Timor to foreign tourists in 1989. But the remaining 'low-intensity' security problem seems to warrant the continued presence of 15,000 Indonesian troops (including local militia).

The cost of the takeover to the East Timorese people has been huge. International humanitarian organisations estimate that about 100,000 people may have died in the hostilities and from disease and famine that followed. It's also estimated that 90% of the population has been relocated since 1975 for 'security reasons' with only 20% of villages now occupying ancestral sites, although some people are being moved back.

There are still complaints about indiscriminate arrests, restrictions of movement and human rights abuses. East Timor is the poorest province in Indonesia, but relatively large amounts of money are being spent by the Indonesian government in an effort to improve roads, electricity and water supplies, and social welfare. Despite this, health care is poor with 123 doctors for the population of 650,000. Technical skills are lacking and malaria is a problem.

Compounding the problems is the alleged predominance of the military in economic life. The military deny this, yet private companies are unwilling to get involved. East Timor's most valuable export is high-quality coffee. Until recently, most of this was collected and exported through Surabaya by PT Denok, a company run by Indonesian-Chinese businesspeople but apparently set up by a group of Indonesian generals with a view to controlling all industry and commerce in East Timor, including the sandalwood trade. Coffee growers complained that they received less for their product than growers in West Timor and this was adding to unrest in the province. This coffee monopoly was officially ended by a governor's decree in 1991, though it remains to be seen how much difference this really makes.

Currently, no permit is required for foreigners to travel to East Timor and travellers are getting right through to Tutuala, East Timor's most easterly point.

The military and political atmosphere has been fairly calm in recent years, but on 12 November, 1991, about 1000 Timorese staged a rally at a cemetery to protest the killing of an independence activist two weeks earlier. Indonesian troops opened fire on the crowd. The number killed was variously reported from 19 to 200. The Indonesian Legal Aid Foundation claimed a death toll of 115. Two US reporters on the scene were beaten by soldiers when they tried to intervene. The shootings triggered a harsh diplomatic protest from Australia, the EC countries and the USA. The Indonesian government has set up a commission to investigate. Whether this will have any effect on travel to the area remains unknown.

Books Probably the best account of events surrounding the Indonesian invasion of East Timor is John Dunn's *Timor – A People Betrayed* (Jacaranda Press, Brisbane, Australia, 1984). Dunn was Australian consul in East Timor from 1962 to 1964; he was also part of an Australian government fact-finding mission to East Timor in June to July 1974 and returned in 1975, just after the Fretilin-UDT war, to lead an Australian relief effort. *Timor, The Stillborn Nation* by Bill Nicol (Widescope International, Melbourne, Australia, 1978) provides something of a balance to Dunn's book: Nicol tends to criticise Fretilin leaders and places much more of the blame on the Portuguese who, he says, provoked the UDT-Fretilin civil war and invited Indonesian military intervention by their attempts to rid themselves of East Timor as fast as possible.

For the inside story from a Fretilin point of view, read *Funu: The Unfinished Saga of East Timor* by Jose Ramos Horta (Red Sea Press, New Jersey, USA, 1987). Horta was a Fretilin leader in 1975 and has since been its UN representative. Also sympathetic to Fretilin is *The War Against East Timor* by Carmel Budiardjo and Liem Soei Liong, (Pluto Press, Leichhardt, Australia, 1984).

KUPANG

Kupang is virtually a booming metropolis compared with the overgrown villages that pass for towns in other parts of Nusa Tenggara. It's the capital of East Nusa Tenggara (Nusa Tenggara Timur or NTT) province which covers West Timor, Roti, Sawu, the Solor and Alor Archipelagos, Sumba, Flores and Komodo. As such it comes fully equipped with footpaths and brightly decorated bemos with sophisticated sound systems.

The centre is busy, noisy and untidy while the wealthier residential areas are in the suburbs. There's a lot of building going on, particularly on the eastern edge of town.

Merpati's regular Darwin to Kupang flights are attracting many short-term Australian visitors from the Northern Territory. It's not a bad place to hang around for a few days – Captain Bligh did when he arrived here after his *Bounty* misadventures.

History

The Dutch East India Company occupied Kupang in the middle of the 17th century, mainly in an attempt to gain control of the sandalwood trade. The Portuguese had built

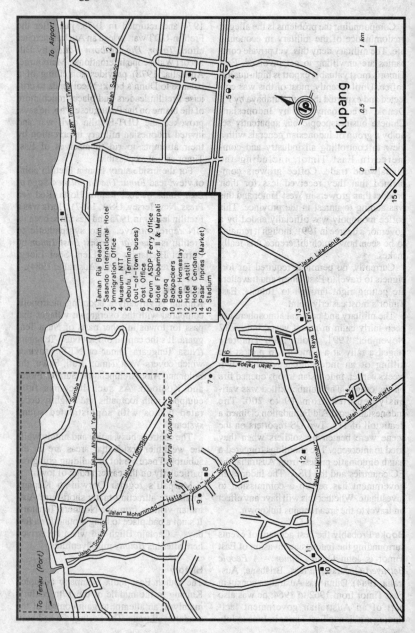

Kupang

1 km
0.5
0

Jalan Timor Timur
Jalan Sasando
To Airport

Jalan Lalamentik

Jalan Raya El Tari

Jalan Palapa

Jalan Jend Suharto

Jalan Ahmad Yani
Jl Sumba
Jalan Tompelo

Jalan Jend Sudirman

Jalan Herman
Jalan Mohammed Hatta
Jalan Soekarno

See Central Kupang Map

To Tenau (Port)

1 Taman Ria Beach Inn
2 Sasando International Hotel
3 Immigration Office
4 Museum NTT
5 Oebufu Terminal
   (out-of-town buses)
6 Post Office
7 Perum ASDP Ferry Office
8 Hotel Flobamor II & Merpati
9 Bourag
10 Backpackers
11 Eden Homestay
12 Hotel Astiti
13 Hotel Cendana
14 Pasar Inpres (Market)
15 Stadium

a fort at Kupang but abandoned it before the Dutch arrived, leaving the Portuguese-speaking Christian mixed-blood mestico population (or the 'black Portuguese' as they were known) to oppose the Dutch. It was not until 1749, after an attack by the mestico on Kupang had been decisively defeated, that the Dutch went more or less unchallenged in west Timor.

Timor was, however, very much a side-show for the Dutch. Supplies of sandalwood had already dwindled severely by 1700, and by the late 18th century Kupang was little more than a symbol of the Dutch presence in Nusa Tenggara. Not until the 20th century did they pay much attention to the interior of the island.

The original inhabitants of the Kupang area were the Helong who, squeezed by the Atoni, had by the 17th century been limited to a small coastal strip at the western tip of the island. Later, partly because of the Dutch-supported migration of people from the nearby island of Roti to Kupang, most of the Helong migrated to the small island of Semau off Kupang. By the mid-20th century they were confined to just one village near Tenau (the port of Kupang) and several villages on Semau.

Orientation

Kupang is hilly. Its downtown area hugs the waterfront. Hotels are scattered throughout the town. One focal point is the junction of Jalan Siliwangi and Jalan Soekarno, where the central, Kota Kupang, bemo station, usually just called Terminal, is located. Most of the restaurants are around here. Kupang's El Tari airport is 15 km east of town and Tenau Harbour is eight km west.

Information

Tourist Office The helpful tourist office is on Jalan Soekarno near the Terminal, and they usually have someone on duty who speaks good English. This is a good place to make contact with guides – through this office, we met Dominggus Rohi, who proved to be a very competent guide and accompanied us throughout Nusa Tenggara. The office is open Monday to Thursday from 7.30 am to 2 pm, Friday from 7.30 am to 1 pm and Saturday from 7.30 am to 12.30 pm.

Post & Telecommunications The main post office, with the poste restante, is at Jalan Palapa 1. It's open Monday to Thursday from 8 am to 2 pm, Friday from 8 to 11 am and Saturday from 8 am to 1 pm. To get there, take a No 4 bemo from downtown. There's a sub-post office on Jalan Soekarno, a short walk from the Terminal. The telecom office is on Jalan Urip Sumohardjo.

Money The Bank Dagang Indonesia is the best place to change money, and is open Monday to Friday from 7 am to noon and from 1 to 2.30 pm and Saturday from 7 to 11 am. Bank Negara Indonesia 1946 on Jalan Sumatera is open from 7.30 am to 2.30 pm Monday to Friday and from 7.30 am to 11.30 am on Saturday. Pitoby Travel at Jalan Siliwangi 75 gives about 150 rp less for the US dollar but it's open on Sundays. A money changing office opens at Kupang airport when flights from Darwin come in and gives same the rate as the banks.

Markets

The main market is the rambling Pasar Inpres off Jalan Suharto in the south of city. To get there, you can take bemo Nos 1 or 2 and walk the short distance to the market from Jalan Suharto. There's a lesser market on the seafront off Jalan Garuda.

Museum NTT

The interesting East Nusa Tenggara Museum is on Jalan Perintis Kemerdekaan on the eastern edge of the city. It has exhibits of arts, crafts and artefacts from all over the province. There are helpful English-speaking guides and most of the labels are in Indonesian and English. This is a good place to get an introduction to Nusa Tenggara if you've just arrived, or to pull together what you've seen if you're leaving. To get there, take a No 10 bemo from the Terminal. It's open Monday, Thursday and Saturday from 9 am

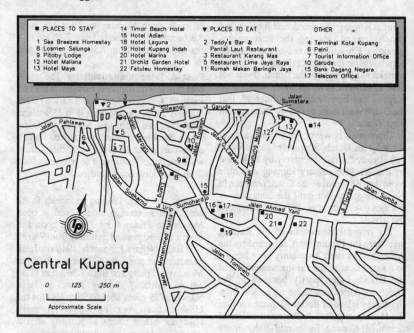

■ PLACES TO STAY	14 Timor Beach Hotel	▼ PLACES TO EAT	OTHER
1 Sea Breezes Homestay	16 Hotel Adian	2 Teddy's Bar &	4 Terminal Kota Kupang
8 Losmen Salunga	18 Hotel Laguna	Pantai Laut Restaurant	6 Pelni
9 Pitoby Lodge	19 Hotel Kupang Indah	3 Restaurant Karang Mas	7 Tourist Information Office
12 Hotel Maliana	20 Hotel Marina	5 Restaurant Lima Jaya Raya	10 Garuda
13 Hotel Maya	21 Orchid Garden Hotel	11 Rumah Makan Beringin Jaya	15 Bank Dagang Negara
	22 Fatuleu Homestay		17 Telecom Office

Central Kupang

to noon. Entry is free, but give a donation when you leave.

Pulau Semau

Semau, visible from Kupang, is an interesting island to wander around and has some good beaches where you can snorkel and freshwater springs. You may be able to organise a boat from one of the fishing villages along the beach outside Kupang or from Tenau. Teddy's Bar in Kupang runs day trips to Semau. The cost for the one-hour each way boat trip and a barbecue lunch is 17,500 rp. Departure is at 10 am and return at 4 pm. You can stay overnight in the bungalows run by Teddy's Bar, in which case the trip will cost 35,000/60,000 rp for singles/doubles, including transport to the island and three meals daily.

Monkey Island (Pulau Kera)

This small island is also visible from Kupang. Taman Ria Beach Inn organises

trips the the island, or talk to the people operating the fishing boats.

Pantai Lasiana

Lasiana is about 12 km east of town and a busy picnic spot on Sunday. A few stalls sell drinks and snacks or you can buy a *kelapa muda* (young coconut). The beach doesn't look much in the wet season, but it makes a pleasant outing from Kupang during the week. If you walk over the headland through the lontar palm grove, you'll find more beaches where hotel development is planned. To get to Lasiana, take bemo No 17 (300 rp) from the Terminal. About three or four km along the Soe road beyond the airport turn-off, there's a road to the left with a sign 'Welcome to Lasiana Beach' above it. Walk down the road for about one km.

Baun

A small, quiet village 25 km south of Kupang in the hilly Amarasi district, Baun is a centre of ikat weaving and has a few Dutch buildings. You can visit the *rumah raja*, the last raja's house, now occupied by his widow. She loves to chat with foreigners and will show you some of her interesting weavings and her rose garden. If your Indonesian is good enough, you can learn a lot about the area's history from her, particularly about WW II. The house is a short walk straight ahead from where the bemo drops you in Baun. Market day in Baun is Saturday. From Baun to the south coast and back is a good day's hike – reportedly, there's a surf beach down there.

To get to there, take a bemo from Inpres market (700 rp) to Baun.

Places to Stay – bottom end

Accommodation in Kupang is spread out, but the efficient bemo system makes everywhere easily accessible. Prices are being driven up absurdly by air-conditioning which even budget hotels are installing, even though it's cool at night and few foreigners want it. However, there are still some remaining good options at the bottom end.

Taman Ria Beach Inn (☎ 31320), at Jalan Tim Tim 69 three km from the Terminal, is popular for its cheap dorm prices – 2000 rp per person in a four-bed room or 3500 rp in an eight-bed room. Singles/doubles with shared bath are 7500/10,000 rp, and a private mandi jacks the price up to 10,000/12,000 rp. Taman Ria fronts the beach. On the grounds is Ozzy Rock Cafe with a bar, which cranks into noisy action at about 9.30 pm. If you don't need early nights Taman Ria is fine. To get there, catch a No 10 bemo.

The very popular *Backpackers* at Jalan Kancil 37B, Air Nona, is about four km from the city centre. It's part of the International Network Group which has hostels in Darwin, Sydney, Los Angeles and elsewhere. The cost is 3000 rp per person in doubles or small dorms with outside bath. It's a friendly if basic place, but the setting is peaceful and it even has a small swimming pool. They don't do food but there's a cheap gado-gado warung where Jalan Kancil meets

the main road. To get there from the Terminal, catch a No 3 bemo.

Just a one minute jog from the Backpackers is *Eden Homestay* (☎ 21921) at Jalan Kancil 6. They have bungalows with private bath and charge just 3000 rp per person. You can swim in the large pond nearby.

Fatuleu Homestay (☎ 31374) is a new place conveniently close to the centre. Rooms with shared bath are 5000 rp per person, or you can enjoy the luxurious doubles with private bath for 15,000 rp. It's very clean and good value.

Sea Breezes Homestay is on Jalan Ikan Tongkol (Tuna Fish St) next to Teddy's Bar. It's very basic, but the location is very convenient and the friendly owner speaks good English, plus there are nice views over the sea. Singles/doubles are 5000/8000 rp.

Places to Stay – middle

Many of these places have a range of prices so the bottom, middle and top end overlap to some extent.

The central *Pitoby Lodge* (☎ 32910) on Jalan Kosasih 13 has budget rooms for 14,625/19,500 rp; economy for 23,400/29,250 rp; and standard rooms for 29,250/39,000 rp. The management speak good English, rooms are very clean and the decor tasteful, but none of the rooms have private bath.

Also centrally located is *Losmen Salunga* (☎ 21510), Jalan Kakatua 20, where all rooms have private bath and start at 13,750/19,250 rp.

Facing out to sea at Jalan Sumatera is the spacious *Timor Beach Hotel* (☎ 31651). This place is also known by its Indonesian name, Hotel Pantai Timor. Economy rooms with fan are 9000/12,500 rp and air-con inflates the price to 22,000/27,500 rp. All rooms have private bath. Even if you don't stay here, enjoying a meal or drink at the restaurant is recommended for the fine sea views.

Nearby and also with a sea view is *Hotel Wisma* (☎ 22172). An economy room with outside bath is 8000 rp, but singles/doubles with attached shower are 11,500/16,500 rp and air-con rooms are 18,500/23,500 rp.

Just next door is *Hotel Maliana*
(☎ 21879). All rooms have private bath and
start at 19,250/24,200 rp. Also next door is
the brand new *Hotel Maya* (☎ 22697), Jalan
Sumatera 31. Standard rooms are 22,500/
27,500 while family rooms with air-con,
bathtubs and real hot water go for 50,000 rp.

A few blocks back from the sea front is
Hotel Laguna (☎ 21559) at Jalan Gunung
Kelimutu 36. With shared bath, economy
singles/doubles are 6600/9900 rp. Air-con
doubles with an attached bathroom are
27,500 rp. This place is often full.

You can also try next door at the *Hotel
Kupang Indah* (☎ 21919), Jalan Kelimutu
21A. All rooms have attached bath. With a
fan only, singles/doubles start at 7500/9000
rp and air-con pushes the price up to
15,000/17,500 rp. Also on the same street at
number 40, is *Hotel Adian* (☎ 21913), which
has standard rooms for 11,000/13,750 rp and
air-con rooms for 19,250/22,000 rp.

Hotel Cendana (☎ 21541) is at Jalan Raya
El Tari 23, about four km from the centre. It's
a beautiful hotel, but there is no place nearby
to buy food or anything else, though there's
a decent restaurant in the hotel. Take bemo
Nos 1 or 2 to Jalan Raya El Tari, then walk
or change to bemo No 7. All rooms have
attached mandi. An economy room with
breakfast is 10,000/16,000 rp and air-con
doubles the price to 20,000/30,000 rp. The
staff speak good English.

Hotel Marina (☎ 22566) at Jalan Jenderal
Ahmad Yani 72 is a very new and clean
place. With no fan, no air-con and no bath,
an economy single is 11,000 rp. Air-con
costs 22,000/27,500 rp and VIP rooms go for
44,000 rp.

Also worth considering is *Hotel Astiti*
(☎ 21810), Jalan Jenderal Sudirman 146. It's
a quiet place where all rooms have air-con
and private bath. Economy singles/doubles
are 22,500/27,500; standard, 27,600/32,600
rp; special class costs 33,600/39,600 rp.

Places to Stay – top end

Hotel Flobamor II (☎ 21346) at Jalan Sudirman 21 next to the Merpati office, features

comfy air-con rooms with hot water bath.
Singles/doubles are 49,500/66,000 rp.

Kupang's ritziest accommodation is the
sparkling new *Orchid Garden Hotel*
(☎ 21707, fax 31399), Jalan Gunung Fatuleu
2. They have it all: swimming pool, international telephone and fax, bathtubs, hot water,
refrigerator, etc. All this grandeur costs
107,640/123,340 rp for singles/doubles.

Sasando International Hotel (☎ 22224) at
Jalan Kartini 1 is a plush resort that sees few
customers due to its peculiar location; it's on
a windy hilltop to the south of the main road
to the airport. Because it's not close to anything, prices have dropped and it's a bargain
for this level of luxury. Economy singles/
doubles are 30,000/37,500 rp; standard costs
50,000/57,500; deluxe rooms are
55,000/63,000 rp.

Places to Eat

Kupang is no gourmet's delight but there are
several reasonable places to eat. The best is
probably the *Restaurant Lima Jaya Raya* at
Jalan Soekarno 15, near the Terminal. It has
a long menu of Chinese and Indonesian
dishes including sea cucumber, frogs' legs
and hens' feet. The restaurant has air-con and
the Chinese owner likes to entertain by
playing an old lute-like instrument.

Teddy's Bar at Jalan Ikan Tongkol 1-3 has
good food including a few Western dishes.
This place is the centre of tourist nightlife
with a few hostess-like types floating around
and· sometimes crowds of Kupang
schoolkids lurking outside to watch the
antics of drunken Darwinites.

Next door, the *Pantai Laut Restaurant* has
good food and amiable staff. *Restaurant
Karang Mas* at Jalan Siliwangi 88, a short
walk from the Terminal, is on the seafront
but more interesting for its look-at-the-
sunset location than its food. It's a bit of a
travellers' hangout, a good place for a cold
beer and a snack.

On Jalan Garuda, the eastward continuation of Jalan Siliwangi, the *Rumah Makan
Beringin Jaya* has good Padang food at reasonable prices and air-con.

You'll see night warungs around town,

particularly along the street leading down to the bridge off Jalan Soekarno, just a short walk from the Terminal. Besides the usual gado-gado and sate, try *bubur kacang* (mung beans and black rice in coconut milk). In case you're intersted, a few of these warungs sell dogmeat. There are also stalls set up off Jalan Garuda almost opposite the Rumah Makan Beringin Jaya.

Things to Buy

Timorese ikat is colourful with a huge variety of designs, and there are lots of other embroidered textiles. Purists will be disappointed that natural dyes have all but disappeared from Timor, though you may have some luck in Soe, Kefamenanu, Baun or other rural towns and villages or at Kupang's market – Pasar Inpres – where country people often bring weavings to sell.

Several shops in Kupang sell ikat, handicrafts, old silver jewellery, ornamented bamboo sirih boxes and more – bizarrely shaped lontar leaf hats from Roti make a fun purchase. These shops also have ikat from other parts of East Nusa Tenggara including Sawu and Roti. Prices are quite high and bargaining won't bring them down dramatically, but it's still cheaper to buy the Timorese stuff in Timor than in Bali or elsewhere. Try *Dharma Bakti*, at Jalan Sumba 32, out towards Jalan Tim Tim. *Toko Sinar Baru* on Jalan Siliwangi opposite the Terminal has interesting stock, but is hard to shift on prices. Look for large Sawu blankets or a selendang (shawl) – Sawu designs are distinctive and elegant but natural dyes are rarely used. You can watch ikat weavers at work in Kupang at Ibu Bunga's Sentra Tenun Ikat on Jalan Tifa, about one km south-west of the Terminal. Locals will give you directions. Cloths, shoes and bags are on sale here. Sometimes the shop at Kupang airport has handicrafts for sale at cheaper prices than the city shops.

Outside Kupang, woven sarongs are cheaper but always check the work carefully. Close inspection may reveal flaws such as the two halves not lining up exactly.

Getting There & Away

Kupang is the transport hub of Timor, with buses and flights to and from the rest of the island, plus planes and regular passenger boats to the rest of Nusa Tenggara and beyond.

Air Merpati flies to and from Darwin twice a week for as little as A$350 return. Garuda offers a slightly more expensive flight. Kupang is a gateway city, so you can enter and exit Indonesia here without a visa.

Merpati links Kupang to Alor (87,000 rp), Atambua (73,000 rp), Bajawa (118,000 rp), Balikpapan, Bima (196,000 rp), Denpasar (201,000 rp), Dilli (73,000 rp), Ende (86,850 rp), Jakarta (395,000 rp), Kendari, Labuhanbajo (164,950 rp), Larantuka (81,000 rp), Lewoleba (86,000 rp), Mataram, Maumere (65,000 rp), Roti (36,000 rp), Ruteng (122,000 rp), Sawu (73,000 rp), Surabaya (267,000 rp), Tarakan, Ujung Pandang (169,000 rp), Waingapu (122,400 rp), Waikabubak-Tambolaka (164,950 rp) and Yogyakarta.

Bouraq connects Kupang to Bandung, Denpasar, Jakarta, Maumere, Surabaya and Waingapu.

Merpati (☎ 21121, 21961) is at Jalan Sudirman 21, next to the Hotel Flobamor II. Bemos Nos 1 and 2 go there. The office is open Monday to Saturday from 8 am to 4 pm, Sunday and holidays from 9 am to 3 pm. Bouraq (☎ 21421) is almost opposite at Jalan Sudirman 20. Garuda (☎ 21205) is more central at Jalan Kohsasi 13. There are also numerous air ticket agents around town, including Pitoby Travel (☎ 21222) at Jalan Siliwangi 75, which is open Sunday.

Bus Kupang's main bemo terminal (Terminal Kota Kupang) is *not* where the buses depart for long-distance journeys. For out-of-town buses, you need to take a No 10 bemo to Oebufu, a station in the eastern part of the city near the Museum NTT. Buses to Soe (two hours) cost 3000 rp, to Kefamenanu (five hours) 5000 rp and to Atambua (eight hours) 7500 rp (day), 6000 rp (night).

From Kupang to Dilli, most people stay

overnight in Atambua. For more details, see the Dilli section.

There's an agent for the Paris Indah night bus to Kefamenanu and Atambua on Jalan Siliwangi.

Boat Regular ships to Flores, Sawu, Roti, Alor, Sumba and further afield leave from the port of Tenau, eight km west of Kupang. From the Kupang station, bemo Nos 12 or 13 (500 rp) will take you straight to Tenau harbour and drop you right outside the harbour master's office (☎ 21790) at Jalan Yos Soedarso 23.

Pelni and the ferry company Perum ASDP both have ticket offices in Kupang. Pelni is at Jalan Pahlawan 3 within walking distance of the Terminal. The *Kelimutu* leaves Kupang every second Sunday, reaching Semarang on Java a week later then returning by the same route in reverse. The complete *Kelimutu* schedule is in the Getting Around chapter near the beginning of this book. From Kupang the *Kelimutu* stops at Ende, Waingapu, Bima, Ujung Pandang, Lembar, Padangbai, Surabaya, Banjarmasin, and Semarang. Tickets prices (in rp) are:

Destination	1st	2nd	Ekonomi
Bima	105,500	84,000	36,000
Ende	45,000	35,000	16,000
Ujung Pandang	124,700	93,300	39,700
Waingapu	65,250	51,300	21,000

Pelni also runs the KM *Elang* which loops every 10 days or so round Timor and the small islands to the north. A typical route is Kupang, Larantuka, Kalabahi, Kupang again, Oekussi, Atapupu, Dilli, Kisar in southern Maluku, Kalabahi, Kupang.

Pelni's *Baruna Eka* and/or *Baruna Fajar* do about one circuit a week round Kupang, Sawu, Ende, Waingapu, Sawu, Kupang, sometimes with extra stops such as Maumbawa in Flores, south of Bajawa. The ships usually spend the day in port and sail overnight. The trip from Kupang to Sawu takes nine hours and costs 11,500 rp. Kupang to Ende takes two nights and one day for

14,500 rp. Kupang to Waingapu is three nights and two days.

The Perum ASDP ferry office (☎ 21140) at Jalan Cak Doko 20 sells tickets the day before departure for the ferries *Kerapu I*, *Kerapu II* and *Madidihang* to Larantuka (Flores), Kalabahi (Alor), Sawu and Roti. The office is open from 8 am to 4 pm, and a No 4 bemo from downtown gets you there. The Larantuka ferry leaves Tenau on Monday and Thursday at 3 pm. The fare is 11,500 rp. It's a 12-hour overnight trip, sometimes via Lembata or Adonara. See under Larantuka for more on this ferry.

The Kalabahi ferry leaves Tenau on Tuesday and Saturday around midday. It's about a 12-hour trip and the fare is 13,900 rp. The Sawu ferry leaves on Thursday afternoons and costs 11,500 rp. There are ferries to Roti on Monday, Wednesday and Saturday mornings. The four-hour trip costs 4200 rp.

The mission ship *Ratu Rosario*, which plies the Kupang-Surabaya route, makes a loop every three weeks and visits many of the islands of Nusa Tenggara.

Other Transport You can rent cars or motorcycles or fix up tours to places like Semau island, Soe, the surf beach near Baun, or Roti at Teddy's Bar.

Getting Around
To/From the Airport Kupang's El Tari airport is 15 km east of the city centre. A taxi from the airport into the city is a fixed 7500 rp.

To get a bemo from the airport, walk out of the terminal and follow the road to your left a full km to the junction with the main highway. The fare to town is 300 rp. From the city centre, bemo Nos 14 and 15 go by the airport.

Bemo The bemo system is efficient but loud, with music played at full blast and the bass set to maximum. However, if you're into heavy metal, Kupangites have pretty good taste in music, at least compared to the rest of Indonesia. Some bemo names we've seen include LA Disco and Madonna.

Kupang is too spread out to do much walking. The hub of the bemo routes is the Terminal Kota Kupang, simply known as 'Terminal'. All bemos within town cost 250 rp and they stop running by 9 pm. Bemos are numbered and the main bemo routes are as follows:

Nos 1 & 2 Kuanino-Oepura; passing by the following hotels: Maya, Maliana, Timor Beach, Fatuleu, Orchid Garden, Marina, Flobamor II and Astiti.

No 3 Airnona-Bakunase; the best bemo for reaching Backpackers and Eden Homestay.

No 4 Oebobo-Airnona-Bakunase; goes by the ferry office and main post office.

No 5 Oebobo-Oepura

No 6 Oebobo-Oebufu; goes to the stadium but *not* to Oepura bus terminal.

No 7 Walikota-El Tari-Oepura; most useful for getting from Hotel Cendana to Oebufu bus terminal.

No 10 Kelapa Lima-Walikota; Terminal to Taman Ria Beach Hotel.

No 11 Perumnas; only useful for reaching the Timor Beach Hotel from the Terminal.

No 12 Tenau

No 13 Bolok

Nos 14 & 15 Penfui; useful for getting to the airport.

No 16 Baumata; to the natural cave and spring-water swimming pool.

No 17 Tarus; goes to Pantai Lasiana.

CAMPLONG

Camplong, 41 km from Kupang on the Soe road, has some caves, a small forest and an artificial lake. The Camplong convent runs a reasonable penginapan. Rooms with attached mandi are 10,000 rp single, including breakfast and dinner.

SOE

Soe, with its backdrop of hills and cooler temperatures, makes a pleasant change from Kupang. At over 800 metres elevation and 11° south of the equator, average night temperatures in July reach down to 14°C, but it's toasty enough in the daytime for shorts and T-shirts. The road from Kupang passes through rugged countryside, reminiscent of Australia's bush though most of the eucalyptus trees have been chopped down for firewood. Soe is a sprawl of wooden and iron-roofed houses, but there's a large market where you'll see people in their traditional garb.

Like most of rural Timor, Soe district is very poor. Apples used to provide the area with a steady income, but in 1988 a bug killed all the trees. There is now replanting under way.

A number of Australian expatriates live in Soe and Kefamenanu, around 100 km further east. Australian aid projects include building small dams around Soe to cope with dry season water shortages. Health education projects are also planned.

Lopo, the local beehive-shaped houses, give the region a distinctive character but they have been banned by the authorities who consider them unhealthy, as they're small and smoky. The locals, however, believe that their new houses are equally unhealthy, as they're cold – so they construct new lopos behind the approved houses. Another smaller type of lopo, which acts as a meeting place, has no walls and a toad-stool-like roof.

Orientation

Soe's bus and bemo terminal is on the far side of Soe if you're coming from Kupang. Accommodation is on and near Jalan Diponegoro in the town centre, a km or so back from the terminal. The market is a km in the opposite direction from the terminal. To get to the hotels, turn left out of the bus station and walk uphill past the post office, then turn right at the first junction.

Markets

There are village markets worth visiting from Soe. Niki Niki, 34 km to the east along the main road, is the site of some old royal graves. Its busy market is on Wednesdays when people come in from miles around – it's supposed to be a good place to buy weavings. One reader's letter reported visiting Ayotupas which has a 'great' market. To get there, hop on a truck in Niki Niki. The uncomfortable trip on a shocking road may still be worth it. Oenlasi is 58 km north-east of Soe, high up in the rugged mountains.

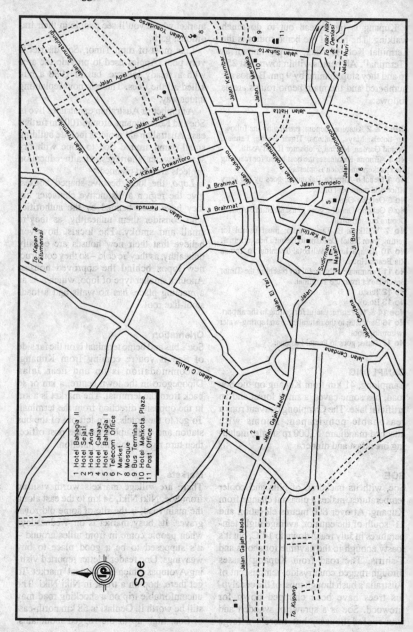

Soe

1 Hotel Bahagia II
2 Hotel Sejati
3 Hotel Anda
4 Hotel Cahaya
5 Hotel Bahagia I
6 Telecom Office
7 Market
8 Mosque
9 Bus Terminal
10 Hotel Mahkota Plaza
11 Post Office

Buses or trucks go there from Soe, at least on Tuesdays for the weekly market.

Kapan, 21 km north of Soe, has its interesting market on Thursdays when the roads are blocked with stalls. The village is situated on steep slopes from where you can see Gunung Mutis (2470 metres).

Fatumenasi

This town, 20 km beyond Kapan on the slopes of Gunung Mutis, doesn't have a market but has great views of the surrounding rocky, alpine landscape. Some trucks run between Kapan and Fatumenasi, or charter a jeep from Kapan for 20,000 rp – try the Chinese shopowner there.

Places to Stay & Eat

Hotel Mahkota Plaza, at Jalan Jenderal Soeharto 11, is a large place right opposite the bus terminal. All rooms include private bath and there is a good restaurant inside. Singles/doubles are 11,000/16,500 rp.

Hotel Bahagia I at Jalan Diponegoro 72 is one of the more upmarket places to stay. Clean singles/doubles with shared mandi are 11,000/13,200 rp; rooms with attached mandi start at 13,750/16,500 rp. Its restaurant is one of the best in town.

Under the same management is the *Hotel Bahagia II* where all rooms are 22,000 rp. The rooms have air-con – just why its needed at this elevation is a mystery.

Around the corner from Hotel Bahagia I is the basic but very friendly *Hotel Anda*, Jalan Kartini 5. Rooms are cheap at 4000 rp with an attached mandi. The hotel is run by an interesting and talkative English/Dutch/German-speaking owner from Roti who used to work with Save the Children on Java. They cook reasonable meals and throw in an occasional snack.

Just next door is *Hotel Cahaya* next door where some rooms have attached mandi and some are without, but all cost 4000 rp per person.

Hotel Sejati at Jalan Gajah Mada 18 has a wide range of accommodation. Economy rooms with common bath are 5500/7150. Standard rooms with attached mandi are

7250/11,000 rp while 1st class costs 8800/13,750 rp.

There are a few warungs and rumah makan near the market, but the best meals seem to be served in either the *Hotel Mahkota Plaza* or *Hotel Bahagia I*.

Things to Buy

There are good weavings to be had in Soe itself. The shop attached to the Wisma Bahagia has an excellent but expensive collection. Bargaining in Bahasa Indonesia will drop the price a little. Locals come around to the losmens to show you weavings which are much cheaper, but sometimes poor in quality. You can watch women weaving in the kampungs on the edge of the town – you're likely to be invited there.

Getting There & Away

Buses from Kupang cost 3000 rp and the 110-km journey takes three to four hours. It's best to set off early and get a 7 am bus as the chances are your bus will fill up quickly and leave sooner. If you ask, your bus can drop you off at a losmen in Soe before going on to the bus terminal.

Buses to Kefamenanu (2500 rp) run frequently from early in the morning until afternoon.

In Soe, bemos run around town and to nearby villages. Within Soe, the bemo fare is 200 rp.

KEFAMENANU

Kefamenanu, 217 km from Kupang, is cool and quiet but apart from some pleasant walks to surrounding hills, there's little to hold you. The town had a reputation in the past as a place to buy fine rugs. Locals bring around reasonable ikats to the losmens and you could strike a bargain. Oelolok, a weaving village 26 km from 'Kefa' by bus and a further three km by bemo, has a Tuesday market.

Places to Stay

Losmen Ariesta (☎ 7), Jalan Basuki Rachmat 29, has big, bright and airy rooms and is good value. Economy rooms with outside mandi cost 8250 rp. Standard rooms with attached bath cost 13,750 rp and VIP rooms go for 27,500 rp. The restaurant here serves good food. Get to this place by bemo from the terminal.

The new and relatively upmarket place in town is *Losmen Cendana* (☎ 168), Jalan Sonbay about 100 metres from the Pertamina petrol station. Single rooms with fan cost 11,000 and 16,500 rp, while air-con makes it 33,000 rp. Breakfast is included.

Losmen Soko Windu (☎ 122) is on Jalan Kartini, a short bemo ride from the bus terminal. It's basic but cheap at 5500 rp per person for a room with shared bath. Breakfast is included.

Losmen Sederhana on Jalan Patimura is far from the bus terminal but there are bemos. Singles/doubles with attached toilet go for 7500/10,000 rp.

Losmen Bahtera is a basic dungeon a long ways from the terminal on Jalan Ketumbar. Rooms with shared bath are 4000 rp.

Getting There & Away

There are two bemo terminals in town. 'Terminal Bus Kefa' is where you get buses to Soe, Kupang and Atambua. The market (pasar) is a bemo terminal only. Buses leave Kupang early in the morning. From Kefa to Kupang there are several buses in the morning and a few at night. The journey takes five hours if there's no stop in Soe. To or from Soe costs 2500 rp and takes two hours. There are regular buses to Atambua (2500 rp, three hours).

OEKUSSI

This former Portuguese coastal enclave north-west of Kefamenanu is part of East Timor province. When East Timor was re-opened to tourists in January 1989, travellers were only permitted to visit Oekussi on condition that they passed straight through. The situation should have eased by now.

ATAMBUA & BELU

Atambua is the major town at the eastern end of West Timor. It's a pleasant enough place with amiable people. Overland travellers to East Timor usually break the long bus journey between Kupang and Dilli by overnighting here.

Atambua is the capital of Belu (formerly Tetun) province which borders East Timor. The district is mainly dry-farmed using traditional time-consuming methods though there are some wet paddy lands on the south coast. Belu has some beautiful scenery and unspoilt villages.

Some get as far as Betun, 60 km south of Atambua, where there are a couple of losmens and restaurants. A few intrepid travellers visit the nearby villages of Kletek, Kamanasa and Bolan – you can see flying foxes and the sun set over the mountains at Kletek.

Places to Stay

There are five losmen near the centre within walking distance of each other and a sixth hotel which requires a bemo ride. All losmen include a free breakfast.

Losmen Minang (☎ 135) is cheap, clean and very central at Jalan Sukarno 12A. Singles/doubles are 5500/8800 rp with breakfast included. You can buy tickets here for the Atambua-Dilli bus.

About 100 metres to the south-west on Jalan Sukarno is *Losmen Nusantara* (☎ 117). All rooms have attached baths and singles/doubles are 10,000/15,000 rp with breakfast thrown in free.

From Losmen Minang, 100 metres to the north-east at Jalan Jenderal Gatot Subroto 3 is *Losmen Kalpataru* (☎ 351). This is one of the more expensive places in town with singles for 12,500 rp with private bath. Ironically, doubles have shared bath and cost 12,000 rp. The manager speaks some English.

Just next to the Losmen Kalpataru at Jalan Jenderal Gatot Subroto 12 is *Losmen Liurai* (☎ 84). Rooms with shared bath are 3300 rp per person, while excellent and clean singles with private bath are 8250 rp.

Losmen Merdeka (☎ 197) at Jalan Merdeka 37 is reasonably good standard with singles/doubles for 6600/11,000 rp. All rooms have an attached bath. Nearby at Jalan

Merdeka 7 is *Losmen Sahabat* where singles with outside bath are 4400 rp.

You'll have to take a bemo or make a long walk to reach *Losmen Klaben* at Jalan Dube Sinanaet 4. Rooms with attached mandi are 6600/11,000 rp.

Getting There & Away

Air Merpati has one flight weekly between Atambua and Kupang for 73,000 rp, and also one flight weekly between Atambua and Dilli for 43,000 rp.

Bus Buses from Kupang to Atambua cost 7500 rp. Atambua to Dilli is 6500 rp and buses leave early in the morning, reaching Dilli around 3 or 4 pm. You can easily arrange to have the bus pick you up at your hotel in the morning. The journey may not be straightforward in the wet season. For more details of buses to Atambua from Kupang, see the Kupang section.

Heading east towards Dilli, expect trouble during the wet season when roads are sometimes cut. Much bridge building and road improvements were going on during our last visit, but if you're going overland to Dilli, expect a bone-jarring ride.

Boat Atapupu, 25 km from Atambua, is a major port for the export of cattle to other parts of Indonesia and to Hong Kong and Singapore. You might find boats to other islands here.

MALIANA, ERMERA & MAUBARA

Maliana is the first town inside East Timor. *Losmen Purwosari Indah* is the only place to stay. Ermera, about 2½ hours south-west of Dilli, is next and has no accommodation. This was the main coffee town of Portuguese Timor.

Maubara on the coast west of Dilli has an old European-built fort. This was the centre of one of the most important old kingdoms in Portuguese Timor and it was here in 1893 that the first of a series of revolts took place, eventually leading to bloody pacification of the island by the Portuguese.

DILLI

Dilli was once the capital of Portuguese Timor. When the English scientist Alfred Russel Wallace spent several months here in 1861, he noted Dilli as:

...a most miserable place compared with even the poorest of the Dutch towns...After three hundred years of occupation there has not been a mile of road made beyond the town, and there is not a solitary European resident anywhere in the interior. All the government officials oppress and rob the natives as much as they can, and yet there is no care taken to render the town defensible should the Timorese attempt to attack it.

In the early 1970s, before the Indonesian invasion, Dilli was a pleasant, lazy place. It's still slow-paced, though it appears relatively prosperous with lots of new public buildings. Shops are open early in the morning, but everything closes up for an afternoon siesta from noon until 4.30 pm. People go to bed early and most stores shut down by 8 pm.

The dry season is *really* dry in this part of Timor, but this makes for spectacular scenery with rocky, brown hills dropping right into a turquoise sea lined with exotic tropical plants.

Information

Tourist Office The Tourist Office (☎ 21350), or Dinas Pariwisata, is on Jalan Kaikoli.

Money Bank Summa, just to the south of the New Resende Inn, is the best place to change money.

Places to Stay – bottom end

Dilli accommodation is somewhat more expensive than what you'd pay in Kupang for the same standard.

The bottom end belongs to *Penginapan Harmonia* (☎ 22065), also known as 'Mona Lisa' because that's the name of its restaurant. It's a good, quiet place and the friendly manager speaks English. Rooms with common bath are 5000 rp person. The only

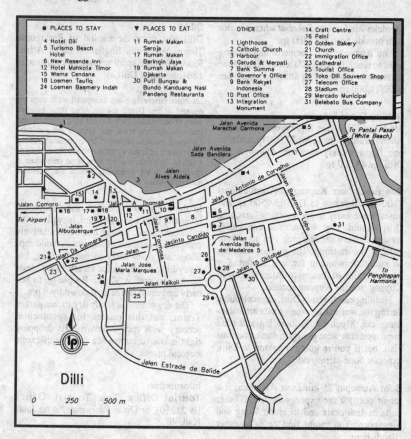

■ PLACES TO STAY	▼ PLACES TO EAT	OTHER	14 Craft Centre
4 Hotel Dili	11 Rumah Makan	1 Lighthouse	16 Pelni
5 Turismo Beach	Seroja	2 Catholic Church	20 Golden Bakery
Hotel	17 Rumah Makan	3 Harbour	21 Church
6 New Resende Inn	Beringin Jaya	6 Garuda & Merpati	22 Immigration Office
12 Hotel Mahkota Timor	19 Rumah Makan	7 Bank Summa	23 Cathedral
15 Wisma Cendana	Djakarta	8 Governor's Office	25 Tourist Office
18 Losmen Taufiq	30 Puti Bungsu &	9 Bank Rakyat	26 Toko Dili Souvenir Shop
24 Losmen Basmery Indah	Bundo Kanduang Nasi	Indonesia	27 Telecom Office
	Padang Restaurants	10 Post Office	28 Stadium
		13 Integration	29 Mercado Municipal
		Monument	31 Belebato Bus Company

Dilli

0   250   500 m

drawback is that it's four km from the centre. Taxis want 1000 rp to go there.

Losmen Taufiq (☎ 22152) on Jalan Americo Thomas is another good cheapie and has the advantage of a very central location. With shared bath, singles/doubles are 7500/12,000 rp. A room with attached mandi costs 10,000/15,000 rp.

Losmen Basmery Indah (☎ 2731) is on Jalan Estrada De Balide opposite the University of Timor Timur. It's also relatively cheap at 8250 rp per person with an outside bath, but singles/doubles with private bath go for 8250/16,500 rp.

Places to Stay – middle

Of best value is the lovely *Hotel Dilli* (☎ 21871) on the beachfront at Jalan Avenida Sada Bandeira 25, a short walk east of the town centre. All rooms are doubles, and with an attached bath and ceiling fan the tariff is 16,500, 18,000 or 20,000 rp depending which standard you choose. Air-con rooms are available for 30,000 rp.

A short walk further away from the centre, also on Jalan Avenida Marechal Carmona, the *Turismo Beach Hotel* (☎ 22029) is more expensive but continues to get rave reviews. Budget singles/doubles are 11,000/18,150 rp, but air-con rooms are 32,250/35,200 rp. There are VIP rooms at 45,650/50,600 rp and suites for 61,050/66,000 rp. The higher priced rooms include a balcony and seaview.

Wisma Cendana (☎ 21141) on Jalan Ameriko Thomas is a government-run hotel which seems to explain why no one cares that the rooms are often empty. Nevertheless, it's spotlessly clean and centrally located. Standard doubles are 25,000 rp and VIP rooms go for 35,000 rp. All rooms have air-con and attached bath.

Places to Stay – top end
New Resende Inn (☎ 22094) is centrally located on Jalan Avenida Bispo Medeiros. It's luxuriously air-conditioned and has standard singles/doubles for 35,000/40,000 rp while deluxe rooms are 44,000/49,000 rp. The hotel restaurant serves good Indonesian, Chinese and Western food.

Hotel Mahkota Timor (☎ 21283, 21656) on Jalan Alves Aldeia is so new that the paint wasn't dry on the walls when we visited. Plush standard rooms are 45,000/50,000 rp, while deluxe is 55,000/60,000 rp and suites go for 75,000 rp.

Places to Eat
For some reason, East Timor can import directly from overseas without goods going through Jakarta, so you can buy Singapore Tiger beer and even Portuguese wines like Mateus.

The top-rated restaurant in town is *Rumah Makan Djakarta* on Jalan Albuquerque in the centre of town. The setting is congenial and the food is good, but prices are relatively high.

Slightly lower prices but less fancy decor can be found at *Rumah Makan Seroja* on Jalan Alves Aldeia. This place is known for its Chinese food.

The *Turismo Beach Hotel* serves Western and Indonesian food in a beautiful garden setting.

Getting There & Away
Air Merpati flies daily from from Kupang to Dilli (73,000 rp). Some return flights to Kupang continue on to Denpasar and Surabaya, or you can change planes at Kupang and continue on to Jakarta the same day. Merpati has less frequent flights linking Dilli with Oekussi, Atambua and Suai on the south coast of East Timor. Merpati (☎ 21088) and Garuda (☎ 21880) share an office in the New Resende Inn on Jalan Avenida Bispo Medeiros.

Bus From Kupang, you must first take a bus to Atambua and spend the night there, continuing to Dilli the following morning. For details of Kupang-Atambua buses see the Kupang section. In Atambua, buy bus tickets to Dilli in the Losmen Minang the night before departure and they will pick you up at your hotel. Buses from Atambua to Dilli cost 6500 rp and leave around 7 am. The actual ride takes about 4½ hours on a bad road. However, you may be subjected to a tedious sightseeing tour (keliling) of Atambua as they pick up more passengers and finally get going an hour or more after you hop in, and the same thing happens when you arrive in Dilli.

Going the other way, in Dilli buy your tickets the night before at the Rumah Makan Beringin Jaya next to Losmen Taufiq. Again, expect an hour of keliling before actual departure.

Buses from Dilli to Baukau depart between 6 and 7 am. The journey takes four hours and costs 3000 rp. Buy tickets the night before at Belebato Bus Company and catch the bus at the Mercado (Pasar), or have them arrange to pick you up at your hotel and go keliling.

Boat The large Pelni ship *Kelimutu* stops in at Dilli on every other journey (about once a month). See the Getting Around chapter at the beginning of this book for the complete schedule.

Pelni's KM *Elang* loops every 10 days or so round Timor and the small islands to the north. One route is Kupang, Oekussi, Atapupu, Dilli, Kisar in southern Maluku, Kalabahi, Kupang. Recently, a once-weekly

Pelni ship has started running from Dilli to Kalabahi on Alor Island (6500 rp).

When buying boat tickets in Dilli, you need a photocopy of your passport and Indonesians need a photocopy of their ID cards.

Getting Around
To/From the Airport Dilli's Comoro Airport is five km west of the town centre and a taxi to your accommodation costs 5000 rp. You can also get there for 200 rp on bus A or B.

Bemo & Taxi Bemos cost 200 rp any place within the city limits. The best way to get around is by taxis which cost a flat 750 rp within the town.

SAME
A spectacular route runs through the rugged interior to Same south of Dilli. This was a centre of late 19th and early 20th century revolts led by Boaventura, the liurai of Same.

BAUKAU
The second-largest centre of what was Portuguese Timor, the charmingly run-down colonial town of Baukau (formerly Baucau) has many Portuguese buildings and Japanese caves left over from WW II. Baukau once had an international airport eight km west of the centre, but it's now used by the Indonesian military. The altitude makes Baukau pleasantly cool and the beaches, five km sharply downhill from the town, are breathtakingly beautiful. To get to the beaches you can walk down and take the risk of having to walk back up – or charter a bemo for around 5000 rp for a couple of hours.

Dilli to Baukau is a four-hour bus trip (3000 rp) along the coast. The bus stops briefly at Manatuto along the way. The road is unsealed and pretty rough all the way from Manatuto to Tutuala at the eastern end of Timor.

Places to Stay & Eat
The Portuguese-built *Hotel Flamboyant* is the only hotel. It may have been good 15 years ago but now nothing seems to work

although the beds are fine and the views beautiful. There is no food available but there's one restaurant in town. Bicycle rentals are available for a pricey 15,000 rp per day.

BAUKAU TO TUTUALA
There's an old Portuguese fort at Laga, on the coast about 20 km beyond Baukau. Lautem, a further 35 km, is the next town where there are lots of traditional houses. From Lautem the road improves dramatically for 15 km until it reaches Lospalos. Lospalos to Tutuala, on the eastern tip of Timor, is about 30 km and you should be able to get a bemo if it's not too late in the day. Tutuala has interesting houses built on stilts, plus spectacular views out to sea. While Timorese houses are usually built out of timber, bamboo and palm leaves the design varies greatly from region to region.

VIKEKE
A road heads south over the mountains from Baukau to Vikeke which is close to the south coast. There is a bus from Dilli but few travellers make the effort to visit Vikeke as the south coast is less scenic than the north.

Roti & Sawu

Between Timor and Sumba the small dry islands of Roti and Sawu are little visited but, with their successful economies based on the lontar palm, have played a significant role in Nusa Tenggara's history and now preserve some interesting cultures.

The Lontar Economy
The traditional Rotinese and Sawunese economies have for centuries centred on the lontar palm. The wood from this multipurpose tree can be used to make houses, furniture, musical instruments, mats, baskets and even cigarette papers. Its juice can be tapped and drunk fresh, or boiled into a syrup and diluted with water – and this syrup formed the staple diet. The juice can be

further boiled into palm sugar and the froth from the boiling juice can be fed to pigs and goats kept in small coral-walled enclosures (doing away with the time-consuming fencing of fields required for cattle). The lontar palm is also drought and fire-resistant and there was no annual period of hunger on Roti or Sawu as there was on the other islands of Nusa Tenggara. Meanwhile, vegetables could be grown in dry fields or in small garden plots, kept fertilised with animal manure or lontar leaves.

Because the lontar palm only required two or three months of work each year, and since the women were the gardeners and handicrafts people, the men had plenty of time for other activities. Thus the Rotinese and Sawunese became the entrepreneurs of Nusa Tenggara, especially on Sumba and Timor to which many of them emigrated with Dutch encouragement. By the 20th century, the Rotinese dominated both the civil service *and* the local anti-colonial movements on these islands.

ROTI (ROTE)

Off the west end of Timor, Roti (also spelled Rote) is the southernmost island in Indonesia. The lightly built Rotinese speak a language similar to the Tetum of Timor. Traditionally, Roti is divided into 18 domains. In 1681 a bloody Dutch campaign placed their local allies in control of the island, and Roti became a source of slaves and supplies for the Dutch base at Kupang. In the 18th century, the Rotinese started taking advantage of the Dutch presence, gradually adopted Christianity and, with Dutch support, established a school system which, with the time left available for education by the lontar economy, eventually turned them into the region's educated elite.

The Rotinese openness to change is the main reason their old culture is no longer so strong as Sawu's – though animistic beliefs and rites linger behind their Protestantism. At some festivals, families reportedly cut separate chunks out of a live buffalo then take them away to eat.

Ikat weaving on Roti today uses mainly black, red and yellow chemical dyes but the designs can still be complex: typical are floral and patola motifs, and/or a wide central black stripe with several patterned and coloured stripes either side of it. In former times the motifs were different for each of Roti's 18 domains, and patola motifs were status symbols. One tradition which hasn't disappeared is the wearing of wide-brimmed lontar leaf hats with a curious spike sticking up near the front – perhaps representing a lontar palm, an old Portuguese helmet or a mast. Rotinese also love music and dancing.

The tiny island of Ndao off west Roti is another lontar-tapping and ikat-weaving centre. In the dry season, Ndao men take off for other islands to sell ikat and work as gold and silversmiths.

Baa

Roti's main town is on the north coast. The main street is close to the ocean and a couple of churches stand beside the central square. *Nembrela Beach Hotel* has its own generator, costs 6000 rp per person and meals are served at extra cost. *Hotel Ricki* on the square near the mosque is adequate with rooms at

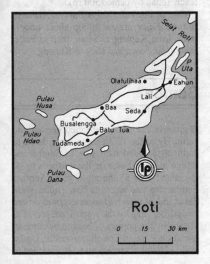

Roti

0   15   30 km

6000 rp per person, but there's no food and crowds of kids peer in at the windows. Alternatively, there's the slightly newer *Hotel Kesia*. There are some coral beaches near Baa. Some houses have boat-shaped thatched roofs with carvings (connected with traditional ancestor cults) at the ends. There's plenty of good fresh fish to be bought if someone will cook it for you.

Getting There & Away

Air Merpati has two flights a week to/from Kupang for 36,000 rp.

Boat Boats to Roti depart from Bolok Harbour in Kupang on Monday, Wednesday, Friday and Saturday at 9 am and return the same day. Reach Bolok Harbour from central Kupang by taking bemo Nos 12 or 13 (750 rp). The four-hour boat trip costs 4200 rp. In Roti, the ferries dock about an hour's bemo ride from Baa. Smaller boats also make the crossing.

Getting Around

There are only a few buses or bemos on Roti, but it's possible to rent a motorbike in Baa.

SAWU (SABU)

Mid-way between Roti and Sumba, but with closer linguistic links to Sumba, the low, bare little island of Sawu (also spelled Sabu) is still a stronghold of animistic beliefs, collectively known as *jingitiu*. These persist even though Portuguese missionaries first arrived before 1600 and the Dutch continued their work.

Sawu's roughly 40,000 people are divided into five traditional domains and the main settlement, Seba on the north-west coast, was the centre of the leading domain in Dutch times. Sawunese society is divided into clans named after their male founders, but also into two 'noble' and 'common' halves determined by a person's mother's lineage: the halves are called *hubi ae* (greater flower stalk) and *hubi iki* (lesser flower stalk). Sawunese women have a thriving ikat-weaving tradition – their cloth typically has stripes of black or dark blue interspersed by stripes with floral motifs, clan or hubi emblems.

There are three places to stay in Sawu: *Ongko Da'i Homestay*, *Makarim Homestay* and *Petykuswan Homestay*. All three cost 5,000 rp per person without meals and 10,000 rp with. Seba has a market and a handful of trucks provides the island's public transport, though you can also hire motorcycles for 10,000 rp per day. A group of stones at Namata near Seba is a ritual site: animal sacrifices, with a whole community sharing the meat, take place around August to October. Another festival in the second quarter of the year sees a boat pushed out to sea as an offering – in Timu in the east, it may carry a buffalo.

Getting There & Away

Air Merpati flies from Kupang to Sawu and back twice a week for 73,000 rp each way.

Boat A Perum ASDP ferry to Sawu leaves Kupang's Bolok Harbour every Wednesday at 4 pm. The fare is 11,500 rp for the nine-hour trip. There are also large ships which depart occasionally from Tenau Harbour, near Kupang. From central Kupang, you can reach Tenau by bemo (500 rp).

One of the Pelni ships *Baruna Artha* or *Baruna Fajar* makes a loop about once a week from Kupang to Sawu, then to Ende, Waingapu, Sawu and back to Kupang.

Sumba

A great ladder once connected heaven and earth. By it, the first people came down to earth; they found their way to Sumba and settled at Cape Sasar on the northern tip of the island – or so the myth goes. Another Sumbanese tale recounts how Umbu Walu Sasar, one of their two ancestors, was driven away from Java by the wars. Transported to Sumba by the powers of heaven he came to live at Cape Sasar. The other ancestor, Umbu Walu Mandoko, arrived by boat, travelled to

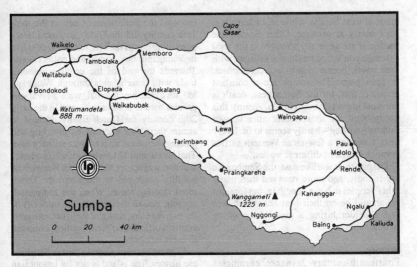

the east and settled at the mouth of the Sungai (river) Kambaniru.

Such myths may come as near the truth as any version of the origins of a people who are physically of Malay stock with a tinge of Melanesian; whose language falls into the same bag that holds the Bimanese of east Sumbawa, the Manggarai and Ngada of west Flores and the Sawunese of Sawu; whose death and burial ceremonies are strongly reminiscent of Torajaland in Sulawesi; and whose brilliant ikat textiles, fine carved stone tombs and high, thatched clan houses suggest common origins with similar traditions scattered from Sumatra to Maluku.

Wherever they came from, the island the Sumbanese have ended up on lies far from Indonesia's main cultural currents, south of Flores and midway between Sumbawa and Timor. Its isolation has helped preserve one of the country's most bizarre cultures, particularly in its wetter, more fertile and remoter western half which is home to about two-thirds of its 400,000 people.

Right up to this century, Sumbanese life has been punctuated by periodic warfare between a huge number of rival princedoms. Though Christianity and (less so) Islam have

now made inroads, more than half the people in the west and about a third in the east still adhere to the animist *marapu* religion, and old conflicts are recalled every year at west Sumba's often violent Pasola festivals – semi-mock battles between teams of mounted horsemen.

The 'mock' battles sometimes become real, as in August, 1991 when two villages went to war. Over 80 homes were burnt down. The authorities had to intervene, and two police and one army officer were killed. While such incidents are rare, it should serve as a reminder to make local enquiries before heading out into the bush.

Many Sumbanese men still carry long-bladed knives in wooden sheaths tucked into their waistbands; they wear scarves as turbans and wrap their brightly coloured sarongs so that they expose the lower two-thirds of their legs and have a long piece of cloth hanging down in front. Bahasa Indonesia apart, East and West Sumbanese speak different dialects of one language. The eastern one is called Kambera.

The last 20 years have seen an increasing flow of visitors to Sumba, attracted chiefly by the ikat cloth of east Sumba. The ikat made in west Sumba, while still interesting, isn't nearly as exciting. Other Sumbanese traditions are generally stronger in the west – though you'll find traditional villages, with their exotic houses, tombs and ceremonies, in both parts. The tombs are a constant reminder that, for the Sumbanese, death is the most important event in life. Against this background the most recent attraction of Sumba – surfing – hardly seems to fit. Every year, however, a few more Western surfies come in search of different waves.

Despite their warlike past, the Sumbanese are friendly, and more reserved than many other peoples in Nusa Tenggara, but foreigners should be on their best behaviour here and consider hiring a guide for visiting remote villages.

History

Fourteenth-century Javanese chronicles place Sumba under the control of the Majapahits. After that empire declined the island is supposed to have come under the rule of Bima in Sumbawa, then of Gowa in southern Sulawesi. But Sumbanese history is mostly a saga of internal wars, mainly over land and trading rights, between a great number of petty princedoms. A ruler's authority rested on his descent from the legendary hero-founder of the princedom together with the prestige and wealth of his clan. The most powerful clans claimed direct descent from the legendary original settlers, Sasar and Mandoku. The traditional social order was legitimised in lengthy all-night recitations. Despite their mutual hostility, princedoms often depended on each other economically. The inland regions produced horses, lumber, betel nuts, rice, fruit and dyewoods, while the much-valued ikat cloth was made on the coast, where the drier climate was suitable for cotton growing. The coastal people also controlled trade with other islands.

The Dutch at first paid little attention to Sumba because, like the rest of Nusa Tenggara, it lacked commercial possibilities. The sandalwood trade conducted in the 18th century was constantly interrupted by wars

amongst the Sumbanese. Only in the mid-19th century did the Dutch arrange a treaty permitting one of their representatives to live in Waingapu, buy horses and collect taxes. Towards the end of the century Sumba's trade with other islands through Waingapu led to extensive internal wars as various princes tried to dominate it – and in the early 20th century the Dutch finally decided to secure their own interests by invading and placing the island under direct military rule. That lasted until 1913 when a civilian administration was set up, although the Sumbanese nobility continued to reign and the Dutch ruled through them. When the Indonesian republic ceased to recognise the authority of the native rulers, many of them became government officials, so their families continued to exert influence.

Climate has also played a part in Sumbanese history. The island is dry by Indonesian standards, especially in the east which is much more like Timor and Australia than the lush islands to the north. Its extensive grasslands made it into one of the leading horse-breeding islands in Indonesia. Horses are still used as transport in the more rugged regions; they are a symbol of wealth and social status and have traditionally been used as part of the bride-price. Brahmin bulls, first brought to Sumba in the 1920s, are also bred.

Culture

Old beliefs fade, customs die and rituals change: the Sumbanese still make textiles, but no longer hunt heads; 20 years ago the bride-price may have been coloured beads and two buffaloes, today it might include a bicycle. Churches are now a fairly common sight and in some areas the following traditions are dying – but in others, particularly in the west, they thrive.

Religion The basis of traditional Sumbanese religion is *marapu* – a collective term for all spiritual forces including gods, spirits, and ancestors. The most important event in a person's life is death, when he joins the invisible world of the marapu, from where he can influence the world of the living.

Marapu mameti is the collective name for dead people. The living can appeal to them for help, especially to their own relatives – but they can also be harmful if irritated. The *marapu maluri* have always been marapu (unlike human beings who become marapu when they die). Their power is sometimes concentrated on certain places or objects, much like the Javanese idea of *semangat*.

Death Ceremonies On the day of burial horses or buffaloes are killed to provide the deceased with food for their journey to the land of the marapu. Ornaments and a sirih (betel nut) bag are also buried with the body. The living must bury their dead as richly as possible to avoid being reprimanded by the marapu mameti. Without a complete and honourable ceremony the dead cannot enter the invisible world, and roam about menacing the living. It was said the dead travel to Cape Sasar to climb the ladder to the invisible world above.

One Sumbanese custom – which parallels the Torajan customs of central Sulawesi – is the deliberate destruction of wealth. Traditionally a major goal of the family is the accumulation of wealth: buffaloes, horses, textiles and jewellery. A family would gain prestige by sponsoring religious festivals at which this wealth would be displayed and many buffaloes slaughtered. Funerals may be delayed for several years until enough wealth has been accumulated for a second burial accompanied by the traditional rites and the erection of a massive stone slab tomb. In such cases the dragging of the tombstone from outside the village is an important part of the procedure. Everyone takes part – sometimes hundreds are needed to move the block of stone – and the family of the deceased feeds them. A *ratu* (priest) sings for the pullers, urging them on with songs which are often answered in chorus by the group. The song functions as an invocation to the stone. Once upon a time, important people's slaves would be buried with them.

When the Indonesian republic was founded, the government tried to stop the destruction of livestock by introducing a slaughter tax, as in Toraja. This reduced the number of animals killed but didn't alter basic attitudes. The Sumbanese, like the Torajans, believe you *can* take it with you!

Villages A traditional village usually consists of two more or less parallel rows of houses facing each other, with a square between. In the middle of the square is a stone with another flat stone on top of it, on which are made offerings to the village's protective marapu. These structures, spirit stones or *kateda* can also be found at the main entrance to the village, keeping out the angry spirits of evil and disease, and other outside marapu. Kateda are also found in the gardens and rice fields and mark the places where people call on the agricultural marapu, and bring them offerings when planting, weeding and harvesting.

The village square also contains the large stone-slab tombs of important ancestors, often finely carved, though nowadays often made of cement.

In former times the heads of slain enemies would be hung on a dead tree in the village square while ceremonies and feasts took place. This skull-tree is called *andung* which means 'monument' and it's often pictured on east Sumbanese textiles. The andung represents the war marapu and the ceremony of hanging the heads is a celebration of victory.

A traditional Sumbanese dwelling is a large rectangular structure raised on piles; it houses an extended family. The thatched – nowadays often corrugated iron – roof slopes gently upwards from all four sides, then rises sharply toward the centre, and is supported on four central pillar posts. Along the front of the house is a verandah at least a metre wide and about one to 1½ metres above the ground.

Inside the house, a cooking hearth is set in the middle of the floor between the four main roof pillars. Above it in a kind of loft are placed objects representing the marapu maluri. Rituals accompanying the building of a house include an offering, at the time of planting the first pillar, to find out whether or not the marapu agree with the location; one method is to slaughter a chicken and examine its liver. On every important occasion a Sumbanese attempts to cultivate good relations with the invisible world to ensure a secure and peaceful life. If this harmony is disturbed, sickness, drought and bad harvests might follow. Many houses are decked with buffalo horns or strings of pig-jaws from past sacrifices.

Visiting Villages A very awkward situation can arise when you visit traditional villages in Sumba, especially west Sumba. If the villagers ask you to pay to take photos, or even just to visit, should you?

Some Sumbanese villages are completely unaccustomed to tourists, and even those that get a steady stream seem to have difficulty knowing how to handle them. This is hardly surprising for a society which has little understanding of the Westerner's desire simply to observe and explore 'exotic' cultures.

If you're interested in their weavings or other artefacts, the villagers can probably put you down as a potential trader. If all you want to do is chat a bit and look around they may be puzzled about why you've come, and if you simply turn up with a camera, little of the local language and less time, they're not only likely to think you're nuts but may be offended too.

On Sumba, giving betel nut (sirih) is the traditional way of greeting guests or hosts, and if you have time to get friendly with villagers it's a great idea to take some with you. Offer it to the kepala desa or the other most 'senior' looking person around. You can buy it at Waingapu and Waikabubak markets among other places. Most foreigners find it pretty disgusting stuff – it gives you a mild buzz and a bright red mouth.

If you are offered betel nut, never refuse it! Some foreigners have really caused offence by saying, 'No, I don't want to buy it'. If you don't want to chew betel nut, then just put it in your pocket and offer some cigarettes in return – make sure you've stocked up on cigarettes.

Some villages have grown used to foreigners arriving without sirih and without any apparently sensible purpose. In such places a gift of 1000 rp or a pack of cigarettes has become a usually acceptable substitute; in return you should be able to take pictures and may be offered a drink. In off-the-beaten-track kampungs, offering 1000 rp is also OK, especially if you make clear that you're offering it because you don't have any sirih. This way you still conform to the give-and-take principle. Some places have seen so many fleeting visits by people they can't converse with that they have lost interest and hospitality will be thin; a few villages have even come out and said they no longer want tourists. Just a few have become decidedly commercial and will ask you for as many rupiah as they can get, sometimes using intimidation and (usually hollow) threats.

Some villages are under a kind of government supervision as protected monuments. In these places there'll usually be a kiosk or at least a semi-official person who will ask you for a fee of 1000 rp or 2000 rp. Where the money goes is anybody's guess.

Whatever the circumstances, taking a guide is a very big help. A guide smoothes over the language difficulties and will know when someone is simply trying to con you for money. No matter where you go, taking the time to chat with the villagers and establish some kind of warmth with them, helps them to treat you more as a human being and guest than as a customer or alien. The more time you have to spend in each place, rather than just dashing lens-in-hand from one kampung to the next, the better.

Ikat The ikat woven by the women of the eastern coastal regions of Sumba is probably the most dramatic in Indonesia. Not only are the colours predominantly bright – indigo blue and earthy *kombu* orange-red – but unlike the more abstract patterns on Flores, the Sumba motifs are pictorial history, reminders of tribal wars and an age which ended with the coming of the Dutch – the skulls of vanquished enemies dangle off trees, mounted riders wield spears.

Ikat motif

Traditionally ikat cloth was used only on special occasions: at rituals accompanying the harvest and the reception of visitors, as gifts to other families, as offerings to the sponsors of a festival and as clothing for leaders, their relatives and attendants. Less than 90 years ago, only members of Sumba's highest clans and their personal attendants could make or wear it. Death was threatened for those who violated the class monopoly. The most impressive use of the cloth was at important funerals where dancers and the guards of the corpse were dressed in richly decorated costumes and glittering head-dresses. The corpse itself was dressed in the finest textiles and then bound with so many of them that it resembled a huge mound. The first missionary on Sumba, D K Wielenga, described a funeral he witnessed in 1925:

The brilliant examples of decorated cloths were carefully kept till the day of burial. The prominent chief took 40 to 50 to the grave with him and the raja was put to rest with no less than 100 or 200. When they appeared in the hereafter among their ancestors, then they must appear in full splendour. And so the most attractive cloths went into the earth.

The Dutch conquest broke the Sumbanese nobility's monopoly on the production and use of ikat, and opened up a large external market for it. Collected by Dutch ethnographers and museums since the late 19th century (the Rotterdam and Basel museums have fine collections), the large cloths became popular in Java and Holland. To cater for the new market, production expanded. Furthermore the trade in horses and, later, in beef cattle brought increased riches to some of the Sumbanese nobility whose demand for textiles consequently increased. By the 1920s, visitors were already noting a fall in standards and the introduction of non-traditional design elements – rampant lions from the Dutch coat of arms, fluttering flags, bicycles and steamships.

A Sumbanese woman's ikat sarong is known as a *lau*; a *hinggi* is a large rectangular cloth used by men as a sarong or shawl.

Motifs The skull tree is the most readily identifiable of the amazing range of motifs that appear on Sumba ikat today. Figures of skull trees on the textiles usually also include its stone base and the horns of sacrificed buffaloes attached to the tree.

Deer – whose antlers were exported in large quantities from Sumba in the early 20th century – and the dogs and horsemen that hunted them are also found on textiles. Snakes often appear as *nagas* – the crowned snake-dragon with large teeth, wings and legs. Turtle motifs also appear – turtles were caught on Sumba's southern beaches and used for food while the shell was exported or used for making combs.

Sumba's famous horses often appear with riders holding long spears. Oddly enough buffaloes, which have been equally important with possibly hundreds slaughtered at the burial of a Sumbanese raja, have rarely been depicted on ikat.

Humans, male and female, adult and child, are included. Sometimes male figures wear the gold forehead decoration known as a *lamba*, which may represent a boat. On Sumba the lamba was a preserve of the royal class. Boat motifs also appear: although the

Sumbanese aren't a seagoing people, many coastal families trace their ancestry from a founder who arrived on a boat. Other motifs which have appeared on Sumba ikat include trees, shrimps, squid, fish, seahorses, scorpions, beetles, centipedes, spiders, horseflies, lizards, crocodiles, apes, chickens, fighting cocks, hawks and eagles. Dragons have also been depicted, possibly inspired by motifs taken from Chinese porcelain long before Europeans arrived. Even elephants have appeared on Sumba ikat!

WAINGAPU

Now the largest town on Sumba, with 25,000 people, Waingapu became the administrative centre after the Dutch took over the island in 1906. It had long been the centre of the trade controlled by the coastal princedoms, with textiles and metal goods being brought in by traders from Makassar, Bima and Ende, and the much-prized Sumba horses, dyewoods and lumber being exported.

Waingapu is the main entry point to Sumba but the island's chief attractions lie elsewhere, in the west and south-east. The town does, however, have a large group of ikat traders who run stores or hang around outside hotels. If you're interested in buying ikat have a look at what they offer before heading out to the villages. You can get an idea of the range of quality, design and price – and if you don't find what you want in the villages, come back to Waingapu. Prices in the town are generally higher than in the actual weaving centres – but not that much higher, and there's more to choose from. Bargaining's equally tough anywhere. The Hotel Sandle Wood has a good range of ikat for sale, and the owner's son has a separate, well-stocked shop out the back of the hotel, on Jalan Metawai.

Prailiu, two km out of Waingapu and just to the right off the road south to Melolo, is an ikat-weaving centre. Kawangu, 10 km from Waingapu and about 300 metres to the right off the same road, has some stone-slab tombs. Traditional houses may be seen at Maru, on the coast heading north-west from Waingapu. You can easily reach Prailiu by frequent bemos.

Orientation & Information

Waingapu has two centres, about a km apart: the northern one focuses on the harbour, the southern one on the bus station. Both have markets, and places to stay; banks and offices are divided between the two. The Bank Rakyat Indonesia on Jalan Yani will change major travellers' cheques (it's the only bank on the island that will), as well as some foreign currencies. It's open from 8 am to noon Monday to Thursday and Saturday, and from 7 to 11 am on Friday. The post office on Jalan Hasanuddin is open from 7 am to 2 pm Monday to Thursday, to 11 am Friday and to 1 pm Saturday.

Places to Stay

Losmen Permata is a small but pleasant place with only five rooms. This hotel would have had an outstanding harbour view except that the owners put the windows on the wrong side of the building! Nevertheless, it's OK and becoming popular. The price is 3300 rp per person for a room with attached mandi.

Hotel Sandle Wood (☎ 117) at Jalan Panjaitan 23 near the bus terminal is the top place in town with some fine new rooms. Economy singles/doubles with shared bath are 6600/11,000 rp, while excellent '1st class' rooms with private bath cost 11,000/16,500 rp. VIP rooms with air-con go for 22,000/33,000 rp. This is a sharp place whose Chinese owners are constantly upgrading the facilities.

Just down the road from the Sandle Wood is the amiable *Losmen Kaliuda*, a small, quiet and new place with a pleasant garden. Clean singles/doubles with shared bath are 7000/8800 rp, or 8000/11,000 rp for rooms with attached bath.

Hotel Elim (☎ 462) at Jalan Ahmad Yani 55 is somewhat old and faded, but it's still the number two place in town. All rooms have attached bath. Upstairs rooms with fans and mosquito nets go for 12,100/13,310 rp, more basic downstairs ones for 5500/6050 rp

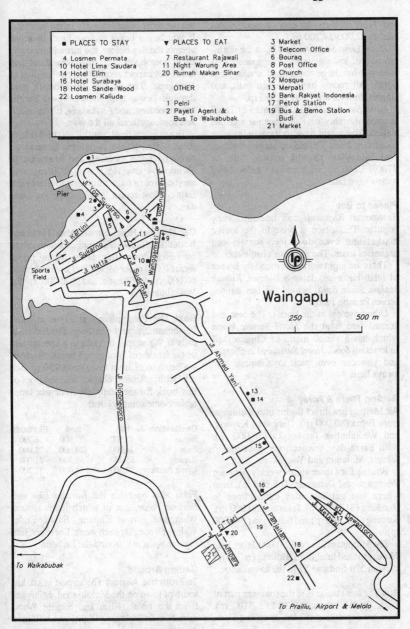

PLACES TO STAY
4 Losmen Permata
10 Hotel Lima Saudara
14 Hotel Elim
16 Hotel Surabaya
18 Hotel Sandle Wood
22 Losmen Kaliuda

PLACES TO EAT
7 Restaurant Rajawali
11 Night Warung Area
20 Rumah Makan Sinar

OTHER
1 Pelni
2 Payeti Agent &
   Bus To Waikabubak
3 Market
5 Telecom Office
6 Bouraq
8 Post Office
9 Church
12 Mosque
13 Merpati
15 Bank Rakyat Indonesia
17 Petrol Station
19 Bus & Bemo Station
   Budi
21 Market

Waingapu

0   250   500 m

To Waikabubak

To Prailiu, Airport & Melolo

and 7150/7865 rp. Air-con singles/doubles start at 22,000/24,200 rp.

Hotel Lima Saudara (☎ 83), in the northern part of town at Jalan Wanggameti 2, is tatty but has large rooms and a nice front porch. All rooms have attached bath, and singles/doubles are 7500/14,150 rp.

Hotel Surabaya (☎ 125) at Jalan El Tari 2 is uncomfortably near the mosque and bus station. You might have to bargain for your room rate here. Officially, singles/doubles cost 5500/9900 rp with outside bath, or 7700/13,200 rp with private bath. Most rooms have fans.

Places to Eat

Restaurant Rajawali has become very popular. This place is wise to the tourist market and even does jeep rentals and organises tours. The food isn't bad either.

There are night warungs around the corner of Jalan Hatta and Jalan Sudirman. *Rumah Makan Sinar Budi*, behind the bus station, serves Padang food.

Otherwise eat at the hotels. The best and dearest fare is at the *Hotel Sandle Wood* which has a varied menu of Chinese and Indonesian food. *Hotel Surabaya* is cheaper and you can even pick up Chinese take aways here.

Getting There & Away

Air Merpati has direct flights into Waingapu from Bima (80,000 rp), Denpasar, Kupang, and Waikabubak-Tambolaka (50,000 rp), with same-day connections possible to Jakarta, Mataram and Yogyakarta.

Bouraq flies three times weekly between Waingapu and Denpasar (165,000 rp), from where you get same-day connections to Bandung (317,000 rp), Jakarta (430,000 rp), Kupang (122,400 rp) and Surabaya (198,000 rp).

The Merpati office (☎ 323) is at Jalan Yani 73 next to the Hotel Elim. Bouraq (☎ 363) is at Jalan Yos Sudarso 57 in the town centre.

Bus The bus station is in the southern part of town. To Waikabubak (136 km, 3100 rp), there are departures at 7 am, noon and 3 pm,

but the most buses are early in the morning. If you buy a ticket at your hotel or a bus agent's the day before, the bus will pick you up at your hotel. The trip takes about five hours but expect another hour of keliling in Waingapu. The road to Waikabubak goes through Lewa, long the centre of Sumba horsebreeding, and Anakalang. It's an excellent road, surfaced all the way.

Buses also head south-east to Melolo, Rende, Baing and Nggongi. Several go throughout the morning and afternoon to Melolo (64 km, 1½ hours, 1500 rp), with maybe three or four continuing to Rende and Baing. Most return to Waingapu the same day.

Car The Elim Hotel, Sandle Wood Hotel and Restaurant Rajawali all rent cars with driver for out- of-town trips. Some asking prices were 50,000 rp for Melolo or Lewa and back, 60,000 rp for Rende and 100,000 rp for Waikabubak.

Boat The Pelni office (☎ 27) is at Jalan Pelabuhan 2, near the harbour. The *Kelimutu* calls at Waingapu. It docks at a special pier on the far side of Waingapu's regular harbour – a bemo to or from town costs 250 rp. See the Getting Around chapter near the front of this book for the complete *Kelimutu* timetable. Some sample fares:

Destination	1st	2nd	Ekonomi
Bima	49,300	37,600	16,700
Ende	34,000	28,000	13,000
Kupang	65,250	51,300	21,000
Ujung Pandang	93,300	74,000	31,200

Pelni also operates the *Baruna Eka* and *Baruna Fajar*, one of which loops around Waingapu, Sawu, Kupang, Sawu, Ende, Waingapu roughly each week. For other, less regular boats ask around the harbour.

Getting Around

To/From the Airport The airport is six km south of town on the Melolo road. Minivans from the hotels Elim and Sandle Wood usually meet incoming flights and will give you a free ride if you stay with them. The taxi drivers will tell you that these vans don't exist – go out in the car park and look for yourself. On departure, these hotels will also give you a free ride back to the airport.

Taxi drivers will ask for 3000 rp to go to/from the airport, but they can be bargained to 2000 rp.

Bemos to the airport are infrequent, but if you find one expect to pay around 300 rp.

Bemo A bemo to any destination around town costs 200 rp.

SOUTH-EAST SUMBA
Some of the villages of south-east Sumba have splendid stone tombs (as well as less exciting concrete ones) and produce some of the island's best weaving, but the traditional way of life is not as strong as it is in the west of the island. You can buy weavings in the villages, but take plenty of patience with you if you want prices below those of the Waingapu merchants.

Melolo
If you don't want to visit the south-east in a day trip from Waingapu, the small town of Melolo, 62 km from Waingapu and close to some of the more interesting villages, has accommodation possibilities. On Thursday afternoon and Friday morning there's a market at Lumbukori, on a hilltop about three km out of Melolo.

Places to Stay & Eat *L D Gah Homestead*, owned by the same people as the Taman Ria Beach Inn in Kupang, has a couple of rooms at 3000 rp per person. It's a primitive place to stay, marginally better than an ill-equipped camping trip. Bus drivers can drop you here and the hotel can arrange for you to rent a motorbike or pushbike to get out to the villages. Basic meals are available or try the *Rumah Makan Anda* for goat and rice. There might be families in Melolo which take in travellers, or try the kepala desa.

Getting There & Away Buses to Melolo from Waingapu run about hourly until

around 4 pm; it's 1500 rp for the 1½-hour trip. The road is paved and crosses mainly flat grasslands. From Melolo the road continues south to Baing. Another road from Melolo crosses the mountains to Nggongi – trucks run along this road except during the rainy season.

Rende
Seven km towards Baing from Melolo, Rende has an impressive line-up of big stone-slab tombs and makes some of the best ikat in the world. You may be asked 2000 rp as a sort of admission/hospitality fee and photo-licence. If you sit and chat with the villagers rather than just stride in and start pointing your camera, they might not ask you for anything – but you might want to make a small gift anyway, at least some cigarettes. Some of the finest ikat weaving goes on here and the people are usually happy to explain their methods to you, but prices are high. Though Rende still has a 'raja', other traditions are declining owing to the cost of ceremonies and the breakdown of the marapu religion here.

The largest tomb at Rende is for a former chief and consists of four stone pillars two metres high, supporting a rectangular slab of stone about five metres long, 2½ metres wide and a metre thick. Two stone tablets stand atop the main slab and are carved with human, buffalo, deer, lobster, fish, crocodile and turtle figures. A number of traditional-style Sumbanese houses face the tombs.

Places to Stay It is possible to stay with the raja, but remember that this is a royal family, not hotel staff. Act accordingly!

Getting There & Away Three or four buses a day go from Waingapu to Rende, starting around 7 am each morning. The trip takes about two hours and costs 1200 rp.

Umabara & Pau
Like Rende, these two villages near Melolo have traditional Sumbanese houses, impressive tombs and weavings. At Umabara the largest tombs are those of relatives

of the present 'raja' – who speaks some English and is quite friendly. Apart from serving you coffee he may also offer you betel nut. The moment a Sumbanese opens his or her mouth you'll see that the custom of betel nut chewing is alive and well! Again, expect to pay 1000 rp if you're looking for hospitality and/or want to take photos. Apart from ikat you may also be shown *hikung* cloth, in which decorative patterns are woven, not dyed, into the fabric.

Getting There & Away Leave Melolo by the main road in the Waingapu direction, and soon after crossing the river on the edge of town, turn left along a dirt road. About a 20-minute walk up here is a horse statue, where you fork right for Umabara or left for Pau, both just a few minutes further. A trail also links the two villages. From Waingapu, ask the bus driver to drop you off at the turning from the main road.

Mangili

This village 38 km from Melolo, a 20-minute walk off the road to Baing, is another high-quality ikat weaving centre, though its people don't seem very interested in bargaining with travellers. About six buses a day from Waingapu and Melolo pass the Mangili turn-off with the first leaving Waingapu at about 7 am and passing through Melolo from 8.30 to 9 am. Altogether it takes around two hours from Melolo to Mangili and the fare is 1000 rp. If you take the first morning bus down to Mangili, you should be able to spend about two hours there before taking the same bus back.

Kaliuda

This town is reputed to have the best ikat in all of Indonesia. However, you might have trouble finding what you want here – much of the best stuff gets bought up in large quantities and shipped off to Bali! Still, it's worth a look. Kaliuda is a few km from Ngalu, which is on the main road from Waingapu to Baing.

Baing

There's good surf in the first few months of the year near this village at the end of the road south. The same buses as for Mangili carry on to Baing, about 24 km and one hour further, usually returning the same day.

SOUTH CENTRAL SUMBA

This part of the island is little explored and requires a jeep trip and often some hiking.

Lumbung

The main attraction here is the spectacular 25-metre waterfall. Although it is not extremely high, the volume of water is huge and it's crystal-clear. At present, you can drive to within eight km of the falls and then must walk, but road building is continuing, so eventually this trip won't require much exercise. A guide is advisable, though you can ask directions to the falls (air terjun).

Praingkareha

Like Lumbung, the big attraction is a waterfall, only this one is over 100 metres high. There is a beautiful pool at the base of the falls. By tradition, women are forbidden to look into it, but an exception is made for foreigners!

Getting here is still an expedition, though continuing road building will eventually make it easier. You can drive a jeep to within 20 km, then you have to walk. Out of necessity, this is an overnight trip, but you can stay at the kepala desa's house. A guide is needed and can be hired for 5000 rp per day.

Tarimbang

If you're looking for that perfect wave, then you might want to give this place a try. Tarimbang has a beautiful surfing beach, but access is by jeep only and you'll probably have to camp if you want to spend the night.

WAIKABUBAK

At the greener western end of Sumba, where the tropical trees and rice paddies contrast with the dry grasslands around Waingapu, is the neat little town of Waikabubak. More a collection of kampungs with the gaps

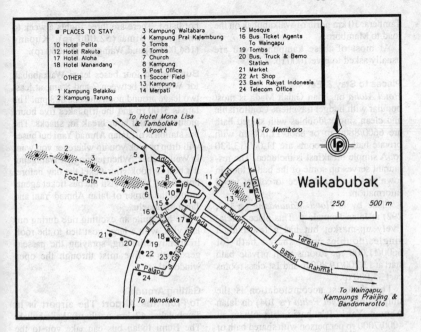

■ PLACES TO STAY	3 Kampung Waitabara	15 Mosque
	4 Kampung Prai Kalembung	16 Bus Ticket Agents
10 Hotel Pelita	5 Tombs	To Waingapu
12 Hotel Rakuta	6 Tombs	19 Tombs
17 Hotel Aloha	7 Church	20 Bus, Truck & Bemo
18 Hotel Manandang	8 Kampung	Station
	9 Post Office	21 Market
OTHER	11 Soccer Field	22 Art Shop
	13 Kampung	23 Bank Rakyat Indonesia
1 Kampung Belakiku	14 Merpati	24 Telecom Office
2 Kampung Tarung		

between them filled in, it has clusters of traditional clan houses and small graveyards of old stone-slab tombs carved with buffalo horn motifs. About 600 metres high and cooler than the east, it's a good base for exploring the traditional villages of west Sumba.

Information

The Bank Rakyat Indonesia on Jalan Gajah Mada will change US and Australian cash – but *not* travellers' cheques. It's open from 8 am to noon Monday to Thursday and Saturday, and from 7 to 11 am Friday. The post and telecom offices are open from 7 am to 2 pm Monday to Thursday, until 11 am Friday and 1 pm Saturday.

Tombs & Traditional Kampungs

Large stone-slab tombs are dotted around Waikabubak and several traditional kampungs occupy ridge or hilltop positions around the town. These kampungs have become accustomed to the eccentric behaviour of tourists, so you can see some traditional culture here without so easily offending somebody. The three most interesting kampungs are Praijjing, Tarung and Bondomarotto.

Kampung Praiijing is especially scenic, with five levels of neat traditional homes.

Kampung Tarung, reached by a path off Jalan Maadaelu marked by a large number of tombs at the junction, is the scene of an important month-long ritual sequence, the Wula Podhu, each November. This is an austere period and even weeping for the dead is forbidden. Rites mainly consist of offerings to the spirits, drum and gong beating and some dancing. The day before it ends, hundreds of chickens are sacrificed and on the final day people sing and dance day-long. Tarung has some fine tombs and its monuments are under official protection.

Another major kampung worth visiting is

Tambera, 10 km north of Waikabubak on the road to Mamboro.

At most of these kampungs, you are usually asked to give 1000 rp.

Places to Stay & Eat

Hotel Aloha on Jalan Gajah Mada is most popular with budget travellers. Comfortable and clean singles/doubles with shared bath are 6600/8800 rp or 8800/11,000 rp with private bath. VIP rooms are 11,000/13,530 rp. A simple breakfast is included. The restaurant serves up some of the better food in town and is a good place to collect travel information.

Close by is *Hotel Manandang* (☎ 197, 292) at Jalan Pemuda 4. This place is relatively up-market but has a few budget singles/doubles with shared bath for 6600/11,000 rp. Rooms with private bath start at 13,200/19,800 rp and 1st-class rooms cost 33,000 rp.

The cheapest accommodation is the simple little *Hotel Pelita* (☎ 104) on Jalan Ahmad Yani. It's basic, but clean, at 4000/7000 rp per person with shared bath or 7500/12,000 rp with inside mandi.

Hotel Rakuta on Jalan Veteran has rooms, beds and mandis that are vast by Nusa Tenggara's standards, but the place is musty and out of the way. Singles and doubles are both 5000 rp.

Hotel Mona Lisa on Jalan Adhyaksa is the luxury resort of Waikabubak, but it's 2½ km from town and mainly used by tour groups. Singles/doubles cost a breathtaking 48,750/74,100 rp, while family rooms are 87,750 rp. Off-season discounts of up to 20% can be negotiated. The Chinese owner has first-rate knowledge of western Sumba and organises tours to the villages.

There are lots of basic rumah makan along Jalan Ahmad Yani and some warungs set up here at night, but hotels are the best places to eat.

Getting There & Away

Air The Merpati agent is on Jalan Ahmad Yani. If you're checking the Merpati timetable, look under Tambolaka; Waikabubak is not listed. There are three flights a week to and from Bima (52,000 rp), Kupang (164,000 rp) and Waingapu (50,000 rp).

Bus Around four buses leave Waikabubak for Waingapu between 7 and 8 am, at least two leave around noon and one at 3 pm. The fare is 3100 rp and the trip takes five hours including a half hour break for snacks. The bus station is off Jalan Ahmad Yani but buses will drop or pick you up wherever you want in Waikabubak. When leaving for Waingapu, it's best to book your ticket the day before: hotels may help or visit the bus ticket agents around the corner of Jalan Ahmad Yani and Jalan Maadaelu.

We had quite an exciting ride during our last visit, with a large goat tied to the roof, frequently urinating, spraying the passengers with a fine mist through the open windows!

Getting Around

To/From the Airport The airport is in Tambolaka, 42 km north of Waikabubak. The Bumi Indah bus can take you to the airport for 1500 rp, but it is not very reliable. It goes once each flight day at 7 am, but if it hasn't left by 7.30 am, you'd better get a taxi which will cost a whopping 35,000 rp. It's not a bad idea to check the flight list at Merpati the day before to find out who else is going and where they are staying, so at least you can share the taxi and split the cost. If the bus is running, it will pick you up at your hotel.

Bus Minibuses, bemos and trucks make their way out to most other towns and villages in west Sumba – for details, see under the separate places. They tend to do an enormous amount of keliling to find passengers before leaving Waikabubak. It's best to get one early, when they're likely to fill up quicker.

Car & Motorcycle The Hotel Aloha rents motorbikes for 15,000 rp a day. You would be wise to have a guide and could probably find someone to go with you for 5000 rp or so, maybe for free if you just find someone who wants to practice English.

The hotels Aloha, Manandang and Mona Lisa all have vehicles and drivers available to take you around. Jeeps can usually hold three people while vans can take five or more. Rented jeeps and vans include the driver who can also serve as your guide. Some popular destinations with quoted prices include:

Destination	Fare (rp)
Anakalang	50,000
Bondokodi	80,000
Lamboya	75,000
Lewa	75,000
Malata	75,000
Mamboro	75,000
Rua	60,000
Tambolaka	45,000
Waingapu	100,000
Wanokaka	55,000

AROUND WEST SUMBA

The traditional village culture of west Sumba is one of the most intact in Indonesia. Kampungs of high-roofed houses still cluster on their hilltops (a place of defence in times past) surrounding the large stone tombs of their important ancestors. Away from the few towns, women still go bare-breasted and men in the traditional 'turban' and short sarong can be seen on horseback. The agricultural cycle turns up rituals, often involving animal sacrifices, almost year-round and ceremonies for events like house building and marriage can happen any time. Some kampungs are totally unaccustomed to foreigners – taking betel nut and cigarettes is a good way to get a decent reception.

Pasola Festival

The most famous of Nusa Tenggara's festivals sees large teams of colourfully-clad west Sumba horsemen engaging in semi-mock battles. Its pattern is similar to that of other ritual warfare that used to take place in Indonesia – the cause being not so much a quarrel between the opposing forces but the need for human blood to be spilt to keep the spirits happy and bring a good harvest.

Despite the blunt spears that the horsemen now use and efforts at supervision by the Indonesian authorities, few holds are barred; injuries and sometimes deaths still occur.

The Pasola is part of a series of rituals connected with the beginning of the planting season. It takes place in four different areas in February or March each year and its exact timing is determined by the arrival on nearby coasts of a certain type of seaworm called *nyale*. Priests examine the nyale at dawn and from their behaviour predict how good the year's harvest will be. Then the pasola can begin: it's usually fought first on the beach then, later the same day, further inland. The opposing 'armies' are drawn from coastal and inland dwellers.

The nyale are usually found on the eighth or ninth day after a full moon. In February Pasola is celebrated in the Kodi area (centred on Kampung Tosi) and the Lamboya area (Kampung Sodan); in March it's the turn of the Wanokaka area (Kampung Waigalli) and the remote Gaura area west of Lamboya (Kampung Ubu Olehka).

Anakalang & Around

Kampung Pasunga, beside the Waingapu road at Anakalang, 22 km from Waikabubak, boasts one of the Sumba's most impressive tomb line-ups. The grave of particular interest consists of a horizontal stone slab with a vertical slab in front of it. The vertical slab took six months to carve with figures of a man and a woman. The tomb was constructed in 1926; five people are buried here and 150 buffalo were sacrificed during its construction. There seems to be a standard charge of 1000 rp for a close look at these tombs and/or photos but you can see them fairly well from the road.

Anakalang has a market on Wednesday and Saturday and is the scene of the *Purung Takadonga*, a mass marriage festival held every two years. The exact date is determined by the full moon. At Kampung Matakakeri, a 15-minute walk down the road past Anakalang market, are more traditional houses and tombs. Check in at the *Departemen Kebudayaan* (Cultural Department) hut

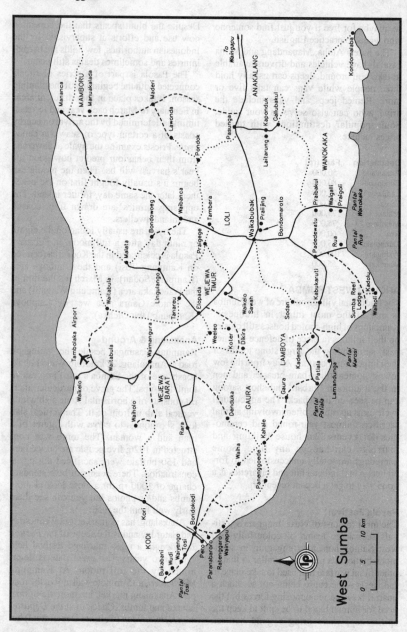

West Sumba

0   5   10 km

at the entrance to the kampung: there seems to be no 'fee' here but you'll probably get a guide who'll ask for a tip. One of the Matakakeri tombs is Sumba's heaviest, weighing in at 70 tonnes. The construction of this one is said to have taken three years, 250 sacrificed buffaloes, and 2000 workers who chiselled it out of a hillside and dragged it to the site. It commemorates a 19th-century raja with the snappy name of Umbusapipateduk. Lai Tarung, the hilltop ancestral village of 12 local clans, now almost deserted but partly renovated with government money is a 15-minute side-trip from Matakakeri. Several tombs are scattered around and there's a ceremonial building with carved stone columns. You'll probably be asked into a kind of 'showroom' traditional house – we couldn't work out whether it's really lived in or not.

At Gallubakul (formerly Prai Bokul), 2½ km on down the road from Kampung Matakakeri, the Umbu Sawola tomb is a single piece of carved rock about five metres long, four metres wide and nearly a metre thick. The villagers often ask 5000 rp to let you take photos – some people manage to bargain them down, others leave. A handful of travellers have gone beyond Gallubakul following the road on to the Wanokaka area south of Waikabubak.

Getting There & Away Regular minibuses run between Waikabubak and Anakalang – fewer after about 1 pm. The trip takes about one hour and costs 500 rp. A bus from Waingapu to Anakalang is 2100 rp.

South of Waikabubak

The Wanokaka district, centred around Waigalli, about 20 km south of Waikabubak towards the coast, has numerous traditional kampungs and is the scene of one of the March Pasolas. The Watu Kajiwa tomb in Praigoli is said to be the oldest in the area. Kampung Sodan, centre for the Lamboya Pasola further west, was burnt down in 1988 (accidentally, it seems) but will probably be rebuilt. Pantai Rua on the south coast has a

beach with swimming spots and there's surf at Pantai Marosi near Lamandunga.

The Sumba Reef Lodge is an expensive foreign-owned venture on the south coast. Reportedly, the American manager is nonplused with Australian surfies who have been sneaking onto the private beach.

Getting There & Away Trucks and bemos rattle irregularly down the rough roads to Wanokaka District (500 rp) and to Lamboya District (500 rp) via Pandedewatu. Be at Waikabubak bus station as early as you can (6 am) if you want to catch one. Better, start asking the day before – otherwise walk, hitch, or rent a vehicle.

Kodi

Kodi is the westernmost region of Sumba. The small town of Bondokodi, about two km from the coast, is the centre of this district, and the area has become a popular place with travellers. The coastline is spectacularly beautiful with some superb beaches. There is a unique freshwater pool right by the seashore. The kampung houses have even higher roofs than elsewhere in west Sumba, and there are some unusual tombs and statues. If you're on foot you won't see much of the area unless you stay a couple of days.

To get to the kampungs, you go either north or south along the paved road from Bondokodi market. To reach Tosi, about six km north and the scene of the Kodi Pasola in February, head north along the road for a km until you see a track on your left. Follow it for five km, past a series of tombs. You'll soon see Tosi's roofs on your right. From Tosi it's a 10-minute walk to the beach. A track runs beside the beach all the way south to the river mouth near Wainyapu.

If you head south from Bondokodi market for a km, you'll see a dirt track on your right. Take that and keep forking to the right, and you'll reach Paronabaroro after about two km. This kampung is more interesting than Tosi with even higher roofs, stone statues and an elaborate house complete with pig jaws hanging from its verandah, numerous buffalo horns, separate rooms and even a door with a lock! Pantai Radukapal, a beach with white sand, clear water and strong currents, is about a km from Paronabaroro.

From Pantai Radukapal it's roughly two km south along the coast to Wainyapu, on the far side of a river mouth. A dirt track runs along beside the beach to the river mouth. The view here will take your breath away. The seas glisten, coconut palms fringe the shoreline and Wainyapu's tall roofs peep above the treeline. On the near side of the river mouth are some unusual stone tombs and the kampung of Ratenggaro. You can wade across the river mouth to Wainyapu. You can also reach Wainyapu by inland tracks from Paronabaroro or by following the paved road south from Bondokodi and turning off somewhere beyond the Paronabaroro turning.

Places to Stay At Pantai Pero, there are two homestays, the basic *Abdullah* or the better-appointed *Harum Story*. Both cost 7500 rp per person, or 10,000 rp with three meals. At

Harum Story, when they ask you if you are interested in buying wood carvings or ikat, immediately say no unless you want to be inundated by every vendor in west Sumba!

Getting There & Away From Waikabubak there are two direct buses a day departing in the morning. One is run by the Hotel Mona Lisa, but you can book it in town.

Wejewa Timur

This area less than 20 km west of Waikabubak sees relatively few tourists, in part because there is no transport other than motorcycle or rented jeep. It's an attractive region with very friendly people who still maintain their traditional culture. The villages of Weeleo and Kater, both near Elopada, make interesting day trips.

Waikelo

Occasional boats go to Sumbawa, Flores or even further afield from this small port north of Waitabula.

Kalimantan

Some people go to Kalimantan expecting to see half-naked, heavily tattooed Dayaks striding down the streets of Balikpapan, Samarinda or Pontianak. Sorry to disappoint you but the parts of Kalimantan near harbours and airports have been impaled on a drill bit and carved up with a chain saw. Your first impressions are likely to be of oil refineries and timber mills. Tourism is just taking off; most Westerners in Kalimantan work for foreign companies like Union or Standard Oil.

To see the pre-colonial, pre-Javanised, pre-multinational Kalimantan requires travelling well into the interior. The Bugis, Javanese, Banjarmasis and Chinese dominate the coast, while about a million Dayaks – the island's original inhabitants and former head-hunters – live in the vast, jungle-covered hinterland along the island's many rivers.

HISTORY

Kalimantan is the southern two-thirds of the island of Borneo. Northern Borneo consists of the Malaysian states of Sarawak and Sabah and the independent sultanate of Brunei. Of the seven million people on Borneo, 5½ million live in Kalimantan, most in settlements and cities along its river banks. The mountains stretching across

Borneo's interior feed its rivers, which carry immense quantities of silt to the coast. Heavy rainfall and poor drainage have produced a broad rim of dense, inhospitable swamps along much of the island's shores.

Like Sumatra and Java, Kalimantan was once a cultural crossroads. Hinduism reached Kalimantan by about 400 AD and Hindu temple remains have been unearthed in southern Kalimantan near Amuntai and Negara on Sungai Negara. There are Sanskrit tablets in the museum at Tenggarong in East Kalimantan.

Kalimantan was a stopover point on the trade routes between China, the Philippines and Java and Chinese settlements were established on the island long before Europeans came to the Indonesian archipelago. The coastal ports were Islamic by around the 15th or 16th centuries and some of the sultanates, such as Kutai and Banjarmasin, became major trading centres.

In the early 17th century, Kalimantan became a scene of conflict between the British and the Dutch. Much to the annoyance of the Dutch, the British set up bases in Java, Sumatra and south-west Kalimantan. Banjarmasin was reputed to be a great source of pepper so the British turned their attention there, since the Dutch had control over the spice islands further east. Trade with Banjarmasin seemed promising but when the

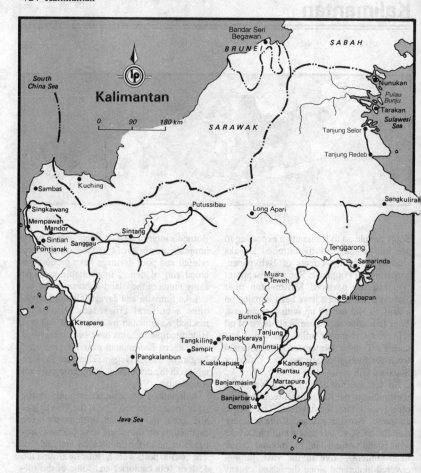

Kalimantan

South China Sea

Bandar Seri Begawan

BRUNEI

SABAH

Nunukan

Pulau Bunju

Tarakan

Sulawesi Sea

SARAWAK

Tanjung Selor

Tanjung Redeb

Sangkulirang

Sambas

Kuching

Putussibau

Long Apari

Singkawang

Mempawah

Mandor

Sintang

Tenggarong

Sintian

Sanggau

Samarinda

Pontianak

Muara Teweh

Balikpapan

Ketapang

Buntok

Tanjung

Tangkiling

Palangkaraya

Amuntai

Sampit

Kandangan

Pangkalanbun

Kualakapuas

Rantau

Banjarmasin

Martapura

Banjarbaru

Cempaka

Java Sea

British stationed a guard ship at the mouth of Sungai Barito and recruited Bugis mercenaries to guard their warehouses, the Banjarmasin rulers felt threatened. War with the British erupted in 1701. The Banjarmasis were defeated and had to tolerate the British presence until 1707, when the latter were finally ejected.

By the 19th century, British and Dutch interests in Borneo had changed markedly. The British interest was mainly strategic as the north and west coasts flanked the sailing routes between China and India. The Dutch interest was mainly colonial.

To the north of the Java Sea, Borneo was a hideout for pirates and, although the interior was unknown and presumed to have little commercial value, the Dutch had some interest in controlling the south and west coasts. By the late 1820s and 1830s the Dutch had concluded treaties with various small west-coast states. Parts of the Banjarmasi sultanate were signed over to the Dutch in the early part of the 1800s but the

Dutch didn't establish garrisons or administrative offices.

In 1838 the Dutch were jolted by the arrival of an Englishman named James Brooke. Brooke, a self-styled adventurer, arrived in Borneo with an armed sloop to find the Brunei aristocracy facing rebellion from the inland tribes. Brooke quelled the rebellion. In gratitude, so the story goes, he was given power over Kuching (in what is now Sarawak) in 1841. Brooke put down the inland tribes, suppressed their head-hunting, eliminated the dreaded Borneo pirates who infested the coast, and founded a personal dynasty of white rajas that lasted until the Japanese invasion in WW II.

With Brooke's arrival, the spectre of intervention by other European powers suddenly became a reality for the Dutch. In the 1840s and 1850s the Dutch put down several internal disputes and established new treaties with local rulers. From 1846 they opened coal mines in South and East Kalimantan and gradually the island became more commercially important. War broke out between the Dutch and the Banjarmasis in 1859, but after four years the Banjarmasis were defeated and the Dutch instituted direct rule, although some fighting continued until 1905.

The current division of Borneo between Indonesia and Malaysia originates from the British-Dutch rivalry. After WW II the Brooke family handed Sarawak over to the British government, putting Britain in the curious position of acquiring a new colony at the time it was shedding others. Sarawak remained under British control when Malaya (the part of Malaysia formed by the Malay Peninsula) gained independence in 1957.

Sabah was another story. Once part of the Brunei sultanate, Sabah came under the influence of the British North Borneo Company after being avoided for centuries because of its pirates. In 1888, north Borneo's coast became a British protectorate, although fighting did not end until the death of the Sabah rebel leader, Mat Salleh, in 1900. After WW II, the administration of Sabah was handed to the British government. In 1963, Sarawak and Sabah joined with the Malay Peninsula – and, temporarily, Singapore – to form the nation of Malaysia.

The border between Sarawak, Sabah and Kalimantan became the scene of fighting during Indonesia's Confrontation with Malaysia under Sukarno. Even after Confrontation was abandoned, anti-Malaysian Chinese guerrillas of the Sarawak People's Guerrilla Troops, originally trained and armed by Indonesia, remained in Kalimantan until the early 1970s. A joint Malaysian-Indonesian military operation suppressed them, although it is said Dayak tribesmen played a key role guarding the border and removing support the guerrillas may have had in the villages.

Towards the end of the 19th century the outer islands, rather than Java, became the focus of Dutch commercial exploitation of the archipelago. Rubber and oil became increasingly important and products like pepper, copra, tin and coffee were developed in the outer islands. The existence of oil deposits in north Sumatra's Langkat area had been known since the 1860s and they were commercially exploited by the Dutch by the 1880s. By early this century oil was also being drilled in Kalimantan.

To finance drilling in East Kalimantan, a British company was set up in London: Shell Transport & Trading Company. In 1907 Shell merged with the Royal Dutch Company for the Exploitation of Petroleum Sources in the Netherlands Indies (the first company to start drilling in Sumatra) to form Royal Dutch Shell, giving the Dutch the greater share.

Shell expanded rapidly and soon oil was produced everywhere from California to Russia. The Russian properties were confiscated in 1917 but by 1930 Shell was producing 85% of Indonesia's oil. Today the countries in which Shell operates read like a United Nations' roll-call. In the 1920s US companies began taking up major oil concessions in Indonesia, followed by the Japanese in 1930.

Economic value aside, East Kalimantan is set to become one of Indonesia's prime transmigration targets. Although Kalimantan is

Indonesia's second-biggest province and covers an area 30% greater than Java, its population is minute by comparison. Until now, the Samarinda and Balikpapan areas have accounted for most of the East Kalimantan transmigration, still less than 5% of the national total. The figure is expected to grow and new immigrants will have to settle further away from the cities. The plan is to send new settlers to the forest districts north of Samarinda and, after ripping down the natural forest, to develop these areas as rubber producers.

It's arguable that such transmigration projects indicate a shift away from the idea of reducing the population crush on Java and Bali, and that transmigration is now directed at the economic development of the outer islands. So far most major outer island developments have occurred independently of government-sponsored transmigration. Transmigration tied to estate crop development such as rubber is perhaps the first attempt to link the programme to regional development.

Not everyone goes to Kalimantan on government-sponsored transmigration schemes. A major group in East Kalimantan are the Bugis of southern Sulawesi, continuing a transmigration tradition 400 years old, although most have settled since independence. The Kahar Muzakar rebellion in 1951 spurred Bugis movement from Sulawesi. After the rebellion was suppressed another wave of Bugis transmigrants joined their relatives in Kalimantan, tempted by the prospect of a better life. Some returned to Sulawesi after the disastrous fire which swept East Kalimantan and Sabah in 1982-83.

If you're heading back from Sulawesi to Java then a detour to the east or south coasts of Kalimantan can be worthwhile, particularly to Banjarmasin and Samarinda.

FLORA & FAUNA

The strangest inhabitants of Kalimantan are the orang-utan, whose almost human appearance and disposition puzzled both Dayaks and early European visitors. The English Captain Daniel Beeckman visited Borneo early in the 18th century and in his book *A Voyage To & From the Island of Borneo* wrote:

They grow up to be six foot high; they walk upright, have longer arms than men, tolerable good faces (handsomer I am sure than some Hottentots that I have seen) large teeth, no tails nor hair, but on those parts where it grows on human bodies; they are very nimble footed and mighty strong; they throw great stones, sticks and billets at those persons that offend them. The natives do really believe that these were formerly men, but metamorphosed into beasts for their blasphemy. They told me many strange stories of them....

Orang-utan

The orang-utan is not the only strange creature inhabiting the interior of this vast but increasingly less mysterious island. The deep waters of Sungai Mahakam are home to freshwater dolphin, and there are gibbons in the jungles, proboscis monkeys and crab-eating macaques in the mangrove swamps, and crocodiles, clouded leopards, giant butterflies and hornbills, including the legendary black hornbill.

The Dayaks traditionally believe that the black hornbill carries the human soul, but because of its feathers and huge beak it was almost hunted into extinction.

PEOPLE

There are three main ethnic groups in Kalimantan today: the recently arrived coastal Malay/Indonesians who follow Islam and live in towns, cities and settlements at the mouths of rivers; the Chinese, who have controlled trade in Kalimantan for centuries; and the Dayaks, the collective name for the interior tribes who originally inhabited the island.

The Dayaks

The tribes do not use the term Dayak. It's a slightly pejorative term used by Indonesians, or indigenous peoples converted to Islam (such as the Banjars and the Kutais) to differentiate non-Muslim from Muslim inhabitants. Enlightened Indonesians call them *orang gunung* or mountain people. The tribes prefer to be identified by their separate tribal names, such as Kenyah, Iban and Punan.

The Dayaks were coastal dwellers until the arrival of Malay settlers drove them inland to the highlands and river banks. Some also live in neighbouring Sabah and Sarawak. They have definite ethnic commonalities and are generally light-skinned, somewhat Chinese in appearance and may be descendants of immigrants from southern China or South-East Asia. Tribal dialects show linguistic similarities.

Traditionally, the Dayaks live in communal longhouses, called *lamin* in East and West Kalimantan. In South Kalimantan, communal houses are called *balai* and in Central Kalimantan they are called *betang*. They are one room deep and up to 300 metres long. Although they may be either a short, wide rectangle or a large square, in English both types are called longhouses.

A group of small longhouses or one large longhouse make up the traditional village. Longhouses are built on wooden piles up to three metres high as protection against wild animals, flooding and, in the past, enemies. Stairs of notched logs leading to the house can be pulled in as needed. Domestic animals (usually pigs or chickens) are kept below the house. The longhouses are traditionally divided into separate family quarters, with either a communal verandah running the length of the building or a central verandah between two rows of family quarters. The verandah is the main thoroughfare and the place where women pound rice and repair fishing nets, and where meetings are held and ceremonies performed.

Traditional Dayak agriculture is slash-and-burn farming. Since this drastically reduces soil fertility, villages constantly move to find new land, dismantling and reassembling the entire lamin in a new location.

The most striking feature of many Dayak men and women is their pierced ear lobes stretched with the weight of heavy gold or brass rings. This custom is increasingly rare among the young; older Dayaks, influenced by missionaries, often trim their ear lobes as a sign of conversion.

It was once the custom for all women to tattoo their forearms and calves with bird and spirit designs. Tattooing of young women has almost disappeared, except in tribes deep in the interior. However, it is still seen among men.

Many Dayaks are modifying their traditions under pressure from the Indonesian government and European missionaries. Neither the Muslims nor the Christians seem content to leave the indigenous belief systems, the backbone of these tribal cultures, alone.

Not all Dayaks live in villages. The Punan are nomadic hunter/gatherers who still move through the jungles, although some stay in longhouses at the height of the rainy season and many have settled in permanent riverside villages. The word 'punan' is common to many inland dialects and means upriver or headwaters.

To other Dayaks the Punan are the ultimate jungle dwellers. As logging and ethno-religious evangelism push them deeper into the interior, they can be difficult to find. Over the border in East Malaysia they are known as the Penan, and actively protest against the destruction of their forest homes by government-backed lumber interests.

BOOKS

Two recent publications are highly recommended reading for those planning extensive travel in Kalimantan. *Stranger in the Forest* (Houghton Mifflin Co, Boston and Century Hutchinson, London, 1988) is an inspiring account of Eric Hansen's six-month journey by boat and on foot across Borneo in 1982.

The hilarious *Into the Heart of Borneo* (Vintage Departures, New York, 1987) by Redmond O'Hanlon recounts the almost slapstick adventures of the author, a British naturalist, and the English poet James Fenton, as they made their way to Gunung Batu in Kalimantan, via Sarawak. Both books give a good feel for interior travel in Borneo.

GETTING THERE & AWAY

To enter or exit Indonesia via Kalimantan by air, sea or land you'll need an Indonesian visa as Kalimantan's entry and exit points don't seem subject to the no-visa rule. The exception to this is a visa-free entry to Pontianak by air. At the time of writing, there are plans to admit visa-free visitors coming from Malaysia to Singkawang and Pontianak by road (ask the status of this at the Indonesian consulate in Kuching). Tarakan, Banjarmasin and Balikpapan now seem to accept all new arrivals as long as they have advance tourist visas.

If you don't intend heading inland, Kalimantan is probably best seen as a detour between Java and Sulawesi. The East and South Kalimantan cities of Samarinda and Banjarmasin are particularly worth seeing.

On the other hand, if you plan to spend some time exploring the interior, Banjarmasin or Pontianak are probably your best entry points. They can be reached quickly from Singapore or Jakarta, therefore eating up less of your visa time.

To/From Singapore

Air Garuda has three flights a week in either direction between Singapore, Pontianak and Balikpapan. There is also a daily service (with a change of planes in Jakarta) between both Singapore and Banjarmasin, and Singapore and Balikpapan.

Sempati also has daily flights between Singapore and Balikpapan, with a change of planes in Jakarta. Sempati flies three times a week (with a connection) between Singapore and Banjarmasin.

Union Oil has an office at Balikpapan's airport and charters direct flights to Singapore. The cheapest fare between Singapore and Kalimantan is via Pontianak for about US$150.

To/From Malaysia

Rules about crossing the border between Malaysia and Kalimantan seem to change constantly. At the time of writing, this crossing should become easier if relations between Malaysia and Indonesia continue to improve. Up until now, some people got through, some didn't. Sometimes it was OK to fly, but not to go by boat. Experiences vary widely, as letters we've received indicate:

In Manila the Indonesian Embassy would not give us a visa to cross via Kalimantan. We had a mileage ticket which goes Sandarkan, Tawau, Tarakan, Samarinda, etc. We had to change our flight ticket to come in via Jakarta or Denpasar before they would give us a visa. However we met a Danish couple who crossed the border with no problems. They said the Indonesian consul in Tawau was very nice and there were no hassles...

Air Supposedly to get airline tickets for Kalimantan to Sarawak, or Kalimantan to Sabah flights, you need a passport which is valid for six months after your arrival date, a special visa for east Malaysia, a return ticket from Sarawak and US$1000. There's one slight problem: the Malaysian embassy in Jakarta might not give you the special visa! The Malaysian consulate in Pontianak say you can pick up your visa in Pontianak, however. To be absolutely safe, get the east Malaysia visa in your own country first.

MAS flies twice weekly between Pontianak and Kuching in Sarawak for US$74. Bouraq flies between Tarakan to Tawau in Sabah four times a week for 122,000 rp.

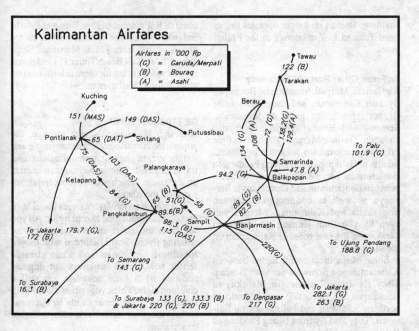

Kalimantan Airfares

Airfares in '000 Rp
(G) = Garuda/Merpati
(B) = Bouraq
(A) = Asahi

Kuching

151 (MAS) 149 (DAS)

Pontianak 65 (DAT) Sintang Putussibau

75 (DAS) 103 (DAS)

Palangkaraya

Ketapang

84 (G) 65 (B) 51 (G) 58 (G)

Pangkalanbun 89.6 (B)

96.3 (B) Sampit
115 (DAS)

To Jakarta 179.7 (G),
172 (B)

To Semarang
143 (G)

To Surabaya
16.3 (B)

To Surabaya 133 (G), 133.3 (B)
& Jakarta 220 (G), 220 (B)

Tawau
122 (B)

Tarakan

Berau

134 108 (A) 72 (G) 138.2 (G)
(A) 129.4 (A)

To Palu
101.9 (G)

Samarinda
47.8 (A)
Balikpapan

94.2 (G)

89 (G)
82.5 (B)

Banjarmasin

To Ujung Pandang
188.8 (G)

220 (G)

To Denpasar
217 (G)

To Jakarta
282.1 (G)
263 (B)

MAS flies the same route once a week for 136,000 rp.

Land At present, the border between Pontianak and Kuching is definitely open to foreigners with advance (paid) visas who want to cross by land on daily buses. If you want to cross by land, check with the Indonesian immigration office and the Malaysian Consulate in Pontianak first – it is possible that by the time you read this the one-month advance (paid) visa will be unnecessary to enter or leave Indonesia by land via this border.

Travelling from Pontianak to Kuching by bus costs 30,000 rp if booked by SJS Travel in Pontianak.

Boat To leave Indonesia by sea via Nunukan in East Kalimantan (to Tawau, Sabah), you'll need an exit permit from the immigration office in Jakarta if you entered Indonesia at a visa-free port. The exit permit isn't neces-

sary if you entered Indonesia on a one-month advance (paid) visa.

At this writing most people seem able to cross between Kalimantan and Sabah or Sarawak as long as their paperwork is in order. Advance visas for Indonesia are now reportedly available in Kuching and Kota Kinabalu.

There are longboats from Tarakan to Nunukan (12 hours, 11,000 rp), and speedboats from Nunukan to Tawau (four hours, 21,000 rp). Buy tickets from CV Tam Bersaudara on Jalan Pasar Lingkas in Tarakan. The boats usually depart daily between 7 and 8 am, although they may not run on Sunday.

To/From the Philippines

Air Presuming you can make it from Tarakan to Tawau, there are on-again and off-again flights between Tawau and Zamboanga in the southern Philippines. Check with Sabre Air Services in Tawau and don't count on anything. Bouraq no longer operates flights from Tarakan to Zamboanga in the Philippines.

To/From Other Parts of Indonesia

Air Garuda, Merpati, Sempati and Bouraq all fly into Kalimantan and there are lots of flights from other parts of Indonesia. Sempati and Bouraq flights are usually cheaper. Garuda/Merpati flights include Jakarta to Banjarmasin, Jakarta to Pontianak, Jakarta to Balikpapan and Ujung Pandang to Banjarmasin. Merpati also has connections between Banjarmasin and Denpasar via Surabaya as well as connections between Yogyakarta and Kalimantan. Merpati will even fly you from Kupang (in Timor) to Tarakan on the east coast of Kalimantan on the same day.

Some of the most useful flights between Kalimantan and Sulawesi are with Bouraq. They fly from Ternate (in Maluku) to Balikpapan via Gorontalo and Manado in northern Sulawesi, and Palu in central Sulawesi. They also fly from Ujung Pandang to Balikpapan and Banjarmasin and are slightly cheaper than Merpati. There are also connections from Ujung Pandang to Pontianak, Samarinda and Tarakan. Sempati also has a flight between Ujung Pandang and Banjarmasin.

Boat There are shipping connections with Java and Sulawesi, both with Pelni and other shipping companies.

The Pelni liners *Kelimutu*, *Kerinci* and *Kambuna* pull into various ports on the South and East Kalimantan coast on their loops out of Java around Kalimantan and Sulawesi. The *Lawit* also plies the waters between Sumatra's major ports, Jakarta and Pontianak. Pelni fares are quite low. For example, economy class fares from Jakarta to Banjarmasin are 82,000 rp, to Balikpapan 63,500 rp, and to Pontianak 33,500 rp. From Surabaya to Banjarmasin, economy fares are 25,100 rp and to Balikpapan, 33,600 rp.

There are also regular passenger-carrying cargo ships between the ports on the east

coast of Kalimantan to Pare Pare and Palu in Sulawesi – see the relevant sections for details. Apart from Pelni, Mahakam Shipping at Jalan Kali Besar Timur 111 in Jakarta may be worth trying for more information on other ships to Kalimantan.

GETTING AROUND

Although Kalimantan's area is huge, the population is sparse and the dense jungle and rough terrain make communications and travel difficult. Life in Kalimantan centres on the rivers, which are the most important roads on the island.

If there are no navigable rivers travel is, in most cases, impossible except by air. All you see from the air is endless jungle cut by winding rivers. Small outboard motorboats, speedboats, longboats and some sizeable ferries now cruise the rivers but dugouts paddled by a lone boatman are still a common sight. Thick vegetation cloaks both sides of the rivers, broken only by the occasional village, small riverside town or timber concession.

Apart from the area around Pontianak and the stretch from Samarinda to Banjarmasin there are few real roads and the boats and ferries that ply the numerous rivers and waterways are the most popular forms of long-distance transport. Each of Kalimantan's four provinces has at least one major river into the interior that serves as a slow-moving highway: in East Kalimantan there are the Mahakam and Kayan rivers; in South Kalimantan, the Barito; in Central Kalimantan, the Barito and the Kahayan; in West Kalimantan, the Kapuas and the Melawai.

There are also plenty of flight connections to inland and coastal destinations and some shipping along the eastern coast. Going upriver into some of the Dayak regions is now relatively easy from Pontianak and Samarinda, but the further you go off the beaten canal the more time you'll need. For serious forays into the interior, even along the main rivers, you must allow about two weeks minimum per province.

Air

There are flights around the coastal cities and into the interior of Kalimantan with the regular airline companies. Merpati carries the bulk of traffic, although there are many flights with DAS (Dirgantara Air Service), Asahi, Bouraq and Deraya Air Taxi.

Other possibilities include planes run by the oil companies and those by the missionaries. If you're in the right place at the right time, and ask the right person, you may be able to pick up a ride, providing they don't mind the look of you.

DAS's small prop aircraft fly to all sorts of places, with daily flights from Pontianak to inland West Kalimantan towns like Sintang or south-east to the coastal town of Ketapang. They also have flights between Palangkaraya and Banjarmasin or Buntok. Deraya Air Taxi flies in and out of Pangkalanbun in Central Kalimantan to Pontianak, Palangkaraya and Banjarmasin. In East Kalimantan, Merpati has the best interior routes and Asahi makes the most runs between Balikpapan and Samarinda.

Boat

There are small boats, speedboats, ferries and houseboats plying the rivers between some of the major towns and cities – like the daily ferries and speedboats between Banjarmasin and Palangkaraya or the longboats between Tarakan and Berau or Nunukan.

There are a number of variations on the river ferry theme. The *feri sungai* (river ferry/cargo boat, also known as a *kapal biasa*) carries both cargo and passengers; the *taxi sungai* (river taxi) carries cargo downstairs and has an upper level with rows of wooden bunks (sometimes with mattresses and pillows); and the *bis air* (water bus) has rows of seats.

Along Sungai Kapuas in Pontianak are the bandung, large cargo-cum-houseboats that take up to a month to move upriver to Putussibau. A bis air does the same distance in about four days. A *longbot*, as the name indicates, is a longboat – a narrow vessel with two or three large outboard motors at the rear and bench seats in a covered passenger cabin. You commonly see these carrying passengers on the major waterways of Kalimantan.

Speedboats *(speed* or *speedbot)* commonly ply the Barito, Kapuas, Kahayan and Kayan rivers and seem to be appearing elsewhere. Don't get too hung up on the terminology, as what may be called a bis air in one province may be a taxi sungai in another.

East Kalimantan

Kalimantan Timur, or Kal-Tim for short, is the most populated and developed province in Kalimantan. Lumber, oil, mining and, to a small extent, tourism, have wrought irreversible changes upon the coastal areas and far into the interior. In the interior, once thriving Dayak cultures, including Punan, Banuaq, Iban and Kenyah, are fast transforming in the face of logging, oil exploration and missionary activity. Still, with time and effort you can reach places that rarely see a foreign face.

The Mahakam and Kayan rivers are the main aquatic thoroughfares.

BALIKPAPAN

Apart from the clean, comfortable and highly insulated Pertamina, Union Oil and Total residential areas, Balikpapan is mostly grubby and decayed back streets, ravaged footpaths and rampaging Hondas and Yamahas. The suburban area bounded by Jalan Randan Utara and Jalan Pandanwanyi north of the oil refinery is built on stilts over the muddy isthmus, with uneven, lurching wooden walkways between the houses.

The huge oil refinery dominates the city and flying in you'll see stray tankers and offshore oil rigs. This is the centre of Kalimantan's oil business and the chief city of the province. There are five Garuda flights from Jakarta to Balikpapan every day, a five-star hotel which could easily be ranked as

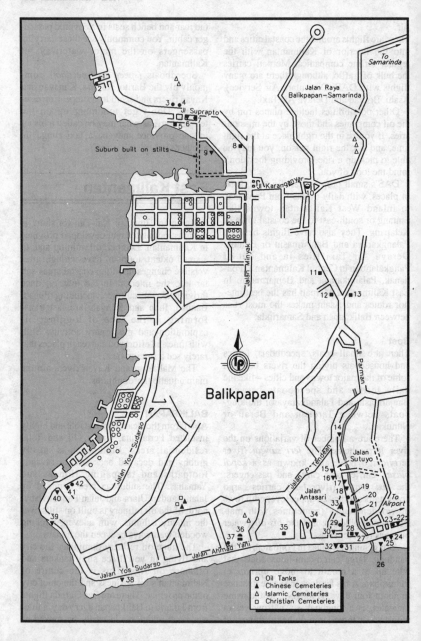

Balikpapan

To Samarinda

Jalan Raya
Balikpapan–Samarinda

Jl Suprapto

Suburb built on stilts

Jl Karanganyar

Jalan Minyak

Jl Parman

Jalan P. Tendean

Jalan Sutuyo

Jalan
Antasari

Jalan Yos Sudarso

Jalan Ahmad Yani

Jalan Yos Sudarso

To Airport

o	Oil Tanks
▲	Chinese Cemeteries
△	Islamic Cemeteries
□	Christian Cemeteries

PLACES TO STAY		24	Hap Koen Restaurant
		26	Pasar Baru
5	Penginapan Segara	27	Kentucky Fried Chicken
8	Blue Sky Hotel	30	Restaurant Atomic
11	Penginapan Mama	32	Restaurant Salero Minang
12	Hotel Aida	38	Benua Patra Restaurant & Bar
13	Hotel Murni	39	Restaurant/Bar Samudra Indah
20	Hotel Budiman	40	Sari Bundo Restaurant
21	Hotel Benakutai		
23	Penginapan Royal		**OTHER**
25	Penginapan Fajar		
28	Bahtera Hotel	1	PT Nurlina Office
31	Hotel Gajah Mada	2	Speedboats & Longboats to
34	Balikpapan Hotel		Banjarmasin Bus Station
35	Hotel Sederhana	3	Depot Tuhung Agung
		4	Depot Banjar Indah
PLACES TO EAT		7	Bank Expor Impor Indonesia
		10	Rapak Bus & Bemo Station
6	Warungs	19	Bouraq Airlines
9	Fruit Market	29	Asahi Airlines
14	New Shangrila Restaurant	33	Antasari Cinema
15	New Holland Icecream & Steakhouse	36	Post Office
16	Dynasty Restaurant	37	Immigration Office
17	Restaurant Sinar Minang	41	Pelni Office
18	Bondy Restaurant	42	Harbour Master's Office
22	Restaurant Roda Baru		

one of the hundred best in the world, and nearly as many US, Australian and European voices as there are Japanese motorcycles.

Since the oil glut of the early '80s, Balikpapan's economy has taken a serious downturn and the number of expatriates working on fat oil-company contracts has declined.

Orientation & Information

A good landmark is the enormous Hotel Benakutai on Jalan Pengeran Antasari, near the shorefront. Heading east from Jalan Pengeran Antasari along the shorefront is the airport road; heading west is Kelandasan which runs into Jalan Ahmad Yani. Heading north, Jalan Pengeran Antasari merges into Jalan Sutuyo, Jalan Parman and Jalan Panjaitan. Most of the hotels and offices can be found along these streets.

The immigration office is on the corner of Jalan Ahmad Yani and Jalan Sudirman. The shop in the foyer of the Hotel Benakutai sells Indonesian and English-language newspapers, and foreign news magazines.

Money The Bank Negara Indonesia on Jalan Pengeran Antasari changes major travellers' cheques and cash currencies. The bank is open Monday to Friday from 8 am to noon and 1.30 to 3 pm, and on Saturday from 8 to 11 am. The branch office at Seppingan Airport also changes cash and travellers' cheques.

Post The post office on Jalan Ahmad Yani is open Monday to Friday from 8 am to 6 pm and on Saturday, Sunday and holidays from 8 am to 5 pm. The airport post office is open Monday to Thursday from 8 am to 2 pm, Friday from 8 to 11 am, Saturday from 8 am to 1 pm, and Sunday and holidays from 8 am to noon.

Another post office is on Jalan Suprapto, next to the Blue Sky Hotel; it's open Monday to Thursday from 8 am to 2 pm, Friday from

8 to 11 am, Saturday from 8 am to 1 pm, and is closed on Sunday and holidays.

Places to Stay – bottom end

What little cheap accommodation there is in Balikpapan is often permanently full. Most of what's readily available is in the mid-range and priced from about 40,000 rp.

The best bet is probably the *Penginapan Royal* near the Pasar Baru, at the start of the airport road near the Jalan Pengeran Antasari corner. It's spartan but fairly clean and at a good location with singles/doubles for 4000/6500 rp with shared mandi. Rooms at the back should be quiet, but avoid those facing the noisy main street.

The *Hotel Sederhana* on Kelandasan Ulu is decent and has a new section. Singles/doubles without bath are 13,600/15,800 rp in the old wing and 36,300/42,400 rp in the all air-con new wing with bath and breakfast.

There's a string of places on Jalan Panjaitan, including the adequately clean *Hotel Aida* (☎ 21006) with economy singles/doubles from 12,000/15,000 rp, standard rooms at 14,000/17,000 rp and air-con rooms at 26,000/29,000 rp. Close by, the *Hotel Murni* has rooms for 14,000/17,500 rp and looks OK, but get a room at the back away from the main street. On the same street the *Penginapan Mama* looks passable but always seems to be full – meaning they don't want to mess with foreigners. If you can get a room here it costs 4000 rp with shared mandi.

Places to Stay – middle

The *Hotel Gajah Mada* (☎ 21046), at Jalan Gajah Mada 108, is decent. Air-con singles/doubles with big beds and attached bathroom cost 42,400/48,400. The terrace off the second floor overlooks the sea.

The *Hotel Balikpapan* (☎ 21490/1/2/3) at Jalan Garuda 2 is a pleasant place with a bar tucked away from the main road. Rooms are overpriced; standard rooms are more expensive and not as good value as the Hotel Gajah Mada's. Doubles range from standard at 66,500 rp, superior at 72,600 rp and deluxe at 78,650 rp.

The *Hotel Budiman* (☎ 22583, 21163) on Jalan Pengeran Antasari has rooms with air-con and TV for 42,550 rp, plus tax and service.

The *Mirama* (☎ 22960) at Jalan Sutoyo 16 has a good location, a restaurant, chemist, and barber shop. Its air-con rooms cost 47,500 rp for standard, 70,000 rp for first class, 82,000 rp for superior and 95,000 to 105,000 rp for suites.

The best attribute of the *Bahtera Hotel* (☎ 22603) is its central location near the Benakutai at Jalan A Yani 2. However, because its attached disco provides guests with more options than drinks and dance, the hotel can get a bit noisy. All rooms have air-con and TV; economy 'medium' rooms cost 42,400 rp, standard rooms 48,400 rp and superior rooms 60,500 rp.

The *Blue Sky Hotel* on Jalan Suprapto is comfortable and clean but expensive. Standard/superior/deluxe doubles cost 78,000/90,000/126,000 rp and suites cost from 156,000 rp. As you might expect at these prices, all rooms are air-con and have TV. There is also a sauna, gymnasium and billiard tables.

Places to Stay – top end

Balikpapan's *Hotel Benakutai* (☎ 21804, 21813) on Jalan Pengeran Antasari costs from 147,000 rp for a single to 392,000 rp for a suite plus 21% service and tax. An office building/shopping centre is attached and of course there's an international-style bar/restaurant.

Places to Eat

Balikpapan can be recommended for its seafood Padang places, although Padang food tends to be expensive here compared with other parts of Indonesia.

At modest prices for Balikpapan, try the *Restaurant Masakan Padang Simpang Raya* next to the Hotel Murni on Jalan Panjaitan. The *Restaurant Salero Minang* at Jalan Gajah Mada 12B (as well as a smaller branch on Jalan Sutoyo) is similarly priced, as is the *Restaurant Sinar Minang* on Jalan Pengeran Antasari. This place serves *udang galah* (giant river prawns) and is marginally better than the Salero Minang. Near the harbour, *Sari Bundo* serves decent Padang fare.

If you are hankering for Chinese food try the *Atomic*, conveniently located on a little alley off Jalan Antasari near the Benakutai, the *Dynasty* on Jalan Sutoyo, or the *Hap Koen* which is a bit further out at Jalan A Yani 19 RT 36. The food at all these eateries is decent and the prices moderate.

Although more expensive than the establishments already mentioned, for expats and locals alike, one of the most popular restaurants in town is the *New Shangrila* (☎ 23124). It is located on the extension of Jalan Sutoyo where its name changes to Jalan Gunung Sari Hilir. There's excellent Cantonese and Shanghai-style fare and a savoury hot-plate special with pigeon eggs, vegetables and your choice of meat, chicken or seafood. Get there before 7 pm or you may have a considerable wait. It's a cheap bemo ride or at least a 25-minute walk from the Benakutai.

For a seafood meal which is not cheap, but well worth spending a bit more on, dine at the *Bondy* on Jalan Sutoyo. It is an easy walk from the Benakutai. Don't be deceived by the ice-cream shop at the front (great for desserts) – walk back to the alfresco dining patio and pick out a fish you want freshly barbecued. Delicious! Depending on the size of the fish, you can expect to pay 8000 to 14,000 rp. Carnivores can order steak here, but further up Jalan Sutoyo you will find grilled fillets the speciality of the *New Holland Icecream & Steakhouse*.

If you are willing to spend an average of 30,000 rp for an excellent meal with a splendid view of the ocean, visit the *Benua Patra* on Jalan Yos Sudarso, beyond the hospital complex. A potpourri of cuisines, including Western, Japanese, Korean and Chinese, are skilfully prepared here and oriented to please the palate of expats.

Western breakfasts in the Benakutai Hotel's coffee shop are surprisingly reasonable. The two other restaurants in the hotel serve excellent Western and Chinese fare at moderate to expensive prices.

More unusual (for the decor) is the *Restaurant Roda Baru*, near the Penginapan Royal, where you eat beneath a chandelier amidst a rockery with plaster storks.

The cheapest eats are at the numerous warungs and food trolleys open during the evening along Jalan Dondong, near the Hotel Benakutai. There's a *Kentucky Fried Chicken* on Jalan A Yani. The *Depot Banjar Indah*, which serves udang galah, and the *Depot Tuhung Agung* are both on Jalan Suprapto and are cheapies worth visiting if you're staying in the north-west corner of town.

Entertainment

Apart from watching the twinkling lights of the oil refinery at night you could try getting drunk in one of Balikpapan's dwindling number of bars and discos.

Try the *Benua Patra Restaurant & Bar* on Jalan Yos Sudarso. It has a large bar and dance floor – some nights there's a band and other nights an up-market disco. For a raunchier disco scene, there's the dancing emporium attached to the Bahtera Hotel on Jalan A Yani. There's a 4000 rp cover charge plus a one-drink minimum unless you are staying at the hotel.

Further west, Jalan Ahmad Yani becomes Jalan Yos Sudarso and rounds the peninsula, where you'll come to a couple of smaller bar/disco affairs. There's usually a cover charge and a drink minimum.

Getting There & Away

Air Garuda/Merpati is diagonally opposite the Hotel Benakutai. Bouraq (☎ 21107, 21087) has an office near the Hotel Benakutai on Jalan Pengeran Antasari, next to Hotel Budiman. Asahi Airlines (☎ 22044) is across the street and to the left of the Hotel Benakutai.

Garuda/Merpati has flights from Balikpapan to: Banjarmasin, Batam, Kupang, Maumere, Medan, Samarinda, Semarang, Solo, Jakarta (282,100 rp), Surabaya (198,150 rp), Ujung Pandang and Yogyakarta. There are same-day connecting flights to Ambon, Bandung, Berau, Datadawai,

Denpasar, Kendari, Long Ampung, Long Bawan, Nunukan, Palangkaraya, Tanjung Selor and Tarakan.

Garuda flies to and from Singapore via Pontianak three times a week for 418,300 rp.

Bouraq flies Balikpapan-Jakarta on slower Bouraq planes for about 264,000 rp.

Asahi has bought out the Merpati landing rights to Samarinda and now has the most frequent flights between Balikpapan and Samarinda at 47,800 rp.

Union Oil has an office at Balikpapan airport and they charter planes for direct flights from Balikpapan to Singapore (there is a separate Singapore-bound terminal).

Bus From Balikpapan you can head either north to Samarinda or south to Banjarmasin. Buses to Samarinda (2800 rp, two hours) depart from a bus stand in the north of the city accessible by a bemo for 300 rp. You buy your ticket on the bus.

Buses to Banjarmasin (15,000 rp or 20,000 rp for air-con, 12 hours) depart from the bus station on the opposite side of the harbour to the city. To get there, take a colt from the Rapak bus station to the pier on Jalan Mangunsidi. Charter a speedboat to take you to the other side (the speedboat drivers will mob you). It costs 1200 rp per person, or around 4000 rp to charter, and takes 10 minutes. Alternatively, a motorised longboat costs 800 rp and takes 25 minutes. The Banjarmasin bus station is immediately behind the speedboat and longboat dock. There are also a couple of warungs here. It may be a good idea to go to the station the day before you want to leave, buy a ticket and find out when the bus departs.

Boat The Pelni liners *Kerinci* and *Kambuna* call in regularly and connect Balikpapan to: Tarakan, on the east coast of Kalimantan; Pantoloan, Toli Toli and Ujung Pandang in Sulawesi; Surabaya; and Jakarta. For fares (in rp) from Balikpapan, see the table below.

In Balikpapan the Pelni office (☎ 22187) is on Jalan Yos Sudarso. For regular ships to Surabaya try PT Ling Jaya Shipping (☎ 21577) at Jalan Yos Sudarso 40 and PT Sudi Jaya Agung (☎ 21956) at Jalan Pelabuhan 39. Fares are around 30,000 rp.

Also worth considering are the regular ships to Pare Pare in Sulawesi. Go to the office of PT Nurlina at the pier where speedboats and longboats depart for the Banjarmasin bus station. Departures for Pare Pare are almost daily and the fare is around 27,000 rp.

Getting Around

To/From the Airport Seppingan Airport is a 15-minute fast drive from Pasar Baru along a surfaced road. A taxi from the airport to town costs a standard 7500 rp if you buy your taxi ticket in the terminal. Walk outside and bargain your fare down to around 6000 rp.

In town you should be able to charter a bemo to the airport for less – from Pasar Baru for 4000 to 5000 rp. Chartered bemo or taxi seems to be the only way to the airport. There are a couple of rumah makan at the airport.

Bemo Bemos ply the streets; 300 rp gets you anywhere around town. The chief station is the Rapak bus and bemo station at the end of Jalan Panjaitan. From here bemos do a circular route around the main streets. (Guys with motorcycles also hang around the Rapak station and will take you anywhere as a pillion passenger).

Destination	I	II	III	IV	Ekonomi
Jakarta	224,500	165,000	123,500	97,000	63,500
Surabaya	117,800	87,800	64,800	51,800	33,600
Ujung Pandang	81,300	62,000	47,600	34,500	23,700
Tarakan	66,500	44,000	37,400	31,300	25,200

Top: Coast of Komodo Island, Nusa Tenggara (JN)
Bottom: Komodo Dragon at Banu Nggulung, Komodo Island, Nusa Tenggara (JN)

Top: 'Just hanging around', Kalimantan (AS)
Bottom: River boat activity, Pontianak, Kalimantan (AS)

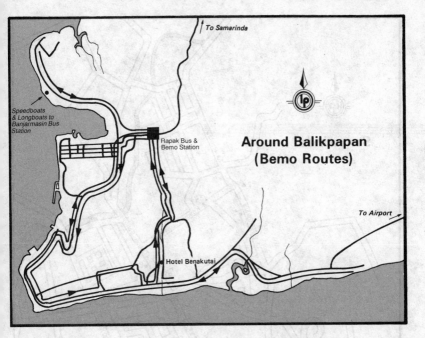

Speedboats & Longboats to Banjarmasin Bus Station

To Samarinda

Rapak Bus & Bemo Station

Around Balikpapan (Bemo Routes)

To Airport

Hotel Benakutai

SAMARINDA

Balikpapan for oil, Samarinda for timber; this is another old trading port on one of Kalimantan's mighty rivers. If you want to look at a timber mill there's a giant one on the road to Tenggarong, not far from Samarinda. Samarinda is also the most convenient starting point for inland trips up Sungai Mahakam to the Dayak areas. The riverbank around Samarinda is pitted with factories and warehouses, and numerous cargo ships ply the water.

Most of the people who have settled in Samarinda are Banjars from South Kalimantan, so the main dialect is Banjarese. There are also many Kutais, the indigenous people of this area, most of whom are now Muslims.

On the south side of the Mahakam, in the part of town called Samarinda Seberang (across from Samarinda), you can visit cottage industries where Samarinda-style sarongs are woven. The traditional East Kalimantan wraparound is woven of *daun doyo* (dried leaves from the doyo tree).

Orientation & Information

The main part of Samarinda stretches along the north bank of Sungai Mahakam. The best orientation point is the enormous mosque on the riverfront. Jalan Yos Sudarso runs east from here and Jalan Gajah Mada runs west. Most of the offices and hotels are along these two streets or in the streets immediately behind them.

The Hotel Mesra allows day guests to use their large, well-kept pool for 2500 rp per day.

Tourist Office The Tourist Office (☎ 21669) is informative when it comes to Samarinda itself but less knowledgeable when it comes to travels into the interior. It is located just off Jalan Kesuma Bangsa at Jalan A I Suryani 1 (signposted 'Kantor Pariwisata').

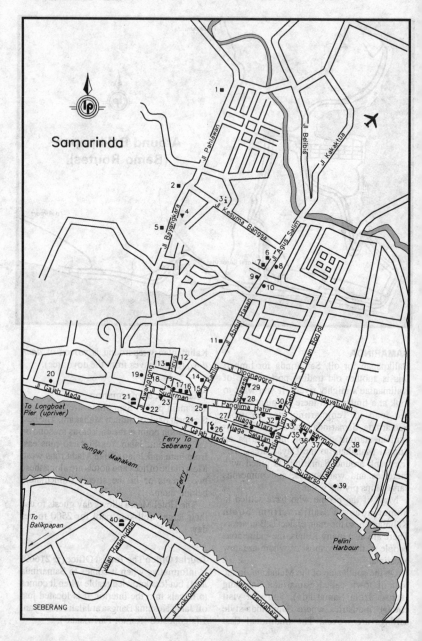

PLACES TO STAY		28	California Fried Chicken
		29	Haur Gading Restaurant
1	Kota Tepian Hotel	33	Sari Wangi Restaurant
2	Hotel Mesra	35	Restaurant Gumarang
5	Hotel Lamin Indah	36	Lezat Restaurant
6	Hotel Andhika		
7	Penginapan Maharani		OTHER
11	Hotel Rahayu		
12	Wisma Pirus	3	Tourist Office
13	Hotel Hayani	15	Mesra Indah Shopping Centre
14	Hotel Hidaya	18	Bank Expor/Impor Indonesia
16	Hotel Djakarta I	19	Telephone Office
17	Hotel Sewarga Indah	20	Bank of Indonesia
25	Hidayah I Hotel	21	Post Office
31	Pondok Indah	22	Bank Rakyat Indonesia
32	Sukarni Hotel	24	Pasar Pagi
		26	Mesjid Raya (Grand Mosque)
▼ PLACES TO EAT		27	Citra Niaga Plaza
		30	Bank Negara Indonesia
4	Lembur Kuring Restaurant	34	PT EMKL & PL
8	Mirasa Restaurant	37	Bouraq Office
9	Soto Madura	38	Bank Dagang Negara
10	Depot Prambanan	39	Mahakam Cinema
23	Sweet Home Bakery	40	Post Office

For good information on East Kalimantan trekking and river journeys contact Jailani, a Kutai guide, through Hotel Rahayu, Jalan K H Abdul Hasan 17, Samarinda.

Money The Bank Negara Indonesia is on the corner of Jalan Sebatik and Jalan Panglima Batur. It changes only US dollars (cash and travellers' cheques). It is open Monday to Thursday from 8 am to 12.30 pm, Friday from 1.30 to 4.30 pm, and Saturday from 8 to 11.30 am.

The Bank Dagang Negara on Jalan Mulawarman is the only bank in Samarinda that changes travellers' cheques in currencies other than US dollars. It's open during the same hours as the BNI.

Post The main post office is on the corner of Jalan Gajah Mada and Jalan Awanglong, opposite the Bank Rakyat Indonesia.

Things to See
Beside the Mahakam Cinema is an old **Chinese temple**, which is worth a stroll

around if you have some spare time. About 500 metres north of the Hotel Mesra is a large **morning market**, open from 5 to 10 am. Arrive before 7 am to see it at its best.

Places to Stay – bottom end
The *Hotel Hidayah* on Jalan K H Kahlid is central and its spartan but clean singles/doubles cost from 6000/12,000 rp, while doubles with mandi cost 15,500 rp. Rooms upstairs are quieter (away from the noisy TV in the foyer) than those at the front. Rates include a small breakfast.

This budget inn should not be confused with its new mid-range cousin, the *Hidayah I Hotel* (☎ 31210) on Jalan Tenungung (Jalan Kahlid changes to this name as it approaches the river). Pleasant singles/doubles with private bath and a fan cost 15,200/18,200 rp, air-con doubles are 20,300 rp and suites cost 35,300 rp. Next door, another new hotel, the *Aida*, is being built and, according to its owner, prices will be similar to those of the Hidaya I.

Further up Jalan Kahlid where it becomes Jalan Abdul Hassan as you head away from the river, and beyond the *Penginapan Siar* (which doesn't accept foreigners), is the basic *Hotel Rahayu* (☎ 22622) at No 17. Rooms here are 7200/12,000 rp including breakfast, 15,600/19,200 rp with mandi. New rooms with correspondingly higher prices are being built.

The *Hotel Andhika* (☎ 22358, 23507) at Jalan Haji Agus Salim 37 has clean and quiet economy singles/doubles with shared mandi at 10,900/17,000 rp including breakfast. More expensive standard rooms with private mandi are 20,000/25,000 rp and air-con rooms start at 24,000/30,000 rp. They have an attached coffee shop/restaurant serving Chinese, European and Indonesian food.

Next door to the Andhika is *Penginapan Maharani*, the cheapest accommodation open to foreigners in Samarinda. Very basic rooms, without attached mandi, cost 5500/11,000 rp.

Two recent discoveries are the pleasant *Wisma Pirus* (☎ 21873) and *Hotel Hayani* (☎ 22653). Both hotels are on Jalan Pirus, off Jalan Jenderal Sudirman.

The staff at Wisma Pirus are friendly and the owner is a Balinese who has information on East Kalimantan travel. Rooms without mandi in the old wing cost 10,000//14,600 rp. Rooms with mandi are 15,200/20,000 rp (including tax and service). The air-con new wing has singles/doubles/triples with attached bath for 50,000/60,000/70,000 rp. The Pirus is very clean and quiet.

The Hayani across the street is also good, with singles/doubles for 15,200/20,600 rp (all with mandi) and bigger rooms for 17,500/22,400 rp. The hotel also has a budget restaurant.

The *Hotel Djakarta I* (☎ 22624) is a larger cheapie right on Jalan Jenderal Sudirman between Jalan Veteran and Jalan K H Kahlid. Adequate rooms cost 10,000/18,000 rp without mandi, or 20,000 rp with mandi. They have a few air-con doubles for 25,000 rp. There is a good travel agency in front of this hotel.

An economical choice if you want to stay near Samarinda's airfield is *Hotel Rahmat Abadi* (☎ 23462) at Jalan Serindit 215, just across from the mouth of Jalan Pipit, which leads to the terminal. Rooms start at 9000/12,800 rp with breakfast.

Down the street towards the town centre is the cheaper *Penginapan Putra Tapin* with basic but clean rooms for 7500 rp.

Places to Stay – top end

Samarinda's top hotel is the *Hotel Mesra* (☎ 21011), at Jalan Pahlawan 1. The hotel comes complete with a large, clean swimming pool, tennis court, giant chess set, coffee shop and excellent restaurant. You may also dine right next to the swimming pool.

Singles range from a surprisingly low 50,000 rp right up to 83,000 rp. Doubles range from 65,000 to 98,000 rp. There are also luxurious cottages at 134,000 rp. There is a 21% service/tax charge.

The Mesra is on the north-west edge of town in a hilly area that sometimes gets a nice breeze. The staff are very friendly here and the ambience quite attractive.

There are two other up-market hotels in town, but neither of these is really comparable with the Mesra. The new *Kota Tepian* (☎ 32510) at Jalan Pahlawan 4 is air-con and has economy rooms for 30,000 rp and standard to deluxe doubles for 45,000 to 65,000 rp. Suites cost 105,000 rp.

The *Hotel Sewarga Indah* (☎ 22066) at Jalan Jenderal Sudirman 11 has all air-con rooms starting at 47,800 rp for economy doubles, with larger doubles ranging from 55,700 rp (standard) to 96,000 rp (deluxe). The tariff includes breakfast and tax/service. The rooms here are nothing to rave about; the only advantage this hotel has over its competitors is its location in the centre of Samarinda.

Places to Eat

Samarinda is a great place if you like eating, and especially if you like fruit. Along Jalan Mas Tenggarong people sit carving giant nangka into manageable segments. A zurzat will cost you 650 rp and there are pineapples, bananas and salaks aplenty.

Samarinda's chief gastronomic wonder is the udang galah found in the local warungs. The prawns are caught by local fisherfolk using big rattan baskets. The standard price for udang galah in the markets is 12,000 rp per kg, which should yield roughly seven to 10 giant prawns, depending on the size. Two or three of these suckers are a meal for most individuals. Ask your hotel's kitchen staff to grill them for you.

One of the better places for decent local food at decent prices is the *Citra Niaga* hawkers' centre off Jalan Niaga, east a block or two from the Mesjid Raya. There's an excellent range of seafood, Padang, satay, noodle and rice dishes, *ayam panggang* (roast chicken) and fruit juices as well as beer (usually warm). Ayam panggang is a local speciality and shouldn't be missed. It seems like the kind of place where it might be a good idea to establish prices in advance, although we weren't ever ripped off.

At the Mesra Indah shopping centre close to the Hotel Hidayah on Jalan K H Kahlid, are two decent food centres and, upstairs overlooking the street, an ice-cream parlour.

If you like pastries for breakfast, try the *Sweet Home Bakery* at Jalan Jenderal Sudirman 8, west of Jalan Pirus on the left. For excellent Chinese breakfasts your best bet is the spotless *Depot AC*, located behind the Wella Beauty Salon off Jalan Mulawarman. They serve very tasty bubur ayam, nasi bebek, nasi ayam and nasi tahu – all made with top grade Thai rice and quite inexpensive. The Depot AC is only open mornings.

If you prefer Indonesian nasi soto or nasi sop for breakfast, there's the efficient *Warung Aida* on the south side of Jalan Panglima Batur at the Jalan Kalimantan intersection. For savoury beef soup at lunch or dinner, eat at *Soto Madura* on Jalan A Salim. Also on Jalan A Salim, a cheap place for satay and *ayam goreng* is *Depot Prambanan*. Nearby is another Indonesian budget eatery, *Mirasa*. Those craving a taste of home will find a *California Fried Chicken* joint on Jalan Sulawesi.

For good, albeit not cheap, Chinese fare dine at *Lezat* on Jalan Mulawarman. The *Sari Wangi* on Jalan Niaga Utara is not quite the quality of Lezat, but it's somewhat cheaper and has some decent Chinese seafood dishes. Locals praise *Lembur Kuring* for its moderately priced grilled seafood and chicken. If you are hankering for Padang-style food, visit *Restaurant Gumarang* on Jalan Veteran.

For a splurge, locals reckon the best hotel restaurants are at the Mesra, Sewarga Indah and the Andhika, in that order. In addition to its attractive wood panelled restaurant serving excellent European, Indonesian and Chinese cuisine, the Mesra often has a barbecue grill for pool-side dining. The fanciest restaurant in town is the *Haur Gading Restaurant* off Jalan Sulawesi. They specialise in seafood, and the udang galah are 4000 rp each.

Those who really want to treat themselves to terrific grilled fish should catch an ankutan or taxi to the *Alpha Omega Restaurant* on the outskirts of town at Jalan Srinoti 10. It's worth the trip, as you choose your own fish Sundanese-style from pools near your table and dine alfresco beneath a thatch roof.

The warung across from the airport terminal has good, inexpensive rice dishes, including nasi rawon, nasi pecel and nasi sop. The airport cafeteria is more expensive and limited in variety.

Entertainment

Several bars and discos are tucked away throughout the Kaltim Theatre complex across from the sleazy Sukarni Hotel (always full because it's strictly a brothel). Most are fairly hard-core hostess bars, but the *Blue Pacific* is a slightly up-market discotheque where couples are welcome. The cover charge is 5000 rp and includes a small bottle of beer and peanuts. Take care climbing the metal stairs to the upper floors – they're in an advanced state of decay.

For young Indonesians the place to dance the night away is the 'floating disco', Tepian Mahakem, picturesquely situated at the foot of the Mahakam bridge. There is a 4000 rp cover charge.

Getting There & Away

Air The Garuda/Merpati and Asahi offices are on the east side of Jalan Iman Bonjol, a couple of blocks north of Bank Negara Indonesia.

Asahi has several flights daily to Balikpapan (47,800 rp) which connect with Garuda and Merpati flights to other domestic destinations including Bandung, Kupang, Maumere, Semarang, Surabaya, Ujung Pandang and Yogyakarta. Asahi has very useful flights to the upriver villages of Long Lunuk (Data Dawai), Long Ampung and Tanjung Selor. See the Dayak Villages section for flight details. Asahi also flies to Berau (108,000 rp) and Tarakan (129,200 rp).

Bouraq (☎ 21105) is at Jalan Mulawarman 24 and they book daily flights to Tarakan (on small Bali Air planes, 118,200 rp; on Bouraq 129,400 rp), Berau (on Bali Air only, 108,500 rp), Banjarmasin (132,300 rp), Jakarta (291,800 rp) and Surabaya (two flights daily, 241,200 rp).

Bus From Samarinda you can head west to Tenggarong or south to Balikpapan. The long-distance bus station is at Seberang on the south side of Sungai Mahakam. To get there take a longboat from the pier at Pasar Pagi on Jalan Gajah Mada. The crossing takes a few minutes, costs 300 rp, and there are boats that take motorcycles across. The bus station is immediately behind the boat dock on the other side. Alternatively, there are bemos running between the centre of town and the bus station for 500 rp.

From Seberang there are buses daily to Tenggarong (1500 rp, one hour) and to Balikpapan (2800 rp bus, two hours) along well-surfaced roads.

Taxi You can be driven direct to your destination in Balikpapan in less than two hours by shared taxis for 7500 rp. Taxis embark from a parking lot across from the Sukarni Hotel. The drawback here is that they don't leave until they have four passengers or until a passenger is willing to pay for any empty seats.

Boat Pelni are at Jalan Yos Sudarso 40/56 or ask at the nearby Terminal Penumpang Kapal Laut Samarinda and the Direktorat Jenderal Perhubungan Laut – both on Jalan Yos Sudarso. However, Balikpapan and Tarakan are the nearest harbours for Pelni passenger ships, which don't operate in or out of Samarinda. Various shipping offices are along the same street, like PT Perusahaan Pelayaran Lokal and PT EMKL.

There are many non-Pelni boats from Samarinda to other ports in East Kalimantan. Possible destinations include Berau, also known as Tanjung Redep, (40,000 rp, about 36 hours) and Tarakan (49,000 rp, about two days and two nights). If you can't get a ship to Tarakan then take one as far as Berau. From there it's easy to get a boat to Tarakan.

Occasional boats go to Donggala, Palu, Pare Pare and Pantoloan on the west coast of Sulawesi. There should be one or two ships a week to at least one of these places although you may have to hunt around the shipping agencies. The KM *Tanjung Slamat* and the KM *Harapanku III* sail to Pare Pare on Tuesday, Wednesday and Saturday for 41,500 rp per person. Another possibility is to try and catch a Bugis schooner across to Sulawesi.

The KM *Dewi Mutiara* sails to Surabaya twice weekly for 37,000 rp.

Riverboat Boats up the Mahakam leave from the Sungai Kunjang ferry terminal south-west of the town centre. To get there take a green city minibus A (called taxi A) west on Jalan Gajah Mada, and ask for 'feri'. The regular fare is 500 rp but if you get in an empty taksi they may try to make you charter. If you don't want to charter, insist on 'harga biasa'.

A riverboat to Tenggarong costs 750 rp and takes three hours. For other destinations further up the Mahakam, see the Dayak Villages section.

Getting Around

To/From the Airport The airport is quite literally *in* the suburbs. You might think you're hard up if a freeway gets slapped down over your nature strip, but how many people have Twin Otters landing in their backyards?

A taxi counter is in the terminal. Pay 7500 rp for a taxi into the centre of town or walk a few minutes down Jalan Pipit to Jalan Serindit and catch a public taxi/colt (route B) for 300 rp all the way down Jalan Kakaktua to the waterfront.

You should be able to catch a colt to the airport from the corner of Jalan KH Kahlid and Jalan Panglima Batur. Be wary of getting into empty colts unless you want to end up chartering them. If colt drivers believe you are going to the airport, they will try to charge you outrageous sums. To avoid being ripped-off, say you are going to the Rahmat Abadi Hotel, pay 300 rp and make the short walk to the airport.

Public Taxi City colts, called taxis, run along several overlapping routes designated A, B and C. Most short runs cost 300 rp. It's a standard 300 rp to the ferry pier for boats going upriver and 300 rp to the airfield.

AROUND SAMARINDA

Pampang Dayak Village

Pampang Village, 26 km from Samarinda, is a government-settled village of fairly Westernised Kenyah Dayak. The tourist office can arrange for transport to the village (not cheap) and for traditional dances (expensive). You can arrange for either car or taxi rental on your own.

Kutai Game Reserve

This wildlife conservation home of orangutan and other exotic species can be visited either via a tour booked through agencies in Balikpapan and Samarinda, or on your own. Other than a monument to Bontang's location on the equator, some wooden houses on stilts, and an immense liquefied natural gas plant, there is little reason to spend much time in the town.

Guide service costs about 12,000 rp. Allow at least two days for your visit to the reserve from Samarinda.

Places to Stay If you stay overnight in Bontang, the best place is the comfortable *Equator Hotel* (☎ 22939). Air-con bungalows start at 30,000 rp with TV and attached mandi.

There are also a few cheap hotels in town but most budget travellers stay at the basic government *Kutai Guesthouse* in the reserve where a bed costs 3000 rp. There is some basic Indonesian food here, but it is recommended that you bring some of your own.

Getting There & Away Independent travellers can take a bus from Samarinda to Bontang for 2500 rp for the three-hour trip and then charter a boat from the PHPA office (50,000 rp for the round trip). A road from Bontang is being constructed to the reserve and may be completed by the time you read this.

TENGGARONG

On Sungai Mahakam, 39 km from Samarinda, Tenggarong was once the seat of the sultanate of Kutai. Today it's a little riverside town cut by dirty canals. Like many small towns along the Mahakam, wooden walkways lead from each house to the toilet shacks built on stilts over the waterways. Both river and canals function as a combined toilet/bath/washbasin/well.

Orientation & Information

The chief attraction of Tenggarong is the former sultan's palace museum. Some travellers prefer to start long river trips from here, although you'll have more seating choice on boats from Samarinda.

Tourist Office A tourist office next to the sultan's palace has information on river trips and the Kutai Nature Reserve.

Sultan's Palace (Mulawarman Museum)

The former sultan's palace is now a museum. It was built by the Dutch in the 1930s in

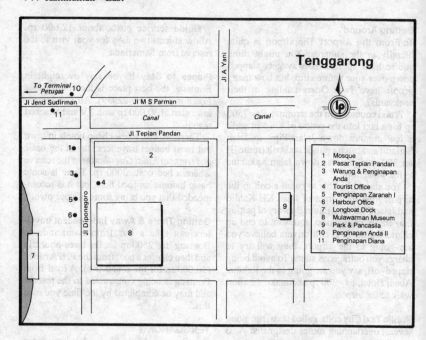

Tenggarong

To Terminal Petugas 10

Jl Jend Sudirman
11

Jl M S Parman

Canal   Canal

Jl Tepian Pandan

Jl A Yani

1
2
3
4
Jl Diponegoro
5
6

8

7

9

1 Mosque
2 Pasar Tepian Pandan
3 Warung & Penginapan Anda
4 Tourist Office
5 Penginapan Zaranah I
6 Harbour Office
7 Longboat Dock
8 Mulawarman Museum
9 Park & Pancasila
10 Penginapan Anda II
11 Penginapan Diana

futurist, monolithic, modernist style. It holds a collection of artefacts from the days of the sultan and many Dayak artefacts.

The palace is closed on Monday; it's open Tuesday to Thursday from 8 am to 2 pm, Friday from 8 to 11 am, Saturday from 8 am to 1 pm and Sunday and holidays from 8 am to 2 pm. The sultan's fine porcelain collection is only exhibited on Sundays (although if you pay the guard a 'tip' he might show you the porcelain on other days). Admission to the museum is 400 rp. On some Sundays, there is Dayak dancing here; it can be arranged on other days for a good sum – say 100,000 rp.

Erau Festival

Once a year, Dayak travel from various points in Kalimantan to celebrate the Erau Festival in the town of Tenggarong. Although the festival has become somewhat touristy, it will give you a good opportunity to see the Dayak in their traditional finery perform tribal dance and ritual ceremonies.

The festival is usually held the last week in September and goes on for five days. Contact the tourist office in Samarinda for the exact dates. Tourist agencies in Balikpapan and Samarinda should also know when it is held.

Places to Stay

Down on the waterfront there are two places right on the boat dock. The *Penginapan Zaranah I* (☎ 148) has rooms for 3000/6000 rp. The *Warung & Penginapan Anda* (☎ 78) costs 4000/7500 rp.

Up the road and around the corner on Jalan Jenderal Sudirman are the similarly priced *Anda II* and *Penginapan Diana*. The Diana is the pick of the lot, with large rooms and a restaurant downstairs that looks decent.

Places to Eat

A couple of rumah makan and warungs are around the market and the boat dock, but none is memorable. Try the *Rumah Makan Ibunda* in the Pasar Tepian Pandan – it's a Padang place, so expect to pay a couple of thousand rupiah for a decent meal, but the food is OK.

Getting There & Away

Colts to Tenggarong leave Samarinda's Seberang bus station, across the river from the main part of Samarinda. The one-hour trip costs 1500 rp and the colt pulls into the Petugas station on the outskirts of Tenggarong. From here you have to get a taxi kota (another colt) into the centre of Tenggarong for 300 rp.

Guys with motorcycles will also take you into town for 500 rp. The city taxis run between 7 am and 6 pm. It takes about 10 minutes to get from Petugas station to Pasar Tepian Pandan, where you get off for the boat dock, palace and tourist office.

There are no direct buses or colts from Tenggarong to Balikpapan. Boats from Samarinda to Tenggarong leave from the Sunggai Kunjang pier outside town. The boat costs 750 rp, takes about three hours, and docks at Tenggarong's main pier.

DAYAK VILLAGES

Probably the best starting point for visits to inland Dayak villages is Samarinda. Longboats leave from here to ply the Mahakam, Kedang Kapala and Balayan rivers. Asahi Airlines flies from here to Long Ampung, close to the mouth of the mighty Sungai Kayan.

There is also the relatively acculterated Kenyah Dayak village of Pampang 26 km from Samarinda. You can travel there in a rented car or the yellow shared taxis departing from Samarinda's Segiri station (if and

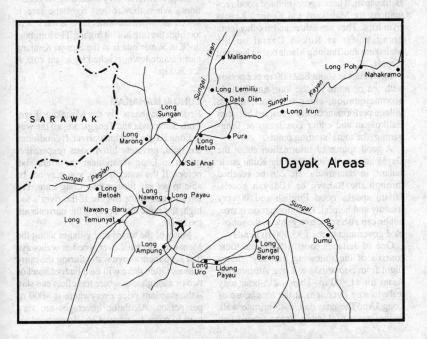

SARAWAK

Malisambo

Long Poh

Nahakramo

Long Lemiliu
Data Dian

Long Sungan

Long Irun

Long Marong

Long Metun

Pura

Sai Anai

Dayak Areas

Long Betoah

Long Nawang

Long Payau

Nawang Baru

Long Temunyat

Dumu

Long Sungai Barang

Long Ampung

Long Uro

Lidung Payau

when there are sufficient passengers to fill the taxi).

Organised Tours

Let's face it, not everybody has the time or hardiness to do solo trekking in East Kalimantan. The tourist offices in Samarinda and Tenggarong can arrange official government guides at around 35,000 rp per day, not including food, accommodation, or transport.

It may be less expensive and more organised overall to go with one of the private tour companies based in Samarinda or Balikpapan. In Samarinda, see the guide Jailani (see the paragraphs below) if you are willing to rough it, or the management of the Mesra Hotel can set up a tour for you.

In Balikpapan, see Kaltim Adventure (ask to see Tour Manager Antoni) in Komplex Balikpapan Permai (☎ 33408), or PT Tomaco Tours (☎ 21747) in the Hotel Benakutai building, Jalan P Antasari, Balikpapan. These agencies have good reputations for Mahakam and Kedang Kepala river trips. They have three and six-day tours going as far as Rukun Damai on the Mahakam and Tanjung Manis on the Kedang Kepala.

Rates start at about 882,000 rp per person with ten or more on the tour, and include accommodation, river transport, meals, village performances and transport between Balikpapan and either Loa Janan or Tenggarong, the tours' starting points.

A good source of information about the Dayak areas in the interior is the Kutai guide Jailani, in Samarinda. He can be reached through the Rahayu or Hidayah hotels. Jailani speaks good English and is very friendly and helpful. His information is free, but he can also serve as a guide at the scheduled government fee of 35,000 rp per day.

One of Jailani's most picturesque tours consists of the following itinerary: first a flight from Samarinda to Long Ampung on Asahi for 41,800 rp. Then a 2½-hour easy walk to stay overnight at the longhouse of Long Uro. The next day, a 45-minute walk to the lamin of Lidung Payau where you catch a boat back to Long Ampung for your flight back to Samarinda. Hardy travellers may include a difficult five-hour jungle walk from Lidung Payau to Long Sungai Barang.

Getting There & Away

Boat Longboat trips are a slow but very relaxing way to travel into the interior. Generally, you sleep on a covered deck with an unobstructed view of every sunset and sunrise. Every few hours, boats without cooking facilities pull in at a village dock and those who haven't brought their own food get off to eat in a warung.

Some boats have warungs on board and an upstairs sleeping area with mattresses and lockers. Either way it's a good idea to bring snacks and plenty of bottled water. Also, take reading or writing material to help pass the time when you tire of viewing river life – birds, monkeys, fisherfolk, and people bathing.

Longboat fares vary according to conditions. When they're just right the fare is lower, and when the water level is too low or too high the fare is a bit higher. The longboat dock in Samarinda is at the Sungai Kunjang pier outside town, reached by a taxi kota A for 500 rp.

SUNGAI MAHAKAM

Regular longboats ply the Mahakam River from Samarinda and Tenggarong all the way to Long Bagun, 523 km upriver. If conditions are right, privately hired boats (expensive) go on to Long Apari near the Malaysian border. If the water is low, you may not be able to get any further than Long Iram, 114 km short of Long Bagun. If the river's too high, the same may apply if the currents are too swift.

Many of the towns and villages along the Mahakam are built over wooden walkways that keep them above water during the rainy season. Often there will be a budget hotel or two or a longhouse where travellers can stay – the standard price everywhere is 4000 rp per person. Alcoholic beverages are very hard to come by upriver so, if you need to,

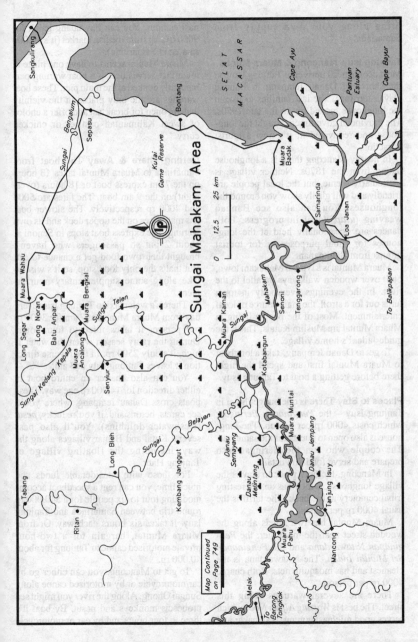

Map Continued on Page 749

bring along your own supply from Samarinda.

Tanjung Isuy, Mancong & Muara Muntai

Most people head upriver to Tanjung Isuy on the shores of Danau Jempang in Banuaq Dayak territory. The last families to live in the longhouse moved out in the late 1970s. The provincial government bought the longhouse and renovated it; it's now a tourist attraction.

In nearby Mancong there is a longhouse dating from the 1870s. Neither village is particularly scenic, but the local people are friendly and will gladly show you around the longhouses. You can also see Banuaq weaving *(ulap doyo)* in progress. Folk dances are occasionally held at the longhouses for ritual purposes or for tourist groups from Balikpapan.

Muara Muntai is a typical Mahakam town, built over wooden walkways parallel to the river. In the evenings everybody in town turns out for a stroll, the main source of local entertainment. Most of the people living in Muara Muntai are Muslim Kutais. This is the guide Jailani's home village.

To get to Danau Jempang, take a longboat to Muara Muntai first and spend the night there before getting a boat to Tanjung Isuy.

Places to Stay There is one budget hotel in Tanjung Isuy – the *Penginapan Beringan*, which costs 4000 rp per person. The longhouse is also open to guests for the same rate. The couple who run the Beringan also prepare and serve food downstairs.

In Mancong, the only place to stay is the village longhouse, which has an interesting tribal cemetery at the back. The tariff is the usual 4000 rp per person.

Muara Muntai has two hotels along the wooden street near the main pier: the *Penginapan Nitawardana* and the *Penginapan Sri Muntai Indah*. The Nitawardana is the cleanest and has mosquito nets. Both charge 4000 rp per person.

There are several warungs along this street. The best is *Warung Alfian Noor* which serves good mie/nasi goreng, ikan bakar and nasi campur. You can buy udang galah for 9000 rp a kg from the fish market (it's 12,000 rp a kg in Samarinda).

Muara Muntai seems to have one place in town that serves beer – a boat warung permanently docked at the main pier. These boat warungs are the only places in the vicinity that are open for breakfast and offer a choice of sweet Kalimantan pastries or chicken curry.

Getting There & Away The boat from Samarinda to Muara Muntai takes 13 hours on the 7 am express boat or 18 hours (overnight) on the 9 am boat. The fares are 5000 and 4000 rp respectively. The slower boat has mattresses on the upper deck and its own warung. The express boat stops in Senoni at about 2 pm so passengers who haven't brought their own food get a chance to eat. But that's the only food stop, so it's wise to take along some supplementary nourishment.

There's a water taxi to Tanjung Isuy every day from Muara Muntai at 7 am for 3000 rp per person. It takes three to four hours. During the rainy season when the water is high, it's only 2500 rp. In the reverse direction it leaves Tanjung Isuy at 3 am.

You can also charter an entire boat in either direction for 14,000 rp one way. These boats cross Danau Jempang, where you'll see egrets, herons and, if you're lucky, *pesut* (freshwater dolphins). You'll also pass several Kutai and Banjar villages along the way, including the floating village of Tanjung Haur.

For those with considerable funds and much time, you can rent a speedboat accommodating four to six people for a 540,000 rp round trip between Samarinda and Tanjung Isuy. It takes six hours each way. Or from Muara Muntai, bargain for a two-hour private motorised canoe to Tanjung for about 40,000 rp.

To get to Mancong, you can either go by car/motorcycle or by motorised canoe along Sungai Ohong. Along the river you might see proboscis monkeys and pesut. By boat it's three to four hours and by car or motorcycle it's only half an hour along a very chancy road.

If it's very rainy, canoe may be your only choice. Allow 25,000 rp return for a car, 18,000 rp return for a motorcycle, or 14,000 rp each way by boat.

Melak & Eheng

Melak is famous for its 5000-acre orchid forest, where 27 different species of orchid grow, including the extremely rare *Cologenia pandurata* or black orchids. The best time to see the orchids is January to February, when the rains are profuse. The Kersid Luwai Orchid Reserve is about 16 km from Melak and may be reached via jeep or ojek charter.

Most of the people of Melak are Tanjung Dayaks, animists who worship the thunder god Belare. Female shamans of the Tanjung, called *balian*, go into ritual trance on auspicious occasions. Inquire whether any funerals, weddings or harvest celebrations are being held while you are there – they can be pretty spectacular. They often include the ritual slaughter of water buffalo.

If you need a guide, travellers have recommended Mr Agus Noto, who can be contacted through the hotel Rahmat Abadi in Melak.

In nearby Eheng there is an unusually long Banuaq lamin and cemetery. Some 200 Dayak reside in Eheng's 65-metre longhouse. You can walk there, or rent a jeep or ojek from Melak.

Places to Stay There are five different

hotels in Melak, the best of which is the clean, well-run *Rahmat Abadi*. A bed there costs 4000 rp per person, as usual.

In Eheng, you may be allowed to stay in the friendly Banuaq longhouse. Near Eheng, in the village of Barong Tongkok, there is a spartan hotel called *Barong Tongkok* costing 4000 rp per person. It is preferable to stay in the local lamin for about 8000 rp a day for room and board.

Getting There & Away Longboats from Samarinda leave for the 325-km trip at 9 am and arrive in Melak at around 10 am the next day. The fare is 8000 rp per person.

Long Iram

This is the end of the line for many would-be explorers because of river conditions or lack of time. Long Iram has recently become a sort of backwater boom town as a result of gold mining. Gold fever has driven local prices up considerably and this is the only town along the upper Mahakam where the standard budget hotel price is 6000 rp.

There are several small Dayak villages nearby and some longhouses, but traditions are not very strong.

A few intrepid travellers have trekked overland west of Long Iram (a week to 10 days) to a tributary of Sungai Barito in Central Kalimantan, and from there worked their way downriver to South Kalimantan and Banjarmasin. There is a road from the village of Tering, near Long Iram, to Tanjung Balai in Central Kalimantan.

You may be able to hitch a ride on a

logging truck to Tanjung Balai, and from there to Muara Teweh. From there regular longboats ply the Barito all the way to Banjarmasin.

Getting There & Away Long Iram is 409 km from Samarinda. The longboat fare is usually 11,500 rp and the trip takes about 33 hours.

Datah Bilang to Muara Merak

If conditions allow you to ferry upriver beyond Long Iram, places of interest include Datah Bilang, where there are two Bahau Dayak (lamin), one of which is heavily decorated with typical Dayak artwork. A reader has recommended the Dayak village of Long Hubung, 45 minutes north of Datah Bilang by motor canoe (7500 rp per person). Yusram, the kepala desa, welcomes visitors to this traditional village.

Between Datah Bilang and Long Bagun is Rukun Damai, surrounded by virgin rainforest, and home to the Kenyah Dayak, many of whom still hold fast to their traditions. There are five Kenyah lamin, including one 250 metres long.

Downstream less than 25 km is Muara Merak, a Punan Dayak settlement. There is good trekking in this area, especially along the Merak to the north-east. With a Punan guide hired in Muara Merak, you could trek overland east for three to four days to Tabang and then travel down the Belayan River to Kotabangun, where you can catch longboat services back to Samarinda.

Long Bagun to Long Apari

Long Bagun is the end of the line for regular longboat services from Samarinda along the Mahakam. A longboat from Samarinda to Long Bagun (conditions permitting) takes three days, two nights and two days going up, and two nights coming down. The boat docks in Long Iram one night each way while the crew and passengers sleep, since night navigation can be dangerous this far upriver. The fare is 15,500 rp.

From Long Bagun you must charter motorised canoes from village to village or trek through the forests. River conditions must be optimum because of river rapids between Long Bagun and the next major settlement, Long Pahangai.

Under normal conditions, it's a one-day canoe trip from Long Bagun to Long Pahangai, then another day to Long Apari, from where the Mahakam is no longer motor-navigable. **Long Lunuk**, between Long Pahangai and Long Apari, is a good place from which to visit Kenyah villages.

Data Dawai

If you want to start your trip from the top, you can fly to Data Dawai, an airstrip near Long Lunuk. Asahi Airlines flies every Sunday and Thursday for 42,000 rp each way. From there you can work your way downriver back to Samarinda, or trek overland to the Apo-Kayan highlands.

One way to save a considerable amount of money going downriver is to buy a canoe and paddle. The price will depend on the size and condition of the canoe – a decent used canoe costs 35,000 to 75,000 rp without an engine. If you want an engine it will cost considerably more, as much as double.

Apart from saving you money, having your own canoe means you can stop when and where you want along the way. However, *do not* attempt to navigate the rapids between Long Pahangai and Long Bagun on your own. In fact, it would be best not to start a self-paddled trip above Long Bagun. Downriver from Long Bagun it's a pretty straightforward trip as long as you check in at villages along the way to make sure you haven't taken a tributary of the Mahakam by mistake, as there is the occasional fork.

The flight from Samarinda to Data Dawai/Long Lunuk took one hour and twenty minutes. In Samarinda travel agents said there was no space, but we called the airport directly and they said there were seats. Because there are no computer hookups for Asahi, travel agents tend to say flights are full, even if they aren't.

At Long Lunuk, we stayed with Luhat Brith and his family; 5000 rp included three meals. He took us upriver to Long Apari with two other travellers for 200,000 rp! This is probably high and other travellers should negotiate hard here. A guest register showed people paying between 100,000 rp and 400,000 rp for this trip. It helps financially to go with at least four other travellers as you are not likely to encounter other foreigners here.

Long Apari is the uppermost village on the Mahakam. This is the last stop for longboats and it is *beautiful*. The longboat trip from Long Lunuk takes five to six hours. It's tiring and a layover in Long Apari is recommended. We joined villagers for a night of dancing with hornbill feathers and they loved it as much as we did. Dinner was forgettable – greasy babi and bony ikan – so travellers should consider bringing their own.

We met some guides who offered to take us to Malaysia for 1,000,000 rp. We didn't try to bargain this down, but it probably can be lowered considerably. They said it would take four days, part by boat and part by trekking. We didn't do this, but it sounded great. Instead, we went downriver to Long Bagun and took a boat to Samarinda for 32,000 rp each.

SUNGAI KEDANG KEPALA

There are regular longboat services up the Kedang Kepala, which branches north off the Mahakam near Muara Kaman, from Samarinda to Muara Wahau. This trip takes three days and two nights and goes via the Kenyah and Bahau villages of Tanjung Manis, Long Noran and Long Segar. The longboat fare from Samarinda to Muara Wahau is 16,500 rp.

In Tarakan, we met a US man and a Swedish woman who had taken a boat north from Muara Wahau to Miau Baru, where they stayed with the Dutch-speaking kepala desa and his English-speaking son, Wilson. They then travelled by local school bus to a lumber camp four km north, where they hitched a ride on a jeep to the Dayak village of Marapun two hours away. From Marapun they got a 12-hour boat ride up the Kelai to Tanjung Redep, which was another 10 hours by boat from Tarakan.

SUNGAI BELAYAN

Another adventurous trip is up Sungai Belayan to Tabang. The Belayan branches north-west off the Mahakam at Kota Bangun and longboats take about three days to reach Tabang from Samarinda.

You can also reach Tabang on foot from the town of Muara Merak on the Mahakam.

You can hire a Punan guide in either Tabang or Muara Merak to lead you north of Tabang into extensive virgin rainforests that are nomadic Punan territory.

SUNGAI KAYAN

South of Tarakan is Tanjung Selor at the mouth of the mighty Sungai Kayan. Asahi flies from Samarinda to Tanjung Selor on Tuesday, Friday and Saturday for 121,500 rp.

There are regular longboat services up the Kayan as far as the Kenyah villages of Mara I and Mara II, but a section of rapids further on prevents boats from reaching the headwaters of the Kayan in the mythicised Apo-Kayan highlands.

Asahi has a government-subsidised flight to Long Ampung in the Apo-Kayan area twice weekly for 41,800 rp. There is good trekking in the Apo-Kayan headlands; you could also trek overland to the Mahakam headwaters from here in about a week with a guide from Long Ampung. The Kutai guide, Jailani, (based in Samarinda) leads easy or vigorous treks to Dayak lamin from Long Ampung (see the Dayak Villages section).

Kenyah godly mask of the Apo Kayan area

TARAKAN

Just a stepping stone to other places, Tarakan is an island town close to the Sabah border. It was the site of bloody fighting between Australians and Japanese at the end of WW II. Unless you're really enthusiastic about Japanese blockhouses, or want to try exiting Indonesia to Sabah, there's little of interest. It's not a bad town, just dull. Some of the houses have old Japanese cannon shells painted silver and planted in their front yards like garden gnomes.

The battle at Tarakan was one of a series of battles fought by Australian soldiers in Indonesia and New Guinea from mid-1944 onwards. There's an interesting argument put forward by Peter Charlton in *The Unnecessary War – Island Campaigns of the South-West Pacific 1944-45* (MacMillan, Australia, 1983) that these battles had no value in the defeat of the Japanese. By that time the Japanese in Indonesia were already effectively defeated, reluctant to fight, incapable of being either evacuated or reinforced, had to live off the land and fought only when they were forced to.

The capture of Tarakan (after six weeks of fighting and the deaths of 235 Australians) was carried out to establish an air base which was never used. After the Tarakan operation Indonesia was effectively bypassed, yet in July 1945 an assault was made on Balikpapan. This last large amphibious landing of the war managed to secure a beach, a disused oil refinery, a couple of unnecessary airfields and the deaths of 229 Australians.

Information

Money Bank Dagang Negara on Jalan Yos Sudarso will change some travellers' cheques and foreign currency.

Places to Stay

There's a line of cheap and middle-range hotels along Jalan Jenderal Sudirman (also known as Jalan Kampung Bugis). These

1	Nirama Hotel
2	Rumah Makan Cahaya
3	Losmen Jakarta
4	Losmen Herlina
5	Rumah Makan Sarang Kepeting
6	Depot Theola
7	Aneka Restaurant
8	Barito Hotel
9	Orchid Hotel
10	Depot Gembira
11	Wisata Hotel
12	Juita Theatre
13	Bank Negara Indonesia
14	Bouraq
15	Tarakan Theatre
16	Bank Dagang Negara
17	Hotel Tarakan Plaza
18	Restaurant Pheonix
19	Japanese Blockhouse
20	Merpati
21	Bank Rakyat Indonesia
22	Perginapan Alam Indah
23	Bali Air Agent
24	CV Tam Bersaudara
25	Hotel Bunga Muda
26	Post Office

Jl Jen Sudirman

Tarakan

← To Airport

Jl Mulawarman

Jl Yos Sudarso

Pier

include the *Losmen Jakarta* (☎ 21919) at 112, which has little boxes for rooms but is otherwise not bad at 6500/8200 rp for singles/doubles. Experience the local way of life by filling your mandi with a hand-pump.

The *Losmen Herlina* is basic but habitable at 5500/6400 rp for singles/doubles but avoid the dark, dismal downstairs rooms. Preferable, although more expensive, is the *Indah* on Jalan Yos Sudarso, where singles/doubles cost 8500/13,000 rp.

The *Barito Hotel* (☎ 21212) on Jalan Jenderal Sudirman 133 has basic but clean rooms for 7700/9400 rp, or 13,000 rp with attached mandi and fan. There are a couple of air-con rooms for 21,500 rp. All rooms include a towel with soap and shampoo and a breakfast of coffee/tea and Chinese rolls, a nice change from the usual slabs of white bread. A laundry is off the second floor on a terrace. Next door, the *Orchid Hotel* (☎ 21664) has rooms at 6500/11,500 rp, but the mandis could be cleaner.

Further along Jalan Jenderal Sudirman near the junction with Jalan Mulawarman the *Wisata Hotel* (☎ 21245) is basic but pleasant with rooms at 10,500/14,000 rp. Rooms at the rear will probably be very quiet. Nearby is the slightly more up-market *Hotel Mirama* (21637) where rooms with air-con, TV and hot water cost from 24,000 rp.

Number one in town is the big *Hotel Tarakan Plaza* (☎ 21870) on Jalan Yos Sudarso, which comes complete with restaurant and expatriates held up by a bar. Air-con

doubles cost 62,000 rp and suites cost 94,000 rp. Further down Jalan Yos Sudarso towards the Pelni harbour is the *Hotel Bunga Muda* (☎ 21349) at No 78, a newish concrete block with fairly clean rooms at 8500/11,000 rp.

There are two hotels on Jalan Sulawesi (on the outskirts of town) to try if you want air-con at middle-range prices. The *Bahtera* (☎ 21821) and the smaller *Oriental* (☎ 21348) have decent air-con rooms starting at 24,000 rp. Note one potential problem: the hotels are situated next to a seedy disco where local prostitutes accompany timber workers back to their rooms, making for a possibly noisy evening.

Places to Eat

The *Rumah Makan Cahaya* on Jalan Jenderal Sudirman (across from the Losmen Jakarta) is pretty good; the menu includes *cumi cumi* (octopus) goreng at 2400 rp, cap cai goreng at 1800 rp, and nasi goreng at 1450 rp. The *Rumah Makan Sarang Kepeting* near Losmen Herlina on the same road has good crab dishes.

At night the happening place is *Depot Theola* on Jalan Jenderal Sudirman, where they serve the local speciality, *nasi lalap* (battered, fried chunks of chicken served with rice and soup). They also have cold beer, ice cream, fruit juices and jamu drinks. There are only one or two tables downstairs, but there's an upstairs area with several more. They'll be glad to play your cassettes on their stereo.

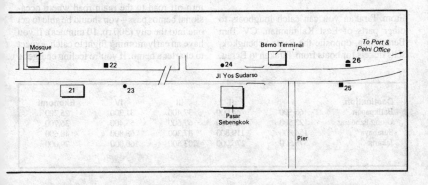

The *Nirwana* on the airport side of Jalan Yos Sudarso has an OK restaurant for alfresco dining, but most patrons come here after 11 pm for the bar, disco and other diversions.

Cheap warungs are at the junction of Jalan Sudirman and Jalan Yos Sudarso and stalls sell reasonably priced imported apples and oranges.

Getting There & Away

Air The easiest way to reach Tarakan is with Bouraq, Asahi or Merpati flights from Balikpapan or Samarinda. The early Merpati flight from Tarakan to Balikpapan continues on to Ujung Pandang, Maumere and Kupang.

In Tarakan, Merpati is at Jalan Yos Sudarso 8. Bouraq (☎ 21248, 21987) is at Jalan Yos Sudarso 9B, across from the Tarakan Theatre. Bali Air, owned by Bouraq, flies Tarakan-Berau and Tarakan-Samarinda. Asahi has an office in the Hotel Tarakan Plaza.

Daily flights between Tarakan and Balikpapan on Bouraq are 138,200 rp. Bouraq also flies to Tawau in Sabah three times weekly for 122,000 rp. MAS flies to Tawau once a week for 136,000 rp.

Boat The Pelni office is at the port – take a colt almost to the end of Jalan Yos Sudarso. The Pelni ship *Kerinci* calls into Tarakan on its regular run around Kalimantan and Sulawesi. Adult fares from Tarakan (in rp) are shown in the table below.

From Tarakan you can catch longboats to other parts of East Kalimantan. CV Tam Bersaudara, opposite the Pasar Sebengkok, sells tickets for boats from Tarakan to Berau.

Departures are at around 6 am daily. Also inquire at the office at the start of the pier just over the bridge from Pasar Sebengkok. Other longboat destinations are: Tanjung Selor (7000 rp), Nunukan (11,500 rp) and Pulau Bunju (7000 rp).

For boats to Nunukan and on to Tawau in the east Malaysian state of Sabah, go to the Pelabuhan Tarakan. Longboats leave daily at around 9 am and arrive in Nunukan 12 hours later for 11,000 rp per person.

In Nunukan you can catch a speedboat to Tawau for 21,000 rp – it takes about four hours. You can also spend the night at the *Losmen Nunukan* for 5000 rp and get a speedboat the next day. Or get a speedboat to Tawau from Tarakan for 35,000 to 40,000 rp, which only takes about five hours.

There is an Indonesian immigration office in Nunukan where you must get your exit stamp. Note that if you got a two-month tourist visa on arrival in Indonesia, you will need an exit permit from the immigration office in Jakarta or the Nunukan office won't stamp your passport. If you got a one-month tourist visa before coming to Indonesia, they can stamp your passport without an exit permit from Jakarta. Hopefully, by the time you read this the improving political and trade relations with Malaysia will make border crossings here much easier.

Getting Around

To/From the Airport Buy tickets for taxis at the taxi counter in the airport terminal – it's 3500 rp to the city. Or walk down the airport turn-off road to the main road where occasional bemos pass – you should be able to get one into the city (300 rp, 10 minutes). If you have an early morning flight to catch, expect to charter a bemo. If you're feeling energetic

Destination	I	II	III	IV	Ekonomi
Balikpapan	66,500	44,000	37,400	31,300	25,200
Ujung Pandang	122,500	98,400	67,600	55,400	36,700
Surabaya	154,800	119,800	87,300	68,800	48,600
Jakarta	375,500	276,000	203,500	160,000	79,000

and not carrying much you could even walk into town from the airport.

Colt Transport around town is by colt. A 250 rp flat rate gets you just about anywhere.

South Kalimantan

The province of Kalimantan Selatan, Kal-Sel for short, is an area of about 37,600 sq km with a population of approximately 2.5 million. It is Kalimantan's smallest province. Kal-Sel is an important centre for diamond mining, rattan processing and, of course, lumber. It is also the centre of Banjarese culture and a good starting point for treks into Central and East Kalimantan.

Traditional Banjarese clothing is made from *kain sasirangan*, cloth produced by a striking tie-dyeing process that uses motifs reminiscent of Javanese *jumputan* batik. The traditional Banjar-style house is the *bubungan tinggi* or tall roof design and the best examples can be seen in the town of Marabahan, 50 km north of Banjarmasin on Sungai Barito. There are a few remaining bubungan tinggi houses are around Banjarmasin and Banjarbaru.

In the mountainous north-eastern interior of South Kalimantan is a group of Dayaks said to be descendants of the original Banjarese race. These original Banjars may have been families from the Barito delta area who fled to the mountains to avoid Muslim conversion in the 15th and 16th centuries. Communal houses (balai) hold up to 30 or more families and serve as a ritual centre for these mountain villages.

BANJARMASIN

This is yet another 'Venice of the East' and the Banjarmasis are indeed up to their floorboards in water. Much of Banjarmasin is planted on swamp land, with a vast number of houses perched on stilts. The city is a short distance up from the mouth of the Barito at its confluence with the Martapura and is criss-crossed by numerous smaller rivers and canals lined with stilt houses, and even houses built on bundles of floating lashed logs. It is far and away Kalimantan's most interesting city.

Banjarmasin is also an important seaport for the shipping of lumber, rattan and other Kalimantan products. Several harbours are along the Barito, one for large cargo and passenger ships, one for longboats going up and down the river, one for Buginese and Javanese pinisi, etc.

Orientation

Banjarmasin is big, but just about everything you'll need is packed into the city centre around the Pasar Baru. There are several cheap hotels along Jalan Ahmad Yani near the banks of Sungai Martapura. Sungai Barito lies to the west of the city centre.

Information

Money Several banks and government offices are along Jalan Lambung Mangkurat. As usual, Bank Dagang Negara has the best rates for travellers' cheques.

Tourist Office At the time of writing, the South Kalimantan tourist office is at Jalan D I Panjaitan 3, near the Grand Mosque. But there are plans to relocate it to the top of the BNI Bank Building at Arjuna Plaza. The staff are very helpful and generous with information. This is also headquarters for the South Kalimantan Tourist Guide Association which has over 30 members, including ten adventure/jungle guides.

The going rate for guides is about 20,000 to 30,000 rp per day for local tours (including trips to nearby Pulau Kaget, Martapura, or Cempaka) or 40,000 to 50,000 rp per day for jungle tours (eg to Loksado). A highly recommended local guide is Johansyah Yasin (Johan). He can be contacted through the tourist office or at the Borneo Homestay at Jalan Pos 123.

At the Tourist Office, Akhmad Arifin (Ifin) speaks fair English and is a knowledgeable guide, but he is only available on weekends.

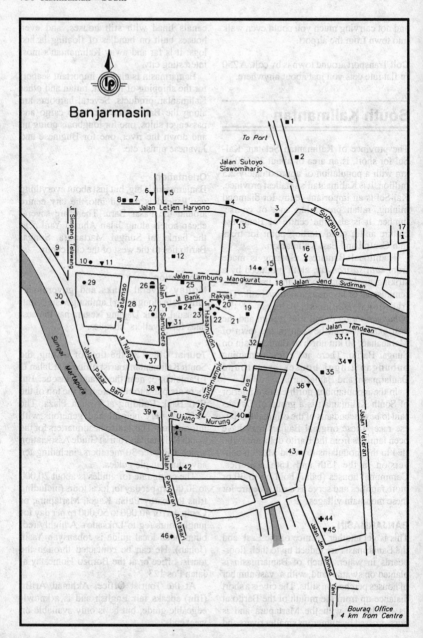

Banjarmasin

To Port

Jalan Sutoyo
Siswomiharjo

Jalan Letjen Haryono

Jalan Lambung Mangkurat

Jalan Jend Sudirman

Jl Bank

Rakyat

Jalan Tendean

Jalan Pasar Baru

Jl Sudimampir

Jl Pos

Murung

Jalan Veteran

Jalan Pangeran Antasari

Jalan Jen Ahmad Yani

Bouraq Office
4 km from Centre

Post & Telecommunications The office for long-distance phone calls is also on Jalan Pos and the main post office is further west at the Jalan P Samudera intersection.

Bookshops Detailed blueprint maps of South and Central Kalimantan are available at Toko Cenderawasih Mas, Jalan Hasanuddin 37, between the Garuda office and Jalan Pos. Across the street a bookshop sells week-old copies of *Newsweek* and *Asiaweek*.

Travel Agencies A good travel agency in Banjarmasin is Adi Travel (☎ 3131), Jalan Hasanuddin 27. It's run by the friendly and informative Pak Mariso who, along with his staff, speaks English. It's the only agency that accepts credit cards.

Mesjid Raya Sabilal Muhtadin
On Jalan Jenderal Sudirman, this is a giant modern art mosque with a copper-coloured

flying saucer dome and minarets with lids and spires. The interior is quite striking and visitors must pay a small fee.

Canal Trips
Banjarmasin should be seen from water level, otherwise it looks just like any Indonesian city. Hire someone to take you around the river and canals in a canoe. It costs 5000 rp per hour in a motorised canoe, or *klotok*. One or two hours should be more than enough. Johan at Borneo Homestay will provide one, or ask around the wharf near the junction of Jalan Lambung Mangkurat and Jalan Pasar Baru. Don't hire a speedboat – they go too fast to observe or photograph anything.

Everything revolves around the waterways, which are lined with closely packed stilt houses. Stairs lead from each house to wooden platforms at water level. People squat on these platforms for everything from washing to defecating. Bugis schooners can be seen tied up to the docks or under construction on the riverbanks. River ferries head inland loaded with cargo, motorcycles and people.

Look for *pasar terapung* or floating markets on the river – these are groups of boats, large and small, to which buyers and sellers paddle in canoes. Trading begins early and is over by 9 or 10 am. At the meeting of the Kuin and Barito rivers is a particularly fine floating market every morning from around 5 to 8 am. There are canoe cafes among the hundreds of boats that converge here, and you can get a nice breakfast of scented tea and Banjarese pastries.

The kampung of Muara Mantuil is a floating village of houses and shops built on logs lashed together. It's on a tributary of the Barito not far from Trisakti Harbour.

Pulau Kembang

The island is 20 minutes from the town centre by boat and home to a large tribe of long-tailed macaques who congregate at an old Chinese temple near shore. On Sundays the temple becomes a virtual circus when Chinese families give the monkeys huge offerings of eggs, peanuts and bananas.

You can buy bags of peanuts to feed the macaques, but it is suggested that you keep them in your pockets, withdrawing one peanut at a time. The reason for this will become quite clear should you hold the bag in your hand, as the aggressive simians often jump on the visitor and steal all their peanuts in one fell swoop.

There are also long-nosed proboscis monkeys in the interior of Pulau Kembang, but they're more difficult to approach than those on Pulau Kaget because of the dominating macaques.

Either Borneo Homestay's klotok or a boat hired on the waterfront can combine a tour of the canals with Pulau Kembang.

Pulau Kaget

About 12 km downstream from Banjarmasin is an island reserve inhabited by the comical long-nosed proboscis monkeys. Indonesians call them *kera belanda* or Dutch monkeys because of their long noses, red faces and pot bellies.

Borneo Homestay or the Tourist Office can tell you the best time to leave Banjarmasin (this depends upon the tide, at 2.30 to 3 pm or early in the morning) so you can reach the island when the monkeys come out to feed. Because they're very shy creatures the boat pilots usually cut the engines and glide beneath tree perches so the monkeys won't flee.

Speedboats at the pier at the end of Jalan Pos ask 45,000 to 50,000 rp for a round trip, or you can pay 20,000 to 25,000 rp for a round trip in a klotok. It's two hours each way.

Ramadan Cake Fair

During Ramadan, the Muslim fasting month, Banjarmasin is the site for the festive *pasar wadai* or cake fair. Dozens of stalls sell South Kalimantan's famous Banjarese pastries near the city hall or the grand mosque.

Muslims don't eat these delicious pastries until after sundown of course, but non-believers can gorge themselves all day.

Places to Stay – bottom end

The *Borneo Homestay* (☎ 66545), on Sungai Martapura at Jalan Pos 123, is pleasant and a good information centre. Johan and Lina, two of the nicest people you will meet in your travels, run the show. Johan speaks very good English and knows South and Central Kalimantan well. Travellers recommend his tour services.

Accommodation is simple but clean here, with a pleasant verandah overlooking the river. A small single/double costs 4500/6500 rp.

The Adi travel agency has opened a new budget lodge, *Diamond Homestay* (☎ 3131) at Jalan Simpang Hasanuddin 58. Go into the travel agency at Hasanuddin 27 and they will show you the nearby alley where the homestay is situated. This pleasant place charges 10,000/15,000/20,000 rp for singles/doubles/triples with fan and shared mandi. The staff can set up tours of the area.

A couple of acceptable places are on the east side of the river. The *Hotel Rahmat* (☎ 4429) at Jalan Ahmad Yani 9 is sizeable with a friendly manager, and singles/doubles cost 7500/12,000 rp with shared mandi. Close by at No 114, the *Hotel Kuripan* has singles/doubles for 7000/8000 rp in the old wing and air-con singles/doubles with attached mandi for 24,200/30,300 rp in the new building signposted *Kuripan II* (☎ 3313).

The very central *Losmen Abang Amet* on Jalan Penatu has rooms for 5000 rp. It's friendly but always seems to be full and in truth does not accept foreigners. Some of the cheaper hotels don't take foreigners since the local police charge proprietors 1000 rp per guest to process the required paperwork.

There are two ultra cheapies which do, although you would have to be truly desperate to lodge at either. The spartan *Mestika* at Jalan Haryono 78 has singles for 3500 rp and doubles for 5500 rp. The mandis are pretty grotty here. Next door at No 178 is the *Beauty*. A beauty it's not, but it is preferable to the Mestika, with singles/doubles at 6500/7500 rp. There are rooms with private bath for 8000/8500 rp.

There are two other cheap places which, while basic, are passable. The *Sinar Amandit* on Jalan Ujung Murung has singles/doubles for 5000/6000 rp and the *Hotel Kalimantan* on Jalan Haryono near Jalan Telawang (not to be confused with the luxury hotel of the same name) has singles/doubles for 5500/8250 rp.

Somewhat preferable, but more expensive is the *Wisma Banjar*, located 100 metres from the Grand Mosque on Jalan Suprapto. Singles/doubles with shared mandi cost 8000/12,000 rp.

Places to Stay – middle & top end

The new *Barito Palace* (☎ 67301) at Jalan Haryono 16-20 is one of Banjarmasin's two top hotels. This luxury establishment boasts an excellent restaurant and swimming pool. All air-con singles/doubles with satellite colour TV start at 98,000/117,000 rp for standard and 127,000/147,000 rp for larger

superior rooms. Deluxe rooms are 156,000 rp and suites range from 196,000 rp to 490,000 rp.

The *Kalimantan* (☎ 66818) on Jalan Lambung Mangkurat is Banjarmasin's other international-class hotel. It too has a restaurant and pool as well as a karaoke bar. Standard singles/doubles cost 127,000/147,000 rp and larger rooms are 176,000/196,000 rp. Suites range from 294,000 to 1,176,000 rp.

Once Banjarmasin's number-one hotel, the *Hotel Maramin* (☎ 8944), at Jalan Lambung Mangkurat 32, now lags behind the Barito Palace and Kalimantan. Correspondingly, it's less expensive as its rooms start at 78,000 rp. The hotel has a bar, restaurant and convention facilities, so a lot of businesspeople stay here.

In the middle range, the comfortable *Hotel Sabrina* (☎ 4442, 4721), at Jalan Bank Rakyat 21, has singles/doubles for 15,000/118,000 rp with fan, 20,000/25,000 rp with fan and shower, and 27,000/30,000 rp with air-con and TV. The *Perdana Hotel* (☎ 3276) at Jalan Katamso 3 has economy singles/doubles with private mandi for 19,400/23,000 rp, two-bedded doubles from 25,500 rp and air-con singles/doubles at 37,600/43,600 rp.

The city has a very nice government guesthouse near the Mesjid Raya, the *Wisma Batung Batulis*, which has large air-con singles/doubles with hot water for 39,100/52,700 rp. Foreigners are welcome to stay whenever one of the 18 rooms is free.

Also well located, near the Grand Mosque, the *Metro* (☎ 2427) at Jalan Sutoyo 102 has fan-cooled rooms with private mandi at 16,000 rp and 19,000 rp and air-con rooms at 24,000 rp. The *Sampaga* (☎ 2753) is at least a half-hour walk from the centre at Jalan Sutoyo 128. It has pleasant all air-con singles/doubles for 36,300/48,400 rp.

Places to Eat

Banjarmasin has a wide variety of eating places. Behind the Hotel Rahmat on Jalan Veteran is a string of moderately priced Chinese rumah makan – like the *Rumah*

Makan Sari Wangi at 70, the *Flamingo* across the road, and *Rumah Makan Simpang Tiga* at 22.

A warung next to the Hotel Rahmat serves delicious *nasi kuning*, a kind of South Kalimantan-style chicken biryani, on Sunday. Across the street is another no-name warung that serves cheap and tasty *soto banjar*, also a local speciality.

The *Warung Raihana*, a few stalls down (away from the river), serves some of the best *mie kuah* in Banjarmasin for only 650 rp. Look for the place wallpapered with kung-fu movie posters. Several other nighttime warungs are nearby and in the Pasar Baru area.

For breakfast, the *Depot Miara*, on the corner diagonally opposite from the Flamingo on Jalan Veteran, has good bubur ayam, as does the *Rumah Makan Jakarta* on Jalan Hasanuddin near the Garuda office. For excellent Western, Chinese and Banjarese pastries check out the famous *Utarid* (also called the Menseng) bakery at Jalan Pasar Baru 22-28, near the Jalan Antasari bridge. The Utarid has cakes, whole wheat bread, biscuit mix and ice cream.

Next to the bridge is a building with a rooftop cafe, *Depot Taman Sari*, where you can bring pastries from the Utarid and have coffee or tea – they don't mind. The Depot Taman Sari is a good place for evening libations, with the odd breeze and views of the Martapura and surrounds.

If you're on a very tight budget, eat at the tea stalls along Jalan Niaga Utara between Jalan Katamso and Jalan P Samudera near Pasar Baru. Banjarmasin is famous for its unique pastries – try the *roti pisang* (moist, round banana cakes). There is a friendly tea stall next to the Jalan A Yani bridge, near Borneo Homestay.

For authentic Banjar seafood eat at *Kaganangan*, at Jalan Samudera 30. It is open from 7 am till late. As with most Indonesian regional cuisine, you pay only for what you eat. Udang galah is 3200 rp, a plate of *saluang goreng* (fried smelt) 700 rp, and baked *papuyu* (a local fish) 1000 rp. Vegetable soup is free.

Opposite the Kaganangan is the similar *Cenderawasih Restaurant* where you can also enjoy local specialities at reasonable prices. For good local Banjar soup served cheaply, try the *Soto Acil Inun* on Jalan Haryono, near the Barito Palace Hotel. It is only open in the morning.

On Jalan Lambung Mangkurat, there is an excellent medium-range seafood place called the *New Masakan Jakarta*. For good Padang food, try *Kobana* at Jalan Pangeran Samudera 93A.

The Arjuna Plaza complex on Lambung Mangkurat offers some superlative non-Indonesian fare for those willing to spend more. Carnivores will love the *Rama Steak House* where grilled fillets begin at 10,000 rp. Cheaper here are char-broiled hamburgers (around 4000 rp) and hot dogs (less than 3000 rp). Or if you are in the mood for savoury Chinese cuisine, dine here at the *Shinta Restaurant*. Japanese businesspeople congregate at the Arjuna's *Hakone Restaurant* for a taste of home.

The Mitra Plaza shopping complex also has a good Japanese restaurant, the *Eiyu*. The Mitra's *Hero Supermarket* is a good place to stock up on goods for trekking and the complex also has several fast food places, including the aptly named *Hero Fast Food*.

Those craving Western fare will find the Kalimantan Hotel complex on Jalan Lambung Mangkurat harbouring a *Kentucky Fried Chicken* joint and a *Swenson's Ice Cream*.

Getting There & Away

Air Garuda/Merpati (☎ 4203, 3885) is at Jalan Hasanuddin 31 and open Monday to Thursday from 7 am to 4 pm, Friday from 7 am to noon and from 2 to 4 pm, Saturday from 7 am to 1 pm, and Sunday and holidays from 9 am to noon.

Bouraq (☎ 2445, 3285) is inconveniently situated at an office 4 km from the centre on Jalan Yani. DAS (☎ 2902) is across the road from Garuda at Jalan Hasanuddin 6, Blok 4.

Merpati flies from Banjarmasin to Balikpapan (89,000 rp), Jakarta (220,000 rp), Kota Bangun, Palangkaraya, Solo,

Pangkalanbun, Semarang, Surabaya (133,000 rp), Ujung Pandang, Sampit and Muara Teweh. With same-day connecting flights you can also get to Ambon, Bandarlampung, Bandung, Denpasar and Mataram.

Adi Travel at Jalan Hasanuddin 27 is a good place to buy air tickets and offers some discounts. Sample fares ex-Banjarmasin are: Jakarta via Sempati (twice a week) 186,400 rp; Balikpapan (three times a week) via Sempati 76,950 rp; Pangkalanbun via DAS (one flight daily) 114,900 rp.

Bus Buses and colts depart frequently from the Km 6 station for Martapura and Banjarbaru. Night buses to Balikpapan (15,000 rp or 20,000 rp with air-con) leave daily between 4 and 4.30 pm and arrive in Panajan, just across the river from Balikpapan, about 12 hours later. You have to get a speedboat across the river (1200 rp).

Regular day buses go via Rantau, Amuntai and Tanjung and there are buses to other destinations in the south-east corner of the island.

You can break up the trip from Banjarmasin to Balikpapan halfway by spending the night in Tanjung. From Banjarmasin to Tanjung costs 7500 rp and takes five hours. Tanjung to Panajan/ Balikpapan costs 7500 rp and takes six hours.

Boat All sorts of vessels leave from Banjarmasin. From here you can travel by ship to another island or head inland by river.

Passenger Ship Ships leave for Surabaya about twice a week and the trip takes about 24 hours. The ships dock at Pelabuhan Trisakti. To get there take a bemo from the taxi kota station on Jalan Samudera for 250 rp. The bemo will take you past the harbour master's and ticket offices.

The harbour master's office (**☎** 4775) is on Jalan Barito Hilir at Trisakti. Opposite is a line of shops with several agents for boat tickets to Surabaya. The fare from Banjarmasin to Surabaya on Pelni's *Keli-*

mutu is 27,000 rp in economy class, 72,000 rp in 2nd class and 87,500 rp in 1st class. Going to Semarang on the *Kelimutu* costs 32,000 rp in economy, 77,000 rp in 2nd class and 103,500 rp in 1st class.

Another agent for these ships is at the Km 6 bus station, and others can be found off Jalan Pasar Baru near the Antasari bridge. The Pasar Baru agents also sell less expensive passenger tickets for cargo boats that leave about every two days – fares are usually 23,000 to 27,000 rp to Surabaya.

The government's *Karakatau* to Pangkalanbun in Central Kalimantan leaves every other day and costs around 24,000 rp. The trip takes a day and a half and tickets can be purchased from Pelni.

To sail between Banjarmasin and Pontianak, take the boat from Banjarmasin to Pangkalanbun in Central Kalimantan (there are usually three or four a week), then another from Pangkalanbun to Ketapang on Kalimantan's west coast. From here, you can ferry over to Pontianak. The trip should cost about 40,000 rp. (You'll save a lot of time if you fly.)

Ships occasionally sail from Banjarmasin to Jakarta, but don't rely on anything.

Ferry & Speedboat Heading inland, one of the more obvious courses to take is from Banjarmasin to Palangkaraya, a journey of 18 hours in a bis air or about six to seven hours in a speedboat. You go up three rivers – the Barito, Kapuas and the Kahayan, and through the two artificial canals that link them.

Speedboats to Palangkaraya leave from a dock at the end of Jalan Pos, near the traffic circle. From Banjarmasin to Palangkaraya is 21,000 rp and there are boats daily. Note that the speedboats can get pretty crowded with upwards of 20 passengers. Buy tickets from the office at the dock.

River ferries to Palangkaraya depart from the wharf at the end of Jalan Sudimampir daily and cost 11,000 rp. Long-distance bis air which journey up the Barito leave from the Taxi Sungai station near the Banjar Raya fish market. To get there take a yellow colt

(250 rp) to the end of Jalan Jenderal Sutoyo west of the city centre. The end of the route is the town of Muara Teweh in Central Kalimantan, 56 hours away and costing only 12,500 rp. The tariff includes the price of a bed.

Getting Around

To/From the Airport Banjarmasin's Syamsudin Noor Airport is 26 km out of town on the road to Banjarbaru. To get there take a bemo from Pasar Baru to the Km 6 station. Then catch a Martapura-bound colt, get off at the branch road leading to the airport and walk the short distance to the terminal.

Alternatively, a taxi all the way to the airport will cost you 9000 rp. They cluster near the Garuda office and the Sabrina Hotel.

From the airport to the city, buy a taxi ticket at the counter in the terminal. Alternatively, walk out of the airport, through the car park, past the post office and the MIG aircraft, turn left and walk down to the Banjarmasin to Martapura highway. From here pick up one of the Banjarmasin to Martapura colts into Banjarmasin.

If you're travelling light you could hire a guy on a motorcycle to take you to the airport – these guys hang out at the Km 6 station and at the taxi kota station on Jalan Samudera.

Local Transport You can hire a boat operator to navigate the canals. Without a water-pump motor, expect to pay no more than about 5000 rp per hour.

On dry land, the area around Pasar Baru is very small and easy to walk around. You don't need wheels since the hotels, taxi terminal, airline offices etc are all grouped together. For longer trips there are bemos, becaks, ojek and bajaj – this is one of the few places outside Jakarta where you see bajaj. A bajaj from the centre to Banjar Raya harbour is around 1500 to 2000 rp; by ojek it would cost 1000 rp.

The bemos congregate at the taxi kota station at the junction of Jalan Samudera and Jalan Pasar Baru. They go to various parts of town including the Km 6 station, which is the departure point for buses to Banjarbaru,

Martapura and Balikpapan. The standard taxi kota fare from Pasar Baru to Km 6 or anywhere in town is 250 rp.

Banjarmasi becak drivers aren't predatory but they do ask hefty prices and are hard to bargain with. The bajaj drivers work the same way.

Guys with taxi motorcycles (ojeks) wait at Pasar Baru and Km 6 and will take you anywhere. If you're travelling light this is a good way to get to the airport.

BANJARBARU

The chief attraction of this town, on the road from Banjarmasin to Martapura, is its museum collection of Banjar and Dayak artefacts and statues found at the site of Hindu temples in Kalimantan.

Museum

The museum is on the Banjarmasin to Martapura highway. Ask the colt driver to drop you off. The museum is open to the public on Saturday and Sunday from 8.30 am to 2 pm. If you can't make it on the weekend go anyway, with the exception of Monday. Someone will probably open the place and show you around. Dance performances are held every Sunday at 9 am.

Exhibits include a replica of Banjar river boat equipment used in traditional Banjar circumcision ceremonies (including an antibiotic leaf and, would you believe, a cut-throat razor!), cannons, swords and other artefacts from wars with the Dutch, a small cannon used by British troops in Kalimantan, Dayak and Banjar swords, knives and other pointy things.

Probably the most interesting exhibit is items excavated from the Hindu Laras Temple and Agung Temple in East Kalimantan, including a Nandi bull and a Shiva lingam. The remains of the Laras Temple (Candi Laras) are in Magasari village, near the town of Rantau, 100 km from Banjarmasin. Agung Temple is near Amuntai, 150 km from Banjarmasin. Unless you're a hard-core archaeology freak, it's not worth going all the way to these villages to view what are mainly heaps of rubble – most of the good stuff is in the museum.

Getting There & Away
There are frequent colts to Banjarbaru from Banjarmasin's Km 6 station.

MARTAPURA
Continuing on from Banjarbaru you come to Martapura. On a good day – Fridays are best – the large market is a photographer's paradise, with every type of food on sale and lots of colourfully dressed Banjarmasi women. The Banjarmasis are big people. This is one of the few places in Indonesia where you commonly see plump women.

A section of the market sells uncut gems, silver jewellery and trading beads – the choice, both strung and unstrung, is excellent. Be prepared to bargain diligently for good prices, although the vendors seem honest about the quality and age of their merchandise.

The market is behind the Martapura bus station. A few minutes' walk diagonally across the sports field near the bus station is a diamond polishing factory and shop – ask for the Penggosokan Intan Tradisional Kayu Tangi.

Places to Stay
Backing on to the market is the *Wisma Penginapan Mutiara* on Jalan Sukaramai. It's quite decent and pleasant with rooms starting at 4000/5000 rp.

Getting There & Away
Frequent colts leave from the Km 6 station in Banjarmasin. The fare is 750 rp and it takes about 45 minutes along a good surfaced road.

CEMPAKA
Kalimantan is said to be endowed with fabulous diamond and gold mines. Most of those accessible to the public are small concessions. The big multinationals (mostly Australian) have guarded claims deep in the interior. Cempaka is one place where you can see some of the smaller diamond and gold

digs. The mines are, in fact, silt-filled, waterlogged holes dug from muddy streams. The diggers spend the day up to their necks in water, diving below and coming up with a pan full of silt which is washed away to separate the gold or diamond specks. Note that the diamond mines and polishing centres are generally closed on Friday.

Getting There & Away
The main stream is behind Cempaka village, 43 km from Banjarmasin. Bemos leave infrequently from Martapura; otherwise charter a bemo from Martapura bus station. The round trip costs 5000 rp with a brief stop at the creek. Ask at the Km 6 station in Banjarmasin for colts direct to Cempaka. The stream is not far off the road from Martapura. If you get a public bemo you can walk from the road to the mine.

NEGARA
The north-western section of South Kalimantan is mostly swamp, but a group of Banjars have made this area their homeland. Negara is typical of many towns and villages built over the swamp and is easily accessible. A visit gives you a chance to see how the swamp inhabitants have adapted to the local geography.

One amazing local custom is the raising of water buffalo herds on wooden platforms. Apart from trading in water buffalo the locals make a living fishing for serpent fish, a popular freshwater fish eaten throughout South-East Asia. They have a distinctive method of catching the fish – they use live baby ducks as bait.

There is a basic little hotel in Negara where you can stay for 3000/4000 rp with a shared mandi.

Getting There & Away
To get to Negara from Banjarmasin you can catch a bus via Kandangan. The trip costs 3000 rp and takes 2½ hours to Kandangan, then 1700 rp and one hour to Negara. Otherwise take one of the twice-weekly boats direct from the Banjarmasin river taxi pier for 6200 rp. The boat leaves Banjarmasin at

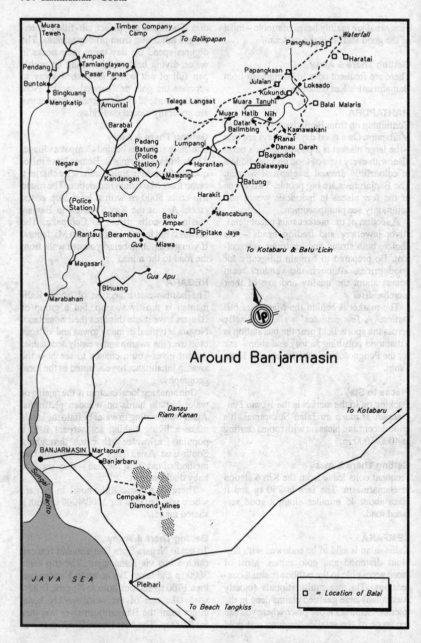

To Balikpapan

Muara
Teweh

Timber Company
Camp

Panghujung □   *Waterfall*

□ Haratai

Papangkaan

Ampah
Tamianglayang
Pasar Panas

Pendang

Buntok

Bingkuang
Mengkatip

Amuntai

Telaga Langsat

Julaian

Kukundu   Loksado

□ Balai Malaris

Muara Tanuhi

Barabai

Muara Hatib   Nih

Datar
Balimbing

Padang
Batung
(Police
Station)

Kamawakani

Lumpangi

Ranai

Danau Darah

□ Bagandah

Negara

Kandangan

Harantan

□ Balawayau

Mawangi

□ Batung

(Police
Station)

Bitahan

Harakit

Batu
Ampar

Mancabung

Rantau
Berambau
Miawa

Gua

□ Pipitake Jaya

Magasari

Gua Apu

To Kotabaru & Batu Licin

Binuang

Marabahan

Around Banjarmasin

To Kotabaru

Danau
Riam Kanan

BANJARMASIN   Martapura
              Banjarbaru

Cempaka
Diamond Mines

Sungai
Barito

JAVA SEA

Pleihari

To Beach Tangkiss

□ = *Location of Balai*

around 2 pm and takes a day and a night to reach Negara via the Barito and Negara rivers.

LOKSADO

East of Kandangan in the Muratus Mountains is a collection of villages that are the remnants of an animist Banjar society that may have moved here from the Barito delta to avoid the Islamic tide of the 15th and 16th centuries. About 20 villages are spread over about 2500 sq km between Kandangan and Amuntai to the west and the South Kalimantan coast to the east.

Loksado is an important market village in the area and a good base from which to explore. One of the best times to be in Loksado is market day on Wednesday, when villagers from all over the area come to buy and sell.

Malaris

A 30-minute walk through a bamboo forest south-east of Loksado is the village of Malaris, where 32 families (about 150 people) live in a large balai.

Trekking

Before trekking in the Loksado area, you must first check in at the police post in Padang Batung, a town between Kandangan and Mawangi on the road to Loksado. They will ask to see your hotel registration form from Banjarmasin – this shows your registration with the South Kalimantan authorities – before giving you a permit for the Loksado area.

Places to Stay

Loksado has basic hotels for 3000 rp per person. Many of the villages in this area – such as Niih, to the south-west of Loksado – will take guests for 1000 to 2000 rp per night.

If you spend the night in Kandangan, you can stay at the *Losmen Sentosa*, near the bus station, for 3000/4000 rp or at the *Loksado Permai Inn* where better rooms cost 6500/9000 rp with bath, or 4000/5500 rp without.

Getting There & Away

It's a full day's trip to Loksado from Banjarmasin. If you ride on the back of a chartered dirt bike for the Mawangi-Lumpangi leg, you can make Loksado by nightfall. If you plan to walk this section, you should spend the night in Kandangan and start from there.

Buses to Kandangan leave the Km 6 station in Banjarmasin throughout the day. The fare is 3000 rp and the trip takes from 2½ to three hours. In Kandangan you can get a local bus (1000 rp) to Mawangi or charter an ojek for 2500 rp and ask to stop on the way to Loksado at the police post in Padang Batung to register. (No permit is necessary – this is said to be just for your own protection should you become lost while trekking.) By bus it's about 30 minutes to Mawangi; by motorcycle it's 15 to 20 minutes.

From Mawangi it's a steep one-hour motorcycle ride to Lumpangi (5000 rp) if the road is dry enough, or a three-hour walk if it's not.

From Lumpangi, you can either hike along the jeep track straight through town or take a path over a bridge to the right. The footpath is about half an hour shorter than the jeep road, has more shade and passes through the villages of Datar Balimbing and Niih. The walk along the jeep track takes four hours to reach Loksado and can be quite hot, as there are few trees along the way. The main village along this road is Muara Hatib, which is a bit of a tourist trap since all the 4WD tours from Banjarmasin stop here.

Coming back from Loksado, most trekkers charter a bamboo raft and pole down Sungai Riam Kiwa to Kandangan. Rafts can be arranged in Loksado and Malaris for about 45,000 rp per raft, or in Niih for 30,000 to 35,000 rp. If you leave Loksado on market day (Wednesday) you may be able to share a raft with local people for much less. It's an all-day trip and some sections of the river are quite rough – be sure to put things you want to keep dry in a watertight bag.

Another interesting route in or out of Loksado, if you have time, is a trail between Malaris and Rantau through twelve villages that are conveniently spaced about an hour apart. Allow about four days to reach Rantau comfortably. Several of these villages have balai where you can spend the night.

SUNGAI BARITO

From Banjarmasin, you can travel by riverboat up Sungai Barito all the way to Muara Teweh in Central Kalimantan and then by speedboat to the Dayak village of Puruk Cahu. From Puruk Cahu a logging road leads to Long Iram in East Kalimantan.

A bis air from Banjarmasin to Muara Teweh costs 13,000 rp and takes about 56 hours. There are several budget hotels in Muara Teweh where you can stay for about 5000 rp. You can charter a speedboat to Puruk Cahu for 25,000 rp one way, which takes about 2½ hours. You can stay in longhouses in Puruk Cahu.

Central Kalimantan

Geographically speaking, Kalimantan Tengah is Kalimantan's largest province. It is also the least populated. The northern part is quite mountainous, while the southern part

is mostly swamp and mangrove forests. In between is thick, almost uninterrupted rainforest.

The main attractions in Kal-Teng are the mountains north of Muara Teweh and Tanjung Puting National Park in the south near Pangkalanbun. Every few years a major inter-tribal Dayak festival called Teweh takes place in the mountains of Central Kalimantan. During Teweh the bones of ancestors who have been waiting in state or in temporary graves are finally buried. This translates into a month of feasting, drinking and ritual dancing.

The major river thoroughfares in Kal-Teng are the Barito, the Kahayan, the Arot and the Sampit.

PALANGKARAYA

The story goes that Palangkaraya was considered during the Sukarno period for development as Kalimantan's capital city. It is a surprisingly large inland town on Sungai Kahayan surrounded by an extraordinarily flat expanse of jungle.

The town's chief attraction is the road connecting it to the nearby village of Tangkiling. Built by the Russians during the Sukarno period, this surfaced road leads 35

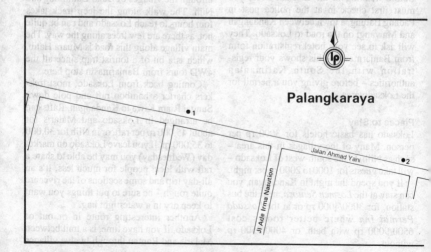

km to nowhere and appears to have no use whatsoever to justify the extravagance of building it.

Places to Stay

There's a cluster of cheap hotels by the dock where the longboats, river ferries and speedboats depart for Banjarmasin.

The *Losmen Putir Sinta* (☎ 21132) at Jalan Nias 2 has good clean singles/doubles with fan and mandi for 8500/11,000 rp. Across the road the *Losmen Mahkota* (☎ 21672) at No 5 has rooms from 7000 to 12,000 rp, but be forewarned that they may ask more for foreigners.

The overpriced *Hotel Virgo* (☎ 21265) at Jalan Ahmad Yani 7B has fan-cooled rooms starting at 15,000 rp and air-con rooms for 30,000 rp. If you are going to spend on a hotel in the middle price range, the *Adidas* (☎ 21770), at Jalan Ahmad Yani 90 is preferable. Decent air-con rooms here range in price from 38,000 to 43,000 rp. For an air-con hotel near the docks, try the *Rachman* (☎ 21428) at Jalan Murjani, where singles/doubles with mandi cost 21,000/23,000 rp.

The town's single luxury hotel, the *Dandang Tingang* (☎ 21805) is quite a walk from the centre at Jalan Yos Sudarso 11, but transport is provided to the downtown sector. The hotel includes a restaurant, bar and disco. All air-con rooms start at 39,000 rp and range to 127,000 rp.

Places to Eat

For moderately priced Indonesian fare, try the *Sampaga* at Jalan Murjani 100 or the *Hotel Virgo Restaurant* at Jalan Ahmad Yani 7B. Close to the Hotel Virgo, you will find decent Padang food at *Simpang Raya*. For Chinese food at moderate prices, try the *Tropicana* on Jalan Darma Sugondo or the *Depot Gloria* on Jalan Murjani. The *Empat Lima* at Jalan Ahmad Yani 63 is best known for its barbecued seafood.

Lots of cheap rumah makan and warungs

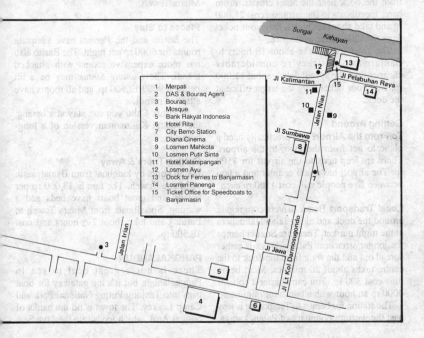

1 Merpati
2 DAS & Bouraq Agent
3 Bouraq
4 Mosque
5 Bank Rakyat Indonesia
6 Hotel Rita
7 City Bemo Station
8 Diana Cinema
9 Losmen Mahkota
10 Losmen Putir Sinta
11 Hotel Kalampangan
12 Losmen Ayu
13 Dock for Ferries to Banjarmasin
14 Losmen Panenga
15 Ticket Office for Speedboats to Banjarmasin

are around the dock and near the hotels. Back from the river, Jalan Halmahera and Jalan Jawa turn into night markets with many food trolleys. Several rumah makan are along Jalan Ahmad Yani, and some serve udang galah.

Getting There & Away

Air Garuda/Merpati has an office at Jalan Ahmad Yani 69A. DAS has an office at Jalan Milono 2 and Bouraq is located at Jalan Ahmad Yani 84.

Bouraq flies from Palangkaraya to Banjarmasin and Sampit twice daily and to Pangkalanbun daily. Merpati connects Palangkaraya with Balikpapan, Banjarmasin, Jakarta, Sampit, Semarang, Muara Teweh and Surabaya. DAS has flights to smaller towns and flies daily to Pangkalanbun.

Boat For details on getting from Banjarmasin to Palangkaraya see the Banjarmasin section. Boats out of Palangkaraya leave from the dock near the hotel cluster. From here, speedboats to Banjarmasin cost 21,000 rp and take about six hours. Buy your ticket from the little office at the pier.

The river ferries take about 18 hours to Banjarmasin but they're considerably cheaper than the speedboats – about 11,000 rp. Buy your ticket from the larger office at the dock.

Getting Around

To/From the Airport You practically need a plane to get from the town to the airport. There are jeep taxis to the airport for 7500 rp. The airport has a taxi counter and a taxi between five people will cost 1500 rp each.

Local Transport Becak drivers congregate around the dock and along Jalan Halmahera at the night market. There are Suzuki bemos for longer stretches. Palangkaraya is rather spread out and the walk from the dock to the centre takes about 20 minutes. Most bemo runs cost 300 rp. You can charter a colt for 4000 rp an hour with a two-hour minimum.

The station for bemos to Tangkiling is *way* past the western boundary of Palangkaraya.

It's a long way and it seems to take ages to catch a bemo. There are frequent bemos for the 25-minute trip from the station to Tangkiling.

MUARA TEWEH

Muara Teweh is the last longboat stop on Sungai Barito. Beyond Muara Teweh, travel by speedboat to Puruk Cahu in the foothills of the Muller Range. Hire Dayak guides for treks into the mountains in Puruk Cahu. Near Gunung Pancungapang, at the border of Central and East Kalimantan, a cement pillar marks the geographical centre of Borneo.

Trekking

From Muara Teweh trek overland to Long Iram in East Kalimantan, then catch a longboat down Sungai Mahakam to Samarinda. The trek takes up to two weeks and can be done on your own, following logging roads. You can trek along more interesting footpaths if you hire a guide in Banjarmasin or Muara Teweh.

Places to Stay

The *Barito* and the *Permai* have adequate rooms for 6000 rp per night. The Barito also has more expensive rooms with attached mandi. The *Gunung Sintuk* may be a bit better at 9000/12,500 rp, and all rooms have attached mandi.

In Puruk Cahu you can stay at a betang, the Central Kalimantan version of a longhouse.

Getting There & Away

It's 56 hours by longboat from Banjarmasin to Muara Teweh. The fare is 13,000 rp per person and most boats have beds and a warung. Speedboats from Muara Teweh to Puruk Cahu take about 2½ hours and cost 18,500 rp.

PANGKALANBUN

There is not a great deal to see in Pangkalanbun but it's the gateway for boat trips into Tanjung Puting National Park and Camp Leakey. The town is on the banks of Sungai Arot, which feeds into the Java Sea,

Top: Martapura, Kalimantan (AS)
Left: Floating market, Banjarmasin, Kalimantan (JC)
Right: Kuta, Lombok (HF)

Top: Traditional houses in Tanatoraja, Sulawesi (LH)
Bottom: Painted engravings on a traditional house, Tanatoraja, Sulawesi (TW)

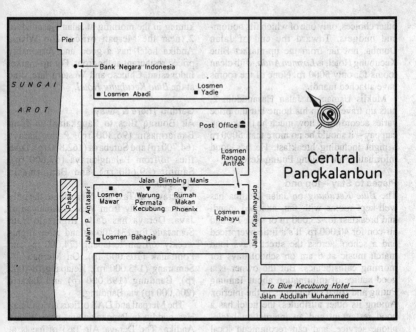

Central
Pangkalanbun

and it's a fairly important harbour for the cargo boats that ply the Kalimantan coast. Get a police letter here if you want to enter the Tanjung Puting National Park (see the Tanjung Puting section later in this chapter).

Orientation & Information

Pangkalanbun is little more than an overgrown village with a small downtown area next to the Pelabuhan Penumpang (passenger pier).

Most businesses, banks, the post office and the Deraya Air Taxi office are located along two parallel streets, Jalan Kasumayuda and Jalan P Antasari. There are also several cafes, a few hotels and a large, swampy market.

The better hotels and the DAS and Merpati offices are east of the downtown area away from the river.

The Bank Negara Indonesia near the passenger pier on Jalan P Antasari will change US-dollar travellers' cheques.

Places to Stay – bottom end

The new budget inn, *Losmen Yadie*, has decent doubles with fan and mandi for 8500 rp. The proprietor is a good source of information on Tanjung Puting Reserve and he sells both plane and boat tickets.

The *Losmen Rahayu* and the *Losmen Rangga Antrek* are both on Jalan Kasumayuda, not far from the post office. The Rahayu is the cheaper of the two with adequate rooms at 5000/7500 rp. The Rangga Antrek is larger and more of a local hangout – rooms with mandi are 8000/14,000 rp.

Over on Jalan P Antasari are the *Abadi* and the *Bahagia* hotels. Both are 5000/6000 rp for basic rooms without mandi, 8000 rp with bath and fan. The Bahagia is the cleanest.

Connecting these two main roads is Jalan Blimbing Manis, where you'll find several good warungs and the *Losmen Mawar*. The Mawar has small, basic rooms for 5000 rp without mandi, 7000 rp with.

About 1½ km east of the centre are several

other choices, only one of which fits bottom-end budgets. Toward the end of Jalan Domba, not far from the up-market Blue Kecubung Hotel, is *Losmen Anda*, with clean rooms for only 5000 rp. None of the rooms have attached mandi.

Muklis Usman, at Jalan Hasanuddin 2, puts up travellers in his home but the price varies according to how much he thinks you can pay – it should be no more than 5000 rp a night including breakfast. He has good information on Tanjung Puting Reserve.

Places to Stay – top end

The *Blue Kecubung* on Jalan Domba has well-kept rooms with fan, attached mandi and breakfast for 25,000 rp or with TV and air-con for 40,000 rp. It's a little overpriced and a school across the street plays loud march music at 6 am on school days for morning callisthenics. But the owner is a good source of information about Tanjung Puting and tribal ceremonies in the interior. Among its other attributes, the hotel has a good restaurant and an international tele-phone service, and can recommend local guides.

Further along Jalan Domba is the smaller *Wisma Sampurga* where rooms with mandi cost 10,000 rp. They also have more expen-sive air-con rooms.

Best value in the upper end is *Wisma Andika*, around the corner from Losmen Anda on Jalan Hasanuddin, to the west. It's very clean, the staff are helpful and the res-taurant good. Rooms are 15,000 rp with attached bath, or 27,000 rp with air-con.

Places to Eat

On Jalan Blimbing Manis there's a very good Chinese warung, the *Rumah Makan Phoenix*. On the same street towards Jalan P Antasari, *Warung Permata Kecubung* has a similar menu but is slightly more expensive. Near the Losmen Abadi on Jalan P Antasari is *Warung Pahala*, a tea stall with good ice drinks. They sell the local speciality, *es kolak*, a kind of pineapple/coconut smoothie.

If you're staying in the Jalan Domba area away from the centre, you can get good nasi kuning in the morning at Jalan Hasanuddin 2, near the Merpati office. The Wisma Andika hotel has a good and reasonably priced restaurant at the front. For up-market Indonesian, Chinese and Western fare, dine at the *Blue Kecubung Hotel*.

Getting There & Away

Air Bouraq flies to Pangkalanbun from Banjarmasin (96,300 rp), Palangkaraya (64,700 rp) and Surabaya (162,800 rp). DAS flies to/from Palangkaraya (67,600 rp), Sampit (89,600 rp), and Banjarmasin (114,900 rp).

Deraya Air Taxi and Merpati are the only services that fly from West Kalimantan or Java. Deraya has daily flights to/from Semarang for 131,400 rp and three flights weekly to/from Ketapang (74,000 rp) and Pontianak (103,000 rp). On Merpati it's Semarang (143,000 rp), Ketapang (84,000 rp), Bandung (198,000 rp) and Jakarta (206,000 rp) via Bandung.

The Merpati and DAS offices are on Jalan Hasanuddin in Pangkalanbun, near Wisma Andika. The Deraya Air Taxi office is at Jalan P Antasari 51 near the swampy market.

You can also book flights at the Blue Kecubung and Wisma Andika hotels. You pay cash rupiah for your tickets wherever you book them.

Boat The Pelni passenger ship *Krakatoa* comes here twice a month from Semarang and Banjarmasin, the passage taking about a full day and night. The economy fare is about 27,000 rp. There are also many cargo boats with berths or at least deck space. Passage can be booked at the Pelabuhan Penumpang.

Every few days there's a boat to Banjarmasin or Pontianak and occasionally to Semarang. A typical fare to Pontianak is 32,000 rp including meals. The trip takes three days and two nights. For an added 14,000 rp you can usually get a bed in a crew cabin; otherwise you sleep on the deck. There are boats to Banjarmasin at least three times every two weeks. The fare is around 25,000 rp and takes anywhere from one to two days.

Getting Around

To/From the Airport From the airport, it's 8000 rp to your destination in town. If you are going direct to Kumai, you may charter a taxi at the airport for 24,000 rp – this includes a stop at the police station for your necessary registration to the reserve.

TANJUNG PUTING NATIONAL PARK

Tanjung Puting National Park is 305,000 hectares of tropical rainforest, mangrove forest and swamp. It is home to a vast variety of flora and fauna, including crocodiles,

hornbills, wild pigs, bear cats, crab-eating macaques, orang-utan, proboscis monkeys, pythons, dolphins and mudskippers (a kind of fish that can walk and breathe on land).

This is also a habitat for the dragon fish, an aquarium fish worth 700,000 rp and highly valued by Chinese collectors throughout South-East Asia. Unfortunately, both the dragon fish and the crocodiles are occasionally prey to poachers.

Orientation & Information

A trip into the park begins in the town of

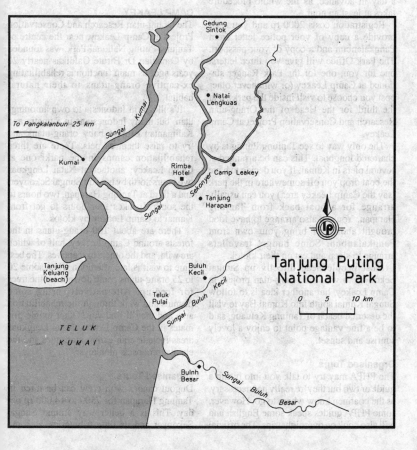

Tanjung Puting National Park

Kumai, on the banks of Sungai Kumai about 25 km south-east of Pangkalanbun. However, the first step to entering the park is to get a police letter in Pangkalanbun. Visit the *Kantor Polisi* in Pangkalanbun with a copy of the first page of your passport and a copy of the photo page to obtain your letter/ permit.

When you arrive in Kumai go first to the police station and drop off a copy of your police letter/permit and a copy of your passport. Next, you must register at the PHPA office in Kumai. If you're not planning to spend the night in the park it's best to register a day in advance, as the whole procedure takes at least an hour.

Registration costs 2000 rp and you *must* provide a copy of your police letter from Pangkalanbun and a copy of your passport. The Park Office will give you three letters: one for you, one for the Park Ranger stationed at Camp Leakey (or whichever other post you choose to visit inside the park), and the third for the Head of the Orang-utan Research and Conservation Project at Camp Leakey.

The only way to see Tanjung Puting is by chartered longboat. This can be arranged at several piers in Kumai. If you decide to have the boat drop you off somewhere in the park (say the Camp Leakey area) you can usually arrange for a boat back from Tanjung Harapan. You can also arrange to have food brought aboard or bring your own from Pangkalanbun. Some budget travellers arrange to sleep and eat on their klotok.

Most people head directly up Sungai Sekonyer to visit the orang-utan project in Camp Leakey, but another idea is to follow Sungai Kumai south into Kumai Bay to visit the deserted beach of Tanjung Keluang, said to be a fine vantage point to enjoy a lovely sunrise and sunset.

Organised Tours

The PHPA may try to talk you into hiring a guide or two but they're really not necessary, as the boatmen know where to go. However, some PHPA guides speak some English and will also cook on overnight trips. The official PHPA guide rate nationwide is a bargain 7500 rp per day, but they may ask more. Use your discretion.

Places to Stay

There are two small budget hotels in Kumai, the *Losmen Kumara* near the river on the main road from Pangkalanbun and the *Losmen Cempaka* adjacent to the market. Both are quite basic, with rooms with shared mandi from 6000 rp to 9000 rp. There are warungs near the market and also a store to purchase food supplies for your venture to the park.

CAMP LEAKEY

The Orang-utan Research and Conservation Project at Camp Leakey, near the centre of Tanjung Puting National Park, was founded by Canadian Dr Birute Galdikas nearly 20 years ago. Its main function is rehabilitating ex-captive orang-utans to their natural habitat.

It's illegal in Indonesia to own an orangutan, but many Indonesians in Sumatra and Kalimantan capture baby orang-utans and try to raise them as pets. There are three rehabilitation camps in the park: one at Camp Leakey; another at Natai Lengkuas two hours north by boat on Sungai Sekonyer; and a third at Tanjung Harapan, two hours to the south. It takes four hours to get from Kumai to Camp Leakey by klotok.

There are about 100 orang-utans in the forests around Camp Leakey, half of which are wild, and the others ex-captives. The best time to visit is late afternoon when some 20 to 25 orang-utans come down from the trees for feeding. Alternatively, bring some peanuts and walk through the rehabilitation area and they'll find you. Other jungle primates in the Camp Leakey-Natai Lengkuas areas include crab-eating macaques and the elusive proboscis monkeys.

Organised Tours

Dugout canoes with crew can be hired in Tanjung Harapan for 7500 to 14,000 rp per day. This is a better way around Sungai Sekonyer and its little tributaries, as some sections are very narrow. The canoes are also much quieter so you're likely to see more wildlife. It's not unusual to see three to four-metre crocodiles in this area – keep your hands in the boat.

Places to Stay

Although budget travellers sleep on their *klotok*, those who can afford it may opt for greater comfort by staying at the *Rimba Hotel* located near Sekonyer village near Tanjung Harapan. A double room with attached mandi costs 90,000 rp, including meals.

Getting There & Away

Colt Kumai is about half an hour away from Pangkalanbun by colt. You can catch colts to Kumai (800 rp) near the market by Sungai Arot in Pangkalanbun, or on the road to Kumai, which skirts the north end of Pangkalanbun. This is the same road that goes to the airport.

Boat Longboats from Kumai take about two hours to reach Tanjung Harapan, four hours to Camp Leakey, or six hours to Natai Lengkuas. Rental rates vary with the size and condition of boats but should cost between 45,000 and 65,000 rp a day, including crew. Most boats can take up to 10 people easily. It's wise to get a longboat with a roof to keep off sun and rain. It's the same rate for one way and return. A boat to Tanjung Keluang alone should cost about 25,000 rp return.

West Kalimantan

Kalimantan Barat's major distinction is that it is home to Indonesia's longest waterway, Sungai Kapuas (1143 km). Kal-Bar is Kalimantan's third-least populated province, although it has the highest concentration of Chinese people of any province in Indonesia. The populations of its two largest towns, Pontianak and Singkawang, are 35% and 70% Chinese respectively.

Whether it's a result of the industriousness of the Chinese, as the locals claim, or the relative proximity of prosperous Kuching in Sarawak to the north, West Kalimantan is the business and educational centre of Indonesian Borneo.

In spite of all the activity on the coast, Kal-Bar's interior is relatively unexplored. There are many Punan, Iban and Kenyah Dayak villages in the mountainous eastern part of the province.

PONTIANAK

Situated right on the equator, Pontianak lies astride the confluence of the Landak and Kapuas Kecil rivers. The city was founded in 1771 by Syarif Abdul Rahman Al-Kadri of Saudi Arabia. The economic hub of Kalimantan, Pontianak is surprisingly large, with a giant indoor sports stadium, a sizeable university and a couple of big girder bridges spanning Sungai Landak.

Like Banjarmasin it really needs to be seen from the canals that criss-cross the city. Walk over the bridge from Jalan Gajah Mada for a sweeping view of the river and houses and brilliant orange sunsets that make Balinese sunsets look pathetic!

As the city has a large proportion of Chinese, there are many Chinese shops selling porcelain, Chinese vases and amphoras, gold and jewellery.

From Pontianak you can take a trip north along the coast to Pasir Panjang, a lovely stretch of beach with clean, white sand and calm water, just back from the Pontianak to Singkawang road. The Mandor Nature Reserve is to the north-east.

This is also the starting point for boat trips up the Kapuas, which terminate in Putussibau in the north-eastern corner of the province.

Orientation & Information

The main part of the city is on the southern side of the Kapuas Kecil where it meets the Landak. Here you'll find several markets, the main bemo station (Kapuas Indah), several hotels, the airline and Pelni offices, banks, etc.

A short distance from the Kapuas Indah

station there are many small motor boats and a vehicle ferry to Pasar Lintang on the opposite side of the river, which is the site of Sintian Terminal, the main long-distance bus station.

The Pontianak immigration office (☎ 4512) is at Jalan L Sutoyo, off Jalan A Yani.

Tourist Office The West Kalimantan tourist office is way out at Jalan Ahmad Sood 25. They have a good provincial map and provide official guides for river and jungle trips. Otherwise, the staff are not particularly helpful. Far more convenient are the friendly and knowledgeable English-speaking staff at Hotel Makot – they're an excellent source for information.

Post The post office is on Jalan Rahadi Usman near the Kartika Hotel and open Monday to Friday from 8 am to 7 pm (but closed Friday from 11 am to 2 pm), Saturday from 8 am to 1 pm and Sunday from 9 am to 2 pm.

Foreign Embassies The Malaysian Consulate at Jalan A Yani 42 issues tourist visas

West Kalimantan

0   90   180 km

for east Malaysia (Sarawak and Sabah) for 14,000 rp per application. This allows you to fly from Pontianak to Kuching, Sarawak, without restrictions. Consulate hours are from 7 am to 3 pm Monday to Saturday; it's closed from 11 am to 1.30 pm on Friday.

Negotiations are underway to allow access to Sarawak without restrictions, so by the time you read this a visa may not be necessary – check with the consulate.

To cross by land you'll need the East Malaysian visa and an exit permit from the Pontianak immigration office or the Jakarta immigration office. Again, as relations between the two countries improve, these requirements may be lifted.

Mesjid Abdurrakhman
This was the royal mosque of Syarif Abdul Rahman (in Indonesian, Abdurrakhman), who reigned as Sultan of Pontianak from 1771 until his death in 1808. It's a very large mosque in the Malay or Sumatran style with a square tiered roof, and made entirely of wood. Beautiful inside and out, it's worth the short canoe trip across Sungai Landak from the pinisi harbour. Charter a boat for 500 to 700 rp or wait for a shared canoe taxi for only 100 rp per person.

Istana Kadriyah
About 100 metres behind the sultan's mosque is his former palace, now an interesting museum displaying the personal effects of the sultan's family. Eight sultans reigned after the death of the first in 1808. The last died in 1978.

The palace caretaker is the gracious Syarif Yusuf Alkadri, a descendant of the sultan's family. His features are very Arabic and he is proud to pose for photos. Visiting hours are from 8.30 am to 6 pm daily. There is no admission fee to the istana, but a donation is encouraged.

For an interesting experience of life along Pontianak's riverfront, take a walk from the mosque along the wooden planks that serve as sidewalks for the local stilt houses. You will find the people of the *kampung* extremely friendly and curious, for few tourists pass this way. Take your camera. The locals, particularly the kids, love to be photographed.

Pinisi Harbour
If you follow Jalan S Muhammad south along the Kapuas Kecil you eventually come to the pinisi harbour, where you can see East Javanese and Sulawesi-style sailing schooners.

Also docked in this area are the large houseboats, or *bandung*, peculiar to West Kalimantan. Bandungs function as floating general stores that ply their way up and down the Kapuas, trading at villages along the way. Their family owners live on board. A typical run up the Kapuas might last as long as a month.

Museum Negeri Pontianak (Pontianak National Museum)
Located near Tanjungpura University, south of the city centre on Jalan Ahmad Yani, this

Pontianak (Orientation)

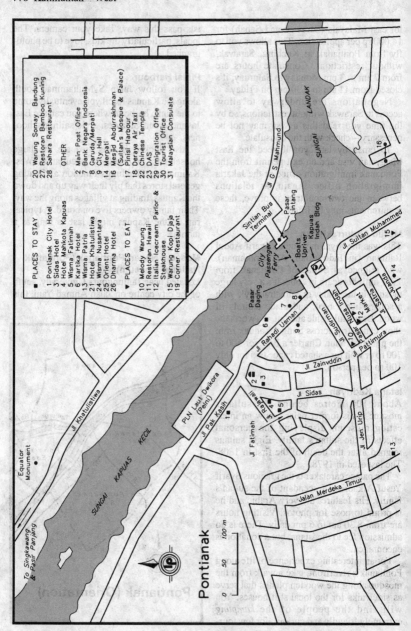

Pontianak

0   50   100 m

Equator
Monument

To Singkawang
& Pasir Panjang

SUNGAI KAPUAS KECIL

Jl Khatulistiwa

PLN Laut Dwikora
(Peni)

Jl Pak Kasih

Jl Fatimah

Jl Rahadi Usman

Jl Zainuddin

Jl Sidas

Jl Tanjungpura

Jl Pattimura

Jl Sultan Muhammad

Jalan Merdeka Timur

Jl Jen Urip

SUNGAI KAPUAS

SUNGAI LANDAK

Jl G S Mahmund

Sintian Bus Terminal

Pasar Lintang

City Passenger Ferry

Pasar Daging

Boats Upriver

Kapuas Indah Bldg

Market

PLACES TO STAY
- Pontianak City Hotel
1 Sidas Hotel
4 Hotel Mahkota Kapuas
5 Wisma Fatimah
6 Kartika Hotel
13 Wisma Patria
21 Hotel Khatulistiwa
24 Wisma Nusantara
25 Orient Hotel
26 Dharma Hotel

PLACES TO EAT
10 Melody Warung
11 Restoran Hawaii
12 Italian Icecream Parlor &
   Steakhouse
15 Warung Kopi Djaja
19 Corner Restaurant
20 Warung Somay Bandung
27 Restoran Bamboo Kuning
28 Sahara Restaurant

OTHER
2 Main Post Office
7 Bank Negara Indonesia
8 Garuda/Merpati
9 City Hall
14 Merpati
16 Mesjid Abdurrakhman
   (Sultan's Mosque & Palace)
17 Pinisi Harbour
18 Deraya Air Taxi
22 Chinese Temple
23 DAS
29 Immigration Office
30 Tourist Office
31 Malaysian Consulate

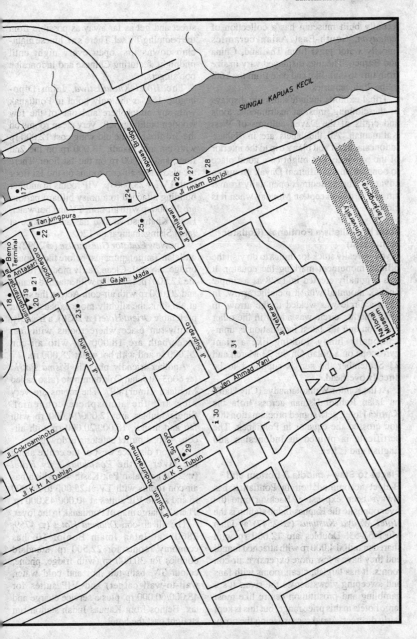

SUNGAI KAPUAS KECIL

Kapuas Bridge

Jl Imam Bonjol

▲ 26 ▲ 27 ▲ 28

■ 24

● 17

Jl Tanjungpura

■ 22

● 25

Jl Pahlawan

Jl Bernio

Jl Sisingamangaraja – Bernio Terminal

● 18

▲ 20 ● 21
● 19

Jl Diponegoro

Jl Antasari

Jl Gajah Mada

● 23

Jl Letjamang

Jl Suprapto

Jl Veteran

● 31

National Museum

Jl Cokroaminoto

Jl Jen Ahmad Yani

Jl Sutoyo

i 30

Jl K H A Dahlan

● 29

Jl K S Tubun

Jl Sultan Abdurrakhman

Universitas

Tanjungpura

recently built museum has a collection of *tempayan*, South-East Asian ceramics (mostly water jugs) from Thailand, China and Borneo. The jugs displayed vary in size from tiny to tank-like and date from the 16th to the 20th centuries.

Tribal exhibits include dioramic displays of the clothing, musical instruments, tools and crafts of the Dayak cultures of West Kalimantan. All the labels are in Bahasa Indonesia, but if you plan a trip to the interior of the province, this might be a good place to bone up on the different Dayak groups in advance. The museum is open daily from 9 am until 1 pm, except on Monday when it is closed.

Tugu Khatulistiwa Pontianak (Equator Monument)

If you're really stuck for things to do visit the official monument marking the equator. It was originally erected in 1928 as a simple obelisk mounted with a metallic arrow. In 1930 a circle was welded to the arrow, in 1938 another circle was added in the other direction and it's latest incarnation is unintentionally funny, looking like a giant gyroscope on a pillar. On the 23 March and 23 September the sun is supposed to be directly overhead.

At the Kantor Walikotamadya (City Hall), on Jalan Rahadi Usman across from the Kartika Hotel, get a signed proclamation that you crossed the equator in Pontianak. The certificate is printed in Indonesian and English and is free.

Places to Stay – middle & bottom end

Budget accommodation in Pontianak has always been expensive. Backing onto the river opposite the Kapuas Indah station is the *Hotel Wijaya Kusuma* (☎ 2547) at Jalan Musi 51-53. Doubles are 12,000 rp with shared mandi, 14,000 rp with attached mandi and they have a few more expensive air-con rooms. It has largish, clean rooms with fans and sweeping views across the river. It's a gambling and prostitution centre like most large hotels in this price range, but this is kept fairly discreet. Avoid rooms facing the noisy

street and get as far away as possible from the booming TV set. There's a Chinese nightclub downstairs, open every night until midnight, featuring Chinese and Indonesian pop singers.

The *Hotel Khatulistiwa*, Jalan Diponegoro 151, is the only hotel in Pontianak with any atmosphere and one of the few wooden buildings left. Very clean rooms on the 3rd floor of the old wing cost 12,000 rp with fan and mandi, 13,000 rp on the 2nd floor, and 15,000 rp on the 1st floor. There are also a few air-con rooms on the 1st floor with TV for 23,000 rp. VIP rooms in another building attached to a noisy billiard parlour are 28,000 rp with air-con, TV and hot water. Hotel Khatulistiwa also has an entrance at Jalan Sisingamangaraja 126.

The *New Equator Guesthouse* (☎ 2092) is on Jalan Tanjungpura just before the Kapuas bridge at No 91. Clean, fairly modern rooms are 12,500 rp, 15,000 rp with attached mandi and 20,000 rp with air-con. Across the street at No 45 is the slightly more expensive but preferable *Orient Hotel* (☎ 2650), a friendly, family-run place where rooms with fan/ video/bath are 18,000 rp, with air-con 24,000 rp and with hot water 28,000 rp.

Another friendly place is *Wisma Patria* (☎ 6063) at Jalan Cokroaminoto (also called Merdeka Timur) 497. The rooms are very nice and the atmosphere congenial. Single/doubles are 12,000/14,000 rp with fan and mandi, 18,000/20,000 rp with air-con. A good buffet cafeteria is downstairs.

A short distance west of the centre along the river is the *Pontianak City Hotel* (☎ 2495) at Jalan Pak Kasih 44, which has air-con rooms with TV at 25,000 to 36,000 rp and some VIP suites at 40,000/43,000 rp. There's a large map of Pontianak in the foyer.

The all air-con *Dharma Hotel* (☎ 4759, 2860), at Jalan Imam Bonjol 10, has economy rooms for 22,500 rp, standard doubles for 30,000 rp (with fridge, phone, colour TV, bath tub, hot and cold water, wall-to-wall carpet) and VIP suites for 48,000/60,000 rp, plus a service charge and tax. Bemos from Kapuas Indah station run straight past the hotel.

There are two other adequate but nothing-special hotels in the middle range which you might consider if for some reason their location appeals to you. The *Sidas Hotel* (☎ 34337) at Jalan Sidas 11A, near Hotel Mahkota, has air-con rooms for 25,000/30,000 rp and *Wisma Nusantara* (☎ 34217) on Jalan Letjend Suprapto has air-con singles/doubles for 23,000/27,000 rp.

Places to Stay – top end
The two top hotels in Pontianak are the *Hotel Mahkota Kapuas* and the *Kapuas Permai Hotel*. The Mahkota (☎ 36022), the newest and best, is well located in the centre of town at Jalan Sidas 8. Comfortable, nicely decorated rooms with air-con and hot-water bath and shower start at 55,000 rp for a studio with a double bed, or 68,000/78,000 rp for standard singles/doubles. Suites cost 172,500 rp and the two-bedroom Presidential Suite with built-in wet bar is 385,000 rp. The Mahkota has a couple of bars, an excellent restaurant and a discotheque. They plan to add a swimming pool. The manager here is the gracious Tahan Sinaga, a veritable fountain of information on local travel and customs.

The *Kapuas Permai Hotel* (☎ 6122) is further down Jalan Imam Bonjol past the Dharma Hotel towards the airport. It's on sprawling grounds with a little shopping mall that includes a travel agency. They have an amazing 100-metre swimming pool that's well tended. There are three kinds of accommodation: rooms in the main building for 55,000/62,000 rp, cottages for 42,000 rp and drive-in apartments with their own carports for 58,000 rp. The cottage and drive-in apartment areas get very swampy when it rains and mosquitoes are a problem. Rooms smell musty. Stay here only if you want to do some serious lap swimming. Otherwise, the Mahkota is better top-end value.

The *Kartika Hotel* (☎ 29256), on the river across from City Hall, is an up-market version of the Hotel Wijaya Kusuma. It is a recreational hotel for businessmen. Rooms start at 52,000 rp for a single and go as high as 70,000 rp for a double with a river view

or 98,000 rp for an executive suite. The rooms are nice enough but the service is said to be inept.

Places to Eat
The best places to eat are the countless warungs. Good ones in the Kapuas Indah station offer udang galah, ayam goreng, mixed vegetables and nasi putih for around 2500 rp to 3500 rp. Try the night warungs and gerobak makanan on Jalan Pasar Sudirman for *satay kambing* (goat satay) and steaming plates of rice noodles, *kepiting* (crab), udang, ikan, vegetables – all fried up in a wok for 1800 rp.

More foodstalls are along Jalan Asahan. For pastries and thick fruit juices, try the *New Holland Bakery* next door to the Hotel Wijaya Kusuma near the Kapuas Indah station. On the road to the car ferry to Pasar Lintang is Pontianak's night-time martabak headquarters with numerous food trolleys dedicated to the pursuit of the perfect stuffed crepe.

The clean little *Somay Bandung* in the theatre complex on Jalan Sisingamangaraja near Jalan Pattimura serves delicious Chinese-style bubur ayam for 850 rp and the house speciality, *somay*, a tasty concoction of potatoes, tofu, hard-boiled egg and peanut sauce for 1000 rp. They also serve good ice drinks. Nearby, aptly named *Corner Restaurant* serves good, inexpensive breakfasts as does the *Melody Warung* opposite the market on Jalan Pattimura.

West Kalimantan grows good coffee and there are great *warung kopi* in Pontianak. Try the *Warung Kopi Djaja (Jaya)* at Jalan Tanjungpura 23. The coffee is particularly good here – they roast their own beans. They have delicious Indonesian pastries, including some of the best pisang goreng in Indonesia, served with a special custard sauce. You can buy bags of freshly ground Djaja coffee here, or with a day's notice they'll sell you a heat-sealed bag of whole roasted beans for 8000 rp per kg.

Along Jalan Diponegoro are several more formal restaurants and a good Chinese night market. Padang food fans shouldn't miss

Rumah Makan Beringin at No 115. There is also an *American Fried Chicken* and a *Pioneer Fried Chicken* on this street as well as the large *Haramani* supermarket.

Expats claim the best Chinese food in town is at the *Restoran Bambu Kuning* near the Dharma Hotel on Jalan Imam Bonjol. Ask for the *ikan jelawat*, a local freshwater fish. The highly regarded *Sahara Restaurant* is nearby. The *Restoran Hawaii* on Pasar Nusa Indah is another good choice for Chinese and somewhat cheaper. Nearby on the same street is the *Italian Ice Cream Parlor & Steakhouse* where you can get a variety of Western food. Also good, albeit not cheap, for Western fare is the restaurant of Hotel Mahkota Kapus.

Getting There & Away

Air Garuda/Merpati (☎ 21026) is at Jalan Rahadi Usman 8A and is open Monday to Friday from 8 am to 4 pm, Saturday from 8 am to 1 pm, Sunday and holidays from 9 am to noon. DAS (☎ 583) is at Jalan Gajah Mada 67 and Bouraq (☎ 2371) is at Jalan Tanjungpura 253.

Flights between Pontianak and Jakarta cost 179,700 rp on Merpati, 172,000 rp on Bouraq and 167,000 rp on Sempati. All three airlines have daily flights.

With same-day connections, Merpati flies from Pontianak to Bandarlampung, Jakarta, Batam, Ketapang, Pangkalanbun, Padang, Medan, Putussibau, Balikpapan and Sintang.

Garuda flies to/from Singapore three days a week for 205,000 rp. The flight takes an hour. To/from Kuching (twice a week on MAS) costs US$74.

Deraya Air Taxi flies three times a week from Pontianak to Sintang (65,000 rp) and has four flights to Pangkalanbun (103,000 rp). Deraya flies mainly Cessnas. DAS flies daily to Sintang (88,500 rp), Putussibau (149,000 rp), Ketapang (75,000 rp) and Nangapinoh (128,000 rp).

Bus From Pontianak you can catch the bus north along the coast to Singkawang (about 3½ hours, 4000 rp). Colts depart every hour from about 6 am from the Sintian Terminal.

Colts also leave here further north to Sambas or north-east to Mandor (1½ hours, 2000 rp).

Daily buses head inland to Sintang. These leave the ferry pier on the city side of the river around 8 am, take 10 hours to reach Sintang, and the fare is usually 12,000 rp. When the roads are wet the fare may increase to as high as 15,000 rp. You can also fly or ferry on Sungai Kapuas to Sintang. See the section on Kapuas river trips for more information on travel to Sintang.

To reach Kuching in Sarawak by bus you have to change twice, first at Entikong at the border, than again in Serian (Sarawak) for the final leg to Kuching. The total fare from Pontianak to Kuching is 30,000 rp. Given the improving relations between Malaysia and Indonesia a through service to Kuching will probably soon develop.

Boat Pelni is on Jalan Pak Kasih on the southern bank of the river at the Pelabuhan Laut Dwikora. For other ships ask at the entrance to the port adjacent to the Pelni office.

Pelni's *Lawit* does the two-day, two-night Pontianak to Jakarta trip every 10 days. Economy class is 33,500 rp including food; 1st and 2nd class are 128,500 rp and 91,500 rp respectively. At least two non-Pelni cargo ships also take passengers on this run daily. The average fare is 23,000 rp but you may have to sleep on deck.

There may be occasional cargo ships but there are no regular passenger ships on the Pontianak-Singapore route. There are no Pontianak-Banjarmasin ships – you have to go to Pangkalanbun or Surabaya first and get ships from there to Banjarmasin. Pontianak-Pangkalanbun-Banjarmasin costs about 47,000 rp by cargo boat.

River Boat See the Kapuas River Trips section for details on trips into the interior of West Kalimantan by riverboat. Most riverboats leave from the Kapuas Indah station (Lalulinta Sunggai dan Feri) near the Hotel Wijaya Kusuma. Some, like the houseboat bandungs, leave from the pinisi harbour near the end of Jalan Sultan Muhammed.

Bandungs don't usually take passengers, but they may make exceptions for curious foreigners. There are a few deluxe bandungs available for rent by up-market tourists.

Car Although renting a car in Pontianak is relatively expensive it's a way to see coastal West Kalimantan at your own pace. Most roads are in good condition and traffic is relatively light. At Citra Tours & Travel (☎ 4248) at Jalan Pak Kasih 6, you can rent an L300 minibus or kijang (Indonesian jeep) for 120,000 rp per day with a driver. The L300s can hold up to 10 people.

Getting Around

To/From the Airport A counter at the airport sells tickets for taxis into town for 10,000 rp. Or walk down the road in front of the station building bringing you to the main road in Pontianak and from here you should be able to get a colt. It is a half-hour drive from the airport to the Kapuas Indah station.

Local Transport The two main bemo stations are in the middle of the city: the Kapuas Indah station near the waterfront, and the other on Jalan Sisingamangaraja. There are taxis for hire next to the Garuda office and becaks aplenty – the drivers overcharge but they're not too difficult to bargain with. Should you wish to tour the city and environs with a taxi, the tariff is 6600 rp per hour with a two-hour minimum.

Outboard motorboats depart from piers next to the Kapuas Indah building on the river. They cross the river to the Pasar Lintang and Sintian Terminal for 200 rp per person. A car and passenger ferry just north of here will take you to Pasar Lintang at the same cost.

KAPUAS RIVER TRIPS

Pontianak is the launching point for riverboat services along Indonesia's longest river. Boats of all sizes and shapes journey the Kapuas, but the standard is a double-decker *bandung* with beds on the upper deck. A riverboat to Sintang (about 700 km from Pontianak) costs 15,000 rp per person and

takes two days and one night. This includes basic meals and there are warungs aboard most boats.

An interesting side trip off Sungai Kapuas is from Sintang along Sungai Melawai to Nangapinoh. There are a couple of hotels in Nangapinoh for 4000 to 6000 rp. From Nangapinoh catch boats further south on the Sayan River to the villages of Kota Bahru and Nangasokan. The journey entails riding sections of thrilling rapids and nights spent in Dayak villages. Boat fares from Nangapinoh to Nangasokan should be about 12,000 rp. Allow a week to do the trip from Sintang. You can fly back to Pontianak from Nangapinoh.

The terminus of all riverboat services, over 1000 km up the Kapuas, is Putussibau. From here you can travel overland to East Kalimantan and the headwaters of Sungai Mahakam, then catch a series of riverboats all the way to Samarinda on the east coast. The fare to Putussibau is 29,000 rp and the trip takes four days and three nights. Meals are included but you're well advised to supplement the meagre fish and rice diet with food from Pontianak.

Once you arrive in Putussibau visit the office of the bupati (lord mayor) and register your presence. He can also give you a letter of introduction for trekking beyond this point. Near Putussibau in the village of Melapi is a traditional Iban longhouse.

Putussibau to Long Apari

The hardy and intrepid can begin a river and jungle trek east across the West/East Kalimantan borders through the Muller Range to Long Apari at the headwaters of the Mahakam. If you make it all the way to Samarinda, you'll become one of the very few Westerners to have accomplished a true trans-Kalimantan journey from west to east. But the journey is arduous and expenses can be considerable.

The first step is to arrange a knowledgeable guide or two in Putussibau – the bupati can assist. If guides cannot be found in Putussibau, you can postpone this until you reach the village of Tanjung Lokan, where guides may be easier to locate. Do not attempt the trip beyond Tanjung Lokan alone, as the trails are not well marked.

While still in Putussibau, you'll have to stock up on provisions for yourselves and your guide(s) – allow about 75,000 rp for the essentials: rice, sugar, coffee and canned fish. Then charter a longboat or motor canoe for 300,000 to 450,000 rp – bargain hard – to make the one-day trip further upriver to Nangabungan. From Nangabungan you must charter a smaller canoe (prahu) for 75,000 rp for another day's travel to Tanjung Lokan.

In Tanjung Lokan find a guide or guides to lead you through the jungle into East Kalimantan. The walk takes about six days and guides will ask for around 60,000 rp each. Once you reach the logging camp west of Long Apari, the guides will turn around and head back to Tanjung Lokan and you must offer them a substantial amount of rice for their return journey.

From the logging camp it's a four-hour walk plus a three-hour boat ride to the village of Long Apari. You should be able to charter a prahu for the trip for about 35,000 rp. From Long Apari it's a short boat ride down the Mahakam to Long Lunuk where there's an airstrip with regular flights on Asahi Airlines for 42,000 rp to Samarinda. Otherwise spend a leisurely week gliding downriver to Long Bagun and Samarinda via the regular public riverboat service.

SINGKAWANG

A predominantly Chinese town, Singkawang is known as the Hong Kong of Indonesia. If you've travelled along the west coast of West Malaysia, the atmosphere and colonnaded shop architecture will seem familiar. If nothing else, it's probably the cleanest town in Indonesia. It's a day trip from Pontianak and the drive is quite beautiful with lush palm trees most of the way.

The main attraction of Singkawang is nearby Pasir Panjang beach, a two to three km stretch of clean, white sand and calm water with few people. At the south end, a whisky-coloured river flows into the sea.

1 Mosque
2 Hotel Diponegoro
3 Hotel Pelita
4 Hotel Khatulistiwa Plaza
5 Chinese Temple
6 Hotel Bandung
7 Hotel Makota
8 Bus Station
9 Hotel Sahuri

Singkawang

To Pontianak

Pasir Panjang is a 20-minute drive out of Singkawang just off the Singkawang to Pontianak road. There's a little warung on the beach serving bottled drinks and nasi gudeng.

On the road to Singkawang you could stop at Pulau Kijing, a seaside picnic spot just before the town of Sungaiduri, also called Seiduri for short. (Several towns along here shorten Sungai to Sei.)

East of Singkawang 12 km is Gunung Puting, Nipple Mountain (once you see it, you'll know how it got its name), which is a minor hill resort complete with neo-colonial hotel. The largest flower in the world, the Rafflesia, grows wild on these slopes.

The bank next door to the Hotel Diponegoro will cash US-dollar travellers' cheques.

Places to Stay

In Singkawang the *Hotel Bandung* on Jalan Pasar Tengah (Sejahtera), a 10-minute walk from the bus station, is basic but generally clean, although you could get a lot of street noise. Singles/doubles are 5500/8000 rp with shared mandi/toilet.

A block or two away is the *Hotel Khatulistiwa Plaza* (☎ 21697) at Jalan Selamat Karman 17 with fairly nice rooms from 9500 rp with attached mandi/toilet. Across the road the *Hotel Pelita* has run-down overpriced rooms with small attached mandi/toilet for 8500 rp. The staff here are surly.

The best hotel in this price range is the scrupulously clean *Hotel Diponegoro* (☎ 21430) at Jalan Diponegoro 32, on the corner diagonally opposite to the Hotel Khatulistiwa Plaza. The 9200 rp rooms are a little small but all have fans and spotless mandis. Slightly larger rooms are 10,600 rp and for 21,500 rp you get air-con. Downstairs, an airy restaurant serves good satay.

The cheapest hotel in town is *Losmen Singkawang* on a lane off Jalan Sejahtera, south of the centre. Dingy rooms are 5000 rp with shared mandis only. Nearby in the Kal-Bar Theatre complex is the *Hotel Kal-Bar* which is strictly a brothel and gambling venue – no foreigners allowed.

South of town in a quiet residential area is Singkawang's best middle range accommodation, the *Hotel Palapa* (tel 21449) on Jalan Tahir Singkawang. It's a pleasant, clean place, if a little isolated, with standard rooms for 17,500 rp, air-con for 24,000 rp.

The top accommodation in town is the new *Hotel Makota* (☎ 36022) on Jalan Diponegoro 1. Under the same ownership as the Makota Kapuas in Pontianak, this luxurious all air-con hotel boasts a swimming pool and disco. It has studios for 55,000 rp, standard singles/doubles for 68,000/78,000 rp and some pricey suites. Numerous affluent Chinese businesspeople stay here.

At the Pasir Panjang beach, 12 km south of Singkawang, there's a very shabby hotel with rooms for an outrageous 15,000 rp. At the north end of the beach is a recreational park called Taman Pasir Panjang Indah, where there's another *Hotel Palapa*. Adequate rooms are 19,000/38,000 rp on weekdays, 32,000/50,000 rp on weekends. You can also camp among the casuarina trees that line the beach.

Places to Eat

Since this is the Hong Kong of Indonesia, Chinese food is your best bet. The *Rumah Makan Tio Ciu Akho* at Jalan Diponegoro 106 serves some of the best *kwetiaw goreng* in all of Indonesia, loaded with shrimp, squid, wheat gluten and freshly made fishballs. Most of their dishes are prepared in the savoury Chiu Chao (Chao Zhou, Tae Jiu) style and the beer is ice-cold. Look for the giant wood stove in front, reminiscent of the Chinese warungs of Ipoh, West Malaysia.

Also on Jalan Diponegoro are the *Bakso 68* and *Bakso 40* noodle shops, serving variations on bakso (Chinese meatballs) with mie (wheat noodles), bakmi (egg noodles) and kwetiaw (rice noodles). The *Rumah Makan Indonesia* on the same street serves – what else – Indonesian (mostly Javanese) food, a rarity in this town.

Along Jalan Johan Godang at the Jalan Diponegoro intersection is a string of good Chinese warung kopi, all with Bentoel International signboards – the *Mexico, Malang, Asoka* and *Tahiti*. The Mexico has the best selection of pastries.

Along Jalan Niaga (Pasar Lama) you'll find three or four decent Padang-style places serving Banjarese and Sumatran food. In front of the cinema, on Jalan Pasar Hilir (Budi Utomo), is a Chinese night market.

If you are willing to splurge for delicious seafood, locals say the *Restaurant Dadap* on Jalan Ali Anhang is the best eatery in town. The Hotel Makota also has an excellent up-market restaurant.

Getting There & Away

Colts to Singkawang leave Pontianak's
Sintian Terminal (4000 rp, 3½ hours). It's a
nicely surfaced road plied by lunatic colt
drivers trying to break land, water and air
speed records all at once.

From Singkawang, it's 650 rp as far as
Pasir Panjang and takes about 15 to 20
minutes. To Gunung Poteng catch a Beng-
kayang bus east for the 12-km trip (650 rp).
Let the driver know where you're going and
he'll let you off at the foot of the hill. Or offer
him a little extra to take you up the hill to
Wisma Gunung Poteng, the only hotel.

You can also get colts north-east to
Sanggau (5200 rp), south to Pontianak (4000
rp), north to Pemangkat (650 rp) and Sambas
(2200 rp) or east to Mandor (2200 rp).

Sulawesi

The strangely contorted island of Sulawesi sprawls across the sea between Borneo and Maluku. Three great gulfs between the narrow, mountainous peninsulas – Bone, Tolo and Tomini – give the island its characteristic mutilated-octopus shape. When the Portuguese first came by in the early 16th century they sighted so many narrow points of land they presumed they were passing by an archipelago.

Protected by mountains and for the most part walled in by thick jungle, the interior of the island has provided a refuge for some of Indonesia's earliest inhabitants, some of whom have managed to preserve elements of their idiosyncratic cultures well into the 20th century. The Muslim Makassarese and Bugis of the south-west peninsula and the Christian Minahasans of the far north are the dominant groups of Sulawesi. They have also had the most contact with the West, but it's the Christian-animist Toraja, of the Tanatoraja district of the central highlands, who attract large numbers of visitors every year.

Strange cultures are not the only thing that makes Sulawesi so interesting; the landscape is strikingly beautiful and the island, a transition zone between Asian and Australian fauna, is home to some peculiar animals. The *babirusa*, or 'pig-deer', has long legs and tusks which curve upwards like horns, while the rare *anoa* is a metre-high dwarf buffalo.

Few visitors get further than the Ujung Pandang-Tanatoraja area; travel to other parts of the island is still difficult or time-consuming. Nevertheless, the Minahasa area of the northern peninsula is interesting and there are stunning coral reefs off the coast of Manado, the chief city of the region. Huge areas of central Sulawesi are almost untouched by tourism.

GETTING THERE & AWAY
Air
Garuda, Merpati, Mandala and Bouraq all fly to Sulawesi, with most connections via Ujung Pandang. There are international flights to Manado in North Sulawesi, which is also an approved gateway for visa-free stays.

Sea
Manado's Bitung seaport is an approved gateway to enter Indonesia without a visa.

The Pelni liners *Kerinci*, *Kambuna*, *Rinjani*, *Tidar*, *Kelimutu* and *Umsini* do regular loops out of Java.

GETTING AROUND
The south-western peninsula has the best transport, while the south-eastern peninsula has very poor transport and is seldom visited by tourists. The road connecting southern and central Sulawesi (between Mangkutana

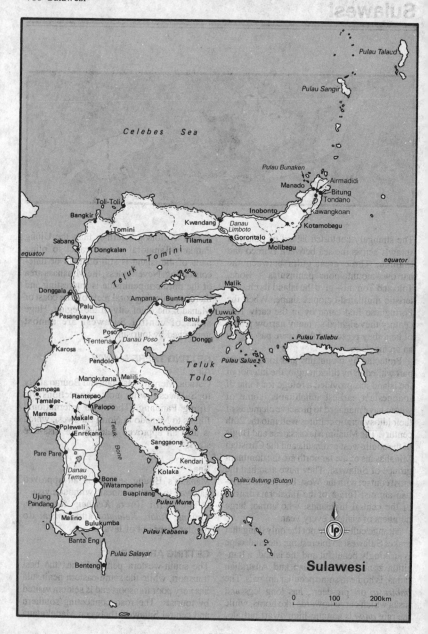

Sulawesi

0   100   200km

and Pendolo) is tenuous, but the road between Pendolo, Poso and Palu is quite OK. Elsewhere it's best to fly or take a boat. Otherwise, be prepared for rough roads which occasionally flood out.

Air

There are numerous flights around Sulawesi, chiefly by Merpati and Bouraq, although Garuda also flies several routes.

Boat

Apart from the coastal connections there are other ships which allow you to skirt some of the harder sections. These include the regular passenger ships from Poso in central Sulawesi to Gorontalo on the northern peninsula, which stop off at various ports on the way. There are ships along the western and northern coasts between Palu and Manado that call in at places like Toli-Toli, Paleleh and Kwandang.

South-Western Peninsula

The south-west is a lush, mountainous region of caves, waterfalls and large (but surprisingly shallow) lakes. The 6.5 million people – 60% of the total population of Sulawesi – include about four million Bugis, two million Makassarese and around 500,000 Toraja. Irrigated-rice agriculture is particularly important. Coffee, cotton and sugar cane are also important crops.

Descendants of the region's earliest tribes still existed until fairly recently. Groups like the Toala (the name means 'forest people') had dwindled to a single village near Maros by the 1930s and have now vanished altogether. In his book, *A Pattern of Peoples*, Robin Hanbury-Tenison relates how poisonous darts were shot at prospectors from the Inco Mining Company. More often, men toting blowpipes and wearing bark loin cloths, and bare-breasted women, would emerge from the surrounding cover and make friendly approaches. Tenison's book also relates other curious stories, including those of tribes who lived on boats in the swamps and rivers in central Sulawesi. They were possibly related to the *orang laut* ('people of the sea') found in many places in Indonesia.

Toraja mythology suggests that their ancestors came by boat from the south, sailed up the Sungai (river) Sadan and initially dwelled in the Enrekang region, before being pushed into the mountainous central regions by the arrival of other groups. The Bugis and the Makassarese are the main groups of the south-western coastal regions. The Makassarese are concentrated in the southern tip, centred on the port of Makassar (now known as Ujung Pandang). Bugis territory was originally further north, extending all the way to the Gulf of Bone and adjoining the lands of the southern Toraja. The Bugis and Makassarese have similar cultures, the main difference between them being language. Both are seafaring people who for centuries were active in trade and piracy, sailing to Flores, Timor and Sumba and even as far south as the north coast of Australia. Islam became their dominant religion in the 17th century but the Makassarese retained vestiges of their old animistic beliefs into the 20th century.

History

Much of Sulawesi's history has been the conflict between the Toraja in the mountains and the people of the coastal region, who were much more open to foreign influences. Pushed northwards, the Toraja people built their villages high in the mountains of central Sulawesi to guard against the marauding Bugis of the lowlands. Despite the constant threat they never formed a united front against the common enemy; each tribe occupied a valley or some other fairly well-defined pocket of territory, and at most only a group of villages would band together for protection. Complicating the story was the continuing rivalry between the Bugis and the Makassarese.

The coming of the Dutch upset this

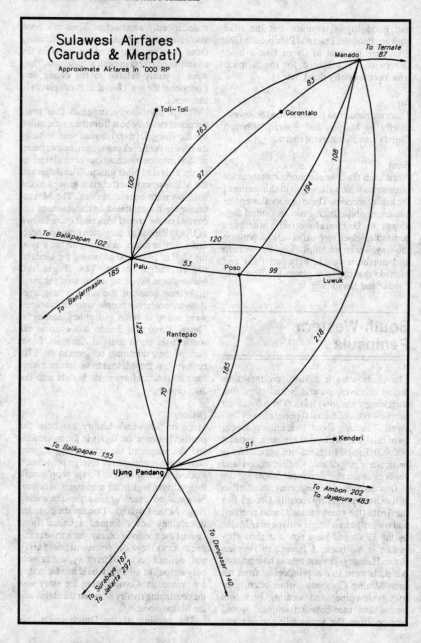

Sulawesi Airfares
(Garuda & Merpati)
Approximate Airfares in '000 RP

To Ternate 87

Manado

To Balikpapan 102

83

Gorontalo

Toli–Toli

163

97

108

194

100

120

Palu

53

Poso

99

Luwuk

To Banjarmasin 185

129

Rantepao

185

218

70

To Balikpapan 155

Kendari

91

Ujung Pandang

To Ambon 202
To Jayapura 483

To Surabaya 187
To Jakarta 297

To Denpasar 140

balance. The southern peninsula was divided into petty kingdoms, the most powerful being the Makassarese kingdom of Gowa (centred on the port of Makassar) and the Bugis kingdom of Bone on the east coast of the peninsula. Around 1530, before its conversion to Islam, Gowa started to expand its power. By the middle of the century it had established itself at the head of a loosely united empire and had emerged as a major trading power in eastern Indonesia. The king of Gowa adopted Islam in 1605 and between 1608 and 1611 Gowa attacked and subdued Bone, spreading Islam to the whole Bugis-Makassarese area.

The VOC set up its first south Sulawesi trading post in 1609 but soon found that Gowa was a considerable hindrance to its plans of total domination of the whole archipelago. The Sultan of Gowa cooperated with the English, French, Danish, Spanish, Portuguese and Asian traders in thwarting the VOC's attempts at gaining a spice monopoly. Peace treaties in 1637, 1655 and 1660 failed to end Gowa's hostility towards the VOC.

The Dutch found an ally in the Bugis prince Arung Palakka, one of the most famous warriors of 17th-century Indonesia. In 1660 Palakka was among a group of perhaps 10,000 Bugis from Bone who rebelled against Gowanese overlordship but were defeated. Palakka took refuge on the island of Butung off the south-eastern peninsula. With Dutch blessing they moved to Batavia in 1663. Three years later a large Dutch fleet, carrying 600 European troops, Ambonese soldiers and Palakka and his Bugis, set sail for Sulawesi. Just as the Dutch had hoped, the return of Palakka encouraged the Bugis of Bone and Soppeng to rise against the Makassarese. A year of fighting ensued on land and sea, and Sultan Hasanuddin of Gowa was forced to sign the Treaty of Bungaya in 1667. Even then the fighting did not end and the Sultan was not finally subdued until the middle of 1669.

The Treaty of Bungaya relieved Bone and the other Bugis states of their allegiance to Gowa. The Makassarese fort at what is now Ujung Pandang was turned over to the VOC and renamed Fort Rotterdam. Gowa's power was broken and in its place Bone, under Palakka, became the supreme state of southern Sulawesi. Makassarese claims to Minahasa, Butung and Sumbawa were abandoned and European traders (other than the VOC) were expelled.

However, by the 18th century there was new rivalry between the Bugis and Makassarese, and between Bone and the other Bugis states. After the brief British interlude following the Napoleonic wars, the Dutch were confronted with a Bugis revolt led by the Queen of Bone. This was suppressed but rebellions continued to break out. Not until 1905-06 was Makassarese and Bugis resistance finally broken. In 1905 the Dutch also subdued the Toraja people, again in the face of bitter resistance. There was still some minor resistance right up until the early 1930s.

The 20th century has had a mixed effect on the people of south-western Sulawesi. Under the Dutch the Toraja came down from their hilltop forts into the valleys and adopted wet-rice cultivation. The efforts of the missionaries have given a veneer of Christianity to their traditional animist beliefs and customs although extravagant funeral ceremonies continue. The majority of Bugis and Makassarese continue living as rice farmers but they remain Indonesia's premier seafaring people. Their schooners carry goods between Java, Kalimantan and Sulawesi and probably comprise the biggest sailing fleet in the world today; you can still see these ships being built in places like Bulukumba. The people are still staunchly Islamic and also independently minded − a revolt against the central government in Java took place in 1957. The reputation of the Bugis as the most kasar (rough and coarse) people in the archipelago remains a persistent stereotype.

UJUNG PANDANG

Ujung Pandang, the capital of southern Sulawesi and the Makassarese, is a major port. The Muslim Bugis are known for their magnificent prahus that trade extensively

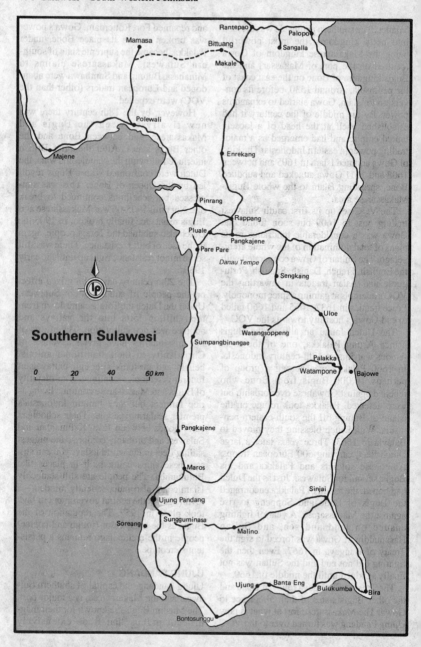

Southern Sulawesi

0   20   40   60 km

throughout the Indonesian archipelago. You can see some of these prahus at Paotere Harbour, a short becak ride north of the city centre. However, it's nowhere near as impressive as the awesome line-up at the Pasar Ikan in Jakarta, where they off-load timber from the outer islands.

The impressive Fort Rotterdam still stands as a reminder of the Dutch occupation, and there are many other Dutch buildings, including the Governor's residence on Jalan Jenderal Sudirman. Ujung Pandang is also the last resting place of Sultan Hasanuddin and of the Javanese prince, Diponegoro. In the surrounding countryside are the palace of the Gowanese kings, waterfalls where the naturalist Alfred Wallace collected butterflies, and cave-paintings left by the first inhabitants of Sulawesi perhaps 5000 years ago.

History

Once known as Makassar, this great city-port of 800,000 people on the south-western limb of Sulawesi has for centuries been the gateway to eastern Indonesia and the spice islands of Maluku. From Makassar the Dutch could control much of the shipping that passed between western and eastern Indonesia. Although the weaker kingdoms of southern Sulawesi occasionally rose in revolt and the pirates were a constant nuisance, the amount of direct territorial control required to maintain this hegemony was very small. Well into the 19th century the borders of the sultanate of Gowa were just a few km from the port of Makassar, and the only other parts of Sulawesi under direct Dutch control were a few ports on the Gulf of Tomini and the Minahasa region in the northern peninsula.

Early accounts of Makassar describe it as a fine town. In the mid-1800s the naturalist Alfred Wallace found Makassar 'prettier and cleaner' than any of the towns he had previously seen in the east.

Orientation

Ujung Pandang is a busy port with its harbour in the north-west corner of the city.

The streets immediately back from the harbour – like Jalan Nusantara – are where you'll find Pelni and Ujung Pandang's Chinatown. Heading due south along Jalan Nusantara brings you to Fort Rotterdam, which is pretty much the centre of town.

Information

Tourist Office The tourist office (☎ 21142) is on Jalan Pangerang Andi Petta Rani, which is a long way out of town and leads off from the airport road. You can get there by bemo. There is also a tourist information office at the airport.

Money The Bank Rakyat Indonesia is on Jalan Jenderal A Yani near the Garuda office. Bank Negara Indonesia is on Jalan Nusantara. The moneychanger in the airport terminal gives the same rates as the banks and is open on Sunday.

Post & Telecommunications The post office is on the corner of Jalan Supratman and Jalan Slamet Riyadi, south- east of the fort. Telephone and telex offices are at Jalan Balaikota and Jalan Veteran.

Benteng Ujung Pandang (Fort Rotterdam)

One of the best preserved examples of Dutch architecture in Indonesia, Fort Rotterdam continues to guard the harbour of Ujung Pandang. A Gowanese fort dating back to 1545 once stood here, but that failed to keep out the Dutch. The original fort was rebuilt in Dutch style after the Treaty of Bungaya in 1667. Parts of the crumbling wall have been left pretty much as they were, an interesting comparison to the restored buildings. The fort now bears the rather more nationalistic title of Benteng (Fort) Ujung Pandang.

Of the two museums in the fort, the larger, more interesting one is open Tuesday to Thursday from 8 am to 1.30 pm, Friday from 8 to 10.30 am, and Saturday and Sunday from 8 am to 12.30 pm. It's closed on Monday and holidays. It has an assortment of exhibits including rice bowls from Tanatoraja, kitchen tools from south Sulawesi,

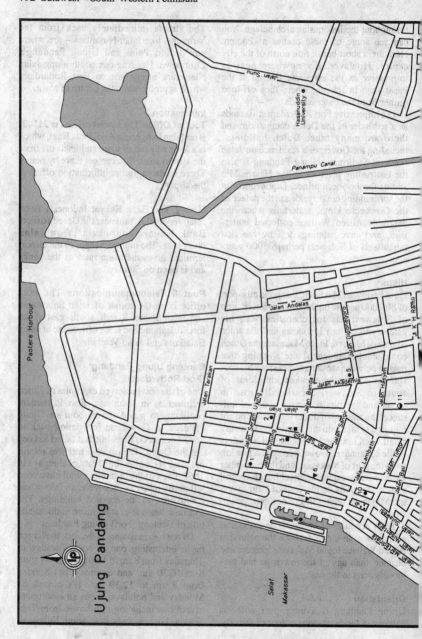

Ujung Pandang

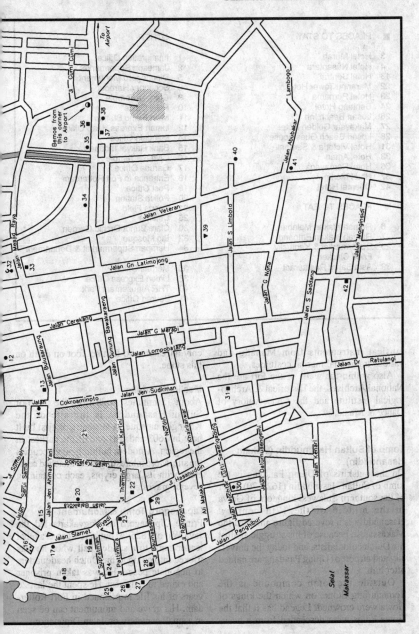

■ PLACES TO STAY

3	Hotel Murah
4	Hotel Nusantara
13	Hotel Sentral
22	Marannu Tower Hotel
23	Hotel Purnama
24	Benteng Hotel
26	Losari Beach Inn
27	Makassar Golden Hotel
28	Losari Beach Guesthouse
31	Hotel Victoria & Sempati
33	Hotel Aman
36	Hotel Ramayana
37	Hotel Marlin
42	Oriental Hotel

▼ PLACES TO EAT

6	Rumah Makan Malabar
7	Rumah Makan Empang
29	Supermarket & Kentucky Fried Chicken
39	Asia Bahru Restaurant

OTHER

1	Immigration Office
2	Jameson Supermarket
5	Diponegoro Monument
8	Schooner Harbour
9	Chinese Temple
10	Pelni Office
11	Main Bemo Station
12	Liman Express Head Office
14	Mandala Office
15	Bank Rakyat Indonesia
16	Chinese Temple
17	Garuda Office
18	Entrance to Fort Rotterdam
19	Post Office
20	Police Station
21	Sports Field
25	Cinema
30	Clara Bundt Orchid Garden
32	Big Mosque
34	Harapan Supermarket & Department Store
35	Merpati Office
38	Liman Express Office
40	THR Amusement Park
41	Bouraq Office

musical instruments from Manado and various traditional marital costumes.

Also within the walls of the fort are the National Archives, the Historical & Archeological Institute and the Conservatory of Dance & Music.

Tomb of Sultan Hasanuddin (Makam Hasanuddin)

On the outskirts of Ujung Pandang is the tomb of Sultan Hasanuddin (1629-70), ruler of the southern Sulawesi kingdom of Gowa in the middle of the 17th century. Hasanuddin is a revered figure amongst the Makassarese because of his struggle against the Dutch colonialists, and today the university and airport of Ujung Pandang are named after him.

Outside the tomb compound is the Tomanurung Stone, on which the kings of Gowa were crowned. Legend has it that the Gowa kings were descended from a heavenly ancestor who first set foot on earth on this stone.

Mesjid Katangka

About 15 minutes' walk from the tomb of Sultan Hasanuddin is the site of the Katangka mosque. A mosque was first built here in 1603 and was one of the earliest in the region. A modern building now occupies the site. More interesting is the attached cemetery with its large crypts, each containing several graves.

Diponegoro Tomb & Monument

Prince Diponegoro of Yogyakarta led the Java War of 1825-30 but his career as a rebel leader came to a sudden halt when he was tricked into going to the Dutch headquarters to negotiate peace. He was taken prisoner and exiled to Sulawesi. He spent the last 26 years of his life imprisoned in Fort Rotterdam. His grave and monument can be seen in a small cemetery on Jalan Diponegoro.

Paotere Harbour

This anchorage is where the Bugis (or Pinisi) sailing ships berth, although the line-up is nowhere near as impressive as that at the Pasar Ikan in Jakarta.

Chinese Temples

You'll notice a fairly large number of light-skinned Indonesians in Ujung Pandang, who are in fact ethnic Chinese. Chinese temples can be seen along Jalan Sulawesi, but the most ornate is the brilliantly coloured building at the corner of Jalan Sulawesi and Jalan Serui Sama.

Clara Bundt Orchid Garden

This well-known orchid garden and shell collection is hidden away in a compound at Jalan Mochtar Lufti 15. It's a little oasis in the middle of Ujung Pandang. There's a huge collection of shells including dozens of giant clams, and a small plantation of orchids grown in pots and trays. Admission is free; just knock on the door and someone will let you in. Some of the shells and orchids are for sale.

Places to Stay – bottom end

Ujung Pandang is none too cheap, at least by Indonesian standards. The cheapest places are pretty dismal, and they don't take foreigners anyway.

Just south of the fort is the *Hotel Purnama* (☎ 23830) at Jalan Pattimura 3-3A, which seems like the best deal in this price range. Singles/doubles with private bath start at 12,000/15,000 rp. The nearby *Benteng Hotel* (☎ 22172) at Jalan Ujung Pandang 8 is not as pleasant but is similarly priced at 12,500 rp for a double.

There are some cheap places in the streets immediately north-east of the fort. Bottom of the line is the *Hotel Nusantara* (☎ 23163) at Jalan Sarappo 103, where singles/doubles go for 5000/8000 rp. The rooms are hot, noisy little sweat-boxes with masonite-thin walls. Since there's not much to get dirty the rooms themselves are clean. Just across the road at number 60 is the slightly better appointed *Hotel Murah* (☎ 23101) where small,

windowless rooms with private bath cost 12,500 rp.

Heading east from the waterfront the *Hotel Sentral* at Jalan Bulusaraung 7 is pretty run-down, with rooms for 8000 rp. Further on is the *Hotel Aman* on Jalan Mesjid Raya, across the road from the large mosque. Rooms cost 8000 rp and are cell- like with little cot beds. The bathrooms are scungy and virtually unuseable, and the front rooms are noisy.

Places to Stay – middle

Probably the best place, and also very popular with travellers, is the *Hotel Ramayana* (☎ 22165) on Jalan Gunung Bawakaraeng, where rooms start from 13,750 rp. It's clean, conveniently located and is generally a pleasant place to stay. Single rooms for 19,800 rp and up have air-con and private bath with plentiful hot water.

Diagonally opposite the Hotel Ramayana is the comfortable *Hotel Marlin* (☎ 317795) at Jalan Gunung Bawakaraeng 120. Singles/doubles without air-con are 15,000/18,000 rp. With air-con the price rises to 21,000/24,000 rp.

On the waterfront there's the *Losari Beach Inn* (☎ 817041) on Jalan Pasar Ikan. The upper floors give a fine view of the sea, but the 'beach' is quite ugly. Singles/doubles are officially 55,400/63,000 rp, but they give a 30% discount during the slow season (most of the time?) which brings the tariff down to 39,300/44,100 rp. The price includes breakfast, and the rooms have comfy double beds, carpet, television and sparkling clean bathrooms.

Hotel Afriat is a 10-minute walk from the airport terminal, facing the main road into Ujung Pandang. It's similar to the Hotel Ramayana. Rooms cost from 15,000 rp, or 19,000 rp with air-con.

Places to Stay – top end

Makassar Golden Hotel (☎ 314408, fax 317999) at Jalan Pasar Ikan 50 is an enormous five-star hotel. Standard singles/doubles cost 97,500/126,750 while deluxe rooms go for 146,250/175,500. There is also a combined tax and service charge totalling 21%.

Marannu Tower Hotel (☎ 21470) at Jalan Sultan Hasanuddin 3 was closed for renovation at the time of this writing, but should reopen by the time you read this. Prices should be similar to those at the Makassar Golden Hotel.

Places to Eat

Home to two of Indonesia's foremost seafaring peoples, this place has good seafood in abundance. Ikan bakar (barbecued fish) and *cumi cumi bakar* (barbecued octopus) are especially popular. Because of the sizeable Chinese population Ujung Pandang is also a good place for Chinese food and for practising your Mandarin. Other options include *soto makassar*, which is a soup made from buffalo innards and sold in the warungs.

There are good, cheap restaurants along Jalan Sulawesi. *Rumah Makan Malabar* at Jalan Sulawesi 290 specialises in Indian food and serves simple curries and crispy martabak.

Asia Bahru Restaurant, near the corner of Jalan Latimojong and Jalan G Sala, specialises in seafoods and when you order a big fish you get a very big fish! A seafood alternative is the *Rumah Makan Empang* at Jalan Siau 7 by the harbour, which serves very good dishes and is excellent value.

Rumah Makan Ujung Pandang at Jalan Irian 42 is an air-con restaurant with a mixed Chinese and Indonesian menu, and very large servings – satays come piled high on the plate.

Try the dozens of evening food trolleys along the waterfront south of the Makassar Golden Hotel, or the warungs around the THR Amusement Park for a slab of ikan bakar with cucumber, peanut sauce and rice.

The great food hunt might lead you to *Kentucky Fried Chicken* diagonally opposite the Marannu Tower Hotel. Even if you decide not to sample the Colonel's finger-lickin' chicken, there is a great supermarket on the ground floor of the same building.

Things to Buy

Jalan Sombu Opu, which is a street to the south of the fort and one block east of the waterfront, has a great collection of jewellery shops. Toko Kerajinam at 20 is good for touristy souvenirs. CV Kanebo, on the corner with Jalan Pattimura, has crafts from all over Indonesia.

Ujung Pandang is supposed to be a good place for buying Kendiri filigree silver jewellery. This is made in Ujung Pandang, not in Kendari on the south-eastern peninsula of Sulawesi as the name would suggest.

Other possible buys include Toraja handicrafts, Chinese pottery, Makassarese brasswork, silk-weaving and mounted butterflies from Bantimurung.

Getting There & Away

Ujung Pandang is the gateway to southern Sulawesi and is connected to many other parts of Indonesia by air and sea. There are numerous buses to various destinations on the south-western peninsula, although for most people the next stop is the Tanatoraja district in the central highlands.

Air Garuda (☎ 22705) is at Jalan Slamet Riyadi 6; Merpati (☎ 4114) is at Jalan Gunung Bawakaraeng 109; Bouraq (☎ 83039) is at Jalan Veteran Selatan 1; Mandala is on Jalan Jenderal Sudirman; Sempati (☎ 311556) is in the Hotel Victoria, Jalan Jenderal Sudirman 24.

Garuda offers daily international flights to Singapore. Merpati and Garuda combined have numerous domestic flights out of Ujung Pandang. With connecting flights, you can reach the following places:

Destination	Fare (rp)
Ambon	202,000
Balikpapan	155,000
Bandung	315,000
Banjarmasin	315,000
Biak	366,000
Buton	150,000
Denpasar	140,000
Dilli	243,000
Gorontalo	266,000
Jakarta	297,000

Jayapura	483,000
Kendari	91,000
Kupang	169,000
Luwuk	254,000
Manado	218,000
Manokwari	386,000
Maumere	129,000
Nabire	456,000
Palu	129,000
Pomalaa	102,000
Poso	185,000
Samarinda	204,000
Semarang	246,000
Solo	232,000
Sorong	253,000
Surabaya	187,000
Tanatoraja	77,000
Tarakan	288,000
Ternate, Timika	393,000
Toli-Toli	234,000
Yogyakarta	240,000

Bouraq offers good coverage on the minor routes between various cities in Sulawesi. From Ujung Pandang, Bouraq flies to the following places: Balikpapan (155,000 rp), Banjarmasin (239,000 rp), Gorontalo (222,000 rp), Manado (218,000 rp), Palu (129,000 rp), Samarinda (200,000 rp) and Ternate (301,000 rp).

Mandala has flights to Jakarta (235,000 rp), Surabaya and Ambon (163,000 rp).

Sempati also flies from Ujung Pandang to Denpasar and Surabaya, with a connecting flight to Jakarta and Singapore.

Bus The long-distance bus terminal is a few km out on the road heading towards the airport. You can get there by bemo for 250 rp.

From Ujung Pandang most people head direct for Rantepao, the centre of the Tanatoraja region. The road from Ujung Pandang to Rantepao is surfaced all the way. Liman Express, at Jalan Laiya 25 near the market, is probably the best of the companies running daily minibuses and buses there. This company also has another ticket office diagonally opposite the Hotel Ramayana. There are daily buses to Rantepao via Pare Pare. The trip takes 10 to 12 hours and costs 8000 rp. Take the day-bus to Tanatoraja because the scenery as you enter Tanatoraja from the lowlands is spectacular.

Liman also has buses from Ujung Pandang to Palopo and Malili. A number of other companies run buses, minibuses to Tanatoraja and other parts of south-western Sulawesi.

There are alternative paths to Rantepao. You could head south along the coast to Banta Eng and Bulukumba, turn north to Watampone (Bone), and head north to Palopo, which is a three-hour bus ride from Rantepao. Stop off along the way at Sengkang and Soppeng. Such a route takes you through some of the larger Bugis and Makassarese towns. Or take the direct route along the west coast and stop off at the port of Pare Pare.

Shared taxis to places like Pare Pare leave from Jalan Sarappo, in the same block as the Hotel Nusantara. There are also shared taxis to other places in the vicinity of Ujung Pandang.

As in other parts of Indonesia there is a great love of abbreviation. Tator means Tanatoraja, Pol-mas is Polewali-Mamasa Regency and Sul-sel is Sulawesi Selatan (Sulawesi South).

Boat Pelni (☎ 27961) is at Jalan Martadinata 38 on the waterfront. The modern Pelni liners *Kambuna, Kerinci, Kelimutu, Rinjani, Tidar* and *Umsini* make regular stops in Ujung Pandang on their various loops around Indonesia. For full timetables for these ships see the Boat section in the Getting Around chapter.

Typical economy and 1st-class fares from Ujung Pandang are given in the following table. Second, 3rd and 4th-class fares range between these two extremes.

Destination	1st	Ekonomi
Ambon	118,000	31,000
Balikpapan	81,000	23,000
Belawan	269,000	74,000
Bitung	149,000	45,000
Ende	125,000	36,000
Kupang	124,700	39,700
Padang	236,000	63,000
Pantoloan	87,000	27,000
Tanjung Priok	172,000	45,000

Other possibilities include the cargo ships which leave Ujung Pandang for various destinations around Indonesia and in other South-East Asian countries. For inter-island shipping try PT PPSS at Jalan Martadinata 57. If they're not helpful, find out what ships are in port and where they're going, and bargain directly with the captain of the ship.

For foreign ports like Singapore try PT Samudera Indonesia at Jalan Pasar Ikan 1, PT Trikora Lloyd at Jalan Martadinata 26 and PT PRI at Jalan Nusantara 32. There are other agencies along Jalan Nusantara but note that Ujung Pandang is not an official Indonesian entry/exit port.

Getting Around
To/From the Airport Bemos to Ujung Pandang's Hasanuddin Airport (22 km out of town) leave from the main bemo station on Jalan Cokroaminoto. If you're staying at the Ramayana Hotel they run past the large intersection just east of the hotel. A taxi from the airport to the city centre is 10,000 rp with bargaining, or take a becak or walk a few hundred metres to the main road and catch a bemo to the city for 1000 rp.

Local Transport Ujung Pandang is too big to do much walking and if you stay in hotels on the outskirts, like the Ramayana, or want to visit places like the THR Amusement Park, you'll need the becaks and bemos. The main bemo station is on Jalan Cokroaminoto. Bemos will get you to places like Paotere Harbour, the tourist office, airport, and some of the sights on the outskirts of the city such as the Hasanuddin Tombs and the old palace at Sungguminasa.

Becak drivers are hard bargainers and it seems almost impossible to get those legs moving for under 500 rp! They're fearless drivers with your life in the frontline – getting into the traffic or cutting across streets during peak hour is a truly horrendous experience!

AROUND UJUNG PANDANG
Sungguminasa
Once the seat of the Sultan of Gowa, Sung-

guminasa is 11 km from Ujung Pandang. The former residence of the sultan is now the Museum Ballalompoa and houses a collection of artefacts similar to those in the Fort Rotterdam museums. Although the royal regalia, which includes a stone-studded gold crown, can be seen on request, it is the palace itself which is the real attraction. It is constructed of wood and raised on stilts; the same architectural style inspired the palaces you see in Sumbawa Besar and Bima on Sumbawa Island, over which the Makassarese once ruled. To get to Sungguminasa take a bemo from the central bemo station. It's a half-hour trip and the palace can be seen from the road.

Bantimurung
About 45 km from Ujung Pandang, the Bantimurung Waterfalls are set amidst lushly vegetated limestone cliffs. Bantimurung is crowded with Indonesian day-trippers on weekends and holidays; at other times it's a wonderful retreat from the congestion of Ujung Pandang. Entrance to the park costs 800 rp.

Past the 15-metre waterfall there's a cave at river level. Bring a torch (flashlight) to look inside the cave. Scramble along the rocks past the waterfall and get onto the track, but you will encounter an admission gate where you must pay an additional 800 rp.

There are many other caves in these cliffs but apart from the scenery the area is also famous for its numerous beautiful butterflies. The naturalist Alfred Wallace collected specimens here in the mid-1800s.

Getting There & Away To get to Bantimurung take a bemo from Ujung Pandang's central bemo station. The trip takes a bit over an hour. If you can't find a direct bemo then take one to Maros (1000 rp, one hour) and another from there for the rest of the way (500 rp, half an hour).

Gua Leang Leang
A few km before the Bantimurung turn-off is the turn-off for the Leang Leang Caves,

noted for their paintings thought to date back at least 5000 years. The paintings are images of human hands made by placing the hand up against the rock wall and spitting a mixture of red ochre and water around them. To get there, take a bemo from Ujung Pandang to Maros, and another from there to the turn-off then walk the last couple of km – or charter a bemo from Maros.

Malino

Malino is a hill town 74 km east of Ujung Pandang on the slopes of Gunung Bawakarang, where the Dutch influence is still highly visible. Deer-hunting on horse-back in these parts was once a favoured sport of the Makassarese royalty. The Takapala Waterfall is nearby.

Banta Eng

Traditional boat-building can be seen at Banta Eng (also known as Bontain or Bantaeng) on the south coast, 123 km from Ujung Pandang. Boats are also built in the Bugis and Makassarese villages in the region of Bulukumba which is a further 30 km from Banta Eng.

PARE PARE

The second-largest city in southern Sulawesi is a smaller, more manageable version of Ujung Pandang. Pare Pare is a seaport through which a good deal of the produce of southern Sulawesi (rice, corn, coffee, etc) is shipped out. It's a pleasant stopover between Tanatoraja or Mamasa and Ujung Pandang. There are also frequent ships to the east coast of Kalimantan and to northern Sulawesi from here.

Orientation

Pare Pare is stretched out along the water-front. Most of what you need (hotels, restaurants, etc) is on a couple of streets immediately back from the harbour.

Money Bank Negara Indonesia is the only bank in town that changes money. It's right next to the large mosque (see map).

1 Cinema
2 Restaurant Asia
3 Hotel Siswa
4 Warung Sedap
5 Statue
6 Cinema
7 Park
8 Bank Negara Indonesia
9 Mosque
10 Tanty Hotel
11 Post Office
12 Harbour Master's Office
13 Hotel Gandaria
14 Pelni Office
15 Cinema
16 Penginapan Palanro & Penginapan AM
17 Restaurant Sempurna
18 Bus & Bemo Station

Pare Pare

To Ujung Pandang

Places to Stay

Hotel Gandaria (☎ 21093) at Jalan Bau Massepe 171 is the best in town. It's excellent value, very clean and comfortable, and run by friendly people. Economy/deluxe single rooms with attached toilet and shower cost 11,000/22,000 rp, with the latter price including breakfast.

Tanty Hotel (☎ 21378) on Jalan Hasanuddin 5 is clean though basic, but has a quiet, back street location. There's no sign on the outside except one that says 'Office'. Rooms average 8000 rp.

Hotel Siswa (☎ 21374) at Jalan Baso Daeng Patompo 30 is a great rambling rundown place about 20 minutes walk from the bus station. The rooms, which are thinly partitioned but should be OK for a night or two, cost 5000/10,000 for basic/deluxe. The bathrooms leave a lot to be desired.

Penginapan Palanro and the *Penginapan A M* (☎ 21801) are next to each other in the same building at Jalan Bau Massepe 154 and 152. They're similar in standard with thinly partitioned pigeon holes for rooms that go for 5000 rp.

Places to Eat

Restaurant Sempurna on Jalan Bau Massepe is pretty good value with both Indonesian and Chinese food. *Restaurant Asia* is spanking clean and has good Chinese food, but their seafood dishes are overpriced. *Warung Sedap* is a good ikan bakar place next door to the Asia. There are many small warungs along the main street in the vicinity of the Hotel Siswa.

Getting There & Away

Bus Pare Pare is on the road from Ujung Pandang to Rantepao. By road from Ujung Pandang takes three to four hours and costs 4000 rp. From Pare Pare, most travellers head north-east to Rantepao (five hours), but a few hardy souls go south-east to Sengkang.

Alternative destinations are north-west to Polewali or even further to Majene. The bus companies have ticket offices at the bus station.

Boat The main reason to come to Pare Pare is to catch a ship to the east coast of Kalimantan. There are daily boats to one port or another. There are also ships once or twice a week from Pare Pare along the coast to Pantoloan (the port of Palu) and to northern Sulawesi. Given the state of the road through central Sulawesi it could be worth backtracking from Rantepao to Pare Pare in order to get to north Sulawesi.

Pelni (☎ 21017) is at Jalan Andicammi 130. The harbour master's office is on the waterfront on Jalan Andicammi, and several shipping companies have their offices here. There are also numerous ticket offices and agents on the main street in the centre of town.

SENGKANG

Inland and south-east of Pare Pare is the Bugis town of Sengkang, which has only recently been discovered by tourists and is still little visited.

Scenic Danau Tempe, a large lake, is the main attraction, and is best admired by taking a boat trip. Boats can be chartered for 10,000 rp per boat (not per person).

The other main attraction of Sengkang is the silk-weaving industry. You can visit the silk factories and get things made to order. Most visitors buy ready-made silk products at bargain prices in the town's silk market.

Places to Stay

The nicest place is *Hotel Apada*. The friendly manager speaks English and can arrange tours of the lake and silk weaving factories. Double rooms go for 15,000 rp. The hotel is one km from Danau Tempe.

Similarly priced is *Hotel Alsalam*. Its chief advantage is that it's only about 100 metres from the lake.

Getting There & Away

Sengkang is readily accessible from Pare Pare by bus or bemo. If you're coming from or going to Rantepao, the bemo goes through Palopo and takes about six or seven hours.

WATAMPONE (BONE)
Also known as Watangpone, this is a Bugis town and was once the centre of the powerful Bone kingdom. The town lies south-west of Sengkang.

Things to See
Not far from town is the Museum Lapawawoi which is run by a prince – well, a former prince – who'll give you an explanation of the collection in Dutch.

Some 34 km north-west is Uloe. Seven km from Uloe is Gua Mampu, which is the largest cave in south Sulawesi. Legends and stories are told of the many rock formations resembling people and animals.

Getting There & Away
Bus Watampone can be reached by bus from Ujung Pandang, a pretty ride through mountainous country taking about six hours. A number of companies have buses on the route.

Boat You can take a ship to Kolaka on the south-east peninsula of Sulawesi – for details see the Kolaka section.

BULUKUMBA & BIRA
In the vicinity of Bulukumba you can see traditional boat-building in Bugis and Makassarese villages. The nearby town of Bira has a beautiful white-sand beach.

Places to Stay
For cheap accommodation try the quiet *Sinar Jaya* on Jalan Sawerigading 4, or travel on for an hour's drive to stay at the losmen in Bira.

Getting There & Away
From Watampone you can take a minibus to Bulukumba on the southern tip of the peninsula (you may have to change buses in Sinjai). From Bulukumba you can take a bus

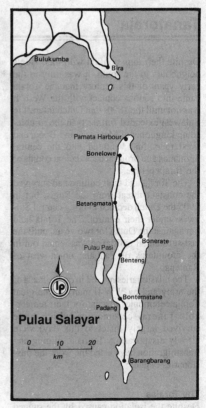

(153 km) to Ujung Pandang, or a motorboat to Pulau Salayar.

PULAU SALAYAR
This long, narrow island lies off the tip of the south-west peninsula of Sulawesi and is inhabited by Bugis-Makassarese people. Benteng is the chief settlement. South-east of Salayar are the Bonerate islands, which are also inhabited by Bugis people.

Getting There & Away
Take a bus from Ujung Pandang to Bira (east of Bulumkumba) and a boat from Bira to Benteng. Boats from Bira go to Pamatata Harbour at the northern end of Pulau Salayar.

Tanatoraja

Despite their long conflict with their Bugis neighbours to the south, it was only in the early years of this century that the Toraja came into serious contact with the West. It was not until the 1890s that Dutch interest in Sulawesi extended further than the troublesome kingdoms of Makassar and Bone, and Westerners first ventured into the central highlands and brought back their accounts of the Toraja people.

The Toraja and their culture had survived the constant threat from the Bugis, but in 1905 the Dutch decided to bring central Sulawesi under their control. The Toraja held out against the Dutch for two years, until the last substantial resistance was wiped out in the mountains of Pangala, north-west of Rantepao.

The missionaries moved in on the heels of the army and by WW II many of the great Toraja ceremonies (except for their remarkable funeral ceremonies which have survived largely intact to this day) were already disappearing. Tourism, mining and transmigration have aided the work the missionaries began.

The Torajas

Despite the isolation caused by the rugged landscape of central Sulawesi, similar cultures have existed in the territory bordered by the Bugis to the south-west, the Gorontalo district in the north, and the Loinang and Mori peoples in the east. The people in this vast area are collectively referred to as the Toraja. The name is derived from the Bugis word *toriaja*, meaning 'men of the mountains' or 'people of the interior', but the connotations of the name are something like 'yokel' or 'hillbilly' – rustic, unsophisticated, oafish highlanders.

The Bugis traded Indian cloth, Dutch coins and porcelain with the Toraja in return for coffee and slaves. The Bugis are even said to have introduced cock-fighting to the Toraja, who incorporated the sport into the death rituals of their noble class. Islam brought a new militancy to the Bugis and under Arung Palakka they attacked the Toraja in 1673 and 1674. However, Islam never spread much further than the southern Toraja areas because, it is said, of the people's fondness for pork and tuak (palm wine)!

Customarily the Toraja have been split by ethnologists into western, eastern and southern groups. To some extent these divisions represent the varying degrees of influence the old kingdoms of Luwu, Gowa and Bone have had on the Toraja. It *doesn't* reflect any political organisation amongst the Toraja. In the past there has been no organisation beyond the level of the local village or small groups of villages. Sometimes villages would band together in federations to resist the Bugis invaders, and these federations in effect became mini-states. However, there have never been any large Toraja states.

Of all the Toraja peoples the best known to the Western world are the southern Toraja, also known as the Sadan or Saqdan Toraja. These people live in the northern part of south-west Sulawesi, in the mountainous limestone country through which the Sungai (river) Sadan cuts a deep valley. Their main concentration is in the area called Tanatoraja, about 300 km north of Ujung Pandang, where the chief towns are Rantepao and Makale. Tanatoraja has become the chief tourist destination in Sulawesi but, like Bali, the tourist trade is peripheral. The vast majority of the Toraja make a living from farming or raising livestock.

The introduction of wet-rice cultivation after the Dutch conquest has sculpted and terraced the slopes of the steep mountainsides, with streams originating near the hilltops harnessed to flow in a succession of little waterfalls before escaping once more into the natural rivers below. Toraja villages were once built on the summits of hills, sometimes surrounded by fortified walls with the settlement itself reached by tunnels. This was partly for protection, partly because the original clan ancestors were supposed to have arrived from heaven on hilltops. The

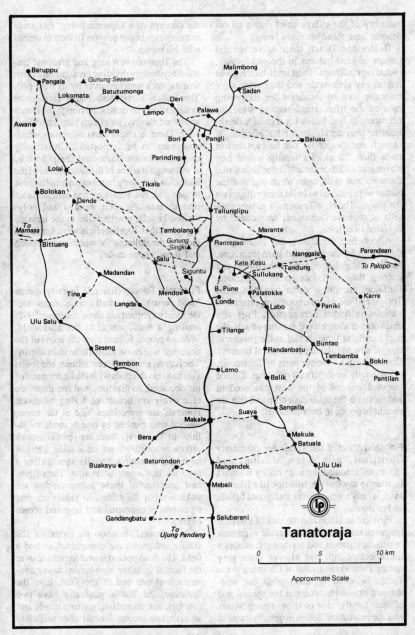

Malimbong

Baruppu
Pangala
▲ Gunung Sesean
Batutumonga
Lokomata
Sadan
Deri
Palawa
Lempo
Awan
Pana
Pangli
Balusu
Bori
Parinding
Lolai
Tikala
Bolokan
Dende
Tallunglipu
Marante
Tambolang
Gunung
Singki
Rantepao
Nanggala
Parendean
To Mamasa
Bittuang
Salu
To Palopo
Madandan
Siguntu
Kete Kesu
Tandung
Tina
Mendoe
Sullukang
Karre
Langda
B. Pune
Palatokke
Paniki
Ulu Salu
Londa
Labo
Seseng
Tilanga
Buntao
Rembon
Randanbatu
Tembamba
Bokin
Lemo
Balik
Pantilan
Sangalla
Makale
Suaya
Bera
Makula
Buakayu
Baturondon
Batuala
Ulu Uai
Mangendek
Mebali
Gandangbatu
Salubarani
To
Ujung Pandang

Tanatoraja

0   5   10 km

Approximate Scale

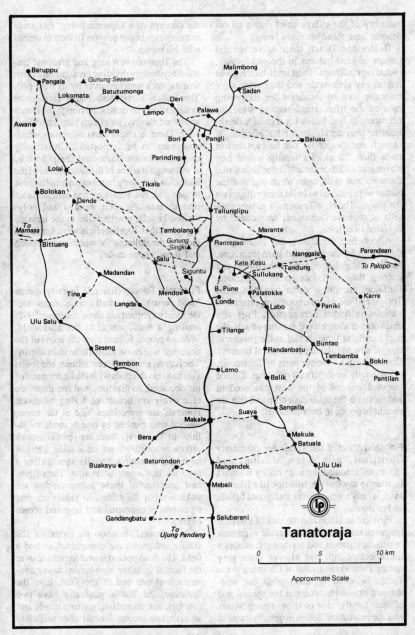

authority of the village chief rested on his descent from these heavenly beings.

Before the Dutch there were several groups of head-hunters in the archipelago, including the Toraja. Their head-hunting was not on any great scale and their raids were basically tests of manhood for the young men of the tribe. Head-hunting was also necessary to find heads for a chief's death-feast to provide slaves for his afterlife. If enough enemies could not be captured in raids then the chief's family would buy slaves and sacrifice them. Under Dutch rule the wars and raids came to an end and the Sadan were ordered to build their villages on the plains. Today, a Tanatoraja village consists of separate farmsteads surrounded by irrigated rice fields.

Also before the Dutch, the Toraja grew their crops by the slash-and-burn technique, hunting and gathering food in the forests and grazing their buffaloes on bare hillsides. Buffaloes are still a status symbol for the Toraja, and are of paramount importance in various religious ceremonies. Pigs and chickens are slaughtered at many rituals, the pigs mostly at funerals and at the consecration of new *tongkonan* (traditional houses). Dogs are eaten in some parts of Tanatoraja, occasionally as sacrificial offerings. Coffee (reputedly some of the best produced in Indonesia) is the main cash crop and fish are caught in ponds in the rice fields.

Religion Most of the Toraja are ostensibly Christians, with a few Muslims and 'animists' amongst them. In reality it would be truer to say that Christianity, like Islam in Java, is only a veneer over traditional beliefs and customs.

Physical isolation and the lack of a written language resulted in considerable variations in beliefs, customs and mythology, although the ancestor cult has always been very strong. Prior to the arrival of Christianity the Toraja believed in many gods but worshipped one in particular as the special god of their family, clan or tribe. Puang Matua was the nearest the Toraja originally came to

the concept of a supreme being, and early missionaries began prayers in their churches with his name.

The Toraja have a long and involved creation mythology dividing creation into three worlds, each watched over by its own god. The Sadan Toraja also had a rigid caste system and a slave class. Although the Dutch abolished slavery, its effects continued long after. There is also a class of nobles which continues to be important. Christianity undermined some traditional Toraja beliefs.

Although it is one of the five articles of the Pancasila that every Indonesian must believe in *one* god, the Toraja gained official sanction to maintain their animist and polytheistic beliefs, possibly due to the tenuous argument that Toraja beliefs were similar to those of the Balinese for whom an exception had already been made.

Funerals *Tomate* (funeral) literally means 'dead person', and of all Toraja ceremonies the most important are those concerned with sending a dead person to the afterworld. Without proper funeral rites the spirit of the deceased will cause misfortune to its family. The funeral sacrifices, ceremonies and feasts also impress the gods with the importance of the deceased, so that the spirit can intercede effectively on behalf of living relatives. Funerals are sometimes held at the *rante*, funeral sites marked by one or more megaliths. In Tanatoraja there are several arcs or groups of roughly hewn stone slabs, some as high as four metres, usually surrounding a big rock like a sacrificial altar. The origins and purpose of these stone circles are unknown but the efforts to raise even one stone was phenomenal and involved scores of men.

At a funeral, bamboo pavilions for the family and guests are constructed around a field. The dead person is said to preside over the funeral from the high-roofed tower constructed at one end of the field. Like the Balinese, the Toraja generally have two funerals, one immediately after a death, and an elaborate second funeral after sufficient time has elapsed to make the preparations and raise the necessary cash. Until the final feast the corpse remains in the house where the person died. Food is cooked and offered to the dead person; those of noble birth have attendants who stay in their immediate presence from the hour of death to the day of their final progress to the tomb.

The souls of the dead can only go to Puya, the afterworld or realm of the dead, when the entire death ritual has been carried out. A spirit's status in the afterlife is the same as its owner's status in the present life; even the souls of animals follow their masters to the next life – hence the animal sacrifices at funerals. The story also goes that the soul of the deceased will ride the souls of the slaughtered buffaloes and pigs to heaven. The trip to Puya requires a strong buffalo because the long and difficult journey crosses hundreds of mountains and thousands of valleys.

Sons and daughters of the deceased have an equal chance to inherit their parents' property, but their share depends on the number of buffaloes they slaughter at the funeral feast. Buffalo have traditionally been a symbol of wealth and power – even land could be paid for in buffaloes. A modelled buffalo head, fitted with real horns, is the figurehead of traditional Toraja houses, buffalo motifs are carved or painted on the walls of houses, and horns decorate gable poles.

The more important the deceased the more buffaloes must be sacrificed: one for a commoner, four, eight, 12 or 24 as you move up the social scale. The age of the deceased also determines the number of animals slaughtered; only one pig may be killed for a young child or infant. Pigs are sacrificed at all rituals as pig meat is the food of the dead in the afterlife, as well as for the guests at the funeral ceremony.

The Dutch imposed limits on the number of buffaloes that could be slaughtered at a funeral, since the temptation to honour the dead and impress the living by extravagant sacrifices was so great that whole families would be bankrupted. Today the Indonesian government is also trying to limit the destruction of wealth by taxing each slaughtered animal. However, the funeral ceremonies of today seem to have lost none of their ostentation – they are still a ruinous financial burden on families.

Funerals can be spread out over several days and involve hundreds of guests. The wooden effigies alone can cost nearly a year's wages for many Indonesians. Bamboo pavilions are constructed specially for the occasion, with a death tower at one end. After the guests display their presents of pigs and buffaloes, the traditional Mabadong song and dance is performed. This is a ceremonial re-enactment of the cycle of human life and the life story of the deceased. It also bids farewell to the soul of the deceased and relays the hope that the soul will arrive in the afterworld safely. Cigarettes are circulated, and pork and rice dishes (washed down with alcoholic tuak) are served to the guests by immaculately clad women, their hair tied back in large buns, playing the part of waitresses and squishing barefoot through the thick mud of the compound. The following day, in the early morning, buffalo fights may be held.

Funeral ceremonies last from one to seven days, depending on the wealth and social status of the deceased. For the longest and most ostentatious ceremonies months, or even years, may be required to accumulate sufficient money, plan the ceremony and to allow time for relatives living far away to make arrangements to return home to take part. Hundreds of buffaloes and pigs might be slaughtered at such a funeral; there would be buffalo fights and *sisemba* kick-fighting, and maybe cock fights at the end of the ceremony. The Mabadong would be performed, and maybe other dances like the Maranding, a war dance performed at the burial service of a patriotic nobleman to remind the people of his heroic deeds. Another dance is the Makatia, which reminds the people of the deceased's generosity and loyalty. Songs may also be sung, and these are meant to console the bereaved family or convey their grief to the other guests at the funeral.

Graves & Tau Tau Like the Sumbanese, the Toraja believe you can take it with you and the dead generally go well equipped to their graves. Since this led to grave plundering the Toraja started to hide their dead in caves (of which there are plenty around) or hew niches out of rock faces.

These caves were hollowed out by specialist cave builders who were traditionally paid in buffaloes – and since the building of a cave would cost several buffaloes only the rich could afford it. Although the exterior of the cave grave looks small, the interior is large enough to entomb an entire family. The coffins would go deep inside the caves, and you can see, sitting in balconies on the rock face in front of the caves, the *tau tau* – life-size, carved wooden effigies of the dead.

Tau tau are carved only for the upper classes. Their expense alone rules out their use for poor people. Traditionally the statues only showed the sex of the person, not the likeness, but now they attempt to imitate the likeness of the person's face. The making of tau tau appears to have been a recent innovation, possibly originating in the late 19th century. The type of wood used reflects the status and wealth of the deceased, jackfruit (nangka) wood being the most expensive. After the deceased has been entombed and the tau tau placed in front of the grave, offerings are placed in the palm of the tau tau.

Apart from cave graves there are also house graves – houses made of wood in which the coffin is placed when there is no rocky outcrop or cliff face to carve a niche in. Most of the hanging graves in which the wooden coffins were hung from high cliffs have rotted away. Sometimes the coffins may be placed at the foot of a mountain. Babies who died before teething were placed in hollowed-out sections of living trees.

Most tau tau seem to be in a permanent state of disrepair but in a ceremony after harvest time the coffins are supposed to be wrapped in new material and the clothes of the tau tau replaced. Occasionally left lying around the more obscure grave caves is the *duba-duba*, a platform in the shape of a traditional house which is used to carry the coffin and body of a nobleman to the grave.

Houses One of the first things you notice about Tanatoraja is the size and grandeur of the tongkonan, the traditional houses, raised on piles and topped with a massive roof. Throughout Indonesia a house is more than just a home. Each of the scores of Indonesian ethnic groups have their own distinctive form of architecture and the design of a traditional house has a deep symbolic quality. Such houses are called rumah adat, which translates as 'traditional house', but actually connotes an emotional tie with a whole range of customs, a social organisation, laws, religion and mythology. The tongkonan houses of Tanatoraja are closely bound up with Toraja traditions; one of their important functions is as a constant reminder of the authority of the original noble families whose descendants alone have the right to build such houses.

In many parts of Indonesia traditional houses are no longer being built and the skills to make them are being lost. More and more traditional houses are being replaced by houses built on the modern Javanese model of brick and cement walls and galvanised iron roofs. Often this is simply because of cost and comfort but they may also be a conscious denial of the traditions of the past and a means of identifying with the dominant Javanese influence in Indonesia.

Whether the tongkonan house will also die out remains to be seen. For the moment the tourist trade has inspired the renovation of some older houses and even the construction of new ones purely for the benefit of visitors. There are a number of villages in the region still composed entirely of traditional houses but only a small percentage of the Tanatoraja population lives in traditional-style houses. Most of these houses have rice barns, surrounded by several ordinary bungalows on stilts, like the houses of the Bugis and Makassarese.

The roof, rearing up at either end, is the most striking aspect of a tongkonan house and is somewhat similar to the Batak houses of north Sumatra. Some people think that the house represents the head of a buffalo and the rising roof represents the horns. Others suggest that the roof looks more like a boat and that the raised ends represent the bow and the stern. The houses all face north – some say because it was from the north that the ancestors of the Toraja came, others because the north (and the east) are regarded as the sphere of life, the realm of the gods.

The high gables are supported by poles and the wall panels are decorated with painted engravings of a geometrical design, of which the stylised buffalo head is the most striking. Other designs may include the entire buffalo, or two buffaloes fighting horns to horns. On these panels red is meant to symbolise human life, as red is the colour of blood; white is the colour of flesh and bone and a symbol of purity; yellow represents god's blessing and power; black symbolises death and darkness. Traditionally the colours were all natural – black is the soot from cooking pots, yellow and red are coloured earth, and white is lime. Tuak was used to improve the staying power of the colours. Artisans would decorate the houses and be paid in buffaloes. A realistic carving of a buffalo's head decorates the front part of the house. Numerous buffalo horns are attached to the front pole which supports the gable.

The beams and supports of the Toraja houses are cut so that they all neatly slot or are pegged together; no metal nails are used. The older houses have roofs of overlapping pieces of bamboo but newer houses use corrugated metal sheets. Standing on thick solid piles, the rectangular body of the house is small in contrast to the roof, and consists of two or three dark rooms with low doors and small windows. If necessary the whole house can actually be put on runners and moved to another location.

Toraja houses always face a line-up of rice barns – wealthy owners may have whole fleets of barns. The barns look like miniature houses and, like the living area in a house, the rice storage area is surprisingly small considering the overall size of the structure.

The barn has a small door at one end and the surface of the walls and the high gables are usually decorated. The rice storage chamber is raised about two metres off the ground on four smooth columns of wood, polished to prevent rats climbing up them. About 60 cm from the ground is a wooden sitting platform stretched between the pillars. The boat-shaped roof shelters an area about twice the size of the rice chamber.

The Toraja have a number of ceremonies connected with the construction of a tongkonan house. Construction is preceded by the sacrificial killing of a chicken, pig or buffalo; its successful completion is celebrated with a large feast in which many pigs and at least one buffalo are killed.

Toraja dancing is graceful but less complicated than Balinese or Javanese, and the accompaniment is primarily to the beat of a large drum (or sometimes to taped music). What the dance lacks in complexity is more than made up for by the enthusiasm of members of the audience who dash onto the dance ground and stuff 5000 and 10,000 rp notes into the performers' head-bands.

Sports As on the islands of Sumbawa and Lombok, there's a unique form of man-to-man combat in Tanatoraja, an unarmed contest called sisemba. The aim of the game is to kick your opponent into submission. It's something like Thai boxing except that use of the hands is banned, and you can't kick your opponent when he is down (very sporting). More a feat of strength and endurance now, the original aim of the contest was to instil courage in Toraja children and youth – a useful attribute for a people once hemmed in by their coastal enemies and occasionally at war with each other.

The fights are held at the time of the rice harvest or just after (June to early August), which is also the most popular time for funerals and house ceremonies. Fights are held between individuals or teams of two or more and the women look on and cheer their favourites. When the men of one village challenge another anything up to 200 a side is possible.

The Toraja had another contest known as the *sibamba,* in which the contestants used wooden clubs to hit each other, protecting themselves from the blows with a bull-hide shield (very similar to the contests found on Lombok, eastern Bali and Sumbawa). Apparently it was banned during the Dutch rule. A more docile sport is the game known as *takro,* which uses a rattan ball which is kicked and bounced over a bamboo stick about a metre high and fixed parallel to the ground. It's something like volleyball but uses only two or three players, and only the head and hands can touch the ball.

RANTEPAO

Rantepao, with a population of roughly 15,000, is the largest town and commercial centre in Tanatoraja. It's also the major travellers' centre in Sulawesi. The places to see are scattered around the lush, green countryside surrounding Rantepao. At 700 metres elevation, this area has pleasant, cool evenings.

Information

Tourist Office The tourist office is on the south side of town. They're open from 7.30 am until 2 pm Monday to Saturday. They're helpful, have a good map of the area and keep a list of dates and locations of the funeral ceremonies.

Money The Bank Rakyat Indonesia and Bank Danamon are opposite each other on Jalan Jendral Ahmad Yani. Bank Danamon gives slightly better rates, but both give lower exchange rates than banks in Ujung Pandang. The best exchange rates are available from the moneychanger at the Hotel Indra. Abadi is the name of a moneychanger at the intersection of Jalan Jendral Ahmad Yani and Jalan Pangeran Diponegoro, but his rates are even lower than the banks.

Post & Telecommunications The post office is on Jalan Jenderal Ahmad Yani opposite the Bank Rakyat Indonesia. The telecom office is next to the post office.

Books The locally produced *A Guide to Toraja* by A T Marampa is available in some Rantepao shops in English, German and French. It lists dances, ceremonies and some local walks, and is quite a useful little book.

Also locally produced is *Toraja – An Introduction to a Unique Culture* by L T Tangdilintin & M Syafei in their own unique and impenetrable style. Much more readable is *Life & Death of the Toraja People* by Stanislaus Sandarupa. These books are sold in the souvenir shops on the main street in Rantepao.

White Stranger – Six Moons in Celebes by Harry Wilcox was first published in 1949. This British army officer spent six months in the Rantepao district in the late 1940s, after the Dutch had re-occupied the area and included it in their state of East Indonesia. Wilcox lived in the village of Labo to the south-east of Rantepao.

Organised Tours

Travel agents in Bali organise brief tours to Tanatoraja. A typical four-day trip costs around US$250 per person plus air fare. In Bali try the travel agencies at the larger tourist hotels in Kuta, Legian and Sanur. Trekking tours to Tanatoraja and Mamasa can also be organised.

Things to See

The height of the tourist season in Tanatoraja is July and August – the European holiday period – when Rantepao is packed out with foreigners; French, German and Japanese tour groups descend on the place in plague proportions and hotel prices suddenly sky-rocket.

The best time to visit Tanatoraja is in the gap between the end of the rainy season and the onset of the tourist season. The rainy season usually begins in December and ends in March – although there can still be a considerable amount of rain after that. Then the rice crops are harvested (from May to August) and the ceremonies begin.

The buffalo and pig market *(bolu)* is held every six days. Enquire at your hotel or the

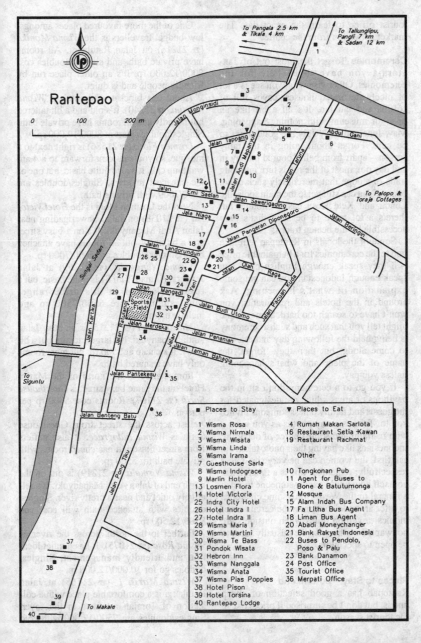

Rantepao

0   100   200 m

To Pangala 2.5 km
& Tikala 4 km

To Tallunglipu,
Pangli 7 km
& Sadan 12 km

Jalan Manginsidi

Jalan Tappang

Jalan Andi Mapanyuki

Jalan Emi Saelan

Jala Niaga

Jalan Landorundun

Jalan Mangadi

Jalan Ratulangi

Jalan Jend Ahmad Yani

Jalan Merdeka

Jalan Penanian

Jalan Taman Bahagia

Jalan Pantekesu

Jalan Benteng Batu

Jalan Pong Tiku

Jalan Kartika

Sungai Sadan

Jalan Tappang

Jalan Taruna

Jalan Abdul Gani

Jalan Sawerigading

Jalan Pangeran Diponegoro

Jalan Beringin

Jalan Olah Raga

Jalan Pasar Kuda

Jalan Budi Utomo

To Palopo &
Toraja Cottages

To Siguntu

To Makale

Sports Field

■ Places to Stay	▼ Places to Eat
1 Wisma Rosa	4 Rumah Makan Sarlota
2 Wisma Nirmala	16 Restaurant Setia Kawan
3 Wisma Wisata	19 Restaurant Rachmat
5 Wisma Linda	
6 Wisma Irama	**Other**
7 Guesthouse Sarla	
8 Wisma Indograce	10 Tongkonan Pub
9 Marlin Hotel	11 Agent for Buses to
13 Losmen Flora	Bone & Batutumonga
14 Hotel Victoria	12 Mosque
25 Indra City Hotel	15 Alam Indah Bus Company
26 Hotel Indra I	17 Fa Litha Bus Agent
27 Hotel Indra II	18 Liman Bus Agent
28 Wisma Maria I	20 Abadi Moneychanger
29 Wisma Martini	21 Bank Rakyat Indonesia
30 Wisma Te Bass	22 Buses to Pendolo,
31 Pondok Wisata	Poso & Palu
32 Hebron Inn	23 Bank Danamon
33 Wisma Nanggala	24 Post Office
34 Wisma Anata	35 Tourist Office
37 Wisma Pias Poppies	36 Merpati Office
38 Hotel Pison	
39 Hotel Torsina	
40 Rantepao Lodge	

tourist office to learn the exact day. The market is two km from the centre.

Ceremonies To get the most out of Tanatoraja you have to be here for the ceremonies. Otherwise what you see is a lot of nicely decorated houses, caves full of coffins and tau tau. It's all a bit like an open-air museum with nothing happening. May, June and early July are good times to be here. Forget about going in the rainy season – apart from being poured on day in and day out, most of the roads turn into long trails of sludge that mercilessly suck down bemos. You can still get to the main spots like Londa and Kete Kesu easily enough, but there's a lot more to be seen that's only accessible by the beaten tracks.

Some of the locals in Rantepao will take you to the ceremonies for a bargainable price – if they speak enough English or if you speak enough Indonesian you can get some explanation of what's happening. Ask around in the hotels and restaurants; you won't have to search too hard. Some people might tell you that such and such a ceremony is being held the following day and ask you to come along, but then they 'forget' the name of the place and what's happening unless you pay.

If you go to a ceremony don't sit in the pavilions or areas which are designated for the guests and family unless someone invites you to. Take as many photos as you want – with restraint and some degree of decorum; Indonesians like having their photo taken but ask first; the women can be very shy. Dress respectfully; remember this is a funeral, ask yourself how you'd expect someone to act at a funeral in the West. Bring some cigarettes to offer around. There may be certain ceremonies or certain times when outsiders are not wanted – otherwise they usually seem to be open to spectators.

Places to Stay – bottom end
Rantepao has a good selection of cheap hotels, but don't be surprised if prices rise in the tourist season.

One of the more favoured places amongst low-budget travellers is the *Wisma Monika* (☎ 21216) on Jalan Ratulangi. All rooms have private bath, and singles/doubles cost 8000/12,000 rp. It's an older place run by friendly people and is quiet.

About one block to the south is *Wisma Martini* (☎ 21240). It's old and a bit tattered but friendly and all rooms have private bath. Singles/doubles start at 8000/10,000 rp.

Losmen Flora (☎ 21586) is right next to a mosque, so you can look forward to a 4 am wake-up call. It's also quite basic, but one of the cheapest in town. Singles/doubles are 4000/7000 with private bath.

Near the Losmen Flora is the *Hotel Victoria* (☎ 21038) on Jalan Sawerigading near Jalan Andi Mapanyuki. It's on a busy street and a bit noisy, but all rooms have attached bath. Singles/doubles are 5000/7000 rp.

Wisma Nanggala (☎ 21269) at Jalan Jenderal Ahmad Yani 81 is quite basic, but a reasonable deal in this price range. Singles/doubles are 6500/7500 rp and include private bath.

Marlin Hotel (☎ 21215) is on busy Jalan Andi Mapanyuki. It's large and airy but a bit noisy. It's cheap at 5500 rp, but most rooms only have a shared bath.

Immediately to the north of the Marlin Hotel on the same busy street is *Guesthouse Sarla* (☎ 21167). Rooms cost 5000 rp per person.

Just across the street from Guesthouse Sarla is *Wisma Indograce*. It also suffers from street noise but has cheap rooms with private bath for 5500 rp.

Wisma Nirmala (☎ 21319) is out on the north end of Jalan Andi Mapanyuki. It's relatively quiet and near a pretty river. Singles/doubles with attached bath will cost you 8500/12,500 rp.

Further to the north, across the river, is *Wisma Rosa* (☎ 21075). It has a quiet location and friendly management. Singles/doubles go for 10,000/12,000 rp.

Wisma Maria I (☎ 21165) at Jalan Ratulangi is a comfortable place with a collection of Torajan artefacts in the foyer. Singles/doubles are 7500/12,000 with cold water baths, or 13,000/20,000 rp with hot water.

Wisma Linda (☎ 21113) is on Jalan Abdul Gani, a quiet back street with lots of greenery. Singles/doubles go for 5000/8000 rp.

Places to Stay – middle

The *Hotel Indra I* (☎ 21163) at Jalan Landorundun 63 is very pleasant, with a central courtyard garden. There are actually two hotels – *Indra I* and *Indra II*, the former costing 21,000 rp for a single with attached bath. There is a moneychanger here, and a very good restaurant. Almost next door at number 55, the *Indra City Hotel* is under the same management and has good carpeted singles/doubles at 39,000/50,700. It's clean and entirely habitable but lacks the pleasant garden that distinguishes some of the other hotels in this town.

Pondok Wisata is a large, new place on Jalan Pembangunan with spotless singles/doubles for 20,000/25,000 rp, or 45,000 rp for a large room with balcony.

Just a few doors to the south on the same street is *Hebron Inn* (☎ 21519), a clean and quiet place where singles/doubles are 45,000/49,000 rp.

Around the corner is *Wisma Te Bass* (☎ 21415), an old but pleasant place run by a couple – the husband speaks English and the wife speaks Dutch. Singles/doubles are 12,000/15,000, all with private bath.

Just a little further south at the end of the street is *Wisma Anata* (☎ 21356) where all rooms are triples. For one or two persons, it costs 20,000 rp and for three it's 25,000 rp.

Wisma Irama (☎ 21371) at Jalan Abdul Gani 16 is a beautiful and quiet hotel with a large garden. It's on the north-east outskirts of town. The cheaper rooms have attached bath with cold showers and cost 15,600 rp. Deluxe rooms with hot showers go for 35,000 rp.

Places to Stay – top end

Hotel Indra II (☎ 21442) is the new wing of the Hotel Indra complex, and costs 62,000/78,000 rp for beautiful singles/doubles facing a courtyard garden.

Rantepao's main tourist hotel is the *Toraja Cottages* (☎ 21089, 21475) on Jalan Pangeran Diponegoro, three km out of town, with rooms starting at 80,000 rp.

Places to Eat

There are various restaurants, rumah makan and warungs around Rantepao, some of them catering mostly to the tourist trade, others to the locals.

Restaurant Setia Kawan (☎ 21264) at Jalan Andi Mapanyuki 32 does good Indonesian and Chinese food.

The *Hotel Indra I* has a reasonably cheap and good Indonesian restaurant – the mie goreng is especially recommended. Just to the south of the Hotel Indra on Jalan Ratulangi is *Rumah Makan Mambo* which does good Indonesian and Toraja food. *Rumah Makan Sarlota* on the northern end of Jalan Andi Mapanyuki is also popular with travellers.

Restaurant Rachmat on Jalan Abdul Gani at the traffic circle caters mainly to tourist groups. The food is quite expensive, although servings are usually quite large.

If you want to self-cater, Toko Remaja is the main grocery store and department store in town. It's adjacent to Bank Damamon. Going to the ceremonies is a good chance to try black rice cooked in coconut milk, and vegetables with pork and buffalo meat cooked in bamboo tubes over an open fire.

The kids demanding candy ('gula gula mister') can be very persistent. To indulge your own sweet tooth, head for Rantepao market. Try *wadi bandung*, a sweet rice-and-grated-coconut confection wrapped in paper; or kajang goreng, an almost over-sweet concoction of peanuts and treacle (hard) wrapped in a dry palm leaf; or a baje, a sticky rice and molasses mixture rolled in a dry palm leaf like a Christmas cracker.

Tuak Rantepao market has local food and there is a whole section devoted to the sale of the alcoholic drink known as *tuak*. Although known as 'palm wine', tuak is actually sap from the sugar palm, which the Torajas call *induk*. Every few months the palm, with its huge, dark metallic-green fronds and untidy black-haired trunk, produces a great cluster of round, dark fruit. The stem is pierced close to the fruit and if sugary sap flows from the wound the fruit cluster is cut off and a receptacle is hung to catch the juice dripping from the amputated stump.

The sap can be boiled down to produce crystalline sugar or it can be left to ferment to produce tuak, which is also known as *toddy* in India. Buy it by the bamboo-tube full in the market or drink it by the glassful at night in the warungs outside. Tuak is carried into town in long bamboo containers frothing at the top, is left to ferment all day and then consumed at night. It comes in a variety of strengths, ranging from lemonade-coloured to the stronger orange or red.

Southern Sulawesi grows the most extraordinary variety of bananas: from tiny, sweet specimens grown in Nanggala to the goliaths found on the lowlands and which you'll see sold in warungs on the way up from Ujung Pandang. Tanatoraja is also noted for its fine-quality coffee; there are several plantations here and you also see the plants growing wild.

Entertainment

The *Tongkonan Pub* on Jalan Andi Mapanyuki offers the only real nightlife in town. It's open from around 8 pm until midnight or 1 am.

Things to Buy

Woodcarving, weaving and basketry are the main crafts of Tanatoraja – some villages are noted for particular specialities. Woodcarvings include panels carved like the decorations on traditional houses and painted in the four traditional colours – black, white, yellow and brown. Bamboo containers with designs carved and burnt on them are decorative as well as functional – ideal for keeping spaghetti. Other artefacts sold in the souvenir shops include mini replicas of Toraja houses with incredibly exaggerated overhanging roofs. Other interesting pieces include hand-spun Toraja weaving and necklaces made of plant seeds.

All these things can be bought either in the villages or in the shops in Rantepao, most of which are in the large bus terminal at Jalan Andi Mapanyuki and Jalan Landorundun.

Getting There & Away

The entrance to Rantepao is impressive: huge, rocky cliffs rise out of a sea of green rice paddies and forests studded with Toraja houses. On the way up to Rantepao by road from Ujung Pandang you see pine, clove, grapefruit, papaya, coconut and cassava (tapioca) trees, as well as Bugis stilt-houses.

Air There is an airport at Makale, 25 km south of Rantepao. Merpati has three flights a week between Ujung Pandang and Makale and the fare is 70,000 rp.

Bus There are regular buses between Ujung Pandang and Rantepao. In Rantepao the offices of the bus companies are around Jalan Andi Mapanyuki in the centre of town. The three main bus companies on the Rantepao-Ujung Pandang route are Fa Litha, Liman and Alam Indah. Departures in each direction are typically at 7 am, 1 pm and 7 pm. The trip from Ujung Pandang (330 km) takes nine to 10 hours and costs 8000 rp. Pare Pare to Rantepao takes five hours and costs 4500 rp.

Buses head north from Rantepao through central Sulawesi to Pendolo, Tentena, Poso and Palu. Ticket agents are at the intersection of Jalan Landorundun and Jalan Andi Mapanyuki in the centre of town. The biggest bus company on this route is Bina Wisata, which runs two buses weekly on Tuesday and Saturday. Fares from Rantepao to Pendolo, Tentena and Poso are all 20,000 rp. To Palu, it's 25,000 rp. Travelling times from Rantepao are: Pendolo, 10 hours; Tentena, 11½ hours; Poso, 12½ hours; Palu, 20 hours. You can also make this trip by bemo – see the section on Pendolo for details.

Bemos run downhill to the coastal city of Palopo (3000 rp), taking two hours for the journey but 2½ hours in the other direction. There are buses from Rantepao to Soroako on Danau (lake) Matana and the road is surfaced all the way. The trip takes about 10 hours and the fare is around 6000 rp.

Getting Around

To/From the Airport A direct bus from the Merpati ticket office in Rantepao to the airport guarantees that you will reach your flight on time, but the bus costs a steep 7500 rp.

Local Transport Central Rantepao is small and easy to walk around. Becaks hang around the bus terminals, but you probably won't have much use for them.

Bemos run from Rantepao to various destinations in the surrounding region. Bemos run almost continuously from Rantepao to Makale and you can get off at the signs for Londa or Lemo and walk. There are also frequent bemos towards Palopo for the sights in that direction.

Fares from Rantepao are: Nanggala 500 rp, Londa turn-off 400 rp, Tilanga turn-off 400 rp, Lemo turn-off 400 rp, Makale 500 rp and Sadan 800 rp.

Motorcycles can be rented from the Marlin Hotel for 3000 rp per hour. Allow for two days of recovery after one day of riding! It might be cheaper for a group to charter a bemo or a jeep.

Apart from the roads to Makale, Palopo, Sadan, Kete Kesu and a few other places, most of the roads around Rantepao are terrible. Some are constructed out of compacted boulders – you don't get stuck but your joints get rattled loose. If trekking, bring good footwear to negotiate the mud and the rocks. Take a water bottle, something to eat, a torch (flashlight) in case you end up walking at night, and an umbrella or raincoat. Even in the dry season it's likely to rain in the afternoon.

AROUND RANTEPAO

The following places (distance in km from Rantepao) are all within fairly easy reach on day trips, but you can make longer trips staying overnight in villages or camping out. If you stay in villages don't exploit the Toraja

hospitality – make sure you pay your way. Guides are useful if you have a common language, but in some ways it's better without a guide. The Toraja are friendly and used to tourists so they rarely bother you and it's great to get out on your own into the beautiful countryside around Rantepao. If you're really short on time you could hire a bemo and whip round the main sites in a day or two – but that's not the way to see this place!

Mamasa

Mamasa to Bittuang (58 km) is one of the best treks in the area, but it isn't easy. Most travellers walk from Mamasa to Bittuang (58 km), which takes three days. Mamasa is at 1200 metres above sea level and is therefore quite chilly at night, so come prepared. The track is easy to follow, and there are plenty of villages along the way where you can stay. You can do this trek in either direction, but from Mamasa to Bittuang is a little easier since it's mostly downhill. You can reach Mamasa by taking a bus from Pare Pare to Polewali and then onwards to Mamasa. Bittuang is connected by road to Makale, from where there are frequent bemos to Rantepao.

Gunung Sesean

At 2150 metres above sea level, this is not the highest peak in Sulawesi, but it's certainly the most popular with climbers. The summit is accessible via a trail which begins in the town of Batutumonga, which is about a four-hour walk to the north-west of Rantepao. You can spend the night in Batutumonga, and from there, the return trip to the summit takes five hours. A guide might be useful, but the trail is so well established that you can probably manage on your own.

Karasbik (1 km)

On the outskirts of Rantepao, just off the road leading to Makale, the traditional-style houses here are arranged in a horseshoe around a cluster of megaliths. The complex of houses may have been erected some years ago for a single funeral ceremony, but some are now inhabited. In the past, temporary houses would be built around a rante for use at a funeral and when the funeral was finished these would be demolished or burnt.

Kete Kesu (6 km)

Just off the main road south of Rantepao, the village of Kete Kesu is reputed for its wood-carving.

On the cliff face behind the village are some grave caves and some very old hanging graves. The rotting coffins are suspended on wooden beams under an overhang. Others, full of bones and skulls, lie rotting on the ground. If you continue along the vague trail heading uphill you'll come to another grave cave. There are no tau tau, just coffins and bones, similarly neglected. One of the houses in the village has several tau tau on display.

The houses at Kete Kesu are decorated with enough handicrafts to fill a souvenir floor at Harrods; the village is a tourist museum, no one seems to live here anymore and there are surfaced paths to the main caves, but it's still an interesting site.

Take a bemo from Rantepao to Kete Kesu. From Kete Kesu you can continue walking to Sullukang and then along the track to Palatokke.

Buntu Pune

On the way to Kete Kesu, stop by at Buntu Pune where there are two tongkonan houses and six rice barns. The story goes that one of the two houses was built by a nobleman named Pong Marambaq at the beginning of this century. During the Dutch rule he was appointed head of the local district, but planned to rebel and was subsequently exiled to Ambon where he died. His corpse was brought back to Toraja and buried at the hill to the north of this village.

Sullukang

Just past Kete Kesu and off to the side of the main road is the village of Sullukang. There is a rante here, marked by a number of large, rough-hewn megaliths.

Palatokke (9 km)

In this beautiful area of lush rice paddies and traditional houses there is an enormous cliff face containing several grave caves and hanging graves. Access to the caves is difficult but the scenery alone makes it worthwhile.

There is a story amongst the Toraja that Palatokke is the name of a person who was able to climb the rock face, his palms being like that of a gecko which could cling easily to the wall. When he died, it is said, his corpse was put into an *erong* (wooden coffin) and hung on these cliffs. In another part of Tanatoraja there is a story that Palatokke refers to a group of people who were able to climb the rock face like geckos. These people are said to have been a special class of workers whose job it was to hang the erong of noblemen on the cliff face by climbing the cliff without using ladders!

From Palatokke you could walk to Labo and on to Randanbatu, where there are supposed to be more graves, then continue to Balik, Sangalla, Suaya and Makale.

Londa (6 km)

Two km off the Rantepao to Makale road is this very extensive burial cave at the base of a massive cliff face. A bemo from Rantepao heading towards Makale will drop you at the turn-off to Londa, from where it's a short walk.

The entrance to the cave is guarded by a balcony of tau tau. Inside the cave is a collection of coffins, many of them rotted away, with the bones either scattered or thrown into piles. Other coffins hold the bones of several family members – it's an old Toraja custom that all people who have lived together in one family house should also be buried together in a family grave. There are other cave graves in Tanatoraja where no coffin is used at all – the body is wrapped in cloth, placed in a niche in the rock face and then the door of the niche is tightly closed. A local myth says that the people buried in the Londa caves are the descendants of Tangdilinoq, chief of the Toraja at the time when they were pushed out of the Enrekang region by new arrivals and forced to move into the highlands.

Kids hang around outside the Londa caves with oil lamps to guide you around (1000 rp). Unless you've got a strong torch you really *do* need a guide with a lamp. Inside the caves, the coffins (some of them liberally decorated with graffiti) and skulls seem to have been placed in strategic locations for the benefit of sightseers. Still, it's an interesting site and a beautiful location.

Close to the Londa graves is Pabaisenan (Liang Pia) where the coffins of babies can be found hanging from a tree.

Lemo (11 km)
This is probably the most interesting burial area in Tanatoraja. The sheer rock face has a whole series of balconies for the tau tau. The biggest balcony has a dozen figures – white eyes and black pupils, outstretched arms – like spectators at a sports event. One tall figure stands on a slightly depressed section of floor so it can fit in.

There is a story that the graves are for descendants of a Toraja chief who, hundreds of years ago, reigned over the surrounding district and built his house on top of the cliff into which the graves are now cut. Because the mountain was part of his property only his descendants could use it. The chief himself was buried elsewhere, as the art of cutting grave caves had not been developed then.

It's a good idea to go early in the morning so you get the sun on the rows of figures – by 9 am their heads are in the shadows. A bemo from Rantepao will drop you off at the road to Lemo. From there it's a 15-minute walk to the tau tau.

Suaya & Tampangallo (25 km)
Apart from those at Lemo, it is becoming increasingly difficult to see many tau tau in Rantepao. This is because so many of them have been stolen by grave robbers that the Toraja have taken to keeping the remaining ones in their own homes.

One place where you can still see substantial numbers of tau tau is at Tampangallo, due east of Makale and very close to Suaya. Coming from Sangalla, there's a signpost about a km before you get to Suaya. Turn off the road and walk about 500 metres through the rice paddies to a place where there are over 40 tau tau.

The local graves belong to the chiefs of Sangalla, descendants of the mythical divine being, Tamborolangiq, who is believed to have introduced the caste system, the death rituals and techniques of agriculture into Torajan society. The former royal families of Makale, Sangalla and Menkendek all claimed descent from Tamborolangiq who is said to have descended from heaven by a stone staircase.

Tilanga (11 km)
There are several cold and hot springs in the Toraja area and this natural cool-water swimming pool is very pretty. It's an interesting walk along the muddy trails and through the rice paddies from Lemo to Tilanga, but keep asking directions along the way. The natural pool at Tilanga is uphill from a derelict concrete swimming pool and decaying changing rooms. Other natural swimming pools in the Rantepao area include the hot spring at Makula, 20 km east of Makale on the road to Sangalla. Another is Sarambu Sikore at the base of a waterfall in Mamullu.

From Tilanga you can continue to Londa.

Singki (1 km)
This rather steep hill is just west across the river from Rantepao. There's a slippery, somewhat overgrown trail to the summit with its panoramic view across the town and the surrounding countryside. Rantepao looks surprisingly large from high up. From Singki you can continue walking down the dirt road to Siguntu, an interesting walk past the rice fields.

Siguntu (7 km)
This traditional village is on a slight rise to the west of the main road. The path is not obvious so keep asking directions. The walk

from Rantepao via Singki and Siguntu to the main road at Alang Alang near the Londa burial site is pleasant. Stop on the way at the traditional village of Mendoe, six km from Rantepao and just off the Siguntu to Alang Alang road. At Alang Alang, seven km from Rantepao where a covered bridge crosses the river, you could head to Londa or back to Rantepao or Makale or, alternatively, remain on the west side of the river and continue walking to the villages of Langda and Madandan.

Marante (6 km)

This very fine traditional village lies close to the road to Palopo. Near Marante there are stone and hanging graves, with several tau tau, skulls on the coffins and a cave with scattered bones.

From Marante you can cross the river on the suspension bridge and walk to the village of Ba'ta, which is set in attractive rice-paddy country.

Nanggala (16 km)

In the same direction but further off the Palopo road, this traditional village has a particularly grandiose traditional house and an impressive fleet of 14 rice barns! The rice barns have a bizarre array of motifs carved into them, including soldiers with guns, Western women and automobiles. Bemos from Rantepao take you straight there for 300 rp.

Paniki & Buntao

From Nanggala you can walk to Paniki and Buntao, a very long walk along a dirt track up and down the Toraja hills. The trail starts next to the rice barns. It's a three-hour walk from Nanggala to the Paniki district, and along the road you'll see coffee-plantation machines grinding and packing coffee into sacks. It's a long, tedious trudge and can be very hot, so take lots of water. From Paniki it's a two-hour walk to the Buntao turn-off; there are supposed to be some house graves with tau tau there. Alternatively, catch a bemo to Rantepao. Buntao is about 15 km

from Rantepao. Two or three km beyond Buntao is Tembamba, which has more graves and is noted for its fine scenery.

Sangalla (22 km)

From this junction you can head south-east to Makula, west to the Rantepao to Makale road, or north to Labo and the road to Kete Kesu. There are occasional bemos from Makale and Rantepao to Sangalla. At Makula there is a hot spring and bath-house.

Sadan (13 km)

Sadan is the weaving centre of Tanatoraja and the women have a tourist market where they sell their weaving. All of it is handmade on simple, back-strap looms. You can see the women making the cloth using this technique. There are bemos direct to Sadan along a surfaced road for 500 rp.

Pangli (7 km)

To the north of Rantepao, Pangli has tau tau and house graves. House graves are an interesting innovation used when there are no rock faces available for carving out burial niches. Graves are dug in the earth and a small Toraja-style house is built over the top. Each grave is used for all the members of the family and the bodies are wrapped in cloth and entombed without coffins.

Palawa (9 km)

This traditional village a km or two north of Pangli has tongkonan houses and rice barns.

Bori (8 km)

Bori is the site of an impressive rante. A km south is Parinding, which has tongkonan houses and rice barns.

Lempo (15 km)

West of Palawa, Lempo is a traditional village set in an area of stunning paddy fields.

Batutumonga (23 km)

Situated on the slopes of Gunung Sesean, this is a good viewpoint from where you can see a large part of Tanatoraja. Occasional bemos from Rantepao (more on market day) take 1½ to two hours along an abominable road.

You can walk from either Lokomata or Batutumonga to Rantepao. One traveller described it as 'a beautiful walk and probably one of the highlights of my trip (it is all downhill too). The path is easy to follow as virtually all tracks lead to Rantepao and there are many small villages on the way down, so ask for directions.'

Alternatively, you could take the bemo up from Rantepao to Lokomata, walk back down the same road to the Rantepao to Sadan road, and catch a bemo back to Rantepao. This is a very pleasant downhill walk of about five hours through some of the finest scenery in Tanatoraja.

Places to Stay There is a losmen at Batutumonga called the *Batutumonga Guesthouse*, which has very basic accommodation for 6000 rp per person per night, including breakfast and dinner. It's more or less dormitory accommodation. There are spectacular views overlooking Rantepao, and it's often very cold at night. This would be an excellent base for exploring other villages in the area.

Lokomata (26 km)
A few km past Batutumonga there are cave graves in one large rocky outcrop, and more beautiful scenery. To the south-east of Lokomata is Pana, where there are very old graves amidst bamboo.

Pangala (35 km)
This traditional village is noted for its fine dancers.

Sungai Sadan Whitewater Rafting
The canyon of the Sungai (river) Sadan makes for an interesting whitewater rafting trip that can be completed in one day. There are over 20 rapids, though none of them terribly dangerous.

All equipment, transport and guides can be provided by Sobek Expeditions (☎ (0423) 22143) in Makale near Rantepao. You can also make bookings in Ujung Pandang at Wira Karya Tours (☎ (0411) 312298, fax 314652), Jalan Gunung Lokon 25. The cost per person is 87750 rp.

MAKALE
Makale is the county seat of Tanatoraja, and some travellers stay here when Rantepao gets packed out with visitors. Like Rantepao, it's a good base for exploring the area but guides are a little harder to find. Makale is a fairly small town built around an artificial lake and set amidst cloud-shrouded hills. The old part of town has many Dutch houses and a good market.

Places to Stay
There are a couple of simple but clean places near the town centre.

Wisma Bungin (☎ 22255) at Jalan Pongtiku 35 is a modern-looking place and the best deal in town, with rooms for 4500 rp per person. All rooms have private bath.

Losmen Indra (☎ 22022), Jalan Merdeka 11, is on the south side of town. It's a clean place with friendly people. Singles and doubles with shared bath are 10,000 rp, or 15,000 with private bath.

Losmen Merry (☎ 22013) is one of the cheaper alternatives, with single rooms for 3500 rp with shared bath.

Losmen Litha (☎ 22009) is dismal looking and on a noisy street. The small rooms with shared bath go for 4000 rp per person.

Further to the north on Jalan Pongtiku is *Losmen Marga* (☎ 22011) which looks a bit tattered but has friendly management and rooms with private bath for 5000 rp per person.

About three km north of the centre is the elegant *Wisma Puri Artha* (☎ 22047) where singles/doubles are 38,500/45,500 rp. Just next door is Makale's expensive tourist resort, the *Marannu City Hotel* (☎ 22028) where singles/doubles go for 95,000/108,000 rp. This place comes complete with tennis courts and a swimming pool.

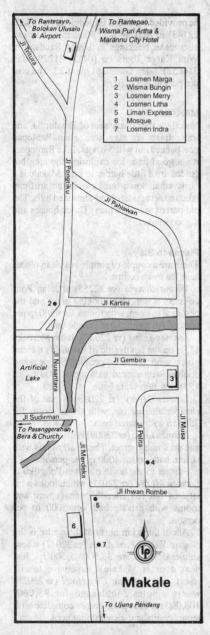

1 Losmen Marga
2 Wisma Bungin
3 Losmen Merry
4 Losmen Litha
5 Liman Express
6 Mosque
7 Losmen Indra

Makale

Places to Eat

One of the disadvantages of Makale is the lack of restaurants. There's not much and what there is is cheap but forgettable. There are several cheap noodle shops on Jalan Merdeka near the mosque.

Getting There & Away

Air Merpati has flights three times a week from Makale to Ujung Pandang; the fare is around 45,000 rp.

Bus There are bemos all through the day from Rantepao and the trip takes 40 minutes and costs 500 rp. From Makale you can get buses to the same places (and for the same prices) as you can from Rantepao. The offices and agents for the buses are all in the middle of town. Liman Express is at Jalan Ihwan Rombe 3. Buses Merry is at the Losmen Merry. Buses Litha is at the Losmen Litha.

PALOPO

This Muslim port town is the administrative capital of the Luwu district. Before the Dutch this was once the centre of the old and powerful Luwu kingdom and the former palace is now the miniscule Museum Batara Guru. It's at Jalan Andi Jemma 1 and contains relics of the royal era.

On the waterfront is a Bugis village and a long pier where you can get a closer look at the fishing boats.

Overall there's not much to this place, but Palopo is a possible staging point for the trip to Pendolo and Poso in Central Sulawesi.

Places to Stay

The *Palopo Hotel* (☎ 209) at Jalan Kelapa 11 is opposite the bus station and therefore convenient for transport. Economy singles/doubles are 5000/10,000 rp, while rooms with air-con go for 15,000/17,000. All rooms have an attached bath.

Buana Hotel (☎ 664) is an attractive-looking place with a very friendly manager. Economy rooms are 7500 rp while standard rooms are 8500 to 15,000 rp. The VIP rooms are 20,000 rp. All rooms have private bath.

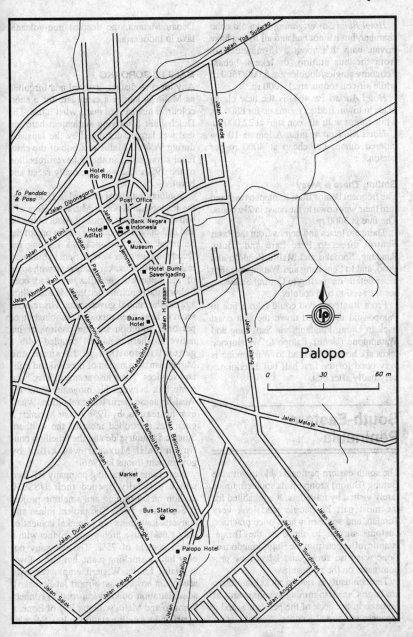

To Pendolo
& Poso

Hotel
Rio Rita

Jalan Diponegoro

Post Office

Jalan Kartini

Hotel
Adifati

Bank Negara
Indonesia

Museum

Jalan Ahmad Yani

Jalan Patimura

Jalan Alemma

Hotel Bumi
Sawerigading

Jalan Manemmungen

Buana
Hotel

Jalan Khadichlan

Jalan Remuten

Palopo

0   30   60 m

Jalan Yos Sudarso

Jalan Carade

Jalan H Hasan

Jalan Ci Lalang

Jalan Malaja

Market

Jalan Durian

Jalan Narqka

Jalan Lagaligo

Bus Station

Jalan Belimbing

Palopo Hotel

Jalan Jend Surdirman

Jalan Merdeka

Jalan Anggrek

Jalan Salak

Jalan Kelapa

Hotel Bumi Sawerigading is an old echo chamber, but it's not bad and all rooms have private bath. It's about a 15-minute walk from the bus station, or take a becak. Economy singles/doubles are 5,000/7500 rp while air-con rooms are 15,000 rp.

Hotel Adifati (☎ 467) is the new classy place in town. Budget rooms go for 8800 rp, while rooms with air- con start at 22,000 rp.

Hotel Rio Rita at Jalan A Jemma 10 is a tattered dump, but cheap at 4000 rp per person.

Getting There & Away

The frequent bemos from Rantepao twist and turn their way down to the coast in 2½ hours. The fare is 3000 rp.

There are buses and bemos from the Pasar Sentral direct to Pare Pare and Ujung Pandang, Soroako and Malili, Pendolo and Poso, and to Sengkang and Watampone. For more details on the trip to Central Sulawesi, see the section on Pendolo.

From Rantepao you could take a bus to Palopo and then head down the east coast back to Ujung Pandang, via Sengkang and Watampone (Bone). Palopo to Watampone takes six hours. The road to Watampone is very good for the first half but deteriorates very badly after that.

South-Eastern Peninsula

The south-eastern peninsula, along with the Butung (Buton) group off its southern tip, is rarely visited by travellers. It's inhabited for the most part by people who look very Torajan, and some of whom once practised customs similar to those of the Toraja. Islamic influence from the Bugis kingdom of Bone was also strong and Islam now predominates on the peninsula.

The peninsula is rich in nickel and there are large Canadian mining developments at Soroako in the neck of the peninsula, and a Japanese venture at Kendari. Soroako is on Danau Matana, the deepest non-volcanic lake in Indonesia.

MALILI & SOROAKO

Any town as distant, isolated and forgotten as Malili is hardly a candidate for a short colourful history, but that's what it has. The Dutch built a thriving settlement here but that was largely destroyed by the Japanese during WW II. Malili was one of the chief rebel strongholds in the Sulawesi rebellion of the 1950s and was repeatedly razed and burnt.

Southern Sulawesi rebelled in 1950 under the leadership of Kahar Muzakar. He was a native of the Luwu region of south Sulawesi and had played a founding role in one of the Sulawesi youth organisations fighting the Dutch on Java after WW II. Sent to Sulawesi in June 1950, Muzakar teamed up with some of the Sulawesi guerrillas who had been fighting the Dutch and led them in a rebellion against the central government. His reasons seem to have been mixed: a combination of personal ambition for the control of his native southern Sulawesi coupled with a general opposition to Javanese and Minahasan domination of the civil and military services. There also seems to have been some link between his movement and the West Javanese Darul Islam rebellion. Whatever his reasons, by 1956 Kahar Muzakar's guerrillas controlled most of the southern Sulawesi countryside and the rebellion continued until Muzakar was killed by government troops in 1966.

Next came the mining company PT Inco which officially opened their US$850 million nickel mining and smelting project at Soroako in 1977. The project mines and converts low-grade ore (a nickel content of only 1.6%) into a high-grade product with a nickel content of 75%. The company not only built a smelting plant, but also a town at Malili for its Western employees with schools, a hospital, an airport (at Soroako), administration buildings, a road to connect Soroako and Malili with the Bay of Bone, a wharf and a satellite station to link Soroako directly with its offices in Ujung Pandang and Jakarta.

Getting There & Away

One benefit of the mine as far as travellers bound for central Sulawesi are concerned is the brilliant road between Palopo and Soroako via Malili. There are bemos and buses from Rantepao to Malili and Soroako. There is an airport at Soroako but all flights are charters.

KOLAKA

A port town on the west coast of the south-eastern peninsula, Kolaka is readily accessible by boat from Watampone (Bone).

To get there, take a bemo from Watampone south-east to the harbour at Bajowe. The ferry leaves nightly and the trip to Kolaka takes about 12 hours. From the harbour in Kolaka there are hordes of minibuses eager to take you to Kendari.

KENDARI

This is a mining town on the east coast of the south-eastern peninsula with little of interest. Desa Mata, about five km away, has an OK beach.

Places to Stay & Eat

There are a couple of fairly cheap losmens and a few more expensive places. *Wisma Maiwali* is on the road into town from Kolaka. On the main road are *Wisma Mutiara*, *Wisma Nirwana* and *Penginapan Noer Indah*. By the harbour, near the cinema, are more losmen including the *Penginapan Kendari* and the expensive *Wisma Andika*.

There's good food at the night-time foodstalls at the waterfront, about a km from the harbour. There are also a lot of dingy places near the market.

Getting There & Away

Air Because it's a mining town Kendari is well connected by air to other parts of Indonesia. Merpati (☎ 109, 360) is at Jalan Sudirman 29; Garuda (☎ 21729) is at Jalan Diponegoro 59. There are daily flights to Ujung Pandang (87,000 rp).

Bus A minibus from Kolaka to Kendari takes you to a place 13 km before Kendari. From there you have to take two different bemos to get into town.

Boat From Kendari you can get ships to Surabaya – try the Meratus shipping company. They have about two ships per month on this route. The trip takes about four days and nights and the crew members on the ships will rent out their cabins. There are also daily boats between Kendari and Baubau on Butung Island.

BUTUNG GROUP
Baubau

This is the main settlement on Butung (Buton) and is on the south-west coast. It was once a fortified town, the seat of the former sultanate of Wolio which reigned over the scattered settlements on Buton and the neighbouring islands of Muna, Kabaena, Wowini and Tukangbesi, as well as the adjacent mainland, until they came under direct Dutch rule around 1908 to 1910.

The people of this island group are all closely related culturally and speak similar languages. As in the south-eastern peninsula of Sulawesi, most of the cultural influences seem to have come from the Bugis; the Butonese are Muslims and they were noted sailors and traders who emigrated widely, especially to Maluku. The island group was also once a pirate bastion and a centre of the slave trade.

Getting There & Away

There are daily boats from Kendari to Baubau. Ships between Ambon and Ujung Pandang sometimes stop at Baubau.

Central Sulawesi

The inhabitants of the interior of the eastern peninsula of central Sulawesi are traditionally known to the coastal dwellers as the Loinang – the term is somewhat derogatory. The highlanders are a mixed bunch, some

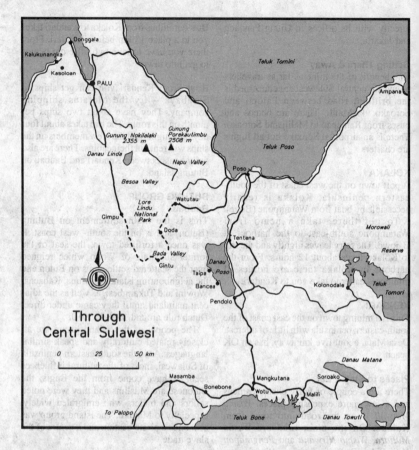

Through Central Sulawesi

0   25   50 km

more akin to the inhabitants of central Sulawesi, while others appear to have mixed with later immigrants from Ternate.

History

Both Christianity and Islam started planting roots in the eastern peninsula in the early 1900s when the Dutch took over the area. However, the town of Palu is known to have been settled – and Islamised – over 200 years ago. One of the earliest Western visitors to this region was the unfortunate Bostonian Captain David Woodard. In the early 1790s Woodard, along with four other sailors,

became separated from their ship and were taken prisoner by the inhabitants of the coast just to the south of what is now Donggala, a town near Palu. They spent 2½ years in captivity before escaping to Makassar, and the story is recorded in the book *The Narrative of Captain David Woodard & Four Seamen* published in 1805. Woodard was held in Palu (Parlow) for eight months and described it as:

a fine town, containing perhaps five hundred houses...Round and near the town are rice-fields, which are occasionally overflowed with water from the river, by means of canals...The inhabitants smoke opium, which they purchase from the Dutch.

Woodard also noted their Muslim aversion to pork, the great distances over which their trading prahus voyaged, and events from the bloody war between Palu and Donggala to the north.

Prior to the Dutch intrusion, the sultanate of Ternate held sway over these areas, as it did over other parts of eastern Sulawesi. Off the tip of the eastern archipelago are the Banggai Islands, whose inhabitants also seem to be a diverse mixture. At one time a royal dynasty of Javanese origin ruled here, subject to the sultanate of Ternate. After the Dutch took over in 1908 native rulers were set up to run the islands.

Although the period of Dutch rule was brief, the first Europeans settled in central Sulawesi some 200 years ago. At this time the Dutch had established two settlements on the Bay of Tomini: the northern coast settlement of Gorontalo and another on the south coast called Priggia or Priggy, up country from the coast near what is now Poso. Along with Makassar and Gowa these were the principle Dutch settlements of the time. The rest of the island was controlled by the native tribes, although in the late 1780s or early 1790s the Dutch also attempted to take Toli-Toli (because of its fine harbour), but without success.

PENDOLO

Here it is, a sleepy paradise about to be jarred awake by mass tourism. Pendolo is a small village on the southern shore of beautiful Danau Poso (Lake Poso), and the reason it escaped development was, simply, the horrible road connecting it to the outside world. The road was only surfaced in 1991, and the Indonesian government is now fixing the bridges, which are still in a somewhat sorry state. Keeping this road open will be a continuous challenge – it's a shelf carved out of the mountainsides and subject to frequent landslides. If transport improves, more travellers will arrive; Danau Poso is probably

destined to become another Lake Toba. Don't forget, you read it here first.

Things to See
The lake and its lovely beach are the main attractions. You can swim, there are boat rides on the lake and the surrounding countryside has some decent walks. The lake is 600 metres above sea level so the climate is pleasantly cool in the evening without being too cold. The area is also famous for its wild orchids. The locals are mostly Christians who were brought in with a transmigration scheme.

Places to Stay
The *Pondok Wisata Victory* has the best location overlooking the beach. Rooms with shared bath are 2500 rp, while a room with private bath goes for a modest 3500 rp.

Pondok Wisata Masamba is also very close to the beach. Rooms with shared bath are 2500 rp, while an attached bath will cost you 4000 rp.

Penginapan Danau Poso is about 100 metres back from the beach. The management are very friendly and it has good rooms for 2500 and 3500 rp.

Getting There & Away
Bus From Rantepao, Bina Wisata is the best bus company. They run two buses weekly on Tuesday and Saturday and the fare is 20,000 rp. The travelling time is 10 hours.

Tentena, on the north shore of the lake, is a much larger town than Pendolo. You can reach Tentena by bus, bemo or boat. Right near the beach at Pendolo is a sign indicating the Jawa Indah bus company. The fare to Tentena is 2500 rp and to Poso it's 5000 rp. From Poso, there are flights to elsewhere in Sulawesi as well as Java and Bali.

Bemo From Rantepao, there are normally no direct bemos, but you can make the trip in about 11 hours by taking three separate bemos. First get a bemo from Rantepao to Palopo, then to Mangkutana and finally to Pendolo.

Another option is to charter a bemo. A

bemo can normally hold about seven passengers and will cost 175,000 to 200,000 rp to make this journey. Split amongst seven people, this works out to 25,000 to 28,600 rp, not much more than the bus. A little bit of bargaining with the bemo drivers is probably a good idea. When researching this edition, a group of us chartered a bemo from Laurenz (☎ 21082, 21385) in Rantepao. He speaks good English and proved to be a competent driver and guide. Also try asking around the Hotel Indra, Wisma Irama and other hotels in Rantepao.

Boat It is possible to cross the lake between Pendolo and Tentena by small outrigger motor boat or on a large ferry that holds from 30 to 70 people. Boats from Tentena depart at least once daily at 5 pm, but there are plans to add more runs per day depending on demand. From Pendolo to Tentena, departures are currently at sometime between 7 am and 9 am. The fare is 1500 rp.

TENTENA

Tentena, on the north shore of Danau Poso, has long had good roads connecting it to the outside world. As a result, it's far more developed and noisy than Pendolo. Unfortunately, Tentena lacks a beach and is much inferior to Pendolo as a peaceful lakeside resort. However, there are good views over the lake and Tentena is a useful transit point.

From Tentena there are bemos to the nearby village of Taripa. Across the big covered bridge are some interesting caves near the missionary airstrip. Another possibility is to head to the remote jungles of Lore Lindu National Park.

Places to Stay

The *Hotel Wasantara* by the lake is a large and cheery place. The economy rooms have shared bath and go for 3500 rp per person. Standard room with private bath at 13,500 rp and small bungalows can be rented for 16,500 rp.

Nearby is *Pamona Indah*, a huge, fancy place with plush wood-panelled decor. The cheapest double rooms go for 12,500 rp, but

with TV, hot water and other amenities the price escalates to 40,000 rp.

Losmen Rio is a dismal edifice that charges 2500 rp – OK for the desperate. Considerably better is *Penginapan Wisata Remaja* where doubles have attached bath and go for 7500 rp to 10,000 rp.

Wisma Panorama is on a hill set back from the lake and affords fine views. It's a pleasant place to stay and costs 15,000 rp for a double with attached bath.

Getting There & Away

Tentena is 57 km from the coastal city of Poso. Bemos and buses make the run in about 1½ hours.

LORE LINDU NATIONAL PARK

Covering an area of 250,000 hectares, this large and remote national park has been barely touched by tourism. It's a wonderful area for trekking – the park is rich in exotic plant and animal life, including incredible butterflies larger than your hand. It is also home to several indigenous tribes, most of whom wear colourful costumes, at least for traditional ceremonies. Other attractions include ancient cultural relics such as stone-carved cisterns, mostly in the Bada, Besoa and Napu valleys. It's even possible to climb remote peaks, which reach as high as 2613 metres above sea level.

There are two main approaches to the park: from Palu to the north, or from Tentena on the east side of the park. From Palu, it's 100 km or 2½ hours by car south to Gimpu, from where the road deteriorates into a track requiring 4WD. The other approach, from Tentena, usually takes visitors by road through Poso, then another 50 km to the isolated village of Gintu. It is also possible to fly to Bada Valley in a Cessna aircraft operated by the Missionary Aviation Fellowship (MAF), which is based in Tentena. Roads within the park consist chiefly of mud and holes, and transport is usually by jeep, on horseback and on foot.

Getting to the park is a bit of an expedition and not something you can do on your own. A permit and a guide are required. This doesn't have to be horribly expensive, especially if you can organise a group. The government tourist office can put you on to some licensed tour operators, though they tend to recommend their most expensive friends. The name of the game is 'negotiate'! Prices quoted were from as low as 50,000 rp per person per day all the way up to 200,000 rp. In Tentena, enquire at the Pomona Indah Hotel. Some of the cheapest tours we've seen have been organised through Milano Ice Cream (a restaurant in Palu). You can also book tours in Palu with Katriall Tours & Travel Service (☎ 21020), Jalan Hasanuddin 10. Most trips to the park take about three or four days.

Although all food is supplied, it's wise to bring other necessities such as mosquito repellent and sunblock (UV) lotion.

MOROWALI RESERVE

This nature reserve was established in 1980 on the east side of Teluk Tomori. Aside from the scenic beauty, the area is inhabited by the Wana people who still live mostly by hunting and gathering, and slash-and-burn agriculture.

Organised treks of the area take about four days and can be organised in Tentena, Poso or Palu. In Tentena, enquire about trips at the Pomona Indah Hotel.

The route goes east from Poso to Kolonodale by bus (eight to 12 hours). Most visitors spend the night in Kolonodale at the Losmen Sederhana or the more luxurious Hotel Tomor Indah. From there it's a two-hour boat trip across Tomori Bay and a two-km trek to the first Wana village, then a four-hour trek to the next village. There are opportunities to see the tangkasi tiny monkey and maleo birds. Trips usually also include a canoe trip on a lake and exploration of a sea cave with paintings of human hands on the walls.

POSO

Poso is the main town and port on the northern coast of central Sulawesi. For most travellers it's only a rest stop and transit point. However, it's quite a pleasant town,

amazingly clean and prosperous-looking. The southern side of town is the new section and looks much like a suburb in Australia or the USA, with manicured lawns and neat houses.

From Poso you can head west to Palu and continue on to northern Sulawesi, or take a ship across Teluk Tomini (Tomini Bay) to Gorontalo on the northern peninsula. An unexplored alternative is to head out to the peninsula that juts eastwards out of central Sulawesi into the Maluku Sea.

The city itself is not rich in sights, and about the only thing to do is head for the beaches which, unfortunately, are not within walking distance. Pantai Madale is five km from Poso and costs 250 rp by bemo. Pantai Toini, seven km and 500 rp from town, is somewhat nicer. Pantai Matako is 20 km from Poso and the bemo fare is 1000 rp.

Places to Stay

Anugrah Inn (☎ 21820), Jalan P Samosir 1, is on the southern edge of town, convenient only if you're arriving/departing at the Jawa Indah bus terminal or the Merpati office. It's a very friendly and quiet place with double rooms for 10,000 and 20,000 rp.

Hotel Nels (☎ 21013) is in the northern part of town on Jalan Yos Sudarso. It's an old but amiable place. There is one economy room for 2500 rp, but the other singles/doubles have private bath and go for 7500/8500 rp.

Hotel Kalimantan (☎ 21420), Jalan Haji Augus Salim 14, is also quite old but big, bright and airy. It's also quite cheap at 5500 rp for a single with attached bath.

A few minutes' walk up the road at the corner of Jalan Haji Agus Salim and Jalan Imam Bonjol is the *Penginapan Sulawesi* (☎ 21294) which has singles for 2000 rp. It's a small, old hotel and the rooms are basic little boxes, but it's clean.

The most elegant lodging in Poso is the *Bambu Jaya Hotel* (☎ 21570), Jalan Haji Agus Salim 101. The economy rooms are 15,000 rp, while a room with air-con is 22,000 rp. Suites are 40,000 to 65,000 rp.

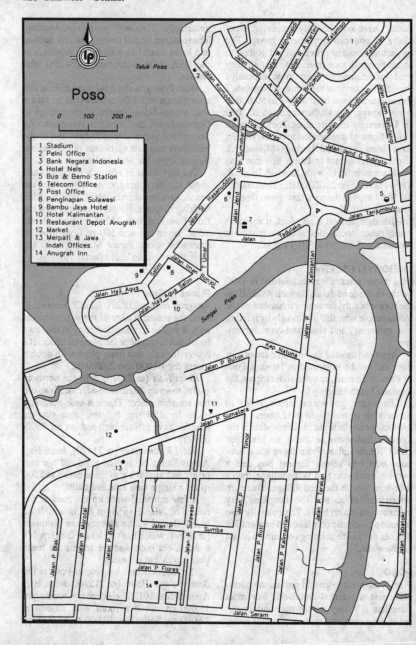

Teluk Poso

Poso

0   100   200 m

1 Stadium
2 Pelni Office
3 Bank Negara Indonesia
4 Hotel Nels
5 Bus & Bemo Station
6 Telecom Office
7 Post Office
8 Penginapan Sulawesi
9 Bambu Jaya Hotel
10 Hotel Kalimantan
11 Restaurant Depot Anugrah
12 Market
13 Merpati & Jawa
    Indah Offices
14 Anugrah Inn

Jalan Komodor
Jalan Jend W Monginsidi
Jalan Jend R A Kartini
Jalan Brigjend
Kalamso
Kalamso
A Yani
Jalan Jend Sudirman
Jalan Sam Ratulangi
Yos Sudarso
Jalan Jend G Subroto
Urip Sumoharjo
Jalan St Hasanuddin
Jalan Jend
Jalan Tanjumbulu
Tadulako
Jalan
Salim
Jalan Iman Bonjol
Umar
Jalan Haji Agus
Jalan Haji Agus Salim
Sungai Poso
Kalimantan
Jalan P
Kep Natuna
Jalan P Buton
Jalan P Sumatera
Jalan P
Timor
Jalan P Tarakan
Jalan P Morotai
Jalan P Bali
Jalan P Sulawesi
Jalan P
Sumba
Jalan P
Roti
Jalan P Kalimantan
Jalan P Tabaroki
Jalan P Blak
Jalan P Flores
Jalan Seram

There is a terrace in the back with chairs and great views of the sea.

Places to Eat

Restaurant Depot Anugrah (☎ 21586) is a Chinese-Indonesian restaurant offering good cheap food. It's on Jalan P Sumatera on the south side of town.

Getting There & Away

Air Merpati (☎ 21274) on Jalan P Sumatera is on the south side of town across from the market (Pasar Sentral). There are direct flights to Palu for 53,000 rp and Luwuk for 99,000 rp, with possible same-day connections to Surabaya (325,000 rp) and Ujung Pandang (178,000 rp). The airport is 13 km from Poso at Kasiguncu.

Bus There are regular buses from Poso to Tentena on the northern shore of Danau Poso. Buses from Palu bound for Rantepao and Palopo come through Poso, but don't count on being able to get on board.

There are at least eight buses daily between Poso and Palu, and some run at night. The trip takes eight hours and costs 10,000 rp. Bina Wisata Sulteng bus company has its ticket office right inside the Merpati office, and Jawa Indah is right next to it. Or you can catch a bemo or bus from the main bus terminal on Jalan Tanjumbulu.

There are also buses from Poso heading east to Ampana (six hours) and Kolonedale near the Morowali Reserve. The roads are in poor condition and heavy rains may cause landslides – be prepared to wait a long time.

Boat Ships depart Poso for Gorontalo, on the northern peninsula, at least once a week and the trip takes about two days. Buy your ticket at Pos Keamanan Pelabuhan at the port. The ships usually stop at various ports along the coast or in the Togian Islands – including Ampana, Wakui, Dolong and Pagimana. On these ships you can sometimes rent a cabin or a bunk from the crew.

There are occasional ships to Ujung Pandang, Bitung (the port of Manado) and Surabaya. Enquire at the harbour master's office at Jalan Pattimura 3, and at the Pelni office which is next door on the same street.

Getting Around

It's fortunate that Poso isn't a very large city, because there are no becaks to be seen! Bemos ply the streets but you can reach most important places on foot.

PALU

The capital of Central Sulawesi Province, Palu is a Bugis town and major port at the end of Palu Bay, on the west coast of Sulawesi. It's larger and noisier than Poso, but also reasonably prosperous and clean.

One of the more interesting things about Palu is the climate. It's possibly the driest place in Indonesia, with only about four or five good rainstorms a year. On the outskirts of town you'll see huge prickly pear cactus and other desert vegetation. However, there is still plenty of tropical vegetation in the area, partly because of ground water from the mountains. Not surprisingly, days are hot, nights are tolerably cool and the brilliant sunshine is amenable to sunbaking and snorkelling.

Orientation

Like Poso, Palu is spread out and the street names constantly change. The airport is on the south-eastern outskirts, and the town is split neatly in two by the Sungai Palu.

Information

Tourist Office The tourist office (kantor pariwisata) is on Jalan Cik Ditiro, but there is no English sign. They have a couple of decent brochures. The office is open vaguely from 7.30 am until around 2 pm.

Post & Telecommunications

The post office is on Jalan Sudirman and the Warpostal is adjacent to the Central Hotel on Jalan Kartini.

Things to See & Do

The Central Sulawesi Museum (☎ 22290), or Museum Negeri Propinsi Sulawesi Tengah, is at Jalan Sapiri 23. The museum

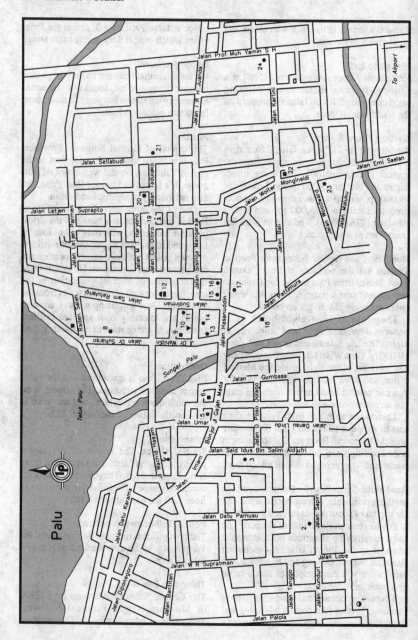

Palu

Teluk Palu

To Airport

Jalan Prof Muh Yamin S H
Jalan Setiabudi
Jalan Letjen Parman
Jalan Letjen Suprapto
Jalan M T Haryono
Jalan Cik Ditiro
Jalan Sam Ratulangi
Jalan Sudirman
Ji Dr Wahidin
Jalan Dr Suharso
Ji Raden Saleh
Jalan Singa Mangaraja
Jalan Hasanuddin
Jalan I R H Juanda
Jalan Kartini
Jalan Emmy Saelan
Jalan Wolter Monginsidi
Jalan Moh Hatta
Jalan Maluku
Jalan Bali
Jalan Pattimura
Jalan Tadulako
Sungai Palu
Jalan Gumbasa
Jalan Poso
Jalan Dolago
Jalan Danau Lindu
Jalan D
Bonjol Ji Gajah Mada
Jalan Umar
Ji Wachid Hasyim
Jalan Imam
Jalan Said Idus Bin Salim Aldjufri
Jalan Datu Karana
Jalan Bantilan
Jalan Diponegoro
Jalan Datu Pamusu
Jalan W R Supratman
Jalan Tanggo
Jalan Kunduri
Jalan Sapiri
Jalan Lobe
Jalan Palola

■ Places to Stay

6	Hotel Pasifik
7	Palu Golden Hotel
8	Hotel Karsam
9	Purnama Raya Hotel
18	Hotel Pattimura
20	New Dely Hotel
22	Central Hotel, Warpostal & Buana Hotel

▼ Places to Eat

10	Restaurant New Oriental
13	Golden Bakery
14	Milano Ice Cream & Jameson's Supermarket

Other

1	Terminal Inpres
2	Central Sulawesi Museum
3	Garuda Office
4	Ancient Mosque
5	Pelni Office
11	Bank Negara Indonesia
12	Post Office
15	Merpati Office
16	Bank Expor Impor Indonesia
17	Jawa Indah Office
19	Tourist Office
21	Tadulako University
23	Bouraq Office
24	Immigration Office

houses cultural relics, natural history exhibits and a collection of books in Dutch, Indonesian and English. It opens from about 8.30 am until about noon. Pantai Palu (Palu Beach) is not especially clean or nice, but it's better than nothing. Fortunately, there is an excellent beach nearby at Donggala.

Places to Stay – bottom end

The *Hotel Karsam* (☎ 21776), at Jalan Dr Suharso 15 near Pantai Palu, is a pretty good deal with singles/doubles for 5500/10,000 rp, although it's about a 15-minute walk from the centre.

Purnama Raya Hotel (☎ 23646) is centrally located at Jalan Dr Wahidin 4, and has singles/doubles for 7500/10,000 rp, all with

private bath. It's clean and friendly though can be a bit noisy.

Hotel Pasifik, Jalan Gajah Mada 130, is centrally located but supernaturally noisy. Booming TVs, blasting tape players, barking dogs, squawking roosters and a nearby mosque (equipped with stereo loudspeakers!) all combine to create an incredible eardrum-shattering cacophony. However, it's a great place if you're deaf, with rooms starting from 5000 rp with shared bath.

Places to Stay – middle

The *New Dely Hotel* (☎ 21037), Jalan Tadulako 17, is clean, quiet and good value with single rooms for 15,000 to 25,000 rp. It's right near the tourist office, about a 10 minute walk from the centre.

Buana Hotel (☎ 21475), Jalan Kartini 8, is a respectable place and one of the better deals in this price range. Single rooms with private bath start at 15,000 rp, while more luxurious accommodation goes for 20,000 and 30,000 rp.

Central Hotel (☎ 23794) is next to the Buana Hotel. It's a quiet and spotlessly clean place with English-speaking staff. Singles/doubles with shared bath are 20,000/25,000 rp, while giant-sized deluxe rooms are 50,000/55,000 rp.

Hotel Pattimura (☎ 21775), Jalan Pattimura 18, is a decent place with its own restaurant. Standard rooms are 24,500 rp while 1st class will cost you 35,000 rp.

Places to Stay – top end

Palu Golden Hotel (☎ 21126), Jalan Raden Saleh 22, is Palu's top hotel. It's at Pantai Palu, which is not exactly lovely for swimming, but the views are OK. At 100,000 rp and up for a double, it's not surprising that they have plenty of vacancies.

Places to Eat

Jalan Hasanuddin II is a busy market street with many places to eat. Here you will find *Milano Ice Cream* (☎ 23857), open from 8 am to 2 pm, and from 5 until 10 pm. The food is good, the ice cream is outstanding, but drinks are a bit expensive. However, the main reason most travellers stop in here is to chat with the owners, Peter and Maureen Meroniak, who organise trekking tours and operate a beachside hotel in Donggala (See Donggala – Places to Stay).

Restaurant New Oriental (☎ 23275) is also on Jalan Hasanuddin II, and serves excellent Chinese food in addition to Indonesian dishes.

Golden Bakery is just around the corner on Jalan Dr Wahidin. It's excellent for breakfast and midnight snacks. It's no place to visit if you're on a diet – plenty of tempting cakes, rolls and pastries.

If you want to self-cater, Jameson's is the best supermarket in the busy Jalan Hasanuddin area. An even larger supermarket is Sentosa (☎ 21738), Jalan W Monginsidi 59, near the Bouraq office and right next to the Central Hotel.

Getting There & Away

From Palu (or the nearby ports of Pantoloan, Wani or Donggala) you can take a ship to the east coast of Kalimantan, to northern Sulawesi or Pare Pare in southern Sulawesi. Palu is connected by road to Poso in central Sulawesi and to Gorontalo in northern Sulawesi.

Air Aside from the usual daytime office hours, Merpati, Garuda and Bouraq also sell tickets in the evening from about 7 pm until the staff feel like going home.

Bouraq (☎ 22563), Jalan W Monginsidi 58, offers the most extensive flight network from Palu, with fares as shown in the following table.

Destination	Fare (rp)
Balikpapan	102,000
Bandung	403,000
Banjarmasin	185,000
Gorontalo	97,000
Jakarta	394,000
Manado	163,000
Samarinda	146,000
Semarang	309,000
Surabaya	258,000
Tarakan	235,000
Ternate	246,000
Ujung Pandang	129,000
Yogyakarta	337,000

Garuda (☎ 21095) is on Jalan Said Idus Aldjufrie, south of the intersection with Jalan Gajah Mada. Merpati (☎ 21295) is at Jalan Hasanuddin 33. Merpati offers direct flights to Buol (119,000 rp), Luwuk (120,000 rp), Manado (163,000 rp), Poso (53,000 rp), Toli-Toli (100,000 rp) and Ujung Pandang (129,000 rp). With same-day connections, you can also reach Ambon, Bandung, Biak, Jakarta (418,000 rp), Jayapura, Kendari, Surabaya and Yogyakarta.

Bus Buses to Poso, Palopo, Rantepao, Gorontalo and Manado all leave from the Inpres station. At Masomba station you can get buses to inland cities. Palu to Gorontalo takes 1½ days over a bone-jarring road. Palu to Poso costs 10,000 rp and takes about eight hours.

Boat There are three ports near Palu. Larger vessels dock at Pantoloan which is north-east of Palu, and some dock at Donggala which is north-west of Palu. Smaller ships dock at Wani, two km past Pantoloan.

In Palu, the Pelni office is upstairs at Jalan Gajah Mada 86. They also have an office at Pantoloan, opposite the road to the wharf. The offices of the other shipping companies are at the various ports. Pelni ships dock at Pantoloan.

Two large, modern Pelni liners, the *Kerinci* and the *Kambuna*, stop in at Pantoloan. For a complete timetable of these ships, see the Getting Around chapter.

You can avoid the long and winding road through central Sulawesi by taking a ship from Palu to Ujung Pandang or Pare Pare.

Getting Around

To/From the Airport Palu's Mutiara airport is seven km from town. It's 10 minutes by bemo and costs 1000 rp. A taxi will cost you 5000 rp.

Local Tranport Transport round town is by bemo – 300 rp gets you anywhere. The best place to catch a bemo is along Jalan Gajah Mada. Inpres station has bus and bemo connections to Donggala and other areas around Palu. Karampe station has buses to the harbour at Pantoloan.

DONGGALA

As the administrative centre under the Dutch, Donggala was once the most important town and port in central Sulawesi. That all came to an end as the harbour silted up; the ships switched to the harbours on the other side of the bay and Palu became the regional capital.

Today Donggala is a quiet backwater, with an excellent beach north of town.

The main attractions are sun, sand and water. North of town are the beaches, where there are opportunities for snorkelling, scuba diving and sailing. There are lots of Europeans here, but it's still very relaxed except on Sunday, when Indonesians descend on the place in droves.

Places to Stay

Milano Beach Cottage attracts a steady stream of travellers. The losmen is run by a German expatriate, Peter Meroniak, and his Indonesian wife, Maureen. Singles/doubles are 15,000/25,000 rp, including three meals. They also rent equipment for snorkelling (4500 rp per day), scuba diving (35,000 rp per 45 minutes) and sailboats. You can contact Peter and Maureen at Milano Ice Cream in Palu (see Palu – Places to Eat) and they can arrange transport to the beach.

Getting There & Away

Bemo & Taxi From Palu, you can catch a 'sedan' to Donggala (*taksi Donggala*) for 1250 rp. Bemos cost 1000 rp and depart from Terminal Inpres. The ride takes 40 minutes. It's another 20 minutes on foot to the beach, or you can take a taxi for 200 rp.

Boat From Donggala you can also catch a ship to northern or southern Sulawesi.

KASOLOAN & KALUKUNANGKA

This area to the west of Palu is off the main tourist track, but makes for fascinating trekking. The people who live in the hills around Kasoloan and Kalukunangka lead traditional lives – they wear little clothing and still use blow guns. Despite the blow guns, the locals are quite used to trekkers and there is no danger.

Aside from the local culture, there is more of interest. There is a very large cave filled with thousands of bats. The locals eat them, and part of the thrill for travellers is a chance to sample bat stew (*enak*).

A visit to this area requires about three to four days. The trek itself is fairly easy and even suitable for older children. A guide is necessary – see the information about visiting Lore Lindu National Park for details.

Northern Sulawesi

The Dutch have had a more enduring influence on this isolated northern peninsula than anywhere else in the archipelago. This influence was established while the Bugis and the Makassarese were trying to repel the Dutch from the south- western peninsula. The greatest economic development in Sulawesi has also taken place in the north.

Unlike the more insular kingdoms of Java and Bali and the isolated hill-peoples of central Sulawesi, northern Sulawesi was once strongly oriented to the sea and had a long history of trade and contact with the outside world. Together with the Sangir-Talaud islands, it also formed a natural bridge to the Philippines, providing a causeway for the movement of peoples and cultures back and forth between Indonesia and the Philippines. Languages and physical features related to the Philippines can be found in north Sulawesi amongst the Minahasans at the tip of the peninsula, and the inhabitants of the Sangir group.

The three largest distinct groups of people in north Sulawesi are the Minahasans, the Gorontalese and the Sangirese. Like much of Indonesia, north Sulawesi was once divided into numerous kingdoms and Toraja-type customs may once have predominated, although the institutions and rituals of the royalty seem to have been imported from Islamic Ternate in Maluku, or from Mindanao in the Philippines.

History

At the time of the first contact with Europeans the sultanate of Ternate held some sway over north Sulawesi, and the area was often visited by seafaring Bugis traders from south Sulawesi. The Spanish and the Portuguese, the first Europeans to arrive, landed in north Sulawesi in the 16th century. The main Portuguese trade route rounded south Sulawesi at the port of Makassar, but also included the Sulu Islands (off the north coast of Borneo) and the port of Manado (tip of north Sulawesi). The Spanish set themselves up in the Philippines. Although they had sporadic contacts with north Sulawesi, the Spanish and Portuguese influence was limited by the power of Ternate.

The Portuguese left reminders of their presence in the north in subtle ways. Portuguese surnames and various Portuguese words not found elsewhere in Indonesia, like *garrida* for an enticing woman and *buraco* for a bad man, can still be found in Minahasa. In the 1560s the Portuguese Franciscan missionaries made some converts in Minahasa, and the Jesuit priest Mascarenhas had great success in the Sangir-Talaud islands. At the same time, however, Islam was arriving from Ternate.

By the early 17th century the Dutch had toppled the Ternate sultanate, and with that out of the way they set about eclipsing the Spanish and Portuguese. As was the usual pattern in the 1640s and 50s, the Dutch teamed up with the local population to throw out their European competitors. In 1677 the Dutch occupied Pulau Sangir and, two years later, the Dutch governor of Maluku, Robert Padtbrugge, visited Manado at the tip of the northern peninsula.Out of this visit came a treaty (some say a forced one) with the local Minahasan chiefs, which resulted in domination by the Dutch for the next 300 years.

Although relations with the Dutch were often less than cordial (a war was fought around Tondano between 1807 and 1809) and the region did not actually come under direct Dutch rule until 1870, the Dutch and the Minahasans eventually became so close that the north was often referred to as 'the 12th province of the Netherlands'. For the most part the history of northern Sulawesi is the history of the Minahasans, who have dominated events on the peninsula for the last century.

Portuguese activity apart, the Christianisation of the region really began in the early 1820s when a Calvinist group, the Netherlands Missionary Society, turned from an almost exclusive interest in Maluku to the Minahasa area. The wholesale conversion of the Minahasans was almost complete by

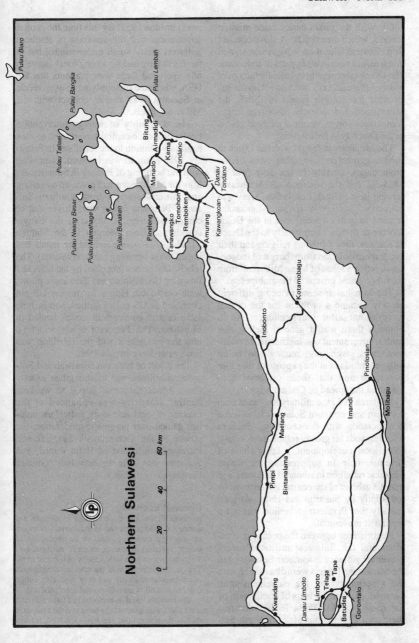

Northern Sulawesi

0   20   40   60 km

Pulau Biaro

Pulau Lembah

Pulau Bangka

Pulau Talise

Pulau Neang Besar

Pulau Mantehage

Pulau Bunaken

Bitung
Airmadidi
Manado
Kema
Tondano
Danau Tondano
Pineleng
Tomohon
Tanawangko
Remboken
Amurang
Kawangkoan

Kotamobagu

Inobonto

Pinolosian

Imandi

Mopugad

Maelang

Pimpi
Bintanalama

Kwandang

Danau Limboto
Limboto
Telaga
Tapa
Batudaa
Gorontalo

1860. With the missionaries came mission schools, which meant that, as in Ambon and Roti, Western education in Minahasa started much earlier than in other parts of Indonesia. The Dutch government eventually took over some of these schools and also set up others. Because the schools taught in Dutch, the Minahasans had an early advantage in the competition for government jobs and places in the Dutch East Indies Army.

The Minahasans fought with the Dutch in subduing rebellions in other parts of the archipelago, notably in the Java War of 1825-30, and the tradition of Minahasans serving in the Dutch East Indies Army was maintained until WW II. The Minahasans seemed to gain a special role in the Dutch scheme of things. Their loyalty to the Dutch as soldiers, their Christian religion and their geographic isolation from the rest of Indonesia all led to a sense of being 'different' from the other ethnic groups of the archipelago.

The Minahasan sense of being different quickly became a problem for the central government after independence. As in Sumatra there was a general feeling that central government was inefficient, development was stagnating, money was being plugged into Java at the expense of the outer provinces and that these circumstances favoured the spread of Communism.

In March 1957 the military leaders of both southern and northern Sulawesi launched a confrontation with the central government with demands for greater regional autonomy, more local development, a fairer share of revenue, help in suppressing the Kahar Muzakar rebellion in southern Sulawesi, and that the cabinet of the central government be led jointly by Sukarno and Hatta. At least initially the 'Permesta' rebellion was not a separatist movement.

Negotiations between the central government and the Sulawesi military leaders prevented violence in southern Sulawesi, but the Minahasan leaders were dissatisfied with the agreements and the movement split. Inspired, perhaps, by fears of domination by the south, the Minahasa leaders declared their own autonomous state of North Sulawesi in June 1957. By this time the central government had the situation in southern Sulawesi pretty much under control but in the north they had no strong local figure to rely upon and there were rumours that the USA, suspected of supplying arms to rebels in Sumatra, was also in contact with the Minahasa rebels.

The possibility of foreign intervention finally drove the central government to seek a military solution to the rebellion. In February 1958 Manado was bombed, coinciding with the bombing of Padang in Sumatra. By May the Minahasans had given up on getting any military support from southern Sulawesi. Permesta forces were driven out of central Sulawesi, Gorontalo, the Sangir islands and from Morotai in the Maluku islands (from whose airfield the rebels had hoped to fly bombing raids on Jakarta). The rebels' few planes (supplied by the USA and flown by US, Filipino and Taiwanese pilots) were destroyed. Hopes for further US aid crumbled as US policy shifted, and in June 1958 central government troops landed in Minahasa. The Permesta rebels withdrew into the mountains and the rebellion was finally put down in mid-1961.

The effect of both the Sumatran and Sulawesi rebellions was to strengthen exactly those trends they had hoped to weaken: central authority was enhanced at the expense of local autonomy, radical nationalism gained over pragmatic moderation, the power of the Communists and Sukarno increased while that of Hatta waned, and Sukarno was able to establish 'Guided Democracy' in 1959.

Coconut Economy

Northern Sulawesi's three million inhabitants are among the most prosperous in Indonesia. Cloves are an important cash crop, used in the production of kretek cigarettes. However, much of northern Sulawesi is covered by a solid canopy of coconut trees. The coconut palm is one of the most important plants in the tropical economy, not only producing edible fruit but also oil, waxes, fibres and other products.

The coconut 'meat' is enclosed in a light-coloured inner shell, which eventually turns into the hard, dark shell of the ripe nut that you see in the West. It takes a year for the nut to reach maturity, at which point the hard-shelled nut within the fibrous husk is about 12 cm in diameter and full of sweet liquid and hard, white flesh. Copra is the dried flesh and the second-most important export product of northern Sulawesi. Coir is the fibre from the husk of the coconut.

Like bamboo, the uses of the coconut tree are manifold. You can eat the meat, drink the juice, dry the meat for export as copra, burn the dried husks as fuel, build your house with coconut timber, use the fronds to thatch the roof or make mats and baskets, burn the oil to provide lighting at night or put it in your hair to keep it moist and glossy, use the leaf as a sieve to strain the sago flour that is the staple of the Maluku Islands, make rope and mats with the fibre, use the thin centre spine of the young coconut leaf to weave hats, or bag your midday meal of rice in a palm leaf.

Coconut oil, made from copra, is used instead of cooking fat, and is also used in the manufacture of soaps, perfumes, face creams, hair dressings, and even nitro-glycerine.

GORONTALO

The Gorontalese include the people of the city of Gorontalo as well as a large slice of the surrounding region, including Kwandang to the north and Toli-Toli to the west. Perhaps 500,000 people live in the Gorontalo district, the vast majority of them Muslims. The city of Gorontalo itself has a population of around 115,000 and the feel of a large country town.

Islam probably arrived here when the Ternate sultanate held sway over the tribes of the Gorontalo region before the Dutch took over. Gorontalo is the chief town of the Gorontalo district and the second-largest in north Sulawesi. It's a port on the west shore of Teluk Gorontalo and to the south of Danau Limboto, a fertile rice-growing region.

Orientation

Although rather spread out, most of the hotels, shops and other life-support systems are concentrated in a small central district. The bus station and main market are at the north end of town, within easy walking distance of the centre.

Things to See

There really isn't much to this town, but there is evidence of its European past. Gorontalo's local hero is Nani Wartabone, an anti-Dutch guerilla, and there is a large statue of him dressed like a boy scout in the sports field adjacent to the Hotel Saronde.

On the outskirts of Gorontalo are some European-built fortresses. There's some confusion over whether it was the Dutch or the Portuguese who built them. On a hill at Dembe overlooking Danau Limboto is Benteng (Fort) Otanaha, which was probably built by the Portuguese; you can see the remains of three towers. To get there take a bendi to the path up the hill from Jalan Belibis, or take an opelet (bemo) from the bus station, though these are infrequent. There's a sign at the foot of the path pointing to the fort. The Otanaha fortress overlooks a lake and there is another fortress on the shore of the lake to the south-east.

Pantai Indah is the name of the local beach on the southern side of the city. You can get there by bendi or opelet.

Air Panas Lombongo (Lombongo Hot Springs) are 40 km from Gorontalo and reachable by opelet. There's a swimming pool filled with hot springs water and a nearby river with cold water.

Places to Stay – bottom end

Penginapan Teluk Kau at Jalan Jenderal S Parman 42 has large rooms with high ceilings, big double beds and singles/doubles for 8000/12,000 rp. However, it's run-down, incredibly noisy and hardly worth the price. Some other crumbling losmen on this same street include *Asia Jaya* and *Asia Baru*, all similarly priced and in shoddy condition.

Places to Stay – middle

If you value your sanity, you'll spend a little bit more for accommodation rather than staying in Gorontalo's decrepit losmen.

Hotel Saronde (☎ 21735), Jalan Walanda Maramis 17, is the best in town. Singles/doubles with fan are 12,100/18,700 rp, while big, beautiful air-con rooms are 20,900/28,600 rp. Breakfast is included.

Hotel Wisata (☎ 21736) at Jalan 23

Januari 19 is an excellent place, and is also the location of the Merpati office. Singles/doubles come in three standards: economy for 9000/14,500 rp, standard for 13,500/21,000 rp, 1st class for 20,000/30,000 and deluxe for 25,000/36,000 rp.

Hotel Inda Ria (☎ 21296) at Jalan Jenderal A Yani 20, has three standards of rooms for 17,500, 20,000 and 25,000 rp. The cheaper rooms only have shared bath, but otherwise it's a very congenial place.

Places to Stay – top end

Hotel Saronde II (☎ 21735) at Jalan Walanda Maramis 17 is attached to the already-mentioned Hotel Saronde. Double rooms come in at least three standards for 40,700, 43,450 and 55,000 rp. All rooms are big and bright with refrigerator, colour TV and air-con.

Places to Eat

Near the Pasar Sentral at the north end of town, the *Rumah Makan Padang* on Jalan Sam Ratulangi is a decent place and relatively cheap as padang places go. There are some very cheap warungs in the Pasar Sentral.

In the centre of town the *Rumah Makan Dirgahayu* on Jalan Pertiwi serves up goat satay with peanut sauce (tersida sate kambing spesial). Also in the centre, the *Rumah Makan Olympic* has decent-sized helpings of seafood.

Getting There & Away

Air The Merpati office (☎ 21736) is in the Hotel Wisata at Jalan 23 Januari 19; Bouraq (☎ 21070) is at Jalan Jenderal Ahmad Yani 34 next to the Bank Negara Indonesia.

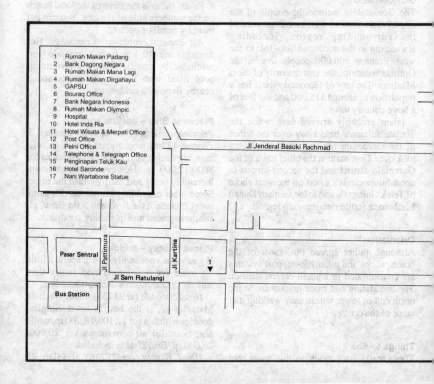

1 Rumah Makan Padang
2 Bank Dagong Negara
3 Rumah Makan Mana Lagi
4 Rumah Makan Dirgahayu
5 GAPSU
6 Bouraq Office
7 Bank Negara Indonesia
8 Rumah Makan Olympic
9 Hospital
10 Hotel Inda Ria
11 Hotel Wisata & Merpati Office
12 Post Office
13 Pelni Office
14 Telephone & Telegraph Office
15 Penginapan Teluk Kau
16 Hotel Saronde
17 Nani Wartabone Statue

Jl Jenderal Basuki Rachmad

Jl Pattimura

Jl Kartina

Pasar Sentral

Jl Sam Ratulangi

Bus Station

Merpati flies daily between Gorontalo and Manado, from where you can make same day connections to Ambon, Jakarta, Ternate and Ujung Pandang.

Bouraq flies non-stop from Gorontalo to both Manado (78,000 rp) and Palu (92,000 rp), with possible same-day connections to Balikpapan, Samarinda, Surabaya, Tarakan, Ternate and Ujung Pandang.

Bus There are regular buses to Manado. If the road is dry it takes only 12 hours; if it's wet, good luck. There are direct buses to Palu and Poso in central Sulawesi, a 1½ day journey.

Boat Pelni (☎ 20419) is at Jalan 23 Januari 31, and there's also an office at the port in Kwandang. Another shipping line, Gapsu

(☎ 88-173), has an office at Jalan Pertiwi 55 in central Gorontalo, and also at Gorontalo Harbour on Jalan Mayor Dullah (☎ 198).

The port of Kwandang, two hours by bus from Gorontalo, is a stop for the large Pelni liner *Umsini*. See the Getting Around chapter for the *Umsini* timetable. Smaller ships to Poso and Bitung, usually with various stops along the way, depart from Gorontalo Harbour.

Getting Around
To/From the Airport The shared Merpati and Bouraq bus will transport you from town to the airport 32 km away. It's an half-hour drive and costs 4000 rp per person. You can go to the Merpati or Bouraq office and arrange to have the bus pick you up at your hotel on the day of departure.

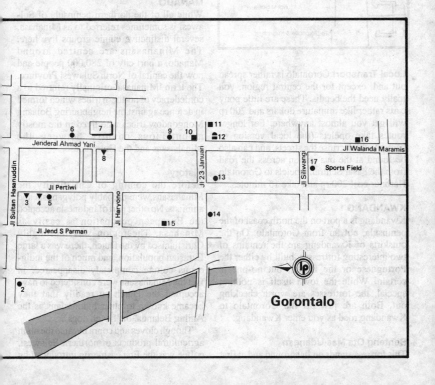

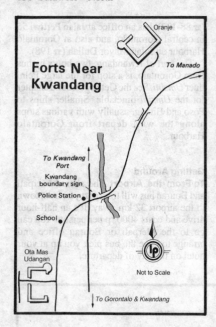

Forts Near Kwandang

Oranje

To Manado

To Kwandang Port

Kwandang boundary sign

Police Station

School

Ota Mas Udangan

Not to Scale

To Gorontalo & Kwandang

Local Transport Gorontalo is rather spread out and, except for the central region, you really need the bendis. These are little pony carts rather like miniature dokars and 200 rp will get you almost anywhere. For longer routes take opelets (the local version of bemos) which cruise the streets, and can also be found at the bus station across the road from the Pasar Sentral. Opelets to Gorontalo Harbour cost 200 rp and take 15 minutes.

KWANDANG

Kwandang is a port on the north coast of the peninsula, not far from Gorontalo. On the outskirts of Kwandang are the remains of two interesting fortresses, built by either the Portuguese or the Dutch, but no-one is certain. While the town itself is nothing special, the fortresses are worth checking out. Both are just off the Gorontalo to Kwandang road as you enter Kwandang.

Benteng Ota Mas Udangan

This fortress stands on flat ground and at first glance appears to be ill-placed to defend anything. One suggestion is that the ocean once came right up to the fort, but has since receded. All that remains of the once-sizeable fort are the ruins of a tower alongside the road, a gateway further back, and traces of the walls.

Benteng Oranje

Benteng Oranje (Fort Orange) lies on a hill some distance back from the sea and just a short walk from the Gorontalo to Kwandang road. It's been partly restored, though Benteng Ota Mas Udangan is probably the more interesting of the two.

Getting There & Away

To get to Kwandang, take a bus from Gorontalo bus station (two hours, 2000 rp).

MANADO

While all of the northern peninsula of Sulawesi is sometimes referred to as Minahasa, several distinctive ethnic groups live here. The Minahasans are centred around Manado, a port city of 280,000 people and now the capital of North Sulawesi Province. The term 'Minahasa' originally referred to a confederacy of northern tribes which formed in defence against the neighbouring Bolaang Mongondow tribes who lived in the mostly mountainous country between the Minahasans and the Gorontalese.

History

Before the coming of Christianity the Minahasans were probably polygamists and animists. No other part of Indonesia accepted the European occupation as easily as Minahasa. The region was thoroughly Christianised by the Dutch, there was a large Eurasian population, and much of the indigenous culture completely disappeared. In fact the Minahasans were considered to have accepted the Dutch so readily that they became known to other Indonesians as the Anjing Belanda, or 'Dutch dogs'.

Though cloves and copra became the main agricultural products of northern Sulawesi, coffee was the first cash-crop introduced by

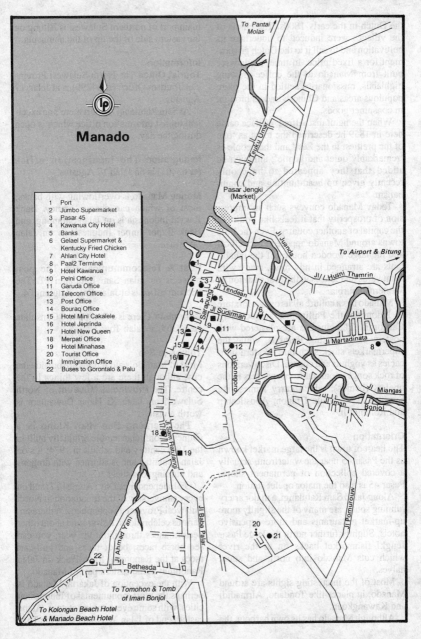

Manado

1 Port
2 Jumbo Supermarket
3 Pasar 45
4 Kawanua City Hotel
5 Banks
6 Gelael Supermarket & Kentucky Fried Chicken
7 Ahlan City Hotel
8 Paal2 Terminal
9 Hotel Kawanua
10 Pelni Office
11 Garuda Office
12 Telecom Office
13 Post Office
14 Bouraq Office
15 Hotel Mini Cakalele
16 Hotel Jeprinda
17 Hotel New Queen
18 Merpati Office
19 Hotel Minahasa
20 Tourist Office
21 Immigration Office
22 Buses to Gorontalo & Palu

the Dutch in the early 1800s. The chiefs of the villages were induced to undertake its cultivation and to sell it to the Dutch government for a fixed price. In time, roads were built from Manado to the coffee-growing highlands, missionaries settled in the more populous areas and Chinese traders brought in consumer goods.

When the naturalist Alfred Wallace came here in 1859 he described the town as 'one of the prettiest in the East' and the people as 'remarkably quiet and gentle', although he added that they appeared to have only recently given up head-hunting and cannibalism.

Today Manado conveys such an impression of prosperity that it feels like you're in the capital of another country. Even the little towns around Manado appear to be well off and the large wooden houses of the inhabitants are arranged in tidy rows, many with front yards and fences in the best tradition of Western suburbia.

Manado has a culture all its own, a mixture of Indonesia, the Philippines and southern California. The cinemas are plastered with posters of gun-toting Rambos, while the supermarkets stock such rare Western delicacies as yoghurt and cheese. Disco versions of rock songs boom out from speakers in the opelets (bemos), which carry names like Sweet Steven, White Dragon, Apostleship and Rommel Jr.

Orientation

The heart of town is the large market known as the Pasar 45 near the waterfront, actually a covered collection of permanent shops. Pasar 45 is also the major opelet station.

Along Jalan Sam Ratulangi, a major artery running south, are many of the slightly more up-market restaurants and more expensive hotels. Slightly further north the large Pasar Jengki fishmarket backs on to the river which cuts Manado into north and south halves.

Most of the interesting sights are around Manado, in places like Tondano, Airmadidi and Kawangkoan.

Although Manado has its own harbour, the main port of northern Sulawesi is Bitung on the eastern side of the tip of the peninsula.

Information

Tourist Office The North Sulawesi Provincial Tourism Office (☎ 64299) is at Jalan 17 Agustus.

At Sam Ratulangi Airport there's an excellent tourist information office which is open during the day.

Immigration The immigration office (☎ 63491) is on Jalan 17 Agustus.

Money Manado is overflowing with banks, most of which can change money. Bank Rakyat Indonesia is on Jalan Sarapung, and Bank Expor Impor Indonesia is on Jalan Sudirman.

Post & Telecommunications The post office is on Jalan Sam Ratulangi 21. The telecom office is at Jalan Sam Ratulangi 4.

Consulate There is a Philippines Consulate (☎ 62365) at Jalan Toar 3.

Things to See

Most of Manado's attractions are outside the city, although there are a few things in the centre. The **Provincial Museum** of North Sulawesi on Jalan Ki Hajar Dewantara is worth a visit.

The **Kienteng Ban Hian Kiong** is a Chinese Confucian temple originally built in the 19th century and rebuilt in 1974; it's on Jalan Panjaitan and is adorned with dragons and burning joss sticks.

On Independence Day (August 17) and on every anniversary of the foundation of North Sulawesi Province (September 23) there are various celebrations. Ask around about other performances throughout the year; you can see horse races, bendi races and bull-cart races at the Ranomuut Race Track on Jalan Ranomuut in the eastern part of Manado.

With the exception of Jakarta, Manado is perhaps the most monumental of Indonesian cities, with some eye-catching statues. At the eastern end of Jalan Yos Sudarso is the **Toar**

Lumimuut Monument, depicting the original ancestors of the Minahasans, Lumimuut and her combined son and husband, Taor. The **Monument of Ibu Walanda Maramis**, a pioneer of the Indonesian women's movement, is also on Jalan Yos Sudarso and her tomb is in the village of Maumbi in the Airmadidi district. The Monument to the Worang Battalion commemorates an army battalion which fought against the Dutch during the independence wars; it's on Jalan Sam Ratulangi near the Pasar 45. The **Sam Ratulangi Monument** honours the first governor of Sulawesi under the republican government. The **Monument of the Allied Forces** is on Jalan Sarapung, beside the Central Protestant Church of Manado, and commemorates the allied victory over Japan in WW II.

Places to Stay – bottom end

The one drawback of Manado is the lack of good, cheap accommodation. In Manado, 'cheap' begins at around 9000 rp and mid-range at 30,000 rp.

The most popular place with budget travellers is *Hotel Kawanua* (☎ 63842), Jalan Sudirman 40. The name is unfortunate, because everyone you ask directs you to the similarly named Kawanua City Hotel, the most expensive place in town. Tell people you want to go to *Kawanua kecil* (little Kawanua). Singles with shared bath are 9000 rp, while double rooms with private bath are 15,000 to 20,000 rp.

Ahlan City Hotel (☎ 63454) is in the same neighbourhood at Jalan Sudirman 103. It's basic but clean. Singles with shared bath are 8300 rp, while singles/doubles with attached bath cost 11,000/13,750 rp. They have one cheap room on the ground floor for 5000 rp.

Hotel Jeprinda (☎ 64049) at Jalan Sam Ratulangi 33 is clean and cheery, with singles/doubles for 21,000/25,000 rp. The manager speaks reasonably good English.

Hotel Mini Cakalele (☎ 52842) is at Jalan Korengkeng 40, a street running off Jalan Sam Ratulangi south of the main post office. Doubles are 17,600 rp with fan and 24,750 rp with air-con. It's clean and comfortable.

Hotel Minahasa (☎ 62059) at Jalan Sam Ratulangi 199 is an elegant-looking hotel with an old colonial feel to it. The friendly manager speaks Dutch and English. Spotlessly clean singles/doubles with fan and attached bath are 18,000/22,500 rp. With air-con they're 23,000/28,000 rp.

Places to Stay – middle

The *Hotel New Queen* (☎ 65979, fax 64440) at Jalan Wakeke 12-14 is one of the best mid-range places in Manado. It's on a quiet side street and is very clean and comfortable. Singles/doubles start from 36,800/49,900 rp. All rooms have air-con, refrigerator and colour TV.

Kolongan Beach Hotel (☎ 51001) is seven km south of the city and is the last stop for many of the opelets. The main advantage of staying here is that it's a good place for snorkelling and diving. With fan, singles/doubles are 23,000/27,000 rp, and with air-con they're 29,000/33,000 rp.

Places to Stay – top end

The *Kawanua City Hotel* (☎ 52222, fax 65220) at Jalan Sam Ratulangi 1 is Manado's number one establishment, complete with swimming pool. Singles/doubles begin at 107,000/126,000 rp plus a 21% tax and service charge.

The *Manado Beach Hotel* (☎ 67001, fax 67007) is 22 km south of the city and reachable by taxi or a long bus ride. Singles/doubles start at 117,000/136,500 rp plus a 15% service charge.

Places to Eat

Manado is famous for *rintek wuuk* – spicy dog meat (*gulei anjing* in Bahasa Indonesia), or just plain RW for short. Some other traditional Minahasan delights include *kawaok* which is fried forest rat, or *tikus utan goreng*. Top it off with some *lawa pangang* (stewed bat) and wash it down with *tinutuan* (vegetable porridge).

There's a string of eating houses all the way along Jalan Sam Ratulangi serving up a mixed bag of Chinese and Indonesian food. For those who need it, there's a *Kentucky*

Fried Chicken on Jalan Sudirman, right above the *Gelael Supermarket* which itself is well worth a visit for the fine yoghurt. Another outstanding supermarket is *Jumbo* near the Kawanua City Hotel.

Getting There & Away

Manado has an international airport. You can enter and exit Indonesia via Manado without an Indonesian visa.

Air Garuda (☎ 62242) is at Jalan Diponegoro 15; Bouraq (☎ 62757) is at Jalan Sarapung 27; Merpati (☎ 64027) is at Jalan Sam Ratulangi 135. Sempati (☎ 60282) has an agent in the Kawanua City Hotel and there is a sales desk in the airport.

Bouraq has some of the more useful flights, including those listed below.

Destination	Fare (rp)
Balikpapan	224,000
Bandung	482,000
Banjarmasin	306,000
Gorontalo	75,000
Jakarta	472,000
Palu	154,000
Samarinda	267,000
Semarang	426,000
Surabaya	358,000
Tarakan	354,000
Ternate	82,000
Ujung Pandang	207,000
Yogyakarta	409,000

Merpati has direct flights from Manado to the following places.

Destination	Fare (rp)
Ambon	212,000
Biak	310,000
Gorontalo	83,000
Jakarta	491,000
Jayapura	369,000
Kendari, Luwuk	112,000
Mangole	149,000
Melangguane	125,000
Naha	94,000
Palu	163,000
Poso	194,000
Sorong	185,000
Ternate	87,000
Ujung Pandang	218,000

There are same-day connections to Bandung 529,000 rp, Denpasar 338,000 rp and Surabaya 373,000 rp.

Garuda also has international flights connecting Manado with Amsterdam, Frankfurt, Jeddah, London, Melbourne, Paris, Singapore, Sydney and Zurich.

Sempati flies from Manado to Surabaya and Jakarta, with a possible same-day connection to Singapore.

Bus From Manado's Gorontalo bus station there are daily buses to Gorontalo. The fare is 9000 rp and the trip normally takes about 12 hours, but that depends entirely on the weather. The vehicles have to ford two rivers which sometimes flood. Don't be surprised if it takes 24 hours or longer to get between the two cities. There are also daily buses to Palu, which take two days and one night and cost 25,000 rp.

Boat There are plans afoot to start a regular boat service from Manado to Davao in the Philippines. It wasn't in operation at the time of this writing, but might be by the time you get there.

Pelni (☎ 62844) is at Jalan Sam Ratulangi 3. They have a number of ships calling into Bitung or Manado, including the modern liners *Kambuna* and *Umsini*, which pull into Bitung once every two weeks. The complete timetable is in the Getting Around chapter. Some destinations and fares (in rp) include:

Destination	1st	Ekonomi
Balikpapan	123,000	42,000
Ujung Pandang	149,000	45,000
Tanjung Priok	383,000	97,000

If the Pelni office in Manado can't give you a place on the ship, ask at their office in Bitung.

From Manado it's easy to take ships along the coast of Sulawesi as far south as Pantoloan (the port of Palu) and Pare Pare. These ships stop off at various ports on the way including Kwandang, Paleleh, Leok and Toli-Toli. There are regular ships on this run, including the *Mauru*, whose Manado office is at the entrance to the harbour terminal.

For other ships along the northern peninsula and also for ships to the islands of Tahulandang, Siau and Sangir, enquire at the shipping offices near the port in Manado.

From Manado or Bitung there are ships to Ternate in the Maluku islands. The fare is around 20,000 rp (see the Ternate section for details). There are also weekly ships from Bitung to Poso, in central Sulawesi, via Gorontalo, Pagimana and Ampana.

Getting Around

To/From the Airport The local bemos are called opelets or mikrolets. Opelets from Sam Ratulangi Airport go to Paal2 (or Paal Paal) (350 rp), and from there you can get another opelet to Pasar 45 (250 rp) or elsewhere in the city. A taxi from the airport to the city costs 5000 rp. The airport is 13 km from Manado.

Local Transport Transport around town is by opelet or mikrolet for a flat fare of 250 rp. Destinations are shown on a card in the front windscreen, *not* on the side of the van. There are various bus stations around town for destinations outside Manado. Mercifully, the vehicles do not do endless picking-up rounds!

There are several bus/opelet stations from which you can get opelets to destinations around town and to other parts of Minahasa and northern Sulawesi. Pasar 45 is the central opelet station. The other important stations are:

Gorontalo Bus Station for buses to Gorontalo. Take a Sario opelet from Pasar 45, and tell the driver you want to go to the bus station, because the opelet has to make a detour to do this.
Pasar Paal2, the station for opelets to the airport, Bitung and Airmadidi. To get to Pasar Paal2 take a Paal2 opelet from Pasar 45. Paal2 is sometimes written as Pal2.
Pasar Karombasan, the station for opelets to Tomohon, Tondano and Kawangkoan. To get to Pasar Karombasan take a Wanea opelet from Pasar 45. There are also opelets from Pasar Karombasan to Langowan, Kotamanbagu, Inobonto, Amurang, Belang and Remboken.

The Wanea and Sario opelets from Pasar 45 will take you straight down Jalan Sam Ratulangi, which is useful for the Merpati office and the restaurants and hotels along this road. Sario opelets can also be caught at the southern end of the large bridge over which Jalan Sisingamangaraja runs. Banjer and Paal2 opelets usually pass here from Pasar 45.

The E Gogola opelets from Pasar 45 take you to Jalan Eddy Gogola, which is the location of the immigration office; the tourist office is close by. These opelets go out along Jalan Diponegoro so they're also useful for getting to the telephone office and to Garuda.

There are no becaks in Manado. There are some bendis in the city (most are found in the small towns in the surrounding region) but they're not terribly numerous and not very convenient for long distances around the city.

AROUND MANADO
Pulau Bunaken

Manado's main attractions are the stunning coral reefs off nearby Pulau Bunaken. You can hop across on one of the regular motorboats, although you need your own boat to see the reefs at their best.

To get a boat to Bunaken go to the Toko Samudera Jaya in the Kuala Jengki market; the shop is hidden behind the stalls so ask directions. The shop backs onto the river and steps lead down to water level; outboard-powered outrigger longboats zip back and forth all through the day, take half an hour and cost 1000 rp.

You may be able to hire a boat in Bunaken village to take you out to the reefs, or else walk from the village to the long pier which you'll see as you arrive. Climb down the steps at the end of the pier and you're right on the reef.

The other alternative is to hire your own boat to get further out. If you hire a boat in Manado you can go back whenever you want. It's probably easiest to charter a boat at the Toko Samudera; it costs about 25,000 rp for them to take you out to the reef in the morning, paddle around for a few hours and back to Manado in the afternoon. It's worth every last rupiah!

There are no losmen or penginapan on Bunaken, though you could ask the kepala desa if there's anything available, or you could probably camp. At Liang around the other side of the island from the village there are huts where the tour groups pull in for lunch. There's another beautiful stretch of reef diagonally opposite Liang, with a sudden and quite spectacular drop, but it's so far out you need a boat to get to it.

The travel agency PT Polita Express (☎ 52231, 52768) at Jalan Sam Ratulangi 74 organises trips and scuba diving tours to Bunaken Island. The Nusantara Diving Club (☎ 3988) and Barracuda Diving Resort (62033), both north of Manado at Pantai Molas (Molas Beach) also run diving tours to Bunaken and other islands.

Snorkels and masks can be bought from Toko Akbar Ali on the western boundary of the Pasar 45.

Other Reefs

There are other coral reefs around the Minahasan peninsula. Manado Tua, or 'Old Manado', is a dormant volcano you can see off the coast. The Portuguese and Spanish once based themselves here to trade between northern Sulawesi and Maluku. Nowadays, like Bunaken Island, it's the coral reefs that pull in visitors. Other coral reefs lie off Pulau Mantehage and Bitung. The boatmen *say* there are no sharks in the waters around Bunaken, but sharks have been reported at the neighbouring islands of Manado Tua and Mantehage, and at Bitung.

Airmadidi

Airmadidi means 'boiling water'. Legend has it that there was a bathing place here and nine angels flew down from heaven on nights of the full moon to bathe and frolic in it. One night a mortal man succeeded in stealing a dress belonging to one of them – unable to return to heaven she was forced to remain on earth.

That has nothing to do with the real attraction of the place – the odd little pre-Christian

tombs known as *warugas*. They look like small Chinese temples and the corpses were placed in a squatting position with household articles, gold and porcelain – most have been plundered. There's a group of these tombs at Airmadidi Bawah, a 15-minute walk from Airmadidi opelet station.

Opelets go to Airmadidi from Manado's Paal2 terminal (400 rp). From Airmadidi you can also take an opelet to Tondano (1000 rp, 45 minutes) or to Bitung (1000 rp, 40 minutes). You can see more warugas at Sawangan, Likupang, and at Kema on the south coast near Bitung.

Kawangkoan

Northern Sulawesi did not escape WW II. The region was occupied by the Japanese between January 1942 and August 1945, and in 1945 the Allied advance into Indonesia resulted in the bombing of the main towns in northern Sulawesi, including Manado where there was considerable damage. During the occupation the Japanese dug caves into the hills surrounding Manado to act as air-raid shelters and storage space for ammunition, food, weapons and medical supplies.

One such cave is three km out of Kawangkoan on the road to Kiawa. There are opelets to Kawangkoan from Pasar Karombasan (the Wanea terminal) in Manado.

Tondano

Danau Tondano, a crater lake in an extinct volcano, is 30 km south-west of Manado. It's 600 metres above sea level, making it pleasantly cool, scenic and an excellent place to visit. In addition, some of the best Japanese caves are just outside Tondano on the road to Airmadidi. A bus from Airmadidi to Tondano will get you to the caves in 45 minutes. From the caves you can hitch or walk (one hour) to Tondano opelet station and get an opelet back to Pasar Karombasan in Manado. Opelets from Tondano to Tomohon take 30 minutes.

Tomohon

Several km out of the hill town of Tomohon on the road to Tara Tara are more Japanese caves. Take an opelet from Pasar Karombasan (Wanea terminal) to Tomohon and another opelet towards Tara Tara. There are also opelets between Tomohon and Tondano, and between Kawangkoan and Tomohon. Tomohon is the site of a Christian college and a centre for the study of Christian theology in Minahasa.

Batu Pinabetengan

This stone, scratched with the vague outline of human figures, is said to be the place where Minahasan chiefs held meetings. It is said that it was at this site that the chiefs divided up the land between the different tribes. The locals sometimes pronounce 'Batu Pinabetengan' as 'Watu Pinawetengan' – *watu* means 'stone' and *weteng* means 'divide', meaning this was the place where the division of land was carried out. *Mina-esa* (from which the name Minahasa is derived) means 'to become one' or 'united'.

The scratchings on the stone have never been deciphered though it is thought that they may record agreements concerning the division of land amongst the tribes, and the political unification of Minahasa in the early meetings between the chiefs.

The stone is close to Pinabetengan village, about 40 km from Manado and five km from Kawangkoan. To get there, take an opelet to Kawangkoan from Manado's Wanea station, then a bendi from Kawangkoan to Desa Pinabetengan. The bendi will take you as far as the turn-off road that leads to Batu Pinabetengan and then you have to walk the last half hour.

Tara Tara

About 30 km south of Manado and eight km from Tomohon, Tara Tara is one of the centres of Minahasa art.

BITUNG

Sheltered by Pulau Lembah, Bitung is the chief port of Minahasa and lies to the east of Manado. Many ships dock at Bitung rather than at Manado. Because of the port facilities, there are also many factories here. Overall, the town is not very attractive, but

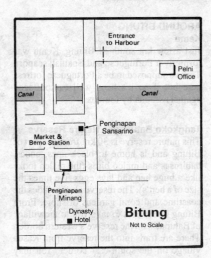

there are some nice beaches along the way. The Pelni office (☎ 21167) is on Jalan Jakarta, within the harbour compound.

Places to Stay & Eat

Penginapan Sansarino near the main market has rooms for 10,000 rp and a downstairs restaurant.

Penginapan Minang (☎ 21333) is a dark hovel above a restaurant by the same name at Jalan Sam Ratulangi 34. Rooms go for 15,000 rp with attached mandi.

The fanciest place in town is *Dynasty Hotel* (☎ 22111), Jalan Yos Sudarso 10. Doubles cost 50,000 to 60,000 rp.

Getting There & Away

Bitung is 50 km from Manado and is connected by a surfaced racetrack along which kamikaze opelet drivers break land, water and air speed records all at once. There are regular departures from Manado's Paal2 terminal; the fare is 1000 rp and the trip takes about an hour. The opelet drops you off at the Mapalus terminal just outside Bitung, where you catch another opelet into town (250 rp, 10 minutes).

AROUND BITUNG
Kema
Just a few km south of Bitung, Kema was formerly a Portuguese and Spanish seaport. There's supposed to be a Portuguese fortress here but if so it's been well camouflaged against assaults by tourists.

Tangkoko Batuangas Nature Reserve
This nature reserve is 30 km from the port of Bitung and is home to black apes, anoas, babirusas and maleo birds (the maleo looks like a huge hen and lays eggs five times the size of a hen's). The reserve also includes the coastline and coral gardens offshore. From Bitung hire a boat to take you to the village of Batuputih on the reserve's western border. There are trails into the reserve from Kasua village on the south-east border. You may need a permit from PHPA in Manado.

SANGIR-TALAUD
Strewn across the straits between Indonesia and the southern Mindanao region of the Philippines are the islands of Sangir-Talaud. These small and volcanically active islands are at the end of the long chain of volcanoes that stretches from the western highlands of Sumatra, east through Java and Nusa Tenggara and then north through the Banda islands of Maluku to north-east Sulawesi. One of the more recent volcanic eruptions in northern Sulawesi was that of Gunung Api on Pulau Siau in 1974, which compelled the temporary evacuation of the entire population of the island (then 40,000 people).

The main islands in the Sangir group are Sangir Besar, Siau, Tahulandang and Biaro. The Talaud group consists of Karakelong, Salibabu, Kabaruan, Karatung, Nanusa and Miangas. Despite their tiny size, around 300,000 people live on these islands! The

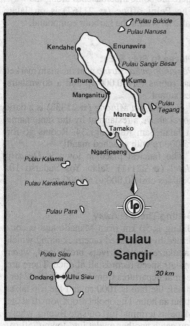

Pulau Sangir

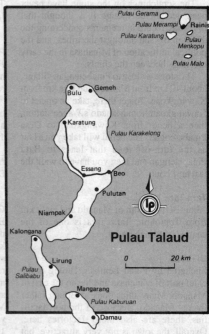

Pulau Talaud

capital of the Sangir-Talaud group is Tahuna on Sangir Besar.

History

Once upon a time these islands were subject to strong Islamic influence from the Ternate sultanate to the east. That was checked by the Christian missionaries who followed in the wake of the Dutch takeover in 1677. Most of the population was converted to Christianity. Prior to the arrival of the missionaries, ancestral spirits were important, and some women (and occasionally men) became possessed by spirits. Human sacrifice at some ceremonies was also reported.

Not only did the Dutch bring a new religion but they also encouraged the local population to raise coconuts (for copra) and nutmeg. The island economy came to rely heavily on trade in these products, chiefly carried on with Ternate and Manado. Today the main industries are copra and cloves.

Getting There & Away

Air Merpati has almost daily flights to Naha which is the airfield 20 km from Tahuna.

Boat For ships to these islands ask at the shipping offices near the entrance to the harbour terminal in Manado.

There are usually about three ships a week between Manado and Siau and Tahuna. Some of these ships go to Siau and Tahuna and then to the ports along the northern peninsula of Sulawesi. Also ask about ships to Beo and Lirung on Karakelong.

Maluku (The Moluccas)

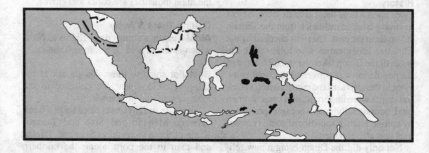

From Halmahera in the north, to Wetar off the north-east end of Timor, are the thousand islands of Maluku (or the Moluccas). Sprawled across a vast area of ocean but making up only a tiny proportion of Indonesia's land area, what these islands lack in size they more than make up for in historical significance. These were the fabled 'spice islands' to which Indian, Chinese, Arab and later European traders came in search of the cloves, nutmeg and mace which grew here and nowhere else; and it was these islands which bore the brunt of the first European attempts to wrest control of the Indonesian archipelago and the lucrative spice trade.

The destinations of most visitors to the region are: Ambon, the capital of Maluku province, just south of the large island of Seram; the cluster of islands south-east of Ambon known as the Bandas; and the two adjacent northern islands of Ternate and Tidore off the west coast of Halmahera. Although spices are still produced in these islands it's the fine tropical scenery, the relics of the early European invasion, some excellent snorkelling and diving, plus some enticing beaches which draw visitors today. Maluku is one of Indonesia's remotest provinces and its lesser known islands offer infinite scope for getting right off the tourist trail.

HISTORY

Before the arrival of the Europeans, the sultanate of Ternate held tenuous sway over some of the islands and parts of neighbouring Sulawesi and Irian Jaya, but there was little political unity – when the Portuguese reached the Indonesian archipelago Maluku was known to them as the 'land of many kings'.

The spice trade, however, goes back a lot further than the Portuguese and Dutch. The Roman encyclopedist Pliny described trade in cinnamon and other spices from Indonesia to Madagascar and East Africa and from there to Rome. By the 1st century AD Indonesian trade was firmly established with other parts of Asia, including India and China, and spices also reached Europe via the caravan routes from India and the Persian Gulf.

Apart from Marco Polo and a few wandering missionaries, Portuguese sailors were the first Europeans to set foot on Indonesian soil. Their first small fleet and its 'white Bengalis' (as the local inhabitants called them) arrived in Melaka in 1509; their prime objective was the spice islands. For a hundred years previously the Portuguese had been pushing down the west African coast and when Vasco de Gama's ships rounded southern Africa and reached Calicut in India in 1498 the Portuguese suddenly got a whiff of the huge

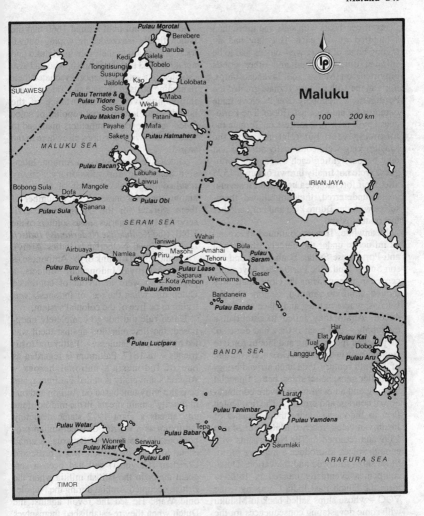

Maluku

0   100   200 km

SULAWESI

Pulau Morotai
Berebere
Daruba
Kedi   Galela
Tongitisungi   Tobelo
Susupu   Kao
Jailolo   Lolobata
Pulau Ternate &   Maba
Pulau Tidore
Soa Siu   Weda
Pulau Makian   Patani
Payahe   Mafa
Saketa   *Pulau Halmahera*
MALUKU SEA

IRIAN JAYA

Pulau Bacan
Labuha
Laiwui
Bobong Sula   Mangole
Dofa   *Pulau Obi*
Sanana
Pulau Sula   SERAM SEA

Wahai
Taniwel
Airbuaya   Piru   Masohi   Amahai   Bula
Namlea   Tehoru   *Pulau*
Pulau Buru   *Pulau Lease*   *Seram*
Leksula   Saparua   Werinama   Geser
Kota Ambon
Pulau Ambon
Bandaneira
Pulau Banda

Har
Elat   *Pulau Kai*
Tual   Dobo
Pulau Lucipara   Langgur   *Pulau Aru*
BANDA SEA

Larat
Pulau Tanimbar
Pulau Wetar   *Pulau Yamdena*
Tepa
Wonreli   Serwaru
Pulau Kisar   *Pulau Babar*
Pulau Leti   Saumlaki
TIMOR   ARAFURA SEA

profits to be made from the Asian trade. Because the trade was almost exclusively in the hands of Muslims they had the added satisfaction (and excuse) that any blow against their commercial rivals was a blow against the infidels. A master plan was devised to bring all the important Indian Ocean trading ports under Portuguese control. The capture of Melaka in 1511, fol-

lowing the capture of Goa on the west Indian coast, preceded the Portuguese attempt to wrest control of the Spice Islands: Ternate and Tidore, Ambon, Seram and the Bandas.

Ternate and Tidore, the rival clove-producing islands of Maluku, were the scene of the greatest Portuguese effort. They were ruled by kings who controlled the cultivation of cloves, and who policed the region with fleets of war boats with sails and more than a hundred rowers each. But they had no trading boats of their own – cloves had to be shipped out, and food and other goods imported, on Malay and Javanese ships. Early in the 16th century Ternate granted the Portuguese a monopoly over its clove trade in return for help against Tidore. The Portuguese built their first fortress on Ternate the following year, but relations with the Muslim king were continually strained and they began fighting each other. The Portuguese were not finally thrown out until 1575 after their fort had been besieged for several years; undeterred, they ingratiated themselves with the Tidore king and built another fort on that island.

Meanwhile, Ternate continued to expand its influence under the fiercely Islamic and anti-Portuguese Sultan Baab Ullah and his son Sultan Said. The Portuguese never succeeded in monopolising the clove trade; they moved south to Ambon, Seram and the Bandas, where nutmeg and mace were produced. Again they failed to establish a monopoly – and even if they had done so, they lacked the shipping and labour force to control trade in the Indian Ocean. By the end of the 16th century, the Dutch arrived bringing better guns, better ships, better financial backing and an even more severe combination of courage and brutality. The first Dutch fleet to Indonesia, under the command of Jacob van Neck, reached Maluku in March 1599 and returned to The Netherlands with enough spices to produce a massive profit. More ships followed and the various Dutch companies eventually merged in 1602 to form the Dutch East India Company – the VOC – whose ships sailed back to Maluku with some devastating consequences for the inhabitants of the Bandas, most of whom were exterminated.

By 1630 the Dutch were established on Ambon in the heart of the spice islands and had their headquarters at Batavia in the west. Melaka fell to them in 1641, but a monopoly of the spice trade eluded them for many years; they first had to fight the Ternateans, and the Ambonese with their Makassarese allies. It was not until around 1660 that the Dutch finally succeeded in wiping out all local opposition to their rule in Maluku and not until 1663 that the Spanish, who had also established a small presence, evacuated their remaining posts in Ternate and Tidore. Inevitably, however, the importance of the islands as an international supplier of spice faded, as European competitors managed to set up their own plantations elsewhere in the world.

Dutch rule was centred in Ambon. Intensive schooling and missionary activity resulted in a high standard of education among the Ambonese. A large number of them worked for the Dutch in the civil service, as missionaries and as soldiers of the KNIL (the *Koninklijke Nederlandse Indisch Leger* – Royal Netherlands Indies Army). The Dutch liked to think of the Ambonese as their most loyal Indonesian subjects, a people who were in favour of continued Dutch rule when the rest of Indonesia was trying to be free of the colonial system.

Dutch rule did not go completely unopposed; the first rebellion against them was led by Thomas Matulessy – 'Pattimura' to his friends – in 1817. Pattimura is regarded as one of Indonesia's national heroes – Ambon's university is called Pattimura, and so is the army unit based on Ambon and one of the city's main streets. In the middle of the city stands a giant 1972 statue depicting Pattimura as a warrior of superhuman proportions. He came from Saparua, a small island just east of Ambon, was a professed Christian (Calvinist) and had been a sergeant-major in the British militia when the British occupied Ambon during the Napoleonic Wars. He led the revolt against the Dutch when they re-established themselves after the British left. The uprising lasted only a few months and ended with the capture and execution of Pattimura.

There were several other revolts in Maluku over the next 50 years and it was not until the 1890s that the Dutch managed to recruit the Ambonese as soldiers in any great numbers – indeed, many fought against the Dutch in the Indonesian independence wars.

Further problems arose in Ambon in 1949, when the Dutch finally quit Indonesia, but what really happened is obscured in the smog of history. There are numerous theories: some say Ambonese soldiers revolted against Indonesian rule because they preferred continued Dutch control to Javanese domination, others suggest that these soldiers were deliberately sent back (armed) to Ambon by Dutch officers opposed to independence for Indonesia, but others believe that the majority of the Ambonese population wanted no part of the independence struggle.

Whatever happened, in April 1950 an independent Republic of the South Moluccas (the RMS, *Republik Maluku Selatan*) was proclaimed in Ambon supported, it appears, by most of the 2000 or so Ambonese KNIL troops on the island. In July, Indonesian government troops occupied Buru and parts of Seram and at the end of September the first landings on Ambon took place. By the middle of November most resistance on Ambon had been put down and in early December the RMS government fled to the Seram jungles (where many RMS troops had already gone).

At this time there were still several camps of Ambonese KNIL soldiers and their families in Java. Initially the Dutch intended to demobilise them and send them back to Ambon, but it was feared that this would virtually be sending them to their deaths. Instead, the Dutch government moved them (about 12,000 people) to The Netherlands. It was hoped that once the RMS was suppressed they could be sent back to Indonesia. Meanwhile, they were treated as political refugees, dumped in a camp, and demobilised from the KNIL. They and their descendants (now over 40,000) have been in The Netherlands ever since.

On Seram the remainder of the RMS forces clashed every now and then with Indonesian troops. In 1952 the RMS president and a number of ministers of the RMS government were captured; they were tried in Jakarta in 1955 and given relatively mild sentences ranging from three to 10 years'

imprisonment (perhaps a gesture of reconciliation on Sukarno's part). The fighting on Seram continued into the mid-1960s.

The impossible dream of an independent 'South Moluccas' still has its adherents among the Malukans in The Netherlands. One of their more memorable actions was a headline-grabbing train hijack in the mid-1970s, in which the hijackers shot and killed several innocent passengers. This triggered a severe public backlash, with many Dutch calling for their expulsion. Although the enmity has died down, many Malukans in The Netherlands have created some tight-knit communities that refuse to be assimilated into the mainstream Dutch society, in preparation for their 'return home'.

Today Maluku is politically stable and 'Indonesianised' although, with its slightly Polynesian feel, it remains different from other parts of Indonesia. Despite its location in Indonesia's remote outer provinces, Ambon has as cosmopolitan an air as anywhere east of Denpasar, and its people maintain a sense of their own distinctness from other Indonesians. Maluku's distance from the centres of national activity prompted the Suharto government to pick Pulau Buru, west of Ambon, as the site of a stark internment camp for most of the 1970s for the 10,000-plus survivors of its 'anti-Communist' purges.

Spices are still grown on many Maluku islands but they are no longer the mainstay of the economy. Large-scale fishing, logging and mining, controlled jointly by foreign companies and the Indonesian government, are growth industries but show scant regard for the environment. Agriculture is important, with coffee, rice, sago, fruit, sugarcane, maize and copra the major products. Tourism is slowly increasing but, despite its obvious potential, it's not yet a big money-earner.

CLIMATE

Timing a visit to Maluku is a bit different from going to the rest of Indonesia. The dry season in Maluku is generally from September to March, with average temperatures of 34 to 38°C. The wet season is from April to

August, with average temperatures of 18 to 20°C. There's not much point visiting the region in the wet season; the rain *pounds* down endlessly and since the seas are rough, there's less inter-island sea transport.

In some parts, local variations complicate the picture. On Seram, for example, the south coast follows the general Maluku pattern with its wet season from April to August, with particularly rough seas in July and August – but the north coast has its wet season from September to March and associated strong winds blow from January to March. Aru in far south-east Maluku has its wet season from September to April, in tune with most of Indonesia, but not with Maluku.

STAPLES & SPICES

Sago

The staple food of much of Maluku and other parts of eastern Indonesia is sago, from the sago palm. After 15 years the sago palm produces a flower spike; if the flower is allowed to mature, the fruit will feed off the starchy core of the trunk, leaving it a hollow shell. When the palm is cultivated, the tree is cut down when the flower spike forms and the starchy pith of the trunk is scooped out, strained and washed to remove the fibres from the starch.

There's enough starch from one trunk to feed a whole family for months. Sago bread is commonly sold in Maluku in the form of thick wafers. *Papeda*, a unique native dish, is made by pulverising and straining the pulp from the sago palm and then boiling it up to make a glutinous porridge-like mass which is eaten hot. You can also use sago combined with brown sugar to make a sort of fudge; sago wafers and fried fish make a filling meal.

Every scrap of the sago palm is used for making something, the bark for the outer walls of houses, the leaves for roofs and the wood for house frames.

Cassava

Also known as mandioca, tapioca, manioc or yuca, cassava is another tropical staple, par-

Sago palm

ticularly among the poor in areas where cereals and potatoes won't grow. It's extracted from the tuberous roots of a South American plant which was brought to Indonesia by the Portuguese.

These roots grow well in poor soils: they are easy to plant, harvest and store, they can be planted at different times of the year to ensure a year-round crop, the yield of starch per hectare is more than from any other crop, and it is not susceptible to many diseases. The drawback is that most of the root is starch, with only a tiny amount of protein and fat, although the leaves have a high protein content. The tapioca pellets familiar to Westerners are actually cassava starch pellets forced through a mesh then heated while being shaken or stirred on a plate.

Nutmeg & Mace

Nutmeg and mace are both produced from the fruit of the nutmeg tree. The fleshy, yellow-brown fruit resembles an apricot and splits in half when it's ripe, exposing a scarlet seed-covering which is dried to produce mace. Nutmeg is made from the seed itself. Although both contain much the same type of chemicals, differences in the quantity of these chemicals account for their different tastes. A 17th-century Spanish historian wrote that these spices:

...correct stinking Breath, clear the Eyes, comfort the Stomach, Liver, and Spleen, and digest Meat. They are a Remedy against many other Distempers, and serve to add outward Lustre to the Face...

Cloves

Cloves come from a tree also native to the spice islands; today they are used mainly as food flavouring, but clove oil can also be used as an anaesthetic (try applying some to your gums). The word 'clove' comes from the French word *clou* which means 'nail' and refers to the dry, unexpanded, nail-shaped flower bud. The buds are picked just before the flower bud opens. Once the flower bud opens, its value as a spice is lost, because the composition of its oils changes.

FLORA & FAUNA

Maluku is a transition zone between Asia and Australia/New Guinea and there are some flora and fauna unique to the province. Vegetation is luxuriant and includes some Australian species, such as *kayu putih* or eucalypts, as well as the usual tropical Asiatic species. Maluku hardwoods are prized by timber companies. Clove and nutmeg trees are spread throughout central Maluku, sago and coconut trees through the entire province. Ambon and Tanimbar are famous for their wild orchids, while Ternate has some of the most brilliantly coloured bougainvillea you'll ever see.

Maluku's seas teem with life, including dugongs, turtles, trepang, sharks and all manner of tropical and shell fish. On land there are few Asiatic-type mammals such as monkeys but there are also small marsupials such as the cuscus and the bandicoot. Miniature tree kangaroos, wallabies, crocodiles and monitor lizards are found on the southeastern island groups of Aru and Kai. Wild pig and deer are common, but they are introduced. Insect life abounds and butterflies are particularly brilliant.

Maluku is well known for its exotic birdlife, particularly Seram's, whose colourful birds are being smuggled out at an alarming rate – you can see some of them in the Ambon pasar. In Maluku there are 22 different varieties of parrots, numerous lories, black cockatoos, kingfishers, varieties of pigeons, the huge flightless cassowary and, on Aru, a couple of varieties of the famous birds of paradise, including the greater bird of paradise and bower birds.

Birds of Paradise

The first exotic bird of paradise specimens reached Europe in 1522 aboard the last surviving ship of Magellan's round-the-world fleet. The skins of these birds had been presented to the sailors by the King of Bacan, an island in Maluku off south-west Halmahera – and were said by the king to have come from a 'terrestrial paradise'. These specimens, like others which came to Europe in later years, had had their legs and wings removed by the native skinners to emphasise the plumes; hence the belief that the birds never alighted on the ground but stayed airborne (despite the lack of wings). It was not until the 18th century that this and other myths were disproved, although the romantic aura was never quite dispelled and the first specimen's scientific name, *Paradisea apoda*, even indicates its legless form! Of the more than 50 species now known, most live in Papua New Guinea and Irian Jaya, although a few are found in outlying Maluku islands like Aru.

BOOKS

The 19th-century naturalist Alfred Russel Wallace spent six years, much of it in Maluku, roaming the Indonesian archipelago. His record of the journey *The Malay Archipelago* still makes fascinating reading. Another Victorian writer, Anna Forbes, in her *Unbeaten Tracks in Islands of the Far East*, presents a lively account of her time in

Bird of paradise

deals mainly with Ambon, where she lived and worked for a couple of years in the 1970s. She found that many adat customs, including the *pela* law – the traditional Ambonese bond between two or more villages for mutual protection and help in crises – were adhered to and that magic and witchcraft were still alive. She also observed that adat marriages were often carried out in conjunction with Christian and/or civil marriages.

Dieter Bartel's fascinating book *Guarding the Invisible Mountain*, based on research in central Maluku in 1974 and 1975, also discusses the key role of the pela alliances.

GETTING THERE & AWAY

Ambon is the transport hub for all Maluku, and is well served by Merpati, Garuda and Mandala airlines, with flights to both Irian Jaya and western Indonesia. There are also regular flights from Sulawesi to Ternate in northern Maluku.

The Pelni passenger liners *Rinjani*, *Tidar* and *Umsini* call at Ambon (and the *Tidar* also at Ternate) on their fortnightly runs between western Indonesia, Sulawesi and Irian Jaya. Other irregular ships also link these ports with the rest of the Indonesian archipelago.

GETTING AROUND

If you're planning to do a lot of travel in Maluku, you need either time or money – preferably both! Merpati has a number of flights out of Ambon and Ternate to various destinations around Maluku.

Transport by sea between adjacent islands is generally fairly easy but time-consuming. There are regular passenger ferries between Ambon, Saparua and Seram, and frequent motorboats every day making the short hop between Ternate and Tidore, as well as regular passenger ships from Ternate to various places on Halmahera.

Long distance sea transport around the islands becomes more of a problem. There are semi-regular boats from Ambon to Banda and others like the *Niaga XVIII* doing loops round northern and southern Maluku from

Indonesia, much of it spent on Ambon and Tanimbar. Marika Hanbury-Tenison's *A Slice of Spice* details a visit to Ambon and the wilds of Seram in the early 1970s. Lawrence & Lorne Blair's exciting *Ring of Fire* (Bantam Press, 1988) has chapters on the Bandas and Aru. For an accurate picture of the tourist scene in Banda today, read the relevant chapter of Annabel Sutton's *The Islands In Between* (Impact Books, London, 1989). In his novel *Gifts of Unknown Things* (Hodder & Stoughton, London, 1983), Lyall Watson has used a fictitious island in Maluku as the setting for some intriguing, mystical events. See the introductory Facts for The Visitor chapter for more on some of these books.

Shirley Deane's *Ambon, Island of Spices* (John Murray, London) touches on the Lease Islands, Seram, the Bandas, Kai and Aru but

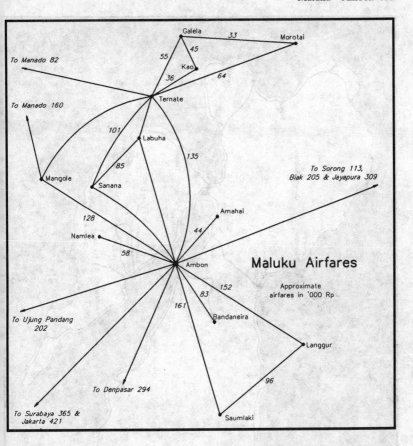

Maluku Airfares

Approximate
airfares in '000 Rp

Ambon. In general, conditions on these are fairly primitive.

Ambon

Barely a dot on a map of Indonesia, the island of Ambon is the economic and transport centre of Maluku. Its landscape is dramatic and mountainous, with little flat land for cultivation or roads. There are a few good beaches, coral reefs and plenty of opportunities for hiking and exploring Ambon's abundant insect, bird and plant life and its culture. Don't be deceived by its largely Christian and increasingly modern veneer – adat customs and practices plus magic and superstition still exist. To appreciate the island, you need to get out into the villages, where there's a definite Polynesian feel. Ambon reeks with history, especially at places like the old European fort at Hila on the north coast.

The island is just 48 km by 22 km, with a larger northern portion known as Leihitu and a smaller arrow-head shaped southern portion known as the Leitimur Peninsula.

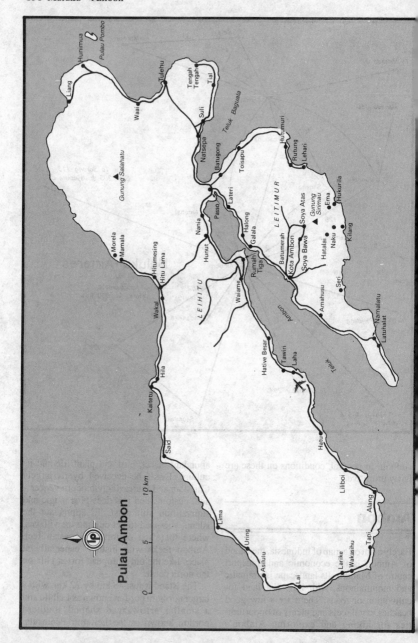

Pulau Ambon

They're separated for most of their length by Teluk Ambon and are connected only by a narrow isthmus at Passo. Kota Ambon, the capital, lies on the Leitimur Peninsula, on the southern side of Teluk Ambon.

Although Ambon is in the 'Ring of Fire' there are no active volcanoes. Most Ambonese still live in villages strung along the coasts. There are no rice paddies, but many sago and spice plantations (rice is grown on neighbouring Seram). Village craftspeople stitch clove twigs into stick figures and large, intricate mounted ships. Others pound the trunks of spiky sago palms to extract the sludgy pulp, which forms the staple Maluku diet, while the leaves are woven into baskets.

You may get to see the Bulu Gila or crazy bamboo dance, a feature of Ambonese magic (but not adat), where men in a trance are somehow taken over by the bamboo that they are holding. *Arumbae*, or gondola races between traditional carved boats with sailors decked out in colourful costumes, are fairly common on Teluk Ambon.

History

Ambon had the misfortune to be located almost at the dead centre of the spice islands. As early as the 14th century, central Maluku found the rest of the world thrust upon it because of the demand for its spices.

The original trade intermediary between central Maluku and western Indonesia was the sultanate of Ternate, which brought Islam to central Maluku and also seems to have had some influence in reducing the incidence of head-hunting. Other colonisers settled along the coasts of these islands – like the Javanese who set up a base at Hitu on the north coast of Ambon. At this time, though Ambon grew no spices, it was an important way-station between Ternate and the nutmeg-producing Bandas.

The Ternateans were displaced on Ambon by the Portuguese; they stayed until 1605 when the Ambonese teamed up instead with the newly arrived Dutch. When the Portuguese fort (in what is now Kota Ambon) was about to be attacked, the Portuguese appear simply to have surrendered and sailed away;

the Dutch occupied the fort, renamed it Victoria and made Ambon their spice-island base.

While the Portuguese probably didn't have much effect on the political fortunes of the Maluku kingdoms, or on the overall structure of trade, there was one man among them who initiated what would be a permanent change in eastern Indonesia. This was the Spaniard Francis Xavier (later canonised) who co-founded the Jesuit order. In 1546 and 1547 Xavier worked as a missionary in Ambon, Ternate and Morotai and laid the foundations for permanent missions there. After his departure from Maluku, others continued his work and by the 1560s there were perhaps 10,000 Catholics in the area, mostly on Ambon. By the 1590s there were said to be 50,000 to 60,000, and these Christian communities survived through the succeeding centuries.

The Portuguese left other signs of their presence: the romantic *keroncong* ballads sung to the guitar are of Portuguese origin. A considerable number of Indonesian words are from Portuguese and many family names still found on Ambon are Portuguese. But overall, given the grandeur of their original designs to conquer the trade of Asia, the Portuguese legacy in Maluku was insignificant: though they had introduced Christianity into the region, it was the Dutch who nurtured it and made Ambon the centre of administration and missionary work for all Maluku.

The Dutch influence is still obvious today – notice the demure blouses that women wear with their pink and white-checked sarongs and the considerable numbers of Dutch and Dutch/Moluccan tourists; if you speak Dutch, you're sure to be invited into some local homes.

In WW II Kota Ambon was bombed and the island was attacked by the Japanese. Australian forces helped to defend Ambon but were defeated. Those who survived were interned in Japanese prisoner-of-war camps, where many died of starvation and disease. Australians are liked on Ambon and the maintenance of the Australian War Cemetery in Kota Ambon is funded by the Australian government.

KOTA AMBON

The post-independence RMS rebellion having faded into history, Ambon today is a much more peaceful place. The only substantial urban area on the island is the city of Ambon (Kota Ambon), the capital of Maluku, built around a natural harbour where the Portuguese established Fort Victoria some 400 years ago. The city was bombed heavily during WW II and battles were fought here during the RMS rebellion. Today it's a busy port and the bay is full of boats of all kinds.

The central area is reasonably prosperous and there are a large number of churches and Chinese merchants living here. The western part of the city is consideably poorer, mostly a drab collection of concrete blocks.

A church on Jalan Anthoni Rhebok exhibits one of those massive murals for which Ambon is memorable; a huge painting on the rear wall depicts the cross as a bridge for hordes of people to walk from earth to heaven.

Becaks add colour and quiet to certain parts of the city. Tuesdays and Fridays see white becaks in action, Mondays and Thursdays yellow, while red is the colour for Wednesdays and Saturdays. Becaks of all three colours operate on Sundays. Many of the pedallers are from Sulawesi and some have becaks of all three colours to get round the restrictions. You hear quite a lot of rock music in Ambon; the Ambonese are well known for their love of music.

Orientation & Information

On the south side of Teluk Ambon, Kota Ambon is hemmed in by the hills to the south and stretches along the waterfront for several km. The main street for shops and offices is Jalan A Y Patty and hotels are two or three blocks back (south) from here. The bemo and bus terminal and main market – the latter especially busy and colourful early in the morning – are in a relatively new complex on reclaimed coastal land about half a km

east. The main harbour is at the end of Jalan Yos Sudarso, a short walk from Jalan A Y Patty.

Tourist Office The tourist office is on the ground floor of the governor's office (Kantor Gubernor). It's open Monday to Thursday from 8 am to 2.30 pm, Friday from 8 to 11.30 am and Saturday from 8 am to 1 pm. Reasonable maps of the island are sold here and you can rent snorkelling gear.

Immigration Should you need to visit the city immigration office (☎ 42128), it's at Jalan Batu Capeo 57/5, way out in the south-west of Kota Ambon. Bemos from the bemo/bus terminal near the new main market will take you straight there.

Money Bank Negara Indonesia 1946 on Jalan Said Perintah is the best place to change money (faster service), but you can also change at Bank Expor Impor Indonesia and Bank Dagang Negara, both on Jalan Raya Pattimura.

Post & Telecommunications The post office is on Jalan Raya Pattimura and the telecom office is directly across the road.

Fort Victoria

Originally built by the Portuguese in 1575 but renamed by the Dutch, this used to be on the waterfront but, owing to a relatively recent land reclamation project, it's now back from the coastline. Parts of the fort are still standing while others have been replaced by new buildings used by the military. You need a permit from them to visit the fort, which is surrounded by Taman Victoria, a park which always seems to be closed.

Siwalima Museum

Among the model boats made of turtle shell, sago palm and cloves, this museum also houses ancestor statues from south-east Maluku and ancestor skulls from northern Buru. The captions are in both English and Indonesian and it's definitely worth a visit.

Guided tours in English seem to be compulsory.

The museum is just off the road leading west from Kota Ambon to the village of Amahusu. Take an Amahusu bemo (200 rp) from the terminal. Tell the driver you want the museum. It's about a 10-minute ride then a five to 10-minute walk uphill to the museum. Opening hours are Sunday from 10 am to 3 pm; Tuesday, Wednesday and Thursday from 9 am to 2 pm and Saturday from 9 am to 1 pm.

War Cemeteries

The WW II cemetery is in the suburb of Tantui, about two km from the centre of Kota Ambon. The cemetery is for Australian, Dutch, British and Indian servicemen killed in Sulawesi and Maluku and there is row upon row of marker stones and plaques. A Tantui bemo (200 rp) from the terminal takes you straight past the cemetery. Just down from this cemetery is the Indonesian Heroes Cemetery dedicated to Indonesian servicemen killed fighting the Maluku rebels during the 1950s and 1960s.

Other Attractions

The Pattimura Monument stands at one end of the sports field. Pattimura is said to have been betrayed by one of the village chiefs on Saparua who took him prisoner and delivered him to the Dutch on Ambon. The monument stands on the site where he and his followers were hanged.

On a hill overlooking Kota Ambon is the Martha Christina Tiahahu memorial, honouring another revered Maluku freedom fighter. Tiahahu's father supported Pattimura against the Dutch and the story goes that after they were both captured, her father was executed on Pulau Nusa Laut and she was put onto a ship to be sent to Java; grieved by her father's execution she starved herself to death and her remains were buried at sea.

Nearby is the Karang Panjang tourist village where you may see 'traditional' ceremonies and watch sago being processed. The village is surrounded by gardens of varieties of coconut trees, orchids, bamboo species and fruit trees. To get there, catch a Karang Panjang bemo (200 rp) from the bemo/bus terminal.

Places to Stay – bottom end

In a case of poetic justice, Kota Ambon – once heavily exploited by the Europeans – has learned how to exploit tourists with a vengeance. This is the most expensive city in Indonesia for accommodation, and if you get a single room for 10,000 rp you're doing well. However, when they're not too busy, many hotels can be persuaded to give a discount. Discounts can range up to 20% so it's worth asking.

Hotel Gamalama (☎ 52720) on Jalan Anthony Rhebok is about as cheap as you'll find. It's a a decent place in the quieter, more leafy part of town. Singles/doubles are 10,000/15,000 rp with an attached bathroom.

Penginapan Beta (☎ 53463), Jalan Wim Reawaru 114, has verandahs, a hint of tropical foliage and some possibility of a cool breeze. Singles/doubles with mandi and fan start at 13,200/20,900 rp.

Hotel New Silalou (☎ 53197) at Jalan Sedap Malam 4 has adequate rooms with shared bath, and is clean and friendly. Singles/doubles are 10,000/20,000 rp including breakfast.

Next door to the Beta, at Jalan Wim Reawaru 115, the *Hotel Transit Rezfanny* (☎ 42300) has singles with shared mandi, for 14,000 rp. A room with private bath costs 22,500 rp and one with air-con will cost you 35,000 rp.

Hotel Elenoor (☎ 52834) at Jalan Anthony Rhebok 30 has singles starting from 15,000 rp including breakfast. It's a nice place but no one here speaks a word of English.

Wisma Game is on Jalan Ahmad Yani near the Garuda office. Singles start at 12,000 rp.

Places to Stay – middle

The *Hotel Hero* (☎ 42978) on Jalan Wim Reawaru is a new and shiny place and is definitely recommended. Economy rooms are 38,500 rp; standard rooms 45,000 rp;

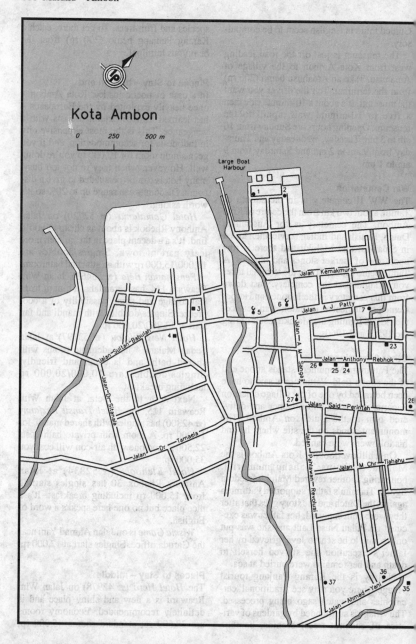

Kota Ambon

0   250   500 m

Large Boat
Harbour

Jalan Kemakmuran

Jalan A J Patty

Jalan—Sultan—Babulah

Jalan—A M Sangaji

Jalan—Anthony Rebhok

Jalan—Dr—Sitanala

Jalan—Said—Perintah

Jalan—Dr—Tamaela

Jalan Pahlawan—Revolusi

Jalan—M Chr Tiahahu

Jalan Ahmad—Yani

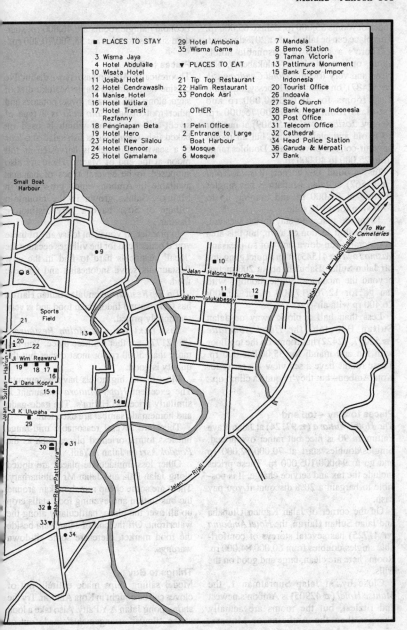

■ PLACES TO STAY	29 Hotel Amboina	7 Mandala
	35 Wisma Game	8 Bemo Station
3 Wisma Jaya		9 Taman Victoria
4 Hotel Abdulalie	▼ PLACES TO EAT	13 Pattimura Monument
10 Wisata Hotel		15 Bank Expor Impor
11 Josiba Hotel	21 Tip Top Restaurant	Indonesia
12 Hotel Cendrawasih	22 Halim Restaurant	20 Tourist Office
14 Manise Hotel	33 Pondok Asri	26 Indoavia
16 Hotel Mutiara		27 Silo Church
17 Hotel Transit	OTHER	28 Bank Negara Indonesia
Rezfanny		30 Post Office
18 Penginapan Beta	1 Pelni Office	31 Telecom Office
19 Hotel Hero	2 Entrance to Large	32 Cathedral
23 Hotel New Silalou	Boat Harbour	34 Head Police Station
24 Hotel Elenoor	5 Mosque	36 Garuda & Merpati
25 Hotel Gamalama	6 Mosque	37 Bank

Small Boat
Harbour

To War
Cemeteries

Jalan Halong–Mardika

Jalan Tulukabessy

Jalan W. W. Mongisidi

Sports
Field

Jl Wim Reawaru

Jl Dana Kopra

Jl K Ulupaha

Jalan – Sultan – Hairun

Jalan Rijali

Jalan Raya–Pattimura

superior rooms 55,000 rp; deluxe 65,000 rp. This place can be talked into a 20% discount.

There's a group of reasonable hotels along, or just off, Jalan Tulukabessy. The clean and very friendly *Hotel Cendrawasih* (☎ 52487), on Jalan Tulukabessy, has standard rooms for 45,000/60,000 rp and 1st-class rooms for 60,000/75,000 rp. Nearby, *Josiba Hotel* (☎ 52509) at number 19 is old and plain-looking, but all rooms have air-con and private bath. Doubles range from 25,000 to 40,000 rp.

Just around the corner, *Wisata Hotel* (☎ 53567) at Jalan Mutiara 3 has singles starting at 33,000 rp and ranging up to 77,000 rp for a VIP suite.

There are places to stay in the western, more-Muslim section of town, but this area is generally run-down and not so pleasant. *Wisma Jaya* (☎ 41545) is on a quiet gang just off Jalan Sultan Babulah, about 200 metres beyond the mosques. Singles/doubles with fan go for 12,700/17,600 rp, or 20,400/26,400 rp with air-con.

Less than half a block away on Jalan Sultan Babulah, the *Hotel Abdulaile* (☎ 52057, 42422) has rooms on the top floor with fan and mandi for 35,000/45,000 rp. These rooms have a sea view – a rarity for Kota Ambon– but they're quite a climb up.

Places to Stay – top end
The *Hotel Mutiara* (☎ 97124) at Jalan Raya Pattimura 90 is nice but rather overpriced. Singles/doubles start at 70,000/82,000 rp and go to 94,000/105,000 rp. These prices include the tax and service charge. It is possible to bargain a 20% discount if you pay cash.

On the corner of Jalan Kapten Ulupaha and Jalan Sultan Hairun, the *Hotel Amboina* (☎ 41725) has several storeys of comfortable singles/doubles from 60,000/84,000 rp. Rooms here are clean, large and good on the frills.

Close by, at Jalan Supratman 1, the *Manise Hotel* (☎ 42905) is Ambon's newest and ritziest, but the rooms are actually cheaper than the Amboina or Mutiara.

Economy single rooms are 46,800 rp; standard singles/doubles are 58,500/70,200 rp.

Places to Eat
Theoretically, Ambon has its own distinctive cuisine based on the staple Maluku diet of sago, along with cassava, sweet potatoes and other root dishes. *Colo colo* is a type of sweet-and-sour sauce which is used on baked fish, *kohu kohu* is fish salad and *laor* is a sea-worm which is harvested at full moon at the end of March. There are also supposed to be several types of bananas available in Ambon which grow only in Maluku. Salaks grown in the mountain village of Soya have a very distinctive flavour.

In practice, if you want to try any of these you'd better head for the villages because the 'local' cuisine is hard to find in the city. Restaurants serve Indonesian and Chinese food.

Tip Top Restaurant on Jalan Sultan Hairun has Chinese and Indonesian food and is very reasonably priced.

Just next door is *Halim Restaurant* (☎ 52177), another Chinese place. You pay more than 5000 rp for most dishes but the quality is good.

Most of the big hotels have restaurants. The excellent *Hotel Mutiara* restaurant is similarly priced to Halim's. The gado-gado and homemade sambal are excellent.

There are several reasonable mid-range but less tourist-oriented places such as the *Pondok Asri* on Jalan A Yani.

Other less immaculate places are dotted along Jalan Pala and Jalan Mr Latuharhary. There are some cheap rumah makan around the bus station and evening food stalls crop up all over the place, particularly along the waterfront. Off the end of Jalan Pala beside the food market, there are some sit-down warungs.

Things to Buy
Model sailing ships made entirely out of cloves can be bought in Kota Ambon. Try the shops along Jalan A Y Patty. Also take a look at the 'flower arrangements' made out of

mother of pearl. Avoid the turtle-shell fans, ashtrays, lampshades and any other turtle-shell products. Look around for handwoven clothes from south-eastern Maluku. Ambon is a supplier of good eucalyptus oil and there are some interesting animist carvings from South Maluku, available at the hotel shops and from hawkers.

You'll see Ambonese women carrying loads in chocolate-brown baskets. These are finely woven and worth buying if you're into baskets. Try the villages or just make an offer when you spot one in use.

Getting There & Away

Air Kota Ambon is the gateway to Maluku, connected by air and sea to western and eastern Indonesia and the other islands of Maluku. Merpati (☎ 53480, 42480) and Garuda (☎ 52481, 52572) share an office on Jalan Jenderal Ahmad Yani. Flights include the following:

Destination	Fare (rp)
Amahai	44,000
Balikpapan	354,000
Bandung	493,000
Biak	205,000
Denpasar	294,000
Jakarta	421,000
Jayapura	309,000
Kendari	290,000
Kupang	368,000
Manado	160,000
Mangole	128,000
Maumere	327,000
Namlea	58,000
Palu	327,000
Semarang	424,000
Solo	414,000
Sorong	113,000
Surabaya	365,000
Tarakan	487,000
Ternate	135,000
Timika	295,000
Ujung Pandang	202,000
Yogyakarta	419,000

Merpati's subsidiary, Indoavia, runs flights to obscure destinations around Maluku. They fly to/from Langgur (Kai islands) daily, and to/from Banda (83,000 rp) three times weekly. Indoavia (☎ 42260, 53816) is at Jalan Anthony Rhebok 28. Office hours are Monday to Saturday from 9 am to 3 pm and Sunday from 10 am to 2 pm.

Mandala (☎ 42551), with its office on Jalan A Y Patty, flies to and from Jakarta, Surabaya and Ujung Pandang most days. Mandala flights are cheaper than Garuda's.

Boat The Pelni office (☎ 53161, 52049) is in the main harbour complex entered from the west end of Jalan Yos Sudarso. Pelni's passenger liners *Rinjani*, *Tidar* and *Umsini* call in here. See the Getting Around chapter for the full schedule. Some sample fares from Ambon:

Destination	1st	2nd	Ekonomi
Sorong	64,000	37,000	19,000
Surabaya	188,000	101,000	48,000
Ujung Pandang	118,000	89,000	31,000

Other distinctly less comfortable Pelni ships, some taking cargo as well as passengers on deck (you may be able to rent a small cabin from a crew member), circle various parts of Maluku with irregular schedules from Kota Ambon. The people in the Pelni office are helpful and there's usually someone who speaks reasonable English. See the relevant island sections for more info. From the same main harbour, other boats also leave for places like Sorong, Bali, Banjarmasin, even Port Moresby or Japan.

Smaller boats to destinations around Maluku leave from a second harbour near the end of Jalan Pala. Common destinations include the north coast of Seram, Buru, Bacan and Obi. A board at the harbour entrance shows what's going where and when. There are fewer small boats in the monsoon (roughly from June to September for much of Maluku). Boats to the south coast of Seram leave from the east coast of Ambon; see the Seram section for details.

Getting Around

To/From the Airport Ambon airport is 48 km out of the city on the other side of the bay. A taxi to the city costs 15,000 rp, a public bemo 1000 rp per person. Beware of rip-offs

– drivers may ask for much more. If you take a public bemo from the bus/bemo terminal to the airport allow lots of time: it's normally about an hour's drive but allow for rubber time.

There's a taxi stand on the corner of Jalan Pala and Jalan Slamet Riyadi, and you can charter vehicles from the terminal, but you're less likely to be ripped off if you get your hotel to organise it. If you fly with Mandala, they run their own bus (usually once daily, at variable times) to coincide with their flights. The hotel bus leaves from the Mandala office on Jalan A Y Patty, and costs 3 5000 rp.

Local Transport Getting around town is fairly easy. Walking will do for the compact central area; it's about a 10-minute walk from the Penginapan Beta to the terminal. Otherwise there are becaks: the correct fare for around town is 500 rp but with foreigners they will usually ask at least 1000 rp.

For places at the edge of town, like the Museum Siwalima or the war cemeteries, you need the city bemos. Catch these either on the street or from the bemo station (easier). If you try to catch one on the street, you may find yourself waiting around in the sun for ages as vehicles don't usually leave the station until they're full.

Kota Ambon's bus and bemo station spreads over a square and two or three streets near the market at the east end of the city waterfront. There are frequent departures for Soya, Latuhalat, Natsepa, Waai and Liang. There's a taxi stand at the corner of Jalan Pala and Jalan Slamet Riyadi.

A vehicle and passenger ferry crosses Teluk Ambon at Galala village, cutting short the circuitous road route. Bemos and taxis sometimes use it as a short cut to the airport. The fare is 200 rp per person, five times more for cars. The ferry runs every day.

Much of Pulau Ambon is hilly and inaccessible except on foot so there are plenty of opportunities for hiking. As yet, there's nowhere organised to rent motorbikes or bicycles.

AROUND AMBON
Leitimur Peninsula Villages
Paths connect the villages in the hills on the Leitimur peninsula to each other or to Kota Ambon. Try walking from the city to Soya on Gunung Sirimau or catch a bemo from the terminal, a 20-minute (350 rp) ride in rickety vehicles. The bemos drop you at Soya Atas and then it's a one-km walk up to the summit of Gunung Sirimau – the last section is quite steep. There are great views from the top – over Kota Ambon in one direction, over Passo and the east coast in another. On the way up there are also good views down to the south coast. The villages of Hatalai, Ema and Naku on the southern slopes of the mountain may also be worth investigating.

Coast & Beaches
Latuhalat & Namalatu These south-coast beaches have good scuba diving and snorkelling on the coral reefs offshore. To get there take a bemo from the Kota Ambon station (about 45 minutes, 500 rp). Namalatu has a lovely beach and there are secluded coves between it and Latuhalat. Even on a Sunday, the busiest day, Namalatu is relaxed and pleasant. There are a few rooms available for 15,000 rp in the old governor's house – extensions are planned. Ask for directions. The beachside warung at Namalatu is only open during the day.

Natsepa This beach, on the east coast 14 km from Kota Ambon, is littered with concrete tables and cigarette advertising but it's OK for a swim – avoid Sundays when it gets really crowded. Take a bemo from the station; it takes about 45 minutes and costs 1000 rp. On weekends there's an entrance fee of about 400 rp to the beach. There are a few basic rooms where you can stay almost on the beach, right next door to the cafe. Rooms with mandi cost from 25,000 rp. There's no food available at night, but during the day there are plenty of snack stalls, some selling *rujak*, an Ambonese favourite consisting of sliced fruit, chilli, palm sugar and peanut sauce – delicious and cheap.

Top: Tau Tau, wooden effigies of the dead, Kete Kesu, Tanatoraja, Sulawesi (AS)
Bottom: Tau Tau, Lemo, Sulawesi (TW)

Top: Fort Belgica, Bandaneira, Maluku (AS)
Bottom: On the beach, Ai Island, Banda Islands, Maluku (JN)

Waai North of Natsepa, 31 km from Kota Ambon, this beach has an underwater cave beneath a mountain spring which is the home of sacred eels and sacred carp. The villagers flick the water surface to draw the creatures from their underground cave, enticing them with eggs. There are also some good murals in the church at Waai.

Toisapau This small beach, 18 km from Kota Ambon, is on the opposite side of Teluk Baguala from Natsepa and within reach of outriggers and motorboats from the village of Passo.

Halong On the south side of Teluk Ambon, this is the finishing point for the annual Darwin-Ambon yacht race, which takes about five days, each July. The usual prostitute population is moved out of Halong for three weeks when the yachts arrive. Kota Ambon is now Darwin's twin city.

Hila

This village on the north coast 42 km from Kota Ambon is the site of a fortress that was originally Portuguese and an old Christian church. Bemos from the city terminal cost 1200 rp and take from 1½ to two hours.

The fortress was built right on the coast to guard the straits between Ambon and Seram, which are at their narrowest here. It was originally built of wooden palisades by the Portuguese at the end of the 16th century, and was later rebuilt by the Dutch and renamed Fort Amsterdam. The main tower and fragments of the wall remain (the cannons have gone) and the interior of the tower has been taken over by enormous tree roots which have wrapped themselves all over the walls from top to bottom. There are more forts west along the coast from here.

The church is just a few minutes' walk from the fort. Built in 1780, it is the oldest in Ambon, though it has virtually been rebuilt over the years from the stumps up. There's a Dutch-inscribed plaque on the outside wall. Although it is not the oldest church in Maluku, it is the oldest that is still standing and in use.

Wapauwe is an old mosque near Hila – the original mosque dated back to the early 15th century and, according to folktales, is said to have been dragged down from the hills. It's still an active place of worship.

Hila has a twin village called Kaitetu.

Liang

There's a very Muslim village on the coast here, 32 km from Kota Ambon. The round trip by bemo costs 3000rp. If you're adventurous you can walk west along the coast, or into the hills where there's some primary rainforest with many butterfly and orchid species. Wear adequate footwear as there are snakes and lizards. The last bemo returns to the city at 4 pm; if you get stuck, walk south and pick up a bemo at the turn-off to Hunimua – one of the departure points for ferries to Seram.

Pulau Pombo

The coral around this tiny, attractive island off north-east Ambon is nowhere near as good as the coral gardens off Manado in northern Sulawesi but it could make for a pleasant few hours. Take care, though, becuse the water over the reef is very shallow.

To get there take a bemo from the Kota Ambon terminal to the village of Tulehu (one hour, 1000 rp). The bemo will drop you at the wharf from where you can hire a speedboat to Pulau Pombo. The ride takes 20 minutes and is expensive at 50,000 rp for the round trip. There's a small beach on Pulau Pombo, sheltered by the reef. You could have the boat drop you off in the morning and pick you up in the afternoon or the next day. There's a small derelict shelter on the island, but bring your own food and water. You might also be able to get a boat from Waai to take you out to the island. If you're offered a local fishing boat check it out carefully – one traveller almost drowned en route to Pombo because his guide had forgotten to bring a bailer, the need for which only became apparent some distance from the shore.

THE LEASE GROUP

Formerly the Uliassers, this small group of islands east of Ambon onsists of Haruku, Saparua, Nusa Laut and Molana, Saparua being the largest and most populated. Saparua is very hilly and is a centre of nutmeg and clove production. Its main claim to fame is that it was the source of the revolt against the Dutch led by Pattimura who was later betrayed, handed over to the Dutch and hanged in Ambon. Visitors to Saparua can view Pattimura's battledress at Haria.

Saparua is also the name of the island's main town midway along the south coast. It has a large twice-weekly market. Nearby is the well-restored Fort Duurstede which Pattimura captured shortly before his betrayal; there are more forts in much poorer condition on other parts of the coast.

The island has good beaches and coral – try Pantai Waisisil. At Mahui, there's an expensive hotel geared to people on diving holidays. Distinctive local pottery can be seen in the village of Ouw, east of Saparua town. The pretty village of Bool on the coast west of Saparua specialises in bricklayers. As on the other Lease islands, there are hot springs on Saparua. The few roads inland are poor.

Boats to Saparua (1500 rp) depart daily from Tulehu on the east coast of Ambon and dock at Porto from where you can take a bemo into Saparua town and on to Ouw. The boats often stop at Haruku en route to Saparua and may continue to south Seram. Bigger boats from Hurnala, just north of Tulehu, stop off at Saparua en route to southern Seram. There's a ferry to Amahai on Seram from a village near Mahui.

Seram

Maluku's second-largest island (17,151 sq km), Seram is wild, mountainous, heavily forested and well watered. The Malukans call it Nusa Ina, or Mother Island, as it's believed that this is where the ancestors of central Maluku came from. Most of the island is untouched due to its rugged terrain, but logging has now begun with a vengeance and Seram's famed birdlife is being smuggled out in huge numbers. There's also a

large oil centre at Bulu on the north-east coast.

Much of the centre has difficult access and is home to the indigenous Alfuro peoples, some of whom have only relatively recently given up head-hunting. One tribe, the Bati of the southern mountains, can fly, so the story goes. They number 2000 and are supposed to have piercing eyes with the power to dominate and whisk a victim into the skies. Apparently, such is their power, the victim is quite happy to accompany them. Their flying is seasonal, but there's always one active group. Most Ambonese and Seramese believe in the powers of the Bati. The south and west coasts are populated by Malays and there are transmigrants from Java and Sulawesi. Both the Dutch and Indonesian governments resettled numbers of the native people on the coast.

Seram is a birdwatcher's paradise, though other wildlife is restricted to cuscus and bandicoots plus introduced deer and pigs. Butterfly species are particularly bright in colour. The birdlife includes lories, parrots, cockatoos, kingfishers, pigeons, cassowaries, hornbills, friar birds and other honeyeaters, megapodes and white eyes.

Seram receives a lot of rain throughout the year but while the centre is always wet, the north has a wetter season from around October to March, and the south from March to October. Boat schedules become erratic during the rough monsoon seas.

History

Before the 15th century, Seram had commercial links with the Javanese Hindu kingdoms. In 1480, Ternatean influence and Islam reached Seram and the matrilineal system of succession was replaced by the patrilineal. Portuguese missionaries arrived in the 16th century and then, in the early 17th century, the Dutch established four coastal trading posts. The Dutch controlled Seram, though they didn't bother with the wild interior, from about 1650 until it was occupied by the Japanese in 1942 and used as an air base.

Today Seram is becoming 'Indonesian-ised', with oil and timber both being exploited. Copra, rice, spices and a few other crops are grown for export. During the clove season, from October to January on the south coast, it seems the whole population is busy collecting, drying and shipping the spice. The indigenous peoples of the interior still do some hunting and gather forest products such as wild sago.

South Coast

The south coast is heavily populated by Maluku standards. Masohi is the main centre and accommodation is available but expensive. Try the *Wisma Lestari*, with good rooms and meals included. There are also the *Penginapan Maharani* and the *Penginapan Ole-Sioh*. Amahai is a smaller place between Masohi and the kampung of Soahuku where the ferry arrives from Tulehu on Ambon. It has one losmen, a few houses, a school and a post office. Bemos go from the harbour to Masohi.

Bemos and minibuses run short distances east and west from Masohi and are useful for getting you part of the way to indigenous villages or maybe the beaches. Janeero and Bonara are 'traditional' villages of the Nuaulu people in the Masohi area, but on the surface they're nothing special.

Bemos heading east terminate at Tamilu, 36 km from Amahai's port. To get to Piliani, the slightly inland southern entry point to Manusela National Park, or to villages on the coast beyond Tamilu, you have to walk or catch a boat – motorboats go from Amahai to Tehoru and on to Saunulu and Hatemete at least three times a week. Some start their journeys at Tulehu on Ambon. You could arrange for local boats to take you where you want.

The ferry from Hunimua on Ambon docks at Waipirit, the port for Kairatu, a sizeable town towards the west end of the south coast, but there appear to be no roads between Kairatu and Masohi.

Manusela National Park

A large chunk of Seram's centre is marked as Manusela National Park and supposedly protected, but the park management has to contend with locals who want to use the area for purposes other than conservation. The park comprises a wide lowland plain in the north, a central enclave with the small villages of Manusela, Solumena and Kanikeh in an isolated inner valley at about 700 metres, and a giant mountain range in the south. Gunung Manusela (3000 metres) on the park's eastern border is Seram's highest mountain. There are some beautiful white, sandy beaches and excellent coral off the north coast. The island receives very few visitors and a trek through its interior or a shorter walk along parts of the north or south coasts is a real 'off-the-beaten track' experience. You may need a permit from the PHPA before trekking in Seram. There are PHPA offices at Air Besar near Wahai on Seram and on Ambon at Balai KSPA VIII, Jalan Laksdya Leo Wattimena, Passo.

Walking across Seram to or from Wahai on the north coast through the park is tough going, but is the highlight of a trip to the island – it's less visited than the Balim Valley in Irian Jaya. There are no facilities at all in the park and villagers have little spare food so you must be self-sufficient. It's recommended that you take a guide (for maybe 10,000 rp per day, plus food). Good maps of the park are difficult to find but some can be obtained from the Botanical Gardens Office at Bogor in Java. Keep asking directions as you go.

From the south coast you can walk into the park from Hatu or from Saunulu via Piliani; it's about 1½ hours' walk from Saunulu. This locally named 'route of sorrow' rises to 2500 metres en route to Manusela village in the inner valley, one to three days' walk away – depending how fit you are. From Manusela it's another three or four days to Wahai. The villages in the interior are almost untouched apart from churches and schools. Check in with the head of the village, the *bapak raja*, who usually has room for guests – what you pay is up to you.

Wahai is the starting point into the park from the north. The PHPA park office is a half-hour walk along the road east of Wahai,

past Air Besar, near the schools. There are three routes of varying difficulty into Manusela. One is via Solea village, 15 km from Wahai – take the path near the park office. From there you walk upriver and over Gunung Kobipoto (1500 metres) via Solumena in the inner valley and out via Manusela to the south coast. Reaching Solumena takes from three days to a week. Or walk south-west from Wahai through Melinani, Wassa and Roho to Kanikeh in the inner valley, and out via Manusela to the south coast – this is another hard route taking from three to six days as far as Kanikeh. The easiest way would be to take a truck east from Wahai to Pasahari then a logging truck south to Kaloa from where it's a one-day walk to Manusela.

North Coast

Wahai With a population of 1500, this is the main town on the north coast. Roads extend short distances east to Kalisonta and west to Rumah Sokat – catch trucks to get there. You can stay in rooms at Mr Tan Tok Hong's shop on Jalan Sinar Indok. There is also Pak Leo's place, next to the post office and opposite a church.

Sawai West of Wahai, this is a friendly Muslim village with a small offshore island also called Sawai. You can paddle out there or hire a motorised dugout canoe. Locals use the island for fishing and making coconut oil, and have built small houses, which you can rent cheaply. There is no fresh water on the island.

There's stunning snorkelling off the north coast and amazing beaches – try Asele, one hour east of Wahai!

Getting There & Away

Air Theoretically, Indoavia flies from Ambon to Amahai weekly for 44,000 rp, but the flights have a knack for being cancelled.

Boat The main boats serving Seram's north coast leave from Kota Ambon – check both the small and large boat harbours there. Boats include the *Wahai Star*, the *Tiga*

Berlian and the *Taman Pelita*. Boats stop in at small villages on the way – passengers go ashore by dugout – and usually at Sawai, Wahai and then go on to Bula, the eastern oilfield, but not always. Ambon to Wahai is about a 30-hour trip.

Boats to Amahai on the south coast go from Tulehu and Hurnala on Ambon, usually via Saparua. Some continue to Tehoru, Saunulu and Hatemete. To Amahai takes about four hours and to Tehoru, about eight hours. From Hunimua on Ambon, a ferry goes three times daily to Waipirit, the port of Kairatu.

The Bandas

South-east of Ambon lies the tiny cluster of islands known as the Bandas. The group consists of about a dozen small islands of which the seven main ones are Neira, Gunung Api, Banda Besar (Lonthor), Hatta (Rozengain), Sjahrir (Pisang), Ai and Run. Bandaneira on the island of Neira is the chief township.

One of the most beautiful clusters of islands in Indonesia, the Bandas are littered with deserted forts and deteriorating Dutch villas which are now being restored. The locals are friendly; there's a single cinema and only a handful of motor vehicles. Superb deserted beaches and excellent snorkelling and diving around the numerous coral reefs (the best coral's off the islands of Karaka, Sjahrir and Ai) are major pluses. There is even a still-active volcano to climb, Gunung Api. The Bandas are well worth the effort to get there: no tourist bungalows line the beaches, there's virtually no pollution and no touts hassle you to buy anything! The atmosphere is possibly the most laid-back and relaxed in all of Indonesia.

For centuries the Bandas were the centre of production of nutmeg and mace, and from the 16th century onwards the Portuguese, Dutch and the English all vied for their control. Today, with the centre of production moved to other parts of the world, the Bandas have fallen into obscurity, though they're slowly being rediscovered by a steady trickle of tourists. Try not to miss these islands!

History

By the time Europeans arrived the native Bandanese had adopted Islam and lived in little coastal communities, virtually village republics. Each one was presided over by its *orang kaya* – a term which signified leading citizens, chiefs or village elders.

The ordinary people earned their livelihood by gathering the ripe fruit of the nutmeg tree and processing it into commercial nutmeg (from the seed of the fruit) and mace (the fibre around the seed). These spices were sold on the spot to resident or visiting Malay, Chinese and Arab traders who traded them on through Asia to Europe. The value of the goods doubled every time they changed hands.

Portuguese ships landed in Banda in 1512 and stayed for a month. Meanwhile, the rival sultans of Ternate and Tidore heard of the impressive Portuguese firepower and sent emissaries to encourage them to travel north and join an alliance. Ternate won the race, and thus by chance it was Ternate (the centre of clove production), and not Banda, which became the first foothold of the Portuguese in Maluku.

For almost 90 years the Portuguese had Maluku to themselves until a Dutch fleet sailed in in 1599, with orders to seek out spices at their source and circumvent the Portuguese monopoly. Part of the fleet sailed to Banda, loaded a cargo of spices, alarmed the Portuguese and sailed back to Holland. Soon afterwards the Dutch forced the Portuguese out of the spice trade but they still had other rivals: in 1601 the English East India Company had set up a fort on the island of Run in the Bandas and in 1606 the Spanish got into the act by taking Ternate and Tidore.

From 1605 to 1616, the history of the Bandas is largely one of the successive arrivals of intimidating Dutch fleets, while the English interlopers appear to have had better relations with the Bandanese, helping them

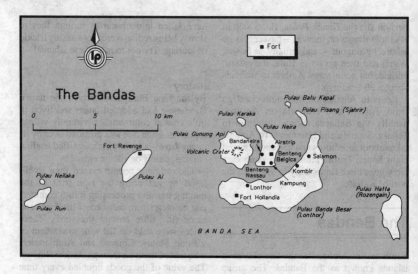

to fight off Dutch attacks and frustrating the Dutch desire for a spice trade monopoly.

The turning point came in 1619. Jan Pieterszoon Coen, the new VOC governor-general, envisaged a Dutch commercial empire in the east the would-be grandeur of which would match the extent of his violent ruthlessness. Coen intended to control all trade in the region from India to Japan; his first step was to shift the centre of Dutch activity to Batavia in Java. Next he seized control of the Bandas, got rid of the unhelpful Bandanese and started producing nutmeg using imported slaves and labourers, with Dutch overseers.

In early 1621, Coen sailed from Batavia to Banda with 13 large ships, about 1900 soldiers, 100 Japanese mercenaries and 300 Javanese convicts to serve as rowers and porters. He attacked Lonthor Island, the most important of the group, and almost totally wiped out the native Bandanese population. Coen now returned to Batavia and announced that the VOC would accept applications for land grants in Banda if the applicants would settle permanently in the islands and produce spices exclusively for the company, at fixed prices. The company

would import rice and other necessities, provide slaves to work on the plantations and defend the islands against attack.

Relations between the VOC and the licensed planters known as the *perkenier* were often bitter, but by the late 1620s the islands were beginning to produce nutmeg and mace in quantities which soon exceeded those of earlier years. The surviving Bandanese – mostly enslaved – were obediently teaching their skills to imported slaves from a variety of regions. The mixed origins of the people on these tiny islands are still apparent.

The perkeniers and regional traders certainly smuggled out a good deal of the spices but Coen had established something close to the long-sought monopoly of the spice trade. It was not until the Napoleonic Wars, almost 200 years later, that this was finally broken. The Bandas, like other Dutch-held parts of the archipelago, were occupied by the English during the Napoleonic Wars and nutmeg seedlings were shipped off to Sri Lanka, Bengkulu in Sumatra and Penang in Malaysia. By 1860, these areas were almost as important as Banda for producing nutmeg and mace. The invention of refrigeration, however, which allowed meat to be kept without the heavy use of spices, spelt the end of the spice trade.

After the return of Dutch rule to Maluku in the 1820s, their monopolistic slave-based policies were gradually altered but the perkeniers prospered – while they spent most of their time in debt, they also spent most of their money on extravagant houses and lifestyles in Bandaneira.

The islands' economy, so precariously dependent on a single product, declined with the loss of the Dutch spice monopoly and as spices started to be grown in other parts of Indonesia. Today, the centres of Indonesian nutmeg production are in Sulawesi and Java. Grenada in the Carribean is the major international centre. The Bandas still produce nutmeg and mace for use in Indonesia, but for the most part the islands have been forgotten by the rest of the world.

Books

While you're in Bandaneira, buy a copy of Willard Hanna's *Indonesian Banda* – it's sold at the Bandaneira museum. It takes you cannon shot by cannon shot through the history of the islands, from the time the first European ships sailed in until the late 1970s.

NEIRA

Bandaneira on Pulau Neira is the only town in the Bandas. In its heyday, it was a town of spacious mansions built and rebuilt over the centuries, with floors of polished marble or brightly coloured tiles, and elegant European-style furnishings. The perkeniers spent huge sums of money on their Neira mansions, converting the town into a showpiece enclave of the Netherlands East Indies. When the naturalist Henry Forbes visited Bandaneira in 1881, he was 'charmed with its clean aspect, its green parks with gravelled walks, and pretty dwellings'.

It was a self-indulgent life for the perkeniers, though not a carefree one. Over the centuries, the islands were visited by a series of misfortunes. After the Dutch left, when the marble cracked and the tiles broke, there were no funds for repairing them. Today, a major effort is under way to restore the old

mansions of Bandaneira, a very expensive task. A new programme has been proposed, in which retired foreigners will be permitted to restore the mansions and live in them until their death.

This is a place for scrambling around old forts, walking in the hills, climbing the volcano or daytripping to other islands' unspoilt beaches and coral reefs. At the north end of Neira itself, Malole is a small beach on the east side. There's coral about 50 metres offshore. Though there are better places to swim and snorkel on other islands, Malole is a pleasant hour's stroll from Bandaneira along a shady path.

Bandaneira has no bank so bring plenty of cash with you. If you're staying at the Laguna, Maulana, Sjahrir or Museum hotels, you can change cash and travellers' cheques.

Museum

Notable buildings in Bandaneira include the Museum (Rumah Budaya). It's an old Dutch villa which also doubles as a hotel and houses a small collection of cannon, muskets, helmets, old coins, maps, china and paintings – including one depicting the massacre of Bandanese by the Dutch in 1621.

Next door to the museum is a restored house claiming to be the Rumah Pengasingan (Exile House) of Sutan Sjahrir, the Indonesian independence hero. It has a few Sjahrir memorabilia – mainly photos – but it *wasn't* where he lodged during his exile to Banda by the Dutch in the 1930s.

Dutch Church

The fine Dutch Church on Jalan Gereja dates from 1852 when it replaced an earlier stone building which was destroyed by an earthquake. There's a whole crowd of people buried beneath the floor. The church's clock no longer works; its hands are stuck where they were at the moment of the Japanese invasion of 1942.

Benteng Nassau

On low ground in front of the massive Benteng (Fort) Belgica, the original stone foundations of Benteng Nassau were built

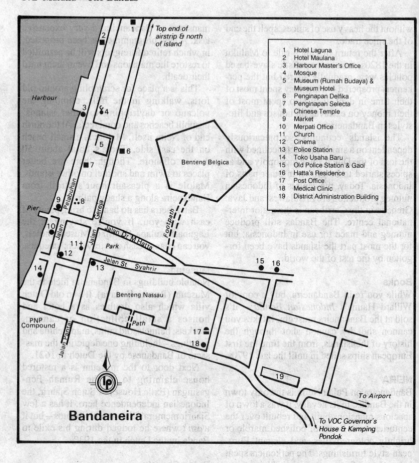

1   Hotel Laguna
2   Hotel Maulana
3   Harbour Master's Office
4   Mosque
5   Museum (Rumah Budaya) &
    Museum Hotel
6   Penginapan Delfika
7   Penginapan Selecta
8   Chinese Temple
9   Market
10 Merpati Office
11 Church
12 Cinema
13 Police Station
14 Toko Usaha Baru
15 Old Police Station & Gaol
16 Hatta's Residence
17 Post Office
18 Medical Clinic
19 District Administration Building

Bandaneira

by the Portuguese around 1529 when they sent troops from their base in Ternate to make a show of force in Banda. The fort, however, wasn't completed and the foundations were abandoned. In 1608 a powerful Dutch fleet under Admiral Pieterszoon Verhoeven arrived with orders to annex the Bandas. When negotiations stalled Verhoeven simply confronted the Bandanese with a *fait accompli* by landing soldiers on Pulau Neira and constructing a fort on the old Portuguese foundations.

Benteng Nassau was restored for use as a warehouse in the early 19th century but eventually lapsed into ruins. Both it and Benteng Belgica were restored superficially in the early 20th century by colonial officials more conscious of their picturesque aspects than their military history. Today the area around the fort is much overgrown – only three walls and a gateway remain and an old cannon lies on the ground.

Benteng Belgica

The construction of this fort began in 1611 under the direction of Pieter Both who had been appointed governor-general of the region with the assignment of creating a monopoly, and kicking out the English. Both sailed to Maluku with 11 ships and 500 soldiers and after pausing at Ambon continued to Banda. With the prospect of a Banda-English alliance, his men erected the imposing Benteng Belgica on the ridge overlooking Benteng Nassau. Belgica was maintained as a military headquarters until around 1860.

Belgica is pentagonal with towers at each corner, cannons which point out to sea from the battlements, and walls which have been disfigured by graffiti. There is now a project in progress to fully restore it. With Gunung Api towering in the distance, the fort's setting is quite beautiful.

Hatta & Sjahrir's Residence

In the late 1930s the Bandas achieved a dim sort of reflected glory as the place of exile for two of Indonesia's top young nationalist leaders, whose political passions the Dutch hoped would be calmed by the serenity of the islands. Mohammed Hatta and Sutan Sjahrir were moved here from Boven Digul, an infamous detention camp in New Guinea. They took up residence in the very spacious house – now restored – next to the prison.

Hatta was a Sumatran, born in 1902. After independence he became vice president but resigned in 1956 because of conflicts with Sukarno. He continued to be respected, but for a decade after 1956 took no active part in government. An economist educated in Holland, he was attracted to slow and careful national development, based on hard work and thriftiness. Despite being a Muslim, and influenced by Marxism, he was still considered pro-Western and a moderate.

Sjahrir was also a Sumatran, born in 1909, and of much the same intellectual and rationalist bent as Hatta. He formed the PSI (Partai Socialis Indonesia) in 1945, but it lacked mass appeal and was eventually banned by Sukarno for its involvement with the Sumatran rebellion of the late 1950s. Sjahrir was imprisoned.

VOC Governor's House

The old VOC governor's residence is just back from the waterfront on the way down to Kampung Pondok on the eastern edge of Bandaneira. It's an imposing building but now seemingly disused.

OTHER ISLANDS

Gunung Api

Jutting out of the sea directly in front of Bandaneira Harbour, this volcano has been a constant threat to Banda. For three centuries from the first Dutch visit to Banda in 1599, it seemed recurrently on the point of blowing itself apart much as Krakatau did in the 19th century. Hot ash from eruptions set fire to thatch-roofed Dutch houses so the Dutch learnt the hard way to use stone, plaster and tile. In Neira stone shelters were erected in case the main buildings were destroyed. Sulphurous fumes sometimes settled over Neira and were held responsible for illness and the high mortality rate.

In one awful hour in April 1778, there occurred simultaneously an especially destructive volcanic eruption, an earthquake, a tidal wave and a hurricane – resulting in great destruction of the nutmeg trees and a massive drop in production.

Since then Gunung Api has erupted twice in the 19th century – in 1901 and again in May 1988 when two people were killed; over 300 houses on its north and south flanks and 120,000 coconut trees were destroyed. On this most recent occasion its caldera grew from 50 to 400 metres wide and is now 200 metres deep. All but a few brave or crazy souls were evacuated to Ambon until the danger of further eruptions subsided.

It's only a short paddle across to Gunung Api from Neira in a canoe. The climb to the top of the volcano is very interesting. Climbers who reach the summit are now issued certificates.

Pulau Karaka

Off the north end of Gunung Api, Karaka only has a small beach but there are some fine coral reefs in shallow water near the shore. It's close enough to paddle from

Bandaneira in a dugout canoe and takes about an hour in a two-person canoe.

Taman Laut (Sea Garden)

Between Neira and Lonthor islands, only about 150 metres out from the VOC governor's house and close enough to paddle out to in a canoe, the coral here is nowhere near as good as at Pulau Karaka.

Banda Besar (Lonthor)

A walk around this island makes a very interesting day trip. There's a good beach (but smaller than the one on Pulau Pisang) with coral offshore on the south side of Banda Besar behind Fort Hollandia. Fort Hollandia was erected after Jan Pieterszoon Coen's capture of Lonthor, now Banda Besar, in 1621. The fort is placed high on the central ridge of the island, commanding the surrounding seas. It was once enormous, but an earthquake wrecked it in 1743 and what little remains is derelict and overgrown. A long flight of steps leads up to it.

Pulau Pisang (Sjahrir)

Pulau Pisang is so called because it's banana-shaped. About 45 minutes by motorboat (8000 rp return) from Bandaneira, it has a good sandy beach and some pretty coral (with a big drop-off) with colourful fish. You can wander uphill to the small village behind the beach.

Pulau Ai

Ai is a good two hours by boat from Neira but definitely worth visiting. It has an overgrown fort near the village on the north-east side. Facing Gunung Api, about one km east of the fort, there's a long sandy beach with wonderful snorkelling.

Pulau Run

Beyond Ai, Run was once the centre of English activity in the Bandas. In early 1615, John Jourdain, the English East India Company's leader in Banten, Java, having set up a post at Makassar, ordered several ships to Maluku to harass the Dutch. In late 1616 the English built a stone fort on a spit of half-exposed coral rock on Pulau Neilakka, which lies off Run. Both islands lacked fresh water other than rainwater and any food except fish, so they were vulnerable to prolonged blockade.

When Coen seized Run the English continued to hold out on Neilakka – but Coen had the nutmeg plantations on Run destroyed to make sure that the English could not continue trading. The English stayed for almost a decade. Unable to make a profit, virtually forgotten and fearing for their lives after the 'Ambon massacre' of 1623 (in which the English merchants in Ambon were seized, tortured and executed or expelled by the Dutch for allegedly plotting to take over the town), they packed up in 1628 and withdrew to Banten.

Under the Treaty of Breda in 1667, the English abandoned their claim to Banda while the Dutch relinquished none other than the small island of Manhattan in what would one day become the centre of New York City.

Places to Stay – bottom end

All accommodation is in Bandaneira. *Hotel Sharir*, *Penginapan Delfika*, *Penginapan Selecta* and *Museum Hotel* all cost 20,000 rp per person including three meals, but they can be persuaded to give a discount (especially in the case of the Selecta) if they're not full. You may also be able to get rates with fewer or no meals if you want. Prices usually don't include 10% tax so it's best to check first.

The Delfika, an old Dutch house painted green, purple and white and run by a friendly family, is the cleanest. It has good home cooking – tuna is the mainstay of the diet in Banda and it's amazing how many different ways it can be dished up. The Delfika has a pleasant garden and a verandah facing the street. Snorkelling gear can be rented for 4000 per day even if you're not staying there.

You can stay with a family for 15,000 rp including food – the local justice department will arrange this.

Places to Stay – top end

The two top-end hotels, the *Hotel Laguna*

and the *Hotel Maulana*, plus the Museum Hotel and Sharir Hotel, are owned by Des Alwi, a Bandanese who became a protege of Mohammed Hatta during Hatta's exile in Banda and was educated in Europe. Alwi has put a lot of effort into developing tourism in the Bandas, including getting the airport built. His most recent project is restoring the old Dutch villas.

The Hotel Laguna is on the waterfront and has air-con. There's one nice big room upstairs. They ask 48,750 rp a double plus 20,000 rp per person for food but can be bargained down.

Hotel Maulana is even more expensive with singles/doubles from 68,250/97,500 rp plus 24,000 per person for meals. Both hotels rent compressed air tanks, snorkels, masks and fins, and speedboats. They can arrange cruises, visits to nutmeg plantations and take you deep-sea fishing.

The 10% tax, common throughout Malaku, is added to most prices.

Places to Eat

The Bandaneira pasar has a good range of fruit and salad vegetables, but bargain hard – they're getting used to tourists. Many of the shops bake their own bread rolls, which you can buy straight from the oven in the mornings. The food at losmen is mainly good and filling but, if you want more, there are a couple of little restaurants like the *Rumah Makan Nusantara*, which has basic Indonesian fare.

Getting There & Away

Air Merpati's subsidiary, Indoavia, flies from Ambon to Banda on Monday, Wednesday and Saturday. The fare is 83,000 rp. There is heavy demand for these flights and it's usually necessary to book ahead. At the time of this writing, negotiations were under way with several other airlines to open additional routes, so make enquiries in Ambon.

The approach to Banda is spectacular – you fly right over Gunung Api. A shop on Jalan Pelabuhan is the agent for Indoavia in Bandaneira.

Boat Various semi-regular boats – perhaps one every five days or so – make the overnight trip from Ambon to Banda. Boats are grubby and crowded, though it's possible to negotiate a cabin.

Getting Around

To/From the Airport By road it's a 45-minute walk from the town to the airport or you can take an opelet. If walking, you can take a short cut by heading north from the Museum Hotel. The road turns into a dirt trail and takes you to the top end of the airstrip – it's a 20-minute walk.

Local Transport Bandaneira is very small; it's a five-minute walk from the museum to the PT Perkebunan Pala Banda, formerly the government nutmeg factory (PNP), and 10 minutes further to the District Administration building (Kantor Kecamatan). The only road on Neira leads to the airport. There are no becaks, but opelets will take you anywhere in town for 100 to 200 rp.

Bicycles can be rented from Hotel Maulana if you're staying there or at one of Des Alwi's other three hotels. The cost is 2000 rp per day.

Motorboats from the pasar and Kampung Pondok, a 10-minute walk east of the town, go fairly regularly to Pulau Lonthor (800 rp for locals). There aren't any regular boats to the other islands. Ask at the losmens, Bandaneira harbour or Kampung Pondok about renting boats. Prices depend on bargaining. A dugout with a man to paddle it costs around 10,000 rp per day. You might be able to take one out yourself but you can only reach places near Neira such as Taman Laut, Lonthor, Gunung Api and Karaka. Pulau Pisang is too far to paddle to.

If you hire a canoe to go out alone and snorkel it's easy enough to get out of the canoe and into the water, but virtually impossible to get back in without capsizing the canoe. The people insist there are no sharks in the waters immediately around Neira, but watch out around some of the outlying islands.

Motorised fishing boats (*kapal motor*) to

Pulau Karaka cost around 10,000 rp for a half-day. To Pulau Pisang costs 20,000 rp for the day, probably more for a group, perhaps 30,000 rp for eight. To Pulau Ai will cost maybe 60,000 rp for a small group, and to Run about 80,000 rp.

The Delfika offers a day trip round Karaka, Malole, Pisang, and Taman Laut. The owner of the Selecta can also be persuaded to run travellers around by boat.

Speedboats, available from Des Alwi's hotels, cost 280,000 rp per day.

Southern Maluku

Probably the most forgotten islands in Indonesia, the islands of southern Maluku are dispersed across the sea between Timor and Irian Jaya. The three main groups, all southeast of Banda, are Kai, Aru and Tanimbar. West of Tanimbar, two arcs of smaller islands stretch across to Timor – a southern, less fertile arc consisting of the Babar and Leti groups, Kisar and Wetar and a northern arc of volcanic, wooded islands (Serua, Nila, Teun, Damar and Romang).

Southern Maluku is inhabited mostly by people of mixed Malay and Papuan stock with the Papuan features more noticeable on the islands closer to Irian Jaya. The Makassarese and the Bugis traded in this region, and the Dutch came here in the 17th century in the interests of maintaining their spice monopoly, but the islanders were long noted for their hostility to outsiders and propensity for head-hunting, even cannibalism in some instances. Christian missionaries helped to pacify the area, and Islam also established itself in many parts. More recently, there's been logging and fishing by all and sundry. Trepang and pearls, once plentiful, are becoming scarce.

Southern Maluku has some deserted white sandy beaches, good snorkelling and diving, colourful and exotic birdlife, unique flora and fauna (all at risk), and traditional cultures quite unaffected by tourism. Its people are known for their boatbuilding, woodcarving, ikat weavings and shell artifacts.

ARU

The closest of the island groups to Irian Jaya, Aru is best known as home to the threatened birds of paradise, a species whose males display their full plumage during their courting season from May to December. There are also other fantastic birds, small kangaroos, wallabies, cuscus and crocodiles. Sea life includes dugongs and turtles. The southeastern part of the group is a marine reserve. Many parts of the islands are swampy. The main town is Dobo on the small, northern island of Wamar; as yet there isn't an airport – Langgur on Kai is the closest one. Unlike some of the other southern Maluku islanders, the people of Aru have the reputation of being peaceful. Despite the influence of Islam and Christian missionaries, animism persists; Aru is supposed to have more *suanggi* (witches) than anywhere else in Maluku.

KAI

Like Aru, the beautiful Kai islands are uplifted coral reefs which are mountainous and heavily forested. The two main islands are Kai Kecil and Kai Besar. Tual on Pulau Dullah is the main town, but the airport is five km away at Langgur on Kai Kecil. Birds and butterflies are prolific. The islanders have a reputation for being happy, talkative and excitable. They are also excellent boatbuilders and decorate their boats with woodcarvings, shells and cassowary 'hair'. Some travellers have reported finding rock paintings on some of the coastal cliffs and good coral off Dullah. The religious breakup is one-third Islam, one-third Christian and one-third animist. Malaria and cholera are widespread.

TANIMBAR

The Tanimbar group, the most southerly of Maluku, consists of 66 islands. The main town is Saumlaki on Pulau Yamdena, the biggest of the group. The island's interior is uninhabited. In the past, the islanders had a reputation for being ferocious. Though Catholicism is the major religion today, much of the original culture is maintained. Woodcarvings, common decorations on boats and houses, are related to ancestor worship. You'll probably also see smaller woodcarvings of human figures with thin, graceful limbs. Rituals and dances remain an integral part of planting and harvest, weddings and funerals.

At Sanglia Dol, on the east coast of Yamdena, a 30-metre-high stone staircase leads up from the beach to a large, boat-shaped, carved stone platform 18 metres long. Such structures were once a feature of many Tanimbar villages and may link these islands with other megalithic ('big stone') cultures in Indonesia, such as those on Nias and Sumba islands.

Tanimbar and the islands west to Timor produce Maluku's best ikat weavings, with traditional symbols and motifs predominating. Tanimbar's gold and silversmiths were highly skilled: they melted down, recast and beat gold jewellery and coins into elaborate headpieces. There are at least five separate languages, including one related to Tetum, which is spoken on Timor. There's said to be good diving off Pulau Nustabun. A road is being built along the east coast of Yamdena but most travel is by boat.

THE SOUTH-WEST ISLANDS

The islands between Tanimbar and Timor are lightly populated, Kisar, Leti and Babar having the most people. Now largely Christianised, except for Islamic Kisar, the people here were head-hunters and warlike with a phallic, animist religion.

Kisar produces excellent ikat weavings. The island has never had extensive cultural dominance from elsewhere so the traditional motifs on its ikat are very old and probably unique. They include human, animal, and bird-and-rider motifs. Today, commercial and natural cotton and dyes are used together. *Kain sinun* is a special Kisar textile with the tree of life motif and the figure of a man with arms raised. Sinun is usually black or dark blue, while other ceremonial ikat fabrics usually have bright colours in stripes.

Animistic woodcarvings are produced on Dawera (in the Babar group), Moa and Lakor (both in the Leti group), and Wetar.

Places to Stay

There are losmen in Tual and Saumlaki. In Dobo you can stay at the mission for a small fee. Tepa on Babar has the new and cheap *Hotel Sumber Jaya*. Away from the main towns, check in with the kepala desa.

Getting There & Away

Air These islands are probably the last place anyone thinks of when Indonesia comes to mind. Merpati's subsidiary Indoavia runs several flights a week from Ambon to Langgur (152,000 rp) on Kai and to Saumlaki (161,000 rp) on Yamdena, or you can fly between Langgur and Saumlaki (96,000 rp).

Boat Pelni's *Niaga VIII*, *Dhuta Nusantara* and *Nasuna* are among the ships covering southern Maluku from Ambon. Sometimes they just go from Ambon to Banda, Tual (Kai), Banda and back to Ambon; at other times they make longer round trips lasting from 11 to 18 days. Ambon to Kai via Banda takes about 2½ days. Other possible ports of call include Dobo; Saumlaki; Tepa, Lelang, Kroing and Masela (Babar Group); Damar; Romang; Wetar; Kisar; and Leti, Moa and Lakor (Leti Group).

From Timor, Pelni's *Elang* sometimes includes Kisar on its loops out of Kupang, often also calling at Dili and Kalabahi (Alor).

Transport around the islands is mostly on foot or by boat.

Northern Maluku

The main town and communications hub of the scattered islands of northern Maluku is Ternate on the small island of the same name, one of a chain of volcanic peaks poking out of the ocean off the west coast of the large

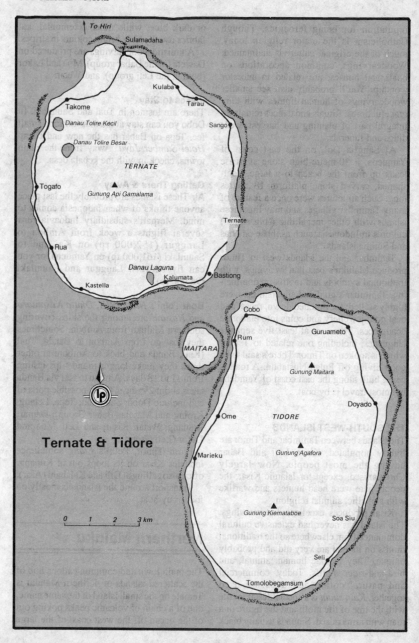

To Hiri

Sulamadaha

Kulaba

Takome   Tarau

Danau Tolire Kecil   Sango

Danau Tolire Besar

TERNATE

Togafo

▲
Gunung Api Gamalama

Ternate

Rua

Danau Laguna

Kalumata   Bastiong

Kastella

MAITARA

Cobo

Rum   Guruameto

▲
Gunung Maitara

Ternate & Tidore

Doyado

Ome   **TIDORE**

▲
Gunung Agafora

Marieku

0   1   2   3 km

▲
Gunung Kiemataboe

Soa Siu

Seli

Tomolobegamsum

island of Halmahera. Apart from Ternate and neighbouring Tidore, northern Maluku is little-visited but certainly offers scope for adventurous travellers.

TERNATE

For centuries the sultanate of this little island was one of the most important in Maluku, with influence south as far as Ambon, west to Sulawesi and east to Irian Jaya. Islam was probably brought here in the middle of the 15th century by Javanese merchants. Ternate's prosperity came from its abundant production of cloves, which allowed it to become a powerful regional military force. Rivalry with the neighbouring sultanate of Tidore resulted in frequent wars and only in 1814 was peace finally established.

Ternate was one of the first places where the Portuguese and Dutch established themselves in Maluku and it's dotted with the ruins of old European fortifications. Even the Spanish got into the act as the chief foreign power in Ternate and Tidore for much of the 17th century.

Today the town of Ternate is, in contrast to Ambon, a relaxed place only occasionally alarmed by rumblings from the huge volcano, Gamalama, to which it clings. The population is strongly Muslim but surprisingly liberal: women wear snappy modern fashions here in the middle of nowhere, at odds with the usual Islamic code of female dress. Calls to Allah from the numerous mosques must compete, on Saturday nights, with amplified Muslim pop music as someone up on the hillside celebrates something into the early hours.

Orientation

The town of Ternate stretches several km along the waterfront. The former Sultan's palace is at the northern end of town and beyond that is the airport. The huge Benteng Oranye (Fort Orange) is near the main bemo station and market. The harbour (Complex Pelabuhan) is at the southern end of town. Further south is another port, Bastiong, from where boats go to Tidore. If you're in a hurry

you can do a loop around the island in just a few hours, taking in all the main sights.

Information

There's a useful tourist information office or *dinas pariwisata* (☎ 21494) hidden inside the Kantor Bupati complex on Jalan Pahlawan Revolusi.

Kedaton (Palace) of the Sultan of Ternate

This interesting creation, looking more like a European country mansion than a palace, lies just back from Jalan Sultan Babulah, the road to the airport. The ill-kept building now houses a museum with little to see – just a few Portuguese cannons, Dutch helmets and armour. To get there take a bemo for 125 rp from the bemo station on Jalan Pahlawan Revolusi.

Benteng Oranye (Fort Orange)

Continuing clockwise from the sultan's palace, this fort dates from 1637 and is a Dutch construction. It's right in the middle of Ternate, opposite the bemo station. It has forlorn-looking cannons and sadly crumbling walls overgrown with weeds, but you'll get some idea of its importance from its great size; this is quite an interesting building to walk around.

Benteng Kayuh Merah

At the southern end of Ternate, a km beyond Bastiong (where you catch motorboats to Tidore) and just before Desa Kayuh Merah, is the small fort of Benteng Kayuh Merah. Constructed in 1510, it's right on the beach with waves splashing its walls.

Danau Laguna

This volcanic, spring-fed lake is just past Ngade and much of it is covered in lotuses. A big whitewashed wall surrounds part of it and it appears to be some sort of official park. If the main entrance is closed there's a dirt track which leads down to the lake from the start of the wall as you come from Ternate. Just past the main entrance to the lake is Taman Eva (entry fee 500 rp), a popular spot

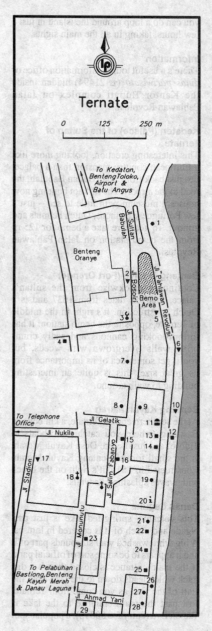

Ternate

0   125   250 m

To Kedaton,
Benteng Toloko,
Airport &
Batu Angus

Benteng
Oranye

Jl Sultan Babullah

Jl Bosoiri

Jl Pahlawan Revolusi

Bemo
Area

To Telephone
Office

Jl Gelatik

Jl Nukila

Jl Stadion

Jl Salim Fabanyo

Jl Monunutu

To Pelabuhan
Bastiong, Benteng
Kayuh Merah
& Danau Laguna

Jl Ahmad Yani

on Sundays with its pleasant gardens and splendid views across the bay to Tidore. You can scramble down to the rocks below and dive into the sea. You can reach Danau Laguna by bemo (300 rp).

Benteng Kastella

Continuing clockwise round the island from Danau Laguna, the road cuts straight through what's left of this fort, which is covered in moss and undergrowth and grazed over by goats. Tree roots have wrapped themselves around the ruins of the main tower. A bemo from Ternate to Kastella will cost you 500 rp. There's a sandy beach but it's not very attractive.

Danau Tolire

Actually, there are two volcanic crater lakes here, Danau Tolire Kecil (Lake Tolire Little) and Danau Tolire Besar (Lake Tolire Big). Both are on the north-western side of the island. Bemos to this stretch of the island are not plentiful and you may have to wait.

Sulamadaha

Sulamadaha, near Ternate's northern tip, has the best beach (black sand) on the island. However, part of it has big waves and a strong current – take care! Walk to the left for 15 minutes, over the rocks and headland to a tiny coral beach where the water is calm and safe for swimming. It's a popular Sunday picnic spot but is almost deserted, except for a few waifs, during the week. On Sundays it costs 200 rp to go onto the beach; there are a few drinks and snacks stalls. Boats leave here several times daily for the small island of Hiri, off the northern tip of Ternate (500 rp). Bemos from Ternate to Sulamadaha are 350 rp.

Just before the main beach as you come from Ternate, on the left, is the friendly *Penginapan Pantai Indah* with clean rooms at 18,000 rp per person including three good meals, but it's a tiny place. Get someone to take you to the nearby hot-water well for a cliff-top mandi – it's a luscious experience. The track to the well is about 100 metres on the left, back towards Ternate from the penginapan.

Batu Angus (Burnt Rocks)

North of Ternate, Batu Angus is a volcanic lava flow caused by an 18th-century eruption of Gamalama. A massive river of jagged volcanic rocks like a landscape on another planet pushes right into the sea. Take a bemo to just past Tarau village to see this.

Benteng Toloko

This small fort is in better condition than the others. A path leads off the airport road (north of the sultan's palace but south of the airport) down to Dufa Dufa and the Benteng Toloko which lies on a rocky hill above the beach.

Gunung Api Gamalama

This active volcano is, in fact, the entire island of Ternate. The most recent eruptions were in 1980 and 1983. Take a bemo up the mountainside as far as possible and then walk. In early 1991, a Swiss visitor disappeared while climbing the mountain and was never found, so it might be a good idea to take along a guide. You'll definitely need a guide (villagers from Marikrobo will volunteer) to find the impressively large 350-year-old clove tree, *cengkeh afo* on the slopes. The tree is now dead after having been split by lightning. It is possible and worthwhile to climb right up to the crater.

Places to Stay – bottom end

Many places operate on a room-plus-meals basis, and breakfast is almost always included.

The pleasant *Wisma Sejahtera* (☎ 21139), on Jalan Salim Fabanyo, has singles with fan for 9000 rp without meals.

Wisma Alhilal (☎ 21404), at Jalan Monunutu 2/32, is plain but run by a friendly family. Rooms with fan and attached mandi and toilet are 8000 rp per person including a small breakfast.

On Jalan Pahlawan Revolusi, opposite the entrance to the harbour, the basic *Peningapan Yamin* has singles for 8000 rp. The penginapans *Sentosa* and *Rachmat* further up the same road are similarly priced.

Places to Stay – middle

Hotel Nirwana (☎ 21787), at Jalan Pahlawan Revolusi 58, is a fine place to stay and the economy rooms even qualify as budget accommodation. All rooms have private bath and are quiet. Prices for singles/doubles are: economy 10,000/15,000 rp; standard 20,000/25,000 rp; standard with air-con 30,000/35,000 rp; VIP 35,000/40,000 rp.

Hotel Indah (☎ 21334), at Jalan Bosoiri 3, is pleasant enough and costs 18,000 rp for a single with fan or 25,000 rp for a room with air-con. All rooms have private bath and breakfast is included.

Chrysant Hotel (☎ 21580), at Jalan Ahmad Yani 131, is quiet and popular.

Singles/doubles with fan and mandi are 10,000/15,000 rp, and with air-con they're 20,000/30,000 rp.

Hotel El Shinta (☎ 21059), almost next door to the Nirwana, has three standards: economy for 15,000/20,000 rp, standard for 25,000/35,000 rp and VIP (with hot water and air-con) for 30,000/50,000 rp. The economy rooms are overpriced, as they don't have attached mandis.

Hotel Merdeka on Jalan Monunutu costs 18,000 rp per person without meals. It looks like it must have been Dutch-built.

Places to Stay – top end

The *Hotel Neraca* (☎ 21668), Jalan Pahlawan Revolusi 30, is the newest and fanciest place in town. Rooms come in different standards from 30,000 to 50,000 rp, and all are excellent.

Places to Eat

About a 10-minute walk west of the centre, the *Restaurant Siola* (☎ 21377) on Jalan Stadion has the best food in Ternate in definitely the most salubrious surroundings. They serve Chinese food, but seafood is another speciality and even the asparagus and corn (*jagung*) soups swim with crabmeat. With a bowl of rice, these soups are a meal in themselves.

The upstairs restaurant in the *Hotel Neraca*, Jalan Pahlawan Revolusi 30, is not expensive but has good food and pleasant surroundings with a view of the ocean. On the same street is the *Restoran Garuda*, which comes complete with karaoke in the evening.

Rumah Makan Gamalama, at Jalan Pahlawan Revolusi, is a good cheap place. *Rumah Makan Roda Baru* further down Jalan Pahlawan Revolusi is fairly cheap as Padang places go.

There are more cheap eats at the *Rumah Makan Anugerah* on Jalan Bosoiri, across the road from the bemo station. Cheapest of all are the night stalls that set up around the Merpati office – the martabaks are especially worth trying.

Getting There & Away

Air Merpati flies non-stop from Ternate to Ambon (135,000 rp), Galela (55,000 rp), Gebe (93,000 rp), Kao (36,000 rp), Manado (87,000 rp) and Morotai (64,000 rp). The flights to and from Ambon are often full, so book at least several days in advance.

Bouraq has non-stop flights from Ternate to Manado for 82,000 rp, from where you can easily make same-day connections to Balikpapan, Banjarmasin, Gorontalo, Jakarta, Palu, Samarinda, Surabaya, Tarakan and Ujung Pandang.

The Merpati office (☎ 21651) is at Jalan Bosoiri 81 and there's a Garuda agent in the same building, though Garuda doesn't fly to Ternate. The office is open daily, including Sunday, from 8 am to noon. Bouraq (☎ 21668) is somewhat inconveniently located on Jalan Stadion and is open every day from 8 am to 7 pm. There's a more central Bouraq agent in the Neraca Hotel (☎ 21327) at Jalan Pahlawan Revolusi 30.

Boat The harbour master's office (☎ 21129) and the Pelni office (☎ 21434) are just inside the Complex Pelabuhan on the corner of Jalan Ahmad Yani and Jalan Pahlawan Revolusi.

The Pelni liners *Tidar* and *Umsini* call at Ternate. See the Getting Around chapter at the beginning of this book for the complete route and schedule.

It is possible to reach Ternate from either Manado or Ambon. PT Teratai Murni's ship, *Delta Teratai*, departs every Monday from Manado Harbour at 5 pm. It arrives at Ternate on Tuesday morning and leaves the same afternoon for the Sula islands, arriving in Ambon on Thursday. It leaves again the same day for the return trip. The fare from Manado to Ternate is 20,000 rp.

Other shipping offices inside the harbour entrance include PT Perusahaan Peliaran Lokal, with boats to Daruba on Morotai and Tobelo on Halmahera, PT Pelayaran Rakyat and PT Peramut with boats to Morotai, Galela on Halmahera and Manado on Sulawesi.

Other possibilities out of Ternate include

ships to Surabaya, Sorong in Irian Jaya and even Singapore. Enquire at the harbour master's and Pelni offices.

Getting Around

To/From the Airport The airport is at Tarau, north of Ternate township. Charter a bemo for 3000 rp – the ride takes 10 minutes. Or walk a km down to the main road from the airport terminal and pick up a public bemo for 200 rp.

Bemo Ternate town is small and you can walk to all places in the central area. You can also take bemos. These cost 200 rp (flat rate) to anywhere around town or to Bastiong, the sultan's palace, or the airport. There are also bendis, usually costing 500 rp to any place in the central area. There are no becaks.

A surfaced road rings the island and public bemos cover it – though less frequently in the more distant reaches. They also climb part-way up Gamalama from Ternate town. One way of seeing the sights quickly would be to charter a bemo, as the ring-road links Ternate township with Batu Angus, Sulamadaha, Danau Tolire, Benteng Kastella, and Benteng Kayuh Merah. It takes a bit less than two hours to do a non-stop circle around the island – a charter would cost 3500 rp per hour.

TIDORE

Tidore has had very similar influences from the outside world to Ternate. Islam arrived in the middle of the 15th century and at the end of that century, the first ruler to take the title of 'sultan' assumed command. Tidore once claimed parts of Halmahera and a number of islands off the west coast of Irian Jaya. For a couple of centuries it rivalled Ternate for control of the spice trade. Today, Soa Siu is the main township on the island; Rum is the harbour for boats from Ternate.

Things to See

The town of Soa Siu is small, with none of the nightlife of Ternate. There's a fort above the road as you enter Soa Siu, but you need a local to show you the vague track leading up to it. The jungle has almost gobbled it up and you'd really have to be an enthusiast to come here. There is another fort near Rum. There are hot springs at Desa Ake Sahu, which can be reached by bemo.

Places to Stay

Few travellers actually stay here, but in Tidore there is a budget place called *Penginapan Jang*.

Getting There & Away

To get to Tidore from Ternate, take a bemo from Ternate township to Bastiong (200 rp). Boats powered by outboard motor depart frequently from the Pasar Impris at Bastiong for Rum on Tidore; they take about half an hour and cost 500 rp. From Rum, take a bemo for 1000 rp to the main town of Soa Siu (a 45-minute ride). The boats operate from about 7 am until 6 pm, but you'd better depart Tidore by 4 pm unless you plan to spend the night there.

Getting Around

Bemos operate from around 6 am until 6 pm. There are no becaks.

HALMAHERA

Shaped something like a mini version of Sulawesi, Halmahera was once under the sway of the old Ternate and Tidore sultanates who split the island between them. The inhabitants are a curious mixture. The mainly Muslim coastal people are, like the people of Ternate and Tidore, a mix of Portuguese, Gujarati (from western India), Arab, Malay and Dutch – a result of the long contact with foreign traders who came to this area in search of spices. There are still some indigenous tribes in the interior of Halmahera's northern peninsula and on the east coast. Much of their traditional culture remains intact. Strangely, the native languages spoken by north Halmaherans, Ternatans and Tidorese seem to have more in common with those of Australian Aborigines and the people of inland Irian Jaya and the Andaman islands in the Indian Ocean,

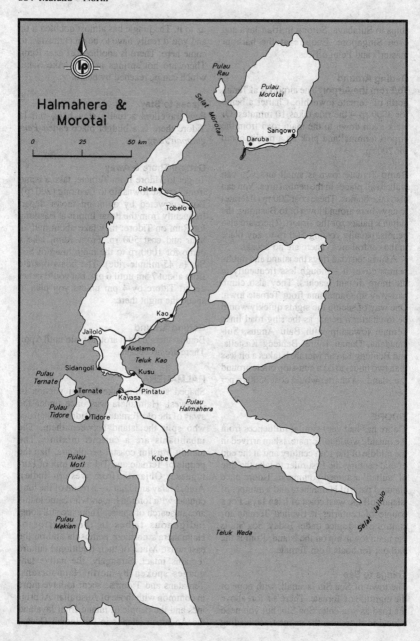

Halmahera & Morotai

0   25   50 km

Pulau Rau

Pulau Morotai

Selat Morotai

Sangowo
Daruba

Galela

Tobelo

Kao

Jailolo

Akelamo

Teluk Kao

Sidangoli

Kusu

Pulau Ternate

Pulau Tidore

Ternate

Kayasa

Pintatu

Tidore

Pulau Halmahera

Pulau Moti

Kobe

Pulau Makian

Teluk Weda

Selat Jailolo

than with the other languages of Indonesia and the Philippines.

Halmahera is little-developed, although its seas and forests are starting to be plundered like those in the rest of Maluku, with the profits largely leaving the area. There are a number of plywood mills, but these provide employment for Javanese rather than locals. The northern peninsula is the most populated and developed part, but it has mountains, volcanoes and untouched jungle as well as some coconut plantations on the coast. Tobelo, the main town on the island, only got electricity in 1985 and TV in 1987.

Only a handful of tourists visit this area of beautiful, white- sand beaches, excellent coral and clear waters (especially on and around the small islands in Teluk Kao and Pulau Morotai off north-east Halmahera). There's also diving to WW II wrecks off Morotai.

Places to Stay

In Tobelo, the *Pantai Indah* is best because it's on the seafront. Prices run at 18,000 to 25,000 rp per person and excellent meals are available. Rooms have attached mandi and a balcony with a sea view, but downstairs rooms are cheaper. The fanciest place in town is the *President Hotel* but it's not on the beach. Prices range from 15,000 to 50,000 rp. Also in the town are *Penginapan Karunia* and *Penginapan Megaria*.

In Kao there's the *Penginapan Dirgahaya*, which also serves meals. The owner is very helpful.

On Morotai, there's a penginapan at Daruba. It costs 15,000 rp per person including meals.

Getting There & Away

Air Merpati flies between Ternate and Galela (57,000 rp) four times weekly, Ternate and Kao (37,000 rp) twice weekly and Ternate and Morotai (65,000 rp) once weekly. There are also flights between Kao and Galela (45,000 rp).

Boat From Ternate Harbour there are boats daily to Sidangoli and most days to Jailolo on the west coast of Halmahera – see the Ternate section for details. From Sidangoli you can take a bus to Kao, Tobelo and Galela. There are also boats thrice weekly from Ternate to Tobelo via Daruba on Morotai. These leave Ternate at around 6 pm, taking around 12 hours to reach Daruba. Ask about other boats for Halmahera at the shipping offices at Ternate harbour and at Bastiong.

Getting Around

Tobelo, the biggest town, is about an hour by bus from Galela. The central and southern parts of the island have few roads and much more difficult access compared with the northern peninsula.

Irian Jaya

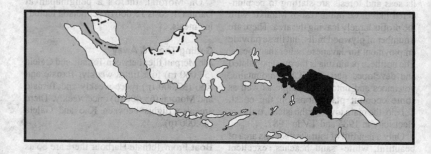

It's a different place from Indonesia, with a different people. Culturally and ethnically most of the people of Irian Jaya are classed as 'Papuan' – related to the people of neighbouring Papua New Guinea and similar to the Melanesians of the south Pacific. The terms 'Melanesian' and 'Papuan' are often used interchangeably. Although there does seem to be some distinction between the lighter-skinned coastal dwellers and the darker-skinned highland dwellers, the dividing line is a hazy one.

The people *are* far removed from the Malayan people of the Indonesian islands to the west; the Papuans are dark skinned, woolly haired, the men heavily bearded, their facial features reminiscent of the Australian Aborigines. They live in some of the most rugged terrain on earth, an island of soaring snow- capped mountains, almost impenetrable jungle, mangrove swamps and broad river valleys. Communications have always been so difficult that the different tribes have lived – for the most part – in isolation from each other, resulting in a diversity of cultures and languages that defies any attempt at neat pigeon-holing. The Papuans have no connection in appearance, culture or language with the predominantly Malay Indonesians, their sole historical link being that their homeland once formed part of the Dutch East Indies, and even then the interior was mostly just a huge blank on a map.

For visitors, Irian Jaya presents spectacular mountains and jungle, wonderful birdlife, intriguing and little-known peoples who have had minimal contact with the outside world, and some great trekking opportunities. More travellers are now getting to Irian Jaya, particularly with direct Garuda flights to Biak from Los Angeles. Most visitors include a trip to the Balim Valley, the only part of the interior which is regularly open, and two or three tourists generally arrive each day in Wamena.

HISTORY

Irian Jaya [in 1974] is being 'discovered' and brutally dragged into the sphere of influence of the technocrats – strange people everywhere; self-seeking people, who have no feeling for this country apart from what they can get from it; mechanical, emotionless people, mouthing cliches as they tear the place apart: very sad and disturbing. There is going to be a great turmoil here very shortly...
Robert Mitton, *The Lost World of Irian Jaya*

When the Portuguese sighted the island now divided between Irian Jaya and Papua New Guinea, they called it 'Ilhas dos Papuas', the Island of the Fuzzy-Hairs, from the Malay word *papuwah*. Later Dutch explorers called it 'New Guinea' because the black-skinned people reminded them of the people of

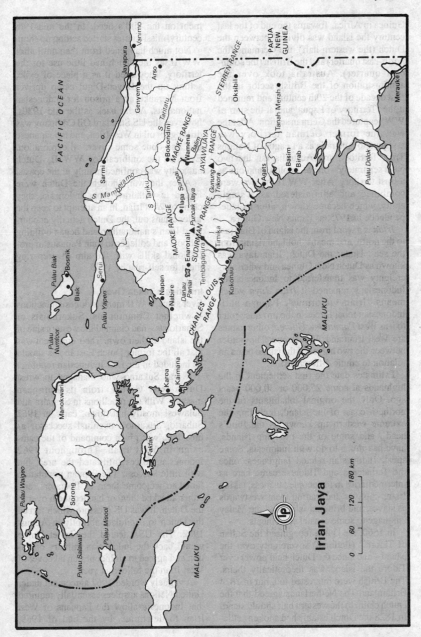

Irian Jaya

0   60   120   180 km

Guinea in Africa. Towards the end of the last century the island was divided between the Dutch (the western half), the Germans (the north-east quarter) and the British (the south-east quarter). Australia took over the administration of the British sector in the first decade of the 20th century and renamed it the 'Territory of Papua' and at the start of WW I captured the German section. After the war, the former German territory was assigned to Australia as a League of Nations Trust Territory, and Australia ran the two parts separately – one as a colony and one as a trust territory. After WW II the two were combined and administered as a single entity, which became known, after its independence in 1975, as Papua New Guinea.

Irian is a word from the island of Biak just to the north, and means 'hot land rising from the sea'. Under the Dutch, Irian Jaya was known as Dutch New Guinea and when sovereignty was transferred to Indonesia the Indonesians renamed it *Irian Jaya* which means 'Irian victorious'. Papuan anti-Indonesian rebel forces in the province refer to it as *West Papua New Guinea*; other names are West Irian and West Papua. The border between the two halves of the island bears no relation to ethnic differences.

Estimates date the first settlement in the highlands at some 25,000 or 30,000 years ago. Only the original inhabitants of the northern coast of the island, including the extreme western tip known as the 'bird's head', and some of the off-lying islands, have had much to do with Indonesia. Some speak Indonesian-related languages; once the Ternateans and Tidorese came here as intermediaries in the people business, taking Irians captives and trading them westwards as slaves, and bringing Islam and the Malay language to some coastal settlements.

In 1660, the Dutch recognised the Sultan of Tidore's (fictional) sovereignty over the island – and since the Dutch held power over Tidore the island was theoretically theirs. The British were interested too, but in 1824 Britain and The Netherlands agreed that the Dutch claim to the western half should stand. In 1828 the Dutch established a token settlement on the bird's head. In the mid-19th century, missionaries started setting up shop.

Not much happened from then until after WW II, as the Dutch had little use for the territory. They used it as a place of exile, setting up the Boven-Digul camp upriver from Merauke as a prison for Indonesian nationalists. As far back as the mid-1930s, however, the US Standard Oil Company was drilling for oil in West Irian, and the Japanese had also done some covert oil exploration. Even at the outbreak of WW II, Dutch authority was confined mainly to the coasts.

After the war, though the Dutch were forced to withdraw from Indonesia, they clung to West Irian. In an attempt to keep the Indonesians out, the Dutch actually encouraged Irian's nationalism and began building schools and colleges to train Papuans in professional skills with the aim of preparing them for self-rule by 1970.

Indonesia Takes Over

Ever since WW II many Indonesian factions – whether Communists, Sukarnoists or Suhartoists – had claimed the western side of the island as their own. Their argument was that all the former Dutch East Indies should be included in the new Indonesian republic.

It was Sukarno who managed to wrest Dutch New Guinea from its European masters. With the rebellions in Sumatra and Sulawesi mostly put down, early in 1962 Suharto, Sukarno's eventual successor as president, was given command of the campaign in West Irian. Throughout 1962 Indonesian forces infiltrated the area, but with little success. The Papuan population failed to welcome them as liberators, and either attacked them or handed them over to the Dutch. It was US pressure which forced the Dutch to capitulate abruptly in August 1962. The USA feared the Soviet Union would back the Indonesian military operation and agreed to an Indonesian takeover of West Irian the following year.

A vaguely worded 1962 agreement under United Nations auspices essentially required that Indonesia allow the Papuans of West Irian to determine, by the end of 1969, whether they wanted independence or to remain within the Indonesian republic. This 'Act of Free Choice' (or 'Act Free of Choice' as it became known) was held in 1969, 'supervised' by the UN. The Indonesian government announced that it would use the procedure of *musyawarah* under which a consensus of 'elders' is reached. While it was claimed that this accorded with the traditions of the nation it was also easy to hand-pick and pressurise the assemblies of elders. In July 1969 the Indonesian government announced that the assemblies in Merauke, Jayawijaya and Paniai districts, in which the greater part of the West Irian population lives, had unanimously decided to become part of Indonesia.

Papuan Opposition

Even before the Act, the Indonesians faced violent opposition from the Papuans. In 1967 aircraft were used to bomb and strafe Arfak tribespeople threatening Manokwari town on the bird's head but the fighting continued into 1969. In the same year rebellions broke out on the island of Biak and at Enarotali in the highlands. In 1977 there was serious conflict in the highlands around the Balim Valley and Tembagapura, site of the US-run Freeport copper mine. Bombs damaged Freeport installations and cut the pipeline which takes copper concentrates to the coast. In 1981 there was heavy fighting in the Enarotali region, and in early 1984 the consequences of an attempted uprising centred on Jayapura sent thousands of Irians fleeing into PNG. These were not the only uprisings, nor were they the last: the pattern is mainly one of intermittent incidents, depending mainly on the levels of resentment against the Indonesians and of organisation of the resistance forces. In 1988 somewhere between 15 and 40 transmigrants from Sulawesi were killed in an attack at Arso, south-east of Jayapura.

The Irians are provoked by a number of factors, among them the taking of their land for logging, mining or other commercial purposes (often done in a superficially legal way, accompanied by pressure and threats);

transmigration, which is bringing large numbers of western Indonesians to Irian Jaya, to live in close proximity to the people whose former land they occupy and whose potential jobs they take in the towns; the typical Indonesian attitude to the Irians, which is at best patronising; attempts to 'Indonesianise' the locals by schooling, propaganda, and even some efforts to make them forsake their traditional attire and wear 'proper clothes'; extremely brutal Indonesian responses to conflict, protest or even uncooperativeness (reportedly including mass reprisals, strafing villages from the air, torture and arbitrary killings) and total intolerance of political dissent. Additionally, the Irians never use their rivers as a toilet, an Indonesian habit which has brought the Irians dysentery, giardiasis and other serious waterborne diseases.

The chief anti-Indonesian guerrilla force is known as the OPM (Organisasi Papua Merdeka – Free Papua Movement). It appears to have been set up just after West Irian was handed over to the Indonesians, but there seems to be neither a single leader nor a unified command. The number of active members goes up and down: in the late '80s there were perhaps 500, mainly in the northeast of Irian Jaya. Sometimes there appears to be rivalry between different OPM factions. They have limited weapons other than spears, machetes, bows and arrows. In the mid '80s an OPM group managed to 'occupy' a 10-km wide strip of territory on the Indonesian side of the PNG border near Mindip Tanah, south of the highlands, but activity there has since waned. Incidents that do occur nevertheless still generate tales of courage, glory and unity, feeding the 'war of independence' mentality of many Papuans. However, if you harbour any romantic fantasies of joining the OPM and liberating Irian Jaya, it might be wise to keep in mind that the OPM has kidnapped Westerners on several occasions, though so far only on the Papua New Guinea side of the border.

Refugees

Because the PNG-Indonesia border straddles

tribal territories, some people in the centre of the island have always wandered back and forth across it. But since the Indonesian take-over many more have crossed as a result of Indonesian (or sometimes OPM) violence or the fear of it. The biggest exodus came in 1984 when over 10,000 people fled to PNG after the abortive OPM uprising that year. Many of these were from Jayapura and included intellectuals, public servants, police, army deserters, students and their families.

Most of these refugees have ended up in camps not very far inside PNG territory – camps whose connections with the OPM provoke tension between the PNG and Indonesian governments. Indonesia complains about the camps harbouring OPM activists; PNG complains about Indonesian armed incursions into its territory in pursuit of the OPM. There have been attempts by both sides to get refugees to go back to Irian Jaya – some have even been forced to do so by PNG – but most are reluctant for fear of what will happen to them. In 1987 there were an estimated 11,000 Irians in camps in PNG. The following year, after the Arso attack mentioned earlier, about 1000 were airlifted from the South Blackwater camp near Vanimo on PNG's north coast to the East Awin camp, south of the highlands and further from the border, where they had to mix with 2000 refugees from southern Irian Jaya who had already been at East Awin since 1987. East Awin has poor soil and a shortage of fresh water. Conditions in the camps are generally poor and there have been reports of starvation. The problem is too large to be solved by the PNG government, which has to tread warily with its powerful neighbour and receives little help on the issue from outside.

When PNG protested in October 1988 at three incursions over the border by Indonesian troops, which apparently culminated in their taking five villagers hostage but later releasing them, Indonesia's response was that such events might continue as long as Melanesian separatists operated in the border area.

Transmigration & Environment

The Indonesian policies which provoke Papuan unrest continue. In 1988, according to official figures, 113,634 of Irian Jaya's 1.2 million people had arrived on government transmigration schemes. Another 180,000 or so western Indonesians had come as independent settlers. So far the transmigrants are mostly grouped near main towns like Jayapura, Merauke, Manokwari, Nabire and Sorong, but there are others up towards the border north of Merauke and in the Fakfak area. Also there are reports of plans to open up the Central Highlands and the Mappi area, on the swampy west coast south of Agats, to transmigrants.

The government has grandiose plans for moving far larger numbers in – the target (not reached) for 1984 to 1989 was about 600,000. Some reports even talk of an ultimate target of four million. A number of observers, noting the poor locations and lack of planning for many existing settlements, have concluded that the main thrust of transmigration to Irian Jaya is less for the benefit of the transmigrants than to make the province truly Indonesian, by populating it with Indonesians and turning the Irians into a minority in their own land.

The environment is being exploited at a lightning pace and land concessions to western Indonesian and/or foreign companies threaten the survival of some tribes. The forests of the Asmat district on the west coast are being clear-felled by three companies, using the Asmat people – under conditions which have often been tantamount to slavery – to fell and strip the trees and float them downstream for the concessionaires to collect. There is no reforestation. Erosion and flooding of the low-lying land is expected to increase, eventually destroying the sago palms on which the Asmat depend for food. In the Sungai (river) Digul area, south of the Central Highlands, the US Scott Paper Company and its Indonesian partner Astra, which in 1987 were granted forest concessions 1½ times the size of Bali, plan to produce 1000 tonnes of woodchip and 4000 tonnes of wood pulp a day.

GEOGRAPHY

The landscape is part of what a visit to Irian Jaya is about. One of the last wildernesses, it has a rugged, varied and dramatic geography. Flying across the bird's head from Ambon to Biak over wide, snaking rivers surrounded by thick vegetation gives you a taste of the treats ahead. Approaching Jayapura's Sentani Airport, you see stunningly beautiful lakes girdled by hills. Equally exciting is the view, from the plane en route to the Balim Valley, of the Sungai Taritatu, a tributary of the giant Mamboramo.

A central east-west mountain range is the backbone of Irian Jaya and Papua New Guinea. It reaches its maximum altitude in the west, with Puncak Jaya the highest peak (5050 metres). This and other Irian Jaya peaks such as Puncak Mandala have permanent snowfields and small glaciers. Alpine grasslands, jagged bare peaks, montane forests which include pines, foothill rainforests, ferocious rivers, gentle streams, stunning rock faces and gorges add to the varying landscape of the highlands. The most heavily populated and cultivated areas of the Irian highlands are the Paniai lakes district and the Balim Valley to the east.

South of the mountains is a coastal plain, widest in the east at the border with Papua New Guinea; there are sago swamps and low-lying alluvial plains (of fine-grained fertile soil consisting of mud, silt and sand deposited by flowing water), though it gets drier and more savannah-like in the far eastern section around Merauke. The northern coastal plain is much narrower and less swampy, with larger-than-life tropical vegetation – real jungle! There are coconut-fringed white sandy beaches on the north

coast and the offshore islands of Biak, Yapen and Waigeo.

CLIMATE

The coastal climate is hot, humid and rainy most of the year. The highlands have warm to hot days and cool to very cold evenings, depending on the altitude. Plenty of rain falls in the highlands too but it's often confined to the evenings. Wetter and drier seasons vary from valley to valley in the highlands. In the Balim Valley, from May to July is the driest time; from September to November is the wettest and windiest. From January to March is a good time for trekking as it's neither too muddy nor too hot. The south coast has a distinct dry season from July to October, and the north coast tends to have slightly less rain at this time too.

FLORA & FAUNA

Irian Jaya's flora is as varied as its geography. Much of the land is covered in impenetrable tropical rainforest, with the usual luxurious collection of Asiatic species and some endemic to the island, which is in the transition zone between Asia and Australia. The south coast's vegetation includes mangroves and sago palms plus eucalypts, paperbarks and acacias in the drier eastern section. Highland vegetation ranges from alpine grasslands and heaths to pine forests, bush and scrub that is unique.

Land animals are largely confined to marsupials, some indigenous, others also found in Australia. These include marsupial 'mice' and 'cats', bandicoots, ring-tailed possums, pygmy flying phalangers, big cuscuses, tree kangaroos and, in the south, wallabies. Reptiles include snakes, frill-necked and monitor lizards and crocodiles. The spiny

Saltwater crocodile

anteater is also found. Insects are abundant, particularly the colourful butterflies. Despite large-scale plunder, Irian Jaya's exquisite birdlife is still most famous . There are more than 600 species including numerous bird of paradise species, bowerbirds, cockatoos, parrots and lorikeets, kingfishers, crowned pigeons and cassowaries.

Pulau Yapen is supposed to be one good place to see birds of paradise. The males are renowned for their ostentatious plumage and long, brightly coloured tail feathers which are employed in energetic dances with the objective of enamouring a mate. Dances can be individual or in groups – they are a fascinating sight but are difficult to come across. The best time is early in the morning from May to December. The females' plumage is dull, fortunate for the species as they have been left alone to continue their breeding; the males, though now 'protected', have been hunted to near-extinction.

Teluk Cendrawasih – the bay between Biak and the mainland – is one of the richest marine life areas in Indonesia. It's a feeding ground for sea turtles and dugongs, and its coral islands are nesting sites for many seabirds.

BOOKS

Irian Jaya's unique landscape, flora and fauna and intriguing peoples (particularly the Dani of the Balim Valley) have inspired several excellent books. One is Peter Matthiessen's *Under the Mountain Wall* (Collins Harvill, London, 1989), based on his long visit to the Balim in 1961. In beautifully written semi-fiction he chronicles daily life among the Kurulu tribe including work, relaxation, war, feasts and funerals, somehow capturing the magic of the area before it was swamped by change. *Gardens Of War* by R Gardner & K Heider (Andre Deutsch, London, 1969) also covers the same area at a similar time.

Robert Mitton's *The Lost World of Irian Jaya* (Oxford University Press, Melbourne, 1983) looks like a coffee-table book and is priced like one but is probably *the* classic book on the province. Mitton spent six years,

on and off, in Irian Jaya in the '70s, studying and exploring while working for a mining company. The book was compiled from his letters, diaries, maps and photographs after his sudden death from leukaemia in 1976. The book bitterly criticises the reckless way in which the Irians have been shoved into the modern world.

Indonesia's Secret War: The Guerilla Struggle In Irian Jaya by Robin Osborne (Allen & Unwin, 1985) is an excellently documented account of events up to 1984, and *West Papua: the Obliteration of a People* by Carmel Budiardjo & Liem Soei Liong (TAPOL, London, 1988) is also worth reading. George Monbiot's *Poisoned Arrows* (Michael Joseph, London, 1989) details a remarkable journey by the 24-year-old author to the wilds of Irian Jaya with the objective of uncovering the truth about transmigration, the plight of the refugees and the true nature of the OPM resistance. He travelled without permits to restricted areas and even ventured into Asmat territory through its back door via an overland and river route from Wamena.

Another interesting book is *The Asmat* (Museum of Primitive Art, New York, 1967), a collection of photographs of the Asmat people (who live on the south coast of Irian Jaya) and their art, taken by Michael Rockefeller in 1961. Rockefeller disappeared on his second trip to Irian Jaya after his boat overturned at the mouth of the Sungai Eilanden (Betsj). His body was never found and there are various accounts of what became of him, the usual story being that he was eaten by natives.

Ring of Fire by Lawrence & Lorne Blair devotes a chapter to two visits to the Asmat and also tackles the Rockefeller mystery.

VISAS & PERMITS

The paperwork you need to visit Irian Jaya, and the places you can go to once you get there, fluctuate according to a number of variables including the level of conflict between the native people and the Indonesian colonists, and between Indonesia and Papua New Guinea. Other recent visitors to

Irian Jaya are the most reliable source of information, but the situation has been relatively relaxed in recent years and may improve. There is now a PNG consulate in Jayapura and Indonesia is planning to open one up in Vanimo or Wewak.

Entering Irian Jaya

If you arrive at Biak Airport – most likely on a Garuda flight from the USA – you get the regular two-month tourist pass stamped in your passport. To enter by sea or at any other airport – for example, flying in to Jayapura from PNG – you'll need an Indonesian visa. You can get this from Indonesian consulates and embassies in other countries and it is usually good for 30 days, though it's worth asking for more. The visa *might* be extendable at an *imigrasi* office in Indonesia.

At the time of writing, the only place you could get an Indonesian visa in PNG was the embassy in Port Moresby. It will probably take a few days, a few kina and a couple of passport photos; you may have to show an onward ticket from Jayapura and a ticket out of Indonesia. At least once, the Indonesians have stopped issuing visas at Port Moresby, so it would be worth getting yours before you arrive in PNG, if you can. There are both tourist and visitor visas (both have at different times excluded visits to the highlands); which type is better or easier to get seems to depend on which way the wind is blowing. Your visa might come with a two-day Jayapura transit pass, which means you should report to the Jayapura police within two days of arriving.

From Indonesia Some people take the precaution of getting a *surat jalan* (travel permit), for the parts of Irian Jaya that they plan to visit, from the Jakarta police chief, although at the time of writing there didn't seem to be any restrictions on going to Irian Jaya at least by regular means (eg with Garuda, Merpati or Pelni passenger liners). But you'll still have to get another surat jalan in Irian Jaya itself in order to go outside the main coastal towns.

Travel Permits – around Irian Jaya

Unless some political upheaval alters the picture, you can travel to the main coastal cities – Jayapura, Biak, Sorong and probably Merauke – without any permit, but to go elsewhere you need a surat jalan. This you obtain from a head police station – supposedly in either Jayapura, Biak, Sorong or Merauke, but Jayapura is the HQ for Irian Jaya and is less likely to suffer from any 'must contact our superiors' delays (though if you don't get what you want there, you just might get it somewhere else). If you're heading to Wamena, the most convenient place to get your surat jalan is in Sentani, the small city near Jayapura's airport.

The surat jalan is free and takes maybe half an hour to issue. You must provide two passport photos and state where you want to go and for how long. Questions you're likely to be asked include your religion (say you're a Christian) and profession (don't be a journalist). There appears to be no limit on how long you can stay in the areas you're allowed to visit, so long as you don't overstay your Indonesian visa or tourist pass.

Some parts of Irian Jaya are off limits to foreign tourists and you won't get a permit for them. The situation is fluid (presumably depending on the level of tension or OPM activity, or other things Indonesia wants to hide in any given area): head police stations will tell you where you can and can't go. In 1991, only the following areas were absolutely off limits to foreigners: Oksibil, Kiwirok, Admisibil, Iwur and the Papua New Guinea border.

For other areas, you have to get permission from specific police offices. To enter Akimuga, you have to get permission from the police in Timika. To enter Enarotali, Ilaga, Moanemani and Waghete, you must get permission in Nabire. For Mamberamo, you get permission in Jayapura. If you want to climb Gunung Trikora (worthwhile!) you can get permission in Wamena.

It's worth taking a few photocopies of your surat jalan: it may save you a few hours sitting in small police stations later while dozy cops write your details into their books.

Once you arrive in the town you have a permit for, you're supposed to report within 24 hours to the police, who will stamp your surat jalan and probably tell you where, officially, you can go within their area. You may also be told to report again to the police each time you enter a new district within the area – such as the Jiwika district in the Wamena area. Some travellers manage to stray beyond official boundaries and visit places they 'shouldn't', because police are pleasantly thin on the ground away from the main centres.

Leaving Jayapura for PNG

Though PNG issues visas on arrival to tourists entering at Port Moresby, it doesn't at Vanimo – which is where you fly into from Jayapura. So you need to get your PNG visa in advance. PNG has opened a consulate in Jayapura, though if you want to be prepared you can get your visa in Jakarta.

Since Jayapura is not an officially designated Indonesian exit/entry point, you should, strictly speaking, have entered Indonesia on a visa, rather than the regular two-month tourist pass, if you want to leave the country through Jayapura. In the past some Indonesian immigration officials have required the aid of items like US$80 *and* a bottle of whisky to help them iron out this little bureaucratic wrinkle for you, but since 1988 they have seemed to be more human, and it *may* be possible to exit from Jayapura to PNG, even if you entered Indonesia on a tourist pass.

MONEY

Make sure you change plenty of money before heading into the interior. It's especially important that you get plenty of 100 rp notes. In remote villages, the people actually want 100 rp notes simply because they're red in colour! Rupiah can usually be obtained in Wewak from the Westpac Bank, although the exchange rate is not as good as in Indonesia. You can get rupiah in banks in Jayapura, Biak, Wamena and probably other main towns and, for a reasonable rate, at the MAF office at Sentani Airport.

Cigarettes are also a form of money in Wamena and other parts of Irian Jaya. The locals love them, and they can be traded or just given away to make friends. Stock up on the cheapest brand and carry a cigarette lighter, even if you don't smoke.

GETTING THERE & AWAY

Air

Garuda's thrice-weekly flights from Los Angeles to Jakarta and vice-versa stop en route at Honolulu, Biak and Denpasar. There's a once-weekly border-hop flight on Wednesday from Vanimo in Papua New Guinea to Jayapura and back, in a tiny plane of the little PNG airline Douglas Airways. Book through the Papua New Guinea consulate in Jayapura. Vanimo is connected to Wewak and Port Moresby by internal PNG flights (usually same-day) and you can book right through between Jayapura and these places. From Jayapura to Wewak, it used to be US$40 cheaper, and may still be, to fly first to Vanimo then buy another ticket on to Wewak from there. From Port Moresby a ticket to Jayapura costs around 400 kina (about US$450).

There are occasional mission flights from Jayapura to PNG, but your chances of getting on one are close to zero. There are also aircraft operated by various mining companies, and both mission and mining planes occasionally fly to Australia.

Biak is the air transport hub of Irian Jaya, and there are plenty of domestic flights connecting Biak to the rest of Indonesia. If you catch the early flight from Jayapura to Biak, you can even get to Jakarta the same day.

Boat

Two Pelni passenger liners, the *Umsini* and the *Rinjani*, serve Irian Jaya. For a complete schedule of these two ships, see the Getting Around chapter at the beginning of the book.

Other cheaper, less comfortable ships link Jayapura, Sorong, Biak and possibly other ports with the rest of Indonesia with their customary irregularity. As usual it's a case of hanging around and seeing what's available. Surabaya is a fairly frequent departure point

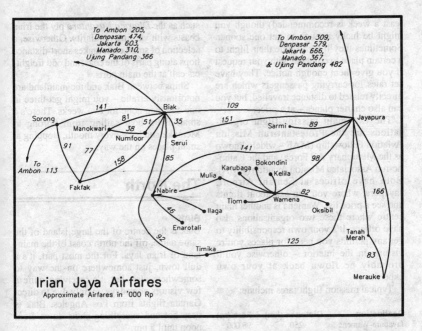

Irian Jaya Airfares
Approximate Airfares in '000 Rp

To Ambon 205,
Denpasar 474,
Jakarta 603,
Manado 310,
Ujung Pandang 366

To Ambon 309,
Denpasar 579,
Jakarta 666,
Manado 367,
& Ujung Pandang 482

Sorong
Biak 141
109
Jayapura
Manokwari 81 51 35 151 Sarmi 89
91 38 Numfoor Serui 141
To 77 158 85 Bokondini 98
Ambon 113 Karubaga Kelila
Fakfak Mulia 82 166
Nabire Tiom Wamena Oksibil
46 Ilaga
Enarotali Tanah
92 Merah
Timika 125 83
Merauke

(every couple of days) for ships to Maluku and Irian Jaya. Ask the harbour master at Jalan Kalimas Baru 194.

To/From PNG

Officially, there is no land or sea crossing between Irian Jaya and PNG. They're worried about guerilla activities in the border area, so just strolling across the border or even taking a small boat from Jayapura to Vanimo is not allowed at present.

GETTING AROUND

Unless you're into mounting full-scale expeditions and are adept at cutting your way through jungle with a machete, or like shuffling your way around coasts in slow, dirty boats, then flying is the only way to get around Irian Jaya. There are roads in the immediate vicinity of the urban areas and a good paved one extending westwards along the coast from Jayapura, but other than these few stretches there is – as of yet – nothing. A

trans-Irian highway is being built from Jayapura to Merauke via Wamena, but no one knows when it will be finished and few have confidence that it will be kept in working order if it is.

Air

If you want to go inland you have to fly. Merpati carries the bulk of the traffic from the major centres to other parts of the coast and interior.

For getting to remote parts that even Merpati doesn't reach – or occasionally as a substitute if Merpati is full – you can use flights run by the various missionary groups in Irian Jaya. These cover a truly amazing network of maybe 200-plus airstrips – nearly all grass and many on steep slopes in narrow valleys – all over Irian Jaya with tiny planes and occasionally helicopters, flying where and when the missions need them to.

They *will* accept passengers if they have room, but book as far ahead as possible (at least a week is recommended) though you might be lucky enough to get one sooner. Sometimes they'll try to time their flight to a certain place to coincide with your request if you give them enough notice. They have set rates for carrying passengers which are directly related to distance travelled, but you can also charter planes – at a price.

The two main mission-flight organisations are the Protestant-run Mission Aviation Fellowship (MAF – widely known as the Missionary Air Force) and the Catholic-run Associated Mission Aviation (AMA). Both have offices at Sentani Airport, Jayapura, where you can ask about flights and see a price list. Wamena is another main centre where these two organisations also have offices. It's your own responsibility to get any permits you need for places you're visiting in the interior – otherwise you'll probably be flown back at your own expense.

Typical mission flight fares include:

Destination	Distance (km)	Fare (rp)
Jayapura-Wamena	250	98,000
Nabire-Enarotali	120	46,000
Wamena-Pass Valley	40	15,600
Wamena-Bokondini	60	24,000
Wamena-Angguruk	80	31,000
Wamena-Ilaga	160	62,000
Wamena-Oksibil	210	82,000
Merauke-Senggo	330	129,000

Over short distances, mission fares are similar to Merpati's, but for longer flights they're considerably dearer. The cheapest charters are small Cessnas for around 300,000 rp an hour – which gives you a 25-minute flight if you're just going one way, since you also have to pay for the plane's turnaround time and its flight back to where you came from. Helicopters seat four people and can be chartered for 1,560,000 rp per hour.

Boat

Pelni's *Umsini* (see the Getting Around chapter for details) will take you between Jayapura and Sorong in comfort if you wish, and other more basic Pelni passenger ships

such as the *Dharma Nusantara* ply the Irian coasts with varying regularity. Otherwise, a selection of small craft makes short-distance hops along parts of the coast and odd freighters call at the main ports.

Ships between Biak and the mainland are notoriously erratic – you might get three in one day then none for two weeks. There's a small Pelni boat sailing from Sorong to Merauke and back every month, stopping at small places on the way.

The North

BIAK

Biak is the centre of the large island of the same name, off the north coast of the mainland of Irian Jaya. For the most part, it's a dull town, just somewhere on the way to somewhere else, but it's receiving quite a few visitors nowadays, mainly due to direct Garuda flights from Los Angeles. Biak is very hot and everything shuts down from noon until 5 pm.

The most interesting place in town is the central Pasar Panir where lorikeets and cockatoos are sometimes for sale. When a Pelni ship goes through, half the crew seem to buy one to sell later in Java, and at the end of a flight from Biak to Jakarta you can witness the odd spectacle of cages and boxes of live birds rolling out on the luggage conveyer belts.

If you want to make a trip to Biak worthwhile then leave the town and explore the island, which feels very Polynesian, especially if you have come from western Indonesia. At Ambroben village, about four km from the town, are some caves that were built by the Japanese during WW II; more caves are dotted around the island. You can easily make the half-hour bemo trip east to Bosnik, which was the former Dutch centre on the island. There are some WW II relics, a reasonable beach and views across to the Owi islands. Pantai Korim is on the north coast, about 40 km from the town.

Near Bosnik, Parieri Reserve has some

Top: Dani hut, Balim Valley, Irian Jaya (AS)
Bottom: River crossing near Wamena, Balim Valley, Irian Jaya (AS)

Top: Market in Wamena, Balim Valley, Irian Jaya (AS)
Left: Mummy at Akima, Balim Valley, Irian Jaya (AS)
Right: Crossing the river near Wamena, Balim Valley, Irian Jaya (AS)

original stands of forest. On the north-west tip of the island, Biak Utara Reserve is larger and includes 15 km of beach. It's well forested, with lots of parrots and cockatoos. Separated from Pulau Biak by only a very narrow channel, Pualau Superiori is just about all reserve and includes mangrove and montane forests. Apparently its birdlife has been less exploited than Biak's.

Orientation & Information
Biak is a fairly compact town. Jalan Prof M Yamin runs from the airport and connects with Jalan Ahmad Yani. The latter is Biak's main street, with many of the hotels, restaurants and offices. The other main street, Jalan Imam Bonjol, cuts at right angles through Jalan Ahmad Yani.

Money The Bank Expor Impor Indonesia at the corner of Jalan Ahmad Yani and Jalan Imam Bonjol is open Monday to Friday from 8 am to 2 pm, Saturday from 8 to 10 am and is closed Sunday. Get there a good hour before it closes if you want to change money.

Police & Immigration The head police station is on Jalan Selat Makassar opposite the Pasar Panir. Biak is a very good place to get permits (surat jalan) for the Balim Valley and other places in the interior of Irian Jaya. Two photographs are required. Permits are issued in 10 minutes and cost 2000 rp.

The immigration office is at the corner of Jalan Ahmad Yani and Jalan Imam Bonjol.

Places to Stay – bottom end
Penginapan Solo (☎ 21397) at Jalan Monginsidi 4 is the cheapest in town. Singles/doubles are 7700/15,400 rp with a shared bath. It's reasonably clean and well run.

Places to Stay – middle
Losmen Maju (☎ 21218) at Jalan Imam Bonjol 45 has singles/doubles with fan for 15,750/24200 rp and air-con rooms for 38,750/55,400 rp. Rooms are basic but clean, with fan and attached mandi.

Hotel Mapia (☎ 21383) on Jalan Ahmad Yani is comfortable but has definitely seen better days. Rooms with fan and attached mandi start at 16,950/23,000 rp; air-con rooms cost 26,650/33,3000 rp. Lunch and dinner both cost 5000 rp.

Places to Stay – top end
Hotel Irian (☎ 21139, 21839) is across the street from the airport terminal and adjacent to the Merpati office. It's a beautiful hotel with a large seaside garden, bar and spacious restaurant, but this luxury does not come cheaply. Economy singles/doubles cost 27,850/48,400 rp; standard rooms with air-con are 46,000/72,700 rp and VIP suites are 60,550/84,700 rp. Transit passengers sometimes get to stay here for free if Merpati's 'rubber time' schedule causes them to miss a flight connection.

Hotel Titawaka (☎ 21835) is memorable for the miniature Sulawesi Toraja-style house built over its foyer – just a little incongruous in Irian Jaya! It's at Jalan Selat Makassar 3 and is quite comfy if not cheap. Economy rooms are 33,900/58,100 rp, standard rooms costs 51,450/78,650 rp and VIP suites go for 60,500/90,750 rp. The price includes three meals, tax and transport to the airport.

Also run by the same friendly family, who speak English and Dutch, is the pleasant *Wisma Titawaka* (☎ 21658) at Jalan Monginsidi 24. Singles/doubles cost 50,850/78,000 rp, which includes three meals and an afternoon snack. The nearby *Titawaka Home* (☎ 21891) at Jalan Monginsidi 14 costs 78,000 rp for a double, but is currently contracted out to Garuda. Perhaps it will reopen to the public someday. The Titawaka Home has a TV room and is on the beach, with a view of Pulau Yapen.

Places to Eat
There are evening foodstalls on the road leading from the Bank Expor Impor to the sea. *Restoran Cleopatra* opposite the Hotel Mapia is one of the best in town, and has a varied menu in English featuring good Chinese food, chicken and seafood dishes. *Restaurant 99* and *Restaurant New Garden*

on Jalan Imam Banjol are both OK. There are some cheap places along Jalan Ahmad Yani like the *Rumah Makan Anda*, the *Restaurant Megaria* and the *Restaurant Himalaya*. If you want to do self-catering, the *Indah Supermarket* is not bad.

Getting There & Away

Air Biak is one of Indonesia's gateway cities, so you can enter or exit the country here without a visa. Garuda has four flights weekly between Biak and Los Angeles via Hawaii. Garuda also flies daily between Biak and Singapore (948,400 rp). There are also less frequent flights from Biak to Bangkok, Amsterdam, Frankfurt, London, Paris, Rome and Zurich.

Merpati and Garuda have domestic flights from Biak to:

Destination	Fare (rp)
Ambon	205,000
Bandung, Denpasar	474,000
Fakfak	158,000
Jakarta	603,000
Jayapura	109,000
Kupang	536,000
Manado	310,000
Manokwari	81,000
Maumere, Nabire, Numfoor	51,000
Palu, Serui	35,000
Sorong	141,000
Surabaya	541,000
Timika & Ujung Pandang	366,000

Garuda (☎ 21416, 21331) is on Jalan Ahmad Yani near the corner of Jalan Imam Bonjol in the middle of Biak. The Merpati office (☎ 21213, 21386) is out of town, just across the road from the airport terminal. If you're in the town, PT Sentosa Tosiga at Jalan Ahmad Yani 36 is a good agent for Garuda and Merpati. There's another Merpati agent in town just off Jalan Imam Bonjol.

Boat Biak has shipping connections with western Indonesia, Pulau Yapen to the south, and mainland Irian Jaya, but these tend to be erratic – though you may be able to find

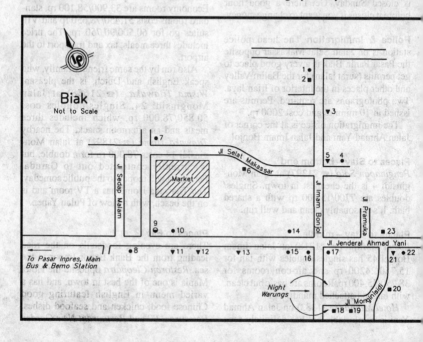

fairly frequent small passenger ships to Manokwari on the bird's head. See the Irian Jaya introductory sections for more details.

The Pelni office is on Jalan Ahmad Yani, a short distance west of the Garuda office. The harbour entrance is nearby.

Getting Around

To/From the Airport A bemo from the airport to any place in the centre costs 300 rp, although the drivers try to charge foreigners 1000 rp. Bemos to the airport run regularly up and down Jalan Ahmad Yani and Jalan Prof M Yamin. A taxi from the airport to the centre costs 5000 rp. You could walk into the city from the airport if you're feeling energetic (not likely in this heat!). Walking takes about 40 minutes, depending on how heavy your pack is.

Local Transport The main bemo and bus terminal is right by the Pasar Inpres. Clearly

marked boards indicate where vehicles are heading. Bemos to Bosnik cost 600 rp. Buses go to Pantai Korim on the north coast.

For Parieri Reserve, take a bemo to Adibai and then walk. To get to Biak Utara Reserve, it may be more feasible to charter a bemo in Biak but trucks do go to Warsa, about six km from the reserve's eastern boundary. From Warsa, a road continues around the island's northern tip. For Superiori Reserve, boats go from Biak to Sowok on the south-west coast of Pulau Superiori and take four to five hours – you may be able to make a shorter journey to a village on the south-east coast.

PT Sentosa Tosiga at Jalan Ahmad Yani 36, opposite the Hotel Mapia, does a few Biak tours.

JAYAPURA & SENTANI

Jayapura is the name now given by the Indonesians to the capital of Irian Jaya. In Dutch times it was known as Hollandia, and

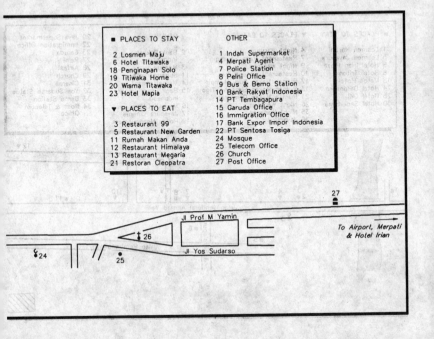

was deliberately placed just a few km from the border with German New Guinea, to emphasise the Dutch claim to the western half of the island.

Apart from relics of WW II there are few sights as such in Jayapura. In April 1944 the Allies stormed ashore up the road at Hamadi and captured the town after only token resistance from the Japanese. It was in Jayapura that General MacArthur assembled his fleet for the invasion of the Philippines.

Built on hills which slope down to the sea, the city is squeezed on to every available bit of semi-level land. At night it's a pretty sight from above, with the lights of fishing boats winking out on the bay, but during the day it's heavily polluted and unattractive. There's very little that's Melanesian about the place. It is dominated by Indonesians and looks little different from any other medium-sized Indonesian city. Nearby are large Indonesian transmigration colonies, like the

Genyem settlement just to the south at Nimboran.

Jayapura is stinking hot, though not as bad as Biak. Everything normally closes between around noon and 4 pm. There's no reason to come here unless you have to deal with the Merpati office, a bank or some other bureaucratic institution. Sentani, a small town 36 km from Jayapura, where the airport is located, is in many ways a better place to stay – it's quieter, less polluted and, for some reason, cooler than Jayapura itself.

Orientation & Information

In Jayapura, just about everything you want – most of the hotels, the shops, the head police station, the airline offices – is confined to a very small area near the waterfront. The two main streets are Jalan Ahmad Yani and, parallel to it, Jalan Percetakan.

If you want to seek advice or information from missionaries, try the Inter-Mission

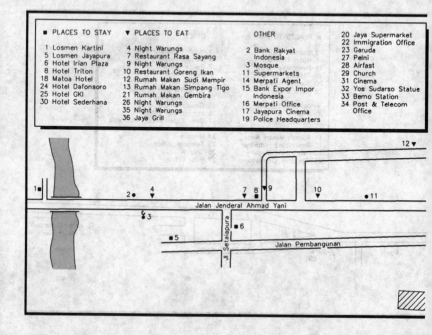

■ PLACES TO STAY	▼ PLACES TO EAT	OTHER	20 Jaya Supermarket
1 Losmen Kartini	4 Night Warungs		22 Immigration Office
5 Losmen Jayapura	7 Restaurant Rasa Sayang	2 Bank Rakyat	23 Garuda
6 Hotel Irian Plaza	9 Night Warungs	Indonesia	27 Pelni
8 Hotel Triton	10 Restaurant Goreng Ikan	3 Mosque	28 Airfast
18 Matoa Hotel	12 Rumah Makan Sudi Mampir	11 Supermarkets	29 Church
24 Hotel Dafonsoro	13 Rumah Makan Simpang Tigo	14 Merpati Agent	31 Cinema
25 Hotel GKI	21 Rumah Makan Gembira	15 Bank Expor Impor	32 Yos Sudarso Statue
30 Hotel Sederhana	26 Night Warungs	Indonesia	33 Bemo Station
	35 Night Warungs	16 Merpati Office	34 Post & Telecom
	36 Jaya Grill	17 Jayapura Cinema	Office
		19 Police Headquarters	

12 ▼

1 ■   2 ●   4 ▼   7 8 ▼ 9   10 ▼   ● 11

Jalan Jenderal Ahmad Yani

● 3

Jl. Setiapura   ■ 6

■ 5   Jalan Pembangunan

Business Office at Jalan Sam Ratulangi 11, almost opposite the Mess GKI. The PHPA is at Jalan Tanjung Ria II, Base G. Its postal address is Kotak Pos 545, Jayapura.

Money The Bank Expor Impor Indonesia on Jalan Ahmad Yani gives the best exchange rates and fast service. The Hotel Dafonsoro and some travel agents also change money but at a poor rate.

Post

The post office is open Monday to Thursday from 8 am to 2 pm, Friday from 8 to 11 am and Saturday from 8 am to 1 pm.

Immigration The immigration office is on Jalan Percetakan in the middle of town. It's open from Monday to Thursday from 7.30 am to 2.30 pm, Friday from 7.30 to 11 am and Saturday from 7.30 am to 1 pm.

Travel Permits If you're staying in Sentani, most of the hotels can arrange your surat jalan without you having to track down the police. Just ask at the front desk and they can have the police come to you with forms and a portable typewriter to make out the permit. This extra service costs about 2000 rp.

The head police station, where you obtain permits for the interior, is on Jalan Ahmad Yani.

Consulate Kantor Papua Guinea do visas and sell air tickets to Papua New Guinea. It's a couple of km north of town towards the Numbai Hotel and can be reached by bemo or taxi. Opening hours are Monday to Friday from 6 am to noon and from 1 to 5 pm. It's closed on weekends.

Hamadi

This suburb is about a 15-minute drive from the centre of town. Its market place is

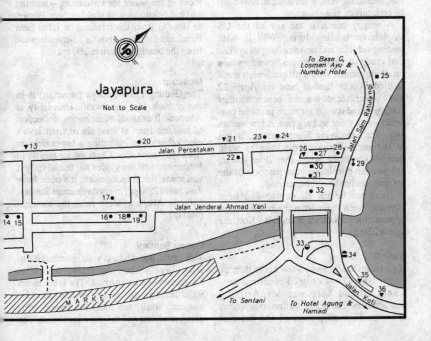

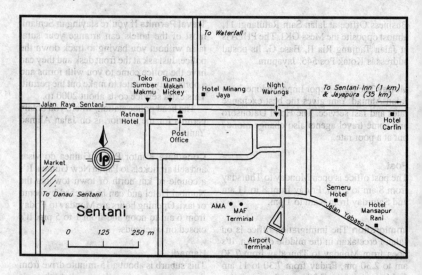

To Waterfall

Toko Sumber Makmu

Rumah Makan Mickey

Hotel Minang Jaya

Night Warungs

To Sentani Inn (1 km) & Jayapura (35 km)

Jalan Raya Sentani

Ratna Hotel

Post Office

Hotel Carfin

Market

To Danau Sentani

Sentani

Semeru Hotel

AMA MAF Terminal

Jalan Yabaso

Hotel Mansapur Rani

Airport Terminal

0   125   250 m

---

stocked with every conceivable variety of fish, including yellow fin tuna, massive 40-kg cod, turtles and sharks.

A nearby beach is the site of the US amphibious landing during WW II, with landing vehicles and tanks rusting away. The first group of landing barges lies opposite a small monument with a plaque which reads 'Allied Forces landed here on April 22 1944'. Further down the beach another landing barge is used for more peaceful purposes – as a toilet and pig pen. A few metres away sits a decaying Sherman tank. To get to the second group you have to walk through a military base – they'll let you in, but you have to leave your passport at the entrance and collect it on leaving.

There are bemos all day to and from Hamadi; catch them from the bemo station opposite the post office or on Jalan Koti, the fare is 250 rp.

Base G

If you want to idle away a few hours then try Pantai Base G – so named because somewhere around here was MacArthur's headquarters. The beach is a disappointment; although it's mostly deserted and peaceful there is too much broken coral and too many rocks in the water for swimming – and the surf can be strong, with real dumpers. Bemos to Base G from the terminal or Jalan Sam Ratulangi drop you about a 15-minute walk from the beach; the fare is 300 rp.

Museum

The Gedung Loka Budaya (museum) is in the grounds of Cendrawasih University at Abepura. It exhibits a fascinating collection of artifacts from at least six of Irian Jaya's nine kabupatens, including a big collection from the Asmat area. Captions are mostly in Indonesian and the guides are useful only if you speak fluent Indonesian. It's open from 7.30 am to 2.30 pm every day except Sunday. Take an Abepura bemo from the terminal (400 rp).

Danau Sentani

This magnificent lake is your introduction to Irian Jaya when you arrive by air at Jayapura's Sentani Airport. The lake covers 9630 hectares but as yet is untouched by tourism. You'll see local houses on stilts along its shores and the occasional boat. The

Sentani people are known for their wood-carvings and pottery. Ask at your losmen about renting boats on the lake. Sentani town has a lazy feel compared with Jayapura, but there's actually quite a lot of activity, particularly with the large numbers of expatriates – mainly missionaries – living there. From the town you can walk to waterfalls and tropical forests or clamber up hills.

Places to Stay – bottom end
Sentani Sentani is more pleasant than Jayapura as it's quieter, less polluted and cooler. Since you can now get your surat jalan in Sentani, there is little need to go to Jayapura unless you need to arm wrestle with the Merpati office or visit the Papua New Guinea consulate. Touts from the various hotels in Sentani greet incoming passengers at the airport.

Ratna Hotel (☎ 91435) on Jalan Raya Sentani 7 is one of the best places to stay. It's a new place and very centrally located. Singles/doubles with fan are 16,500/28,000 rp, or 28,000/36,000 rp with air-con. All rooms have private bath.

Just around the corner is *Hotel Minang Jaya* (☎ 91067). Prices are exactly the same as the Ratna Hotel. It's clean enough and the staff are friendly.

Hotel Mansapur Rani (☎ 91219) is closer to the airport at Jalan Yabaso 113. Turn right just outside the airport and walk about 400 metres. It's a large and popular place, and all rooms have an attached mandi. With fan, singles/doubles are 13,750/25,000 rp and air-con pushes the price up to 36,000 rp. The price includes a snack and two drinks.

Just next door is *Semeru Hotel*. It was brand new and not quite ready to open when we visited, but prices should be similar to its neighbour, Hotel Mansapur Rani. All rooms come with private bath.

Sentani Inn (☎ 91440) on Jalan Raya Sentani is about 1½ km in the Jayapura direction from the airport. Singles/doubles with air-con cost 23,500/30,000 rp, without air-con 15,000/24,000 rp. Prices include breakfast.

Jayapura Hotel prices in Jayapura itself are a black hole for your wallet.

The bottom of the price barrel belongs to *Losmen Jayapura* (☎ 21216), a spartan place where singles/doubles go for 8800/15,400 rp. Some rooms have an attached bath.

Hotel Sederhana (☎ 22157, 31561) at Jalan Halmahera 2 is good value and very centrally located. The rooms are clean enough, with fan and shared mandi, and cost 11,000/19,800 rp, more with meals. There are more expensive rooms with private mandi and air-con from 17,600/19,800 rp. There is an added 10% tax and service charge.

Hotel GKI (☎ 21574), pronounced 'Geki', is a bit of a walk on the north side of town at Jalan Sam Ratulangi 6. There's a pleasant outdoor sitting area, but the main drawback is that no rooms have private bath. Singles/doubles are 15,000/26,000 rp including breakfast.

Losmen Ayu (☎ 22263) at Jalan Tugu II 101 has good rooms with singles starting at 20,000 rp. Heading away from the centre, Jalan Tugu II is about 500 metres along Jalan Sam Ratulangi from its intersection with Jalan Percetakan.

Losmen Kartini (☎ 22371) at the west end of Jalan Ahmad Yani might be cheap but we can't tell – the manager was outright hostile and refused to tell us the room prices, let alone let us stay there. Some travellers have managed to stay here previously though.

Places to Stay – middle
Sentani *Hotel Carfin* (☎ 91478) is about 500 metres east of town on Jalan Raya Sentani. It's a strange place. Although it's brand new, expensive and designed to attract well-moneyed tourists, most (but not all) of the rooms come with shared bath only. Singles/doubles with fan cost 20,000/25,000 rp, and with air-con cost 32,000/40,000 rp. There is an additional 10% tax and service charge. Unless you get one of the rooms with private bath, it's probably a bad deal.

Jayapura One of the best in the mid-range is the *Hotel Dafonsoro* (☎ 31695) at Jalan

Percetakan Negara 20-24. Air-con rooms are 30,000/36,000 rp, and spiffier ones cost 38,000/48,000 rp. The price includes a big breakfast of eggs, toast and jam and a pot of tea or coffee. It's a busy, friendly place.

Hotel Irian Plaza (☎ 23925) on Jalan Setiapura, off Jalan Ahmad Yani, is clean and offers an attached mandi with all rooms. Room prices are: economy 20,000/26,000 rp; standard 34,000/39,000 rp; deluxe 43,000/50,000 rp.

Hotel Triton (☎ 21218) on Jalan Ahmad Yani has a 'seen-better-times' feel and a restaurant that never seems to be open. Economy singles/doubles are 20,000/30,000 rp while VIP rooms go for 40,000 rp.

Hotel Agung (☎ 21777) at Jalan Argapura 37, half-way between Jayapura and Abepura, is excellent except for its out-of-the-way location. Single/doubles with fan cost 18,000/22,000 rp and air-con tweaks the price up to 28,000/33,000 rp. An Abepura bemo will drop you outside.

Another nice hotel but in an inconvenient location is *Numbai Hotel* (☎ 22185), about three km north of Jayapura. Rooms with fan are 20,000/23,000 rp, or 25,000/31,000 rp with air-con. There are nice sea views and all rooms have an attached mandi.

Places to Stay – top end
In Jayapura on Jalan Ahmad Yani, *Matoa Hotel* (☎ 31633) is the flash place in town. Singles/doubles are a modest 99,400/132,500 rp, while a suite is a trifling 220,850 rp. The restaurant prices are exorbitant.

Places to Eat
Sentani has a couple of good places including the *Rumah Makan Mickey*, the best place in town. A big surprise in Sentani is the well-stocked supermarket, *Toko Sumber Makmu*, where you can buy everything from Skippy peanut butter to Kraft cheese and whole-wheat bread to spread it on. There are several warungs near the main road between the airport turn-off and the market. The market is well stocked with fruit and vegetables. *Sentani Inn* has a restaurant.

In Jayapura itself, the best places to eat are the warungs – not just because they're cheaper than the restaurants, but because they serve the best food. Night foodstalls in front of the Pelni office serve up gado-gado or *tahu lontong* (fried tofu) with hot peanut sauce, *bubur kacang hijau* (mung beans in coconut milk broth) and other Indonesian dishes. Other stalls here specialise in the tastiest fish you'll eat in eastern Indonesia. There are also night warungs around the mosque on Jalan Ahmad Yani and along the waterfront on Jalan Koti.

On Jalan Percetakan, the *Hotel Dafonsoro* offers fairly expensive but ordinary Indonesian dishes, though the nasi and mie goreng are filling and tasty. Try *Cafetaria* with its modern decor a few doors away. Further along the same road the *Rumah Makan Sudi Mampir* does reasonably priced Indonesian and Chinese food and there are also several Padang places, including the smart-looking *Simpang Tigo*.

If you want to splash out, the *Jaya Grill*, on the waterfront on Jalan Koti, is good; it's frequented by missionaries.

Things to Buy
Souvenir shops in central Jayapura sell handicrafts from the Balim Valley and are cheaper than in the Balim Valley itself! Who knows, maybe the stuff comes from a factory in Taiwan.

Getting There & Away
Air From Jayapura (assuming you have a permit) you can fly to just about anywhere there's a landing strip in the northern half of Irian Jaya and to many places in the south. You can also fly to western Indonesia and east to PNG.

As usual, Merpati has the most flights, including:

Destination	Fare (rp)
Ambon	309,000
Biak	109,000
Denpasar	579,000
Jakarta	666,000
Manokwari	197,000
Manado	367,000
Merauke	166,000

Mulia, Nabire	141,000
Sarmi	89,000
Senggeh	22,000
Serui	151,000
Sorong	249,000
Surabaya	657,000
Timika	125,000
Ujung Pandang	482,000
Wamena	68,000

Garuda (☎ 21220) has its office next door to the Hotel Dafonsoro at Jalan Percetakan 20-24. It's open Monday to Friday from 8 am to 12.30 pm and from 1.30 to 4 pm, Saturday from 8 am to 1 pm and is closed on Sunday.

Theoretically, it is possible to buy air tickets from the Merpati office at Sentani Airport, but they are seldom open, don't have a computer and the telephone lines are usually busy so they can't confirm a booking with the Jayapura main office. However, if they have seats, you can buy tickets at the check-in counter about an hour before departure.

In Jayapura, Merpati (☎ 21913, 21810, 21327) is at Jalan Ahmad Yani 15, and is open Monday to Thursday from 7 am to 2 pm, Friday from 7 to 11 am, Saturday from 7 am to 2 pm and Sundays and holidays from 10 am to noon. The office is busy, often jam-packed, making it difficult to buy a ticket. It's usually easier to book from the Merpati agent on Jalan Ahmad Yani just west of the Bank Expor Impor Indonesia (see the Jayapura map), but beware of overbooked flights.

MAF (Mission Aviation Fellowship) is at Sentani Airport. It's open every day from 5.30 am to noon and from 2 to 4 pm. AMA (Aviation Mission Association) is next to the MAF terminal. It's open from 5 am to 1 pm Monday to Saturday and closed on Sunday.

Airfast is a cargo carrier which flies to Wamena and sometimes takes just a few passengers if they have room. You can find them at Sentani Airport, though they also have an office in Jayapura on Jalan Sam Ratulangi (see map).

Boat The Pelni passenger liner *Umsini* regularly plies between Jakarta and Jayapura with numerous stops along the way. See the Getting Around chapter for the complete *Umsini* schedule. There are also other occasional ships to elsewhere on the coast of Irian Jaya or to western Indonesia.

The Pelni office (☎ 21270) is near the waterfront in the centre of Jayapura, at Jalan Halmahera 1. The closest harbour master's office (☎ 21923, 22018) to the city is on Jalan Koti, on the way out towards Hamadi. There's another harbour master's office (☎ 21634) further along this road.

Getting Around

To/From the Airport A taxi from the airport to Sentani costs 4000 rp – ridiculous considering you can walk from the airport to the centre in 10 minutes. Most hotels provide free transport to and from the airport if you stay there.

Sentani Airport is 36 km from Jayapura. A taxi from the airport to Jayapura costs a hefty 17,500 rp. Alternatively, you can walk into Sentani to the main road and then catch a bemo.

Bemo From Sentani to Jayapura, you have to change bemos in Abepura and then continue to Jayapura. The total fare is 1250 rp: 750 rp to Abepura and 500 rp from Abepura to Jayapura. It takes about an hour in total.

Bemos within the local area of Sentani or Jayapura cost 300 rp to any place in town.

The Balim Valley

Like an island in the sky, the Balim Valley was totally isolated from the rest of the world until recent times. The first White men chanced upon the Balim Valley in 1938, a discovery which came as one of the last and greatest surprises to a world that had mapped, studied and travelled the mystery out of its remotest corners. Explorer Richard Archbold, who landed on nearby Danau Habbema in a seaplane, wrote:

From the air the gardens and ditches and native-built

walls appeared like the farming country of Central Europe. Never in all my experience in New Guinea have I seen anything to compare with it...The agricultural pursuits of natives I saw in other parts of New Guinea were the helter-skelter efforts of children compared with those of the inhabitants of the Grand Valley...they showed an understanding of the basic principles of erosion control and drainage. From the neat stone fences surrounding their carefully weeded fields it was easy to imagine that we were in New England rather than in an isolated valley of the last Stone Age man...

Archbold found that the fencing and irrigation works had all been built by the inhabitants of the valley using stone tools and sharpened sticks. Sweet potatoes were the main crop – taro, spinach, cucumbers and beans were also grown, while bananas and tobacco could also be found in the local compounds. The reaction of the valley's inhabitants was friendly:

Whilst temperamental at times, the natives as a whole remained friendly throughout our stay. Some offered themselves as carriers and helped bring supplies down from Danau Habbema in return for small cowrie shells. Others brought bananas, sweet potatoes, and often pigs to trade. As a medium of exchange, steel implements did not interest them so much as shells or mirrors. Apparently they regarded their crude stone instruments as far superior.

One of the native inhabitants showed him a steel-headed axe, perhaps having found its way to the highlands along the trade routes from the coast. Archbold found men using spears, bows and arrows and stone axes, and wearing penis gourds, cuscus-fur headdresses, necklaces of cowrie shells and boar's tusk nose ornaments. He also noted that they were 'ingenious' engineers, capable of building strong suspension bridges of forest vines with split-timber decking which could support large numbers of people. WW II prevented further exploration and not until 1945 was attention again drawn to the valley, when a plane crashed there and the survivors were rescued. The first missionaries arrived in 1954, the Dutch government established a post at Wamena in 1956 and changes to the Balim lifestyle followed.

Today the Indonesians have added their own brand of colonialism, bringing schools, police, soldiers and shops and turning Wamena into a town. But local culture has in many ways proved very resilient, helped perhaps by the absence of alcohol, which is banned in Balim Valley. The Indonesians have received some criticism for this, but seeing the havoc wreaked by alcohol in nearby Papua New Guinea, perhaps the prohibition in parts of Irian Jaya is not such a bad idea.

Try not to miss Balim Valley. It remains one of Indonesia's most fascinating and beautiful destinations, and the best way to see it is to explore on foot.

Geography

The Balim Valley is one of four densely settled basins in the mountain backbone of Irian Jaya and Papua New Guinea. The others are the Wahgi and Asaro valleys in PNG and the Paniai lakes region in Irian Jaya.

The Sungai Balim starts from east and west points 120 km apart. The eastern arm rises near the summit of Gunung Trikora (4750 metres), not far west of Wamena, and flows west away from Wamena. From the confluence of the east and west arms, near Kuyawage, the river travels east then turns south into what's known as the Balim Grand Valley, 1554 metres above sea level (at Wamena Airport), and about 60 km long and 16 km wide, with Wamena roughly at its centre. The valley probably contained a lake at one stage and its flat expanse slows the river and allows sediment to be deposited during floods. From the Grand Valley the river continues south through the massive Balim Gorge – in which it drops 1500 metres in less than 50 km, forming a spectacular series of cataracts – and on down to the Arafura Sea on the south-west coast.

In the Balim Valley a sophisticated system of agriculture using drainage and irrigation systems developed. In other places in the highlands, shifting agriculture has been practised – the land is cultivated for several years and then left to regenerate. By perhaps 5000 years ago, horticulture and pig-raising

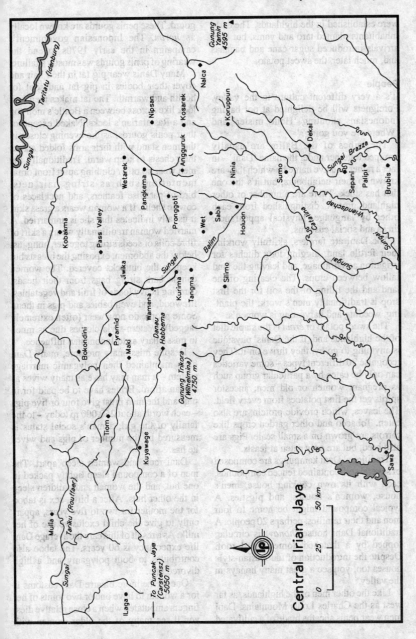

Central Irian Jaya

0   25   50 km

were established in the highlands. The early inhabitants planted taro and yams, but later arrivals introduced sugar cane and bananas and, much later, the sweet potato.

People

It's a very different culture in the valley. Foreigners will be delighted at not having Indonesians shouting 'Hello mister' and 'Where are you going?'

The tribes of the Balim are usually grouped together under the name 'Dani' – in fact a rather abusive name by which they are known to their neighbours, but it's the one that has stuck. There are a number of other highland groups, distinguished from each other by language, physical appearance, dress and social customs.

The Dani are farmers, skilfully working their fertile land, digging long ditches for irrigation and drainage, and leaving the land fallow between crops. The clearing of the land and the tilling of the soil for the first crop is traditionally men's work; the planting, weeding and harvesting is women's.

The sweet potato or *erom* is the staple diet of the highlands and, if the Danis' physique is anything to go by, they thrive on it. They recognise 70 different types – some varieties can only be eaten by a particular group such as pregnant women or old men; ancestor spirits get the first potatoes from every field. The leaves, which provide protein, are also eaten. Tobacco and other garden crops like carrots are grown on a small scale. Pigs are also bred, but are only eaten at feasts.

Traditional Dani kampungs are composed of several self-contained fenced compounds, each with its own cooking house, men's house, women's houses, and pigsties. A typical compound might be home to four men and their families, perhaps 20 people. A traditional Dani house (*honay*) is circular, topped by a thatched dome-shaped roof. Despite the introduction of Indonesian-style houses too, you see a great many honays in the valley.

Like the other men of the highlands, as far west as the Charles Louis Mountains, Dani men wear penis sheaths made of a cultivated gourd. These penis gourds are known locally as *horim*. The Indonesian government's campaign in the early 1970s to end the wearing of penis gourds was mostly a failure.

Many Danis wear pig fat in their hair and cover their bodies in pig fat and soot for health and warmth. The fat makes their hair look like a cross between a Beatle's mop-top and a Rastafarian's locks. Naked except for their penis gourds, as the evening closes in the men stand with their arms folded across their chests to keep warm. Traditionally, the men wear no other clothing apart from ornamentation such as string hair nets, bird-of-paradise feathers, and necklaces of cowrie shells. If a woman wears a grass skirt it usually indicates that she is unmarried. A married woman traditionally wears a skirt of fibre coils or seeds strung together, hung just below the abdomen, exposing the breasts but keeping the buttocks covered. The women dangle bark string bags from their heads, carrying heavy loads of fruit and vegetables, firewood, and even babies and pigs in them. Some people do now wear (often extremely ragged) Western-style clothes due as much to missionary as to Indonesian influence.

Despite missionary pressure, many Dani have maintained their polygamic marriage system – a man may have as many wives as he can afford. Brides have to be paid for in pigs and the man must give four or five pigs – each worth about 250,000 rp today – to the family of the girl; a man's social status is measured by the number of pigs and wives he has.

Dani men and women sleep apart. The men of a compound sleep tightly packed in one hut, and the women and children sleep in the other huts. After a birth, sex is taboo for the mother for two to five years, apparently to give the child exclusive use of her milk. As a result of this care the average Dani life expectancy is 60 years. The taboo also contributes to both polygamy and a high divorce rate.

One of the more bizarre Dani customs is for a woman to have one or two joints of her fingers amputated when a close relative dies; you'll see many of the older women with fingers missing right up to the second joint. Cremation was the traditional method of disposing of the body of the deceased, but sometimes the body would be kept and dried. At present, there are five villages in the valley which have these smoked 'mummies' which you can pay (4000 rp) to see and photograph. The five villages are Akima, Jiwika, Kimbim Pommo and Wasalma.

Fighting between villages or districts seems to have been partly a ritual matter to appease the ancestors and attract good luck, and partly a matter of revenge and settling scores. In formal combat the fighting is carried out in brief clashes throughout the day and is not designed to wreak carnage. After a few hours the opposing groups tend to turn to verbal insults instead. The Indonesians and missionaries have done their best to stamp out Dani warfare, but with only partial success: an outbreak between the Wollesi and Hitigima districts in 1988 led to about 15 deaths.

The merits of the changes wrought by these outsiders are, at the least, debatable. A typical – though not universal – Indonesian attitude to the Dani is a colonialist mixture of fear and contempt, but at least the Indonesians don't appear to have made any systematic attempt to wreck Dani culture. But there have been rumblings of plans to start transmigration to the Balim Valley. Among the missionaries, the Catholics have a reputation for being more tolerant of traditional ways than the Protestants. Quite a number of missionaries in the highlands have been killed in return for their efforts. By and large, they're friendly to travellers and are excellent sources of information if you get talking to them.

The Dani around the Wamena area are generally more traditional than those to the north and north-west, where Christianity has taken firmer root. The western Dani apparently regarded White missionaries as their snake ancestors reincarnated and were suitably impressed by the aeroplanes bringing in amazing loads of goods.

The ugliest year in the Balim's modern history was 1977, when a lot of fighting between the Indonesians and the Dani took place in and around the north of the Grand Valley. While the Dani were armed with spears, bows and arrows, the Indonesians are said to have bombed and strafed villages from the air, even dropping some chiefs to their deaths from helicopters. The scale of fighting and the number of Dani killed depends on which report you believe; estimates range from 30 to 600 dead. What started it all is also uncertain: possibilities that have been advanced include Dani anger with missionaries, provoked by frustration that Christianity wasn't bringing the material rewards they had expected; Indonesian soldiers trying to stop inter-Dani fighting; Dani resentment at 'Indonesianisation' campaigns and efforts to get them to vote in that year's national elections, and OPM activists coming up from the coast to rouse the highlanders. There's still little love lost between the Dani and their rulers today.

If you speak some Indonesian you'll be able to get around OK. The northern and western Dani speak a dialect of Dani distinct from that in the Wamena area. In the Wamena area, a man greeting a man says *nayak*; if greeting more than one man *nayak lak*. When greeting a woman, a man says *la'uk*; if greeting more than one woman *la'uk nya*. Women say *la'uk* if greeting one person, *la'uk nya* if greeting more than one person. *Wam* means pig, *nan* is eat, *i-nan* is drink. At first meeting many Dani are friendly, some are shy and occasionally they seem sullen. Long handshakes, giving each person time to really feel the other's hand, are common. In the Grand Valley most people demand 100 to 200 rp if you want to take their photo, but sometimes 1000 rp if they're dressed up in feathers or other ceremonial costume. The major sequence of festivals in the Grand Valley, including young men's initiation rites, mock battles and multiple marriages, takes place every five years and is next due in 1993.

WAMENA

Wamena is an Indonesian colony – a collection of neat rows of tin-roofed bungalows. The main airfield in the highlands is at one side of the town, and a siren blows to warn people off the runway whenever a plane is about to use it. Wamena has the main market in the valley, so lots of Dani come in from the surrounding villages to trade. Some men may put on the simple savage act to get a few cigarettes from you. Smoking is rampant in the valley, even among the Dani women.

Wamena is peaceful and cool, with a beautiful backdrop of mountains, and it's intriguing to watch the endless stream of tribal people wandering around. Even here in the town, this is a very different world! Accommodation in Wamena is expensive – in fact most things are very expensive compared with in the rest of Indonesia, since they have to be flown up here. Petrol is more than twice as expensive here.

Orientation & Information

Your surat jalan from Jayapura will probably be checked and stamped at Wamena Airport, saving you the trouble of having to report to the police station. It must be stamped again at the airport on departure. A surat jalan for Wamena is also good for most places around Wamena. You usually have to report to the police again each time you come to a new village with a police station. The Wamena police station has a map on its wall of the main Balim Valley and another showing most of the villages in the central highlands, plus a list of where you're not supposed to go.

The post office is near the airport and open Monday to Thursday from 8 am to noon, Friday from 8 to 10 am and Saturday from 8 to 11 am. The Bank Rakyat Indonesia near the airstrip is open Monday to Friday from 7.30 am to noon and Saturday from 7.30 to 11 am. You can also change money at Bank Expor Impor Indonesia.

Places to Stay

There are plenty of clean and comfortable places to stay, but at this time no hotel in Wamena has hot-water bathing facilities. Given the bracing mountain climate and icy water, your early morning bath is going to be an invigorating experience!

Hotel Syahrial Jaya (☎ 31306), Jalan Gatot Subroto 51, is the cheapest place in town. It's a five-minute walk from the airport. Singles/doubles with attached mandi cost 10,000/20,000 rp, but doubles in the new wing go for 30,000 rp. The only problem is that some travellers have expressed extreme dissatisfaction with the owner – apparently there have been big arguments over the quoted price and what was finally charged at checking-out time. Perhaps you should get the manager to write down the price on paper when you check in, or just pay in advance and get a receipt.

Hotel Anggrek (☎ 31242) on Jalan Ambon near the airport is comfortable and conveniently located. Pleasant downstairs singles/doubles with private mandi cost 35,000/40,000 rp; smaller upstairs rooms with shared mandi and toilet are 20,000/30,000 rp.

Nayak Hotel (☎ 31067) is on Jalan Angkasa, directly opposite the airport terminal. Singles/doubles are 30,000/40,000 rp, which includes breakfast. The rooms are large and all have an attached bath.

Hotel Sri Lestari (☎ 31221) is opposite the market on Jalan Trikora. It's clean and the people are friendly, and the rooms are large though nothing fancy. Singles/doubles without private mandi are 19,000/27,000 rp, with private mandi 22,000/33,000 rp. Boiled water is supplied and prices include a light breakfast.

Marannu Jaya Hotel (☎ 31257) on Jalan Trikora is a new place with plush-looking carpeted floors, and each room has a TV and private bath. Singles/doubles are 30,000/40,000 rp.

Baliem Palace Hotel (☎ 31043) at the end of Jalan Trikora is also new and very clean. The large rooms have attached mandi with Western-style bathtubs. Singles/doubles are 30,000/45,500 rp.

Hotel Baliem Cottages (☎ 31370) is on Jalan Thamrin, a good 10-minute walk from the airport. It's a government-run hotel and was once a fancy place but has gone to seed, though plenty of tour groups still put up there. The hot water plumbing system, once

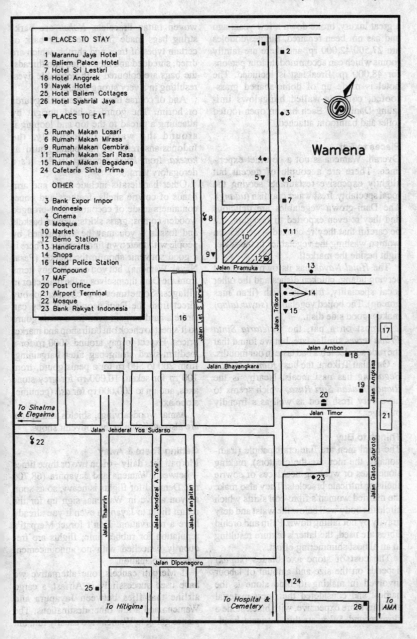

PLACES TO STAY

1 Marannu Jaya Hotel
2 Baliem Palace Hotel
7 Hotel Sri Lestari
18 Hotel Anggrek
19 Nayak Hotel
25 Hotel Baliem Cottages
26 Hotel Syahrial Jaya

PLACES TO EAT

5 Rumah Makan Losari
6 Rumah Makan Mirasa
9 Rumah Makan Gembira
11 Rumah Makan Sari Rasa
15 Rumah Makan Begadang
24 Cafetaria Sinta Prima

OTHER

3 Bank Expor Impor Indonesia
4 Cinema
8 Mosque
10 Market
12 Bemo Station
13 Handicrafts
14 Shops
16 Head Police Station Compound
17 MAF
20 Post Office
21 Airport Terminal
22 Mosque
23 Bank Rakyat Indonesia

Wamena

Jalan Pramuka
Jalan Let S Darwis
Jalan Trikora
Jalan Ambon
Jalan Bhayangkara
Jalan Angkasa
Jalan Timor
Jalan Gatot Subroto
Jalan Jenderal Yos Sudarso
Jalan Thamrin
Jalan Jenderal A Yani
Jalan Panjaitan
Jalan Diponegoro

To Sinatma & Elegaima

To Hitigima

To Hospital & Cemetery

To AMA

a great luxury, broke down a few years ago and has not been repaired. Singles/doubles are 27,500/42,000 rp, and there are family rooms which can accommodate four persons for 48,000 rp. Breakfast is included. The hotel is made up of dome-shaped grass-roofed, concrete-walled bungalows imitating Dani huts. Each has an open-roofed toilet and bathroom attached.

Places to Eat

Overall, Wamena is not a gourmet experience. There are a couple of decent but slightly expensive restaurants serving the local speciality, freshwater crayfish (udang). The Dani-grown vegetables are delicious and they're even exported to Jayapura, but be careful that they're cooked – we've seen women washing the vegetables in the sewer right beside the market!

The Hotel Nayak has its own restaurant serving udang, chicken dishes and the other local speciality, fried goldfish (ikan mas goreng). The boiled vegetables (sayur lalap) make a good side dish.

Almost on a par, the Cafetaria Sinta Prima serves similar fare, but we found that the rude service left a bad taste in our mouths.

On Jalan Trikora, the busy Rumah Makan Begadang has nasi meals. Nearby is the Rumah Makan Sari Rasa, which seems to have very fresh food as well as a friendly manager.

Things to Buy

The Dani men are fine craftspeople (traditionally, the men are the creators), making stone axes or weaving necklaces of cowrie shells or intricate bracelets. They also make the married women's fibre-coil skirts which circle the body well below the waist and defy gravity by not falling down. Palm and orchid fibres are used, the latter's texture resulting in an almost shimmering effect.

The cost of stone axe blades (kapak) depends on the size and amount of labour involved in making it; blue stone is the hardest and considered the finest material and thus more expensive, with black stone a close second. Sekan are thin, intricate, hand-woven rattan bracelets. Noken are bark-string bags made from the inner bark of certain types of trees and shrubs, which are dried, shredded and then rolled into threads; the bags are coloured with vegetable dyes, resulting in a very strong smell.

And of course there are the penis gourds or horim. The gourd is held upright by attaching a thread to the top and looping it around the waist. Incidentally, the Indonesians refer to the penis gourd as koteka, from kotek meaning 'tail' – it's a derogatory term.

Other handicrafts include head and arm bands of cowrie shells, feathers and bone; containers made of coconuts; four-pronged wooden combs; grass skirts; woven baskets and fossils – you may be approached by people with their own finds for sale. There is a good souvenir shop in the market (Pasar Nayak Wamena), but you can also buy items from the Dani themselves in the market or in villages. Sometimes it's cheaper to buy direct from the Dani people, but they can strike a hard bargain even for a penis gourd so it's best to check out both shop and market prices. Expect to pay around 4000 rp for a medium-sized string bag after bargaining, from 200 to 500 rp for a penis gourd, from 100 rp for sekan, 10,000 rp for grey stone axes, and up to 200,000 rp for asli (genuine) stone axes.

Asmat woodcarvings, shields and spears are also available in the souvenir shops.

Getting There & Away

Merpati flies daily – often two or three times – between Wamena and Jayapura (68,700 rp). Demand for flights is heavy, so as soon as you arrive in Wamena, sign up for the return flight to Jayapura even if you already have a reservation. Don't forget Merpati's reputation for rubber time; flights are frequently cancelled with no announcement and no explanation.

If Merpati cancels, one alternative we have used successfully is Airfast, a cargo airline that flies between Jayapura and Wamena and a few other destinations. The planes going to Wamena are usually full, but they come back empty and will take a few passengers for 80,000 rp per person. They don't sell tickets and don't make reservations, but enquire at their office right next to the Merpati terminal in Wamena. Flying in a cargo plane is great fun, but you carry your own luggage and don't expect meals, flight attendants or a non-smoking section.

Merpati also flies at least once weekly from Wamena to Bokondini, Karubaga, Kelila, Mulia, Oksibil and Tiom in the highlands, and back. The Merpati desk at Wamena Airport opens a few hours before their planes are due to leave.

The MAF and AMA have offices in Wamena and fly to numerous destinations – it's a case of waiting for a flight that has seats to where you want to go. Book as far ahead as you can – even if you're prepared to charter a plane, you might have to wait a week or so before one becomes available. To reach some places in the interior from Wamena, it's sometimes quicker to fly back to Jayapura and then out again with Merpati. The MAF office is next to the Wamena airport building and is usually open Monday to Friday from 5.30 am to 5 pm, closed on Saturday and Sunday. The AMA office is at the southern end of the airstrip.

For more information on Merpati and mission flights, see the Irian Jaya introductory Getting Around section. Gigantic Hercules cargo planes owned by the Indonesian air force make frequent runs down to Jayapura and Biak, but they take only Indonesian passengers – foreigners can forget it.

Getting Around

This is a small town and all hotels in Wamena are within walking distance of the airport. Taxis are available, but the pushy drivers are mostly interested in having you charter them for the entire day for around 60,000 rp.

AROUND & BEYOND THE BALIM VALLEY

Getting out and wandering the valleys and hills brings you into close contact with the Dani and makes even Wamena seem a distant

metropolis! This is great hiking country, but travel light because the trails are muddy and slippery. You have to clamber over stiles, maybe cross rivers by dugout canoe or log raft, and traverse creeks or trenches on quaint footbridges or a single rough plank or slippery log.

You can take all-day or half-day trips out of Wamena, longer treks around the Balim Valley, staying in villages as you go, or cross the mountains to remoter areas where you may have to camp some of the time.

Walking in the Balim Valley

Guides In Wamena, you'll almost certainly be approached by people offering to guide you on walks. You don't have to have a guide, but taking one usually makes things easier *and* more interesting. They can tell you the options of where to go, facilitate communication with locals, find places to stay and generally keep you informed. In addition, you'll get to know a local person.

Young Danis expect around 10,000 rp a day, maybe more for distant or strenuous treks. A porter – useful if you have several days' food to take – gets from 5000 rp. For this they'll also make fires and cook for you and find places to stay. You provide their food and will probably have to keep them supplied with cigarettes too. If you're happy with them at the end of the trip, a bonus won't go amiss. It's not a bad idea to test out a Dani guide on a short walk or two before hiring him for a longer trip. A few Danis are licenced guides who have become well established in the business and manage to get 30,000 rp or more a day. In addition, a number of Indonesian travel companies can provide trekking guides for Irian Jaya. These guides are experienced, have good contacts with the Dani and speak good English, but they don't come cheap. The name of the game is 'negotiate'. Quoted prices for a five-day walk for two people were US$75 per day all-inclusive. One well-established guide who has started his own trekking agency is Justinus Daby. He can usually be found greeting incoming flights at Wamena Airport, or you can write to him at PO Box

100, Wamena Airport, Wamena 99511, Irian Jaya. Sam Chandra at Cafetaria Sinta Prima also does tours but his prices are even higher.

What to Bring If you need sun block, bring it. You can get most other things you need from Wamena's market and shops: there's no shortage of food and you can buy pots, pans, hats, mosquito coils, umbrellas and blankets. Take a torch if you want to enter any of the caves in the area. Some Grand Valley villages have kiosks selling things like biscuits, bottled drinks, noodles and rice – heading north the last are at Meagaima on the east side and just beyond Pyramid on the west. Otherwise you can usually get plenty of sweet potatoes, but don't rely on much else except occasional eggs or fruit. The nights are always cold and usually wet, so bring warm clothes and raingear. If you need a tent, bring your own or find a guide who's adept at constructing ad hoc forest shelters (many are).

Places to Stay There are losmen in a few places and in many villages you can get a wooden bed in the house of a teacher or a leading family, usually for 5000 to 10,000 rp per person, sometimes including food. Sleeping on the floor of Dani huts is also quite possible, but make sure you've been invited before entering the compound or any particular hut. Missions can put you up in one or two places, but in general you're advised to try elsewhere.

Getting Around You can fly to a large number of places in the highlands and walk back. Merpati goes weekly from Wamena to Bokondini, Kelila and Karubaga. Bokondini also has an MAF flight most days. Other places with airstrips include Angguruk, Danime, Dekai, Holuon, Ibele, Ilaga, Ilugua, Kobakma, Kuyawage, Maki, Ninia, Pass Valley, Sungai Pitt, Pronggoli, Pyramid, Senggo, Soba, Sumo, Tiom and Wolo.

Bemos, known locally as taxis, run to some places around Wamena during daylight hours, more often in the morning, from opposite the market. How far and how often

they go depends on the state of the roads and the number of people likely to be travelling the route. You can also charter bemos.

The best road out of Wamena heads north to Homhom, bridges the Sungai Balim at Pikhe, then continues to Akima (500 rp by bemo), Tanah Merah (10 km from Wamena, 700 rp), Jiwika (15 km, 800 rp), Waga Waga (21 km, 1000 rp) and Uwosilimo (1800 rp), where it plunges east into the mountains – it's intended eventually to get to Jayapura from here! Bemos to Jiwika leave roughly hourly – to Waga Waga, usually their furthest limit, they're rarer. The other bemo routes from Wamena are south to Hepuba, Hitigima (1000 rp) and Sugokmo (2000 rp); and west to Sinatma (two km, 200 rp, about every half-hour). There are now also bemos to Kimbim (2000 rp).

Grand Valley – central & south

Sinatma This is an hour or two's stroll west of Wamena. Walk along Jalan Yos Sudarso to where it turns right at a small shop, where you go straight on past a church over the fields. Near a small hydro power station you can cross the raging Sungai Wamena by a hanging bridge and walk down the far side to Wauma where you meet the main road into Wamena from the south.

Hitigima There are saltwater wells *(air garam)* near the village of Hitigima, an easy two to three-hour walk along the main road south from Wamena. To extract the salt, banana stems are beaten dry of fluid and put in a pool to soak up the brine. The stem is then dried and burned and the ashes collected and used as salt.

The road to Hitigima is a flat stroll past hills with neat chequerboards of cultivated fields enclosed by stone walls. From Wamena walk down Jalan A Yani, over the bridge and straight on, the Sungai Balim making occasional appearances by the roadside as you go. Hitigima is slightly above the road on the west side. The turning is marked by a small green sign saying 'SD Hitigima 500m, Kurima 6 km'. The village has a

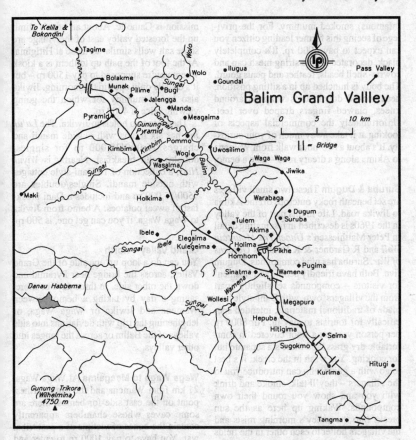

Balim Grand Valley

0 5 10 km

|| = Bridge

To Kelila & Bokondini
Tagime
Wolo
Sungai
Ilugua
Goundal
Pass Valley
Bolakme
Munak
Pilime
Bugi
Jalengga
Pyramid
Manda
Meagaima
Gunung
Pyramid
Pommo
Kimbim
Wogi
Uwosilimo
Waga Waga
Wasalma
Balim
Jiwika
Maki
Sungai
Holkima
Warabaga
Dugum
Suruba
Ibele
Tulem
Akima
Ibele
Elegaima
Kulegeima
Holima
Homhom
Pikhe
Pugima
Sungai
Sinatma
Wamena
Danau Habbema
Sungai
Wollesi
Megapura
Hepuba
Hitigima
Seima
Sugokmo
Gunung Trikora
(Wilhelmina)
4750 m
Kurima
Hitugi
Tangma

school as well as a mission, and the salt wells are a further 45 minutes or so above Hitigima.

Kurima & Hitugi From Hitigima the road continues south to Sugokma. That's as far as bemos go, but you can easily walk to Kurima (two hours), where there's a police post and a hanging bridge over the Balim leading to Hitugi (about three hours away). From Hitugi two trails lead north to Pugima, one nearer the river, the other more mountainous. You'd need two days to do a Wamena, Kurima, Hitugi, Pugima, Wamena circle.

Pugima The village of Pugima lies behind the first low line of hills as you look east across Wamena airstrip. It's a two to three-hour walk from the town. Take the rough road from the southern half of the airstrip past Wesagaput kampung. At the river, turn south along the bank to the Kupelago Manunggal XIII bridge (a half-hour walk from Wamena). The path on the other side of the bridge leads to Pugima.

Akima This nondescript village, about seven km north of Wamena just off the Jiwika road, is also known as Momi after its famous (or infamous) smoked mummy. For the privilege of seeing this former leading citizen you can expect to pay 4000 rp. It's completely black, decorated with a string mesh cap and cowrie-shell beads, feather and penis gourd. The body is hunched up in a sitting position, head tucked down, arms wrapped around knees, clawed fingers draped over feet. Unfortunately the commercial aspects of looking at it take away much of your curiosity. It's about a two-hour walk from Wamena to Akima along a dreary road – take a bemo.

Suruba & Dugum These two small villages are set beneath rocky outcrops off the Akima to Jiwika road. Life in this part of the valley in the 1960s is described in fascinating detail in Peter Matthiessen's *Under The Mountain Wall* and R Gardner & K Heider's *Gardens of War*. Suruba has nine compounds, Dugum five. Both have friendly people and 'losmen' for visitors – compounds set slightly apart from the villagers' own, with Dani-style huts made of traditional materials, intended specifically for tourists to stay in. For 8000 rp per person you get a floor covered in comfortable dry grass, and there's a separate hut for cooking. You wash in the creek. It's best to go with a guide who can introduce you to the villagers – they'll talk, smoke and drink with you and show you round their own compounds. Waking up here as the sun breaks into the valley's morning mists and the villagers holler to each other in the fields is a magical moment.

To reach Suruba, walk a few minutes east off the Jiwika road at Tanah Merah, 10 km from Wamena. For Dugum continue a km beyond Tanah Merah then do the same. Bemos from Wamena will drop you at the turnings.

Jiwika There's a busy Sunday morning market at the largish village of Jiwika (pronounced 'Yiwika'), 20 km from Wamena. Kurulu, the long-time chief here, was once such a powerful man in the valley that the Indonesians named the whole district surrounding Jiwika after him. The Jiwika mission is Catholic. About an hour's climb up the forested valley east of the village are some salt wells similar to those at Hitigima. At the foot of the path up to them is a kiosk where you're supposed to pay 1500 rp – but it's usually only open in the morning. Jiwika also has a mummy for which the going viewing price is 4000 rp.

There are two hotels in Jiwika. The *La'uk Inn* has six rooms with outside mandi and charges 15,000/20,000 rp for singles/ doubles with breakfast. Nearby is *Wiyuk Huts*, a collection of 10 Dani-style cottages with outside mandi. Singles/doubles are 7500/15,000 rp and includes a Dani breakfast of sweet potatoes. A bemo from Jiwika to Waga Waga, if you can get one, is 500 rp.

Grand Valley – north

You can do a loop up one side of the Grand Valley, across the bridge near Pyramid and down the other side, in three days or more, saving a day by taking a bemo between Wamena and Jiwika or Waga Waga, or lengthening the trip with deviations into side valleys of the Balim or across the ranges into other valleys.

Waga Waga to Meagaima At Waga Waga, 21 km from Wamena and the usual furthest point on the east side for bemos, there are some caves whose chambers apparently contain the bones of victims of a past tribal war. You have to pay 1000 rp to enter and aren't likely to see them. The caves at Uwosilimo, two hours' walk along the open, truck-infested road from Waga Waga, are better. You'll need someone to show you the entrance, which is to the right of the 'Jayapura' road just after it turns off east shortly before Uwosilimo. Locals will probably ask you for 1000 rp to enter the caves, which are said to be three km long, with a river and a boat somewhere deep inside.

From Uwosilimo it's 1½ hours' walk through wooded country to the tiny village of Meagaima on a rise overlooking the Sungai Balim. Before Meagaima, another track leads down to the Sungai Balim, which you can cross by canoe to Pommo, where there's another mummy (4000 rp).

Wolo Valley & Beyond This is one of the most beautiful and spectacular side-valleys of the Balim. From Manda, half an hour north of Meagaima, the gently rising river-side track to Wolo village is about 2½ hours' walk. Wolo, inspired by a strong strain of Evangelical Protestantism, is a non-smoking place with lovely flower gardens. It won the 1988 'Most Progressive Village in Irian Jaya' title for a string of self-initiated projects including fish farming and a mini hydro scheme that provides street lights. Two villagers went to Jakarta to meet Suharto. It's said that in the upheavals of 1977, Indonesian troops and Dani enemies from the Jiwika area came up the valley burning and looting and left not a house standing. The honays have been rebuilt in neat rows, with a dramatically sloping airstrip at one side of the village.

From Wolo there are two-hour walks to a waterfall in the hills to the north, or up the Sungai Wolo to where it emerges from another cave. The main track up the Wolo Valley, however, leads to Ilugua (about 2½ hours). About two-thirds of the way to Ilugua, a side track to the right leads round a huge sinkhole and down to Yogolok cave and Goundal, a tiny kampung on the floor of an awesome canyon. From Goundal you can continue on to Ilugua – a full day's walk from Wolo. To see Goundal from the top of the canyon precipice, take a 10-minute side track to the right off the main Ilugua track about 20 minutes before Ilugua. You need a guide to help you find these side-tracks.

The Danau Archbold area, home to the few thousand Gem-speakers, is down around 1000 metres and about 1½ days' walk north-east of Ilugua via Babu. Kobakma is about 15 km east of Danau Archbold.

Meagaima to Kimbim It's about 3½ hours' flat walking west from Meagaima to the bridge over the Balim just north of Pyramid, through Manda, past Jalengga, through Pilimo (a pretty place beside the Balim) and Munak. Pyramid, a major mission and education centre near a pyramid-shaped hill about 35 km from Wamena, is about 1½ hours south of the bridge. Kimbim, with a police station and a Saturday morning market, another two hours south, is a better place to stay.

Kimbim to Wamena This is a fairly dull stretch down the open west side of the main Balim valley – about eight hours' walk through Holkima, Elegaima and Sinatma. There's a lower-lying, usually muddier, route from Pyramid to Wamena via Miligatnem, Musatfak and Homhom.

North & West of the Grand Valley

The north end of the Grand Valley and the regions around it are more heavily Christianised (mainly by Protestants) than the Wamena area. They were also the centre of conflict and destruction in 1977.

North Directly north of the Grand Valley it's up-and-down walking. From Bolakme, just north of the bridge near Pyramid, it's about seven hours via Tagime to Kelila, which is at about 1300 metres but you climb to over 2000 metres on the way. Kelila has a police station. From Kelila down to Bokondini, a missionary centre, is about 2½ hours (four or five hours coming back).

The following information on the walk round the Bokondini-Karubaga area and back to Pyramid comes from a reader: Bokondini to Wunen, about eight hours with an exhausting ascent; Wunen to Karubaga, seven hours over one moderate mountain (you can stay and eat at *Karubaga Guesthouse*; Karubaga to Wunggilipur (on the way to Kangime), one hour; Wunggilipur to Jugwa, seven hours over a high mountain; and Jugwa to Pyramid, 10 hours over mountains.

Western Dani West along the Balim upstream from Pyramid is the country of the western Dani, who call themselves Lani.

There are tracks to Maki, the first main village, from Kimbim, Pyramid and

Bolakme. Between the Sungai Pitt and Kuyawage the Balim disappears underground for two km. Ilaga is about 60 km west of Kuyawage, beyond the western Balim watershed. West of Sungai Pitt the going is often swampy.

Danau Habbema From Ibele, west of the main Wamena to Pyramid track, it's two days up to the lake, at 3450 metres. Habbema is below the 4730-metre Gunung Trikora. The 1938 Archbold expedition set up a big camp beside Danau Habbema, ferrying men and supplies in by seaplane. You'll need to camp if you come up here.

Yali Country

East and south of the Dani region are the Yali people, who have rectangular houses and whose men wear 'skirts' of rattan hoops, their penis gourds protruding from underneath. Missionaries are at work here, but the Indonesian presence is thinner than in the Balim Valley. Bordering the Yali on the east are the Kim-Yal, amongst whom cannibalism was still practised at least in the 1970s.

Reaching Yali country on foot involves plenty of ups and downs on steep trails. Pronggoli, the nearest centre from Wamena as the crow flies, is three days' hard walking by the most direct route, with camping needed en route. From Pronggoli to Angguruk takes a day. Easier but longer is a southern loop through Kurima, Tangma (where there's a hanging bridge over the Balim), Wet, Soba (the last Dani village, in a side-valley off the Balim Gorge), Ninia, then north to Angguruk. This takes about seven days. Along the way you can stay in teachers' or village houses. In Angguruk and Pronggoli the missions can often put you up.

Pass Valley, a settlement in the north of the Yali area, is 1½ days' walk from Jiwika. A steep four-hour walk past the Jiwika salt wells leads to Watlangu, from where it's a long day to Pass Valley.

South

It's about two weeks' walk from Wamena down to Dekai via Soba, Holuon and Sumo.

From Dekai it could be possible to canoe downriver as far as Senggo on the fringes of the Asmat region – though you might need a special surat jalan from Wamena to go that far.

Gunung Trikora

For the adventurous and physically fit, there is the possibility of climbing snow-clad Gunung Trikora. At 4750 metres, Trikora is just 300 metres shy of Puncak Jaya, Irian Jaya's highest peak. Good equipment and a guide are needed. A special permit is also required but it can be obtained in Wamena.

Other Destinations

Almost anywhere in Irian Jaya will probably be of interest, if you're permitted to go there. Despite the exploitation of the land and its people, it remains one of the earth's last wildernesses. The towns may be unappealing but you might find some of the nearby mining sites or transmigration colonies of interest. The nature reserves, while mostly requiring expedition-type efforts to reach, would also be rewarding. Robert Mitton's *The Lost World of Irian Jaya* is a good source of info on several areas.

MERAUKE

Merauke, at the south-east corner of Irian Jaya, is the last major town in Indonesia – *dari Sabang ke Merauke* is the slogan denoting the spread of Indonesian territory. It has long dry seasons and eucalypts – a more Australian landscape than anywhere else in Irian Jaya. Despite uninviting red soils 30,000 or more transmigrants had been moved to the Merauke area by 1988. Several of the transmigrant centres have faced severe problems resulting in large numbers seeking work in Merauke itself. There are possibilities of river trips from Merauke to elsewhere in southern Irian Jaya. Places to stay include the *Hotel Asmat* and the cheaper *Hotel Abadi* and *Wisma Praja*.

Flora & Fauna Rawa Biru-Wasur Reserve, 60 km east of Merauke on the southern border with PNG, contains a blue-coloured swamp *(rawa biru)*, acacia and eucalypt trees, long grass and giant termite hills. Cockatoos, parrots, crowned imperial pigeons, cassowaries, wallabies, crocodiles and dugongs are among the reserve's wildlife. You can get there by jeep from Merauke in the dry season.

TANAH MERAH

Inland, to the far north of Merauke, is Tanah Merah, which means 'red earth'. The Dutch called it Boven Digul and this was the site of their prison camp for Indonesian nationalists – both Hatta and Sjahrir spent time here before being sent to the Banda islands.

AGATS

Agats, on the south-west coast, is a jumping-off point for visiting the Asmat people, once cannibals and head-hunters. The Asmat live in the lowland swamps where the Sungai Balim (known here as the Sirets or Eilanden) reaches the sea as a wide, muddy tidal river. The Indonesian takeover has overturned the Asmat lifestyle. Traditionally they were mainly nomadic, living in temporary shelters for a few months then moving on as food in an area was depleted. Now the push is towards permanent settlements with schools, missionary stations and clinics. The area has been sold out to timber companies who use the Asmat to fell their own forests, often by coercion and for no pay – no wonder the area has been off limits to tourists for several years.

The Asmat are master carvers, famous for their two to three-metre tall *Bisj* poles – tree trunks carved with crouching, interlocked phallic figures. They also decorate ceremonial shields, sago bowls, canoe paddles and intricate prows for their dugout canoes. You can buy their fantastic work in Biak, Wamena and Jayapura or, at more exorbitant prices, in Bali and Jakarta.

FREEPORT MINE & PUNCAK JAYA

Tembagapura is the town serving the Free-port Copper Mine at Gunung Bijih (formerly Mt Ertzberg), just a little north-west of Puncak Jaya (Mt Carstensz). At 5050 metres, Puncak Jaya is the highest peak between the Andes and the Himalayas. The mine's crushing plant is 3700 metres high. The Dutch geologist Dozy in 1936 described Ertzberg as 'a mountain of copper ore' but it was not until the late 1960s that anyone attempted to mine it. At that time the Suharto government's desire for foreign capital led to a reappraisal of even the most remote reserves and an agreement allowing the Freeport Company from the USA to mine.

Tembagapura is 10 km south of the mine, about 70 km south-east of Enarotali and 50 km north-east of Timika. The road connecting the mine and the town passes through a 900-metre-long tunnel. The road south from Tembagapura to the coast passes through a second tunnel 1500 metres long.

On snow-capped Puncak Jaya you could stand on a glacier in the tropics and see the sea. The surrounding area is rugged with other peaks and more small glaciers. It's been reported that one can reach the summit by some routes without serious mountaineering gear, but take serious advice before you try. Four climbers who went missing in the area in 1987 were believed to be victims of the OPM. For a long time after, it was impossible to get a permit to enter the area, let alone climb the mountain. Now it is possible, but permission must be obtained in Jakarta. Ilaga is the starting point for assaults on the mountain.

DANAU PANIAI

On the western edge of the central highlands, these lakes surrounded by mountains are legendary for their beauty. The district is home to the Ekagi people, who are very short in stature. Enarotali, on the east side of Danau Paniai, is the town.

SORONG

At the tip of the bird's head this is a big Pertamina oil and timber base, but really nothing more than a stopover unless you visit the Raja Ampat Islands Reserves off the coast. By 1987 there were 30,000 transmigrants in the Sorong area. Sorong Airport is 32 km from the town, on another island linked to the mainland by ferry, but there are plans to build another closer to the town.

Some places to stay include *Hotel Bangaria* and *Penginapan Indah*, about 200 metres from the harbour on the main road.

There's an island off the town where you can go for walks – you can reach it by boat from the dock. The PHPA office is at Jalan Pemuda 40 (postal address: PO Box 353, Sorong). They can advise you about visiting the Raja Ampat Reserves which take in parts of Pulau Waigeo (known for its birdlife, including two bird of paradise species), Pulau Batanta and Pulau Salawati.

MANOKWARI

The Manokwari area, on the north-eastern tip of the bird's head, is mountainous but has fertile lowlands. Some 100,000 people (including many transmigrants) are spread along the coast and in near the town. Sago and cassava are the major crops but soybeans, rice, vegetables and groundnuts are also grown and there are coffee, coconut and oilpalm plantations. The town has a clean beach with white sand and clear water, plus lots of trees, good shops including a bakery, a hospital and a cinema.

Places to stay include the *Hotel Arfak* (☎ 21293) at Jalan Brawijaya 8, 12 km from the airport. It's an old Dutch building on a hill with a bay view, beside a military camp.

Glossary

abangan – nominal Muslim, whose beliefs owe more to older, pre-Islamic mysticism

adat – traditional laws and regulations

agung – high, noble

air – water

Airlangga – 11th-century king of considerable historical and legendary importance in Bali

air panas – hot springs

air terjun – waterfall

aling aling – guard wall behind the entrance gate to a Balinese family compound; demons can only travel in straight lines so the aling aling prevents them from coming straight in through the front entrance

alun-alun – main public square of a town or village

anak – child

andong – horse-drawn passenger cart

angklung – musical instrument made of differing lengths and thicknesses of bamboo suspended in a frame

anjing – dog

arak – colourless distilled palm-wine firewater

Arja – particularly refined form of Balinese theatre

Arjuna – hero of the *Mahabharata* epic and a popular temple gate guardian image

ayam – chicken

Ayodya – Rama's kingdom in the *Ramayana*

Babad – early chronicle of Balinese history

babi – pork

Bahasa Indonesia – Indonesia's national language

bajaj – motorised three-wheeler taxi found in Jakarta

bakar – barbequed

bakmi – rice-flour noodles

bakso – meatball soup

balai – communal house in South Kalimantan

bale – Balinese pavilion, house or shelter; a meeting place

Bali Aga – 'original' Balinese, who managed to resist the new ways brought in with Majapahit migration

balian – female shaman of the Tanjung Dayak people in Kalimantan

banjar – local area of a Balinese village in which community activities are organised

banyan – see waringin

bapak – father; also a polite form of address to any older man

barat – west

Baris – warrior dance

barong – mythical lion-dog creature, star of the Barong dance and a firm champion of good in the eternal struggle between good and evil

barong landung – enormous puppets known as the 'tall barong'; these can be seen at an annual festival on Serangan, Bali

barong tengkok – Lombok name for portable form of gamelan used for wedding processions and circumcision ceremonies

batik – cloth made by coating part of the cloth with wax, then dyeing it and melting the wax out. The waxed part is not coloured and repeated waxings and dyeings builds up a pattern.

becak – trishaw (rickshaw)

bemo – popular local transport. Traditionally a small pickup-truck with a bench seat down each side in the back, these are now disappearing in favour of small minibuses

bendi – two-person dokar used in Sulawesi

bensin – petrol

berempah – traditional Sumbawan bare-fisted boxing

betang – communal house in Central Kalimantan

bhaga – miniature thatched-roof house dedicated to the ancestors of the Ngada people of Flores

bis – bus

blimbing – starfruit

bouraq – winged horse-like creature with the head of a woman; also the name of the domestic airline which mostly services the outer islands

Brahma – the creator; one of the trinity of Hindu gods

brem – fermented rice wine

bubur ayam – Indonesian porridge of rice or beans with chicken

bukit – hill

bun upas – morning frost (lit. poison dew)

bupati – government official in charge of a regency (kabupaten)

camat – government official in charge of a district (kecamatan)

candi – shrine, or temple, of originally Javanese design, also known as a prasada

candi bentar – split gateway entrance to a Balinese temple

cap – metal stamp used to apply motifs to batik

cap cai – fried vegetables, sometimes with meat

catur yoga – ancient manuscript on religion and cosmology

cumi cumi – squid

dalang – storyteller of varied skills and considerable endurance who operates the puppets, tells the story and beats time in a wayang kulit shadow puppet performance

danau – lake

delman – horse-drawn passenger cart

desa – village

Dewi Sri – rice goddess

dokar – horse cart, still a popular form of local transport in many towns and larger villages

dukun – faith healer and herbal doctor or mystic

durian – fruit that 'smells like hell and tastes like heaven'

dwipa mulia – moneychanger

fu yung hai – sweet and sour omelette

gado-gado – traditional Indonesian dish of steamed bean sprouts, vegetables and a spicy peanut sauce

Gajah Mada – famous Majapahit prime minister

Gambuh – classical form of Balinese theatre

gamelan – traditional Javanese and Balinese orchestra, usually almost solely percussion, with large xylophones and gongs

Ganesh – Shiva's elephant-headed son

gang – alley or footpath

Garuda – mythical man-bird, the vehicle of Vishnu and the modern symbol of Indonesia; also the name of Indonesia's international airline

gereja – church

gili – islet or atoll

gringsing – rare double ikat woven cloth of Tenganan

gua – cave (in Bali, 'goa')

gunung – mountain

haji, haja – Muslim who has made the pilgrimage to Mecca. Many Indonesians save all their lives to make the pilgrimage, and a haji (man) or haja (woman) commands great respect in the village.

halus – 'refined', high standards of behaviour and art; characters in wayang kulit performances are traditionally either halus or kasar

harga biasa – usual price

harga touris – tourist price

homestay – small family-run losmen

hutan – forest

huta – Batak village

ibu – mother; also polite form of address to any older woman

ikan – fish

ikat – cloth in which the pattern is produced by dyeing the individual threads before weaving

Jaipongan – relatively modern, West Javanese dance incorporating elements of pencak silat and Ketuktilu

jalan – street or road

jalan jalan – to walk

jalan potong – short cut

jam karet – 'rubber time'

jamu – herbal medicine; most tonics go under this name and are supposed to cure everything from menstrual problems to baldness

jembatan – bridge

jeruk – citrus fruit

jidur – large cylindrical drums played widely throughout Lombok

jukung – prahu

kabupaten – regency

kacang – peanuts

kain – cloth

kaja – towards the mountains

kamar kecil – toilet, usually the traditional hole in the ground with footrests either side

kantor – office, as in kantor imigrasi (immigration office) or kantor pos (post office)

kasar – rough, coarse, crude; the opposite of halus

Kawi – classical Javanese, the language of poetry

kebaya – Chinese long-sleeved blouse with plunging front and embroidered edges

kebun – garden

kecapi – Sundanese (West Javanese) lute

kelapa – coconut

keliling – driving around (buses and bemos) to pick up passengers

kelod – towards the sea

kepala desa – village head

kepala stasiun – station master

kepeng – old Chinese coins with a hole in the centre, which were the everyday money during the Dutch era and can still be obtained quite readily from shops and antique dealers for just a few cents

kepiting – crab

ketoprak – popular Javanese folk theatre

Ketuktilu – traditional Sundanese dance in which professional female dancers (sometimes prostitutes) dance for male spectators

kina – quinine

klotok – canoe with water-pump motor used in Kalimantan

Konfrontasi – catchphrase of the early '60s when Sukarno embarked on a confrontational campaign against Western imperialism, and expansionist policies in the region, aimed at Malaysia.

kopi – coffee

kraton – walled city palace and traditionally the centre of Javanese culture. The two most famous and influential kratons are those of Yogyakarta and Solo.

kretek – Indonesian clove cigarette

kris – wavy-bladed traditional dagger, often held to have spiritual or magical powers

Kuningan – holy day celebrated throughout Bali 10 days after Galungan

ladang – non-irrigated field, often using slash-and-burn agriculture, for dry-land crops

lamin – communal house in East and West Kalimantan

langsam – crowded, peak-hour commuter train to the big cities

lesehan – traditional style of dining on straw mats

longbot – high-speed motorised canoe used on the rivers of Kalimantan

lontar – type of palm tree. Traditional books were written on the dried leaves of the lontar palm

lopo – beehive-shaped house found on Timor

losmen – basic accommodation, usually cheaper than hotels and often family-run

lumpia – spring rolls

Mahabharata – great Hindu holy book, telling of the battle between the Pandavas and the Korawas

Majapahit – last great Hindu dynasty in Java, pushed out of Java into Bali by the rise of Islamic power

mandi – usual Indonesian form of bath, consisting of a large water tank from which you ladle water to pour over yourself like a shower

marapu – collective term for all spiritual forces including gods, spirits and ancestors

martabak – pancake found at foodstalls everywhere; can be savoury but is usually very sweet

Merpati – major domestic airline

meru – multi-roofed shrines in Balinese temples; they take their name from the Hindu holy mountain, Mahameru

mesjid – mosque

mie goreng – fried noodles, usually with vegetables, and sometimes meat

mikrolet – small taxi; a tiny opelet

menara – minaret, tower

moko – bronze drum from Alor (Nusa Tenggara)

muezzin – those who call the faithful to the mosque

muncak – 'barking deer' found on Java

naga – mythical snake-like creature

nanas – pineapple

nasi – cooked rice. Nasi goreng is the ubiquitous fried rice. Nasi campur is rice 'with the lot' – vegetables, meat or fish, peanuts, krupuk. Nasi gudeg is cooked jackfruit served with rice, chicken and spices. Nasi rames is rice with egg, vegetables, fish or meat. Nasi rawon is rice with a spicy hot beef soup.

ngadhu – parasol-like, thatched roof; ancestor totem of the Ngada people of Flores

nusa – island, as in Nusa Penida

Odalan – temple festival held every 210 days, the Balinese 'year'

ojek – motorcycle becak

opelet – small intra-city minibus, usually with side benches in the back

opor ayam – chicken cooked in coconut milk

Padang – city and region of Sumatra which has exported its cuisine to all corners of Indonesia. Padang food consists of spicy curries and rice, and is traditionally eaten with the right hand. In a Padang restaurant a number of dishes are laid out on the table, and only those that are eaten are paid for.

paduraksa – covered gateway to a Balinese temple

pak – shortened form of bapak

pandanus – palm plant used to make mats

pantai – beach

Pantun – ancient Malay poetical verse in rhyming couplets

pasanggrahan – lodge for government officials where travellers can usually stay

pasar – market

pasar malam – night market

pasar terapung – 'floating market' consisting of groups of boats to which buyers and sellers paddle to in boats

patih – prime minister

patola – ikat motif of a hexagon framing a type of four-pronged star

peci – black Muslim felt cap

pedanda – high priest

pelan pelan – slowly

Pelni – Pelayaran Nasional Indonesia, the national shipping line with major passenger ships operating throughout the archipelago

pemangku – temple priest

pencak silat – form of martial arts originally from Sumatra but now popular throughout Indonesia

penginapan – simple lodging house

perbekel – government official in charge of a village (desa)

peresehan – popular form of one-to-one physical combat peculiar to Lombok, in which two men fight armed with a small hide shield for protection and a long rattan stave as a weapon

Pertamina – huge state-owned oil company

pinang – betel nut

pinisi – Makassar or Bugis schooner

pisang goreng – fried banana

pompa bensin – petrol station

pondok – guesthouse or lodge

porhalaan – bamboo divining calendar

prahu – traditional Indonesian outrigger boat

prasada – see candi

Pulaki – sparsely populated, dry and hilly west end of Bali

pulau – island

puputan – fight to the death

pura – temple

pura dalem – temple of the dead

puri – palace

pusaka – sacred heirlooms of a royal family

rafflesia – gigantic flower found in Sumatra, with blooms spreading up to a metre

raja – lord or prince

Ramadan – Muslim month of fasting, when devout Muslims refrain from eating, drinking and smoking during daylight hours

Ramayana – one of the great Hindu holy books, stories from the *Ramayana* form the keystone of many Balinese and Javanese dances and tales

rangda – witch; evil black-magic spirit of Balinese tales and dances

rattan – hardy, pliable vine used for handicrafts, furniture and weapons such as the staves in the spectacular trial of strength ceremony, peresehan, in Lombok

Ratu Adil – the Just Prince who, by Javanese prophecy, will return to liberate Indonesia from oppression

rebab – two-stringed bowed lute

rijstaffel – Dutch for 'rice table'; a banquet of Dutch-style Indonesian food

rintek wuuk – spicy dog meat; a Minahasan (Sulawesi) delicacy

roti – bread; usually white and sweet

Rudat – traditional Sasak dance overlaid with Islamic influence

rumah adat – traditional house

rumah makan – restaurant or warung (lit. eating house)

rumah sakit – hospital

sambal – chilli sauce

Sanghyang – trance dance in which the dancers impersonate a local village god

Sanghyang Widi – Balinese supreme being, never actually worshipped as such; one of the 'three in one' or lesser gods stands in

santri – orthodox, devout Muslim

saron – xylophone-like gamelan instrument, with bronze bars struck with a wooden mallet

sarong – all-purpose cloth, often sewed into a tube, and worn by women, men and children

Sasak – native of Lombok

satay – classic Indonesian dish; small pieces of charcoal-grilled meat on a skewer served with spicy peanut sauce

sawah – an individual rice field, or the wet-rice method of cultivation

sayur – vegetable

selat – strait

selatan – south

selendang – shawl

selimut – blanket

Sempati – domestic airline which flies to Kalimantan, southern Sumatra and Java

Shiva – one of the trinity of Hindu gods

sirih – betel nut, chewed as a mild narcotic

sisemba – form of kick-boxing popular with the Torajan people of Sulawesi

songket – silver or gold-threaded cloth, hand woven using floating weft technique

sop, soto – soup

sudra – lowest or common caste to which most Balinese belong

stasiun – station

suling – bamboo flute

sungai – river

syahbandar – harbour master

tahu – soybean curd (tofu)

taman – 'garden with a pond'; ornamental garden

tari topeng – type of masked dance peculiar to the Cirebon area

tarling – musical style of the Cirebon area, featuring guitar, suling and voice

tau tau – life-sized carved wooden effigies of the dead placed on balconies outside cave graves in Torajaland, Sulawesi

taxi sungai – cargo-carrying river ferry with bunks on the upper level

teluk – bay

telur – egg

tempe – fermented soybean cake

timur – east

tomate – Torajan funeral ceremony

tongkonan – traditional Torajan house

topeng – wooden mask used in funerary dances

tuak – acoholic drink fermented from palm sap or rice

uang – money

udang – prawn

ular – snake

utara – north

Vishnu – one of the trinity of Hindu gods

wali songo – nine holy men who brought Islam to Java

Wallace Line – imaginary line between Bali and Lombok which marks the end of Asian and the beginning of Australasian flora and fauna.

wantilan – open pavilion used to stage cockfights

waringin – holy banyan tree found at many temples; a large and shady tree with drooping branches which root and can produce new trees. It was under a banyan (bo) tree that the Buddha achieved enlightenment

waruga – pre-Christian Minahasan (Sulawesi) tomb

warung – food stall; a sort of Indonesian equivalent to a combination of corner shop and snack bar

wayang kulit – shadow-puppet play

wayang topeng – masked dance drama

wayang wong – masked drama playing scenes from the *Ramayana*

Wektu Telu – religion, peculiar to Lombok, which originated in Bayan and combines many tenets of Islam and aspects of other faiths

wisma – guesthouse or lodge

Index

TEXT

Map references are in **bold** type.

Thanks

Thanks also to those travellers who took the time and trouble to write to us about their experiences in Indonesia. Writers (apologies if we've misspelt your name) to whom thanks must go include:

Christian Adams (USA), S L Adelson (C), Kees Admiraal (NL), Nassir Alkatiri (Indo), Fred Ameling (NL), Jan Andersen (DK), Julie Anderson (USA), Paul Andresen (DK), Judith Appteloy, Claire Aylmer (UK), Nicola Bache (UK), Craig Baker (USA), Dee & Dave Bale (AUS), Peter J Balfry (UK), Paul Ballantyne (UK), Jean & E Barben (CH), Bill Barlow (C), Tim Baron (UK), Jennifer Basye (USA), Lynn Bates (UK), Roland Bauernfeinol (D), Jane Benham (UK), Dietrich Bents (D), Jan Berglund (S), Mallee Bhanji, Roger Biefer (CH), John Billingham (UK), Lucy Bingham (UK), B B Bitty (Indo), Lars Bjornholt (DK), Stephen Blaas, Stephen Blake (NZ), Fons Bloemen (NL), Marit & Jorgen Blystad (N), Ben Bodenhoff (C), Markus Bonggasau, Bruce Bonnell (USA), Jefferson Boone (USA), Arnaud Boonen (B), Darko Bosnjar, Peter N J Bot (NL), Marco Bottasso (F), Don Branagan (AUS), Roderick Brazier (AUS), Derrick Browne (AUS), Lone Brun-Jensen (DK), Julia Bucknall (UK), Albert Bukit, Jonathan Burdett (UK), Markus Burkhari (D), Bonnie D Bush (USA), Caspar Byleveld (NL), Robert Campbell (AUS), Jay Cappell (USA), J Carlsen (UK), Rod Carnochan (C), Todd Carpenter (USA), Anna Cassilly (USA), C Andrew Causey (USA), David Chandlee (AUS), Susan Chandler (UK), Thierry Chausse (C), Mike Chester (AUS), Doug Coggins (USA), Nuala Connolly (UK), Martin Copland (AUS), Tony Copland (AUS), John Cottle (USA), Versey Critchton (UK), John Currie (AUS), Luc Cuypers (C), Hans Damen (NL), N Arden Danekas (USA), Jamnes Danenberg (UK), Elaine Daniels, Paul Davenport (AUS), Mike Davies (C), Stephanie Davies (AUS), Andy & Alison Dawson (UK), Francis Dawson (AUS), Luc De Moyette (B), Jan de Riele (NL), Ann de Schryver (B), Jan Dekker (NL), Tobb Dell'Oro (USA), Simon Denyer (UK), Will Derks (NL), Alex Derom (B), Claire & Ian Dick (UK), Ursel Digdoyo, Els Dingemanse (NL), Andrew Dinwoodie (UK), S P Doherty (UK), Pat & Jim Donovan (USA), Marianne Doos (S), Larry Dougherty (USA), Barry Downs, Simon Driver (AUS), Fiona Duncan (UK), D B Duncan (AUS), Megan Durnford (C), Ineke Dykstra (NL), Keith Ellis (UK), Michael Elmore, Walter Emberger (A), Hendrika Fahey (AUS), Tim Farey (USA), Steve Farram (AUS), Len Feinstein (USA), Chris Feirebend (USA), Sabine Feldwieser (D), Mirjam Ferkenius (NL), Ione Fett (AUS), Michele Ford (AUS), Michelle Forde (AUS), Tom & Karen Forland (USA), Jane & Alan Fowler (UK), Lisa Freaney, Jeremy Friar (UK), Antje Friedrich (D),

Howard F Fries (USA), Peter Frylink (AUS), Charles Gannon (IRL), Clare Garevel (UK), Stuart Garland (AUS), Roger Gates (USA), Le Gilbert (USA), Steven Gilman (USA), Jodi Glimm (C), Alan Gordon (UK), Yoga Goutama (Indo), Maggie Greathead (AUS), David Green (UK), Mel Greenblatt (UK), Paul Greening, Stan Gregory (USA), Mark Gregory (UK), Alfred Groot (NL), Maxine Grudiot (D), B Grunbauer (NL), Thomas Grundel (D), Klaus & Dori Grunning (D), Sebastian Hagebaum (D), Malcolm Haines (AUS), Brenda Haiplik (C), Jim Hall (USA), Soren Hansen (DK), Michael Harris (AUS), Tim Harris, Fiona Harrison (UK), Helen Harrison, Bruce Hart (AUS), Aang Hasanudin (Indo), John Hassett (IRL), Stan Hawkins (D), Susan Hay (USA), Paul Haymes (UK), Ann Healy (AUS), Carl J Hefner (USA), C Heij (NL), Kees J Heij (NL), Vonny Helberg, Rudy Hermawan Victoria Herriott (UK), Alfred Heuperman (AUS), Anders Hiller (S), Linda & Lotte Hoffmann (DK), Rik Hofman (NL), Mark Hoggard (USA), Margit Holshauser (D), Christopher Howe (UK), Paul Howlett (UK), Aviva S Hoyer MD (USA), Winona Hubbard (USA), Janet Huddleston (NZ), David & Greeba Hughes (UK), Mark Huis (NL), Herbet Hurwitze (USA), Yeo Soo Hwa, Tineke Indradjaya (Indo), Martin Ireland (UK), Bonnie Irvine (C), Alex Ismunandar (Indo), Vesna & Natko Jakic (Yug), Nel Jans (AUS), Tom Janssen (NL), Menno Janssen (NL), Jacco Jasperse (NL), Sean Jenner (NZ), Chris Johnson (AUS), Kirsten Jorgensen (DK), Emma Joynson (UK), Zen Jufri (Indo), Bruno Kahn (F), Soren Kahns (DK), Paul Karp (AUS), C & D Kelly (AUS), Andy Keogh (AUS), Fiona Kerlogue (UK), Kath Kerr (AUS), Tom Ketley (C), Paul Key, Ray Kitson (AUS), Jan Kleinman (USA), Fred Kleinveld (NL), Brian Kliesen (USA), Rolf Knuttsam, Jens Kofod (DK), Kiros Kokkas (G), Wayne Kosh (AUS), Hugh Lailey (UK), Christy Lanzl (USA), Jenny Leckley (UK), Mike Lee (UK), Tzu Hong Lee (S), Leah Leneman (UK), Marie Lippens (B), Jodi Lipson (USA), Richard Little (C), Jenny & Peter Littlewood (UK), Irmi Lochner (D), Kate Lodge (UK), Rosemary Lyndall (AUS), Graeme MacRae Nicola Maher (AUS), John Maidment (UK), Anders Malm (S), Ken Malvern (UK), Marampan Mamasa (Indo), Barita O Manullang (USA), Daniel Marchisio (F), Philip Marks (UK), Dieter Marohl (D), Elliot Marscelli (USA), Jim Marson (USA), Martin & Anny (UK), Saleh Maswi (Indo), Rita Maver, Lisa & Pat McCarthy (UK), John McCarthy (AUS), Noel McWhinnie (AUS), Ty Melvyn (UK), Anna Michielsen (USA), Gergely Miklos (Hun), Craig Miles (UK), Warren Mills (AUS), Lui Misconi (AUS), Melinda Misuraca, C Moehiker (NL), E Molenaar (NL), Kelvin Moody (NZ), Sean Moore (C), Neil Moore (UK), Enrique Morales (F), H G Morgan (AUS), Peter Morice (NZ), Don Morrisey (UK), Wayne Morriss (NZ), Chris Morton (UK), Denys Morton (UK), Steve Mossholder (USA), Ny

Muharti (Indo), K B Mullins (USA), L J Naef (CH), Made Taman Nd (Indo), Paul Nicholls (UK), Bob Noorda (AUS), Dorothee Noyon (USA), T H Nuretty (Indo), Carol O'Donoghue, Maree & Julie O'Gorman (AUS), Betsy O'Neill (USA), David Odell (USA), Y Rsa & Mikael Oman (S), Rachel Oram (UK), Jens Otto (D), Jackie Pagett, Martin Paludan-Muller, Daniele Passalacqua (I), Henrik Pedersen (DK), Barry Pell (USA), Yves Penduff (F), Martin J Perry (UK), Colleen Peters (AUS), Christopher Phillips (UK), Albert Pieters (NL), Gary & Mary Pinkus (USA), Jan Pock-Steen (DK), Clive Porter (UK), Lee Purdie (AUS), Kate Purnell (AUS), Viki & Tony Ramsay (AUS), Ken & Julie Ransford (USA), Chris Reid (AUS), Bente Remm (C), Diana M Rendall (UK), A Rijsdijk (NL), Didi Suradin Rini (Indo), J Robert (USA), Mary Jo Roberts (IRL), D Roberts (USA), Paul Robertson (AUS), Perry Robinson (AUS), Gottfried Roelcke (D), Elizabeth Romano, Bruno Rosenberg, Giuseppe Rossini (I), Jean Rowland (AUS), Anwar Said (AUS), Fernando Sala (I), Esron & Louise Samosir (AUS), Indra Saputra (Indo), Edi Sastri (Indo), E L Scharenquivel (AUS), Martin Schell), Eva Scherb (USA), Manya Schilperoort (Tw), Glen Schlueter, Gerard Schlund (F), Katja Schroder (D), B I Scott (AUS), David Searcy (USA), Leon Sebek (C), E B Seemann (UK), Eva Sherb, Jonathan Simon (USA), Sarah Smith (UK), Laurie Smith (C), Julie Smith (AUS), Trevor Smith (UK), Julie Smith (AUS), Jackie Smith (UK), David South (AUS), Douglas Stanley (USA), Peter Streit (AUS), Jill Strudwick (UK), Coenraad Strumphler, Louise Sudet (C), Heru Sutomo (Indo), Inge Svenhat, Andrew Symms, Di Taylor, Eric Telfer (USA), Emmy & Anton Thie (NL), Dieter Thieser (D), Keith & Birgid Thompson (C), Thon (Indo), Hans Thybo (DK), Steve Tibbett (USA), Alan Tibbett (UK), Steve Tibbetts (USA), Wayan Tony (Indo), Margaret Traeger (AUS), Doug Ulene (USA), Elaine Ulph (UK), Denis & Mary Umstot Rob van Bohee-men (NL), Tom Van Den Akker (NL), Johan van der Stoop (NL), Ad van Oosten (NL), Moses Vaughan (USA), Eddie Veenhoven (NL), Trish Veitch (A), Alex Velberg Clary Verbunt (AUS), J Verhoeven (NL), Joost Voeten (NL), Riccardo Voltan (I), Friederike Wartenberg (D), Daniela Watson (UK), Daniel Watson (UK), Tineke Wedzinga (NL), Luke Weldon (UK), James Welsh (UK), Stephan Westgarth (UK), Beth Wetzler (UK), Jero Wijenja (Indo), Albert Wijngaard (NL), Peter Wilkins, Robert A Wilkinson (USA), C A Williams (UK), Stephen Williams (UK), Russell Wills (NZ), Gavin Wilson (UK), Erik Wimmer (S), Deb Winters (UK), Henrik Wisborg (DK), Ron With (AUS), Casper Witteman (NL), Kit Mui Wong (S), Des Woods (NZ), Marianne Wood-ward (UK), Juliet & John Wooldridge (UK), Sandra Wooltorton, Phil & Linda Wotherspoon (AUS), Julia Wynn (UK), Nel Yans (NL), David Yates (AUS), R A Zambardino (UK), Jurgen Zeitner (D), Fione Zon-neveld (NL), Quirien Zyden (NL)

A – Austria, AUS – Australia, B – Belgium, C – Canada, CH – Switzerland, D – Germany, DK – Denmark, F – France, IRL – Ireland, I – Italy, Indo – Indonesia, N – Norway, NL – Netherlands, NZ – New Zealand, S – Sweden, UK – United Kingdom, US – United States of America

Keep in touch!

We love hearing from you and think you'd like to hear from us.

The Lonely Planet Newsletter covers the when, where, how and what of travel. (AND it's free!)

When...*is the right time to see reindeer in Finland?*
Where...*can you hear the best palm-wine music in Ghana?*
How...*do you get from Asunción to Areguá by steam train?*
What...*should you leave behind to avoid hassles with customs in Iran?*

To join our mailing list just contact us at any of our offices. (details below)

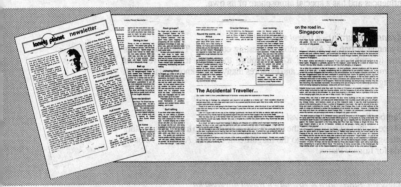

Every issue includes:

- *a letter from Lonely Planet founders Tony and Maureen Wheeler*
- *travel diary from a Lonely Planet author - find out what it's really like out on the road*
- *feature article on an important and topical travel issue*
- *a selection of recent letters from our readers*
- *the latest travel news from all over the world*
- *details on Lonely Planet's new and forthcoming releases*

Also available Lonely Planet T-shirts. 100% heavy weight cotton (S, M, L, XL)

LONELY PLANET PUBLICATIONS
Australia: PO Box 617, Hawthorn, 3122, Victoria (tel: 03-819 1877)
USA: Embarcadero West, 155 Filbert Street, Suite 251, Oakland, CA 94607 (tel: 510-893 8555)
UK: Devonshire House, 12 Barley Mow Passage, Chiswick, London W4 4PH (tel: 081-742 3161)

Guides to South-East Asia

South-East Asia on a shoestring
The well-known 'yellow bible' for travellers in South-East Asia covers Brunei, Burma (Myanmar), Cambodia, Hong Kong, Indonesia, Laos, Macau, Malaysia, the Philippines, Singapore, Thailand and Vietnam.

Bali & Lombok - a travel survival kit
This guide will help travellers to experience the real magic of Bali's tropical paradise. Neighbouring Lombok is largely untouched by outside influences and has a special atmosphere of its own.

Myanmar (Burma) - a travel survival kit
Myanmar is one of Asia's most interesting countries. This book shows how to make the most of a trip around the main triangle route of Yangon–Mandalay–Bagan, and explores many lesser-known places such as Bago and Inle Lake.

Cambodia - a travel survival kit
As one of the last nations in the region opens its doors to travellers, visitors will again make their way to the magnificent ruins of Angkor. Another first for Lonely Planet!

Malaysia, Singapore & Brunei - a travel survival kit
Three independent nations of amazing geographic and cultural variety – from the national parks, beaches, jungles and rivers of Malaysia, tiny oil-rich Brunei and the urban prosperity and diversity of Singapore.

Philippines - a travel survival kit
The friendly Filipinos, colourful festivals, and superb natural scenery make the Philippines one of the most interesting countries in South-East Asia for adventurous travellers and sun- seekers alike.

Thailand - a travel survival kit
This authoritative guide includes Thai script for all place names and the latest travel details for all regions, including tips in trekking in the remote hills of the Golden Triangle.

Vietnam, Laos & Cambodia - a travel survival kit
This comprehensive guidebook has all the information you'll need on this most beautiful region of Asia – finally opening its doors to the world.

Singapore - city guide

Singapore offers a taste of the great Asian cultures in a small, accessible package. This compact guide will help travellers discover the very best that this city of contrasts can offer.

Bangkok - city guide

Bangkok has something for everyone: temples, museums and historic sites; an endless variety of good restaurants, clubs, international culture and social events; a modern art institute; and great shopping oppurtunities. This pocket guide offers you the assurance that you will never be lost...or lost for things to do in this fascinating city!

Also available:

Thai phrasebook, *Thai Hill Tribes* phrasebook, *Burmese* phrasebook, *Pilipino* phrasebook, *Indonesian* phrasebook, *Papua New Guinea Pidgin* phrasebook, *Mandarin Chinese* phrasebook and *Vietnamese* phrasebook.

Lonely Planet Guidebooks

Lonely Planet guidebooks cover every accessible part of Asia as well as Australia, the Pacific, South America, Africa, the Middle East, Europe and parts of North America. There are five series: *travel survival kits*, covering a country for a range of budgets; *shoestring guides* with compact information for low-budget travel in a major region; *walking guides*; *city guides* and *phrasebooks*.

Australia & the Pacific
Australia
Bushwalking in Australia
Islands of Australia's Great Barrier Reef
Fiji
Melbourne city guide
Micronesia
New Caledonia
New Zealand
Tramping in New Zealand
Papua New Guinea
Papua New Guinea phrasebook
Rarotonga & the Cook Islands
Samoa
Solomon Islands
Sydney city guide
Tahiti & French Polynesia
Tonga
Vanuatu

South-East Asia
Bali & Lombok
Bangkok city guide
Myanmar (Burma)
Burmese phrasebook
Cambodia
Indonesia
Indonesia phrasebook
Malaysia, Singapore & Brunei
Philippines
Pilipino phrasebook
Singapore city guide
South-East Asia on a shoestring
Thailand
Thai phrasebook
Vietnam, Laos & Cambodia
Vietnamese phrasebook

North-East Asia
China
Mandarin Chinese phrasebook
Hong Kong, Macau & Canton
Japan
Japanese phrasebook
Korea
Korean phrasebook
North-East Asia on a shoestring
Taiwan
Tibet
Tibet phrasebook
Tokyo city guide

West Asia
Trekking in Turkey
Turkey
Turkish phrasebook
West Asia on a shoestring

Middle East
Arab Gulf States
Egypt & the Sudan
Egyptian Arabic phrasebook
Iran
Israel
Jordan & Syria
Yemen

Indian Ocean
Madagascar & Comoros
Maldives & Islands of the East Indian Ocean
Mauritius, Réunion & Seychelles